BRITISH IMPRINTS
RELATING TO NORTH AMERICA
1621–1760

AN ANNOTATED CHECKLIST

BRITISH IMPRINTS
RELATING TO NORTH AMERICA
1621–1760

AN ANNOTATED CHECKLIST

R. C. SIMMONS

THE BRITISH LIBRARY
1996

© 1996 R. C. Simmons

First published 1996 by
The British Library
Great Russell Street
London WC1B 3DG

ISBN 0 7123 0363 4

Typeset by Carnegie Publishing Ltd
Printed in England on permanent paper by
Redwood Books Ltd, Trowbridge

CONTENTS

Preface	vii
Introduction	ix
Structure and Nature of the Entries	xxiii
Abbreviations	xxiv
Library Symbols	xxvi
Chronological Checklist	1
Title Index	255
Author Index	337

PREFACE

During the compilation of this checklist, I have been helped by many persons and institutions. Research grants from the Bibliographical Society of America, the British Academy, the United States Information Service and the University of Birmingham Faculty of Arts Research Fund have enabled me to visit and work in many superb collections. In addition, I have benefitted from fellowships and financial support from the American Antiquarian Society, Worcester, Massachusetts, the Henry E. Huntington Library, San Marino, California, and the John Carter Brown Library, Providence, Rhode Island. I am most grateful to all these institutions.

I have made use of the following libraries and archives and I am indebted for the assistance given me by their staffs: American Antiquarian Society, Worcester, Massachusetts; Andover-Newton Theological Library, Cambridge, Massachusetts; Bodleian, Oxford; Birmingham University Library; The British Library; Cambridge University Library; Central Library, Manchester; Chetham's Library, Manchester; Dr. William's Library, London; Edinburgh University Library; Glasgow University Library; Goldsmith's Library, University of London; Guildhall Library, London; Henry E. Huntington Library, San Marino, California; Houghton Library, Cambridge, Massachusetts; John Carter Brown Library, Providence, Rhode Island; John Rylands Library, Manchester; Mitchell Library, Glasgow; National Library of Scotland, Edinburgh; Scottish Register Office, Edinburgh; Society of Friends Library, London; William L. Clements Library, Ann Arbor, Michigan.

The staff of Trinity College Library, Dublin and Mr. Hugh Amory of the Houghton Library replied helpfully to my written queries. I am grateful to them, to Robin Alston of The British Library and University College, London, and to Mr David Way, Publishing Manager, The British Library for their assistance.

The Master and Fellows of Gonville and Caius College, Cambridge elected me to a visiting fellowship in 1993, thereby enabling me to finish this project in congenial and stimulating company and incomparable surroundings.

My greatest obligation is to Dennis C. Landis of *European Americana* for answering many queries and for allowing me access to his files, including to prepublication materials for the years 1651–1700. Norman Fiering, Director and Librarian of the John Carter Brown Library, has aided me in numerous ways. I am very grateful for his support.

R.C.S.
University of Birmingham

INTRODUCTION

Part of this introduction is based, with permission, on my essay 'Americana in British Books, 1621–1760' which appeared in Karen O. Kupperman, ed. *America in European Consciousness* (Chapel Hill, University of North Carolina Press for the Institute of Early American History and Culture, 1994), pp. 361–387.

This chronological checklist is designed as a guide for historians and others needing information about one kind of source material. It was not compiled as an exercise in bibliography and its compiler is a historian not a bibliographer. The aim was to produce a useable guide to a substantial, a relatively neglected (in comparison with manuscript sources), and a not uninteresting corpus of material.[1]

Several recent publications have been of enormous assistance. The *Eighteenth-Century Short-Title Catalogue (ESTC)* of books printed from 1701 to 1800 in the English language lists the holdings of libraries around the world and is now available on CD-ROM.[2] For the historian this is a better finding aid than STC and Wing precisely because it is *not* a short-title catalogue. I suppose one may call it a medium-title catalogue, since it abbreviates the longer titles without losing much relevant detail. In these days of increasingly used computer searches, it will probably be advisable for bibliographical guides to include complete titles in order to allow different search strategies. In the case of British imprints relating to the Americas, the intensive use of *ESTC* should lead to the possibility of publishing a full British Americana down to 1800. It was especially useful as a finding list to British Library class marks and enabled me to consult hundreds of works which would not otherwise have been easily traceable. Similarly useful is the Library of Congress *National Union Catalog of pre–1956 imprints*,[3] a monument to functionality, organising efficiency and painstaking scholarship, which provided U.S. locations for many of the books in the check list.

The card index of the John Carter Brown Library, Providence, Rhode Island, which probably has the strongest single collection of seventeenth- and eighteenth-century British imprints relating to North America outside the British Library, is also of inestimable assistance to students of early Americana.

An earlier reference work was Sabin's *Dictionary*, well known to every student of early Americana.[4] His policy of inclusion was generous. I have examined most of the uncertain or unclear Sabin entries and eliminated some which he included but which seemed to me not to have been relevant. I have also, with a few exceptions, not included works of which no copy seems to be extant. Sabin's volumes

---

1 For guides to complementary manuscript sources see *A Guide to the manuscripts relating to America in Great Britain and Ireland*, edited by John W. Raimo (London, Published for the British Association for American Studies by Meckler Books/Mansell Publishing, c1979).

2 *The Eighteenth-Century Short Title Catalogue, the British Library Collections*, ed. R. C. Alston, 113 microfiches, 1 pamphlet (London, British Library, 1983). *The Eighteenth-Century Short Title Catalogue*, 1990, 2 vols. of microfiches, London, British Library, 1991). The CD-ROM version became available in 1992.

3 Library of Congress, *National Union Catalog of pre–1956 Imprints*. 685 vols. (London and Chicago, 1966–1980).

4 *A dictionary of books relating to America, compiled by Joseph Sabin and others* (New York, 1868–1936; reissued, New York, Scarecrow Press, 1966).

are now being superseded for the period to 1750 by *European Americana*.[5] The first volume, which appeared in 1980, covered the years 1493 to 1600. Subsequent volumes have so far extended this cover to the years 1601 to 1650, 1701 to 1725 and 1726 to 1750 *European Americana* is the central twentieth-century bibliographical contribution to its subject. The question perhaps arises as to how this current checklist can in fact add anything to *European Americana*, with its avowed policy of listing every imprint published in Europe relating to the Americas.

There are three things (at least) to say about this. First *European Americana*, a work of the highest importance and utility, which should open new ground in the study of European-American relationships, does exclude one category of imprint which is nevertheless central to American and European cultural history and transatlantic contacts. The European publications, whether reprints or originals, of American authors, unless those publications themselves contained material relating to the Americas, are omitted. However, the history of the European printings of works by, for example, John Cotton, Cotton Mather, Benjamin Franklin, and Jonathan Edwards is an intrinsic component of 'European Americana'. Information on where such works were first printed or reprinted in Europe, of how widely and how often, is essential in any study of cross-cultural relationships (Scotland and New England in the eighteenth century, for example) or for any study of publishing history. The present check list attempts to provide this information for Great Britain.

Second, *European Americana* conceives of 'Europe' as an organising principle. Admittedly, there were certain European 'best-sellers' and the multi-country approach of *European Americana* does allow their precise identification in a way that has not before been possible. But apart from these most of the works published in more than one country were usually surveys of botany, medicine, geography and other subjects that mostly contained only incidental or very general references to the Americas. The vast majority of imprints in *European Americana* were indeed published only in one country and most printed works relating to America are best understood within national contexts. A *national* approach seems to be appropriate, and more convenient for users, and it is obviously adopted in the present checklist.

Third, I have been able to add to the listings contained in *European Americana*, by making some more-or-less intensive searches in specific collections. Although the compilers of *European Americana* were able to take excellent steps in this direction, they were forced by constraints of time and available resources to work mainly from information provided to them or accessible in printed catalogues. Guided by a particular wish to look closely at American references in cheap popular literature (chapbooks, garlands, and broadsides especially), which are under catalogued, my special investigations have been made so far in superb but little used collections of chapbooks and ballads in various libraries in England and Scotland, including the holdings not only of the Bodleian, of the British Library and of Cambridge University Library but of the National Library of Scotland and of provincial English libraries in such cities as Manchester and Newcastle. (The Bibliographical Society of America has supported the extension of this research into the period after 1760 and important items for the period of the American Revolution have been found). Of related interest is the penetration of a consciousness of America into popular entertainments. The *Compleat Country Dancing-Master. . .* (London, 1718, 1735) contains 364 dances, including 'America', 'Indian Queen' and other New World titles.

---

5 *European Americana, a chronological guide to works printed in Europe relating to the Americas, 1493–1776*, Vol. I, *1493–1600*, Vol. II, *1601- 1650*, both volumes edited by John Alden with the assistance of Dennis C. Landis (New York, Readex Books, 1980 and 1982), Vol. V, *1701–1725*, Vol. VI, *1726–1750*, both volumes edited by Dennis C. Landis (New York 1987 and 1988).

Scottish material in general has also been investigated in some depth. Some of the sermons given before the Society in Scotland for Propagating Christian Knowledge and other printed Scottish Americana rest in the manuscript collections of the Scottish Register Office in Edinburgh and seem not to have been recorded from that source in *ESTC* or *European Americana*. The location of printed items in collections of mainly manuscript materials in England and Scotland is something that presents a difficulty to historical bibliographers. Other items, not listed in *European Americana*, are in specific collections in the National Library of Scotland. Among these *A succinct view of the Society in Scotland for propagating Christian knowledge. . .* (Edinburgh, 1738) discusses the conversion of Indians in 'our colonies in North-America', and various printed circulars plead for money from the Church of Scotland to support this and other missionary work.

Wales had no printing presses until the early eighteenth century and their output was in mainly in Welsh. I am not aware that any study was made of this Welsh language literature for *European Americana* and I have not investigated it myself. Future studies will be considerably facilitated by the publication of E. Rees, *Libri Walliae. A Catalogue of Welsh Books and Books printed in Wales 1546–1820* 2 vols. (Aberystwyth, 1987).

There may also be a need for the further investigation of Americana in British dramatic works. There were representations of the New World in masques and pageants as well as in plays in the later sixteenth and the earlier seventeenth centuries and these may be under recorded. *European Americana* lists books of which no extant copies are known. But its format precludes it from listing such lost plays and masques as the *Conquest of the West Indies* (1601/2) or *The Masque of Amazons* (1618) or *A tragedy of the plantation of Virginia* (licensed for acting in August, 1623/4).[6] Representations of the New World occurred in masques and pageants as well as in plays in the later sixteenth and the earlier seventeenth centuries and these are probably under recorded. Then and later such popular pageants as those forming part of the Lord Mayor's procession in London may also have been important in providing a broad audience with depictions of New World themes. To cite only two examples, the theme of the pageant for Sir James Edward's mayoralty in October 1678, designed by Thomas Jordan, celebrated the reduction of barbarous peoples through commerce in every part of the world and included many depictions of blacks and Indians while Sir John Peake's pageant in 1686 included representations of Europe, Africa, Asia and America.[7] Some contemporary printed materials relating to these annual events have survived.[8] Whether or not the costumes and properties worn and used at these pageants were based on any real acquaintance with genuine New World artefacts, or even included any of these, is an interesting speculation and might be worth further enquiry. Some artefacts could, of course, be seen in various cabinets of curiosities in London.[9] Later

---

6   G. M. Sibley, *The lost plays and masques* (Ithaca, 1933), pps. 30, 123, 183.

7   *The triumph of London: performed on Tuesday, October XXIX, 1678.* (London, 1678) ; *London's yearly jubilee perform'd on Friday, October XXIX, 1686. . .* (London, 1686).

8   August W. Staub and Robert W. Pinson, 'Fabulous wild men: American Indians in European pageants, 1493–1700,' *Theatre Survey*, XXV, 43–54 (May, 1984). For Lord Mayor's pageants in London and civic pageantry in London and elsewhere, see David M. Bergeron, *English Civic Pageantry 1558–1642* (London, 1971). John Nichols, *London Pageants* (London, 1831) lists Lord Mayor's Pageants to 1708. See also F. C. Brown, *Elkanah Settle, His life and Works* (Chicago, 1910) and R.T.D. Sayles, *Lord Mayor's Pageants of the Merchant Taylor's Company in the 15th, 16th and 17th centuries* (London, 1931).

9   See Christian F. Feest, 'The Collecting of American Indian Artifacts in Europe, 1493–1750' in Karen O. Kupperman, ed. *America in European Consciousness* (Chapel Hill, University of North Carolina Press for the Institute of Early American History and Culture, 1994)

seventeenth- and eighteenth-century plays[10] also need specialised attention; my investigations of these have been limited. Similarly, there are undoubtedly many more American references in the poetry of the period than I have located or sought to locate.

Chronological coverage

The period 1621–1760 was chosen for two reasons. Until 1621 the works printed in the British Isles relating to North America were small in number and they are well documented and discussed.[11] After 1760, for obvious reasons, the number became very great; nevertheless the publications of the revolutionary period are also well documented.[12] In contrast, although excellent chronological guides exist to some specialised aspects of British imprints issued in the years 1621–1760, no systematic national listing has been undertaken. The compiler's realization of this state of affairs, while undertaking other investigations in seventeenth- and eighteenth-century Anglo-American history, and his 'discovery' of items which, while not 'unknown', seem never to have been adequately assessed or studied, led him to this undertaking. So too did the wish to try to complement the extraordinarily useful chronological American bibliography of Charles Evans.[13]

The entries in this checklist total 3212. Some contain material that is unique and central to our knowledge of particular episodes and events, others rather marginal material. The *general* pattern of publication, not unexpectedly, shows the increasing quantity of printed material relevant to North America appearing in the British Isles, as the colonies became larger, more populous and more important to the affairs of the mother country. Certain decades also produced relatively higher numbers of imprints for particular reasons: the 1640s because of the interchange of arguments and ideas between English, Scottish and New England commentators on church government, arising from the situation in the mother country; the 1740s because of the transatlantic exchanges resulting from the Great Awakening; the 1750s because of the struggle with France for trade and colonies.

Some categories and themes

One great difference between British Americana before about 1620 and after was, of course, its quantity. Indeed in the sixteenth century much British Americana was adapted or translated from works first published in continental Europe. Only from the 1570s did the voyages of Frobisher and Gilbert begin the process that led to the flowering of English works with American themes and even in the last three decades of the sixteenth century indigenous British Americana was still outnumbered

---

10 See, for example, Pierre Danchin, *The prologues and epilogues of the Restoration, 1660–1700: a complete edition*, 6 vols. (Nancy, 1981–1988).

11 J. Parker, *Books to Build an Empire: A Bibliographical History of British overseas interests to 1620* (Minneapolis, 1965) ; and in *European Americana*, Vols I and II.

12 Thomas R. Adams, *The American controversy, a bibliographical study of the British pamphlets about the American disputes, 1764–1783* (Providence, New York, Brown University Press, Bibliographical Society of America, 1980) 2 vols. and Thomas R. Adams and Colin Bonwick, *British pamphlets relating to the American Revolution. . . 1764–1783* (Microform Academic Publishers, East Ardsley, n.d) [49 reels of microfilm].

13 *American Bibliography: A Chronological Dictionary of all books, pamphlets and periodical publications printed in the United States of America, 1639–1800*, compiled by Charles Evans and others, 14 vols. (Chicago and Worcester, 1909–1959) with supplements by R. P. Bristol (Charlottesville, Virginia).

by translations or borrowings from continental European sources. This was both an indication of the relative contemporary balance of national strengths in the New World and a reflection of the general cultural dependence of the British Isles on Italy, Spain and France. Such continental books, beginning with Sebastian Brant's *Shyppe of Fooles* in 1509 and including texts by Thevet, Oviedo, Las Casas, Acosta, Du Bartas, Gómara, and Alemán constituted a high percentage of all British Americana before 1601. From about 1630 they comprised a diminishing percentage of works published in the British Isles relating to America.

Britain indeed (probably in the second half of the seventeenth century) became a net exporter of works with American themes. Yet some of the British works with the widest republication outside of the British Isles actually contained little American material. The medical works of John Allen, Walter Harris and Charles Sydenham are such cases. Allen's *Synopsis universae medicinae practicae* was first published in London in 1719. By 1750 it had been reprinted a total of fourteen times, four issues appearing in Paris, three in Amsterdam, two in Venice, one in Leipzig and four more in London, one in Bautzen. But its American references seem to be limited to the (by then) hackneyed question of syphilis and the probability that the disease was transmitted by Spaniards to Europe. At the other extreme Daniel Defoe's works were obviously fully conscious of the New World and reprinted throughout Europe. William R. Chetwood's fictional Americana was also popular outside Britain.[14]

If the diffusion of knowledge about or the practice of activities concerning America are among the factors to be related to places of publication, within the British Isles the predominance of London is always significant. Yet the steady rise of provincial publishing is also noticeable. ESTC lists about 108,000 British entries 1701–1760 of which about 25,800 were printed outside of London. The provincial printings that appear in my checklist are slightly more than ten percent of total printings, still not a negligible figure.[15] By the 1740s at least this provincial output reflected the intensifying impact of the New World on provincial middle- and even lower-class consciousness, especially consciousness of the Americas as an aspect, even as an engine, of the beneficial growth of commerce.

This increasing volume of provincial printing certainly reflected the wide interest in the events leading to the French and Indian war and in the war itself. An extensive circulation throughout the British Isles of works relating to the war from simple broadside verses or cheap garlands[16] to expensive atlases and other descriptive works illustrates the extent to which it both familiarised large numbers

---

14   Chetwood, William Rufus, *The voyages, dangerous adventures and imminent escapes of Captain Richard Falconer: containing the laws, customs and manners of the Indians of America. . . Intermixed with the voyages and adventures of Thomas Randal. . . His being taken by the Indians of Virginia, etc.* (London, 1720) ; *The voyages and adventures of Captain Robert Boyle. . .* (London, 1726) ; *The voyage, shipwreck, and miraculous escape of Richard Castleman. . . With a description of Pennsylvania. . . and. . . Philadelphia. . .* (London, 1726)

15   I have not included as provincial imprints books printed in London for provincial booksellers.

16   The following are some examples of cheap 'popular' works: *A New song* (Edinburgh, 1755). A broadside. Concerns recruiting of Scots troops for French and Indian war. *Great Britain's glory; being a loyal song on the taking of Cape Breton from the French the 26th of July by Admiral Boscawen. . .* (London?, 1758?). *The Northumberland garland. Containing four excellent new songs* (London, 1759) with verses on 'Britain's conquest' mentioning Cape Breton, Crown Point, Senegal, etc. and 'Quedec's [sic] mighty fall.' *The Soldier's delight. Being a choice collection of songs* (London, Aldermary Church Yard, 1759?). A garland. Contains 'Britannia's glory' with verses on Boscawen, Amherst and Cape Breton. *Chapter of Admirals. To which are added. . . Patrick O'Neal's return from drubbing the French. An Anacreonic song (London, 1760?)*, a chapbook. A mockery of Irish boasting. *The Highlander's march a garland. Composed of several new songs viz. 1. The Highlander's march to America. . .* (Edinburgh, 1760?). Damaged part of an 8p. chapbook. 'O the French like Foxes do lie in the Wood', etc. *A Hint to the fair sex. A garland, containing six new songs* (Leominster, Worcester, Gloucester, 1760). A chapbook. Patriotic verses refer to Amherst, Wolfe, etc.

of Britons with matters of trade, colonies and empire and produced an outpouring of patriotism which also identified British successes with the providentially-directed victory of Protestantism. Many British provincial cities and towns first produced a first edition of a work relating to America in or after 1754, including Aberdeen, Belfast, Canterbury, Coventry, Leominster, Liverpool, Portsmouth, Shrewsbury, Tewkesbury and Wells. Of the total items in this checklist about eighteen per cent were printed from 1751 through 1760. There is certainly room for a bibliographical survey and for reprints of works relating to the origins of the war and to the war itself, similar to those produced by Thomas R. Adams and Colin Bonwick for British books in the years of the American Revolution.[17]

The continuing importance of the historic capitals of Ireland and Scotland also merits comment. Outside of London, Edinburgh and Dublin had the largest number of printings, demonstrating the continuing and increasing importance of old national capitals both as centres of printing and of American contacts. Moreover, the third largest number of first printings outside of London occurred in Glasgow, certainly a result of the growth of that port city's burgeoning commercial and personal links to North America. In these cities not only were certain popular London books reprinted but indigenous works made their first appearances, so that by the 1760s it becomes necessary to consider not only Americana in British books but Americana in English, Scottish and Irish books.

In the case of Scotland in the seventeenth century such indigenous productions were mainly tracts aimed at promoting emigration to the Americas; in the eighteenth century works that reflected the activities of the Scottish churches and the considerable repercussions of the Great Awakening in Scotland seen in Glasgow and Edinburgh imprints. There were also such works as the poetical survey of the Seven Years' War, *Britain, a poem; in three books...* (Edinburgh, 1757) ('Behold the ghost of Braddoc [sic], brave in fight,/With generous Halket, stalking round/Ohio's red streams, unburied, unavenged' etc. etc) which show well how the disloyal Scots of the 'forty-five became transformed into the loyal highlanders of a decade later! Nor should Scottish popular literature be overlooked. For example, *The jovial gamester's garland, Composed of several excellent new songs...* (Edinburgh, 1750?) tells of the 'betray'd Maid' who was betrayed to Virginia and 'served seven years to Captain Gulshaw laird.' In Ireland there was a concentrated interest in emigration. *A Letter from a gentleman in the North of Ireland, to a person in an eminent post under his majesty; concerning the transportation of great numbers from that part of the kingdom to America* (Dublin, 1729) seems to have slipped out of *European Americana*. There is a single copy of it in Trinity College, Dublin, one of many Irish imprints dealing with the same topic. In both Scotland and Ireland, works also appeared on the problem of developing specific beneficial, mainly commercial, links with the Americas while avoiding English constraints.

Out of numerous books, pamphlets, broadsides, chapbooks, garlands, parliamentary bills, court briefs, and so on, it is only possible to mention a few other publications, some because they represent important categories among British imprints, others because they are more obscure but interesting. Drama, poetry and fiction, for example, are relatively strongly represented. As well as works that are still widely read such as Daniel Defoe's novels, many are largely forgotten like the Abbé Prévost's *The life of Mr Cleveland natural son of Oliver Cromwell, written by himself. Giving a particular account of... his great sufferings in Europe and America...* or William Moraley's *The infortunate: or, the voyage and adventures of William Moraley... Containing, whatever is curious and remarkable in... Pennsylvania and New Jersey... several adventures through divers parts of America...* (Newcastle-upon-Tyne, 1743). The first novel written

---

17   See Thomas R. Adams, *The American controversy, a bibliographical study of the British pamphlets about the American disputes, 1764–1783*, 2 vols. (Providence and New York, 1980). Thomas R. Adams and Colin Bonwick, *British pamphlets relating to the American Revolution... 1764–1783* (Microform Academic Publishers, East Ardsley, n.d) [49 reels of microfilm].

by a North-American woman author, Charlotte Lennox's *The life of Harriot Stuart, written by herself* (London, 1751) is partly set in New York, where Lennox was born. Anthony Aston's, *The Fool's Opera; or, the taste of the age. Written by Mat. Medley. . . To which is prefix'd, a sketch of the author's life, written by himself* (London, 1730) describes his experiences as an actor in the West Indies and North America. The sketch is appended not prefixed in the British Library copy. Several eighteenth-century poems and collections of poems, such as William Donaldson's *North America, a descriptive poem. Representing the voyage to America; a sketch of that beautiful country; with remarks upon the political humour and singular conduct of its inhabitants. . .* (London, 1757) or John Dyer's, *The fleece: a poem. In four books* (London, 1757), which contains substantial American references, are less well known than similar kinds of seventeenth-century works. This whole category of material has not been looked at in much depth by historians.[18]

Popular and of very great importance in forming a view of America were numerous works on kidnapping and transportation. The operations of confidence tricksters, of 'spirits' and 'crimps' who either with kindly cunning or with great brutality kidnapped boys and girls, young men and women to servitude as labourers in the colonies had entered the literature of British America at an early period. During the seventeenth century references to it remained generally in the broadside and chapbook section of the market, as, for example, in the *Kid-napper trapan'd. . . being a pleasant relation of a man that would have sold his wife to Virginia. . .* (London. 1675?) but who found himself taken up or in the story of an innocent in the big city, or *The Trappan'd Welsh man, sold to Virginia* (London, 1685?) who on his first marvelling visit to London was entrapped by a pretty woman. Other references were to real cases, for example William Lauder's process against four fellow Scots for trepanning his son to Boston in 1716.[19]

In the eighteenth century, fact, fiction and fantasy contributed to and mingled in more substantial works. The kidnapping theme was often found in sometimes lurid fictions. In Penelope Aubin's account of *The life of Charlotta du Pont* (London, 1723), a lovely 13 year-old virgin was kidnapped and sent to Virginia on the instructions of her wicked stepmother's lover, Captain Farley. In Edward Kimber's *The history of the life and adventures of Mr. Anderson. Containing his strange varieties of fortune in Europe and America. . .* (London, 1754), a young boy of respectable family is seized by a seafaring man on the pavements of genteel London and then exposed to the lust of a homosexual sea captain before his sale to a Maryland planter. Other publications referred to true or purportedly true kidnappings. The most famous was certainly that of James Annesley who claimed to be the legitimate heir to the Earldom of Annesley, which had passed (illegally he said) to his uncle, Richard, in 1727. Annesley stated that he had been kidnapped as a young boy and sent as a 'common slave' to North America before finding his way back to Ireland via Jamaica in Admiral Vernon's fleet. Accounts of his life and a subsequent trial of his claims certainly entered the best seller lists, with regional and provincial reprintings (and European translations) and inspired a number of supplemental and auxiliary accounts and satires.[20] All these publications still repay study and the question of the derivation of the American background and other material in them has not been fully explored.

Equally popular were accounts, also both fictional and 'true' of rogues and unfortunates, sent forcibly but legally to the New World. Several of the printed Newgate 'confessions' involved persons

---

18   David S. Shields, *Oracles of Empire: Poetry, politics and commerce in British America 1690–1760* (Chicago, 1990) is a pioneering work, surveying some of the major British poetry.
19   William Lauder, *Memorial or state of the process at the instance of William Lauder of Wine-Park. . .* (n.p. 1718?). A seemingly unique copy of this pamphlet is in the John Carter Brown Library.
20   For a popular, if under-researched, treatment see Andrew Lang, *The Annesley Case* (Edinburgh and London, 1912).

who at one point had been transported, including those of James Dalton who, from a humble background, claimed to have been sentenced five times to transportation to Virginia, to have arrived there on four of these—on the other occasion as the result of various adventures he ended up in Spain—and once to have journeyed voluntarily to the Chesapeake. At least two of the criminals whose confessions were published claimed to be old Etonians, one William Parsons[21] was a confidence trickster who had been taken up by Governor Fairfax of Virginia, the other Henry Simms, the son of a favoured upper servant, spoiled by his employer's patronage. *The life of Henry Simms, alias young gentleman Harry* (London, 1747) took his story to his to his death at Tyburn on June 17, 1747 and recounted his 'extraordinary adventures. . . at home and abroad.' A recent study, drawing in part on contemporary printed accounts, suggests that many of those hanged in eighteenth-century London, had had experience of one kind or another in the Americas and comments on the cosmopolitan nature of the London proletariat, which included many American blacks.[22]

Such generally masculine accounts were widely read but probably the most famous eighteenth-century real life transportee and certainly the most famous fictional one were both women. Elizabeth Canning (1734–1773) was sentenced to transportation in 1754 after a sensational trial, which divided London society, involving her claimed perjury in a previous court case about her alleged kidnapping.[23] Her later virtuous behaviour there was reported in *Virtue triumphant; or, Elizabeth Canning in America; being a circumstantial narrative of her adventures, from her setting sail for transportation, to the present time. . .* (London, 1757) and was said to have included running away from a New York family in order to escape the advances of the head of the household (after which she was captured by Indians) and her eventual marriage after which she became an accomplished charitable worker. Another publication, a remarkable broadside, includes a coloured depiction, the *Sceene of sceenes* (London, 1755), Canning's 'dream for the good of her native country', which was said to have occurred shortly after she arrived in Boston (not New York). Here the spin off of a factual event into fictitious reconstructions demonstrates a typical eighteenth-century genre.

The real fictional character was, of course, Daniel Defoe's *Moll Flanders* (London, 1722) who journeyed twice to Virginia, once as a voluntary emigrant and once as a transportee and who found there the wealth and gentility which she could not obtain in England. Her adventures were quickly used by the chapbook makers. A useful study might be made of the way in which they handled the American content and altered Defoe's story.

The largest group of involuntary migrants to the new world were African slaves. Most works appearing before 1760 accepted the naturalness of slavery, though some called for the catechising, baptism and humane treatment of slaves. In the eighteenth century Edmund Gibson, Bishop of London, took seriously his responsibility for the ecclesiastical oversight of the American plantations; his letters to the master and mistresses of slaves were published in 1727. Some of the writings of American clergy, such as Thomas Bacon of Maryland and Samuel Davies of Virginia, who stressed slaveowners' duties to propagate Christianity, were reprinted in London. However a few works— Richard Baxter's *A Christian directory: or, A summ of practical theology* of 1673, for example, which contains

---

21 Anon., *A genuine, impartial, and authentick account of the life of William Parsons, esq; executed at Tyburn, Monday Feb. 11, 1751, for returning from transportation.* . . (London, 1751).

22 Peter Linebaugh, *The London Hanged. Crime and Civil Society in the Eighteenth Century* (London, 1991). See also Lincoln B. Faller, *Turned to account. The forms and functions of criminal biography in late seventeenth- and eighteenth-century England* (Cambridge, 1987). There has been no detailed study of English seventeenth- and eighteenth- century criminal biographies that seeks to elucidate all the New World material in them.

23 For a recent reexamination, see John Treherne, *The Canning Enigma* (London, 1989).

a typical chapter on the duties of masters towards their servants, of which the second section is 'Directions to Masters in Forain Plantations who have Negro's and other Slaves; being a solution of several cases about them'—discuss whether blacks are 'reasonable creatures' and refer to the 'natural liberty' of all humans.

Unless there is material in the numerous accounts of the travels of members of the Society of Friends in North America and the West Indies or in the official letters sent between Friends' meetings in America and Britain, such discussions of slavery as a moral or ethical question were rare. Nor was the justification of the African trade questioned. Malachy Postlethwayt's tract of 1745, *The African trade, the great pillar and support of the British plantation trade in America*, argued in part for its continuation in terms of control over the American plantations which dependence on the supply of slaves by British merchants made certain. Readers who sought novel challenges to slavery were forced to look to the Frenchman, Montesquieu, whose *Esprit Des Lois* first appeared in an English publication in 1750, or to the Scottish philosophers, George Wallace and Francis Hutcheson. The latter's *A System of Moral Philosophy* was published in Glasgow and London in 1755. Five years later J. Phillmore published his attack on the slave trade and on slavery in the plantations, *Two Dialogues on the Man-Trade*. These writings are part of the prehistory of the great flowering of antislavery arguments and sentiments that appeared after about 1770. Perhaps the most remarkable related book of the period was Thomas Bluett's *Some memoirs of the life of Job, the son of Solomon the high priest of Boonda in Africa; who was a slave about two years in Maryland; and afterwards being brought to England, was set free, and sent to his native land in the year 1734...* (London, 1734), the biography of an enslaved African who finally benefitted from his noble pedigree.

Stories of adventure, whether true or invented, were important in the corpus of British Americana. Besides the themes of transportation and kidnapping, other exotica arose naturally from the double hazards of maritime travel—exposing individuals to the threats of both shipwreck and piracy—and, if the crossing was safely completed, those arising from the new world environment itself. The sea voyage also figured in pietistic contexts because of its analogy with the passage of the soul. On land, encounters, friendly or otherwise, with native Americans were also commonplace occurrences in such works. In John Dennis's play published in 1704, *Liberty Asserted*, Indians occupied the stage for the first 32 pages of dialogue, while many fictional or individual accounts of America included pages of description of various Indian communities and the writer's personal experiences with native Americans. This was the continuation, or imitation, of a tradition that can be dated back at least to the adventures of Captain John Smith and of Pocahontas. Other narratives, such as Peter Williamson's widely circulated *French and Indian cruelty; exemplified in the life... of P. W. ... written by himself...*, published in York in 1757, in Glasgow in 1758 and in London in 1759, reflected the author's experience or alleged experience in warfare with the Indians, dwelling on the tortures which they inflicted and their savagery. I have treated some aspects of the theme of the 'savage' in British Americana elsewhere but another look at eighteenth-century sermons, drama and poetry rather than at works directly treating the Amerindian suggests itself as highly desirable from my readings in a large number of these sources.[24]

Williamson's work also dealt with his captivity among the Indians and 'captivity narratives' have, of course, been seen as an important American genre. However they were not widely republished in the British Isles. Although Mary Rowlandson's 1682 work, *A true history of the captivity and restoration of Mrs Mary Rowlandson, a minister's wife in New England...* was reprinted in London in the same year

---

24 See R. C. Simmons, *Savagery, Enlightenment, Opulence*, (The University of Birmingham, 1989)

as the first editions published in Massachusetts,[25] it was not reprinted in the eighteenth century. The first American female captivity narrative to be reprinted after 1700 seems to have been that by Elizabeth Hanson, in 1760, *An account of the captivity of Elizabeth Hanson, now or late of Kachecky; in New-England: who, with four of her children and servant-maid, was taken captive by the Indians, and carried into Canada...* a work first published in 1728 in Philadelphia. Only a handful of others appeared before 1800 and these do indicate the growing impact of the wars in North America from the late 1750s. But certainly before 1760 works dealing with Europeans captured by the Moors were more frequent and these reflect the point that contemporary Britons were more interested in the slavery and captivity of Europeans among the Moors than European captivity in North America. The release of English captives from Morocco in 1721 was celebrated by a service in St. Paul's Cathedral.[26] Many plays and novels, of course, treated this theme.

The numerical importance of works on religion, theology and church government, associated especially with Puritanism and with the Society of Friends in the seventeenth century, continued during the eighteenth, reinvigorated by the effects of the transatlantic wave of revivalism of the late 1730s and the 1740s. Jonathan Edwards's account of conversions at Northampton *A faithful narrative of the conversion of many hundred souls in Northampton... New England. In a letter to Dr. B. Colman... and published with a preface by Dr. Watts and Dr. Guyse...* was published in Edinburgh and London in 1736 and his famous *Sinners in the hands of an angry God* was reprinted in Edinburgh in 1745. Numerous works by or about George Whitefield appeared almost simultaneously in England and America. Whitefield continued, perhaps expanded, the habit of leading clerics who sought publication and republication for the sake of reputation as well as for the advancement of religion. Evident throughout the period is the large number of printed sermons. The Church of England was most strongly represented by the annual sermon before the Society for the Propagation of the Gospel, to which was usually appended an account of the work of the Society overseas with a strong North American section. Many of the sermons before the Georgia Trustees also contained North American material as did some of those before the Scottish Society for Propagating Christian Knowledge, the less well-known Scottish missionary body, founded in 1709 in Edinburgh. It badly needs a modern study. Nor have I seen any assessment of *The females advocate: or, an essay to prove that the sisters in every church of Christ, have a right to church-government as well as the brethren* (London, 1718), a work which cites Cotton Mather on the New England churches but is not listed in *European Americana*.

All these series of sermons merit reassessment in the light of new historical approaches to non-Europeans, especially to the Amerindian and the African, and to the poor. Questions of commerce and liberty have also not been looked at in the sermon literature which is where many contemporaries would have become acquainted with them. Excellent examples are the sermons delivered throughout Britain on 29 November 1759 on the capture of Quebec, a unique window into contemporary views of providence, empire, commerce and liberty at the peak of British eighteenth-century imperial success. Thirty-six have been located, many in single copies in libraries as far apart as the Huntington, California and the Rylands, Manchester. A short study of these sermons is now being finished.[27]

---

25 For a discussion of the publishing history see E. Z. Derounian, 'The publication, promotion, and distribution of Mary Rowlandson's Indian Captivity Narrative in the seventeenth century,' *Early American Literature*, Vol 23, No. 5 (1988) pps. 239–261.

26 E.g. William Berriman, *The great blessings of redemption from captivity. A sermon preached at the cathedral church at St. Paul, December 4, 1721. Before the captives redeem'd by the late treaty with the Emperor of Morocco* (London, 1722).

27 R.C. Simmons, 'God and Victory: The Quebec Thanksgiving Sermons of 29 November 1759' (in progress).

More esoteric and more vulgar fare was provided by works relating to the prophecies, to horrible acts allegedly committed under the delusions of religion, and by tales of supernatural horror, including Richard Chamberlayne's *Lithobolia: or, the stone throwing devil. . . account. . . of. . . infernal spirits. . . and the great disturbance they gave to George Walton's family, at. . . Great Island in. . . New Hantshire [sic] in New-England. . .* (London, 1698). New England witchcraft naturally also featured not only in the Mathers' eagerly promoted specific accounts but in general works on witchcraft and magic.[28]

Some of the most frequently reprinted works were those first published in the seventeenth century. Thomas Shepard's *Sincere Convert* was first printed in London in 1640 and republished about nineteen times by 1692; it seems to have received its last printing in Edinburgh in 1714. Shepard's *Sound Beleever*, another work dealing with the conditions of religious conversion, first published in London in 1645, was also popular until the third quarter of the seventeenth century. George Herbert's *The Temple*, with its famous lines on religion and the 'American strand' was also frequently reprinted in the seventeenth century. The 'Bay Psalm Book' had appeared in many British editions by 1760.

The closest rivals to these works of devotion seem to have been works of geography. Peter Heylyn's *Microcosmus; or a little description of the great world. . .* had reached eight editions by 1639; his *Cosmographie in four books. . .* first published in 1652, was reprinted many times to 1703. In both books the text relating to North America hardly changed over the years.[29] The same was true of Patrick Gordon's book, discussed below. Nathaniel Crouch's *English empire in America* (London, 1685) also had about eleven editions through 1760. Some explanation of the extraordinary popularity of Bernard Le Bovyer de Fontenelle's *A discourse of the plurality of worlds. . .*, the text of which appeared under numerous slightly changed titles from 1687 for the next one hundred years, is also needed.

Other works went into many editions over a shorter period. Accounts of military successes were always popular; Thomas Prince's *Extraordinary events the doings of God and marvellous in pious eyes. . . seen on. . . taking the city of Louisbourg, on the Isle of Cape Breton. . .* (1747), first printed in Boston in 1746, appeared in at least five London and one Belfast and one Edinburgh editions in the same year. John Brown's attack on luxury and corruption, which he linked to British failures in the war against the French, *An estimate of the manners and principles of the times. . .*, first printed in 1757, had reached eight or nine editions by the end of 1758.

Calculations based on British North Americana printed between 1621 and 1760 suggest that about half of the works listed were printed in one edition and about another quarter in two or three. The remainder ranged up to about thirty editions. But the number of editions is of course no guide to the number of copies printed; the number of copies per edition could number from about 250 upwards. Without direct information about the publishing history of individual imprints, sometimes found in printers' or publishers' records or other sources, there is no way of discovering the size of editions or assessing the readership for different works. What does seem clear is that some frequently

---

28 Richard Baxter, *The certainty of the world of spirits, fully evinced by the unquestionable histories of apparations and witchcrafts. . .* (London, 1691), William Turner, *A compleat history of the most remarkable providences, both of judgement and mercy, which have hapned [sic] in this present age. . .* (London, 1697), John Beaumont, *An historical, physiological and theological treatise of spirits, apparitions, witchcrafts. . .* (London, 1705), Richard Boulton, *A compleat history of magick, sorcery, and witchcraft. . .* (London, 1715), Francis Hutchinson, *An historical essay concerning witchcraft. . . And also two sermons. . .* (London, 1718), Richard Boulton, *The possibility and reality of magick, sorcery and witchcraft. . . In answer to Dr. Hutchinson's Historical essay. . .* (London, 1722) all contain more or less substantial sections on New England witchcraft.

29 John Huber Walker, 'A descriptive bibliography of the early printed works of Peter Heylyn' (Ph.D. diss, The University of Birmingham, 1978).

issued works were little changed over time and must have presented an inaccurate and antique view of America to their readers, perhaps with an effect on their attitudes and beliefs. Patrick Gordon's *Geography anatomized: or, a compleat geographical grammer. . .* was first published in London in 1693 and seems to have been issued in more than twenty issues/editions with slight title alterations to 1754 with the text hardly altered.[30]

Works first printed in North America

The years to 1760 saw the increasing republication in the British Isles—mainly in London—of works first printed in North America. The first British North American imprint to have been reprinted in the mother country seems to have been *The Capitall Lawes of New-England* of 1643, issued in London during the intense debate, involving the religious practices of New England, among others, over forms of church and civil government during the first decade of the English Revolution. The second was the second edition (1647) of the Bay Psalm Book, *The Whole book of psalmes, faithfully translated into English metre; whereunto is prefixed a discourse. . .*, although Wing, Holmes and Wilberforce Eames mention the possibility that this and some other subsequent 'Cambridge' editions were of Cambridge, Massachusetts, it seems now to be widely accepted that Cambridge, England or Amsterdam was the place of publication. All or part of the preface to the Bay Psalm Book had in fact been reprinted in 1644 in London in Nathaniel Holmes's *Gospel Musick*. It is fairly clear that from the 1640s the publication—though it is not clear if the same was true of its use—of the New England form of psalms was frequent in England and in Scotland.[31]

Although numerous works by (mainly) divines living in New England were first published in London in the 1640s and 1650s, no other direct republication of a work first printed in North America seems to have happened until 1652, when a version of the Massachusetts Platform of Church Discipline attributed to Richard Mather (Cambridge, Mass.,1649) was printed in London by W. Bentley for J. Ridley. According to Holmes this was technically flawed and was suppressed.[32] Only one copy is now extant. A second more successful version, printed by Peter Cole, appeared in the following year with a forward by Edward Winslow. Seven years later, in 1660, Quakers—voracious customers of the printing shops—had a declaration of the Massachusetts General Court justifying the trials and executions of Quakers in Boston reprinted in London, in *A True relation of the proceedings against certain Quakers, at the generall court of the Massachusetts. . . October 18, 1659. . .*. In the same year John Norton's apologia for the prosecutions of the Quakers in New England, *The heart of New-England rent at the blasphemies of the present generation*, was also reprinted in London.

---

30 Patrick Gordon, *Geography anatomized: or, a compleat geographical grammer. . .* (London, 1693) appeared in a second enlarged edition in 1699 and then from 1701–1760 in more than twenty issues/editions with slight title alterations. *European Americana* lists editions in 1702, 1704, 1708, 1711, 1716, 1719, 1722, 1725, 1730, 1733, 1735, 1737, 1740, 1741, and 1744. *ESTC* has also London, 1728 (11th edition, corrected and enlarged), 1749 (19th edition) and 1754 (20th edition) and Dublin, 1739 (15th edition, corrected) and 1747 (16th edition). For a discussion of the size of editions and related points on eighteenth-century books see Marjorie Plant, *The English Book Trade, an economic history of the making and sale of books*, 3rd. ed., (London,1975) and John Feather, *The provincial book trade in eighteenth-century England* (Cambridge, 1985). An accessible source, with frequent and representative references to sizes of editions, is James E. Tierney ed., *The correspondence of Robert Dodsley, 1733–1764*, (Cambridge, 1988).

31 Thomas J. Holmes, *The Minor Mathers. A list of their works* (Cambridge, Mass., 1940) ; Wilberforce Eames, *A list of editions of the Bay Psalm Book or New England version of the Psalms* (New York, 1885). I am grateful to Mr Hugh Amory of the Houghton Library for providing me with information on the printing of the Psalms.

32 Holmes, *Minor Mathers*, 51B.

INTRODUCTION

The frequency of London reprints of New England works hardly increased after the Restoration of Charles II. Three works appeared, in 1666, including Michael Wigglesworth's *The day of doom: or, A description of the great and last judgement*. This would be reprinted again in 1673 and 1687 in London and in 1711 in Newcastle-upon-Tyne. The Newcastle imprint was probably the first reprint outside of London of a book first published in North America. Despite their presumed allure for nonconformists, Wigglesworth's verses were not to be reprinted again in Great Britain until 1774 when an edition appeared in Norwich. In 1675–6 several accounts of the serious Indian war in New England, King Philip's war, appeared in London, either closely adapted, or directly reprinted, from Boston originals. The first 'captivity' narrative to be reprinted in Britain was that of Mary Rowlandson, *A true history of the captivity and restoration of Mrs Mary Rowlandson, a minister's wife in New England. . .* in 1682, and has been mentioned above.

By the 1680s another category of British reprint was becoming more common—that of works by individuals whose wish for literary or other forms of recognition led them to seek as many British printings as possible both for their previously unpublished or their previously American-published writings. Increase Mather's first London reprint was in 1684 when G. Calvert issued his essay on 'illustrious providences' published earlier in the same year in Boston. This had a degree of success and was republished in London in 1687. Thereafter his British reprints were frequent. Cotton Mather followed his father's example. His works on the New England witchcraft cases were reprinted in London and Edinburgh, while he either had certain Boston publications reprinted in London or arranged for some of his writings to be first printed there. Some of his works continued to be printed or reprinted in the British Isles upto the time of his death in 1728. One of the Mathers' London contacts and agents was John Dunton who had visited New England and published an account of his travels.[33] The Mathers' example was to be followed by other clergy in the following years.

By the latter decades of the seventeenth century the Massachusetts printing press was no longer the only one in British North America. Probably the first work from another American press to be reprinted in London was provoked by Leisler's rebellion in New York. Although the title page of *A modest and impartial narrative of several grievances. . . that the peaceable and most considerable inhabitants of New-York. . . lye under, by the extravagant and arbitrary proceedings of Jacob Leisler and his accomplices. . .* claimed that this tract had been first 'printed at New York', its actual place of first publication had been Philadelphia. An earlier justification of the Protestant Revolution of 1689 in Maryland, *The Declaration of the reasons and motives for the present appearing in arms of their majesties protestant subjects in Maryland* was also 'reprinted' in London, but despite this claim on the title page no evidence has been found of a first printing in Maryland. A popular and entirely different work, the Rev. J. Dickinson's *God's protecting providence, man's surest help and defence. . .*, a story of shipwreck and cannibals, was first printed in Philadelphia in 1699 and reprinted in London in 1700, 1701, 1720 and 1759. After 1700 there were frequent reprintings of New York and Philadelphia publications, later to be joined by those of the presses located in the colonial south. These included many works relating to political controversies in the colonies which, for various reasons, it was felt might advantageously be reprinted in London. Among other topics were Indians and Indian converts and the dispute relating to the treatment of smallpox. But, as we shall see, works relating to religion and the churches predominated during much of the eighteenth, as they had in the seventeenth century. There were also increasing republications of American pieces concerned with military relations between France and Britain in the new world, such as the patriotic sermons of the Rev. Samuel Davies of Virginia. Of these militaria,

---

33 See S. Parks, *John Dunton and the English book trade. A study of his career with a checklist of his publications* (New York, 1976).

The Journal of Major George Washington..., first printed in Williamsburg in 1754 and reprinted by Thomas Jefferys in London in the same year, is the most celebrated. By the 1750s also, quite substantial historical works were being reprinted in London, including William Stith's *The history of the first discovery and settlement of Virginia...* (Williamsburg, 1747, London 1753) and William Douglass's two volume *A summary, historical and political of the first planting, progressive improvements and, and present state of the British settlements in North America* (Boston, 1749, 1753, London, 1755).

Exclusions

Pilot books of maps and charts, maps, atlases, and general collections of voyages are not exhaustively listed. Nor have I sought to list every work of general British history, though these may have some sections on colonisation. Most periodical publications, certainly all magazines, such as the *Gentleman's Magazine*, are excluded. Some of the more important botanical works are listed, as are sales catalogues of American plants, common by the eighteenth century, but readers wishing for fuller listings of these are referred to other excellent specialised reference works including *European Americana*.[34] A number of other categories were also generally not included. These were: a) editions of treaties b) works, except for royal proclamations, relating to tobacco after it reached Britain c) works relating to the Royal African Company, which had marginal North American references. First-rate modern bibliographies (Arents, Fage,[35] Hanson, 'Goldsmith's-Kress', *European Americana* etc. (see the list of sources, below) provide excellent guides to all these categories. Nor was any systematic search made of poetry and dramatic works, though those that were found were included.

Unless they contained material about North America, works by temporary residents who were not born in the colonies and which were published after their residence had finished were not included. For example, Nathanael Ward returned to England from New England at the start of the Civil Wars and published many tracts. These are not listed since they contain no American references. But his writings published in London while he lived in Massachusetts are. The works of those born in North America, who settled permanently in Britain, are listed only if they contained North American references. This was not a significant exclusion: the writings of the prolific Pennsylvania-born James Ralph and of the woman writer, Charlotte Lennox, daughter of Lieutenant-Governor James Ramsay of New York, are the main cases in point.[36]

---

[34] British horticulturists and botanists are dealt with by Blanche Henrey, *British botanical and horticultural literature before 1800, comprising a history and a bibliography of botanical and horticultural books printed in England, Scotland and Ireland from the earliest times to 1800*, 3 vols. (London, 1975). See Henry Lowood, 'The New World and the European Catalog of Nature' in Karen O. Kupperman, ed. *America in European Consciousness* (Chapel Hill, University of North Carolina Press for the Institute of Early American History and Culture, 1994) for the theme of 'managing new information' about natural history.

[35] J. D. Fage, *A guide to original sources for precolonial western Africa published in European languages* (University of Wisconsin-Madison, 1987).

[36] R. W. Kenny, 'James Ralph. An 18th-century Philadelphian in Grub Street,' *Pennsylvania Magazine of History and Biography*, LXIV (1940). Charlotte Lennox has entries in both the *Dictionary of National Biography* and the *Dictionary of American Biography*.

STRUCTURE AND NATURE OF THE ENTRIES

My aim has been to provide a useable checklist, not a bibliographical catalogue. Entries are listed alphabetically by year of publication, under the actual, the attributed or the assumed author. In some cases, because of vagaries of pagination, etc. the total number of *pages* has been estimated or roughly counted and is given in square brackets. *Titles* have in many cases been shortened and seventeenth- and eighteenth-century capitalization has not always been followed; nor was it possible to check every entry against the original imprint for accuracy of punctuation, etc. Where the work was *first* published in North America, a cross reference is provided to Evans or Bristol and to the date and place of American publication. An attempt has been made to provide one or more British and American *locations* for each entry.

Subsequent and different issues and/or editions

Each entry refers a) to the first edition of the imprint and b) any issues/editions subsequent to the first (whether issued in the same year or in subsequent years) which are noted for the period to 1760. In a very few cases, however, additional volumes of the same work not published in the same year as the first volume are given separate entries. To have given each new or separate edition/issue its own entry would have added enormously to the size and cost of the checklist and made it too complex and too large for a single compiler to handle, without necessarily adding to its usefulness.

Checking of entries

It was not possible to inspect every work listed. However, many hundreds were looked at, especially to discover the exact nature of their North American relevance or to establish certain details of publication or pagination, etc. The British Library (still incomparable for the depth of its holdings in this period) was the main source of material, closely followed by the John Carter Brown Library. The collections and reference facilities of the American Antiquarian Society and the Henry E. Huntington Library were also invaluable.

ABBREVIATIONS

ALDIS — Aldis, H.G., *A list of books printed in Scotland before 1700*... (Edinburgh, 1970).

ARENTS — New York Public Library. Arents Tobacco Collection. *Tobacco; A Catalogue.* (New York: New York Public Library, 1958–69).

BAER — Baer, Elizabeth, *Seventeenth-Century Maryland; a Bibliography.* (Baltimore, 1949).

BRADSHAW — *A catalogue of the Bradshaw Collection of Irish books in the University Library, Cambridge.* 3 vols. (Cambridge, 1916).

BRIGHAM — Brigham, C. S., *British Royal Proclamations relating to America, 1603–1783* in *Transactions and Collections of the American Antiquarian Society.* Vol. XI (Worcester, Mass., 1911).

BRISTOL — See EVANS.

CRAWFORD — *Handlist of Proclamations issued by royal and other constitutional authorities, 1714–1910.* (Wigan, 1913).

CHURCH — Church, E. D. *A catalogue of books relating to the discovery and early history of North and South America, forming a part of the library of E.D. Church.* 5 vols. (New York, 1907).

DEXTER — Dexter, H.M. *The congregationalism of the last three hundred years, as seen in its literature.* (New York, 1880).

EA — *European Americana, a chronological guide to works printed in Europe relating to the Americas, 1493–1776.* Vol. I, 1493–1600, Vol. II, 1601–1650, both volumes edited by John Alden with the assistance of Dennis C. Landis (New York, Readex Books, 1980 and 1982). Vol. V: 1701–1725; Vol. VI: 1726–1750, both volumes edited by D.C. Landis, (New York, 1987, 1988).

EAMES — Eames, Wilberforce, *The Bay Psalm Book: being a facsimile reprint of the first edition, printed by Stephen Daye at Cambridge, in New-England...* (New York, 1908).

ESTC — *ESTC on CD-ROM [The Eighteenth-Century Short-Title Catalogue].* (London: British Library, 1992).

EVANS — *American Bibliography: A Chronological Dictionary of all books, pamphlets and periodical publications printed in the United States of America, 1639–1800.* Compiled by Charles Evans and others, 14 vols. (Chicago and Worcester, 1909–1959) with supplements by R. P. Bristol (Charlottesville, Virginia, 1962-).

FORD — Ford, P.L., *List of some briefs in appeal cases which relate to America tried before the Lords Commissioners of Appeals...* (Brooklyn, 1889).

FOXON	Foxon, D. J., *English verse, 1701–1750, a catalogue.* 2 vols. (London, 1975).
GOLDSMITH'S	*London University Goldsmith's Library of Economic Literature Catalogue.* 2 vols. (London, 1970, 1975).
GOVE	Gove, P.B., *The Imaginary Voyage in Prose Fiction.* (New York, 1941).
GUERRA	Guerra, F., *American Medical Bibliography, 1639–1783.* (New York, 1962).
HANSON	Hanson, L. W., *Contemporary printed sources for British and Irish economic history, 1701–1750.* (Cambridge, 1963).
HIGGS	Higgs, H., *Bibliography of Economics 1751–1775.* (Cambridge, 1935).
HOLMES CM	Holmes, T. J., *Cotton Mather; a bibliography of his works.* 3 vols. (Cambridge, Mass., 1940).
HOLMES IM	Holmes, T.J., *Increase Mather; a bibliography of his works.* 2 vols. (Cambridge, Mass., 1931).
HOLMES MM	Holmes, T.J., *The minor Mathers; a list of their works.* (Cambridge, Mass., 1940).
KRESS	Harvard University. Kress Library of Business and Economics. *Catalogue.* 5 vols. (Boston, Baker Library, 1940–1964).
KRESS SUPP.	Supplements. (Boston, Baker Library, 1967).
LARKIN	J. F. Larkin and Paul L. Hughes, *Stuart royal proclamations.* Vol. 1, *Royal proclamations of King James 1, 1603–1625.* (Oxford, 1973) ; Vol.2, *Royal proclamations of King Charles I, 1625–1646.* (Oxford, 1983).
NUC	Library of Congress, *National Union Catalog of pre–1956 Imprints.* 685 vols. (London and Chicago, 1966–1980).
SABIN	Sabin, Joseph and others, *Bibliotheca Americana. A dictionary of books relating to America.* 29 vols. (New York, 1868–1936) reissued, New York, Scarecrow Press, 1966).
SMITH	Smith, Joseph, *A descriptive catalogue of Friends' books, or books written by members of the Society of Friends.* 2 vols. (London, 1867).
SMITH, AQ	Smith, Joseph, *Bibliotecha anti-Quakeriana; or a catalogue of books adverse to the Society of Friends.* (London, 1873).
STC	Pollard, A. W. and Redgrave, G. R. comps. *A short-title catalogue of books printed in England, Scotland, & Ireland and of English books printed abroad, 1475–1640.* (London, Bibliographical Society, 1926) and 2nd edition revised and enlarged by Jackson, W.A., Ferguson, F.S. and Panzer, K. F. 3 vols. (London, 1976–1991).
STEELE	Crawford, J.L, Earl of, *Bibliotheca Lindesiana. . . A bibliography of royal proclamations of the Tudor and Stuart sovereigns and of others. . . 1485–1714.* 2 vols. (Oxford, 1910).
WING	*Short-title catalogue of books printed in England, Scotland, Ireland, Wales, and British America, and of English books printed in other countries, 1641–1700.* Compiled by Donald Wing. 3 vols. (second revised edition, New York, 1972–1988).

LIBRARY SYMBOLS

British, Irish and European Library Symbols

ABu;	Aberdeen University
AN;	National Library of Wales, Aberystwyth
AWn;	National Library of Wales, Aberystwyth
BAT;	Bath, Avon County Library, Bath Reference Library
BBN;	Birmingham. Selly Oak. Bevan-Naish Library, Woodstock College
BC;	Birmingham Central
BLI;	Blickling, Blickling Hall
BMu;	Birmingham University
BN	Paris. Bibliothèque Nationale
BR;	Bristol Reference Library
BRG;	Brighton Central
BRu;	Bristol University
C;	Cambridge University Library
Cgc;	Cambridge. Gonville and Caius College
Cj;	Cambridge. Jesus College
Ck;	Cambridge. King's College
Cm;	Cambridge. Magdalene College
Cpe;	Cambridge. Peterhouse
Cq;	Cambridge. Queens' College
Csj;	Cambridge. St. Johns
Ct;	Cambridge. Trinity College
CYc;	Canterbury Cathedral
D;	Dundee University
DA;	Eire. Dublin. Royal Irish Academy
DCH;	Derbyshire. Chatsworth
DM;	Eire. Dublin. Narcissus Marsh's
DPR;	Eire. Dublin. Public Record Office
Dt;	Eire. Dublin. Trinity College
DUc;	Durham Cathedral
E-NRO;	Scotland. Edinburgh National
E;	Scotland. Edinburgh. National Library of Scotland
EN;	Scotland. Edinburgh. National Library of Scotland
Ep;	Scotland. Edinburgh Central Library
ES;	Scotland. Edinburgh Signet Library
Eu;	Scotland. Edinburgh University Library
GH;	Scotland. Glasgow. Hunterian Museum. University of Glasgow

GK;	Keynes
Gp;	Scotland. Glasgow, Mitchell
Gu;	Scotland. Glasgow University
LAM;	Lampeter. St. David's University College
LANu;	Lancaster University
LEu;	Leeds University
LIN;	Lincoln. Cathedral
LVu;	Liverpool University Library,
L;	London. British Library
Lce;	London, Customs and Excise
Ldc;	London Draper's Company
Ldhs;	London, Department of Health
Ldw;	London, Dr. William's
Lfr;	London. Society of Friends
Lg;	London. Guildhall
Lhl;	London, House of Lords
Lke;	London, Royal Botanic Garden's, Kew
Lli;	London, Lincoln's Inn
Lll;	London. London Library
Llp;	London. Lambeth Palace
Lmh;	London. Congregational Library
Lpro;	London. Public Record Office
Lrag;	London. Royal Agricultural Society
Lrcs;	London. Royal College of Surgeons
Lrcw;	London. Royal Commonwealth Society
Ls;	London. Sion College
Lsa;	London. Society of Antiquaries
Lsb;	London. St. Bride's Printing Company
Lse;	London. London School of Economics
Lu;	London. University of London
Lub;	London. Royal Holloway and New Bedford
Luk;	London. King's College
Luu;	London. University College
Lv;	London. Victoria and Albert
MRc;	Manchester. Chetham's
MRu;	Manchester. John Rylands University
MY;	Ireland. Maynooth. St. Patrick's College
NCp;	Newcastle upon Tyne Central Library
NO;	Norwich. Norfolk and Norwich Literary Institution
Npl;	Norwich. Public
O;	Oxford. Bodleian
Oa;	Oxford University Archives
Ob;	Oxford. Balliol
Oc;	Oxford. Christ Church
Om;	Oxford Merton
Or;	Oxford. Regent's Park College

BRITISH IMPRINTS RELATING TO NORTH AMERICA

Ot;   Oxford. Trinity College
Ow;   Oxford. Worcester College
MAL;   Essex. Maldon. Plume
R;   Rothamsted. Agricultural Experimental Station
REu;   Reading University Library
SC;   Salisbury Cathedral
WARE;   Hertforshire. Ware. St. Edmund's College
WCA;   Windsor. St George's Chapel

North American Library Symbols

CaAEU   University of Alberta
CaBVaU   University of British Columbia
CaBViPA   Victoria. Provincial Archives
CaOHM   Ontario. McMaster University, Mills Memorial Library
CaOTP   Toronto. Public
CaOTU   Toronto. University of Toronto
CaQMBN   Bibliothèque Nationale de Quebec
CaQMM   McGill University
CU   California. Berkeley. University of California
CU-BANC   California. Berkeley. Bancroft
CCC   California. Claremont College
CU-A   California. Davis. University of California
CLL   California. Los Angeles County Law
CLU   California. Los Angeles. University of California
CLU-C   California. Los Angeles. William A. Clark Memorial
CLU-M   California. Los Angeles. Biomedical
CLU-S/C   California. Los Angeles. University of California Special Collections
CSt   California. Palo Alto. Stanford University
CU-Riv   California. Riverside. University of California
C   California. Sacramento. State Library
C-S   California. San Francisco. Sutro
CSmH   California. San Marino. Henry E. Huntington
CU-SB   California. Santa Barbara. University of California
Ct   Connecticut. Hartford. Connecticut State
CtHT-W   Connecticut. Hartford. Watkinson Library, Trinity College
CtW   Connecticut. Middletown. Wesleyan University
CtY   Connecticut. New Haven. Yale University
CtY-D   Connecticut. New Haven. Yale Divinity School
DeU   Delaware. Newark. University of Delaware
DFo   District of Columbia. Folger
DLC   District of Columbia. Library of Congress
DN   District of Columbia. Department of the Navy
DNAL   District of Columbia. National Library of Agriculture
DNLM   District of Columbia. National Library of Medicine
DWT   District of Columbia. Wesley Theological Seminary

FMU	Florida. Coral Gables. University of Miami
FU	Florida. Gainesville. University of Florida
GEU	Georgia. Atlanta. Emory University
GHi	Georgia. Savannah. Georgia Historical Society
GU	Georgia. Athens. University of Georgia
GU-DeR	Georgia. Athens. University of Georgia. De Renne
I	Illinois. Springfield. State Library
ICJ	Illinois. Chicago. John Crerar
ICN	Illinois. Chicago. Newberry
ICRL	Illinois. Chicago. Center for Research Libraries
ICU	Illinois. Chicago. University of Chicago
IEG	Illinois. Evanston. Garrett Theological Seminary
IU	Illinois. Urbana. University of Illinois
InU	Indiana. Bloomington. Indiana University
InU-L	Indiana. Bloomington. Indiana University Law
InU-Li	Indiana. Bloomington. Indiana University. Lilly
IaU	Iowa. Iowa City. University of Iowa
KEmT	Kansas. Emporia. State Teachers College
KU	Kansas. Lawrence. University of Kansas
KU-S	Kansas. Lawrence. University of Kansas. Spencer Research
MeB	Maine. Bowdoin College
MdBJ-G	Maryland. Baltimore. Johns Hopkins University. John Work Garret
MdBJ-W	Maryland. Baltimore. Johns Hopkins University. Welch
MdBP	Maryland. Baltimore. Peabody Institute
MdHi	Maryland. Baltimore. Maryland Historical Society
MA	Massachusetts. Amherst. Amherst College
MU	Massachusetts. Amherst. University of Massachusetts
M	Massachusetts. Boston. Massachusetts State Library
MB	Massachusetts. Boston. Boston Public
MBAt	Massachusetts. Boston. Boston Athenaeum
MBH	Massachusetts. Boston. Massachusetts Horticultural Society
MBM	Massachusetts. Boston. Boston Medical Library
MH	Massachusetts. Cambridge. Harvard University
MH-AH	Massachusetts. Cambridge. Andover Theological
MH-A	Massachusetts. Cambridge. Arnold Arboretum
MH-L	Massachusetts. Cambridge. Harvard Law
MHL	Massachusetts. Cambridge. Harvard Law School
MH-Z	Massachusetts. Cambridge. Harvard Zoological
MH-BA	Massachusetts. Cambridge. Harvard, Business School
MHi	Massachusetts. Boston. Massachusetts Historical Society
MSaE	Massachusetts. Salem. Essex Institute
MShM	Massachusetts. South Hadley. Mount Holyoke College
MWA	Massachusetts. Worcester. American Antiquarian Society
MWH	Massachusetts. Worcester. College of the Holy Cross
MWiW-C	Massachusetts. Williamstown. Chapin Library, Williams College
MiD	Michigan. Detroit. Public Library

MiU-C	Michigan. Ann Arbor. William L. Clements
MiU	Michigan. Ann Arbor. University of Michigan
MnU	Minnesota. Minneapolis. University of Minnesota
MoU	Missouri. Columbia. University of Misssourri
N	New York. Albany. New York State Library
NBL	New York. Brooklyn. Brooklyn Law School
NC	North Carolina. Raleigh. State Library
NcD	North Carolina. Durham. Duke University
NcU	North Carolina. Chapel Hill. University of North Carolina
Nh	New Hampshire State Library
NjP	New Jersey. Princeton. Princeton University
NjPT	New Jersey. Princeton Theological Seminary
NjR	New Jersey. Rutgers University
NHC	New York. Hamilton. Colgate University
NHi	New York. New York City. New-York Historical Society
NIC	New York. Ithaca. Cornell University
NN	New York. New York City. New York Public
NN-RB	New York. New York City. New York Public - Rare books
NNBG	New York. New York City. Botanical Gardens
NNC	New York. New York City. Columbia University
NNG	New York. New York City. General Theological Seminary
NNH	New York. New York City. Hispanic Society of America
NNNAM	New York. New York City. New York Academy of Medicine
NNPM	New York. New York City. Pierpoint Morgan
NNU	New York. New York City. New York University
NNUT	New York. New York City. Union Theological Seminary
NPV	New York. Poughkeepsie. Vassar College
NRCR	New York. Rochester. Colgate Rochester Divinity School
NRU	New York. Rochester. University of Rochester
NRU-M	New York. Rochester. University of Rochester. Medical
O	Ohio. Ohio State University
OC	Ohio. Cincinnati. Public Library
OCH	Ohio. Cincinnati. Hebrew Union College
OChHi	Ohio. Ross County Historical Society
OCl	Ohio. Cleveland. Public Library
OClW-Hi	Ohio. Western Reserve Historical Society
OClW	Ohio. Case Western Reserve University
OClWHi	Ohio. Cleveland. Western Reserve Historical Society
OCU	Ohio. Cincinnati. University of Cincinnati
OHU	Ohio. Hebrew Union College
OO	Ohio. Oberlin. Oberlin College
OU	Ohio. Columbus. Ohio State University
OkTG	Oklahoma. Tulsa. Thomas Gilcrease Foundation
OkU	Oklahoma University. Tulsa
OrU	Oregon. Eugene. University of Oregon
P	Pennsylvania State Library

PBL	Pennsylvania. Lehigh. Lehigh University
PHC	Pennsylvania. Haverford. Haverford College
PHi	Pennsylvania. Philadelphia. Pennsylvania Historical Society
PL	Pennsylvania. Lancaster. County Library
PP	Pennsylvania. Philadelphia. Free Library of Philadelphia
PPAmP	Pennsylvania. Philadelphia. American Philosophical Society
PPAN	Pennsylvania. Philadelphia. Pennsylvania Academy of Natural
PPC	Pennsylvania. Philadelphia. College of Physicians
PPJ	Pennsylvania. Philadelphia. Jefferson Medical College
PPl	Pennsylvania. Philadelphia. Library Company of Philadelphia
PPL	Pennsylvania. Philadelphia. Library Company of Philadelphia
PPPrHi	Pennsylvania. Philadelphia. Presbyterian Historical Society
PPRF	Pennsylvania. Philadelphia. Rosenbach
PPULC	Pennsylvania. Philadelphia Union Library Catalog
PSC-Hi	Pennsylvania. Swarthmore. Friends Historical Society
PSC	Pennsylvania. Swarthmore. Swarthmore College
PSt	Pennsylvania. University Park. Pennsylvania State
PU	Pennsylvania. Philadelphia. University of Pennsylvania
PU-L	Pennsylvania. University of Pennsylvania
R	Rhode Island State Library
RHi	Rhode Island. Providence. Rhode Island Historical Society
RPB	Rhode Island. Providence. Brown University
RPJCB	Rhode Island. Providence. John Carter Brown
ScCC	South Carolina. Charlestown. College of Charleston
TNF	Tennessee. Nashville. Fiske University
TxDaM-P	Texas. Southern Methodist University
TxHU	Texas. Houston Public
TxU	Texas. Austin. University of Texas
Vi	Virginia. Richmond. Virginia State Library
ViRA	Virginia. Richmond. Virginia Academy of Medicine
ViU	Virginia. Charlottesville. University of Virginia
ViW	Virginia. Williamsburgh. William and Mary College
ViWC	Virginia. Williamsburgh. Colonial Williamsburgh
WU	Wisconsin. Madison. University of Wisconsin

A VOYAGE INTO NEVV-ENGLAND.

CHAP. I.

Containes my discouery of diuerse Riuers and Harbours, with their names, and which are fit for Plantations, and which not.

THe first place I set my foote vpon in *New England*, was the Iles of *Shoulds*, being Ilands in the Sea, about two Leagues from the Mayne.

Vpon these Ilands, I neither could see one good timber tree, nor so much good ground as to make a garden.

The place is found to be a good fishing place for 6. Shippes, but more cannot well be there: for want of convenient stage-roome, as this yeares experience hath proued.

The Harbour is but indifferent good. Vpon these Ilands are no Savages at all.

The next place I came vnto was *Pannaway*, where one *M. Tomson* hath made a Plantation, there I stayed about one Moneth, in which time, I sent for my men from the East: who came over in diverse Shipps.

At this place I met with the Governour, who came thi-

British Imprints Relating to North America 1621–1760

CHRONOLOGICAL CHECKLIST

1621#1
ENGLAND AND WALES. SOVEREIGN. JAMES I. *A proclamation for suppressing the lottery in Virginia and all others...* [8 March 1621]. London. B. Norton and J. Bill. s.sh. F. [1620/1]
Note: SABIN 99843, STC 8660, LARKIN I, 212, EA 621/49.
Locations: Lsa; RPJCB, CSmH

1621#2
ENGLAND AND WALES. SOVEREIGN. JAMES I. *Whereas wee are credibly informed...* London. For R. Wood, etc. s.sh. F. 1621
Note: Brief for wife of Capt. Henry Challons, captured by Spanish en route for Virginia. STC 8652, STEELE 8562, EA 621/48.
Locations: Lsa

1621#3
HEYLYN, Peter. *Microcosmus; or A little description of the great world...* Oxford. J. Lichfield and J. Short, [417]p. 4to. 1621
Note: SABIN 31656, STC 13276, EA 621/55. Other editions Oxford, 1625, 1627, 1629, 1631, 1633, 1636, 1639, EA 625/117, 627/60, 629/74, 631/55, 633/58, 636/35, 639/62–3. See also Heylyn, *Cosmographie*, below, 1652.
Locations: L; RPJCB, CSmH

1621#4
SCOTT, Thomas. *A relation of some speciall points concerning the state of Holland...* London. E. Allde, 19p. 4to. 1621
Note: STC 22083, EA 621/113. Title page states 'The Hague' but a London imprint. Translated from Dutch. Mentions Dutch West India Company.
Locations: L; CSmH, DFo, MH

1621#5
SPARKE, Michael. *Greevous grones for the poore. Done by a well-wisher, who wisheth, that the poore of England might be so provided for, as none should neede to go a begging within this realme...* London. [28]p. 4to. 1621
Note: SABIN 88961, STC 12391, EA 621/51. Sometimes attributed to Thomas Deller. Dedicated to and issued in the interests of the Virginia Company.
Locations: ICN, MiU-C

1621#6
A true relation of of [sic] *a wonderfull sea fight betweene two... Spanish ships... and a small... English ship... in her passage to Virginia...* London. For N. B[utter], 21p. 8vo. 1621
Note: SABIN 97140, STC 22130, EA 621/133. Also, in 1621, an abridgement, *A notable and wonderfull sea-fight...* L; CSmH (EA 621/91).
Locations: CSmH, ViU

1621#7
UNITED PROVINCES. STATES GENERAL. *Orders and articles granted by the... States General of the United Provinces, concerning the erecting of a West India Companie...* London. 18p. 4to. 1621
Note: SABIN 57498, STC 18460, EA 621/76.
Locations: L; CSmH

1621

1621#8
UNITED PROVINCES. STATES GENERAL.
Letters patent graunted by the states of the United Netherlands Provinces, to the West Indian company of merchants... London or the Hague, s.sh. F. [1621]
Note: STC 18459.5.
Locations: L;

1621#9
VIRGINIA COMPANY. *A note of the shipping, men, and provisions, sent and provided for Virginia, by... Earle of Southampton and the Company, this yeare, 1620.* [London]. p. 3p. 4to. [1621]
Note: SABIN 55947, STC 24842a, EA 621/139.
Locations: L; NN

1621#10
WINNE, Edward. *A letetr [sic] written... to Sir G. Calvert his Majesties principall secretary: from Feryland in Newfoundland...* London. B. Alsop, 21p. 8vo. 1621
Note: SABIN 104786, STC 25854, EA 621/140. Contains an account of the country.
Locations: L; NIC

1622#1
BACON, Francis. *The historie of the raigne of King Henry the seventh.* 1622 London. W. Stansby, 248p. F.
Note: STC 1159–60, EA 622/10. For many subsequent English and Latin editions see EA and WING. Cabot and North America.
Locations: L; CSmH, NiU-C, DLC

1622#2
BONOEIL, John. *His majesties gracious letter to the Earle of South-hampton, treasurer, and to the Councell and Company of Virginia heere: commanding the present setting up of silke works, and planting of vines in Virginia...* London. F. Kyngston, [12], 88p. 4to. 1622
Note: SABIN 31998, 99886, STC 14378, EA 622/2o.
Locations: L; RPJCB

1622#3
BRERERWOOD, Edward. *Enquiries touching the diversity of languages and religions through the chief parts of the world...* London. J. Bill, 203p. 4to. 1622
Note: SABIN 7732, STC 3619, EA 622/24. First edition, 1614. Other editions 1624, 1635 (EA 635/30), 1674.
Locations: L; RPJCB

1622#4
BRINSLEY, John. *Consolation for our grammar schooles, or a Comfortable encouragement for laying of a sure foundation of all good learning... More specially for all those of an inferiour sort... for Ireland, Wales, Virginia...* London. R. Field for T. Man, 84p. 4to. 1622

Note: SABIN 7996, 16037, STC 3767, EA 622/25.
Locations: L; RPJCB

1622#5
BROOKE, Christopher. *A poem on the late massacre in Virginia. With particular mention of those men of note that suffered in that disaster.* London. G. Eld for R. Milbourne, 23p. 4to. 1622
Note: SABIN 100510, EA 622/26.
Locations: Lpro; OkTG

1622#6
COOKE, John. *Greene's Tu quoque, or the cittie gallant.* London. T. Dewe, 87p. 4to. 1622
Note: First published 1614. STC 5674–5, EA 622/39. Also 1627 or 1628, EA 628/36. Mentions Virginia.
Locations: L; MH, CSmH, DFo

1622#7
COPLAND, Patrick. *A declaration how the monies... were disposed, which was gathered (by Mr Patrick Copland...)... (towards the building of a free schoole in Virginia)...* London. F. K., 7p. 4to. 1622
Note: SABIN 99884, STC 5726, EA 622/40.
Locations: Lpro; CSmH

1622#8
COPLAND, Patrick. *Virginia's God be thanked, or A sermon of thanksgiving for the happie successe of the affayres in Virginia this last yeare. Preached by Patrick Copland... 18. of April 1622...* London. J. D. for W. Sheffard and J. Bellamie, 36p. 4to. 1622
Note: SABIN 16691, STC 5727, EA 622/41.
Locations: L; RPJCB

1622#9
COUNCIL FOR NEW ENGLAND. *A brief relation of the discovery and plantation of New-England: and of sundry accidents therein occurring...* London. J. Haviland for W. Bladen, 36p. 4to. 1622
Note: SABIN 52619, STC 18483, EA 622/44. Treats the years 1607–1622. Reprinted in 1627 as *A historical discoverie and relation...*, EA 627/32: (L;).
Locations: L; RPJCB, DFo, CSmH

1622#10
CUSHMAN, Robert. *A sermon preached at Plimmoth in New-England December 9. 1621 in an assemblie of his majesties faithfull subjects, there inhabiting... with a preface, shewing the state of the country, and condition of the savages...* London. J. D. for J. Bellamie, 19p. 4to. 1622
Note: SABIN 18132, STC 6149, EA 622/45.
Locations: O; RPJCB

1622#11
DONNE, John. *A sermon upon the VIII. verse of the I. chapter of the Actes of the Apostles. Preached to the*

honourable company of the Virginian plantation. London. A. Mat[thewes] for T. Jones, 49p. 4to. 1622
Note: SABIN 20601, STC 7051–2, EA 622/49. Sermon preached on 13 November 1622. Reprinted twice in 1624 in his *Three sermons*. . . (EA 624/49 and EA 624/50).
Locations: L; RPJCB

1622#12
DRAYTON, Michael. *A chorographicall description of. . . Great Britain. . . Digested into a poem. . .* London. J. Marriott, etc, 303p. F. 1622
Note: STC 7228, EA 622/50. First published in 1612 as *Poly-Olbion*. Mentions Madoc and America.
Locations: L; CSmH, DLC, CtY

1622#13
ENGLAND AND WALES. SOVEREIGN. JAMES I. *By the King. A proclamation prohibiting interloping and disorderly trading to New England in America. . . the sixty [sic] of November. . . [1622].* London. B. Norton and J. Bill, s.sh. F. 1622
Note: STC 8692, LARKIN I, 233, EA 622/61.
Locations: L; RPJCB

1622#14
FOTHERBY, Martin. *Atheomastix clearing foure truthes against atheists.* London. N. Okes, 362p. F. 1622
Note: STC 11205, EA 622/56. Refers to Indians, New Albion, etc.
Locations: L; CSmH, DLC, CtY

1622#15
MALYNES, Gerard. *The maintenance of free trade.* London. J. Legat for W. Sheffard, 105p. 8vo. 1622
Note: STC 17226, KRESS 391, EA 622/81. Limits on imports of Spanish tobacco may help Virginia and Bermudas.
Locations: L; CtY, MH-BA

1622#16
MISSELDEN, Edward. *Free trade. or, The meanes to make trade flourish.* London. J. Legat for S. Waterson, 134p. 8vo. 1622
Note: STC 17986–7, KRESS 392, EA 622/89–90. Mentions Virginia and tobacco. Another edition in 1622: L; DFo, MH, CtY.
Locations: C; Oc;

1622#17
Mourning Virginia. London. H. Gosson. [1622]
Note: SABIN 100489, EA 622/92.
Locations: NO COPY LOCATED.

1622#18
More excellent observations of the estate and affaires of Holland. . . London. E. A. for N. Bourne and J. Archer, 37p. 4to. 1622
Note: STC 13573, SABIN 102898, EA 622/91. Translated from Dutch. Trade to America and Dutch West India Company.
Locations: L; RPJCB, CSmH

1622#19
Mourt's relation. A relation or journall of the beginning and proceedings of the English plantation setled at Plimoth in New England, by certaine English adventurers both merchants and others. . . London. J. Bellamie, 72p. 4to. 1622
Note: SABIN 51198, STC 10074, EA 622/93. Edited by George Mourt (or Morton).
Locations: L; DLC, MiU-C, CSmH

1622#20
SCOT, Thomas. *Phylomythie or phylomythologie. . . Second edition, much inlarged.* London. J. Legat for F. Constable 2pts, 8vo. 1622
Note: STC 21871, 21871a, EA 622/129–30. Mentions America and tobacco. Another edition in 1622. First published in 1616.
Locations: L; CSmH, DFo, MH

1622#21
SMITH, John. *New Englands trials. Declaring the successe of 80 ships employed thither within these eight yeares. . . With the present estate of that happie plantation, begun but by 60 weake men in the year 1620. . .* London. W. Jones, 32p. 4to. 1622
Note: SABIN 82835, STC 22793, EA 622/138. Second edition; first printed in 1620.
Locations: L; RPJCB

1622#22
VIRGINIA COMPANY. *The inconveniencies that have happened to some persons which transported themselves from England to Virginia, without provisions necessary to sustaine themselves. . .* London. F. Kyngston, s.sh. F. 1622
Note: SABIN 99887, STC 24844, EA 622/75.
Locations: L; RPJCB, MiU-C

1622#23
VIRGINIA COMPANY. *A note of the shipping, men, and provisions, sent and provided for Virginia, by. . . Earle of Southampton, and the Company, and other private adventurers, in the yeere 1621. . .* London. 4p. F. [1622]
Note: SABIN 99888, STC 24843, EA 622/166.
Locations: Lsa; NN, CSmH

1622#24
WATERHOUSE, Edward. *A declaration of the state of the colony and affaires in Virginia. With a relation of the barbarous massacre in the time of peace. . . treacherously executed by the native infidels upon the English, the 22 of*

March last... London. G. Eld for R. Mylbourne, 54p. 4to. 1622
Note: SABIN 99885, STC 25104, EA 622/170. With an account of North-West passage, etc.
Locations: L; DLC, RPJCB

1622#25
WHITBOURNE, Sir Richard. *The copy of a reference... [12 April 1622]* London. F. Kingston, [4]p. 4to. [1622]
Note: STC 25375a2. Reference from James I and others allowing Whitbourne to collect money. Cf. also Bishop's briefs for the same, 1622–3, (STC 25375.a.4–25375.a.8.).
Locations: L; CSmH

1622#26
WHITBOURNE, Sir Richard. *A discourse and discovery of New-found-land, with many reasons how a plantation may there be made...* London. F. Kingston, 107p. 4to. 1622
Note: SABIN 103331–2, STC 25373, 25373a, BAER 2, 3, EA 622/171. An expanded reissue of first edition of 1620. Another issue in 1623 (EA 623/152).
Locations: L; O; DFo, CSmH

1622#27
WHITBOURNE, Sir Richard. *A discourse containing a loving invitation... to all such as shall be adventurers, either in person, or purse, for the advancement of his Majesties most helpfull plantation in the New-found-land, lately undertaken...* London. F. Kyngston, 46p. 4to. 1622
Note: SABIN 103333, STC 25375, EA 622/172–3. Another issue with additions relating to Maryland in 1622: L; CSmH, DFo.
Locations: Dt; MiU-C

1623#1
A., W. *A letter from W. A., a minister in Virginia, to his friend T. B., merchant, of Gracious street, London, declaring the advantages to those minded to transport themselves thither.* London. 8p. 4to. 1623
Note: SABIN 40349, EA 623/64.
Locations: NO COPY LOCATED.

1623#2
BACON, Francis. *Historia vitae & mortis.* London. J. Haviland for M. Lownes, 454p. 8vo. 1623
Note: STC 1156, EA 623/7. Mentions Virginia, etc. Two different translations in 1638, STC 1157, 1158, EA 638/9–10.
Locations: L; DLC, CtY, CSmH

1623#3
C., T. *A short discourse of the New-found-land; Contaynig [sic] diverse reasons and inducements, for the planting of that countrey...* Dublin. Society of Stationers, 30p. 4to. 1623
Note: SABIN 80620, STC 4311, EA 623/131.
Locations: L; RPJCB

1623#4
SCOTT, Thomas. *The Belgicke pismire.* London. J. Dawson, [12]p. 4to. 1623
Note: SABIN 78358, STC 22070, EA 623/122. Mentions colonies, new world Indians, and danger of war spreading to Asia, Africa, and America.
Locations: L; CSmH, DFo

1623#5
SCOTT, Thomas. *An experimentall discoverie of Spanish practises or the counsell of a well-wishing soldier.* London. 54p. 4to. 1623
Note: STC 22077, EA 623/123–6. Four issues in 1623. Mentions Drake, Cabot etc. A second edition in 1624.
Locations: L; DFo

1623#6
SMITH, John. *The generall history of Virginia, the Somer Iles, and New England, with the names of the adventurers, and their adventures...* London. [J. Dawson]. [4]p. F. [1623]
Note: SABIN 82823, STC 22789, EA 623/133. A prospectus.
Locations: Lsa; DLC

1624#1
ABBOT, George. *A briefe description of the whole worlde...* London. J. Marriot, [174]p. 4to. 1624
Note: SABIN 21, STC 30, WING A60–2, EA 624/1. Other editions 1634, 1635, 1636, 1642, 1664, 1656. EA 634/1, 635/1, 636/1, 642/1. First published 1599. Contains section 'Of the northerne part of America'.
Locations: L; DLC, MBAt, NN

1624#2
ALEXANDER, William, 1st Earl of Stirling. *An encouragement to colonies.* London. W. Stansby, 47p. 4to. 1624
Note: SABIN 739, 91853, STC 341, 341a, EA 624/156. Reissued in 1630, as *The mapp and description of New-England...* (STC 342, EA 630/174): L; CSmH.
Locations: L; CSmH

1624#3
Boanerges. or The humble supplication *of the ministers of Scotland.* London. 34p. 4to. 1624
Note: STC 3171, 3171.3, EA 624/20, 21. Place of publication stated as 'Edenburgh' but EA states to be London. Impact of Spanish tobacco sales on Virginia. Another issue in 1624.
Locations: L; CSmH, CtY, DFo

1624#4
EBURNE, Richard. *A plaine path-way to plantations.* London. G. P[urslowe] for J. Marriot, [120]p. 4to. 1624
Note: SABIN 21752, STC 7471, EA 624/53.
Locations: Lrag; CSmH, RPJCB

1624#5
ENGLAND AND WALES. COMMISSIONERS FOR VIRGINIA. *By his majesties commissioners for Virginia...* London. F. Kingston, s.sh. F. 1624
Note: STC 24844.3, EA 624/64. Notice for weekly sittings for advice on emigration and trade.
Locations: L; DLC

1624#6
ENGLAND AND WALES. SOVEREIGN. JAMES I. *By the King. A proclamation concerning tobacco.* London. B. Norton and J. Bill, 4p. F. 1624
Note: SABIN 99844, STC 8738–9, STEELE 1385, LARKIN I, 257, EA 624/65–6. Another edition in 1624: Lsa
Locations: L; RPJCB, CSmH

1624#7
Good newes from Virginia, sent from James his towne this present moneth of March, 1623, by a gentleman in that country. To the tune of, All those that be good fellowes. London. J. Trundle, [2]p. F. [1623/4?]
Note: STC 24830. 2. EA 624/63 dates to 1624.
Locations: Lpro;

1624#8
GUNTER, Edmund. *The description and use of his Majesties dials in White-Hall Garden.* London. B. Norton and J. Bill, 59p. 4to. 1624
Note: STC 12524, EA 624/68. Mentions time difference with Virginia.
Locations: L; RPJCB, DFo, CSmH

1624#9
LEVETT, Christopher. *A voyage into New-England begun in 1623 and ended in 1624. Performed by Christopher Levett, his majesties woodward of Somersetshire, and one of the Councell of New England...* London. W. Jones, 38p. 4to. 1624
Note: SABIN 40751, STC 15553.5, EA 624/77. Another issue, 1628, (EA 628/66): L; RPJCB.
Locations: L;

1624#10
SCOTLAND. PRIVY COUNCIL. *Proclamation on institution of Nova Scotia baronets.* [Edinburgh]. 1624
Note: STEELE 1413, EA 624/123.
Locations: NO COPY LOCATED.

1624#11
SMITH, John. *The generall historie of Virginia, New-England, and the Summer Isles...* London. J. D. and J. H. for M. Sparke, 248p. F. 1624
Note: SABIN 82823–82830, STC 22790, BAER 7, EA 624/152. Other editions in 1625, 1626, 1627, 1631, 1632. See STC 22790a, 22790b, 22790c, 22790c. 5, 22790d, EA 625/210, 626/128, 631/102, 632/99.
Locations: L; MiU-C

1624#12
WINSLOW, Edward. *Good newes from New-England: or A true relation of things very remarkable at... Plimoth.* London. J. D. for W. Bladen and J. Bellamy, [67]p. 4to. 1624
Note: STC 25855–6, SABIN 104795, EA 624/174–5. Another issue in 1624.
Locations: L; CSmH, CtY, RPJCB

1625#1
BACON, Francis. *The essayes or counsels, civill and morall...* London. J. Haviland for H. Barret, 340p. 4to. 1625
Note: STC 1147–8, WING B283–296, EA 625/12–13. 'Of Plantations' included. Two issues in 1625. Later editions 1629, 1632, 1639, 1642, 1163, 1664, 1669, 1673, 1680, 1689, 1691, 1696, 1701, etc. EA 629/11, 632/8, 639/6, 642/8, 701/22–5.
Locations: L; DLC, ICN, MH

1625#2
DITCHFIELD, Master. *Considerations touching the new contract for tobacco, as the same hath been propounded by Maister Ditchfield, and other undertakers.* London. 11p. 4to. 1625
Note: SABIN 20328, STC 6918, EA 625/68.
Locations: L; CSmH

1625#3
DU BARTAS, Guillaume de Salluste. *Part of Du Bartas, English and French... Englished...* London. J. Haviland, [273]p. 4to. 1625
Note: STC 21663, EA 625/73. Section on colonies.
Locations: L; DFo, CSmH, CtY

1625#4
ENGLAND AND WALES. SOVEREIGN. CHARLES I. *A proclamation for setling the plantation of Virginia.* London. B. Norton and J. Bill, 2p. F. 1625
Note: SABIN 99848, STC 8774–5, LARKIN II, 10, EA 625/105–6. Another edition in 1625: Lsa
Locations: L; DFo, CSmH

1625#5
ENGLAND AND WALES. SOVEREIGN. CHARLES I. *A proclamation touching tobacco.* London. B. Norton and J. Bill, 2p. F. 1625
Note: SABIN 99846, STC 8767, LARKIN II, 6, EA 625/108.
Locations: L; DFo

1625#6
ENGLAND AND WALES. SOVEREIGN. JAMES I. *A Proclamation. For the utter prohibiting the importation of. . . all tobacco. . . not of. . . Virginia and the Summer Islands. . .* London. B. Norton and J. Bill, 4p. F. [1624/5]
Note: SABIN 99845, STC 8751, LARKIN I, 265, EA 625/107.
Locations: L; CSmH

1625#7
GORDON, Robert. *Encouragements. For such as shall have intention to bee under-takers in the new plantations of Cape Breton. . .* Edinburgh. J. Wreittoun, 34p. 4to. 1625
Note: SABIN 27967, STC 12069, EA 625/100.
Locations: L; RPJCB, CSmH

1625#8
HAGTHORPE, John. *England's-exchequer. or A discourse of the sea. . .* London. M. Flesher for N. Butter and N. Bourne, 49p. 4to. 1625
Note: SABIN 29522, STC 12603, EA 625/113. Commodities and colonies.
Locations: L; CSmH

1625#9
LESCARBOT, Marc. *Nova Francia, or the description of that part of New France, which is one continent with Virginia. . .* London. A. Hebb, 307p. 4to. [1625]
Note: SABIN 40176, STC 15492, EA 625/128. First published in 1609.
Locations: L; CSmH

1625#10
MORRELL, William. *New-England, or a brief enarration of the ayre, earth, water, fish and fowles of that country. . . in Latine and English verse.* London. J. D[awson] 24p. 4to. 1625
Note: SABIN 50786, STC 18169, EA 625/155. With description of the natives.
Locations: L; CSmH

1625#11
PURCHAS, Samuel. *Purchas his pilgrimes.* London. W. Stansby for H. Fetherstone, 4 vols. F. 1625
Note: SABIN 66683, 66686, STC 20509, BAER 8, EA 625/173. Also with title *Hakluytus posthumus, or Purchas his pilgrimes.*
Locations: L; DLC, RPJCB, CSmH

1625#12
SCOTLAND. PRIVY COUNCIL. *Proclamation completing number of Nova Scotia baronets.* [Edinburgh]. 1625
Note: STEELE 1432, EA 625/199.
Locations: NO COPY LOCATED.

1625#13
VAUGHAN, William. *Cambrensium Caroleia. . .* London. G. Stansbeius, 110p. 8vo. 1625
Note: SABIN 98691, STC 24604–5, BAER 10, EA 625/246. Latin poems, some dedicated to Baltimore. Newfoundland map.
Locations: L; DFo, CSmH

1626#1
PURCHAS, Samuel. *Purchase his Pilgrimage. Or Relations of the world and all ages and places discovered.* London. W. Stansby for H. Fetherstone, 1047p. F. 1626
Note: SABIN 66682, STC 20508, 20508. 5. EA 626/100–10l. First published in 1613. A second issue in 1626 (L; RPJCB, MH)
Locations: L; MiU-C, MWiW-C

1626#2
SANDYS, George. *Ovid's Metamorphosis Englished by G. S. . .* London. W. Standsby, 326p. F. 1626
Note: STC 18964, SABIN 76456, EA 626/95. Partly translated by Sandys in Virginia.
Locations: L; RPJCB, DLC, CSmH

1626#3
VAUGHAN, William. *The golden fleece divided into three parts. . . the errours of religion, the vices and decayes of the kingdome. . . the wayes to get wealth, and to restore trading.* London. W. Stansby and others for F. Williams, 4 pts., 4to. 1626
Note: SABIN 98693, STC 24609, KRESS 430, BAER 12, EA 626/143. Newfoundland.
Locations: L; CSmH

1627#1
DRAYTON, Michael. *The battaile of Agincourt.* London. A. Mathews for W. Lee, 218p. F. 1627
Note: STC 7190, EA 627/35. Includes epistle to George Sandys on his departure for Virginia.
Locations: L; DLC, CtY, CSmH

1627#2
ENGLAND AND WALES. SOVEREIGN. CHARLES I. *A proclamation for the ordering of tobacco. . .* London. B. Norton and J. Bill, s.sh. F. 1627
Note: SABIN 99850, STEELE 1516, STC 8864, LARKIN II, 73, EA 627/50.
Locations: L; CSmH, DFo

1627#3
**ENGLAND AND WALES. SOVEREIGN.
CHARLES I.** *A proclamation touching the sealing of tobacco.* London. B. Norton and J. Bill, s.sh. F. 1627
Note: SABIN 65936, 99849, STC 8857, LARKIN II, 66, STEELE 1509. EA 627/51.
Locations: L; CSmH

1627#4
**ENGLAND AND WALES. SOVEREIGN.
CHARLES I.** *A proclamation touching tobacco.* London. B. Norton and J. Bill, 3p. F. [1626/7]
Note: SABIN 99848, STC 8853, LARKIN, II, 63, STEELE 1505, EA 627/52.
Locations: L; DFo, CSmH, MH-BA

1627#5
PURCHAS, Samuel. *Purchas his pilgrim. Microcosmus, or The historie of man.* London. 818p. 8vo. 1627
Note: SABIN 66677n, STC 20504, EA 627/92. Mention of Indians; nothing directly North American; first published 1619.
Locations: L; RPJCB, CtY

1627#6
SMITH, John. *A sea grammar, with the plaine exposition of Smith's Accidence for young seamen enlarged...* London. J. Haviland, 86p. 8vo. 1627
Note: STC 22794, SABIN 82839, EA 627/108. References to North American Indians.
Locations: O; RPJCB, CSmH, NN

1627#7
SPEED, John. *A prospect of the most famous parts of the world. Together with that large theater of Great Brittaines empire.* London. J. Dawson for G. Humble, [86]p. F. 1627
Note: SABIN 89228n, STC 23039g.7, 23040, EA 627/110. Other editions in 1631 and 1646. EA 631/107, 646/142-3.
Locations: L; C; MH, DLC

1628#1
HAYMAN, Robert. *Quodlibets, lately come over from New Britaniola, Old Newfound-land. Epigrams and other small parcels, both morall and divine... All of them composed and done at Harbor-Grace in Britaniola, anciently called Newfound-land.* London. Elizabeth All-de for R. Mitchell, 64p. 4to. 1628
Note: SABIN 31037, STC 12974, EA 628/55.
Locations: L; DLC, MiU-C

1629#1
Leather: a discourse, tendered to *the high court of Parliament...* London. T. C. for M. Sparke, 27p. 4to. 1629
Note: STC 15344, EA 629/82. Mentions Virginia, Newfoundland.
Locations: L; CSmH, CtY, DFo

1629#2
PARKINSON, John. *Paradisi in sole paradisus terrestris...* London. H. Lownes and R. Young, 612p. F. 1629
Note: STC 19300, WING P495, EA 629/121. A garden of flowers. Many American plants. Later editions 1635, 1656.
Locations: L; O; C; CSmH, MH

1630#1
COTTON, John. *God's promise to His plantation, 2 Sam. 7. 10; in a sermon.* London. W. Jones, 20p. 4to. 1630
Note: SABIN 17065, STC 5854, EA 630/49, 634/44. Another edition in 1634.
Locations: L; DLC, NN

1630#2
COUNCIL FOR NEW ENGLAND. *A proposition of provisions needfull for such as intend to plant themselves in New England, for one whole yeare. Collected by the adventurers, with the advice of the planters.* London. F. Clifton, s.sh. F. 1630
Note: SABIN 66013, STC 18486, EA 630/134.
Locations: L; LNC;

1630#3
**ENGLAND AND WALES. SOVEREIGN.
CHARLES I.** *A proclamation forbidding the disorderly trading with the salvages in New England...* London. R. Barker, etc. 2p. F. 1630
Note: SABIN 65938, STC 8969, LARKIN, II, 142, STEELE 1627, EA 630/76.
Locations: L; MH, CSmH

1630#4
GOODALL, Baptist. *The tryall of travell... In three bookes epitomized...* London. J. Upton, 80p. 4to. 1630
Note: SABIN 27842, STC 12007, EA 630/75. Another edition in 1639, EA 639/45. References to American discoverers, etc.
Locations: L; DLC, MiU-C

1630#5
HIGGINSON, Francis. *New-Englands plantation. Or, A short and true description of that countrey...* London. T. C. and R. C. for M. Sparke, 4to. 1630
Note: SABIN 31739, 31740, STC 13449-51, EA 630/80-2. Second issue (DM; CSmH) and a third issue with additions (L; CSmH, ICN) in 1630.
Locations: O; CSmH, MWiW-C; RPJCB

1630

1630#6
PHILLIPS, George?. *The humble request of his majesties loyall subjects, the governour and company late gone for New-England; to the rest of their brethren, in and of the Church of England...* London. J. Bellamie, 10p. 4to. 1630
Note: SABIN 104846, STC 18485, EA 630/101.
Locations: O; DLC, RPJCB

1630#7
SHARPE, Edward. *England's royall fishing revived.* London. W. J. for N. Bourne [47]p. 4to. 1630
Note: STC 21487, KRESS 470, EA 630/160. Mentions Virginia timber. First published 1615 as *Britaines busse...*
Locations: Lg; DLC, MH, CSmH

1630#8
SMITH, John. *The true travels, adventures, and observations of Captaine John Smith, in Europe, Asia, Affrika, and America, from anno Domini 1593. to 1629...* London. J. H. for T. Slater, 60p. F. 1630
Note: SABIN 82851, 82852, STC 22796, EA 630/162.
Locations: L; RPJCB, MiU-C

1630#9
TAYLOR, John. *All the workes of John Taylor the Water-poet...* London. J. Beale, etc. for J. Boler, 2pts. F. 1630
Note: STC 23725, EA 630/178. Virginia, Powhatan, etc. mentioned.
Locations: L; CSmH, DLC, MH

1630#10
VAUGHAN, William. *The Newlanders cure. As well of those violent sicknesses... as also by a cheape and new-found dyet, to preserve the body sound and free from all diseases...* London. N. O. for F. Constable, 143p. 8vo. 1630
Note: SABIN 98694, STC 24619, BAER 16, EA 630/194.
Locations: L; RPJCB

1630#11
WHITE, John. *The planters plea. Or the grounds of plantations examined, and usual objections answered. Together with a manifestation of the causes mooving such as have lately undertaken a plantation in New-England...* London. W. Jones, 84p. 4to. 1630
Note: SABIN 17075, 103396, STC 25399, EA 630/216.
Locations: L; RPJCB, MiU-C

1631#1
ENGLAND AND WALES. SOVEREIGN. CHARLES I. *A proclamation concerning tobacco...* London. R. Barker, 2p. F. [1630/1]
Note: SABIN 99851, STC 8971, LARKIN, II, 144, EA 631/45.
Locations: L; NN, CSmH

1631#2
LLOYD, David. *The legend of captaine Jones.* London. R. Young for J. M., 163p. 4to. 1631
Note: Cf SABIN 41683. STC 16614, WING L2630–35, EA 631/64, 648/91. Also 1648 (continued from the first part), 1656, 1659, 1671. Verse satire on Captain John Smith. Mentions Virginia, etc. See Alden T. Vaughan, 'John Smith Satirized...' *William and Mary Quarterly*, October, 1988, 712–732.
Locations: L; MH

1631#3
SMITH, John. *Advertisements for the unexperienced planters of New-England, or any where. Or, the path-way to experience to erect a plantation.* London. J. Haviland, 40p. 4to. 1631
Note: SABIN 82815, STC 22787, EA 631/101.
Locations: L; RPJCB, MiU-C

1631#4
STOW, John. *The annales... of England... Continued unto 1631. By Edmund Howes.* London. J. Beale, etc. for R. Meighen, 1087p. F. 1631
Note: STC 23340, EA 631/109. Account of Virginia.
Locations: L; DLC, MH, MnU

1632#1
HOOKER, Thomas. *The soules preparation for Christ, or a treatise of contrition...* London. M. F. for R. Dawlman, 456p. 4to. 1632
Note: SABIN 32856, STC 13735–8. Other seventeenth-century editions in 1635, 1638, 1643, 1658.
Locations: L; O; C;

1633#1
GERARD, John. *The herball or Generall historie of plantes... very much enlarged and amended by Thomas Johnson.* London. A. Islip, etc. 1630p. F. 1633
Note: STC 11751, EA 633/39, 636/25. First published 1597; reissued 1636.
Locations: L; DLC, MH, CtY

1633#2
HERBERT, George. *The temple...* Cambridge. T. Buck, R. Daniel, 4, 192p. 12mo. 1633
Note: SABIN 31457, STC 13183, WING M1516–1524. Second edition and two other variants, Cambridge, 1633. Also Cambridge, 1635, 1641, 1638 and eight London issues 1647–1695. Contains 'The Church Militant...' - Christianity passing to and the '*American* strand'.
Locations: L; CSmH

1633#3
JAMES, Thomas. *The strange and dangerous voyage of Captaine Thomas James, in his intended discovery of the Northwest Passage into the South Sea...* London. I. Legatt for I. Partridge, 230, [22]p. 4to. 1633

Note: SABIN 35711, STC 14444, EA 633/62. Another edition in 1740, SABIN 35712, EA 740/169.
Locations: L; MiU-C

1633#4
NASH, Thomas. *Quaternio, or A fourefold way to a happie life...* London. J. Dawson, 280p. 4to. 1633
Note: STC 18382, EA 633/83. Some American references.
Locations: L; CSmH, CtY, MH

1633#5
SCOTLAND. PARLIAMENT. *The acts made in the first parliament of our... soveraigne Charles... at Edinburgh...* Edinburgh. R. Young, 66p. F. 1633
Note: STC 21902, EA 633/110. Act xxviii relates to Earl of Stirling and Nova Scotia. Reissued in 1640s. See EA 64-/11.
Locations: L; CSmH, DLC, MH

1633#6
WHITE, Andrew. *A declaration of the Lord Baltemore's plantation in Mary-land, nigh upon Virginia: manifesting the nature, quality, condition, and rich utilities it contayneth.* London. B. Alsop and T. Fawcet, 8p. 4to. 1633
Note: SABIN 1033351, STC 25375a, EA 633/128. Cf. BAER 2o.
Locations: WARE;

1634#1
ENGLAND AND WALES. SOVEREIGN. CHARLES I. *A commission for the well governing of our people, inhabiting in New-found-land...* London. R. Barker, etc, 22p. 4to. [1633/4]
Note: STC 9255, EA 634/59.
Locations: L; DFo, DLC, RPJCB

1634#2
ENGLAND AND WALES. SOVEREIGN. CHARLES I. *A proclamation concerning tobacco...* London. R. Barker, etc. 2p. F. 1634
Note: STC 9016, LARKIN, II,184, EA 634/60.
Locations: L;

1634#3
ENGLAND AND WALES. SOVEREIGN. CHARLES I. *A proclamation restraining the abusive venting of tobacco...* London. R. Barker, etc. s.sh. F. [1633/34]
Note: STC 9011-2, LARKIN II, 179, EA 634/61-2. Another edition: Lpro
Locations: L; NN

1634#4
HERBERT, Sir Thomas. *A relation of some yeares travaile, begunne anno 1626...* London. W. Stansby and J. Bloome, 225p. F. 1634

Note: STC 13190, SABIN 31471, EA 634/68. Contains a discourse on Madoc's discovery of America.
Locations: L; RPJCB, CtY DLC

1634#5
MOFFETT, Thomas. *Insectorum, sive minimorum animalium theatrum.* London. T. Cotes and sold by B. Allen, 326p. F. 1634
Note: STC 17993-3a-3b, EA 634/89-91. Scattered American references, including Virginia. Two other issues in 1634.
Locations: L; MH, MiU, NNNAM

1634#6
STAFFORD, Robert. *A geographicall and anthologicall description of all the empires...* London. N. Okes for S. Waterson, 55p. 4to. 1634
Note: STC 23137, EA 634/130. First published in 1607.
Locations: L; RPJCB, CSmH, DLC

1634#7
WHITE, Andrew. *A relation of the successfull beginnings of the Lord Baltemore's plantation in Mary-land... extract of certain letters written from thence... The conditions of plantation propounded by his lordship for the second voyage intended this present yeere, 1634.* London. 14p. 4to. [1634]
Note: SABIN 45316, STC 4371, BAER 21, EA 634/114. Another edition in 1635 with title *A relation of Maryland...* (EA 635/108): L; RPJCB, MiU-C.
Locations: L; DLC, RPJCB

1634#8
WOOD, William. *New Englands prospect. A true, lively, and experimentall description of that part of America, commonly called New England...* London. T. Cotes for J. Bellamie, 98p. 4to. 1634
Note: SABIN 105074, STC 25957-9, EA 634/141. Other issues 1635, 1639, EA 635/134, 639/126.
Locations: L; RPJCB, MiU-C

1634#9
YOUNG, Thomas. *Englands bane: or, The description of drunkennesse.* London. W. Jones for T. Bailey, 24p. 8vo. 1634
Note: STC 26117, EA 634/142. Mentions Virginia Indians and tobacco; first published in 1617.
Locations: L; DFo

1635#1
FOX, Luke. *North-West Fox or, Fox from the North-west passage...* London. B. Alsop and T. Fawcett, 269p. 4to. 1635
Note: SABIN 25410, STC 11221, EA 635/47.
Locations: L; MiU-C

1635#2
PAGITT, Ephraim. *Christianographie. or The description of the multitude and sundry sort of Christians in the world not subject to the Pope*... London. T. Paine, W. Jones for M. Costerden, xxiv, 156, 72p. 4to. 1635
Note: STC 19110–12, EA 634/96. Other editions 1636, 1640, EA 636/73, 640/141 and 1674, WING P173.
Locations: L; RPJCB

1635#3
SELDEN, John. *Mare clausum, seu De dominio maris libri duo*... London. W. Stansby for R. Meighen, 304p. F. 1635
Note: SABIN 78971, STC 22175, KRESS 512, EA 635/114, WING S2431-2. Also 1652, 1663. Reply to Grotius's *Mare liberum*... with some American references.
Locations: L; CSmH, MH, RPJCB

1635#4
SWAN, John. *Speculum mundi. or A glasse representing the face of the world.* Cambridge. T. Buck and R. Daniel, 504p. 4to. 1635
Note: STC 23516, EA 635/116. Also 1643, 1665, 1670, 1698 WING S6238–40A, 1665 and 1670, EA 643/116. Discusses origin of New World and American tobacco areas.
Locations: L; DLC, MH, CSmH

1636#1
HEYLYN, Peter. *A coale from the altar*... London. A. Matthews for R. Milbourne, 78p. 4to. 1636
Note: STC 13270–1. Other editions, 1636, 1637. Answer to letter, supposedly by John Cotton.
Locations: L; DFo, MH

1636#2
LUPTON, Donald. *Emblems of rarities; or Choice observations out of worthy histories*... London. N. Okes, 478p. 12mo. 1636
Note: STC 16942, EA 636/44. Brief account of America.
Locations: L; DLC, CSmH, MiU

1636#3
MALYNES, Gerard de. *Consuetudo, vel, Lex mercatoria, or, The antient law-merchant.* London. A. Islip, 333p. F. 1636
Note: STC 17222–3, KRESS 518, EA 636/46–7, WING M364–5. Substantial references to North America and colonisation. Other issues in 1636, 1656, 1685, 1686.
Locations: O; CSmH, MH, DFo

1636#4
PEACHAM, Henry. *Coach and sedan*... London. R. Raworth for J. Crouch, 55p, 4to. 1636
Note: STC 19501, EA 636/77–8. Two issues in 1636. Mentions New England rattlesnakes.
Locations: L; CSmH, DFo

1636#5
SANDYS, George. *A paraphrase upon the Psalmes of David*... London. A. Hebb, 271p. 8vo. 1636
Note: SABIN 76464, STC 21724, WING B2428, 2522, 2522A, EA 636/98, 638/107, EA 648/142–3/. Also 1638, 1648, and 1676 as *A paraphrase upon the divine poems.* Mentions Indian massacres.
Locations: L; DLC, CtY, CSmH

1637#1
ENGLAND AND WALES. SOVEREIGN. CHARLES I. *Proclamation against the disorderly transporting his majesties subjects*... *to America.* London. R. Barker, etc. s.sh. F. 1637
Note: STC 9086, SABIN 65939, LARKIN II, 237, EA 637/50.
Locations: L; MB, MH

1637#2
HEYLYN, Peter. *Antidotum Lincolniense. Or, an answer to a book entituled, The holy table, name and thing*... London. B. Alsop, T. Fawcett, [374]p. 4to. 1637
Note: SABIN 31653, STC 13267. A second edition in 1637. Indirect references to John Cotton.
Locations: L; CSmH, CtY

1637#2A
HOOKER, Thomas. *The soules humiliation*... London. I. L. for A. Crooke, 224p. 4to. 1638
Note: SABIN 32851–3. STC 13728–30. Two editions in 1638, another 1640. Also 1658?
Locations: L; O; RPJCB, CtY.

1637#3
HOOKER, Thomas. *The soules implantation*... London. R. Young, [320]p. 4to. 1637
Note: SABIN 32855, STC 13731, 13732. Another edition in 1640. L; CSmH.
Locations: L;

1637#4
HOOKER, Thomas. *The soules ingrafting into Christ*... London. J. H[aviland] for A. Crooke, 30p. 4to. 1637
Note: SABIN 32856, STC 13733.
Locations: L; CSmH

1637#5
MORTON, Thomas. *New English Canaan or New Canaan. Containing an abstract of New England, composed in three bookes*... London. [Amsterdam. J. F. Stam] for C. Greene, London. 188p. 4to. [1637?]
Note: SABIN 51028n, STC 18203, EA 637/70. The first edition was also Amsterdam, 1637 (L; RPJCB, CSmH). See EA 637/69.
Locations: L; DCH;

1637#6
NORWOOD, Richard. *The sea-mans practice, contayning a fundamentall probleme in navigation...* London. B. Alsop, etc for G. Hurlock, 88p. 4to. 1637
Note: STC 18691, EA 637/75. Mentions, Indians, New England, Virginia, etc. Another edition 1732, EA 732/174.
Locations: L; CtY, DFo

1637#7
VINCENT, Philip. *A true relation of the late battell fought in New England, between the English, and the salvages: with the present state of things there.* London. M. P. for N. Butter and J. Bellamie, 23p. 4to. 1637
Note: SABIN 99760–99763, STC 24758, EA 637/101. Another issue and another edition in 1638, EA 638/24.
Locations: L; RPJCB, MiU-C

1638#8
BLOYS, William. *Adam in his innocence.* London. R. Young for G. Latham, 279p. 12mo. 1638
Note: STC 3139, EA 638/19. Mentions North-West passage.
Locations: L; MH, DFo

1638#9
ENGLAND AND WALES. SOVEREIGN. CHARLES I. *By the King. A proclamation to restraine the transporting of passengers and provisions to New England, without licence... [1 May 1638.]* London. R. Barker, etc. s.sh. F. 1638
Note: SABIN 65939n, STC 9113, LARKIN II, 261, STEELE 1772, EA 638/48.
Locations: Lpro; DFo

1638#10
ENGLAND AND WALES. SOVEREIGN. CHARLES I. *A proclamation concerning tobacco...* London. R. Barker, etc. 4p. F. [1637/8]
Note: SABIN 99852, STC 9109, LARKIN, II, 257, STEELE 1769, EA 638/47.
Locations: L;

1638#10A
HOOKER, Thomas. *Foure learned and godly treatises.* London. T. Cotes for A. Crooke, 293p. 12mo. 1638
Note: SABIN 32838, STC 13725.
Locations: O; NjPT, MH

1638#11
HOOKER, Thomas. *The soules exaltation...* London. J. Haviland for A. Crooke, [313]p. 4to. 1638
Note: SABIN 32850, STC 13727.
Locations: L; CSmH

1638#12
HOOKER, Thomas. *The soules possession of Christ...* London. M. F.[lesher] for F. Eglesfield, 170, 47p. 12mo. 1638
Note: SABIN 87293, STC 13734.
Locations: C;

1638#13
HOOKER, Thomas. *The soules vocation or effectual calling to Christ...* London. J. Haviland for A. Crooke, 668p. 4to. 1638
Note: STC 13739.
Locations: L; CSmH, MH

1638#13A
HOOKER, Thomas. *Three godly sermons...* London. M. Parsons for J. Stafford, 139p. 12mo. 1638
Note: STC 13739.5. Also, a variant, *Three sermons...* STC 13739.7.
Locations: L; RPJCB

1638#14
HOOKER, Thomas. *The unbeleevers-preparing for Christ...* London. T. Cotes for A. Crooke, 204p. 4to. 1638
Note: SABIN 32862, STC 13740.
Locations: L; MWA

1638#15
HUES, Robert. *A learned treatyse of globes... made English... by John Chilmead.* London. Assignes of T. P. for P. Stephens, etc. 1638
Note: STC 13907-8, EA 638/54. Reissued in 1639: L; DLC, RPJCB.
Locations: L;

1638#16
ROBERTS, Lewes. *The merchants mappe of commerce...* London. R. O. etc. for R. Mabb, 3pts. [676]p. F. 1638
Note: SABIN 71906, STC 21094, EA 638/102. Describes 'America and the provinces thereof'. Also editions in 1671, 1677, 1700, WING R1599–1601.
Locations: L; RPJCB, CSmH, DLC

1638#17
UNDERHILL, John. *Newes from America; or A new and experimentall discoverie of New England; containing, a true relation of their war-like proceedings... with a figure of the Indian fort, or palizado...* London. J. D. for P. Cole, 44p. 4to. 1638
Note: SABIN 97733, STC 24518, EA 638/122.
Locations: L; RPJCB, MiU-C

1639#1
BANCROFT, Thomas. *Two bookes of epigrammes and epitaphs...* London. J. Okes for M. Walbanke, [87]p. 4to. 1639

1638/9

Note: STC 1354, EA 639/11. Mention of New England and North-West passage.
Locations: L; DLC, CSmH, CtY

1639#2
ENGLAND AND WALES. SOVEREIGN. CHARLES I. *A proclamation concerning tobacco...* London. R. Barker, etc. 3p. F. [1638/9]
Note: STC 9138–9, LARKIN II, 282, STEELE 1798, EA 639/46.
Locations: O; Lsa;

1639#3
MAYNE, Jasper. *The citye match. A comoedye.* Oxford. L. Lichfield, 64p. F. 1639
Note: STC 17750, EA 639/77. Brief references to New England.
Locations: L; CtY, CSmH, DLC

1639#4
PAGITT, Ephraim. *A relation of the Christians in the world...* London. J. Okes, 79p. 4to. 1639
Note: STC 19113, EA 639/87.
Locations: L; NN, NNUT

1639#5
PLATTES, Gabriel. *A discovery of subterraneall treasure, viz, Of all manner of mines and mineralls from the gold to the coal.* London. J. Okes, for J. Emery, 60p. 4to. 1639
Note: SABIN 63360, STC 20000, WING P2410–12, EA 639/94. Also 1653, 1679, and 1684. Mentions North American gold and silver.
Locations: L; CSmH, CtY, MH-BA

1640#1
DONNE, John. *LXXX sermons.* London. M. Fletcher for R. Royston and R. Marriott, 826p. F. 1640
Note: STC 7038, EA 640/74. Mentions North-West passage.
Locations: L; DLC, CtY, CSmH

1640#2
GLAPTHORNE, Henry. *Wit in a constable. A comedy.* London. J. Okes, for F. C., 64p. 4to. 1640
Note: STC 11914, EA 640/84. Mentions New England, tobacco.
Locations: L; CSmH, CtY, DLC

1640#3
HOOKER, Thomas. *The Christian's two chief lessons...* London. T. Badger for P. Stephens and C. Meredith, 22, 303p. 4to. 1640
Note: SABIN 32831, STC 13724.
Locations: L; CSmH

1640#4
PARKINSON, John. *Theatrum botanicum: The theater of plants.* London. T. Cotes, 1755p. F. 1640
Note: STC 19302, EA 640/143.
Locations: L; DLC, CSmH, CtY

1640#5
HOOKER, Thomas. *The paterne of perfection: exhibited in Gods image on Adam...* London. For R. Young and A. Clifton, 12mo. 1640
Note: STC 13726. Another issue in 1653?
Locations: L; O; NN, NjPT

1640#6
SHEPARD, Thomas. *The sincere convert: discovering the small numbers of true believers; and the great difficulty of saving-conversion.* London. T. Paine for M. Symmons, 267p. 8vo. 1640
Note: STC 22404. 7–9, EA 640/168–70. Three issues in 1640. WING S3118–3131B also lists London, 1641, 1642, 1643, 1646, 1648, 1650, 1650 (EA 641/136, 642/122, 643/115, 647/156, 648/158, 650/195–6), 1652, 1655, 1657, 1659, 1664, 1667, 1669, 1672, 1680, 1680, 1692; Edinburgh, 1647, 1653, 1674, 1678, 1695; Glasgow, 1667. Also Edinburgh, 1714 and Glasgow, 1734, EA 714/129, 734/203.
Locations: L; RPJCB

1640#7
VAUGHAN, William. *The church militant, historically continued.* London. T. Paine for H. Blunden, 345p. 12mo. 1640
Note: STC 24606, EA 640/188. In verse. Many American references.
Locations: L; CSmH, CtY, DLC

1641#1
BAILLIE, Robert. *The unlawfulnes and danger of limited episcopacie.* London. T. Underhill, 47p. 4to. 1641
Note: WING B460. Discusses New England church practices.
Locations: L; O; RPJCB

1641#2
CASTELL, William. *A petition of W. C. exhibited to the high court of Parliamen[t] now assembled, for the propagating of the gospel in America, and the West Indies; and for the setling of our plantations there.* London. 19p. 4to. 1641
Note: SABIN 11397, WING C1230, EA 641/25.
Locations: L; MH

1641#3
CHAUNCY, Charles (1592–1672). *The retraction of... written in his own hand before his going to New England, in the yeer, 1637.* London. viii, 40p. 4to. 1641

Note: SABIN 12308, WING C3740. Retracts his submission made in 1635 before the Court of High Commission.
Locations: L; RPJCB

1641#4
CHIDLEY, Katherine. *The justification of the independent churches of Christ. Being an answer to Mr Edwards his booke.* London. W. Larner, [82]p. 4to. 1641
Note: SABIN 12687, WING C3832. New England references.
Locations: L; CtY

1641#5
COTTON, John. *An abstract or [sic] the lawes of New England as they are now established.* London. F. Coules, W. Ley, 17p. 4to. 1641
Note: SABIN 17042, 52595, WING C6408, EA 641/31.
Locations: L; RPJCB

1641#6
COTTON, John. *A coppy of a letter of Mr Cotton of Boston, in New England, sent in answer of certaine objections made against their discipline and order there.* London. 6p. 4to. 1641
Note: SABIN 17057, WING C6422, EA 641/32.
Locations: L; RPJCB

1641#7
COTTON, John. *God's mercie mixed with his justice, or, his people's deliverance in times of danger. . . in severall sermons.* London. G. M. for E. Brewster and H. Hood, 135p. 4to. 1641
Note: SABIN 17064, WING C6433. Reissued in 1658 as *The Saint's support. . .* (WING C6456).
Locations: L; MH

1641#8
COTTON, John. *The way of life. Or, God's way and course, in bringing the soule into, keeping it in, and carrying it on, in the wayes of life and peace. . . in foure severall treatises.* London. M. F. for L. Fawne and S. Gellibrand, 481p. 4to. 1641
Note: SABIN 17087, WING C6470.
Locations: L; CtY

1641#9
DAVENPORT, John. *An exhortation to the restoring of brotherly communion.* London. R. B. for R. Balfour and J. Williams, 12mo. 1641
Note: WING D359.
Locations: Lmh; CM; NNUT

1641#10
EDWARDS, Thomas. *Reasons against the independent government of particular congregations. . . as also against the toleration of such churches.* London. R. Cotes for J. Bellamie and R. Smith, xx, 56p. 4to. 1641
Note: WING E233.
Locations: L; CtY, CSmH, NjP

1641#11
EVELYN, Robert. *A direction for adventurers. . . with small stock to get two for one, and good land freely. . . true description of the healthiest, pleasantest, and richest plantation of New Albion, in North Virginia.* London. [8]p. 4to. 1641
Note: SABIN 63312, WING E3524, EA 641/39.
Locations: CSmH

1641#12
HALL, Joseph. *A survay of that foolish, seditious, scandalous, prophane libell, The protestation protested.* London. 40p. 4to. 1641
Note: WING H418, EA 641/56. Replies to H. Burton's *The protestation protested* (1641). Mentions New England and Virginia.
Locations: L; RPJCB, CSmH, CtY

1641#13
HOMES, Nathaniel. *The new world, or the new reformed church. Discovered out of the second epistle of Peter the third chap. verse 13.* London. T. P. and M. S. for W. Adderton, 79p. 4to. 1641
Note: WING H2570. Mentions New England churches.
Locations: L; CtY

1641#14
HOOKE, William. *New Englands teares, for old Englands feares. . . sermon. . . July 23. 1640.* London. E. G. for J. Rothwell, H. Overton, 23p. 4to. 1641
Note: SABIN 32810, 32811, WING H2624–6, EA 641/62–4. Two more editions in 1641.
Locations: L; RPJCB

1641#15
HOOKER, Thomas. *The danger of desertion: or a Farwel sermon.* London. G. M. for G. Edwards, 29p. 4to. 1641
Note: SABIN 32834, WING H2645, EA 641/65–6. Another edition in 1641.
Locations: L; RPJCB

1641#16
The memorialls of Margaret de Valoys, first wife to Henry the fourth, King of France. London. R. H. 229p. 8vo. 1641
Note: SABIN 44536, WING N595. Other editions 1645, 1647, 1661, 1665. Canadian references.
Locations: L; CSmH

1641#17
A pack of patentees. opened. shuffled. cut. dealt. and played. London. 15p. 4to. 1641

1641

Note: WING P156, EA 641/99. Mentions Virginia and St. Kitts.
Locations: L; CSmH, MH

1641#18
PAGIT, John. *A defence of church-government exercised in prebyteriall, classical and synodall assemblies.* London. T. Underhill, xxxii, 256p. 4to. 1641
Note: WING P166. Contains an answer to Davenport's *Apologeticall Reply*, (Rotterdam, 1636).
Locations: L; NNC, MH, MWA

1641#19
PYM, John. *A speech delivered in Parliament, by a worthy member thereof.* London. R. Lowndes, 40p. 4to. 1641
Note: WING P4284, EA 641/118-9. Mentions effects in colonies of taxes. Another edition in 1641.
Locations: L; CSmH, RPJCB, MH

1641#20
ROBERTS, Lewes. *The treasure of traffike. or a discourse of forraigne trade.* London. E. P. for N. Bourne, [103]p. 4to. 1641
Note: SABIN 71910, WING R1602, KRESS 595, EA 641/124.
Locations: L; RPJCB, DLC, CtY

1641#21
ROBINSON, Henry. *England's safety, in trades encrease.* London. E. P. for N. Bourne, 62p. 4to. 1641
Note: SABIN 72083, WING R1671, KRESS 597, EA 641/125. Mentions English colonies.
Locations: L; CtY, CSmH, MH-BA

1641#22
TAYLOR, John. *The complaint of M. Tenter-hooke the projector.* London. E. P. for F. Cowler, s.sh. F. 1641
Note: WING T443, EA 641/141. Mentions American tobacco growing areas.
Locations: L;

1642#1
BALL, John. *An answer to two treatises of Mr John Cann, the leader of the English Brownists in Amsterdam.* London. R. B. to be sold by J. Burroughes, 144, 92p. 4to. 1642
Note: SABIN 2937, WING B558. Marginal New England references.
Locations: L; MH

1642#2
CALVERT, George. *The answer to Tom-Tell-Troth. The practise of princes and the lamentations of the kirke.* London. 30p. 4to. [1642/3]
Note: WING B611, EA 642/10. Mentions Greenland, Indies, etc.
Locations: L; RPJCB, MH

1642#3
CHAUNCY, Charles (1592–1672). *The doctrine of the sacrament.* London. G. M. for T. Underhill, 2, 20p. 8vo. 1642
Note: WING C3737E.
Locations: O; PPL

1642#4
COTTON, John. *A brief exposition of the whole book of Canticles, or, the Song of Solomon.* London. P. Nevil, 264p. 8vo. 1642
Note: SABIN 17047, WING C6410. Another edition in 1648.
Locations: L; RPJCB, MH

1642#5
COTTON, John. *The churches resurrection, or the opening of the fift and sixt verses of the 20th. chap. of the Revelation.* London. R. O. and G. D. for H. Overton, 30p. 4to. 1642
Note: SABIN 17054, WING C6419, EA 642/46.
Locations: L; MH, CtY

1642#6
COTTON, John. *A modest and cleere answer to Mr Ball's discourse of set formes of prayer.* London. For H. Overton, 49p. 4to. [1642?]
Note: SABIN 17070, WING C6444-5. Another issue in 1642.
Locations: L; RPJCB, MB

1642#7
COTTON, John. *The powring out of the seven vials: or, An exposition of the 16. chapter of the Revelation.* London. R. S. for H. Overton, 171p. 4to. 1642
Note: SABIN 17074, WING C6449-50, EA 642/47-8. Other editions in 1642, 1645, EA 645/206.
Locations: L; RPJCB, MH

1642#8
COTTON, John. *The true constitution of a particular visible church.* London. For S. Satterthwaite, 13p. 4to. 1642
Note: WING C6468.
Locations: L; RPJCB, MH

1642#9
DAVENPORT, John. *The profession of faith of. . . Mr J. D. . . Made publiquely before the congregation at his admission into one of the churches of God in New-England.* London. J. Hancock, 8p. 4to. 1642
Note: SABIN 18709, WING D364, EA 642/50.
Locations: L; RPJCB, CtY, CSmH

1642#10
DAVENPORT, John. *The saints anchor-hold.* London. W. L. for G. Hurlocke, 8p. 4to. 1642

1643

Note: Cf. SABIN 18710, WING D364–6. Other editions 1661, (L;), 1662, 1682, 1701.
Locations: MB, CtY

1642#11
LECHFORD, Thomas. *Plain dealing: or, Newes from New-England... A short view of New-Englands present government, both ecclesiastical and civil.* London. W. E. and J. G. for N. Butter, 80p. 4to. 1642
Note: SABIN 39640–1, WING L809–10, EA 642/71. Reprinted in 1644 as *New-England's advice to Old-England...* (EA 644/93): L; RPJCB.
Locations: L; RPJCB

1642#12
Newes from New-England: of a most strange and prodigious birth, brought to Boston in New-England... Also other relations of six strange and prodigious births. London. J. G. Smith, 8p. 4to. 1642
Note: SABIN 54970, WING N984, EA 642/91.
Locations: L;

1642#13
TAYLOR, John. *The devil turn'd Round-head: or, Pluto become a Brownist.* London. 8p. 4to. [1642]
Note: SABIN 94477, WING T449, EA 642/127. References to New England.
Locations: L; CtY

1643#1
ASHE, Simeon and BALL, John. *A letter of many ministers in Old England, requesting the judgement of their reverend brethren in New England concerning nine positions... together with the answer thereunto returned anno 1639. And the reply made... and sent over unto them... 1640.* London. T. Underhill, 90p. 4to. 1643
Note: SABIN 2171, 40355, WING B583A and L1573A, EA 643/9. Reissued in 1644 as *A Tryall of the new-church way...*, WING T2229, EA 644/16.
Locations: L; DLC, RPJCB, MH

1643#2
CANNE, Abednego. *A new wind-mil, a new.* Oxford. L. Lichfield, 6p. 4to. 1643
Note: SABIN 10688, WING N797, EA 643/27. Pseudonymous attack on Puritans with New England references. EA states London imprint.
Locations: L; CtY

1643#3
The capitall lawes of New-England. London. B. Allen, s.sh. F. 1643
Note: WING C479, EA 643/82. First printed Cambridge, Mass., 1642 (EVANS 10).
Locations: L;

1643#4
COTTON, John. *The doctrine of the church.* London. For S. Satterthwaite, ii, 14p. 4to. 1643
Note: WING C6428–30. Other editions 1643, 1644.
Locations: O; CtY

1643#5
COTTON, John. *A letter of Mr. John Cottons, teacher of the church of Boston in New-England, to Mr [Roger] Williams.* London. B. Allen, 13p. 4to. 1643
Note: WING C6441, EA 643/37.
Locations: L; RPJCB, MH

1643#6
DAVENPORT, John. *An answer of the elders of the severall churches in New-England unto nine positions... written in the yeer 1639.* London. T. P. and M. S. for B. Allen, [29]p. 4to. 1643
Note: SABIN 46776. Paged continuously with R. Mather's *An Apologie...* below, 1643.
Locations: L; DLC, RPJCB

1643#7
ELIOT, John. *New Englands first fruits; in respect. First of the conversion of some, convictions of diverse, preparation of sundry of the Indians. 2. Of the progresse of learning, in the colledge at Cambridge in Massacusets Bay.* London. R. O. and G. D. for H. Overton, 26p. 4to. 1643
Note: SABIN 52758, WING E519, EA 643/87.
Locations: L; DLC, RPJCB

1643#8
ENGLAND AND WALES. LORDS AND COMMONS. *An ordinance of the Lords and Commons... whereby Robert earle of Warwicke is made governour in chiefe, and lord high admirall of all those islands and other plantations... of America... and a committee... [to assist him and advance Protestant religion... 3 Nov 1643.].* London. J. Wright, 6p. 4to. 1643
Note: SABIN 57510, WING E2104, EA 643/58.
Locations: L; RPJCB, CSmH

1643#9
ENGLAND AND WALES. SOVEREIGN. CHARLES I. *A proclamation to give assurance unto all his majesties subjects in the islands and continent of America.* [Oxford. L. Lichfield], s.sh. F. 1643
Note: STEELE 2512, LARKIN, II, 458, WING C2701, EA 643/61.
Locations: O;

1643#10
HUIT, Ephraim. *The whole prophecie of Daniel explained, by a paraphrase, analysis and briefe comment...* London. H. Overton, 368p. 4to. 1643

1643

Note: SABIN 33630, WING H3359. Huit was 'pastor to church at Windsor in New-England.'
Locations: DLC, MiU-C

1643#11
The humble petition of divers inhabitants of New-England. London. 2p. F. 1643
Note: WING H3455. Brief dated 2 February 1642 with parliament's approval for London parish collections 'for the transporting and transplanting of poore Children driven out of Ireland, and other poore fatherless Children.' With letter of recommendation from Thomas Welde and Hugh Peter.
Locations: Lg;

1643#12
LAMBE, Thomas. *A confutation of infants baptisme, or an answer to a treatise written by Georg [sic] Phillips, of Wattertowne in New England...* London. 51p. 4to. 1643
Note: WING L209.
Locations: Dt; NHC

1643#13
MATHER, Richard. *An apologie of the churches in New-England for church-covenant... Sent over in answer to Master Bernard, in the yeare 1639...* London. T. P. and M. S. for W. Allen, 46p. 4to. 1643
Note: SABIN 52610, WING M1267, HOLMES, MM, 38. Paged continuously with Davenport, *An Answer*, above, 1643.
Locations: L; RPJCB

1643#14
MATHER, Richard. *Church government and church-covenant discussed, in an answer of the elders of the severall churches in New England...* London. R. O. and G. D. for B. Allen, [170]p. 4to. 1643
Note: SABIN 46776, WING M1269, HOLMES, MM, 38.
Locations: L; RPJCB

1643#15
MEDE, Joseph. *The key of the revelation, searched and demonstrated... whereunto is added A conjecture concerning Gog and Magog by the same author...* London. Printed by J. L. for Phil. Stephens, 151p. 4to. 1643
Note: WING M1600, 1601. Second edition in 1650. Discussion of whether 'the people of America are the Colonies of Magog, by reason of the short passage through the Ocean.'
Locations: L; O; MH, CtY

1643#16
Observations upon Prince Rupert's white *dogge, called Boye, carefully taken by T. B...* London. 10p. 4to. 1643

Note: SABIN 2558, WING B194, EA 643/91. Minor references to New England.
Locations: L; MH, CtY

1643#17
STEUART, Adam. *Some observations and annotations upon the Apologeticall narration, submitted to Parliament...* London. For C. Meredith, 71p. 4to. [1643 or 1644]
Note: SABIN 56461, 91383, WING S5492, EA 644/148–9. Another edition in 1644. New England references.
Locations: L; RPJCB, CtY

1643#18
TAYLOR, John. *A letter sent to London from a spie at Oxford.* Oxford. H. Hall, 14p. 4to. 1643
Note: WING T474, EA 643/117. Mentions New England.
Locations: O; C; CSmH

1643#19
WILLIAMS, Roger. *A key into the language of America: or, An help to the language of the natives in... New-England... with brief observations of the customes... of the afore-said natives...* London. G. Dexter, [205]p. 8vo. 1643
Note: SABIN 104339, WING W2766, EA 643/125.
Locations: L; RPJCB, MiU-C

1644#1
C. C. the covenanter vindicated *from perjurie...* London. T. Paine, 90p. 4to. 1644
Note: SABIN 16354, WING C176. New England references.
Locations: L; CtY, MiU-C

1644#2
CASTELL, William. *A short discoverie of the coasts and continent of America, from the equinoctiall northward, and of the adjacent isles... Whereunto is prefixed the authors petition to this present Parliament...* London. 2pts. 4to. 1644
Note: SABIN 11398, WING C1231, EA 644/39.
Locations: L; DLC, RPJCB, CtY

1644#3
A coole conference between the Scottish commissioners cleared reformation, and the Holland ministers Apologeticall narration... London. 18p. 4to. 1644
Note: WING C6044a, C6045, EA 644/48.
Locations: L; O; CSmH, CtY

1644#4
COTTON, John. *The keyes of the kingdom of heaven, and power thereof, according to the word of God...* London. M. Simmons for H. Overton, 59p. 4to. 1644
Note: SABIN 17067, WING C6437–40, EA 644/49–51. Three other issues in 1644.
Locations: L; DLC, CtY

1644

1644#5
COTTON, John. *Sixteene questions of serious and necessary consequence, propounded unto Mr John Cotton...* London. E. P. for E. Blackmore, 14p. 4to. 1644
Note: SABIN 81490, WING C6458, EA 644/52. Reprinted 1647 as *Severall questions... propounded by the teaching elders...* (WING C6455, 6455, EA 647/57).
Locations: L; O; NN

1644#6
EDWARDS, Thomas. *Antapologia: or, A full answer to the Apologeticall narration...* London. G. M. for J. Bellamie, 307p. 4to. 1644
Note: SABIN 21991, WING E222–224A, EA 644/58–9. Other editions 1644, 1646. EA 646/52–3.
Locations: L; O; MH, RPJCB

1644#7
FORBES, Alexander. *An anatomy of independency, or, A brief commentary, and moderate discourse upon the Apologeticall narration...* London. R. Bostock, 52p. 4to. 1644
Note: Cf. SABIN 27953. WING F1439, EA 644/64.
Locations: L; CSmH

1644#8
GOODWIN, John. *M. S. to A. S. with a plea for libertie of conscience against the cavils of A. S.* London. F. N. for H. Overton, 110p, 4to. 1644
Note: SABIN 74624, WING G1180, EA 644/66. Many New England references.
Locations: L; CSmH, CtY, RPJCB

1644#9
GOODWIN, John. *A reply of two of the brethren to A. S. wherein you have observations on his considerations... upon the Apologeticall narration...* London. M. Simmons for H. Overton, 112p. 4to. 1644
Note: SABIN 69679, WING G1198, EA 644/67. A second edition corrected and enlarged in 1644: L; MH.
Locations: L; CtY

1644#10
GOODWIN, John. *A short answer to A. S. alias Adam Stewart's second part of his overgrown duply to the two brethren...* London. 4, 36p. 4to. 1644
Note: WING G1201.
Locations: L; NN-UT

1644#11
HOLMES, Nathaniel. *Gospel musick. or, The singing of David's Psalms, etc., in the publick congregations, or private families asserted, and vindicated...* London. H. Overton, 30p. 4to. 1644
Note: SABIN 28050, WING H2567, EA 644/79. Reprints 'A discourse of our worthy brethren of New England', part of *The Whole Book of Psalmes*, Cambridge, Mass., 1640. See, *The whole book of psalmes*, below, 1647.
Locations: L; CSmH

1644#11A
HOOKER, Thomas. *The faithful covenanter: A sermon... By... Mr. Tho. Hooker... now in New England.* London. C. Meredith, 43p. 4to. 1644
Note: SABIN 32837, WING H2648.
Locations: L; MH, InU, CtY

1644#12
MATHER, Richard. *A modest and brotherly answer to Mr. Charles Herle his book, against the independency of churches...* London. H. Overton, 58p. 4to. 1644
Note: SABIN 46781, WING M1274, HOLMES MM, 50.
Locations: L; RPJCB

1644#13
PARKER, Thomas. *The true copy of a letter: written by Mr. Thomas Parker... in New-England... touching the government practised in the churches of New-England.* London. R. Cotes for R. Smith, 4p. 4to. 1644
Note: SABIN 58770, WING P482, EA 644/124.
Locations: L; RPJCB

1644#14
RATHBAND, William. *A briefe narration of some church courses held in opinion and practise in the churches lately erected in New England.* London. G. M. for E. Brewster, 55p. 4to. 1644
Note: SABIN 67947, WING R298, EA 644/130.
Locations: L; RPJCB

1644#15
RATHBAND, William. *A most grave, and modest confutation of the errors of the sect commonly called Brownists...* London. E. Brewster and G. Badger, 22, 71p. 4to. 1644
Note: SABIN 67948, WING R299.
Locations: L; MH, CtY

1644#16
RUTHERFORD, Samuel. *The due right of presbyteries... wherein is examined 1. The way of the church of Christ in New England.* London. E. Griffin for R. Whitaker, and A. Crooke, 468p. 4to. 1644
Note: SABIN 74456, WING R2378, EA 644/137.
Locations: L; CtY, DLC, RPJCB

1644#17
STEUART, Adam. *An answer to a libell intituled, A coole conference...* London. 62p. 4to. 1644
Note: SABIN 91381, WING S5489, EA 644/146. Many New England references.
Locations: L; NN

1644

1644#18
STEUART, Adam. *The second part of the duply to M. S. alias Two brethren...* London. J. Field, 194p. 4to. 1644
Note: SABIN 91382, WING S5491, EA 644/147.
Locations: L; RPJCB, CtY, CSmH

1644#19
WELD, Thomas. *An answer to W. R. his Narration of the opinions and practises of the churches lately erected in New-England...* London. T. Paine for H. Overton, 68p. 4to. 1644
Note: SABIN 102551, WING W1262, EA 644/166.
Locations: L; RPJCB

1644#20
WILLIAMS, Roger. *The bloudy tenent, of persecution, for cause of conscience, discussed, in a conference between truth and peace...* London. 247p. 4to. 1644
Note: SABIN 104331–2, WING 2758–9, EA 644/167–8. Two issues in 1644.
Locations: L; RPJCB

1644#21
WILLIAMS, Roger. *Mr Cottons letter lately printed, examined and answered: by Roger Williams of Providence in New-England.* London. 47p. 4to. 1644
Note: SABIN 17082, 104341, WING W2767, EA 644/169.
Locations: L; O; RPJCB, CtY

1644#22
WILLIAMS, Roger. *A paraenetick or humble addresse to the Parliament and assembly for (not loose, but) Christian libertie.* London. M. Simmons for H. Overton, 14p. 4to. 1644
Note: SABIN 58510, 104342, WING W2768–9. Two issues in 1644.
Locations: L; O; RPJCB, MiU-C

1644#23
WILLIAMS, Roger. *Queries of highest consideration proposed to Mr Thomas Goodwin... And to the Commissioners of the General Assembly (so-called) of the Church of Scotland...* London. 13p. 4to. 1644
Note: SABIN 104343. WING W2770 ascribes to Roger Williams. Mentions New England.
Locations: L; MWA, CSmH, RPJCB

1644#24
WINTHROP, John. *Antinomians and Familists condemned by the synod of elders in New-England...* London. For R. Smith, 2, 66p. 4to. 1644
Note: SABIN 104843, 104848, WING W3094, EA 644/170–2. The same text as *A short story of the rise, reign, and ruine of the Antinomians... of New-England* (WING W1269), which appeared in two editions in 1644 (both in MH and RPJCB) with a preface by Thomas Weld, who is sometimes listed as the author. Another edition in 1692 (WING W1270).
Locations: L; Dt; RPJCB, MH, NN

1645#1
BAILLIE, Robert. *A dissuasive from the errours of the time: wherein the tenets of the principall sects, especially of the Independents, are drawn together in one map...* London. S. Gellibrand, 252p. 4to. 1645
Note: SABIN 4059, WING B456, EA 645/12. Other issues 1646, 1655.
Locations: L; MH

1645#2
BASTWICK, John. *The second part of that book called Independency not God's ordinance: or the post-script...* London. J. Macock for M. Spark, [106]p. 4to. 1645
Note: WING B1069. Mentions New England Puritans.
Locations: L; O; DFo, CtY

1645#3
CAWDREY, Daniel. *Vindiciae clavium, or, A vindication of the keyes of the kingdome of heaven... Being some animadversions on a tract of Mr J[ohn]. C[otton]. called, The keyes of the kingdome of heaven... As also upon... The way of the churches of New-England...* London. T. H. for P. Whaley, 90p. 4to. 1645
Note: SABIN 11616, WING C1640, EA 645/33.
Locations: L; MH

1645#4
COTTON, John. *The covenant of Gods free grace... Whereunto is added A profession of faith... by John Davenport...* London. M. Simmons, 40p. 4to. 1645
Note: SABIN 17058, WING C6423–4, EA 645/40–1. Two issues in 1645.
Locations: L; MBAt

1645#5
COTTON, John. *The way of the churches of Christ in New-England.* London. M. Simmons, 116p. 4to. 1645
Note: SABIN 17090, WING C6471–2, EA 645/43–4. Another edition in 1645.
Locations: L; MH

1645#6
EATON, Samuel and TAYLOR, Timothy. *A defense of sundry positions & scriptures alledged to justifie the Congregationall way...* London. M. Simmons for H. Overton, 130p. 4to. 1645
Note: SABIN 29402, WING E118–20, EA 645/49. Another edition in 1646, EA 646/51.
Locations: L; CSmH

1645#7
GILLESPIE, George. *Wholesome severity reconciled with Christian liberty. or, The true resolution of a present*

controversie concerning liberty of conscience... London. C. Meredith, 40p. 4to. 1645
Note: SABIN 17046, WING G765, EA 645/55. Sometimes attributed to John Cotton.
Locations: L; RPJCB

1645#8
HOLLINGWORTH, Richard. *An examination of sundry scriptures, alleadged by our brethren (of New England) in defence of some particulars of their church-way...* London. J. R. for L. Fawne, 30p. 4to. 1645
Note: SABIN 29401, WING H2491-2, EA 645/67-8. Another issue in 1645.
Locations: L; CSmH

1645#9
HOOKE, William. *New-Englands sence, of old-England and Ireland sorrowes. A sermon preached upon a day of generall humiliation in the churches of New-England.* London. J. Rothwell, 34p. 4to. 1645
Note: SABIN 32809, WING H2623, EA 645/69.
Locations: L; RPJCB, MH, CSmH

1645#9A
HOOKER, Thomas. *A briefe exposition of the Lord's prayer...* London. M. Bell for B. Allen, 90p. 4to. 1645
Note: SABIN 32830, WING H2642. Another issue in 1645?
Locations: RPJCB, CSmH, NcD

1645#9B
HOOKER, Thomas. *An exposition of the principles of Religion.* London. R. Dawlman, 58p. 12mo. 1645
Note: SABIN 32832, WING H2647D
Locations: L; RPJCB

1645#9C
HOOKER, Thomas. *Heaven's treasury opened in a fruitfull exposition of the Lords Prayer.* London. R. Dawlman, 197p. 12mo. 1645
Note: SABIN 32939, WING H2650.
Locations: L; RPJCB

1645#10
HOOKER, Thomas. *The immortality of the soule...* London. 2, 21p. 4to. 1645
Note: SABIN 32841, WING H2651.
Locations: L; Dt; RPJCB

1645#11
HOOKER, Thomas *The saint's guide...* London. For John Stafford, 12mo. 1645
Note: WING H2655.
Locations: L; O; MH, CtY

1645#12
HUDSON, Samuel. *The essence and unitie of the church catholike visible.* London. G. Miller for C. Meredith, 4, 52p. 4to. 1645
Note: SABIN 33495, WING H3265, EA 645/72. References to John Cotton's books.
Locations: L; MH

1645#13
Independency accused by nine severall *arguments; written by a godly learned minister.* London. H. Overton, 34p. 4to. 1645
Note: WING P71, EA 645/75. Discusses New England civil magistrates' powers in theological matters.
Locations: L; RPJCB, CtY, MH

1645#14
PAGITT, Ephraim. *Heresiography: or, A description of the hereticks and sectaries of these latter times...* London. Marie Okes, sold by R. Trot, 131p. 4to. 1645
Note: SABIN 31483, WING P174-182, EA 645/94-5. Discusses New England antinomians. Other editions 1645, 1646, 1647, 1648, 1654, 1661, 1662. EA 647/142, 648/122.
Locations: L; CSmH, CtY, MH

1645#15
PHILLIPS, George. *A reply to a confutation of some grounds for infants baptisme: as also concerning the form of a church...* London. M. Simmons for H. Overton, 154p. 4to. 1645
Note: WING P2026. Phillips was minister at Watertown, Mass. Preface by Thomas Shepard.
Locations: L; CSmH, DLC, NN

1645#16
SHEPARD, Thomas. *New Englands lamentations for old Englands present errours and divisions...* London. G. Miller, 6p. 4to. 1645
Note: SABIN 80211, WING S3113, EA 645/108.
Locations: L; O; DLC, MH

1645#17
SHEPARD, Thomas. *The sound beleever. Or, a treatise of evangelicall conversion.* London. R. Dawlman, 352p. 8vo. 1645
Note: SABIN 80239. WING S3132-40 lists other issues/editions in 1649, 1652, 1653, 1659, 1670, 1671 and Edinburgh, 1645, 1650, 1658.
Locations: L; CtY

1645#18
STEUART, Adam. *Zerubbabel to Sanballat and Tobiah: or, the first part of the duply to M. S. alias Two Brethren... concerning Independents...* London. J. Field, (8), [112]p. 4to. 1645

1645

Note: SABIN 91384, WING S5495.
Locations: L; CtY

1645#19
WELD, Thomas. *A brief narration of the practices of the churches in New-England, in their solemne worship of God...* London. M. Simmons for J. Rothwell, 18p. 4to. 1645
Note: SABIN 51775, 52617, 102552, WING W1263, EA 645/122. Other editions 1647, 1651, EA 647/206.
Locations: L; RPJCB

1645#20
WHEELWRIGHT, John. *Mercurius Americanus, Mr Welds his Antitype, or, Massachusetts great apologie examined...* London. 24p. 4to. 1645
Note: SABIN 103223, WING W1605, EA 645/123. Antinomian crisis. See Winthrop, *Antinominians...*, above, 1644, which this work discusses.
Locations: L; RPJCB, DLC, CtY

1646#1
BOOTHBY, Richard. *A briefe discovery or description of the most famous island of Madagascar.* London. E. G. for J. Hardesty, 72p. 4to. 1646
Note: WING B3743, EA 646/25. Some discussion of Indian wars in New England and Virginia. Another edition in 1647, EA 647/39.
Locations: L; RPJCB, CSmH, CtY

1646#2
BULKELEY, Peter. *The gospel-covenant; or The covenant of grace opened... Preached in Concord in New-England...* London. M. S. for B. Allen, 383p. 4to. 1646
Note: SABIN 9096, 9097, WING B5403–5, EA 646/31. Other editions 1651, 1653, 1674.
Locations: L; DLC

1646#3
CALVERT, Cecil. *A moderate and safe expedient to remove jealousies and feares, of any danger... by the Roman Catholickes of this kingdome...* London. 16p. 4to. 1646
Note: SABIN 49802, WING M2322, BAER 27, EA 646/96.
Locations: LIL; RPJCB

1646#4
CLARKE, Samuel. *A mirrour or looking-glasse, both for saints and sinners... By... examples...* London. R. Cotes for J. Bellamie, 227p. 8vo. 1646
Note: SABIN 13447–8, WING C4548–52, EA 646/39. Some New England lives. Other editions 1654, 1656, 1657.
Locations: L; MH

1646#5
CORNWELL, Francis. *A conference Mr. John Cotton held at Boston with the elders of New-England...* London. J. Dawson, F. Eglesfield, 2pts. 8vo. 1646
Note: SABIN 17055, WING C6335, EA 646/43. By John Cotton?
Locations: L; MB

1646#6
COTTON, John. *The controversie concerning liberty of conscience in matters of religion, truly stated...* London. R. Austin for T. Banks, 14p. 4to. 1646
Note: SABIN 17056, WING C6420. Another edition, 1649.
Locations: L; RPJCB

1646#7
COTTON, John. *Gospel conversion together with some reasons against stinted forms of praising God...* London. J. Dawson, 80p. 8vo. 1646
Note: WING C6435–6, EA 646/44.
Locations: L; RPJCB

1646#8
COTTON, John. *Milk for babes...* London. J. Coe for H. Overton, 13p. 8vo. 1646
Note: WING C6443. See Cotton, *Spiritual milk*, below, 1657.
Locations: L; CSmH

1646#9
EDWARDS, Thomas. *Gangraena: or a catalogue and discovery of many of the errours...* London. R. Smith, 184p. 8vo. 1646
Note: WING E228–30, EA 646/54–7 for bibliographical details. Catalogue of and attack on religious sects, including New England congregationalism. Second and third editions 'much enlarged' also in 1646: L; CtY.
Locations: L; RPJCB, DLC, ICN

1646#10
EDWARDS, Thomas. *The second part of Gangraena.* London. T. R. and E. M. for R. Smith, 182p. 4to. 1646
Note: WING E234–5, EA 646/58–60. Two other editions in 1646. Many New England references.
Locations: L; NNUT

1646#11
EDWARDS, Thomas. *The third part of Gangraena.* London. For R. Smith, 295p, 4to. 1646
Note: WING E237, EA 646/61. New England references.
Locations: L; MH, CtY, DFo

1646#12
ENGLAND AND WALES. LORDS AND COMMONS. *Two ordinances of the Lords and Commons... the one dated November 2. 1643... the other*

March 21. 1645... London. J. Wright, 6p. 4to. [1645/6]
Note: WING E2418, EA 646/75. Appointing Committee for the better governing of and advancement of Protestant religion in American plantations.
Locations: L; RPJCB, MH, MiU-C

1646#13
GORTON, Samuel. *Simplicities defence against seven-headed policy. or, Innocency vindicated...* London. J. Macock for L. Fawne, 111p. 4to. 1646
Note: SABIN 28044, 28045, WING G1308, EA 646/74. New England church controversies.
Locations: L; RPJCB

1646#14
HOLLINGWORTH, Richard. *Certain queres [sic] modestly (though plainly) propounded... to such as affect the Congregationall-Way...* London. R. Raworth for L. Fawn, 31p. 4to. 1646
Note: WING H2488, 2488A. Directed against S. Eaton's and F. Taylor's *A defense of sundry positions...* above, 1645. Many New England references.
Locations: L; O; MH, CSmH, RPJCB

1646#14A
HOOKER, Thomas. *Heautonaparnumenos: or a treatise of self-denyall...* London. W. Wilson for R. Royston, 70p 4to. 1646
Note: SABIN 32840, WING H2649.
Locations: NN; MH, CLU-C

1646#15
MAINWARING, Randall. *The case of Mainwaring, Hawes, Payne and others, concerning a depredation... upon the ship Elizabeth, going... to Virginia...* London. 17p. 4to. 1646
Note: SABIN 44055, WING M296, EA 646/35.
Locations: L; RPJCB, CSmH

1646#16
PARKER, Thomas. *The visions and prophecies of Daniel...* London. R. Raworth and J. Field for E. Paxton, 156p. 4to. 1646
Note: SABIN 58771, WING P480–1. Another edition in 1646. The Rev. Thomas Parker was of Newbury, Berkshire and of New England.
Locations: L; O; MH, MiU-C, NNUT

1646#17
PETER, Hugh. *Mr Peters last report of the English wars...* London. M. S. for H. Overton, 15p. 4to. 1646
Note: WING P1707, SABIN 61195.
Locations: L; MH

1646#18
RUTHERFORD, Samuel. *The divine right of church-government and excommunication...* London. J. Field for C. Meredith, 2pts, [750]p. 4to. 1646
Note: SABIN 74455, WING R2377, EA 646/133. Discusses Indians, America, Roger Williams.
Locations: L; CtY, NNUT, ICU

1646#19
TWISSE, William. *A treatise of Mr Cottons... concerning predestination...* London. J. D. for A. Crooke, 288p, 4to. 1646
Note: SABIN 17088, 97545, WING C6464, T3425, EA 646/147. A reply to Cotton, not the treatise.
Locations: L; RPJCB, DLC, CtY

1646#20
WILLIAMS, Roger. *Christenings make not Christians, or A brief discourse concerning that name heathen, commonly given to the Indians.* London. Jane Coe for J. H., 21p. 8vo. [1645 i.e. 1646]
Note: SABIN 104334, WING W2761, EA 646/156.
Locations: L;

1646#21
WINSLOW, Edward. *Hypocrosie unmasked: by a true relation of the proceedings of the Governour and Company of the Massachusetts against Samuel Gorton...* London. R. Cotes for J. Bellamy, 103p. 4to. 1646
Note: SABIN 104796, WING W3037, EA 646/157. Reissued in 1649 as *The dangers of tolerating levellers in a civil state...* (EA 649/130): L; MB, RPJCB.
Locations: L; RPJCB, MiU-C

1646#22
WORKMAN, Giles. *Private-men no pulpit men: or, A modest examination of lay-mens preaching...* London. F. Neile for T. Underhill, 28p. 4to. 1646
Note: SABIN 105475, WING W3583, EA 646/158–9. Another edition, F. N. for T. Langford at Gloucester, 1646.
Locations: L; MH, RPJCB

1647#1
ASPINWALL, William. *Certain queries concerning the ordination of ministers.* London. M. Simmons for H. Overton, 3, 42p. 4to. 1647
Note: WING A4005.
Locations: L; O; MH, RPJCB

1647#2
BAILLIE, Robert. *Anabaptism, the true fountaine of independency... a second part of The disswasive from the errors of the time...* London. M. F. for S. Gellibrand, 179p. 4to. 1647
Note: SABIN 2762, WING B452, EA 647/11.
Locations: O; MB, RPJCB

1647

1647#3
BIBLE. OLD TESTAMENT. PSALMS. *The whole book of psalmes, faithfully translated into English metre; whereunto is prefixed a discourse...* [London or Amsterdam?]. 274p. 12mo. 1647
Note: WING B2427, HOLMES MM 53AA, EA 647/26, EVANS 20, SABIN 66430. Second issue, first non-Massachusetts edition, of *The Whole book of psalmes, faithfully translated...*, Cambridge, Mass. 1640 (STC 2738, SABIN 66428, EVANS 4), also known as the 'Bay Psalm Book.' However, this may be an Amsterdam edition. Later English and Scottish editions had the usual title of *The psalms, hymns, and spiritual songs of the Old and New-Testament, faithfully translated into English metre*. For several editions before 1700 there is some uncertainty about place and year of publication:

[1648?] EA 648/16, HOLMES no entry, WING no entry, SABIN no entry. Possibly an Amsterdam edition c. 1680.

1652 London, for J. Blague. HOLMES MM 53BB, SABIN 66432 (no copy known). Mentioned only in White Kennett's catalogue.

c. 1658 Cambridge [or Amsterdam?] WING B2488, HOLMES MM 53CC, SABIN 66434 dates as 1665, EVANS 96, EAMES dates as 1658 and EA as c.1658). Possibly Amsterdam and later.

166-. Cambridge. EA lists without further references.

1664? WING B2487 dates circa 1664, HOLMES no entry, SABIN No entry. Possibly Amsterdam edition, c. 1680. This is rejected by EA and may not exist.

c. 1669 Cambridge [or Amsterdam]. Printed for Hezekiah Usher of Bostoo [sic]. WING B2470B, HOLMES MM 53DD, SABIN 66433, EVANS 49, EAMES dates as 1669.
1671 London, WING B2505A, HOLMES MM 53EE, SABIN 66436.

1680 London, the fifth edition. WING B2538A, HOLMES MM 53FF, SABIN 66437.

c1682? Cambridge [or Amsterdam], cf WING B2538A, HOLMES MM 53GG. SABIN 66435 lists as Holland or Edinburgh without assigning a date.

1688 London, the sixth edition. RPJCB only.

1694 London, WING B2590A, HOLMES MM 53HH, SABIN 66438.

1697 London, WING B2602B, HOLMES MM 53II, SABIN 66439.

1701 London, the ninth edition, EA 701/38, HOLMES MM 53JJ, SABIN no entry.

1706 London, the tenth edition, EA 706/23, HOLMES MM 53KK, SABIN 66441n (no copy known).

1709 London, the eleventh edition, EA 709/18, HOLMES MM 53LL.

1713 London, the twelfth edition, EA 713/10, HOLMES MM 53MM, SABIN 66441n.

1719 London, the thirteenth edition, EA 719/8, HOLMES MM 53NN, SABIN 66441n.

1725 London, the fifteenth edition, EA 725/22, HOLMES MM 53OO, SABIN 66441n.

1725 London, the sixteenth edition, EA 725/23, HOLMES MM 53PP.

1729 London, the seventeenth edition, EA 729/24, HOLMES MM 53QQ, SABIN 66441n.

1737 London, the seventeenth edition, EA 737/34, HOLMES MM 53RR, SABIN 66441n.

1741 London, the eighteenth edition, EA 741/17, HOLMES MM 53SS, SABIN 66441n.

1754 London, the eighteenth edition, HOLMES MM 53TT, SABIN 66441n.

1732 Edinburgh, the sixteenth edition, EA 732/34, HOLMES MM 53CCC, SABIN 66441n.

1738 Edinburgh, the sixteenth edition, EA 738/23, HOLMES MM 53DDD.

1741 Edinburgh, the eighteenth edition, EA 741/18, HOLMES MM 53EEE, SABIN 66441n.

1748 Edinburgh, the nineteenth edition, EA 748/17, HOLMES MM 53FFF.

[1754] Edinburgh, the twentieth edition, HOLMES MM 53GGG.

1756 Edinburgh, the twenty-first edition, HOLMES MM 53HHH.

1759 Edinburgh, the twenty-second edition, HOLMES MM 53III.

1721 Glasgow, the seventeenth edition, EA 721/18, HOLMES MM 53AAA.

1726 Glasgow, EA 726/18, HOLMES MM 53BBB. A copy is reported in ESTC at MSae.

Locations: L; RPJCB

1647#4
CHILD, John. *New-Englands Jonas cast up in London: or, A relation of the proceedings of the court at Boston in New-England against divers honest and godly persons...* London. T. R. and E. M., 22p. 4to. 1647
Note: SABIN 12705, WING C3851, EA 647/48.
Locations: L; O; DLC, RPJCB

1647#5
COTTON, John. *The bloudy tenent, washed...* London. M. Simmons for Hannah Allen, 196, 144p. 4to. 1647
Note: WING C6409, SABIN 17045, 17077, EA 647/56.
Locations: L; O; CSmH, RPJCB

1647#6
COTTON, John. *The grounds and ends of the baptisme...* London. R. C. for A. Crooke, vii, 196p. 4to. 1647
Note: SABIN 17066, WING C6436.
Locations: L; O; CSmH, MH

1647#7
COTTON, John. *Singing of psalmes...* London. M. S. for Hannah Allen and J. Rothwell, 72p. 4to. 1647
Note: SABIN 17081, WING C6456.
Locations: L; O; CSmH, MH, RPJCB

1647#8
ENGLAND AND WALES. PARLIAMENT. *Die Sabatti 23 Januarii 1646. Whereas the severall plantations in Virginia, Bermudas, Barbados, and other places of America...* London. J. Wright, s.sh. F. 1647
Note: WING E2186, E2496, STEELE 2677, EA 647/72. Goods for plantations may be exported without paying customs. Dated 23 January 1646/7.
Locations: L; CSmH, RPJCB

1647#9
HART, John. *Trodden down strength, by the God of strength, or Mrs Drake revived...* London. R. Bishop for S. Pilkington, 193p. 12mo. 1647
Note: SABIN 20864, WING H960. Material on Thomas Hooker.
Locations: L; CSmH

1647#10
A letter to Mr. Tho. Edwards... Scavenger Generall, throughout Great Britaine, New-England, and the United Provinces... London. T. Veere, 10p. 4to. 1647
Note: SABIN 21911, WING L1721.
Locations: L; MH

1647#11
MATHER, Richard. *A reply to Mr Rutherford.* London. J. Rothwell and H. Allen, 109p. 4to. 1647
Note: SABIN 46782, WING M1275, HOLMES, MM, 54, EA 647/98. Deals inter alia with New-England synodical propositions.
Locations: L; DLC, MH, CtY

1647#12
Moro-Mastix: Mr John Goodwin whipt with his own rod. Or the dissecting of the sixteenth section of his book... so far as it... mentions a... disputation in Christ-Church parish... London. T. Underhill, 15p. 4to. 1647
Note: SABIN 50773, WING M2807, EA 647/108. Attack on New England churches.
Locations: L; O; MH, CtY

1647#13
NOYES, James. *The temple measured: or, a brief survey of the temple mystical, which is the instituted church of Christ...* London. E. Paxton, 95p. 4to. 1647
Note: SABIN 56220, WING N1460.
Locations: L; O; RPJCB, MH, CtY

1647#14
SEAMAN, Lazurus. *The DIATRIBE proved to be PARADIATRIBE, Or A Vindication of the judgement of Reformed Churches...* London. T. R. and E. M. for J. Rothwell, 96p. 4to. 1647
Note: WING S2174. Cites New England church practice relating to ordination.
Locations: L; MH, NNUT, TxU

1647#15
SHINKIN ap SHONE. *The honest Welch-cobler, for her do scorne to call her selfe the simple Welch-cobler...* London. 'M. Shinkin, printer to S. Taffie', 8p. 4to. 1647
Note: SABIN 32778, WING W780, EA 647/159. Satire on N. Ward's *Simple cobler of Aggawam*, below, 1647.
Locations: L; CtY, NN

1647#16
T[ANNER], R[obert]. *A brief treatise of the use of the globe celestiall and terrestiall...* London. T. Forcet for W. Lugger, 36p. 8vo. 1647
Note: WING T45, EA 647/182. Discusses geographical divisions of America.
Locations: L; DLC, MB

1647#17
TAYLOR, John. *The Kings most excellent majesties wellcome to his own house...* London. 6p. 4to. 1647
Note: EA 647/184. Verse. Mentions New England, Virginia, Bermudas, etc.
Locations: L; CSmH, MH, PU

1647#18
WARD, Nathaniel. *The simple cobler of Aggawam in America. Willing to help 'mend his native country...* London. J. D. and R. I. for S. Bowtell, 80p. 4to. 1647
Note: SABIN 101323, WING W786-90, EA 647/200-4. Four more issues in 1647.
Locations: L; RPJCB, MiU-C

1647#19
WARD, Nathaniel. *A word to Mr. Peters, and two words for the Parliament and Kingdom. Or, an answer to a scandalous pamphlet, entituled, A word for the armie...* London. F. Neile, for T. Underhill, 38p. 4to. 1647
Note: SABIN 101330, WING W792. Refers to New England.
Locations: L; RPJCB, CtY

1647

1647#20
WILSON, John. *The day-breaking, if not the sun-rising of the gospell with the Indians in New-England.* London. R. Cotes for F. Clifton, 25p. 4to. 1647
Note: SABIN 22146, 80207, WING S3110, EA 647/207.
Locations: L; RPJCB, CSmH, DLC

1647#21
WINSLOW, Edward. *New-Englands salamander, discovered by an irreligious and scornefull pamphlet, called New-England's Jonas...* London. R. Cotes for J. Bellamy, 29p. 4to. 1647
Note: SABIN 104797, WING W3088, EA 647/208.
Locations: L; RPJCB

1648#1
ALLIN, John and SHEPARD, Thomas. *A defence of the answer made unto the nine questions or positions sent from New-England...* London. R. Cotes for A. Crooke, 211p. 4to. 1648
Note: SABIN 921, WING A1036, EA 648/6.
Locations: L; C; DLC, RPJCB

1648#2
The British bell-man. Printed in the year of the saints fear. Anno Domini, 1648... London. 20p. 4to. 1648
Note: WING B4823, EA 648/28. References to New England.
Locations: L; O; RPJCB, MH

1648#3
COBBET, Thomas. *A just vindication of the covenant and church-estate of children of church members...* London. R. Cotes for A. Crooke, 296p. 4to. 1648
Note: SABIN 13867, WING C4778, EA 648/42.
Locations: O; C; NNUT, RPJCB

1648#4
COTTON, John. *The way of congregational churches cleared.* London. M. Simmons for J. Bellamie, xii, 104, 44p. 4to. 1648
Note: SABIN 17091, WING C6469, EA 648/51–2. Another issue in 1648.
Locations: L; O; RPJCB, MH

1648#5
An endevour after the reconcilement of that... difference between the godly Presbyterians and the godly Independents... London. M. S. for J. Bellamy, 4, 90p. 4to. 1648
Note: SABIN 17062, WING E727.
Locations: L; CSmH

1648#6
HOOKER, Thomas. *A survey of the summe of church-discipline. Wherein, the way of the churches of New-England is warranted out of the Word.* London. A. M. for J. Bellamy, xxxvi, 296, 90, 46, 60p. 4to. 1648
Note: SABIN 32860, WING H2658, EA 648/83. Also issued (EA 648/84) with Cotton's *The way of congregational churches...*, above, 1648.
Locations: L; RPJCB

1648#7
JOHNSON, Edward. *Good news from New-England: with an exact relation of the first planting that countrey... With the names of the severall towns, and who be preachers to them.* London. M. Simmons, 25p. 4to. 1648
Note: SABIN 27832, WING G1062, EA 648/85. A poem.
Locations: L; O; RPJCB, CSmH

1648#8
MEDE, Joseph. *The works of the pious and profoundly learned Joseph Mede...* London. Roger Norton for R. Royston, 923p. 4to. 1648
Note: WING M1585–89. Other editions, 1664, 1672, 1677. Contains material on Gog, Magog, and America, especially New England.
Locations: L; CtY, MWA, DFo

1648#9
NORTON, John. *Responsio ad totam quaestionum syllogen à... Guilielmo Apollonio...* London. R. B. for J. Crooke, 170p. 8vo. 1648
Note: SABIN 55888, WING N1322, EA 648/110. Many New England references.
Locations: O; RPJCB, DLC, CSmH

1648#10
PLANTAGENET, Beauchamp. *A description of the province of New Albion. And a direction for adventurers with small stock to get two for one, and good land freely...* London. 35p. 4to. 1648
Note: SABIN 19724, 63310–11, WING P2378, EA 648/129. Another edition in 1650, WING P2379, EA 650/165.
Locations: L; RPJCB

1648#11
Remonstrance on behalf of the merchants trading to Spain, East Indies, and Newfoundland. London. F. 1648
Note: SABIN 69584, EA 648/136.
Locations: NO COPY LOCATED.

1648#12
RUTHERFORD, Samuel. *A survey of the spirituall antichrist.* London. J. D. and R. I. for A. Crooke, 2pts, [613]p. 4to. 1648
Note: SABIN 74459, WING R2394, EA 648/140. Discussion of New England.
Locations: L; RPJCB, CtY, CSmH

1648#13
SHEPARD, Thomas. *Certain select cases resolved. Specially, tending to the right ordering of the heart, that we may comfortably walk with God in our general and particular callings.* London. M. Simmons for J. Rothwell, xxiv, 248p. 12mo. 1648
Note: SABIN 80199, WING S3103. Other editions in 1648, 1650, 1655.
Locations: L; MH

1648#14
SHEPARD, Thomas. *The clear sun-shine of the Gospel breaking forth upon the Indians in New England...* London. R. Cotes for J. Bellamy, 38p. 4to. 1648
Note: SABIN 80205, WING S3109, EA 648/157.
Locations: L; RPJCB, MiU-C

1648#15
SHEPARD, Thomas. *The first principles of the oracles of God...* London. M. Simmons, [78?]p. 12mo. 1648
Note: WING S3112. Other editions 1650, 1655. Reprinted Boston, 1747.
Locations: C; MWA, CtY

1648#16
WALKER, Clement. *The history of Independency...* London. 174p. 4to. 1648
Note: WING W329, EA 648/196. Also issued in 1648 as *Relations and observations...*, (EA 648/197). Republished in 1649 and 1650. See the discussion in EA 649/127–9 and EA 650/227–8. Contains references to Independents' connexions with America.
Locations: L; CSmH, DFo, MH

1648#17
WOODBRIDGE, Benjamin. *Church members set in joynt. Or, a discovery of the unwarrantable and disorderly practice of private Christians, in usurping the peculiar office and work of Christ's own pastours, namely publicke preaching...* London. E. Calamy for Edmund Paxton, viii, 32p. 4to. 1648
Note: WING W3423. The first published book of a Harvard graduate. Answer to E. Chillenden's *Preaching without ordination...* London, 1647.
Locations: L; O; MH, NNUT, CtY

1649#1
BULLOCK, William. *Virginia impartially examined, and left to publick view, to be considered by all judicious and honest men...* London. J. Hammond, 66p. 4to. 1649
Note: SABIN 9145, WING B5428, EA 649/35. Also discusses Maryland.
Locations: L; O; DLC, RPJCB

1649#2
ENGLAND AND WALES. PARLIAMENT. *An act for the promoting and propagating the gospel of Jesus Christ in New-England.* London. E. Husband, [7]p. F. 1649
Note: SABIN 52600, EA 649/119. From a collection of Parliamentary acts, or printed separately by the Society for the Propagation of the Gospel in New-England?
Locations: L; RPJCB, DLC, CtY

1649#3
HOOKER, Thomas. *The covenant of grace opened: wherein these particulars are handled...* London. G. Dawson, ii, 85p. 4to. 1649
Note: WING H2644.
Locations: L; O; CtY, RPJCB

1649#4
LISLE, Francis. *The kingdoms divisions anatomized...* London. J. Clowes for H. Allen, 13p. 4to. 1649
Note: SABIN 39934, WING L2369, EA 649/75. Refers to events in New England.
Locations: L; MH, CLU-C, NNUT

1649#5
A perfect description of Virginia: being, a full and true relation of the present state of the plantation... Also, a narration of the countrey, within a few dayes journey of Virginia, west and south... London. R. Wodenoth, 19p. 4to. 1649
Note: SABIN 60918, WING P1486, EA 649/95.
Locations: L; RPJCB, MiU-C

1649#6
RUTHERFORD, Samuel. *A free disputation against pretended liberty of conscience...* London. R. Ibbitson for A. Crooke, 410p. 4to. 1649
Note: SABIN 74457, WING R2379, EA 649/106. References to Roger Williams and New England.
Locations: L; RPJCB, CtY, MH

1649#7
SHEPARD, Thomas. *Theses Sabbaticae. Or, The doctrine of the Sabbath.* London. T. R. and E. M. for J. Rothwell, xx, [380]p. 8vo. 1649
Note: SABIN 80257, WING S3144–7. Other editions in 1650, 1655.
Locations: L; RPJCB

1649#8
To our reverend and deare brethren the ministers *of England and Wales.* [Cambridge]. s.sh. F. 1649
Note: EA 649/36. Broadside signed by Cambridge University officers, etc. exhorting collections for Society for Propagation of the Gospel in New-England.
Locations: Ow;

1649

1649#9
To our reverend brethren the ministers of the Gospel in England and Wales. [Oxford?]. s.sh. F. 1649
Note: SABIN 58037, EA 649/86. Broadside signed by Vice-Chancellor of Oxford University and others exhorting collections for Society for Propagation of the Gospel in New-England.
Locations: Ow;

1649#10
WINSLOW, Edward. *The glorious progress of the Gospel, amongst the Indians in New England. Manifested by three letters.* . . London. E. Winslow, printed by H. Allen, 28p. 4to. 1649
Note: SABIN 22152, WING W3936, EA 649/131. Letters by J. Eliot and T. Mayhew.
Locations: L; RPJCB

1650#1
BRADSTREET, Anne. *The tenth muse lately sprung up in America. Or severall poems.* . . *Also a dialogue between old England and new, concerning the late troubles.* London. S. Bowtell, 207p. 8vo. 1650
Note: SABIN 7296, WING B4167, EA 650/37.
Locations: L; DLC, RPJCB

1650#2
CHEWNEY, Nicholas. *Anti-Socinianism, or a brief explication.* . . *for the confutation of.* . . *gross errors and Socinian heresies, lately published by William Pynchion.* . . London. J. M. for H. Twyford and T. Dring, [240]p. 4to. 1650
Note: WING C3804.
Locations: L; RPJCB, DLC

1650#3
COTTON, John. *Of the holinesse of church-members.* . . London. F. N. for H. Allen, 95p. 4to. 1650
Note: SABIN 17073, WING C6448, EA 650/54.
Locations: L; O; DLC, RPJCB

1650#4
ENGLAND AND WALES. PARLIAMENT. *An act for charging of tobacco brought from New-England with custome and excise.* London. 2p. F. [1650]
Note: SABIN 52599, WING E1004a, EA 650/76.
Locations: L; RPJCB, NN

1650#5
ENGLAND AND WALES. PARLIAMENT. *An act prohibiting trade with the Barbada's, Virginia, Bermudas and Antego.* . . *[30 October 1650].* London. E. Husband and J. Field, [9]p. F. 1650
Note: SABIN 145, EA 650/77.
Locations: L; RPJCB, ViU

1650#6
HUDSON, Samuel. *A vindication of the essence and unity of the Church Catholike visible.* . . *in answer to.* . . *Mr Hooker.* . . London. A. M. for C. Meredith, 30, 265p. 4to. 1650
Note: SABIN 33496, WING H3266, EA 650/97.
Locations: L; O; MH, CtY

1650#7
MATHER, Richard. *A catechisme or, the grounds and principles of Christian religion, set forth by way of question and answer.* . . London. J. Rothwell, 124p, 8vo. 1650
Note: WING M1268, HOLMES, MM, 36.
Locations: L; O; MH, RPJCB, CtY

1650#8
MATHER, Richard. *A heart-melting exhortation, together with a cordiall consolation, presented in a letter from New-England.* . . London. A. M. for J. Rothwell, 84p. 12mo. 1650
Note: SABIN 46780, WING M1273, HOLMES, MM, 42, EA 650/123.
Locations: O; CtY, ViU

1650#9
PARKER, Thomas. *The copy of a letter written by Mr. Thomas Parker, pastor of the church in Newbury in New-England, to his sister.* . . *Novemb. 22. 1649.* . . London. J. Downame, J. Field, E. Paxton, 20p. 4to. 1650
Note: SABIN 58769, WING P475.
Locations: L; MH

1650#10
ROBINSON, Henry. *Briefe considerations concerning the advancement of trade.* London. M. Simmons, 10p. 4to. [1649 i.e. 1650]
Note: SABIN 72083n, WING R1667, KRESS 797, EA 650/184.
Locations: L; DFo, CSmH, MH-BA

1650#11
SANDERSON, William. *Aulicus coquinariae; or Vindication, in answer to a pamphlet.* . . London. For Henry Seile, 205p. 8vo. 1650
Note: SABIN 31654, WING S645. Observations on Raleigh, America, etc., often ascribed to Peter Heylyn. EA dates to 1651.
Locations: L; CSmH

1650#12
SIBELIUS, Caspar. *Of the conversion of five thousand and nine hundred East Indians.* . . *with a post-script of the Gospel's good successe also amongst the West-Indians, in New-England.* . . London. J. Hammond, 8, 38p. 4to. 1650

Note: SABIN 56742, 80815, WING S3748, EA 650/197. Reissued in 1656.
Locations: L; RPJCB

1650#13
THOROWGOOD, Thomas. *Jewes in America, or, Probabilities that the Americans are of that race...* London. W. H. for T. Slater, 136p. 4to. 1650
Note: SABIN 44194, WING T1067-8, BAER 32, EA 650/210. Reissued in 1652 as *Digitus Dei: new discoveryes...* (MBAt, RPJCB). Another edition in 1660.
Locations: L; RPJCB

1650#14
To the supreme authority of this nation, the Commons of England assembled in Parliament... The humble petition of the merchants and others of the cities of London and Bristol... [London]. s.sh. F. [1650]
Note: SABIN 101433, WING T1738. EA dates to 1651. For restraint on growing tobacco in England to benefit thousands of families in the plantations. Signed by five London and one Bristol merchant.
Locations: L;

1650#15
A treatise of New England published in anno Dom. 1637. and now reprinted. London. 16p. 4to. 1650
Note: SABIN 96741, EA 650/211. No copy of the Treatise of 1637 is known.
Locations: MH

1650#16
WILLIAMS, Edward. *Virginia's discovery of silkewormes, with their benefit. And the implanting of mulberry trees...* London. T. H. for J. Stephenson, 75p. 4to. 1650
Note: SABIN 104192, WING W2659, EA 650/230. Issued separately and as part of *Virgo triumphans...*, below, 1650.
Locations: L; RPJCB

1650#17
WILLIAMS, Edward. *Virgo triumphans: or, Virginia richly and truly valued; more especially the south part thereof: viz the fertile Carolina, and no lesse excellent isle of Roanoak...* London. T. Harper for J. Stephenson, 47p. 4to. 1650
Note: SABIN 104193, WING W2661, EA 650/231. A second edition *Virginia: more especially the south part thereof...* in 1650 (EA 650/232).
Locations: L; RPJCB, CSmH, DLC

1651#1
BLAND, Edward. *The discovery of New Brittaine. Began August 27. Anno Dom. 1650... From Fort Henry... in Virginia... to the fals of Blandina... in*

1651

New Brittaine... London. T. Harper for J. Stephenson, 16p. 4to. 1651
Note: SABIN 52518, WING B3155, BAER 54.
Locations: L; DLC, RPJCB

1651#2
CARTWRIGHT, William. *The ordinary, a comedy.* London. For. H. Moseley, 90p. 8vo. 1651
Note: WING C714. Rogues escape to New England, where the orthodox will be their easy prey. Reprinted in *Comedies, tragi-comedies...* London, 1651, WING C709.
Locations: L; Lg; CSmH, CLU-C

1651#3
CAWDREY, Daniel. *The inconsistencie of the independent way, with scripture, and it self. Manifested in a three fold discourse...* London. A. Miller for C. Meredith, 219 p. 4to. 1651
Note: SABIN 11615, WING C1629.
Locations: L; RPJCB

1651#4
CHAPPEL, Samuel. *A diamond or rich jewel, presented to the Common wealth of England, for inriching the Nation.* London. J. Clowes, 20p. 4to. 1651
Note: WING C1955. To the 'Counsel for regulating trade' from Captain Samuel Chappel of Freminton, in the County of Devon, merchant. A fanciful program for increasing trade, converting heathen, exploring 'back side of plantations in the South Sea' etc. Chappel had been imprisoned for debt.
Locations: L; Es; CtY, DFo

1651#5
COLLINGES, John. *Vindiciae ministerii evangelici...* London. R. Tomlins, 89p. 4to. 1651
Note: WING C5346-7. Another edition in 1651. New England familists, antinomians and libertines.
Locations: O; LCL; MH, CtY;

1651#6
Copy of a petition from the governor and company of the Sommer Islands... with a short collection of the most remarkable passages from the original to the dissolution of the Virginia Company. And a large description of Virginia. London. E. Husband, 30, 20p. 4to. 1651
Note: SABIN 100450, WING C6187.
Locations: L; RPJCB

1651#7
COTTON, John. *Christ the fountaine of life...* London. R. Ibbitson, 256p. 4to. 1651
Note: SABIN 170530, WING C6417.
Locations: C; RPJCB, MH

1651#8
ENGLAND AND WALES. PARLIAMENT. *An act for increase of shipping, and encouragement of the navi-*

1651

gation of this nation... the ninth of October, 1651... London. J. Field, 5p. F. 1651
Locations: MiU-C

1651#9
GARDYNER, George. *A description of the new world. Or, America islands, and continent: and by what people those regions are now inhabited...* London. R. Leybourn, 187p. 8vo. 1651
Note: SABIN 26659, WING G221.
Locations: L; MiU-C

1651#10
HARTLIB, Samuel. *Samuel Hartlib, his legacie; or an enlargement of the discourse of husbandry used in Brabant and Flanders...* London. H. Hills, for R. Wodenothe, 8, 131p. 4to. 1651
Note: SABIN 30702, WING H989–991. Also 1652, 1655. Reissued as *The compleat husbandman* (1659). Many references to New England. By Robert Child?
Locations: L; NNUT

1651#11
HELWIG, Cristoph. *Christophori Helvici, v. c. theatrum historicum...* Oxford H. Hall, F. 1651
Note: WING H1411–3, EA 687/75. First published in Latin, in 1609. This 1651 edition mentions New England. Also 1662 (Latin) and 1687 in English with section on English colonies.
Locations: L; O; MH, CtY, CSmH

1651#12
HOBBES, Thomas. *Leviathan, Or the matter, forme, and power of a Commonwealth.* London. A. Crooke, 396p. F. 1651
Note: WING H2246–50. Other editions, 1651, 1676, 1681 etc. Virginia and English colonisation as well as savages of America.
Locations: L; O; CSmH, MHL, CtY

1651#13
HOOKER, Thomas. *The saints dignitie and dutie...* London. By G. D. for F. Eglesfield, 245p. 4to. 1651
Note: WING H2654.
Locations: L; O; MH, CtY

1651#14
LEACH, Edmund. *A short supply or amendment to the propositions for the new representative, for the perpetual peace... of this nation... written and proposed by Edmund Leach of New-England, merchant.* London. J. Macock, 8p. 4to. 1651
Note: SABIN 39504, WING L769.
Locations: L; CtY, MB

1651#15
WHITFIELD, Henry. *The light appearing more and more towards the perfect day. Or, a farther discovery of the present state of the Indians in New England...* London. T. R. and E. M. for J. Bartlet, 46p. 4to. 1651
Note: SABIN 103688, 103689, WING W1999.
Locations: L; DLC

1651#16
WOODNOTH, Arthur. *A short collection of the most remarkable passages from the originall to the dissolution of the Virginia Company.* London. R. Cotes for E. Husband, 20p. 4to. 1651
Note: SABIN 104974, WING W3243, KRESS 842.
Locations: L; RPJCB, CSmH

1652#1
CLARK, John. *Ill newes from New England: or A narrative of New-Englands persecution... Also four proposals to... Parliament and Councel of State, touching the way to propage [sic] the gospel... both in Old England and New...* London. H. Hills, 76p. 4to. 1652
Note: SABIN 13307, WING C4471.
Locations: L; O; DLC, RPJCB

1652#2
FIRMIN, Giles. *Separation examined: or, a treatise wherein the grounds for separation from the ministry and churches of England are weighed and found to be too light...* London. By R. I. for S. Bowtell, 111p. 4to. 1652
Note: WING F964. Firmin lived in New England from 1632 to c.1647. He makes frequent references to New England congregationalism.
Locations: L; O; MH, RPJCB

1652#3
HARTLIB, Samuel. *Glory to be God on High... A rare and new discovery of a speedy way... for the feeding of silk worms in the woods, on the mulberry-tree-leaves in Virginia...* London. For R. Wodenothe, 12p. 8vo. 1652
Note: WING H988.
Locations: L; RPJCB, MH, MB

1652#4
HEYLYN, Peter. *Cosmographie in four books...* London. H. Seile, [1250]p. F. 1652
Note: SABIN 31655, WING H1689–98A. BAER 48. Book IV, part 2 is the 'chorography and history of America'. BAER discusses the second edition of 1652 and further issues, 1657, 1657, 1665, 1666, 1666, 1669, 1670, 1673, 1674, 1674, 1677, 1682 with text hardly changed.
Locations: L; RPJCB, CtY, NN

1652#5
Invocation of Neptune, and his *attendant Nereids, to Britannia, on the dominion of the sea.* London. 1p. F. 1652?

1652

Note: From Nedham's translation of Selden's *Mare Clausum*? Mentions north-west discoveries. Reprinted 1760?
Locations: L;

1652#6
LEACH, William. *First, a bitt and a knock for undersheriffs. . . secondly, with a preservative against fraudulent executors. . . by William Leach. . . and explained by Edmund Leach of New-England, merchant. . .* London. E. Cotes, 24p. 4to. 1652
Note: SABIN 39510, WING L773.
Locations: L;

1652#7
LESTRANGE, Hamon. *Americans no Jewes, or improbabilities, that the Americans are of that race. . .* London. W. W. for H. Seile, 80p. 4to. 1652
Note: SABIN 40231, WING L1186.
Locations: L; RPJCB

1652#8
LILLY, William. *An easie and familiar method whereby to judge the effects depending on eclipses. . .* London. Company of Stationers and H. Blunden, 44p. 4to. 1652
Note: WING L2219. The second part of his *Annus tenebrosus*; also sold separately. Mentions gospel and America.
Locations: L; O; C; CSmH, CtY, DFo

1652#9
MATHER, Richard. *A platform of church discipline. . .* London. W. Bentley for J. Ridley, 32p. 4to. 1652
Note: HOLMES, MM, 51B. Poor edition which was suppressed. First published Cambridge, Mass., 1649 (EVANS 25).
Locations: NN

1652#10
PYNCHON, William. *The Jewes Synagogue: or, a treatise concerning the ancient orders and manners of worship used by the government truly and plainly stated.* London. For J. Bellamie, 4, 90p. 4to. 1652
Note: SABIN 66869, WING P4309.
Locations: L; MH

1652#11
ROBINSON, Henry. *Certain proposalls in order to the peoples freedome and accommodation in some particulars. . .* London. M. Simmons, 27p. 4to. 1652
Note: WING R1670, KRESS 858. Advocates enlargement of foreign plantations and prohibition of export of money to them.
Locations: L; O; DFo, CtY

1652#12
SHEPARD, Thomas. *Subjection to Christ in all his ordinances and appointments, the best means to preserve our liberty. . .* London. T. R. and E. M. for J. Rothwell, 195p. 8vo. [1652?]
Note: WING S3141–3.
Locations: L; DLC, RPJCB, MH

1652#13
STOAKES, John. *A great victory obtained by the English against the Dutch. . . Also, the number of ships. . . richly laden from the east-Indies, the Straights, Virginia and the Barbadoes.* London. G. Horton, 8p. 4to. 1652
Note: WING S5691.
Locations: L; DLC, MiU, NCH

1652#14
STONE, Samuel. *A congregational church is a catholike visible church. . .* London. P. Cole, 51p. 4to. 1652
Note: SABIN 92113, WING S5734.
Locations: L; RPJCB, MiU-C

1652#15
TAYLER, Silvanus. *Common-good: or, the improvement of commons, forests, and chases, by inclosure. . .* London. F. Tyton, 60p. 4to. 1652
Note: WING T552. Enclosure will lead to employment for many hundred thousand labouring men, many of whom go to the plantations 'where the Air is no whit agreeable to their constitutions, and so they quickly return to their dust. . .'
Locations: L; O; CtY, DFo, MH

1652#16
TAYLOR, John. *The impartialiste satyre. . .* London. 14p. 4vo. 1652
Note: WING T469–70. Also 1653 (Lg; CSmH). Execution of Charles I. Scots and 'the Levites of New-England's brood,/Have made old England drunke with English blood.'
Locations: Lv;

1652#17
WHITFIELD, Henry. *Strength out of weaknesse; or A glorious manifestation of the further progresse of the gospel among the Indians in New-England. . .* London. M. Simmons for J. Blague and S. Howes, [46]p. 4to. 1652
Note: SABIN 92797, WING W2001A–2003. Four issues in 1652. Reprinted in 1657 as *The banners of grace and love displayed*, (WING B674).
Locations: L; RPJCB, NN

1652#18
WILLIAMS, Roger. *The bloody tenant yet more bloody: by Mr. Cotton's endevour to wash it white in the blood of the lambe. . .* London. G. Calvert, 320p. 4to. 1652
Note: SABIN 104333, WING W2760.
Locations: L; RPJCB, MiU-C

1652#19
WILLIAMS, Roger. *Experiments of spiritual life and health, and their preservatives in which the weakest child of God may get assurance of his spirituall life.* . . London. 50p. 4to. 1652
Note: SABIN 104335, WING W2762.
Locations: L; RPJCB

1652#20
WILLIAMS, Roger. *The fourth paper, presented by Major Butler, to the. . . committee of Parliament, for the propagating of the gospel.* . . London. G. Calvert, 23p. 4to. 1652
Note: SABIN 104336, WING W2763.
Locations: L; RPJCB

1652#21
WILLIAMS, Roger. *The hireling ministry none of Christs, or, A curse touching the propagating of the gospel of Jesus.* . . London. 36p. 4to. 1652
Note: WING W2765.
Locations: L; RPJCB, MH

1652#22
WOODBRIDGE, Benjamin. *Justification by faith: or a confutation of that antinomian error, that justification is before faith.* . . London. J. Field for E. Paxton, 36p. 4to. 1652
Note: WING W3424–5. Another edition in 1653: O; CT, MH.
Locations: L; RPJCB, MH

1653#1
ASPINWALL, William. *A brief description of the fifth monarchy, or kingdome that shortly is to come into the world.* . . London. M. Simmons for L. Chapman, 14p. 4to. 1653
Note: SABIN 2218, WING A4004.
Locations: L; DLC

1653#2
BROWNE, John. *A brief survey of the prophetical and evangelical events of the last times.* . . London. G. Dawson, 48p. 4to. 1653
Note: SABIN 8655, WING B5117. References to English in America.
Locations: L; O; NNUT

1653#3
COBBET, Thomas. *The civil magistrates power in matters of religion modestly debated. . . with a brief answer to a certain slanderous pamphlet. . . Ill news from New-England.* . . London. W. Wilson for P. Stephens, 108, 52p. 4to. 1653
Note: SABIN 13865, WING C4776.
Locations: L; O; RPJCB, CSmH

1653#4
The Common-wealth's great ship. . . London. M. Simmons for T. Jenner, 32p. 4to 1653
Note: WING C5577. Contains Navigation Act and an account of the Dutch in New Netherland supplying Indians with arms.
Locations: L; Lg; MH, RPJCB

1653#5
DAVENPORT, John. *The knowledge of Christ.* . . London. L. Chapman, 87p. 4to. 1653
Note: SABIN 18707, WING D361.
Locations: L; O; MH, CtY

1653#6
DENHAM, Sir John. *Certain verses written by severall of the authors friends; to be reprinted with the second edition of Gondibert.* London. 24p. 8vo. 1653
Note: WING D991–2. Another edition in 1653. Virginia and slaves mentioned.
Locations: L; CK; CSmH, CtY

1653#7
ELDERFIELD, Christopher. *Of regeneration and baptism, Hebrew and Christian, with their rites, etc.* London 4to. 1653
Note: WING E329. Not seen. EA includes.
Locations: O; CS; CLU-C, NNUT

1653#8
ELIOT, John. *Tears of repentance: or, A further narrative of the progress of the gospel amongst the Indians in New England.* . . London. P. Cole, 47p. 4to. 1653
Note: SABIN 22166, WING E520, HOLMES MM 56. With letter by Richard Mather. Two other editions in 1653.
Locations: L; C; RPJCB, MiU-C

1653#9
EVERARD, John. *Some gospel-treasures opened: or the holiest of all unvailing.* London. By R. W. for R. Harford, 8vo. 1653
Note: WING E3531–33, EA 679/50. Also 1657 and 1659. Variant title, *The gospel-treasury opened.* Urges missionary work among Indians.
Locations: L; CS; MH, DFo, CtY

1653#10
FIRMIN, Giles. *A sober reply to the sober answer of reverend Mr Cawdrey. . . also, the question of Reverend Mr Hooker concerning the baptisme of infants.* . . London. J. G. to be sold by R. Littlebury, 59p. 4to. 1653
Note: WING F966.
Locations: L; O; NN, DFo, MB

1653#11
HOWELL, James. *A German diet: or, the ballance of Europe.* . . London. H. Moseley, 187p. F. 1653

Note: WING H3079. A debate on the merit of the European nations; references to Spanish and British claims in America, to Drake and California, etc.
Locations: L; O; DLC, MH, CtY

1653#12
The Lord Baltemores case, concerning *the province of Maryland.* London. 20p. 4to. 1653
Note: BAER 38.
Locations: L; MHi, NN

1653#13
MATHER, Richard. *A platform of church discipline. . . agreed upon by the elders and messengers. . . at Cambridge in New-England. . .* London. Printed in New-England and reprinted in London. Peter Cole, [41]p. 4to. 1653
Note: SABIN 63332, WING P2398, HOLMES, MM, 51. With epistle by Edward Winslow. First printed Cambridge, 1649 (EVANS 25).
Locations: L; O; RPJCB, CtY

1653#14
NORTON, John. *A discussion of that great point in divinity, the sufferings of Christ. . .* London. A. M. for G. Calvert and J. Nevill, 270, 2p. 8vo. 1653
Note: WING N1317. Norton was teacher at Ipswich, Mass. Contains 'The copy of a letter written from New England, in answer to a letter which they had received from some brethren in Old England, in the behalfe of Mr Pinchin.'
Locations: L; NN, RPJCB, MH

1653#15
ROSS, Alexander. *The history of the world: the second part. . .* London. J. Clark, 647p. F. 1653
Note: WING R1981 and R1956 and 1956A. Another edition in 1652. To 1641, with a chronology. Virginia, New England, etc.
Locations: L; O; CLU-C, MiU, RPJCB

1653#16
ROSS, Alexander. *Pansebeia: or, a view of all religions in the world. . . throughout Asia, Africa, America, and Europe.* London. J. Young, for John Saywell, 587p. 12mo 1653
Note: SABIN 73313, WING R1971–8. Other editions in 1655, 1658, 1664, 1670, 1671, 1672, 1673, 1675, 1683, 1696.
Locations: L; CtY

1653#17
SHEPARD, Thomas. *A treatise of liturgies. . . in answer to. . . Mr. John Ball. . .* London. E. Cotes for A. Crooke, ii, 212p. 4to. 1653

Note: SABIN 80259, WING S3148. EA ascribes to John Allin.
Locations: L; O; RPJCB, NNUT, CtY

1653#18
A total rout, or a *brief discovery of a pack of knaves and drabs. . .* London. Printed for R. L., s.sh. F. 1653
Note: WING T1951. Virginia references.
Locations: L;

1654#1
ASPINWALL, William. *An explication and application of the seventh chapter of Daniel. . .* London. R. I. for L. Chapman, 44p. 4to. 1654
Note: WING A4006.
Locations: L; O; NNUT

1654#2
ASPINWALL, William. *Thunder from heaven against the back-sliders. . .* London. For L. Chapman, 39p. 4to. 1654
Note: WING A4009.
Locations: L;

1654#3
Britannia triumphalis; a brief history *of the warres and other state-affaires of Great Britain. . .* S. Howes, 207p. 8vo. 1654
Note: WING B4817. Also 1656. Revolt of Virginia and Carybe islands in 1649.
Locations: L; O; CSmH, MH, DFo

1654#4
COBBET, Thomas. *A practical discourse of prayer. . . by Thomas Cobbet, minister of the word at Lyn.* London. T. M. for R. Smith, 551p. 8vo. 1654
Note: SABIN 13868, WING C4779. Other editions in 1654, 1657.
Locations: L; MH

1654#5
ENGLAND. *A collection of all the proclamations, declarations, articles and ordinances. . .* London H. Hills, [725]p. F. 1654
Note: WING E876. Dec. 16 1653–Sept 2 1654. Articles of Peace with United Provinces, 1 April 1654.
Locations: L; MiU

1654#6
COTTON, John. *A briefe exposition with practicall observations upon the whole book of Ecclesiastes.* London. T. C. for R. Smith, 277p. 8vo. 1654
Note: SABIN 17049, WING C6413. Another edition, 1657.
Locations: L; O; RPJCB, CSmH

31

1654

1654#7
COTTON, John. *Certain queries published by a friend.* . . London. M. S. for J. Allen and F. Eglesfield, 22p. 4to. 1654
Note: SABIN 17052, WING C6416. Perhaps always printed with separate title page as part of *The covenant of grace.* . . below, 1655.
Locations: L; LCL; RPJCB, CSmH

1654#8
COTTON, John. *The new covenant, or, a treatise, unfolding the order and manner of giving and receiving the covenant of grace.* . . London. M. S. for F. Eglesfield and J. Allen, 198p. 4to. 1654
Note: SABIN 17072, WING C6447. Perhaps always part of *The covenant of grace.* . . , below, 1655.
Locations: L; O; RPJCB, MH

1654#9
COTTON, John. *The result of a synod.* . . London. M. S. for J. Allen and F. Eglesfield, 75p. 4to. 1654
Note: SABIN 70107, WING C6453. Perhaps always part of *The covenant of grace.* . . below, 1655.
Locations: L; O; RPJCB, MH

1654#10
EATON, Samuel. *The Quakers confuted.* . . London. R. White for T. Brewster, (15), 79p. 4to. 1654
Note: WING E125.
Locations: L; MiU-C

1654#11
ELIOT, John. *A late and further manifestation of the progress of the gospel amongst the Indians, in New-England.* . . Pub. by the corporation. . . *for propagating the gospel there.* . . London. M. S., 23p. 4to. 1654
Note: SABIN 22162, WING E517.
Locations: L; O; RPJCB, MH

1654#12
JOHNSON, Edward. *A history of New England. From the English planting in the yeere 1628 untill the yeere 1652.* . . London. N. Brooke, 236p. 4to. 1654
Note: SABIN 36203, WING J771. Running title *Wonder-working providence of Sion's Saviour, in New England.*
Locations: L; RPJCB, MiU-C

1654#13
NORTON, John. *The orthodox evangelist; Or, a treatise wherein many great evangelical truths.* . . *are briefly discussed.* . . London. J. Macock for H. Cripps and L. Lloyd, 331p. 8vo. 1654
Note: SABIN 55887, WING N1320. Another edition in 1657.
Locations: L; RPJCB

1654#14
PYNCHON, William. *The time when the first sabbath was ordained.* . . London. By R. I. to be sold by T. N. [295]p. 4to. 1654
Note: SABIN 66873, WING P4313.
Locations: L; O; DLC, RPJCB, MH

1655#1
Articles of peace, friendship and *entercourse.* . . London. H. Hills and J. Field, [16]p. F. 1655
Note: 3 Nov. 1655 at Westminster with France. Article 25 concerns forts in America. Published as part of a series?
Locations: L;

1655#2
ASPINWALL, William. *A premonition of sundry sad calamities.* . . London. L. Chapman, 39p. 4to. 1655
Note: WING A4008.
Locations: L; MH

1655#3
ASPINWALL, William. *The work of the age.* . . London. R. I. for L. Chapman, 56p. 4to. 1655
Note: WING A4010.
Locations: L; NNUT

1655#4
BAILLIE, Robert. *The disswasive from the errors of the time, vindicated from the exceptions of Mr Cotton and Mr Tombes.* . . London. E. Tyler for S. Gellibrand, 88p. 4to. 1655
Note: WING B458.
Locations: L; O; MH, RPJCB

1655#5
COTTON, John. *An abstract of laws and government.* . . *Collected and digested by.* . . *Mr. John Cotton.* . . *published after his death, by William Aspinwall.* . . London. M. S. for L. Chapman, 35p. 4to. 1655
Note: SABIN 17043, WING C6407.
Locations: O; CtY, MH

1655#6
COTTON, John. *A brief exposition with practicall observations upon the whole book of Canticles.* London. T. R. and E. M. for R. Smith, xvi, 238p. 8vo. 1655
Note: WING C6412.
Locations: L; LCL; DLC, RPJCB

1655#7
COTTON, John. *The covenant of grace.* . . *Whereunto are added: Certain queries.* . . *also a discussion of the civil magistrates power.* . . London. M. S. for F. Eglesfield and J. Allen, 315p. 8vo. 1655
Note: WING C6425, C6426. Another edition in 1655.
Locations: L; O; RPJCB, CSmH

1655#8
COTTON, John. *An exposition upon the thirteenth chapter of the Revelation.* London. M. S. for L. Chapman, x, 262p. 4to. 1655
Note: SABIN 17063, WING C6431. Another edition in 1656.
Locations: L; LCL; MB, CtY

1655#9
ENGLAND. LORD PROTECTOR. *A declaration of his highnes by the advice of his council...* London. H. Hills and J. Field, [26]p. F. 1655
Note: WING C7081, SABIN 46141. Mentions Virginia, Florida, etc. and Spanish interference with American shipping. Dated 26 October 1656.
Locations: L; LL; C; MH, RPJCB

1655#10
HAMMOND, John. *Hammond versus Heamans. Or, an answer to an audacious pamphlet... by... Roger Heamans... his murthers and treacheries committed in the Province of Maryland...* London. 17p. 4to. [1655]
Note: WING H619, BAER 40, CHURCH 537.
Locations: L; RPJCB

1655#11
HARTLIB, Samuel. *The reformed common wealth of bees. Presented in severall letters and observations... With the reformed Virginian silk-worm...* London. For G. Calvert, 62, 40p. 4to. 1655
Note: SABIN 30701, WING H997, KRESS 925. Part of proposals intended to diversify Virginia's economic life.
Locations: L; O; MH, CtY, NN

1655#12
HARTLIB, Samuel. *The reformed Virginian silk-worms, or, a rare and new discovery... for the feeding of silk-worms... on the mulberry tree-leaves in Virginia...* London. J. Streater for G. Calvert, 40p. 4to. 1655
Note: SABIN 30700, WING H1000. A reprint of part II of *The reformed common wealth of bees*, above, 1655.
Locations: L; RPJCB

1655#13
HEAMAN, Roger. *An additional brief narrative of a late bloody design against the Protestants in Ann Arundel County, and Severn, in Maryland in the Country of Virginia...* London. L. Chapman, 15p. 4to. 1655
Note: WING H1305, BAER 41.
Locations: L; RPJCB

1655#14
IRELAND. BY THE LORD DEPUTY AND COUNCIL. *Proclamation that if any protected person is murdered and the murderers go free four papists shall be transported in their place to America* [18 April 1655].
Note: STEELE II, 553.
Locations: NO COPY LOCATED.

1655#15
LANGFORD, John. *A just and cleere refutation of a false and scandalous pamphlet, entituled, Babylon's fall in Maryland, etc... To which is added a law in Maryland concerning religion, and a declaration concerning the same.* London. 35p. 4to. 1655
Note: SABIN 38886, WING L387, BAER 42.
Locations: L; DLC, RPJCB

1655#16
N., N. *America: or an exact description of the West Indies...* London. R. Hodgkinsonne for E. Dod, 484p. 8vo. 1655
Note: WING N26, 26A. SABIN 51678, BAER 43, 49, Reissued in 1657. Contains North American material. By Thomas Peake?
Locations: L; O; RPJCB, NN

1655#17
PRICE, Laurence. *The mayden's of London, brave adventures, or, a boon voyage intended for the sea...* London. For F. Grove, s.sh. F. [1655]
Note: 1655 or 1656. WING P3373, SABIN 100486.
Locations: L; O;

1655#18
PYNCHON, William. *A farther discussion of that great point in divinity the sufferings of Christ...* London. lii, 439p. 4to. 1655
Note: SABIN 66868, WING P4308.
Locations: LCL; NNUT

1655#19
STRONG, Leonard. *Babylon's fall in Maryland; a fair warning to Lord Baltimore. Or, a relation of an assault made by divers Papists... against the Protestants... to whom God gave a great victory...* London. [15]p. 4to. 1655
Note: SABIN 92940, WING S5994, BAER 44.
Locations: L; DLC, MBAt

1655#20
***Virginia and Maryland. Or, the** Lord Baltamore's [sic] printed case, uncased and answered. Shewing, the illegality of his patent and usurpation of royal jurisdiction and dominion there...* London. 52p. 4to. 1655
Note: SABIN 100546, WING F1457, BAER 45.
Locations: L; CSmH

1656#1
ASPINWALL, William. *The legislative power is Christ's...* London. L. Chapman, iv, 52p. 12mo. 1656
Note: SABIN 2219, WING A4007.
Locations: L; O; RPJCB

1656#2
BRECK, Edward. *An answer to a scandalous paper... therein is found many lies and slanders, and false accusations against those people called Quakers...* London. G. Calvert, 24p. 4to. 1656
Note: SABIN 66910, WING B4339. Dated from Dorchester, in New England.
Locations: L; DLC, RPJCB

1656#3
A censure of that learned and reverend... *Mr John Cotton... upon the way of Mr Henden, of Benenden, in Kent...* London. J. G. for S. Stafford, 56p. 4to. 1656
Note: SABIN 17051, WING C6415.
Locations: L; O; RPJCB

1656#4
COBBET, Thomas. *A fruitfull and usefull discourse...* London. S. G. for J. Rothwell, 12, 243p. 8vo. 1656
Note: SABIN 13866, WING C4777. On parents' and childrens' duties.
Locations: L; O; RPJCB

1656#5
COTTON, John. *A practical commentary, or an exposition... upon the first epistle generall of John...* London. R. I. and E. C. for T. Parkhurst, 43p. F. 1656
Note: SABIN 17076, WING C6641. Second edition, 1658.
Locations: L; O; RPJCB, CtY

1656#6
EVANS, Arise. *Light for the Jews, or the means to convert them...* London. Printed for the author, 8vo. 1656
Note: WING E3461. 'The winde-breath and lyes of sectuaries coming from New-England, Holland, and other places east from us, has spoiled the glory of our Nation.' A second title page dated 1664
Locations: L; O; MH, OHU

1656#7
HAMMOND, John. *Leah and Rachel, or, The two fruitful sisters Virginia, and Mary-land: their present condition, impartially stated and related...* London. T. Mabb for N. Bourn, 32p. 4to. 1656
Note: SABIN 30102, WING H620, BAER 46.
Locations: L; DLC, RPJCB

1656#7A
HOOKER, Thomas. *The application of redemption, by the effectual work of the word, and spirit of Christ...* London. Peter cole, 702, 32p. 4to. 1656
Note: See WING H2639–41 for other variant issues in 1657 and 1659.
Locations: L; DLC

1656#8
HOOKER, Thomas. *A comment upon Christ's last prayer in the seventeenth of John...* London. P. Cole, 532p. 4to. 1656
Note: SABIN 32832, WING H2634.
Locations: L; RPJCB

1656#9
JESSEY, Henry. *A narrative of the late proceed's [sic] at White-Hall concerning the Jews...* London. L. Chapman, 14p. 4to. 1656
Note: WING J696. Postscript: 'The late progress of the Gospel among the Indians in New-England.'
Locations: L; O; RPJCB, CtY, NN

1656#10
New-Haven's settling in New-England. And some laws for government: published for the use of their colony... London. M. S. for L. Chapman, 81p. 4to. 1656
Note: SABIN 53017, WING N645B.
Locations: MBAt, MWA, NN

1656#11
TRADESCANT, John. *Musaeum tradescantianum: or, A collection of Rarities preserved at South-Lambeth neer London.* London. John Grismond, to be sold by Nathanael Brooke, 179p. 8vo. 1656
Note: WING T2005–7. Other editions 1660, 1661. Birds and animals from Virginia, Indian artefacts, etc. etc. This collection later formed part of the Ashmolean Museum, Oxford.
Locations: L; O; C; MH, NN, CtY

1656#12
VANE, Henry. *A healing question propounded and resolved... in order to love and union amongst the honest party...* London. T. Brewster, 24p. (3)p. 4to. 1656
Note: SABIN 98498, 98499, WING V68. Another edition in 1660.
Locations: L; MH

1656#13
WOODBRIDGE, Benjamin. *The method of grace...* London. T. R. and E. M for E. Paxton, 4to. 1656
Note: WING W3426.
Locations: L; O; CtY, DFo, MH

1657#1
ASPINWALL, William. *The abrogation of the Jewish sabbath.* London. J. C. for L. Chapman, 40p. 4to. 1657
Note: WING A4003A.
Locations: L; MH

1657#2
A book of the continuation *of forreign passages...* London. M. S. for T. Jenner, 61p. 4to. 1657
Note: WING B3716. On articles of peace in 1654 and 1655. Forts in America.
Locations: L; MH, NN, RPJCB

1657#3
BOS, Lambert van den. *Florus Anglicus or an exact history of England, from the reign of William the Conqueror to the death of Charles I.* London For S. Miller, 217 1p. 8v0. 1657
Note: WING B3773–6. 'Gabat' and new countries to the west, New England and Virginia. Other editions 1658, 1660, 1662.
Locations: L; O; DFo, CtY, CSmH

1657#4
CLARKE, Samuel. *A geographicall description of all the countries in the known world... and of the four chiefest English plantations in America...* London. R. I. for T. Newberry, F. 1657
Note: WING C4516–7. Another edition, 1671.
Locations: O; C; LCL; DLC, MH, RPJCB

1657#5
COLES, William. *Adam in Eden: or, Nature in Paradise. The history of plants, fruits, herbs and flowers...* London. J. Streeter for N. Brooke, 629p. F. 1657
Note: WING C5807–8. Virginia hemp and five-leaved ivy, water agrimony of New England, etc. etc. Another edition in 1657.
Locations: L; O; MH, CtY, DFo

1657#6
COTTON, John. *Spiritual milk for Boston Babes.* London. H. Cripps, 8vo. 1657
Note: WING C6462A. First published Cambridge, Mass., 1656 (EVANS 42, WING C6462). Another edition, 1672, WING C6461.
Locations: Oc;

1657#7
ENGLAND. PARLIAMENT. *An act giving a licence for transporting fish in forreigne bottoms.* London. H. Hills and J. Fields, 3p. F. 1657
Note: WING E1138. Fish from Newfoundland and New England may be transported without paying any customs or duties. Dated 17 September 1656.
Locations: L; L; O; MH, CtY

1657#8
GATFORD, Lionel. *Publick good without private interest...* London. For H. March, 76p. 4to. 1657
Note: SABIN 26760, WING G337, BAER 47. Maryland.
Locations: RPJCB, NN

1657#9
GORTON, Sam. *An antidote against the common plague of the world. Or, an answer to a small treatise... intitul'd Saltmarsh returned from the dead...* London. J. M. for A. Crook, 296p. 4to. 1657
Note: WING G1305, 1305A. Dated at Narragansett Bay, October 20, 1656.
Locations: L; MB

1657#10
IRELAND. LORD DEPUTY AND COUNCIL. *Proclamation voiding all orders and licences for transportation of idle and vagabond persons to the West Indies.* [4 March 1656/7].
Note: STEELE II, 588.
Locations: NO COPY LOCATED.

1657#11
PARKER, Thomas. *Methodus gratiae divinae in traductione hominis peccatoris ad vitam, septuaginta thesibus succincta et elaborate explicate.* London. A. Roper, 62p. 8vo. 1657
Note: WING P477. Edited and published by Parker's son, Robert Parker.
Locations: L; O; MH, MiU-C

1657#12
PURCHAS, Samuel. *A theatre of politicall flying insects. Wherein especially the nature... of the bee, is discovered and described...* London. R. I. for T. Parkhurst, 207p. 4to. 1657
Note: SABIN 66688, WING P4224. A discussion of bees, hornets, etc. with some American references.
Locations: L; O; RPJCB

1657#13
TATHAM, John. *London's triumphs, celebrated the nine and twentieth day of... October, 1657...* London. J. Bell, 11p. 4to. 1657
Note: WING T226. The four parts of the world represented, each 'having four attendance answerable to the natives of their severall countries.'
Locations: L;

1658#1
ALLEN, Thomas. *A chaine of scripture chronologie from the creation of the world to the death of Jesus Christ.* London. By M. S. 8, 240p. 4to. 1658
Note: SABIN 872, WING A1047A. Other editions 1659, 1668.
Locations: MB

1658#2
The coat of armes *of Sir John Presbyter.* London. s. sh, F. 1658
Note: WING C4764–5. Also 1661. The third part of the coat is 'of the countrey of New England; she beares for her

1658

armes, a prick-ear'd Preach-man, pearcht upon a Pulpit, holding forth to the people a Schismaticall Directory.'
Locations: L; O

1658#3
COTTON, John. *A defence of Mr John Cotton from the imputation of selfe contradiction.* . . Oxford. By H. Hall for T. Robinson, [183]p. 8vo. 1658
Note: WING C6427. Reply to works by D. Cawdrey.
Locations: L; O; DLC, MH, RPJCB

1658#4
FAGE, Robert. *A description of the whole world.* . . London. J. Owsley, 70p. 4to. 1658
Note: SABIN 23646, WING F82aA–82B, F83, BAER 63, 69. Other editions in 1663, 1666, 1667, 1671. Little on North America in this edition; perhaps more in later ones?
Locations: L; CtY, RPJCB

1658#5
FIRMIN, Giles. *Of schism. Parochial congregations in England, and ordination.* . . London. T. C. for N. Webb and W. Grantham, 158p. 8vo. 1658
Note: SABIN 24401. WING F958. Firmin was 'late of New England' and discusses various New England writers.
Locations: L; O; DLC, MH, RPJCB

1658#6
GORGES, Ferdinando. *A brief narration of the original undertakings.* London. E. Brudenell, for N. Brook, 236p. 4to. 1658
Note: WING G1303. Also reprinted as Part ii of *America painted.* . . , below, 1659. An unacknowledged reprint of Johnson's *A History of New England*, above, 1654.
Locations: CSmH, MH, CtY, RPJCB

1658#7
HOLYOKE, Edward. *The doctrine of life, or of mans redemtion [sic].* . . London. T. R. for N. Ekins, 426p. 4to. 1658
Note: SABIN 32666, WING H2534.
Locations: L; DLC

1658#8
HUDSON, Samuel. *An addition or postscript to the Vindication.* . . London. J. B. for A. Kemble, 4, 52p. 4to. 1658
Note: SABIN 33497, WING H3263. Relates to John Cotton.
Locations: L; O;

1658#9
The king of Spain's cabinet council divulged. . . for obtaining the universal monarchy. London. J. H. for J. S. 158p. 8vo. 1658
Note: WING K574. Spanish cruelties: Florida, Virginia, West-Indies, New Spain, etc.
Locations: L; Cgc; DFo, CtY

1658#10
NORTON, John. *Abel being dead yet speaketh; or, The life and death of. . . Mr. John Cotton.* . . London. T. Newcomb for L. Lloyd, 51p. 4to. 1658
Note: SABIN 41005, 55881, WING N1313.
Locations: L; RPJCB

1658#11
RUTHERFORD, Samuel. *A survey of the Survey of that summe of church discipline, penned by Mr Thomas Hooker, late pastor. . . in New England.* . . London. J. G. for A. Crook, 521p. 4to. 1658
Note: WING R2395.
Locations: L; O; DLC, MH, CtY

1658#12
WHEELWRIGHT, John. *A brief, and plain apology by John Wheelwright: Wherein he doth vindicate himself, from al [sic] those errors. . . layed to his charge by Mr. Thomas Welde.* . . London. Edward Cole, 29p. 4to. 1658
Note: WING W1604. See Winthrop, *Antinomians.* . . , above, 1644. Also Sargent Bush, Jr., 'John Wheelwright's Forgotten Apology,' *New England Quarterly*, LXIV, No. 1, March 1991, 22–45.
Locations: EN;

1659#1
BEVERLEY, John. *Unio reformantium sive examen Hoornbecki de indepentismo apologeticum.* . . London. S. Thompson, 185p. 8vo. 1659
Note: SABIN 5111, WING B2118. Numerous references to writings by New Englanders. Another edition in 1659.
Locations: L; O; MB, CtY

1659#2
BLAND, John. *Trade revived, or a way proposed to restore, increase, inrich, strengthen and preserve the decayed. . . trade of this our English nation.* . . London. For T. Holmwood, 57p. 4to. 1659
Note: WING B3158–9, KRESS 1009. Also 1660 (L;).
Locations: CSmH, MH

1659#3
CARYL, Joseph? *Peters patern. . . a funeral sermon preached at the internment of Mr Hugh Peters.* . . London. 13p. 4to. 1659
Note: WING C784. A satire?
Locations: L; RPJCB, MH

1659#4
CHARKE, Ezekiel. *A pretended voice from heaven, proved to bee the voice of man, and not of God.* . . London A. Kembe, 126p, 4to. 1659

Note: WING C2069. Cites Cotton, Noyes, New England Platform of Church Discipline, etc.
Locations: L; LCL; NNUT

1659#5
CHAUNCY, Charles (1592–1672). יהוה צדקנו *or the doctrin [sic] of the justification of a sinner in the sight of God.* . . London. R. I. for A. Byfield, 306p. 4to. 1659
Note: SABIN 12307, WING C3739.
Locations: L; C; RPJCB, MH

1659#6
CLARKSON [or CLAXTON], Laurence. *The Quakers downfal. . . also a brief narration of the Quakers conference with us the second of July 1659. wherein we made it appear, that all their sufferings in New-England, or any other nation, they suffer justly as evil doers. . .* London. For the author to be sold by W. Learner, 72p. 4to. 1659
Note: WING C4582, SMITH AQ, 125–6.
Locations: Lfr; DLC, MH

1659#7
COTTON, John. *A treatise of the covenant of Grace. . .* London. J. Cottrel for J. Allen, 250p. 8vo. 1659
Note: SABIN 17085, WING 6465. Other editions, 1662, 1671.
Locations: L; O; CtY

1659#8
CYRANO DE BERGERAC, Savinien. *Selemnarchia. Or the government of the world in the moon.* London J. Cottrel, to be sold by H. Robinson, 8vo. 1659
Note: WING C7719. Canadian references.
Locations: L; O; CtY, MH

1659#9
DAVENPORT, John. *A catechisme containing the chief heads. . . for the church of Christ at New-Haven. . .* London. J. Brudenell, J. Allen, 54p. 8vo. 1659
Note: WING D357.
Locations: L; CtY

1659#10
ELIOT, John. *The Christian commonwealth: or, The civil policy of the rising kingdom of Jesus Christ. . .* London. L. Chapman, 35p. 4to. [1659]
Note: SABIN 22144, WING E505.
Locations: L; O; RPJCB, MiU-C

1659#11
ELIOT, John. *A further accompt of the progresse of the gospel amongst the Indians in New-England, and of the means used effectually to advance the same. . .* London. M. Simmons for Corporation of New England, 35p. 4to. 1659

Note: SABIN 22149, WING E510. Another edition in 1660. Contains Abraham Pierson's *Some helps for the Indians. . .*, first published Cambridge, Mass, 1658 (EVANS 52).
Locations: L; O; DLC, RPJCB

1659#12
FOWLER, Robert. *A Quakers Sea-Journal: being a true relation of a voyage to New-England. Performed by Robert Fowler of the Town of Burlington in Yorkshire, in the year 1658.* London. F. Cassinet, 8p. 4to. 1659
Note: SABIN 25318, WING F1376, SMITH II, 656.
Locations: L;

1659#13
FOX, George. *The secret workes of a cruel people made manifest. . .* London. 1, 26p. 4to. 1659
Note: WING F1899. SMITH, II, 512 ascribes to John Rous and others. Attack on New England Puritans.
Locations: Lfr; CSmH, MH, RPJCB

1659#14
FOX, George. *To the councill of officers of the Armie, and the Heads of the nation; and for the inferior officers and souldiers to read.* London. 8p. 4to. 1659
Note: WING F1955. Refers to the New Inquisition set up in New-England.
Locations: L; C; RPJCB, CtY, DFo

1659#15
GODFREY, Edward. *To the right honourable the Parliament of the Commonwealth of England. . . Humble petition of Edward Godfrey. . . and sundry others. . . of the Provinces of Mayne and Liconia. . .* London. s.sh. F. [1659]
Note: WING T1706A.
Locations: Lpro; CSmH

1659#16
GORGES, Ferdinando. *America painted to the life. The true history. . .* London. E. Brudenell, for N. Brooke, 4pts. 4to. 1659
Note: SABIN 28020, WING G1300, 1301, 1302, BAER 50, KRESS 971. See CHURCH 559 for discussion of parts and editions. Two other editions, 1659: (1) L; DLC, MH (2) L; O; DLC, MH.
Locations: L; DLC, MH

1659#17
HOWGILL, Francis. *The heart of New-England hardned [sic] through wickednes. . .* London. T. Simmons, 40p. 4to. 1659
Note: SABIN 33362, WING H3166.
Locations: L; MiU-C

1659#18
HOWGILL, Francis. *The popish inquisition newly erected in New-England, whereby their church is manifested*

A Quakers Sea-Journal:

BEING A TRUE
RELATION
Of a Voyage to
NEW-ENGLAND.

Performed by ROBERT FOWLER of the Town of *Burlington* in *Yorkshire*, in the Year 1658.

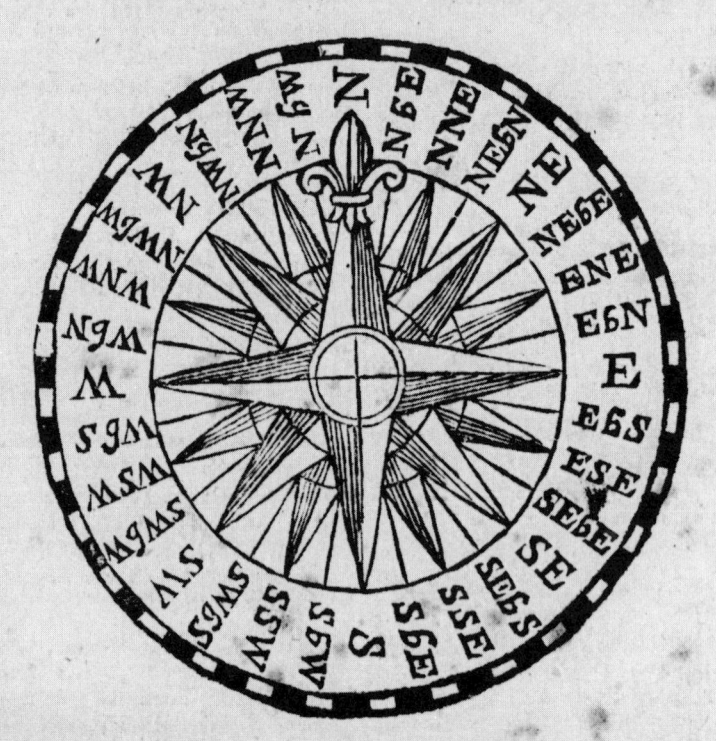

London, Printed for *Francis Coffinet*, at the Anchor & Mariner in Tower-street. Anno 1659.

to be a daughter of mysterie Babylon... London. T. Simmons, 72p. 4to. 1659
Note: SABIN 33363, WING H3177.
Locations: L; CSmH

1659#19
MASSACHUSETTS GENERAL COURT. *A declaration of the General Court of the Massachusetts... October 18. 1659. Concerning the execution of two Quakers... Reprinted in London...* London. s.sh. F. 1659
Note: WING M1001. First printed Cambridge, Mass., 1658 (EVANS 51).
Locations: L; O; MH

1659#20
MATHER, Richard. *A disputation concerning church-members and their children, in answer to XXI. questions...* London. J. Hayes for S. Thomson, 31p. 4to. 1659
Note: SABIN 20274, WING M1271a, HOLMES, MM, 40.
Locations: L; DLC, RPJCB

1659#21
MATTHEWS, Marmaduke. *The messiah magnified by the mouths of babes in America...* London. A. M. for S. Miller, 52p. 8vo. 1659
Note: WING M1324.
Locations: L;

1659#22
MATTHEWS, Marmaduke. *The rending church-member regularly called back, to Christ, and to his church...* London. A. M. for S. Miller, 45p. 8vo. 1659
Note: WING M1325.
Locations: O;

1659#23
MOXON, Joseph. *A tutor to astronomie and geographie: or an easie...* London. J. Moxon, 224p. 4to. 1659
Note: WING M3021-27A. Other editions 1665, 1670, 1674, 1698, 1699. An accompaniment to globes he produces which incorporate latest discoveries, e.g. California and north-west.
Locations: L; MH, CtY, CLU-C

1659#24
NEWCOMEN, Matthew. *Irenicum; or, an essay towards a brotherly peace and union, between those of the Congregational and Presbyterian way...* London. For N. Webb and W. Grantham; (14), 75p. 4to. 1659
Note: SABIN 35063, WING N910. Largely relates to New England.
Locations: L; O; MH, CtY

1659#25
NICOLSON, William. *An apology for the discipline of the ancient church... especially... our mother the Church of England...* London. W. Leake, 12, 241, 6p. 4to. 1659

Note: SABIN 55261, WING N1110. References to New England.
Locations: L; O; NNUT

1659#26
NORTON, Humphrey. *New-England's ensigne: it being the account of cruelty, the professors pride, and the articles of new faith; signified in characters written in blood...* London. T. D. for G. Calvert, 120p. 4to. 1659
Note: SABIN 52756, WING N636.
Locations: L; RPJCB, MiU-C

1659#27
PETAVIUS, Dionysius or PETAU, Denis. *The history of the world... Together with a geographicall description...* London. J. Streater, to be sold by G. Sawbridge, 610p. F. 1659
Note: WING P1677, 1677A,B,C,D. Four other editions in 1659. Sections on America, including discussion of New England church government.
Locations: L; CT; NN, CtY, NcU

1659#28
PIERCE, Thomas. *The new discoverer discover'd... By way of an answer to Mr. Baxter...* London. J. G. for R. Royston, 309p. 4to. 1659
Note: WING P2186. Mrs Hutchinson and New England antinomians.
Locations: L; O; CSmH, RPJCB, CtY

1659#29
PINDER, Richard. *Bowells of compassion towards the scattered seed... Written to the scattered people in America...* London. M. W. 11p. 4to. 1659
Note: SABIN 62918, WING P2261.
Locations: Lfr; PHC

1659#30
ROUS, John. *New-England a degenerate plant. Who having forgot their former sufferings, and lost their ancient tenderness, are now become famous among the nations in bringing forth the fruits of cruelty...* London. 20p. 4to. 1659
Note: SABIN 73483, WING R2043.
Locations: Lfr; O; CSmH, RPJCB, CtY

1659#31
ROUS, John. *The sins of a gainsaying and rebellious people laid before them... Written at the command of the Lord...* London. M. W. 4p. 4to. 1659
Note: SABIN 73484, WING R2044.
Locations: Lfr; PHi

1659#32
STEPHENSON, Marmaduke. *A call from death to life, and out of the dark wayes and worships of the world...* London. T. Simmons, 32p. 4to. 1659

1660

Note: SABIN 91318, WING S5466.
Locations: L; RPJCB, MiU-C

1660#1
BAKER, Daniel. *Yet one warning more, to thee, O England. . . with a very tender lamentation. . . which may echo and ring again in the ears of New-England. . .* London. R. Wilson, 37p. 4to. 1660
Note: SABIN 2817, WING B489.
Locations: L; RPJCB

1660#2
BISHOP, George. *The warnings of the Lord to the men of this generation.* London. By M. Inman, London and R. Moon in Bristol, 44p. 4to. 1660
Note: WING B3016. Quakers in and near Salem, Mass. and cruel laws of New England.
Locations: L; Lfr; CSmH, DLC, CtY

1660#3
BROME, Alexander. *The Rump: or, a collection of songs and ballads. . .* London. For H. Brome and H. Marsh, 228p. 8vo. 1660
Note: WING B4850A–54 lists editions with variant titles also in 1662, 1664, 1668. See also WING R2275. These collections contain a few pieces about New England.
Locations: L; CtY

1660#4
COTTON, John. *Some treasure fetched out of rubbish.* London. 75p. 4to. 1660
Note: SABIN 17083, WING C6459.
Locations: L; O; RPJCB, MH

1660#5
ELLWOOD, Thomas. *An alarm to the priests, or, a message from heaven. . .* London. R. Wilson, 8p. 4to. 1660
Note: WING E612. Persecuting spirit is badge of antichrist, e.g. that of Independents against Quakers in New England.
Locations: L; O; DFo, CtY

1660#6
EVELYN, John. *Sylva, or a discourse of forest trees, and the propagation of timber in his majesty's dominions.* London. J. Martyn and Ja. Allestry, [xii, 255]p. 1660
Note: WING E3516–8. Also 1670, 1679, 1706, 1729, EA 706/84, 729/85.
Locations: L; CtY, MH

1660#7
ENGLAND AND WALES. PARLIAMENT. *A subsidy granted to the King, of Tonnage and Poundage, and other sums of money payable upon merchandize exported and imported. Together with a book of rates. . .* London. John Bill and Chr. Barker, 140pp., 12mo. 1660

Note: WING E2314. Other editions relate to subsequent Acts. American goods are listed.
Locations: L; MH-BA, InU

1660#8
FIRMIN, Giles. *Presbyterial ordination vindicated. In a brief and sober discourse concerning episcopacy. . .* London. N. Webb, 48p. 4to. 1660
Note: WING F961. Cites Norton in a discussion of New England practices.
Locations: L; RPJCB, MH, CSmH

1660#9
FLETCHER, Henry. *The perfect politician.* London. I. Cottrel, for W. Roybould and H. Fletcher, 8vo. 1660
Note: WING F1334–6, EA 680/74–5. Two issues of second edition in 1680; another edition in 1681. Life of Cromwell with American references.
Locations: L; O; DLC, MH, CtY

1660#10
For the King and both houses of Parliament. . . London. T. Simmons, 34p. F. 1660
Note: WING F1436, SMITH II, 658, BAER 51. Refers to Quaker sufferings in England and America.
Locations: L; Lfr; RPJCB, MB

1660#11
FOX, George. *An epistle general to them who are of the royal priest-hood and chosen generation. . . to be sent abroad among the saints. . . in Old and New England. . . Barbados, and Virginia. . .* London. T. Simmons, 16p. 4to. 1660
Note: SABIN 22694, WING F1802–3. Another issue in 1660 (Lfr; CtY).
Locations: Lfr; MH, RPJCB, MiU-C

1660#12
FOX, George. *The promise of God proclaimed. . . preached by the apostles and by his servants and messengers sent forth since for Barbados, New-England, Virginia. . . to go to them all. . .* London. T. Simmons, s.sh. F. 1660
Note: WING F1888A.
Locations: PHi

1660#13
GARFIELD, John. *The wandring whore continued. A dialogue between Magdalena. . .* London. 15p. 4to. 1660
Note: WING W705 is *The wandering whore's complaint*, 1663 (O;) 'If the trade were as constant and certain, as it is profitable, there would be fewer whores go to Barbadoes and Virginia. . .' Published in parts. Various parts and editions.
Locations: Lg; CSmH

1660#14
HOWGILL, Francis. *The deceiver of the nations discovered. . . his cruel works of darkness. . . in Maryland in Virginia. . .* London. T. Simmons, 27p. 4to. 1660

Note: SABIN 33361, WING H3158, BAER 52.
Locations: Lfr; DLC, RPJCB

1660#15
LE BLANC, Vincent. *The world surveyed: or, the famous voyages and travailes of Vincent Le Blanc...* London. J. Starkey, 407p. F. 1660
Note: WING W3588A, L801–801A. Also 1672, 1675. Chapters on New France, Virginia, Florida.
Locations: L; O; CSmH, DLC, MH

1660#16
MASSACHUSETTS GENERAL COURT. *The humble petition and address of the General Court sitting at Boston in New England, unto Prince Charles the second: presented Feb. 11, 1660.* London. 8p. 4to. 1660
Note: WING H3426, EVANS 61. Evans and Wing give [Boston] as place of publication.
Locations: L; O; MH, RPJCB, CtY

1660#17
MAYHEW, Thomas. *Upon the joyfull and welcome return of Charles the second... to his... government over these his majesties kingdoms and dominions...* London. A. Roper, 13p. 4to. 1660
Note: SABIN 47153, WING M144.
Locations: L; O; MH, CtY

1660#18
NICHOLSON, Joseph. *The standard of the Lord lifted up in New-England...* London. R. Wilson, 24p. 4to. 1660
Note: SABIN 55230, WING N1109.
Locations: L; RPJCB, MiU-C

1660#19
NORTON, John. *The heart of New-England rent at the blasphemies of the present generation... doctrine of the Quakers...* London. J. H. for J. Allen, 95p. 8vo. 1660
Note: SABIN 55884, WING N1319. First printed Cambridge, Mass., 1659 (EVANS 56).
Locations: L; MiU-C

1660#20
NOTTINGHAM, Heneage. *An exact and most impartial accompt... of the trial... of nine and twenty regicides...* London. A. Crook and E. Powel, 287p. 4to. 1660
Note: WING N1403–4. Other editions in 1660 and 1679. Trial of Hugh Peter. He came out of New England to stir up the war.
Locations: L; O; DLC, MH, DFo

1660#21
PENINGTON, Isaac. *An examination of the grounds or causes, which are said to induce the court of Boston... to make that order against the Quakers...* London. L. Lloyd, 99p. 4to. 1660
Note: SABIN 59659, WING P1166.
Locations: L; RPJCB

1660#22
PETER, Hugh. *A dying father's last legacy.* London. For G. Calvert and T. Brewster, 122p, 12mo. 1660
Note: WING P1697. Other issues 1660, 1661, 1683. Also Boston, 1717. Spiritual advice, followed by a short and interesting autobiography with many New England references.
Locations: L; CT; MH, RPJCB

1660#23
PETER, Hugh. *The tales and jests of Mr Hugh Peters, collected in one volume...* London. S. D., 22p. 4to. 1660
Note: SABIN 61196, WING P1721.
Locations: L; O; MH, NN

1660#24
PINDER, Richard. *The captive... visited with the day-spring from on high... Given forth especially for the scattered people in America...* London. T. Simmons, 45p. 8vo. 1660
Note: SABIN 62919, WING P2262.
Locations: Lfr; PSC-Hi

1660#25
SHEPARD, Thomas. *The parable of the ten virgins opened and applied: being the substance of divers sermons on Matth. 25. 1, — 13...* London. J. H. for J. Rothwell and S. Thomson, 240, 203p. F. 1660
Note: SABIN 82735, WING S3114. Reprinted 1695.
Locations: L; RPJCB

1660#26
SMITH, Humphry. *New-England's pretended Christians, who contrary to Christ, have destroyed the lives of men.* London. R. Wilson, s.sh. F. 1660
Note: WING S4080.
Locations: L; Lfr;

1660#27
A true relation of the *proceedings against certain Quakers, at the generall court of the Massachusetts... October 18, 1659...* London. A. W., s.sh. F. 1660
Note: WING T3019.
Locations: L; CSmH

1660#28
UNDERHILL, Thomas. *Hell broke loose: or, an history of the Quakers, both old and new...* London. S. Miller, 50p. 4to. 1660
Note: WING U43–4. Chapt. 6 is on New England Quakers.
Locations: L; O; NN, MH, RPJCB

To the Kings most Excellent Majesty,

The humble Remonstrance of John Blande of London Merchant, on the behalf of the Inhabitants and Planters in Virginia and Mariland,

MOST HUMBLY representing unto Your Majesty the inevitable destruction of those Colonies, if so be that the late Act for encrease of Trade and Shipping be not as to them dispenc'd with; for it wil not onely ruinate the Inhabitants and Planters, but make desolate the largest, fertilest, and most glorious Plantations under Your Majesties Dominion; the which, if otherwise suspended, will produce the greatest advantage to this Nations Commerce, and considerablest Income to Your Majesties Revenue, that any part of the world doth to which we trade.

And that the prejudice which this Act bringeth to those Colonies may appear to Your Majesty, I shall presume to desire, that the following particulars in order to the discovery thereof may be taken into consideration, as it hath reference to the Territories of *Virginia* and *Mariland*, and then to those persons that first were the promoters of the same, for debarring the Hollanders trading to those Plantations, in the long Parliament, with their specious pretences alleged for the obtaining thereof, which are as followeth.

First, That the Hollanders will not permit us to trade into their Indian Territories, therefore we should not admit them to trade in ours.

Secondly, That the Hollanders admission into *Virginia* and *Mariland* spoiled our Commerce, not onely there, but in *England*, and hindred the increase of our Shipping.

Thirdly, That the Hollanders trading into those Colonies lessen'd our Customes here in *England*.

Before I come to shew how invalid the Pretences of the aforesaid persons be, as to the intent for which they were alleged, being onely colourable, and to hinder the Hollanders trade thither, that they might still keep the trade which they had ingrossed in their own hands.

First, I will say something concerning the Persons that did solicit and procure the prohibition of the Hollanders from trading into those Plantations.

Secondly, Wherefore the said Act against the Dutch was procured by them, and is still sought to be continued.

Thirdly, I shall take into consideration those three Motives, or Pretences, urged by the Ingrossers of the *Virginia* and *Mariland* trade, for the debarring the Hollanders from trading thither; and so speaking to each of them, demonstrate plainly, that what is alleg'd thereby to be an advantage to those Colonies, is quite contrary, and will in time utterly ruinate them, the Commerce, our Customes, and Shipping here in *England*.

To the First, concerning the Persons that procured the prohibition of the Hollanders from trading into *Virginia* and *Mariland*, I give this account of them.

They are no Merchants bred, nor versed in forein parts, or any Trade, but to those Plantations, and that from either Planters there, or Whole-sale Tobacconists and Shop-keepers retailing Tobacco here in *England*, who know no more what belongs to the Commerce of the World, or managing new discovered Countries, such as *Virginia* and *Mariland* are, than children new put out Prentice, Can it then be Rational, that such persons judgments should be taken or relyed upon for passing so important an Act?

To the Second Particular, Why these men procured this Act, prohibiting the Hollanders trade into those Colonies at first, and its continuance now, was, and is, because they would keep still in their own hands that Trade which they had ingrossed, and have no body come there to hinder them, and that for the following reasons.

First, That for whatever goods they carried out of *England* to those Plantations, the Inhabitants should pay to them what prices and rates they pleased to require, else they should have nothing at all of them to supply their necessities.

Secondly, To force the Planters to deliver them such Tobaccoes, which by the labour and sweat of their browes they had made, at the rates they themselves trading thither would have it, whereby they got that oftentimes of the poor Planters for a half-penny, which they made us pay for here in *England* by Retale three or four shillings.

Thirdly, That if they could not get the Planters Tobaccoes at their own rates, but that the Planters would ship it themselves for *England*, then would not the Traders thither let the Planters have any Tunnage in their Ships to *England*, except it were at such high freight, as the Tobacco comming for *England* could never yield what would satisfie the same; so that if they could not get the Planters Tobacco for nothing in the Country, They would have it for nothing when arrived in *England*.

Fourthly, That seeing the Hollanders could not go to *Virginia* and *Mariland*, the Traders thither might carry it to *Holland* from those Colonies themselves, and so get (besides having the Tobacco for little or nothing of the Planters) the Duties the Hollander used to pay in the Countrey for what he exported thence; and also the Custom, which ought by their own rule to have been paid in *England*.

By which I hope its apparent, that it was nor is not their love to the Plantations, the Commerce, or to encrease the Duties in *England*, that caused them to seek the Hollanders prohibition from *Virginia* and *Mariland*, but their own private interests, not regarding if the Colonies and all in them perished, so they might keep the said Trade still: Surely then such men are not meet Judges for debarring of the Hollanders from trading to those Plantations.

To the third Particular, wherein it is to be considered, how destructive those three motives and pretences (urged) for the obtaining this Act of prohibition to the Hollanders from trading to *Virginia* and *Mariland* are to those Colonies, the Commerce, and Your Majesties Customes here in *England*, I declare as followeth.

To the First, in which it is alleged, That being the Hollander permits not us Trade in their Indian Dominions, why should we admit him Trade in ours?

A good reason it were, and justly retaliated, if *Virginia* and *Mariland* were stoared with, and did produce
such

1661#4

1661#1
BACON, Francis. *A letter of advice written by Sr. Thomas Bacon to the Duke of Buckingham...* London. For R. H. and H. B. 14p. 4to. 1661
Note: WING B299–300. Advice on trade and colonisation, treatment of Indians, etc. 'Never before published.'
Locations: L; O; MH, CtY, CSmH

1661#2
BISHOP, George. *An epistle of love to all the saints.* London. R. Wilson, 27p. 4to. 1661
Note: WING B2992.
Locations: L; O; MH, MiU-C

1661#3
BISHOP, George. *New England judged... and the summe sealed up of New-England's persecutions...* London. R. Wilson, 176p. 4to. 1661
Note: SABIN 5628–9, WING B3003, BAER 53, SMITH I, 279.
Locations: L; O; MH, MiU-C

1661#4
BLAND, John. *To the Kings most excellent majesty, the humble remonstrance of John Blande... on the behalf of the inhabitants and planters in Virginia and Mariland...* London. 4p. F. [1661]
Note: SABIN 100529, WING B3157, BAER 54.
Locations: L;

1661#5
BURROUGH, Edward. *A declaration of the sad and great persecution of and martyrdom of the people of God, called Quakers, in New-England...* London. R. Wilson, 32p. 4to. 1661
Note: SABIN 9455, WING B5994.
Locations: L; C; DLC, CtY

1661#6
ENGLAND AND WALES. SOVEREIGN. CHARLES II. *A proclamation for the due observation of certain statutes made for the suppressing of rogues, vagabonds... [9 May 1661.]* London. Bill and Barker, 3p. F. 1661
Note: STEELE 3300, BRIGHAM 109, WING C3476. Mentions transportation to colonies, etc.
Locations: L; O; MH, DFo

1661#7
***For the King and both** houses of Parliament...* London. 12p. F. 1661
Note: SMITH I, 456, II, 660, BAER 55. References to Quaker sufferings in England and America.
Locations: O; MB, MH, DLC

1661#8
FOX, George. *To Friends in Barbadoes, Virginia, Maryland, New-England, and elsewhere.* London. 4p. 4to. 1661
Note: SABIN 25356, WING F1953, SMITH I, 669, BAER 61. Reprinted in *A Collection of many select and Christian epistles...*, below, 1698.
Locations: Lfr; CT; DLC, PHC

1661#9
***The history of the life** and death of Hugh Peters, that archtraytor, from the cradell to the gallowes.* London. F. Coles, 13p. 4to. 1661
Note: SABIN 61197, WING H2167.
Locations: L;

1661#10
MAYLINS, Robert. *A letter which was delivered to the King...* London. G. Calvert, s.sh. F. 1661
Note: SABIN 47156, WING M1447, SMITH I, 169, BAER 56. Asks for repeal of laws against Quakers.
Locations: Lfr; DLC

1661#11
***Merry drollery, or a collection** of jovial poems, merry songs...* London. J. W. for P. H., 175p. 8vo. [1661?]
Note: WING M1860–2. Other editions with slightly varying titles and contents in 1670, 1691. Items about New England and emigration.
Locations: O; CtY

1661#12
NOYES, James. *Moses and Aaron: or, the rights of church and state...* London. T. R. for E. Paxton, 96, 24p. 4to. 1661
Note: WING N1457. An exposition of congregationalism by Noyes, sometimes minister at Newbury, Mass. Dedication to Charles II by Thomas Parker. Written from Newbury.
Locations: O; NNUT, RPJCB

1661#13
PEACHAM, Henry. *The compleat gentleman... third impression, much inlarged...* London. E. Tyler, for R. Thrale, 455p. 4to. 1661
Note: WING P943. Enlarged by Thomas Blount with references to American cosmography.
Locations: L; CtY, DLC, MH

1661#14
PERROT, John. *Beames of eternal brightness, or branches of everlasting blessings, to be spread over India and all the nations of the earth, by John, who is called a Quaker.* London. For R. Wilson, 40p. 4to. 1661
Note: SABIN 4116, WING P1613. 'India' includes North America.
Locations: O; C; MH, CtY

1661

1661#15
ROBINSON, William. *An appendix to. . . New England judged; being certain writings (never yet printed) of those persons which were there executed. . .* London. R. Wilson, 31p. 4to. 1661
Note: SABIN 5629, WING R1721.
Locations: L; LF;

1661#16
ROFE, George. *A true believers testimony of the work of true faith. . .* London. R. Wilson, 96p. 8vo. 1661
Note: SABIN 72602, WING R1790. Written in Pennsylvania and Maryland.
Locations: Lfr; BBN;

1661#17
SMITH, William. *To the King's most excellent majesty. . . an essay for recovery of trade.* London. T. Milbourn, 49p. F. 1661
Note: WING S4267. Part III 'For the advancement of fishing and plantations.'
Locations: L;

1662#1
BROOKSOP, Joan. *An invitation of love. . . With a word to the wise. . . and a lamentation for New-England. . .* London. R. Wilson, 15p. 4to. [1662]
Note: SABIN 8372, WING B4983.
Locations: L; RPJCB

1662#2
CLARKE, Samuel. *A collection of the lives of ten eminent divines. . .* London. W. Miller, 535p. 4to. 1662
Note: WING C4506. Other editions. New England material, including life of John Cotton. Other biographical works by Clarke issued in 1677 also included the life of Cotton.
Locations: L; RPJCB

1662#3
COALE, Josiah. *A song of the judgements and mercies of the lord: wherein the things seen in secret, are declared openly. . .* London. 20p. 8vo. 1662
Note: WING C4756. Reprinted 1663: L; CLU-C, PHi and 1669: L; CtY, RPJ, CSmH. Written on Long Island in America.
Locations: Lfr;

1662#4
ENGLAND AND WALES. SOVEREIGN. CHARLES II. *A proclamation declaring. . . a free port at his city of Tanger. . . [16 November 1662.]* London. Bill and Barker, 2p. F. 1662
Note: WING C3284, STEELE 3369. Tangiers, a free port, except for ships from English plantations, etc.
Locations: L; Lsa; CSmH, MH

1662#5
ENGLAND AND WALES. TREATIES. *Articles of peace and alliance. . .* London. Assigns of J. Bill and C. Barker, 48p. 4to. 1662
Note: WING C2896, 2896A. With the United Provinces, 4 September, 1662. English and Latin texts. Also Edinburgh, 1667.
Locations: L; O; MH, RPJCB, CtY

1662#6
GRAVE, John. *A song of Sion. Written by a citizen thereof, whose outward habitation is in Virginia. . . with an additional postscript from another hand.* London. R. Wilson, 12p. 4to. 1662
Note: SABIN 28334, WING G1604. Postscript by M. M. attributed to Martin Mason.
Locations: L; O; CSmH, RPJCB

1662#7
GRAY, Robert. *Virginia's cure: or an advisive narrative concerning Virginia. Discovering the true ground of that churches unhappiness. . .* London. By W. Godbid for H. Brome 22p. 4to. 1662
Note: SABIN 26274, WING G1624. 'As it was presented to Bishop of London Sept. 2, 1661'. Authorship also ascribed to the Rev. Roger Green.
Locations: L; LLL; MH, NN, RPJ

1662#8
HOWGILL, Francis. *The rock of ages exalted above Rome's imagined rock. . .* London. For G. C., 110p. 8vo. 1662
Note: WING H3178. Christianity rising in America.
Locations: L; Lfr; MH, NN, RPJCB

1662#9
HOWGILL, Francis. *A testimony concerning the life, death, trials, travels. . . of Edward Burroughs. . .* London. W. Warwick, 25p, 4to. 1662
Note: SABIN 33364, WING T809. Another edition in 1663.
Locations: Lfr; CtY

1662#10
LLOYD, Owen. *The panther-prophesy, or, a premonition to all people. . .* London. 7p. F. 1662
Note: WING P2665. Cf. SABIN 40120. Account of vision occurring to Lloyd who was living in Virginia in 1643 and lost his fortune there. Reprinted in Dutch in 1688.
Locations: L; LW; MH, DFo

1662#11
MITCHEL, Jonathan. *Propositions concerning the subject of baptism and consociation of churches. . . by a synod. . . of the churches in Massachusetts-colony. . . anext the answer of the dissenting brethren and messengers of the churches of New-England. . .* London. 40p. 4to. 1662

Note: SABIN 66059, WING M2291. First (?) printed Cambridge, Mass., 1662 (EVANS 68). Also contains *Anti-Synodalia Scripta Americana* by Charles Chauncy, reprinted in Cambridge, Mass. in 1664 (EVANS 86).
Locations: L; O; MH, RPJCB

1662#12
MORYSON, Francis. *The lawes of Virginia now in force...* London. E. Cotes for A. Seile, 86p. F. 1662
Note: SABIN 100380, BAER 58, WING M2849.
Locations: L; RPJCB, DLC

1662#13
RIGGE, Ambrose. *A visitation of tender love (once more) from the Lord unto Charles the II...* London. 8p. 4to. 1662
Note: SABIN 13816, SMITH I, 433. WING R1500. The author is sometimes given as Josiah Coale. Preface by A. K. Coale from 'New-England, this 25th of the 3rd month, 1662' against New England cruelties to the Quakers.
Locations: L; Lfr; CSmH, PSC

1662#14
Short notes and observations drawn *from the present decaying condition of this kingdom in point of trade...* London. 14p. 4to. 1662
Note: WING S3608A. Advocates free trade to Virginia.
Locations: LU; MnU, ViU, NN

1662#15
SIKES, George. *The life and death of Sir Henry Vane, Kt. Or, a short narrative of the main passages of his earthly pilgrimage...* London. 162p. 4to. 1662
Note: SABIN 80993, WING S3780.
Locations: L; LL; DLC, MH, CtY

1662#16
STILLINGFLEET, Edward. *Origines sacrae: or, A rational account of the grounds of the Christian faith.* Cambridge. University Press, for H. Mortlock [at London], 424p. fol. 1662
Note: WING S5616–20A lists five other editions, 1663, 1668, 1675, 1680, 1680. Bk 3, chapt. 4 includes passage on the peopling of America by Indians, estimating the period of their presence there at no more than 800 years. Editions also in 1701, 1702, 1709, 1724, EA 701/247, 702/185, 709/148, 724/168.
Locations: O; C; CtY

1663#1
BERKELEY, Sir William. *A discourse and view of Virginia. By Sir William Berkeley (governor of Virginia).* London. 8, 12p. 4to. [1663]
Note: SABIN 4889, WING B1975, BAER 59.
Locations: L; O; CSmH, NjP

1663#2
BOYLE, Robert. *Some considerations touching the usefulnesse of experimental naturall philosophy.* Oxford. H. Hall, for R. Davis, 2 vols on one, 4to. 1663
Note: WING B4029–31. New world medicines, maize, New England maple. A second edition, Oxford, 1664.
Locations: L; O; CSmH, DLC, DFo

1663#3
YONGE, William. *England's shame: or the unmasking of a political atheist... the life and death of... Hugh Peters...* London. D. Maxwell for T. Sadler, (31) 88p. 16mo. 1663
Note: SABIN 106018, WING Y44.
Locations: L; MH

1664#1
BILLING, Edward. *A faithful testimony for God and my country.* London. For the author, 12p. 4to. 1664
Note: WING B2900. Quaker trials; their transportation to Virginia not allowed.
Locations: L; O; DFo, MH

1664#2
BUSHNELL, Edmund. *The compleat ship-wright.* London. W. Leyburn for G. Hurlock, 4to. 1664
Note: WING B6252–6255A, EA 678/14. Also 1669 (2), 1678, 1688, 1699. Shipwrights to New England and Virginia.
Locations: O; CM

1664#3
A catalogue of the damages *for which the English demand reparation from the United Provinces...* London. H. Brome, 75p. 4to. 1664
Note: WING C1371. With a list of United Provinces' demands from the English. Ship seizures, mainly slavers, but some Newfoundland and New England.
Locations: L; O; C: MH, DFo, CtY

1664#4
The cry of the innocent *and oppressed for justice.* 39p. 4to. 1664
Note: WING C7450. Quaker trials; judge stated that they should not be transported to New England or Virginia.
Locations: L; O; Lfr; MH, PH, CtY

1664#5
DAVENPORT, Thomas. *A brief manifestation of the state and case of the Quakers presented to all people... also to all planters or occupiers of land in the English and forreign plantations...* London. 8p. 4to. 1664
Note: SABIN 44277, WING D372.
Locations: L; CtY

1664

1664#6
DOWNING, Sir George. *A discourse written by Sir Geo. Downing vindicating his royal master.* . . London. J. M. 21p. 8vo. 1664
Note: WING 2106–7. Another edition with additions in 1672.
Locations: L; ICN

1664#7
FORSTER, John. *England's happiness increased, or, a sure and easie remedy against all succeeding dear years; by a plantation of the roots called potatoes.* . . London. A. Seile, 30p. 8vo. 1664
Note: WING F1601. References to Virginia potatoes.
Locations: L; O; NN, WDA

1664#8
HILTON, William. *A relation of a discovery lately made on the coast of Florida, (from lat. 31 to 33 deg. 45 min. north lat.).* . . *with proposals made.* . . *to all such persons as shall become the first settlers.* . . London. J. C. for S. Miller, 34p. 4to. 1664
Note: SABIN 31919, WING H2043. Carolinas.
Locations: L; DLC, RPJCB

1664#9
HOMES, Nathaniel. *Miscellanea; consisting of three treatises.* . . London. Printed for the author, [106]p. F. 1664
Note: WING H2568. America and habitation of Gog and Magog.
Locations: L; LL; Llp;

1664#10
HUBERT, Robert. *A catalogue of many natural rarities.* . . *to be seen at the place called the Musick-House near the west end of St. Paul's church.* . . London. T. Ratcliffe, for the author, 62p. 12mo. 1664
Note: WING H3243. Virginia rattle snake and antivenom, Florida sloth, etc.
Locations: L; O; CSmH, CtY

1664#11
MUN, Thomas. *England's treasure by forraign trade.* . . London. J. G. for T. Clark, 88p. 8vo. 1664
Note: WING M3073–4, KRESS 1139. Also 1669 and 1698 as *England's benefit.* . . Mentions our 'fishing plantations' in New-England, Virginia, Greenland, the Summer Islands and New-found-land.
Locations: L; O; MH, DFo, CtY

1664#12
PHILIPOT, Thomas. *Original and growth of the Spanish monarchy.* . . London. W. G. for R. Taylor, 264p. 8vo. 1664
Note: WING P1998. Section on Spain and America, including California and Florida.
Locations: L; O; NN, RPJCB, CtY

1665#1
CODRINGTON, Robert. *His majesties propriety, and dominion on the Brittish seas asserted: together with a true account of the Neatherlanders insuportable insolencies.* . . London. T. Mabb for A. Kembe and others. 176p. 8vo. 1665
Note: WING C4602–3. New Netherland and New England. Also attributed to R. Clavell. Another edition, 1672.
Locations: L; O; RPJCB

1665#2
CLIFFE, Edward. *An abreviate of Hollands deliverance by, and ingratitude to the Crown of England.* . . London. Printed 1685, 68p. 4to. 1665
Note: WING C4700. Section on Dutch West India Company and North America.
Locations: L; RPJCB, CtY, DFo

1665#3
DOWNING, Sir George. *A reply of Sir George Downing.* . . *to the remarks of the deputies of the Estates-general, upon his memorial of December 20. 1664.* . . London. 104p. 4to. 1665
Note: SABIN 20787, WING D2109.
Locations: L; O; CtY, MiU-C

1665#4
ENGLAND AND WALES. SOVEREIGN. CHARLES II. *Proclamation dispensing with clauses in Navigation Act [22 March 1664/5].* London. Bill and Barker, s.sh. F. 1665
Note: STEELE 3414. Suspends navigation acts until further notice. Allows foreign seamen in ships trading directly and exclusively to plantations, etc. STEELE 3415 is another edition: Lpro
Locations: L; Lsa;

1665#5
FLECKNOE, Richard. *The mariage of Oceanus and Brittania.* London. 44p. 8vo. 1665
Note: WING F1230A. A masque. Africa, Asia, America represented.
Locations: L; CSmH

1665#6
HEAD, Richard and KIRKMAN, Francis. *The English rogue, described in the life of Meriton Latroon. A witty extravagant. Being a compleat history of the most eminent cheats of both sexes.* . . London. H. Marsh, 131p. 8vo. 1665
Note: WING H1245–52 lists 13 other editions/issues. Part I in 1665, 1666, 1667, 1668, 1669, 1672, 1680; part II, 1668, 1671, 1680; part III, 1671, 1674; part IV, 1671, 1680. He trepanned a young girl to Virginia. See S. Gibson, 'A bibliography of Francis Kirkman', *Oxford Biblio. Soc. Pubs.* New series, vol. I, 1947 (Oxford

46

1949) for a detailed discussion of authorship, editions, etc.
Locations: L; DLC, MH, CtY

1665#7
REA, John. *Flora: seu, De florum cultura...* London. By J. G. for R. Marriott, fol. 1665
Note: Also London 1676, 1702. WING R421–2, EA 702/163.
Locations: L; MH

1665#8
SPRAT, Thomas. *Observations on Monsieur de Sorbier's voyage into England...* London. J. Martyn and J. Allestry, 298p. 8vo. 1665
Note: WING S5035–6. Also 1668, 1672, 1677. Criticism of author's failure to discuss western colonies, tobacco and silk in Virginia, etc.
Locations: L; CtY, DFo, MH

1665#9
WAKELY, Andrew. *The mariner's compass rectified...* London. W. Leybourn for G. Hurlock, 8vo. 1665
Note: WING W273–4A. Other editions, 1694 and 1699. Tables of latitude and longitude for the world.
Locations: C; SC; CtY

1666#1
ALSOP, George. *A character of the province of Maryland... also a small treatise on the wilde and naked Indians... Together with a collection of historical letters.* London. T. J. for R. Pring, 118p. 8vo. 1666
Note: SABIN 963, WING A2901, BAER 60.
Locations: L; GH; RPJCB, MiU-C

1666#2
A brief description of the *province of Carolina on the coasts of Floreda...* London. R. Horne, 10p. 4to. 1666
Note: SABIN 10961, WING B4571.
Locations: L; O; RPJCB, MiU-C

1666#3
COUCH, Robert. *New-Englands lamentation for the late firing of the city of London.* London. N. Brooke. Printed Cambridge in New England. Reprinted London s.sh. F. [1666?]
Note: WING C6509.
Locations: L;

1666#4
DANFORTH, Samuel. *An astronomical description of the late comet.* London. Reprinted in London, P. Parker, 28p. 8vo. 1666
Note: SABIN 18474, WING D73. First printed Cambridge, Mass., 1665 (EVANS 99).
Locations: L; RPJCB, CSmH

1666#5
PENINGTON, Isaac. *To friends in England, Ireland, Scotland, Holland, New-England...* London. 12p. 4to. 1666
Note: WING P1211
Locations: L; Lfr; DLC, CtY, PH

1666#6
THOROWGOOD, Thomas. *Vindiciae Judaeorum, or a true account of the Jews...* London. 3pts. 4to. 1666
Note: WING T1069A, SABIN 95653. An enlarged edition of his *Jews in America*, London, 1650, 1660. References to John Eliot, etc.
Locations: DU;

1666#7
WIGGLESWORTH, Michael. *The day of doom: or, A description of the great and last judgement...* London. J. G. for P. C., 9p. 12mo. 1666
Note: WING W2100–3. Other London editions, 1673, 1687; also Newcastle, 1711. First printed Cambridge, Mass., 1662 (EVANS 71). No other British edition until Norwich, 1774?
Locations: L; O;

1667#1
BISHOP, George. *New England judged. The second part... a relation of the cruel and bloody sufferings of... Quakers, in the jurisdiction chiefly of the Massachusetts...* London. 147p. 4to. 1667
Note: SABIN 5630, WING B3004, SMITH I, 282, BAER 62.
Locations: L; O; MH, MiU-C

1667#2
CHAMBERLAYNE, Edward. *Englands wants; or several proposals probably beneficial to England, humbly offered to... both houses of Parliament.* London. For J. Martyn, 43p. 4to. 1667
Note: WING C1839, KRESS 1195. Other editions 1668, 1685, 1689 Advocates a college 'de propagande fide' to convert Indians bordering on English plantations.
Locations: L; O; MH, CtY

1667#3
ENGLAND AND WALES. TREATIES. *Articles of peace and alliance...* London. At the Savoy, 31p. 4to. 1667
Note: WING C2897–9. With United Provinces at Breda, 21/31 July 1667. Another edition in 1667; also Edinburgh, 1667.
Locations: L; O; MH, RPJCB

1667

1667#4
ENGLAND AND WALES. TREATIES. *Articles of peace and alliance.* . . London. Assigns of J. Bill and C. Barker, 58p. 4to. 1667
Note: WING C2895. With France at Breda, 21/31 July 1667. Articles X, XI concern Acadia.
Locations: L; O; MH, CtY, DFo

1667#5
ENGLAND AND WALES. SOVEREIGN. CHARLES II. *A proclamation for recalling dispensations in the Navigation Acts [23 August 1667].* London. Assigns of Bill and Barker, s.sh. F. 1667
Note: WING C3408, STEELE 3499, KRESS 1190. Cancels dispensations granted in proclamation of 22 March 1665, above, 1665.
Locations: L; O; CSmH, DLC

1667#6
GLANVILL, Joseph. *Some philosophical considerations touching the being of witches.* . . London. E. C. for J. Collins, 62p. 4to. 1667
Note: WING G832. Compares the agents of the Devil to 'seducing Fellows we call spirits, who inveigle children by their false and flattering Promises, and carry them away to the Plantations of America, to be servilely employed there in the works of their Profit and Advantage.' Also Indians as witches. The same appears in his *A blow at modern Sadducism* (1668), his *Essays on several important subjects*, (1676) and his *Saducismus triumphatus: or full and plain evidences concerning witches* (1681).
Locations: L; O; CtY, DFo, MH

1667#7
Strange newes from Virginia, being a true relation of a great tempest. London. W. Thackery, 7p. 4to. 1667
Note: SABIN 92715, WING S5910.
Locations: RPJCB

1668#1
BISHOP, George. *A looking glass for the times, etc. to which is added the report from the Lords of the Committee of Councils, and the King's Orders relating to Quakers in New England.* London. 236p. F. 1668
Note: SABIN 24948, WING B2998.
Locations: L; RPJCB

1668#2
COTTON, John. *Spiritual milk for babes.* London. P. Parker, 4to. 1668
Note: SABIN 17084, WING C6460. Perhaps a reprint of Cotton's *Milk for Babes*, above, 1646. Another edition, 1672, WING C6461.
Locations: MB

1668#3
GLANVILL, Joseph. *Plus ultra: or, the progress and advancement of knowledge since the days of Aristotle.* London. J. Collins, 149p. 8vo. 1668
Note: WING G820. Geography and discoveries.
Locations: L; O; DLC, MH, CtY

1669#1
MATHER, Increase. *The mystery of Israel's salvation, explained and applyed.* . . London. J. Allen, 181p. 8vo. 1669
Note: SABIN 46707, WING M1230, HOLMES, IM, 78.
Locations: L; O; E; DLC, MH, MiU-C

1669#2
PATRICK, Simon. *A continuation of the friendly debate. By the same author.* London. R. Royston, 454p. 8vo. 1669
Note: WING P779, 779A, 779B. Two other editions in 1669. Attacks New England ministerial writings.
Locations: L; CLC, CtY, MH

1669#3
A representation to king and parliament, of. . . *Quakers in New-England.* . . London. s.sh. F. 1669
Note: WING R1109A.
Locations: MH

1669#4
ROBINSON, William. *Several epistles given forth by two of the Lord's faithful servants, whom he sent to New-England.* . . *William Robinson, William Leddra.* . . London. 12p. 4to. 1669
Note: SABIN 72199, WING R1722.
Locations: L; RPJCB

1669#5
SHRIGLEY, Nathaniel. *A true relation of Virginia and Mary-land; with the commodities therein, which in part the author saw, the rest he had from credible persons.* . . *anno 1669.* London. T. Milbourne for T. Hudson. 5p. 4to. [1669]
Note: SABIN 80748, WING S3697, BAER 64.
Locations: L; DLC, RPJCB

1670#1
BLOME, Richard. *A geographical description of the four parts of the world.* . . London. T. N. for R. Blome, 64p. F. 1670
Note: SABIN 5968, WING B3214, BAER 65, KRESS 1225. Fourth part refers to America. Reissued in 1680?
Locations: L; O; NN

1670#2
CLARKE, Samuel. *A true, and faithful account of the four chiefest plantations of the English in America.* . . *Virginia, New-England, Bermudas, Barbados.* . . *as also.* . .

48

the natives of Virginia, and New-England. . . London. R. Clavel and others, 9p. F. 1670
Note: WING C4558.
Locations: CSmH, MH, DLC

1670#3
DENTON, Daniel. *A brief description of New-York; formerly called New-Netherlands.* . . London. J. Hancock and W. Bradley, 21p. 4to. 1670
Note: SABIN 19611 WING D1062, BAER 66.
Locations: L; DLC, RPJCB

1670#4
DYRE, William. *To the King's most excellent majesty. The humble petition of William Dyre gent.* . . London. 3p. F. [1670?]
Note: WING D2949A. William Dyer, Quaker, of Rhode Island.
Locations: L;

1670#5
ENGLAND AND WALES. FARMERS OF HIS MAJESTIES CUSTOMS. *Index Vectigalium; or, an abbreviated collection of the Laws, Edicts, Rules and Practices, touching the Customs.* . . London. J. Macock, G. Richards, 93pp. F. 1670
Note: WING E916B. Material on American goods and Acts of Trade relating to colonies.
Locations: L;

1670#6
ENGLAND AND WALES. TREATIES. *A treaty for the composing of differences, and the establishing of peace in America, between the Crowns of Great Britain and Spain.* London. Assigns of J. Bill and C. Barker, 11p. 4to. 1670
Note: WING C3616A-B. The Treaty of Madrid, 8/18 March 1670.
Locations: L; CSmH, RPJCB

1670#7
FIRMIN, Giles. *The real Christian, or a Treatise of effectual calling.* . . London. For. D. Newman, 327p. 4to. 1670
Note: WING F963. References to Thomas Shepard, Richard Hooker, etc.
Locations: L; O; MH, CtY, DFo

1670#8
HOLDER, Christopher. *The faith and testimony of the martyrs and suffering servants of Christ Jesus persecuted in New England vindicated.* . . London. 11p. 4to. 1670
Note: WING H2384, SABIN 32480, SMITH I, 963, EA 678/66.
Locations: Lfr; MRu; CSmH, MH, RPJCB

1670#9
LOCKE, John. *The fundamental constitutions of Carolina, in number a hundred and twenty.* . . *dat. the first day of March, 1669.* London. 25p. F. 1670
Note: WING L2743A. Another edition in 1682: WING L2744: NN.
Locations: Lpro; RPJCB

1670#10
OGILBY, John. *America: being the latest, and most accurate description of the new world.* . . London. By T. Johnson for the author, 674p. F. 1670
Note: SABIN 58809, WING O164–5. Variant issue 1671: L; O; DLC, MH. See discussion in BAER 67, 70.
Locations: CT; NPL; MH, PBL

1670#11
PENN, William. *Truth rescued from imposture. Or a brief reply to. . . a pretented answer, to the tryal of W. Penn, and W. Mead, etc.* . . London. [20]p. 4to. 1670
Note: SABIN 97265, WING P1392.
Locations: L; RPJCB

1670#12
The royal fishing revived. Wherein is demonstrated from what causes the Dutch have upon the matter ingrossed the fishing trade of his majesty's seas. . . London. 12p. 4to. 1670
Note: SABIN 73788, WING R2128, KRESS 1272. Some American references.
Locations: L; MH

1670#13
The true lover's joy: or, a dialogue between a seaman and his love. London. P. Brooksby, s.sh. F. 1670
Note: WING T2747. Date is a guess (Brooksby published 1670–1696). Inconsequential reference to Virginia.
Locations: L; CM;

1671#1
BAXTER, Richard. *A defence of the principles of love, which are necessary to the unity and concord of Christians.* . . London. N. Simmons, 104, 183p. 8vo. 1671
Note: WING D1234. Postscript discusses New England church affairs.
Locations: L; O; MH, MiU-C

1671#2
BETHEL, Slingsby. *The present interest of England stated.* . . London. Printed for D. B., 35p. 4to. 1671
Note: WING B2072–3. Trade needs religious toleration; plantations exhaust men and money. Second edition, 1681.
Locations: L; O; MH, CtY, DFo

1671#3
BOHUN, Ralph. *A discourse concerning the origine and properties of wind. With a historicall account of*

1671

hurricanes. Oxford. W. Hall for T. Bowman, 302p. 8vo. 1671
Note: SABIN 6146, WING B3463.
Locations: L; O; DLC, CtY

1671#4
COALE, Josiah. *The books and divers epistles of the faithful servant of the Lord Josiah Coale...* London. [344]p. 4to. 1671
Note: SABIN 13814, WING C4751, SMITH I, 435, BAER 68.
Locations: L; RPJCB

1671#5
COKE, Roger. *A treatise wherein is demonstrated, that the Church and state of England, are in equal danger with the trade of it.* London. J. C. for H. Brome and R. Horne, 151p. 4to. 1671
Note: WING C4984. Peopling of America, etc. damages the wealth of England.
Locations: L; O; MH, CtY

1671#6
A description of a great sea-storm, that happened to some ships in the gulph of Florida, in September last... London. T. Milbourn for D. Newman, s.sh. F. 1671
Note: SABIN 9706, WING D1142.
Locations: L; CSmH

1671#7
ELIOT, John. *A brief narrative of the progress of the gospel amongst the Indians in New-England, as in the year 1670...* London. J. Allen, 11p. 4to. 1671
Note: SABIN 2242, WING E504.
Locations: L; C; DLC, RPJCB

1671#8
PETTUS, John. *St. Foine improved.* London. S. G. and E. G. for N. Brooke, 20p. 4to. 1671
Note: WING P1909–10, ARENTS, 317. Also 1674. Urges cultivation of St. Foine grass. Refers to those adventuring lives and fortunes in the colonies and to economic advantages of trade.
Locations: O; R; DLC, NN

1671#9
Some considerations touching the present debate between owners and fishermen, relating to the New-found-land trade. By the impartial pen of an eye witness... Oxford. 21p. 4to. 1671
Note: WING S4496A, KRESS 1301.
Locations: MH

1672#1
BLOME, Richard. *A description of the island of Jamaica...* London. T. Millbourn and sold by J. Williams Junior, 192p. 8vo. 1672

Note: SABIN 5966, WING B3208, BAER 71. Describes the English plantations in America. Reprinted 1678.
Locations: L; RPJCB

1672#2
BURROUGH, Edward. *The memorable works of a son of thunder and consolation... Edward Burroughs...* London. [896]p. F. 1672
Note: SABIN 9642, WING B5982. Material on Friends in North America.
Locations: L; O; DLC, MH

1672#3
DAVENPORT, John. *The power of Congregational churches asserted and vindicated.* London. R. Chiswell, and to be sold by J. Usher of Boston, x, [164]p. 12mo. 1672
Note: SABIN 18708, WING D362. Another edition in 1672.
Locations: L; MH

1672#4
HUGHES, William. *The American physitian; or, a Treatise of the roots, plants, trees, shrubs, fruits, herbs, etc. growing in the English plantations in America...* London. J. C. for W. Crook, 159p. 12mo. 1672
Note: SABIN 33605, WING H3332.
Locations: L; RPJCB

1672#5
JOSSELYN, John. *New Englands rarities discovered; in birds, beasts, fishes, serpents, and plants of that country...* London. G. Widdowes, 114p. 8vo. 1672
Note: SABIN 36674, WING J1093. Another edition in 1674.
Locations: L; RPJCB, MiU-C

1672#6
LEDERER, John. *The discoveries of John Lederer, in three several marches from Virginia, to the west of Carolina, and other parts of the continent...* London. J. C. for S. Heyrick, 27p. 4to. 1672
Note: SABIN 39676, WING L835, BAER 72.
Locations: L; DLC, RPJCB

1672#7
STUBBE, Henry. *A justification of the present war against the United Netherlands...* London. H. Hills and J. Starkey (8) 80p. 4to. 1672
Note: SABIN 93225, WING S6050–1, KRESS 1321. Incidental American references. Also 1673.
Locations: L; DLC

1672#8
JORDAN, Thomas. *London triumphant: Or, the City in jollity and splendour...* London. W. G. for N. Brook and J. Playford, 20p. 4to. 1672

Note: WING J1036. Page 9, 'the description of America', pps. 9–11, 'speech by America.'
Locations: L; O; MH, CtY, CSmH

1673#1
BAXTER, Richard. *A Christian directory: or, A summ of practical theology, and cases of conscience...* London. R. White for N. Simmons, 928, 214p. F. 1673
Note: WING B1219–20. Title page dated 1672. Second edition in 1678. Chapter XIV includes slaves in the plantations.
Locations: L; MH, DFo, CtY

1673#2
BAXTER, Benjamin. *Forgery detected, and Innocency vindicated. Being a full discovery of an horrid... slander raised on the Anabaptists of New-England...* London. By J. D. for F. Smith, 4to. 1673
Note: WING F1558.
Locations: L; O; MH, NN

1673#3
BLOME, Richard. *Britannia: or A geographical description of the kingdom's of England, Scotland and Ireland, with the Isles and territories there to belonging...* London. T. Roycroft for R. Blome, 464p. F 1673
Note: WING B3207–8, SABIN 5965, EA 677/26. Another edition in 1677.
Locations: L; O; DLC, MH, CtY

1673#4
FOX, George. *An epistle to all professors in New-England, Germany, and other parts of the called Christian world...* London. 16p. 4to. 1673
Note: WING F1806.
Locations: L; RPJCB

1673#5
The grand concern of England explained; in several proposals offered to the consideration of parliament... London. 92p. 4to. 1673
Note: WING G1491. Dangerous loss of population through emigration, especially to colonies.
Locations: L; O; CtY, MH, DLC

1673#6
HEDWORTH, Henry. *Controversy ended: or the sentence himself given against himself by George Fox... ratified and aggravated by W. Penn...* London. F. Smith, 27p. 8vo. 1673
Note: WING H1351. Attack on Fox and Penn, whose American voyages are mentioned.
Locations: L; Lfr; NNUT, RPJCB

1673#7
LISOLA, François. *Englands appeale from the private cabal at White-hall to the great council of the nation...* London. 52p. 4to. 1673
Note: WING L2372, 2372 A-C, 2373. Six issues in 1673. Also 1689. British Library catalogue lists as by P. Moulin. French threat to plantations, trade, etc.
Locations: L; O; C; MH, NCU, IU

1673#8
A list of the names and stocks, of the governour and company of the adventurers of England trading to Hudson's bay... London. s.sh. F. [c. 1673]. 1673
Locations: L;

1673#9
PARKER, Samuel. *Mr Baxter baptiz'd in bloud, or, a sad history of the unparallel'd cruelty of the Anabaptists in New England...* London. 6p. 8vo. 1673
Note: SABIN 4003, WING P466, B1170. Fictitious. (?)
Locations: LG; RPJCB

1673#10
The present state of Ireland... London. By M. D. for C. Wilkinson and T. Burrell, 281p. 8vo. 1673
Note: WING P3267. Dutch and arming of Indians in New Netherland; Irish colonial trade.
Locations: L; O; Dt; MH, DFo, CtY

1673#11
STUBBE, Henry. *A further justification of the present war against the United Netherlands...* London. H. Hills and J. Starkey, 136p. 4to 1673
Note: WING S6046. Commerce and America.
Locations: L; O; C; MH, DFo, CtY

1674#1
CODDINGTON, William. *A demonstration of true love unto you the rulers of the colony of the Massachusetts...* London. 20p. 4to. 1674
Note: SABIN 14121, 41726, WING C4875. SMITH I, 439 states an edition in 1672.
Locations: L; Lfr; RPJCB, MiU-C

1674#2
ENGLAND AND WALES. SOVEREIGN. CHARLES II. *A proclamation for protection of Royal African Company [30 November 1674].* London. Assigns of Bill and Barker, 2p. F. 1674
Note: STEELE 3604, BRIGHAM 120. Governors to enforce restrictions on African trade to plantations.
Locations: L; O;

1674#3
EVELYN, John. *Navigation and commerce, their original and progress...* London. T. R. for B. Tooke, 120p. 8vo. 1674
Note: WING E3504, KRESS 1358. Mentions British plantations and American fishery.
Locations: L; O; MH, DFo, CtY

1674

1674#4
GELLIBRAND, Henry. *An epitome of navigation...* London. A. Clark for W. Fisher, 8vo. 1674
Note: WING G474–7, EA 680/82, EA 695/78. Tables of latitude and longtitude for America. Other editions 1680, 1695, 1698
Locations: O;

1674#5
JANEWAY, James. *Mr James Janeway's legacy... twenty seven famous instances of God's providences in and about sea-dangers and deliverances... a sermon on the same subject...* London. For D. Newman (8), 134p. 8vo. 1674
Note: SABIN 35752, WING J473–5. Largely about New England. Other editions, 1675, 1680, 1683.
Locations: CT; RPJCB

1674#6
JOSSELYN, John. *An account of two voyages to New England, wherein you have the setting out of a ship, with the charges; the prices of all necessaries...* London. G. Widdows, 279p. 8vo. 1674
Note: SABIN 36672, WING J1091–2, BAER 76, 79. Another edition, 1675.
Locations: L; RPJCB, MiU-C

1674#7
MATHER, Increase. *Some important truths about conversion, delivered in sundry sermons...* London. R. Chiswell, 248p. 8vo. 1674
Note: WING M1253, HOLMES IM, II, 124A. Reprinted Boston, 1684.
Locations: O; E; NN, RPJCB, CSmH

1674#8
MERITON, George. *A geographical description of the world...* London. W. Leake, 444p. 12mo. 1674
Note: SABIN 47971, WING M1790–2, BAER 77. Reprinted in 1679. Has a description of Maryland which is not in first edition of 1671.
Locations: MH, MiU, CtY

1674#9
A net for a night-raven; or, A trap for a scold. London. F. Coles, T. Vere, J. Wright, s.sh. F. [1674?]
Note: SABIN 100502, WING N470A. The date is very approximate.
Locations: O; NN

1674#10
The non-conformists plea for uniformity*... judgement of... provincial assembly... and... preachers, English, Scottish, and New English, concerning toleration and uniformity...* London. H. Brome, 8p. 4to. 1674
Note: SABIN 55420, WING N224.
Locations: L; O; MH, CtY

1674#11
REYNELL, Carew. *The true English interest.* London. G. Widdowes, 92p. 8vo. 1674
Note: SABIN 70402, WING R1215, R1215A, KRESS 1369. Argues for New England and Virginia settlers to move south; to find gold and silver and to consume English goods. Also 1679.
Locations: L; O; DLC, RPJCB, MH

1675#1
A brief and true narration *of the late wars risen in New-England: occasioned by the quarrelsom [sic] disposition... of the barbarous, savage and heathenish natives there...* London. J. S. 8p. 4to. 1675
Note: SABIN 52616, WING B4535.
Locations: L; RPJCB, MiU-C

1675#2
CAREW, George. *Severall considerations, offered to the Parliament, concerning the improvement of trade...* 8p. 4to. 1675
Note: WING C551. New England, Barbados, etc. should have been annexed to Crown; Holland as staging post for English migration to America.
Locations: L;

1675#3
CARKESSE, Charles (compiler). *The Act of Tonnage and Poundage, and Book of Rates; with several statutes at large relating to the Customs... With an abridgment of several other statutes concerning the Customs, etc.* London. Assigns of John Bill and Christopher Barker, 325pp. 12o. 1675
Note: Published in revised and expanded editions in 1684, 1689 (MH-BA), 1702, 1726, 1728, 1731. Supplement, 1737. EA 702/37, 726/33, 728/26, 731/35, 737/51.
Locations: L; MnU

1675#4
COKE, Roger. *England's improvements. In two parts...* London. J. C. for B. H. Brome and others, 115p. 4to. 1675
Note: SABIN 14241, WING C4978, KRESS 1380. Emigration to America.
Locations: L; O; MH, CtY

1675#5
ENGLAND AND WALES. SOVEREIGN. CHARLES II. *By the King. A proclamation for prohibiting the importation of commodities of Europe into any of his majesties plantations in Africa, Asia, or America... not laden in England [and for putting all other laws relating to plantation trade into execution, 24 November 1675].* London. Assigns of J. Bill and C. Barker. s.sh. F. 1675

Note: WING C3378, BRIGHAM 126, STEELE 3619, KRESS SUPP 1421.
Locations: L; O; MH, CSmH

1675#6
FENWICK, John. *Friends, These are to satisfie you... that New Cesarea, or New Jersey... is a healthy, pleasant and plentiful country... dated this 8th of the 1st month, 1675.* London. s.sh. F. 1675
Note: WING F718C, SABIN 24081, SMITH I, 602-3.
Locations: PHi

1675#7
FOX, George. *Cain against Abel, representing New England's Church hirarchy [sic], in opposition to her Christian Protestant dissenters...* London. 48p. 4to. 1675
Note: WING F1754.
Locations: O; RPJCB, MiU-C

1675#8
The kid-napper trapan'd... being a pleasant relation of a man that would have sold his wife to Virginia... London. For P. B. 8p. 4to. 1675
Note: SABIN 37720, WING K421A.
Locations: NN

1675#9
A list of the adventurers of England trading into Hudson's Bay and of their respective shares in the general stock. November 1, 1675. London. s.sh. F. 1675
Note: WING L2412A.
Locations: L; DLC

1675#10
Mock Songs and joking poems... London. W. Birch, 142p. 8vo. 1675
Note: WING M2301. Virginia and Jamaica voyages.
Locations: L; O; MH, NN

1675#11
A new discoverie of an old traveller lately arrived from Port-Dul... London. 6p. 4to. 1675
Note: WING N624. EA states reference to severity of laws against immoral conduct in New England.
Locations: CtY

1675#12
The present state of NEW-ENGLAND, with respect to the Indian War. Wherein is an account of the true reason thereof... Licenced December 13, 1675... London. D. Newman, 9p. F. 1675
Note: SABIN 65324, WING P120A. Another edition in 1676.
Locations: Lg; DLC, RPJCB

1675#13
The Quakers farewel to England, or their voyage to New Jersey, scituate on the continent of Virginia, and bordering upon New England. To the tune of, the independents voyage to New England... London. J. G. s.sh. F. 1675
Note: SABIN 66937, WING Q23.
Locations: L; O;

1675#14
A testimony against John Fenwick, concerning his proceeding about New-Cesaria, or New-Jersey... Also John Fenwick's letter of condemnation sent to Friends; upon their testifying against his proceedings... London. s.sh. F. 1675
Note: SABIN 24082, WING T804
Locations: Lfr;

1675#15
WHARTON, Edward. *New-England's present sufferings, under their cruel neighbouring Indians. Represented in two letters, lately written from Boston to London.* London. B. Clark, 7p, 4to. 1675
Note: SABIN 10300, WING W1536. Second issue in 1675.
Locations: RPJCB, CSmH

1676#1
A continuation of the state of New-England; being a further account of the Indian warr... London. T. M. for D. Newman, 20p, F. 1676
Note: SABIN 52623, WING C5971.
Locations: Lg; O; DLC, RPJCB

1676#2
ENGLAND AND WALES. SOVEREIGN. CHARLES II. *By the King. A proclamation for the suppressing a rebellion lately raised... Virginia... [27 October 1676.]* London. Assigns of J. Bill and C. Barker 2p. F. 1676
Note: BRIGHAM 130
Locations: Lpro;

1676#3
A farther brief and true narration of the late wars risen in New-England... with an account of the fight, the 19th of December last, 1675. London. T. D. for M. K. 12p. 4to. 1676
Note: SABIN 52638, WING F529.
Locations: O; RPJCB, NN

1676#4
FOX, George. *Gospel family order, being a short discourse concerning the ordering of families, both of whites, blacks, and Indians...* London. 22p. 4to. 1676
Note: SABIN 25351, WING F1829, SMITH, I, 675, BAER 82. Reprinted Philadelphia, 1701 (EVANS 972).
Locations: Lfr; MH, MiU-C

1676#5
GLANVILL, Joseph. *Seasonable reflections and discourses, in order to the conviction and cure of the... age...* London. R. W. for H. Mortlock, 8vo. 1676
Note: WING G830, EA 676/83. Mentions wild Americans.
Locations: L; O; C; CLC, CtY, DFo

1676#6
The grand pyrate, or the life and death of Capt. George Cusack the great sea-robber... London. J. Edwin, 31p, 4to. 1676
Note: SABIN 18078, WING G1505. Cusack visited New England and Virginia.
Locations: L; CSmH. RPJCB

1676#7
GROOME, Samuel. *A glass for the people of New-England, in which they may see themselves and spirits, and if not too late repent, and turn away from their abominable ways...* London. 43p. 4to. 1676
Note: SABIN 28926, WING G2065.
Locations: Lfr; RPJCB

1676#8
HARTSHORNE, Richard, and others. *A further account of New Jersey. In an abstract of letters lately writ from thence, by several inhabitants there resident.* London. 13p. 4to. 1676
Note: WING H1007.
Locations: L; RPJCB, CSmH

1676#9
The historians guide, in two parts... Summary account of all... remarkable passages in his majesty's dominions from 1600 until 1676... London. W. Crook, 122p. 8vo. 1676
Note: SABIN 32044, WING C4519. Later editions published 1679, 1688, 1690 as *The historian's guide, or England's remembrancer...* take the events described to the year of publication.
Locations: L; O; MB, CSmH

1676#10
HOWGILL, Francis. *The dawnings of the gospel-day, and its light and glory discovered...* London. [742]p. F. 1676
Note: SABIN 33360, WING H3157, SMITH I, 997, BAER 83. Contains several of his writings on New England.
Locations: L; O; DLC, MH, DFo

1676#11
LUPTON, Donald. *A most exact and accurate map of the whole world: or, The orb terrestrial described in four plain maps, (viz.) Asia, Europe, Africa, and America.* London. J. Garret, 195p. 4to. 1676
Note: WING L3492.
Locations: L; Cj; ICN, DFo

1676#12
MATHER, Increase. *A brief history of the war with the Indians in New-England. From June 24. 1675... to August 12, 1676...* London. R. Chiswell, 51p. 4to. 1676
Note: SABIN 46641, WING M1188, HOLMES, IM, 16. First published or contemporaneously published Boston, 1676 (EVANS 220, 221).
Locations: L; O; RPJCB, MH

1676#13
MOLLOY, Charles. *De jure maritimo et navali: or a treatise of affaires maritime...* London. J. Bellinger and G. Dawes, 452p. 8vo. 1676
Note: WING M2395-99, KRESS 1417. Other editions 1677, 1678, 1682, 1688, 1690, two issues in 1701, editions in 1707, 1722, 1744, EA 701/186, 707/111, 722/132, 744/151. A discussion of slavery and rights of 'planters' with incidental American references.
Locations: L; DLC, NN, MH-BA

1676#14
News from New-England, being a true and last account of the present bloody wars carried on betwixt the infidels, natives, and the English Christians, and converted Indians of New-England... London. J. Coniers, 6p. 4to. 1676
Note: SABIN 55060, WING N983. Another issue in 1676.
Locations: L; RPJCB, MiU-C

1676#15
ORCHARD, N. *The doctrine of devils, proved to be the grand apostacy of the times...* London. Printed by the author, vi, 205p. 8vo. 1676
Note: WING O366A. Dutch translation of 1691 states written by a predicant in New England. Attacks the butchery of witches.
Locations: L; O; MH, DFo, CtY

1676#16
PENN, William. *The description of the province of West-Jersey, in America: as also proposals to such who desire to have any propriety therein.* London. s.sh. F. [1676]
Note: SABIN 59692, WING P1276.
Locations: Lfr;

1676#17
S., N. *A new and further narrative of the state of New-England, being a continued account of the bloudy Indian-war from March till August, 1676...* London. J. B. for D. Newman, 14p. F. 1676
Note: SABIN 52445, WING S120.
Locations: L; RPJCB

1676#18
SPEED, John. *An epitome of Mr. J. Speed's theatre of the empire...* London. For T. Basset and R. Chiswell, 146p. 8vo. 1676
Note: WING S4886. Includes Africa, America etc.
Locations: L; O; NN, MH, RPJCB

1676#19
TOMPSON, Benjamin. *New England's tears for her present miseries: or, A late and true relation of the calamities of New-England since April last past...* London. N. S., 14p. 12mo. 1676
Note: SABIN 96156, WING T1867. First printed Boston, 1676 as supplement to *New England's crisis...* (EVANS 225).
Locations: RPJCB, CSmH

1676#20
TOMPSON, Benjamin. *Sad and deplorable newes from New England...* London. For H. J. 16p. 4to. 1676
Note: WING T1868A.
Locations: L; CtY

1676#21
*A **true account of the** most considerable occurences that have hapned [sic] in the warre between the English and the Indians in New England...* London. B. Billingsley, 10p. F. 1676
Note: SABIN 97085, WING T2385.
Locations: L; RPJCB, MiU-C

1677#1
The Charter of Maryland. London. 24p. 8vo. [after 1676]. 1677
Note: WING M896, 896A, BAER 80. EA lists 1679? and 1685?. Same text as 1632 charter.
Locations: RPJCB

1677#2
ENGLAND AND WALES. SOVEREIGN. CHARLES II. *Articles of peace between... Charles II... and several Indian Kings and Queens... 29th day of May, 1677...* London. J. Bill, etc., 18p. 4to. 1677
Note: SABIN 2145, 34614, 100005, WING C2909.
Locations: L; RPJCB, CSmH

1677#3
The Four gospels and the *Acts of the Holy Apostles, translated into the Malayan tongue...* Oxford. H. Hall, 14, 221p. 4to. 1677
Note: SABIN 25281, WING B2796. References to New England. Dedicated to Robert Boyle.
Locations: O; C; ICN, CtY

1677#4
HALE, Matthew. *The primitive origination of mankind, considered and examined according to the light of nature.*
London. W. Godbib for W. Shrewsbury, 380p. F. 1677
Note: WING H258, EA 677/101, 678/59. Madoc and America; Biblical legends among Indians.
Locations: L; RPJCB, MH

1677#5
HOLYOAKE, Thomas. *A large dictionary, in three parts.* London. W. Rawlins, etc., 3 vols. F. 1677
Note: WING H2535, EA 677/107. Section on exploration of America, etc.
Locations: L; CSmH, NjP, MH

1677#6
HOUGHTON, John. *England's great happiness: or, A dialogue between content and complaint...* London. J. M. for E. Croft, 22p. 4to. 1677
Note: WING H2922, EA 677/113. Lands in America.
Locations: L; RPJCB, CtY, DLC

1677#7
HUBBARD, William. *The present state of New-England. Being a narrative of the troubles with the Indians... To which is added a discourse about the war with the Pequods in the year 1677...* London. T. Parkhurst, 131, 88p. 4to. 1677
Note: SABIN 33446, WING H3212. First printed Boston, 1677, (EVANS 231).
Locations: L; RPJCB

1677#8
HUGHES, William. *The flower garden enlarged... To which is now added a treatise of all the roots, plants, trees, shrubs, fruits, herbs, etc., growing in his majesties plantations, etc.* London. For C. Wall, xii, 102p. 12mo. 1677
Note: WING H3338-9. Another edition in 1683 (the 'third-edition'): L; LRHS; LWML
Locations: L; Oc; IU

1677#9
HUTCHINSON, Richard. *The warr in New-England visibly ended. King Philip that barbarous Indian now beheaded, and most of his bloudy adherents submitted to mercy...* London. J. B. for F. Smith, 2p. F. 1677
Note: SABIN 50536, 101454, WING H3834. Another issue in 1677, printed by J. B. for D. Newman.
Locations: L; CSmH

1677#10
KEITH, George. *The way cast up, and the stumbling-blockes removed...* Edinburgh? 8vo. 1677
Note: WING K218, EA 677/121. Mentions New England's bloody persecutors.
Locations: L; RPJCB, DLC, CtY

55

1677

1677#11
LEE, Samuel. *Eleothriambos, or, The triumph of mercy...* London. J. Hancock, 200p. F. 1677
Note: WING L895. 'The Europeans purchase whole territories with a few beads, knives and Hammers of the naked Indians.'
Locations: L; O; MH, RPJCB, CtY

1677#12
The life of Michael Adrian *de Ruyter Admiral of Holland.* London. J. B. for D. Newman, 115p. 12mo. 1677
Note: WING L2035. His operations in American waters, including Newfoundland.
Locations: L; Ct, MH, DFo, CSmH

1677#13
More news from Virginia, being *a full and true relation of all occurrences in that countrey, since the death of Nath. Bacon with an account of thirteen persons that have been tried and executed...* London. W. Harris, 7p. 4to. 1677
Note: SABIN 100488, WING M2712A.
Locations: ViU

1677#14
NALSON, John. *The countermine: or, a short but true discovery of the dangerous principles, and secret practices of the dissenting party...* London. J. Edwin, 317p. 8vo. 1677
Note: WING N96-100. Other editions 1677, 1678, 1684. References to New England.
Locations: L; O; CtY, DLC, CSmH

1677#15
The present state of Christendome *and the interest of England, with regard to France.* London. J. B. for H. Brome, 28p. 4to. 1677
Note: WING P3257. France, America and West Indies. Universal dominion and universal commerce.
Locations: L; O; DFo, CSmH, RPJCB

1677#16
SELLER, John. *A mapp of New Jersey, in America... The description of the province of West-Jersey... As also, Proposals to such as desire to have any property there.* London. J. Seller and W. Fisher. 1677
Note: BAER 88. With text.
Locations: L; RPJCB, MdBJ-G

1677#17
SHIRLEY, John. *The life the valiant and learned Sir Walter Raleigh, Knight...* London. J. D. for B. Shirley, etc. 243p. 8vo. 1677
Note: WING S3495. Brief mention of Virginia.
Locations: L; O; MH, CtY, RPJCB

1677#18
Strange news from Virginia; being *a full and true account of the life and death of Nathanael Bacon Esquire.* London. W. Harris, 8p. 4to. 1677
Note: SABIN 2679, 92715-6, WING S5911.
Locations: L; RPJCB, MiU-C

1677#19
The true state of the *case between John Fenwick Esq., and John Eldridge and Edmund Warner, concerning Mr. Fenwick's ten parts of his land in West New Jersey in America.* London. 9p. 12mo. 1677
Note: SABIN 24083.
Locations: PHi

1677#20
VOSSIUS, Isaac. *A treatise concerning the motion of the seas...* London. By H. C. for H. Brome, 189p. 8vo. 1677
Note: WING V706. Relates sailing routes to ocean currents; American ocean currents and tides.
Locations: L; O; MH, NN, DFo

1678#1
BROWNE, John, Quaker. *In the eleventh month, on the nineth day... the Spirit of the Lord then signified... saying, Arise and take up a lamentation over New England... With a warning to the rulers of Boston... by Margaret Braister...* London. s.sh. F. 1678
Note: SABIN 8654, SMITH I, 329, WING B5120A.
Locations: Lfr;

1678#2
CROUCH, Nathaniel. *Miracles of art and nature, or, a brief description of the several varieties of birds, beasts, fishes, plants, and fruits of other countreys...* London. W. Bowtel, 120p. 12mo. 1678
Note: SABIN 9502n, WING C7345, C7349-50A. EA 678/28, 683/41, 685/51, 699/50. Also with variant title *Surprizing miracles of nature and art...* 1683, 1685, 1690, 1699. Chapters on America, Florida, etc.
Locations: L; GU; RPJCB, DFo, CtY

1678#3
A discourse showing the great *advantages that new-buildings, and the enlarging of towns and cities do bring to a nation...* London. 22p. 4to. 1678
Note: WING D1620. References to emigration to America.
Locations: L; DLC, CtY

1678#4
FOX, George. *An answer to several new laws and orders made by the rulers of Boston in New England...* London. 7p. 4to. 1678
Note: WING F1744.
Locations: O; RPJCB

1678#5
FOX, George. *Something in answer to a letter (which I have seen) of John Leverat Governor of Boston to William Coddington. . . dated 1677. . .* London. 12p. 4to. [1678?]
Note: WING F1912, SMITH I, 627.
Locations: Lfr; RPJCB, PHi

1678#6
FOX, George, and BURNYEAT, John. *A New-England fire-brand quenched, being something in answer unto. . . book entituled: George Fox digged out of his burrows, etc. . .* London. 233, 255p. 4to. 1678
Note: WING F1864-6. The second part issued in 1678 (L; RPJCB). Another edition in 1679.
Locations: ORP; RPJCB, CSmH

1678#7
WILLUGHBY, Francis. *The ornithology of Francis Willughby. . .* London. By A. C. for J. Martyn, F. 1678
Note: WING W2880. Some American birds, e. g. Virginia nightingale. He designed a voyage to the New World but died first. Edited by John Ray? Latin version in 1686 (WING W2879).
Locations: L; O; DFo, CSmH, MH

1679#1
Description du pays nommé Caroline. London. 3p. F. [1679?].
Locations: L; CSmH

1679#2
DUGDALE, Richard. *A narrative of the wicked plots carried on by Seignior Gondamore for advancing the popish religion and Spanish faction. . .* London. T. B. to be sold by R. Clavel, 16p. F. 1679
Note: WING D2472. Spanish policy towards Virginia, Bermuda, and West Indies. Also 1744.
Locations: L; CtY, DFo, CSmH

1679#3
FOX, George. *Caesar's due rendred unto him according to his image and superscription.* London. 35p. 4to. 1679
Note: WING F1753, EA 679/54. New England persecutions of Quakers.
Locations: Lfr; RPJCB, NN

1679#4
SELLER, John. *Atlas minimus, or a book of geography.* London. J. Seller, 48p. and maps, 12mo. 1679
Note: WING S2465. Short section on English colonies, including Pennsylvania.
Locations: L; O; CSmH, DLC, CtY

1680#1
BETHEL, Slingsby. *The interest of princes and states.* London. J. Wickins, 354p. 8to. 1680

Note: WING B2064-67, EA 680/14, 681/10. Also 1681, 1689, 1694. Newfoundland and English trade, etc.
Locations: L; O; RPJCB, MH, CtY

1680#1A
A congratulatory poem upon the *noble feast made by the ancient and renouned families of the Smiths.* London. Printed for F. Smith, s.sh. F. [1680].
Note: Captain John Smith of Virginia.
Location: L;

1680#2
The fair traders objections, against *the bill, entituled, a bill for preventing clandestine trading, as it relates to the plantations of Virginia and Maryland.* London. s.sh. F. [168-]
Note: SABIN 100466, WING F102a, BAER 135.
Locations: L; NN

1680#3
G., R. *The vain prodigal life, and tragical penitential death of Thomas Hellier. . . executed according to law at Westover, in Charles-City, in the Country of Virginia. . . 5th August 1678. . .* London. S. Crouch, 4, 40p. 4to. 1680
Note: SABIN 3252, WING V19. See *William and Mary Quarterly*, January, 1982.
Locations: RPJCB, CSmH

1680#4
GODWIN, Morgan. *The Negro's and Indian's advocate, suing for their admission into the church. . . To which is added, A brief account of religion in Virginia.* London. J. D. 7, 174p. 8vo. 1680
Note: SABIN 27677, WING G971.
Locations: L; RPJCB, MiU-C

1680#5
LEIGH, Edward. *The gentlemans guide, in three discourses. First, of travel. . .* London. For R. Whitwood, 87p. 8vo. 1680
Note: WING L996. Favourable remarks on John Eliot and his method of converting the Indians; review of travel and voyage literature.
Locations: BC; LIU; DLC, DFo, CSmH

1680#6
MARTINDELL, Anne. *A relation of the labour, travail and suffering of that faithful servant of the Lord Alice Curwen. . .* London. 55p. 4to. 1680
Note: WING M857.
Locations: Lfr; RPJCB

1680#7
MORDEN, Robert. *Geography rectified: or, a description of the world. . .* London. Printed for R. Morden and T. Cockerill, [418]p. 4to. 1680

1680

Note: SABIN 50535, WING M2619–2622a, BAER 95, 128, 153, 207. Discussion of America. Reissued 1688, 1693, 1700.
Locations: RPJCB, MH, DLC

1680#8
PETYT, William. *Britannia languens; or a discourse of trade.* London. T. Dring and S. Crouch, 310p. 8vo. 1680
Note: SABIN 12707, WING P1946, KRESS 1521.
Locations: L; DLC

1680#9
RICH, Robert. *The epistles of Mr Robert Rich to the seven churches.* . . London. F. Smith, 116p. 4to. 1680
Note: WING R1356. Condemns religious persecution in New England
Locations: L; O; Lfr; MH, DFo, PH

1680#10
RUSSELL, John. *A brief narrative of some considerable passages concerning the first gathering, and further progress of a Church of Christ, in gospel-order, in Boston in New-England. . . dated in Boston, 20th, 3rd month, 1680. . .* London. (4), 15p. 4to. [1680 or 1681].
Note: SABIN 74288. Not found in WING. E. C. STARR, *A Baptist bibliography* (New York, 1947) R5021. W. T. WHITLEY, *A Baptist Bibliography* (London, 1916) gives a location at Baptist College, Bristol.
Locations: Lfr;

1680#11
The Virginia trade stated. . . London. s.sh. F. [n. d.] 1680
Note: SABIN 100570, STC 24838, EA 650/223. Date is a guess, but internal references to King's customs and re-export of tobacco suggest later date than that assigned by EA.
Locations: L;

1681#1
An abstract or abbreviation of *some few of the many (later and former) testimonys from the inhabitants of Jersey, and other eminent persons.* . . London. T. Milbourn, 32p. 4to. 1681
Note: SABIN 5303, WING A147.
Locations: L; RPJCB, CSmH

1681#2
BAXTER, Richard. *Faithful souls shall be with Christ.* . . London. N. Simmons, 60p. 4to. 1681
Note: WING B1265, EA 681/9. Mentions John Eliot.
Locations: L; RPJCB, CtY

1681#3
The Charter granted by Charles *II, to William Penn, Esq. Proprietor and Governor of Pennsylvania (4th March 1681).* London. 4p. F. 1681

Note: SABIN 59968.
Locations: NO COPY LOCATED.

1681#4
A conference between a Bensalian *Bishop and an English doctor, concerning church-government.* London. T. Parkhurst and J. Collier, 17p. F. 1681
Note: WING C5725, EA 681/29. Transportation of religious malcontents to America.
Locations: L; O; RPJCB, MH

1681#5
COLLINGES, John. *The history of conformity.* London. A. Maxwell and R. Roberts, [32]p. 4to. 1681
Note: WING C5319–20, EA 681/27. Also 1689. References to New England.
Locations: L; O; CSmH, CtY, MH

1681#6
ENGLAND AND WALES. PRIVY COUNCIL.
At the Court. . . 16 February 1680[–1]. To regulate and encourage trade with the colonies. London. Assigns of J. Bill, etc., 2p. F. 1681
Note: STEELE I, 3726, KRESS SUPP 1505. Deals with Irish exports, etc.
Locations: L; MH-BA

1681#7
ENGLAND AND WALES. SOVEREIGN. CHARLES II. *Proclamation. Grant of Pennsylvania to William Penn [2 April 1681.]* London. Assigns of Bill, etc, 1p, F. 1681
Note: WING C3633, STEELE 3727, BRIGHAM 133.
Locations: L; O; CSmH, MiU

1681#8
FLEMING, Robert. *The fulfilling of the Scripture, or an essay shewing the exact accomplishment of the word of God in his works of providence.* . . London. 8vo. 1681
Note: WING F1268, 1269, 1269A. The 'third edition.' First published in Holland. Also two issues in 1693. Complete in 1726 2nd pt. 1674, 3pt 1678. Intended voyage of Scottish ministers in Ireland to New England in 1636.
Locations: L; Lg; LW; MH, CtY, CSmH

1681#9
The French intrigues discovered. With *the method and art to retrench the potency of France.* . . London. R. Baldwin, 31p. F. 1681
Note: WING F2185, EA 681/50. Newfoundland.
Locations: L; O; CSmH, MH

1681#10
GODWIN, Morgan. *A supplement to the Negro's and Indian's advocate: Or, some further considerations and proposals for the effectual and speedy carrying on of the Negro's Christianity.* . . London. By J[ohn] D[arby]. 12p. 4to. 1681

Note: SABIN 27678, WING G973.
Locations: CSmH, DLC, RPJCB

1681#11
GREW, Nehemiah. *Musaeum regalis societatis. Or a catalogue and description of the natural and artificial rarities belonging to the Royal Society and preserved at Gresham Colledge.* London. W. Rawlins, 385p. in 2pts. F. 1681
Note: WING G1952–1955. Other editions, 1685, 1686 (2), 1694. Plants and trees from Virginia, New-England 'stuff', Indian artefacts, etc.
Locations: L; O; C; CtY, MH, DFo

1681#12
HARRIS, Benjamin. *The case of Benjamin Harris, bookseller, lately come from New England. . .* London. s.sh. F. 1681
Note: SABIN 30463, WING H842A.
Locations: NN

1681#13
HICKES, George. *Peculium Dei. A discourse about the Jews. . .* London. W. Kettilby, 32p. 4to. 1681
Note: WING H1858, EA 681/60. References to Massachusetts laws.
Locations: L; O; NN, CtY, MH

1681#14
NALSON, John. *The character of a rebellion, and what England may expect by one. . .* London. B. Tooke, 18p. F. 1681
Note: WING N91. Refers to effects of rebellion on the American colonies.
Locations: L; DLC, MH

1681#15
NESSE, Christopher. *The signs of the times: or, wonderful signs of wonderful times. . . a faithful collection of. . . signs and wonders. . . in the heavens, on the earth and on the waters. . . this last year 1680.* London. L. Gurtiss, 84p. 4to. 1681
Note: SABIN 52342, WING N463. Some New England references.
Locations: CtY, MH, CLU-C

1681#16
PENINGTON, Isaac. *The works of the long-mournfull and sorely distressed Isaac Penington. . .* London. B. Church, [965]p. F. 1681
Note: WING P1149. Various pieces relating to New England and Quakers.
Locations: L; O; CtY, DFo, MH

1681#17
PENN, William. *A brief account of the province of Pennsylvania, lately granted by the King, under the great seal of England, to William Penn and his heirs and assigns.* London. B. Clark, 8p. F. 1681

Note: SABIN 59680, WING P1225. Another issue in 1681: SABIN 59681
Locations: L; MH, PHi

1681#18
PENN, William. *Some account of the province of Pensilvania in America. . .* London. B. Clark, 10p. F. 1681
Note: SABIN 59733, WING P1365.
Locations: L; RPJCB, MiU-C

1681#19
The present state of the colony of West-Jersey, in America. London. s.sh. F. 1681
Note: WING P3271A
Locations: PHi

1681#20
To the Parliament of England, the case of the poor English protestants in Mary-land under the arbitrary power of their popish governour the Lord Baltimore. . . [London?]. 4p. F. [1681?]
Locations: RPJCB

1681#21
WILLIAMS, Roger, mariner. *To the King's most excellent majesty, the humble petition of. . .* London. s.sh. F. [1681]
Note: SABIN 104344, WING W2271. Relates to Newfoundland.
Locations: RPJCB

1682#1
The articles, settlement, and offices of the Free Society of Traders in Pennsylvania: Agreed upon by divers merchants and others for the better improvement and government of trade in that province. London. B. Clark, [14]p. F. 1682
Note: SABIN 59897, WING A3885, KRESS SUPP 1539.
Locations: L; O; MH, RPJCB

1682#2
ASH, Thomas. *Carolina; or A description of the present state of that country, and the natural excellencies thereof. . .* London. W. C., 40p. 4to. 1682
Note: SABIN 2172, WING A3934.
Locations: L; O; DLC, RPJCB

1682#3
BAXTER, Richard. *Mr. Baxter's vindication of the church of England. . .* London. W. Kettilby, 37p. 4to. 1682
Note: WING B1449, EA 682/9. Discusses New England churches.
Locations: L; RPJCB, MH, CtY

1682

1682#4
BLOME, Richard. *Cosmography and geography in two parts.* London. S. Roycroft for R. Blome, 494p. F. 1682
Note: SABIN 76720, WING V101–4, BAER 101, 105, 146. Text on North America. Other issues 1683, 1693.
Locations: C; CSmH, DLC, NN

1682#5
BUGG, Francis. *De Christiana liberate, or liberty of conscience. . . In two parts. . . To which is added, a word of advice to the Pensilvanians.* London. E. Presser 143, 228p. 8vo. 1682
Note: WING B5370.
Locations: L; C; MH, MiU-C

1682#6
CALVERT, Philip. *A letter from the chancellour of Mary-land, to Col. Henry Meese, merchant in London: concerning the late troubles in Maryland. . . From Patuxent riverside, this 28 December, 1681.* London. A. Banks, 2p. F. 1682
Note: WING C320, BAER 102.
Locations: L; O; RPJCB, MdHi

1682#7
CHAMBERLAYNE, Peregrine. *Compendium geographicum: Or, a more exact, plain, and easie introduction into all geography. . .* London. For William Crook, 186p. 8vo. 1682
Note: WING C1860–1, EA 682/42. Also 1685 (L; CtY). Mainly Europe. pp. 10–12, America; p. 17, St Lawrence.
Locations: L; Cpe; CSmH

1682#8
COLLINS, John. *Salt and fishery. A discourse thereof. . .* London. A. Godbid and J. Playford, 164p. 4to. 1682
Note: WING C5380, KRESS 1553. Newfoundland material.
Locations: L; RPJCB, MH, CSmH

1682#9
CRIPPS, John. *A true account of the dying words of Ockanickon, an Indian King. . . by John Cripps of Burlington, N. J.* London. B. Clark, 8p. 4to. 1682
Note: SABIN 17510, WING O127–8. Another edition in 1683. Reprinted Philadelphia, 1741 (EVANS 4660). Also Boston, 1717?
Locations: L; O; RPJCB, MH

1682#10
CROUCH, Nathaniel. *Admirable curiosities, rarities and wonders. . .* London. T. Snowden for N. Crouch, 232p. 12mo. 1682
Note: WING C7306–8, 7308A, EA 682/54. Florida. Other editions 1684, 1685, 1697.
Locations: L; O; MH, NjP

1682#11
CROUCH, Nathaniel. *Wonderful prodigies of judgement and mercy. . .* London. [189]p. 12mo. 1682
Note: SABIN 9502, WING C7361–2. Other editions 1685 (MH, DFo), 1693, 1699. New England, etc. references.
Locations: L; O;

1682#12
ENGLAND AND WALES. SOVEREIGN. CHARLES II. KING IN COUNCIL. *Whereas. . . by reason. . . abuses of a lewd sort of people called spirits, in seducing many of his majesties subjects to go on shipboard. . . [December 13 1682].* London. Assigns of J. Bill, etc. 2p. F. 1682
Note: STEELE 3737.
Locations: L; O; CtY

1682#13
F., R. *The present state of Carolina with advice to the setlers. . .* London. J. Bringhurst, 36p. 4to. 1682
Note: SABIN 23586, 87919, WING F52a.
Locations: L; RPJCB, CSmH

1682#14
The Frame of the government *of the province of Pennsylvania in America; together with certain laws agreed upon in England by the governour and divers freemen of the aforesaid province. . .* London. [A. Sowle], 11p. 8vo. 1682
Note: SABIN 59697, WING P1292–3. Another edition in 1691: Lfr; MiU-C, PHi. Reprinted Philadelphia, 1689.
Locations: L; O; RPJCB, MH

1682#15
GASCOYNE, Joel. *A true description of Carolina.* London. J. Gascoin and R. Greene, [4]p. 4to. 1682
Note: SABIN 97115, WING G284.
Locations: DLC, RPJCB

1682#16
GIBBON, John. *Introductio ad latinam blasonium. . .* London. J. M. for the author, 165p. 8vo. 1682
Note: WING G650, EA 682/77. The author lived in Virginia. Indians, Carolina, New England and heraldry.
Locations: L; O; DFo, CLC, CtY

1682#17
GODWIN, Morgan. *The revival: or Directions for a sculpture, describing the extraordinary care and diligence of our nation, in publishing the faith among the infidels in America, and elsewhere; compared with other both primitive and modern professors of Christianity. . .* London. J. Darby, s.sh. 4to. 1682

Note: SABIN 703215, WING G972. The sculpture is depicted in a drawing. References to New England and to the shame of slavery.
Locations: O; RPJCB

1682#18
JOSSELYN, John. *A description of New-England in general.* . . London. To be sold by J. Seller. 4p. 4to. [1682?]
Note: SABIN 52692, 79026, WING S2470 gives the author as John Seller. Extracted from Josselyn's *Account of two voyages*, above, 1674.
Locations: L; MH

1682#19
LODDINGTON, William. *Plantation work the work of this generation. Written in true-love to all such as are weightily inclined to transplant themselves and their families to any of the English plantations in America.* . . London. B. Clark, 18p. 4to. 1682
Note: SABIN 63318, WING L2804.
Locations: L; RPJCB, PHi

1682#20
PECHEY, John? *Some observations made upon the Virginian nutts, imported from the Indies: showing their admirable virtue against the scurvy.* . . London. 7p. 4to. 1682
Note: SABIN 56480, 86678, WING P940.
Locations: L; CSmH, NN

1682#21
PENN, William. *An epistle, containing a salutation to all faithful friends, a reproof to all the unfaithfull; and a visitation to the enquiring, in a solemn farewell to them all in the land of my nativity.* London. A. Sowle, 8p. 4to. [1682]
Note: WING P1283, SMITH, II, 302.
Locations: L; O; RPJCB, CtY

1682#22
Proposals by the proprietors of East-Jersey *in America; for the building of a town on Ambo-Point, and for the disposition of lands.* . . *And for the encouragement of artificers and labourers.* . . London. B. Clark, 6p. 4to. 1682
Note: SABIN 1000, WING P3717.
Locations: RPJCB

1682#23
RAY, John. *Methodus plantarum nova.* . . London. H. Faithorne and J. Kersey, 166p. 8vo. 1682
Note: WING R396. Some American references, e. g. Virginia acacia.
Locations: L; O; MH, CtY, DFo

1682#24
ROWLANDSON, Mary. *A true history of the captivity and restoration of Mrs Mary Rowlandson, a minister's wife in New England. . . annexed, a sermon. . . by Mr. Joseph Rowlandson.* . . London. Printed first at New-England: and reprinted at London. Joseph Poole, 46p. 4to. 1682
Note: SABIN 73579, WING R2094. First printed Boston and Cambridge, 1682 (EVANS 331-2). For a discussion of the publishing history see E. Z. Derounian, 'The publication, promotion, and distribution of Mary Rowlandson's Indian Captivity Narrative in the seventeenth century,' *Early American Literature*, Vol 23, No. 5 (1988) pps. 239-261.
Locations: L; RPJCB

1682#25
SOMERS, Nathan. *Proposals for clearing land in Carolina, Pennsylvania, East Jersey, West Jersey: or any other parts of America.* . . *August 9, 1682.* London. J. Bringhurst, s.sh. F. 1682
Note: SABIN 10977, 86801, WING S4646.
Locations: L;

1682#26
STEERE, Richard. *The history of the Babylonish cabal; or the intrigues.* . . *of the Daniel-Catchers. In a poem.* London. R. Baldwin (4), 36p. 4to. 1682
Note: SABIN 91183, WING S5397. Steere lived on Long Island.
Locations: L; CtY

1682#27
A testimony concerning our dear *and well-beloved friend and brother in the truth, William Coale.* . . London. A. Sowle, 16p. 8vo. 1682
Note: SABIN 13817, WING T808, BAER 103, SMITH I, 437. Coale lived in Maryland and most of the testimonies were written by residents of the colony.
Locations: Lfr;

1682#28
W., J. *A letter from New-England concerning their customs, manners and religion. Written upon occasion of a report about a Quo Warranto brought against the government.* London. R. Taylor, 9p. F. 1682
Note: SABIN 52641, WING W59.
Locations: O; RPJCB

1682#29
WHITELOCKE, Bulstrode. *Memorials of the English affairs.* . . London. N. Ponder, 704p. F. 1682
Note: WING W1986. Inconsequential mention of colonial matters.
Locations: L; O; C; DFo, CtY, MH

1682

1682#30
WILSON, Samuel. *An account of the province of Carolina in America. Together with an abstract of the patent, and several other necessary and useful particulars, to such as have thoughts of transporting themselves thither.* London. G. Larkin for E. Smith, 27p. 4to. 1682
Note: SABIN 104685, WING W2932-3. A second edition, corrected, in 1682.
Locations: L; DLC, RPJCB

1683#1
An abstract of a charter *granted by his majesty...* London. J. Playford, F. 1683
Note: WING C2885. Pennsylvania charter.
Locations: LL; MH

1683#2
A brief account of the *province of East: New: Jersey in America: Published by the Scots Proprietors having interest there. For the information of such as may... desire to transport themselves or their families thither...* Edinburgh. J. Reid, 15p. 4to. 1683
Note: SABIN 53079, WING B4518, BAER 107, ALDIS 2370.
Locations: L; E; RPJCB, NN

1683#3
Britanniae Speculum; or a short *view of the ancient and modern state of Great Britain... and of all other dominions and territories now in... possession of... King Charles II.* London. T. Milbourn for C. Hussey, 295p. 12mo. 1683
Note: SABIN 8071, WING B4819.
Locations: L; O; CSmH, MiU-C

1683#4
BROWNE, Sir Thomas. *Certain miscellany tracts.* London. For C. Mearne, 215p. 8vo. 1683
Note: WING B5151-2. Another edition 1684 (L; O; CtY, MH). Includes the prophecy 'When New England shall trouble New Spain'. Also included in *The works of the learned Sir Thomas Browne...*, (London 1686). (L; O; MH, CtY, DFo).
Locations: O; Ob; MH, CSmH, NNUT

1683#5
CLARKE, Samuel. *The lives of sundry eminent persons in this later age. In two parts.* London. T. Simmons, 216p. F. 1683
Note: WING C4538. Includes Richard Mather.
Locations: L; MH, DFo; CtY

1683#6
CRAFFORD, John. *A new and most exact account of the fertile and famous colony of Carolina... the whole being the compendious account of a voyage made... Begun in October 82, and finished this present year, 1683.* Dublin. N. Tarrant, 7p. 4to. 1683
Note: SABIN 17334, WING C6770A.
Locations: NNC, NN

1683#7
CRISP, Thomas. *The second part of Babel's builders unmask't.* London. 16p. 4to. 1683
Note: WING C6953, SMITH, I, 478, EA 683/37. Quakers in New England and Barbados.
Locations: Lfr; Csj; NN-RB

1683#8
CROUCH, Nathaniel. *The strange and prodigious religions customs and manners, of sundry nations...* London. H. Rhodes, 228p. 12mo. 1683
Note: SABIN 18237, WING C7348.
Locations: L; O; CtY, CLU-C

1683#9
ENGLAND AND WALES. PRIVY COUNCIL. *At the Court at Whitehall, the 20th of July, 1683.* London. Assigns of J. Bill, and by Henry Hills, s.sh. F. 1683
Note: SABIN 45929, WING E2893, EA 683/76. Quo Warranto against the Massachusetts charter.
Locations: L; O; RPJCB, MH

1683#10
ENGLAND AND WALES. SOVEREIGN. CHARLES II. *His majesty's declaration concerning the province of East-New Jersey.* Edinburgh. Heir of A. Anderson, s.sh. F. 1683
Note: WING C2963, ALDIS 2449. 5, STEELE, 2559.
Locations: EN;

1683#11
ENGLAND AND WALES. SOVEREIGN. CHARLES II. *To the Governor and Council of East New Jersey and the inhabitants etc. ordering their obedience to the proprietors, the Earl of Perth, John Drummond, Robert Barclay, Robert Gordon and others.* London. Assigns of J. Bill, etc. s.sh. F. 1683
Note: Possibly the same as *His majesties declaration concerning the province of East-New-Jersey...*, above, 1683.
Locations: RPJCB (facsimile)

1683#12
FORD, Philip. *A vindication of William Penn, proprietary of Pennsylvania, from the late aspersions... 12th. 12 Month, 1682...* London. B. Clark, 2p. F. 1683
Note: SABIN 25067, WING F1470, SMITH I, 621.
Locations: L; CSmH

1683#13
LOCKHART, George. *A further account of East-New-Jersay by a letter write to one of the proprietors therof, by a countrey-man, who has a great plantation there...* Edinburgh. J. Reid, 7p. 4to. 1683

Note: WING L2777A, ALDIS 2380.5.
Locations: E; RPJCB

1683#14
A modest examination of the resolution of this case of conscience... London. T. Parkhurst, 35p. 4to. 1683
Note: WING M2364. Cites New England church practices.
Locations: L; O; CSmH, NN, DFo

1683#15
MURET, Pierre. *Rites of Funeral. Ancient and modern, in use through the known world...* London. For R. Royston, 126p. 8vo. 1683
Note: SABIN 51443, WING M3098-9. Also 1695. Includes 'Funerals of the Americans.'
Locations: L; O; MH, NNUT, DFo, RPJCB

1683#16
PASKELL, Thomas. *An abstract of a letter from Thomas Paskell of Pensilvania to his friend J. J. of Chippenham.* London. J. Bringhurst, 2p. F. 1683
Note: SABIN 58991, WING P647.
Locations: L; RPJCB

1683#17
PENN, William. *A letter from William Penn, proprietary and governour of Pennsylvania... to the committee of the Free Society of Traders of that province, residing in London. Containing a general description of the said province...* London. J. Sowle, 14p. F. 1683
Note: SABIN 59712, WING P1319. Three other issues in 1683.
Locations: L; DLC, RPJCB

1683#18
PETTY, William. *The third part of the present state of England... To which is likewise added England's guide to industry: or, the improvement of trade for the good of all people in general.* London. R. Holt for T. Passinger and B. Took, 362p. 12mo. 1683
Note: WING C1844. This was included, with a separate title page, as part of Edward Chamberlayne's *The present state of England.* Part III. and Part IV. (London, 1683). Sections on America, Virginia, New England, etc.
Locations: L; O; CK; ICN, DFo, CtY

1683#19
REID, John. *The Scots gard'ner in two parts...* Edinburgh. David Lindsay and partners, 125p. 4to. 1683
Note: WING R764. Virginia strawberry, tobacco planting etc.
Locations: L; Lg; CtY, DFo, MH

1683#20
SMITH, Humphry. *A collection of the several writings... of Humphrey Smith, who dyed... 4th day of the 3d moneth... 1663...* London. A. Sowle, (48), 340p. 4to. 1683
Note: SABIN 82734, WING S4051. Includes 'To New England's pretended Christians'.
Locations: L; CtY

1683#21
SYLVESTRE DUFOUR, Philippe. *Moral instructions of a father to his son, upon his departure for a long voyage...* London. W. Crook, [114]p. 12mo. 1683
Note: WING M2455. Dedicated to Sir Thomas Grantham with references to Bacon's rebellion in Virginia. By Jacob Spon.
Locations: L; Ls; RPJCB, CtY

1683#22
TENISON, Thomas. *An argument for union, taken from the true interest of those dissenters in England, who profess, and call themselves Protestants...* London. T. Basset etc., 43p. 4to. 1683
Note: WING T688. New England intolerance.
Locations: L; O; CSmH; DFo, RPJCB

1683#23
Three letters of thanks to the Protestant reconciler. 1. From the Anabaptists at Munster. 2. From the congregations in New-England. 3. From the Quakers in Pensilvania. London. B. Took, 26p. 4to. 1683
Note: SABIN 95739, WING T1098.
Locations: O; RPJCB

1683#24
WILLIAMS, John. *The case of lay-communion with the Church of England considered...* London. D. Newman, 75p. 4to. 1683
Note: WING W2691-2. Also 1684. New England churches and separatism.
Locations: L; O; MH, DFo, NN

1683#25
WISWALL, Ichabod. *A judicious observation of that dreadful comet, which appeared on November by J. W. in New-England...* London. J. Darby, 15p. 8vo. 1683
Note: SABIN 104922. Reprinted Boston, 1759.
Locations: DLC, MB

1684#1
ANTROBUS, Benjamin. *Some buds and blossoms of piety...* London. A. Sowle, 80p. 4to. 1684
Note: SABIN 1721, WING A3523, Foxon A268. Other editions 1691, 1716, 1743. EA 716/9, 743/14. Material on New England.
Locations: Lfr; DLC, PHi

1684#2
Carolina described more fully than heretofore, being an impartial collection from the several relations of that place... from divers letters of the Irish settlers there... the

1684

charter with the Fundamental constitutions. . . the charges of transporting persons and goods. Dublin. 56p. 4to. 1684
Note: SABIN 10963, WING C606.
Locations: RPJCB, NN, CSmH

1684#3
CAUSTON, Peter. *Tunbridgalia: or, The pleasures of Tunbridge. A poem. In Latin and English.* London. 17p. 4to. 1684
Note: WING C1552A, C1553A, C1554. Refers to American expedition led by Sir William Phips and to Virginia tobacco. Also 1686 (two editions), 1688, Tunbridge, 1705, EA 705/38.
Locations: L; –

1684#4
A complete collection of all the laws of Virginia now in force. . . London. T. J. for J. P. to be sold by T. Mercer, 326p. F. 1684
Note: SABIN 100381, WING V636, BAER 113. Compiled by John Purvis.
Locations: L; DLC, MH, RPJCB

1684#5
FOWLER, Edward. *A defence of The resolution of this case. . .* London. J. H. for B. Aylmer, 52p. 4to. 1684
Note: WING F1697, 1967A, EA 684/58–9. Another edition, 1684. New England references.
Locations: L; O; DFo, CtY, MH

1684#6
H., N. *The pleasant art of money-catching.* London. For J. Dunton, 12mo 1684
Note: WING H100. Also London 1705, EA 705/138.
Locations: L; MH, NC

1684#7
MATHER, Increase. *An essay for the recording of illustrious providences, wherein an account is given of many remarkable and memorable events. . . especially in New-England. . .* London. Printed at Boston. London. G. Calvert, 372p. 8vo. 1684
Note: WING M1208, HOLMES, IM, 52. Another London issue in 1687. First printed Boston, 1684 (EVANS 372, 373).
Locations: O; DLC, RPJCB

1684#8
PENN, William. *Information and direction to such persons as are inclined to America, more especially those related to the province of Pennsylvania.* London. 4p. F. [1684?]
Note: SABIN 59707, WING P1302. Reissued in 1686; also 1750 (NN).
Locations: PHi, NHi

1684#9
Sad and dreadful news from New England, being a true relation of the barbarous cruelty lately committed by the Spaniards upon the English. . . London. For Langley Curtis, 4p. 4to. 1684
Note: WING S236. New England sailors; attested before Boston magistrates.
Locations: L; O; CSmH, DLC

1684#10
TRYON, Thomas. *The countryman's companion. . .* London. 184p. 8vo. [1684]
Note: SABIN 97285, WING T3176. Contain's the 'planter's speech. . . ' below, 1684.
Locations: L; RPJCB

1684#11
TRYON, Thomas. *The planter's speech to his neighbors and country-men of Pennsylvania, East and West-Jersey, and to all such as have transported themselves into new colonies. . .* London. A. Sowle, 73p. 8vo. 1684
Note: SABIN 97288, WING T3191. First published as part of *The countryman's companion*, above, 1684.
Locations: O; CSmH

1685#1
An Advertisement concerning East-New-Jersey. Edinburgh. J. Reid, senior, bds. F. 1685
Note: WING A609A dates to 1685, EA 683/1.
Locations: NLS; RPJCB

1685#2
B., R. [i. e. CROUCH, Nathaniel.] *The English empire in America: or, A View of the dominions of the Crown of England in the West-Indies. . .* London. For N. Crouch, 212p. 12mo. 1685
Note: B., R. = Robert Burton. SABIN 9499, WING 7319–21, BAER 115, 142, 183. Other editions 1692, 1696, 1698, 1704, 1711, 1728, 1735, 1739, 1760, and Dublin, 1735, 1739. EA 704/38, 711/47–8, 728/45, 729/65, 735/75, 739/86.
Locations: L; RPJCB, MH

1685#3
BARBON, Nicholas. *An apology for the builder; or, a discourse shewing the causes and effects of the increase of building.* London. C. Pullen, 37p. 4to. 1685
Note: SABIN 1765, WING B705, KRESS 1608. American references. Another issue in 1689: L; DLC, RPJCB.
Locations: L;

1685#4
BOYLE, Robert. *Of the reconcileableness of the specifick medicines to the corpuscular philosophy. . .* London. S. Smith, 225p. 8vo. 1685

Note: WING B4013, EA 685/31. Another issue. References to English and Spanish colonies.
Locations: L; MH, CLU-C, MnU

1685#5
BUDD, Thomas. *A true and accurate account of the disposal of the one hundred shares or proprieties of the province of West-New-Jersey, by Edward Bylling*. . . London. s.sh. F. 1685
Note: SABIN 8955, WING B5360A.
Locations: PHi

1685#6
BUTLER, Nathaniel. *Six dialogues about sea-services.* London. M. Pitt, 404p. 8vo. 1685
Note: WING B6288, EA 685/37. Also 1688 as *Colloquia maritima*, WING B6287, EA 688/52. References to superiority of colonial diets; Virginians should produce foodstuffs not tobacco.
Locations: L; RPJCB, CtY, MH

1685#7
The cov–ous mother, or, the *terrible overthrow of Two Loyal Lovers.* London. J. Deacon, s.sh. F. [1685?]
Note: WING C6635, EUING, no 42. A mother arranged for her daughter to be sold 'to be a Slave', we may presume in Virginia!
Locations: GU; MH

1685#8
CROUCH, Nathaniel. *England's monarchs.* . . London. N. Crouch, 234p. 12mo. 1685
Note: WING C7314–7, EA 685/47–8, 687/41, 691/49, 694/46. Raleigh, New England, etc.
Locations: L; CtY, MH, ICN

1685#9
DUVAL, Pierre. *Geographia universalis: The present state of the whole world.* . . London. H. Clarke for F. Pearse, 482p. 8vo. 1685
Note: WING D2919–20. Second edition in 1691. New England and New York mentioned as parts of Canada. Black slavery and some Indians tribes discussed.
Locations: L; C; DLC, CSmH, MH

1685#10
ENGLAND AND WALES. SOVEREIGN. JAMES II. *A proclamation to prohibit his majesties subjects from trading within the limits assigned to the Royal African Company.* . . *[1 April 1685].* London. Assigns, etc. s.sh. F. 1685
Note: WING J371, STEELE 3791, BRIGHAM 137, KRESS 1615. Governors in plantations to enforce prohibition.
Locations: L; O; CSmH, MH

1685#11
ENGLAND AND WALES. SOVEREIGN. JAMES II. *A proclamation. Continuing officers in colonies. [6 February 1684/5.]* London. Assigns, etc. s.sh. F. 1685
Note: STEELE 3774, BRIGHAM 135. Cf. WING J369.
Locations: L; O;

1685#12
ENGLAND AND WALES. TREATIES. *Several treaties of peace and commerce.* . . London. Assigns of T. Bill, H. Hills and T. Newcomb, 269p. 4to. 1685
Note: WING C3604A, C3605, EA 685/80, 686/69. American references. Also 1686.
Locations: WCA; CJ; MH, RPJCB, CtY

1685#13
Form of a certificate for *a ship that gives bond in the plantations to return to England, Wales, or Berwick only.* London. s.sh. [1685]
Locations: DLC

1685#14
Form of a certificate for *a ship that hath produced a certificate in the plantations of bond given in England, to return to England, Wales, or Berwick only.* London. s.sh. [1685]
Locations: DLC

1685#15
GAYA, Louis de. *Nuptial rites, or, the several marriage ceremonies practised amongst all the nations of the world.* . . London. T. S. for the author, 104p., 12mo. 1685
Note: WING G402. Title page gives author as 'I. S. S.'. The same material with slight stylistic changes is found in *Matrimonial Ceremonies display'd wherein are exhibited, the various customs.* . . (1687) and *Marriage ceremonies: or, the ceremonies used in marriages in all parts of the world.* . . (1697), WING G399–400. Other issues 1698, 1703, 1744, and five editions in 1748, EA 703/60, 744/100, 748/70–74. Sections on customs of Canada, Florida, Caribbean, and Latin American territories.
Locations: L;

1685#16
GODWIN, Morgan. *Trade preferred before religion, and Christ made to give way to Mammon.* . . *a sermon relating to the plantations.* . . London. B. Took, 3, 12, 24p. 4to. 1685
Note: WING G974, KRESS SUPP. 1581.
Locations: L; O; DLC, RPJCB, CtY

1685#17
HAYNE, Samuel. *An abstract of all the statutes made concerning aliens.* . . *Also, all the laws made for securing our plantation trade to our selves. With observations thereon,*

1685

proving that the Jews. . . break them all. . . London. 38p. 4to 1685
Note: WING H1216, KRESS 1621.
Locations: L; MH-BA

1685#18
MAURICE, Henry. *The antithelemite, or an answer to certain queries. . . and to the Considerations of an unknown author concerning toleration.* London. For S. Smith, 76p. 4to. 1685
Note: SABIN 46954, WING M1359. References to Roger Williams and New England.
Locations: L; O; RPJCB, MH

1685#19
NALSON, John. *Toleration and liberty of conscience considered, and proved impracticable, impossible. . . sinful and unlawful.* London. T. Dring, 40p. 4to. [1685?]
Note: WING N115 References to New England; also toleration does not encourage trade.
Locations: L; O; EN; MH, NNUT, DFo

1685#20
PENN, William. *A further account of the province of Pennsylvania and its improvements. For the satisfaction of those that are adventurers, and enclined to be so.* London. 20p. 4to. [1685]
Note: SABIN 26246, 59701, WING P1294, BAER 118. Another issue in [1685?].
Locations: L; RPJCB, MiU-C

1685#21
PERTH, James Drummond. *An advertisement concerning the province of East-New-Jersey in America. Published for information of such as are desirous to be concerned therein. . .* Edinburgh. By J. Reid, 22p. 4to. 1685
Note: WING P1672, ALDIS 2529, CHURCH 695. Four variants in 1685.
Locations: ABu; EN; RPJCB, CSmH, NN, RPJCB

1685#22
PILKINGTON, R. *The skilful doctor; or the compleat mountebank. . .* London. G. Conyers, s.sh. F. 1685
Note: WING P2232C, P2232D. Another edition in [1686]. Inconsequential reference to Virginia and tobacco.
Locations: O; CM;

1685#23
REYNELL, Carew. *A necessary companion; or the English interest discovered and promoted. . .* London. Printed and sold by W. Budden, etc. 92p. 8vo. 1685
Note: WING R1214A. Chapter 31 'Of plantations'.
Locations: L; Lu; MH, CtY, DFo

1685#24
SCOTT, George. *A brief advertisment, concerning East-New-Jersey, in America.* Edinburgh? J. Reid?, 3p. F. 1685?
Note: WING S2034A.
Locations: RPJCB

1685#25
SCOTT, George. *The model of the government of the province of East-New-Jersey in America.* Edinburgh. J. Reid to be sold by A. Ogston, 272p. 12mo. 1685
Note: SABIN 78186, WING S2036, BAER 120, ALDIS 2605. Another issue in 1685.
Locations: L; RPJCB

1685#26
SELLER, John. *An almanack for the provinces of Virginia and Maryland. . .* London. 62p. 12mo. [1684–5]
Note: BAER 112. Another issue 1685, or later: WING A2376, BAER 121 (MdBJ-G).
Locations: DLC, MdBJ-G

1685#27
SELLER, John. *New-England almanack. . . for xxx. years.* London. Sold by the author, 12mo. 1685
Note: WING A2380
Locations: MH

1685#28
SELLER, John. *A new systeme of geography. . .* London. 110p. 8vo. [1685]
Note: WING S2477–9, BAER 122. Reissued 1690, 1694. Short references to North American colonies.
Locations: CT; DLC

1685#29
The trappan'd Welsh man, sold to *Virginia.* London. C. Dennisson, s.sh. F. [1685]
Note: WING T2051A. The date is a guess. Dennisson was most active in the 1680s.
Locations: Cm;

1685#30
A voyage to Virginia: or, the valliant souldiers' farewel to his love. . . London. s.sh. F. [1685]
Note: WING V745 gives the date of [1690] but this is included in a 1685 list of ballads and the date may be much earlier.
Locations: L; O;

1685#31
The woman outwitted: or, the weaver's wife cunningly catched in a trap, by her husband, who sold her for ten pounds, and sent her to Virginny. . . London. By W. O. and to be sold by C. Bates, s.sh. F. [1685]
Note: WING W3320. The date is a guess.
Locations: L; CSmH

1686#1
ENGLAND AND WALES. SOVEREIGN. JAMES II. *Treaty of peace, good correspondence and neutrality in America, between. . . James II. . . of Great Britain, and. . . Lewis XIV, the most Christian king: concluded the 6/16th day of Novemb. 1686. . .* London. 20p. 4to. 1686
Note: WING J393.
Locations: L; RPJCB

1686#2
ENGLAND AND WALES. SOVEREIGN. JAMES II. *Whereas. . . by reason. . . abuses of a lewd sort of people, called spirits, in seducing many of his majesties subjects to go on shipboard, where they have been. . . carried by force to. . . plantations in America. . . [March 26 1686.]* London. C. Bill, etc. 2p. F. 1686
Note: STEELE 3830, WING C2896, E2896, KRESS SUPP 1599, EA 686/68. Reissue of order in council of 1682, above, 1682.
Locations: L; O;

1686#3
PETTY, William. *An essay concerning the multiplication of mankind: together with another essay in political arithmetick.* London. For M. Pardoe, 50p. 8vo. 1686
Note: WING W1923–4. Also 1698. In fact contains only a sketch for the essay. Treatment of 'encrease of people and colonies.'
Locations: L; O; MH, TU

1686#4
RAY, John. *Historia plantarum; species hacteus editas aliasque insuper multas naviter inventas et descriptas complectens. . .* London. M. Clark, H. Faithorne, 983p. F. Volume I. 1686
Note: SABIN 68027, WING R394–5A. Volume II was published in 1688. Another edition in 1693. Volume III was published (S. Smith and B. Walford) in 1704, EA 704/126.
Locations: L; O; MH, DLC

1686#5
A relation of the invasion *and conquest of Florida by the Spaniards, under the command of Fernando de Soto. . .* London. J. Lawrence, 272p. 8vo. 1686
Note: WING R840. Part of the work is a translation from a French version of 1685 by Citri de la Guette of the Portuguese *Relaçam verdadeira. . .*
Locations: L; DLC, MiU-C

1686#6
WILLUGHBY, Francis. *Ornithologia libri tres. . .* London. Impensis, J. Martyn, 307p., plates. F. 1686
Note: WING W2879. Some American birds, e. g. Virginia nightingale.
Locations: O; MH, CtY, DFo

1687#1
BLOME, Richard. *The present state of his majesties isles and territories in America, viz. Jamaica. . . New Jersey, Pensilvania. . . Carolina, Virginia, New-England, Tobago, New-foundland, Mary-land, New-York. With new maps. . .* London. H. Clark for D. Newman, 262, 42p. 8vo. 1687
Note: SABIN 5972, WING B3215, BAER 124, KRESS 1647.
Locations: L; O; MiU-C, RPJCB

1687#2
CLEVELAND, John. *The works of John Cleveland. . .* London. R. Holt for O. Blagrave, 514p. 8vo. 1687
Note: SABIN 13662, WING C4654. Royalist poet. Some references to Puritans, New England, etc. which may also have appeared in earlier editions of his poems. Another edition in 1699.
Locations: L; O; CtY, MH

1687#3
CYRANO DE BERGERAC, Savinien. *The comical history of the. . . states and empires of the moon and the sun.* London. H. Rhodes, 2pts. 8vo. 1687
Note: WING C7717, EA 687/43. References to Canada. First published Paris, 1662.
Locations: L; CtY, CSmH, NN

1687#4
FONTENELLE, Bernard Le Bovyer de. *A discourse of the plurality of worlds. . .* Dublin A. Cook and S. Helsham for W. Norman, 86p. 4to 1687
Note: WING F1411. 1412, 1412A, 1416, 1417, 1418. 'Translated by Sir W. D. Knight.' From Fontenelle's *Entretiens sur la pluralité des mondes*, first issued Paris, 1686. Some discussion of beliefs of American Indians, Columbus, etc. The same text appears in *A discovery of new worlds. . .*, (two London editions in 1688) and in *A plurality of worlds* (1688, 1695) and probably in *The theory or system of several new inhabited worlds*, (1700), WING F1412, 1412A, F1416–18. Aphra Behn was also a translator and it seems that a text may appear in her collected works. Subsequently published as *Conversations on the plurality of worlds* and under other slightly varying titles, London, 1700, 1702, 1707, 1710, 1715, 1718, 1719, 1728, 1728, 1757, 1757, 1760; Dublin, 1728, 1737; Glasgow, 1749; Edinburgh 1753. The London 1737 (and I suppose subsequent editions) adds a sixth discourse. EA 702/79, 707/55, 749/105, 710/431, 715/70, 718/58, 719/56 1728/70 728/72 737/92–93.
Locations: L; MH, CtY

1687#5
FRANCK, Richard. *A philosophical treatise of the original and production of things. Writ in America in a time of solitudes. . .* London. J. Gain, 170p. 8vo. 1687

1687

Note: SABIN 25467, WING F2065. Another edition in 1707, EA 707/57.
Locations: L; DLC

1687#6
MATHER, Increase. *A testimony against several prophane and superstitions customs, now practised by some in New-England...* London. [31]p. 8vo. 1687
Note: WING M1256, HOLMES, IM, 130A. Reprinted Boston, 1688
Locations: O; MH, CSmH, MWA

1687#7
MORE, Nicholas. *A letter from Doctor More, with passages out of several letters from persons of good credit, relating to the state and improvement of the province of Pennsylvania...* London. 11p. 4to. 1687
Note: WING M2684.
Locations: L; RPJCB

1687#8
RANDOLPH, Bernard. *The present state of the Islands in the Archipelago, (or Arches) Sea of Constantinople, and Gulf of Smyrna...* Oxford. 2, 108p. 4to. 1687
Note: SABIN 67811, WING R234. References to New England.
Locations: L; DLC

1688#1
BOHUN, Edmund. *A geographical dictionary, representing the present and ancient names of all countries...* London. C. Brome, 806p. 8vo. 1688
Note: SABIN 6145, 26972, WING B3452–5, BAER 147, 162, EA 688/33. Other issues in 1691, 1693, 1695. A few North American territories, e. g. New England, Carolina, New Albion. Bohun died in South Carolina, where he was Chief Justice.
Locations: L; CtY, DLC, MiU

1688#2
BOYLE, Robert. *Some receipts of medicines, for the most part parable and simple... sent to a friend in America.* London. 26p. 12mo. 1688
Note: WING B4043, EA 688/40. Also 1703.
Locations: L;

1688#3
COMPANY FOR MINES AND MINERALS IN NEW-ENGLAND. *An alphabetical list of the subscribers in nomination for deputy-governor and assistants for the first government of the company...* London. s.sh. F. 1688
Note: WING A2899B. Dated 8 September 1688.
Locations: CtY

1688#4
CROUCH, Nathaniel. *The kingdom of darkness...* London. For N. Crouch, 12mo. 1688

Note: WING C7342. Also 1705, 1728, EA 705/49, 728/47. References to Massachusetts.
Locations: L; MH, MHi

1688#5
Curious enquiries. Being six brief *discourses...* London. R. Taylor, 24p. 4to. 1688
Note: BAER 127, WING C7678. WING C7677 (entry cancelled) is 1687 edition of which no copy is known. Material on emigration to America.
Locations: L; CtY, NN, MdBJ-G

1688#6
ENGLAND AND WALES. SOVEREIGN. JAMES II. *By the King. A proclamation for the more effectual reducing and suppressing of pirates and privateers in America... [20 January 1687/8.]* London. Charles Bill, etc. 2p. F. 1688
Note: SABIN 65939n, WING J355, BRIGHAM 140, STEELE 3857, EA 688/111.
Locations: L; O; RPJCB, MiU-C

1688#7
ENGLAND AND WALES. SOVEREIGN. JAMES II. *Proclamation prohibiting trade within limits of the Hudson's Bay Company. [31 March 1688.]* London. C. Bill etc., s.sh. F. 1688
Note: WING J3666, KRESS SUPP 1630, STEELE 3862.
Locations: L; MH

1688#8
HOLME, Randle. *The academy of armory.* Chester. Chester, for the author, [1197]p. F. 1688
Note: WING H2513, ARENTS 400. Brief references to Indians, more to tobacco. Another edition in 1701.
Locations: L; O; CSmH, DLC, CtY

1688#9
LEUSDEN, John. *The book of psalmes with the new translation in English...* London. S. Smith, 240p. 12mo. 1688
Note: SABIN 66452, WING B2569A. Also WING B2744 (?) Dedicated to John Eliot, with other New England references, based on information from Increase Mather. Another issue in 1688, WING L2745.
Locations: L; CtY, RPJCB

1688#10
LOVE, John. *Geodaesia: or, The art of surveying and measuring of land...* London. John Taylor, [xxii], 196p., tables. 1688
Note: WING L3191. Other editions in 1715, 1720, 1731; EA 715/120, 720/155, 731/136. Section on laying out lands in America has reference to Carolina.
Locations: L; CtY, MH

1688#11
MATHER, Increase. *De successu evangelii apud Indos in Nova-Anglia epistola.* . . London. J. G., 1, 13p. 8vo. 1688
Note: WING M1197. First published Boston, 1687 (BRISTOL, B82).
Locations: L; O; C; MWA, MH

1688#12
MATHER, Increase. *A narrative of the miseries of New England, by reason of an arbitrary government erected there.* . . [London R. Baldwin?]. 8p. 4to. [1688]
Note: SABIN 171231, WING M1231, 1231a, HOLMES, IM, 79B First printed, (or reprinted?), Boston, 1688 (EVANS 450). Reprinted Boston, 1775. WING lists an edition by R. Janeway, reprinted Boston, 1688.
Locations: GH; MH, RPJCB, ViU

1688#13
A model for erecting a bank of credit; with a discourse in explanation thereof. Adapted to the use of any trading countrey. . . more especially for his majesties plantations in America. London. J. A. for J. Cockeril, 38p. 8vo. 1688
Note: WING M2312, KRESS SUPP 2670. Last page signed 'N. A.'
Locations: L; MB, RPJCB

1688#14
PERRAULT, Claude. *Some memoires for a natural history.* . . London. J. Streater, to be sold by T. Basset, 267p. F. 1688
Note: WING P1582A. Canadian beaver and stag.
Locations: L; O; MH, DFo, DLC

1688#15
POPPLE, Will. *A letter to Mr Penn. With his answer.* London. A. Wilson, 20p. 4to. 1688
Note: WING P2961. Refers to Penn kidnapping 'A monk out of your American province.'
Locations: O; Lfr; RPJCB, CtY, NN

1688#16
Septima pars patentium de Anno Regis Jacobi Secundi Quarto. London. 6p. F. [1688]
Note: SABIN 99889, WING J386B. Printed caption 'Grant of the Northern Neck in Virginia to Lord Culpepper' [By James II].
Locations: RPJCB, MH, NN

1688#17
A third collection of papers relating to the present juncture of affairs in England. London. R. Janeway, 38p. 4to. 1688
Note: WING T900 and 901 See also C5169A and C5683A. Another edition in 1689. William of Orange had 200 blacks wearing fur caps and white feathers from the New Netherland in America when he entered Exeter. Also 200 Finlanders and Laplanders.
Locations: L; O; CtY, DFo, MH

1688#18
WIDDERS, Robert. *The life and death, travels and suffering of Robert Widders.* . . London. [28]p. 4to. 1688
Note: SABIN 103883, WING L2019, SMITH II, 926, BAER 129. References to journeys in America.
Locations: L; RPJCB, MH, PHC

1689#1
An abstract of some of the printed laws of New England which are either contrary or not agreeable to the laws of England. . . London. 4p. F. [1689 or 1690]
Note: Possibly always found as part of *Considerations humbly offered to the Parliament.* . . , below, 1689.
Locations: Lpro;

1689#2
ATWOOD, William. *Wonderful predictions of Nostredamus, Grebner, David Pareus and Antonio Torquatus, wherein the grandeur of their present majesties, the hapiness of England, and the downfall of France and Rome, are plainly delineated.* . . London. For J. Robinson, 27p. F. 1689
Note: WING N1401. Atwood was Chief Justice of New York.
Locations: L; O; DFo, CtY

1689#3
BINGLEY William. *An epistle of love and tender advice, to friends and brethren in America, or elswhere.* . . London. For. A. Sowle, 14p. 4to. 1689
Note: WING B2196, SMITH, I, 271, EA 689/16.
Locations: L; Lfr; MH, PH

1689#4
BYFIELD, Nathaniel. *An account of the late revolution in New-England. Together with the declaration of the gentlemen, merchants, and inhabitants of Boston, and the country adjacent.* . . London. R. Chiswell, 20p. 4to. 1689
Note: SABIN 52597, WING B6379–80. Another edition, Edinburgh, 1689. First printed Boston, 1689 (EVANS 462).
Locations: L; O; DLC, RPJCB

1689#5
CALVERT, George. *Case of Charles Lord Baltemore, a minor, with relation to his government of Maryland, granted by King Charles I, to Cecil Lord Baltemore, in 1632, which was settled on the marriage of Lady Charlotte Lee with Benedict Lord Baltemore.* London. s.sh. 1689
Note: SABIN 10083.
Locations: NO COPY LOCATED.

1689

1689#6
CLARKE, Samuel. *A new description of the world, or a compendious treatise. . . of Europe, Asia, Africa and America. . .* London. For Henry Rhodes, 236p. 12mo. 1689
Note: WING C4554, 4554A, BAER 130, 167, EA 689/34, EA 696/43. Fourth section concerns America. Reissued in 1696: L; MB, RPJCB. Other editions in 1708, 1712. EA 708/21, 712/36.
Locations: L; LCL; RPJCB, MB, MH

1689#7
A compleat collection of papers. In twelve parts. . . London. J. D. for R. Clavel, 12 parts in one vol., 4to. 1689
Note: SABIN 9317, WING C5638A. Includes 'Narrative of the miseries of New England' by Increase Mather. See Mather, above, 1688.
Locations: L; RPJCB

1689#8
Considerations humbly offered to the parliament shewing that those charters relating to the plantations. . . London. 4p. F. [1689 or 1690]
Note: See *An abstract of some of the printed laws*, above, 1689.
Locations: Lpro;

1689#9
DRYDEN, John. *The prologue and epilogue to the History of Bacon in Virginia.* London. For J. Tonson 4p. F. 1689
Note: WING B2332.
Locations: O; C; CLU-C, ICN, RPJCB

1689#10
ENGLAND AND WALES. SOVEREIGN. WILLIAM AND MARY. *Their majesties declaration against the French King. . . [7 May 1689.]* London. Bill and Newcomb, s.sh. F. 1689
Note: WING W2502, STEELE 3999 BRIGHAM 147. Grievances cited include invasion of New York and Hudson's Bay, etc.
Locations: L; O; MH

1689#11
FLAVELL, John. *England's duty, under the present gospel liberty. . .* London. For M. Wotton, 42, 454, 71p. 8vo. 1689
Note: WING F1159A. With a preface by Increase Mather.
Locations: L; LW; MH, Mhi, CtY

1689#12
A full and impartial account of all the secret consults. . . of the Romish party in Ireland. . . London. R. Chiswell, 152p. 4to. 1689

Note: WING F2282-3, EA 689/71, 690/56. Also 1690. Colonial references.
Locations: L; O; MH, MnU

1689#13
HAWLES, Sir John. *Remarks upon the trials of Edward Fitzharris. . .* London. J. Tonson, 104p. F. 1689
Note: WING H1188, EA 689/88. New England laws.
Locations: L; ICN, NN, CtY

1689#14
A law of Maryland concerning religion. London. s.sh. F. [1689?]
Note: SABIN 45181, WING M897, BAER 132.
Locations: Lpro; NN

1689#15
MASSACHUSETTS GOVERNOR, COUNCIL AND CONVENTION. *Two addresses from the governour, council and convention of the Massachusetts colony. . . Presented to his majesty at Hampton-Court, August 7, 1689. . .* London. R. Baldwin, 4p. F. 1689
Note: SABIN 9708, 97547, WING M1025A.
Locations: MHi, NN

1689#16
MATHER, Cotton. *Early piety, exemplified in the life and death of Nathaniel Mather. . .* London. J. Astwood for J. Dunton, [158]p. 8vo. 1689
Note: HOLMES, CM, 100, WING M1096. Another edition in 1689 with preface by Matthew Mead: L; RPJCB. Reprinted Boston, 1690 (EVANS 536).
Locations: MWA, NN

1689#17
MATHER, Cotton. *Right thoughts in sad hours, representing the comforts and duties of good men under all their afflictions; and particularly that one, the untimely death of Children. . .* London. J. Astwood, (6) 54p. (2), 8vo. 1689
Note: HOLMES, CM, 334, WING M1147.
Locations: O; MB

1689#18
MATHER, Increase. *A brief discourse concerning the unlawfulness of the Common-prayer worship and the laying the hand on, and kissing the booke in swearing.* Reprinted London, 43p. 8vo. 1689
Note: WING M1186, HOLMES, IM, 15B. A reprint of the first edition, Cambridge, Mass., 1686 (EVANS 490).
Locations: O; MWA, MB

1689#19
MATHER, Increase. *A brief relation of the state of New England, from the beginning of that plantation to this present year, 1689. . .* London. R. Baldwin, 18p. 4to. 1689

Note: HOLMES, IM, 17, WING M1189.
Locations: L; DLC

1689#20
MATHER, Increase. *A further vindication of New-England from false suggestions in a late scandalous pamphlet, pretending to shew, The inconvenience of joyning the plantation-charters with those of England.* London. s.sh. F. 1689
Note: WING M1214, HOLMES, IM, 59.
Locations: ViU

1689#21
MATHER, Increase. *New-England vindicated from the unjust aspersions cast on the former government there, by some late Considerations, pretending to shew, that the charters in those colonies were taken from them on account of their destroying the manufactures and navigation of England.* London. 8p. 4to. [1689]
Note: WING M1233, HOLMES, IM, 81a.
Locations: L; DLC, MWA, ViU

1689#22
News from New-England: in a letter... London. For J. Dunton, s.sh. F. 1689
Note: WING N983A.
Locations: ICN, ViU

1689#23
PITMAN, Henry. *A relation of the great sufferings and strange adventures of Henry Pitman...* London. A. Sowle and to be sold by J. Taylor, 38p. 4to. 1689
Note: WING P2298. Transported after Monmouth rebellion. Escaped via Carolina and New York.
Locations: L; BR; CSmH, NN, RPJCB

1689#24
A proclamation for Newfoundland. Whereas, William and Mary [have been proclaimed King and Queen of England, France and Ireland and of the dominions and territories thereunto belonging. We therefore... do hereby proclaim them.] London. J. Starkey and A. Churchill, s.sh. F. 1689
Note: Cf. STEELE 3957.
Locations: NO COPY LOCATED.

1689#25
PROTESTANT ASSOCIATION. *The declaration of the reasons and motives for the present appearing in arms of their majesties protestant subjects in Maryland.* London. Maryland printed... Reprinted in London, and sold by Randal Taylor, 8p. 4to. 1689
Note: SABIN 19180, WING P3823, BAER 134.
Locations: O; DLC, RPJCB, MdBJ-G

1689#26
A seventh collection of papers relating to the Parliament and the penal laws... London. 36p. 4to. 1689

Note: WING S2743. Includes queries to Penn, with reference to liberty of conscience for Indians and reference to Carolina religious laws.
Locations: L; O; C: CSmh, DFo, CtY

1689#27
A short discourse, shewing the great inconvenience of joyning the plantation charters with those of England, etc. Containing a full answer to a late pamphlet intituled New-England Vindicated... London. 4p. F. [1689]
Note: WING S3585.
Locations: L; Lpro; V

1689#28
A sixth collection of papers relating to the present juncture of affairs in England. London. R. Janeway, (2), 34p. 4to. 1689
Note: SABIN 9372, 81492, WING S3929. Many New England references. Reissued by J. Dunton, 1689. Cf. HOLMES, IM, 79B.
Locations: DLC, RPJCB, CSmH

1689#29
To the Right Reverend, and Reverend the Bishops, and Clergy of the Province of Canterbury... in Convocation... petition of many divines, and others of the classical, congregational, and other persuasions, in the name of themselves and brethren both of Old England and New... London. 8p. 4to. 1689
Note: SABIN 96029, WING T1717.
Locations: MRu; RPJCB, CLU-C, NNUT

1689#30
WILLARD, Samuel. *A brief discourse concerning that ceremony of laying the hand on the Bible in swearing.* London. By J. A. 4, 8p. 4to. 1689
Note: WING W2268. Preface by Increase Mather.
Locations: O; MB, MWA, CtY

1689#31
WORLIDGE, John. *The second parts of Systema agriculturae, or The mystery of husbandry...* London. G. Grafton, 191p. F. 1689
Note: ARENTS, Suppl. Part IX states that this edition unlike earlier ones contains a discussion of Virginia tobacco planting. Another edition in 1697. Cf. WING W3598–3602.
Locations: NN, CLU-C

1690#1
The answer to The call to humiliation, or, A vindication of the Church of England, from the reproaches of W. Woodward... London. A. Roper, 46p. 4to. 1690
Note: WING A3394, 3394A, EA 690/8, 691/4. Also Ludlow, 1691 (CN, NN, DFo). Pennsylvania Quakers.
Locations: MiU

1690

1690#2
BARBON, Nicholas. *A discourse of trade, by N. B...* London. T. Milbourne, 92p. 8vo. 1690
Note: WING B707, EA 690/15. Predicts an oceanic British empire.
Locations: L; MH, CtY

1690#3
BEHN, Aphra. *The widdow ranter, or, the history of Bacon in Virginia. A tragi-comedy.* London. J. Knapton, 56p. 4to. 1690
Note: SABIN 4372, WING B1774. With prologue by John Dryden. Her collected plays were published in 1702, 1716, 1724, 1731, EA 702/20, 716/17, 724/7, 735/31 and her Works (Volume II of which are her plays) in 1711.
Locations: L; O; DLC, MH

1690#4
The case of the felt-makers, against the bill now depending, for confirming the charter of the Hudson's Bay Company. London. s.sh. F. [c. 1690]
Locations: L;

1690#5
The case of the owners and proprietors of the ship and goods, Charles, seized by order of the Hudson's bay company, as the said ship was sailing on the high seas, in or near Hudsons-straits... London. s.sh. F. [1690?]
Note: KRESS SUPP 1695.
Locations: L; MH-BA

1690#6
CHILD, Josiah. *A discourse about trade.* London. A. Sowle, 238p. 8vo. 1690
Note: WING C3853, KRESS 1725. Discusses nature of plantations, etc. Other editions with title *A new discourse of trade... the nature of plantations, and their consequences in relation to the kingdom are seriously discussed...* London, 1693, 1694, 1698, 1718, 1736, and twice in 1740(?); and Glasgow, 1751. EA 718/35, 736/61, 740/61–2.
Locations: L; CT; RPJCB, MH

1690#7
D., C. *New England's faction discovered; or a brief and true account of their persecution of the Church of England...* London. For J. Hindmarsh, 8p. 4to. 1690
Note: SABIN 18229, 52757, WING D6.
Locations: O; DLC, RPJCB

1690#8
DEFOE, Daniel. *Taxes no charge: in a letter from a gentleman, to a person of quality...* London. R. Chiswell, 28p. 4to. 1690
Note: WING D848A. Taxes can employ poor at home; against Virginia and plantation trade which 'we with so little reason so much boast of.'
Locations: L; O; Lfr; MH, PH, CtY

1690#9
A dialogue about the French government... between Tom and Dick, two seamen... London. For R. Taylor, 2p. F. 1690
Note: WING D1289. Reference to French and Hudson's Bay.
Locations: L; CSmH, ICN

1690#10
HUDSON'S BAY COMPANY. *The case of the Hudson's-Bay Company. Reasons for the continuance of the former act.* London. s.sh. F. [1690]
Note: Stresses Company as defence against the French.
Locations: L;

1690#11
A list of such the names of the nobility... of England and Ireland... attainted for high treason... together with... copies of the acts of the said pretended Parliament... London. R. Clavel and J. Watts, 70p. 8vo. 1690
Note: WING L2409, EA 690/70. Irish Parliament of 7 May 1689, in which Irish navigation act, etc. was passed.
Locations: L; C; CtY, MH, CSmH

1690#12
LOCKE, John. *An essay concerning humane understanding.* London. E. Holt for T. Basset, F. 1690
Note: WING L2738–42. Reference to Virginia.
Locations: L; O; C; CSmH, MH, DFo

1690#13
LOCKE, John. *Two treatises of government.* London. For A. Churchill, 8vo. 1690
Note: WING L2766–8. References to Carolina, etc. Other editions in 1694 and 1698, etc.
Locations: L; O; C; MH, CtY, DFo

1690#14
MATHER, Increase? *A vindication of New-England.* [London?], 1690
Note: WING 486. EVANS 452 states [Boston, 1688] but internal evidence suggests 1690 and it may be a London imprint.
Locations: RPJCB, MH, MWA

1690#15
MATHER, Increase. *The wonders of free-grace: Or, A compleat history of all the most remarkable penitents that have been executed at Tyburn, and elsewhere, for these last thirty years...* London. For John Dunton, 180, 32p. 12mo. [1690?]
Note: WING W3378B, HOLMES, IM, 115C, SABIN 46735n. Cf. Mather, *A sermon occasioned by the execution... March 11th 1686...*, Boston, 1686. (EVANS 417).
Locations: L; O; NN, V

1690#16
A modest and impartial narrative of several grievances. . . that the peacable and most considerable inhabitants of New-York. . . lye under, by the extravagant and arbitrary proceedings of Jacob Leisler and his accomplices. . . *London.* Printed at New York, reprinted London, 26p. 4to. 1690
Note: WING M2353. Also printed Philadelphia, 1691 (EVANS 570). No New York edition located.
Locations: L; Lpro; O;

1690#17
N. N. *A short account of the present state of New-England. Anno Domini 1690.* London. 12p. 4to. 1690
Note: WING N57.
Locations: Llp; O; RPJCB

1690#18
Newes from New-England in a letter written to a person of quality. . . London. J. Dunton 2p. F. 1690
Note: WING N983A.
Locations: ICN, ViU

1690#19
PALMER, John. *An impartial account of the state of New England; or, the late government there, vindicated. . .* London. E. Poole, 40p. 4to. 1690
Note: SABIN 58359, WING P246. First printed Boston, 1689, as *The present state. . .*, (EVANS 495).
Locations: L; DLC, RPJCB

1690#20
PENN, William. *Some proposals for a second settlement in the province of Pennsylvania.* London. A. Sowle, s.sh. F. 1690
Note: SABIN 59735, WING P1371.
Locations: L; DLC

1690#21
PETTY, William. *Political Arithmetick, or a discourse concerning, the extent and value of lands people. . .* London. For R. Clavel and H. Mortlock, 117p. 8vo. 1690
Note: WING P1932–3. Another edition in 1691. Also Glasgow, 1751. Included in his *Essays in political arithmetick,* 1711 and 1755. Contains considerable American material, including a discussion of trade, colonial demography and economics of slavery.
Locations: L; O; MH, CtY, DFo

1690#22
Reasons humbly offered against the bill, for continuing a former act, for the confirming to the Hudson's bay company, their priviledges and trade. . . London. 3p. F. [1690?]
Note: KRESS SUPP 1710. Indorsed 'Reasons against the Hudsons Bay Company.'
Locations: L; MH-BA

1690#23
Saint Paul the tent-maker: in a discourse shewing how religion has in all ages, been promoted by the industrious mechanick. London. R. Baldwin, 26p. 4to. 1690
Note: WING S348. Substantial discussion of New England and differences in Indian conversions between it and slave plantations.
Locations: L; O; CSmH, DLC, CtY

1690#24
THOMAS, Dalby. *An historical account of the rise and growth of the West-Indies collonies.* London. J. Hindmarsh 30, 54p. 4to. 1690
Note: SABIN 32506, BAER 137, KRESS 1749. Material on Chesapeake tobacco.
Locations: L; O; RPJCB, MH

1691#1
BAXTER, Richard. *The certainty of the world of spirits, fully evinced by the unquestionable histories of apparations and witchcrafts. . .* London. T. Parkhurst and J. Salusbury, 252p. 8vo. 1691
Note: WING B1214–5. Two issues in 1691. Material on Cotton and Increase Mather's 'New England instances.'
Locations: L; CSmH, NN, Njp

1691#2
BETHEL, Slingsby. *The providences of God, observed through several ages, towards this nation.* London. For R. Baldwin, 60p. 4to. 1691
Note: WING B2074–6. Also 1694 (L;), 1697. Anti-Stuart history, with colonial references.
Locations: EN; CSmH, MBAt, CtY

1691#3
BLOUNT, Sir Thomas Pope. *Essays on several subjects.* London. For R. Bently, 179p. 8vo. 1691
Note: SABIN 5999, WING B3348. Other editions 1692, 1697. References to American curiosities.
Locations: L; O; CtY

1691#4
BURNYEAT, John. *The truth exalted in the writings of that eminent and faithful servant of Christ, John Burnyeat, collected into this ensuing volume. . .* London. T. Northcott, 264p. 4to. 1691
Note: SABIN 9417, WING B5968, BAER 138. Travels in America.
Locations: L; O; CSmH, MH

1691#5
COMPANY FOR PROPAGATION OF THE GOSPEL IN NEW ENGLAND AND THE PARTS ADJACENT IN AMERICA. *Rules and orders respecting the Charity left by the will of the hon. Robert Boyle. . .* [London]. 9p. 8vo. [1691?]

1691

Note: Boyle died in 1691.
Locations: Lg;

1691#6
The conformists reasons for hearing *and joining with the nonconformists...* London. 8p. 4to. 1691
Note: WING C5805, EA 691/44, References to New England churches. Reissued 1703 as *Reasons humbly offered to the conformists...*
Locations: L; RPJCB, CtY, DFo

1691#7
ECHARD, Laurence. *A most compleat compendium of geography...* London. T. Salisbury, 168p. 12mo. 1691
Note: WING E148–9A, EA 691/52–3, 693/64. Two issues in 1691; also 1693. Chapter IV is about America.
Locations: L; Cgc; DFo;

1691#8
The humble address of the *publicans of New England, to which king you please; with some remarks upon it...* London. 39p. 4to. 1691
Note: SABIN 33688, WING H3386. Sometimes ascribed to, but not by, Increase Mather. See *New England Quarterly*, vol. 51 (June, 1978), pps. 241–9.
Locations: L; RPJCB

1691#9
The interest of the nation *as it respects all the sugar-plantations abroad.* London. B. Motte, 11p. 4to. 1691
Note: WING I269. Discusses loss of manufacturing and of shipping through high duties; workmen will go to Virginia, etc.
Locations: L; Lu; MH, RPJCB, CtY

1691#10
KEITH, George. *The presbyterian and independent churches in New-England and elsewhere brought to the test...* London. For Thomas Northcott, 6, 223p. 8vo. 1691
Note: WING K191. First published Philadelphia, 1689 (EVANS 472).
Locations: L; O; RPJCB, MBAt

1691#11
MATHER, Cotton. *Late memorable providences relating to witchcrafts and possessions...* London. T. Parkhurst, 144p. 8vo. 1691
Note: WING M1118, HOLMES, CM, 228. First printed Boston, 1689, as *Memorable providences...* (EVANS 486); and reprinted under that title, Edinburgh, 1697: DLC, RPJCB, CSmH.
Locations: L; RPJCB, MiU-C

1691#12
MATHER, Cotton. *The life and death of the renown'd Mr John Eliot...* London. John Dunton, 138p. 8vo. The second edition. 1691
Note: SABIN 46382, WING M1120–1, HOLMES, CM, 409. First printed Boston, 1691 (EVANS 568) as *The triumphs of the reformed religion in America. The life of the renowned John Eliot...*; a third edition, London, 1694. Reprinted in John Wesley's *A Christian Library* (Bristol, 1749–55)
Locations: L; O; RPJCB, MH

1691#13
MATHER, Increase. *A brief account concerning several of the agents of New-England...* London. 24p. 4to. 1691
Note: WING M1184, HOLMES, IM, 14A. Includes 'An extract of a letter (written by some of the most eminent nonconformist divines in London) concerning the new charter...'.
Locations: O; CSmH, RPJCB, MH

1691#14
MATHER, Increase. *Reasons for the confirmation of the charters belonging to the several corporations in New-England.* London. 4p. 4to. [1691]
Note: SABIN 46724, WING M1242, HOLMES, IM, 109.
Locations: MHi

1691#15
MIEGE, Guy. *The new state of England under their majesties K. William and Q. Mary...* London. H. C. for J. Wyat, 12mo. 1691
Note: WING M2019, 2019A, 2020–2. In three parts. Second part comments on slavery; third part has lists of officials, including colonial governors. Other issues in 1691, 1693, 1694, 1699.
Locations: L; O; CtY, DFo, CSmH

1691#16
RAY, John. *The wisdom of God manifested in the works of the creation...* London. S. Smith, 8vo 1691
Note: WING R410–11. Also 1692, 1701, 1727, 1735, EA 701/217, 727/193 735/191 744/186.
Locations: L; MH

1691#17
Reasons for the confirmation of *the charter belonging to the Massachusetts colony in New-England.* London. 4p. 4to. [1691?]
Note: WING M1241.
Locations: MBAt, MHi

1691#18
SAVAGE, Thomas. *An account of the late action of the New-Englanders, under... Sir William Phips, against the French at Canada...* London. T. Jones, 15p. 4to. 1691

Note: SABIN 76746, WING 5771.
Locations: L; RPJCB, MH

1691#19
Some letters and an abstract *of letters from Pennsylvania, containing the state and improvement of that province. Published to prevent mis-reports.* London. A. Sowle, 12p. 4to. 1691
Note: SABIN 60621, WING S4515.
Locations: CSmH, MH, RPJCB

1691#20
STOUGHTON, William. *A narrative of the proceedings of Sir E. Androsse printed in the year 1691...* London. F. 1691
Note: WING S763 lists a London edition in 1691. First published Boston, WING S762, EVANS 572.
Locations: RPJCB

1691#21
To the King's most excellent *majesty. The humble address of divers gentry, merchants, and others... in Boston, Charlestown and places adjacent...* London. H. Hills, 8p. 4to. 1691
Note: SABIN 6474, 95946, WING T1501.
Locations: Lpro; RPJCB, V

1691#22
VOKINS, Joan. *Gods mighty power magnified: as manifested... in his faithful handmaid Joan Vokins...* London. T. Northcott, 9p. 8vo. 1691
Note: SABIN 100683, SMITH II, p. 844, WING V685. Travels in America.
Locations: L; CtY

1691#23
WOOD, Anthony. *Athenae Oxoniensis...* London. T. Bennet, 2 vols. F. 1691
Note: WING W3382, 3383A. Volume II was published in 1692. Lives of Richard Hakluyt, William Berkeley, Thomas Hariot, Benjamin Woodbridge, Anthony Ashley Cooper, etc. etc.
Locations: L; O; CtY, DFo, MH

1692#1
BOYLE, Robert. *General heads for the natural history of country great or small; drawn out for the use of travellers and navigators...* London. For T. Taylor and S. Holford, 138p. 12mo. 1692
Note: SABIN 7139, WING B3980. Virginia, West Indies, etc.
Locations: L; NN, RPJCB, MH

1692#2
The charter granted by Their *majesties King William and Queen Mary, to the inhabitants of the... Massachusetts Bay.* London. 13p. F. 1692

Note: WING M997A. EVANS 616 notes Boston, 1692, printed at London and reprinted in Boston, by R. Harris. Unique copy at NN.
Locations: NN

1692#3
CHAUNCY, Isaac. *Neonomianism unmask'd: or, the ancient gospel pleaded, against the other, called a new law, or gospel.* London. J. Harris, 40p. 4to. 1692
Note: WING C3754, C3754A, C3755, EA 692/43. Refers to New England antinomians. Also published in parts.
Locations: L; LW; RPJCB, DLC, MH

1692#4
The covenant of grace, not *absolute but conditional...* London. D. Newman, 73p. 4to. 1692
Note: SABIN 17211, WING C6618. New England antinomianism.
Locations: L; O; MB, CtY

1692#5
FIRMIN, Giles. *Weighty questions discussed...* London. For the author, 28p. 4to. 1692
Note: WING F969, EA 692/61. Many New England references.
Locations: L; O; NNUT-MC

1692#6
FLAVELL, John. *An exposition of the Assemblies catechism...* London. For T. Cockerill, 224p. 12mo. 1692
Note: WING F1160–61. Second edition, 1695; also Edinburgh, 1695. With a preface by Increase Mather.
Locations: L; O; MB, PPL

1692#7
KEITH, George. *An account of the great divisions amongst the Quakers in Pensilvania, etc. As appears by their own book... printed 1692... intituled... The plea of the innocent...* London. J. Gwillim and R. Baldwin, 26p. 4to. 1692
Note: SABIN 37178, WING K136.
Locations: L; RPJCB

1693#1
BAYARD, Nicholas and LODOWICK, Charles. *A journal of the late actions of the French at Canada. With the manner of their being repulsed...* London. R. Baldwin, 22p. 4to. 1693
Note: SABIN 4035, WING B1458. Probably a reprint of *A Narrative of an attempt*, Philadelphia or New York, 1693 (EVANS 632).
Locations: L; RPJCB

1693#2
BLOUNT, Sir Thomas Pope. *A natural history: containing many not common observations; extracted out of*

the best modern writers... London. For R. Bently, 469p. 12mo. 1693
Note: WING B3351, ARENTS 416. Includes information on the Virginian method of planting and curing tobacco.
Locations: DLC, MH, CtY

1693#3
BUGG, Francis. *New Rome arraigned, and out of her own mouth condemned*... London. For the author and to be sold by F. Dunton, R. Baldwin, F. Guillim, 68p. 4to. 1693
Note: SMITH I, 336, WING B5376–7, BAER 148, 154. Discusses Keith and Philadelphia. Second corrected edition in 1694.
Locations: L; C; DLC, MH

1693#4
The case of the Hudson's-*Bay Company*. [London?]. s.sh. 1/2o. [1693?]
Note: Refers to an expedition against French last year to prevent trade being lost.
Locations: RPJCB

1693#5
DALE, Samuel. *Pharmacologia, seu Manuductio ad materiam medicam*... London. Sam. Smith and Benj. Walford, 12mo. 1693
Note: WING D126. Also 1710, 1713, 1737, EA 710/32, 713/52, 737/62.
Locations: L; O; NC, DFo

1693#6
FIRMIN, Giles. *Panourgia. A brief review of Mr Davis's vindication*... London. J. Lawrence, 32p. 4to. 1693
Note: WING F959, EA 693/69. New England references.
Locations: L; RPJCB, MH, NN

1693#7
GORDON, Patrick. *Geography anatomized: or, a compleat geographical grammer*... London. J. R. for R. Mordern and T. Cockerill, 208p. 12mo. 1693
Note: WING G1287–8. Second enlarged edition in 1699. More than twenty issues/editions with slight title alterations, 1701 - 1760. EA has 702/93, 704/70, 708/51, 711/86, 716/60, 719/70, 722/91, 725/86, 730/108, 733/107, 735/111, 737/103, 740/146, 741/97, 744/106. ESTC has also London 1728 (11th edition, corrected and enlarged), 1749 (19th edition) and 1754 (20th edition) and Dublin, 1739 (15th edition, corrected) and 1747 (16th edition). Text relating to the Americas seems to have been hardly changed.
Locations: L; DLC, CtY

1693#8
KEITH, George. *The Christian Quaker: or, George Keith's eyes opened. Good news from Pensilvania*... London. Printed Pennsylvania. Reprinted London. B. Keach, 12p. 4to. 1693
Note: SABIN 37186, WING K153.
Locations: L; RPJCB

1693#9
KEITH, George. *A farther account of the great divisions among the Quakers in Pensilvania, etc. As appears by another of their books*... *intituled, Some reasons and causes*... London. J. Dunton, 23p. 4to. 1693
Note: WING K166.
Locations: L; MiU-C

1693#10
KEITH, George. *The tryals of Peter Boss, George Keith, Thomas Budd, and William Bradford, Quakers*... *at Philadelphia in Pennsylvania, the ninth, tenth and twelfth days of December, 1692*... London. R. Baldwin, 34p. 4to. 1693
Note: SABIN 37226, WING T2254, BAER 151, SMITH II, 27. First printed Philadelphia, 1693 (EVANS 642) as *New-Englands spirit of persecution*...
Locations: O; DLC, RPJCB

1693#11
KEITH, George and BUDD, Thomas. *More divisions among the Quakers*... London. First printed beyond the sea, and now reprinted, and to be sold by R. Baldwin, 22p. 4to. 1693
Note: SABIN 37202, WING K182, SMITH II, 28, BAER 149. Previously published in Philadelphia in 1692 as two titles: *The Christian Faith of a people* and *False Judgements reprehended*..., (EVANS 600, 610).
Locations: L; DLC, RPJCB, NN

1693#12
M., C. *A true account of the tryals, examinations, confessions, condemnations, and executions of divers witches, at Salem, in New-England*... London. J. Conyers, 8p. 4to. 1693
Note: SABIN 46563, WING M12a, Cf. HOLMES, CM, III, p. 1133. Signed C. M. but not by Cotton Mather, although based on his *Wonders*, below, 1693.
Locations: RPJCB, NN

1693#13
MATHER, Cotton. *The wonders of the invisible world: being an account of the tryals of several witches lately excuted [sic] in New England*... London. J. Dunton, 106p. 4to. 1693
Note: SABIN 46604, WING M1174–6, HOLMES, CM, 454. First printed Boston (EVANS 657). Holmes states that both the Boston and London editions were published in 1692, although their title-pages are post-dated to

1693. Two abridged editions of the same title were published in London in 1693: SABIN 46605–6 (1) J. Dunton, 64p. O; NN. (2) J. Dunton. L; RPJCB, CSmH. Cf. WING F2546.
Locations: L; DLC, RPJCB, NjP

1693#14
MATHER, Increase. *A further account of the tryals of the New-England witches. With the observations of a person who was upon the place... To which is added, Cases of Conscience concerning witchcraft and evil spirits...* London. For J. Dunton, [54]p. 4to. 1693
Note: WING F2546, HOLMES IM, 22-B. Part I is 'A true narrative of some remarkable passages relating to sundry persons afflicted by witchcraft' 'collected by' Deodat Lawson, which was first published Boston, 1692 (EVANS 613). Part II is Cases of Conscience, by Increase Mather, with separate t. p. which was first published Boston, 1693. A 'further account' is a short letter and Holmes states that this is the only fresh material in the book. See also A. B. Cook, 'Damaging the Mathers...', *New England Quarterly*, LXV, No. 2, June, 1992.
Locations: L; O; MH, NN

1693#15
MOYLE, John. *Chirurgus marinus; or, The sea chirurgion...* London. For Eben. Tracy and H. Barnard, 12mo. 1693
Note: WING M3028A. Bk 3, chapt. 1 ('Of the scurvy') cites author's experience of scurvy on voyages to Newfoundland. An edition in 1702, EA 702/136.
Locations: L; O; MH, CtY

1693#16
RAY, John. *Synopsis methodica animalium quadrupedum et serpentini generis...* London. S. Smith and B. Walford, 336p. 8vo. 1693
Note: WING R405. New England moose, great grey Virginia squirrel, etc.
Locations: L; O; CtY, DFo, MH

1693#17
SAINT LO, George. *England's safety: or, A bridle to the French king...* London. W. Miller, 48p. 4to. 1693
Note: WING S341–2. Also 1693. Newfoundland references.
Locations: L; O; CtY, DFo, CtY, MH

1693#18
WHITEHEAD, George. *The Christian doctrine and society of the people called Quakers, cleared from the reproach of the late division of a few in some parts of America...* London. T. Northcott, 20p. 8vo. 1693
Note: SABIN 12913, 66917, WING W1905.
Locations: Lfr; CtY

1693#19
WILLIAMS, John. *A brief discourse concerning the lawfulness of worshipping God by the Common-Prayer...* London. R. Chiswell, 4, 36p. 4to. 1693
Note: WING W2682–4. Also 1694, 1696. Reply to I. Mather's *A brief discourse*, above, 1689.
Locations: O; Llp; NNUT, CSmH, MWA

1694#1
BUGG, Francis. *Quakerism withering, and Christianity reviving or, A brief reply to the Quakers pretended vindication...* London. J. Dunton and J. Guillam, 72p. 8vo. 1694
Note: WING B5386.
Locations: L; O; MH, CtY

1694#2
BULKLEY, Thomas. *To the right honourable William, Earl of Craven... being proprietors of Carolina, and the Bahama Islands...* London. 16p. 4to. [1694?]
Note: WING B5408.
Locations: RPJCB

1694#3
COKE, Roger. *A detection of the court and state of England during the last few reigns...* London. 2 vols. 8vo. 1694
Note: WING C4973–5. EA 694/34. Other editions 1696 and 1697. American impact on British economy, etc.
Locations: L; C; RPJCB, CtY, MH

1694#4
CRISP, Thomas. *Animadversions on George Whitehead's book...* London. J. Dunton, 40p. 4to. 1694
Note: WING C6947, SMITH I, 479, EA 694/45. Quakers in Pennsylvania.
Locations: Lfr; O; CSmH, CtY, MH

1694#5
ELLWOOD, Thomas. *An epistle to Friends... and warning them to beware of that spirit of contention... in George Keith, and some few others... who have made a break... from Friends in some parts of America...* London. T. Sowle, 73p. 8vo. 1694
Note: SABIN 22350, WING E620.
Locations: L; DLC, RPJCB

1694#6
ELLWOOD, Thomas. *A further discovery of that spirit of contention and division... in George Keith, etc. Being a reply to two late printed pieces of his...* London. T. Sowle, 128p. 8vo 1694
Note: SABIN 22351, WING E623.
Locations: BBN; DLC, RPJCB

1694

1694#7
FOX, George. *A journal, or historical account of the life, travels, sufferings. . . of. . . George Fox. . . The first volume. . .* London. T. Northcott, 733p. F. 1694
Note: SABIN 25352, WING F1854, SMITH I, 691. Another issue in 1693. Other editions in 1709 (EA 709/60), 1765. Volume I of his *Collected Works*.
Locations: L; C; DLC, MiU-C

1694#8
HANNAY, Robert. *A true account of the proceedings. . . of. . . Quakers in London. . . to. . . end. . . divisions and differences among some of the people called Quakers in America, with the proceedings of the yearly meeting at Burlington, New Jersey.* London. R. Lewis, 2, 16p. 4to. 1694
Note: SABIN 30235, SMITH I, p. 912, WING H656.
Locations: L; O; CSmH

1694#9
HOUGHTON, Thomas. *Royal institutions: being proposals for articles to establish and confirm laws. . . of silver and gold mines. . . in. . . Africa and America.* London. T. Houghton, 126p. 12mo. 1694
Note: WING H2935, EA 694/87. Reissued as *The golden treasury*, 1699.
Locations: L; RPJCB, NN, CSmH

1694#10
KEITH, George. *The causeless ground of surmises. . . in relation to the late religious differences and breaches among some of the people called Quakers in America.* London. R. Levis, 16p. 4to 1694
Note: WING K149, SABIN 37182, SMITH II, 29, EA 694/98.
Locations: L; O; RPJCB, PHi

1694#11
KEITH, George. *A further discovery of the spirit of falshood [sic] and persecution in Sam. Jennings and his party. . . in Pensilvania. . .* London. R. Levis, 52p. 4to. 1694
Note: WING K170, SABIN 37196, SMITH II, 28, EA 694/99.
Locations: L; RPJCB, PHi, DLC

1694#12
KEITH, George. *A seasonable information and caveat against a scandalous book of Thomas Ellwood, called, An epistle to Friends.* London. R. Levis, 40p. 4to. 1694
Note: WING K203, SABIN 37214, SMITH II, 29, EA 694/100. Quakers in America.
Locations: Lfr; O; RPJCB, PHi, DLC

1694#13
JANNEY, Thomas. *An epistle from James Janney to Friends of Cheshire, and by them desired to be made publick. . .* London. T. Sowle, 8p. 4to. 1694
Note: WING J480A, SMITH II, p. 7. From his house near the Falls of the Delaware in Pennsylvania.
Locations: Lfr; CSmH

1694#14
JENNINGS, Samuel. *The state of the case. . . betwixt the. . . Quakers, in Pennsylvania. . . and George Keith. . .* London. T. Sowle, 5p. 8vo. 1694
Note: SABIN 36048, WING J670.
Locations: O; RPJCB

1694#15
The judgement given forth by *twenty eight Quakers against George Keith, and his friends, with answers to the said judgement. . .* London. R. Baldwin 22p. 4to. 1694
Note: WING J1173.
Locations: O; RPJCB

1694#16
MATHER, Cotton. *Ornaments for the daughters of Zion, or The character and happiness of a virtuous woman. . .* London. T. Parkhurst, 130p. 12mo. 1694
Note: WING M1134, HOLMES, CM, 266. First printed Cambridge, Mass., 1691 (BRISTOL, B137).
Locations: L; MiU-C

1694#17
MORERI, Louis. *The great historical geographical, genealogical and poetical dictionary. . .* London. For H. Rhodes, L. Meredith, etc. fol. 1694
Note: WING M2725, BAER 157. Another edition in 1701, EA 701/189.
Locations: L; O; C; DLC, CtY

1694#18
PECHEY, John. *The compleat herbal of physical plants. . .* London. H. Bonwicke, 349p. 8vo. 1694
Note: WING P1021. Virginian snake root, etc.
Locations: L; O; MH, DFo, CtY

1694#19
Reasons for the reversal of *Leister's attainder. Humbly presented to the. . . House of Commons.* London. 2p. F. [1694]
Note: SABIN 39936, 68277.
Locations: NN

1694#20
WORLIDGE, John. *Mr. Worlidge's two treatises.* London. For M. Wotton, 191p. 8vo. 1694
Note: WING W3607. Colonial agricultural products and their benefits for trade expansion.
Locations: O; EN; DLC, MH, DFo

1695

1695#1
An answer to the reasons against Leisler's bill... offerd to the, consideration of the... Commons. London. 2p. [1695]
Note: SABIN 39936, WING A3439A. Cf. SABIN 68285n.
Locations: NN

1695#2
BEKKER, Balthasar. *The world bewitch'd...* London. R. Baldwin, 264p. 8vo. 1695
Note: WING B1781, B1781A, EA 695/17. Chapter X is on America. *The world turn'd upside down*, London 1700 is a reissue.
Locations: L; DLC, MH, ViU

1695#3
BRAY, Thomas. *Proposals for the incouragement and promoting of religion...* London. [8]p. F. [1695]
Note: SABIN 66036, WING B4296, BAER 163, 165, 173, 175, 177, 178 discusses several issues in 1695, 1696/7, 1697, 1699.
Locations: Oc; RPJCB, CSmH, MH

1695#4
BREWSTER, Francis. *Essays on trade and navigation. In five parts. The first part.* London. For T. Cockerill, xi, 126p. 8vo. 1695
Note: SABIN 7778, WING B4434, KRESS 1867. No more published. Material on Newfoundland and New England fisheries.
Locations: L; O; DLC, RPJCB

1695#5
Captain Leisler's case. **London.** s.sh. F. [1695?]
Note: SABIN 39936.
Locations: NN

1695#6
CARY, John. *An essay on the state of England, in relation to its trade.* Bristol: printed by W. Bonny for the author, and are to be sold in London by J. Crouch etc., 178p. 8vo. 1695
Note: WING C730, EA 695/30. American and African trades are most profitable to the kingdom.
Locations: L; NN, CtY, MH

1695#7
COKE, Roger. *Reflections upon East-Indy and Royal African companies...* London. 25p. 4to. 1695
Note: WING C4980, EA 695/38. References to Newfoundland fisheries.
Locations: L; LG, MH, DFo

1695#8
CRISP, Thomas. *The discovery of the accursed thing found in the Foxonian Quakers camp...* London. J. Gwillam, 40p. 4to. 1695
Note: WING C6949, EA 695/51. Pennsylvania references.
Locations: L; O; CSmH, DLC

1695#9
A description of the four parts of the world, viz. Europe, Africa, Asia, America, with the several kingdoms, etc. Edinburgh. Reprinted 1695, 12mo. 1695
Note: WING D1158, EA 695/60. A chapbook. First edition not located. Perhaps based on Blome, *A description*, above, 1670. There were certainly editions down to the 1760s, e. g. at Bodleian.
Locations: EN;

1695#10
ELLWOOD, Thomas. *Truth defended: and the friends thereof cleared, from the false charges... by George Keith... in two books...* London. T. Sowle, 171p. 8vo. 1695
Note: WING E629.
Locations: L; BBN; RPJCB, MiU-C

1695#11
HATTON, Edward. *The merchant's magazine: or, Trades-man's treasury...* London. Printed for and sold by Chr. Coningsby, 4to. 1695
Note: WING H1147–8. Also 1697, 1701, 1707, 1712, 1719, 1726, EA 701/144, 707/64, 712/107, 719/76, 726/103.
Locations: L; CtY, NNC

1695#12
HOUGHTON, Thomas. *A book of funds...* London. R. Baldwin, 32p. 4to. 1695
Note: WING H2924, EA 695/86. Convicts should be shipped to America, Africa, and East-Indies.
Locations: L; O; CtY, DFo, NNC

1695#13
The irregular and disorderly state of the plantation trade, discussed and humbly offered to... the Lords and Commons... London. 4p. F. [1695?]
Note: WING I1049A, KRESS SUPP 1860.
Locations: L; O; MH-BA

1695#14
KEITH, George. *Gross error and hypocrisie detected, in George Whitehead, and some of his brethren...* London. W. Kettilby, 23p. 4to. 1695
Note: WING K172, SABIN 37198, SMITH II, 30, EA 695/93. Quakers in America.
Locations: L; RPJCB, CtY, NN, MH

1695#15
KEITH, George. *The pretended yearly meeting of the Quakers... the evil and wicked practises of them in Pensilvania...* London. R. Levis, 12p. 4to. 1695
Note: WING K193, EA 695/94.
Locations: Lfr; O; RPJCB, NN, CSmH

1695#16
KEITH, George. *The true copy of a paper... together with a short list of... vile and gross errors... (being of the same sort and nature... charged on some in Pensilvania...* London. For R. Lewis, 32p. 4to. 1695
Note: SABIN 37222, WING K220.
Locations: LF, O; DLC; RPJCB

1695#17
LODDINGTON, William. *Tythe no gospel maintenance, for gospel ministers...* London. T. Sowle, 28p. 8vo. 1695
Note: SABIN 41763, WING L2808.
Locations: Lfr; PHi

1695#18
MATHER, Cotton. *Batteries upon the kingdom of the Devil. Seasonable discourses upon some common but woful, instances, wherein men gratifie the grand enemy of their salvation.* London. N. Hiller, [208]p. 8vo. 1695
Note: WING M1083, HOLMES, CM, 26. Reissued in 1695 as *Seven select lectures, of Mr Cotton Mather of New-England...,* HOLMES, CM, 352, (MH, RPJCB).
Locations: L; RPJCB

1695#19
MATHER, Cotton. *Brontologia sacra: the voice of the glorious God in the thunder...* London. J. Astwood, [44]p. 4to. 1695
Note: WING M1086, HOLMES, CM, 41.
Locations: MB, RPJCB

1695#20
MAYHEW, Matthew. *The conquests and triumphs of grace...* London. For N. Hiller, 68p. 8vo. 1695
Note: SABIN 47152, WING M1437. First printed Boston, 1694, (EVANS 701).
Locations: RPJCB, ViU

1695#21
OWEN, Griffith? *Our ancient testimony renewed... occasioned... by several unjust charges... by G. Keith... Given forth... at Philadelphia...* London. T. Sowle, 16p. 8vo. 1695
Note: SABIN 57908, WING O591, SMITH II, 249.
Locations: O; Lfr; RPJCB, NNUT, PHi

1695#22
P., L. *Two essays sent from Oxford to a nobleman in London, concerning some errors about the creation, general flood and peopling of the world...* London. R. Baldwin, 47p. 8vo. 1695
Note: SABIN 58061, 97555n, WING P77. Refers to North America. Reprinted in *Somers Tracts*, 3rd Coll., vol. III, pp. 291–308, (1751).
Locations: L; O; C; NN

1695#23
PECHEY, John? *Some observations made upon the herb cassiny; imported from Carolina; shewing its admirable virtues in curing the small pox...* London. 8p. 4to. 1695
Note: SABIN 86676, WING P933.
Locations: L; CSmH

1695#24
PENINGTON, John. *An apostate exposed, or George Keith's contradicting himself...* London. T. Sowle, 29p. 16mo. 1695
Note: WING P1223. References to Keith in America and to his writings against Cotton Mather.
Locations: L; O; DLC, CSmH

1695#25
PENINGTON, John. *Certain certificates received from America, on behalf of Samuel Jennings...* London. T. Sowle, 43p. 8vo. 1695
Note: SABIN 59664, WING P1224.
Locations: L; DLC

1695#26
PETIVER, James. *Musei Petiveriani prima [-octavia].* London. S. Smith and B. Walford, 8vo. 1695
Note: Issued in parts from 1695. WING P1870, SABIN 61288. Descriptions of American plants, animals, etc. See EA 703/117 (final part). All parts issued with general title page in 1705: EA 705/137.
Locations: L; MH

1695#27
PUFENDORF, Samuel von. *An introduction to the history of the principal states...* London. M. Gilliflower and T. Newborough, 8vo. 1695
Note: WING P4177–4179. Also 1697, 1699, 1700, 1702, 1705, 1706, 1711, 1719, 1728, 1748, EA 702/156, 705/50, 706/184, 711/164, 719/122, 728/148 748/162. With account of colonies.
Locations: Om; DLC, MH-L

1695#28
Reasons humbly offered in behalf *of the plantations, against the bill for settling the trade to Affrica...* London. s.sh. F. 1695
Note: WING R544cA. Guiny Negroes are 'more to the climate of Virginia and Maryland.'
Locations: L; MH

1695#29
Reasons humbly offer'd to the... *Commons... against the passing the bill for the reversing the Attainder of Jacob Leisler, Jacob Milburn, Abraham Governour and others.* London. 2p. F. [1695]
Note: SABIN 39936, 68285, WING R558D.
Locations: DLC, NN, N

1695#30
Thesaurus geographicus. A new body of geography... London. A. Swall and T. Child, 506p. F. 1695
Note: WING T869. Contains 'A general and particular description of America.'
Locations: L; O; CSmH, DFo, RPJCB

1695#31
You are desired to accompany the Corps of Sir William Phipps from Salters Hall... to the parish-church of St. Mary Woolnoth, [and bring this ticket with you.] London. s.sh. 1695
Locations: DLC

1696#1
BAXTER, Richard. *Reliquiae Baxterianiae: or Mr Richard Baxter's narrative of... his life...* London. T. Parkhurst and others, [780]p. F. 1696
Note: SABIN 4013, WING B1370. Original New England material.
Locations: L; MH

1696#2
BUGG, Francis. *The Quakers set in their true light...* London. Printed for the author. To be sold by C. Brome and J. Guillim, 48p. 4to. 1696
Note: WING B5388-90, SMITH I, 337, BAER 166. Diatribe against Quakers with American references. Other issues in 1696 and 1697.
Locations: Lfr; CtY, MH

1696#3
The case of the French Protestant refugees, settled in and about London, and in the English plantations in America. London. s.sh. F. [1696]
Note: WING C1080A. Huguenot protest against Act of Trade of 1696.
Locations: MH, NNC, CtY

1696#4
The case of the Hudson's Bay Company of England, In referrence to the Canada Company of France, and their servant Gabriel de la Forest... London. s.sh. F. [1696?]
Note: Cf. WING C1089.
Locations: Lg; Lpro;

1696#5
The case of the Hudson's-Bay-Company. The Kings of England by right of discovery... London. s.sh. F. [1696?]
Note: Cf. WING C1089, H3276A.
Locations: Lg; Lpro; DLC

1696#6
COKE, Roger. *A supplement to the first edition of The detection of the court of England.* London. A. Bell, 216p. 8vo. 1696

Note: WING C4981, EA 696/47. Canada, Virginia, New England.
Locations: L; E; CtY, MH, DFo

1696#7
COOLE, Benjamin. *The Quakers cleared from being apostates...* London. T. Sowle, 95p. 8vo. 1696
Note: WING C6047, EA 696/65, SMITH, AQ, 459. Quakers in New England and Pennsylvania.
Locations: L; RPJCB, MH, DFo

1696#8
CROESE, Gerard. *The general history of the Quakers...* London. J. Dunton, 3pts. 8vo. 1696
Note: SABIN 17584, WING C6965, BAER 169, SMITH, I, 480-1. Includes Pennsylvania.
Locations: L; O; RPJCB, CSmH

1696#9
DICKINSON, James. *A salutation of love to the seed of God everywhere.* London. T. Sowle, 4p. 4to. 1696
Note: WING D1388, SABIN 20034, SMITH I, 530, EA 696/78. Written on board ship en route to America.
Locations: L; Lfr; CSmH, MH, PHC

1696#10
ELLWOOD, Thomas. *An answer to George Keith's narrative of his proceedings at the Turner's Hall.* London. T. Sowle, 23p. 8vo. 1696
Note: WING E613, SMITH I, 566, EA 696/86. Keith and Pennsylvania.
Locations: L; CtY, RPJCB, NN

1696#11
ENGLAND AND WALES. PARLIAMENT. *An act for preventing frauds and regulating abuses in the plantation trade.* London. [17]p. 4to. 1696
Note: KRESS SUPP 1943.
Locations: MH-BA

1696#12
HUDSON'S BAY COMPANY. *Upon Wednesday the 18th day of November 1696.* London. s.sh. F. 1696
Note: WING H3267B.
Locations: MiU-C

1696#13
An impartial account of the present state of the Hudson-Bay Company, as they stand incorporated... London. s.sh. F. [1696?]
Note: WING I74.
Locations: Lpro;

1696#14
KEITH, George. *The anti-Christs and Saducees detected among a sort of Quakers; or Caleb Pusie, of*

1696

Pennsylvania, and John Pennington... London. 44p. 4to. [1696]
Note: SABIN 37180, WING K138.
Locations: L; O; DLC, RPJCB

1696#15
KEITH, George. *An exact narrative of the proceedings at Turner's Hall*... London. B. Aylmer and J. Dunton, 62p. 4to 1696
Note: WING K161, SABIN 37191, SMITH II, 32, EA 696/115. Quakers in Pennsylvania.
Locations: L; RPJCB, NN, MH

1696#16
KEITH, George. *George Keith's challenge to William Penn and Geor. Whitehead; two eminent Quakers*... London. 8p. 16mo. 1696
Note: SABIN 37184.
Locations: NO COPY LOCATED.

1696#17
KEITH, George. *A just vindication of my earnest expostulation*... London. J. Bradford, 7p. 4to. 1696
Note: WING K178, SMITH II, 31–2, EA 696/116. Quakers in Pennsylvania.
Locations: O; NN, CSmH

1696#18
LESLIE, Charles. *The snake in the grass... discovering the deep and unexpected subtilty... of the principal leaders of those people called Quakers*... London. C. Brome, 271p. 8vo. 1696
Note: SABIN 85363–5, WING L1156. Incidental references to Pennsylvania Quakers.
Locations: L; RPJCB

1696#19
A letter to George Keith, *concerning his late religious differences with William Penn and his party*... [London]. 4p. 4to. 1696
Note: WING L1704A.
Locations: NN, RPJCB

1696#20
MOCQUET, Jean. *Travels and voyages into Africa, Asia, and America, and the East and West-Indies*... London. For W. Newton, J. Shelton, W. Chandler, 352p. 8vo. 1696
Note: WING M2310. Translated from the French by Nath. Pullen. The voyages were early seventeenth century but the preface mentions, Florida, Virginia, New France, etc.
Locations: L; O; DLC, CtY

1696#21
PENINGTON, Edward. *Some brief observations upon George Keith's earnest expostulations*... London. T. Sowle, 24p. 12mo. 1696
Note: SABIN 59657, WING P1146. Pennsylvania references.
Locations: L; RPJCB

1696#22
PENINGTON, John. *The people called Quakers cleared by Geo. Keith, from the false doctrines charged on them by G. Keith*... London. T. Sowle, 47p. 12mo. 1696
Note: SABIN 59665, WING P1129. Pennsylvania references.
Locations: L; RPJCB

1696#23
PUSEY, Caleb. *A modest account from Pensylvania, of the principal differences in point of doctrine, between George Keith and*... London. T Sowle, 68p. 8vo. 1696
Note: WING P4248, SABIN 66739, SMITH II, 438–9.
Locations: L; O; Lfr; RPJCB, DLC, CSmH

1696#24
YOUNG, Samuel. *Vindiciae anti-Baxterianiae, or some animadversions on a book, entitled Reliquiae Baxterianiae, or the life of Mr. R. Baxter*... London. To be sold by R. Standfast, [333]p. 12mo. 1696
Note: SABIN 4014, WING Y89.
Locations: L; MH, CLU-C

1696#25
YOUNG, Samuel. *William Penn and the Quakers either impostors, or apostates*... London. J. Lawrence, 4, 134p. 12mo. 1696
Note: WING Y90. By 'Trepidantium Malleus'. A few Pennsylvania references. Another edition in 1697.
Locations: L; Lfr; MH, CtY

1697#1
BRAY, Thomas. *Bibliotheca parochialis Part I.* London. E. H. for R. Clavel, 130p. 4to. 1697
Note: SABIN 7474, WING B4290, BAER 175. No more parts published. Revised enlarged edition in 1707.
Locations: L; RPJCB, CSmH

1697#2
BRAY, Thomas. *An essay towards promoting all necessary and useful knowledge.* London. E. Holt for R. Clavel, 22p. 4to. 1697
Note: SABIN 7476, WING B4293, BAER 176.
Locations: L; O; DLC, RPJCB

1697#3
BRAY, Thomas. *A short discourse upon the doctrine of our baptismal covenant*... London. E. Holt for R. Clavel, 190p. 8vo. 1697
Note: WING B4297.
Locations: P; RPJCB

1697#4
BRAY, Thomas. *Supplement to the Bibliotheca parochialis.* London. R. Clavel, 4to. 1697
Note: WING B4299B.
Locations: Oc;

1697#5
BUGG, Francis. *A brief history of the rise, growth, and progress of Quakerism.* London. 196p. 8vo. 1697
Note: SABIN 9072, WING B5367, EA 697/28, *The second part of The picture of Quakerism*, 1697.
Locations: L; Lfr; MH, RPJCB

1697#6
BUGG, Francis. *The picture of Quakerism drawn to the life. In 2 parts...* London. W. Kettleby and W. Rogers. [22]p. 8vo. 1697
Note: SABIN 9072, WING 5381. Concerns Keith and Pennsylvania.
Locations: L; O;

1697#7
CRISP, Thomas. *A just and lawful tryal of the Foxonian chief priests...* London. For T. Crisp and sold by B. Aylmer, 132p. 8vo. 1697
Note: WING C6952, SMITH, I, 480, EA 697/44. Attack on Penn, George Whitehead, etc.
Locations: L; O; RPJCB, PSC-Hi

1697#8
DEFOE, Daniel. *An essay upon projects.* London. By R. R. for T. Cockerill, 336p. 8vo. 1697
Note: WING D832. Sir William Phips's salvage of a sunken ship in Caribbean Sea; references to Pennsylvania, Carolina, East and West Jersey, and to Hudson's Bay Company. Republished in 1700 as *Several essays relating to academies*, WING D845, EA 700/69 and in 1702 as *Essays upon several subjects: or, Effectual ways for advancing the interest of the nation*, EA 702/59–60.
Locations: L; O; MH, CtY

1697#9
KEITH, George. *George Keith's explications of divers passages contained in his former books.* London. B. Aylmer and R. Baldwin, 44p. 4to. 1697
Note: WING K163, SMITH II, 32, EA 697/97. Quakers in Pennsylvania.
Locations: L; MH, CSmH, NN

1697#10
MATHER, Cotton. *Pietas in patrium: the life of his excellency Sir William Phips, Knt...* London. S. Bridge for N. Hiller. 132p. 12mo. 1697
Note: WING M1118, HOLMES, CM, 279.
Locations: L; DLC; RPJCB

1697#11
RANDOLPH, Edward. *A discourse how to render the plantations on the continent of America, and Islands adjacent; more beneficial... to this Kingdom.* London. 2p. F. 1697
Note: BAER 174. Printed version of a paper presented in 1696.
Locations: MdBJ-G

1697#12
TURNER, William. *A compleat history of the most remarkable providences, both of judgement and mercy, which have hapned [sic] in this present age...* London. J. Dunton, 634p. F. 1697
Note: WING T3345. References to New England witches and Indians.
Locations: L; MH, MiU-C

1697#13
YOUNG, Samuel. *The Foxonian Quakers, dunces, lyars and slanderers...* London. For W. Marshall and J. Marshal, 134p. 12mo. 1697
Note: WING Y79A. Attack on Penn, 'King of Pensilvania'.
Locations: L; O; RPJCB, DFo

1698#1
An account of Monsieur de la Salle's last expedition and discoveries in North America... Made English from the Paris original. London. J. Tonson and others, 255p. 8vo. 1698
Note: WING A210A.
Locations: L; O; DLC, RPJCB

1698#2
BRAY, Thomas. *Apostolick charity, its nature and excellence consider'd... Preached... Decemb. 19. 1697. at the ordination of some Protestant missionaries to be sent into the plantations... A general view of the English colonies in America, with respect to religion...* London. W. Downing for W. Hawes, 36p. 4to. 1698
Note: SABIN 7473, WING B4285, BAER 182, 189, 190, 195 for discussion of five issues in 1698, 1699, 1700.
Locations: Dt; DLC, RPJCB

1698#3
BUGG, Francis. *The pilgrim's progress, from Quakerism, to Christianity...* London. W. Kettilby, 175p 4to. 1698
Note: WING B5382–3, EA 698/27, 700/34. Second edition in 1700. Quakers in Pennsylvania.
Locations: L; O; CtY, DFo, MH

1698#4
BULKLEY, Thomas. *The monstrous injustice and unmercifulness of Nicholas Trott, late governour of the Bahama-Islands in America...* London. 16p. 4to. 1698

1698

Note: WING B5407A. Trott later went to South Carolina.
Locations: NN

1698#5
CHAMBERLAYNE Richard. *Lithobolia: or, the stone throwing devil... account... of... infernal spirits... and the great disturbance they gave to George Walton's family, at... Great Island in... New Hantshire [sic] in New-England...* London. E. Whitlocke, 16p. 4to. 1698
Note: SABIN 11786, WING C1862.
Locations: L; O; RPJCB, MH

1698#6
DAVENANT, Charles. *Discourses on the publick revenues, and on the trade of England...* London. J. Knapton. 2vols. 8vo. 1698
Note: SABIN 18686, WING D306. Section on plantation trade.
Locations: L; O; DLC, RPJCB

1698#7
FOX, George. *A collection of many select and Christian epistles, letters and testimonies...* London. T. Sowle [527]p. F. 1698
Note: SABIN 25347, WING F1764, SMITH I, 691, BAER 184. Vol II of *Works*. Many American references.
Locations: L; RPJCB, DLC, CtY

1698#8
HENNEPIN, Lewis. *A new discovery of a vast country in America, extending above four thousand miles, between New France and New Mexico...* London. M. Bentley and others, 512p. 8vo. 1698
Note: SABIN 31370, WING H1450. Other editions in 1698, 1699. See EA 698/93, 698/95. Abridged edition, *A discovery...* in 1720, EA 720/119. O; DLC, RPJCB, MiU-C. KRESS SUPPL 2051 is Part Two, published separately in 1698.
Locations: L; RPJCB

1698#9
JOHNSON, Samuel. *A confutation of a late pamphlet intituled, A letter ballancing the necessity of keeping a land-force...* London. A. Baldwin, 35p. 4to. 1698
Note: WING J824, EA 698/111. New England references.
Locations: L; DLC, MH, NjP

1698#10
KEITH, George. *The arguments of the Quakers, more particularly, of George Whitehead, William Penn... against baptism and the supper...* London. C. Brome, 89p. 4to. 1698
Note: WING K142, SMITH II, 33, EA 698/116. Quakers in America.
Locations: L; RPJCB, DLC, CtY

1698#11
KEITH, George. *A third narrative of the proceedings at Turners-Hall...* London. C. Brome, 68p. 4to. 1698
Note: WING K223, SABIN 37191, SMITH II, 32–3, EA 698/117. Quakers in America.
Locations: L; DLC, NN, MH

1698#12
LISTER, Martin. *A journey to Paris in the year 1698...* London. J. Tonson, 245p., plates, 8vo. 1698
Note: WING L2524A–2527. Three other editions in 1699. Visits to collections with American objects; also a grammar of the 'Algonquin Tongue.'
Locations: GK; MBM

1698#13
MATHER, Cotton. *Eleutheria: or, An idea of the Reformation in England: and a History of Non-Conformity in and since that Reformation. With predictions of a more glorious reformation and revolution at hand.* London. I. R. and sold by A. Baldwin, 135p. 8vo. 1698
Note: WING M1101, HOLMES, CM, 107. Also Edinburgh, 1698: New College Library.
Locations: MB, MHi

1698#14
PERRY, Micaiah. *Further reasons for inlarging the trade to Russia, humbly offered by the merchants and planters trading to and interested in the plantations of Virginia and Maryland...* London. s.sh. F. [1698]
Note: WING F2565, BAER 186, KRESS SUPP 1852.
Locations: L; O; MH

1698#15
Proposals for settling a colony in Florida. London. s.sh. F. [1698]
Note: SABIN 66035.
Locations: L; N

1698#16
SCOTLAND. PRIVY COUNCIL. *Proclamation discharging transporting of persons to the plantations of forraigners... [27 December 1698].* Edinburgh. Heirs and successors of A. A., s.sh. F. 1698
Note: WING W2453A, STEELE II, 3167. Prohibits carrying of Scots to foreign plantations.
Locations: EN; DLC

1698#17
Several living testimonies given forth... London. For T. Sowle, 8vo. 1698
Note: WING S2782. Contains George Fox's testimony about Robert Lodge who went to New England.
Locations: L; Lfr; MH, PSC

1698#18
SIDNEY, Algernon. *Discourses concerning government...* London. Booksellers of London and Westminster, 462p. F. 1698
Note: WING S3761. Also 1704. African, American and Asian barbarity and human nature.
Locations: L; O; CtY, MH, DFo

1698#19
STORY, Thomas. *A word to the well-inclined of all persuasions. Together with a copy of a letter from William Penn to George Keith...* London. T. Sowle, 8p. 4to. 1698
Note: SABIN 92330, WING S5755.
Locations: Lfr; RPJCB

1698#20
THOMAS, Gabriel. *An historical and geographical account of the province and country of Pensilvania; and of West-New-Jersey in America...* London. A. Baldwin, 102p. 8vo. 1698
Note: SABIN 95359, WING T964, BAER 188.
Locations: L; DLC, RPJCB

1698#21
TOLAND, John. *The militia reform'd...* London. J. Darby and sold by A. Bell, 8vo. 1698
Note: WING T1766A, 1766B. Second edition, 1699. Members of freeman militia should qualify for public office by serving in two campaigns by land or sea, including 'West Indies' or one in East Indies.
Locations: L; Lu; MH, CtY, DFo

1698#22
TRENCHARD, John. *A short history of standing armies...* London. For T. Baldwin, 32p. 8vo. 1698
Note: WING T2115-7. Second edition in 1699 (L;). Charles II let French seize British plantations in North America.
Locations: AN; LSD; DLC, MiU, DFo

1698#23
TRYON, Thomas. *Some general considerations offered, relating to our present trade...* London. J. Harris, 26p. 4to. 1698
Note: WING T3195. For encouraging plantation and other trade by lowering duties, etc.
Locations: L; Lu; MH, RPJCB, DFo

1698#24
The two charters granted by *King Charles IId. to the proprietors of Carolina. With the first and fundamfntal [sic] constitutions of that colony.* London. R. Parker, 60p. 4to. [1698]
Note: WING C3622, SABIN 10980. Another edition in 1705: (RPJCB, MiU-C), EA 705/31.
Locations: L; RPJCB, DLC

1698#25
TYSON, Edward. *Carigueya, seu Marsupiale Americanum, or the Anatomy of an Opossum, dissected at Gresham-college.* London. S. Smith and B. Walford, 60p and figures., 4to. 1698
Note: WING T3597. 'This Animal was brought from Virginia, and presented to the Royal Society, by William Bird, Esq.' It died of an ulcer.
Locations: L; O; NN, NRU, CtY

1698#26
YOUNG, Samuel. *An apology for Congregational divines...* London. For J. Harris, 190p. 12mo. 1698
Note: WING Y76, SABIN 106097A. Mentions Cotton, Norton etc. and New England and Quakers.
Locations: LW; CSmH, CtY, RPJCB

1699#1
BECKHAM, Edward. *A brief discovery of some of the blasphemous and seditious principles and practices of the people, called Quakers.* London. J. Harris, 32p. 4to. 1699
Note: WING B1652, EA 699/7, SMITH, AQ. 66. Discusses Pennsylvania.
Locations: L; RPJCB, CtY, DFo

1699#2
BEESTON, William. *Proclamation by the Rt. Honourable William Beeston, Kt. Governor of Jamaica... 8th day of April 1699. Reprinted in Edinburgh exactly according to the Originals,* 4p. F. 1699
Note: WING B1695. Includes proclamations by Governors of New York and Massachusetts against giving assistance to Darien scheme.
Locations: E; RPJCB

1699#3
BELLERS, John. *Essays about the poor, manufactures, trade, plantations and immorality...* London. T. Sowle, 26p. 4to. 1699
Note: WING B1828, KRESS 2107.
Locations: L; O; CtY, MH

1699#4
BERNARD, Jacques. *The acts and negotiations, together with the particular articles at large, of the general peace concluded at Ryswick.* London. R. Clavel, T. Childe, 8vo. 1699
Note: WING B1994, EA 699/10. Newfoundland, etc.
Locations: L; RPJCB

1699#5
COOLE, Benjamin. *Sophistry detected, or, an answer to George Keith's synopsis...* Bristol. W. Bonny, 46p. 4to. 1699

Note: WING C6047B. Discussion of Keith and Penn and Keith and America.
Locations: L; O; PH, PSC

1699#6
CURSON, Henry. *A compendium of the laws and government. . . of England and dominions, plantations, and territories thereto belonging.* London. Assigns of R. and E. Atkins for J. Walthoe, 642p. 12mo. 1699
Note: SABIN 15046, WING C7686, BAER 191. Reprinted 1716: SABIN 18009, EA 716/42.
Locations: L; EN; DLC, CtY

1699#7
ENGLAND AND WALES. PARLIAMENT. LORDS. *The humble address of the Lords. . . to his majesty, in relation to the petition of Charles Desborow, employed in the trade to Newfoundland. . .* London. For C. Desborow, 8p. 4to. 1699
Note: SABIN 19686, WING E2801.
Locations: L; O; DLC, RPJCB

1699#8
An essay against the transportation and selling of men to the plantations of forreigners; with special regard to Scotland. . . Edinburgh. 24p. F. 1699
Note: WING E3227C, GOLDSMITHS 3569, ALDIS 3846, EA 699/63. Sales to New England colonies.
Locations: LUG

1699#9
LEEDS, Daniel. *A trumpet sounded out of the wilderness of America. . .* London. Printed by W, Bradford: New York; sold by B. Aylmer and C. Brome, London, 151p. 8vo. 1699
Note: WING L916. First printed New York, as *News of a Trumpet,* EVANS 786.
Locations: L; O; NN

1699#10
A letter from a gentleman in America, to his friend in Scotland. . . London. 1p. F. 1699
Note: WING L1382A. Darien scheme. Dated 'Bolston [sic] November 8th 1698' [sic].
Locations: MiU, RPJCB

1699#11
MATHER, Cotton. *The serious Christian: or three great points of practical Christianity. . . By an American.* London. B. Harris, (4), 116p. 12mo. 1699
Note: WING M1149, HOLMES, CM, 347.
Locations: MB, ViU

1699#12
MATHER, Increase. *Two plain and practical discourses. Concerning 1. Hardness of Heart. . .* London. For J. Robinson, to be sold by Samuel Phillips in Boston, in New-England. 12mo. 1699

Note: WING M1258.
Locations: LW; CSmH, DLC, MHi

1699#13
PATERSON, William. *An abstract, of a letter from a person of eminency and worth in [New] Caledonia, to a friend in Boston in New England. . .* Edinburgh. Printed by John Reid, s.sh. F. 1699
Note: WING P709A, 709B. Also Glasgow and Boston, 1699 (EVANS 892).
Locations: EN;

1699#14
PETTY, William. *Several essays in political arithmetick.* London. R. Clavel and H. Mortlock, 276p. 8vo. 1699
Note: SABIN 61308, WING P1937. Other editions in 1711, 1751, 1755. EA 711/161. Discussion of colonial trade.
Locations: O; MH

1699#15
The seaman's opinion of a standing army in England, in opposition to a Fleet at Sea, as the best security of this nation. London. A. Baldwin, 22p. 4to. 1699
Note: WING S2189, 2189A, 2190, 2190A. Three other editions in 1699. References to New England.
Locations: L; O; CLC, MH, CSmH

1699#16
A sober dialogue between a country friend, a London friend, and one of G. K.'s friends, concerning the great differences. . . betwixt many Quakers. . . London. B. Aylmer, 16p. 8vo. 1699
Note: SABIN 85662, WING S4408.
Locations: Lfr; RPJCB

1699#17
Some considerations; humbly offered to demonstrate how prejudicial it would be to the English plantations. . . London. 2p. F. 1699
Note: WING S4486. Criticisms of the Royal African Company for failure to deliver slaves to Virginia and Maryland.
Locations: L; MH, NN, CtY

1699#18
TRYON, Thomas. *Englands grandeur, and way to get wealth; or, promotion of trade made easy. . .* London. J. Harris and G. Conyers, 2, 26p. 4to. 1699
Note: SABIN 97286, WING T3178,
Locations: L; MiU-C

1699#19
WARD, Edward. *A trip to New-England. With a character of the country and people, both English and Indians.* London. 16p. F. 1699
Note: SABIN 10132, 101286, WING W764.
Locations: O; RPJCB, MiU-C

1699#20
WOODWARD, Josiah. *An account of the societies for reformation of manners in London and Westminster...* London. For B. Aylmer, 163p. 8vo. 1699
Note: WING W3512–3514A. Other editions, 1699, 1700. Lewd women will transport themselves to plantations.
Locations: L; O; MH, CtY, DFo

1699#21
WYETH, Joseph. *Anguis flagellatus; or, a switch for the snake. Being an answer to the third and last edition of the Snake in the Grass...* London. T. Sowle, (18), 548p. 8vo. 1699
Note: SABIN 105650, WING 3757.
Locations: L; RPJCB, NN

1700#1
BECKHAM, Edward. *The principles of the Quakers further shewn to be blasphemous and seditious...* London. B. Aylmer, 100p. 4to. 1700
Note: WING B1653, EA 700/12. Mrs Hutchinson, the American Jezebel and Pennsylvania Quakers and military defence.
Locations: L; O; RPJCB, CtY, MH

1700#2
BEHN, Aphra. *Histories, novels, and translations. The second volume.* London. S. Briscoe and sold by M. Brown, 4pts. 8vo. 1700
Note: WING B1714, EA 700/14. Contains Behn's translation of Fontenelle.
Locations: L; RPJCB, CtY, CSmH

1700#3
BRAY, Thomas. *The acts of Dr. Bray's visitation. held at Annopolis [sic] in Mary-land, May 23, 24, 25, anno 1700.* London. W. Downing, 17p. F. 1700
Note: SABIN 7472, WING B4282. BAER 194 for discussion of three issues in 1700.
Locations: L; Oc; MH, NN

1700#4
BRAY, Thomas. *A circular letter to the clergy of Maryland...* London. [6]p. F. [1700]
Note: SABIN 7475, WING B4291, BAER 196. Running title 'Letter I'.
Locations: L; O; RPJCB, MH

1700#5
BRAY, Thomas. *A letter from Dr. Bray to such as have contributed towards the propagating Christian knowledge in the plantations...* London. 3p. F. [1700]
Note: SABIN 7478, WING B4293A. BAER 197 states published London; EVANS 90 lists as New York imprint.
Locations: L; RPJCB

1700#6
BRAY, Thomas. *A memorial, representing the present state of religion, on the continent of North-America.* London. W. Downing, 15p. F. 1700
Note: SABIN 7479, WING B4294, BAER 198. Another edition in 1701, EA 701/51.
Locations: L; O; RPJCB, MiU-C

1700#7
BRAY, Thomas. *The present state of the Protestant religion in Maryland, under the government of Francis Nicholson Esq. by Dr Bray...* London. s.sh. F. [1700?]
Note: SABIN 7481, WING P3273. BAER 165J lists this as the second part of *Proposals for the incouragement of religion...*, above, 1695.
Locations: L; RPJCB

1700#8
BRAY, Thomas. *A short account of the several kinds of societies, set up in late years...* London. J. Brudenell, 4p. F. 1700
Note: WING B4296a, BAER 200.
Locations: MH, MdBJ-G

1700#9
BUGG, Francis. *A modest defence of my book, entituled, Quakerism exposed...* London. R. Janeway, jr. xxviii, [116]p. 8vo. 1700
Note: WING B5375. Cf. SMITH I, 144. Mentions schisms in Pennsylvania.
Locations: L; O; MH, RPJCB, CtY

1700#10
CALEF, Robert. *More wonders of the invisible word: or The wonders of the invisible world displayed... To which is added, a postscript relating to a book intitled, The life of Sir William Phips...* London. N. Hillar, R. Collyer, 156p. 4to. 1700
Note: SABIN 9926, WING C288.
Locations: L; O; DLC, RPJCB

1700#11
Case of J. Degrave... and others, owners of the seven sail of transports taken up to carry provisions to Newfoundland. London. s.sh. F. [1700]
Note: SABIN 54977, WING C928.
Locations: L; LL;

1700#12
COOLE, Benjamin. *Honesty the truest policy, shewing the sophistry, envy and perversion of George Keith.* London. Printed for the author, 128p. 8vo. 1700
Note: WING C6046, EA 700/63. Keith in America.
Locations: L; O; RPJCB, DFo, CtY

1700#13
DEFOE, Daniel. *The two great questions consider'd.* London. R. T. for A. Baldwin, 28p. 4to. 1700

1700

Note: WING D850, EA 700/71. French and Spanish America and the British colonies.
Locations: L; O; MH, CtY, DLC

1700#14
DICKINSON, Jonathan. *God's protecting providence, man's surest help and defence. . . remarkable deliverance. . . from devouring waves. . . also from. . . inhumane cannibals of Florida. . .* London. Philadelphia printed, London reprinted, T. Sowle, 89p. 12mo. 1700
Note: SABIN 20015, WING D1390. Reissued in 1700, 1701, 1720, 1759 etc. First printed Philadelphia, 1699 (EVANS 863). See also EVANS 3896, 6651.
Locations: L; Lfr; DLC, MiU-C

1700#15
DONALDSON, James. *The undoubted art of thriving, showing that a million. . . may be raised. . . how the Indian and African Company may propagate their trade, in New York, Jamaica, and other parts of the West Indies. . .* Edinburgh. J. Reid, 135p. 8vo. 1700
Note: SABIN 20589, WING D1856, KRESS 2218.
Locations: L; EN; RPJCB, MH

1700#16
FIELD, John. *The Christianity of the people called Quakers, asserted, by George Keith: in answer to a sheet, called, A serious call to the Quakers.* London. T. Sowle, s.sh. F. 1700
Note: WING F861B. Quakers in America. EVANS 1048 lists this as [Philadelphia?]. cf. SMITH I, 606. Another London edition in 1702, EA 702/76.
Locations: Lfr; PH

1700#17
A full and true discovery *of all the robberies, pyracies. . . of that famous English pyrate Capt James Kelly. . . With an account of his joyning with Capt. Kidd. . . in several parts of the world. . . written with his own hand. . .* London. J. Johnson, 2p. F. 1700
Note: WING F2312.
Locations: L; DLC

1700#18
HEATHCOTE, Samuel. *Heads of some of those advantages this nation might enjoy, by encouraging the tobacco trade to Russia. . .* London. s.sh. F. 1700? 1700
Note: WING H1291A. References to planting in Virginia, 'where there is land enough to produce more Tobacco than all Europe can consume.'
Locations: L; LIU; V

1700#19
HUMFREY, John. *A paper to William Penn, at the departure of that gentleman to his territory. . .* London. T. M. for J. Mortlock, 24p. 4to. 1700

Note: SABIN 58444, WING H3698. Other editions 1720, 1759.
Locations: L; RPJCB, MiU-C

1700#20
KEITH, George. *An account of the Quakers politicks.* London. W. Redmayne, for B. Aylmer and C. Brome, 39p. 4to. 1700
Note: WING K137, SMITH II, 38, EA 700/147. Quakers in America.
Locations: L; O; RPJCB, NN, DLC

1700#21
KEITH, George. *George Keith's fourth narrative, of his proceedings at Turner's Hall.* London. B. Aylmer, 116p. 4to. 1700
Note: WING K167, SMITH II, 35–68, EA 700/148. Quakers in America.
Locations: L; RPJCB, MH, DLC

1700#22
KEITH, George. *A second narrative of the proceedings at Turners-Hall. . .* London. B. Aylmer, 36p. 4to. 1700
Note: WING K204, SABIN 37191, SMITH II, 32, EA 697/78. Quakers in America.
Locations: L; DLC, NN, MH

1700#23
KEITH, George. *A sermon preach'd at Turner's Hall. . . 5th. of May, 1700.* London. W. Bowyer, 32p. 4to. 1700
Note: WING K209, 209A, SMITH II, 36, EA 700/149–50. Quakers in America.
Locations: L; O; MH, RPJCB, DFo

1700#24
KEITH, George. *Two sermons preach'd at the parish-church of St. George. . . London May the 12th. 1700.* London. W. Bowyer for B. Aylmer and C. Brome, 31p. 4to. 1700
Note: WING K226–7, SMITH II, 36, EA 700/151–2. Another issue in 1700. Quakers in America.
Locations: L; RPJCB, CtY, MH

1700#25
LESLIE, Charles. *A defence of a book, intituled The snake in the grass. . .* London. M. Bennet, etc. 241p. 8vo. 1700
Note: WING L1126. Includes, with separate title page, *A collection of several papers which relate to the fore-going*, 93p., mainly concerning Quakers in Pennsylvania.
Locations: L; O; Mh, DFo, CtY

1700#26
LESLIE, Charles. *A parallel between the faith and doctrine of the present Quakers, and that of the chief hereticks in all ages. . .* London. J. Nut, 59p. 4to. 1700

Note: WING P334B, P334C. Another issue in 1700. Pennsylvania, East Jersey and Long Island references; the Nicolaitan heresy.
Locations: L; C; MH, PH, PSC

1700#27
A letter to a member of parliament in the country, concerning the present posture of affairs in Christendom. London. 26p. 8vo. 1700
Note: WING L1674–5. Second edition in 1700. Union of France and Spain will give France oceanic and colonial supremacy.
Locations: L; O; MHL, CSmH, CtY

1700#28
MATHER, Cotton. *A letter of advice to the churches of the non-conformists in the English nation: endeavouring their satisfaction in that point, Who are the true Church of England?* London. A. Baldwin, 4, 130p. 4to. 1700
Note: WING M1119, HOLMES, CM, 195.
Locations: L; RPJCB

1700#29
MATHER, Increase. *The order of the gospel, professed and practised by the churches of Christ in New-England...* London. Reprinted London. A. Baldwin, 86p. 8vo. 1700
Note: WING M1236 SABIN 46714, WING M1236, HOLMES, IM, 84. First printed Boston, 1700 (EVANS 938–9).
Locations: L; RPJCB

1700#30
MUCKLOWE, William. *A bemoaning letter of an ingenious Quaker...* London. A. Baldwin, 45p. 8vo. 1700
Note: SABIN 3532, WING M3303.
Locations: O; RPJCB

1700#31
Old John Uncas and the greater part of the tribe of Mohegan Indians, by Samuel Mason, their Guardian, Appellants... To be heard before... Privy Council... London. 24p. F. 1700
Note: SABIN 15749. Mohegan Indians versus Connecticut.
Locations: RPJCB

1700#32
Remarks upon a late pamphlet, intitul'd The two great questions consider'd. London. Printed in the year 1700, 27p. 4to. 1700
Note: WING R938. No losses to England, except in Newfoundland fisheries and Hudson's Bay Trade, if Philip of Anjou inherits Spanish Crown.
Locations: L; O; NN, DFo, CtY

1700#33
SMITH, Thomas. *England's danger by Indian manufactures.* London. 8p. 4to. [1700?]
Note: WING S4229. Cheap East Indian exports ruin English woollen exports, including those to plantations.
Locations: L; CtY, NNC

1700#34
STODDARD, Solomon. *The doctrine of instituted churches explained and proved from the word of God...* London. R. Smith, 34p. 4to. 1700
Note: SABIN 91945, WING S5708.
Locations: O; RPJCB, MiU-C

1700#35
The trappan'd maiden: or, the distressed damsel... London. By and for W. O. and for A. M. and sold by C. Bates, s.sh. F. [1700?]
Note: WING T2049. The date is uncertain; Bates definitely operated 1709–14; William Onley, 1697–1709.
Locations: L; O; CM;

1700#36
TRYON, Thomas. *Tryon's letters, domestic and foreign to several persons of quality...* London. G. Conyers and E. Harris, 16, 240p. 8vo. 1700
Note: SABIN 97289, WING T3183. American material.
Locations: L; MH

1700#37
WIGHT, Thomas. *Truth further defended, and William Penn vindicated...* London. 8, 179p. 8vo. 1700
Note: SABIN 103939, WING T2108. Reply to *A brief and modest reply, to Mr. Penn's tedious... defence, against the Bishop of Cork.*
Locations: Lfr; MiU-C

1700#38
WYETH, Joseph. *An answer to a letter from Dr. Bray, directed to such as have contributed towards the propagating Christian knowledge in the plantations...* London. T. Sowle, 19p. 4to. 1700
Note: SABIN 105651, WING W3758, SMITH II, 996, BAER 209. Another issue in 1700.
Locations: Lfr; DLC

1701#1
An account of a great fight, between the Christians, and the Quakers, and also how they blew themselves up, with a magazine of there [sic] own gunpowder. [London]. For the author, T.H. s.sh. [1701]
Note: FOXON A8, EA 701/5. In verse. References to Quakers in America.
Locations: MH

1701

1701#2
An account of the Earl *of Bellomont's proceedings at New-York. Offer'd to be proved before the Committee of Trade and Plantations.* . . London. 2p. 1/2o 1701
Note: EA 701/33. First published New York, 1698 (EVANS 834).
Locations: L; CSmH

1701#3
AMERICAN. *An essay upon the government of the English plantations in America. Together with some remarks upon the discourse on the plantation trade. Written by the author of the essay on ways and means. . . By an American.* London. Richard Parker, 32, 86, 2p. 8vo. 1701
Note: SABIN 22976, HANSON 74, KRESS 2296, EA 701/117.
Locations: L; Dt; O; RPJCB, NN, MiU-C

1701#4
The arraignment, tryal, and condemnation *of Captain William Kidd, for murther and piracy.* . . London. J. Nutt, 60p. 2o. 1701
Note: SABIN 37701, EA 701/155.
Locations: L; MiU-C

1701#5
Articles of agreement made the 10th day of *October. . . 1695. Between the. . . Earl of Bellomont. . . and Robert Levingston. . . and Captain William Kidd. . .* London. J. Richardson, 2p. F. 1701
Note: SABIN 16654, EA 701/34–6. Two other editions in 1701.
Locations: L; MHi, PHi

1701#6
B., J. *A letter to a member of Parliament, on the regulation of the plantation trade.* London. 11, 31p. 8vo. 1701
Note: SABIN 40403, HANSON 53, EA 701/163.
Locations: L; O; NN

1701#7
BENNET, Henry, earl of Arlington. *The right honourable the Earl of Arlington's letters to Sir W. Temple, Bar. . . All printed from the originals and never before publish'd.* London. W. N., for T. Bennet, 2 vols, 8vo. 1701
Note: Edited by T. Bebington. References to English and Dutch colonies and to Indians. EA 701/16.
Locations: L; CSmH, CtY, DFo

1701#8
BOWREY, Thomas. *A dictionary of the Hudson's Bay Indian language.* [London]. 7p. F. 1701
Note: SABIN 7098, EA 701/46. ESTC lists under 1710, NUC under [1750?].
Locations: L;

1701#9
BRAY, Thomas. *Catechetical discourses on the whole doctrine of the covenant of grace. . . design'd to be read in the plantations.* London. W. Hawes, 344p. F. 1701
Note: EA 701/50.
Locations: MB

1701#10
BRAY, Thomas. *A memorial representing the present case of the church in Mary-Land, with relation to its establishment by law.* London. 4p. F. 1701
Note: SABIN 7479, EA 701/182.
Locations: RPJCB

1701#11
BRAY, Thomas. *Several circular letters to the clergy of Mary-Land, subsequent to their late visitation, to enforce such resolutions as were taken therein.* London. W. Downing, 21p. 2o. 1701
Note: SABIN 7482, EA 701/52–3. Another abridged edition in 1701.
Locations: L; MH, MdBJ-G

1701#12
BUGG, Francis. *News from New Rome, occasioned by the Quakers challenging of Francis Bug. . . News, Numb. I.* London. R. Janeway, for the author, 56p. 8vo. 1701
Note: SMITH, I, 341, EA 701/57. Mention of William Penn.
Locations: L; RPJCB, CtY, DFo

1701#13
A brief narrative of the *proceedings of William Pen.* London. For J. Nutt, 2p. 2o. 1701
Note: EA 701/54.
Locations: L; ICN

1701#14
BUGG, Francis. *The last will of that impostor, George Fox (with a letter from Josiah Coale of Maryland). . .* London. R. Janeway, s.sh. F. 1701
Note: EA 701/55–6. Another issue in 1701.
Locations: PPULC, PSC-Hi

1701#15
BUGG, Francis. *A seasonable caveat against the prevalency of Quakerism. . . a hint also of arbitrary government in Pensilvania. . .* London. J. Robinson, etc. 118p. 8vo. 1701
Note: SMITH, I, 341, EA 701/58.
Locations: L; DLC, RPJCB

1701#16
The case of the colony *of Connecticott, upon its establishment under the charter of K. Charles II.* London. s.sh. 1/2o. [1701?]

Note: Cf. *The Case of his majesty's colony of Conneticut [sic] in New England, with respect to their Charter*, below, 1715, which is probably misdated.
Locations: L;

1701#17
An elegy on the death of Capt. William Kidd. . . London. A. Baldwin, s.sh. F. [1701]
Note: FOXON E168, EA 701/116.
Locations: MH

1701#18
ENGLAND AND WALES. SOVEREIGN. WILLIAM III. *Charter of incorporation of Society for the Propagation of the Gospel in Foreign Parts, dated 16th June 1701].* London. C. Bill, etc., 4p. 2o. 1701
Note: SABIN 59033, 85933A, EA 701/239. Other variant issues dated 1702 (L; RPJCB) and, at RPJCB, [1703], 1706.
Locations: L; Owo; CSmH

1701#19
ENGLAND AND WALES. SOVEREIGN. WILLIAM III. *Proclamation. For apprehension of pirates [6 March 1700/1].* London. C. Bill, etc. s.sh. F. 1701
Note: STEELE 4288, BRIGHAM 155, HANSON 61. Pirates must be delivered to colonial governors, etc.
Locations: L; LS;

1701#20
FIELD, John. *Light and truth. . . reply to. . . 'A plain discovery of many gross falsehoods, etc. . . ' by George Keith. . .* London. T. Sowle, 7p. 4to. 1701
Note: SABIN 24278, SMITH, I, 606–7. Cf. Whitehead, *Light and truth. . .*, below, 1712.
Locations: L; PHC, PHi

1701#21
A full account of the proceedings in relation to Captain Kidd. In two letters. . . to a kinsman of the Earl of Bellomont. . . London. 51p. 4to. 1701
Note: EA 701/134–5. Other editions, London, 1701. Also Dublin, 1701, *A full account of the actions of the late famous pyrate. . .* Also Dublin, 1702, EA 702/86.
Locations: L; RPJCB, CtY, NN

1701#22
GENTLEMAN IN NEW-ENGLAND. *A poem on the death of His Highness the Duke of Gloucester. Written by a gentleman in New-England.* London. Printed by J. Darby, and sold by B. Lintot, 4p. 2o. 1701
Note: FOXON P597.
Locations: MH

1701#23
HUDSON'S BAY COMPANY. *Sir, may it please you to be at the Hudson's-Bay House. on [blank] the [blank] day of [blank] 170[blank]. . . at a committee there to be held.* [London?]. s.sh. 1701
Note: EA 701/148.
Locations: MH

1701#24
J., F. *A letter from the Grecian coffee-house, in answer to the Taunton-Dean letter to which is added, a paper of queries sent from Worcester.* London. 14p. F. 1701
Note: Concerns trial of Captain Kidd.
Locations: L; DLC, RPJCB, MH

1701#25
KEITH, George. *George Keith's fifth narrative, of his proceedings at Turners-Hall; detecting the Quakers errors.* London. B. Aylmer and C. Brome, 68p. 4to. 1701
Note: SABIN 37191, SMITH, II 39, EA 701/153. Quakers in Pennsylvania. Replies to John Whiting, *Judas. . .* below, 1701.
Locations: L; CtY, MH, RPJCB

1701#26
KEITH, George. *A plain discovery of many gross falshoods, cheats and impostures.* London. B. Aylmer and C. Brome, 46p. 4to. 1701
Note: SMITH, II, 39, EA 701/154. References to Pennsylvania Quakers.
Locations: L;

1701#27
LORRAIN, Paul. *The ordinary of Newgate his account of the behaviour, confessions and dying words of Captain William Kidd, and other pyrates. . .* London. E. Mablet, 2p. 1/2o. 1701
Note: Cf. EA 701/158. 'Executed 23 May, 1701.'
Locations: L; DLC, CSmH

1701#28
LUYTS, Jan. *A general and particular description of America. . . with very particular accounts of the English plantations; and maps. . .* London. 230p. 4to. [1701?]
Note: Cf. EA 701/184–5. SABIN 42744. Extracted from H. Moll, *A System of Geography,* below, 1701.
Locations: DLC, CtY

1701#29
MACKWORTH, Sir Humphrey. *A vindication of the rights of the Commons of England. By a member.* London. J. Nutt, 1701. 40p. F. 1701
Note: EA 701/170–1. Mentions courts in New England and Capt. Kidd. Second edition 1701.
Locations: L; CtY, DFo, RPJCB

1701#30
MATHER, Cotton. *Death made easie and happie. Two brief discourses on the prudent apprehensions of death. . . together with serious thoughts in dying times. . .* London. T. Parkhurst, 106p. 12mo. 1701

Note: HOLMES, CM, 83.
Locations: MB, MA, MWA

1701#31
MOLL, Herman. *A system of geography, or, A new and accurate description of the earth in all its empires, kingdoms and states*... London. T. Childe, [768]p. 2o. 1701
Note: EA 701/184–5. In two parts, of which Part II describes Asia, Africa, and America. Another edition in 1701; and in 1709 as *The compleat geographer*, 'Wherein the descriptions of Asia, Africa and America are compos'd anew.' EA 709/109. A fourth edition in 1722–3, EA 723/106.
Locations: L; C; E; DLC, RPJCB, MiU-C

1701#32
PENN, William. *The allegations against proprietary governments considered, and their merit and benefit to the Crown briefly observed*... London. 4p. F. [1701]
Note: SABIN 59676, WING P1251, SMITH, II, 203. EA 701/206 dates [1701]. WING dates [1687].
Locations: LF; PPAmP, RPJCB

1701#33
PENN, William. *The case of William Penn, esq; as to the proprietary government of Pensilvania; which, together with Carolina, New York, etc is intended to be taken away by a bill in Parliament.* London. s.sh. 1/2o. [1701]
Note: Title from ESTC., EA 701/207 has 'New-Jersey'.
Locations: L; RPJCB

1701#34
PENNSYLVANIA Assembly. *His excellency, Governour Penn's speech, to the assembly, held at Philadelphia in Pensilvania; September the 15th 1701. With their address, and thankful acknowledgements for the same.* London. s.sh. F. 1701
Note: EA 701/208. First printed Philadelphia, 1701 (EVANS 1017).
Locations: DLC, PHC, CtY

1701#35
POVEY, Charles. *The unhappiness of England, as to its trade by sea and land*... London. 142p. 8vo. 1701
Note: SABIN 64744, KRESS 2314.
Locations: RPJCB, CtY, CSmH

1701#36
The proceedings of the Kings commission of the peace... held for the tryal of Captain William Kidd... May 1701. [London]. 4p. F. 1701
Note: SABIN 37705, EA 701/157.
Locations: NO COPY LOCATED.

1701#37
SMITH, Thomas. *An affidavit taken and sworn at York... the 14th. day of Feb: 1701. Setting forth... the hardships of several merchants in the said City trading to his Majesties Dominions in America and the plantations thereunto belonging.* London. s.sh. F. [1701]
Note: HANSON 167, EA 702/177. On the seizure of his ship by the Customs in Pennsylvania.
Locations: Lpro;

1701#38
Some reasons humbly offered to the Honourable the House of Commons for passing the Newfoundland bill. [London. s.sh. 1/2o. [1701?]
Locations: C-S

1701#39
A State of the proceedings in the House of Commons, with relation to the impeached Lords... London. E. Jones and T. Goodwin, [57]p. F. 1701
Note: SABIN 90624. Piracy and Captain Kidd.
Locations: L; RPJCB

1701#40
STEPNEY, George. *An essay upon the present interest of England*... London. J. Nutt, 84p. 4to. 1701
Note: KRESS 2322, EA 701/ 243–5. Discusses consequences of Franco-British union for English liberty, trade, etc. A well-managed war in 'America' could bring great benefits. Other editions London and Dublin.
Locations: L; RPJCB

1701#41
TOMKINS, John. *Piety promoted, in a collection of dying sayings of many of the people called Quakers. With a brief account of some of their labours in the Gospel, and sufferings*... London. T. Sowle, 10p. 12mo. 1701
Note: SABIN 24279, 96142, SMITH, II, 747, EA 701/256. Issued in three parts. L; has 1702, 1703, 1706, 1711, 1721, 1723, 1737, 1754, 1759. EA lists 1702, 1703, two in 1706, two in 1711, 1718, 1721, 1723, 1728, 1740, EA 702/189, 703/153, 706/215–6, 711/77, 711/222, 718/56, 721/191, 723/161, 728/69, 740/30.
Locations: L; PPL, MH, NN

1701#42
A true account of the behaviour, confession and last dying speeches, of Captain William Kidd, and the rest of the pyrates that were executed... 23rd of May, 1701. London. E. Miller, s.sh. F. [1701]
Note: EA 701/158.
Locations: L; DLC

1701#43
WHITEHEAD, George. *Truth prevalent; and the Quakers discharged from the Norfolk rector's furious charge.* London. T.Sowle, 187p. 4to. 1701
Note: EA 701/271. References to religion in America and to Friends and sufferings in old and New England.
Locations: L; CtY, DLC, MHi

1701#44
WHITING, John. *Judas and the chief priests. . . in answer to G. Keith's fourth. . . narrative. . .* London. T. Sowle, 25p. 4to. 1701
Note: SMITH, II, 917, EA 701/272–3. Another edition in 1701. References to Pennsylvania.
Locations: L; RPJCB

1701#45
WOODWARD, Josiah. *An account of the progress of the reformation of manners, in England and Ireland, and other parts of the world. . .* London. J. Downing, 63p. 8vo. 1701
Note: Cf. KRESS 2329, EA 701/276–7, 702/207, 703/174, 704/175, 705/183–4, 706/237. Fourteen editions to 1706, of which that of 1702 and later include America in the title.
Locations: L; CtY, RPJCB, MiU-C

1701#46
WOOLEY, Charles. *A two years journal in New-York: and part of its territories in America. . .* London. J. Wyat, E. Tracy, [104]p. 8vo. 1701
Note: SABIN 104994, EA 701/274–5. Second issue in London: For D. Boys, in Lowth and G. Barton, in Boston.
Locations: L; E; RPJCB, CSmH, ViU

1701#47
WYETH, Joseph. *Remarks on Dr Bray's memorial, etc. with brief observations on some passages in the Acts of his Visitation in Maryland, and on his circular letter to the clergy there. . .* London. T. Sowle, 51p. 4to. 1701
Note: SABIN 10562, EA 701/281.
Locations: L; NIC, MH, RPJCB

1702#1
BEHN, Aphra. *Plays written by the late ingenious Mrs. Behn, entire in two volumes. . .* London. J. Tonson, etc. 2 vols. 8vo. 1702
Note: SABIN 4369, EA 702/20. Vol II contains *The Widdow-Ranter. . .*, with Dryden's preface. Other editions 1711, and as part 2 of her *Works*, 1716, 1724.
Locations: L; MH, ICU, PPL

1702#2
BREWSTER, Sir Francis. *New essays on trade.* London. For H. Walwyn, 128p. 8vo. 1702
Note: KRESS 2335, EA 702/24. References to American fisheries; tables show exports and imports for 1697, including British plantations.
Locations: L; DLC, CtY, DFo

1702#3
BUGG, Francis. *A bomb thrown amongst the Quakers in Norwich, which will. . . set fire on [sic] the combustible matter thorow their whole camp in England, Wales and America.* Norwich. 2p. F. 1702
Note: SABIN 66735n, SMITH, I, 343, EA 702/27–8. Second enlarged edition, Norwich and London, 1702.
Locations: L;

1702#4
BUGG, Francis. *Vox populi: or, A cloud of witnesses, proving the leading Quakers great impostors.* London. R. Janeway, for the author 40p. 8vo. 1702
Note: SMITH, I, 341, EA 702/29–30. Refers to Quakers in North American colonies, particularly in Pennsylvania. Another edition in 1702.
Locations: L; MH, PHi

1702#5
CALAMY Edmund, D. D. *An abridgment of Mr Baxter's History of his life and times. With an account of the ministers who were ejected, after the Restauration. . . and a continuation. . . till. . . 1691. . .* London. 701p. 8vo. 1702
Note: SABIN 9869, EA 702/33. Another edition in 1713 in two volumes.
Locations: L; RPJCB, MH, CSmH

1702#6
COURT VAN DER VOORT, Pieter de la. *The true interest and political maxims of the republick of Holland and West-Friesland. . . Written by John de Witt and other great men in Holland. . .* London. 492p. 8vo. 1702
Note: EA 702/49, 743/57. Remarks on New Netherland. Also, 1743, 1746.
Locations: L; RPJCB, CtY, MH

1702#7
DAVENANT, Charles. *The true picture of an ancient Tory.* London. 64p. 8vo. 1702
Note: EA 702/58. References to Newfoundland and Hudson Bay.
Locations: CLU-C, CtY

1702#8
Dialogue between the ghost of Captain Kidd, and the napper in the Strand, napt. [London]. s.sh. 1/2o. [1702].
Locations: L;

1702#9
EGLETON, John. *A letter written to a member of Parliament, relating to trade.* London. 4p. 4to. [1702]
Note: EA 702/69. Some American references.
Locations: NN

1702#10
ENGLAND AND WALES. SOVEREIGN. ANNE. *A proclamation. [For continuing all officers in their places. 9 March 1701/2].* London. C. Bill and executrix of T. Newcomb, s.sh. F. 1702

1702

Note: STEELE 4313, BRIGHAM, 159. Includes colonies and plantations.
Locations: L;

1702#11
ENGLAND AND WALES. SOVEREIGN. ANNE. *Whereas it hath pleased Almighty God, to call to His mercy our late sovereign lord King William the Third...* London. C. Bill and executors, s.sh. F. 1702
Note: STEELE 4310, BRIGHAM, 159. Dated 8 or 9 March 1701/2. Form of proclamation of accession of Queen Anne for use in the plantations.
Locations: L; MH

1702#12
ENGLAND AND WALES. SOVEREIGN. WILLIAM III. *Whereas we are credibly informed, that in many of our plantations...* London. Printed by J. Downing, 4p. 2o. 1702
Note: EA 702/180–1. Letters patent with reference to provisions for ministers and the incorporation of the Society for the Propagation of the Gospel in Foreign Parts. Another issue in 1702 with a longer list of members.
Locations: L; O; RPJCB

1702#13
HILL, Anthony. *Afer baptizatus: or the negro turn'd Christian... I. The necessity of instruction, and baptizing slaves... a sermon.* London. C. Broome and E. Evett, 55p. 8vo. 1702
Note: SABIN 31807, EA 702/105.
Locations: L; MiU-C, RPJCB, M

1702#14
LESLIE, Charles. *A reply to a book entitul'd Anguis flagellatus, or, A switch for the snake. The opus palmare of the Quakers.* London. C. Brome. etc., 381p. 8vo. 1702
Note: SABIN 40197, EA 702/119. Pennsylvania references.
Locations: L; DLC, RPJCB, PPL

1702#15
A letter from a member of the Society for the propagation of Christian knowledge in London, to a correspondent in the country. London. 3p. F. 1702
Note: EA 702/120.
Locations: L; DLC, RPJCB, CSmH

1702#16
The loyal address of the clergy of Virginia... [London?]. F. R. Maggot, s.sh. F. [1702]
Note: SABIN 42545, FOXON L296, EA 702/123. Although listed as Virginia imprint (EVANS 1057), this was a London parody. See *Virginia Magazine of History and Biography*, April 1959, pp. 164–9 and Foxon. In verse.
Locations: L; RPJCB

1702#17
MATHER, Cotton. *Magnalia Christi Americana: or; the ecclesiastical history of New-England, from its first planting in the year 1620 unto the year of our Lord, 1698...* London. T. Parkhurst, 2 vols. F. 1702
Note: SABIN 46392, HOLMES, CM, 213, EA 702/127.
Locations: L; C; E; DLC, RPJCB, MiU-C

1702#18
A new project to make England a florishing [sic] kingdom. London. 18p. 4to. 1702
Note: EA 702/142. Contains proposal that felons convicted of capital crimes should be enslaved and sent to build warships in America.
Locations: IU, MH-BA, NN

1702#19
NICKOLLS, Thomas. *A turbulent spirit troubled with his own confutations. In reply to George Keith's pretended Answer to seventeen queries...* London. T. Sowle, 35p. 4to. 1702
Note: SMITH, II, 239. References to Penn.
Locations: NN, PHC

1702#20
PETIVER, James. *Gazophylacii naturae et artis decas prima [-quinta].* London. C. Bateman, 96p. 8vo. [1702–1706]
Note: EA 702/152. American plants and animals. For a continuation, see Petiver, below, 1711. Issued in parts.
Locations: L; MH-A, PPAN

1702#21
Proposals for carrying on an effectual war in America, against the French and Spaniards. London. J. Nutt, 24p. 4to. 1702
Note: SABIN 66027, HANSON 182, EA 702/154.
Locations: L; Dt; O; DLC, RPJCB, CtY

1702#22
Reasons prov'd to be unreasonable: or, An answer to the reasons against a war with France. London. 32p. 4to. 1702
Note: EA 702/165. Proposes seizure of Spanish and French possessions in West Indies and Canada. A reply to Defoe's *Reasons*, London, 1701. For a reissue see *Reasons for a war with France*, below, 1715.
Locations: L; CtY, ICN, MB

1702#23
Reflections on the printed case of William Penn, esq; in a letter from some gentlemen of Pensilvania... London. 15p. 8vo. 1702
Note: SABIN 68710, EA 702/166.
Locations: L; MiU-C

1702#24
RIDPATH, George. *The case of Scots-men residing in England and in the English plantations. Containing an account of the reasons in law, why they look upon themselves as entituled to all the priviledges of the natives of England...* London. 12p. 2o. 1702
Note: ESTC lists this edition. HANSON 259, EA 703/134 list Edinburgh, 1703 (E; NN, CtY). Anonymous. By George Ridpath.
Locations: DFo

1702#25
SOCIETY FOR THE PROPAGATION OF THE GOSPEL. *An abstract of the Charter granted to the Society for the Propagation of the Gospel in Foreign Parts; with a short account of what hath been, and what is designed to be done by it.* London. 3p. F. 1702
Note: SABIN 84, EA 702/178. By Thomas Bray?
Locations: L; RPJCB, MdBJ-G

1702#26
SOCIETY FOR THE PROPAGATION OF THE GOSPEL. *The request of the Society for the Propagation of the Gospel. . . concerning fit ministers to be sent abroad for that good purpose.* London. 21p. F. [1702]
Note: SABIN 85945, EA 702/179.
Locations: L; RPJCB, CtY, PHi

1702#27
WILLIS, Richard. *A sermon preach'd. . . 20 February 1701/2. . .* London. M. Wotton, 23p. 4to. 1702
Note: SABIN 104517, EA 702/205. SPG sermon for 1702.
Locations: L; RPJCB

1703#1
***Advertisement. February 4, 1702. There** will be speedily published some New voyages to North-America, perform'd by the Baron de la Hontan. . .* London. H. Bonwick and others, s.sh. 1/2o. [1703]
Note: See LAHONTAN, below, 1703.
Locations: L;

1703#2
ATWOOD, William. *The case of William Atwood, esq; by the late King William. . . constituted chief justice of the province of New York. . . With a true account of the government and people of that province; particularly of Bayard's faction, and the treason of which he and Hutchins stand attainted. . .* London. 23p. F. 1703
Note: SABIN 2346, HANSON 303, EA 703/9.
Locations: L; E; DLC, MiU-C, N

1703#3
BAYARD, Nicholas. *An account of the commitment, arraignment, tryal and condemnation of Nicholas Bayard, Esq; for high treason, in endeavouring to subvert the government of the province of New York in America. . .* London. Printed New York, reprinted London. 31p. F. 1703
Note: SABIN 53436, EA 703/12. First printed New York, 1703 (EVANS 1102).
Locations: L; DLC, RPJCB

1703#4
BISHOP, George. *New England judged. . . in two parts. . . Formerly published by G. Bishop, and now somewhat abbreviated. With an appendix. . . Also an answer to Cotton Mather's abuses of the said people in his late history of New England (by John Whiting), etc.* London. T. Sowle, [710]p. 8vo. 1703
Note: SABIN 5631, SMITH, I, 283, EA 703/16–17. Another edition in 1703.
Locations: L; RPJCB

1703#5
BUGG, Francis. *News from Pensilvania: or a brief narrative of several remarkable passages in the government of the Quakers, in that province. . .* London. 4, 36p. 8vo. 1703
Note: SABIN 9071, SMITH, I, 343, HANSON 304, EA 703/26.
Locations: L; RPJCB

1703#6
COMMELIN, Izaak. *A collection of voyages undertaken by the Dutch East-India Company, for the improvement of trade and navigation. . .* London. W. Freeman, etc., 336p. 8vo. 1703
Note: SABIN 14401, KRESS 2404, EA 703/132. Translated from French; includes account of North-West passage.
Locations: RPJCB, MH-BA

1703#7
DENNIS, John. *A proposal for putting a speedy end to the war, by ruining the commerce of the French and the Spaniards. . .* London. D. Brown, A. Bell, 28p. 4to. 1703
Note: SABIN 66019, KRESS 2382, EA 703/44–5, References to New England, New York, etc. Another edition in 1703.
Locations: L; NN, MH, CtY

1703#8
ECHARD, Laurence. *The gazetteer's or newsman's interpreter. Being a geographical index of. . . Asia, Africa and America.* London. J. Nicholson and S. Ballard, 264p. 12mo. 1703
Note: EA 704/57, 710/37, 718/50, 740/102. L; has 1703, 1706, 1707 (EA 707/49), 1709, 1713?, 1716, 1724 (EA 724/57), 1732 (EA 732/89, sixth ed.), 1738 (EA 738/85, 7th ed.), 1741 (EA 741/167, 8th edition) 1744 (EA 744/85, 9th ed.), 1751. Also Dublin 1740 [1741?] (EA 740/103). First published in 1695. Seems to have included

only Europe until 1703. ESTC lists also other editions London, 1704, 1710, 1718, and Belfast, 1740.
Locations: L; C; MH, CLU-C

1703#9
LAHONTAN, Louis Armand de Lom d'Arce.
New voyages to North-America. Containing an account of the several nations of that vast continent... Done into English... London. H. Bonwicke and others, 2 vols. 8vo. 1703
Note: SABIN 38644, EA 703/86, 735/139–41. Two editions in 1735 of vols. 1 and 2, one edition of volume one.
Locations: L; Dt; O; DLC, RPJCB, MiU-C

1703#10
An universal, historical, geographical, chronological and poetical dictionary. London. J. Hartley, W. Turner, and T. Hodgson, 2 vols, 8vo. 1703
Note: EA 703/159.
Locations: L; DFo, MnU, PPL

1703#11
WARD, Edward. *The second volume of the writings of the author of the London Spy.* London. J. How, 372p. 8vo. 1703
Note: EA 703/171. The 'second edition.' Also 1704, 1706, 1709, EA 704/170, 706/229, 709/171. Contains 'A trip to Jamaica' and 'A trip to New England'.
Locations: L; ICU, DLC

1703#12
WHITING, John. *Truth and inocency defended; against falsehood and envy... In answer to Cotton Mather... his late Church-History of New-England...* London. T. Sowle, 212p. 8vo. [1703]
Note: SMITH, II, 918. Reissue of part of G. Bishop's *New England Judged*. With a 'postcript containing some further sufferings and judgement of God on the persecuted...'
Cf. Bishop, *New England judged*, above, 1703.
Locations: RPJCB, MH-AH

1704#1
An abridgement of the laws in force and use in her majesty's plantations... London. J. Nicholson, etc. 495p. 8vo. 1704
Note: SABIN 81, EA 704/1.
Locations: L; DLC, RPJCB, MiU-C

1704#2
An answer to the reasons offered against restraining the use and wearing of printed callicoes in England, Ireland, and the plantations. London. s.sh. F. [1704?]
Note: HANSON 369, EA 704/11.
Locations: L; CtY-BR

1704#3
The arraignment, tryal, and condemnation, of Capt. John Quelch, and others... for sundry piracies, robberies, and murder... London. B. Bragg, 24p. F. 1704
Note: SABIN 67086, EA 704/123, 705/143. A Boston trial. Second edition in 1705.
Locations: L; MH

1704#4
A Ballad. Addres'd to the Reverend Members of the Convocation, held at Man's Ordinary, at Williamsburgh, in Virginia; to defend G[overno]r N[icholso]n, and form an Accusation against C[ommissary] B[lair]. London. 4p. 4to. 1704
Note: See A. C. GORDON, *Virginian writers of fugitive verse* (New York, 1923), who states this piece was published anonymously in London and circulated in the colony. The P.R.O. reference is CO 5/131 (44(i). Information kindly supplied by Dr. G. Thomas.
Locations: Lpro;

1704#5
BRAY, Thomas. *An introductory discourse to catechetical instruction... In a Pastoral Letter to the clergy of Maryland... containing a Course of Catechising to be observed in the plantations, consisting of Books... for the use of several classes of catechumens... with a preface...* London. J. Brudenell, 46p. 8vo. 1704
Note: SABIN 7477, EA 704/21.
Locations: L; O; NHi

1704#6
BRAY, Thomas. *The whole course of catechetical institution, through three classes of catechumens, consisting of I. An introductory discourse to catechical instruction, being a pastoral letter to the clergy of Maryland, concerning the same...* London. J. Brudenell for W.Hawes, [449]p. 8vo. [1704–1710?]
Note: Cf. SABIN 7483. EA 704/22.
Locations: L; RPJCB, CSmH, MHi

1704#7
BURNET, Gilbert. *Of the propagation of the gospel in foreign parts. A sermon preach'd... Feb. 18. 1703/4...* London. Printed for D. Brown; and R. Sympson [2], 29, [1]p. 4to. 1704
Note: EA 704/25–6. Another edition in 1704. Also issued as part of: *A collection of sermons preached by the Right Reverend Dr. Gilbert Burnet*, London, 1704 and in other collections of his writings.
Locations: L; CSmH, MH-H, RPJCB

1704#8
CAROLINA. *The Copy of an act lately passed in Carolina, and sent over to be continued here... which would be highly prejudicial to her Majesty's interests, destructive to that colony, discouraging to trade...* London. 8p. 4to. 1704

Note: SABIN 10980, 87347. EA lists as part of *Two charters...*, 1705, EA 705/31, for which see above, 1698. This imprint is listed in ESTC.
Locations: L (Dept. of Manuscripts); Dt; ICN, NcU

1704#9
The case of the officers, victuallers and clothiers of the four independent companies of New-York... London. s.sh. F. 1704
Note: HANSON 414, EA 704/27.
Locations: L;

1704#10
CHURCHILL, Awnsham. *A collection of voyages and travels.* London. H.C., for A. and J. Churchill, 4 vols. F. 1704
Note: EA 704/32. Reissued in 1732 with addition of vols. 5 and 6, and in 1744. EA 732/60, 744/62. Vols 5 and 6 reprinted in 1746, EA 746/37. See also Osborne, 1745, below.
Locations: L; RPJCB, CtY, MH

1704#11
DENNIS, John. *Liberty asserted. A tragedy. As it is acted at the New Theatre in Little Lincoln's-Inn-Fields.* London. G. Strahan and B. Lintott, 64p. 4to. 1704
Note: SABIN 19588–9, EA 704/42–3. The action is set in Canada. Frontenac is the leading figure. Another edition in 1704.
Locations: DLC, MH

1704#12
Dictionarium rusticum and urbanicum: or, A dictionary of all sorts of country affairs. London. J. Nicholson, [843]p. 8vo. 1704
Note: EA 704/44–5. Virginia references. Other issues in 1704, 1717, 1726, EA 717/467, 726/69.
Locations: CLU-C, CtY, IU, MB

1704#13
Dictionarium sacrum seu religiosum. A dictionary of all religions, ancient and modern. London. J. Knapton, [392]p. 8vo. 1704
Note: EA 704/46. Includes religions of America. Sometimes attributed to Daniel Defoe.
Locations: L; CSmH, CtY, MH

1704#14
ENGLAND AND WALES. PARLIAMENT. *An act for encouraging the importation of naval stores... from her majesty's plantations in America...* London. C. Bill and executrix of T. Newcomb, 1704
Note: Cf. SABIN 135.
Locations: MHi

1704#15
ENGLAND AND WALES. SOVEREIGN. ANNE. *Proclamation. For settling and ascertaining the current rates of coin in her majesties colonies and plantations in America [18 June 1704].* London. C. Bill, etc. s.sh. F. 1704
Note: STEELE 4373, BRIGHAM 161, HANSON 412, KRESS SUPP. 2281.
Locations: L; DLC, MH

1704#16
Further considerations for encouraging the woollen manufactures of this kingdom, humbly offer'd to the Lords and Commons... London. s.sh. F. [1704?]
Note: HANSON 367, EA 704/66. For denying dyed calicoes and East Indian silks to colonies.
Locations: L;

1704#17
LAWSON, Deodat. *Christ's fidelity the only shield against Satan's malignity... sermon... Salem-village the 24th of March, 1692.* London. Boston printed, London reprinted. R. Tokey, T. Parkhurst, 120p. 12mo. 1704
Note: SABIN 39443, EA 704/88. First printed Boston 1693 (EVANS 643).
Locations: L; DLC, RPJCB, MH

1704#18
MANDEVILLE, Bernard. *Planter's charity.* [London]. 8p. 4to. 1704
Note: EA 704/98. In verse. Considers the lot of slaves brought to America for work in plantations.
Locations: Llp; DFo, InU, MH

1704#19
MARSHALL, Charles. *Sion's travellers comforted.* London. T. Sowle, 230p. 8vo. 1704
Note: SMITH, II, 146, EA 704/106. Preface by William Penn. Contains an epistle to Quakers in Pennyslvania.
Locations: L; CtY, DLC, MH

1704#20
Owaneko, chief Sachem or prince of the Mohegan-Indians in New-England, his letter to a gentleman now in London: faithfully translated from the original in the Indian language. And his case annexed. London. For Daniel Brown, 3, 1p. 4to. 1704.
Locations: L;

1704#21
PATERSON, William. *An essay concerning inland and foreign... trade... showing how a company for national trade, may be constituted in Scotland...* [Edinburgh]. 8p. 4to. [1704]
Note: HANSON 346, EA 705/135.
Locations: Lu; RPJCB, NNC, MH-BA

(1)

OWANEKO,

Chief *Sachem* or Prince

OF THE

Mohegan-Indians, in *New-England,*

HIS

Letter to a Genleman Now in *LONDON:*

Faithfully Translated from the Original in the Indian *Language.*

And his CASE annexed.

MY Loving Friend Mr. *N. H.* I am informed you are bound for *Old England:* Let me Request you to make Me and my Request known to the Great Queen *Ann,* and to her Noble Council; First of Our Hereditary Right to the Soyl and Royalties of our Dominions and Territories, before the *English* came into the Country; insomuch that all due Loyalty and Obedience is not confer'd on us by the *English,* but by the gods; who gave us a Token, as an Earnest and Pledge of Our happy Reign here; and also (as Our Old *Seers* construed) a more ample Reign in the other Region. Wherefore the gods sent to that Royal Family one of their Own Tobacco-Pipes; which strange

A   Wonderment

1704#22
Reasons for leave to import Tarr, *otherwise than from the places of its growth*. London. s.sh. F. [1704?]
Note: HANSON 386.
Locations: LG;

1704#23
Reasons humbly offered against restraining *the using and wearing of printed callicoes in England, Ireland and the plantations*. London. s.sh. F. [1704]
Note: HANSON 368, EA 704/130.
Locations: L; LLI;

1704#24
Reasons offered to. . . *Commons, relating to the bill. . . for laying an additional duty on all commodities imported, as far as it relates to the trade of Virginia and Maryland*. London. s.sh. F. [1704]
Note: HANSON 416, EA 704/131.
Locations: L;

1704#25
SOCIETY FOR THE PROPAGATION OF THE GOSPEL. *An account of the propagation of the gospel in foreign parts, what the Society hath done. . . in her majesty's plantations, colonies and factories. . .* London. J. Downing, 4p. 2o. [1704]
Note: SABIN 98–9, EA 704/149. Compiled by P. Stubs.
Locations: L; DLC, RPJCB, MiU-C

1704#26
SOCIETY FOR THE PROPAGATION OF THE GOSPEL. *Instructions for the clergy employ'd by the Society.* London. 4p. F. [1704]
Note: EA 706/206 is RPJCB dated [1706]. L; dated [1710].
Locations: L; IU

1704#27
SYMSON, Matthias. *Enchiridion geographicum. Or, A manual of geography. Being a description of all the empires, kingdoms, and dominions of the earth.* Edinburgh. 8vo. 1704
Note: SABIN 74625, EA 704/158.
Locations: L;

1704#28
THOMPSON, John, first baron Haversham. *The Lord Haversham's speech in the House of Peers, on Thursday, November 23, 1704.* London. B. Bragg, 4p. 4to. 1704
Note: EA 704/75. Mentions St. Christopher, Newfoundland, and Hudson Bay.
Locations: L; CLU-C, RPJCB, TxU

1705#1
BEAUMONT, John. *An historical, physiological and theological treatise of spirits, apparitions, witchcrafts. . .* London. O. Browne, etc. xiii, 400p. 8vo. 1705
Note: Long section on Cotton Mather, Robert Calef, etc.
Locations: L; CSmH, DLC, CtY

1705#2
BEVERLEY, Robert. *The history and present state of Virginia, in four parts. . . By a native and inhabitant of the place.* London. R. Parker, 213p. 8vo. 1705
Note: SABIN 5112, HANSON 545, KRESS SUPP. 2302, EA 705/21. Second edition, 1722.
Locations: L; DLC, RPJCB

1705#3
BYFIELD, Thomas. *The case of Thomas Byfield, and Company, owners of the ship Dove. . . relating to the bill for importing naval stores from the plantations.* London. s.sh. F. [1705]
Note: HANSON 521.
Locations: Lpro;

1705#4
COCKSON, Edward. *Rigid Quakers, cruel persecutors. . . together with a short abridgement of the history of the Quakers persecutions for religion in Pennsylvania, and the abominable tyranny of new government there.* London. E. Evets, etc., 39p. 8vo. 1705
Note: SMITH, AQ, 127–8, EA 705/43.
Locations: RPJCB, CSmH

1705#5
A collection of State Tracts, *publish'd on occasion of the late revolution in 1688. . .* London. 3 vols. 2o. 1705
Note: SABIN 14390, EA 705/44, 706/49, 707/33. Published 1705-7 to include reign of William and Mary. Some references to New England, Indians, Newfoundland, etc.
Locations: L; DLC, NN, CtY

1705#6
CRULL, Jodocus. *An introduction to the history of. . . Asia, Africa, and America, both ancient and modern, according to the method of Samuel Pufendorf. . .* London. R. J. for T.Newborough, etc. 621p. 8vo. 1705
Note: EA 705/50. Continuation of Pufendorf's *Einleitung zu der Historie der Reiche. . . in Europa*.
Locations: L; C; NNC, RPJCB, NN

1705#7
DEFOE, Daniel. *Party-tyranny: or, an occasional bill in miniature: as now practised in Carolina. Humbly offered to the consideration of. . . Parliament.* London. 30p. 4to. 1705
Note: SABIN 19288, EA 705/53–4. Another issue in 1705.
Locations: L; RPJCB, MH, DLC

1705#8
DUMMER, Jeremiah. *Mr Dummers account of the West India correspondence, how it was propounded, and how since perform'd. Received 15 October 1705.* London. 4p. 1705
Note: EA 705/60. Another edition, [1711?]. See EA 711/67.
Locations: Lpro; DLC

1705#9
DUNTON, John. *The life and errors of John Dunton late citizen of London...* London. S. Malthus, [515]p. 8vo. 1705
Note: SABIN 21344, KRESS SUPP. 2304, EA 705/62. Pp. 115–195 recount his sojourn in New England.
Locations: L; DLC, RPJCB, MiU-C

1705#10
ENGLAND AND WALES. PARLIAMENT. *Act discharging the importation of tobacco.* [Edinburgh]. s.sh. F. [1705]
Note: HANSON 542.
Locations: Lu;

1705#11
HALLEY, Edmond. *Miscellanea Curiosa. Being a collection of some of the principal phaenomena in nature...* London. J. B. for J. Wale, etc., 3 vols. 8vo. 1705
Note: EA 705/89. Published 1705–7, and other editions 1708–23, 1723–7. Vol. III gives an account of Virginia.
Locations: CSmH, MH, DFo

1705#12
HARRIS, John. *Navigantium atque itinerantium bibliotheca: or, A compleat collection of voyages and travels... To which is prefixed, A history of the peopling of the several parts of the world, and particularly of America... In two volumes.* London. T. Bennet, J. Nicholson, and D. Midwinter, 1705, 2 vols, F. 1705
Note: SABIN 30482, HANSON 533, EA 705/90.
Locations: L; CLU, CtY, DLC, RPJCB

1705#13
HOUGH, John. *Of the propagation of the gospel in foreign parts. A sermon preach'd... Feb. 16 1704/5...* London. J. Downing, 25, 41p. 4to. 1705
Note: EA 705/97. SPG sermon for 1705 with appendix on American colonies, etc.
Locations: RPJCB, NN, ICN

1705#14
LAW, John. *Money and trade considered, with a proposal for supplying the nation with money...* Edinburgh. Heirs of A. Anderson, 120p. 4to. 1705
Note: EA 705/111. A second edition in 1720; other editions Glasgow, 1750, 1760.
Locations: L; DLC, CtY, ICN

1705#15
MAKEMIE, Francis. *A plain and friendly perswasive to the inhabitants of Virginia and Maryland, for promoting towns and cohabitation...* London. J. Humfreys, 16p. 8vo. 1705
Note: SABIN 44081, EA 705/118.
Locations: DLC, RPJCB, MiU-C

1705#16
PEMBERTON, Ebenezer. *Advice to a son. A discourse at the request of a gentleman in New-England, upon his son's going to Europe...* London. Printed for Ralph Smith, [2], 25, [1]p. 12mo. 1705
Locations: MWA, DLC

1705#17
NICHOLSON, Francis. *A modest answer to a malicious libel against his excellency Francis Nicholson... or an examination of that part of Mr Blair's affidavit, relating to the school boys of the grammar-school... in Virginia...* London. 55p. 8vo. [1705?]
Note: SABIN 55222, EA 706/173.
Locations: L; ViW

1705#18
SOCIETY FOR THE PROPAGATION OF THE GOSPEL. *An account of the propagation of the gospel in foreign parts. Continued to... 1705...* London. J. Downing, 4p. F. [1705]
Note: EA 705/158. Compiled by P. Stubs.
Locations: RPJCB, IU, CSmH

1706#1
August 1. 1706. Yesterday arriv'd *an express from the West Indies, with the following news from Rhoad-Island, April 5.* London. Printed and sold by B. Bragge, 1p F. 1706
Note: Also news from Boston, New York, etc.
Locations: E; MRu;

1706#2
BLACK, David. *Essay upon industry and trade...* Edinburgh. J.Watson, 40p. 4to. 1706
Note: HANSON 637, KRESS 2492, EA 706/24. Various references to Spanish and English colonies and Greenland.
Locations: L; CtY, ICU, MH-BA

1706#3
BLACK, William. *Remarks upon a pamphlet, intitled, The considerations in relation to trade considered, and a short view of our present trade and taxes reviewed.* London. 8p. 4to. [1706]
Note: SABIN 69520, EA 706/25. The pamphlet was by James Donaldson. See Donaldson, *Considerations*, below, 1706.
Locations: CtY, CSmH, NNC

1706#4
BLACK, William. *Some considerations in relation to trade.* [Edinburgh]. 15p 4to. 1706
Note: HANSON 657, KRESS 2494, EA 706/26. References to trade and emigration to American colonies, Newfoundland fishery, and Darien Company. For a reply, see Donaldson, *Considerations*, below, 1706.
Locations: L; CSmH, CtY, ICU

1706#5
BOONE, Joseph. *The humble address of the right honourable Lords spiritual and temporal, in Parliament assembled, presented to her majesty on. . . the thirteenth day of March, 1705, relating to the province of Carolina, and the petition therein mentioned. With her majesties most gracious answer thereunto.* London. C. Bill, etc. 4p. 2o. 1705 [i.e. 1706]
Note: SABIN 10972, HANSON 690, EA 705/82.
Locations: L; CLU-C

1706#6
The case of the Church of England in Carolina, humbly offer'd to the consideration of both houses of Parliament. In the year 1663... London. 4p. F. [1706]
Note: SABIN 87805, EA 706/37. ESTC lists under 1705.
Locations: L; RPJCB

1706#7
CLARIDGE, Richard. *Melius inquirendum, or, An answer to a book of Edward Cockson. . . mis-intituled, Rigid Quakers cruel persecutors.* London. T. Sowle, 294p. 8vo. 1706
Note: SMITH, I, 412, EA 706/46. Has a defence of Pennyslvania Quakers against charges of tyranny and persecution.
Locations: L; CU-A, DLC, ICN, MH

1706#8
A complete history of England. London. B. Aylmer, R. Bonwicke, S. Smith and others, 3 vols, F. 1706
Note: EA 706/54. Vols 1 and 2 ed. by John Hughes, vol. 3 comp. by White Kennett. Many American references.
Locations: L; CSmH, CtY, DLC

1706#9
CURSON, Henry. *A new description of the world...* London. J. Nutt, 520p. 18o. 1706
Note: EA 706/63. Second edition in 1710: RPJCB.
Locations: L;

1706#10
DEFOE, Daniel. *The case of Protestant dissenters in Carolina, shewing how a law to prevent occasional conformity there, has ended in the total subversion of the constitution in church and state...* London. 42, [2]; 67, [1]p. 4to. 1706

Note: SABIN 10966, EA 706/73. Anonymous. By Daniel Defoe. With an appendix or supplement, with a separate title page, of 14 documents relating to Carolina, compiled by John Ash and others, commencing with 'The first charter granted by King Charles II. to the proprietors of Carolina'. No. 4 is John Ash, 'The present state of affairs in Carolina. . . '.
Locations: L; DLC, NN, CSmH

1706#11
DONALDSON, James. *Considerations in relation to trade considered.* [Edinburgh]. 26p. 4to. 1706
Note: HANSON 658, KRESS 2506. EA 706/75. Replies to William Black's *Some considerations in relation to trade*, [Edinburgh]. 1706. References to tobacco, Newfoundland, fishery, etc.
Locations: L; Lu; CSmH, ICU, NN

1706#12
The first charter granted by King Charles II to the proprietors of Carolina. London. 67p. [1706?]
Note: See Defoe, *The case of...*, above, 1706.
Locations: RPJCB, MB

1706#13
KEITH, George. *A journal of travels from New-Hampshire to Caratuck, on the continent of North-America.* London. J. Downing for B. Aylmer, 92p. 4to. 1706
Note: SABIN 37199, EA 706/141.
Locations: L; DLC, RPJCB, MiU-C

1706#14
KIRKWOOD, James. *Proposals, concerning the propagating of Christian knowledge, in. . . Scotland and forraign parts of the world.* [Edinburgh?]. 4p. F. 1706
Note: EA 706/143. Mentions plantations in America.
Locations: RPJCB

1706#15
The sailor's Warning Piece. . . Being a dreadful relation of 7 English Sailors. . . as also another astonishing relation of the Gloucester Merchant-ship from Virginia... London. H. Hills. 8p. 8vo. [1706 or 1707]
Note: Cannibalism.
Locations: L;

1706#16
SHARP, John. *A sermon preached at Trinity-Church in New-York. . . August 13, 1706. At the funeral of the right honourable Katherine Lady Cornbury...* London. H. Hills, 16p. 8vo. 1706
Note: SABIN 79840–41, EA 706/201. First printed New York, 1706 (EVANS 1280). Another edition in 1708.
Locations: L; Ct; DLC, RPJCB, MiU-C

1706#17
SOCIETY FOR THE PROPAGATION OF THE GOSPEL. *An account of the Society for Propagating*

the gospel in foreign parts. . . with their proceedings and success, and hopes of continual progress. . . London. J. Downing, 97p. 4to. 1706
Note: SABIN 101, EA 706/204.
Locations: DLC, RPJCB, CtY

1706#18
SOCIETY FOR THE PROPAGATION OF THE GOSPEL. *A collection of papers, printed by order. . . viz. the Charter, the request, etc. . .* London. J. Downing, 45p. 4to. 1706
Note: SABIN 85934, EA 706/205, 738/221. Includes 'qualifications of missionaries, instructions for clergy'. Other editions, 1712 (EA 712/205), 1715 (EA 715/163), 1719, (EA 719/141) and 1738 (EA 738/221).
Locations: L; RPJCB, CtY, NN

1706#19
SOUTH CAROLINA. PROPRIETORS, GOVERNOR AND COUNCIL. *An account of the fair and impartial proceedings of the Lords Proprietors, governour and council of. . . South Carolina, in answer to. . . the petition of Joseph Boone and others, and of a paper. . . The Case of the Church of England in Carolina. . .* London. J. Brudenell, 4p. F. 1706
Note: SABIN 87359, EA 706/207.
Locations: RPJCB, MH

1706#20
WHITING, John. *Truth the strongest of all: or, An apostate further convicted, and truth defended; in reply to George Keith's Fifth narrative.* London. J.Sowle, 161p. 4to. 1706
Note: SABIN 103703, SMITH, II, 919, EA 706/234. A reply to Keith's *Fifth narrative*, above 1701 and to other works by him. References to Quakers in New England and Pennsylvania.
Locations: CtY, MH, NN, PHi, RPJCB

1706#21
WILLIAMS, John. *A sermon preached. . . February 15. 1705/6. . .* London. J. Downing for T. Sheed, 39p. 4to. 1706
Note: SABIN 104258, EA 706/235. SPG sermon for 1706. Another edition in 1706.
Locations: L; C; NN, RPJCB, CSmH

1707#1
ARCHDALE, John. *A new description of that fertile and pleasant province of Carolina: with a brief account of its discovery, settling, and the government thereof.* London. J. Wyat, 32p. 4to. 1707
Note: SABIN 1902, HANSON 810, EA 707/9.
Locations: L; DLC, RPJCB, MiU-C

1707#2
BEVERIDGE, William. *A sermon preach'd. . . February 21st 1706. . .* London. 24p. 4to. 1707
Note: SABIN 5110, EA 707/17. SPG sermon for 1707.
Locations: L; DLC, RPJCB

1707#3
COLMAN, Benjamin. *Practical discourses upon the parable of the ten virgins. . .* London. T. Parkhurst, 423p. 8vo. 1707
Note: SABIN 14508.
Locations: L; DLC, RPJCB, CtY

1707#4
COWETA INDIANS. *The humble submission of the kings, princes, generals, etc. to the Crown of England. Lately presented to. . . Sir Nathaniel Johnston, the present governour of Carolina. . .* London. A. Baldwin, s.sh. 1/2o. [1707]
Note: SABIN 33699, EA 707/35–6. 'Communicated to the Benevolent Society of Chyrugeons by a member of theirs and the Royal Society. . .' Another edition in 1707.
Locations: L;

1707#5
DUDLEY, Joseph? *A modest enquiry into the grounds and occasions of a late pamphlet, intituled, A memorial of the present deplorable state of New-England. By a disinterested hand.* London. 30p. 4to. 1707
Note: SABIN 49822, EA 707/110. See HOLMES, CM, 230B.
Locations: L; DLC, RPJCB, ViU

1707#6
DUNTON, John, comp. *The phenix: or, A revival of scarce and valuable pieces from the remotest antiquity down to the present time.* London. J. Morphew, 2 vols. 8vo. 1707
Note: EA 707/48–9. Another issue in 1707; and in *A collection of choice, scarce and valuable tracts*, EA 721/64.
Locations: L; CLU-C, DLC, RPJCB

1707#7
ENGLAND AND WALES. SOVEREIGN. ANNE. *A Proclamation, declaring what ensigns or colours shall be born at sea in merchant ships or vessels belonging to any of her majesties subjects of Great Britain, and the Dominions thereunto belonging. . . [28 July 1707].* London. Bill and executors, s.sh. F. 1707
Note: STEELE I, 4423. Also Edinburgh, 1707, STEELE II, 3318.
Locations: L;

1707#8
FRANCK, Richard. *The admirable and indefatigable adventures of the nine pious pilgrims. . . Written in*

America. . . by a zealous lover of truth. London. J. Hartley, 288p. 12mo. 1707
Note: EA 707/57. Reissued in 1709. Reference to coast of America.
Locations: L; RPJCB

1707#9
An inquiry into the causes of our naval miscarriages; with some thoughts on the interest of this nation, as to a naval war, and of the only true way of manning the fleet. . . London. viii 34p. 4to. 1707
Note: SABIN 34800, EA 707/117–8. Perhaps part of *The Sailor's advocate*, No 2. xiii, 39p. Two editions in 1707, another edition, 1728.
Locations: L; DLC, DFo, RPJCB

1707#10
JUSTICE, Alexander. *A general treatise of monies and exchanges; in which those of all trading nations are particularly describ'd and consider'd. . . By a well-wisher to trade.* London. S. and J. Sprint, J. Nicholson, and R. Smith, 2 pts 4to. 1707
Note: SABIN 26912, HANSON 824, KRESS 2560, EA 707/83. Contains references to New England.
Locations: L; ICJ, InU, NN

1707#11
LE GOBIEN, Charles. *Edifying and curious letters of some missioners of the Society of Jesus, from foreign missions. . .* London. 258p. 18mo. 1707
Note: SABIN 21853, 40697 note, EA 707/79. Revised (?) edition in 1714, as *The travels of several learned missioners of the Society of Jesus. . .* See EA 714/69. Material on Canada.
Locations: DLC, RPJCB, NN

1707#12
MATHER, Cotton. *A memorial of the present deplorable state of New-England, with the many disadvantages it lyes under, by the male-administration of their present governour, Joseph Dudley, Esq., and his son Paul. . . Faithfully digested from the several original letters, papers, and MSS by Philopolites.* London. 41p. 4to. 1707
Note: SABIN 62560, HOLMES, CM, II, 230, EA 707/106. Reprinted, Boston, 1707. Not the same as *The deplorable state. . .*, below, 1708.
Locations: L; Lpro; CSt

1707#13
A short way to know the world: or, The rudiments of geography. London. T. Osborne, 222p. 8vo. 1707
Note: EA 707/137. Part 5 relates to America. Also 1712, 1745, EA 712/203, 745/194.
Locations: DFo, ICU

1707#14
SLOANE, Sir Hans. *A voyage to the islands. . . with some relations concerning the neighbouring continent and islands of America. . .* London. B. M., 2 vols. 2o. 1707
Note: EA 707/138. Vol. II was published in 1725.
Locations: DLC, RPJCB, CtY

1707#15.
A true state of the tobacco trade I. As it relates to the plantations in America,. . . V. As it relates to the incouragement of the said plantations. . . London printed in the year, 1707, 16p. 4to. 1707
Locations: Dt;

1708#1
BELLEGARDE, Jean Baptiste Morvan de. *A general history of all voyages and travels throughout the old and new world. . . by Monsr. Du Perier. . .* London. E. Curll and E. Sanger, 364p. 8vo. 1708
Note: SABIN 4507–8, EA 708/5, 711/16. First published Paris, 1707, under the name Du Perier. Dedication signed Du Perier. Reissued in 1711 as *A complete collection of voyages made into North and South America. . . Translated from the French. . .*
Locations: L; DLC, MB, RPJCB

1708#2
BROKESBY, Francis. *Some proposals towards promoting the propagation of the Gospel in our American plantations.* London. G. Sawbridge, 30p. 4to. 1708
Note: EA 708/13. Also ascribed to M. Godwyn. L; is the author's copy. DLC and ViU have a second expanded edition of 1708 'to which is prefixed Mr. Goodwin's Brief account of religion in the plantations. . .'.
Locations: L; E; O;

1708#3
COOK, Ebenezer. *The sot-weed factor: or, a voyage to Maryland. A satyr. In which is described, the laws, government, courts and constitutions of the country. . .* London. B. Bragg, 21p. 4to. 1708
Note: SABIN 16234, EA 708/24.
Locations: L; DLC, RPJCB

1708#4
The deplorable state of New-England; by reason of a covetous and treacherous governour, and pusillanimous counsellors with a vindication of. . . Mr Higginson, Mr Mason, and several other gentlemen. . . To which is added, An account of the shameful miscarriage of the late expedition against Port-Royal. London. B. Harris, 39p. 8vo. 1708
Note: SABIN 19639, HANSON 941, HOLMES 88A, EA 708/32. Dedication signed A. H. Variously attributed to Sir Henry Ashurst, Alexander Holmes, John Higginson, Cotton Mather, John Wise. Reprinted Boston, '1720' i.e. 1721.
Locations: L; DLC, RPJCB, MHi

SOME PROPOSALS
TOWARDS PROMOTING
THE
PROPAGATION
OF THE
GOSPEL
IN OUR
AMERICAN PLANTATIONS.

Humbly Offered in a LETTER to Mr. *Nelson*.

A Worthy Member of the Society for Propagating the Gospel in Foreign Parts.

To which is added a *POSTSCRIPT*.

LONDON:

Printed for G. Sawbridge, at the *Three-Golden-Flower-D'Luces*, in *Little Brittain*: And Sold by B. Bragg, in *Pater-Noster-Row.* 1708.

(Price Six-Pence.)

1708#5
GEARE, Allen. *Ebenezer: or, a monument of thankfulness. Being a true account of a late miraculous preservation of nine men in a small boat...* London. A. Bettesworth, sold by J. Morphew, 23p. 8vo. 1708
Note: Cf. SABIN 26818, EA 708/48–9. In icy American waters. Two editions in 1708.
Locations: L; RPJCB

1708#6
GREAT BRITAIN. PARLIAMENT. *An act for ascertaining the rates of foreign coins in her majesties plantations in America.* London. J. Baskett. [1708]
Locations: ViU, NjP

1708#7
GREAT BRITAIN. PARLIAMENT. *An act for the encouragement of the trade to America...* London. C. Bill and executrix of T. Newcomb, s.sh. F. 1708
Note: Also London, 1711 (L;).
Locations: RPJCB

1708#8
GREAT BRITAIN. SOVEREIGN. ANNE. *Proclamation. For encouraging trade to Newfoundland. [26 June 1708].* London. Bill and Executors, s.sh. F, 1708
Note: STEELE 4454, BRIGHAM 163, HANSON 882.
Locations: L; E; MH-BA

1708#9
HALL, John. *Memoirs of the right villainous John Hall, the late famous and notorious robber...* London. B. Bragg, 6, 40p. 8vo. 1708
Note: Escaped while being transported to America. At least one other issue in 1708; also 1714.
Locations: L; MH, NIC

1708#10
JANEWAY, James. *A token for mariners, containing many famous and wonderful instances of God's providence in sea dangers and deliverances...* London. H. N., 147p. 12mo. 1708
Note: SABIN 35755, 96107, EA 708/63. Another edition, 1721. Relates principally to America and West Indies.
Locations: L; DLC, MWA

1708#11
MAKEMIE, Francis. *A narrative of the imprisonment of two non-conformist ministers, and prosecution or trial of one of them, for preaching a sermon in...* New York. London. Printed Boston, London reprinted. 48p. 8vo. 1708
Note: EA 708/82. First printed Boston or New York, 1707 (EVANS 1300).
Locations: L; RPJCB, MiU-C

1708#12
OLDMIXON, John. *The British empire in America, containing the history of the discovery, settlement, progress and present state of all the British colonies, on the continent and islands of America. In two volumes...* London. J. Nicholson, etc. 2 vols. 8vo. 1708
Note: HANSON 940, EA 708/95. Second edition in 1741.
Locations: L; E; RPJCB, DFo

1708#13
Reasons humbly offered by the merchants trading to Virginia and Maryland, for incouraging the exportation of tobacco, and bringing in of French wine in return. London. s.sh. F. [1708]
Note: HANSON 921, EA 708/105.
Locations: Lpro;

1708#14
Reasons humbly offered to the honourable the Commons of England in Parliament for laying an easie duty on whale-finns of the fishery of New-England, New York, and Pensilvania. London. s.sh. F.[1708]
Note: EA 708/106.
Locations: MnU, PHi

1708#15
Some observations on extracts taken out of the report from the Lords Commissioners for Trade and Plantations. London. 4p. F. [1708]
Note: SABIN 56494, 86682, HANSON 915, KRESS SUPP. 2395, EA 708/126. Discusses numbers of slaves imported into America.
Locations: L; MH-BA

1708#16
STANLEY, William. *A sermon preach'd... February 20th, 1707/8...* London. J. Downing, 26p. 8vo. 1708
Note: SABIN 90318, EA 708/127–8. SPG sermon for 1708. Two editions in 1708.
Locations: L; RPJCB, CtY, CSmH

1708#17
WHITEHEAD, George. *The power of Christ vindicated, against the magick of apostacy: in answer to George Keith's book... The magick of Quakerism.* London. J. Sowle, 246p. 12mo. 1708
Note: SABIN 103658, SMITH, II, 906, EA 708/148. Includes references to Quakers in North America.
Locations: L; CtY, DLC, RPJCB

1708#18
WHITING, John. *A catalogue of Friend's books; written by many of the people called Quakers...* London. J. Sowle, 238p. 8vo. 1708
Note: SABIN 103700.
Locations: L; DLC, RPJCB, MiU-C

1709

1709#1
Canary-birds naturaliz'd in Utopia. A canto...
London. 32p. 8vo. [1709]
Note: FOXON, C18, EA 709/25–8. Verses against Palatines en route to America. Three other editions in 1709. Foxon disputes the earlier attribution to Francis Hare.
Locations: L; CLU-C; PPL

1709#2
The case of small twist roll tobacco. London. s.sh. F. [1709?]
Note: HANSON 1010, EA 709/29.
Locations: LLI;

1709#3
The case of the petitioner, Richard Budge, late Commander and part-owner of the ship Hope, and sole-owner of her cargo of logwood. London. 3p. F. [1709]
Note: SABIN 8961, 53081, HANSON 1054, EA 709/23. Alleges illegal seizure and sale by Lord Cornbury, governor of New York.
Locations: O;

1709#4
The case of Thomas Lewis, Elizabeth Jorden, Owen Griffith, Elizabeth Mackay, and Thomas Joy, and others... London. s.sh. F. [1709]
Note: SABIN 40855, EA 709/98. Refers to non-payment of money for service in Newfoundland in Captain Moody's company.
Locations: MB

1709#5
DAWES, William. *A sermon preach'd... February 18, 1708-9...* London. J. Downing for Ann Speed, 25p. 4to. 1709
Note: SABIN 18925. SPG sermon for 1709.
Locations: L; RPJCB, MH, NN

1709#6
A deduction of the right and title of the Crown of Great Britain, and therein of... Queen Anne, to all the streights, bays, seas... and places whatsoever, within Hudson-Streights and Hudson-Bay, and of the right and property of the Hudsons-Bay Company... London. 3(1)p. F. [1709]
Note: HANSON 1056, Cf. KRESS SUPP. 2178, EA 709/48. ESTC lists under 1705. Endorsed 'Some account of the violences committed by the French on the English there'.
Locations: L; Lpro; MH-BA, NN

1709#7
DEFOE, Daniel. *A brief history of the poor Palatine refugees lately arriv'd in England.* London. J. Baker, 50p. 8vo. 1709

Note: EA 709/49–50. Remarks on emigration to America and its consequences for Britain. Another edition, Dublin, 1709.
Locations: L; InU, PHi, MH

1709#8
GREAT BRITAIN. PARLIAMENT. *An act for continuing several impositions... and concerning certain drugs of America... to be imported from her majesties plantations.* London. C. Bill and executors of T. Newcomb. 1709
Locations: ViU, MB

1709#9
HENDERSON, Patrick. *Truth and innocence the armour and defence of the people called Quakers... Being an answer to part of a book, entituled, The man of God furnished.* London. J. Sowle, 1709. 79p. 8vo. 1709
Note: SMITH, I, 931, EA 709/75. Replies to Cotton Mather's *The man of God furnished*, first published in Boston, 1708. References to Quakers in New England.
Locations: CtY, MB, PHC, RPJCB

1709#10
KING, WILLIAM. *A voyage to England... as also Observations on the same voyage, by Dr. Thomas Sprat... with a letter of Monsieur Sorbière's concerning the war... in 1652.* London. J. Woodward, 190p 8vo. 1709
Note: EA 709/146. Minor American references.
Locations: L; CtY, DLC, ICN

1709#11
LAWSON, John. *A new voyage to Carolina; containing the exact description and natural history of that country... And a journal of a thousand mile travel'd thro' several nations of Indians...* London. 258p. 4to. 1709
Note: SABIN 39451, 39452, HANSON 1057, EA 709/91, 737/128. Reissued 1714 with new title *The History of Carolina*. Also editions in 1718 and Dublin, 1737.
Locations: L; DLC, RPJCB, MiU-C

1709#12
A letter from a member of the Society for promoting Christian knowledge in London, to his friend in the country, newly chosen a corresponding member of that Society. London. J. Downing, 28p. 12mo. 1709
Note: EA 709/95. Another expanded edition in 1714, EA 714/80.
Locations: L;

1709#13
MATHER, Cotton. *Winthropi Justa. A sermon at the funeral of the Honble John Winthrop, Esq...* London. Printed at Boston in New-England, and reprinted at London, by B. Harris, 18p. 8vo. 1709
Note: SABIN 46601, HOLMES, CM, 452B, 452C, EA 709/103. First published Boston, 1708 (EVANS 1365).

Gov. John Winthrop of Connecticut. Republished 1710, EA 710/94.
Locations: Llp; MHi.

1709#14
MATHER, Increase. *A discourse concerning the maintenance, due to those that preach the gospel. . .* London. Boston printed, London reprinted. 32p. 8vo. 1709
Note: HOLMES, IM, 36, EA 709/104. An abridged edition of first edition, Boston, 1706 (EVANS 1269).
Locations: L; RPJCB

1709#15
MATHER, Increase. *A dissertation concerning the future conversion of the Jewish nation. . .* London. R. Tookey for N. Hillier, 35p. 4to. 1709
Note: SABIN 46668, HOLMES, IM, 42, EA 709/105.
Locations: RPJCB, MiU-C, CSmH

1709#16
MOLL, Herman. *Atlas manuale: or, a new sett of maps of all the parts of the earth, as well Asia, Africa and America, as Europe. . . Mostly perform'd by Herman Moll.* London. Printed for A. and J. Churchill; and T. Childe, [2], [3]p. 8vo. 1709
Note: EA 709/108. Also 1713, 1723, EA 713/124, 723/105.
Locations: L; Ct; DFo, DLC, NN

1709#17
The Palatines catechism, or A *true description of their camps at Blackheath and Camberwell. In a dialogue between an English tradesman and a High-Dutchman.* London. 8p. 8vo. 1709
Note: EA 709/113. Laments costliness of proposal to send Germans to America.
Locations: L;

1709#18
PENN, William. *The case of William Penn, proprietary, and governor in chief of the province of Pennsilvania, and territories, against the Lord Baltimore's pretensions to a tract of land in America, granted. . . in the year 1682.* [London]. s.sh. F. 1709
Note: SABIN 59687, SMITH, II, 320, EA 709/115 states no copy located and EA 709/116 is another issue with more text in 1709 (PPL). ESTC lists the CSmH (72590) copy, s.sh. F.
Locations: CSmH(?)

1709#19
PETIVER, James. *Catalogus classicus et topicus, omnium rerum figuratarum in V. decadibus, seu primo [-secundo] volumine Gazophylacii naturae et artis.* London. C. Bateman, 2 vols. F. 1709
Note: EA 709/117. Part 2 issued in 1711, EA 711/159.
Locations: L; MH-A

1709#20
The present state of the *tobacco-plantations in America.* London. s.sh. 1/2o. [1709]
Note: SABIN 65332, HANSON 942, EA 708/101. Dated in MSS 17 February 1708/9.
Locations: L; Lpro; NN

1709#21
The state of the Palatines, *for fifty years past to this present time.* London. J. Dutton, 8p. 8vo. 1709
Note: Cf. HANSON 1272, EA 709/147. Passage promoting sending Germans to America, noting success of those sent to Carolina. Another edition in 1710, EA 710/140.
Locations: MH

1709#22
A view of the Queen *and kingdom's enemies, in the case of the poor Palatines. . .* London. 16p. 8vo. 1709
Note: KRESS 2765, EA 709/163. Criticism of Palatines, citing Elector's attack on families going to Pennsylvania.
Locations: L; CtY, NIC

1709#23
WHITELOCKE, Sir Bulstrode. *Memorials of the English affairs. . . with some account of his life and writings by William Penn. . .* London. E. Curll, etc. [310]p. F. 1709
Note: SABIN 59715, 103671, EA 709/172-4. Two other issues in 1709. New edition with additions, 1732.
Locations: L; RPJCB, MiU-C, MH

1709#24
WICKS, Michael. *The case of Michael Wicks, Esq. late receiver of the plantation-duty.* London. 2p. F. [1709?]
Note: ESTC dates [1710?].
Locations: NN

1709#25
WILLARD, Samuel (1640–1707). *A thanksgiving sermon preach'd at Boston. . . December, 1705. On the return of a gentleman from his travels.* London. R. Smith, 16p. 8vo. 1709
Note: SABIN 104108. The gentleman was J. Belcher.
Locations: DLC, MB

1710#1
At Punch's theatre. For the *entertainment of the four Indian kings. . . this present Munday [sic], May 1. at seven a-clock.* London. s.sh. 1/2o. 1710
Note: EA 710/45. An advertisement.
Locations: L;

1710#2
A brief account of the *life and death and some of the gospel labours of. . . William Ellis. . .* London. J. Sowle, 31p. 8vo. 1710

1710

Note: SMITH, I, 562, EA 710/18. American travels.
Locations: RPJCB, PHC

1710#3
The epilogue, to be spoken before the four Indian kings, at the Queen's Theatre... the 24th of April. London. B. Bragg s.sh. F. 1710
Note: FOXON E353, EA 710/38.
Locations: Lsa; MH

1710#4
Four Indian Kings. Part I. How a beautiful lady... Part II. The lady's answer... London. 2p. [1710]
Note: EA 710/46–7. Another issue in 1710. ESTC lists two further printings of this title in [London, 1750?] and EA 726/80–84 four printings, undated but after 1726. There were no doubt others before, certainly after, 1760. There is an extensive secondary bibliographical literature.
Locations: DLC, RPJCB, MiU-C

1710#5
The Four Indian King's speech to her majesty. London, April 20. 1710. Yesterday the four princes... London. J. Baker, s.sh. 1/2o. [1710]
Note: SABIN 89182. EA 710/48–54 lists five London editions and one Edinburgh edition, circa 1710. ESTC lists two Edinburgh and two London editions.
Locations: L; E; CsmH, N

1710#6
The four kings of Canada. Being a succinct account of the four Indian princes lately arriv'd from North America... London. J. Baker, 47p. 8vo. 1710
Note: SABIN 25282, EA 710/55.
Locations: C; Eu; DLC, RPJCB, MiU-C

1710#7
God's wonders in the great deep, or the seaman's danger and deliverance exemplified. Containing several wonderful and amazing relations... London. Printed for Robert Gifford, 115p. 12mo. 1710
Note: The third edition. Previous ones not traced. EA 734/87 lists the fourth edition. Many North American references.
Locations: L; E; Lpro;

1710#8
Have at you blind harpers. Three ballads concerning the times. Consisting of, I. The royal embassy: or, A ballad on the progress of the four Indians kings. London. J. Baker, 8p. 8vo. 1710
Note: FOXON H108, EA 710/71.
Locations: C; O; DLC

1710#9
The history and progress of the four Indian kings to the kingdom of England... also the four Indian kings speech to her majesty... London. A. Hinde, 8p. 8vo. 1710
Note: SABIN 32113, EA 710/75.
Locations: L; ICN

1710#10
The history of the four Indian kings from the continent of America, between New-Eengland [sic] and Canada. Who came to begg [sic] Her Majesties protection from the tyraunical [sic] and arbitrary power of France. Together with their being converted to the Christian religion,... As also their speech to Her Majesty... London. E. Midwinter, 7p. 8vo. 1710
Note: EA 710/76.
Locations: C; O; E;

1710#11
HUDSON'S BAY COMPANY. *Hudson's Bay. A general collection of treatys, declarations of war, manifestoes, and other papers relating to peace and war...* London. J. Darby, 44, 448p. 8vo. 1710
Note: SABIN 26872, EA 710/60. Another edition, 1732, EA 732/102.
Locations: OrU

1710#12
A letter from a Dissenter in the city to a Dissenter in the country. Second edition. London. A. Baldwin, 16p. 8vo. 1710
Note: EA 710/89. Attributed to Daniel Defoe and Jeremiah Dummer. Signed at end: Irenaeus Americus.
Locations: CtY, ICN, InU

1710#13
MATHER, Increase. *A sermon shewing that the present dispensations of providence declare that wonderful revolutions in the world are near at hand...* Edinburgh. 32p. 4to. 1710
Note: SABIN 46737, HOLMES, CM, 116, EA 710/95. Reprint of part of *Dissertation wherein the strange doctrines...*, Boston, 1708 (EVANS 1366). Another edition, Edinburgh, 1713: RPJCB, CSmH, ViU
Locations: MWA, RPJCB, CSmH

1710#14
NAIRNE, Thomas. *A letter from South Carolina; giving an account of the soil, air, product, trade... together with the manner of necessary charges of settling a plantation there... by a Swiss gentleman...* London. A. Baldwin, 63p. 8vo. 1710
Note: SABIN 87859, 87860, HANSON 1162, EA 710/101, 732/170. Other editions, 1718, 1732.
Locations: L; DLC, RPJCB, ViU

1710#15
A proposal for propagating the Christian religion... offered to the Queen's most excellent majesty, who

by those. . . means may now be the foundress of a new empire. . . London. s.sh. F. 1710
Note: SABIN 66018, EA 710/112. By George Berkeley?
Locations: NO COPY LOCATED.

1710#16
A proposal humbly offer'd to *the. . . Commons. . . for improving the woollen manufacture, for raising 3000000L on funds never yet impos'd in this reign. . . and for other ends and purposes. . .* London. s.sh. F. 1710
Note: HANSON 1181, EA 710/113. For duties on cloth made in America, etc.
Locations: LLI;

1710#17
Reasons humbly offered against a *clause in the bill for the encouraging the importation of naval stores from the plantations.* [London]. 3p. fol. 1710
Note: EA 710/119.
Locations: PHi

1710#18
Reasons humbly offer'd to the *honourable House of Commons, by the merchants trading in tobacco, against a clause relating to the exportation of goods entitl'd to a drawback. . .* s.sh. 1/2o. [London] [1710]
Note: HANSON 1147, EA 710/118.
Locations: L; MH-BA

1710#19
Reasons humbly offered to the *Honourable House of Commons, for passing the bill for the better encouragement and protection of the trade to America.* London. s.sh. F. [1710]
Note: SABIN 68286, KRESS SUPP. 2507, EA 710/120–1. Another issue in 1710. ESTC lists this as 1707 at NN.
Locations: RPJCB, MH-BA

1710#20
Reasons humbly offered to the *honourable House of Commons, to obviate the objections made by the East-India Company against the amendments made by the Lords, to the bill, for the better encouragement and protection of the American trade.* [London]. s.sh. F. 1710
Note: EA 710/122. Endorsed 'Reasons for passing the amendments made by the Lords to the American bill'. ESTC lists under 1707 at NN.
Locations: NN, PHi.

1710#21
Reasons humbly offered to the right honourable the House of Commons *for passing the clause in the bill for the better encouragement of trade to America; whereby her majesty is empowered to grant. . . the property of such colonies . . . belonging to her enemies in America. . .* London. s.sh. F. [1710]

Note: EA 710/123.
Locations: DLC, NN

1710#22
TAYLOR, John. *An account of some of the labours, exercises, travels and perils by sea and land, of John Taylor, of York. . .* London. J. Sowle (14), 77p. 12mo. 1710
Note: SABIN 94478, EA 710/141.
Locations: L; NN

1710#23
TRIBBECHOV, Johann. *The Christian traveller: A farewel-sermon preach'd. . . on the 20th of January, 1710. To the Palatines. Before their going out of England. . .* London. J. Downing, etc., 27p. 12mo. 1710
Note: SABIN 96958, EA 710/146.
Locations: CtY

1710#24
TRIMNELL, Charles. *A sermon preached. . . Friday the 17th of February, 1709/10. . .* London. J. Downing, 24p. 4to. 1710
Note: SABIN 96976, EA 710/148. SPG sermon for 1710.
Locations: L; DLC, RPJCB, CtY

1710#25
WARREN, William. *Whereas by Her Majesties directions, a monthly correspondence is settled, between Great Britain, and Her Majesties dominions on the mainland of America.* [London]. J. Sowle, s.sh. F. 1710
Note: EA 710/158.
Locations: RPJCB

1710#26
WHITING, John. *A just reprehension of Cotton Mather. London, the 11th of the 12th month, 1709.* London. J. Sowle, s.sh. F. 1710
Note: SMITH, II, 920.
Locations: MH, PHC

1711#1
The case of Great Britain's *manufacturers of iron and steel, for her majesty's plantations and colonies. . .* London. s.sh. F. [1711]
Note: HANSON 1311n, EA 711/33. Another edition of *The case of the honest exporters. . .*, below, 1711, with an additional paragraph.
Locations: L; O; RPJCB, MH-BA

1711#2
The case of the honest *exporters of Great Britain's manufactured iron and steel to her majesty's plantations and collonies.* London. s.sh. F. [1711]
Note: HANSON 1311, EA 711/32.
Locations: LLI;

1711#3
CHAMBERLAYNE, John. *A letter from a member of the Society for propagating the gospel. . . to an inhabitant of the City of London. . .* London. 4p. 4to. [1711]
Note: SABIN 85939, EA 711/119.
Locations: L; RPJCB, NN

1711#4
COMPTON, Henry. *A letter from the Lord Bishop of London, to his clergy within the bills of mortality. . . 14 May 1711. . .* London. 2p. 4to. [1711]
Note: EA 711/44. Collections for the SPG.
Locations: RPJCB

1711#5
DEAN, John. *A narrative of the sufferings of. . . Captain John Dean. . . in the Nottingham-Galley of London, cast away on Boon island, near New England, December 11 1710.* London. R. Tookey for S. Popping, iv, 23p. 8vo. 1711
Note: SABIN 19024–9, EA 711/51–2, 726/58, 727/53, 738/71. SABIN 19029 is *A true account. . .*, S. Popping, 1711. A shorter version was also printed in 1711 by J. Dutton, *A sad and deplorable, but true account* (L;). Editions also in 1722, 1726 (revised and expanded), 1727, 1730, 1738, 1762. Cf. EVANS 1506: *Compassions called for. . . relation of. . . a company lately ship wrecked. . . on the coast of New England* (Boston, 1711). The 'narrative' was reprinted in Boston in 1727, 1728, and 1762(?). Shipwreck and cannibalism.
Locations: L; NN, MH

1711#6
FLEETWOOD, William. *A sermon preached. . . 16th February, 1710/11. . .* London. J. Downing, 42p. 8vo. 1711
Note: SABIN 24690, EA 711/78–9. Two issues in 1711; also edition, 1725. SPG sermon for 1711, with abstract, etc.
Locations: L; DLC, RPJCB, MiU-C

1711#7
GREAT BRITAIN. GENERAL POST OFFICE. *Whereas the Queen has been pleased to direct, that a monthly correspondence be established between this kingdom, and. . . the continent of America, by packet-boats, to pass to, and from Bristol and New-York. . .* London. J. Sowle, s.sh. 4to. 1711
Note: HANSON 1389, EA 711/238. ESTC lists under 1710.
Locations: L; RPJCB

1711#8
GREAT BRITAIN. PARLIAMENT. *An act for establishing a general post office for all her majesties dominions. . .* London. Assigns of T. Newcomb and H. Hills. 1711.
Locations: ViU

1711#9
GREAT BRITAIN. PARLIAMENT. *An act for the preservation of white and other pine trees. . . in. . . New Hampshire, in Massachusetts Bay,. . . Main, Rhode Island, and Providence-Plantation. . .* London. T. Newcomb and H. Hills. 1711
Note: Act also refers to Narragansett country, Connecticut, New York, and New Jersey.
Locations: ViU

1711#10
GREAT BRITAIN. SOVEREIGN. ANNE. *Proclamation. For enforcing act establishing General Post Office in Dominions 23 June 1711].* London. s.sh. F. 1711
Note: STEELE 4498, BRIGHAM 167.
Locations: L;

1711#11
HARE, Francis. *The reception of the Palatines vindicated: in a fifth letter to a Tory member. . .* London. 40p. 8vo. 1711
Note: EA 711/103.
Locations: L; MiU-C, MH, CtY

1711#12
Entry cancelled.

1711#13
LANGMAN, Christopher. *The true account of the voyage of the Nottingham-galley of London, John Dean Commander. . .* London. S. Popping, 36p. 8vo. 1711
Note: SABIN 19029, EA 711/116. Challenges Dean's account in DEAN, John, *A narrative. . .* above, 1711.
Locations: DLC, RPJCB, NN

1711#14
A list of those members of the late parliament, that voted for the passing of the Act for naturalising foreign Protestants; and consequently, for the bringing over the Palatines. . . London. 2p. 2o. [1711]
Note: L; dates 1708.
Locations: L; RPJCB

1711#15
MATHER, Cotton. *Manly Christianity. A brief essay on the signs of good growth and strength in the most lovely Christianity. . .* London. R. Smith, 34p. 8vo. 1711
Note: HOLMES, CM, 219.
Locations: MWA, MH

1711#16
MATHER, Cotton. *The right way to shake off a viper. An essay, on a case, too commonly calling for consideration. What shall good men do, when they are evil spoke. With a preface by Dr. Increase Mather. . .* London. S. Popping, 35p. 8vo. 1711
Note: HOLMES, CM, 335A. Reprinted Boston, 1720.
Locations: MWA, MH

1711#17
MOLL, Herman. *Atlas geographus: or, a compleat system of geography, ancient and modern... With the discoveries and improvements of the best modern authors to this time...* London. John Nutt; and sold by Benjamin Barker and others, 5 vols. 4to. 1711
Note: SABIN 49902, EA 711/140. Published in 5 vols., 1711–1717. Vol. 5 (1717) is *Atlas geographus; or, a compleat system of geography, ancient and modern, for America...* EA 717/110.
Locations: L; C; Dt; CSmH, CU-Riv, MBAt, NN, RPJCB

1711#18
NICHOLSON, Francis. *Journal of an expedition under the command of Francis Nicholson... for the reduction of Port-Royal in Nova-Scotia...* London. R. S., sold by J. Morphew, 24p. 8vo. 1711
Note: SABIN 36703, EA 711/145.
Locations: DLC, MB, MH

1711#19
PETIVER, James. *Gazophylacii naturae et artis decas sexta [-nona].* London. C. Bateman, 12p. F. 1711
Note: EA 711/160. Continues author's 1702–06 work, above, 1702.
Locations: NNBG

1711#20
PITTIS, William. *The history of the present parliament, and convocation. With the debates... relating to the conduct of the war abroad...* London. J. Baker, 368p. 8vo. 1711
Note: SABIN 63102, EA 711/162.
Locations: L; DLC, RPJCB, ICJ

1711#21
PORTER, Joseph. *The holy seed: or, The life of Mr Thomas Beard, wrote by himself: with some account of his death, September 15, 1710...* London. N. Cliff and D. Jackson, [52]p. 8vo. 1711
Note: SABIN 4127. With funeral sermon by Joseph Porter and preface. A second edition (NN), also 1711, is enlarged from his own manuscripts. Third edition (DLC, NN), 1715. Reprinted Boston 1735.
Locations: L;

1711#22
Reasons for encouraging the importation of timber, plank, boards, and other wood, from her majesty's plantations, by taking off the custom, or allowing a bounty money thereon... London. s.sh. F. [1711?]
Note: HANSON 1376, EA 711/170.
Locations: LLI;

1711#23
Remarks on a false, scandalous, *and seditious libel...* London. A. Baldwin, 40p. 8vo. 1711
Note: EA 711/175. References to Hudson's Bay.
Locations: RPJCB

1711#24.
Remarks upon some queries handed *about by the separate traders to Africa...* London. 4p. F. 1711
Note: Substantial references to North American colonies.
Locations: L; C-S; DFo, RPJCB

1711#25
Remarks upon the present negotiations *of peace begun between Britain and France.* London. 35p. 4to. 1711
Note: EA 711/177–8. Another edition in 1711. Discussion of colonial policy, and of relations of North America and West Indies.
Locations: RPJCB

1711#26
Royal remarks: or, The Indian *king's observations on the most fashionable follies now reigning in the kingdom of Great Britain...* London. 55p. 8vo. 1711
Note: EA 711/184. Also 1730?
Locations: L; DFo, CSmH

1711#27
The sailors danger and hardship *at sea. Giving a full and true description of the late expedition to Quebeck... Likewise, a full... account of the blowing up Her Majest's [sic] ship the Edgar... the 15th of October, 1711...* London. s.sh. 1o. [1711 or 1712]
Note: Two large woodcut illustrations.
Locations: O;

1711#28
SETTLE, Elkanah? *A pindaric poem on the propagation of the gospel in foreign parts.* London. 18p. F. 1711
Note: SABIN 79347, EA 711/192.
Locations: L; RPJCB, MH, CSmH

1711#29
STEVENS, John. *A new collection of voyages and travels... None of them before ever printed in English.* London. 2 vols. 4to. 1711
Note: EA 711/207. First published in parts. Vol I contains (in part 2) John Lawson's *New Voyage to Carolina...* (258p.).
Locations: L; DLC, RPJCB, NcD

1711#30
SWIFT, Jonathan. *The conduct of the allies, and of the late ministry, in beginning and carrying on the present war.* London. J. Morphew, 96p. 8vo. 1711
Note: EA 711/210–15. Attacks continental war. Advocates greater expenditure on colonial and maritime war. Also Edinburgh, 1711 and three other London editions.
Locations: L; DLC, CtY

1711

1711#31
TAYLOUR, Joseph. *By Captain Joseph Taylour, commander of her majesty's ship Litchfield, and commander in chief of all her majesty's forces in Newfoundland, to John Collins, esq; hereby appointed Governour... of the Fort and harbour of St. John's...* London. s.sh. 1o. [1711?]
Note: EA 711/42, SABIN 54976. Docket title 'The case of John Collins, esq; Governour of Newfoundland, Jan. 21. 1711'.
Locations: L; Lpro;

1711#32
THOMPSON, Thomas. *Considerations on the trade to Newfoundland.* London. A. Bell, 4p. F. [1711]
Note: SABIN 54979, HANSON 1374, EA 711/46.
Locations: L; DLC, RPJCB

1711#33
TRELAWNY, Jonathan. *A letter from the Lord Bishop of Winchester, to his clergy within the bills of mortality...* London. [3]p. 4to. [1711]
Note: Collections for SPG.
Locations: RPJCB

1711#34
WATTS, Robert. *The duty and manner of propagating the gospel shewn in a sermon... on requiring a collection to be made for the use of the Society for propagating the Gospel in Foreign Parts.* London. J. Downing etc. 30p. 8vo. 1711
Note: SABIN 102176, EA 711/237.
Locations: L;

1711#35
Z., X. *A letter from an old Whig in town, to a modern Whig in the country, upon the late expedition to Canada.* London. J. Morphew, 8p. 4to. 1711
Note: EA 711/122.
Locations: L; RPJCB, MiU-C, NN

1712#1
BRADBURY, Thomas. *The ass: or, the serpent. A comparison between the tribes of Issachar and Dan, in their regard for civil liberty.* London. N. Cliff and D. Jackson; sold by J. Baker and T. Harrison, 22p. 12mo. 1712
Note: SABIN 7208n. EA 712/18. Another edition in 1715, EA 715/32. Reprinted Boston, 1768. Mentions Britain's American colonies.
Locations: L; CSmH, CtY, DLC, MH

1712#2
By order of the Mineral *Master General, at the New-England Coffee-House behind the Royal Exchange, London.* London. s.sh. F. [1712]
Note: HANSON 1621, EA 712/27. Advertisement for opening of subscription list for setting up iron and steel works in New England and copper works in Connecticut.
Locations: Lpro;

1712#3
The case of Job Mathew. London. s.sh. F. [1712]
Note: HANSON 1738, EA 712/153. Money held by him as surety for John Goodwin and partner, tobacco merchants trading to Virginia.
Locations: L;

1712#4
The case of the importers *of common turpentine, from Her Majesty's plantations, briefly stated.* London. s.sh. F. [1712]
Note: HANSON 1672. For exemption from proposed tax.
Locations: Lu; O;

1712#5
COOKE, Edward. *A voyage to the South Sea, and round the world...* London. H.M. for B. Lintot and R. Gosling, A. Bettesworth and W. Innys, 436p. 8vo. 1712
Note: EA 712/41–2. A second edition in 1712, 2 vols. 8vo. (L;). California voyage.
Locations: CtY, RPJCB, ViU

1712#6
COURT VAN DER VOORT, Pieter de la. *The interest of Holland as to their alliances...* London. J. Baker, 39p. 8vo. 1712
Note: Extracted from his *True interest...*, above, 1702, with references to Newfoundland and North American colonies.
Locations: L;

1712#7
DAVENANT, Charles. *A report to the Honourable Commissioners for putting in execution the Act...* London. A. Bell, etc. [157]p. 8vo. [1712]
Note: GOLDSMITH'S 5213, HANSON 1580n, EA 712/101, 715/63, 736/71. Includes a second report with separate title page, etc. Reissued in 1715 (L; CtY, NNC) and in 1736, as *An account of the trade between Great Britain...* Deals with Newfoundland.
Locations: L; C; Dt; CSmH, DFo, ICN

1712#8
DUMMER, Jeremiah. *A letter to a friend in the country, on the late expedition to Canada...* London. A. Baldwin, 22p. 8vo. 1712
Note: SABIN 21199, EA 712/77.
Locations: L; C; RPJCB, MiU-C

1712#9
DUMMER, Jeremiah. *A letter to a noble lord, concerning the late expedition to Canada.* London. A. Baldwin, 26p. 8vo. 1712

Note: SABIN 10507, EA 712/78. Reprinted Boston, 1712.
Locations: L; DLC, RPJCB

1712#10
GAY, John. *The Mohocks; a tragi-comical farce.* London. B. Lintott, 21p. 12mo. 1712
Note: SABIN 26788, but not the smallest allusion to North American Indians! Another edition in 1717.
Locations: L; DLC, MH, CtY

1712#11
GREAT BRITAIN. PARLIAMENT. *An act for continuing an act. . . intituled, An act for encouraging the importation of naval stores from. . . plantations in America. . .* London. [1712]
Locations: MB

1712#12
The History of the peace with France, and the war with Holland, in the year 1672. . . London. A. Baldwin, 71p. 8vo. 1712
Note: SABIN 32195, EA 712/112.
Locations: L; RPJCB, NN, CtY

1712#13
KENNETT, White. *The lets and impediments in planting. . . the gospel. . . A sermon preach'd. . . Friday the 15th of February, 1711/12.* London. J. Downing, 52p. 8vo. 1712
Note: SABIN 37448, EA 712/124–5. SPG sermon for 1712, with abstract, etc. Another edition in 1712.
Locations: L; C; DLC, RPJCB, MiU-C

1712#14
A letter from a West-India merchant to a gentleman at Tunbridg, concerning the part of the French proposals, which relates to North-America, and particularly Newfoundland. . . London. 34p. 8vo. 1712
Note: SABIN 40319, HANSON 1607, EA 712/142.
Locations: L; C; RPJCB, MiU-C

1712#15
Entry cancelled.

1712#16
MARSTON, Edward. *To the most noble prince Henry duke of Beaufort. . . Palatine of the province of South Carolina in America.* London. 12p. 4to. [1712]
Note: SABIN 44822, EA 712/150. Petition for restoration to his rectory, of St. Philip's, Charlestown.
Locations: L; RPJCB

1712#17
MATHER, Cotton. *The old paths restored. . .* London. Boston printed, London reprinted. 24p. 12mo. 1712

Note: HOLMES CM, 262, EA 712/152. First printed Boston, 1711 (EVANS 1509).
Locations: L; CtY, ViU

1712#18
MATHER, Increase. *Some remarks, on a pretended answer, to a discourse concerning the common-prayer worship. With an exhortation to the churches in New-England, to hold forth to their faith without wavering. . .* London. For N. Hillier and for the booksellers in Boston, 2, 36, 10p. 8vo. 1712
Note: SABIN 46747, HOLMES, IM, 226. Answer to John William's *A brief discourse. . .* above, 1693.
Locations: MH, DLC, MB

1712#19
NORRIS, John. *Profitable advice for rich and poor. In a dialogue between James Freeman, a Carolina planter, and Simon Question, a West-Country farmer, containing a description, or true relation of South-Carolina.* London. J. How, 110p. 8vo. 1712
Note: SABIN 55502, HANSON 1623, EA 712/161.
Locations: L; DLC, RPJCB

1712#20
The offers of France explain'd. . . London. A. Baldwin, 26p. 8vo. 1712
Note: GOLDSMITH'S 4968, EA 712/164. Discusses Canada, Hudson's Bay, beaver trade, etc.
Locations: L; Lu; RPJCB, MiU-C

1712#21
PETIVER, James. *Pteri-graphia Americana; icones continens filicum nec non muscos, lichenes, fungos, corallia. . . ex insulis nostra Charibbaeis. . .* London. 3p. F. 20 plates. [1711 or 1712?]
Note: EA 712/171. North American references. Another edition in 1715 (L;). ESTC lists a slightly different title in 1712 and 1715.
Locations: L; MH-A

1712#22
Reasons humbly offered in behalf of the Hudson-Bay Company, that they may be exempted in the clause that will be offer'd for suppressing the insurance offices. London. s.sh. F. [1712]
Note: HANSON 1756, EA 712/118. ESTC lists under 1711.
Locations: L; RPJCB

1712#23
A scheme for improving the mines, the mineral and the battery works, in New England. London. 4p. 4to. [1712]
Note: HANSON 1622, EA 712/197.
Locations: Lpro;

1712

1712#24
Some reasons for a farther encouragement for bringing naval stores from America, for supplying the Royal Navy... London. 4p. F. [1712]
Note: SABIN 86723, EA 712/207. ESTC lists under 1710.
Locations: CSmH

1712#25
The virtues and excellency of the American tobacco plant, for cure of diseases, and preservation of health: And the noxious qualities of the tobacco growing in northern countries. London. R. Parker, 15p. 8vo. 1712
Note: HANSON 1609, EA 712/258.
Locations: L; Vi

1712#26
WHITEHEAD, George. *Light and truth triumphant.* London. Assigns of J. Sowle, 207p. 12mo. 1712
Note: SABIN 103657, SMITH, II, 906, EA 712/262. Includes references to Quakers in Boston.
Locations: L; DLC, MH, RPJCB

1713#1
A calculation of the species and value of the manufactures and products of Great-Britain, Newfoundland, and Ireland, annually exported to the port of Leghorn. London. s.sh. F. [1713]
Note: HANSON 1863, KRESS 2945, EA 713/18
Locations: Lu; O; MH-BA

1713#2
The case of the chaplains of her majesty's navy, most humbly submitted to the honourable House of Commons. London. s.sh. F. [1713]
Note: HANSON 1948. On the lack of vacant livings, even in the plantations. Another version in 1714, HANSON 2111.
Locations: L; O; Lpro;

1713#3
The case of the merchants, and planters, trading to, and residing in, Virginia and Maryland. London. s.sh. F. [1713?]
Note: SABIN 11312, 100440, HANSON 1895, EA 713/23.
Locations: L; RPJCB

1713#4
CROZAT, Anthony. *A letter to a member of the P——t of G—t B—n, occasion'd by the priviledge granted by the French King to Mr. Crozat.* London. J. Baker, 44p. 8vo. 1713
Note: HANSON 1903, EA 713/111. Relates to Louisiana.
Locations: L; RPJCB, MiU-C

1713#5
KENNETT, White. *Bibliothecae Americanae primordia. An attempt towards laying the foundations of an American library, in several books, papers, and writings humbly given to the Society for the propagation of the Gospel in foreign parts...* London. J. Churchill, 275p. 4to. 1713
Note: SABIN 37447, EA 713/104.
Locations: L; C; E; RPJCB, MiU-C

1713#5A
A letter to a West-country clothier and free holder, concerning the Parliament's rejecting the French treaty of commerce... London. J. Baker, 28p. 8vo. 1713
Note: HANSON 1845, KRESS 2854, EA 713/112.
Locations: L; Lu; RPJCB, CSmH

1713#6
MATHER, Cotton. *Reasonable religion: or the truths of the Christian religion demonstrated...* London. N. Cliff, D. Jackson, 135p. 12mo. 1713
Note: SABIN 46477, HOLMES CM, 320, EA 713/119. First printed Boston, 1711 (EVANS 931).
Locations: L; DLC, RPJCB, CSmH

1713#7
MATHER, Increase. *A discourse concerning faith and fervency in prayer...* London. 80p. 8vo. [1713]
Note: SABIN 46655, HOLMES, IM, 32B, EA 713/120–1. First printed Boston, 1701 (EVANS 1471–3). Also Edinburgh, 1713.
Locations: L; RPJCB, MiU-C, NN

1713#8
MOORE, John. *Of the truth and excellency of the gospel. A sermon preach'd... Friday the 20th of February 1712/13...* London. J. Downing, 56p. 8vo. 1713
Note: SABIN 50406, EA 713/125–6. SPG sermon for 1713, with abstract, etc. Another edition in 1713.
Locations: L; DLC, RPJCB, CSmH

1713#9
NEWCOMB, Thomas. *Pacata Britannia. A panegyrick to the queen, on the peace...* London. Printed for R. Gosling, 12p F. 1713
Note: FOXON N269, EA 713/135. References to Four Indian Kings and maritime empire.
Locations: O; CtY, MH

1713#10
OLDMIXON, John. *Torism and trade never agree. To which is added, an account and character of the Mercator... In a letter to Sir G- H-.* London. A. Baldwin, 2, 38p. 8vo. 1713
Note: Comments on Tory persecution which caused a large emigration to colonies with unexpectedly beneficial results for English trade.
Locations: L; CtY, MH-BA, DFo

1713#11
Reasons humbly offr'd [sic] for allowing the merchants, etc. of New-England, New-York, and Carolina, relief upon the dutys paid on prize-goods, as those who have

114

bonded the same in other colonies. London. s.sh. F. [1713?]
Note: HANSON 1928, EA 713/157. NN dates 1716.
Locations: O; NN

1713#12
SOCIETY FOR THE PROPAGATION OF THE GOSPEL. *A second letter from a member of the Society for the Propagation of the Gospel...* London. 4p. 4to. [1713?]
Note: EA 705/153 gives an earlier date than ESTC.
Locations: L;

1713#13
THOMPSON, Thomas. *A salutation of love, and tender invitation, to all people; but more especially to the inhabitants of New-England, Road-Island and Long-Island, to come unto Shiloh...* London. Assigns of J. Sowle, 42p. 8vo. 1713
Note: SABIN 95528, SMITH, II, 738, EA 713/172.
Locations: L; RPJCB, MiU-C, NN

1713#14
TICKELL, Thomas. *A poem, to his excellency the Lord Privy-Seal, on the prospect of peace.* London. For J. Tonson, 20p.F. 1713
Note: FOXON T303-9. References to Four Indian Kings and predictions of empire. Six editions in 1713.
Locations: L; O; CtY, MH

1713#15
A true list of the several ships arrived at Leghorne from Great Britain, Ireland, and Newfoundland, in one year, commencing at Lady-Day, 1712, to Lady-Day, 1713... London, [2]p. 1/2o. [1713]
Note: HANSON 1864, EA 713/174.
Locations: O; Lpro;

1714#1
The Case of the merchants trading in tobacco, with relation to the bill now depending in... Commons, for lessening the drawback on tobacco exported for Ireland. London. s.sh. F. 1714
Note: HANSON 1987, EA 714/19.
Locations: L; Lu; RPJCB

1714#2
The Case of the merchants who export tobacco. London. s.sh. F. [1714]
Note: HANSON 1988, EA 714/20.
Locations: L; Lu; RPJCB

1714#3
The Case of the tobacco-merchants, who are become insolvent, and are bound to her majesty for duties... London. s.sh. F. [1714]
Note: HANSON 2064, EA 714/22.
Locations: L; RPJCB

1714#4
The court of Atalantis... in verse and prose... London. J. Roberts, 310p. 8vo. 1714
Note: EA 714/33–4. Describes Indian country in North America. Fictional; another issue London, 1717 published as *Court tales...*, EA 717/36.
Locations: CSmH, DLC, ICN

1714#5
EDGAR, William. *Vectigalium systema: or, a complete view of that part of the revenue of Great Britain, commonly called Customs. Wherein... IV. The laws relative to the customs, navigation, and trade, are abstracted under proper heads...* London. Printed by John Baskett, and by the assigns of Thomas Newcomb, etc. [6], 330p. 8vo. 1714
Note: Reissued in 1714, second edition, 1718.
Locations: L; C; E; MH-BA, CaOTU, CLU-C

1714#6
ELLWOOD, Thomas. *The history of the life of Thomas Ellwood, or, an account of his birth, education, etc. with divers observations... To which is added a supplement By Joseph Wyeth.* London. Assigns of J. Sowle, 478p. 8vo. 1714
Note: SABIN 22352, SMITH, I, 568, EA 714/43–4. A second edition in 1714.
Locations: L; DLC, RPJCB

1714#7
GRANTHAM, Sir Thomas. *A historical account of some memorable actions, particularly in Virginia...* London. J. Roberts, 71p. 8vo. 1714
Note: SABIN 28323, EA 714/56. Second edition in 1716 (EA 716/62).
Locations: CSmH

1714#8
GREAT BRITAIN. PARLIAMENT. *An act for encouraging the tobacco trade.* London. J. Baskett and others. 1714
Locations: OCl

1714#9
GREAT BRITAIN. SOVEREIGN. GEORGE I. *By the King, a proclamation... for continuing the officers in... plantations [22 November 1714].* London. J. Baskett, etc, s.sh. F. 1714
Note: BRIGHAM, 174 CRAWFORD p. 3.
Locations: L; Lpro;

1714#10
GREAT BRITAIN. SOVEREIGN. GEORGE I. *By the King, a proclamation, requiring all ships and vessels, trading from the plantations in the way of the Algerines, to furnish themselves with passes [4 October 1714].* London. J. Baskett, etc. s.sh. F. 1714

Note: BRIGHAM 172, HANSON 2007, CRAWFORD p. 3.
Locations: L; E;

1714#11
JOUTEL, Henri. *A journal of the last voyage perform'd by Monsr. de La Sale, to the Gulph of Mexico, to find out the mouth of the Missisipi river.* . . London. A. Bell, etc. 205p. 8vo. 1714
Note: EA 714/70. Also published in 1719 as *Mr Joutel's journal of his voyage to Mexico.* . ., (B. Lintot, 205p.): DLC, RPJCB, ViU.
Locations: L; DLC, RPJCB, MiU-C

1714#12
A Letter to the Honourable A——r M——re, Com———ner *of Trade and Plantation.* London. J. Roberts, 39p. 8vo. 1714
Note: HANSON 1991, EA 714/81.
Locations: L; C; RPJCB, MiU-C, NN

1714#13
MATHER, Cotton. *The saviour with his rainbow. A discourse concerning the covenant which God will remember, in the times of danger passing over his church.* London. J. D. 23p. 8vo. 1714
Note: HOLMES, CM, 342, EA 714/88. *Thoughts for the day of rain.* . ., Boston, 1712 (EVANS 1559) includes this essay.
Locations: DLC, ICN, MH

1714#14
Reasons humbly offer'd to the. . . Lords *for passing the bill, entituled, A Bill for relief of merchants, importers of tobacco and wine, concern'd in Bonds given for part of the duties on the same.* London. s.sh. F. [1714]
Note: HANSON 2066, EA 714/116.
Locations: L; LG;

1714#15
Reasons humbly offer'd to. . . Commons, *by the merchants and traders in tobacco, with relation to the bill, now depending, for the lessening the drawback, on tobacco exported to Ireland.* London. s.sh. F. [1714]
Note: SABIN 100517, HANSON 1989, EA 714/115.
Locations: O; RPJCB

1714#16
Reasons humbly offer'd to. . . Commons, *by the tobacco and wine merchants, against payment of interest for the time past on their bonds at the Custom-house, where the principal is paid.* London. s.sh. F. [1714]
Note: HANSON 2065, EA 714/117.
Locations: L; MH-BA

1714#17
Reasons humbly proposed to the Honourable *House of Commons, for laying a duty upon East-India silks, etc. Exported into Her Majesties Dominions; and that no drawback be allowed upon Callicoes, Muslins, etc. when exported to America and Ireland.* . . London. s.sh. F. [1714?]
Note: HANSON 2018, Cf. SABIN 68289, EA 714/118. ESTC lists under 1710.
Locations: L; O;

1714#18
SHARP, John. *De rebus liturgicis oratio pro gradu doctoratûs in S. S. theologia.* . . *A Io. Sharp ecclesiae Anglicanae apud Americanos prebytero.* Aberdeen. 16p. 4to. 1714
Note: Chaplain to royal forces in New York. His doctoral degree at Aberdeen.
Locations: L; NN, MH

1714#19
SOCIETY IN SCOTLAND FOR PROPAGATING CHRISTIAN KNOWLEDGE. *An account of the rise, constitution, and management of the Society.* . . London. R. Tookey, 35p. 8vo. 1714
Note: Second edition enlarged, Edinburgh, 1720.
Locations: L; E; CSmH

1714#20
STANHOPE, George. *The early conversion of islanders, a wise expedient for propagating Christianity. A sermon preached.* . . *19th of Feb. 1713–14.* . . London. J. Downing, 39p. 8vo. 1714
Note: SABIN 90218, 90219, EA 714/137-8. SPG sermon for 1714, with abstract, etc. Another edition in 1714.
Locations: L; DLC, RPJCB, CtY

1714#21
To the honorable the House of Commons. *Reasons (humbly offer'd) against laying a further duty on linnens to be imported in England; and for the exporting linnen directly from Ireland to the English plantations.* London. s.sh. F. [1714]
Note: HANSON 2062.
Locations: MRc;

1714#22
WISE, Robert. *The case of Robert Wise, late of London, tobacco-merchant.* [London]. s.sh. F. 1714
Note: HANSON 2063, ARENTS 478, EA 714/155. Seizure of estates etc.in colonies to satisfy debts. First two paragraphs are identical to those of *The case of the tobacco merchants who are become insolvent*, above, 1714.
Locations: L; N, RPJCB

1715#1
ASHE, St. George. *A sermon preached.* . . *18th February, 1714.* . . London. J. Downing, 76p. 4to. 1715
Note: EA 715/5-7. SPG sermon for 1715, with abstract, etc. Two other editions in 1715.
Locations: L; DLC, RPJCB, NN

1715#2
BANISTER, Thomas. *A letter to the right honourable the Lords Commissioners of Trade and Plantations; or, a short essay on the principle branches of the trade of New-England...* London. 19p. 8vo. 1715
Note: SABIN 22966, HANSON 2147, EA 715/14.
Locations: L; RPJCB, MiU-C

1715#3
BANISTER, Thomas. *Observations on the report of the Committee of Secrecy.* London. J. Roberts, [26]p. 2o. 1715
Note: Also Dublin and Edinburgh, 1715. Effects of peace on Newfoundland, Nova Scotia, etc.
Locations: L; DLC, MH-BA, DFo, CSmH

1715#4
BILTON, Thomas. *Captain Bilton's journal of his unfortunate voyage from Lisbon to Virginia, in the year 1707...* London. A. Bettesworth, E. Curll, 28p. 8vo. 1715
Note: SABIN 5432, EA 715/22.
Locations: RPJCB, MH, ViU, N

1715#5
BOYLE, Robert. *The theological works...* London. W. Taylor, 8vo. 3 vols. 1715
Note: EA 715/29–30. Two issues in 1715. Also *The Works*, 5 vols, 1744, EA 744/35.
Locations: L; O; DLC, MH

1715#6
BOULTON, Richard. *A compleat history of magick, sorcery, and witchcraft...* London. E. Curll, J. Pemberton, W. Taylor, 2 vols. 12mo. 1715
Note: SABIN 15051, EA 715/28. Account of New England witch trials in vol. II.
Locations: L; DLC, RPJCB

1715#7
The case of Charles Lord Baltemore [sic], *a minor, with relation to his government of Maryland.* London. s.sh. F. [1715]
Note: SABIN 10083, EA 715/13.
Locations: O; RPJCB

1715#8
The case of his majesty's colony of Conneticut [sic] *in New-England, with respect to their Charter, which is intended to be taken away by a bill intitled, A Bill for the better regulation of charter and proprietary governments in America, etc.* London. s.sh. F. [1715]
Note: HANSON 2148, EA 715/39.
Locations: O;

1715#9
The case of the merchants trading to New England, and of others residing there, with relation to the bills of exchange drawn for the Canada expedition... London. s.sh. F. [1715?]
Note: To House of Commons for payment of balance due on Canada bills, issued in 1710. Different from HANSON 2244, *The case of the merchants...*, below, 1716.
Locations: RPJCB

1715#10
The case of the province of the Massachusets-Bay in New England, with relation to their charter, and some observations thereon. London. s.sh. F. [1715]
Note: HANSON 2150, EA 715/41.
Locations: O;

1715#11
Charter of Maryland. Dated the 20th June, in 8th of Car. I. 1632. London. 30p. 8vo. [1715]
Locations: RPJCB

1715#12
DEFOE, Daniel. *Some reasons offered by the late ministry in defence of their administration.* London. J. Morphew, 78p. 8vo. 1715
Note: SABIN 86727, EA 715/64. References to America.
Locations: L; NHi, CSmH, NN

1715#13
DISNEY, Daniel. *A compendious history of the rise and progress of the reformation of the church here in England...* London. T. Varnom, J.Osborne, etc., 16, 148p. 8vo. 1715
Note: SABIN 46790. Largely copied from Cotton Mather's *Eleutheria*.
Locations: L; NNUT, MWA, CLU-C

1715#14
EDMUNDSON, William. *A journal of the life, travels, sufferings, and labour of love in the work of the ministry of... William Edmundson, who departed this life... 1712.* London. Assigns of J. Sowle, 327p. 8vo. 1715
Note: SMITH, I, 558, EA 715/67–8. Other editions Dublin, 1715, London, 1774.
Locations: L; DLC, RPJCB, PPL

1715#15
GREAT BRITAIN. PARLIAMENT. HOUSE OF COMMONS. PROCEEDINGS. *A report from the committee of secrecy, appointed by order of the House of Commons to examine several books and papers... relating to the late negotiations of peace and commerce, etc. reported on the ninth of June, 1715...* London. J. Tonson and others, 4, 64, 96pp. F. 1715
Note: SABIN 69729. Material on Newfoundland fisheries. Reprinted Dublin, T. Humes for P. Campbell, 1715: CSmH.
Locations: L;

1715#16
An index to the report of the Secret Committee... In a letter to a friend. London. S. Popping, 26p. F. 1715
Note: HANSON 2140, KRESS 2959, EA 715/83. Includes numerous references to American commerce, especially to Newfoundland fisheries.
Locations: L; MH-BA, NNC

1715#17
MATHER, Samuel. *De Baptismate...* London. J. Clark, 23p. 12mo. [1715]
Note: Cf. HOLMES, MM, 99.
Locations: MBAt, MB

1715#18
NELSON, Robert. *An address to persons of quality and estate...* London. G. James for R. Smith, 267p. 8vo. 1715
Note: KRESS 2966, EA 715/124. Recommends support for and discusses work of SPG.
Locations: L; RPJCB, MB, CtY

1715#19
PITTIS, William. *Reasons for a war with France.* London. A. Moore, 40p. 8vo. 1715
Note: GOLDSMITH'S 5271, EA 715/137-8. Postcript on France and Cape Breton. Another edition in 1715.
Locations: L; Lu; RPJCB, CtY, CSmH

1715#20
Presumptive reasons why the governments of the provinces of South and North Carolina, and the Bahama and Lucaios Islands being proprietary governments... should... be reassumed into the hands of the Crown... offer'd to... the Committee of the House of Commons... London. 2p. F. [1715]
Note: HANSON 2151, EA 715/140.
Locations: Lu; MH

1715#21
THOMPSON, Thomas. *A farewel epistle, by way of exhortation to Friends... On his departure to America...* London. Assigns of J. Sowle, 16p. 8vo. 1715
Note: SMITH II, p. 738.
Locations: L; MH, PSC-Hi

1715#22
A true and exact list of all the malefactors, both men and women, who pleaded to His Majesty's most gracious pardon, at the sessions-house in the Old-Baily, on Saturday the 6th of August, 1715. Also the number of the men and women, who are to be transported to the plantations beyond sea; and the crimes for which each of these criminals were first condemned to die. London printed by J. Read, 6[i.e.5], [1]p. 2o. 1715
Locations: O;

1715#23
Truth, Truth, Truth... London. J. Roberts etc., 23p. 8vo. 1715
Note: SABIN 97268, EA 715/175. Attack on peace and France's retention of colonial possessions.
Locations: L; RPJCB, DFo, ICN

1715#24
WHITING, John. *Persecution expos'd, in some memoirs relating to the sufferings of John Whiting, and many... Quakers...* London. J. Sowle, 245p. 4to. 1715
Note: SABIN 103701, EA 715/184. American references.
Locations: L; DLC, RPJCB, MH

1715#25
WITHALL, Benjamin. *The Case of Benjamin Withall, gent. In his majesty's victualling office...* London. s.sh. F. [1715?]
Note: HANSON 2174, EA 702/206. For money due him as storekeeper at St. John's Newfoundland. The Bodleian provides the 1715 date and has four 'cases' by him.
Locations: O; NHi

1716#1
BASTON, Thomas. *Thoughts on trade, and a publick spirit.* London. For the author, 212p. 8vo. 1716
Note: HANSON 2217, GOLDSMITH'S 5282, KRESS 2981, EA 716/16. Cites the great value to Great Britain of Newfoundland, Greenland fisheries, and Hudson Bay commerce.
Locations: L; CtY, DLC

1716#2
The case of the merchants trading to New-England, and of others residing there, with relation to the bills of exchange drawn for the Canada expedition... London. s.sh. F. [1716]
Note: HANSON 2244, EA 716/32. To House of Commons for balance due on Canada bills, issued in 1710.
Locations: LLI; RPJCB

1716#3
FRANCKE, August Hermann. *Pietas Hallensis: or, an abstract of the marvellous foot-steps of divine providence, attending the management and improvement of the Orphan-House at Glaucha near Hall... Part III. To which is prefix'd, a letter of the author to a... divine in New-England.* London. Printed and sold by J. Downing, [2],xiv,[2],111,[1]p. 12mo... 1716
Note: Another edition in 1716.
Locations: L; NCp; DFo, MdBJ-W, CSmH

1716#4
MARSH, Henry. *A proposal for raising a stock not exceeding forty thousand pounds sterling; by subscriptions for forming a settlement, in a large and convenient river in*

Acadia. And to improve a great space of land on each side the said river. London. Printed for the author, 15,[1]p. 2o. 1716
Note: HANSON 2235, EA 716/84. See also EA 720/171. Another version of this, *A proposal for raising a stock of two millions of pounds sterling;*... was published in 1720.
Locations: L;

1716#5
The objections against paying the remainder of the Canada bills of exchange, answered... London. s.sh. F. [1716]
Locations: MH-BA

1716#6
Secret memoirs of the new treaty of alliance with France. London. J. Roberts,. 36p. 8vo. 1716
Note: EA 716/115–6. Another edition Dublin, 1716. Relinquishment of British right to Cape Breton in exchange for the sole right to Newfoundland.
Locations: L; CSmH, CtY, RPJCB

1716#7
SHERLOCK, Thomas. *A sermon preached... the 17th of February, 1715.* London. J. Downing for J. Pemberton, 54p. 8vo. 1716
Note: EA 716/117–8. SPG sermon for 1716, with abstract, etc. Another edition in 1716.
Locations: L; DLC, RPJCB, CSmH

1716#8
SOCIETY FOR THE PROPAGATION OF THE GOSPEL. *An abstract of the proceedings of the Society for the Propagation of the Gospel... 1715.* London. J. Downing, 38p. 8vo. 1716
Note: EA 716/121.
Locations: L; RPJCB, NN, MH

1717#1
An answer to Reasons (so call'd) against the bill for exporting Irish linen to the British plantations duty-free. London. s.sh. F. [1717]
Note: KRESS SUPP. 2744. ESTC dates [1710?].
Locations: O; MnU

1717#2
CARY, John. *An essay, towards regulating the trade, and employing the poor of this kingdom...* London. Susanna Collins, etc., viii, 162p. 8vo. 1717
Note: EA 717/16. Mentions New England and Newfoundland; discusses emigration and plantations. Second edition in 1719: L; NjP, NN.
Locations: L; NNC

1717#3
The Case of the colony of South-Carolina in America: humbly offered to the consideration of both houses of Parliament. London. s.sh. F. [1717]

Note: HANSON 2297, EA 717/17.
Locations: Lpro; RPJCB

1717#4
CHARMION, John. *AE. M. S. eximij pietate, eruditione, pudentia' viri D. Ebenezrae Pembertoni, apud Bostoniensis Americanos praedicatoris vere evangelici. Epitaphium.* Edinburgh. s.sh. 1/2o. 1717
Note: FOXON C135. Pemberton was a Boston minister who died in 1717. First printed Boston, 1716. Bristol B521.
Locations: E;

1717#5
A Collection of treaties, alliances, and conventions, relating to the security, commerce, and navigation of the British dominions, made since his Majesty's happy accession to the Crown... London. S. Buckley, 146, 2, 62p. 4to. 1717
Note: HANSON 2283.
Locations: L;

1717#6
GREAT BRITAIN. PARLIAMENT. *An act for continuing the liberty of exporting Irish lining [sic] cloth to British plantations in America duty-free...* London; and Dublin. E. Sandys, 12mo. 1717.
Locations: RPJCB, NN (Dublin ed.)

1717#7
GREAT BRITAIN. SOVEREIGN. GEORGE I. *Proclamation. For suppressing pirates in West Indies or adjoining to our plantations [5 September 1717].* London. J. Baskett, s.sh. F. 1717
Note: BRIGHAM 176. CRAWFORD p. 11.
Locations: L;

1717#8
HAYLEY, Thomas. *The liberty of the gospel explained, and recommended. A sermon... 15 February, 1716...* London. J. Downing, 40p. 8vo. 1717
Note: SABIN 31034, EA 717/70–1. SPG sermon for 1717. Another edition in 1717.
Locations: DLC, RPJCB, MiU-C

1717#9
An historical description of Carolina, North, and South... With the advantageous proposals offered by the assembly to such as will settle in that colony. Belfast. J. Blow, 16p. 8vo. 1717
Note: EA 717/76.
Locations: C; ViU, ICRL

1717#10
HUTCHESON, Archibald. *Some considerations relating to the payment of the publick debts, humbly offer'd to the Commons...* London. 23p. 4to. 1717
Note: HANSON 2307, EA 717/139. Discussion of trade.
Locations: L; RPJCB, CtY, InU

1717#11
LEWIS, Thomas. *The scourge in vindication of the Church of England.* London. 368 p,, 12mo. 1717
Note: Cf. SMITH, AQ, 275, EA 717/95. First published as serial Feb.- Nov. 1717, with caption title *The Scourge*. Describes a Presbyterian woman who emigrated to New England to seek religious freedom.
Locations: L; CtY, DLC, RPJCB

1717#12
MONTGOMERY, Sir Robert. *A brief account of the situation and advantages of the new-intended settlement in. . . Azilia; a late erected British province on the South of Carolina.* London. [1717]
Note: EA 717/111.
Locations: RPJCB

1717#13
MONTGOMERY, Sir Robert. *A discourse concerning the design'd establishment of a new colony to the south of Carolina, in the most delightful country in the universe.* London. 30p. 8vo. 1717
Note: SABIN 51194, HANSON 2298, EA 717/112-3. Some copies include 'An appendix to a discourse lately published. . . '. Another edition in 1717.
Locations: L; C; DLC, RPJCB, MiU-C

1717#14
MONTGOMERY, Sir Robert. *Proposal for raising a stock, and settling a new colony in Azilia. . .* London. [1717]
Note: EA 717/114.
Locations: RPJCB

1717#15
MULFORD, Samuel. *A memorial of several aggrievances and oppressions of his majesty's subjects in the colony of New-York. . .* London. 4p. F. 1717
Note: HANSON 2296, EA 717/116. Possibly a reprint of his *Information. . . defence of his whale fishery*, New York, 1716 (EVANS 1841).
Locations: O; DLC, MH, NHi

1717#16
Reasons humbly offer'd. . . against the bill now depending in the. . . Commons, for exporting Irish linnens, to the British plantations in America. London. s.sh. F. [1717]
Note: HANSON 2292.
Locations: O; MH-BA

1717#17
SUTHERLAND, William. *Britain's glory: or, shipbuilding unvail'd.* London. T. Norris and E. Tracy, 2 vols. F. 1717

Note: EA 717/141. Another edition, 1726, EA 726/197. Describes preparing a ship for the West Indies; types of trees and shipbuilding in New England.
Locations: L; DFo, ICJ

1717#18
TIPTON, William. *The case of William Tipton. . .* London. [2]p. F. [1717]
Note: SABIN 95860, EA 717/143. Charges army officers in America with corrupt practices.
Locations: L; MH

1718#1
BISSE, Philip. *A sermon. . . on Friday the 21st February, 1717. . .* London. J. Downing, 44p. 8vo. 1718
Note: SABIN 5633, EA 718/14–15. Another edition in 1718. SPG sermon for 1718, with abstract, etc.
Locations: L; DLC, RPJCB, NN

1718#2
The case of the officers who served in America, at the reduction of Anapolis Royal, and on several other commands. London. s.sh. F. 1718
Note: Docket title 'The case of the British officers who were reduced to half-pay in America near ten months before they received the orders for their disbandment'.
Locations: L;

1718#3
The Compleat Country Dancing-Master. . . London. H. Meere for J. Walsh, 2p. 364p. 12mo 1718
Note: Contains 364 dances, including 'America', 'Indian Queen', etc. *The second book of the compleat country dancing master* was published in 1719. (L; MH, NjP). Another edition in 1735.
Locations: L; (Music); CSmH

1718#4
E., N. *The females advocate: or, an essay to prove that the sisters in every church of Christ, have a right to church-government as well as the brethren.* London. S. Popping, 24p. 4to. 1718
Note: Cites Cotton Mather on New England churches.
Locations: L;

1718#5
FOX, John. *The publick spirit; a poem. . .* London. H. Meere, 24p. 8vo. 1718
Note: FOXON F222, EA 718/60. A panegyric on Sir Francis Nicholson; references to William and Mary College.
Locations: L; MH, ViW

1718#6
FOX, John. *The wanderer. With all the motto's in Latin and English: to which is added The publick spirit, an heroick*

poem. By Mr. Fox. London. Printed by H. Meere, for the author, [8], 183, [9], 37, [5], 24p., 8vo. 1718
Note: SABIN 51126, FOXON F221, EA 718/59. Fox was a Virginian. The work was dedicated to William Byrd II. See Murdock, 'William Byrd and the Virginian author of The Wanderers', *Harvard Studies and Notes in Literature and Philology*, Vol 17, (1935), pps. 129–39.
Locations: L; C; CLU-C, RPJCB, MH, NN

1718#7
GREAT BRITAIN. ARMY. REGULATIONS. *Rules and articles for the better government of his majesty's horse and footguards. . . in Great Britain and Ireland, and dominions beyond the seas. . .* London. J. Baskett, 48p. 8vo. 1718
Note: NUC and L; list editions 1722, 1735, 1737, 1742, 1745, 1746, 1749, 1752, 1753, 1759.
Locations: L; CLL

1718#8
G., J. *Geography epitomiz'd: or, the London gazetteer. Being a geographical and historical treatise of Europe, Asia, Africa and America. . . To which are added, an introduction to geography.* London. Charles Rivington and others, 12, 239, 25p. 12mo. 1718
Locations: L; CLU-C

1718#9
GREAT BRITAIN. PRIVY COUNCIL. *At the Court at St. James, the second day of February, 1717. . . Upon reading this day a report from the. . . Committee for hearing of appeals from the Plantations. . .* London. J. Baskett, assigns of T. Newcomb and H. Hills, 3p. F. 1718
Note: SABIN 57494, 99252. Refers to petition of P. Sonmans and J. Ormstone concerning land in New Jersey.
Locations: NN, NHi, P

1718#10
GREAT BRITAIN. SOVEREIGN. GEORGE I. *Proclamation. For suppressing pirates in West Indies or adjoining to our plantations [21 December 1718].* London. J. Baskett, s.sh. F. 1718
Note: BRIGHAM 178, CRAWFORD p. 13.
Locations: Lpro;

1718#11 •
HOLME, Benjamin. *An epistle from Benjamin Holme, being a salutation to friends in Great Britain and Ireland. . .* London. J. Sowle, 16p. 8vo. 1718
Note: SABIN 32574, SMITH, I, 965, EA 718/84. 'Written from the Bayside in Maryland, the 14th of the 4th month, 1717'.
Locations: L; C; MH, PHC, ViU

1718#12
HUTCHINSON, Francis. *An historical essay concerning witchcraft. . . And also two sermons. . .* London. R. Knaplock, etc., 270p. 8vo. 1718
Note: SABIN 34063, EA 718/89. Second edition with considerable additions, 1720.
Locations: L; DLC, RPJCB, MiU-C

1718#13
KEIMER, Samuel. *A brand pluck'd from the burning. . .* London. W. Boreham, 124p. 12mo. 1718
Note: SMITH, II, 217, EA 718/95. Keimer became a Philadelphia printer. He refers to his sister as having gone to proselytise in Pennsylvania.
Locations: L; DLC, MiU-C

1718#14
LAUDER, William. *Memorial or state of the process at the instance of William Lauder of Wine-Park. . .* London. 24p. 4to. [c.1718]
Note: EA 718/101. Process against Matthew Crawfurd, John Weir, George Forward, and Andrew Gardener of Edinburgh and Glasgow for trepanning Lauder's son, James, to Boston in 1716.
Locations: RPJCB

1718#15
Reasons against making barr-iron in America. London. [4]p. 2o. [1718?]
Note: Cf. EA 720/196. Includes 'Reasons for making pigg-iron in America'.
Locations: L;

1718#16
Reasons hnmbly [sic] offered for the encouragement of making iron and copper, in His Majesty's plantations of America. London. s.sh. F. [1717 or 1718?]
Note: HANSON 2394, EA 718/149. ESTC dates [1717?].
Locations: L; MH-BA

1718#17
Reasons humbly offer'd against encouraging the making of iron in America. London. s.sh. F. [1717 or 1718]
Note: HANSON 2396, KRESS SUPP. 2761, EA 718/151. ESTC dates to 1717.
Locations: L; RPJCB

1718#18
Reasons humbly offered against the encouragement of making iron in his majesty's plantations. London. s.sh. F. [1717 or 1718]
Note: HANSON 2397, KRESS SUPP. 2763, EA 718/150. Almost identical with *Reasons humbly offered against encouraging the making. . .* ', above, 1718. ESTC dates to 1717.
Locations: L;

1718

1718#19
Reasons humbly offered for the encouragement of making iron in his majesty's plantations of America. London. s.sh. F. [1717 or 1718?]
Note: HANSON 2395, KRESS SUPP. 2765, EA 718/152.
Locations: O;

1718#20
SOCIETY FOR THE PROPAGATION OF THE GOSPEL. *A third letter from a member of the Society.* London. 4p. 8vo. [1718].
Note: EA 718/161.
Locations: L; RPJCB

1718#21
A true and exact list, of all the criminals in Newgate, who were transported this day being Thursday the 28th of August. 1718. London. printed by A. Hinde, 1 sheet; 1/2o. 1718
Locations: O;

1718#22
WILKINSON, William. *The baptism of the holy spirit, without elementary water, demonstratively proved to be the true baptism of Christ...* London. J. Sowle, 5p. 8vo. 1718
Note: SMITH, II, 937, EA 718/177. Wilkinson lived in Rhode Island.
Locations: L; CtY, RPJCB, NN

1718#23
WOOD, William. *A survey of trade. In four parts... Together with considerations on our money and bullion...* London. W. Wilkins for W. Hinchcliffe, 373p. 8vo. 1718
Note: SABIN 105078, HANSON 2349, EA 718/179. Other editions 1719, 1720.
Locations: L; Lu; RPJCB, CtY, MiU-C

1718#24
The Worcestershire garland; composed of three excellent new songs. [London]. 8p. 12mo. [1718?].
Note: 'The downfall of piracy' refers to Black Beard Teach at Carolina, the actions of the Virginia governor, etc. Teach was executed in 1718.
Locations: L;

1719#1
CHANDLER, Edward. *A sermon preached... 20th February, 1718...* London. J. Downing, 55p. 4to. 1719
Note: EA 719/23–4. Another edition in 1719. SPG sermon for 1719, with abstract, etc.
Locations: L; DLC, RPJCB, CtY

1719#2
DEFOE, Daniel. *The king of pirates... an account of the famous enterprises of Captain Avery, the mock king of Madagasgar...* London. A. Bettesworth, etc. 93p. 8vo. 1719
Note: SABIN 2487, EA 719/40. A second edition in 1720, EA 720/60.
Locations: L; CSmH

1719#3
GREAT BRITAIN. PARLIAMENT. *An act for continuing an act made in the twelfth year of... Queen Anne... An act for incouraging the tobacco trade.* London. J. Baskett 1719.
Locations: DLC, N

1719#4
HILL, Hannah. *A legacy for children, being some of the last expressions and dying sayings of Hannah Hill, junr., of... Philadelphia... aged eleven years and near three months.* Dublin, S. Fairbrother, 29p. 8vo. 1719
Note: SABIN 31826, EA 719/79. First published Philadelphia, [c.1714] (EVANS 1679).
Locations: PHi, PP

1719#5
A Key to the Church-catechism... recommended as useful for schools and families... London. The author, sold by S. Keble, etc., viii, 314p. 8vo. 1719
Note: SABIN 37670, EA 719/89. Dedicated by 'Philo-Delphus' to Mr. William Trent, merchant in Philadelphia. Designed for the use of our 'poor countrymen dispersed up and down in your vast and spacious Regions'.
Locations: RPJCB, PPL

1719#6
NEW YORK ASSEMBLY. *Acts of Assembly, passed in the province of New-York, from 1691, to 1718.* London. J. Baskett, etc. 292p. 2o. 1719
Note: EA 719/116. First published New York, 1718 (EVANS 2065) as *The laws of his majesties colony of New York.*
Locations: L; DLC, RPJCB, CtY

1719#7
PARKER, George. *The West-India almanack for the year 1719.* London. [60]p. 12mo. 1719
Note: EA 719/155. Includes North American information.
Locations: L;

1719#8
Reasons against a general prohibition of the iron manufacture in his Majesty's plantations. London. s.sh. F. 1719
Note: HANSON 2522, EA 719/128.
Locations: O;

1719#9
Reasons for encourageing the making of iron in our plantations, and the objections answer'd. London. s.sh. F. [1719?]
Note: HANSON 2523, EA 719/129.
Locations: O;

1719#10
The Tryals of Major Stede Bonnet, and other pirates... at the Admiralty Sessions held at Charles-Town... the 28th of October, 1718... London. B. Cowse, vi, 50p, F. 1719
Note: EA 719/12.
Locations: L;

1720#1
Advertisement. There is lately brought forth to this place from America, a savage: being a canibal-Indian... London. J. Bliss, s.sh. 8vo. [1720?]
Locations: L;

1720#2
America. Translated from the French. London. Printed for the translator, 2 vols. 8vo. 1720
Note: SABIN 1007 states mainly relates to Indians and is scarce and was privately printed. Probably a ghost.
Locations: NO COPY LOCATED.

1720#3
B., A. *A Letter to a member of Parliament, for incouraging offices of insurance for ships... particularly for incouraging the British fishery in America, more especially the cod fishing of Nova Scotia.* London. s.sh. F. [1720]
Note: HANSON 2834, EA 720/148.
Locations: O; MB

1720#4
BARNWELL, John. *An account of the foundation, and establishment of a design now on foot, for a settlement on the Golden Islands, to the south of Port Royal in Carolina...* London. 8p. 4to. 1720
Note: SABIN 3572, HANSON 2733, EA 720/11. Or by Sir Robert Montgomery.
Locations: O; RPJCB, MH

1720#5
BLACKAMORE, Arthur. *The perfidious brethren, or, the religious triumvirate: displayed in three ecclesiastic novels...* London. T. Bickerton, etc., 104p. 8vo. 1720
Note: See R. B. Davis, 'Arthur Blackamore: The Virginia Colony and the early English novel', *Virginia Magazine of History and Biography*, Vol 75, 1967, pps. 22–34.
Locations: L; ViU, DLC, CtY

1720#6
BRADBURY, Thomas. *The necessity of contending for revealed religion... to which is prefix'd, a letter from the Reverend Cotton Mather...* London. H. Woodfall, 88p. 8vo. [1720]
Note: SABIN 7208. See HOLMES CM 397, EA 720/30. Reprinted Boston, 1740 (EVANS 4477).
Locations: L; DLC, RPJCB

1720#7
BRADFORD, Samuel. *A sermon preached... 19th February, 1719...* London. J. Wyat, 72p. 8vo. 1720
Note: SABIN 7254, EA 720/31-2. Another edition in 1720. SPG sermon for 1720, with abstract, etc.
Locations: L; DLC, RPJCB, MH

1720#8
The Bubbler's mirrour: or England's *folley*. London. s.sh. 1/2o. 1720
Note: KRESS 3160. Contains 'bubble' for Pennsylvania Company.
Locations: L; MH, NN

1720#9
CHETWOOD, William Rufus. *The voyages, dangerous adventures and imminent escapes of Captain Richard Falconer: containing the laws, customs and manners of the Indians of America... Intermixed with the voyages and adventures of Thomas Randal... His being taken by the Indians of Virginia, etc.* London. W. Chetwood, 387p. 8vo. 1720
Note: SABIN 23723, EA 720/47. Fictitious voyage. Second corrected edition, 1724. Also Dublin, 1752.
Locations: L; D; E; DLC, RPJCB, MiU-C

1720#10
DEFOE, Daniel. *The chimera: or, the French way of paying national debts... the Mississippi stock.* London. T. Warner, 68p. 8vo. 1720
Note: SABIN 12811, EA 720/59.
Locations: L; DLC, RPJCB, MiU-C

1720#11
FISHER, Sally. *Britain's golden mines discover'd: or the fishery trade considered...* London. J. Morphew, 80p. 8vo. 1720
Note: HANSON 2603, EA 720/85. Newfoundland and other fisheries.
Locations: L; Lu; MH, CtY, NNC

1720#12
GENTLEMAN OF AMERICA [SMITH, James?]. *Some considerations on the consequences of the French settling colonies on the Mississippi, with respect to the trade and safety of the English plantations in America and the West Indies...* London. J. Roberts, 60p. 8vo. 1720
Note: HANSON 2717, EA 720/213.
Locations: L; E; ViU, MiU-C

1720#13
GRATTON, John. *A journal of the life of that ancient servant of Christ, John Gratton...* London. J. Sowle, 432p. 8vo. 1720
Note: SABIN 28341, EA 720/110. Includes epistle to friend in Pennsylvania.
Locations: L; DLC, CtY, MH

1720#14
GREAT BRITAIN. PARLIAMENT. *Act for further preventing robbery, burglary... and for the more effectual transportation of felons.* London. J. Baskett and others. 1720
Locations: MiU-C

1720#15
GREAT BRITAIN. PARLIAMENT. HOUSE OF COMMONS. *A bill for the more easy and effectual conviction of persons returning from transportation [to any part of America].* London. 3p. F. [1720?]
Note: EA 72-/2.
Locations: ViU, OU, PSt

1720#16
HENNEPIN, Louis. *A discovery of a large, rich, and plentiful country, in the North America...* London. W. Boreham, 22p. 8vo. [1720]
Note: HANSON 2716, EA 720/119. Abridgement of Hennepin's *A New Discovery...*, above, 1698.
Locations: L; O; DLC, RPJCB, MiU-C

1720#17
LAW, John. *A full and impartial account of the Company of Mississippi, otherwise called the French East-India Company, projected and settled by Mr. Law...* London. R. Francklin, etc., 71p. 8vo. 1720
Note: SABIN 26144, EA 720/94. With account of the Mississippi.
Locations: L; DLC, RPJCB, MiU-C

1720#18
A letter to a Member of Parliament, concerning The naval-store-bill, brought in last session. With observations on the plantation-trade, and methods proposed for rendring it more beneficial... London. 43p. 8vo. 1720
Note: SABIN 40398, HANSON 2706, EA 720/147. Another edition in 1721.
Locations: L; Lu; DLC, RPJCB, CSmH

1720#19
LOCKE, John. *A collection of several pieces never before printed or not extant in his works.* London. J. Bettenham for R. Francklin, 362p. 8vo. 1720
Note: SABIN 41726, EA 720/153. Includes Fundamental Constitutions of Carolina. Another edition in 1739, EA 739/176.
Locations: L; DLC, RPJCB, MB

1720#20
MACKWORTH, Sir Humphrey. *Sir H. Mackworth's proposal in miniature, as it has been put in practice in New-York, in America.* London. W. Boreham, 18p. 8vo. 1720
Note: SABIN 43481, 43482, HANSON 2746, EA 720/163.
Locations: L; Lu; RPJCB, NN, MiU-C

1720#21
Miscellanea Aurea; or the Golden *Medley...* London. A. Bettesworth and J. Pemberton, 214p. 8vo. 1720
Note: EA 720/175. Supposedly set in Carolina mountains. Ascribed to Thomas Killigrew. By Charles Gildon?
Locations: L; DLC, CSmH, NjP

1720#22
MONTGOMERY, Sir Robert. *A description of the Golden islands, with an account of the undertaking now on foot for making a settlement there...* London. J. Morphew, 45p. 8vo. 1720
Note: SABIN 19719, HANSON 2734, EA 720/74.
Locations: L; DLC, MH, RPJCB

1720#23
NEAL, Daniel. *The history of New-England containing an impartial account of the civil and ecclesiastical affairs of the country to... 1700. To which is added the present state of New-England...* London. J. Clark, etc. 2 vols. 8vo. 1720
Note: SABIN 52140, HANSON 2719, EA 720/178. Other editions in 1747, 1748.
Locations: L; DLC, RPJCB, MiU-C

1720#24
PARMYTER, Paroculus. *Observations and reflections on the present practice, errors and mismanagement of the Governors and their Naval Officers, and the Clerks of his Majesty's Navy-Office in some of the American Plantations.* [London]. 42p. 8vo. 1720
Note: The author, described as of Lincoln's Inn, served in New York under Bellomont. CSmH 86487 seems to be an unique copy.
Locations: CSmH

1720#25
PENN, William. *The case of William Penn, Esq; Proprietary-Governor of Pensilvania and of Joshua Gee, Henry Gouldney, Silvanus Grove, John Woods, and others, mortgagees under the said William Penn.* London. 2p. F. [London, 1720?]. 1720
Note: EA 720/181. Heard 16 August 1715? HANSON 2731 is edition with same title dated to 1720, for a bill for the Crown to buy the colony (L;).
Locations: L; Lpro; MH

1720#26
The present state of Mr. Wood's partnership. London. s.sh. F. [1720]
Note: HANSON 2595. Mining in New England.
Locations: L;

1720#27
The Raree show ballad or the English Missisippi...
London. s.sh. F. [1720?]
Note: FOXON R127 lists a variant at E; Nineteen stanzas.
Locations: CSmH

1720#28
Reasons for encouraging the importation of iron from our plantations... London. [4]p. F. [1720?].
Note: SABIN 68264, EA 720/193.
Locations: RPJCB; NNC

1720#29
Reasons for importing naval stores from our own plantations, and the employing of our people there. London. s.sh. 1/2o. [1720]
Note: HANSON 2707, EA 720/194.
Locations: L; E; RPJCB, CSmH

1720#30
Reasons for making of bar, as well as pig or sow-iron in His Majesty's plantations. London. s.sh. F. [1720?]
Note: HANSON 2720, EA 720/195. ESTC dates [1718].
Locations: L; RPJCB

1720#31
Reasons for making pigg-iron, and against making barr-iron in America. London. 3p. F. [1720]
Note: HANSON 2721, EA 720/196.
Locations: L; RPJCB

1720#32
Reasons humbly offer'd by the merchants trading in pitch and tar, from His Majesty's plantations. London. 1 sheet 1/2o. 1720
Locations: C-S;

1720#33
Reasons humbly offered, for not doubling the subsidy on tobacco from Virginia and Maryland... London. 2p. F. [1720]
Note: SABIN 68282, EA 720/197.
Locations: CSmH, MH-BA

1720#34
Reasons most humbly offered to the Honourable the House of Commons, for carrying on an American fishery, upon the coast of New England and North Carolina, for whale, cod, macrell, and herring. London. s.sh. F. [1720]
Note: HANSON 2612.
Locations: L; MB

1720#35
SMITH, Alexander. *The third volume of the Compleat History of the lives and robberies of the most notorious high-way men...* London. S. Briscoe, 362p. 12mo. 1720
Note: EA 719/140, 720/212. First and second volumes seem to have no Americana. This volume has account of Thomas Wynne who goes to Virginia and returns a prosperous planter, and of Captain Kidd. Later editions under variant titles.
Locations: L; ICN, DFo, CSmH

1720#36
State of the Constitution of the colonies. London. 4p. F. [1720?]
Note: SABIN 90609. Deals with extension of English law to plantations.
Locations: NNC

1720#37
A true copy of eight pages out of the History of the present State of Virginia... containing an account of the actions of Francis Nicholson... London. 16p. 8vo. [1720?]
Note: SABIN 97111, EA 720/20. Caption title: 'For the information of such persons who are anxious to know his actions in South Carolina.'
Locations: CtY

1720#38
A true state of the case between the inhabitants of South Carolina, and the Lords Proprietors of that province; containing an account of the grievances under which they labour. London. 4p. F. [1720]
Note: HANSON 2732, EA 720/227.
Locations: Lpro; DLC

1720#39
WALKER, Hovenden. *A journal: or full account of the late expedition to Canada. With an appendix...* London. D. Browne, etc., 304p. 8vo. 1720
Note: SABIN 101050-1, EA 720/236-7. Another edition, *A full account of the late expedition...*, G. Strahan, 1720 at CaOTY and CaQMBN.
Locations: L; C; O; DLC, RPJCB, MiU-C

1721#1
An abstract of the scheme of government so far as it relates to the grantees in trust, for settling the land lying between Nova-Scotia and the province of Maine... London. 4p. F. [1721]
Note: EA 721/1.
Locations: RPJCB, MB, MiU-C

1721#2
The British merchant. London. J. Darby, 3 vols. 8vo. 1721

1721

Note: HANSON 1851 note, EA 721/28. Also 1743, 1748, EA 743/36, 748/23.
Locations: L; CtY, DLC, MH-BA

1721#3
BYRD, William II? *A discourse concerning the plague, with some preservatives against it. By a lover of mankind.* London. J. Roberts, 40p. 8vo. 1721
Note: EA 721/59. Attributed to William Byrd II.
Locations: L; DNLM, MB

1721#4
DUMMER, Jeremiah. *A defence of the New-England charters.* London. W. Wilkins, 80p. 8vo. 1721
Note: SABIN 21197, HANSON 2929, EA 721/63. Reprinted Boston, 1721, 1745.
Locations: L; RPJCB

1721#5
Elegy on the mournful banishment, of James Campbell of Burnbank, to the West Indies. [Edinburgh?] 1p. F. 1721
Note: FOXON E76–7. The 'only son of Mongo Cleeks/Is to be banifht in few weeks, o're to Virginia.' 19 verses. James Campbell of Burnbank and George Fachney were two notorious Edinburgh criminals. Also published as *The life and conversation of James Campbell*, Edinburgh, 1721, FOXON E78, EA 721/165.
Locations: L; E;

1721#6
GRAY, —. *The memoirs, life, and character of the great Mr Law. . . with an accurate. . . account of the establishment of the Misissippi [sic] Company in France. . . Written by a Scots gentleman.* London. S. Briscoe, 41p. 8vo. 1721
Note: SABIN 39311, EA 721/79–80, 726/96. A second edition in 1721; another edition, 1726.
Locations: L; DLC, IU, RPJCB

1721#7
GREAT BRITAIN. PARLIAMENT. HOUSE OF COMMONS. *The humble address of the House of Commons to the King. . .* London. 2p. F. 1721
Note: On the encouragement of naval stores and discouragement of manufactures.
Locations: RPJCB

1721#8
GREAT BRITAIN. SOVEREIGN. GEORGE I. *A Proclamation. At the Court at Kensington, the second day of October, 1721. . .* London. 4p. 2o. [1721]
Note: HANSON 2926. Order in Council to the Commissioners for Trade and Plantations to require colonial governors in America to observe the laws for regulating trade and navigation in respect of illegal trading with Madagascar.
Locations: L; Lpro;

1721#9
The hat-makers case. London. s.sh. F. [1721]
Note: HANSON 2904. On imported beaver skins.
Locations: Lpro;

1721#10
Letter to Mr. Law, **upon** *his arrival in Great Britain.* London. 23p. 8vo. 1721
Note: SABIN 39310, EA 721/103–8. Five other issues in 1721.
Locations: L; DLC, PU

1721#11
MATHER, Cotton. *The Christian philosopher: A collection of the best discoveries in nature, with religious improvements.* London. E. Matthews, 304p. 8vo. 1721
Note: SABIN 46253, EA 721/122. HOLMES, CM, 52.
Locations: L; DLC, RPJCB, MiU-C

1721#12
MATHER, Cotton. *Three letters from New-England, relating to the controversy of the present time.* London. E. Matthews, 30p. 8vo. 1721
Note: HOLMES, CM, 397, EA 721/123. Third letter by Increase Mather. The first letter published previously in London in T. Bradbury's *The necessity of contending. . .* , (1720). See HOLMES, IM, 200.
Locations: L; MH, ICN, MiU-C

1721#13
MATHER, Increase. *Sermons wherein those eight characters. . . called the beatitudes, are opened. . .* Dublin. Boston printed and Dublin reprinted for Henry Shaw, 211p. 8vo. 1721
Note: SABIN 46740, Holmes IM 119B, EA 721/124. First published Boston, 1718 (EVANS 1938). Some New England references.
Locations: L; CSmH, RPJCB

1721#14
A memorial, humbly shewing the past and present state of the land lying waste and un-inhabited between Nova-Scotia, and the Province of Main in New England in America. London. 2p. F. [1721].
Note: SABIN 47634, EA 721/127.
Locations: MB, PPL

1721#15
OWEN, Charles. *The danger of the church and kingdom from foreigners considered. . .* London. T. Bickerton, 38p 8vo. 1721
Note: EA 721/142–3, 744/164. Another edition in 1721. Other editions in 1722, 1744, 1751. Praises trade as wealth, mentioning colonies.
Locations: L; MB, MH-BA, CSmH

1721#16
PENNECUIK, Alexander. *Burnbank's farewel to Edinburgh, at his departure for the Indies, with his last will and testament.* Edinburgh. 1p. 1/2o. 1721
Note: FOXON P151. Anonymous. By Alexander Pennecuik. Verse 'Waes me, auld Reikie, we man part'. See *Elegy*, above, 1721.
Locations: E; CSmH

1721#17
PINFOLD, Charles. *Doctor Pinfold's state of the case of the petitioner's for settling his majesties waste land, lying between Nova-Scotia, and the province of Maine.* . . London. 3p. F. 1721.
Note: EA 721/153.
Locations: MB

1721#18
The sorrowful lamentation, of James Campbell of Burnbank. Who is banished to the West Indians, for carrying on that horrid murder, of Margaret Hall, with his last farewell to Scotland. Edinburgh. 1p. sheet 1/2o. 1721
Note: FOXON S606. Verse. 'They call me Bournbank, a bloody murthering cheet'. See *Elegy*, above, 1721.
Locations: E;

1721#19
SPURRIER, Caleb. *Copy of a letter from Mr. Caleb Spurrier to his correspondent in Cornwall.* [London]. 2p. F. [1721?]
Note: SABIN 89929. Concerns silver mines in New England.
Locations: MH

1721#20
A stiptick for a bleeding nation. London. J. Roberts, 27p. 8vo. 1721
Note: HANSON 3021, KRESS 3440, EA 721/188. Discussion of importation of iron, hemp, pitch, and tar from plantations.
Locations: Lu; CtY, InU, RPJCB

1721#21
TROTT, Nicholas. *The laws of the British plantations in America, relating to the church and clergy, religion and learning. Collected in one volume.* London. B. Cowse, 435p. 2o. 1721
Note: EA 721/195. Another edition in 1725.
Locations: L; Oc; DLC, RPJCB, NNC

1721#22
TROTT, Nicholas. *Mafteah leshon hakodesh clavis linguae sanctae.* . . Oxford. Sold by B. Cowse, London, 60p. 2o. 1721
Note: Lexicon of psalms.
Locations: L; CtY, MB, NcD

1721#23
WADDINGTON, Edward. *A sermon preached.* . . *Friday the 17th of February, 1720.* . . London. J. Downing, 72p. 4to. 1721
Note: SABIN 100900, EA 721/204. SPG sermon for 1721, with abstract, etc.
Locations: L; DLC, RPJCB, MiU-C

1721#24
WILKINSON, William. *An answer to Joseph Jenk's reply to William Wilkinson's treatise, entituled, the baptism of the holy spirit.* . . London. Associates of J. Sowle, 5p. 8vo. 1721
Note: SMITH, II, 938, EA 721/205. Wilkinson lived in Rhode Island.
Locations: CtY, RPJCB, MH

1722#1
BEVERLEY, Robert. *An abridgement of the publick laws of Virginia, in force and use, June 10, 1720.* . . London. F. Fayram, etc., 184p. 4to. 1722
Note: EA 722/183, Two other issues in 1728, EA 728/199–200.
Locations: ViW, CSmH

1722#2
BLAIR, James. *Our saviour's divine sermon on the mount. . . explained.* . . London. J. Brotherton, 5 vols. 8vo. [1722–3]
Note: SABIN 5745, EA 722/19. A second edition in 1740. Blair was Commissary in Virginia.
Locations: DLC, CtY

1722#3
BOULTER, Hugh. *A sermon preached.* . . *16th of February, 1721.* . . London. J. Downing, 61p. 4to. 1722
Note: SABIN 6887, EA 722/24. SPG sermon for 1722, with abstract, etc.
Locations: L; DLC, RPJCB, MH

1722#4
BOULTON, Richard. *The possibility and reality of magick, sorcery and witchcraft. . . In answer to Dr. Hutchinson's Historical essay.* . . London. J. Roberts, 184p. 12mo. 1722
Note: EA 722/25. Chapter four deals with New England witchcraft.
Locations: L; CtY, MH, MB

1722#5
BRADY, Samuel. *Some remarks upon Dr. Wagstaffe's letter, and Mr. Massey's sermon against inoculating the small-pox.* . . London. J. Clark, 40p. 8vo. 1722
Note: EA 722/27. Cites New England.
Locations: L; DLC, RPJCB, MH

1722#6
Burnbank and George Fachney's last shift or, a strange plot at a dead lift. Edinburgh. 1 sheet 1/2o. 1722
Note: FOXON B578. Sometimes attributed to Alexander Pennecuik. Verse 'Whileom I sung two memorable men'. See *Elegy*, above, 1721.
Locations: E;

1722#7
COCK, Christopher. *Catalogue of divers rich and valuable effects, being a collection of Elihu Yale. Part 4... Will be sold by auction on Thursday the 15th of... November...* London. 32p. 8vo. [1722].
Locations: L;

1722#8
A collection of pamphlets: containing the way and manner of inoculating the small-pox both in Britain and New-England. To which is added, a letter by Dr. D. Cumyng. Dublin Printed by George Grierson, [2], 2;45, [1]; 15,[3]p. 8vo. 1722
Note: Works by Colman and Nettleton.
Locations: C; Dt; MH

1722#9
COLMAN, Benjamin. *A narrative of the method and success of inoculating the small pox in New England... With a reply to the objections... in letter from a minister at Boston... a historical introduction by Daniel Neal...* London. E. Matthews and R. Ford, 48p. 8vo. 1722
Note: SABIN 14502, EA 722/43–4. Also Dublin, 1722. Cf. EVANS 2211: *Some observations on the new method...*, (Boston, 1721).
Locations: L; DLC, RPJCB, MH

1722#10
COXE, Daniel. *A description of the English province of Carolana, by the Spaniards call'd Florida, and by the French, La Louisiane...* London. B. Cowse, 122p. 8vo. 1722
Note: SABIN 17279, HANSON 3149, EA 722/56. Other editions 1726, 1727 and 1741, EA 726/52, 727/46, 741/48.
Locations: L; DLC, RPJCB

1722#11
CRAWFORD, J. *The case of inoculating the small-pox consider'd, and its advantages asserted; in a review of Dr. Wagstaffe's letter...* London. T. Warner, 40p. 8vo. 1722
Note: EA 722/57. Postcript 'As to the accounts from New England...'.
Locations: RPJCB, MH, NPV

1722#12
DEFOE, Daniel. *The fortunes and misfortunes of the famous Moll Flanders...* London. W. Chetwood and T. Edling, xiii, 424p. 8vo. 1722
Note: EA 722/64–7. Second and third editions in 1722. Other editions 1744, etc. Transported to Virginia.
Locations: L; MH, CLU-C, PU

1722#13
DOMAT, Jean. *The civil law in its natural order... translated... by William Strahan...* London. J. Bettenham for E. Bell, J. Darby and others, 2 vols. F. 1722
Note: EA 722/77. Two other editions in 1737, EA 737/73–4.
Locations: L; DLC, MiU-C

1722#14
DOUGLASS, William. *Inoculation of the small pox as practiced in Boston.* [London?]. 20p. 12mo. 1722
Note: EA 722/78. Although EA lists as London, ESTC lists as Boston and the British Library copy is Boston printed. GUERRA 764.
Locations: L;

1722#15
GREAT BRITAIN. PARLIAMENT. *Act for encouragement of silk manufacture... for reducing the duties on beaver skins... imported; and for all furs products of the British plantations, into this kingdom only.* London. J. Baskett and others, s.sh. F. 1722.
Locations: MB, MiU-C

1722#16
GREAT BRITAIN. SOVEREIGN. GEORGE I. *Proclamation. Requiring passes formerly granted for ships trading in way of Algerine cruizers to be returned for reissue [19 July 1722].* London. J. Baskett, etc. s.sh. F. 1722
Note: BRIGHAM 180, CRAWFORD p. 22.
Locations: Lpro;

1722#17
HOLME, Benjamin. *An epistle to Friends and tender-minded people in America...* London. Assigns of J. Sowle, 16p. 8vo. 1722
Note: SABIN 32575, SMITH, I, 965, EA 722/96.
Locations: L; RPJCB, NN, PHi

1722#18
LONDON ASSURANCE, CORPORATION OF. *By the Corporation of London Assurance... Proposals for assuring... from loss and damage by fire, in... England... and all other parts of his majesty's dominions beyond the seas.* London. s.sh. F. 1722
Note: HANSON 3183. The Corporation of London Assurance was chartered in 1721. Another issue 1724: Lg; NjP.
Locations: MRc;

1722#19
MAITLAND, Charles. *Mr. Maitland's account of inoculating the small pox vindicated, from Dr. Wagstaffe's misrepresentations...* London. J. Peele, 64p. 8vo. 1722
Note: HOLMES, CM, I, 208, EA 722/118–9. Includes letter from Cotton Mather, which is text of his MS. 'Curiosa variolum'. Another issue in 1722.
Locations: L; RPJCB, MiU-C, NN

1722#20
MASSEY, Isaac. *A short and plain account of inoculation. With some remarks on the main arguments... by Mr. Maitland and others...* London. W. Meadows, 22p. 8vo. 1722
Note: EA 723/99. Also 1723 (RPJCB) with postcript about Boston.
Locations: L; DLC, MH, CtY-M

1722#21
MATHER, Cotton? *An account of the method and success of inoculating for the small-pox in Boston in New-England. In a letter from a gentleman there, to his friend in London.* London. J. Peele, 27p. 8vo. 1722
Note: HOLMES, CM, 3, Cf. SABIN 46213, EA 722/1. Published anonymously. Sometimes attributed to William Tumain.
Locations: L; DLC, RPJCB, MH

1722#22
PASCHOUD, —, schoolmaster. *Historico-political geography; or, A description of the... several countries in the world...* London. J. Read, 2 vols, 8vo. [1722–4]
Note: EA 722/145. Also 1726, EA 726/158. Includes the Americas. Cf. SABIN 58987.
Locations: MnU

1722#23
PENNSYLVANIA PROVINCE. *The particulars of an Indian treaty at Conestogoe, between... Sir William Keith, governor of Pennsylvania, and the deputies of the Five nations...* London. Printed from the copy published in Pennsylvania by A. Bradford; sold at the Pennsylvania Coffee-House in Birchin-Lane. 32p. 8vo. [1722]
Note: SABIN 58936. First printed Philadelphia, 1722 (i.e 1721): EVANS 2342. EA lists only the Dublin edition, 1723 (EA 723/122).
Locations: L;

1722#24
Reasons humbly offered against general certificates for the conveyance of tobacco's, etc. London. s.sh. F. [1722?]
Note: HANSON 3143. ESTC dates 1751 (L;).
Locations: LLI;

1722#25
Reasons humbly offered for regulating the importation of tobacco into this kingdom, for the preservation of the revenue, and the better carrying on of the said trade. London. F. [1722?]
Note: HANSON 3144.
Locations: LLI;

1722#26
The Sailor's advocate...
Note: SABIN 74972. Two numbers published. Partly relates to America. Another edition in 1728.
Locations: L; DLC, NN

1722#27
SEWEL, William. *The history of the rise, increase and progress of the Christian people called Quakers... written originally in low-Dutch... now revis'd...* London. Assigns of J. Sowle, 723p. 2o. 1722
Note: SABIN 79602, SMITH, II, 561, EA 722/161. Second edition corrected 1725, 3rd edition in 2 vols., 1795. Reprinted Philadelphia, 1728.
Locations: L; RPJCB, MiU-C, MB

1722#28
WAGSTAFFE, William. *A letter to Dr Freind; shewing the danger and uncertainty of inoculating the small pox.* London. S. Butler, 69p. 15p. 8vo. 1722
Note: EA 722/185–7. Two other editions in 1722. Cites New England and publishes Douglass's letter from there.
Locations: L; MH, NRCR, InU

1722#29
YONGE, Francis. *A view of the trade of South Carolina, with proposals humbly offer'd for improving the same.* London. 16p. 8vo. [1722?]
Note: SABIN 106016, EA 722/195.
Locations: DLC, RPJCB, ViU

1723#1
AUBIN, Penelope. *The life of Charlotta du Pont, an English lady... Giving an account of how she was trepan'd by her stepmother to Virginia...* London. A. Bettesworth, 282p. 8vo. 1723
Note: EA 723/8. Other editions in 1733, 1736, 1739. EA 733//14, 736/19, 739/10. Fictitious. Included in her *Collected Works*, 3 vols., 1739, EA 739/9.
Locations: L; DLC, RPJCB

1723#2
BLACKAMORE, Arthur. *Luck at last or the happy unfortunate...* London. H. Parker and sold by T. Warner, 112p. 8vo. 1723
Note: Dedicated to David Bray of Virginia. See Blackamore, *Perfidious brethren*, above, 1720.
Locations: TxU, ICN

1723

1723#3
COCK, Christopher. *Catalogue of divers rich and valuable effects, being a collection of Elihu Yale. part 5. A fifth sale of Elihu Yale... Will be sold by auction at his late dwelling-house... on Thursday the 31st of this instant January...* London. 29p. 8vo. [1723]
Locations: L;

1723#4
DEFOE, Daniel. *The history and remarkable life of the truly honourable Col. Jacque, commonly called Col. Jack...* London. J. Brotherton, etc., vii, 399p. 8vo. 1723
Note: EA 723/43–5. Two other issues in 1723. Others 1724, 1738, 1739, 1741, 1743. Kidnapped to Virginia, where he prospered. Some discussion of slavery.
Locations: L; MWiW-C, CLU-C

1723#5
JURIN, James. *A letter to the learned Caleb Cotesworth, M. D. . . containing a comparison between the mortality of the natural smallpox, and that given by inoculation...* London. W. and J.Innys, 31p. 8vo. 1723
Note: EA 723/72. Some account of Boston inoculation.
Locations: L; RPJCB, MH, ICJ

1723#6
LESLIE, Charles. *A short and easie method with the deists... The eighth edition.* London. J. Applebee, for J. Checkley, in Boston, 132p. 8vo. 1723
Note: SABIN 40192, EA 723/77. First published London, 1698, without 'A discourse concerning episcopacy', with references to Congregationalists in New England, here included. Attributed to John Checkley. Also London, 1726, 1727, 1727, 1745. EA lists only 1727, 1738, 727/144, 738/146 so perhaps other editions lack Americana.
Locations: L; CSmH, DLC, RPJCB

1723#7
MARYLAND ASSEMBLY. *Acts of assembly, passed in the province of Maryland, from 1692 to 1715.* London. J. Baskett, 183p. 2o. 1723
Note: EA 723/98. Cf. EVANS 1965: *Laws... 1692... 1718*, (Philadelphia, 1718).
Locations: L; RPJCB, NN, MB

1723#8
MILLAR, Robert. *The history of the propagation of Christianity, and the overthrow of paganism...* Edinburgh. T. Ruddiman, 2 vols. 8vo. 1723
Note: SABIN 48995, EA 723/104, 726/147, 731/145. 'Heathens in America.' Other editions, London, 1726, 1731.
Locations: L; DLC, CtY-D, NjP

1723#9
PHILOPATRIS. *A most humble proposal to the Most Honourable the Lords Regents... for an effectual method to prevent piracy, and make the trade of America safe...* London. J. Morley, 15p. 4to. 1723
Note: SABIN 51095, 62559, EA 723/124. Another issue (?) '. . . and make the trade of America more secure'.
Locations: E; MB, Mhi

1723#10
Entry cancelled

1723#11
TRENCHARD, John. *Cato's letters...* London. W. Wilkins etc. 4 vols. 12mo. [1723–4]
Note: Also 1733, 1748, 1754, and Berwick, 1754. Contains material on colonies.
Locations: L; DLC, MB, CLU

1723#12
WAUGH, John. *A sermon... preached... the 15th February, 1722.* London. J. Downing, 68p. 4to. 1723
Note: SABIN 102178, EA 723/172. SPG sermon for 1723.
Locations: L; DLC, RPJCB, NN

1724#1
A.B.C. *A letter from a gentleman out of England, to his country men, the people called the Galloway Levellers.* [Glasgow?]. s.sh. 1/2o. [1724?]
Note: Refers to the enclosures revolt in Galloway in 1724 and advocates emigration.
Locations: Gu;

1724#2
BERKELEY, George. *A proposal for the better supplying of churches in our foreign plantations, and for converting the savage Americans to Christianity, by a college to be erected in the Summer Islands, otherwise called the Isles of Bermuda...* London. H. Woodfall, 24p. 8vo. 1724
Note: SABIN 66021, EA 724/11, 725/18–19. Two other London and one Dublin edition in 1725.
Locations: L; D; DLC, MH

1724#3
BOCKETT, Elias. *A determination of the case of Mr. Thomas Story, and Mr. James Hoskins, relating to an affair of the Pennsilvania Company...* London. J. Roberts, 11, 1p. 4to. 1724
Note: SABIN 6106, SMITH, I, 291, HANSON 3305, EA 724/12–13. L; lists as by [Benjamin Braine]. Reprinted or first printed Philadelphia, 1724, (EVANS 2502) as *A determination of the affair between Mess. Story and Hopkins...*; a second edition in 1724 by T. Smith (L;).
Locations: L; RPJCB

1724#4
BOCKETT, Elias. *A poem. To the memory of Aquila Rose, who dyed at Philadelphia, August the 22d, 1723...* London. 8p. 8vo. 1724

Note: FOXON B306, SABIN 6107, SMITH, I, 291, EA 724/14. Reprinted Philadelphia, 1740: EVANS 4593.
Locations: L; NN, PHi

1724#5
CLINCH, William. *An historical essay on the rise and progress of the small-pox.* London. Printed for A. R. and sold by T. Warner, 59p. 8vo. 1724
Note: EA 724/40. Second enlarged edition, 1725: L; DLC, RPJCB, CtY.
Locations: L; PPC, PPULC, MWiW-C

1724#6
CROUCH, Henry. *A complete view of the British Customs...* London. J. Osborn and W. Bell, 335p. 8vo. 1724
Note: HANSON 3320, EA 724/44. Other parts and editions 1725, 1726, 1728, 1731, two in 1738, 1745, 1746, 1755, EA 725/46, 726/53, 728/44, 729/65, 731/63, 738/69-70, 745/54, 746/46.
Locations: L; MH-BA, Vi

1724#7
DEFOE, Daniel. *A general history of the robberies and murders of the most notorious pyrates, and also their policies, discipline and government... by Captain Charles Johnson.* London. C. Rivington, etc., 320p. 8vo. 1724
Note: EA 724/50-1. Two editions in 1724. One London and one Dublin edition in 1725, EA 725/56-7. Also two London editions in 1726, EA 726/65-6, abridged edition Dublin, 1727, EA 727/67, abridged edition, London 1729, EA 729/73. Vol II was published in 1728, EA 728/54. SABIN 36190, also cf. SABIN 32181. See also Johnson, *General History*, below, 1734.
Locations: L; DLC, RPJCB, MnU

1724#8
GREENE, Thomas. *A sermon preached... February 21, 1723...* London. J. Downing, 69p. 4to. 1724
Note: EA 724/71-2. A second edition in 1724. SPG sermon for 1724, with abstract, etc.
Locations: L; DLC, RPJCB, CtY

1724#9
HOSKINS, James. *The just defence of James Hoskins, against the proceedings, and judgements, of Westminster monthly meeting...* London. 32p. 8vo. [1724]
Note: SMITH, I, 976, EA 724/81. Pennsylvania Land Company. New England references. Cf. EVANS 2502, *A determination of the case of... Story and... Hoskins*, [Philadelphia, 1724].
Locations: DLC, RPJCB

1724#10
JONES, Hugh. *An accidence to the English tongue...* London. J. Clarke, [85]p. 12mo. 1724.

Note: Jones was the author of *The present state of Virginia*, below, 1724.
Locations: L;

1724#11
JONES, Hugh. *The present state of Virginia. Giving a particular and short account of the Indian, English, and Negroe inhabitants of that colony... from whence is inferred a short view of Maryland and North Carolina...* London. J. Clarke, 151p. 8vo. 1724
Note: SABIN 36511, HANSON 3308, EA 724/85-6. Another edition in 1724.
Locations: L; E; DLC, RPJCB, ICN, MiU-C

1724#12
KIMBER, Isaac. *The life of Oliver Cromwell.* London. J. Brotherton and T. Cox, 374p. 8vo. 1724
Note: EA 724/90. Cromwell and New England. Another edition 1731, EA 731/125.
Locations: L; CtY, MH, IU

1724#13
A letter to a Member of Parliament, relating to the relief of poor insolvent prisoners for debt... And a proposal for strengthning the British plantations in America. London. J. Peele, 21p. 8vo. 1724
Note: HANSON 3402, EA 724/102.
Locations: L; DFo; CSmH

1724#14
MASSACHUSETTS GENERAL COURT. *Acts and laws, passed by... assembly of the province of... Massachusetts Bay... from 1692 to 1719.* London. J. Baskett, 359p. F. 1724
Note: EA 724/111. Cf. EVANS 1686: *Acts and laws of...* (Boston, 1714).
Locations: L; DLC, RPJCB, NN

1724#15
MILLER, Philip. *The gardeners and florists dictionary.* London. C. Rivington, 2 vols. 8vo. 1724
Note: EA 724/115. Other editions 1732, 1733, 1735, 1737-9, 1740-3, etc.
Locations: L; CLU-C, DNAL, TxU

1724#16
NICHOLSON, Sir Francis. *An apology or vindication of Francis Nicholson... governor of South-Carolina, from the unjust aspersions cast on him by some of the members of the Bahama-company.* London. T. Payne, 62p. 8vo. 1724
Note: SABIN 55221, HANSON 3307, EA 724/122.
Locations: L; RPJCB, CSmH

1724#17
PHILIPS, Miles. *The voyages and adventures of Miles Philips... the inhuman treatment he met... at Mexico,*

and the salvage Indians of Canada... London. T. Payne, T. Butler, 216p. 12mo. 1724
Note: EA 724/133. Reprint (or plagiarism) from Hakluyt.
Locations: L; DLC, NN, MiU-C

1724#18
PURRY, Jean Pierre. *Mémoire presenté à Sa. Gr. Mylord Duc de Newcastle... sur l'état présent de la Caroline et sur les moyens de l'améliorer.* London. G. Bowyer and P. Vaillant, 11p. 4to. 1724
Note: SABIN 66725, EA 724/138. Another edition in English, below, 1724.
Locations: DLC, RPJCB

1724#19
PURRY, Jean Pierre. *A memorial presented to... Duke of Newcastle... concerning the present state of Carolina, and the means of improving it.* London. G. Bowyer for P. Vaileant, 11p. 4to. [1724]
Note: SABIN 66725, HANSON 3306, EA 724/139.
Locations: L; DLC, RPJCB

1724#20
SALMON, Thomas. *A critical essay concerning marriage... to which is added, an historical account of the marriage rites and ceremonies...* London. Charles Rivington, 348p. 8vo. 1724
Note: EA 724/156-7. Another edition in 1724. Discussion of American rites.
Locations: L; DLC, MH, NN

1725#1
BLEWITT, George. *An enquiry whether a general practice of virtue tends to the wealth or poverty, benefit or disadvantage of a people...* London. R. Wilkins, 218p. 8vo. 1725
Note: Attack on Mandeville, with some discussion of trade and colonies.
Locations: L; DLC, CtY N

1725#2
BREAKENRIG, Thomas. *Petition for Thomas Breakenrig messenger in Edinburgh; against [blank] Newlands and others.* Edinburgh. 4p. 2o. 1725
Note: SABIN 91649, EA 724/167. Abduction of petitioner's daughter to Virginia into slavery.
Locations: L;

1725#3
The case of the heir at law and executrix of the late proprietor of Pensilvania... London. 4p. F. 1725
Note: SABIN 59959, EA 725/36. Also published as *The case of Hannah Penn...* below, 1730. EVANS 2735 is [Philadelphia, 1726].
Locations: RPJCB, NIC

1725#4
DEFOE, Daniel. *The complete English tradesman.* London. C. Rivington, 447p. 8vo. 1725
Note: EA 725/54. Title page is dated 1726. References to American commerce. This is perhaps an expanded edition of the first edition of 1725 (also dated 1726), of which no copy has been found, EA 725/53. Other editions in 1726, 1727, 1732, 1738, EA 726/59–60, 727/56, 732/80, 738/73.
Locations: L; CtY, NNC

1725#5
DEFOE, Daniel. *A general history of discoveries and improvements, in useful arts, particularly in the great branches of commerce, navigation and plantation...* London. J. Roberts, etc., 307p. 1725
Note: HANSON 3416, EA 725/55. Published in four parts, 1725–6.
Locations: L; E; O; MB, DLC, CtY

1725#6
FRANKLIN, Benjamin. *A dissertation on liberty and necessity, pleasure and pain.* London. 32p. 8vo. 1725
Note: SABIN 25498. Also Dublin 1733.
Locations: L; DLC, CtY, RPJCB

1725#7
GREAT BRITAIN. COMMISSIONERS OF ADMIRALTY. *Orders that tobacco on British ships should be of the growth of British colonies.* London. s.sh. 1/2o. [1725]
Locations: L;

1725#8
MACNENY, Patrick. *The Freedom of commerce of the subjects of the Austrian Nether-lands asserted and vindicated. Being a confutation of the arguments advanced on the part of the East and West-India Companies...* London or Brussels? E. H. Fricx, [63]p. 4to. [1725?]
Note: SABIN 25747, EA 725/129.
Locations: L; DLC, DFo, MnU

1725#9
MATHER, Cotton. *Memoirs of the life of the late reverend Increase Mather... With a preface by... Edmund Calamy...* London. J. Clarke, R. Hett, 88p. 8vo. 1725
Note: HOLMES, CM, 271, EA 725/138. Abridgement by Samuel Mather of *Parentator*, first printed Boston, 1724, (EVANS 2557).
Locations: DLC, RPJCB, CtY

1725#10
SALMON, Thomas. *Modern history, or The present state of all nations.* London. The author, and sold by J. Roberts, 32 vols. 8vo. 1725

Note: EA 725/174–5 has bibliographical details. Published 1725–1739. Vols 28, 29, 30 and 31 have American sections. See EA 736/218, 737/187–8, 738/205. Two other editions in three volumes in 1739 and 1744, EA 739/270, 744/198. Also published in various serial numbers 1724–1738. EA 727/202 is a Dublin edition 1727–1739 in five volumes with title *Modern History, or the present state of all nations including a dissertation on the first peopling of America*, of which vol. 5 has American material, EA 739/271. EA 737/186, 739/272 are volumes 25 and 26 of a Dublin edition of 26 volumes.
Locations: L; RPJCB, DLC

1725#11
WHITEHEAD, George. *The Christian progress of... G. W; historically relating his experience... and service in defence of the truth, and of... Quakers.* London. T. Sowle, 712p. 8vo. 1725
Note: EA 725/211.
Locations: DLC, RPJCB, NN

1725#12
WYNNE, John. *A sermon preached... Feb. 1724.* London. J. Downing, 63p. 8vo. 1725
Note: SABIN 105681, EA 725/216. SPG sermon for 1725, with abstract, etc.
Locations: L; RPJCB, CtY, CLU-C

1726#1
BARNARD, John. *Ashton's memorial: or, an authentick account of the strange adventures... of Mr. Philip Ashton... To which is added, a sermon on Dan. III, 17, by J. Barnard...* London. R. Ford, S. Chandler. 148p. 2o. 1726
Note: SABIN 2207, EA 726/16. Imaginary adventures. First published Boston, 1725, EVANS 2602. See also *New England Quarterly*, LXIII, No 1, (March, 1990).
Locations: L; DLC, MH

1726#2
BOCKETT, Elias. *The wit and honesty of James Hoskins, etc. consider'd in Remarks on their late Pamphlet, call'd the Pa. Bubble. By the translator of the Pattern of Modesty.* London. J. Smith, 83p. 8vo. 1726
Note: SABIN 92329, HANSON 3599, SMITH I, 291, EA 726/19.
Locations: L; RPJCB, PHi

1726#3
BOYLSTON, Zabdiel. *An historical account of the small-pox inoculated in New England, upon all sorts of persons...* London. S. Chandler, 62p. 4to. 1726
Note: SABIN 7141, EA 726/21. Reprinted Boston 1730 in corrected edition (EVANS 3259).
Locations: L; DLC, MH

1726#4
CHETWOOD, William Rufus. *The voyage, shipwreck, and miraculous escape of Richard Castleman... With a description of Pennsylvania... and... Philadelphia...* London. J. Watts, 43p. 8vo. 1726
Note: Cf. SABIN 12553 and EA 726/46. Not listed in ESTC or EA. Perhaps not a separate publication from Chetwood's *Voyages of... Captain R. Boyle*, below, 1726.
Locations: DLC, PHC

1726#5
CHETWOOD, William Rufus. *The voyages and adventures of Captain Robert Boyle... To which is added the voyage, shipwreck, and miraculous escape of Richard Castleman... With a description of the city of Philadelphia and the country of Pennsylvania.* London. J. Watts, 374p. 8vo. 1726
Note: EA 726/46. Other editions 1727, 1728, 1735, Wolverhampton, 1744, 1748, Dublin, 1741, 1759. EA 727/40, 728/35, 735/68, 741/37, 744/61, 748/40.
Locations: L; DLC, CtY, MH

1726#6
A discourse of the laws *relating to pirates and piracies, and the marine affairs of Great Britain.* London. W. Wilkins for J. Peele, 70p. 8vo. 1726
Locations: L; DLC, MB

1726#7
GORDON, George. *An introduction to geography, astronomy, and dialling.* London. J. Senex, 2 pts. 8vo. 1726
Note: EA 726/92. Includes discussion of geography of America. Also 1729, EA 729/109.
Locations: L; FU, ICU, OkU

1726#8
HOSKINS, James. *The Pensilv[ania] Bubble bubbled by the Treasurer, or, an account of his admitting purchasers for shares...* London. For the author, viii, 50p. 8vo. 1726
Note: SABIN 33095, HANSON 3598, EA 726/109.
Locations: L; DLC, RPJCB, NN

1726#9
KER, John. *The memoirs of John Ker of Kersland, in North Britain... with an account of the... Ostend Company...* London. E. Curll, 3 vols. 8vo. 1726
Note: SABIN 37600, EA 726/119–121, 727/122. Vol. II deals in large part with French America. One complete and one other edition in 1726; another edition in 1727.
Locations: L; DLC, RPJCB, ViU

1726#10
LABADIE, ——. *The adventures of Pomponius, a Roman knight, or the history of our own times...* London. E. Curll, 2 vols. 12mo. 1726

1726

Note: EA 726/125. Translated from *Les avantures de Pomponius*. See EA 726/126. John Law and Mississippi Company.
Locations: L; BN; CLU-C, DFo, ICN

1726#11
LEAKE, Stephen. *Nummi Britannici historia: or, An historical account of English money...* London. W. Meadows, 144p. 8vo. 1726
Note: SABIN 56316, HANSON 3619, EA 726/132, 745/116. Describes plantation half-penny, Maryland coin, New-England money. Another edition with additions in 1745.
Locations: L; DLC, MH, NN

1726#12
The life and character of a strange He-Monster, lately arriv'd in London from an English Colony in America. And is often to be seen on the Royal Exchange, Gratis. [London?], 24p. 4to. 1726
Note: EA 726/137. Author was possibly Sir William Keith. See *William and Mary Quarterly*, XXXVIII, No. 2 (April, 1981), 268–94. EVANS 2757 gives Philadelphia, 1726.
Locations: MH-H

1726#13
N., J. *The liberty and property of British subjects asserted: in a letter from an assembly-man in Carolina, to his friend in London.* London. J. Roberts, 39p. 8vo. 1726
Note: HANSON 3604, EA 726/136.
Locations: L; DLC, RPJCB, ViU

1726#14
PENN, William. *A collection of the works of William Penn. In two volumes. To which is prefixed a journal of his life with many original letters and papers...* London. Assigns of J. Sowle, 2 vols. F. 1726
Note: SABIN 59690, EA 726/162.
Locations: L; DLC, RPJCB, CSmH

1726#15
SHELVOCKE, George. *A voyage round the world... in the years 1719, 20, 21, 22 in the Speedwell of London...* London. J. Senex, etc., 468p. 8vo. 1726
Note: HANSON 3594, EA 726/192. References to California.
Locations: L; DLC, RPJCB, MiU-C

1726#16
URING, Nathaniel. *A history of the voyages and travels of Capt. Nathaniel Uring...* London. J. Peele, 384, 135p. 8vo. 1726
Note: SABIN 98124, HANSON 3309n, EA 726/207, 749/271. Includes North America. Another edition in 1749.
Locations: L; DLC, RPJCB, MiU-C

1726#17
WATTS, Isaac. *The knowledge of the heavens and the earth made easy.* London. J. Clark and R. Hett, 219p. 8vo. 1726
Note: EA 726/219. Also 1728, 1736, 1745, EA 728/208, 736/265, 745/222.
Locations: L; CtY, MH, NN

1726#18
WILCOCKS, Joseph. *A sermon preached... 18th of February, 1725.* London. J. Downing, 63p. 4to. 1726
Note: SABIN 103964, EA 726/222–3. SPG sermon for 1726, with abstract, etc. Another edition in 1726.
Locations: L; DLC, RPJCB, NN

1726#19
YONGE, Francis. *A narrative of the proceedings of the people of South-Carolina, in the year 1719... motives that induced them to renounce their obedience to the Lords Proprietors...* London. 40p. 4to. 1726
Note: SABIN 106014, HANSON 3603, EA 726/229.
Locations: L; DLC, RPJCB, CtY

1727#1
BARNARD, John. *Sermons on several subjects...* London. Printed for S. Gerrish and D. Henchman, Cornhill, Boston, 191p. 8vo. 1727
Note: Three sermons by Barnard who was minister at Marblehead, Mass.
Locations: L; DLC, RPJCB

1727#2
BRADLEY, Richard. *Ten practical discourses.* London. J. Cluer and A. Campbell, for B. Creake, 195p. 8vo. 1727
Note: EA 727/22–3. American trees and horticulture. Also Dublin, 1727.
Locations: L; CtY, NIC

1727#3
BRAY, Thomas. *Missionalia; or, a collection of missionary pieces relating to the conversion of the heathen; both the African negroes and American Indians. In two parts.* London. W. Roberts. [c. 300]p. 8vo. [1727–8]
Note: EA 727/165. In fact in five parts, each with own title page.
Locations: L; LEu; DLC, ICN, PPAmP

1727#4
COLLIBER, Samuel. *Columna rostrata: or, a critical history of the English sea-affairs...* London. R. Robinson, 312p. 8vo. 1727
Note: SABIN 14414, EA 727/43. Other editions, 1739, 1741, EA 739/70, 742/53.
Locations: L; DLC, CtY, MH

1727#5
Entry cancelled

1727#6
FORSTER, Samuel. *A digest of all the laws relating to the customs, to trade, and navigation.* London. E. and R. Nutt, and R. Gosling, for G. Strahan, G. Grafton, and T. Ward, 368p. 8vo. 1727
Note: EA 727/76, HANSON 3738. Includes laws relating to American colonies.
Locations: L; DLC, InU, MH-L

1727#7
FURBER, Robert. *A catalogue of English and foreign trees.* London. H. Woodfall, 2pts. 8vo. 1727
Note: EA 727/84. Many American trees and bushes.
Locations: L;

1727#8
HOUGHTON, John, ed. *A collection for the improvement of husbandry and trade... Now revised, corrected, and published... by Richard Bradley.* London. J. Woodman & D. Lyon, 3 vols. 8vo. 1727
Note: EA 727/116-7. First published as a serial, 1692-1703. References to American flora and to English and Spanish colonies in America. Another issue in 1727.
Locations: L; CLU-C, MH-BA, ViW

1727#9
GIBSON, Edmund. *A letter of the Lord Bishop of London to the masters and mistresses of families in the English plantations abroad; exhorting them to encourage and promote the instruction of their Negroes in the Christian faith.* London. J. Downing, 16p. 4to. 1727
Note: Cf. SABIN 27312. EA 727/87.
Locations: RPJCB, CtY, MH

1727#10
GIBSON, Edmund. *Two letters of the Lord Bishop of London: the first, to the masters and mistresses of families in the English plantations abroad... The second, to the missionaries there...* London. J. Downing, 20p. 4to. 1727
Note: EA 727/88, EA 729/103-4. Two other editions in 1729. Also London, 1760. Letter one is Gibson's *A letter...* above, 1727. For encouraging the instruction of the blacks in Christianity.
Locations: C; O; RPJCB, MiU-C, MH

1727#11
GREAT BRITAIN. PARLIAMENT. HOUSE OF COMMONS. *A bill for importing salt, from Europe, into the province of Pensylvania in America.* London. J. Baskett and others, 3p. F. [1727]
Note: HANSON 3718, EA 727/95. Enacted 13 Geo. I. c. 5.
Locations: L; DLC, MiU-C

1727#12
GREAT BRITAIN. SOVEREIGN. GEORGE II. *By the King, a proclamation... continuing officers in His majesty's Plantations... [5 July 1727].* London. J. Baskett, etc. s.sh. F. 1727
Note: BRIGHAM 182.
Locations: LPC; MiU-C

1727#13
HARTWELL, Henry, BLAIR, James and CHILTON, Edward. *The present state of Virginia, and the college; by Messieurs Hartwell, Blair and Chilton... the charter for erecting the said college...* London. J. Wyat, 95p. 8vo. 1727
Note: SABIN 30716, HANSON 3728, EA 727/105.
Locations: L; DLC, RPJCB, MiU-C

1727#14
An honest scheme, for improving the trade and credit of the nation... London. J. Roberts, 72p. 8vo. 1727.
Locations: L; NN, CtY, PU

1727#15
LENG, John. *A sermon preached... on Friday, the 17th of February 1726...* London. J. Downing for R. Knaplock, 65p. 4to. 1727
Note: SABIN 40025, EA 727/142-3. SPG sermon for 1727, with abstract, etc. Another issue in 1727.
Locations: L; DLC, RPJCB, CSmH

1727#16
LIVINGSTONE, John. *A brief historical relation of the life of Mr J. Livingston... written by himself.* Glasgow? 48p. 4to. 1727
Note: EA 727/148. Livingston and other Scots-Irish sailed for New England in 1636 but returned because of bad weather. Another (expanded?) edition, Glasgow, 1754: L
Locations: L; RPJCB

1727#17
MAYHEW, Experience. *Indian converts... lives and dying speeches of... Christianized Indians of Martha's Vineyard... some account of... English ministers... in that and the adjacent islands...* London. Printed for S. Gerrish, Boston, and sold by J. Osborn and T. Longman, London, 310p. 8vo. 1727
Note: SABIN 47124, EA 727/158. Is this a reprint of EVANS 701: *A brief narrative of the success which the gospel hath had, among the Indians of Martha's vineyard...*, (Boston, 1694).
Locations: L; DLC, RPJCB, MiU-C

1727#18
NICOLL, John. *The advantage of Great Britain consider'd in the tobacco trade... humbly offered to the Parliament of Great Britain...* London. 18p. F. 1727

Note: HANSON 3719, EA 727/174.
Locations: Lu; DLC, RPJCB, MH

1727#19
Papers relating to an affidavit *made by... James Blair... against Francis Nicholson... Printed in the year 1727.* London. 104p. 8vo. 1727
Note: Cf. SABIN 55223. EA 727/178.
Locations: L; RPJCB

1727#20
PEMBERTON, Ebenezer.(1671–1717) *Sermons and discourses on several occasions. By the late... Ebenezer Pemberton... in Boston...* London. J. Batley and others, 210p. 8vo. 1727
Note: SABIN 59602, EA 727/181. Also published for S. Gerish, Boston, 1738. With funeral sermon by Benjamin Colman. The funeral sermon was first published Boston, 1717 (EVANS 1928). The sermons and discourses were published at Boston, 1738 and 1741 (EVANS 4295, 4780).
Locations: DLC, RPJCB, MB

1727#21
PULTENEY, William. *A state of the national debt, as it stood December... 1716, with the payments... out of the sinking fund, &c. compared with... 1725.* London. R. Francklin, 56p. 4to. 1727
Note: HANSON 3736, EA 727/14–15. Another edition in 1727. Replies to Nathaniel Gould's *An essay on the publick debts of this kingdom.* 1st publ. 1726. Newfoundland, Canada, etc.
Locations: ICU, NN

1727#22
Remarks on those passages of *the letters of the Spanish ministers... which relate to the hostilities committed by the Spanish Guarda-Costas...* London. J. Peele, 40p. 8vo. 1727
Note: HANSON 3720, EA 727/196. The continental as well as the West Indian colonies suffer from Spanish attacks. Republished as *A View of the depredations and ravages committed by the Spaniards on the British trade and navigation...*, London, 1731 and Dublin, 1731, EA 731/196–7.
Locations: L; CtY, RPJCB

1727#23
ROYAL HOSPITAL FOR SEAMEN AT GREENWICH. *By the commissioners for collecting and receiving the six pence a month out of seamens wages, for the use of Greenwich Hospital, &c. Instructions to be observed by Mr. [blank] receiver... at the port of [blank] in America.* London. 3, [1]p. 2o. [1727?]
Locations: Lpro;

1727#24
SOCIETY FOR THE PROPAGATION OF THE GOSPEL. *The method used by the Society to encourage the distribution of good books...* London. s.sh. F. [1727]
Note: A circular, with an account of the Society signed in MS. by Henry Newman.
Locations: L;

1727#25
VIRGINIA ASSEMBLY. *Acts of Assembly, passed in the colony of Virginia, from 1622, to 1715. Volume I.* London. J. Baskett, 391p. 2o. 1727
Note: EA 727/234. Printed by order of the Lords Commissioners for Trade and Plantations. Another issue in 1728, EA 728/201. No more published.
Locations: Lpro; RPJCB, NN, ViU

1728#1
BROWNE, Sir John. *Seasonable remarks on trade.* Dublin, S. Powell for G. Ewing, 70p. 8vo. 1728
Note: HANSON 3808, EA 728/19. Sir John Browne of Dublin.
Locations: L; CtY, ICN, NN

1728#2
BURRISH, Onslow. *Batavia illustrata: or, A view of the policy and commerce of the United Provinces... of the rise and progress of their East and West India Companies...* London. W. Innys, 580p. 8vo. 1728
Note: KRESS 3740, EA 728/21. Also 1742, EA 742/27.
Locations: L; CtY, MiU, NjP

1728#3
BURY, Richard. *A collection of sundry messages and warnings to the inhabitants of the city of Bristol...* Bristol. 2pts., 4to. 1728
Note: SABIN 9516, SMITH I, 369, EA 728/22. First published 1701–05 (without Americana?). Part ii includes section on Indian war in South Carolina. etc.
Locations: L; MH

1728#4
The case of the merchants, *and planters, trading to, and residing in, Virginia, and Maryland.* London. 2p. F. [1728]
Note: KRESS SUPP. 2143.
Locations: DLC, RPJCB, MH

1728#5
COLMAN, Benjamin. *Some of the glories of our Lord and Saviour... in twenty sacramental discourses, preached at Boston...* London. S. Palmer for T. Hancock at Boston and J. Osborn and T. Cox, London. 304p. 8vo. 1728
Note: SABIN 14525, EA 728/37.
Locations: L; DLC, RPJCB, MiU-C

1728#6
CUTLER, Nathaniel. *Atlas maritimus & commercialis; or, A general view of the world... together with a*

large account of the commerce carried on by sea between the several countries of the world... to which are added sailing directions... with a sett of sea-charts... London. J. and J. Knapton, W. and J. Innys, J. Darby, A. Bettesworth, J. Osborn, T. Longman, J. Senex, E. Symon, A. Johnston, and Executors of W. Taylor, 2pts. F. 1728

Note: Substantial sections on North America.
Locations: L;

1728#7
DEFOE, Daniel. *A plan of the English commerce...* London. C. Rivington, 368p. 8vo. 1728

Note: HANSON 3837, EA 728/51, EA 730/70, 737/69, 738/73, 749/64. Other editions 1730, [1731], 1737, 1738, 1749. Substantial North American references, including to Indians.
Locations: L; MiU-C, DLC, DFo

1728#8
GIBSON, Edmund. *Methodus procedendi contra clericos irregulares in plantationibus Americanis.* London? 16p. 4to. [1728?]

Note: EA 728/78.
Locations: NN, RPJCB

1728#9
GREAT BRITAIN. ROYAL NAVY. *By the Commissioners for Executing the Office of Lord High Admiral of Great Britain and Ireland... His Majesty hath been pleased by his commission bearing date the 9th of August last, to constitute... Robert Byng, Esq; to be his Receiver-General of the rights and perquisites of the Admiralty...* London? [4]p. 2o. [1728]

Note: 6th of May 1728. North American colonial governors to surrender pirates' effects to Byng or his deputies.
Locations: Lpro;

1728#10
GREAT BRITAIN. SOVEREIGN. GEORGE II). *Commissio Regia pro exercendâ jurisdictione spirituali et ecclesiasticâ in plantationibus Americanis.* London. 6p. 4to. [1728]

Locations: Lpro;

1728#11
MARTYN, John. *Historia plantarum rariorum.* London. J. Reily, 52p. 2o. 1728

Note: SABIN 45004, EA 728/129. Also published in translation: *A history of rare plants...* in 3 parts, 1728–1732. EA 728/130.
Locations: L; MH, MH-A, TxU

1728#12
PERSON WHO RESIDED SEVERAL YEARS AT JAMAICA. *Some observations on the assiento trade, as it has been exercised by the South-Sea Company; proving the damage, which will accrue thereby to the British commerce and plantations in America, and particularly to Jamaica...* London. Printed for H. Whitridge, iv,38p. 8vo. 1728

Note: EA 728/178–9. Second edition in 1728 (in two issues?). Sometimes attributed to James Knight.
Locations: L; BLI; E; CSmH, DFo, RPJCB

1728#13
REYNOLDS, Richard. *A sermon preached... 16th February 1727...* London. J. Downing, 32p. 4to. 1728

Note: SABIN 70441, EA 728/160–1. SPG sermon for 1728. Another edition, London, 1728.
Locations: RPJCB, CSmH, CtY

1728#14
SCOTLAND. CHURCH OF SCOTLAND. GENERAL ASSEMBLY. *Edinburgh, November 14, 1728. R.D.B. [Reverend and Dear Brethren]...* [Edinburgh]. [1728]

Note: Circular to presbtyeries, concerning missionary activities in Highlands, etc. Refers to collection for 'the Presbyterian church in New York', among others.
Locations: E;

1728#15
A true state of the Bishop of London's jurisdiction in the plantations abroad. London. 3p. F. [1728?]

Note: SABIN 97149, EA 728/187. ESTC lists under 1715.
Locations: E; MShM, NNG

1728#16
WILSON, Thomas (1655?–1725). *A brief journal of the life, travels, and labours of love, in the work of the ministry of... T. Wilson...* Dublin. S. Fuller, 98p. 8vo. 1728

Note: SMITH II, 946, EA 728/211, 730/21. Also London, 1730.
Locations: DLC, RPJCB, M

1729#1
AMHURST, Nicholas. *Some farther remarks on a late pamphlet, intitled, Observations on the conduct of Great-Britain...* London. R. Francklin, 2, 32p. 8vo. 1729

Note: SABIN 86644, HANSON 3954, EA 729/200.
Locations: L; RPJCB, DLC, CtY

1729#2
The Anti-Craftsmen: being an answer to the Craftsmen extraordinary... London. J. Brindley, 22p. 8vo. 1729

Note: EA 729/8. Defends peace policy. Mentions colonial trade etc.
Locations: Lu; DLC, InU, RPJCB

1729

1729#3
The case of the planters *of Virginia, and the merchants trading thither, humbly represented to the Parliament.* London. s.sh. F. [1729]
Note: HANSON 3962, EA 729/46. Cf. SABIN 100441 where dated [1733].
Locations: L; DLC, CtY

1729#4
The case of the provinces *of the Massachusets-Bay and New Jersy [sic], and the colonies of Connecticut and Rhode Island, and the Providence plantation, with respect to the bill now depending in the honourable House of Commons, intituled, A Bill for preservation of his Majesty's woods in America and for the encouragement of the importation of naval stores. . .* London. s.sh. F. [1729]
Note: EA does not list. See NUC and ESTC which date it [1729].
Locations: Lu; DLC, CtY, NN

1729#5
COWELL, John. *A true account of the Aloe Americana or Africana, which is now in blossom in Mr. Cowell's garden at Hoxton. . .* London. T. Warner, 44p. 8vo. 1729
Note: EA 729/63, SABIN 17238.
Locations: L; Vi, RPJCB

1729#6
DEFOE, Daniel. *A humble proposal to the people of England, for the encrease of their trade. . . By the author of the Compleat Tradesman.* London. C. Rivington, 60p. 8vo. 1729
Note: HANSON 3900, EA 729/70. Improve colonies in order to benefit consumption of English woollens, etc.
Locations: L;

1729#7
DOBBS, Arthur. *An essay on the trade and improvement of Ireland.* Dublin. A. Rhames, etc., 99p. 8vo. 1729
Note: HANSON 3904, EA 729/76. First part. A second part was published in 1731, with title *An essay on the trade of Ireland.'* (NN). Reprinted, two volumes in one, in 1731: L; NNC, ICJ, NcD.
Locations: L; ICJ, NNC

1729#8
EGERTON, Henry. *A sermon preached. . . 21st February 1728. . .* London. J. Downing, etc. 64p. 4to. 1729
Note: SABIN 22045, EA 729/80. SPG sermon for 1729, with account of the Society. Two other issues of sermon alone.
Locations: L; RPJCB, MiU-C

1729#9
GEE, Joshua. *The trade and navigation of Great-Britain considered: shewing that the surest way for a nation to increase in riches, is to prevent the importation of such foreign commodities as may be rais'd at home. . .* London. S. Buckley, 129p. 8vo. 1729
Note: EA 729/99–100, 730/94–5, 731/94, 738/109, 750/137, 139. SABIN 26827, HANSON 3901 and 3901n. Another issue in 1729. Other issues/editions 1730, Dublin, 1730, 1731, 1738. Fifth and sixth editions, Glasgow, 1750, 1760. Also French translation, London, 1750.
Locations: L; MiU-C, MH, NN

1729#10
GIBSON, Edmund. *Lettre pastorale de Monseigneur l'éveque de Londres. . .* Londres, J. P. Coderc, 115p. 8vo. 1729
Note: SABIN 27311, EA 729/102. Contains French translation of Gibson's *Two letters. . .* above, 1727.
Locations: RPJCB

1729#11
GIBSON, ——. *Memoirs of Queen Anne: being a compleat supplement to the history of her reign.* London. A. Millar, 317p. 8vo. 1729
Note: EA 729/101. Supplement to Abel Boyer, *History of. . . Queen Anne*, with some American references.
Locations: L; CtY, MHi

1729#12
GREAT BRITAIN. PARLIAMENT. *An act for better preservation of his Majesty's woods in America, and for the encouragement of the importation of naval stores from thence. . .* London. H. Hills and others, [12]p. F. 1729.
Locations: L; Lpro; MnU, RPJCB, MiU-C.

1729#13
GREAT BRITAIN. PARLIAMENT. *Act for establishing an agreement with seven of the lords proprietors of Carolina, for the surrender of their title. . .* London. Assigns of H. Hills and others. F. 1729
Note: SABIN 87355.
Locations: DLC, RPJCB ViU

1729#14
GREAT BRITAIN. PARLIAMENT. *An act for importing salt from Europe, into the colony of New York. . .* London. H. Hills and others, 2p. F. 1729.
Note: ESTC lists as 1730 at NN.
Locations: DLC, RPJCB, MiU-C

1729#15
GREAT BRITAIN. PARLIAMENT. *An act to continue an act. . . intituled, An act for granting liberty to carry rice from His Majesty's province of Carolina. . .* London. J. Baskett, 2p. F. 1729.
Locations: GU, ViU, NcU

1729#16
GREAT BRITAIN. PARLIAMENT. *An act to repeal a clause in an act made in the ninth year of his late Majesty's reign, which prohibits the importation of tobacco stript from the stalk or stem...* London. Assigns of H. Hills and others, s.sh. F. 1729
Locations: RPJCB, IU, OCl

1729#17
GREAT BRITAIN. PARLIAMENT. HOUSE OF COMMONS. *A bill for better preservation of his majesty's woods in America, and for the encouragement of the importation of naval stores from thence...* London. 12p. F. [1729]
Note: HANSON 3961, EA 729/110.
Locations: L; NN

1729#18
GREAT BRITAIN. SOVEREIGN. GEORGE II. *Proclamation. Requiring passes formerly granted to ships trading in way of Algerine cruizers to be returned for reissue [31 December 1729].* London. Assigns of H. M. Printer and H. Hill, s.sh. F. 1729
Note: BRIGHAM 184, CRAWFORD p. 40.
Locations: LPC; RPJCB

1729#19
HENDERSON, Jacob. *The case of the clergy of Maryland...* London. 8p. 4to. [1729]
Note: EA 729/117.
Locations: RPJCB

1729#20
JAMES II. *Memoirs of the English affairs, chiefly naval, from the year 1660, to 1673.* London. 280p. 8vo. 1729
Note: EA 729/128.
Locations: L; CtY, DLC, MH

1729#21
LACY, B [sic]. *Miscellaneous poems compos'd at Newfoundland, on board His Majesty's ship the Kinsale...* London. For the author, 128p. 8vo. 1729
Note: SABIN 38513, FOXON L6, EA 729/133. Lacy was chaplain on the vessel.
Locations: O; DLC, RPJCB

1729#22
A letter from a gentleman in the North of Ireland, to a person in an eminent post under his majesty; concerning the transportation of great numbers from that part of the kingdom to America. Dublin. W. S. Ansburey, 4p. F. 1729
Note: HANSON 4038. Dated 1 July 1729.
Locations: Dt;

1729#23
PRIOR, Thomas. *A list of the absentees of Ireland.* Dublin. R. Gunne, 80p. 8vo. 1729

Note: HANSON 3906 and note, EA 729/173–5. References to emigration. Two further Dublin editions in 1729, one Dublin and three London editions in 1730, EA 730/194–7.
Locations: L; CtY, NNC

1729#24
SOCIETY IN SCOTLAND FOR PROPAGATING CHRISTIAN KNOWLEDGE. *The state of the Society in Scotland, for Propagating Christian Knowledge, anno 1729. Published by order of the general meeting of the foresaid society.* Edinburgh. Printed by William Brown and John Mosman, 48p. 8vo. 1729
Note: This was accompanied by a s.sh. printed letter, which I have not seen: E; Ry. III.a.19(93).
Locations: L; C; ABu;

1729#25
WATTS, Isaac. *A caveat against infidelity.* London. J. Clark and R. Hett, 178p. 8vo. 1729
Note: EA 729/224. References to America.
Locations: L; CtY, MH

1730#1
ASTON, Anthony. *The Fool's Opera; or, the taste of the age. Written by Mat. Medley... To which is prefixed, a sketch of the author's life, written by himself.* London. T. Payne, 19p. 8vo. [1730]
Note: EA dates [1731?], EA 731/14–15. The 'sketch' describes his experiences in the West Indies and North America. It is appended not prefixed in the British Library copy. Another edition in same year.
Locations: L; DLC, MiU-C

1730#2
BOREMAN, Thomas. *A description of three hundred animals; viz. beasts, birds, fishes, serpents and insects. With a particular account of the whale-fishery...* London. J. T. for R.Ware, 212p. 12mo. 1730
Note: EA 730/30, 732/36, 736/40, 743/32. Juvenilia. Editions in 1732, 1734, 1736, 1739, 1743, and 1753 with variant titles.
Locations: L; PPAN, PPULC

1730#3
CATESBY, Mark. *Proposals for printing an essay towards a natural history of Florida, Carolina, and the Bahama islands; containing twelve coloured plates...* F. [London, 1730?]
Note: SABIN 11511, EA 730/44. A prospectus.
Locations: O;

1730#4
CHECKLEY, John. *The speech of Mr. John Checkley upon his tryal, at Boston in New-England, for publishing the Short and easy method with the deists...* London. J. Wilford, 46p. 8vo. 1730

1730

Note: SABIN 12365, 40192n, EA 730/49, EA 738/57. Another edition in 1738.
Locations: L; RPJCB, MH

1730#5
Considerations on the bill for *prohibiting the exportation of corn, etc. from North America.* London. 3p. F. 1730
Note: EA 730/57.
Locations: L; CSmH, PHi

1730#6
COWELL, John. *The curious and profitable gardener... To which is added, an exact description of the great American aloe... together with the culture of that, and many other rare exotic plants...* London. W. Bickerton and others, 126, 67p. 8vo. 1730
Note: SABIN 17237, EA 730/64. Also 1732, 1733, EA 732/73, 733/71.
Locations: L; C; RPJCB, CU, MBH

1730#7
DALTON, James. *The life and actions of James Dalton, (the noted street-robber.)... With a particular account of his running away with the ship when he was first transported...* London. R. Walker, 46p. 8vo. [1730]
Note: SABIN 18351, EA 730/65. His adventures in Bermudas, Virginia, Carolina, etc.
Locations: L; RPJCB

1730#8
DOUGLASS, William. *A practical essay concerning the small-pox.* London. W. Innys, 99p., 8vo. 1730
Note: EA 730/76. Many American references. First printed, Boston, 1730, EVANS 3275.
Locations: L; CtY, MHi

1730#9
Entry cancelled.

1730#10
An enquiry into the melancholy *circumstances of Great Britain.* London. W. Bickerton, 47p. 12mo. [c.1730]. 1730
Note: Other editions 1740?, 1742?. Advocates bounties to encourage raising of plantation commodities.
Locations: L; NN, NIC, PU

1730#11
The fortunes and misfortunes of *Moll Flanders, who was born in Newgate... 8 years a transport in Virginia.* [London]. Printed and sold in Aldermary Church-Yard, 8p. [1730?]
Note: The date is a guess. A chapbook; also in other editions, some with title *Fortune's fickle distribution... Moll Flanders...* In this version 'She was buried in St. Mary's Church, in James Town, the chief town in Virginia...'.
Locations: C;

1730#12
Fortune's fickle distribution; in three *parts...* Dublin. 124p. 8vo. 1730
Note: EA 730/67. Life of Moll Flander's husband, who died in Virginia. Abridged from Moll Flanders.
Locations: L;

1730#13
GIBSON, Edmund. *Second pastoral letter to the people of his diocese...* London. S. Buckley, 80p. 8vo. 1730
Note: EA 730/96–101. Four other London editions and one Dublin edition in 1730; also London, 1731, EA 731/95. Reprinted in his *Three Pastoral letters*, 1732, EA 732/106.
Locations: L; CtY, NN

1730#14
GREAT BRITAIN. PARLIAMENT. *Act for granting liberty to carry rice from... Carolina... directly to any part of Europe, South of Cape Finisterre.* London. Hills and others, 17p. F. 1730
Locations: DLC, RPJCB, MiU-C

1730#15
HUMPHREYS, David. *An account of the endeavours... by the Society for the Propagation of the Gospel... to instruct... slaves in New York. Together with... Bp. Gibson's letters... Being an extract from... Humphrey's Historical Account of... Society... to the year 1728.* London. 45p. 8vo. 1730
Note: SABIN 33800, EA 730/124.
Locations: DLC, RPJCB, MiU-C

1730#16
HUMPHREYS, David. *An historical account of the Incorporated Society for the Propagation of the Gospel in Foreign Parts... to the year 1728.* London. J. Downing, 356p. 8vo. 1730
Note: SABIN 33801, EA 730/125.
Locations: L; DLC, RPJCB, MiU-C

1730#17
The Indian lover's garland; or, *an account of how one of the Indian king's fell in love with a lady that was walking in St. James's park.* [London]. 8p. [1730]
Note: Chapbook. Date is notional.
Locations: EN; MH

1730#18
The iron-trade of Great-Britain impartially *considered...* London. 4p. F. [173–]
Note: HANSON 6422. Date is approximate.
Locations: NNC, MnU

1730#19
LONDON. SOCIETY OF GARDENERS. *Catalogus plantarum, tum exoticarum tum domesticarum...*

London. Society of Gardeners, C. Rivington, T. Cox and others 90p. F. 1730
Note: EA 730/145. Sometimes attributed to Philip Miller.
Locations: L; CtY, CSmH

1730#20
MIDDLETON, Christopher? *Table of meteorological observations from 1721 to 1729 in nine voyages to Hudson's Bay.* London. 8p. 4to. 1730
Note: SABIN 4858(note).
Locations: RPJCB

1730#21
MILLER, Philip. *Catalogus plantarum officinalium...* London. 152p. 8vo. 1730
Note: EA 730/151. Chelsea Botanical gardens catalogue.
Locations: L;

1730#22
MILLER, Philip. *Catalogus plantarum. Part I.* London. Society of Gardeners, xii, 90p. 21 plates. F. 1730
Note: EA 730/145. Many American references. Other parts published (?).
Locations: L; CtY

1730#23
NEWTON, William. *The life of... White Kennett... with several original letters... papers and records...* London. S. Billingsley, 288p. 8vo. 1730
Note: SABIN 37448, EA 730/164. Material on SPG.
Locations: L; DLC, RPJCB, CSmH

1730#24
PEARCE, Zachary. *A sermon preached... on Friday the 20th of February, 1729...* London. J. Downing, 69p. 4to. 1730
Note: SABIN 59435, EA 730/180–1. SPG sermon for 1730, with abstract, Another edition in 1730.
Locations: L; RPJCB, NN, MH

1730#25
PENN, Hannah. *The case of Hannah Penn, the widow and executrix of William Penn Esq; late proprietor and governour of Pensilvania.* London. s.sh. 1/2o. [1730?]
Note: SABIN 59672. Perhaps the same as *The case of the heir at law...*, above, 1725. EA dates [1720], EA 720/180.
Locations: L;

1730#26
Proposals for printing by subscription, *in one volume in folio, A. De La Motraye's voyages lately performed through Maryland, Virginia, Carolina, Pensilvania, New Jersey, New York, New England, and the chief islands thereunto belonging.* London. s.sh. F. [1730]
Note: EA 730/198.
Locations: RPJCB, MB, NHi

1730#27
Reasons humbly offer'd for permitting *rice of the growth of the British plantations, to be transported to Spain, Portugal, and other places to the southward of Cape Finisterre, without being first brought to England.* London. 3p. F. [1730]
Note: HANSON 4091, EA 730/203.
Locations: L; MiU-C, NcU

1730#28
Reasons humbly offered for taking *off the enumeration of rice, made in His Majesty's plantations in America.* London. 3, 1p. F. [1730]
Note: HANSON 4092, EA 730/204.
Locations: L;

1730#29
Reasons humbly offer'd to the... *House of Commons by the merchants and traders in tobacco, with relation to the bill... for lessening the drawback, on tobacco...* London. s.sh. F. [1730?]
Note: SABIN 100517.
Locations: MRc;

1730#30
Reasons proposed to the House *of Commons for laying a duty on East India stock, and that no drawback be allowed on articles exported to America...* London. s.sh. F. [1730]
Note: SABIN 68289, EA 730/205.
Locations: DLC, RPJCB, MiU-C

1730#31
A review of the short *view; and of the remarks on the treaty with Spain...* London. J. Roberts, 30p. 8vo. 1730
Note: SABIN 70269, EA 730/207.
Locations: L; DLC, MH, CtY

1730#32
A specimen towards a new *and compleat plan for regulating and settling the military power of Great Britain... by incorporating the Land and Sea-Forces, and vesting the American trade in our selves...* London. xx, 43p. 8vo. 1730
Note: SABIN 89127, HANSON 4071, EA 730/241.
Locations: O; RPJCB, MiU-C

1731#1
ALBIN, Eleazar. *A natural history of birds. Illustrated with a hundred and one copper plates...* London. Sold by W. Innys, J. Clarke, and J. Brindley, [108]p. 4to. 1731
Note: EA 731/1, 738/1. Vol. II published in 1734. Reissued in 1738. Contains American birds.
Locations: L; MH-Z

1731

1731#2
ASHLEY, John? *The present state of the British sugar colonies consider'd: in a letter from a gentleman of Barbadoes to his friend in London.* London. J. Wilford, 28p. 4to. 1731
Note: HANSON 4234, EA 731/12–13. Discussion of North American trade, etc. Another issue in 1731.
Locations: L; Lu; DLC, RPJCB, CtY

1731#3
BERNARD, Jean Frederic, editor. *The religious ceremonies and customs of the several nations of the known world...* London. N. Prevost, 7 vols. F. 1731
Note: SABIN 4934, EA 731/173. EA 733/66 lists a second edition *The ceremonies and religious customs...*, 1733–39 (L; DLC, NN) but see also EA 733/221 for issue with title of 1731, seemingly published in parts.
Locations: NRU, MWiCA;

1731#4
The case of the British *northern colonies.* London. 4p. F. [1731]
Note: Begins 'These colonies consist of a large tract of land on the northern continent of America, above 1500 miles in length'. Page 1 ends 'carried on clandestinely, which is'. Tract ends 'in respect of those who are to be impoverished by it.' Possibly a different issue of HANSON 4223, KRESS 3296, EA 731/37, which begins similarly but page 1 ends 'trade'. EA 731/38 lists another (?) issue, with last word on page one as 'common', HANSON 4223n, GOLDSMITHS 6873 (L;). ESTC lists the same title, London, 1731, as beginning 'These colonies are vastly superior in compass of land, trade and. . .' (Lpro; MnU, MiU-C). ESTC also lists a version beginning 'These colonies consist of a very large tract of land above 1500 miles in length. . . ' (L; Lpro; NNC). The British Library classmarks are 357.c.1(16), 357.b.12(59), 356.m.2(99) and 9603.f.12(3).
Locations: L; Lpro; RPJCB, NjR, CSmH

1731#5
The case of the British *sugar colonies.* London. 3, 1p. F. [1731]
Note: SABIN 102822, HANSON 4222, KRESS 3297, GOLDSMITH 6852, EA 731/40. EA 732/50 gives another edition in 1732, with hyphenated 'sugar-colonies.'. Begins: 'Our plantations must always be considered. . .'. Ends 'are eager and intent to destroy the rest' Last word on page 1 is 'ourselves' or 'our selves'. LLI; has 2 printings of this. This imprint needs more elucidation. See also the same title below, 1731, 1733, 1737.
Locations: L; LLI; RPJCB, NNC

1731#6
The case of the British *sugar-colonies.* London. 4p. [1731]

Note: HANSON 4222, KRESS 3927, EA 731/39. Begins 'Our plantations must always be considered. . . '. Ends 'much wealth will be actually sunk and lost to this nation.' Last word on page 1 is 'Commerce'.
Locations: L; LLI; MH-BA, RPJCB

1731#7
The case of the merchants *trading to and from America.* London. [4]p. F. [1731]
Note: HANS0N 4217, EA 731/41. ESTC lists under 1730. For protection against the Spanish.
Locations: LLI; CSmH, PPRF

1731#8
The case of the provinces *of the Massachusetts-Bay, and New-Hampshire, and the colonies of Rhoad-Island with Providence plantations, and Connecticut in New England, and the province of New Jersey, with respect to the Bill. . . for the better securing and encouraging the trade of his majesty's sugar colonies. . .* London. 4p. F. [1731]
Note: HANSON 4225, GOLDSMITHS 6853, EA 731/42.
Locations: L; Lu; DLC, NN, MiU-C

1731#9
CATESBY, Mark. *The natural history of Carolina, Florida, and the Bahama Islands. . . with remarks upon agriculture. . .* London. Sold by W. Innys, etc. 2 vols. 2o. 1731
Note: SABIN 11509, EA 731/47. Vol. II published 1741. Other editions 1754, 1771.
Locations: L; DLC, RPJCB, MiU-C

1731#10
The consequences of the bill *now depending in favour of the sugar colonies, impartially considered.* London. s.sh. F. [1731]
Note: SABIN 102824, HANSON 4226, EA 731/58.
Locations: L; Lu; RPJCB, MiU-C

1731#11
DENNE, John. *A sermon preached. . . the 19th of February 1730 [i.e. 1731].* London. J. Downing, 119p. 4to. 1731
Note: SABIN 19581, EA 731/71. SPG sermon for 1731.
Locations: L; RPJCB, MH, PHi

1731#12
The dispute between the northern *colonies and the sugar islands, set in a clear view.* London. 2p. F. [1731]
Note: HANSON 4229, EA 731/77. ESTC lists under 1732.
Locations: L; Lu; RPJCB, MiU-C, CtY

1731#13
An exact and true list *[of] the names of all the persons that was sentenced to be hanged, trasported [sic]. . . at the*

Old-Bailey... London. Printed for Philoregis, s.sh. 1o [1731]
Note: 281 transportees shown for 4 December 1730 to 15 October 1731.
Locations: L;

1731#14
GORDON, Kenneth. *The petition of Mr Kenneth Gordon of Cluny, advocate. 26 November 1731.* London. 6p. F. 1731
Note: KRESS 3941. KRESS also lists twelve other documents relating to this speculation in the French Mississippi scheme on the account of Sir William Gordon.
Locations: MH-BA

1731#15
GREAT BRITAIN. PARLIAMENT. *Act for importing from his majesty's plantations in America, direct into Ireland, goods not enumerated in any act of parliament...* London. Assigns of his majesty's printer and of H. Hills, 8p. F. 1731
Note: Another issue in 1732.
Locations: DLC, MB, MiU-C

1731#16
GREAT BRITAIN. PARLIAMENT. *An act for the better securing and encouraging the trade of His Majesty's sugar colonies in America.* London. 6p. F. [1731]
Note: HANSON 4220. Not enacted.
Locations: L;

1731#17
HALL, Fayrer. *Considerations on the bill now depending in Parliament, concerning the British sugar-colonies in America...* London. J. Peele 24p. 8vo. 1731
Note: Cf. SABIN 15968, 15971-4. HANSON 4227, EA 731/99-100. Another edition in 1731.
Locations: L; Lu; MHi, MiU-C, MB

1731#18
HALL, Fayrer. *The importance of the British plantations in America to this kingdom...* London. J. Peele, 114p. 8vo. 1731
Note: SABIN 29766, HANSON 4230, EA 731/101.
Locations: L; Lu; DLC, RPJCB, MiU-C

1731#19
HALL, Fayrer. *Observations on the trade carried on between our plantations and the foreign colonies in America: occasioned by a petition lately presented to the Honourable House of Commons. Printed in the Daily Post-Boy, March the 1st, 1730.* London. 6p. F. [1731]
Note: HANSON 4233, EA 731/102.
Locations: LLI; NN

1731#20
HALL, Fayrer. *Remarks upon a book, entituled, The present state of the sugar colonies consider'd...* London. J. Peele, 34p. 8vo. 1731
Note: SABIN 69154, HANSON 4235, EA 731/103.
Locations: L; Lu; RPJCB, MiU-C, CtY

1731#21
HERVEY, John. *Remarks on the Craftsman's vindication of his two honble patrons...* London. J. Peele, 62p. 8vo. 1731
Note: EA 731/108-116. Eight other issues in 1731. References to Canada and Newfoundland.
Locations: Lu; MH, MB

1731#22
HUNT, Jeremiah. *Victory... A sermon... January 31st 1730... Death of Thomas Hollis, Esq...* London. T. Coxe, 32p. 8vo. 1731
Note: SABIN 33871. Hollis was a noted benefactor of Harvard etc. but this item contains no direct references to North America.
Locations: MH, CtY

1731#23
The importance of the sugar *colonies to Great-Britain stated, and some objections against the sugar colony bill answer'd...* London. J. Roberts, 40p. 8vo. 1731
Note: HANSON 4231, EA 731/121.
Locations: L; Lu; RPJCB, MB, CtY

1731#24
KINLOCH, Robert. *The truth and excellency of the gospel-revelation...* Edinburgh. William Brown, 36p. 8vo. 1731
Note: Society in Scotland for the Propagation of the Gospel sermon for 1731. References to New England.
Locations: L; E; MH, MB

1731#25
MILLER, Philip. *The gardeners dictionary.* London. For the author, [843]p. F. 1731
Note: EA 731/146. Other editions, Dublin 1732, 1741, London, 1733, 1735, 1737, 1743, EA 732/161, 733/181, 735/164, 737/153, 741/152, 743/158. A second volume in 1739, of which a second edition in 1740, EA 739/198, 740/211. A third volume in 1740, EA 740/212. Abridged, 1735, 1741, EA 735/164, 741/151. An appendix, 1735, EA 735/163.
Locations: L; MH-A, CLU-C

1731#26
Observations on the case of *the northern colonies.* London. J. Roberts, 31p. 8vo. 1731
Note: SABIN 56510, HANSON 4224, EA 731/153.
Locations: L; Lu; DLC, RPJCB, MiU-C

1731

1731#27
OLLYFFE, George. *An essay humbly offer'd for an act of Parliament to prevent capital crimes.* . . London. J. Downing, 28p. 8vo. 1731
Note: For more severe punishments, including branding of tranportees; also for selling vagrants as slaves to the plantations and for assisted emigrant schemes. A second edition in 1731.
Locations: L; CtY, CLL

1731#28
PREVOST D'EXILES, Antoine François. *The life of Mr Cleveland, natural son of Oliver Cromwell, written by himself. Giving a particular account of. . . his great sufferings in Europe and America.* . . London. E. Symon and N. Prevost, 4 vols., 12mo. 1731
Note: EA 731/163, Other editions with variant titles, 1732, 1734, 1736, 1741, and Dublin 1736 and 1750, EA 732/188, 734/175, 741/180, 750/250. SABIN 13663, 65441. 'A romance, translated from *Le Philosophe Anglais*', GOVE, 279–84.
Locations: DFo

1731#29
PRIOR, Thomas. *Observations on the trade between Ireland, and the English and foreign colonies in America. In a letter to a friend.* London. 20p. 8vo. 1731
Note: HANSON 4236, EA 731/154.
Locations: REu; RPJCB, MH-BA

1731#30
PULTENEY, William. *A proper reply to a late scurrilous libel; intituled Sedition and defamation displayed.* . . London. R. Francklin, 36p. 8vo. 1731
Note: SABIN 66643, KRESS 3911, EA 731/18–19. Some references to trade, war, etc. Another edition, 1731.
Locations: L; MH-BA, RPJCB, CSmH

1731#31
RUDD, Sayer. *A poem on the death of the late Thomas Hollis, Esq., humbly inscribed to Mr John Hollis, brother of the deceased.* . . London. A. Ward, T. Cox, 36p. 8vo. 1731
Note: SABIN 73885, FOXON R327, EA 731/177. Refers to Hollis's American benefactions.
Locations: MH, CtY, MWA

1731#32
SCOTLAND. CHURCH OF SCOTLAND. GENERAL ASSEMBLY. *Edinburgh, 20 May 1731. R.D.B. [Reverend and Dear Brethren].* . . [Edinburgh]. [1731]
Note: Refers to collections and success of that for Presbyterian church in New York.
Locations: E;

1731#33
A short answer to an elaborate pamphlet, entitled, *The Importance of the sugar plantations, etc.* . . *In a letter to a noble peer.* London. 28p. 8vo. 1731
Note: HANSON 4232, EA 731/182.
Locations: L; DLC, RPJCB, CtY

1731#34
WEBB, George. *Batchelors hall. A poem.* . . Dublin. Philadelphia printed and reprinted in Dublin, for James Hoey, 14p. 8vo. [1731?]
Note: FOXON W263. First printed Philadelphia, 1731. EVANS 3485. 'A country so young as ours'.
Locations: L;

1731#35
Z——h, A——r. *Considerations on the dispute now depending before the Honourable House of Commons, between the British, southern and northern plantations.* . . *In a letter to ——.* London. J. Roberts, 30p. 8vo. 1731
Note: HANSON 4228, EA 731/59.
Locations: L; Lu; RPJCB, MiU-C

1732#1
ANDERSON, James. *Royal genealogies.* . . *Part I.* . . *the genealogies of the earliest great families, and most ancient sovereigns of Asia, Europe, Africa and America.* . . London. J. Bettenham, 812p. 2o. 1732
Note: SABIN 1398, EA 732/6, 735/8, 736/4. Second edition, 1735, enlarged second edition, 1736.
Locations: L; DLC, MB

1732#2
Answers to all the objections made to the bill for supporting the sugar colonies. London. 3p. 2o. [1732]
Note: SABIN 102817, EA 732/7. HANSON 4221 gives date 1731.
Locations: L; Lpro; Lu; RPJCB, MiU-C

1732#3
ASHLEY, John. *The British empire in America, consider'd. In a second letter, from a gentleman of Barbadoes.* . . London. J. Wilford, 29p. 4to. 1732
Note: HANSON 4363, EA 732/41. Mostly about Caribbean.
Locations: Lu; O; DLC, RPJCB

1732#4
B., A. *An expostulatory letter to Mr. Daniel Neal, upon occasion of his publishing the History of the Puritans.* . . London. J. Roberts, 30p. 8vo. 1732
Note: EA 732/92. Attacks New England Puritanism.
Locations: L; RPJCB, MiU-C

1732#5
BERKELEY, George. *A sermon preached.* . . *on.* . . *February 18, 1731.* . . London. J. Downing, 78p. 8vo. 1732

144

Note: SABIN 4879, EA 732/21. SPG sermon for 1732.
Locations: L; DLC, RPJCB

1732#6
BESSE, Joseph. *A cloud of witnesses.* . . London. Assigns of J. Sowle, 53p. 8vo. 1732
Note: SMITH I, 251. Extracts from Quaker (including Pennsylvania) writing.
Locations: L; MH, PHC

1732#7
Britannia major: the new scheme, *or essay, for discharging the debts, improving the lands, and enlarging the trade, of the British dominions in Europe and America.* London. J. Noon, 70p. 8vo. 1732
Note: HANSON 4307, EA 732/40.
Locations: L; Lse; DLC, RPJCB

1732#8
The case of the British *northern colonies.* London. 4p. F. [1731]
Note: Cf. HANSON 4223n. KRESS SUPP. 3393, EA 732/49. Begins 'These colonies consist of a very large tract of land above 1500 miles. . . '. Page 1 ends 'upwards of 300 sail of vessels.' Tract ends 'which Duty will be intirely lost if this Bill prevails.' Bound with a bill dated 28 January 1732. The British Library classmark is 357 b 12(60).
Locations: L; Lpro; NNC, MH

1732#9
The case of the merchants *of London, and manufacturers of wheat and biscuit.* London. 1p. F. 1732
Note: HANSON 4333. Petition for bounty on exports of wheat biscuit, particularly to Newfoundland.
Locations: L;

1732#10
The case of the tobacco *planters in his Majesty's Colony of Virginia, as to the bill now depending in the House of Lords, for the more easy recovery of debts in his Majesty's Plantations and colonies abroad.* London. 3, 1p. F. [1732]
Note: HANSON 4375, EA 732/51.
Locations: LLI; RPJCB, DLC, CtY

1732#11
A comparison between the British *sugar colonies and New England, as they relate to the interest of Great Britain. With some observations on the state of the case of New England. To which is added A letter to a Member of Parliament.* London. J. Roberts, 43p. 8vo. 1732
Note: HANSON 4364, EA 732/67.
Locations: L; Lu; DLC, RPJCB, CtY

1732#12
The controversy between the Northern *colonies and the sugar islands, respectively considered.* . . London. s.sh. F. [1732]
Note: HANSON 4365, EA 732/68.
Locations: L; RPJCB

1732#13
CROUCH, Henry. *A complete guide to the officers of His Majesty's customs in the out-ports. Being forms, precedents, and instructions.* . . London. Printed for the author, ix, [1], 345p. 2o. 1732
Note: British Library copy has list of subscribers.
Locations: L; Lce; Lke; CtY, PU-L

1732#14
DUDLEY, Paul. *An essay on the merchandise of slaves and the souls of men.* . . *With an application thereof to the Church of Rome.* London. Printed at Boston in New England and reprinted at London for J. Downing, 35p. 8vo. 1732
Note: SABIN 21087. Other editions, 1732, 1733. First printed Boston, 1731, EVANS 3413. Anti-Catholic, not anti-slavery!
Locations: L; RPJCB, NIC, MH-AH

1732#15
FURBER, Robert. *The flower-garden display'd.* London. J. Hazard and others, 108p. 4to. 1732
Note: EA 732/101. Also, 1734, EA 734/81. Also attributed to Richard Bradley.
Locations: L; CSmH, DLC, NN

1732#16
GREAT BRITAIN. PARLIAMENT. *Act for the more easy securing of debts in his majesty's plantations and colonies in America.* London. J. Baskett, 2p. F. [1732]
Locations: DLC, MB, MiU-C

1732#17
GREAT BRITAIN. PARLIAMENT. *Act to explain an act made in the last session of Parliament, intituled, An act for importing from.* . . *America, directly into Ireland, goods not enumerated.* . . London. J. Baskett, s.sh. F. 1732
Locations: RPJCB, MiU-C

1732#18
GREAT BRITAIN. PARLIAMENT. *An act to prevent the exportation of hats out of any of His Majesty's colonies in America, and to restrain the number of apprentices taken by the hat-makers in the said colonies.* . . London. J. Baskett, 3p. F. 1732
Locations: NN, MiU-C

1732#19
GREAT BRITAIN. PARLIAMENT. HOUSE OF COMMONS. *A bill, intituled, An act for the better*

1732

securing and encouraging the trade of His Majesty's sugar colonies in America. London. 7,1p. 2o. [1732?]
Note: HANSON 4360, EA 732/109–110. Not enacted. Another edition in 1732.
Locations: L; CtY, RPJCB

1732#20
HALL, Fayrer. *Captain Fayrer Hall's evidence, before a Committee of the House of Commons, in April 1731 concerning the sugar colony bill. Remarks on the examination before the Committee of the Honourable House of Commons.* London. 12p. F. [1732]
Note: HANSON 4361, EA 732/117.
Locations: Lpro; MnU

1732#21
HALL, Fayrer. *My Lord, The Bill upon which I was examined last year...* London. F. [1732]
Note: HANSON 4362, EA 732/118. Corrects his evidence on the Molasses Bill. See Hall, above, 1732.
Locations: Lpro;

1732#22
HAMILTON, William. *The truth and economy of the Christian religion. A sermon preached... January 3, 1732.* Edinburgh. R. Fleming for G. Hamilton, 32p. 8vo. 1732
Note: EA 732/120–1. Another edition in 1732? Scottish Society for propagating Christian Knowledge sermon for 1732. Also Edinburgh, 1735, EA 735/116.
Locations: L; C; RPJCB, TxU

1732#23
The hatmakers case. Shewing that the present exporting of beaver hats of the manufacture of the colonies in America, hath been, and is, a very great discouragement to the English hatmakers. London. s.sh. F. [1732]
Note: HANSON 4334, EA 732/122. Against the import of American beaver hats.
Locations: L; Lpro

1732#24
Hurlo-Thrumbo's lucubrations... *Very proper to be bound up with a pamphlet... A true state of the case between the British northern colonies and the sugar-islands...* London. 7p. 4to. 1732
Note: HANSON 4367, EA 732/234.
Locations: Lu;

1732#25
A letter to a gentleman, *concerning the boundaries of the province of Maryland. Wherein is shewn, that no part of the 40th degree of latitude, is, or can be any part thereof.* London. E. Owen, 15p. 8vo. [1732]
Note: SABIN 45914, EA 732/142.
Locations: DLC, RPJCB

1732#26
The lives of the most remarkable criminals, who have been condemn'd and executed; for murder,... or other offences; from the year 1720, to the present time:... Collected from original papers and authentick memoirs. Vol. I... London. Printed and sold by John Applebee; A. Bettesworth and others, xxiii, [1], 480, [12]p. 12mo. 1732
Note: Printed in 3 vols. in 1735 (L;). American references.
Locations: PP

1732#27
MARTYN, Benjamin. *A new and accurate account of the provinces of South-Carolina and Georgia. With many curious and useful observations on the trade, navigation and plantations of Great-Britain...* London. J. Worrall, J. Roberts, 76p. 8vo. 1732
Note: SABIN 56847, EA 732/176, 733/193. Second edition, 1733. Also attributed to James Oglethorpe.
Locations: L; C; DLC, RPJCB, NN

1732#28
MARTYN, Benjamin. *Some account of the designs of the Trustees for establishing the colony of Georgia in America.* London. 4p. F. [1732]
Note: SABIN 86573–4, HANSON 4378 and note, EA 732/155–7. Two other issues/editions in 1732. For an argument that this tract was written by James Oglethorpe, see R.M. Blaine, 'James Oglethorpe and the early promotional literature for Georgia', *William and Mary Quarterly*, XLV, No. 1 (January, 1988).
Locations: L; RPJCB

1732#29
MASSACHUSETTS. GOVERNOR. *A conference of... J. Belcher, Esq... with Edewakenk Chief Sachem of the Penobscut tribe, Loron one of the chief captains of the same tribe...* London. N. Cholmondeley, 28p. 4to. 1732
Note: SABIN 15429, EA 732/158. First printed Boston, 1732 (EVANS 3554).
Locations: L; DLC, RPJCB

1732#30
NEAL, Daniel. *The history of the puritans, or protestant nonconformists... to the death of Queen Elizabeth...* London. R. Hett, 4 vols. 8vo. [1732–4]
Note: SABIN 52142, 52143, EA 732/171. A second edition in 1754 to the Act of Toleration.
Locations: DLC, MH, CtY

1732#31
OGLETHORPE, James Edward. *Select tracts relating to colonies...* London. J. Roberts, 40p. 8vo. 1732

Note: SABIN 78992, HANSON 4372, KRESS 4241, EA 732/221. Contains tracts by Bacon, De Witt, Penn, Child.
Locations: L; Lu; RPJCB, MiU-C

1732#32
PECK, Philip. *Some observations for improvement of trade, by establishing the fishery of Great Britain...* London. For the author, 55p. 8vo. 1732
Note: HANSON 4332, EA 732/178–80. Two more editions in 1732. Discusses colonies.
Locations: L; RPJCB

1732#33
PERSON WELL ACQUAINTED WITH THE SUGAR TRADE. *Some considerations touching the sugar colonies, with political observations in respect to trade...* London. J. Clarke, 24p. 4to. 1732
Note: SABIN 86628, HANSON 4369, EA 732/226.
Locations: L; RPJCB, NN, NNC

1732#34
PUGH, Ellis. *A salutation to the Britains, to call them from many things, to the one thing needful, for the saving of their souls... translated from the British language.* London. Assigns of J. Sowle, 194p. 12mo. 1732
Note: SABIN 66608, EA 732/194, 739/238. First printed Philadelphia, 1727 (EVANS 2950). Pugh lived in Pennsylvania. Another London edition with account of author, 1739.
Locations: CtY, PHC, PSC-Hi

1732#35
ROBERTSON, Robert. *A detection of the state and situation of the present sugar planters, of Barbadoes and the Leeward islands...* London. J. Wilford, 99p. 8vo. 1732
Note: HANSON 4366, EA 732/211. Discusses population of northern colonies and other North American matters.
Locations: L; DLC, RPJCB, CtY

1732#36
S., T. *The principles of the leading Quakers truly represented.* London. J. Roberts, 232p. 8vo. 1732
Note: SMITH, AQ, 38, EA 732/191. Keithian controversy in Pennsylvania.
Locations: L; DLC, RPJCB

1732#36A
A serious call to the *City of London, and thro' them to the whole nation, to the relief of the persecuted Protestants of Saltzburg. With a postscript, giving some account of their sufferings, and the numbers that were forc'd out of their country.* London. J. Noon, 19p. 8vo. 1732
Note: HANSON 4466.
Locations: L; DLC

1732#37
SOCIETY IN SCOTLAND FOR PROPAGATING CHRISTIAN KNOWLEDGE. *An abridgement of the statutes and rules of the Society...* London. R. Fleming, 48p. 8vo. 1732
Locations: L; E; CLU-C, CSmH

1732#38
SOCIETY IN SCOTLAND FOR PROPAGATING CHRISTIAN KNOWLEDGE. *A short state of the Society...* Edinburgh. W. Brown, 32p. 8vo. 1732
Locations: E; Gu; LG; CLU-C, CtY-D

1732#39
Some considerations humbly offer'd upon *the bill now depending in the House of Lords, relating to the trade between the Northern Colonies and the Sugar-Islands. In a letter to a noble peer.* London. 19p. 8vo. 1732
Note: SABIN 15972, 86616, HANSON 4368, KRESS 4046, EA 732/225.
Locations: L; DLC, MH, NN

1732#40
Some observations on the Northern *colonie trade with the French sugar colonies with respect to our acts of Parliament now in force in a letter to a noble Lord.* London. 3, 1p. F. [1732]
Note: HANSON 4370, EA 732/227.
Locations: L; NNC

1732#41
TATE, Robert. *A practical treatise upon several different and useful subjects... IV. A rational way for the promulgation of the gospel in America...* London. J. Roberts, 116p. 4to. 1732
Note: HANSON 4306, EA 732/233.
Locations: L; RPJCB, MH, CSmH

1732#42
A true representation of the *state of the case of the sugar islands... fully answering a paper, entitled, The dispute between the northern settlements and the sugar colonies... March 4, 1731/2...* London. 4p. F. [1732?]
Note: SABIN 97146, EA 732/238. Caption title.
Locations: MWA, RPJCB, MiU-C

1732#43
A true state of the *case between the British Northern-Colonies, and the sugar islands in America... with respect to the bill... in... the House of Lords, relating to the sugar trade.* London. 46p. 4to. 1732
Note: SABIN 97150, HANSON 4371, EA 732/239.
Locations: L; Lpro; DLC, NN, RPJCB

1733#1
B., L. *The real and true case of the planters in Virginia.* London. 3, 1p. F. [1733]

1733

Note: Docket title. Accuses Virginia agent of being ready to use bribery. CSmH 180821.
Locations: CSmH

1733#2
BARCLAY, Patrick. *The universal traveller: or, A complete account of the most remarkable voyages and travels.* London. A. Holbeche and others, 795p. F. 1733
Note: EA 733/18. Also 1735 and Dublin, 1735, EA 735/25–6. Book I deals with the Americas.
Locations: CLU-C, CSmH

1733#3
BESSE, Joseph. *The sufferings of the people call'd Quakers. . . from the year 1650 to the year 1660.* London. Assigns of J. Sowle, 3 vols. 8vo. 1733
Note: SABIN 66904, SMITH I, 252, HIGGS 659, EA 733/26, 738/22. Includes New England Quakers. Vols. II and III, published in 1738. Reprinted in extended (?) form in 1753, in two volumes. Some references give the title as *An abstract of the sufferings. . .*
Locations: L; RPJCB, MiU-C, CtY

1733#4
BURTON, John. *The duty and reward of propagating principles of religion and virtue. . . A sermon preach'd. . . March 15, 1732. . .* London. J. March, 50p. 4to. 1733
Note: SABIN 9492, 83978, EA 733/34. Georgia Trustees anniversary sermon, with the General Account.
Locations: L; Ct; DLC, RPJCB, MiU-C

1733#5
The case of the British *northern colonies.* London. 3p. F. [1733]
Note: EA 733/41, KRESS SUPP. 3425. Cf. HANSON 4223. Begins 'This is the third time. . .'.
Locations: MH-BA, NNC

1733#6
The case of the British *sugar colonies.* London. 3p. [1]p. F. [1733?]
Note: HANSON 4517, who dates to [1733], EA 733/42. Begins 'The British sugar colonies are of the utmost consequence and importance. . .'. Ends 'to save us this most valuable branch of our commerce.' Last word on page 1 is 'And'.
Locations: LLI; NNC

1733#7
The case of the colony *of Rhoad Island, and Providence Plantations, and the province of New Jersey in America; with respect to the bill. . . Commons. . . A bill for the better securing and encouraging the. . . trade of. . . sugar colonies. . .* London. 3p. F. 1733
Note: EA 733/43. Printed for the use of counsel.
Locations: RPJCB

1733#8
The case of the planters *of tobacco in Virginia, as represented by themselves, signed by the President of the Council and Speaker of the House of Burgesses. . . Williamsburg, June 28, 1732.* London. 4p. F. 1733
Note: SABIN 99910, HANSON 4518, EA 733/44–5. Another edition in 1733. For the use of counsel.
Locations: L; RPJCB

1733#9
The case of the planters *of tobacco in Virginia, as represented by themselves; signed by the President of the Council, and Speaker of the House of Burgesses. To which is added, A vindication of the said representation.* London. J. Roberts, 64p. 8vo. 1733
Note: HANSON 4520, EA 733/46–7. Another issue in 1733. The 'Vindication' is by John Randolph.
Locations: L; RPJCB, KEmT, MiU-C

1733#10
The case of the province *of New York, one of the British northern colonies. . .* London. 3p. F. 1733
Note: EA 733/48. Printed for the use of counsel.
Locations: RPJCB

1733#11
The case of the province *of Virginia, one of the British northern [sic] colonies. . .* London. 3p. F. 1733
Note: EA 733/49. Printed for the use of counsel.
Locations: RPJCB

1733#12
A compendious account of the *whole art of breeding, nursing, and the right ordering of the silk-worm. Illustrated with figures engraven on copper: whereon is curiously exhibited the whole management of this profitable insect.* London. J. Worall, 32p. 4to. [1733?]
Note: HANSON 4320, EA 733/28. Dedicated by T. B. to Georgia Trustees. By Thomas Boreman.
Locations: L; DLC, RPJCB, CtY

1733#13
A discourse on trade; more *particularly on sugar and tobacco: shewing the true and natural means of their support, and the unreasonableness of depending upon the legislature for their relief.* London. J. Roberts, 24p. 8vo. 1733
Note: SABIN 20245, HANSON 4522, EA 733/81.
Locations: L; NNC, CSmH

1733#14
E., R. *The Present state of popery in England. . .* London. A. Dodd, 35p. 8vo. 1733
Note: SABIN 65326, EA 733/209–10, EA 733/209–10. A second edition in 1733. References to Maryland, West Indies, etc.
Locations: L; NN, MH, NN

1733#15
Englishmen's eyes open'd; or All made to see.
London. J. Wilford, 77p. 8vo. 1733
Note: EA 733/85, HANSON 4553. Second edition in 1734, EA 734/72. Tobacco planters.
Locations: L; CtY, RPJCB

1733#16
GEORGIA TRUSTEES. *The general account of all monies and effects received and expended by the Trustees for. . . Georgia. . . from. . . ninth. . . June. . . 1732. . . to ninth. . . June. . . 1733.* . . London. 18p. F. [1733]
Note: HANSON 4532, EA 733/103.
Locations: L; RPJCB, GHi

1733#17
GREAT BRITAIN. PARLIAMENT. *Act for better securing and encouraging trade of His Majesty's sugar colonies in America.* London. J. Baskett, 7p. F. 1733
Locations: RPJCB, DLC, MB

1733#18
GREAT BRITAIN. PARLIAMENT. *Act to apply five hundred thousand pounds out of sinking fund. . . by paying off. . . and ten thousand pounds to the Trustees for. . . Georgia.* . . London. J. Baskett, 12p. F. 1733
Locations: MiU-C

1733#19
GREAT BRITAIN. PARLIAMENT. HOUSE OF COMMONS. *A bill, intituled, an act for the better securing and encouraging the trade of His Majesty's Sugar colonies in America.* London. 7p. F. [1733]
Note: EA 733/113.
Locations: L; RPJCB, MB, MiU-C

1733#20
GREAT BRITAIN. PARLIAMENT. HOUSE OF COMMONS COMMITTEE. *The report, with appendix, from committee of. . . Commons appointed to enquire into the frauds and abuses in the customs. . . Published by order of the House of Commons.* London. R. Williamson, R. Bowyer, 103p. 2o 1733
Locations: L; RPJCB, NHi, MiU-C

1733#21
GREAT BRITAIN. SOVEREIGN. GEORGE II. *South-Carolina, George the Second by the grace of God.* . . London. s.sh. F. [1733]
Note: HANSON 4534, EA 733/121. Form of grant of Crown lands. English or American?
Locations: Lpro;

1733#22
A letter to a noble peer, *relating to the Bill in favour of the sugar planters.* London. 22p. 8vo. 1733
Note: HANSON 4525, EA 733/156.
Locations: DLC, RPJCB, PU

1733#23
LINDSAY, Patrick. *The interest of Scotland considered.* . . Edinburgh. R. Fleming, 229p. 8vo. 1733
Note: KRESS 4111, EA 733/158, 736/135. Also London, 1736. Detailed discussion of Scottish-American trade.
Locations: L; RPJCB, CtY, MH-BA

1733#24
MARTYN, Benjamin. *Reasons for establishing the colony of Georgia, with regard to the trade of Great Britain, the increase of our people. . . employment. . . of. . . poor, as well as foreign persecuted Protestants. With some account of the country, and the design of the Trustees.* London. W. Meadows, 48p. 4to. 1733
Note: SABIN 45002, HANSON 4531, EA 733/176–8. Three issues in 1733, one with postcript.
Locations: L; O; DLC, RPJCB, MiU-C

1733#25
NATIVE OF NEW-YORK. *The counterpart to the state dunces. By a native of New-York.* London. W. Mears, 10p. 2o. 1733
Note: Verses. FOXON C442.
Locations: L; DLC, OCU, MB

1733#26
PHILO-AMERICUS. *Some further considerations of the consequences of the bill now depending in the House of Lords, relating to the dispute of the trade of the British colonies in America.* . . London. F. [1733]
Note: HANSON 4528, EA 733/248.
Locations: Lpro;

1733#27
Observations on The case of the planters of Virginia. In a letter to ——. London. 4p. F. 1733
Note: HANSON 4519, SABIN 100505, EA 733/191. For The case. . . , see above, 1729.
Locations: L; RPJCB, NN

1733#28
The practical husbandman and planter. . .
London. S. Switzer, 2 vols. 8vo. 1733
Note: EA 733/208. First issued in parts. Reissued in 1734, EA 734/1723.
Locations: L; Lrag; MH-A, CU

1733#29
A reply to the Vindication of the Representation of the Case of the planters of tobacco in Virginia. In a letter to Sir J. R. from the merchants or factors of London. London. R. Charlton, 56p. 8vo. 1733
Note: SABIN 69714, HANSON 4521, EA 733/160.
Locations: L; Lu; DLC, RPJCB, NN

1733#30
ROBERTSON, Robert. *A supplement to the detection of the state and situation of the present sugar planters...* London. J. Wilford, 92p. 8vo. 1733
Note: HANSON 4529, EA 733/228. Discusses relative wealth of northern and sugar colonies.
Locations: L; NN, CSmH, CtY

1733#31
Short observations on the bill at present depending in favour of the sugar-islanders... London. s.sh. F. [1733?]
Note: HANSON 4527, EA 733/239.
Locations: L;

1733#32
SMALBROKE, Richard. *A sermon preached... February 16, 1732...* London. J. Downing, 83p. 4to. 1733
Note: SABIN 82914, EA 733/242. SPG sermon for 1733, with abstract, etc.
Locations: L; DLC, RPJCB, CSmH

1733#33
SMITH, James. *The misery of ignorant and unconverted sinners. A sermon preached in the High Church of Edinburgh, Monday, January 1. 1733. Upon occasion of the anniversary meeting of the Society in Scotland for propagating Christian knowledge...* Edinburgh. R. Fleming and Co. for A. Martin, 23p. 8vo. 1733
Note: EA 733/243.
Locations: L; E; MH-H, RPJCB

1733#34
SMITH, Samuel. *A sermon preach'd before the Trustees for... Georgia... and Associates of... Bray... February 23, 1730–1...* London. J. March, 42p. 4to. 1733
Note: SABIN 83978, HANSON 4533, EA 733/244. Anniversary sermon. With account of designs of Trustees and Associates.
Locations: NCp; DLC, RPJCB, MiU-C

1733#35
True copies of I. the agreement between Lord Baltimore and Messieurs Penn, dated 10 May 1732. II. The commissions... to mark out the lines... III. The return... of the commissioners on both sides... London. 7p. F. [1733 or 1734]
Note: SABIN 60743, 97106, EA 734/16, 16a. Another edition, [1733 or 1734?]? First printed Philadelphia, 1733, EVANS 3710, SABIN 45073.
Locations: DLC, RPJCB, PPULC

1733#36
VAREN, Bernhard. *A compleat system of general geography...* London. S. Austen, 2 vols. 8vo. 1733

Note: EA 733/270. Also 1734, 1736, EA 734/223, 736/246.
Locations: L; IU, MH

1733#37
VOLTAIRE, François Marie Arouet de. *Letters concerning the English Nation...* London. C. Davis and A. Lyon, 253p. 8vo. 1733
Note: SABIN 100751, EA 733/273–4, 739/326, 740/322, 741/251. Also Dublin 1733, 1739, 1740 and other 'corrected' etc., editions 1741, 1752, 1760.
Locations: L; CSmH, NN, NjP

1734#1
AUTHOR OF 'SOME CONSIDERATIONS TOUCHING THE SUGAR COLONIES'. *Farther considerations touching the sugar colonies, with additional observations in respect to trade... By the author of Some considerations touching the sugar colonies, with political observations in respect to trade.* London. Printed for John Clarke, 34, [2]p. 4to. 1734
Locations: NN, NNC

1734#2
BEST, William. *The relief of the persecuted protestants of Saltzburgh, and the support of the colony of Georgia, recommended in a sermon preach'd... January 13, 1734...* London. W. Innys, R.Manby, 26p. 8vo. 1734
Note: SABIN 5055, EA 734/31. ESTC dates 1735.
Locations: L; Csj; O; DLC, MiU-C

1734#3
BLUETT, Thomas. *Some memoirs of the life of Job, the son of Solomon the high priest of Boonda in Africa; who was a slave about two years in Maryland; and afterwards being brought to England, was set free, and sent to his native land in 1734...* London. R. Ford, 63p. 8vo. 1734
Note: HANSON 4701, EA 734/32.
Locations: L; DLC, RPJCB, MiU-C

1734#4
CAMPBELL, Duncan. *Time's telescope universal and perpetual... with a general view of the four parts of the world.* London. J. Wilcox, 155p. 8vo. 1734
Note: EA 734/41.
Locations: L; MiU, DLC, CtY

1734#5
EBORANOS. *Ways and means whereby his majesty may man his navy with ten thousand able sailors... To which is added a collection of some political essays. By Eboranos.* London. T. Cooper, 8, 67p. 8vo. [1734]
Note: HANSON 4749. Another edition 1735, with title *A collection of political tracts... On transportation laws.* By Thomas Robe(?). NUC dates 1726: MH, NNC, NN (31p.

8vo.). A second edition in 1726 and third edition 1740: MH, NN.
Locations: L;

1734#6
GEORGIA TRUSTEES. *The general account of all monies and effects received and expended by the Trustees for... Georgia... from the ninth day of June... 1733. to the ninth day of June... 1734...* London. 37p. 2o. [1734]
Note: EA 734/85.
Locations: L; RPJCB, NN

1734#7
GRADY, ——. *A description of the famous new colony of Georgia, in South Carolina (establish'd by the present majesty,) of which Colonel David Dunbar is governor; with an account of the inhabitants, climate, soil, birds, beasts and other curious particulars...* Dublin. J. Hoey, 138p. 8vo. 1734
Note: HANSON 4707. De Renne, I, 50 states that 'Georgia' probably refers to part of Nova Scotia, not to the colony of Georgia. EA 734/91. Not listed in ESTC?
Locations: DLC, RPJCB, MiU-C

1734#8
GREAT BRITAIN. COMMISSIONERS FOR TRADE AND PLANTATIONS. *Representation of the Board of Trade relating to the laws made, manufactures set up, and trade carried on, in His Majesty's plantations in America.* London. 20p. F. [1733/4]
Note: SABIN 69997, HANSON 4705, EA 734/92, 749/124. Another edition in 1749. Representation is dated 23 Jan 1733-4. Pursuant to Lord's address of 13 June 1733.
Locations: L; Csj; Lu; RPJCB

1734#9
GREAT BRITAIN. COMMISSIONERS OF CUSTOMS. *Instructions by the Commissioners for managing... his majesty's customs... in England, to [blank] who is established collector of his majesty's customs at [blank] in America.* London. 23p. 2o. [1734?]
Note: With specimen forms.
Locations: L;

1734#10
GREAT BRITAIN. PARLIAMENT. HOUSE OF LORDS. *The Lord's protest in the last session of Parliament, viz... IV. On the representation of the state of the colonies in America... [26 March 1734].* London. T. Tims, 13p. F. [1734]
Note: KRESS SUPP. 3475, EA 734/93.
Locations: L; RPJCB

1734#11
HALES, Stephen. *A sermon preached before the trustees... Thursday, March 21, 1734...* London. T. Woodward, 62p. 4to. 1734
Note: SABIN 29673, EA 734/100. Georgia Trustees anniversary sermon with the General Account.
Locations: L; Cq; DLC, RPJCB, CtY

1734#12
JOHNSON, Charles. *A general history of the lives and actions of the most famous highwaymen, murderers, street-robbers... To which is added, A genuine account of the voyages and plunders of the most notorious pyrates...* London. J. Janeway, 494p. 2o. 1734
Note: SABIN 36194-6, EA 734/111, 736/120, 742/107-9. Also London 1736, 1742 and two Birmingham editions in 1742. The titles vary slightly. A mélange of Daniel Defoe and Alexander Smith. See Smith, above, 1720, Defoe, above, 1724.
Locations: L; DLC, MH, CtY

1734#13
MADDOX, Isaac. *A sermon preached... on Friday the 15th of February, 1733...* London. J. Downing, 74p. 4to. 1734
Note: SABIN 43700n, EA 734/133. SPG sermon for 1734, with abstract, etc.
Locations: L; DLC, RPJCB, NN

1734#14
MIDDLETON, Patrick. *A short view of the evidence upon which the Christian religion... is established...* London. G. Strahan and others, 2pts. 8vo. 1734
Note: EA 734/148. Appendix includes 'state of the Americans'.
Locations: L; MH, RPJCB

1734#15
NEAL, Daniel. *A review of the principal facts objected to the first volume of the History of the Puritans...* London. R. Hett, 87p. 8vo. 1734
Note: SABIN 5217.
Locations: L; DLC, CtY, NN

1734#16
PULTENEY, William. *The politicks on both sides, with regard to foreign affairs, stated from their own writings...* London. H. Haines, 75p. 8vo. 1734
Note: HANSON 4696, SABIN 66642, EA 734/22-3. Also second edition corrected, H. Haines, 72p. Mainly Spanish America.
Locations: L; RPJCB

1734#17
RECK, Philipp G. and BOLTZIUS, John Martin. *An extract of the journals of Mr Commissary Von Reck, who conducted the first transport of Saltzburgers*

1734

to Georgia; and of the Reverend Mr Bolzius, one of their ministers... London. M. Downing for SPCK, 72p. 8vo. 1734
Note: HANSON 4708, EA 734/179.
Locations: L; MiU-C, CSmH

1734#18
RUNDLE, Thomas. *A sermon preached... February 17, 1733/4. to recommend the charity for establishing the new colony of Georgia.* London. T. Woodward, J. Brindley, 24p. 8vo. 1734
Note: SABIN 74132, EA 734/188–9. Another edition in 1734.
Locations: L; Cq; DLC, NN, MiU-C

1734#19
Select trials for murders, robberies, rapes, sodomy, coining,... at the Sessions House in the Old Bailey. To which are added, genuine accounts of the lives, behaviour, confessions and dying speeches of the most eminent convicts... London. printed for J. Wilford, 2 vols. 8vo. 1734
Note: Vol. 2 is dated 1735. Many of the condemned had had experience of the New World, including North America. A second enlarged edition was published in four vols. in 1742.
Locations: L; E; CSt, MHL

1734#20
SEWALL, Joseph. *Christ victorious over the powers of darkness... A sermon preached in Boston, December 12, 1733.* Edinburgh. R. Fleming, 46p. 8vo. 1734
Note: EA 734/202. First published Boston, 1733, EVANS 3723. Ordination of three Society in Scotland for the Propagation of the Gospel ministers in Boston.
Locations: L;

1734#21
SNELGRAVE, William. *A new account of some parts of Guinea, and the slave-trade...* London. J., J., and P. Knapton, 288p. 8vo. 1734
Note: SABIN 85380, HANSON 4702, EA 734/205. Reissued 1754.
Locations: Lu; DLC, RPJCB, ViU

1734#22
SOCIETY FOR PROMOTING CHRISTIAN KNOWLEDGE. *The gentlemen who at the request of the Society... are trustees for... Saltzburg Protestants... appointed to transport them to Georgia...* London. [1]p. F. [1734]
Note: EA 734/207. At head of title 'London, September 18, 1734'.
Locations: L; RPJCB

1734#23
SOCIETY FOR PROMOTING CHRISTIAN KNOWLEDGE. *The Society for promoting Christian knowledge, and the members chosen by them to be trustees for the poor Saltzburgers... to go to Georgia...* London. [3], 3p. F. [1734]
Note: DERENNE, I, 53, EA 734/208. At head of title 'October 4, 1734'.
Locations: L; RPJCB

1734#24
VANDERLINT, Jacob. *Money answers all things: or, an essay to make money sufficiently plentiful...* London. T. Cox and sold by J. Wilford, 170p. 8vo. 1734
Note: HANSON 4723, EA 734/222. Mentions problem of over-emigration to colonies since discovery of America.
Locations: L; DLC, CtY, PHi

1734#25
WALDO, Samuel. *Samuel Waldo - appellant. Hannah Fayrweather, widow and John Fayrweather, executors, respondents. The respondents case. To be heard... 10th of December, 1734.* London. 3p. F. 1734
Note: SABIN 101002. Hearing before Lords Committee of Privy Council on New Hampshire lands.
Locations: MWA

1735#1
ASHLEY, John. *Some observations on a direct exportation of sugar, from the British islands...* London. 23p. 4to. 1735
Note: HANSON 4806, EA 735/18.
Locations: L; DLC, RPJCB, CtY

1735#2
DYCHE, Thomas. *A new general English dictionary... Together with a supplement of the proper names of the most noted foreign kingdoms, provinces, cities, towns, rivers, etc....* London. R. Ware, [c. 900]p. 8vo. 1735
Note: EA 735/88. Includes American place names. Also 1737, 1740, 1744, 1748, 1750, EA 737/56, 740/101, 744/84, 748/57, 750/104.
Locations: BN; CU, NcD

1735#3
An exact list of the lords spiritual and temporal... To which is added, the names of the Trustees for Georgia, and the places of their abode... London. E. Cave, 37, 2p. 12mo. [1734/5]
Note: SABIN 23335 and cf. 27068, DERENNE, I, 48, EA 735/92.
Locations: GU-DeR, MB, RPJCB, ViU

1735#4
GEORGIA TRUSTEES. *An act for maintaining the peace with the Indians in the province of Georgia, prepared by the Honourable trustees for establishing the colony of Georgia in America, and approved by... George the Second,*

in council, on the third day of April. . . 1735. . . London. J. Baskett, 11p. F. 1735
Locations: Lpro; DLC

1735#5
GEORGIA TRUSTEES. *An act for rendring the colony of Georgia more defencible, by prohibiting the importation and use of black slaves or negroes into the same. . . approved by. . . George the Second, in council, on the third day of April. . . 1735. . .* London. J. Baskett, 6p. F. 1735
Locations: Lpro; GU-DeR

1735#6
GEORGIA TRUSTEES. *An act to prevent the importation and use of rum and brandies in the Province of Georgia. . . approved by. . . George the Second, in Council, on the third day of April. . . 1735. . .* London. J. Baskett, [8]p. F. 1735
Locations: Lpro; PHi, GU-DeR

1735#7
GEORGIA TRUSTEES. *Rules for the year 1735.* London. s.sh. 1o. [1735]
Note: 2 July 1735.
Locations: Lpro;

1735#8
GREAT BRITAIN. COMMISSIONERS FOR TRADE AND PLANTATIONS. *Representation from the Commissioners for Trade and Plantations, to the. . . Lords. . . in pursuance of their Lordships addresses to his Majesty of the 1st and 5th of April, 1734. relating to the state of the British islands in America. . .* London. 19p. F. 1734 [i.e 1735].
Note: HANSON 4811, EA 735/112. 'encouragements. . . to engage the inhabitants of the British colonies on the continent in the north to the cultivation of naval stores. . . and of such other products as may be proper. . . '. Dated 14 January 1734/5. Two impressions.
Locations: L; RPJCB, NNC, MiU-C

1735#9
HALL, Fayrer. *A short account of the first settlement of the provinces of Virginia, Maryland, New-York, New-Jersey, and Pennsylvania, by the English. . .* London. 20p. 4to. 1735
Note: SABIN 80586, EA 735/115.
Locations: DLC, RPJCB, MH

1735#10
HARE, Francis. *A sermon preached. . . 21st February, 1734. . .* London. S. Buckley, 86p. 4to. 1735
Note: SABIN 30362, EA 735/117. SPG sermon for 1735, with abstract, etc.
Locations: L; DLC, RPJCB, NN

1735#11
LEDIARD, Thomas. *The naval history of England, in all its branches; from. . . 1066, to the conclusion of 1734. . .* London. J. Wilcox, etc. 2 vols. F. 1735
Note: SABIN 39683, EA 735/145. First published in serial form.
Locations: L; DLC, RPJCB, MiU-C

1735#12
MARTIN, Benjamin. *The philosophical grammar; being a view of the present state of experimental physiology.* London. J. Noon, 322p. 8vo. 1735
Note: EA 735/155. Other editions 1738, 1748, EA 738/161, 748/123. Some American references.
Locations: L; RPJCB, CtY-M

1735#13
MORRIS, Lewis. *The case of Lewis Morris, esq; lord chief justice in of the province of New York. . . to be heard before. . . the lords of the committee of the Privy Council. . .* London. 8p. F. 1735
Note: SABIN 50847. Morris petitioner, William Cosby respondent.
Locations: MH, NN

1735#14
A new voyage to Georgia. *By a young gentleman. . . his travels to South Carolina, and part of North Carolina. . .* London. J. Wilford, 62p. 8vo. 1735
Note: SABIN 27079, HANSON 4812, EA 735/168, 737/157. Second edition in 1737 (L;). With account of Indians and poem by Oglethorpe.
Locations: O; DLC, RPJCB, NN

1735#15
PEARCE, Zachary. *A sermon preached. . . April the 17th 1735 to which is annexed an account of the origin and design of the society for promoting Christian Knowledge. . .* London. M. Downing, 54p. 4to. 1735
Note: SABIN 59436, EA 735/174.
Locations: L; IU, NNC

1735#16
Remarks on the common topicks *of conversation in town, at the meeting of Parliament. . . 1734–5.* London. J. Roberts, 64p. 8vo. 1735
Note: SABIN 69452, EA 735/194. Georgia references.
Locations: L; MH, CSmH, CtY

1735#17
REVOLUTION, William. *The real crisis: or, the necessity of giving immediate and powerful succour to the emperor against France. . .* London. J. Huggonson, 53p. 8vo. 1735
Note: SABIN 70342, EA 735/195. Refers to Sugar Islands, Jamaica and Carolina.
Locations: L; RPJCB, DLC

1735

1735#18
A series of wisdom and *policy being a full justification of all our measures ever since the year 1721... and... our late most honourable convention with Spain...* London. T. Cooper, 63p. 8vo. 1735
Note: SABIN 79227, HANSON 4803, EA 735/219, 739/215, 280–1. Three London editions in 1739, one as *The original series of...*
Locations: L; OU, MiU-C, ViU

1735#19
WILSON, Samuel. *Sermons on the following subjects... with an abstract of Consul Dean's narrative, relating to his suffering shipwreck... in the year 1710.* London. A. Wood, etc., 203p. 12mo. 1735
Note: SABIN 104686, EA 735/251. See also Dean, John, *A narrative...* above, 1711.
Locations: L; C; DLC

1736#1
ALLEN, William. *Ways and means to raise the value of land; or, the landlord's companion: with political discourses on the land-tax, war, and other subjects.* London. J. Roberts, 58p. 8vo. 1736
Note: HANSON 4845, EA 736/2, 742/3. Another edition in 1742 as *The landlord's companion...* Discusses colonial trade, emigration, etc.
Locations: Lu; RPJCB

1736#2
APPLETON, Nathaniel. *Gospel ministers must be fit for the master's use... sermon preached at Deerfield, August 31. 1735... with special reference to the Indians of the Houssatonnic...* Edinburgh. Boston printed, Edinburgh reprinted. Davidson and Traill, xiv, 33p. 8vo. 1736
Note: SABIN 1831, EA 736/11. First printed Boston, 1735 (EVANS 3867).
Locations: DLC, ICN

1736#3
BENNET, John. *The national merchant: or, discourses on commerce and colonies; being an essay for regulating and improving the trade and plantations of Great Britain, by uniting the national and mercatorial interests. etc.* London. J. Walthoe and T. Osborn, 143p. 8vo. 1736
Note: SABIN 4730, HANSON 4877, EA 736/28.
Locations: L; Lu; C; MB, NN, MiU-C

1736#4
BESSE, Joseph. *A full answer to The country-parson's plea against the Quaker tythe-bill.* London. T.Cooper, 96p. 8vo. 1736
Note: SMITH I, 254, EA 736/31. Mentions American Quaker letters.
Locations: L; RPJCB, InU

1736#5
BROWN, William. *The benefit and comfort of the Christian revelation...* Edinburgh. J. Davidson and Co., 26p. 8vo. 1736
Note: Scottish Society for propagating Christian knowledge sermon for 1736. Discusses New England and Georgia.
Locations: E; L; MH

1736#6
The case of the merchants, *and others, of the City of Bristol, trading to the British Colonies in America.* London. s.sh. F. [1736]
Note: HANSON 4981, EA 736/48. Against the duty on spirits.
Locations: L; Ldc; Lu;

1736#7
An exact list of the *Lords spiritual and temporal; to which is added, the Trustees for Georgia.* London. E. Cave, 40p. 16mo. 1736
Note: DERENNE, I, 48.
Locations: GU-DeR

1736#8
The Four Indian Kings garland; *being a faithful... account how... a young lady conquer'd the heart of one of the four Indian Kings.* Hull? J. Ferraby, 8p. [c.1736]. 1736
Note: EA 736/91. Also Newcastle, [1750], EA 750/120. Date is really a guess.
Locations: L; O;

1736#9
GEORGIA TRUSTEES. *The general accompt of all monies and effects recieved and expended by the Trustees for... Georgia... from the ninth day of June... 1735, to the ninth day of June... 1736.* London. 29p. [1736]
Note: SABIN 27406, EA 736/100.
Locations: RPJCB, GHi, MH

1736#10
Georgia, a poem. Tomo Chachi, *an ode. A copy of verses on Mr Oglethorpe's second voyage to Georgia...* London. J. Roberts, 19p. F. [1736]
Note: FOXON G128 discusses authorship. SABIN 27047, EA 736/99.
Locations: L; MiU-C, RPJCB, GU-DeR

1736#11
HODSHON, Read. *The honest man's companion: or, the family's safeguard... some hints relating to the clergy... our plantations...* Newcastle. M. Bryson, 72p. 8vo. 1736
Note: EA 736/111.
Locations: L; DLC, RPJCB, NN

1736#12
KIRKBY, John. *The history of Autonous.* . . London. J. Roberts, 117p. 8vo. 1736
Note: Republished in 1745 as *The capacity and extent of the human understanding.* . . , (L; CtY, MB, MH). An educational treatise set in 'Soteria' which some identify with modern Fort Bragg, California.
Locations: L; MB, MdBP

1736#13
A letter from James Murray, in New-York in America; to the Reverend Mr. Baptist Boyd, minister of the gospel, in the Parish of Aughelow, and County of Tyrone; with his description of the country. . . Dublin. [9]p. 8vo. 1736
Note: HANSON 4897, EA 736/158. Facsimiles (1925)in DLC, MB, NcD
Locations: DA;

1736#14
LYNCH, John. *A sermon.* . . *February 20, 1735.* . . London. J. and R. Pemberton, 73p. 4to. 1736
Note: SABIN 42814, EA 736/140. SPG sermon for 1736, with abstract, etc.
Locations: L; RPJCB

1736#15
Papers relating to the Quakers tythe bill. London. J. Roberts, 4 pts. 8vo. 1736
Note: HANSON 4916, EA 736/173–6. References to New England Quakers. Two more London and one Dublin edition in 1736. Also Dublin, 1737, EA 737/161.
Locations: Lu; MH-BA, WU

1736#16
Ship Victory. Solomon de Medina, Mosesson and others, appellants. Matthew Norris Esq; and Edward Greenly, Esq. Respondents. The Appellants Case. London. 4p. F. 1736
Note: FORD p. 1. Also *The Respondent's Case*, 3p. F. and *Reasons humbly offered on the part of the appellants*, 3p. F. 'To be heard 2 February 1736'.
Locations: NN

1736#17
SOCIETY FOR PROMOTING CHRISTIAN KNOWLEDGE. *Society for promoting Christian knowledge. This presents you by order of the Society.* . . *with the continuation of the account of receipts and disbursements towards relieving.* . . *emigrants from Saltzburg.* . . *[5 June 1736].* London. [3]p. F. [1736]
Note: EA 736/223.
Locations: RPJCB

1736#18
WATTS, George. *A sermon preached before the Trustees.* . . *Thursday, March 18. 1735.* . . London. M. Downing, 27p. 4to. 1736
Note: SABIN 102173, EA 736/264. Georgia Trustees anniversary sermon.
Locations: L; C; DLC, RPJCB, N.

1737#1
BORELAND, Francis. Boreland, Francis, respondent. . . The respondent's case. . . London. 4p. F. [1737]
Note: EA 737/40. Lands in Rhode Island. To be heard before the Privy Council committee.
Locations: RPJCB, N

1737#2
BRICKELL, John. *The natural history of North-Carolina; with an account of the trades, manners, and customs of the Christian and Indian inhabitants.* . . Dublin. J. Carson, 408p. 8vo. 1737
Note: HANSON 5037, EA 737/42, 743/35. Plagiarised from John Lawson. Cambridge copy has list of subscribers. Other editions Dublin, 1739, London, 1743.
Locations: L; C; DLC, RPJCB

1737#3
BURGES, Frances. *Virginia ss. Pleas at the capitol in Williamsburgh.* . . [London?] 4p. F. [1737]
Note: SABIN 99975, EA 737/46. A copy of the record of the appeal of Frances Burges, plaintiff, John Hack defendant to be heard before the Lords of the Committee of the Privy Council for Plantation affairs, November 2, 1737.
Locations: NN

1737#4
BURNET, Gilbert. *A defence of natural and revealed religion.* . . *With a general index.* . . London. A. Bettesworth and C. Hitch, 4 vols. 8vo. 1737
Note: EA 737/63–4. Also Dublin, 1737 and London 1739, EA 739/90.
Locations: L; MH-AH, IU

1737#5
The case of Messieurs Penn, and the people of Pensilvania, and the three lower counties of Newcastle, Kent, and Sussex, on Delaware, in relation to a series of injuries. . . made. . . by Thomas Cressap and others. . . by the direction and authority of the Deputy-Governor of Maryland. London. 8p. 2o.[1737]
Note: EA 737/163. To be heard by Committee of Privy-Council for Plantation Affairs on 23 February, 1737.
Locations: RPJCB, MiU-C, MH, CSmH.

1737

1737#6
The case of the British sugar colonies. London?, 3, [1]p. 2o. [1737?]
Note: Final word on p.1 is 'the'. ESTC states not before 1736.
Locations: L; Lpro; RPJCB

1737#7
The case of the province of Maryland, touching the outrageous riots which have been committed in the borders of that province, by the inhabitants of Pensilvania. London. 3p. F. [1737]
Note: SABIN 45099, EA 737/216. To be heard by the Lords of the Committee of the Council for Plantation Affairs, 23 February 1737. Signed by J. Strange.
Locations: DLC, MdBJ-G

1737#8
CLAGETT, Nicholas. *A sermon preached... February 18, 1736...* London. J. and J.Pemberton, 75p. 8vo. 1737
Note: SABIN 13183, EA 737/59. SPG sermon for 1737, with abstract, etc.
Locations: L; DLC, RPJCB, CtY

1737#9
D., L. *Reasons for a war against Spain. In a letter from a merchant of London trading to America, to a member of the House of Commons...* London. J. Wilford, 40p. 8vo. 1737
Note: HANSON 5033, EA 737/178, 738/196. Second edition, 1738 (RPJCB).
Locations: L; O; DLC, RPJCB, CtY

1737#10
A defence of the examination of a book entituled, A brief account of many of the prosecutions of the people call'd Quakers... London. J. Roberts, 74p. 8vo. 1737
Note: HANSON 5063, EA 737/65. Material on George Keith and Pennsylvania.
Locations: O; DLC, PPL

1737#11
A dialogue between an English-man and a Dutch-man on the subject of trade... London. J. Roberts, 30p. 8vo. 1737
Note: HANSON 5015, EA 737/72.
Locations: Lu; MnU, NNC

1737#12
EDWARDS, Jonathan. *A faithful narrative of the conversion of many hundred souls in Northampton... New England. In a letter to Dr. B. Colman... and published with a preface by Dr Watts and Dr Guyse...* Edinburgh, reprinted for J. Oswald, London, xvi, 132p. 12mo. 1737
Note: EA 737/77–8, 738/86–7. Also London 1737, 1738, Edinburgh, 1738.
Locations: CtY, MWA, NcU

1737#13
GRAY, Christopher. *A catalogue of American trees and shrubs that will endure the climate of England.* London. [1737?]
Note: EA 737/105. Reissued 66p. in 1755. Gray specialised in American trees and plants.
Locations: O;

1737#14
KIRKPATRICK, James. *An epistle to Alexander Pope esq; from South Carolina.* London. J. Brindley, C. Corbett, 18p. F. 1737
Note: SABIN 87820, FOXON K88.5, EA 737/82.
Locations: L; MH, NN

1737#15
A list of the public offices and officers ecclesiastical and civil employed in his majesty's government... London. J. Watson, 72p. 12mo. [1737–42]
Note: Includes colonial agents and governors and other colonial officers. DLC has six numbers, 1737–42. L; lists numbers for 1739, 1740, 1742.
Locations: L; DLC

1737#16
LOGAN, James. *The charge delivered from the bench to the Grand Inquest at a Court... Philadelphia, April 13th, 1736.* London. Philadelphia printed, London reprinted. J. Roberts, 34p. 8vo. 1737
Note: SABIN 41795, EA 737/164. First printed Philadelphia, 1736 (EVANS 4061) 'At a court of Oyer and Terminer and general Gaol delivery'.
Locations: RPJCB, NN, NNU

1737#17
MACKERCHER, Daniel. *A memorial relating to the tobacco trade...* London. (2), 20p. 8vo. 1737
Note: SABIN 100487 says a shorter version of that issued in Virginia. RPJCB says a very different text from Virginia edition. NUC has American imprint only: Williamsburgh, 1737 (EVANS 4154). EA 737/143.
Locations: RPJCB, CSmH

1737#18
MACSPARRAN, James. *Rhode Island. James Mac Sparran... of... Rhode Island, plaintiff and appellant... The appellants case.* London. 4p. F. 1737
Note: EA 737/144. Ecclesiastical land dispute. For the respondent's case, see next item.
Locations: RPJCB

AN EPISTLE TO *Alexander Pope*, Esq; FROM South CAROLINA.

FROM warmer Lands, ally'd to latest Fame,
In gracious CAROLINE's immortal Name;
Part of that Sylvan World *Columbus* found,
Where GEORGE should be rever'd, and You renown'd;
Hear Heav'n-taught Bard! and hearing, spare the Lyre,
Your real Worth, your real Wrongs, inspire.

B   Tho'

1737#19
MACSPARRAN, James. *Rhode Island. The Reverend James McSparran of North Kingston. . . plaintiff. . . The respondent's case.* London. 3p. F. 1737
Note: EA 737/145. Robert Hazard or Hassard was the respondent.
Locations: RPJCB

1737#20
NISBET, James. *The perpetuity of the Christian religion, a sermon preached in the High Church of Edinburgh, Monday January 3d, 1737; upon occasion of the anniversary meeting of the Society in Scotland, for Propagating Christian Knowledge.* Edinburgh, printed by R. Fleming and Company, and sold at the shop of Messieurs Davidson and Trail, 31,[1]p. 8vo. 1737
Note: References to missionary activity in 'western world.'
Locations: E; MH-H

1737#21
PHILLIPS, Gillam. *Gillam Phillips, only brother of Henry Phillips deceased intestate. appellant. Faith Savage widow. . . and others, respondents. The case of Faith Savage.* London. 4p. F. [1737]
Note: SABIN 92694, EA 737/166. See *Acts of the Privy Council Colonial, 1720–1745* (London, 1910), p. 433. A different imprint in 1737, SABIN 62457, EA 737/167 of which no copy is known.
Locations: NN

1737#22
Reasons for encouraging the importation *of iron in bars from His Majesty's plantations in America.* London. s.sh. 1/2o. [1737?]
Locations: Lpro;

1737#23
SAVAGE, Richard. *Of publick spirit in regard to publick works. An epistle to Frederick, Prince of Wales.* London. R. Dodsley, 18p. 2o. 1737
Note: FOXON S102. Another edition 1739; Dublin 1738. Section 'On Colonies' and in praise of Oglethorpe.
Locations: L; ICU, MH, CSmH

1737#24
SOCIETY OF FRIENDS. *From our yearly-meeting, held at Philadelphia, for Pennsylvania, and New Jersey, from the 17th to the 21st day of the 7th month, 1737. To the quarterly and monthly meetings. . . 1737.* Reprinted London. 4p. F. [1737]
Locations: DLC, RPJCB, NN

1738#1
BEARCROFT, Philip. *A sermon preached. . . March 16, 1737–8. . .* London. J. Willis, 22p. 4to. 1738
Note: SABIN 4122, EA 738/17. Georgia Trustees and Associates of Dr. Bray anniversary sermon.
Locations: L; Llp; C; RPJCB, MiU-C, GU-DeR

1738#2
BINDON, David. *A letter from a merchant who has left off trade, to a member of parliament; in which the case of the British and Irish manufacture of linnen, threads, and tapes is fairly stated. . .* London. R. Willock, 84p. 8vo. 1738
Note: SABIN 40309, KRESS 5245, HANSON 5164, EA 738/148–50. Importance of exports to the plantations for home manufactures. Also London and Belfast, 1738. Reprinted 1753.
Locations: L; RPJCB

1738#3
BROWNE, Peleg. *Rhode Island. Peleg Browne, Collector of Customs. . . Rhode Island. . . appellant. James Allen, and Ezekiel Chever. . . respondents. The appellant's case.* London. 4p. F. 1738
Note: EA 738/58. Case before the Privy Council committee, June 1738.
Locations: RPJCB

1738#4
CHEEVER, Ezekiel. *Rhode Island. Peleg Browne. . . Collector of. . . Customs for. . . Newport. . . appellant. Ezekiel Cheevers, of Boston. . . and James Allen. . . respondents. The respondent's case.* London. 4p. F. 1738
Note: EA 738/59. To be heard before Privy Council committee, 12 June 1738.
Locations: RPJCB

1738#5
Common sense: its nature and *use. With the manner of bringing all disputable cases. . . Applied to the Spanish affair.* London. T. Cooper, 30p. 8vo. 1738
Note: HANSON 5179, EA 738/63. Florida, Georgia and Spanish America.
Locations: L; RPJCB

1738#6
CONYBEARE, John. *A sermon preach'd. . . Thursday May 4th 1738. . . to which is annexed. . .* London. M. Downing, 42, 52p. 4to. 1738
Note: Account of SPCK annexed, including Georgia Saltzburgers.
Locations: L; CtY, GU-DeR

1738#7
FERGUSON, C. *A letter addressed to every honest man in Britain. . .* London. J. Cooper, 50p. 8vo. 1738
Note: EA 738/94. Advocates war. References to Georgia and continental colonies.
Locations: RPJCB

1738#8
A general treatise of naval trade and commerce...
London. E. Nutt, etc., 2 vols. 8vo. 1738
Note: SABIN 26913, HANSON 5176, EA 738/110, 740/131. Also London, 1740. Another edition, 1753.
Locations: DLC, PU, MiU-C

1738#9
The German spy. In familiar letters... written by a gentleman... to his friend in England... London. J. Mechell, 436p. 8vo. 1738
Note: EA 738/111. Story of an Indian boy from Pennsylvania. Second edition in 1740, EA 740/132.
Locations: L; DLC, OCL

1738#10
GREAT BRITAIN. PARLIAMENT. HOUSE OF LORDS. *The humble address of the Right Honourable the Lords... in Parliament... presented to His Majesty... the fourth day of May, 1738. With his majesty's answer...* London. J. Baskett, 4p. F. 1738
Note: Concerns American disputes with Spain.
Locations: E; O; RPJCB

1738#11
GREAT BRITAIN. SOVEREIGN. GEORGE II. *His majesty's most gracious speech to both houses of Parliament, on Thursday the first day of February 1738.* London. T. Baskett, 4p. F. 1738
Note: Disputes with Spain.
Locations: RPJCB

1738#12
HERRING, Thomas. *A sermon... February 17, 1737-8...* London. J. and J. Pemberton, 70p. 4to. 1738
Note: SABIN 31285, 31579, EA 738/119-120. SPG sermon for 1738, with abstract, etc. Another issue in 1738.
Locations: L; DLC, RPJCB, MiU-C

1738#13
KEITH, Sir William. *The history of the British plantations in America. With a chronological account of the most remarkable things...* London. S. Richardson, 187p. 4to. 1738
Note: HANSON 5184, EA 738/129. Part work. Relates almost wholly to Virginia. No more published.
Locations: L; C; DLC, RPJCB, MiU-C

1738#14
A letter from John Ray of New York, to Peter Ennis of Colraine, Pedlar. Dublin. 8vo. 1738
Note: HANSON 5185, EA 738/195. On emigration.
Locations: DA;

1738#15
LYNCH, Francis. *Francis Lynch, merchant, appellant. Martin Killikelly, of Dublin, merchant, and Arthur Lynch and company, of Bilbao in Spain, merchants, respondents. The case of the respondents.* London. 3, 1p. F. [1738]
Note: HANSON 5178, EA 738/156. Ship seized in Newfoundland.
Locations: L; RPJCB

1738#16
LYNCH, Francis. *Francis Lynch, of Dublin, merchant, appellant. Martin Killikelly, of Dublin, Merchant, Arthur Lynch and Company, of Bilbao, merchants, Catherine Killikelly, widow... of Luke Killikelly, late of Newfoundland, merchant, deceased, and James and Thomas Lynch, merchants in Cadiz, respondents. The appellant's case.* Dublin. 3p. F. [1738]
Note: HANSON 5177, EA 738/157. Ships seized at Newfoundland. Hearing at the bar of the House of Lords, May, 1738.
Locations: L; C; RPJCB

1738#17
MELON, Jean François. *A political essay upon commerce. Written in French by Monsieur M———. Tr., with some annotation and remarks by David Bindon, esq.* Dublin. P. Crampton, 352p. 8vo. 1738
Note: SABIN 63773, EA 738/165. Another edition, Dublin 1739.
Locations: L; RPJCB, MH, CtY

1738#18
Reflections and considerations occasioned by the petition... to... House of Commons, for taking off the drawback on foreign linens, etc. London. T. Cooper, 28p. 8vo. 1738
Note: HANSON 5165, EA 738/197. Discusses colonies and trade.
Locations: L; DLC, RPJCB, CSmH

1738#19
Remarks on the continuation of Mr. Whitefield's Journal. Pointing out the many direct inconsistencies...
London. 44p. 8vo. 1738
Locations: L; NN, MH

1738#20
Remarks on the trial of John-Peter Zenger... London. J. Roberts, 27p. 4to. 1738
Note: SABIN 106314, EA 738/198. First printed Philadelphia and New York, 1737 (EVANS 4118-20).
Locations: L; Lsb; DLC, RPJCB, NN

1738#21
ROBINS, Benjamin. *The Merchant's complaint against Spain... the pretensions of Spain to Georgia...* London. W. Lloyd, 63p. 8vo. 1738
Note: SABIN 47917, HANSON 5180, EA 738/168.
Locations: L; Lu; RPJCB, CSmH, CtY

1738

1738#22
SOCIETY FOR PROMOTING CHRISTIAN KNOWLEDGE. *An account of the Society for promoting Christian Knowledge.* London. M. Downing, 49p. 4to. 1738
Note: Some account of Saltzburgers in Georgia.
Locations: GU-DeR, MiU-C, CaBVaU

1738#23
SOCIETY IN SCOTLAND FOR THE PROPAGATION OF CHRISTIAN KNOWLEDGE. *A succinct view of the Society in Scotland for propagating Christian knowledge...* Edinburgh. 4p. 8vo. [1738?]
Note: Conversion of Indians in 'our colonies in North-America'.
Locations: E-NRO; O;

1738#24
Some observations on the occasional writer numb. IV. Wherein the following... London. J. Roberts, 32p. 16mo 1738
Note: References to Georgia, Florida and military matters.
Locations: RPJCB, NNC, CtY

1738#25
Some remarks on the present state of the iron-trade of Great Britain. London. s.sh. F. [1738]
Note: HANSON 5154, EA 738/224. For the prohibition of new or larger forges in American colonies.
Locations: Lu;

1738#26
Strenuous motives for an immediate war against Spain... Inscribed to the merchants of Great-Britain trading to America. London. G. Spavan, 35p. 8vo. 1738
Note: HANSON 5181, EA 738/228.
Locations: L; Lu; RPJCB, NjP, NIC

1738#27
TENNENT, John, M. D. *An epistle to Dr. Richard Mead, concerning the epidemical diseases of Virginia, particularly, a pleurisy and peripneumony: wherein is shewn the surprising efficacy of the Seneca rattle-snake root...* Edinburgh. P. Matthie, 102p. 8vo. 1738
Note: SABIN 94711, EA 738/229, 742/193. Another edition, Edinburgh, 1742.
Locations: L; DLC, RPJCB, ViU

1738#28
THOMSON, James. *The works of Mr. Thomson. Volume the second. Containing Liberty: a poem in five parts.* London. A. Millar, 306p. 4to. 1738
Note: Parts 4 and 5 'Britain' and 'The Prospect' celebrate liberty, empire, and colonies, including Georgia. First published in parts, 1735, 1736.
Locations: L; MH, CtY, ViU

1738#29
The tryal of John Peter Zenger, of New-York, printer... With the pleadings and arguments on both sides... London. J. Wilford, 32p. 4to. 1738
Note: SABIN 106307, EA 738/257–62. EA lists editions two, three and four, London 1738, another possible London edition, and an edition Dublin, 1738. Another edition in 1752 (P. Brown, 74p): DLC, RPJCB, CtY. First printed New York, 1736, EVANS 4107: *A brief narrative...*
Locations: L; DLC, RPJCB, MiU-C

1738#30
WHITEFIELD, George. *The almost Christian: a sermon preached... in England. Added, a poem on his design for Georgia.* London. W. Bowyer, etc., 27p. 8vo. 1738
Note: SABIN 103497. Reprinted Boston, 1739. Also Edinburgh, 1741: NcD RPJCB.
Locations: L;- does not contain poem.

1738#31
WHITEFIELD, George. *The eternity of hell torments. A sermon preached at Savannah in Georgia...* London. J. Hutton, 23p. 8vo. 1738
Note: SABIN 103511, EA 738/246. Also Edinburgh, 1741.
Locations: L; RPJCB, GU-DeR, MiU-C

1738#32
WHITEFIELD, George. *The great duty of family religion: a sermon preached...* London and Bristol. W. Bowyer for J. Hutton; and J. Wilson in Bristol. 25p. 8vo. 1738
Note: Preface 'To the inhabitants of Savannah'. Reprinted Boston, 1739.
Locations: L; MiU-C

1738#33
WHITEFIELD, George. *A journal of a voyage from Gibraltar to Georgia...* London. T. Cooper, 34p. 8vo. 1738
Note: SABIN 103532, EA 738/247. A surreptitious publication of the second part of Whitefield's journal.
Locations: L; C; RPJCB, DLC, MiU-C

1738#34
WHITEFIELD, George. *A journal of a voyage from London to Savannah in Georgia. In two parts. Part I. From London to Gibraltar. Part II. From Gibraltar to Savannah.* London. J. Hutton, 58p. 8vo. 1738
Note: SABIN 103534, EA 738/248–50, 739/343–5, 743/232. Second and third and fourth edition, London, 1738. Also three editions, 1739; sixth edition in 1743.
Locations: L; CSmH, MiU-C

1738#35
WHITEFIELD, George. *Thankfulness for mercies received... farewel sermon... on board Whitaker, at anchor*

AN EPISTLE TO Dr. RICHARD MEAD,

CONCERNING THE

Epidemical Diseases of *VIRGINIA*,

PARTICULARLY,

A Pleurisy and *Peripneumony*:

Wherein is shewn the surprising Efficacy of the *Seneca Rattle-Snake Root*, in Diseases owing to a Viscidity and Coagulation of the Blood; such as *Pleurisies* and *Peripneumonies*, these being epidemick, and very mortal in *Virginia*, and other Colonies on the Continent of *America*, and also the *Lee-Ward* Islands.

To which is prefixt,

A Cut *of that most valuable* PLANT:

And an APPENDIX annexed,

Demonstrating the highest Probability, that this Root will be of more extensive Use than any Medicine in the whole *Materia Medica*, and of curing the *Gout, Rheumatism, Dropsy*, and many nervous Diseases.

By JOHN TENNENT.

Natura, fortuna, providentia, fatum, nomina sunt unius Et ejusdem Dei, varie agentis in rebus humanis. SENECA.

EDINBURGH:

Printed by P. MATTHIE, and sold by most Booksellers in Town. M.DCC.XXXVIII.

POLYGALA *Virginiana folijs oblongis floribus in thyrso candidis radice Alexipharmica.* MILLER.

PRESENTEM OSTENDIT QUÆLIBET HERBA DEUM

Seneca
Rattle-Snake Root

near Savannah... May the 17th, 1738... London. J. Hutton, 19p. 8vo. 1738
Note: SABIN 103598, EA 738/251. Two other editions in 1739, EA 739/346–7.
Locations: L; DLC, NN, MiU-C

1739#1
An abridgment of several acts *and clauses of acts of Parliament, relating to the trade and navigation of Great Britain to, from, and in the British plantations in America, and to the duty of governors, and others...* London. J. Baskett, 44p. F. 1739
Note: SABIN 80.
Locations: L; RPJCB, PPL.

1739#2
AMHURST, Nicholas. *French counsels destructive to Great Britain...* London. J. Roberts, 61p. 8vo. 1739
Note: SABIN 56514, EA 739/6. Also Edinburgh, 1739. Letters of colonial traders on Spanish depredations. By 'Caleb D'Anvers'.
Locations: L; RPJCB, DLC, CtY

1739#3
AMHURST, Nicholas. *A letter to the right honourable Sir R W etc., upon the present posture of affairs...* London. J. Brett, 30p. 8vo. 1739
Note: HANSON 5310, EA 739/7. Some discussion of North America.
Locations: L; CtY, PPL

1739#4
Articles of impeachment of high *treason... against Robert, etc...* London. John Trott, 72p. 8vo. 1739
Note: Attacks Walpole's advice for peace. Mentions Newfoundland, Quebec expedition, etc.
Locations: L; ICU

1739#5
An authentick list of the *house of peers; as they voted for and against the Convention...* London. 7p. 8vo. 1739
Locations: L; MH, MnU

1739#6
BERRIMAN, William. *A sermon preach'd before... Trustees for... Georgia... and the associates of... Bray... March 15, 1738–9...* London. J. Carter, 24p. 4to. 1739
Note: SABIN 4986, EA 739/26.
Locations: L; Llp; DLC, RPJCB

1739#7
BOREMAN, Thomas. *A description of some curious and uncommon creatures, omitted in the Description of 300 animals, and likewise in the supplement to that book.* London. R. Ware, 88p. 12mo. 1739
Note: EA 739/41. North American beaver.
Locations: CtY, OO

1739#8
The British sailor's discovery *: or the Spanish pretensions confuted...* London. T. Cooper, 72p. 8vo. 1739
Note: SABIN 8122, HANSON 5293, EA 739/46. Anti-Spanish tract, particularly about colonies.
Locations: L; RPJCB, MH, MiU-C

1739#9
BUTLER, Joseph. *A sermon preached... February 16, 1738–9.* London. J. and P. Knapton, 91p. 8vo. 1739
Note: SABIN 9651, EA 739/52–3. SPG sermon for 1739, with abstract, etc. Another edition, London, 1739.
Locations: L; CtY, MB, MBAt

1739#10
CAMPBELL, Hugh Hume. *A state of the rise and progress of our disputes with Spain, and of the conduct of our ministers...* London. T. Cooper, 76p. 8vo. 1739
Note: SABIN 90630, HANSON 5326, EA 739/190, 740/198. Another edition in 1740.
Locations: L; DLC, RPJCB, MiU-C

1739#11
CARROLL, Charles. *Maryland. Charles Carroll... appellant. John Parran... and Mary Parran... respondents. The appellant's case.* London. 3p. F. 1739
Note: EA 739/56. Calvert County, Maryland inheritance case.
Locations: RPJCB

1739#12
The case of his majesty's *province of New Hampshire upon two appeals...* London. 8p. F. [1739]
Note: SABIN 52803. EA 739/57. Boundary dispute with Massachusetts. Printed for counsel's use. Before Privy Council, 12 November 1739. This is the case on behalf of the New Hampshire House of Representatives. For the unlocated Massachusetts case see EA 739/58. But this may be the same as EA 739/204. See below GREAT BRITAIN. PRIVY COUNCIL, 1739.
Locations: RPJCB

1739#13
The case of the British *sugar colonies.* London. 4p. F. [1739?]
Note: HANSON 5334, EA 739/60. Cf. SABIN 102822. Begins 'The present situation of the trade of the sugar colonies' Ends 'under the Restrictions therein mentioned, shall pass into a Law.' Last word on page 1 is 'linen'. For direct exportation to Mediterranean.
Locations: LLI; Lpro; RPJCB

1739

1739#14
CLAGETT, Nicholas. *A sermon preach'd... Thursday May 3d, 1739...* London. M. Downing, 32p, 51p. 4to. 1739
Note: Account of SPCK annexed. Georgia Saltzburgers.
Locations: L; DLC, GU, MWA

1739#15
COGGESHALL, Daniel. *Rhode Island. Daniel Coggeshall, Esq.,... appellant. Mary Coggeshall... respondent... The appellant's case.* London. 4p. 2o 1739
Note: Of North Kingstone, King's County. To be heard before Lords of Privy Council 5 April 1739. Also *The respondent's case*, 4p. (L;).
Locations: L;

1739#16
The Convention. An excellent new ballad. To which is added the king of Spain's protest, and a new epitaph. London. T. Reynolds, 7p. F. 1739
Note: SABIN 16194, EA 739/74–6. Also London, 1739 and Edinburgh, 1739.
Locations: MH, TxU, CtY

1739#17
COPITHORNE, Richard. *The English cotejo; or the cruelties... charg'd upon the English in a Spanish libel...* London. J. Mechell, 30p. 8vo. 1739
Note: HANSON 5300, EA 739/80. Cruelties of Spanish in America and their attempts to stir up slave rebellions in British colonies.
Locations: L; Lu; RPJCB, NN, CSmH

1739#18
Cotejo de la conducta... His Catholick Majesty's conduct compared with that of his Britannick Majesty... London. T. Cooper, 63p. 8vo. 1739
Note: SABIN 62442, HANSON 5297, EA 739/83–4. Another edition in 1739. In Spanish and English. Translation of Spanish tract justifying Spain's policy towards Georgia, South Carolina, etc.
Locations: Lu; RPJCB, MiU-C

1739#19
COWLEY, J. *A description of the Windward passage, and Gulf of Florida, with the course of the British trading-ships to, and from the island of Jamaica... Illustrated with a chart of the coast of Florida...* London. J. Applebee, 23p. 4to. 1739
Note: HANSON 5298, EA 739/94–5, 741/056. Second edition with additions in 1739: DLC, NN, CtY. Fourth edition in 1741.
Locations: L;

1739#20
A dissertation on the present conjuncture; particularly with regard to trade... London. J. Clarke, 31p. 8vo. 1739
Note: SABIN 20283, HANSON 5299, EA 739/97–8, 740/90. Another edition in 1739 and in 1740.
Locations: Lu; RPJCB, CtY, NNC

1739#21
DOVER, William. *Useful miscellanies, or Serious reflections, respecting mens duty to God.* London. T. Cooper, 92p. 4to. 1739
Note: EA 739/99. Missions to Indians.
Locations: MH, CtY.

1739#22
The English sailors resolution to fight the Spaniards Guarda Costas. London. s.sh. F. [1739?]
Note: References to Georgia and South Carolina.
Locations: C;

1739#23
An exact list of all those who voted for and against the Convention in the House of Commons... London. J. Purser, 42p. 8vo. 1739
Note: HANSON 5301.
Locations: L;

1739#24
An examination of a pamphlet, entitled his Catholic Majesty's manifesto... London. T. Gardner, 59p. 8vo. 1739
Note: HANSON 5306, EA 739/110. References to Carolina, Georgia, etc.
Locations: L; DLC, RPJCB, MiU-C

1739#25
FAIRFAX, Thomas, Lord. *The right honourable Thomas Lord Fairfax, petitioner. against the governor and council of Virginia, in right of the Crown, defendents. The case of the petitioner the Lord Fairfax.* London. 3, 1p. F. [1739]
Note: SABIN 99894, EA 739/322.
Locations: Lpro;

1739#26
FAIRFAX, Thomas, Lord. *Virginia. The right honourable Thomas Lord Fairfax petitioner, the governor and council of Virginia, in right of the Crown defendents. The case on behalf of the Crown.* London. 4p. F. [1739?]
Locations: L;

1739#27
A faithful narrative of the life and character of the Reverend Mr Whitefield... his motives for going to Georgia... London. M. Watson, 2, 25, 1p. 8vo. 1739

Note: SABIN 103623, EA 739/111.
Locations: L; NN

1739#28
GAGE, Thomas. *The speech of the right honourable the Lord Viscount Gage, in parliament, against the convention with Spain.* London. F. Style, 10p. 4to. 1739
Note: SABIN 26321, EA 739/116.
Locations: L; DLC, MH, FU

1739#29
GORDON, Thomas. *An appeal to the unprejudiced, concerning the present discontents occasioned by the late convention with Spain.* London. T. Cooper, 32p. 8vo. 1739
Note: SABIN 1788, EA 739/131.
Locations: L; DLC, RPJCB, MiU-C

1739#30
GREAT BRITAIN. PARLIAMENT. *An act for naturalizing such foreign Protestants, and others... as are settled, or shall settle in any of his majesty's colonies in America.* London. J. Baskett, 3p. F. [1739]
Note: HANSON 5339.
Locations: L; DLC, MB, ViU

1739#31
GREAT BRITAIN. PARLIAMENT. *An act for the more effectual securing and encouraging the trade of his majesty's British subjects to America...* London. J. Baskett, [12]p. F. 1739
Note: Cf. HANSON 5331, A bill..., below, 1739.
Locations: RPJCB

1739#32
GREAT BRITAIN. PARLIAMENT. HOUSE OF COMMONS. *A bill for registering all seamen, watermen, fishermen, lightermen... capable of service at sea, throughout his majesty's dominions...* London. 16p. 2o. [1739]
Note: This bill was brought in November 1739 and dropped in February 1740. It would have allowed colonial governors to press men for naval service.
Locations: L;

1739#33
GREAT BRITAIN. PARLIAMENT. HOUSE OF COMMONS. *A bill, intituled, An act for naturalizing such foreign protestants, and others therein mentioned, as are settled, or shall settle in any of His Majesty's colonies in America.* London. 6p. F. [1739]
Note: HANSON 5339.
Locations: L;

1739#34
GREAT BRITAIN. PARLIAMENT. HOUSE OF COMMONS. *A bill, intituled, An act for the more effectual securing and encouraging the trade of his Majesty's British subjects in America...* London. 10p. 2o. [1739]
Note: HANSON 5331, EA 739/133.
Locations: L; DLC

1739#35
GREAT BRITAIN. PARLIAMENT. HOUSE OF LORDS. *The Lords protest against the convention-treaty.* London. 3p. 2o. [1739]
Locations: L; DLC, RPJCB, InU

1739#36
GREAT BRITAIN. PRIVY COUNCIL. *Andrew Wiggin, and others, petitioners. Against Jonathan Belcher, Esq: -Respondent. The Respondent's case... 12th day of November, 1739.* London. 3p. F. 1739
Note: SABIN 103894, EA 739/204. Relates to New Hampshire boundary dispute.
Locations: MB

1739#37
GREAT BRITAIN. PRIVY COUNCIL. *Maryland. Benjamin Tasker appellant. John Simpson, lessee of William Brent, respondent. The appellants case... to be heard... 25th... January 1739...* London. 4p. F. [1739 or 1740]
Note: EA 739/265. Relates to Kent-Fort, Md.
Locations: NN

1739#38
GREAT BRITAIN. PRIVY COUNCIL. *Maryland. Benjamin Tasker, esq... appellant. John Simpson, lessee of William Brent, respondent. The respondent's case. To be heard... 25th... January 1739...* London. 4p. F. [1739 or 1740]
Note: EA 739/302.
Locations: NN

1739#39
GREAT BRITAIN. PRIVY COUNCIL. *New Hampshire. The (late) House of Representatives there, complainants. Jonathan Belcher esq, the governour there, respondent. The complainants' case... 12th day of November, 1739.* London. 4p. F. 1739
Note: SABIN 52854, EA 739/203. Relates to New Hampshire boundary dispute.
Locations: Nh

1739#40
GREY, Zachary. *An impartial examination of the fourth volume of Mr. Daniel Neal's history of the Puritans.* London. J. Bettenham, for A. Bettesworth and C. Hitch, 2pts. 8vo. 1739
Note: EA 739/134. Replies to Neal's work, mentioning New England Quakers.
Locations: L; RPJCB, CtY, DFo

1739

1739#41
Gulliver's flight: or The man mountain. A dream. London. s.sh. 4to. [1739?]
Note: EA 739/138. Satirizes North Americans, etc.
Locations: RPJCB

1739#42
HAYES, Richard. *The negociator's magazine. . . to which are added, curious calculations of great use in the West-India, Carolina and New-England trades.* . . London. J. Noon, 479p. 8vo. 1739
Note: EA 739/142, 740/152–4, 749/135. First printed 1721 but without American material? Three editions in 1740, also Dublin, 1749. Other editions to 1770 or later?
Locations: L; DLC, PPL

1739#43
His Catholick majesty's manifesto, justifying his conduct in relation to the late convention. . . London. R. Amey and A. Dodd, 53p. 8vo. 1739
Note: SABIN 62443, HANSON 5305. EA 739/295–6. Also Dublin, 1739.
Locations: Lu; RPJCB, ViU, CaBVaU

1739#44
His Catholic majesty's most Christian manifesto. . . London. C. Corbett, 13p. 4to. 1739
Note: GOLDSMITH'S 7732, EA 739/145. A verse satire. References to Carolina, Georgia.
Locations: L; DLC, RPJCB, CSmH

1739#45
The king of Spain's reasons for not paying the 95,000l. stipulated in the convention signed at the Pardo, 14 Jan. 1739. . . London. J. Roberts, 40p. 8vo. 1739
Note: SABIN 37864, HANSON 5307, EA 739/165.
Locations: L; RPJCB, DLC, CtY

1739#46
LAND, Tristram. *A letter to. . . Whitefield. Designed to correct his mistaken account of regeneration. . . now published to prevent his doing mischief among the common people, upon his return from Georgia.* . . London. J. Roberts, 29p. 8vo. 1739
Note: SABIN 38813, EA 739/168.
Locations: L; Llp; NN, TxU

1739#47
LYTTELTON, George. *Considerations upon the present state of our affairs, at home and abroad. In a letter to a member of Parliament from a friend in the country.* London. T. Cooper, 39p. 8vo. 1739
Note: HANSON 5233, EA 739/179–83. Three other London editions, 1739. Also Dublin, 1739.
Locations: L; DLC, RPJCB, MiU-C

1739#48
MERCHANT RETIR'D. *An address to the merchants of Great-Britain: or, a review of the conduct of the administration, with regard to our trade and navigation.* . . London. J. Roberts, 50p. 8vo. [1739]
Note: SABIN 423, HANSON 5291, EA 739/2.
Locations: L; RPJCB

1739#49
The Methodists, an humorous burlesque poem; address'd to. . . Whitefield and his followers: proper to be bound up with his sermons, and the journals of his voyage to Georgia. . . London. J. Brett, 28p. 8vo. 1739
Note: FOXON M226, EA 739/196.
Locations: L; DLC, RPJCB, NN

1739#50
Ministerial prejudices in favour of the Convention, examin'd and answer'd. London. T. Cooper, 30p. 8vo. 1739
Note: HANSON 5311, EA 739/199.
Locations: L; DLC, RPJCB, MiU-C

1739#51
The national dispute; or, The history of the convention treaty: containing the full substance of all the proceedings, debates, journals, pamphlets. . . London. J. Roberts, 312p. 8vo. 1739
Note: HANSON 5312, EA 739/201.
Locations: L; RPJCB, CSmH, MiU-C

1739#52
Observation upon the manifesto of his catholick majesty; with an answer to his reasons for not paying the ninety-five thousand pounds. . . London. T. Cooper, etc., 42p. 8vo. 1739
Note: SABIN 56589, HANSON 5308, EA 739/211–12. Mentions threat to Carolina, Georgia etc. The 'second edition', London, 1739.
Locations: L; RPJCB, NN, CSmH

1739#53
Observations arising from the declaration of war against Spain. . . and the future management of it by Great Britain. . . London. T. Gardner, 56p. 8vo. 1739
Note: SABIN 56464, HANSON 5313, EA 739/210.
Locations: L; DLC, RPJCB, NN

1739#54
Popular prejudices against the convention and treaty with Spain, examin'd and answer'd. . . London. T. Cooper, 30p. 8vo. 1739
Note: SABIN 64143, HANSON 5316, EA 739/231–3. Also another edition, London 1739; and Dublin 1739. 'With remarks on a pamphlet, considerations upon the present state of our affairs. . . ', by G. Lyttleton. Against the war.
Locations: L; DLC, RPJCB, MiU-C

1739#55
A proposal for humbling Spain. Written in 1711. By a person of distinction. And now first printed. . . London. J. Roberts, 72p. 8vo. [1739]
Note: SABIN 66016, HANSON 5320, EA 739/237. Proposal for attack on Buenos Ayres. References to flaws in settlement and land policies in various northern colonies.
Locations: Lu; DLC, RPJCB, MnU

1739#56
The publick having been imposed on, by several very imperfect and erroneous lists. . . London. J. Purser, 4p. F. 1739
Note: List of members of parliament voting for and against Convention, with offices held, etc., including Georgia Trustees.
Locations: L;

1739#57
PULTENEY, William. *A review of all that hath passed between the courts of Great Britain and Spain, relating to our trade and navigation, from the year 1721, to the present convention.* . . London. H. Goreham, 48p. 8vo. 1739
Note: SABIN 70199, HANSON 5322, EA 739/19-20. Another issue in 1739, 60p: DLC, RPJCB, CtY. Georgia references.
Locations: L; MnU, MB

1739#58
Reasons for giving encouragement to the seafaring people of Great-Britain, in times of peace or war. . . London. J. Millan, 40p. 8vo. 1739
Note: HANSON 5321, EA 739/245.
Locations: L; RPJCB, NjP, CSmH

1739#59
A reply to a pamphlet entitled 'Observations arising from the declaration of war against Spain, etc.' London. J. Roberts, 32p. 8vo. 1739
Note: SABIN 69686, EA 739/246.
Locations: L; DLC, RPJCB, CtY

1739#60
A reply to a pamphlet intitled, Popular prejudices against the Convention and Treaty with Spain, examin'd and answered. In a letter to a member of Parliament. London. T. Cooper, 31p. 8vo. 1739
Note: SABIN 69687, HANSON 5317, EA 739/247-8. A second edition in 1739.
Locations: DLC, RPJCB, CtY

1739#61
ROBINS, Benjamin. An address to the electors, and other free subjects of Great Britain. . . In which is contain'd a particular account of all our negociations with Spain. . . London. H. Goreham, 63p. 8vo. 1739
Note: SABIN 72044, HANSON 5290, EA 739/252-6. EA lists four more London editions in 1739.
Locations: L; RPJCB, MiU-C, CSmH

1739#62
ROBINS, Benjamin. *Observations on the present convention with Spain.* London. T. Cooper, 60p. 8vo. 1739
Note: HANSON 5314, EA 739/258-9. Also Dublin, 1739.
Locations: L; DLC, RPJCB, CtY

1739#63
Several new, pressing and weighty considerations for an immediate war with Spain. . . London. C. St. George, 8p. F. 1739
Note: SABIN 47893, HANSON 5324, EA 739/282.
Locations: Ls; RPJCB

1739#64
Some thoughts upon America, and upon the danger from Roman Catholicks there. London. s.sh. F. [1739?]
Note: SABIN 86780, EA dates to 1745, EA 745/197. However, this title probably refers to the naturalisation act of 20 December, 1739.
Locations: RPJCB, CtY, CSmH

1739#65
The true character of the Rev. Mr. Whitefield. London. A. Dodd, Mrs. Cook, and Mrs Bartlet, 34p. 4to. 1739
Note: EA 739/310. Mentions Georgia orphanage.
Locations: RPJCB, ICN

1739#66
TUCKER, Josiah. *The life and particular proceedings of. . . George Whitefield. . . to his embarking for Pensilvania. . .* London. J. Roberts, 96p. 8vo. [1739]
Note: SABIN 103634, EA 739/311.
Locations: L; RPJCB, MH, CtW

1739#67
A view of the political transactions of Great-Britain since the Convention was approv'd by Parliament. In a letter to an absenting member. . . London. T. Cooper, 59p. 8vo. 1739
Note: SABIN 99572, HANSON 5327, EA 739/321.
Locations: L; RPJCB, MiU-C, CtY

1739#68
WALPOLE, Horatio. *The Convention vindicated from the misrepresentations of the enemies of our peace.* London. J. Roberts, 29p. 8vo. 1739
Note: HANSON 5296, EA 739/327-8. Another edition, Dublin, 1739.
Locations: Lu; MiU-C

1739

1739#69
WALPOLE, Horatio. *The grand question, whether war or no war with Spain, impartially consider'd: in defence of the present measures against those that delight in war.* London. J. Roberts, 32p. 8vo. 1739
Note: SABIN 28264, HANSON 5303, EA 739/329–30. Alludes to North America. Also Dublin, 1739.
Locations: L; DLC, RPJCB, MiU-C

1739#70
WATTS, Isaac. *A new essay on civil power in things sacred.* London. M. Steen, 110p. 8vo. 1739
Note: EA 739/331. Locke's laws for Carolina.
Locations: L; MH, CtY

1739#71
WESLEY, John. *An extract of the Rev. Mr John Wesley's journal from his embarking for Georgia to his return to London. . . edited by Nehemiah Curnock.* Bristol. S. and F. Farley, 75p. 8vo. [1739]
Note: SABIN 102654, EA 739/334, 743/230. Covers 14 Oct. 1735 to 1 Feb. 1738. Second and third editions, Bristol, 1743, 1745.
Locations: L; DLC, RPJCB, ViU

1739#72
WHITEFIELD, George. *An account of money, receiv'd and expended by the Rev. Mr Whitefield, for the poor of Georgia.* London. 23p. 8vo. [1739]
Note: SABIN 103493, EA 739/335.
Locations: NcD

1739#73
WHITEFIELD, George. *A continuation of the Reverend Mr Whitefield's journal, during the time he was detained in England by the embargo. . .* London. W. Strahan, 40p. 8vo. 1739
Note: SABIN 103540. The 'fourth journal'. L; has four 'editions' in 1739.
Locations: L; NN, RPJCB, MiU-C

1739#74
WHITEFIELD, George. *A continuation of the Reverend Mr. Whitefield's journal, from his arrival at London, to his departure, from thence on his way to Georgia. . .* London. J. Hutton, 115p. 8vo. 1739
Note: SABIN 103538, EA 739/336–339, 744/244. The 'third' journal. Three other editions in 1739. Also 1744.
Locations: L; RPJCB, DLC, NN

1739#75
WHITEFIELD, George. *A continuation of the Reverend Mr. Whitefield's journal, from his arrival at Savannah, to his return to London.* London. J. Hutton, 44p. 8vo. 1739
Note: SABIN 103535, EA 739/340–42. Two other London editions in 1739.
Locations: L; RPJCB, MH, MiU-C

1739#76
WHITEFIELD, George. *The heinous sin of drunkenness; a sermon preached on board the Whitaker.* London. J. Hutton, 22p. 8vo. 1739
Note: SABIN 103525. Also Glasgow, 1741. Reprinted Philadelphia, 1740.
Locations: MRu; RPJCB, CtY, MiU-C

1740#1
APPLETON, Nathaniel. *The happiness of a holy life, exemplified in the sickness and death of. . . Mrs Martha Gerrish, of Boston in New-England. . . with a collection of. . . letters. . . defending religion. . . her funeral sermon. . .* London. C. Rivington, 207p. 12mo. 1740
Note: SABIN 27166, EA 740/18. First published Boston, 1736 (EVANS 3983) as *The Christian glorying in tribulation. . .*
Locations: MH

1740#2
ARMISTEAD, HENRY. *The case of Henry Armistead, esq;. . . a native of Virginia. . .* London. 2p. 1/2o. [1740?]
Note: Armistead was a native Virginia plantation owner.
Locations: Lpro; DLC (facsimile?)

1740#3
ASHLEY, John. *Memoirs and considerations concerning the trade and revenues of the British colonies in America. With proposals for rendering those colonies more beneficial to Great Britain.* London. C. Corbett, etc. 2vols. 8vo. 1740
Note: SABIN 2192, HANSON 5455, EA 740/19, 743/16. Second part, 1743, with first part reissued. Supplement, 1744.
Locations: L; C; DLC, RPJCB, CSmH

1740#4
BENSON, Martin. *A sermon preached. . . February 15, 1739–40.* London. J. and H. Pemberton, 88p. 4to. 1740
Note: SABIN 4751, EA 740/31–2. SPG sermon for 1740, with abstract, etc. Another edition in 1740.
Locations: L; RPJCB, CtY

1740#5
The bravo turn'd bully; or, *the depredators. A dramatic entertainment. Founded on some late transactions in America.* London. Printed for, and sold by J. Purser. . . [5], 10–55, [1]p. 8vo. 1740
Note: Some references to English colonies.
Locations: L; C; DLC, ICU; MH-H, CSmH

1740#6
BRICE, Ninian. *Ninian Brice, ship-master in Glasgow, and others, Apellants. William Brice, Merchant in Glasgow, Respondent. The Appellants Case.* London. 4p. F. [1740]

168

Note: HANSON 5476, EA 740/48. About a cargo of Wood's halfpence shipped to Boston.
Locations: L; E; CLU-S/C

1740#7
Britain's mistakes in the commencement *and conduct of the present war. By a merchant and citizen of London.* . . London. T. Cooper, 62p. 8vo. 1740
Note: SABIN 8065, EA 740/50–2. Also two Dublin editions, 1740.
Locations: L; DLC, RPJCB

1740#7A
BRYCE, William. *Ninian Bryce, John Orr of Barrowfield, Esq; and John Robertson, Writer in Glasgow appellants. William Bryce, merchant in Glasgow – respondent. The respondent's case.* – London. 4p. 2o. 1740
Note :HANSON 5477, EA 740/49. See Brice, above, 1740.
Location: L; E; CLU-S/C

1740#8
Considerations on the bill for *prohibiting the exportation of corn, &c. from North America.* . . London. 3, 1p. 2o. 1740
Note: The bill was read 21 November 1740.
Locations: L; Lpro; PHi, CSmH

1740#9
CROWE, William. *The duty of public spirit recommended in a sermon preach'd.* . . *March 20, 1739–40.* . . London. John Clarke, 23p. 4to. 1740
Note: SABIN 17692, EA 740/85. Georgia Trustees and Bray Associates anniversary sermon.
Locations: Cq; Oa; RPJCB, MiU-C

1740#10
An essay on the management *of the present war with Spain.* . . London. T. Cooper, 32p. 8vo. 1740
Note: SABIN 22962, HANSON 5428, EA 740/107–8. Another edition, London, 1740.
Locations: L; RPJCB, CSmH, NN

1740#11
FRANSHAM, John. *The world in miniature; or, the entertaining traveller.* . . London. J. Torbuck, etc. 2 vols. 12mo. 1740
Note: SABIN 25670, EA 740/128, 741/88. Second ed. much enlarged, 1741: L; RPJCB, DLC, NN.
Locations: CtY, PHi, MiD

1740#12
French influence upon English counsels *demonstrated from an impartial examination of our measures.* . . London. T. Cooper, 72p. 8vo. 1740
Note: SABIN 25885, EA 740/129.
Locations: L; CSmH, RPJCB

1740#13
GIB, T. *Remarks on the Reverend Mr Whitefield's journal, his many inconsistencies are pointed out and his tenets considered; the whole showing the dangerous tendency of his doctrine.* . . London. Brett, 32p. 8vo. [1740]
Note: SABIN 27271. A Glasgow edition in 1742(?).
Locations: L; DLC

1740#14
GREAT BRITAIN. LORDS JUSTICES. *Proclamation providing for distribution of prize money. [19 June 1740].* London. J. Baskett, s.sh. F. 1740
Note: BRIGHAM 189, CRAWFORD p. 51.
Locations: LPC;

1740#15
GREAT BRITAIN. PARLIAMENT. *An act for the more effectual securing and encouraging the trade of America.* . . London. 10p. F. 1740
Locations: L; MB

1740#16
GREAT BRITAIN. SOVEREIGN. GEORGE II. *By the King.* . . *Whereas by an act passed this present session.* . . *for the more effectual securing and encouraging the trade.* . . *to America, and for the encouragement of seamen to enter His Majesty's service.* . . *[9 April 1740].* London. J. Baskett, s.sh. F. 1740
Note: BRIGHAM 188, CRAWFORD, p. 51.
Locations: L; RPJCB, DLC, NN

1740#17
Great Britain's complaints against Spain *impartially examin'd. And the conduct of each nation, from the treaty of Utrecht to the late declaration of war, compared.* . . London. J. Roberts, 80p. 8vo. 1740
Note: SABIN 28436, HANSON 5429, EA 740/149. 'Chiefly relates to America.'
Locations: L; DLC, RPJCB, CtY

1740#18
GREY, Zachary. *The Quaker and Methodist compared, in an abstract of Geo. Fox's journal, with his will, and the Rev. Geo. Whitefield's journal, with historical notes.* London. J. Millar, 98p. 8vo. 1740
Note: SABIN 28794.
Locations: DLC, PHC, NjPT

1740#19
The Jenny Wren. Part IV. *being a choice collection of favourite songs.* . . London. Aldermary church yard, 8p. 4to. [c.1740??]
Note: Contains 'A new election song' with curious verse on the 'American planter, too often a ranter/In land, stocks and money so wealthy/Who, worse than a Jew/Sells Old England for New. . . '.
Locations: L;

1740

1740#20
JEPHSON, Ralph. *The expounder expounded: or, Annotations upon that incomparable piece, intitled, A short account of God's dealings with the Rev. G—e W——d... by R–ph J–ps–on.* London. W. and T.Payne, 85p. 8vo. 1740
Note: SABIN 36054.
Locations: MiU-C

1740#21
KEITH, Sir William. *A collection of papers and other tracts, written occasionally on various subjects.* London. J. Mechell, 228p. 8vo. 1740
Note: SABIN 37328, HANSON 5385, EA 740/171, 749/154. Second edition in 1749. Several essays on trade and colonies.
Locations: L; DLC, RPJCB, MiU-C

1740#22
KEITH, Sir William. *Some useful observations on the consequences of the present war with Spain.* London. J. Mechell, 28p. 8vo. [1740]
Note: SABIN 37242, HANSON 5431, EA 740/172.
Locations: L; RPJCB, MH

1740#23
A letter to a member *of Parliament. Concerning the present state of affairs at home and abroad...* London. T. Cooper, 60p. 8vo. 1740
Note: SABIN 40399, EA 740/185–7. Two other editions, 1740.
Locations: DLC, RPJCB, MiU-C

1740#24
MURRAY, Sir Alexander. *The true interest of Great Britain, Ireland and our plantations: or, a proposal for making such an union... as that already made betwixt Scotland and England...* London. 52p. F. 1740
Note: HANSON 5508, EA 740/222.
Locations: L; Lu; E; RPJCB, NN, CtY

1740#25
NICOL, John and others. *Copy of three letters, the first written by Dr John Nicol at New York... the second by a dissenting minister in England... the third from a minister in Boston... giving an account of the progress and success of the gospel in foreign parts...* Edinburgh. A. Alison, for J. Duncan, 8p. 8vo. 1740
Note: SABIN 55240, EA 740/80.
Locations: L; RPJCB, NN, NNNAM

1740#26
NICOL, John and others. *Copy of two letters, the first written by a gentleman at New York... the second by a dissenting minister in England... progress and success of the gospel in foreign parts...* Edinburgh. A. Alison for J. Duncan, 8p. 8vo. 1740

Note: SABIN 16729, EA 740/79.
Locations: L; DLC, N

1740#27
Old England for ever, or, *Spanish cruelty display'd; wherein the Spaniards right to America is impartially examined and found defective, their pretensions founded in blood...* London. Booksellers of London and Westminster, 320p. 8vo. 1740
Note: HANSON 5430, EA 740/232.
Locations: L; RPJCB, DLC, CaBViPA

1740#28
The operations of the war *for the first twelve months, examin'd and accounted for: from a late ministerial piece called, the grand question.* London. T. Cooper, 33p. 8vo. 1740
Note: SABIN 57395, EA 740/233–4. Another edition, Dublin, 1740: CtY.
Locations: RPJCB, CSmH, MH

1740#29
PERRIN, William. *The present state of the British and French sugar colonies, and our own northern colonies, considered...* London. T. Cooper, 63p. 8vo. 1740
Note: SABIN 61011, HANSON 5456, EA 740/241.
Locations: L; Lu; DLC, RPJCB, MiU-C

1740#30
The present state of the *revenue and forces... of France and Spain...* London. T. Cooper, 62p. 8vo. 1740
Note: HANSON 5386, EA 740/253–4. Also Dublin, 1740. English colonies will help war effort.
Locations: Lu; RPJCB, N

1740#31
Reasons for an immediate war *against France...* London. R. Amey, 33p. 8vo. 1740
Note: SABIN 68263, EA 740/263–4. French threat to America. Also Dublin, 1740.
Locations: L; InU, RPJCB, CtY

1740#32
Reasons shewing that it is *the landed interest, as well as the interest of the nation to encourage the importation of iron from America; and that the importation of pigs has not lessened the value of the woods in England.* London. s.sh. F. [1740?]
Note: SABIN 68290, EA 740/266.
Locations: DLC

1740#33
SEWARD, William. *Journal of a voyage from Savannah to Philadelphia, and from Philadelphia to England...* London. J. Oswald. Also sold by J. Wilson, Bristol, Gabriel Harris, Jr. in Gloucester... As also by the

170

booksellers in New-England, New-York, Philadelphia and Charles-Town., etc. 87p. 8vo. 1740
Note: SABIN 79495, EA 740/289.
Locations: L; DLC, MiU-C, CtY

1740#34
THOMAS, John, Dean of Peterborough. *A sermon preach'd. . . Thursday May the 8th 1740. . .* London. M. Downing, 29p. 64p. 4to. 1740
Note: EA 740/306. Account of SPCK, with letter from Georgia Saltzburgers.
Locations: L; DFo, MWA, GU

1740#35
The universal pocket-book. . . Containing. . . I. A map of the world. London. T. Cooper, 272p. 12mo. 1740
Note: HANSON 5387, EA 740/312. Text has description of America and postal information. Other editions 1741, 1742, two in 1745, EA 741/233, 742/202, 745/208–9.
Locations: O; DLC, FU

1740#36
WARNE, Jonathan. *The spirit of the martyrs revived in the doctrines of the Reverend George Whitefield, and the judicious and faithful methodists. . . Part I.* London. T. Cooper, 116p. 8vo. 1740
Note: SABIN 101431.
Locations: IU, NNUT

1740#37
WELLER, Samuel. *The trial of Mr Whitefield's spirit. In some remarks upon his fourth Journal. . .* London. T. Gardner, 55p. 8vo. 1740
Note: SABIN 102565, EA 740/325, 745/225. Second edition, 1745. Reprinted Boston, 1741.
Locations: L; DLC, MWA, GU-DeR

1740#38
WESLEY, John. *An extract of the Rev. Mr John Wesley's journal, from February 1, 1737–8, to his return from Germany.* London. W. Strahan, sold by J. Hutton, 90p. 12mo. 1740
Note: SABIN 102655, EA 740/326. References to Georgia. Another edition, Bristol, 1743, EA 743/229.
Locations: L; NcD, TxDaM-P

1740#39
WHITEFIELD, George. *A collection of papers, lately printed in the Daily Advertiser. . .* London. Printed. And sold at the following booksellers and pamphlet-shops. At J. Oswald's; James Buckland; T. Gardner and A. Dodd; E. Cooke and A. Bartlet. Also by J. Wilson in Bristol; Gabriel Harris, junior, in Gloucester; J. Trail in Edinburgh; and by other booksellers, both in town and country. As also by the booksellers in New-England, New-York, Philadelphia, and Charles-Town, 47p. 8vo. 1740
Note: SABIN 103506, EA 740/66, EA 740/327. Contains Whitefield's letters from New Jersey and Georgia to inhabitants of Chesapeake and Carolinas and material on Georgia orphan house. A second edition in 1740 has an added letter to Mr. William Seward from Mr. Joseph Periam. (L; CtY, RPJCB).
Locations: O;

1740#40
WHITEFIELD, George. *A continuation of the Reverend Mr Whitefield's journal from his embarking after the embargo, to his arrival at Savannah in Georgia.* London. W. Strahan for J. Hutton, 88p. 8vo. 1740
Note: SABIN 103542, EA 740/328–9. Another London edition in 1740. First published Philadelphia, 1740. (EVANS 4633). The 'fifth' journal.
Locations: Llp; MRu; RPJCB, CtY, DLC

1740#41
WHITEFIELD, George. *A letter from the Rev. Mr George Whitefield to the religious societies, lately set on foot in several parts of England and Wales.* London. W. Strahan, 28p. 8vo. 1740
Note: 'Wrote on board the Elizabeth, bound from London to Philadelphia.' First printed Philadelphia, [1739] (EVANS 4455). Also Edinburgh, 1740, (L; E;) and 1742.
Locations: Llp; Lmh; DLC, MH, CtY

1740#42
WHITEFIELD, George. *A letter from the Reverend Mr. George Whitefield to a friend in London, dated at New-Brunswick in New-Jersey, April 27, 1740.* London. W. Strahan, 8p. 8vo. 1740
Note: SABIN 103555, EA 740/330. On the orphan house in Georgia. Also printed Boston and Charlestown, 1740 (EVANS 4642–3).
Locations: L; RPJCB, ICN

1740#43
WHITEFIELD, George. *A short account of God's dealings with the Reverend Mr. George Whitefield. . . from his infancy, to the time of his entring into Holy Orders. . . to be published for the benefit of the orphan-house in Georgia.* London. W. Strahan, for J. Hutton, 76p. 8vo. 1740
Note: SABIN 1249, 103518, 103591, EA 740/331, 741/263, 743/233, 744/247. Also Edinburgh, 1741; two editions in Glasgow, 1741, Whitby, 1743, second edition in 1744. Written on board the Elizabeth bound from London to Philadelphia. Also published in 1747 (EA 747/187) as *The full account of the life and dealings with God. . . to which is annexed, a brief account of the rise. . . of the orphan-house in Georgia. . .* , 80p. 12mo.: L; RPJCB, MH.
Locations: L; DLC, RPJCB, NN

1740

1740#44
WHITEFIELD, George. *Three letters. . . III. To the inhabitants of Maryland, Virginia, and North and South Carolina, concerning their Negroes.* Glasgow. J. Duncan, 20p. 8vo. 1740
Note: EA 740/332. First (?) published Philadelphia, 1740 (EVANS 4651).
Locations: L;

1740#45
WILSON, Thomas (1663–1755). *An essay towards an instruction for the Indians; explaining the most essential doctrines of Christianity. . . Together with directions and prayers. . . By the Right Reverend Father in God, Thomas, Lord Bishop of Sodor and Man.* London. Printed; and sold by J. Osborn; and W. Thorn, [6], xl, [4], 248p. 12mo. 1740
Note: SABIN 104690, EA 740/333, 741/264, 742/213, 743/236–7, 747/190. Dedicated to Georgia Trustees. Other editions as *The doctrines of Christianity made easy to the meanest capacities: or, an essay towards an instruction for the Indians;. . .* Another London edition in 1740; also London, 1741 (second edition corrected, with additions), 1742 (third edition), two in 1743, 1747 (sixth edition), 1751, 1754 (eighth edition), 1759 (ninth edition), Dublin, 1760.
Locations: L; E; O; CLU-S/C; MiU-C, MH

1741#1
BATEMAN, Edmund. *A sermon preached. . . March 19, 1740–1. . .* London. J. and H. Pemberton, 21p. 8vo. 1741
Note: SABIN 3918, EA 741/11. Georgia Trustees and Bray Associates anniversary sermon.
Locations: L; NCp; DLC, RPJCB, MiU-C

1741#2
BELL, John. *An epistle to Friends in Maryland, Virginia, Barbadoes, and the other colonies. . . Dear Friends. . . John Bell. Bromley near London, 3d Month 1741.* London. 4p. F. [1741]
Note: SABIN 4454, SMITH, I, 233, EA 741/15.
Locations: DLC, RPJCB, NN

1741#3
C-, H. *A poem. Inscrib'd to the Right Honourable Sir Robert Walpole, on the success of His Majesty's arms in America.* London. Printed for the author; and sold by J. Hazard, and J. Wright, 8p. 2o. 1741
Note: FOXON P546. On the naval victories against Spain.
Locations: RPB-JH

1741#4
CAMPBELL, John. *A concise history of the Spanish America. . .* London. J. Stagg and D. Browne, 330p. 8vo. 1741

Note: HANSON 5559note, EA 741/26, 742/29, 747/28. Reissued in 1742 as *A compleat history. . .* and, in 1747, as *The Spanish empire in America. . .*
Locations: L; Lu; DLC, RPJCB, NN

1741#5
CHRISTIE, Thomas. *A description of Georgia, by a gentleman who has resided there upwards of seven years, and was one of the first settlers.* London. C. Corbett, 8p. F. 1741
Note: SABIN 27037, EA 741/38.
Locations: RPJCB, MH

1741#6
COLMAN, Benjamin. *Souls flying to Jesus Christ, pleasant and admirable to behold. A sermon preached. . . at the opening evening lecture, in. . . Boston. . . October 21, 1740.* London. Boston printed, London reprinted. S. Mason, 30p. 8vo. 1741
Note: First printed Boston, 1741 (EVANS 4490). Also Glasgow, 1741 (L;).
Locations: RPJCB, NN, MH

1741#7
A comparison between the doctrines taught by the clergy of the Church of England, and. . . Whitefield. . . To which is added, The wisdom of fleeing from persecution, exemplified in the conduct of. . . Whitefield at Charles-Town. . . London. A. Smith, 28p. 8vo. 1741
Note: SABIN 15027, EA 741/41.
Locations: OC

1741#8
COXE, Daniel. *A collection of voyages and travels, in three parts. . . [Part III]. . . A description of the English province of Carolana. . .* London. Oliver Payne, 142, 86, 122p. 8vo. 1741
Note: SABIN 17287, 17281, EA 741/47. The *Description* was first published in 1722. (Coxe, above, 1722).
Locations: L; E; CSmH, MB, PHi

1741#9
DOUGLASS, William. *A discourse concerning the currencies of the British plantations in America. Especially with regard to their paper money. . .* London. T. Cooper, etc. 54p. 8vo. [1741]
Note: SABIN 20721, EA 741/63. Also London, 1751. First printed Boston, 1740 (EVANS 4530–2) where attributed to Thomas Hutchinson. ESTC lists under 1740.
Locations: Lhl; RPJCB, CSmH, NN

1741#10
ELIOT, Joseph. *The life of faith, exemplified and recommended, in a letter found in the study of J. Belcher, late of Dedham in New-England. . . To which is added, A few verses by the late Reverend Mr Killinghall, upon reading of it.* London. J. Oswald, 8p. 8vo. 1741

Note: First printed Boston, 1721 (BRISTOL B685), SABIN 4395.
Locations: L; DLC, NN, RPJCB

1741#11
EVANS, Thomas? *An extract of sundry passages taken out of Mr Whitefield's printed sermons, journals, and letters; together with some scruples. . . with a letter from. . . Charles Tennent, to the printer of the Pensilvania gazette.* London. Philadelphia printed, London reprinted. J.Oswald, 52p. 8vo. 1741
Note: SABIN 103622, EA 741/70–72. Two more London editions in 1741. Taken from *The Querists, or an extract. . .*, Philadelphia and Boston, 1740 (EVANS 4856–7). EA lists the same work twice, EA 741/71 and EA 741/259.
Locations: L; RPJCB, NN

1741#12
The false accusers accused; or *the undeceived Englishman: being an important enquiry into the general conduct of the administration. . .* London. J. Roberts, 56p. 8vo. 1741
Note: SABIN 23756, EA 741/78–80. Two further editions in 1741. Defends ministerial foreign policy, including trade and colonial policy.
Locations: L; RPJCB, MH, NIC

1741#13
FINLEY, Samuel. *Christ triumphing, and Satan raging: a sermon. . . first preached at Nottingham in Pensilvania. . .* London. Philadelphia printed, London reprinted for S. Mason, 44p. 8vo. 1741
Note: SABIN 24386, EA 741/83–4. Also Edinburgh, 1741, (DLC, NjP). First printed Philadelphia, 1741, EVANS 4716.
Locations: L; NN

1741#14
A geographical and historical description *of the principal objects of the present war in the West-Indies. viz. Cartagena, Puerto Belo. . . and San Augustin, etc.* London. T. Gardner, etc. 192p. 8vo. 1741
Note: SABIN 26973, EA 741/94.
Locations: L; C; DLC, CtY, RPJCB

1741#15
GREAT BRITAIN. ARMY. REGULATIONS. 1740. *The pay of the garrisons in Ireland Gibraltar Minorca & ye plantations. The half-pay of the officers of the Navy & of the Army. . . Pensions allowed to the widows of the officers. . . The distribution of prize money.* London. J. Millan, s.sh. 1/2o. [1741?]
Note: MiU-C has 1741 edition, EA 741/98. There may be one list for 1740 and another for 1741, so the identity of the editions is not fully established. ESTC dates [1742?].
Locations: L; NN, CSmH, MiU-C

1741#16
GREAT BRITAIN. BOARD OF TRADE. *A list of copies of charters, from the Commissioners for Trade and Plantations, presented to the Honourable the House of Commons, in pursuance of their address to His Majesty, of the 25th of April, 1740.* London. 89p. F. [1741]
Note: SABIN 41430, HANSON 5563, EA 741/99–100. Another edition, London, 1741. Includes charters of Maryland, Connecticut, Rhode-Island, Pennsylvania, Massachusetts, and Georgia, separately paginated.
Locations: L; RPJCB, MiU-C

1741#17
GREAT BRITAIN. CUSTOMS COMMISSIONERS. *Instructions by the Commissioners for Managing and Causing to be Levied and Collected His Majesty's Customs. . . to [blank] who is established collector of His Majesty's customs at [blank] in America.* London. 49, [1]p. 2o. [1741?]
Note: Includes Privy Council proceedings, 2 October 1741.
Locations: Lpro;

1741#18
GREAT BRITAIN. LORD JUSTICES. *Proclamation. Appointing distribution of prizes taken before His Majesty's declaration of war 18 June 1741.* London. J. Baskett, s.sh. F. 1741
Note: BRIGHAM 192, CRAWFORD p. 53.
Locations: LS; LPC;

1741#19
GREAT BRITAIN. LORDS JUSTICES. *Proclamation. Appointing distribution of prizes taken since the declaration of war. [18 June 1741].* London. J. Baskett, s.sh. F. 1741
Note: CRAWFORD p. 3.
Locations: LPC;

1741#20
GREAT BRITAIN. PARLIAMENT. HOUSE OF COMMONS. *A bill, intituled, an act for restraining and preventing several unwarrantable schemes. . . in his majesty's colonies. . . in America.* London. 10p. F. [1741?]
Note: EA 741/101. Anti-land banks.
Locations: RPJCB

1741#21
HOLDEN, Samuel. *Letters of Samuel Holden, Esquire, to Dr. Benjamin Coleman of Boston, New-England.* London. Printed: and sold by the booksellers in the Poultry, and pamphlet shops at the Royal Exchange, 16p. 8vo. 1741
Locations: L; NjP

1741

1741#22
The importance of Jamaica to Great-Britain. . . the advantages. . . to Great-Britain, Ireland, and the colonies in North-America. . . London. A. Dodd, 81p. 8vo. [1741]
Note: SABIN 35588, HANSON 5574, EA 741/123.
Locations: L; DLC, RPJCB, NN.

1741#23
KEIMER, Samuel. *Caribbeana. Containing letters and dissertations, together with poetical essays.* . . London. T. Osborne, etc. 2 vols., 4to. 1741
Note: SABIN 37174, HANSON 5572, EA 741/28. Material on North America.
Locations: L; Lu; RPJCB, MiU-C, DLC, NN

1741#24
A letter from a gentleman in the country, to his friend in Edinburgh, concerning Mr Wh—f—d. . . Edinburgh. 31p. 8vo. 1741
Note: SABIN 103629, EA 741/139, 742/120. Also London, 1742. Attacks George Whitefield.
Locations: L; CtY, I

1741#25
A letter from the famous Dr. Ph—ps Mountebank, to the Reverend Mr G—e Whitefield, A. B. [Edinburgh?]. s.sh. F. [1741?]
Note: SABIN 103630, EA 741/140. Signed 'R–d Ph—ps.' References to Whitefield's Georgia Orphan House collections.
Locations: GU-DeR

1741#26
MARTYN, Benjamin. *An account shewing the progress of the colony of Georgia in America from its first establishment.* London. 71p. 4to. 1741
Note: SABIN 45000, EA 741/147. Reprinted Maryland, 1742.
Locations: L; DLC, RPJCB, MiU-C

1741#27
MARTYN, Benjamin. *An impartial enquiry into the state and utility of the province of Georgia.* London. W. Meadows, 104p. 8vo. 1741
Note: SABIN 45001, HANSON 5569, EA 741/148–9. Second edition, 1741.
Locations: L; DLC, RPJCB, MiU-C

1741#28
The Newsman's interpreter, or a description of several Spanish territories in America; particularly of those places against which, it is supposed, the English have a design. . . Manchester. [J. Berry?], 67p. 12mo. 1741
Note: SABIN 55068, EA 741/161. The second edition. The first edition has not been found. Probably a compilation from the *Lancashire Journal*, a weekly magazine printed by J. Berry, which in turn took material from the *Gentleman's Magazine*.
Locations: L; MRu; MH, RPJCB

1741#29
Observations upon Remarks upon Mr. Whitefield; containing an answer thereto, and a vindication. . . Edinburgh. s.sh. F. 1741
Note: SABIN 103638, EA 741/162. Dated October 26, 1741. References to Whitefield's Georgia Orphan House collections.
Locations: GU-DeR

1741#30
Remarks on Mr. Whitefield.
Note: SABIN 103646. Begins 'Mr. Whitefield I take to be a hot-headed enthusiast. . . ' Contains references to Whitefield's Georgia Orphan House collections.
Locations: GU-DeR

1741#31
SECKER, Thomas. *An extract out* of the bishop of Oxford's sermon before the Society for propagating the gospel in foreign parts. The state of our colonies. London. 8p. 4to. [1741]
Note: EA 741/211.
Locations: RPJCB

1741#32
SECKER, Thomas. *A sermon preached.* . . Feb. 20, 1740–1. . . London. J. and H. Pemberton, 84p. 4to. 1741
Note: SABIN 78717, EA 741/212–3. Other editions in 1741; and 1752, with additional letters (L;). SPG sermon for 1741. With abstract of Society's proceedings, etc.
Locations: L; RPJCB, DLC, CtY

1741#33
A short essay upon trade in general. . . London. J. Huggonson, 60p. 8vo. 1741
Note: HANSON 5549, EA 741/215. References to fashions in American colonies, etc. By Thomas Cowper.
Locations: L; MH-BA, NNC

1741#34
SMITH, Josiah. *The character, preaching, etc. of the Reverend Mr George Whitefield impartially represented and supported.* . . Glasgow. Boston printed, Glasgow reprinted. R. Smith, 16p. 8vo. 1741
Note: EA 741/216. Sermon preached at Charleston, 26 March 1740. First printed Boston and Philadelphia, 1740 (EVANS 4600–1).
Locations: NN, NcD

1741#35
SMITH, Wavell. *Observations occasion'd by reading a pamphlet, intitled, A discourse concerning the currencies of*

the British plantations in America. In a letter to —. London. T. Cooper, 23p. 8vo. 1741

Note: SABIN 56481, 84538, HANSON 5564, EA 741/217. Sometimes attributed to W. Shippen. Refers to W. Douglass's *Discourse...*, above, 1741.

Locations: L; MB, RPJCB, MiU-C

1741#36
SOCIETY FOR THE PROPAGATION OF THE GOSPEL. *A collection of papers...* London. E. Owen, 51p. 4to. 1741

Note: SABIN 85934note, EA 741/218.

Locations: L; DLC, RPJCB, NN

1741#37
SOCIETY IN SCOTLAND FOR PROPAGATING CHRISTIAN KNOWLEDGE. *State of the Society in Scotland, for propagating Christian knowledge... together with some account of this Society's missionaries, for converting the native Indians of America.* Edinburgh. R. Fleming [75]p. 8vo. 1741

Note: SABIN 85994, EA 741/219.

Locations: L; E; CtY, MH, ViU

1741#38
Some considerations on the prohibiting the exportation of corn and provisions from the northern colonies... London?, [2]p. 1/2o. [1741?]

Locations: Lpro;

1741#39
TAILFER, Patrick. *A true and historical narrative of the colony of Georgia in America, from the first settlement thereof until this present present period...* London. Printed by P. Timothy, Charlestown and sold by J. Crokatt, London, xvi, 112p. 8vo. 1741

Note: SABIN 94217, HANSON 5570, EA 741/224. (First?) published Charlestown, 1741 (EVANS 4816–7).

Locations: L; RPJCB, NN, GU

1741#40
TENNENT, Gilbert. *Four letters from Mr. Gilbert Tennent, the Secretary of New-England, and Dr. Colman, concerning the great success of the gospel abroad.* Glasgow. Printed by W. Duncan, 7, [1]p. 8vo, 1741

Note: Contains 'Proposals for printing by subscription The weekly history', Nov. 18th. 1741.

Locations: Gu;

1741#41
TENNENT, John (1706–1732). *The nature of regeneration openeed, and... demonstrated... a sermon... with an expostulatory address... by G. Tennent...* London. Boston printed, London reprinted, J. Oswald xix, 122p. 12mo. 1741

Note: SABIN 94705. First published Boston, 1735 (EVANS 3968).

Locations: L;

1741#42
TENNENT, John, M.D. *Truth stifled, and an appeal to the genius of the ancient Romans. Being the case of Dr John Tennent, with respect to his free publication of his discovery of the farther efficacy of the Senekka Rattlesnake Root, which cures with, great certainty, the American Epidemical Fever... Which also contains enquiries into the operation of the rattle-snake's venom upon the human body...* London. Printed for C. Corbett, 61, [1]p. 8vo. 1741

Note: EA 741/226 gives no locations.

Locations: DNLM, NRU-M

1741#43
Three letters wrote from Boston in *New-England to a correspondent in the Gorbels of Glasgow...* Glasgow. R. Smith, 8p. 8vo. 1741

Note: SABIN 95745, EA 741/227. On Whitefield's and Gilbert Tennent's revivalism. Another edition, (Glasgow?) 1742, EA 742/196.

Locations: MB

1741#44
To the Right Honourable the Lords Commissioners of Trade and Plantations the following supplement to my essay on trade is most humbly offered. London? 6, [2]p. 4to. [1741?]

Locations: Lpro; MH-BA

1741#45
A true and genuine account of the life and doctrine of the Reverend Mr. George Whitefield. Edinburgh (?). s.sh. F. [1741]

Note: EA 741/231, SABIN 103651. Georgia references.

Locations: GU-De

1741#46
TURELL, Ebenezer. *Memoirs of the life and death of... Mrs Jane Turell, who died at Medford, March 26, 1735... to which is added, two sermons... by... B. Colman, D. D.* London. J. Oswald, 172p. 12mo. 1741

Note: SABIN 97451, EA 741/232. Cf. EVANS 3888: *Two sermons...*, New London, 1735; and EVANS 3969: *Memoirs...*, Boston, 1735.

Locations: L; RPJCB, ICN, MH

1741#47
WEBSTER, Alexander. *Supernatural revelation the only sure hope of sinners. A sermon preached...* Edinburgh. R. Fleming and company, 31p. 1741

Note: Also London, 1741. Society in Scotland for the Propagation of the Gospel sermon for 1741.

Locations: L; E; CtY, MH

1741#48
WHITEFIELD, George. *An account of money received and disbursed for the orphan-house in Georgia... To which is prefixed A plan of the building.* London. W. Strahan for T. Cooper, 45p. 8vo. 1741
Note: SABIN 103492, HANSON 5571, EA 741/256.
Locations: L; MRu; DLC, RPJCB, NN

1741#49
WHITEFIELD, George. *A continuation of the Reverend Mr Whitefield's journal, after his arrival at Georgia, to a few days after his second return thither from Philadelphia...* London. W. Strahan for J. Hutton, 58p. 8vo. 1741
Note: SABIN 103545, EA 741/257. The 'sixth' journal.
Locations: L; O; DLC, RPJCB, MiU-C

1741#50
WHITEFIELD, George. *A continuation of the Reverend Mr Whitefield's journal, from a few days after his return to Georgia to his arrival at Falmouth, on the 11th of March 1741. Containing an account of the work of God at Georgia, Rhode-Island, New-England; New-York, Pennsylvania and South Carolina...* London. W. Strahan for R. Hett, 85p. 4to. 1741
Note: SABIN 103550, EA 741/258, 744/243. The 'seventh' journal. Second edition in 1741. Another edition in 1744.
Locations: L; DLC, MH, GU-DeR

1741#51
WHITEFIELD, George. *An extract of the preface to... Whitefield's account of the orphan-house in Georgia. Together with... some letters sent to him from the superintendents... and some of the children.* Edinburgh. T. Lumisden, etc., 27p. 8vo. 1741
Note: SABIN 103513, EA 741/260.
Locations: Gu; RPJCB, NN, GU-DeR

1741#52
WHITEFIELD, George. *A letter to the Reverend John Wesley, in answer to his sermon, entituled, Free-grace...* London. W. Strahan for T. Cooper, 31p. 8vo. 1741
Note: SABIN 103566n, EA 741/261-2. A second edition in 1741. Dated Bethesda, Georgia, 24 December 1740. First? printed Boston, 1740 (EVANS 4647). Another edition, Philadelphia, 1741.
Locations: L; CtY, RPJCB, Vi

1741#53
WHITEFIELD, George. *Orphan-letters. Being a collection of letters wrote by the orphans in the hospital of Georgia. To the Reverend Mr George Whitefield... the great and wonderful success of Mr Whitefield's labours and ministry among them.* Glasgow. R. Smith, 24p. 8vo. 1741
Note: SABIN 103640, EA 741/166.
Locations: NcD, GU-DeR

1741#54
WOTTON, Thomas. *The English Baronetage... To which are added, an account of such Nova-Scotia baronets as are of English families...* London. T. Wotton, 4 vols in five. 8vo. 1741
Locations: L; MH, NjP, CtY

1742#1
BEST, William. *The merit and reward of a good intention. A sermon preached... March 18. 1741-2... in which some notice is taken of a late abusive pamphlet, intituled, A true and historical narrative of the said colony.* London. W. Innys, 32p. 4to. 1742
Note: EA 742/15. Georgia Trustees and Bray Associates anniversary sermon. The pamphlet was by Tailfer, above, 1741.
Locations: Cq; Owo; DLC, RPJCB, MH

1742#2
BISSET, John. *A letter to a gentleman in Scotland, containing remarks upon... Mr George Whitefield.* Aberdeen. 143p. 12mo. 1742
Note: EA 742/16. Whitefield in America. Second and third editions, Glasgow, 1743, EA 743/28-9.
Locations: MH

1742#3
BLENMAN, Jonathan. *Remarks on several Acts of Parliament relating more especially to the colonies abroad; as also on diverse acts of assemblies there...* London. T. Cooper, 125p. 8vo. 1742
Note: SABIN 6012, HANSON 5638, EA 742/17-18. Second edition in 1742. Mainly relates to West Indies.
Locations: L; E; DLC, MWA, RPJCB

1742#4
Bloody news from Carolina: or, *the English sailors tragedy...* London. 8p. 8vo. 1742
Note: SABIN 87802, EA 742/19. Murder by press gang in South Carolina.
Locations: DLC

1742#5
CALDWELL, John. *An impartial trial of the spirit... a sermon preached at New London-derry, October 14th 1741...* Glasgow. Boston printed, and Glasgow reprinted, and sold by Robert Foulis, and by the book sellers in Edinburgh, London, Dublin and Belfast, viii, 47p. 8vo. 1742
Note: SABIN 9905, EA 742/28. Preface states that purpose of republication is to prevent people taking up with superficial religion. First published Boston, 1742: EVANS 4098.
Locations: L; NN, PHi, MWH

1742#6
CAMPBELL, John. *Lives of the admirals... a new and accurate naval history... with passages relating to our*

discoveries, plantations, and commerce. London. 4 vols. 8vo. 1742
Note: EA 742/30, 744/40, 750/44. SABIN 10236. Other editions, 1744, 1750.
Locations: RPJCB, NN, DFo

1742#7
CARTE, Thomas. *A full answer to the Letter from a by-stander...* London. J. Robinson, 214p. 8vo. 1742
Note: HANSON 5647, EA 742/36. Cost of British troops in America.
Locations: L; CSmH, RPJCB

1742#8
CHAUNCY, Charles (1705–87). *A letter from a gentleman in Boston, to Mr. George Wishart, one of the ministers in Edinburgh, concerning the state of religion in New-England.* Edinburgh. 24p. 8vo. 1742
Note: SABIN 12317, EA 742/49.
Locations: DLC, RPJCB, MiU-C

1742#9
CHAUNCY, Charles (1705–87). *The new creature described and considered as the sure characteristick of a man's being in Christ...* Edinburgh. Reprinted for S. Clark, 37p. 12mo. 1742
Note: SABIN 12331, EA 742/48. First printed Boston, 1741, EVANS 4688.
Locations: L; NN, MH

1742#10
CHAUNCY, Charles (1705–87). *The wonderful narrative: or, a faithful account of the French prophets... several other instances of persons under the influence of the like spirit... particularly in New-England...* Glasgow. R. Foulis, xv, 89p. 8vo. 1742
Note: SABIN 105011, EA 742/215. First published Boston, 1742 (EVANS 4915). Attributed to Chauncy or Benjamin Colman.
Locations: L; DLC, NN, MHi

1742#11
The conduct of the late *administration, with regard to foreign affairs.* London. T. Cooper, 80p. 4to. 1742
Note: EA 742/55–6. Also Dublin, 1742.
Locations: RPJCB, OClW

1742#12
EDWARDS, Jonathan. *The distinguishing marks of a work of the spirit of God... lately appeared... in New-England...* London. Boston printed, London reprinted. S. Mason, 76p. 8vo. 1742
Note: SABIN 21934, EA 742/67–9. Also Edinburgh and Glasgow, 1742, London, 1744, EA 744/86. London and Newcastle, 1755. First printed Boston, 1741 (EVANS 4711).
Locations: DLC, RPJCB, CtY

1742#13
The emissary instructed, or the *wiles of popery represented...* Glasgow. Boston printed, Glasgow reprinted. 15p. 8vo. 1742
Note: Also Boston, 1745 (EVANS 5716).
Locations: L;

1742#14
ERSKINE, John. *The signs of the times consider'd: or, the high probability, that the present appearances in New-England, and the west of Scotland, are a prelude of the glorious things promised to the church in the latter ages.* Edinburgh. T. Lumisden and J. Robertson, iv, 34p. 8vo. 1742
Note: SABIN 80911, EA 742/74.
Locations: L; MB, CtY, MH

1742#15
FISHER, James. *A review of the preface to a narrative of the extraordinary work at Kilsyth, and other congregations in the neighbourhood, written by the Reverend Mr James Robe...* Glasgow. J. Bryce, and P. Bryce, 68p. 8vo. 1742
Note: Includes an attack on Jonathan Edwards's *Distinguishing marks...*, above, 1741.
Locations: L; ICU

1742#16
FRIEND IN EDINBURGH. *A letter from a friend in Edinburgh to a gentleman in the country:... concerning the wonderful progress and success of the glorious gospel in diverse parts of America and Britain, and the opposition made thereto.* Edinburgh. Printed by T. Lumisden and J. Robertson, and sold at their printing-house, by J. Traill, and J. Barry in Glasgow, 40p. 8vo. 1742
Locations: E; ICN, NcD

1742#17
GEORGIA TRUSTEES. *The resolutions of the Trustees for... Georgia... this eight day of March... relating to the grants and tenure of lands within the said colony...* London. 4p. F. [1742]
Note: SABIN 27104, HANSON 5641, EA 742/83. Dated 8 March 1741–2. ESTC dates to 1741.
Locations: DLC, MiU-C, GU-DeR

1742#18
GIB, Adam. *A warning against countenancing the ministrations of Mr G. Whitefield...* Edinburgh. E. Duncan, ix, 65p. 8vo. 1742
Note: EA 742/84, 743/105. Also Edinburgh, 1743. Minor American references.
Locations: L; MB, MH, NNUT

1742#19
GLOVER, Richard. *A short account of the late application to Parliament made by the merchants of London*

1742

upon the neglect of their trade... London. T. Cooper, 61p. 8vo. 1742
Note: SABIN 27608, EA 742/177–80. Two other London and one Dublin edition in 1742. Virginia and Carolina.
Locations: L; DLC, RPJCB, CtY

1742#20
GREAT BRITAIN. PARLIAMENT. *Act for further regulating the plantation trade; and for relief of merchants importing prize goods from America.* London. T. and R. Baskett, 7p. F. 1742
Locations: RPJCB, MiU-C

1742#21
GREAT BRITAIN. PARLIAMENT. *Act to revive several acts... turnpikes... and to continue several acts relating to rice to frauds in the customs, to the clandestine running of goods, and to copper ore of the British plantations.* London. T. and R. Baskett, 5p. F. 1742
Locations: MiU-C

1742#22
GREAT BRITAIN. PARLIAMENT. HOUSE OF COMMONS. *A bill to explain and amend... an act made in the sixth year of the reign of... George the first...* London. 8p. F. [1742]
Note: Seeks to extend act of George I relating to the insurance of ships, lending of money on bottomry, etc., to the American colonies.
Locations: RPJCB

1742#23
Entry cancelled.

1742#24
Illuminatio Britannicae; or, a true and faithful narrative of what passed at a conference held at the Admiralty Office... Jany 11, 1740–41... London. 91p. 4to. 1742
Note: SABIN 34329, EA 742/103. North American matters.
Locations: L; RPJCB, MiU-C, CtY

1742#25
In canc' John Penn. Thomas Penn, and Richard Penn Esqrs. Plaintiffs. Charles Calvert Esq. Lord Baltimore... Defendant. The Plaintiffs case. London. 13p. 1o [1742?]
Note: SABIN 34416, EA 740/240. A map is dated 20 October, 1740 but the date of printing was presumably later.
Locations: L; DLC, CSmH, ICN

1742#26
A letter to the Negroes lately converted to Christ in America. And particularly to those, lately called out of darkness... at Mr. Jonathan Bryan's in South Carolina... London. J. Hart, 32p. 8vo. 1742
Note: SABIN 40504, EA 742/125, 743/144. Second edition 1743: MiU-C, CtY, MB.
Locations: NIC

1742#27
M., A. *The state of religion in New-England, since the Reverend George Whitefield's arrival there. In a letter from a gentleman in New-England to his friend in Glasgow. To which is subjoined an appendix...* Glasgow and Edinburgh, Robert Foulis, 44p. 8vo. 1742
Note: SABIN 90595, 90596, EA 742/183–4. Appendix attests facts of letter and is by C. Chauncy, J. Caldwell, J. Barnard, Mr. Turrell, J. Parsons, B. Colman. The second edition is Glasgow and Edinburgh: R. Foulis; London: sold by A. Millar, 1742 'To which is affixed a reply to Mr Whitefield's remarks on the first edition.' Reprinted Boston, 1743.
Locations: RPJCB, MiU-C, NN

1742#28
MACKAY, Hugh. *A letter from Lieut. Hugh MacKay, of General Oglethorpe's regiment.* London. 39p. 8vo. 1742
Note: SABIN 43362, EA 742/131.
Locations: DLC, RPJCB, MB

1742#29
MAUDUIT, Israel. *The parallel... the renewal of our Prussian treaty.* London. W. Nicol, 50p. 4to. 1742
Note: EA 742/136.
Locations: RPJCB, DLC, NN

1742#30
A modest enquiry into the present state of foreign affairs... By a lover of his country. London. M. Cooper, 71p. 8vo. [1742]
Note: SABIN 49823, EA 742/143. Necessity of maintaining Britain's American connection.
Locations: RPJCB, KU

1742#31
OGLETHORPE, James Edward. *An impartial account of the late expedition against St. Augustine under General Oglethorpe. Occasioned by the suppression of the report, made by a committee of the General Assembly in South-Carolina...* London. J. Huggonson, 68p. 8vo. 1742
Note: SABIN 56846, EA 742/104.
Locations: L; DLC, RPJCB, MiU-C

1742#32
OLD DRUMCLOG SOLDIER. *A warning to all the lovers of Christ in Scotland to be upon their guard against the spreading contagion broken out from Mr. Adam Gib,... Also you are to guard against that deistical pamphlet, called, A letter from a gentleman in New-England to his friend in Glasgow,... Done by an old drumclog soldier, who was author of The warm address.* Edinburgh. Printed in the

Swan Close, and sold by the booksellers in Edinburgh and Glasgow, 38p. 12mo. 1742

Note: *A warm address to lukewarm ministers* was by 'a minister of the Church of England'.

Locations: Gu;

1742#33
OLIPHANT, Andrew. *A letter from New-England, concerning the state of religion there.* Edinburgh. 7p. 12mo. 1742

Note: SABIN 57179, EA 742/146.

Locations: MH, PP

1742#34
PENN, John. *In Chancery. Breviate. John Penn, Thomas Penn, and Richard Penn, plaintiffs. . . For the plaintiffs.* London. 116p. 2o. [1742]

Note: SABIN 34416, EA 742/148. Maryland boundary dispute. Charles Calvert, defendant.

Locations: L; RPJCB, MH, PPL

1742#35
PHILALETHES. *The profit and loss of Great-Britain and Spain, from the commencement of the present war to this time, impartially stated. . .* London. T. Cooper, 62p. 8vo. 1742

Note: SABIN 65959, HANSON 5623, EA 742/149.

Locations: L; RPJCB, CSmH

1742#36
ROBE, James. *Mr Robe's first letter to the Reverend James Fisher. . .* Glasgow. R. Smith, 26p. 8vo. 1742

Note: Vindicates Scottish revivals. Mentions New England Awakening.

Locations: L;

1742#37
Select trials at the Sessions House in the Old Bailey, for murder, robberies, rapes, sodomy, coining,. . . To which are added, genuine accounts of the lives, behaviour, confessions and dying speeches of the most eminent convicts. . . From the year 1720, to this time. . . London printed by J. Applebee for James Hodges, 4 vols., 12mo. 1742

Locations: L; CaOHM, BRG, CLL

1742#38
SHERLOCK, Thomas. *A letter from the Lord Bishop of Sarum, to the clergy of his diocese.* London. 7, 1p. 4to. [1742]

Note: About a collection for the SPG.

Locations: L;

1742#39
Some Observations on the conduct *of the famous Mr Whitefield. . .* Edinburgh. 12p. 12mo. 1742

Note: Attacks Whitefield's financial probity in connection with Georgia.

Locations: L;

1742#40
STEBBING, Henry. *A sermon preached. . . February 19, 1741/2. . .* London. E. Owen, 76p. 4to. 1742

Note: SABIN 91002, EA 742/185–6. Another issue in 1742. SPG sermon for 1742, with abstract, etc.

Locations: L; DLC, RPJCB, CtY

1742#41
STEPHENS, Thomas fl. 1742. *An account shewing what money has been received by the Trustees for the use of the colony of Georgia. . .* London. 2p. F. [1742?]

Note: SABIN 27008, HANSON 5642, EA 742/82.

Locations: L; GU-DeR

1742#42
STEPHENS, Thomas fl. 1742. *The hard case of the distressed people of Georgia.* London. 4p. F. [1742]

Note: SABIN 27055, 91307, HANSON 5643, EA 742/187. Dated 26 April, 1742.

Locations: Ls; DLC, RPJCB

1742#43
STEPHENS, William. *A journal of the proceedings in Georgia, beginning October 20, 1737. . . A state of the province, as attested on oath in the court of Savannah, November 10, 1740. . .* London. W. Meadows, 3 vols. 8vo. 1742

Note: SABIN 91313, HANSON 5640, EA 742/188. Most libraries seem only to have two vols.

Locations: EN; GU-De, RPJCB

1742#44
STEPHENS, William. *Journal received February 4, 1741. By the Trustees for establishing the colony of Georgia. . . commencing September 22, 1741, and ending October 28 following.* London. W. Meadows, 44p. 8vo. [1742]

Note: SABIN 91314, EA 742/189. Also printed as part of Stephen's *Journal of the Proceedings*, above, 1742.

Locations: RPJCB, MiU-C, MB

1742#45
STEPHENS, William. *A state of the province of Georgia, attested upon oath. . . in the court of Savannah, Nov. 10, 1740.* London. W. Meadows, 32p. 8vo. 1742

Note: SABIN 27113, 91315, HANSON 5639, EA 742/190. Also printed as part of Stephen's *Journal of the Proceedings*, above, 1742.

Locations: L; DLC, RPJCB, MH

1742#46
TENNENT, John, M. D. *A brief account of the case of John Tennent, M. D.* London. s.sh. F. [1742]

Note: EA 742/192.

Locations: NNNAM

1742

1742#47
TENNENT, John, M. D. *Physical enquiries: discovering the mode of translation in the constitutions of northern inhabitants, on going to, and for some time after arriving in southern climates...* London. T. Gardner, etc. 69p. 8vo. 1742
Note: SABIN 94715, EA 742/194, 749/266. Second edition, 1749 (RPJCB).
Locations: L; MiU-C, ViU, OU

1742#48
The trial of James Annesley *and Joseph Redding, at the Sessions-House in the Old Bailey, on Thursday the 15th July, 1742 for the murder of Thomas Egglestone...* London. Booksellers of London, Westminster and Dublin, 83p. 12mo. 1742
Note: Other issues 1742 (L; CtY, NN); 1744 revised (DLC, MH, NN). See Annesley, *Memoirs*, below, 1743.
Locations: L; NN

1742#49
WESLEY, John. *An extract of the Revd. Mr John Wesley's Journal from August 12, 1738, to Nov. 1, 1739.* Bristol. F. Farley, 98p. 12mo. 1742
Note: SABIN 102656, EA 742/209.
Locations: L; MH, IEG

1742#50
WHITEFIELD, George. *A continuation of the account of the orphan-house in Georgia, from January 1740/1 to June 1742...* Edinburgh. T. Lumisden and J. Robertson, 84p. 8vo. 1742
Note: SABIN 103495, HANSON 5644, EA 742/210.
Locations: L; MHi, RPJCB

1742#51
WHITEFIELD, George. *Some remarks on a late pamphlet intitled, the state of religion in New-England, since the Rev. Mr George Whitefield's arrival there...* Glasgow. Printed by W. Duncan, and sold by the booksellers in London and Glasgow. 32p. 8vo. 1742
Note: SABIN 103594, 103606, EVANS 5312, EA 742/211–12. Second edition London, 1742, retitled *A vindication and confirmation of the remarkable work of God in New-England. Being some remarks on a late pamphlet... The state of religion in New England...* Reprinted Boston, 1743 (EVANS 5313).
Locations: L; MRu; NN, CtY, MH

1743#1
ANNESLEY, James. *Memoirs of an unfortunate young nobleman, in which is continued the history of Count Richard, concluding with a summary view of the tryal. Part the second. By the author of the first.* London. J. Freeman, 235p. 12mo. 1743

Note: SABIN 1600, EA 743/153. Another edition in 1743; also Dublin, 1744. Vol. II of the *Memoirs*. For Vol. III see 1745. Kidnapped to America.
Locations: L; C; CSmH, MWA

1743#2
ANNESLEY, James. *Memoirs of an unfortunate young nobleman, return'd from a thirteen years slavery in America, where he had been sent by the wicked contrivances of his cruel uncle. A story founded on truth...* London. J. Freeman, 277p. 12mo. 1743
Note: SABIN 1599, EA 743/153–155. Part I of the *Memoirs*. Four further London editions of Vol. I in 1743. Also one Belfast (O;) and two Dublin editions, 1743. Vignette on p. 1 of this edition (L; 1452.a.16) is a cherub. For further imprint information and locations of various editions see ESTC.
Locations: L; E; O; DFo, MiU-C, TxU

1743#3
ASHLEY, John. *The second part of Memoirs and considerations concerning the trade and revenues of the British colonies in America...* London. H. Kent for E. Comyns, 127p. 8vo. 1743
Note: SABIN 2193, HANSON 5455n, EA 743/16–17. Vol II of the *Memoirs...*, above, 1740). Also *A supplement*, London, 1743, and second edition (EA 744/11).
Locations: L; DLC, RPJCB, MH

1743#4
BELSHAZZER, Kapha, the Jew. *The book of James...* Dublin, London reprinted. 8p. 8vo. 1743
Note: EA 743/22-4. Annesley case. Attributed to Robert Dodsley. Actual place of publication was London. Two other editions in 1743. One is *The book of the chronicle of James, the nephew.*
Locations: L; MH-L

1743#5
BICKHAM, George. *The British monarchy: or, a new chorographical description of all the dominions subject to the king of Great Britain...* London. 2 vols. F. 1743
Note: SABIN 5222, HANSON 5683, EA 743/27, 748/18, 749/27. Other editions, 1748, 1749.
Locations: DLC, RPJCB

1743#6
BURRINGTON, George. *Seasonable considerations on the expediency of a war with France... To which are added... a short comparison, between the British and French dominions...* London. F. Cogan, 60p. 8vo. 1743
Note: SABIN 9450, HANSON 5687, EA 743/43.
Locations: L; Lu; DLC, RPJCB, NN

1743#7
CADOGAN, George. *The Spanish hireling detected: being a refutation of the several calumnies and falsehoods in*

MEMOIRS
OF AN
Unfortunate Young Nobleman,

Return'd from a

Thirteen Years Slavery in *America*,

Where he had been sent by the Wicked Contrivances of his **Cruel Uncle**.

A STORY founded on Truth, and address'd equally to the Head and Heart.

This is the Heir; come let us kill him, that the Inheritance may be ours.

LUKE xx. 14.

——————*Foul Deeds will rise,*
Tho' all the Earth o'erwhelm 'em, to Mens Eyes.
Spoken by HAMLET of his Uncle.

LONDON:
Printed for J. FREEMAN in *Fleetstreet*; and sold by the Booksellers in Town and Country.
MDCCXLIII.

a late pamphlet, entituled an impartial account of the late expedition against St. Augustine under General Oglethorpe... London. J. Roberts, 68p. 8vo. 1743
Note: SABIN 9829, EA 743/46–7. A second edition in 1743.
Locations: L; DLC, RPJCB, MiU-C

1743#8
The case of his majesty's *province of the Massachusetts Bay, touching the dispute between that province, and the colony of Rhode-Island*... London. 9p. F. [1743]
Note: EA 743/50. To be heard before the Privy Council. See *The case of New Hampshire*, above, 1739.
Locations: RPJCB

1743#9
CRAIG, Campbell. *An authentic journal of the proceedings in the great cause tried at Dublin, between the Honourable James Annesley plaintiff, and a noble person, defendant*... London. J. Warner, 30p. 8vo. 1743
Note: SABIN 1602, EA 743/58–60. At least two further issues/editions with this title in 1743.
Locations: DLC, MnU, NN

1743#10
CRAIG, Campbell. *The trial at bar, between Campbell Craig*... *and*... *Richard earl of Anglesey*... *at the King's Courts, Dublin*... *1743*. London. M. Cooper, 150p. F. 1743
Note: EA 743/61.
Locations: L; MH, NN

1743#11
A description of Holland. . . *Wherein is contained, a particular account of*... *commerce, in*... *America*. London. J. and P. Knapton, 411p. 8vo. 1743
Note: KRESS SUPP. 3673, EA 743/65, 745/174. Another edition in 1745!
Locations: L; Lu; RPJCB, NN

1743#12
DESLANDES, André F. B. *An essay on maritime power and commerce*. London. P. Vaillant, 163p. 8vo. 1743
Note: SABIN 19744, EA 743/66. Translated from first edition, Paris, 1743.
Locations: L; RPJCB

1743#13
EDWARDS, George. *A natural history of birds*... London. For the author. 4 vols. 4to. 1743–51. 1743
Note: EA 743/80, 745/71. Includes American birds. Issued in 4 parts. French translation, London, 1745; also issued as *A natural history of uncommon birds*, 1751.
Locations: L; CtY, MiU, NjP

1743#14
EDWARDS, Jonathan. *Some thoughts concerning the present revival of religion in New-England, and the way it ought to be acknowledged and promoted*... Edinburgh. Boston printed, Edinburgh reprinted. T. Lumisden and J. Robertson, 221p. 8vo. 1743
Note: SABIN 21961, EA 743/81. First printed Boston, 1742 (EVANS 4939).
Locations: DLC, RPJCB, MiU-C

1743#15
An enquiry into the state *of the bills of credit of the province of the Massachusetts-Bay*... *in a letter from a gentleman in Boston to a merchant in London*. London, 52p. 8vo. 1743
Note: SABIN 22649, HANSON 5715, EA 743/93. Possibly an American imprint. EVANS 5217 has same title, Boston, 1743.
Locations: RPJCB, DLC, MiU-C

1743#16
GRADIN, Arvid. *A short history of the Bohemian-Moravian Protestant church of the United Brethren*... London. J. Hutton, 62p. 8vo. 1743
Note: SABIN 28190, EA 743/109.
Locations: L; NN, MH

1743#17
JENNINGS, David. *The origin of death, and of immortal life, considered*... London. J. Oswald and J. Brackstone, 39p. 8vo. 1743
Note: EA 743/128. Sermon occasioned by death of Daniel Neal, who wrote on New England churches.
Locations: L; RPJCB, NN

1743#18
A key to the present *politics of the principal powers of Europe*... London. T. Cooper, 64p. 8vo. 1743
Note: EA 743/133. Some mention of Spain and America.
Locations: L; RPJCB

1743#19
KING, James. *A sermon*... *March 17, 1742–3*... London. J. Clarke, 22p. 4to. 1743
Note: SABIN 37806, EA 743/135. Georgia Trustees and Bray Associates anniversary sermon.
Locations: DUc; DLC, RPJCB, MiU-C

1743#20
KIRKPATRICK, James. *An essay on inoculation, occasioned by the small-pox, being brought into South Carolina in the year 1738*... *with an appendix, containing a faithful account of the event there*. London. J. Hugginson, 60p. 8vo. 1743
Note: SABIN 46997, EA 743/136.
Locations: L; DLC, RPJCB, MiU-C

1743#21
KNOWLES, Admiral Sir Charles. *An account of the expedition to Carthagena...* London. M. Cooper, 58p. 8vo. 1743
Note: SABIN 11128, EA 743/1-5. Refers to contemporary disparagements of New England officers and soldiers. Other London, Dublin and Edinburgh editions in 1743.
Locations: L; DLC, CtY, RPJCB

1743#22
LOCKMAN, John. *Travels of the Jesuits into various parts of the world; compiled from their letters...* London. J. Noon, 2 vols. 8vo. 1743
Note: SABIN 40708, EA 743/131.
Locations: L; RPJCB, DLC, NN

1743#23
MAWSON, Matthias. *A sermon preached... February 18, 1742-3...* London. S. Draper, 72p. 4to. 1743
Note: SABIN 46997, EA 743/152. SPG sermon for 1743, with abstract, etc.
Locations: L; RPJCB

1743#24
MIDDLETON, Christopher. *A vindication of the conduct of Captain Christopher Middleton, in a late voyage on board His Majesty's ship the Furnace, for discovering a North-west passage... In answer to certain objections and aspersions of Arthur Dobbs...* London. J. Robinson, 206p. 8vo. 1743
Note: SABIN 48858, HANSON 5710, EA 743/157, 744/150. Another edition Dublin, 1744.
Locations: L; Cq; Dt; DLC, RPJCB, MH

1743#25
MORALEY, William. *The infortunate: or, the voyage and adventures of William Moraley... Containing, whatever is curious and remarkable in... Pensilvania and New Jersey... several adventures through divers parts of America...* Newcastle. J. White, 64p. 8vo. 1743
Note: EA 743/159.
Locations: NCp; RPJCB, MiU-C

1743#26
NICKOLLS, John. *Original letters and papers of state, addressed to Oliver Cromwell...* London. W. Bowyer, for J. Whiston, 164p. F. 1743
Note: EA 743/167. With letter written by the 'People of New England'.
Locations: L; RPJCB, NN

1743#27
OGLETHORPE, James Edward. *A full reply to Lieut. Cadogan's Spanish hireling... and Lieut. Mackay's letter... wherein the Impartial account of the late expedition to St. Augustine is clearly vindicated...* London. J. Hugginson, 63p. 8vo. 1743
Note: SABIN 56845, EA 743/102.
Locations: RPJCB, DLC, MB

1743#28
PERCEVAL, John. *Faction detected, by the evidence of facts.* Dublin. G. Faulkner, 170p. 8vo. 1743
Note: SABIN 23610, EA 743/82-8, 744/89. L; also has editions two to six, London, 1743; and seventh edition London, 1744. Some of these have additional material. Discusses Spanish threat to Carolinas, Georgia, etc.
Locations: L; DLC, RPJCB, GU-DeR

1743#29
RALPH, James. *A critical history of the administration of Sr Robert Walpole, now earl of Orford...* London. J. Hinton, 535p. 8vo. 1743
Note: HANSON 5686, EA 743/189. Various American references.
Locations: L; RPJCB, ICN, MH-BA

1743#30
A review of the whole *political conduct of a late eminent patriot, and his friends; for twenty years last past...* London. M. Cooper, 156p. 8vo. 1743
Note: SABIN 70279, EA 743/193. Answer to Perceval's *Faction Detected*, above, 1743.
Locations: L; DLC, RPJCB, MiU-C

1743#31
ROBE, James. *Mr Robe's fourth letter to the Reverend James Fisher...* Edinburgh. R. Fleming, J. Traill, 112p. 12mo. 1743
Note: References to Whitefield, North America, etc.
Locations: L;

1743#32
ROBE, James. *Mr Robe's second letter to the Reverend James Fisher...* Edinburgh. T. Lumisden and J. Robertson, 44p. 12mo. 1743
Note: Contains a vindication of Jonathan Edwards, *Distinguishing Marks...* above, 1741.
Locations: L;

1743#33
ROBE, James. *Mr Robe's third letter to the Reverend James Fisher...* Edinburgh. T. Lumisden and J. Robertson, 56p. 12mo. 1743
Note: References to New England and Jonathan Edwards.
Locations: L;

1743#34
Ship Charles... *James Crokatt and others... appellants. His Majesty's Procurator-General, and Peter Warren, Esq., and the Hon. Henry Aylmer, Esq... respondents...* London. 3p. F. 1743

1743

Note: Involved a ship trading between South Carolina and London. Also *The respondents case*. . . , 3p. F.
Locations: NN

1743#35
Ship Le Grand Juste. . . Peter Vincent Duplessis master. . . appellant. . . Bradwarden Thompson, Esq. respondent. The appellant's case. London. 11p. F. 1743
Note: Thompson was captain of HMS *Success*, which had seized the ship. Case was appealed from Boston Vice-Admiralty Court. Also: *The respondent's case*. . . , 4p. F. To be heard 17 January 1743.
Locations: NN

1743#36
SMITH, Josiah. *Four letters etc. taken from the London Weekly History of the progress of the gospel; with a large postcript vindicating the late revival and the promoters.* Edinburgh. 64p. 8vo. 1743
Note: SABIN 25284, 83439, EA 743/98. Relates entirely to Whitefield and Georgia. (From Josiah Smith of Charlestown to William Cooper in Boston?).
Locations: L; MWA, NHi

1743#37
SOUTH CAROLINA ASSEMBLY. COMMITTEE OF BOTH HOUSES. *Appendix to the report of the Committee of both houses of Assembly. . . appointed to enquire into the causes of the disappointment of success, in the late expedition against St Augustine. . .* London. J. Roberts, 79p. 8vo. 1743
Note: SABIN 87351, EA 743/204. For the report see South Carolina Assembly, below, 1743. First published Charlestown, 1742? Not found in EVANS.
Locations: RPJCB

1743#38
SOUTH CAROLINA ASSEMBLY. COMMITTEE OF BOTH HOUSES. *The report of the committee of both houses of Assembly of the province of South-Carolina, appointed to enquire into. . . the late expedition against St. Augustine. . .* London. South Carolina printed, London reprinted, J. Roberts, 112p. 12mo. 1743
Note: SABIN 87350, EA 743/205. First printed Charleston, 1742 (EVANS 5063).
Locations: L; DLC, RPJCB, MiU-C

1743#39
STEPHENS, Thomas *fl. 1742. A brief account of the causes that have retarded the progress of the colony of Georgia. . . attested upon oath. Being a proper contrast to A state of the province of Georgia. . . and some other misrepresentations. . .* London. 21, 101p. 8vo. 1743
Note: SABIN 91305, HANSON 5716, EA 743/207.
Locations: L; MRu: O; DLC, RPJCB, MiU-C

1743#40
SUTHERLAND, Patrick. *From the London Gazette, of December 25, 1742. An account of the late invasion of Georgia, drawn out by Lieutenant P. S. . .* London. 4p. F. [1743]
Note: SABIN 93962, EA 743/209.
Locations: L; RPJCB, GU-DeR

1743#41
TENNENT, Gilbert. *Some account of the principles of the Moravians; chiefly collected from several conversations with Count Zinzendorf; and from some sermons preached by him. . .* London. S. Mason, 48p. 8vo. 1743
Note: SABIN 94707, EA 743/212.
Locations: L; RPJCB, MiU-C

1743#42
TENNENT, John, M. D. *Detection of a conspiracy to suppress a general good in physic, and to promote error. . .* London. For the author, 24p. 8vo. 1743
Note: Refers to his trial for bigamy at Old Bailey.
Locations: DNLM, ViRA

1743#43
WEBSTER, Charles. *The duty of all Christians to read the scriptures. . . in two sermons.* London. For the author, sold by J. Brotherton, 56p. 8vo. 1743
Note: EA 743/228. With account of S.P.C.K. and references to colonies.
Locations: L; ICN, NjPT

1743#44
WHITEFIELD, George. *A continuation of the account of the orphan-house in Georgia, from January 1740/1, to January 1742/3. . .* London. W. Strahan, 132p. 12mo. 1743
Note: SABIN 103496, EA 743/231.
Locations: E; RPJCB, NN, CSmH

1744#1
Authentic papers relating to the expedition against Carthagena. . . London. L. Raymond, 100p. 8vo. 1744
Note: SABIN 2445, 11132, EA 744/14–15. Minor references to North American troops. A second edition in 1744.
Locations: L; DLC, RPJCB, MiU-C

1744#2
BELSHAZZER, Kapha, the Jew. *The second book of James. . .* London. 8p. 8vo. 1744
Note: EA 744/20. Annesley case. Attributed to Robert Dodsley.
Locations: L;

1744#3
BIRCH, Thomas. *The life of the honourable Robert Boyle.* London. A. Millar, 458p. 8vo. 1744

Note: EA 744/28.
Locations: L; DLC, RPJCB, N

1744#4
BISHOP, Matthew. *The life and adventures of Matthew Bishop, of Deddington in Oxfordshire, containing an account of several actions by sea, battles and sieges by land, in which he was present, from 1701 to 1711. . . written by himself.* London. J. Brindley, 283p. 8vo. 1744
Note: SABIN 5613, EA 744/29. New England and the Quebec expedition.
Locations: L; DLC, RPJCB, NN

1744#5
BOSTON. ASSEMBLY OF PASTORS. *The testimony and advice of an assembly of pastors of churches in New England, at a meeting in Boston, July 7, 1743. Occasioned by the late happy revival of religion.* London. Boston printed, London reprinted. J. Oswald, and sold in Glasgow and Edinburgh, 44p. 8vo. 1744
Note: SABIN 94918, KRESS 4736, EA 744/33. First printed Boston, [1743] (EVANS 5136).
Locations: L; DLC, RPJCB, MiU-C

1744#6
BOWEN, Emanuel. *A complete system of geography. Being a description of all the countries.* London. W. Innys and others, 2 vols. F. [1744–7]
Note: EA 744/34. Second (?) edition in 1747, EA 747/22. Claims to bring Moll's *A system of geography* 'down to the present time.'
Locations: Csj; O; MH, ViU

1744#7
BOYD, Elizabeth. *Altamira's ghost; or, justice triumphant. A new ballad. Occasion'd by a certain nobleman's cruel usage of his nephew. Done extempore.* London. Sold by C. Corbett, 8p. 2o 1744
Note: FOXON B340. Annesley case.
Locations: L; CtY, MH

1744#8
BRUCE, Lewis. *The happiness of man the glory of God. A sermon. . . March 15, 1743. . .* London. D. Browne, 53p. 4to. 1744
Note: SABIN 8725, EA 744/36. Georgia Trustees and Bray Associates anniversary sermon. Also a variant issue in 1744.
Locations: L; MiU-C, RPJCB

1744#9
The case of the exporters of tea to Ireland, and the British plantations in America. London. 3p. [1744?]
Note: EA 744/43.
Locations: MiU-C

1744#10
CHAMPIGNY, Jean. *The present state of the country and inhabitants, Europeans and Indians, of Louisiana, on the north continent of America. By an officer of New Orleans to his friend at Paris.* London. J. Millar, 55p. 8vo. 1744
Note: SABIN 42283, EA 744/177–8. Second edition, 1744.
Locations: L; DLC, RPJCB, NN

1744#11
CRAIG, Campbell. *The Trial at bar, between Campbell Craig, lessee of James Annesley, Esq: plaintiff, and. . . Richard Earl of Anglesey, defendant. Before. . . Barons of the Exchequer, at the King's Court, Dublin, in Trinity Term,. . . 1743.* London. R. Walker, 488p. 8vo. 1744
Note: EA 744/69.
Locations: RPJCB, CtY, NN

1744#12
CRAIG, Campbell. *The Trial at large, between James Annesley, Esq. and the Rt. Hon. Earl of Anglesea. . .* London. C. Corbett, 86p. F. 1744
Note: EA 744/70–72. Also printed in 1744 by J. Watson, 336p. (ICN); and Gooding, Newcastle-upon Tyne, 92p. (L; N, NN); and at Reading, etc. (L;).
Locations: ICN, MH-L

1744#13
CRAIG, Campbell. *The Trial in ejectment (at large) between Campbell Craig, lessee of James Annesley. . . and. . . Richard Earl of Anglesea. . . Friday, November 11, 1743. . . published by the permission of. . . Lord Chief Baron Bowes. . .* London. J. and P. Knapton, etc. 259p. F. 1744
Note: Cf. SABIN 1602, EA 744/73–4. Also Dublin, 1744, *The trial in ejectment between. . .*'.
Locations: L; DLC, CtY, RPJCB

1744#14
DECKER, Sir Matthew. *An essay on the causes of the decline of the foreign trade. . .* London. J. Brotherton, 112p. 4to. 1744
Note: HANSON 5780, EA 744/75, 749/61–2, 750/88. Sometimes attributed to William Richardson. Other editions, Dublin 1749, Dublin, 1751; London, 1750; Edinburgh, 1756.
Locations: L; DLC, RPJCB, MH-BA

1744#15
DOBBS, Arthur. *An account of the countries adjoining to Hudson's Bay. . . With an abstract of Captain Middleton's journal, and observations upon his behaviour. . .* London. J. Robinson, 211p. 4to. 1744
Note: SABIN 20404, HANSON 5798, EA 744/80. 'With the addition of several more abstracts concerning discoveries and trade'.
Locations: L; Lu; DLC, RPJCB, MiU-C

1744

1744#16
DOBBS, Arthur. *Remarks upon Capt. Middleton's defence: wherein his conduct during his late voyage for discovering a passage from Hudson's Bay to the South-Sea is impartially examined... With an appendix of original papers...* London. J. Robinson, 171p. 8vo. 1744
Note: SABIN 20406, HANSON 5800, EA 744/81.
Locations: L; RPJCB, MiU-C, CtY

1744#17
Fortunes favourite; containing memoirs of the many hardships and sufferings... of Jacobo Anglicano, a young nobleman... trepanned into slavery. London. 384p. 8vo. 1744
Note: SABIN 1603, EA 744/93. Annesley case.
Locations: DLC, ViU

1744#18
GILBERT, John. *A sermon preached... February 17, 1743–4...* London. J. and H. Pemberton, 76p. 8vo. 1744
Note: SABIN 27352, EA 744/103. SPG sermon for 1744, with abstract, etc.
Locations: L; RPJCB, MiU-C, CtY

1744#19
GRANVILLE, John Carteret. *Surrender of seven eighth parts of Carolina, from Lord Carteret to his majesty...* London. 2, 22p. 4to. [1744?]
Note: SABIN 93911, 10979, EA 744/107. With 'Grant and release of one eighth part of Carolina' below, 1744.
Locations: DLC, RPJCB, NcU

1744#20
GREAT BRITAIN. PARLIAMENT. HOUSE OF COMMONS. *A bill to prevent the issuing of paper bills of credit in the British colonies and plantations in America, to be legal tenders in payments for money.* London. 7p. F. [1744]
Note: HANSON 5808, EA 744/108. Not enacted.
Locations: L; Lpro;

1744#21
GREAT BRITAIN. SOVEREIGN. GEORGE II. *Grant and release of one eighth part of Carolina, from his majesty to Lord Carteret...* London. 22p. 4to. [1744]
Note: SABIN 10971, EA 744/109.
Locations: DLC, RPJCB, NN

1744#22
GREAT BRITAIN. SOVEREIGN. GEORGE II. *Proclamation. Declaration of war against France. [29 March 1744].* London. T. and R. Baskett, s.sh. F. 1744
Note: BRIGHAM 196, CRAWFORD p. 59.
Locations: L; RPJCB

1744#23
GREAT BRITAIN. SOVEREIGN. GEORGE II. *Proclamation. Regarding distribution of prizes [14 June 1744].* London. T. Baskett and R. Baskett. s.sh. F. 1744
Note: BRIGHAM 200–1, CRAWFORD p. 60.
Locations: LPC;

1744#24
HABERSHAM, James. *A letter from Mr Habersham, (superintendent... at the orphan-house in Georgia,) to... Mr Whitefield...* London. J. Lewis, for J. Syms, 16p. 8vo. 1744
Note: SABIN 29468, EA 744/113.
Locations: GU-De, NN

1744#25
The Harleian miscellany: or, A collection of scarce, curious and entertaining pamphlets and tracts... found in the late earl of Oxford's library. London. T. Osborne, 8 vols., 4to. [1744–6]
Note: SABIN 30394, EA 744/115. Several tracts on America.
Locations: L; DLC, CtY, MH

1744#26
HORSLEY, William. *A treatise on maritime affairs: or a comparison between the naval power of England and France...* London. R. Wellington, 94p. 8vo. 1744
Note: HANSON 5782, EA 744/122.
Locations: L; DLC, RPJCB, NN

1744#27
IRELAND. PARLIAMENT. HOUSE OF COMMONS. COMMITTEE. *A report from the Committee appointed to inspect and examine the several returns (made to the House) of the felons and vagabonds ordered for transportation...* Dublin. S. Fairbrother, 72p. 2o. 1744
Note: Dated 9 February 1743 [i. e. 1744].
Locations: L;

1744#28
JENNINGS, David. *An abridgement of the life of... Dr Cotton Mather... Taken from the account... published by his son, the Reverend Mr. Samuel Mather...* London. J. Oswald, J. Brackstone, 143p. 12mo. 1744
Note: SABIN 36038, EA 744/146.
Locations: DLC, RPJCB, CSmH

1744#29
JENNINGS, David. *Instructions to ministers: in three parts... I. Two discourses... by... John Jennings. II. A letter... by... Augustus... Franck... III. An abridgement of the life of Cotton Mather...* London. J. Oswald, J. Brackstone. [262]p. 12mo. 1744

Note: Cf. SABIN 36038. HOLMES, MM 76B, EA 744/125. Life of Mather is taken from Samuel Mather. See Jennings, above, 1744.
Locations: RPJCB, ViU

1744#30
A journal of the expedition to Carthagena, with notes. In answer to a late pamphlet... An account of the expedition to Carthagena. London. J. Roberts, 59p. 8vo. 1744
Note: SABIN 102632, EA 744/128–30. Also Dublin 1744. References to New England soldiers. Second edition with minor additions in 1744: MB, ICN.
Locations: L; DLC, CtY, NN

1744#31
KIMBER, Edward. *A relation, or journal, of a late expedition to the gates of St. Augustine, on Florida; conducted by... James Oglethorpe...* London. T. Astley, 36p. 8vo. 1744
Note: SABIN 10218, EA 744/132. Facsimiles (?) in DLC, RPJCB, etc.
Locations: L; FMU, MiU-C

1744#32
A letter to a nobleman in the country, on the affair of Mr Annesley... London. J. Roberts, 34p. 8vo. 1744
Note: EA 744/138.
Locations: L; MH, DLC, CtY

1744#33
MIDDLETON, Christopher. *A reply to the Remarks of Arthur Dobbs Esq; on Capt Middleton's Vindication of his conduct...* London. G. Brett, 192p. 8vo. 1744
Note: HANSON 5799, EA 744/149.
Locations: L; DLC, RPJCB, MiU-C

1744#34
MOORE, Francis. *A voyage to Georgia. Begun in the year 1735. Containing, an account of the settling the town of Frederica...* London. J. Robinson, 108p. 8vo. 1744
Note: SABIN 50352, HANSON 5811, EA 744/153.
Locations: L; DLC, RPJCB, CSmH

1744#35
PENNSYLVANIA PROVINCE. *The treaty held with the Indians of the Six Nations at Philadelphia, in July 1742.* London. Philadelphia printed, London reprinted. T. Sowle, etc., xii, 37p. 4to. 1744
Note: Cf. EA 744/166. With account of the Six Nations. First printed Philadelphia, 1743 (EVANS 5216, SABIN 60735).
Locations: RPJCB, MiU-C, NN

1744#36
PURRY, Jean Pierre. *A method for determining the best climate of the earth, on a principle to which all geographers and historians have been hitherto strangers...* London. M. Cooper, 60p. 8vo. 1744
Note: SABIN 66727, EA 744/181.
Locations: L; DLC, CU, ICJ

1744#37
RALPH, James. *The history of England: during the reigns of K. William, Q. Anne and K. George I.* London. D. Browne, for F. Coggan and T. Waller, 2 vols., F. [1744–6]. 1744
Note: SABIN 67608, EA 744/183. Many American references. Vol. II issued in 1746, EA 746/173.
Locations: L; RPJCB, CtY, DLC

1744#38
The trial of the Right Honourable Richard Earl of Anglesey... For an assault on the Honourable James Annesley... London. J. and P. Knapton, 41p. F. 1744
Note: Trial was 3 August 1744.
Locations: L; DLC, PP, CtY

1744#39
VERNON, Edward. *Original paprrs [sic] relating to the expedition to Carthagena.* London. M. Cooper, 154p. 8vo. 1744
Note: SABIN 11134, EA 744/224–5. Northern colonial trade to enemy. Another edition in 1744.
Locations: L; RPJCB, CtY, NN

1744#40
WEBB, Daniel. *An essay presented; or a method humbly proposed, to the consideration of... both Houses... by an English woolen manufacturer, to pay the national debts, without a new tax, to inlarge trade in general... to improve all waste uncultivated lands, within his majesty's dominions...* London. J. Robinson, 45p. 4to. 1744
Note: SABIN 102210, HANSON 5750, EA 744/237.
Locations: L; Lu; DLC, RPJCB, MH

1744#41
WESLEY, Charles and John. *A collection of Psalms and Hymns.* London. W. Strahan, 136p. 12mo. 1744
Note: The third edition. Contains 'A hymn for the Georgia orphans and related hymns.' Earlier editions not found; later editions 1748, 1756, 1762; Bristol, 1760.
Locations: L; OO

1744#42
WESLEY, John. *An extract of the Reverend Mr Wesley's journal, from November 1, 1739, to September 3, 1741.* London. W. Strahan, 120p. 12mo. 1744
Note: SABIN 102657, EA 744/238. Another edition 1749.
Locations: L; RPJCB, MH, CU-A

1744#43
WESLEY, John. *A narrative of the late work of God, at and near Northampton, in New-England, extracted from*

1744

Mr Edwards's letter... Bristol. F. Farley, 48p. 12mo. 1744
Note: SABIN 102684, EA 744/87. Second edition, London, 1745. Extracted from Jonathan Edward's letter to Benjamin Colman.
Locations: L; MH, CtY, NjP

1744#44
WHITEFIELD, George. *A brief account of the occasion, process, and issue of a late trial at the assize held at Gloucester.* London. J. Robinson, sold by J. Sims, 15p. 8vo. 1744
Note: EA 744/239–242. Two other London editions and one Bristol edition in 1744. Brief reference to Georgia. Also London, 1748, EA 748/237.
Locations: L; MH, NcD

1744#45
WHITEFIELD, George. *A letter to the Reverend Mr Thomas Church... in answer to his serious and expostulatory letter to... Whitefield...* London. 20p. 8vo. 1744
Note: SABIN 103565, EA 744/245–6. A second edition in 1744 (NN, CtY, MH).
Locations: L;

1744#46
WILLISON, John. *A fair and impartial testimony, essayed in name of a number of ministers...* Edinburgh. T. Lumisden, J. Robertson, 138p. 8vo. 1744
Note: EA 744/248. Minor references to Whitefield and America.
Locations: L; RPJCB

1745#1
The acccomplish'd vagabond, or, The compleat mumper: exemplify'd in the... enterprizes of Bampfylde Carew... Exeter. A. and S. Brice, for selves and Score, Thorn and Tozer, 34p. 8vo. 1745
Note: EA 745/1. American references. Based on Carew, *Life and Adventures*, Exeter, 1745, below.
Locations: CtY

1745#2
An antidote against the infectious contagion of popery and tyranny... Edinburgh. 23p. 12mo. 1745
Note: Some discussion of trade, colonies and Cape Breton.
Locations: CSmH

1745#3
Articles of agreement, for carrying on an expedition, by Hudson's Streights, for the discovery of a North-West passage... March 30, 1745. London. 16p. 8vo. 1745
Note: HANSON 5909, EA 745/6, 746/14. Also Dublin, 1746.
Locations: L; E; RPJCB, MH

1745#4
ASHLEY, John. *The present state of the British and French trade to Africa and America consider'd and compar'd...* London. E. Comyns, 56p. 8vo. 1745
Note: SABIN 65327, HANSON 5904, KRESS 4776, EA 745/175.
Locations: L; DLC, RPJCB, CtY

1745#5
AUCKMUTY, Robert. *The importance of Cape Breton to the British nation. Humbly represented by Robert Auckmuty, judge of his majesty's court of vice-admiralty...* London. W. Bickerton, 7p. 2o. [1745]
Note: SABIN 2357, 10731, HANSON 5915, 5987, EA 745/7. Another edition in 1746 with title *The importance of Cape Breton considered...*, signed 'Massachusettensis': RPJCB, CSmH, NN. Another edition in 1747(?).
Locations: L; RPJCB, MiU-C

1745#6
BEARCROFT, Philip. *A sermon preached... February 15, 1744...* London. E. Owen, 73p. 4to. 1745
Note: SABIN 4122, EA 745/11. SPG sermon for 1745.
Locations: L; DLC; RPJCB, MiU-C

1745#7
CAREW, Bampfylde Moore? *The life and adventures of Bampfylde-Moore Carew, the noted Devonshire stroller and dog-stealer; as related by himself, during his passage to the plantations in America...* Exeter. The Farleys for J. Drew, 164p. 4to. 1745
Note: Cf. SABIN 27615, EA 745/125–6. EA lists another Exeter issue in 1745: CSmH, ICN, MH. Reprinted Philadelphia, 1773. See *An apology for the life of...* below, 1749.
Locations: L; O; ViU

1745#8
The case of the honourable James Annesley, Esq. being a sequel to the memoirs of an unfortunate young nobleman... London. W. Bickerton, 215p. 12mo. 1745
Note: SABIN 1601, EA 745/52. See Annesley, *Memoirs*, above, 1743. This was reissued as Vol III of *Memoirs*, below, 1747.
Locations: NN, NcU, CtY

1745#9
CHAUNCY, Charles (1705–87). *Marvellous things done by the right hand... of God in getting him the victory...* London. Boston printed, London reprinted. M. Cooper, 31p. 8vo. 1745
Note: SABIN 12324, EA 745/44. First printed Boston, 1745 (EVANS 5558). Sermon preached 18 July 1745 on reduction of Cape Breton.
Locations: RPJCB, DLC, MH

THE
LIFE *and* ADVENTURES
OF
Bampfylde-Moore Carew,

THE NOTED

Devonshire Stroller and Dog-Stealer;

As related by Himself, during his Passage to the Plantations in *America*.

CONTAINING,

A great Variety of remarkable Transactions in a vagrant Course of Life, which he followed for the Space of Thirty Years and upwards.

EXON: Printed by the FARLEYS, for JOSEPH DREW, Bookseller, opposite *Castle-Lane*, 1745.
[*Price Two Shillings.*]

1745

1745#10
Considerations on the state of *the British fisheries in America. . . With proposals for their security, by the reduction of Cape-Breton. . . January 1744–5. . .* London. W. Bickerton, 8p. F. 1745
Note: SABIN 16011, HANSON 5884, EA 745/48.
Locations: L; Eu; MiU-C, RPJCB

1745#11
The court and city kalendar; *or, Gentleman's Register, for England, Scotland, Ireland, and America for the year.* London. H. Woodfall and others, 12mo. 1745
Note: SABIN 17171. British Library catalogue lists editions in 1745, 1751, 1756, 1757, 1759, etc., some of which were destroyed in the Second World War. NUC references give no dates.
Locations: DLC, CtY, MB

1745#12
DAWSON, William. *A letter from the Rev. Mr Dawson. . . to the clergy of Virginia in America.* London. 4p. 16mo. 1745
Note: SABIN 104691n, EA 745/55.
Locations: NN, PPL, ViWC

1745#13
A description of the coast, *tides and currents, in Button's Bay and in the Welcome: being the north-west coast of Hudson's Bay. . . a probability, that there is a passage from thence to the western ocean of America.* London. J. Robinson, 24p. 8vo. [1745?]
Note: HANSON 5980 and note, EA 746/49–50. Also Dublin, 1746 and 1755.
Locations: L; E; MH, CaAEU;

1745#14
DICKINSON, James. *A journal of the life, travels, and labour of love in the work of the ministry of. . . James Dickinson. . .* London. T. Sowle Raylton, L. Hinde, 172p. 8vo. 1745
Note: SABIN 20033, SMITH, I, 530, EA 745/65.
Locations: L; RPJCB, DLC

1745#15
DOBBS, Arthur. *A reply to Capt. Middleton's answer to the remarks on his vindication of his conduct, in a late voyage made by him in the Furnace sloop. . . to which is added, a full answer to a late pamphlet published by Capt. Middleton, called Forgery Detected.* London. J. Robinson., 128p. 8vo. 1745
Note: SABIN 20407, 63269, HANSON 5906, EA 745/66.
Locations: L; RPJCB, MH

1745#16
DODDRIDGE, Philip. *The rise and progress of religion in the soul.* London. J. Waugh, 309p. 12mo. 1745
Note: EA 745/67–9. Mentions America. Two other editions in 1745. Also, London, 1748, 1749, and two in 1750. EA 748/53, 749/76, 750/98–9.
Locations: L; NcD

1745#17
DURRELL, Philip. *A particular account of the taking Cape Breton. . . by Admiral Warren, and Sir W. Pepperell, 17th June, 1745, with. . . a letter from an officer of Marines. . . giving an account of the siege of Louisbourg. . .* London. W. Bickerton, 8p. F. 1745
Note: SABIN 21419, HANSON 5916, EA 745/70.
Locations: L; RPJCB, MH

1745#18
EDWARDS, Jonathan. Sinners in the hands of an angry God. . . preached at Enfield, July 8, 1741. . . With a preface by. . . John Willison Minister of the Gospel at Dundee. . . Edinburgh. Boston printed, Edinburgh reprinted. T. Lumisden and J. Robertson, 24p. 8vo. 1745
Note: SABIN 21959, EA 745/72. First printed Boston, 1741 (EVANS 4713).
Locations: L; CtY, RPJCB

1745#19
EDWARDS, Jonathan. *Thoughts concerning the present revival of religion in New England. . . Abridged by John Wesley.* London. W. Strahan, 124p. 12mo. 1745
Note: SABIN 21963, EA 745/73. Abridged version of *Some thoughts,* Boston, 1742 (EVANS 4939) and Edinburgh, 1743, above.
Locations: L; MH, CtY, NNC

1745#20
ESTAUGH, John. *A call to the unfaithful professors of truth. . .* Dublin. 104p. 12mo. 1745
Note: SABIN 23041, EA 745/78–9. First printed Philadelphia, 1744 (EVANS 5390). Also London, 1745.
Locations: L; PHC, CtY, PPL

1745#21
The free and impartial examiner: *being a candid enquiry into the causes of our present melancholy situation, with regard to both domestick and foreign affairs. . .* London. M. Cooper, 52p. 8vo. 1745
Note: SABIN 25701, EA 745/86.
Locations: L; DLC, CtY

1745#22
GIBSON, Edmund. *An earnest dissuasive from intemperance in meats and drinks. . . sermon. . . Lambeth. . .* London. E. Owen, 48p. 8vo. 1745
Note: EA 745/91, 746/69, 750/145. The sixth edition. Seventh edition in 1746, eighth edition, revised and enlarged, 1750. Contains attack on allowing spirits to Indians.
Locations: L; DLC, RPJCB, MiU-C

1745#23
A full and exact description *of the island of Cape Breton, which was taken from the French, by Admiral Warren, upon the 16th of June 1745. together with an account of the great benefit it will be to the British nation.* Edinburgh. 2p. 1/2o. 1745
Locations: E;

1745#24
GIBSON, James. *A journal of the late siege by the troops from North-America, against the French at Cape Breton, the city of Louisbourg...* London. J. Newbery, 49p. 8vo. 1745
Note: SABIN 27315, EA 745/92, 747/61. Second enlarged edition, 1747.
Locations: L; MRu; DLC, RPJCB, NN

1745#25
GREAT BRITAIN. PARLIAMENT. HOUSE OF COMMONS. *A bill for the speedy and effectual recruiting of his majesty's regiments of foot serving in Flanders, Minorca, Gibraltar, and the plantations, and regiments of marines.* London. 19p. 2o 1745
Note: Enacted as 18 Geo. II cap. 10.
Locations: L;

1745#25A
GREAT BRITAIN. PARLIMENT. HOUSE OF COMMONS COMMITTEE. *Report relating to the finding of a north-west passage.* London. 7p. 4to. [1745]
Note: SABIN 69938, HANSON 5910, EA 745/95. Signed John Rankin and Robert Wilson, 1 August 1742.
Locations: L; RPJCB, MiU-C

1745#26
GREY, Zachary. *A serious address to lay-methodists, to beware of the false pretences of their teachers. With an appendix, containing an account of the fatal and bloody effects of enthusiasm, in the case of the family of the Dutartres in South Carolina, which was attended with the murder of two persons, and the execution of four for those murders.* London. W. Russel, 29p. 8vo. 1745
Note: SABIN 28793, EA 745/96.
Locations: L; DLC, NcU, NcD

1745#27
LE SAGE, Alain René. *The adventures of Robert Chevalier, call'd de Beauchene, Captain of a privateer in New-France.* London. T. Gardner and others, 2 vols. 12mo. 1745
Note: SABIN 40158, EA 745/122. Imaginary adventures, translated from French.
Locations: L; DLC, TxU

1745#28
MARTIN, Samuel. *A plan for establishing and disciplining a national militia in Great Britain, Ireland, and in all the British dominions of America.* London. A. Millar, 106p. 8vo. 1745
Note: SABIN 63269, EA 745/134–5. Another issue, 'a new edition' in 1745.
Locations: L; AWn; DLC, RPJCB, NN

1745#29
MIDDLETON, Christopher. *Forgery detected. By which is evinced how groundless are all the calumnies cast upon the editor, in a pamphlet published under the name of Arthur Dobbs...* London. M. Cooper, G. Brett, 33p. 8vo. 1745
Note: SABIN 48855, HANSON 5905, EA 745/141.
Locations: L; DLC, RPJCB, MH

1745#30
MIDDLETON, Christopher. *A rejoinder to Mr. Dobbs's reply to Captain Middleton...* London. M. Cooper, G. Brett, R. Amey, 156p. 8vo. 1745
Note: SABIN 48856, HANSON 5907, EA 745/142.
Locations: L; DLC, RPJCB, MH

1745#31
MIDDLETON, Christopher. *A reply to Mr. Dobbs's answer to a pamphlet, entitled, Forgery detected...* London. M. Cooper, G. Brett, 28p. 8vo. 1745
Note: SABIN 48857, HANSON 5908, EA 745/143.
Locations: L; DLC, CtY, MH

1745#32
The new general history of *birds...* London. J. Osborn, 2 vols., 8vo. 1745
Note: EA 745/154.
Locations: Vi

1745#33
POSTLETHWAYT, Malachy. *The African trade, the great pillar and support of the British plantation trade in America...* London. J. Robinson, 46p. 4to. 1745
Note: SABIN 501, HANSON 5903, EA 745/173. Some discussion of North America. British colonies will be dependent on mother country while they are dependent on blacks supplied by her.
Locations: L; BMu; RPJCB, CtY, DLC

1745#34
A song [on Louis XIV, *Marshal Belle-Isle, and Prince Charles Edward Stuart...].* London. s.sh. F. 1745
Note: Roxburgh Ballads, Vol. 8, p. 291, Rox. Coll. III, 710. References to Cape Breton.
Locations: L;

1745#35
STENNETT, Joseph. *Rabshakeh's retreat. A sermon preach'd. . . December 18, 1745.* London. A. Ward, H. Whitridge and G. Hawkins, 43p. 8vo. 1745
Note: EA 745/200–1. Fast sermon on account of 'present rebellion.' Mentions capture of Cape Breton. Another edition in 1745.
Locations: L; RPJCB, NN, MH

1745#36
TENNENT, John, M. D. *Physical disquisitions: demonstrating the real causes of the blood's morbid rarefaction and stagnation. . .* London. W. Payne, 120p. 8vo. 1745
Note: EA 745/204. Advocates use of the 'Senecka rattlesnake root'.
Locations: MB, NNNAM

1745#37
WHITE, John. *A second letter to a gentleman dissenting from the Church of England.* Ipswich. C. Davis, W. Craighton, at Ipswich, and M. Cooper, 84p. 8vo. 1745
Note: EA 745/227–8, SABIN 103403 note. New England references. Second edition in 1745.
Locations: CtY, MH, IEG

1745#38
WHITE, John. *The third and last letter to a gentleman dissenting from the Church of England.* London. C. Davis, W. Craighton, at Ipswich, and M. Cooper, 85p. 8vo. 1745
Note: EA 745/229–30. American religious practices. Another edition in 1745.
Locations: L; CtY, MH

1746#1
ANDERSON, James. *The history and constitutions of the. . . Free and Accepted Masons.* London. J. Robinson, 230p. 4to. 1746
Note: EA 746/7. Enlarged with American references from first edition, 1723.
Locations: NIC, NN

1746#2
Authentick papers, concerning a late remarkable transaction. London. J. Jones, 50p. 8vo. 1746
Note: EA 746/16. Relates to Admiral Knowles and prize money at New York.
Locations: L; DLC, RPJCB, MiU-C

1746#3
BOLLAN, William. *The importance and advantage of Cape Breton, truly stated, and impartially considered. With proper maps.* London. J. and P. Knapton, 156p. 8vo. 1746

Note: SABIN 6215, HANSON 5986, EA 746/24. Also attributed to Sir William Peperell.
Locations: L; RPJCB, MiU-C

1746#4
A brief relation of the adventures of M. Bampfylde Carew. London. Aldermary, 24p. [1746?]
Note: The date is a guess. A chapbook.
Locations: L; O;

1746#5
The case of his majesty's province of the Massachusetts Bay. . . with respect to the expences. . . in taking and securing Cape Breton. London. 4p. F. [1746]
Note: SABIN 45666, EA 746/33.
Locations: L; LUB; RPJCB

1746#6
COLDEN, Cadwallader. *An explication of the first causes of action in matter, and of the cause of gravitation.* London. J. Brindley, 75p. 8vo. 1746
Note: SABIN 14268. First printed New York, 1745 (EVANS 5564).
Locations: L; KEmT, MiU-C

1746#7
CROKATT, James. *Observations concerning indigo and cochineal. . .* London. 70p. 1746
Note: SABIN 56466, 87904, HANSON 5992, EA 746/45.
Locations: RPJCB, NN

1746#8
A detection of the views of those who would. . . engage. . . in a ruinous expensive land-war. . . London. L. Raymond, 60p. 8vo. 1746
Note: KRESS 4802, HANSON 5970, EA 745/51.
Locations: Lu; RPJCB, DLC

1746#9
GRANVILLE, John Carteret. *The State of the nation consider'd, in a letter to a member of Parliament.* London. W. Webb, 58p. 8vo. [1746]
Note: SABIN 90617, HANSON 6033, EA 746/70–2, 747/65–6. Two other editions in 1746, third and fourth edition in 1747. Attack on ministry for not waging a naval war. Canada, Mississippi, etc. mentioned.
Locations: L; RPJCB, MnU, NN

1746#10
GREAT BRITAIN. PARLIAMENT. HOUSE OF COMMONS. *A bill for explaining and amending an act of the thirteenth year of his majesty's present reign, intituled, an act for the more effectual securing and encouraging the trade of his majesties subjects to America. . .* London. 15, 1p. 2o. [1746]
Note: HANSON 5983, EA 746/73. Not enacted.
Locations: L; CSmH

1746#11
GREAT BRITAIN. PARLIAMENT. HOUSE OF COMMONS. *A bill for the better protecting and securing the trade and navigation of this kingdom, in times of war.* London. 4p. 2o. [1746]
Note: No ship on station in plantations to leave it without express order. Not enacted.
Locations: L;

1746#12
The great importance of Cape Breton, demonstrated. . . by extracts from the best writers. . . With the reasons that induced the people of New-England to subdue this formidable and dangerous rival. . . London. J. Brindley, 72p. 8vo. 1746
Note: SABIN 10724, 10730, 28448, HANSON 5985, EA 746/75. Republished in 1755 as *An accurate description of Cape Breton. . .*: DLC, RPJCB, NN, of which another edition in 1758 (HIGGS 1735).
Locations: O; RPJCB, MiU-C, NN

1746#13
HUTTON, Matthew. *A sermon preached. . . February 21, 1745. . .* London. E. Owen, 74p. 8vo. 1746
Note: SABIN 34109, EA 746/92–3. Another issue in 1746. SPG sermon for 1746, with abstract, etc.
Locations: L; DLC, RPJCB, MH

1746#14
JAMIESON, John. *Unto the Right Honourable, the Lords of Council and Session, the petition of John Jamieson merchant in Glasgow.* Glasgow. F. [1746]
Note: HANSON 5979, EA 746/101. Trade to Virginia.
Locations: O;

1746#15
PEPPERRELL, William. *An accurate journal and account of the proceedings of the New-England land-forces, during the late expedition against the French settlements on Cape Breton. . .* Exeter. A and S. Brice, 40p. 8vo. 1746
Note: SABIN 42173, 60841, HANSON 5984, EA 746/4. Another edition in 1758 as *An accurate and authentic account of the taking of Cape-Breton. . .* Also published in W. Shirley's *A letter. . . to his grace the Duke of Newcastle,* below, 1746.
Locations: L; RPJCB, DLC

1746#16
PHILOLAOS. *Two letters, concerning some farther advantages and improvements that may seem necessary to be made on the taking and keeping of Cape Breton. . .* London. 12p. 12mo. 1746
Note: SABIN 97566, HANSON 5988, EA 746/148.
Locations: L; DLC, RPJCB, NN

1746#17
The present embargo on cheese and butter prevents the same from being exported to any of his majesty's dominions abroad, as likewise to Holland and Hambro. . . London. s.sh. F. [1746]
Note: HANSON 5963.
Locations: LSC

1746#18
PRINCE, Thomas. *Extraordinary events the doings of God and marvellous in pious eyes. . . seen on. . . taking the city of Louisbourg, on the Isle of Cape Breton. . .* London. Boston printed, London reprinted. J. Lewis, 32p. 8vo. 1746
Note: SABIN 65596, EA 746/161–66. First printed Boston, 1746 (EVANS 5681). At least four more London editions in 1746; also Edinburgh and Belfast, 1746.
Locations: L; DLC, MH

1746#19
PRIOR, Thomas. *An authentick narrative of the success of tar-water. . .* Dublin, M. Rhames, for R. Gunne, 249p. 8vo. 1746
Note: EA 746/167–71. Also four London editions in 1746. With American letters. Reprinted Boston, 1749.
Locations: L; RPJCB, CtY, ICJ

1746#20
Reasons most humbly proposed for encouraging the British coinage, and preventing the melting and exporting that which is, and shall be coined for the service of the British dominions and plantations. . . London. s.sh. F. [1746]
Note: HANSON 6007.
Locations: L; NNC

1746#21
RIDLEY, Glocester. *A sermon preached. . . March 20, 1745–6. . .* London. J. Clarke, 21p. 4to. 1746
Note: SABIN 71296, 83978, EA 746/176. Georgia Trustees and Bray Associates anniversary sermon.
Locations: L; Cq; DLC, RPJCB, GU-DeR

1746#22
SALMON, Thomas. *The modern gazetteer: or, a short view of the several nations of the world. . .* London. S. and E. Ballard and others, 466p. 12mo. 1746
Note: SABIN 75823, EA 746/182. Many other editions.
Locations: L; CLU-C, ICN

1746#23
SHIRLEY, William. *A letter from William Shirley. . . to. . . the Duke of Newcastle: with a journal of the siege of Louisbourg. . .* London. E. Owen, 32p. 8vo. 1746
Note: SABIN 80545, EA 746/186, 748/182. First published Boston, 1746 (EVANS 5863). Another edition 1748. See also Pepperrell, *An accurate journal. . .* above, 1746.
Locations: L; RPJCB, NIC, InU

1746

1746#24
SHORT, Thomas. *Medicina Britannica; or, a treatise on such physical plants, as are generally to be found in... Great Britain...* London. R. Manby, J. Cox, 352p. 8vo. 1746
Note: SABIN 80573n, EA 746/187. Reprinted Philadelphia, 1751. American references. Second edition, London 1747 (L;).
Locations: MH-A, CtY, PPL

1746#25
SMITH, Samuel. *Publick spirit, illustrated in the life and designs of the Reverend Thomas Bray D. D.* London. J. Brotherton, 54p. 8vo. 1746
Note: SABIN 83976, EA 746/189. With list of Associates.
Locations: L; RPJCB, CtY, NN

1746#26
TOWGOOD, Micaiah. *The dissenting gentleman's answer to the Reverend Mr White's three letters.* London. R. Hett, 38p. 8vo. 1746
Note: EA 746/193–4. Another edition in 1746. Also 1747; and Belfast 1747, EA 747/173–4.
Locations: L; NjR, CSmH

1746#27
VERNON, Edward. *Original letters to an honest sailor...* London. R. Thomas, 94p. 8vo. 1746
Note: SABIN 57614, 99249n., EA 746/143. Some American material. British Library copy has been reported lost.
Locations: L; DLC, RPJCB, CtY

1746#28
WALLACE, Robert. *Ignorance and superstition a source of violence and cruelty, and in particular the cause of the present rebellion...* Edinburgh. R. Fleming and Company, 39p. 8vo. 1746
Note: Also London, J. Davidson. Society in Scotland for the Propagation of the Gospel sermon for 1746. Extensive discussion of missionary work, with references to Indians in Long Island, etc.
Locations: L; E-NRO; NN, CtY

1746#29
WHITEFIELD, George. *Accounts relating to the orphan house in Georgia.* London. s.sh. F. [1746?]
Note: SABIN 103575, EA 746/210.
Locations: GU-DeR

1746#30
WHITEFIELD, George. *Britain's mercies, and Britain's duty. Represented in a sermon... at Philadelphia... August 24, 1746. And occasioned by the suppression of the late unnatural rebellion...* London. Philadelphia printed, London reprinted. For J. Robinson, 24p. 8vo. 1746

Note: SABIN 103503n, EA 746/211, 747/185. A third edition, Philadelphia printed, Bristol reprinted, 1747. First printed in Boston and Philadelphia, 1746 (EVANS 5883–4).
Locations: L; E; RPJCB, NN, ICN

1747#1
ANNESLEY, James. *Memoirs of an unfortunate young nobleman, return'd from a thirteen years slavery in America... Vol III which completes the work, and is a key to the other two volumes.* London. J. Freeman, 215p. 12mo. 1747
Note: EA 747/112.
Locations: L; C; TxU, MH

1747#2
BICKHAM, George. *A short description of the American colonies, belonging to the crown of Great Britain. Engrav'd by George Bickham...* London. G. and J. Bickham, 22p. F. 1747
Note: SABIN 80618, EA 747/15, 749/28. Other editions in 1749, 1754. Also issued as part of *The British monarchy*, 1748.
Locations: MB, MHi, RPJCB

1747#3
The Christian history; or, a *general account of the progress of the gospel, in England, Wales, Scotland, and America: so far as the Rev. Mr. Whitefield, his fellow-labourers, and assistants are concerned.* London. J. Lewis, 237p. 8vo. 1747
Note: SABIN 103616, EA 747/36. Issued in parts. Possibly reprints some of the *Christian History*, 2 vols. Boston 1744–5. See EVANS 5154, 5482, 5360, 5682.
Locations: L; MRu; RPJCB, GU-DeR

1747#4
COADE, George. *A letter to the honourable the Lords Commissioners of trade and plantations. Wherein the grand concern of trade is asserted and maintained...* London. J. Robinson, 143p. 8vo. 1747
Note: SABIN 13809, KRESS 4848, HANSON 6031, EA 747/37, 748/44. A second edition in 1748.
Locations: L; C; RPJCB, CSmH, CtY

1747#5
COLDEN, Cadwallader. *The history of the five Indian nations of Canada, which are dependent on the province of New-York in America, and are the barrier between the English and French in that part of the world...* London. T. Osborne, 283p. 8vo. 1747
Note: SABIN 14273, HANSON 3727n., EA 747/38, 750/68. First printed New York, 1727 (EVANS 2849). Other editions, 1750; and 1755 (2 vols).
Locations: L; CYc; DLC, RPJCB, MiU-C

1747#6
Considerations relating to the laying any additional duty on sugar from the British plantations. Wherein is shewn, that such duty will be injurious to the commerce and navigation of this kingdom. . . London. Printed for John Clarke, 31, [1]p. 8vo. 1747
Note: EA 747/43.
Locations: C; ICU, MnU, MH-BA, NN, RPJCB

1747#7
CROKATT, James. *Further observations intended for improving the culture and curing of indigo, etc in South-Carolina.* London. 25p. 12mo. 1747
Note: SABIN 17593, 87849, HANSON 6076, EA 747/44.
Locations: L; NNC, RPJCB

1747#8
GREAT BRITAIN. PARLIAMENT. *Act to extend the provisions of an act. . . intituled An act for naturalizing foreign Protestants. . . in. . . his majesty's colonies in America. . . to other foreign Protestants. . .* London. T. and R. Baskett, 4p. F. 1747
Locations: RPJCB, MB, MiU-C

1747#9
HORSMANDEN, Daniel. *A journal of the proceedings in the detection of the conspiracy formed by some white people, in conjunction with negro and other slaves, for burning the city of New-York. . .* London. Printed in New York, reprinted London. John Clarke, viii, 425p. 8vo. 1747
Note: SABIN 33059, EA 747/82. First printed New York, 1744 (EVANS 5413).
Locations: L; DLC, RPJCB, MiU-C

1747#10
HOUSTOUN, James. *Dr. Houstoun's memoirs of his own life-time. Containing. . . VIII. The importance of Cape Breton to the British nation. . .* London. L. Gilliver and J. Owen, 435p. 8vo. 1747
Note: SABIN 33199, HANSON 6067, EA 747/83-4. Reissued in 1747 as *Memoirs of the life and travels of. . .* and in 1753 as *The works of James Houstoun, M. D. . .*
Locations: L; RPJCB, NNC, MiU-C

1747#11
HUTCHESON, Francis. *A short introduction to moral philosophy, in three books. . .* Glasgow. R. Foulis, 347p. 8vo. 1747
Note: HIGGS 630. Second edition, Glasgow, 1753. Discusses slavery and colonial rights.
Locations: L; DLC, MH-BA, ICN

1747#12
HUTCHINSON, J. Mrs. *The private character of Admiral Anson.* London. J. Oldcastle, 22p. 8vo. 1747
Note: EA 747/86-7. 'From a young lady in South Carolina.' Another edition Dublin, 1747 (RPJCB).
Locations: DLC

1747#13
The interest of Great Britain, in supplying herself with iron: impartially consider'd. . . London. 26p. 8vo. [1747?]
Note: KRESS 5531 dates 1756. HANSON 6055 dates same title to [1747?] (L;). An abridgement issued in 1750 (L;).
Locations: L; MH-BA

1747#14
LENNOX, Charlotte. *Poems on several occasions.* London. S. Paterson, 88p. 4to. 1747
Note: EA 747/100. Although EA states that her poems include a satire on New York, I did not find it. See Lennox, *Life of Harriot Stuart*, below, 1751.
Locations: L; MH, CtY

1747#15
LOGAN, James. *Experimenta et meletemata de plantarum generatione. Autore Jacobo Logan. . . Experiments and considerations on the generation of plants. . . Translated from the original Latin.* London. C. Davis, 39p. 8vo. 1747
Note: SABIN 41796, EA 747/103.
Locations: L; DLC, RPJCB, CtY

1747#16
NE–L, Mc-O–-. *A copy of a letter from Quebeck in Canada, to a Pr-M-r in France, dated October 11. 1747.* [London?] 3, [1]p. 2o. [1747?]
Note: Signed Mc-O–- Ne–l.
Locations: MnU

1747#17
Observations on the course of proceeding in admiralty courts in prize causes. London. E. Say, 40p. 4to. 1747
Note: EA 747/120.
Locations: L; CtY, CSmH, ICN

1747#18
An ode to the right honourable Sir Peter Warren. . . occasion'd by the late signal success of the British navy. London. H. Kent, 11p. 4to. [1747]
Note: EA 747/121. Probably relates to his victory at Cape Finisterre and not at Louisbourg.
Locations: RPJCB

1747#19
PRINCE, Thomas. *The salvations of God in 1746. In part set forth in a sermon at the South Church in Boston, Nov. 27, 1746. . .* London. Boston printed, London reprinted. T. Longman, T. Shewell, 36p. 8vo. 1747

1747

Note: SABIN 65610, EA 747/133. First printed Boston, 1746 (EVANS 5856).
Locations: L; RPJCB, NN, MiU-C

1747#20
PRINCE, Thomas. *A sermon deliver'd at the South-Church in Boston. . . August 14, 1746. . . Thanksgiving for. . . glorious and happy victory near Culloden. . .* London. Boston printed, London reprinted. J. Lewis, 39p. 8vo. 1747
Note: SABIN 65612, EA 747/134–5. First printed Boston, 1746 (EVANS 5857). Also Edinburgh, 1747.
Locations: L; DLC, RPJCB, MH

1747#21
RAE, Robert. *Answers for Robert Rae of Little-Govan, to the petition of John Jamieson merchant in Glasgow.* Glasgow. F. 1747
Note: HANSON 6070, EA 747/137. Relates to Virginia.
Locations: O;

1747#22
RANDALL, Joseph. *A brief account of the rise, principles, and discipline of the people call'd Quakers in America, and elsewhere, extracted from a system of geography, lately published.* Bristol. S. Farley, 24p. 12mo. 1747
Note: SABIN 67792, SMITH II, 470, EA 747/138.
Locations: L; Lmh; RPJCB, NN, MiU-C

1747#23
*A **short account of iron**, made in the colonies of Virginia and Maryland, only. With the opinion of the iron-merchants and manufacturers thereon.* London. s.sh. F. [1747]
Note: EA 747/156.
Locations: RPJCB, KU-S

1747#24
*A **short confession of faith** of the Church of Christ at Newport in Rhode Island, under the care of Mr Daniel White. . .* London reprinted for A. Ward, 36p. 12mo. 1747
Note: SABIN 80614. First printed [Philadelphia, 1731?]; also Philadelphia, 1734 (EVANS 3476, 3833).
Locations: RPJCB

1747#25
SIMMS, Henry. *The life of Henry Simms, alias Young gentleman Harry. . . to his death at Tyburn. . . June 17, 1747. . . robberies. . . and extraordinary adventures. . . at home and abroad. . .* London. T. Parker, C. Corbett, 38p. 8vo. 1747
Note: EA 747/157. Written by himself under sentence of death. Old Etonian, transported to Maryland.
Locations: L; RPJCB, MnU, InU

1747#26
STORY, Thomas. *A journal of the life of Thomas Story containing an account of his. . . embracing the principles. . . held by the Quakers. . .* Newcastle. I. Thompson, etc., 768p. 2o. 1747
Note: SABIN 92324, SMITH II, 639, EA 747/166–7. Another issue Newcastle-upon-Tyne, 1747.
Locations: L; DLC, RPJCB, MiU-C

1747#27
THOMAS, John (1691–1766). *A sermon preached. . . February 20, 1746. . .* London. E. Owens, 76p. 4to. 1747
Note: SABIN 95420, EA 747/170–1. Another issue in 1747. SPG sermon for 1747, with abstract, etc.
Locations: L; DLC, RPJCB, NN

1747#28
TOWGOOD, Micaiah. *The dissenting gentleman's second letter to the Reverend Mr White.* London. R. Hett, 90p. 4to. 1747
Note: EA 747/175. Religious persecution and America.
Locations: L; CLU-C

1747#29
WHITEFIELD, George. *Five sermons on the following subjects. . . With a preface by the Rev. Mr. Gilbert Tennent. . .* London. Philadelphia printed, London reprinted. W. Strahan, 138p. 8vo. 1747
Note: EA 747/186. First printed Philadelphia, 1740 (EVANS 4639).
Locations: L; NN, MH

1747#30
WHITEFIELD, George. *A further account of God's dealings with the Reverend Mr George Whitefield, from the time of his ordination to his embarking for Georgia.* London. W. Strahan, 36p. 8vo. 1747
Note: SABIN 103522, EA 747/188. With account of Georgia orphan house annexed. First printed Philadelphia and Boston, 1746 (EVANS 5886–7).
Locations: L; MRu; RPJCB, NN, GU-DeR

1748#1
BRAINERD, David. *An abridgment of Mr. David Brainerd's Journal among the Indians. Or, the rise and progress of a remarkable work of grace among a number of the Indians. . . In the provinces of New-Jersey and Pennsylvania, etc.* London. J. Oswald, and sold by J. Trail and others in Edinburgh, 110p. 12mo. 1748
Note: SABIN 7338, EA 748/25. With dedication by Philip Doddridge. Abridgement of *Mirabilia Dei. . .*, Philadelphia, 1746 (EVANS 5748).
Locations: L; DLC, CtY

1748#2
BROWNRIGG, William. *The art of making common salt, as now practised in most parts of the world; with several improvements proposed in that art, for the use of the British dominions.* London. C. Davis, etc. 295p. 8vo. 1748
Note: HANSON 6137.
Locations: Lu; DLC, N

1748#3
The case re-stated; or, An examine of a late pamphlet, intituled, The state of the nation for the year 1747. London. M. Cooper, 56p. 8vo. 1748
Note: HANSON 6114 and note, EA 748/31–2. Also Dublin, 1748. Conquest of French in Americas.
Locations: L; CtY, DLC, CSmH

1748#4
CLERK OF THE CALIFORNIA. *An account of a voyage for the discovery of a North-West Passage by Hudson's Streights, to the Western and Southern Ocean of America. Performed in the year 1746 and 1747, in the ship California, Capt. Francis Smith, Commander...* London. Joliffe and others, 2 vols., 8vo. 1748
Note: SABIN 20808, 82549, HANSON 6168, EA 748/54–5. Two editions in 1748. By Charles Swaine or Theodorus Swaine Drage?
Locations: L; E; O; DLC, RPJCB, MiU-C

1748#5
ELLIS, Henry. *A voyage to Hudson's-Bay, by the Dobbs galley and California, in the years 1746 and 1747, for discovering a North West Passage with... a short natural history of the country...* London. H. Whitridge, 336p. 8vo. 1748
Note: HANSON 6169, EA 748/59, 749/95. Also Dublin, 1749.
Locations: L; E; O; RPJCB, CSmH, MiU-C

1748#6
GRANVILLE, John Carteret. *The state of the nation for the year 1747, and respecting 1748. Inscribed to a member of the present Parliament.* London. M. Cooper, 68p. 8vo. 1748
Note: SABIN 90618, 90619, HANSON 6032n, EA 748/85–6. Many North American references; also Dublin, 1748.
Locations: DLC, RPJCB, CtY

1748#7
GRANVILLE, John Carteret. *A supplement to the State of the Nation; being free-thoughts on the present critical conjuncture.* London. M. Cooper, 52p. 8vo. 1748
Note: SABIN 9062, HANSON 6117, EA 748/195.
Locations: L; CtY, InU, RPJCB

1748#8
GREAT BRITAIN. PARLIAMENT. *An act for encouraging the making of indico in the British plantations in America.* London. T. Baskett and assigns of R. Baskett, [5]p. F. 1748
Note: Act made in session 1747–8.
Locations: RPJCB

1748#9
GREAT BRITAIN. PARLIAMENT. *Act for permitting tea to be exported to Ireland, and... plantations in America, without paying the inland duties...* London. J. Baskett and others. 8p. F. 1748
Locations: RPJCB, MiU-C, MnU

1748#10
HILL, John. *A general natural history; or, New and accurate descriptions of the animals, vegetables and minerals...* London. T. Osborne, 3 vols., F. 1748
Note: EA 748/93. Many American references.
Locations: L; DLC, CtY

1748#11
Ill-judged bounties tend to beggary on both sides: or, Observations on a paper, intituled, Reasons for laying a duty on French and Spanish indico, and granting a bounty on what is made in the British plantations. London. E. Owen, 14p. 8vo. 1748
Note: HANSON 6166, EA 748/100.
Locations: C; RPJCB, NNC

1748#12
LISLE, Samuel. *A sermon preached... February 19, 1747...* London. E. Owen, 84p. 4to. 1748
Note: SABIN 41422, EA 748/113–4. Another issue in 1748. SPG sermon for 1748, with abstract, etc.
Locations: L; DLC, RPJCB, CtY

1748#13
LITTLE, Otis. *The state of trade of the northern colonies considered; with an account of their produce, and a particular description of Nova Scotia...* London. G. Woodfall, 84p. 8vo. 1748
Note: SABIN 41523, EA 748/115–6. Another issue, 1748 (L; RPJCB). Reprinted Boston, 1749.
Locations: L; C; RPJCB, CSmH, MiU-C

1748#14
LOWNDES, Thomas. *Extract of a letter from Mr Thomas Lowndes, to the honourable the Commissioners for victualling his majesty's navy, dated 18 April, 1748.* London. s.sh. F. [1748]
Note: HANSON 6138. On the unfair testing of his brine salt in Newfoundland.
Locations: L; RPJCB

1748

1748#15
The mitre and crown; or Great Britain's true interest... London. 2 vols. 8vo. 1748
Note: SABIN 49760. Contains a description of Nova Scotia, etc. Published 1748–1750.
Locations: DLC, MiU-C, KU

1748#16
National prejudice, opposed to national interest, candidly considered in the detention or yielding up Gibraltar and Cape-Breton by the ensuing treaty of peace... London. W. Owen, 50p. 8vo. 1748
Note: HANSON 6153, EA 748/132.
Locations: L; DLC, RPJCB, MH

1748#17
Observations on the probable issue of the Congress at Aix La Chapelle. In a letter to a friend. London. R. Montagu, 52p. 8vo. 1748
Note: EA 748/139.
Locations: L; DLC, RPJCB, CtY

1748#18
OSBORNE, Thomas. *A catalogue of the libraries of the several gentlemen undermentioned, viz... II. The Hon. Governor Winthorp [sic] Fellow of the Royal Society...* London. 31, 367, 24p. 8vo. [1748]
Note: GOLDSMITH'S 8379. Sale catalogue which does not differentiate between Winthrop's and the other collections of books to be sold.
Locations: Lu;

1748#19
PHILOTHEUS. *A true and particular history of earthquakes...* London. 176p. 8vo. 1748
Note: SABIN 42592, EA 748/203. Second edition in 1748: T. Osborne, 344p. References to North America.
Locations: L; DLC, RPJCB, PHi

1748#20
The pr–t–st of the m–ch–ts of G—t B——n against the Pr—l-m—-ry A-t— s for a peace lately signed at A-x la Ch-pp–le. London. R. Freeman, 4, 23p. 8vo. 1748
Note: SABIN 66110, HANSON 6155, GOLDSMITHS 8339, EA 748/161.
Locations: L; Lu; MB

1748#21
Reasons for laying a duty on French and Spanish Indico, and granting a bounty on what is made in the British plantations. London. [4]p. F. [1748]
Note: HANSON 6165, EA 748/164. Refers to Carolina and Georgia.
Locations: Lpro; DLC, RPJCB

1748#22
Reasons grounded on facts... London. M. Cooper, 21p. 8vo. 1748

Note: SABIN 68280, HANSON 6182, EA 748/165–6. Discusses sugar trade with North American references. A second edition with additions in 1748: L; RPJCB.
Locations: L; Lu; RPJCB, NN, PPL

1748#23
SALMON, Thomas. *Considerations on the bill for a general naturalization, as it may conduce to the improvement of our manufactures and traffic...* London. W. Owen, 71p. 8vo. 1748
Note: HANSON 6202, EA 748/175.
Locations: L; Lu; DLC, RPJCB, NN

1748#24
Seasonable observations on the naturalization bill... London. A. Dodd, 14p. 4to. 1748
Note: Mentions beneficial effects of German immigrants in America.
Locations: L; NcD

1748#25
Ship King's Meadow. Jamaica... London. 3p. F. 1748
Note: Ship was built in Boston. FORD lists three other briefs i) 11p. F., ii) 4p. F. 3) 3p. F., dated 1748–1753 and related to the case.
Locations: NN

1748#26
Ship South Kingston. Rhode Island. Benjamin Hassard and others, appellants. John Rous, Respondent. The case of the... appellants... London. 3p. F. 1748
Note: Ship condemned for illegal trade in Charleston.
Locations: NN

1748#27
SQUIRE, Samuel. *An historical essay upon the ballance of civil power in England.* London. M. Cooper, 96p. 8vo. 1748
Note: EA 748/189.
Locations: L; CSmH, CtY

1748#28
STANHOPE, Philip Dormer. *An apology for a late resignation in a letter from an English gentleman to... friend at the Hague.* London. J. Freeman, 46p. 8vo. 1748
Note: EA 748/36–39. Three more editions in 1748. References to Cape Breton.
Locations: L; RPJCB, MH, CtY

1748#29
The state of the nation for 1747–8 with a general balance of the publick accompts. London. M. Cooper,(4), 56p. 8vo. 1748
Note: SABIN 90620, HANSON 6116, EA 748/190–2. Two other London and a Dublin edition in 1748. Attacks

failure to send fleet to Canada and other aspects of policy towards North America.
Locations: Lu; DLC, RPJCB, MiU-C

1748#30
THORESBY, Ralph. *The excellency and advantage of doing good. . . a sermon preached. . . to which is annex'd a letter of Samuel Lloyd. . . concerning the nature and goodness of the Georgia silk.* London. W. Meadows, 21p. 4to. 1748
Note: SABIN 95612, EA 748/202. Georgia Trustees and Bray Associates sermon.
Locations: L; DLC, RPJCB, MiU-C

1748#31
WALCOT, James. *The new pilgrim's progress; or, the pious Indian convert. . . Together with a narrative of his. . . travels among the savage Indians for their conversion. . .* London. M. Cooper, W. Owen, and R. Goadby at Yeovil, 316p. 12mo. 1748
Note: SABIN 100991, EA 748/221, 749/280. Another edition in 1749. Fictional. Countries 'adjoining South Carolina'.
Locations: L; DLC, RPJCB, MiU-C

1748#32
WALKER, Robert. *A short account of the rise, progress, and present state of the Society in Scotland for propagating Christian knowledge. With a sermon prefix'd to it; preached. . . Monday January 4. 1748. . .* Edinburgh. T. Lumisden, 79p. 8vo. 1748
Note: Also issued as *A short state of the Society in Scotland. . .* Extensive American references.
Locations: E; Llp; Ot; CSmH ICN

1748#33
WEST, Gilbert. *A defense of the Christian revelation. . .* London. 246p. 8vo. 1748
Note: SABIN 19238, EA 748/233. Printed by voluntary subscription for distribution in the colonies. Preface by Edmund Gibson. Boston reprinted, 1749.
Locations: L; D; DLC, RPJCB, MH

1748#34
WHITE, John. *A second defence of the Three letters to a gentleman dissenting from the Church of England. . .* London. C. Davis and W. Craighton, at Ipswich, 152p. 8vo. 1748
Note: EA 748/234. References to New England Puritans.
Locations: L; RPJCB, MH, NN

1748#35
WHITE, John. *Three letters to a gentleman dissenting from the Church of England.* London. C. Davis, 3pts. 8vo. 1748

Note: EA 748/235–6. Includes reissues of his second and third letters, above, 1745. Another edition in 1748.
Locations: IU, MCE

1748#36
WHITEFIELD, George. *A brief account of the rise, progress and present situation of the orphan-house in Georgia. In a letter to a friend.* Edinburgh. T. Lumisden, 16p. 8vo. 1748
Note: SABIN 103501, HANSON 6173, EA 748/238.
Locations: E; ICN, GU-DeR

1749#1
The advantages of the difinitive [sic] *treaty to the people of Great-Britain demonstrated.* London. W. Webb junior, 26p. 8vo. 1749
Note: HANSON 6255, EA 749/1–2. A second edition in 1749. Continuing the war could have resulted in the capture of Canada, etc. Substantial discussion of North America.
Locations: L; CtY, NNC, CSmH

1749#2
ANNET, Peter. *Social bliss considered: In marriage and divorce. . . with the speech of Miss Polly Baker. . .* London. R. Rose, 108p. 4to. 1749
Note: SABIN 85685, EA 749/10. Fictitious speech of Miss Polly Baker of Connecticut. See also Annet, *A collection. . .*, below, 1750.
Locations: CLU-C, MH, NPV

1749#3
Answers for Andrew Anderson merchant in *Virginia and his factor, to petition of Arthur Nasmith. . . [signed] Arch. Murray. June 1, 1749.* London. 3p. 1749.
Locations: DLC

1749#4
An apology for the life of *Bampfylde-Moore Carew, (son of the Rev. Mr. Carew of Bickley). . . his many comical adventures, travels through America, living with the wild Indians. . .* London. R. Goadby, W. Owen, 343p. 12mo. [1749 or 1750]
Note: SABIN 27615, EA 749/13, 750/16–17. Two further enlarged editions, Sherborne and London, 1750. An edition, 350p. 12mo. London, [1760?] and later editions. Attributed to R. Goadby. Full account of his 'American adventures.' See Carew, *The life and adventures*, above, 1745.
Locations: L; O; RPJCB, CtY

1749#5
BACON, Thomas. *Two sermons, preached to a congregation of black slaves, at the parish church of S. P., in the province of Maryland. By an American pastor.* London. J. Oliver, 79p. 12mo. 1749
Note: SABIN 2687, EA 749/18.
Locations: L; Llp; O; CSmH, RPJCB, MH

1749

1749#6
Both sides of the question: *or, a candid and impartial enquiry into a certain doubtful character in a letter to a General-Officer, remarkably acquited [sic]. . . by a C—t M——l.* London. J. Mechell, 28p. 8vo. [1749]
Note: SABIN 6814, 27017, DERENNE, I, 125–6, EA 749/33–4. Another issue in 1749: RPJCB. Relates to Georgia, South Carolina and expedition against St. Augustine.
Locations: ViU, GU-DeR

1749#7
The case of the Hudson's-Bay *Company.* London. 3p. F. [1749?]
Note: HANSON 6273, EA 749/141.
Locations: L; CYc; CtY, MnU, RPJCB

1749#8
The case of the inhabitants *in Pensilvania. . .* London. s.sh. 1/2o. 1749
Note: HANSON 6288, EA 748/30 dates to 1748; it refers to bill for regulating paper bills of credit, read 3 March 1749.
Locations: L; DLC, CSmH, PPAmP, PPULC

1749#9
A catalogue of some narratives, *vouchers, and other papers. . . from the United Moravian churches.* London. 4p. F. 1749
Note: EA 749/48. Moravians in Georgia, Pennsylvania, etc.
Locations: MiU-C

1749#10
A defence of the Dutch, *against the imputations of fraud, cruelty and perfidiousness. . . the encroachments of France, and the untractableness of Spain. To which is added, a supplement, relative to the settlement of Nova-Scotia.* London. R. Spavan, 35p. 8vo. 1749
Note: HANSON 6257, EA 749/63.
Locations: L; C; E; MiU-C, RPJCB, CtY, NN

1749#11
DOBBS, Arthur. *Reasons to shew, that there is a great probability of a navigable passage to the western American ocean, through the Hudson's streights. . . offered to the consideration of the Lords and Commons. . .* London. J. Robinson, 23p, 8vo. 1749
Note: SABIN 68291, HANSON 6270, EA 749/226.
Locations: L; MRu; DLC, RPJCB, MiU-C

1749#12
DOBBS, Arthur. *A short view of the countries and trade carried on by the Company in Hudson's-Bay, shewing the prejudice of that exclusive trade. . .* London. 3p. F. 1749
Note: HANSON 6274, EA 749/250.
Locations: L; CYc; CSmH, NN

1749#13
DODDRIDGE, Philip. *Reflections on the conduct of divine providence in the series and conclusion of the late war; a sermon.* London. 37p. 8vo. 1749
Note: EA 749/75. Cape Breton and Nova Scotia.
Locations: L; DLC, MH

1749#14
A geographical history of Nova *Scotia. Containing an account of the situation, extent and limits thereof. As also the various struggles between. . . England and France for the possession of that province. . .* London. P. Vaillant, 110p. 8vo. 1749
Note: SABIN 56135, HANSON 6285, EA 749/112. Also 'Londres' i.e. Paris, 1755.
Locations: L; C; O; DLC, RPJCB, MiU-C

1749#15
GEORGE, William. *A sermon preached. . . February 17, 1748.* London. E. Owen, 67p. 4to. 1749
Note: SABIN 26992, EA 749/113. SPG sermon for 1749, with abstract, etc.
Locations: L; DLC, RPJCB, NN

1749#16
Georgia bill of exchange payable *in England. . .* London. s.sh. 8vo. [1749]
Note: DERENNE I, 126–7.
Locations: GU-DeR

1749#17
GIBSON, Edmund. *Five pastoral letters to the people of his diocese.* London. E. Owen, 314p. 12mo. 1749
Note: EA 749/115.
Locations: L; ICN, PPL

1749#18
GILL, John. *The divine right of infant baptism, examined. . .* London. Printed in Boston; London, J. Ward, etc., 112p. 8vo. 1749
Note: EA 749/116. Answer to Jonathan Dickinson's *Brief illustration. . . of the divine right of infant baptism.* Reprinted Boston, 1750.
Locations: L; DLC, RPJCB, MHi

1749#19
GREAT BRITAIN. PARLIAMENT. *Act for encouraging the people known by the name of Unitas Fratrum or United Brethren, to settle in his majesty's colonies in America.* London. T. Baskett and others, 3p. F. 1749
Note: Cf. HANSON 6292, EA 749/129.
Locations: L; PHi, DLC, MiU-C

1749#20
GREAT BRITAIN. PARLIAMENT. *An act for the further encouragment and enlargement of the whale fishery.* London. T. Baskett 1749
Locations: RPJCB

1749#21
GREAT BRITAIN. PARLIAMENT. HOUSE OF COMMONS. *A bill for encouraging the people known by the name of Unitas Fratrum, or United Brethren, to settle in his majesty's colonies in America.* London. 3p. F. [1749]
Note: HANSON 6292, EA 749/125. Enacted.
Locations: L; MiU-C, InU

1749#22
GREAT BRITAIN. PARLIAMENT. HOUSE OF COMMONS. *A bill to regulate and restrain paper bills of credit in the British colonies and plantations in America, and to prevent the same being legal tenders...* London. 7p. F. [1749]
Note: HANSON 6286, EA 749/126. Not enacted.
Locations: L; CSmH, RPJCB

1749#23
GREAT BRITAIN. PARLIAMENT. HOUSE OF COMMONS COMMITTEE. *Papers presented to the committee appointed to inquire into the state and condition of the countries adjoining to Hudson's Bay, and of the trade carried on there.* London. 79p. F. 1749
Note: SABIN 58462, HANSON 6271, EA 749/127.
Locations: L; RPJCB, NN, MiU-C

1749#24
GREAT BRITAIN. PARLIAMENT. HOUSE OF COMMONS COMMITTEE. *A report from the Committee appointed to inquire into the state and condition of the countries adjoining to Hudson's Bay, and of the trade carried on there.* London. 60p. xxxi, F. [1749]
Note: HANSON 6272, EA 749/128.
Locations: L; C; RPJCB, NN, MiU-C

1749#25
GREAT BRITAIN. PARLIAMENT. HOUSE OF COMMONS COMMITTEE. *Report from the committee to whom the petition of the deputies of the united Moravian churches... was referred; together with some extracts of the most material vouchers and papers contained in the appendix to the said report.* London. 156p. F. 1749
Note: SABIN 69853, HANSON 6291, EA 749/129.
Locations: L; RPJCB, MiU-C

1749#26
HARVEST, George. *A sermon preached... March 16, 1748-9...* London. W. Meadows and M. Cooper, 22p. 4to. 1749
Note: SABIN 20767, EA 749/134. Georgia Trustees and Bray Associates anniversary sermon.
Locations: L; LANu; DLC, RPJCB, GU-DeR

1749#27
KIRKPATRICK, James. *The sea-piece, a poetical narration of a voyage from Europe to America. Canto II.* London. M. Cooper, J. Dodsley, 24p. 2o. 1749
Note: SABIN 38008, FOXON K89-91, EA 749/156, 750/179. Describes voyage to South Carolina. An expanded version published in 1750, in five cantos.
Locations: L; MH

1749#28
Ministerial artifice detected, or, A full answer to a pamphlet... The interests of the empress queen, the Kings of France and Spain, etc., betrayed in the preliminary articles at Aix-La-Chapelle. London. A. Hill, 32p. 8vo. 1749
Note: EA 749/184. Discusses French in North America.
Locations: L; RPJCB, MH, NN

1749#29
Miscellaneous reflections upon the peace, and its consequences... London. J. Roberts, 63p. 8vo. 1749
Note: HANSON 6217, EA 749/185. Advocates emigration to America.
Locations: L; RPJCB, NN

1749#30
MORIN, J. *A short account of the life and sufferings of Elias Neau...* London. J. Lewis, 86p. 8vo. 1749
Note: EA 749/188. Neau lived in New York.
Locations: MnU, NN (imperfect)

1749#31
MOULTRIE, John. *Dissertatio medica inauguralis, de febre maligna biliosa Americae... pro gradu doctoratus... Joannes Moultrie, ex Meridionali Carolinae provincia...* Edinburgh. 23p. 4to. 1749
Note: SABIN 51141, EA 749/189. On yellow fever.
Locations: MRu; DLC, RPJCB, NN

1749#32
PERCEVAL, John. *An examination of the principles, and an enquiry into the conduct, of the two b——rs...* London. A. Price, 79p. 8vo. 1749
Note: SABIN 23367, 22638, EA 749/81-88. Seven more editions in 1749.
Locations: RPJCB, MH

1749#33
PERCEVAL, John. *A second series of facts and arguments: tending to prove that the abilities of the two b——s, are not more extraordinary than their virtues...* London. A. Price, 59p. 8vo. 1749
Note: Cf. SABIN 23367, EA 749/89-91. Two more editions in 1749.
Locations: L; DLC, CtY

1749

1749#34
POSTLETHWAYT, Malachy. *A dissertation on the plan, use, and importance, of the Universal dictionary of trade and commerce, translated from the French of... M. de Savary... with additions which more particularly accommodate the same to the trade and navigation of the British empire...* London. J. and P. Knapton, 53p. 4to. 1749
Note: HANSON 6216, EA 749/218. Elaborate prospectus, promising extensive coverage of British and French North America.
Locations: L; DLC, CtY, NN

1749#35
ROLT, Richard. *An impartial representation of the conduct of the several powers of Europe, engaged in the late general war... To... 1748.* London. S. Birt, etc. 4 vols. 8vo. 1749
Note: SABIN 72881, EA 749/231. Printed 1749–50. Second edition in 1754.
Locations: L; DLC, CtY, NN

1749#36
SALMON, Thomas. *A new geographical and historical grammar...* London. W. Johnston, 550p. 8vo. 1749
Note: SABIN 75827, EA 749/234.
Locations: L; RPJCB, ViU, MH

1749#37
SHEPARD, Thomas. *Meditations and spiritual experiences of Mr T. Shepard...* Edinburgh. Boston printed, Edinburgh reprinted, 82p. 8vo. 1749
Note: SABIN 80210, EA 749/246. With some account of Shepard by Thomas Prince. First printed Boston, 1746 (EVANS 6067).
Locations: L; RPJCB

1749#38
Ship Notre Dame de Deliverance... Philip Durell, Esq. and others Appellants. William Bollan... and others Respondents. The Case of Captain John Wickham and others... London. 3p. F. 1749
Note: Relates to siege of Louisbourg. FORD lists twelve other briefs, 1746–50, concerning the case.
Locations: NN

1749#39
A short state of the countries and trade of North America. Claimed by the Hudson's Bay company, under a pretence of a charter... shewing the illegality of said grant... London. J. Robinson, 44p. 8vo. [1748 or 1749]
Note: HANSON 6275, KRESS 4984, EA 749/249.
Locations: CYc; LVu; MRu; DLC, RPJCB, MH

1749#40
A short narrative and justification of the proceedings of the committee appointed by the Adventurers, to prosecute the discovery of the passage to the western ocean of America; and to open and extend the trade, and settle the countries beyond Hudson's Bay... London. J. Robinson, 30p. 8vo. 1749
Note: SABIN 51824, 80665, HANSON 6269, EA 749/248. Attributed to A. Dobbs.
Locations: L; MRu; EU; RPJCB, ICN, MiU-C

1749#41
STENNET, Joseph. *A sermon preach'd at Little-Wild-Street on Tuesday, April 25, 1749. Being the day... for a general thanksgiving... for the peace.* London. J. Ward, J. Oswald, H. Whitridge, 34p. 8vo. 1749
Note: EA 749/258. Acquisitions in America.
Locations: L; RPJCB, MH, CtY

1749#42
A tale of Two Tubs: or, the b——s in querpo... London. Printed for A. Price, jun. in the year, 1749. 1749
Note: FOXON T31–2. Attack on Pelhams. Extensive North American references. Also Dublin, 1749.
Locations: L; O; CtY, CSmH

1749#43
TUCKER, Josiah. *A brief essay on the advantages and disadvantages which respectively attend France and Great Britain, with regard to trade...* London. T. Trye, 79p. 8vo. 1749
Note: SABIN 97328–9, 97342, HANSON 6256, EA 749/269, 750/321. Several other editions, the second with 'large additions', London, 1750; third edition corrected, 1753. Also printed Glasgow, 1756, (and Dublin, 1756?). Some editions have the title *An essay on the advantages...*
Locations: L; C; NNC, CtY, NN

1749#44
UNITED BRETHREN IN CHRIST. *The case of the deputies of the Moravian Brethren.* London. s.sh. F. [1749]
Note: SABIN 97847, HANSON 6290, EA 749/46. For exemptions from laws in order to encourage American settlement.
Locations: L;

1749#45
VERNON, Edward. *Considerations upon the white herring and cod fisheries...* London. M. Cooper, 58p. 8vo. 1749
Note: SABIN 16035, HANSON 6233, EA 749/275–6. Another edition in 1749.
Locations: L; Lu; DLC, RPJCB, CtY

1749#46
WESLEY, John. *An extract of the Reverend Mr John Wesley's journal, from Sept. 3, 1741 to October 27, 1743.* Bristol. F. Farley, 123p. 12mo. 1749
Note: SABIN 102658, EA 749/291–2. Another Dublin edition in [1749?].
Locations: L; MH

1750#1
ANNET, Peter. *A collection of the tracts of a certain free inquirer, noted for his sufferings for his opinions...* London. 460p. 8vo. [1750]
Note: SABIN 1604, EA 750/13. Contains Franklin's 'the speech of Miss Polly Baker' said to have been delivered in Connecticut when she was presented for having a bastard and which induced one of her judges to marry her the next day.
Locations: L; MH, NNC

1750#2
An answer to some considerations on the bill for encouraging the importation of pig and bar iron from America... London. s.sh. F. [1750]
Note: GOLDSMITH'S 8505, EA 750/14.
Locations: Lu; RPJCB

1750#3
BACON, Thomas. *Four sermons, upon the great and indispensible duty of Christian masters and mistresses to bring up their negro slaves in the knowledge and fear of God. Preached at the parish church of St. Peter in Talbot County... Maryland.* London. J. Oliver, 142p. 12mo. 1750
Note: SABIN 2685, EA 750/20.
Locations: L; DLC, RPJCB

1750#4
BLAIR, Hugh. *The importance of religious knowledge to the happiness of mankind. A sermon preached... January 1, 1750...* Edinburgh. R. Fleming for A. Kincaid, 50p, 8vo. 1750
Note: SABIN 5743. Society in Scotland for the Propagation of the Gospel sermon, with some account of the Society, including its North American interests.
Locations: L; E; MH, ICN, PPULC

1750#5
A brief history of the Episcopal Church of the Moravian brethren, from their first beginning. Together with the reasons for and against the privileges granted them by the B——sh P——t, in the year 1749. London. 32p. 8vo. 1750
Locations: O;

1750#6
A brief history of the Protestant Episcopal Church, known by the name of Unitas Fratrum... the reasons for and against the privileges granted them in the British dominions in the year 1749... Dublin. S. Powell, 32p. 12mo. 1750
Note: HANSON 6492, EA 750/33.
Locations: L; DLC

1750#7
The case and tryal of John Peter Zenger, of New-York, printer... London. J. Wilford, 60p. 8vo. 1750
Note: SABIN 106308, EA 750/351.
Locations: DLC, RPJCB, CtY

1750#8
Case of British merchants, owners of ships, and others, relative to the employment and increase of British shipping... London. 7p. F. [1750?]
Note: HANSON 6437, EA 750/48.
Locations: L; MH-BA

1750#9
The case of the British northern colonies. London. 3p. F. [1750]
Note: SABIN 11315, EA 750/49. Begins 'These colonies are vastly superior in compass of land...'.
Locations: CSmH, MiU, MnU

1750#10
CHARLESTON, SOUTH CAROLINA. LIBRARY COMPANY. *A catalogue of the books belonging to the Charles-Town Library Society...* London. W. Strahan for the Society, 22p. 8vo. 1750
Note: TURNBULL, p. 119.
Locations: DLC

1750#11
Considerations on the bill now depending before the honourable House of Commons, for encouraging the importation of pig and bar iron from America, etc. London. F. [1750]
Note: SABIN 15970, HANSON 6455, EA 750/73.
Locations: L; Lu; RPJCB, NcU

1750#12
ELLIS, Henry. *Considerations on the great advantages which would arise from the discovery of the North west passage, and a clear account of the most practical method for attempting that discovery.* London. 8p. 4to. 1750
Note: SABIN 22311, HANSON 6458, EA 750/107.
Locations: RPJCB, MiU-C

1750#12A
ELLWOOD, Thomas. *A collection of poems on various subjects.* London. Printed and sold by Luke Hinde, iii, 62p. 8vo. 1750
Note: Contains 'To a friend in America', p. 18.
Locations: L; MH, CtY

1750

1750#13
An excellent new song; entituled, The farmer's glory. 8p. [1750?]
Note: The date is notional. 'And every new plantation,/with pagan, Turk and Jew/There none can live without/The virtue of the plow' etc.
Locations: L; E;

1750#14
The fortunate transport; or, the secret history of the life and adventures of the celebrated Polly Haycock... London. T. Taylor, 44p. 8vo. [1750?]
Note: EA 750/118–9. Another edition in [1750?]. Transported to Virginia and sold into slavery, etc. 'By a Creole'.
Locations: L; DLC, NN

1750#15
FRANCKLIN, Thomas. *A sermon preached...* March 16, 1749,50... London. R. Francklin, 20p. 4to. 1750
Note: SABIN 25477, EA 750/124. Georgia Trustees and Bray Associates anniversary sermon.
Locations: L; DLC, NN, RPJCB, GU-DeR

1750#16
FRANKLIN, Benjamin. *Reflections on courtship and marriage... in two letters to a friend.* London. Philadelphia printed, London reprinted. C. Corbet, 62p. 8vo. 1750
Note: EA 750/125–6. First printed Philadelphia, 1746 (EVANS 5772–3). Also Edinburgh, 1750, 1752; London 1759.
Locations: DLC, RPJCB, NN

1750#17
A genuine account of Nova Scotia: containing, a description of its situation, air, climate, soil and its produce... his majesty's proposals, as an encouragement to those who are willing to settle there... Dublin. P. Bowes, 16p. 8vo. 1750
Note: SABIN 56134, HANSON 6465, EA 750/143.
Locations: L; MH, MnU, DLC

1750#18
The golden glover's garland... new songs. [London]. [1750?]
Note: Date is notional. A 'Betray'd maiden' was promised that she would be taken from Dublin to Bath; in fact, kidnapped to New England.
Locations: MH

1750#19
GREAT BRITAIN. PARLIAMENT. *Act for encouraging the growth and culture of raw silk in... colonies or plantations in America.].* London. T. Baskett and others, 3p. F. 1750
Locations: RPJCB, MiU-C

1750#20
GREAT BRITAIN. PARLIAMENT. *An act to encourage the importation of pig and bar iron from... colonies in America; and to prevent erection of any mill... in any... colony.* London. T. Baskett, 7p. F. [1750]
Locations: L; RPJCB

1750#21
GREAT BRITAIN. PARLIAMENT. HOUSE OF COMMONS. *A bill, intituled, An act to encourage the importation of pig and bar iron from his majesty's colonies in America; and to prevent the erection of any mill... in any of the said colonies.* London. 7p. F. [1750]
Note: HANSON 6454, EA 750/149. Enacted.
Locations: L; RPJCB, MiU-C

1750#22
HUME, Sophia. *An exhortation to the inhabitants of... South Carolina, to bring their deeds to the light of Christ...* Bristol. S. Farley, 7p. 8vo. 1750
Note: SABIN 33780, SMITH, I, 1019, EA 750/169. First printed Philadelphia 1747; other Philadelphia editions in 1748 (EVANS 5974, 6165, 6166). Also Bristol, 1751, London, 1752, Leeds, 1752, Dublin, 1754.
Locations: L; RPJCB, CtY, NN

1750#23
Jemmy Gay's garland, consisting of a variety of new songs... [London]. [1750?]
Note: Chapbook. 'The true lover's yoke' mentions a 'pretty young gallant with beauty and fame/who from New England lately came...'.
Locations: MH

1750#24
The jovial gamester's Garland, composed of several excellent new songs... Edinburgh? 8p. [1750?]
Note: Date is notional. A 'betray'd Maid' was sent to Virginia and 'served seven years to Captain Gulshaw laird'.
Locations: MH

1750#25
KIMBER, Edward. *The life and adventures of Joe Thompson.* London. J. Hinton and W. Frederick, 2 vols. 12mo. 1750
Note: EA 750/177–8. Also Dublin, 1750. A novel. American, especially Virginia, references.
Locations: L; RPJCB

1750#26
LAMBERT, Claude François. *A collection of curious observations on the manners, customs, usages... of the several nations of Asia, Africa, and America. Translated from the French... by John Dunn...* London. 2 vols. 8vo. 1750

Note: SABIN 38729–30, EA 750/183–4. Reissued as *Curious observations. . .* in [1753]: L; NN, CSmH, RPJCB and in 1754 (MWA) and 1755 (RPJCB). Material on North American Indians, California, etc.
Locations: LEu; DLC, CtY, MiU-C

1750#27
LEAKE, Stephen Martin. *Life of Sir John Leake. . . admiral of the fleet.* London. 464p. 8vo. 1750
Note: EA 750/191. Destruction of French settlements in Newfoundland.
Locations: L; DLC

1750#28
LOCKMAN, John. *The vast importance of the herring fishery, etc to these kingdoms. . .* London. W. Owen, 39p. 8vo. 1750
Note: HANSON 6415 and note, EA 750/197–8. Second edition, 1750.
Locations: L; MH, NIC, ICU

1750#29
LOGAN, James. *Cato Major; or a treatise on old age, by M. Tullius Cicero. With explanatory notes. . .* London. S. Austen, 170p. 8vo. 1750
Note: SABIN 13041. First printed, Philadelphia, 1744 (EVANS 5361). Reprinted Glasgow, 1751: ICB, NIC, RPJCB. With preface by Benjamin Franklin.
Locations: L; MH, CtY, PP

1750#30
LOVER OF LIGHT. *The contents of a folio history of the Moravians or United Brethren. . . humbly dedicated to the pious of every denomination of in Europe and America. . .* London. J. Roberts, 60p. 12mo. 1750
Note: Some minor American references.
Locations: L;

1750#31
MAILLET, Benoît de. *Telliamed: or, Discourses between an Indian philosopher and a French missionary, on the diminution of the sea, formation of the earth, the origin of men. . .* London. T. Osborne, 284p. 8vo. 1750
Note: SABIN 43892, EA 750/204. Discusses different species of men, including those in North America.
Locations: L; CtY, MiU, MH

1750#32
MAYHEW, Jonathan. *Seven sermons upon the following subjects. . .* London. Boston printed, London reprinted. J. Noon, [162]p. 8vo. 1750
Note: SABIN 47051. First printed Boston, 1749 (EVANS 6365).
Locations: L; RPJCB, NN, CtY

1750#33
MONTESQUIEU, Charles Louis de Secondat, Baron Montesquieu. *The spirit of laws.* *Translated from the French of M. de Secondat. . .* London. J. Nourse and P. Vaillant, 2 vols., 8vo. 1750
Note: Discussion of colonies, slavery etc. Other editions Aberdeen, 1756, London, 1756, 1766, etc, etc.
Locations: L; DLC, MiU, CtY

1750#34
***National considerations upon importing iron** in bars from America, etc.* London. s.sh. F. [1750]
Note: HANSON 6456, EA 750/224.
Locations: L; KU-S; RPJCB

1750#35
***The Nova Scotia's garland; furnished** with three merry, new songs. . .* Newcastle? 8p. 12mo. [c.1750?]. 1750
Note: Two pieces on Nova Scotia emigration. Date is a guess.
Locations: L; RPJCB

1750#36
P., W. *The history of witches and wizards: giving a true account of all their tryals in England, Scotland, Sweedland, France and New England; with their confession and condemnation.* London. C. Hitch, L. Haws, R. Ware, etc. 12, 144p. 12mo. [1750?]
Note: The date is tentative.
Locations: L; MH, CSmH, MWiW-C

1750#37
PARSONS, William. *The case of Mr William P——s, an unfortunate young gentleman who is now confin'd in Newgate for returning from transportation. Shewing the true motives which induc'd him to return to England. With the remarkable incident of his being taken at Hounslow. And how he has put off his tryal for three sessions's [sic] and who is now called for tryal this next sessions.* London printed by J. Webb, 8p. 8vo. 1750
Note: William Parsons was executed on February 11, 1751. ESTC lists under 1751.
Locations: ViU

1750#38
PERCEVAL, John. *A representation of the state of the trade of Ireland, laid before the House of Lords of England. . .* Dublin. G. Faulkner and J. Esdall, 28p. 8vo. 1750
Note: Refers to bill to impose duty on exports of Irish sail cloth. Mentions American trade and concept of a trading empire.
Locations: L; CtY

1750#39
PRINCE, Thomas. *The natural and moral government and agency of God, in causing droughts and rains.* London. Boston printed, London reprinted and published by J. Lewis. 34p. 8vo. 1750

THE
Nova Scotia's GARLAND;

Furnished with Three merry

NEW SONGS.

I. The Weavers Wives Resolution, not to go to *Nova Scotia*.

II. An Invitation to the famous and plentiful Island of Pleasure, call'd, *New Scotland*, in the *Northren* Parts of *America*.

III. Gently touch the Warbling Lyre.

Licensed and Entred according to Order.

Note: SABIN 65606, EA 750/251. Boston Thanksgiving Sermon, first printed 1749 (EVANS 6408). Another edition in 1751.
Locations: RPJCB

1750#40
Reasons for the encouragement of making raw silk in America. London. 3p. F. [1750?]
Note: SABIN 68276, EA 745/182. ESTC lists under 1750, which is likely from external evidence.
Locations: L; D; RPJCB

1750#41
Reasons for the present application to Parliament for liberty to import salt from any part of Europe directly into his majesty's colonies in America. London. 3, 1p. F. [1750]
Note: HANSON 6457, EA 750/256.
Locations: L; RPJCB, NN, ViU

1750#42
REVEL, James. *The poor unhappy transported felon's sorrowful account of fourteen years transportation, at Virginia in America. In six parts. Being a. . . history of the life of James Revel, the unhappy sufferer. . .* [London]. Printed and sold in Aldermary Church Yard, Bow Lane, 8p. 8vo. 1750
Note: [1750?]. There are many English and Irish editions, including some later ones that change the transportee's name and/or the scene to Australia.
Locations: L; C; CLU-C, NcU

1750#43
ST. ANDREWS CLUB, CHARLES-TOWN, SOUTH CAROLINA. *Rules of the St. Andrew's Club at Charles-Town, in South Carolina.* London. J. Crokatt, 14p. 8vo. 1750
Note: Cf. SABIN 12087, TURNBULL p. 122. The dating could be more precise. EA dates [1750], EA 750/268.
Locations: PPL

1750#44
The second part of The fortunate transport. *Being a continuation. . . from the time of her arrival in England, to her death.* London. T. Taylor, 45p. 8vo. [1750?]
Note: EA 750/286. Sequel to *The Fortunate Transport*, above, 1750.
Locations: L; CtY

1750#45
SHERLOCK, Thomas. *A letter from the Lord Bishop of London, to the clergy and people. . .* London. Vertue and Goadby, 16p. 8vo. 1750
Note: SABIN 80350, EA 750/288-296. Blasphemous books in the American plantations. Seven other London editions and one Glasgow edition in 1750.
Locations: L; MH, DLC

1750#46
A short view of the encroachments of France in America; and of the British commerce with Spain. London. R. Spavan, 16p. 8vo. 1750
Note: SABIN 80697, HANSON 6462, EA 750/300.
Locations: L; RPJCB, NN, MiU-C

1750#47
A short view of the smuggling trade, carried on by the British northern colonies, in violation of the act of navigation, and several other acts of Parliament. London. 3p. F. [1750]
Note: EA 750/301. ESTC lists under 1751.
Locations: L; DLC, RPJCB, MB

1750#48
The state of the trade and manufactory of iron in Great-Britain considered. London. 5, 1p. 8vo. 1750
Note: SABIN 90633, HANSON 6423, EA 750/309. Abridgement of *The interest of Great Britain, in supplying herself with iron*, above, 1747.
Locations: L; DLC, RPJCB, CtY

1750#49
STUKELEY, William. *The philosophy of earthquakes, natural and religious.* London. C. Corbet, 48p., 32p. 8vo. 1750
Note: EA 750/311–12. Second expanded edition in 1750. Partially an electrical theory of earthquakes, citing Franklin's work.
Locations: L; BN; MB

1750#50
TREVOR, Richard. *A sermon preached. . . Feb. 16, 1749. . .* London. E. Owen, 71p. 4to. 1750
Note: SABIN 96797, EA 750/317. SPG sermon for 1750, with abstract, etc.
Locations: L; DLC, RPJCB, CtY

1750#51
WHITEFIELD, George. *Six sermons on the following subjects. . . With a preface by the Reverend Mr Gilbert Tennent.* London. W. Strahan, etc., x, 159p. 12mo. 1750
Note: SABIN 103593, EA 750/341. The third edition. Probably the same as *Five sermons*, above, 1747 with the addition of *Britain's mercies*, above, 1746.
Locations: L; MRu; DLC

1750#52
The wonders of nature and art; being an account of. . . natural history. London. S. Birt, 4 vols. 8vo. 1750
Note: EA 750/347. Vol 4 relates entirely to America.
Locations: Vi, DeU

1751

1751#1
An abstract of the case *of James Annesley, Esq. Veritas Praevalebit. Printed in the year 1751...* London. xix, 211p. 8vo. 1751
Locations: L; NNC

1751#2
An account of the colony in *Nova Scotia.* London. 2, 21p. 8vo. [1751?]
Note: SABIN 56103.
Locations: RPJCB

1751#3
B., M. *A letter to the West-India merchants, in answer to their petition now before the Honble House of Commons, praying for a prohibition of the trade carried on from the northern colonies, to the French and Dutch West-India settlements. By a fisherman.* London. H. Whittridge, G. Woodefyll, 27p. 8vo. 1751
Note: SABIN 40546, HIGGS 99, KRESS 5094.
Locations: L; DLC, RPJCB, NN

1751#4
BACON, Thomas. *A sermon preached at the parish church of St Peter's, in Talbot County, Maryland: on Sunday the 14th of October, 1750. for the benefit of a charity working school to be set up in the said parish, for the maintenance and education of orphans and other poor children, and negroes.* London. J. Oliver, 28p. 4to. 1751
Note: To be sold for the benefit of the said charity school. Contains proposals, rules, subscription-roll, and other proceedings relating to the charity school.
Locations: L; RPJCB

1751#5
BACON, Thomas. *Six sermons on the several duties of masters, mistresses, slaves, etc. Preached... in Talbot county... Maryland...* London. J. Oliver, 221p. 8vo. 1751
Note: SABIN 2685.
Locations: RPJCB, TNF

1751#6
BARTRAM, John. *Observations on the inhabitants, climate, soil, rivers... In his travels from Pensilvania to Onondago, Oswego and the Lake Ontario in Canada. To which is annex'd, a curious account of the cataracts at Niagara. By Mr Peter Kalm, a Swedish gentleman who travelled there.* London. J. Whiston, B. White, 94p. 8vo. 1751
Note: SABIN 3868, HIGGS 84.
Locations: L; O; C; NN, DLC, RPJCB, MiU-C

1751#7
BEAWES, Wyndham. *Lex mercatoria rediviva: or the merchant's directory... Containing an account of our trading companies and colonies, with their establishments, and an abstract of their charters...* London. R. Baldwin, xvi, 922p. F. [1751]
Note: HIGGS 244. Cf. KRESS 5179. Also Dublin, 1754 and London, 1761, etc.
Locations: L; PU; RPJCB

1751#8
The case of the colony *of Rhode Island, with respect to the bill depending in Parliament to regulate and restrain paper bills of credit...* London. 4p. 2o. [1751]
Note: The bill was read 27 March 1751 and referred to Rhode Island, Connecticut, Massachusetts and New Hampshire.
Locations: L; RPJCB, CSmH, MH-BA

1751#9
CHALKLEY, Thomas. *A collection of the works of Thomas Chalkley. In two parts...* London. L. Hinde, 2 vols. 8vo. 1751
Note: SMITH I, 401, SABIN 11747. First published Philadelphia, 1749, (EVANS 6297).
Locations: L; MH, NNC, CSmH

1751#10
CHALKLEY, Thomas. *A journal, or, historical account of the life, travels and Christian experiences, of... Thomas Chalkley...* London. L. Hinde, 326p. 8vo. 1751
Note: HIGGS 85, SABIN 11749. The 'first edition' was part of his works. Other editions in 1751 and 1766.
Locations: L; RPJCB, DLC, MiU-C

1751#11
COLDEN, Cadwallader. *The principles of action in matter, the gravitation of bodies, and the motion of the planets, explained from their principles.* London. R. Dodsley, 215p. 4to. 1751
Note: Cf. SABIN 14268.
Locations: L; Eu; NN, CtY, MH

1751#12
DAVIES, Samuel. *The substance of a letter from Mr. Davies... to Mr Bellamy of Bethlem, in New England, concerning the state of religion in Virginia...* Glasgow. John Orr, 16p. 8vo. [1751]
Note: First printed Boston, 1751, (EVANS 6657).
Locations: Vi, RPJCB

1751#13
A dissertation on the origin *of the venereal disease; proving that it was not brought from America, but began in Europe by an epidemical distemper. Translated from the original manuscript of an eminent physician.* London. Printed for R. Griffiths, [4], 92p. 12mo. 1751
Note: With a half-title.
Locations: DNLM

1751#14
FRANKLIN, Benjamin. *Experiments and observations on electricity, made at Philadelphia. . . and communicated in several letters to Mr. P. Collinson, of London, F.R.S.* London. E. Cave, 92p. 4to. 1751
Note: SABIN 25505. A second edition was published in 1753 with the addition of 'Supplemental experiments and observations. . . '. A third edition was published as *New experiments and observations on electricity. . .* , (Three parts in one vol., 1760).
Locations: L; DLC, RPJCB, MiU-C

1751#15
GILLIES, John. *An exhortation to the inhabitants of the South Parish of Glasgow. . . Wednesday September 26th, 1750.* Glasgow. John Orr, 2 vols. 8vo. 1751.
Note: In a series, paged continuously with information on David Brainerd, revivals in America, etc.
Locations: Gu; L; (vol I only), C; (vol I only)

1751#16
GREAT BRITAIN. PARLIAMENT. *An act for continuing several laws. . . relating to the praemiums upon the importation of masts, yards, and bowsprits, tar, pitch and turpentine. . .* London. T. Baskett and assigns of R. Baskett, [2]p. F. 1751
Note: Act passed in session 1747–8.
Locations: RPJCB

1751#17
GREAT BRITAIN. PARLIAMENT. *An act for encouraging the making of pot ashes and pearl ashes in the British plantations in America.* London. T. Baskett, 8p. F. 1751
Note: HIGGS 92.
Locations: RPJCB

1751#18
GREAT BRITAIN. PARLIAMENT. *An act to regulate and restrain paper-bills of credit in his majesty's colonies or plantations of Rhode-Island, and Providence plantations, Connecticut the Massachusetts-Bay, and New Hampshire, in America. . .* London. T. Baskett and others, 3p. F. 1751
Note: HIGGS 113.
Locations: L; DLC, RPJCB, MiU-C

1751#19
HARRIS, William. *An historical and critical account of Hugh Peters. After the manner of Mr Beyle.* London. J. Noon and A. Miller, 41p. 8vo. 1751
Note: SABIN 61194.
Locations: L; DLC, RPJCB, MiU-C

1751#20
The importance of settling and fortifying Nova Scotia: with a particular account of the climate, soil and native inhabitants of the country. . . London. J. Scott, 37p. 8vo. 1751
Note: SABIN 56141, HIGGS 83.
Locations: L; E; DLC, RPJCB, MiU-C

1751#21
LENNOX, Charlotte. *The life of Harriot Stuart, written by herself.* London. J. Payne and J. Bouquet, 2 vols. 12mo. 1751
Note: A novel, partly set in New York, where Lennox grew up.
Locations: L; ICN, CtY, MH

1751#22
National expectations on the late change in the ministry. . . London. M. Cooper, 43p. 12mo. 1751
Note: Treats French threat to British colonies.
Locations: L; MB, CSmH, RPJCB

1751#23
Paper currency in North-America. [London?]. s.sh. F. [1751]
Note: Docket title. CSmH 89116.
Locations: CSmH

1751#24
PARSONS, William. *A genuine, impartial, and authentick account of the life of William Parsons, esq; executed at Tyburn, Monday Feb. 11, 1751, for returning from transportation. . .* London. T. Parker, C. Corbett, 70p. 8vo. 1751
Note: SABIN 58922.
Locations: D; RPJCB, NN, ICN

1751#25
PARSONS, William. *Memoirs of the life and adventures of William Parsons, esq; from the time of his entering into life, to his death. . . Written by himself and corrected (with additions) by a gentleman.* London. For F. Stamper, 62p. 8vo. Second and third editions, London, 1751.
Note: DLC has third edition.
Locations: L; NN, IU

1751#26
PARSONS, William. *The trial and remarkable life of William Parsons, who was executed at Tyburn near London, on Monday the 11th of February 17501. for returning from transportation. Publish'd by the minister who attended him while under sentence of death, and at the place of execution. To which is added, two original letters the one, to his father; the other, to his wife.* Newcastle. Sold by Wm. Cuthbert, printer, Newcastle, 16p. 4to. [1751?]
Locations: MHL

1751#27
PHILIPS, Erasmus. *Miscellaneous works consisting of essays political and moral.* London. Mr. Waller, etc. 508p. 8vo. 1751
Note: SABIN 62454. Plantation trade as source of wealth.
Locations: L; C; DLC, CtY

1751#28
POSTLETHWAYT, Malachy. *Observations on trade and taxes; shewing what is required and necessary to rescue and increase the wealth and power of the British nation...* London. For the author, 40p. F. 1751
Note: HIGGS 103.
Locations: MiU-C

1751#29
The present state of the *tobacco-trade, as the late act affects the London-manufacturers considered; in a letter to a friend.* London. M. Cooper, 22p. 8vo. 1751
Note: KRESS 5149.
Locations: E; LVu; RPJCB, NNC, ICU

1751#30
Private virtue and publick spirit *display'd. In a succinct essay on the character of Capt. Thomas Coram...* London. J. Roberts, 28p. 8vo. 1751
Note: Mentions his interest in and plans for Nova Scotia and the production of naval stores; and for the education of Indian girls in North America; and his support for English hatters in their complaints against colonies.
Locations: L; NIC, NNNAM

1751#31
ROCHE, John. *Moravian heresy, wherein the principal errors of that doctrine, as taught throughout several parts of Europe and America... are... proved and refuted.* Dublin, for the author, 332p. 8vo. 1751
Note: An edition wrongly dated MDCXLI (MRu and RPJCB). EA 741/199 says probably printed c.1751. See ESTC for 2 (?) issues.
Locations: L; D; O; CSmH, PPL

1751#32
SAVARY DES BRUSLONS, Jacques. *The universal dictionary of trade and commerce. Translated from the French... by Malachy Postlethwayt.* London. 2 vols., F. [1751, 1755]
Note: HIGGS 11, SABIN 77276. A second edition of volume II was published in 1757.
Locations: DLC, NN, CtY

1751#33
SOCIETY OF FRIENDS. *To the quarterly and monthly meetings of Friends, in Great Britain, Ireland, and America... From the meeting for sufferings in London, the sixth day of the seventh month, 1751...* London. 4p. F. [1751]

Note: SMITH, I, 729. On alteration of year and naming of days and months. Reprinted in Philadelphia, 1751.
Locations: L; Dt; DLC, RPJCB, CtY

1751#34
THOMAS, John (1696–1781). *A sermon preached... February 15, 1750...* London. E. Owen, 80p. 4to. 1751
Note: SABIN 95432. SPG sermon for 1751, with abstract, etc.
Locations: L; DLC, RPJCB, CtY

1751#35
TUCKER, Josiah. *Reflections on the expediency of a law for the naturalization of foreign protestants. In two parts.* London. T. Trye, 32, 68p. 8vo. 1751
Note: HIGGS 70, KRESS 5172. Cites Palatines and Pennsylvania and need to balance German emigration to America with new immigrants.
Locations: L; NN, CSmH, MH-BA

1751#35A
WHITEFIELD, George. *Ten sermons preached on the following subjects...* London. 184p. 12mo. 1751
Note: With a preface by Gilbert Tennent. Includes sermons preached in North America.
Locations: L; PPPrHi

1751#36
WILSON, John. *Address'd to the merchants of London. A genuine narrative of the transactions in Nova Scotia, since the settlement, June 1749, till August the 5th, 1751...* London. A. Henderson, etc. 21p. 8vo. [1751]
Note: SABIN 104650, HIGGS 82, KRESS SUPP. 3906.
Locations: Lrcw; Lse; MH, RPJCB

1752#1
BERKELEY, George. *A miscellany, containing several tracts on various subjects...* London. J. and R. Tonson, 267p. 12mo. 1752
Note: HIGGS 248, KRESS 5183. The first edition, Dublin, 1752 (RPJCB, CtY, MH) is a corrupt text. Contains several of Berkeley's writings on America, including discussions of paper money, his verses on the prospect of the arts and sciences in America, his proposal for the better supplying of churches, etc.
Locations: L; DLC, MH, CtY

1752#2
BONAR, John. *The nature and necessity of a religious education. A sermon... January 6. 1752...* Edinburgh. W. Miller, 54p. 8vo. 1752
Note: Society in Scotland for Propagating Christian Knowledge sermon for 1752. Has state of the Society, including a discussion of Indian society.
Locations: E-NRO; Gu; NjR, NjP

1752#3
The case of the German protestant churches settled in the province of Pensylvania, and in North America. Edinburgh. s.sh. 1/2o. [1752]
Note: Last date mentioned in document at E; is 1751. EVANS 6977 suggests [Philadelphia, 1753]. ESTC lists as [London? 1753?].
Locations: E; L; Lpro; MRu; PHi, PPULC

1752#4
The case of the manufacturers, and others, concerned in the making and vending of beaver hats... London. 4p. F. [1752]
Note: HIGGS 259.
Locations: MnU

1752#5
DAVIES, Samuel. An account of a remarkable work of grace, or the great success of the gospel in Virginia. In a letter... to the Rev. Mr. Bellamy of Bethlem in New-England. London. J. Lewis and J. Englefield, 12p. 12mo. 1752
Note: Cf. EVANS 6657: S. Davies, *The state of religion among the Protestant dissenters in Virginia: in a letter to Rev. Mr Joseph Bellamy*, (Boston, 1751).
Locations: L; DLC, RPJCB, NcD

1752#6
EVANS, Theophilus. The history of modern enthusiasm from the Reformation to the present times. London. W. Owen and W. Clarke, 88p. 8vo. 1752
Note: Chapter 4 on New England witchcraft, chapter 8 on Methodists, Moravians and 'mad enthusiastic freaks in New England'. A second (expanded?) edition in 1757.
Locations: C; O; CSmH, NNC

1752#7
GREAT BRITAIN. LORDS JUSTICES. By the Lords Justices, a proclamation. Hardwicke, C. Hartington, Granville, P. Holdernesse. London. Printed by Thomas Baskett; and by the assigns of Robert Baskett, s.sh F. 1752
Note: STEELE IV, p.80. All officers or persons concerned in the administration of the government of the Colony of Georgia to proceed in the execution of their duties. 'Given at Whitehall the twenty fifth day of June, 1752.'
Locations: Lpro;

1752#8
GREAT BRITAIN. PARLIAMENT. An act for avoiding and putting an end to certain doubts... relating to... wills and codicils, concerning real estates, in... England, and in his majesty's colonies and plantations in America... London. T. Baskett, etc. 8p. F. 1752
Locations: RPJCB

1752#9
GREAT BRITAIN. PARLIAMENT. An act for continuing the act for encouraging the growth of coffee in his majesty's plantations in America... London. T. Baskett, etc., 4p. F. 1752
Locations: RPJCB

1752#10
GREAT BRITAIN. PARLIAMENT. HOUSE OF COMMONS COMMITTEE. Report on the petitions relating to the manufacture of hats... London. 15, 1p. 2o. 1752
Note: New York and Hudson's Bay.
Locations: L; MnU

1752#11
KENNEDY, Archibald. The importance of gaining and preserving the friendship of the Indians to the British interest considered... London. E. Cave, Jr. 46p. 8vo. 1752
Note: SABIN 37392, HIGGS 290. With letter on Indians possibly by Benjamin Franklin. Cf. FORD, 86. First printed New York, 1751, (EVANS 6699).
Locations: L; DLC, RPJCB, MiU-C

1752#12
MOORE, Charles. Prolusio inauguralis, de usu vesicantium, quae cantharides recipiunt, in febribus... Edinburgh. Hamilton, Balfour, Neill, 22p. 4to. 1752
Note: GUERRA states an American author.
Locations: DNLM, NN, PPC

1752#13
OSBALDESTON, Richard. A sermon preached... on Friday February 21, 1752... London. E. Owen, 71p. 4to. 1752
Note: SABIN 57740. SPG sermon for 1752, with abstract, etc.
Locations: L; DLC, RPJCB, CSmH

1752#14
POWNALL, Thomas. Principles of polity, being the grounds and reasons of civil empire... London. E. Owen, 142p. 4to. 1752
Note: SABIN 64830. Pownall served as a colonial governor, but no direct American references.
Locations: L; DLC, RPJCB, MiU-C

1752#15
ROBSON, Joseph. An account of six years residence in Hudson's-Bay, from 1733 to 1736, and 1744 to 1747... London. J. Payne, J. Bouquet, etc., 84, 94p. 8vo. 1752
Note: HIGGS 289. Also sold at Edinburgh, Glasgow and Dublin. Another edition in 1759 (MWA, DLC).
Locations: L; DLC, RPJCB, CtY

1752

1752#16
RUDD, Sayer. *God's promise; a grand incentive to Christian liberality. A sermon preached at Walmer in Kent, on. . . 12 of July 1752.* Canterbury. For the author and sold by S.Birt and J. Smith, 46p. 4to. 1752
Note: On the occasion of a collection for SPG.
Locations: L; CSmH

1752#17
The ruinous condition of the tobacco trade, and the causes thereof mathematically demonstrated. . . London. 21p. 8vo. 1752
Note: HIGGS 118.
Locations: RPJCB, NN

1752#18
SALMON, Thomas. *The universal traveller: or, a compleat description of the several nations of the world. . .* London. R. Baldwin, 2 vols. 2o. [1752–3]
Locations: L; DLC, CtY, InU

1752#19
The Scotch marine, or memoirs of the life of Celestina, who. . . spent two years. . . as a man. . . her marriage afterwards with Cario, a North Briton, in New-England. . . London. J. Robinson, 2 vols in one. 12mo. [1752]
Note: SABIN 78193.
Locations: DLC, MH

1752#20
Ship Catherina. . . John Paasch, master appellant. John Sweet. Commander of the Defiance, Privateer, Respondent. The Appellant's case. London. 4p. F. 1752
Note: The *Defiance* was a Rhode Island privateer; the *Catherina* was condemned in Rhode Island. Also *The Respondent's case*, 7p. F. To be heard 11 June 1752.
Locations: NN

1752#21
Some considerations on the importation and exportation of beaver, with remarks on the hatter's case. London. 2p. 1/2o. [1752]
Note: HIGGS 260.
Locations: L; RPJCB, MnU

1752#22
STERLING, James. *An epistle to the Hon. Arthur Dobbs, esq; in Europe. From a clergyman in America. . .* London. R. Dodsley and M. Cooper, 2, 95p 4to. 1752
Note: In verse. Also Dublin, 1752.
Locations: CSmH, RPJCB, NN

1752#23
THORNTON, William. *The counterpoise. Being thoughts on a militia and a standing army. . .* London. M. Cooper, 4, 60p. 8vo. 1752

Note: References to New England militia. Another edition in 1753.
Locations: L; NN, CtY, CSmH

1752#24
The William Galley, ship. Lords Commissioners of Prizes. . . The appellants case. London. 3, (1) p. F. [1752]
Note: SABIN 104157. Rhode Island privateering.
Locations: NN

1753#1
B., G. *The advantages of the Revolution illustrated, by a view of the present state of Great Britain. . .* London. W. Owen, 38p. 8vo. 1753
Note: SABIN 470, HIGGS 539. References to the thriving state of the American colonies.
Locations: L; MiU-C, CtY, NN

1753#2
BRAINERD, John. *A genuine letter from Mr. John Brainard [sic], employed by the Scotch Society for Propagating the Gospel, a missionary to the Indians in America, and Minister to a congregation of Indians at Bethel, in East Jersey, to his friend in England. . .* London. J. Ward, 16p. 8vo. 1753
Locations: C; O; Ldw; PPL, DLC, RPJCB, NN

1753#3
A complete answer to the clergyman's letter to the right honourable the Earl of — concerning the affair of Elizabeth Canning. In which are contained, many observations that have escaped the notice of the British writers on this subject by a wild indian, suddenly landed in England from California. London. For the author and printed by J. Fuller, 4, 59, 1p. 8vo. 1753
Note: *Clergyman's letter* was by Allan Ramsay.
Locations: L; MH

1753#4
CRESSETT, Edward. *A sermon preach'd. . . February 16, 1753. . .* London. E. Owen, 79p. 4to. 1753
Note: SABIN 17482. SPG sermon for 1753, with abstract, etc.
Locations: L; DLC, RPJCB, NN

1753#5
DURNO, J. *A description of a new-invented stove-grate, shewing its uses. . . over all others. . .* London. J. Towers, 32p. 8vo. 1753
Note: Examines different stoves, fully describing Franklin's and offering improvements on it.
Locations: C; Ct; RPJCB, CtY

1753#6
FOTHERGILL, John. *An account of the life and travels in the work of the ministry, of J. F. To which are*

added, *divers epistles to friends in Great Britain and America...* London. Luke Hinde, xxviii, 338p. 8vo. 1753
Note: SABIN 25270. Reprinted Philadelphia, 1754.
Locations: L; Ldhs; RPJCB, CSmH, MH

1753#7
FREYEN, ANDREAS. *A true and authentic account of A. F., concerning the occasion of his coming among the Herrnhuters or Moravians...* London. J. Robinson and others, 72p. 8vo. 1753
Note: SABIN 71410, HIGGS 652.
Locations: L; NjR, NNUT

1753#8
The general shop book: or, the tradesman's universal director... explaining the domestic and foreign trade of Great Britain and the plantations... London. C. Hitch, etc. 460p. 8vo. 1753
Note: DERENNE I, 130, KRESS 5264.
Locations: L; GU-DeR

1753#9
GREAT BRITAIN. PARLIAMENT. *An act for vesting the parts or shares late belonging to Benjamin Brain, merchant, deceased, of and in one twenty-fourth part of the eastern division of the province of New Jersey in America, in trustees, to be sold for the purposes therein mentioned.* London. 7p. 2o. [1753]
Note: An enacted private act.
Locations: L;

1753#10
GREEN, John. *Remarks, in support of the new chart of North and South America; in six sheets.* London. T. Jefferys, 48p. 4to. [1753?]
Note: SABIN 28538. Issued to accompany *A chart of North and South America...*, (1753).
Locations: L; O; DLC, RPJCB, NN

1753#11
HILL, Aaron. *The works of the late Aaron Hill, Esq; consisting of letters on various subjects, and of original poems...* London. Printed for the benefit of the family. 4 vols. 8vo. 1753
Note: Second edition, 1754. Vol IV contains his 'On giving the name of Georgia to a part of Carolina'.
Locations: L; CtY, ICU

1753#12
HOLME, Benjamin. *A collection of the epistles and works of Benjamin Holme... his life and travels in the work of the ministry, through several parts of Europe and America...* London. L. Hinde, 194p. 8vo. 1753
Note: SABIN 32573. Another edition in 1754.
Locations: L; DLC, RPJCB, FU

1753#13
JAY, James (1732–1815). *Dissertatio medica inauguralis, de fluoro albo...* Edinburgh. Hamilton, Balfour and Neill, 28p. 4to. 1753
Note: SABIN 35826. The author was born in New York City.
Locations: DNLM, CLU-M, OClW-Hi

1753#14
JONES, Hugh. *The Pancronometer, or universal Georgian calendar...* London. E. Cave, J. Payne, W. Clarke, 66p. 4to. 1753
Note: Partly based on scriptures.
Locations: L; PPL

1753#15
MACSPARRAN, James. *America dissected, being a full and true account of all the American colonies... Published as a caution to unsteady people who may be tempted to leave their native country.* Dublin. 48p. 8vo. 1753
Note: HIGGS 544. Letters are dated 1752 and are not noticeably anti-American.
Locations: MWA, DLC, RPJCB, NN

1753#16
MADDOX, Isaac. *A sermon preached before his grace the Duke of Marlborough... March 5 1752... To which is added a postscript, containing an account of the small-pox and inoculation, at Boston in New-England, in the year 1752.* London. H. Woodfall, 32p. 4to. [1753?]
Note: Cf. SABIN 43699, HIGGS 615. The fifth edition, but the first with the postscript.
Locations: L; DNLM

1753#17
MAGENS, Nikolaus. *The universal merchant: containing a rationale of commerce, in theory and practice.* London. W. Owen, 3, 131p. 4to. 1753
Note: KRESS 5283.
Locations: L; DLC, NN

1753#18
MILLAN, John d. 1782. *Arms of the baronets of England, and Nova Scotia. With crests, supporters, mottos, family honours... By John Millan... corrected to September 1753.* London. Printed for said J. Millan, 40p. 12mo. [1753?]
Locations: E; RPJCB

1753#19
RIMIUS, Heinrich. *A candid narrative of the rise and progress of the Herrnhuters, commonly called Moravians...* London. A. Linde, 16, 139, 38p. 8vo. 1753
Note: SABIN 71404. Second edition in 1753; and reprinted Philadelphia, 1753. Mainly deals with Moravians in Germany.
Locations: L; RPJCB

1753

1753#20
A Speech deliver'd by an *Indian chief, in reply to a sermon by a Swedish missionary, in order to convert the Indians to the Christian religion.* London. 8p. 8vo. 1753
Note: SABIN 89174. The missionary was Joen Auren. Signed 'Philanthropos'. First printed [Philadelphia, 1715?] (BRISTOL B494).
Locations: L; ICN

1753#21
STITH, William. *The history of the first discovery and settlement of Virginia. . .* London. Virginia printed, London reprinted. S. Birt, 341p. 8vo. 1753
Note: SABIN 91861, HIGGS 545. With an appendix containing a collection of ancient charters, etc. First printed Williamsburg, 1747, (EVANS 6071).
Locations: L; DLC, RPJCB, MH

1753#22
WALLACE, Robert. *A dissertation on the numbers of mankind in antient and modern times: in which the superior populousness of antiquity is maintained. . .* Edinburgh. G. Hamilton, J. Balfour, 331p. 8vo. 1753
Note: KRESS 5318, HIGGS 619. Material on America and on slavery.
Locations: L; ViU, NN

1753#23
WHITEFIELD, George. *An expostulatory letter, addressed to Nicholas Lewis, Count Zinzendorff. . .* London. G. Keith, etc., 19p. 8vo. 1753
Note: SABIN 103512. A second edition in 1753.
Locations: L; RPJCB, ICN, CtY

1754#1
An abstract of the case *of the Honourable James Annesley. . . humbly submitted to the consideration of all disinterested persons. . .* Dublin. 118p. 8vo. 1754
Locations: D; MH-L, NN

1754#2
BURT, Edward. *Letters from a gentleman in the north of Scotland to his friend in London. . . In two volumes.* London. For S. Birt, 2 vols. in one, 344, 368p. 8vo. 1754
Note: SABIN 6830, HIGGS 892. Letter X is (spurious?) letter from Donald Macpherson, a young lad who was sent to Virginia in 1715, on account of his having joined his chieftain in the cause of his king and country. The letters date from the 1720s and 1730s.
Locations: L; RPJCB, CSmH, ICN

1754#3
C., T. *A scheme to drive the French out of all the continent of America. . .* London. 23p. 8vo. 1754

Note: SABIN 77555. Reprinted Boston 1755, (EVANS 7377).
Locations: L; O; DLC, MiU-C

1754#4
The Canninad. Or, Betty's soliloquy *in Newgate, on the night destin'd for her departure to her American settlement, but luckily proving the eve of her deliverance. A song. To the tune of, A lass that was laden with care.* London printed by C. Sympson, 11, [1]p. 4to. 1754
Note: Transportation of Elizabeth Canning.
Locations: Gu; DLC

1754#5
CARTER, Landon. *A letter from a gentleman in Virginia, to the merchants of Great Britain, trading to that colony.* London. 36p. 8vo. 1754
Note: SABIN 40292.
Locations: Lu; DLC, RPJCB, ViU

1754#6
CRADOCK, Thomas. *A new poetical translation of the Psalmes of David. . .* London. Printed for Mrs. A. Cradock at Wells and sold by R. Ware, London. 186p. 8vo. 1754
Note: Cradock was a Virginia clergyman.
Locations: L; NN, NjP

1754#7
DAVIES, Samuel. *The duties, difficulties and reward of the faithful minister. A sermon, preached at the installation of the Revd. Mr. John Todd, A.B. into the pastoral charge of the Presbyterian congregation, in and about the upper part of Hanover county in Virginia, Nov. 12, 1752. With an appendix. . .* Glasgow. W. Duncan, jr. 18, 114p. 8vo. 1754
Locations: L; NN

1754#8
DAVIES, Samuel. *A sermon preached at Henrico, 29 April 1753. And at Canongate, 26th May 1754.* Edinburgh. W.Gray and W.Peter, 23p. 4to. 1754
Note: Sermon was in support of College of New Jersey.
Locations: L; Vi, PPPrHi, NcU

1754#9
DOBBS, Arthur. *A letter from a Russian sea-officer. . . relative to the new discoveries northward and eastward from Kamatschatka. Together with some observations on that letter, by Arthur Dobbs. . . Governor of North Carolina. . .* London. A. Linde, 83p. 8vo. 1754
Locations: L; DLC

1754#10
DRUMMOND, Robert Hay. *A sermon preached. . . February 15, 1754. . .* London. E. Owen, 87p. 4to. 1754

Note: SABIN 20967. SPG sermon for 1754, with abstract, etc.
Locations: L; DLC, RPJCB, CtY

1754#11
EDINBURGH PHILOSOPHICAL SOCIETY. *Essays and observations, read before a Society in Edinburgh, and published by them.* . . Edinburgh. G. Hamilton and J. Balfour, 2 vols. 8vo. [1754–6]
Note: HIGGS 909. Some American materials. Volume III published in 1771.
Locations: L; DLC, CtY, ICN

1754#12
GILLIES, John. *Historical collections relating to remarkable periods of the success of the Gospel, and eminent instruments employed in promoting it.* Glasgow. R. and A. Foulis, 2 vols. 8vo. 1754
Note: SABIN 27413.
Locations: L; RPJCB, MiU-C, NN

1754#13
GREAT BRITAIN. LORDS COMMISSIONERS FOR OPENING PARLIAMENT. *The speech of the Lord Commissioners to both Houses of Parliament. . . 1 June 1754.* London. T. Baskett, 4p. F. 1754
Note: War and North America.
Locations: RPJCB

1754#14
GREAT BRITAIN. PARLIAMENT. HOUSE OF COMMONS. *A bill for establishing a method to bar entails upon the province of Maryland.* London. [15]p. [1754]
Locations: L; DLC

1754#15
GREAT BRITAIN. SOVEREIGN. GEORGE II. *Whereas some doubts have arisen with regard to the rank and command, which officers and troops raised by the governors of our provinces in North-America, should have. . .* London. 3, (1)p. F. [1754]
Note: 'Orders for settling the rank of the officers of his majesty's forces, when joined, or serving with the provincial forces in North America.' Given at Court, 12 November 1754.
Locations: CSmH

1754#16
HUME, Sophia. *An epistle to the inhabitants of South Carolina; containing sundry observations proper to be consider'd by every professor of Christianity in general.* London. L. Hinde, 114p. 8vo. 1754

Note: SABIN 33781, SMITH I, 1020.
Locations: L; MH, RPJCB, NN

1754#17
JEFFERYS, Thomas. *The conduct of the French, with regard to Nova Scotia; from its first settlement to the present time. . . In a letter to a member of Parliament.* London. T. Jefferys, 77p. 8vo. 1754
Note: SABIN 35975, HIGGS 776. Also Dublin, 1754 and a French translation, London, chez T. Jefferys, 1754 and another edition, Londres [i.e. Paris], chez les frères Vaillant, 1755. Also discusses Virginia.
Locations: L; MRu; DLC, RPJCB, NN

1754#18
JOHNSON, Samuel (1696–1772). *The elements of philosophy. . . to which is added, an original letter concerning the settlement of bishops in America. . . the third edition corrected and enlarged.* London. A. Millar, 271p. 12mo. 1754
Note: First and second editions, Philadelphia and New York, 1752 (EVANS 6859–60).
Locations: L; C; RPJCB, NN, CtY

1754#19
KENNEDY, Archibald. *Serious considerations on the present state of the affairs of the northern colonies.* London. New York printed, London reprinted. R. Griffiths, 24p. 8vo. [1754?]
Note: HIGGS 782. First printed New York, 1754; also Philadelphia, 1754 and New York, 1756, (EVANS 7223–4, 7692).
Locations: L; DLC, NN, RPJCB

1754#20
KIMBER, Edward. *History of the life and adventures of Mr. Anderson. Containing his strange varieties of fortune in Europe and America. . .* London. W. Owen, 288p. 12mo. 1754
Note: SABIN 1380. Another London edition in 1754. Also Dublin, 1754 (L;). Other editions 1780, etc.
Locations: DLC, ViU, CtY

1754#21
KIRKPATRICK, James. *The analysis of inoculation: comprizing the history, theory and practice of it. . .* London. J. Buckland, etc. 429p. 8vo. 1754
Note: Also an edition by J. Millar, xxiv, 288p.
Locations: L; DLC, CtY, RPJCB

1754#22
LAFARGUE, Etienne de. *Histoire géographique de la Nouvelle Ecosse. . .* London. A Londres, 164p. 8vo. 1754
Note: Possibly printed in Paris.
Locations: L; DLC, RPJCB, NN

1754

1754#23
LANCEY, John. *A genuine account of the burning the Nightingale Brig, lately belonging to Thomas Benson...* London. H. Slater, jr., 56p. 8vo. 1754
Note: HIGGS 755. First and second edition (RPJCB) in 1754? Voyage to Maryland and alleged insurance fraud.
Locations: L;

1754#24
MAYHEW, Jonathan. *A sermon preach'd in the audience of His Excellency William Shirley,... the Honourable His Majesty's council, and the... House of Representatives, of the province of the Massachusetts-Bay, in New-England. May 29, 1754...* London. Boston printed: London, reprinted for G. Woodfall, 56p. 8vo. 1754
Note: First printed Boston, 1754, EVANS 7256, *Dr. Mayhew's election sermon. May 29, 1754.*
Locations: L; Omc; MH-AH, MWA, NN

1754#25
McCULLOH, Henry. *General thoughts on the construction, use and abuse of the great offices...* London. R. Baldwin, 29p. 8vo. 1754
Note: HIGGS 794. Some discussion of Britain and America.
Locations: L; RPJCB, MiU-C, CSmH

1754#26
A Memorial of the case of the German emigrants settled in the British colonies of Pensilvania, and the back parts of Maryland, Virginia, etc... London. 20, 8p. 8vo. 1754
Note: SABIN 25554, HIGGS 772. With an appendix. Sometimes mistakenly attributed to Benjamin Franklin.
Locations: L; DLC, RPJCB, CtY

1754#27
NEWTON, Thomas. *Dissertations on the prophecies, which have remarkably been fulfilled, and at this time are fulfilling in the world.* London. J. and R. Tonson and S. Draper, 3 vols. 8vo. 1754
Note: Published 1754–8. Discusses Mede, Gog, Magog, and America, and has a few other New World references. A second edition in 1759–60. Numerous other editions before 1800.
Locations: L; C; Dt; MH, TxU, NIC

1754#28
PEYTON, Valentine. *Dissertatio medica inauguralis de abortu...* Edinburgh. Hamilton, Balfour and Neill, 31p. 8vo. 1754
Note: Peyton was 'Virginiensis'.
Locations: DLC, DNLM

1754#29
PLENDERLEATH, David. *Religion a treasure to men, and the strength and glory of a nation. A sermon... January 7. 1754...* Edinburgh. Hamilton, Balfour and Neill, 80p. 8vo. 1754
Note: Society in Scotland for Propagating Christian Knowledge sermon for 1754, with state of the Society which has section on America.
Locations: E; DLC, MH

1754#30
PLUMARD DE DANGEUL, Louis Joseph. *Remarks on the advantages and disadvantages of France and of Great Britain with respect to commerce...* London. T. Osborn, 273p. 12mo. 1754
Note: SABIN 63940.
Locations: L; DLC, RPJCB, MiU-C

1754#31
R., P. *A Letter to a friend in America; wherein is clearly held forth the peculiar interest that the elect have in the death of Christ, by virtue of a special appointment, in opposition to Arminians.* Edinburgh. xii, 120p. 8vo. 1754
Locations: L; E; ABu; CU-SB

1754#32
The representation of the committee of the English congregations in union with the Moravian church. London. 16p. 8vo. [1754]
Note: Cites good reports of Moravians in colonies. Prepared by the Rev. James Hulton and the Rev. John Gambold.
Locations: L; PHi

1754#33
RIMIUS, Heinrich. *The history of the Moravians, from their first settlement at Herrnhaag...* London. J. Robinson, 208p. 8vo. 1754
Note: Another edition, 1759.
Locations: L; RPJCB, MH, NN

1754#34
RIMIUS, Heinrich. *A solemn call on Count Zinzendorf, the author, and advocate of the sect of Herrnhuters, commonly call'd Moravians...* London. 28p. 8vo. 1754
Note: SABIN 71408. Another edition in 1757. Attacks Zinzendorf for deception in getting settlements for Moravians in colonies.
Locations: L; DLC, CtY, ICN

1754#35
SMITH, William *(1727–1803)*. *Some account of the North-America Indians... To which are added Indian Miscellanies... by a learned and ingenious gentleman of the province of Pennsylvania...* London. R. Griffiths, 68p. 8vo. [1754]
Note: SABIN 84671, HIGGS 770.
Locations: L; DLC, RPJCB, CtY

1754#36
SMITH, William *(1727–1803)*. *The speech of a Creek-Indians [sic], against the immoderate use of spirituous liquors. Delivered in a national assembly of the Creeks, upon the outbreak of the late war. To which are added, 1. A letter from Yariza, an Indian maid. . . 2. Indian songs of peace. 3. An American fable. . . Together with some remarks upon the characters and genius of the Indians. . . customs. . . ceremonies. . .* London. R. Griffiths, 68p. 8vo. 1754
Note: First printed Boston, [1754?], (EVANS 7321). Reissued in 1754 as *Some account of the North-American Indians. . .* (L; RPJCB).
Locations: L; DLC, RPJCB, PHi

1754#37
SOCIETY OF FRIENDS. *To the quarterly and monthly meetings of Friends in Pennsilvania and elsewhere in America. . .* London. 2p. 2o. 1754
Note: SMITH, I, 729. On readjustment of Quaker calendar.
Locations: L; NN

1754#38
STUDENT IN POLITICS. *Proposals to the legislature, for preventing the frequent execution and exportations of convicts. . .* London. M. Cooper, 50p. 8vo. 1754
Note: Advocates a kind of public slavery in England since transportees serve as virtual slaves in America. Attacks capital punishment.
Locations: L; Ct;

1754#39
TENNENT, Gilbert. *To the worthy and generous friends of religion and learning; the petition of Gilbert Tennent and Samuel Davies, in the name of the trustees of the infant college of New-Jersey, and many of the inhabitants of that, and the neighbouring provinces. . .* London. 4p. F. [1754]
Note: SABIN 94708. Petition dated London, Jan. 19, 1754.
Locations: L; NjP

1754#40
TENNENT, Gilbert and DAVIES, Samuel. *A general account of the rise and state of the College, lately established in the province of New-Jersey, in America. . . Originally published in America, an. 1752, by the Trustees. . . now republished. . . with some alterations. . .* London. 7p. F. 1754
Note: SABIN 94691. Also Edinburgh (RPJCB). First edition, New York 1752 (BRISTOL 40640).
Locations: L; MWA

1754#41
WASHINGTON, George. *The journal of Major George Washington, sent by. . . Robert Dinwiddie. . . lieutenant-governor of Virginia, to the commandant of the French forces on the Ohio. . . with a new map. . .* London. Williamsburg printed, London reprinted. T. Jefferys, 32p. 8vo. 1754
Note: SABIN 101710. First printed Williamsburg, 1754 (EVANS 7331).
Locations: L; DLC, RPJCB, MiU-C

1754#42
WESTON, William. *The complete merchant's clerk: or, British and American compting-house. In two parts. . . To which is added, an appendix. . .* London. Printed by Charles Rivington, for R. Griffiths, [308]p. 8vo. 1754
Locations: L; E; NjP, NNC, DLC, RPJCB

1755#1
ANGELONI, Battista *[pseudonym for J. Shebbeare]*. *Letters on the English nation. . .* London. 2 vols. 8vo. 1755
Note: HIGGS 1355. Second edition in 1756 (L;). Substantial North American references.
Locations: L; MHi, DLC, CSmH

1755#2
An answer to a pamphlet, *called, A Second Letter to the People. . . In which the subsidiary system is fairly stated. . .* London. M. Cooper, 35p. 8vo. 1755
Note: SABIN 80056n. Answer to Shebbeare's pamphlet. North America and European treaty systems.
Locations: L; O; CtY, NN, CSmH

1755#3
BATHER, James. *A full and faithful account of the life of James Bather, late. . . of. . . Nightingale Brig. . .* London. R. Griffiths, 31p. 8vo. [1755]
Note: SABIN 3954. References to voyages to North America. Insurance fraud.
Locations: L; NcD, NcU

1755#4
BUTEL-DUMONT, Georges. *Histoire et commerce des colonies angloises, dans l'Amérique septentrionale. . .* London. 336p. 12mo. 1755
Note: SABIN 9602, HIGGS 1029. Published 'A Londres', but probably Paris. Another issue in 1755.
Locations: L; Lu; DLC, RPJCB, MiU-C

1755#5
CHAUNCY, Charles *(1705–87)*. *A letter to a friend; giving a concise, but just, account. . . of the Ohio-defeat. . .* London. Boston printed, London reprinted. J. Noon, 28p. 8vo. 1755
Note: SABIN 12320. Also Bristol, 1755, reprinted by E. Ward on the Tolzey, 30p. 8vo. Signed 'T. W.' First printed Boston, 1755, (EVANS 7381). Also attributed to Timothy Walker.
Locations: RPJCB, MHi

1755

1755#6
CHAUNCY, Charles *(1705–1787)*. *Two letters to a friend, on the present critical conjuncture of affairs in North America; particularly on the vast importance of the victory gained by the New-England militia. . . at Lake-George. . .* London. Boston printed, London reprinted. For T. Jefferys, 54p. 8vo. 1755
Note: First printed as two separate letters, Boston, 1755, EVANS 7381–2.
Locations: L; O; DLC; RPJCB, MiU-C

1755#7
CLARKE, William. *Observations on the late and present conduct of the French, with regard to their encroachments upon the British colonies in North America. . . to which is added, wrote by another hand, Observations concerning the present increase of mankind. . .* London. Boston printed, London reprinted. John Clarke, 54p. 8vo. 1755
Note: SABIN 13471, HIGGS 1003, KRESS 5427. First printed Boston, 1755, (EVANS 7389). The demographic 'Observations' were by Benjamin Franklin.
Locations: L; O; NNC, RPJCB, MiU-C

1755#8
A clear and succinct account of North America, historical, geographical, etc. so far as it respects the arguments of the present time. . . Dublin. R. James, 48p. 8vo. 1755
Note: SABIN 13583. Supports English claims to French colonies and discusses relative colonial populations.
Locations: RPJCB, PHi, PPULC

1755#9
A constituent's answer to the reflexions of a member of Parliament upon the present state of affairs at home and abroad; particularly with regard to subsidies and the differences between Great Britain and France. . . London. J. Robinson, 48p. 8vo. [1755]
Note: Discusses North American war and Britain's trade.
Locations: L; DLC, RPJCB, MiU-C

1755#10
Copies of Pennsylvania assembly's present address to his majesty, and of the royal instructions given in 1740. . . London. s.sh. F. [1755]
Locations: NN

1755#11
Copies of the lieutenant-governor of Pennsylvania, his speeches to the assembly, their addresses in answer thereto, and several messages and answers, between them. London. 18p. F. 1755
Note: SABIN 60025.
Locations: RPJCB

1755#12
CROSS, –. *An answer to an invidious pamphlet, intituled, A brief state of the province of Pennsylvania. . .* London. S. Bladon, 80p. 8vo. 1755
Note: HIGGS 1009.
Locations: L; DLC, CSmH, MiU-C

1755#13
DAVIES, Samuel. *The following verses were composed by a pious clergyman in Virginia, who preaches to seven congregations. . .* London. 4p. 2o. [1755?]
Note: FOXON D62. Cf. *Miscellaneous poems, chiefly on divine subjects. . .*, Williamsburgh, 1751 (EVANS 6834).
Locations: L; DLC, MH, MiU-C

1755#14
DE LA ROCHE, ——. *A letter from Quebeck, in Canada, to M. L'Maine, a French officer. Which contains a particular account of the present designs of the French upon the English in North-America. . .* Edinburgh. Boston printed, Edinburgh reprinted. W. Gray, W. Peter, 11p. 12mo. 1755
Note: Cf. SABIN 72305. First printed Boston, 1754, (EVANS 7225). Spurious propaganda.
Locations: E; NN, MiU-C

1755#15
A description of the English and French territories, in North America: being, an explanation of a new map of the same. Shewing all the encroachments of the French. . . Dublin. J. Exshaw, 28p. 8vo. 1755
Note: SABIN 19716, HIGGS 1249. Another edition, Dublin, 1756 (L;).
Locations: NN, CSmH, MiU-C

1755#16
DODSLEY, Robert. *A collection of poems in four volumes. By several hands.* London. R. and J. Dodsley, 4 vols. 8vo. 1755
Note: Vol. I contains T. Tickell's 'On the prospect of peace' with references to savage Indians; Vol. IV has 'The Rake' by a 'lady in New England'.
Locations: L; CtY, ICN, MiU

1755#17
DOUGLAS, John *(1721–1807)*. *The destruction of the French foretold by Ezekiel; or, a commentary on the thirty-fifth chapter of that prophet. . .* London. M. Cooper, 47p. 8vo. [1755?]
Note: Several pages on America: mountains of Israel represent Alleghanies, etc. A satire on William Romaine and the Hutchinsonian prophets.
Locations: L; MH, OCH

1755#18
DOUGLASS, William. *A summary, historical and political, of the first planting, progressive improvements, and*

218

present state of the British settlements in North-America... London. Boston printed, London reprinted. R. Baldwin, 2 vols. 8vo. 1755

Note: SABIN 20727, HIGGS 999. Cf. HANSON 6074. Another edition, London, 1760. First printed in parts in Boston; complete edition in Boston of Vol I in 1749 and Vol. II in 1753. See EVANS 5936, 6126, 6306–7, 6490, 6662–3, 6992, 7885.

Locations: L; C; Dt; RPJCB, MH, MiU-C

1755#19
ESTRADES, Godefroi Louis. *Letters and negotiations of Count d'Estrades... from MDXXVIII to MDCLXIII, containing an account of... troubles that happened to King Charles I... and the cession of Acadie or Nova Scotia...* London. R. Willock, 319p. 8vo. 1755

Locations: DLC, CSmH, MiU-C

1755#20
The expedition of Major General Braddock to Virginia; with the two regiments of Hacket and Dunbar... extracts of letters from an officer to his friend in London... London. H. Carpenter, 29p. 8vo. 1755

Note: SABIN 7210.

Locations: L; RPJCB, ViU, MiU-C

1755#21
GIBBONS, Thomas. *Sympathy with our suffering brethren... two discourses... To which are prefixed, some serious reflections on the present situation of these nations, and our American colonies.* London. J. Buckland, etc. 80p. 8vo. 1755

Note: SABIN 27292.

Locations: L; DLC, MiU-C, MH

1755#22
GREAT BRITAIN. BOARD OF TRADE. COMMISSION FOR ADJUSTING BOUNDARIES. *The memorials of the French and English commissaries concerning the limits of Nova Scotia or Acadia.* London. 2 vols. 4to. 1755

Note: SABIN 47741–2, HIGGS 1036. Vol. 2 relates to St. Lucia.

Locations: L; C; Dt; NN, RPJCB, MiU-C

1755#23
GREAT BRITAIN. PARLIAMENT. HOUSE OF LORDS. *The humble address of the... Lords... presented to his majesty... November, 1755...* London. J. Baskett. 1755

Note: French and Indian war.

Locations: RPJCB, MiU-C, MB

1755#24
GREAT BRITAIN. SOVEREIGN. GEORGE II. *His majesties most gracious speech to both houses of Parliament... on... the thirteenth day of November 1755.* London. T. Baskett, 4p. F. 1755

Locations: L; RPJCB

1755#25
GREEN, John and JEFFERYS, Thomas. *Explanation for the new map of Nova Scotia and Cape Breton, with the adjacent parts of New England and Canada.* London. T. Jefferys, 22p. 4to. 1755

Locations: L; E; MH, RPJCB

1755#26
GREEN, Thomas. *A dissertation on enthusiasm...* London. J. Oliver, T. Payne, 220p. 8vo. 1755

Note: Some North American references.

Locations: L; ICN, IU, PHC

1755#27
HAYTER, Thomas. *A sermon preached... February 21, 1755...* London. E. Owen, 80p. 4to. 1755

Note: SPG sermon for 1755, with abstract, etc.

Locations: L; DLC, RPJCB, CtY

1755#28
Humorous and diverting dialogues between Monsieur Baboon, a French dancing-master, (but lately come-over:) and Jack Tar, an English sailor. London. C. Corbet, 24p. 8vo. 1755

Note: A crude satire. CSmH 353944.

Locations: O; CSmH

1755#29
HUSKE, Ellis. *The present state of North America... Part I.* London. R. and J. Dodsley, 88p. 4to. 1755

Note: SABIN 30794, 34027, HIGGS 1000. Also Dublin, 1755; and a second edition with emendations, London, 1755. No part two. Reprinted Boston, 1755, with parts two and three.

Locations: L; O; DLC, CtY, NN

1755#30
HUTCHESON, Francis. *A system of moral philosophy, in three books...* Glasgow. A. Foulis; London, A. Millar, 2 vols. 4to. 1755

Note: HIGGS 935, KRESS 5445. Discussion of slavery and colonial rights.

Locations: L; DLC, MH-BA, CtY

1755#31
Ireland disgraced; or, the island of saints become an island of sinners clearly proved in a dialogue... London. P. Wilkie, vi, 75p. 8vo. 1755

Note: Other editions in 1758, 1760. Anglo-Irish politics and American-Irish trade.

Locations: L; RPJCB

1755#32
JONES, John. *A letter to a friend in the country, upon the news of the town.* London. J. Raymond, 47p. 8vo. 1755
Note: SABIN 40382, 40384. Also Bristol, 1755. Discusses French encroachments in North America as part of consistent scheme since Treaty of Utrecht.
Locations: L; RPJCB, MiU-C

1755#33
A Letter from a member of Parliament to. . . the Duke of ****** upon the present situation of affairs. London. M. Cooper, 25p. 8vo. 1755
Note: SABIN 40300, HIGGS 1011, KRESS 5450.
Locations: L; DLC, MiU-C, NN

1755#34
McCULLOH, Henry. *A miscellaneous essay concerning the courses pursued by Great Britain in the affairs of her colonies: with some observations on the great importance of our settlements in America, and the trade thereof.* London. R. Baldwin, 134p. 8vo. 1755
Note: SABIN 43123, HIGGS 995.
Locations: L; MRu; DLC, RPJCB, MiU-C

1755#35
McCULLOH, Henry. *The wisdom and policy of the French in the construction of their great offices. . . With some observations on. . . disputes. . . English and French colonies. . . America.* London. R. Baldwin, 133p. 8vo. 1755
Note: HIGGS 994, 1007
Locations: L; DLC, RPJCB, MiU-C

1755#36
The names of the lords and gentlemen, entrusted with the moneys collected for the use of the German emigrants in Pensilvania, and other provinces of North America. London. s.sh. 1/4o. [1755?]
Locations: L; (Dept of MSS)

1755#37
A new and complete history of the British empire in America. . . London. 3 vols. 8vo. [1755–7]
Note: SABIN 52443. Serial published 1755–7.
Locations: MH, MiU-C

1755#38
A new song. [Edinburgh?] s.sh. F. [1755]
Note: Concerns recruiting of Scots troops for French and Indian war.
Locations: RPJCB

1755#39
OGLETHORPE, William. *The Naked Truth. Number I. . . addressed to the people of Great Britain, Ireland and America.* London. A. Price, 31p. 8vo. 1755

Note: Attributed to Oglethorpe. Ministerial failures in America. Second edition, with additions in 1755 and three more London editions in 1755; also printed in Londres [i.e. Paris], 1755.
Locations: L; E; MiU-C, NN

1755#40
PALAIRET, Jean. *A concise description of the English and French possessions in North-America, for the better explaining of the map published with that title.* London. J. Haberkorn, 71p. 8vo. 1755
Note: SABIN 58308. Also sold in Dublin. A second edition improved, London, 1755.
Locations: L; E; CaAEU, MH, NN

1755#41
PITT, William. *The Monitor: a speech. . . by the Honourable W——m P—t.* London. 12p. 8vo. 1755
Note: Probably spurious. France and North America.
Locations: RPJCB, MiU-C, PU

1755#42
Reflections upon the present state of affairs, at home and abroad. . . In a letter from a member of Parliament to a constituent. . . London. J. Payne, 60p. 8vo. 1755
Note: SABIN 68727, KRESS 5466.
Locations: L; DLC, RPJCB, MiU-C

1755#43
RIMIUS, Heinrich. *A supplement to the candid narrative of the rise and progress of the Herrnhuters, commonly called Moravians. . . in which the political scheme. . . of their patriarch are disclosed. . .* London. A. Linde, xxx, lxxii, 96p. 8vo. 1755
Note: SABIN 71409.
Locations: L; RPJCB

1755#44
ROBERTSON, William. *The situation of the world at the time of Christ's appearance. . . sermon. . . January 6, 1755. . .* Edinburgh. Hamilton, Balfour and Neill, 70p. 8vo. 1755
Note: SABIN 72005. Society in Scotland for Propagating Christian Knowledge sermon for 1755. Other editions, including Edinburgh, 1759 and 1775.
Locations: L; DLC, MH, CtY

1755#45
SAGEAN, Mathieu. *The original manuscript account of the kingdom of Aacaniba, given by the affidavit of Mathieu Sagean a Frenchman. . . Englished by Quin Mackenzie. . .* London. Printed for the translator, 4, 10p. F. 1755
Note: SABIN 74898note. Fictitious relation of the Mississippi.
Locations: L; RPJCB, DLC, NN

1755#46
A sceene of sceenes. Extract *of a letter from a merchant in Boston, to his correspondent in London, dated Nov. 5. 1754.* London. T. Fox. s.sh. F. 1755
Note: SABIN 800053. 'Elizabeth Canning's dream for the good of her native country, which she dreamt soon after her arrival in America'.
Locations: RPJCB, MH

1755#47
SHEBBEARE, John. *A letter to the people of England, on the present situation and conduct of national affairs. Letter I.* London. J. Scott, 58p. 8vo. 1755
Note: HIGGS 982. Several editions in 1755. Also issued as *A first letter to the people of England. . .* , 35p. (CtY, RPJCB). Considerable discussion of North America.
Locations: L; DLC, ICU

1755#48
SHEBBEARE, John. *Lydia, or Filial Piety: a novel. . .* London. J. Scott, 4 vols. 12mo. 1755
Note: Also Dublin, 1756, and later editions. Narrator is North American Indian.
Locations: L; MH, NjP, NIC

1755#49
SHEBBEARE, John. *A second letter to the people of England, on foreign subsidies, subsidiary armies, and their consequences. . .* London. J. Scott, 56p. 8vo. 1755
Note: HIGGS 983, KRESS 5474–5. A second edition has title: *A letter to the people of England on foreign subsidies. . .* Some discussion of North America.
Locations: L; DLC, RPJCB, CSmH

1755#50
Ship Vrow Dorothea. Michael Goolde *Master of the. . . Trelawny Galley. . . Appellants. Pieter Black master of the vrow Dorothea. . . Respondent. The case of the. . . appellants. . .* London. 7p. F. 1755
Note: Dutch ship condemned in Charleston, S. C. Also *The respondent's case*, to be heard 1 May 1755.
Locations: NN

1755#51
SMITH, William (1727–1803). *A brief state of the province of Pennsylvania, in which the conduct of their assemblies. . . is. . . examined, and the true cause of. . . encroachments of French displayed. . . To which is annexed. . . plan for restoring quiet. . . defeating. . . French. . .* London. R. Griffiths, 45p. 8vo. 1755
Note: SABIN 84589, HIGGS 1008, KRESS SUPP. 4028–9. Also Dublin, 1755; second edition, 1755, third edition, 1756.
Locations: L; DLC, RPJCB, MiU-C

1755#52
SMITH, William (1727–1803). *A sermon preached in Christ-Church, Philadelphia before the Provincial Grand Master. . . 24th June 1755. . .* London. Philadelphia printed, London reprinted, 16p. 8vo. 1755
Note: SABIN 84664. First printed Philadelphia, [1755], (EVANS 7571).
Locations: RPJCB, MH, NIC

1755#53
Some material and very important *remarks concerning the present situation of affairs between Great Britain, France and Spain. . .* London. C. Corbett, 47p. 8vo. 1755
Locations: L; DLC, RPJCB, MH

1755#54
State of British and French *colonies in North America, with respect to number of people, forces, forts, Indians, trade and other advantages. . .* London. A. Millar, [150]p. 8vo. 1755
Note: SABIN 90601, HIGGS 1006, KRESS SUPP. 4030.
Locations: L; C; MRu; NN, DLC, RPJCB, MiU-C

1755#55
STEPHENS, Thomas d. 1780. *The method and plain process for making pot-ash, equal if not superior to the best foreign pot-ash. . .* London. R. Griffiths, 36p. 4to. [1755]
Note: HIGGS 1022. Relates primarily to American potash. Reprinted (?) Boston, 1755: EVANS 7575.
Locations: L; CtY, PPL, NN

1755#56
STERLING, James. *Zeal against the enemies of our country pathetically recommended. In a. . . sermon preached before. . . governor of Maryland and both houses of assembly at Annapolis December 13, 1754. . .* London. Annapolis printed, London reprinted. J. Whiston etc, 30p. 8vo. 1755
Note: First printed Annapolis, 1755, (EVANS 7574).
Locations: L; DLC, RPJCB, ViU

1755#57
TRUE BRITON. *French policy defeated. Being, an account of all the proceedings of the French, against the inhabitants of the British colonies in North America, for the last seven years.* London. M. Cooper, 114p. 8vo. 1755
Note: SABIN 25886, HIGGS 1005, 2232. Another edition in 1760, *French policy defeated: being an account of the original and progress. . .* (DLC, ViU).
Locations: L; DLC, RPJCB, MiU-C

1755#58
TUCKER, Josiah. *The elements of commerce, and the theory of taxes. . .* Bristol. 174p. 2o. 1755

Note: HIGGS 937, KRESS 5480. Intended for the instruction of the Prince of Wales. Much on American trade.
Locations: L; NN, MH-BA, CSmH

1755#59
TUCKER, Josiah. *The important question concerning invasions, a sea war, raising the militia. . . impartially stated. . .* London. R. Griffiths, 64p. 8vo. 1755
Locations: DLC, RPJCB, CtY

1756#1
An account of the present state of Nova-Scotia: in two letters to a noble lord: one from a gentleman in the navy newly arrived from thence. The other from a gentleman who long resided there, etc. London. 31p. 4to. 1756
Note: SABIN 56104. The first letter signed 'J. B.', the second 'W. M.'.
Locations: L; DLC, CSmH, RPJCB

1756#2
An address to the British army and navy. Intended to remind our brave warriors of the important interests, in which they are engaged. . . London. J. Buckland, 24p. 8vo. 1756
Locations: L; RPJCB, NN

1756#3
AMERICAN GENTLEMAN. *Poems moral and divine, on the following subjects. . . To which is added, some account of the author.* London. C. Rivington for J. and R. Rivington, 6, 105p. 4to. 1756
Note: MSS in British Library copy gives author as John Moore. Moore was born in Jamaica as was his father, Sir Henry, who became governor of New York in 1765. Contains no real account of his life.
Locations: L; DLC, MWA, NN, CtY

1756#4
An appeal to the sense of the people, on the present posture of affairs. Wherein the nature of the late treaties are inquired into, and the conduct of the M-n—y with regard to M-n—a, A-r-c, etc. . . London. D. Hookham, 54p. 8vo. 1756
Locations: L; MRu; RPJCB, MWA, MiU-C

1756#5
AVERAY, Robert. *Britannia and the Gods in council; a dramatic poem: wherein. . . the causes of the present disputes in Europe and America are debated. . .* London. T. Kinnersley, 32p. 4to. 1756
Note: SABIN 2477, 8067.
Locations: L; DFo, MiU-C

1756#6
BELL, William. *A dissertation on. . . causes. . . to render a nation populous. . .* Cambridge. J. Bentham etc. 36p. 4to. 1756

Note: HIGGS 1155, KRESS 5493. References to North American Indians.
Locations: L; NNC, MH-BA, CtY, N

1756#7
BIRCH, Thomas. *The history of the Royal Society of London for improving natural knowledge. . .* London. 4 vols. 4to. 1756
Note: Published 1756–7. Also 1760. A history to 1687, with North American material.
Locations: L; C; CtY, NjP, DFo

1756#8
The block and yard arm. A new ballad, on the loss of Minorca, and the danger of our American, rights and possessions. London. Tom Smut, s.sh. 1/2o. 1756
Note: Attacks Byng and Newcastle.
Locations: L; MH

1756#9
BLODGET, Samuel. *A prospective plan of the battle near Lake George, on the eighth day of September, 1755. With an explanation thereof; Containing a full, tho' short, history of that important affair. . .* London. Boston printed, London reprinted. T. Jefferys, 2, 5p. 4to. 1756
Note: SABIN 5955, 23418. First printed Boston, 1755, (EVANS 7363).
Locations: L; RPJCB, MH

1756#10
BOWNAS, Samuel. *An account of the life, travels, and Christian experiences in the work of the ministry of Samuel Bownas.* London. L. Hinde, 198p. 8vo. 1756
Note: SABIN 7097, SMITH I, 309. Other editions, 1756, 1761, etc. Reprinted Philadelphia, 1759.
Locations: L; DLC, RPJCB, MiU-C

1756#11
The case of the honourable James Annesley, esq.; humbly offered to all lovers of truth and justice. . . London. 38p. 8vo. 1756
Note: SABIN 63222n. Cf. HIGGS 1330. Another edition in 1758 (L;) has MSS. correspondence and subscription list.
Locations: L; DLC, NN

1756#12
The conduct of the ministry impartially examined. In a letter to the merchants of London. . . London. S. Bladon, 68p. 8vo. 1756
Note: SABIN 15207, HIGGS 1240, KRESS 5501. French and Indian war. Also Dublin, 1756. By Israel Mauduit?
Locations: L; DLC, RPJCB, CtY

1756#13
Considerations on the addresses lately presented to his majesty, on occasion of the loss of Minorca.

In a letter to a member of Parliament. London. M. Cooper, 63p. 8vo. 1756
Note: Discusses mismanagement of war in America.
Locations: L; DLC, CtY, NN

1756#14
Considerations on the present state *of affairs, with some reflections of the Dutch observator.* London. S. Hooper, [74]p. 8vo. 1756
Note: French and Indian war.
Locations: DLC, RPJCB, MiU-C

1756#15
Copies of several publick papers, *which have passed in the province of Pensilvania in the month of November, 1755.* London. 7, 1p. F. 1756
Note: SABIN 60023.
Locations: NN, MiU-C, PHC

1756#16
CORNWALLIS, Frederick. *A sermon preached... February 20, 1756...* London. E. Owen and A. Millar, 71p. 4to. 1756
Note: SABIN 16817. SPG sermon for 1756, with abstract, etc.
Locations: L; RPJCB, FMU

1756#17
The Crisis. London. M. Cooper, [49]p. 8vo. 1756
Note: HIGGS 1260, KRESS 5507. Cf. EVANS 7176. Discusses nature and government of colonies in relation to French. Also Dublin, 1756.
Locations: L; MY; O; DLC, RPJCB, CSmH

1756#18
DAVIES, Samuel. *The good soldier. Extracted from a sermon preached to a company of volunteers, raised in Virginia...* London. 15p. 12mo. 1756
Note: The sermon was first printed, Philadelphia, 1755, (EVANS 7403). Cf. his *Religion and patriotism...*, below, 1756, attributed in ESTC to John Wesley.
Locations: L; Vi, RPJCB

1756#19
DAVIES, Samuel. *Religion and patriotism... sermon... to... volunteers, raised in Hanover county, Virginia, August 17, 1755.* London. Philadelphia printed, London reprinted. J. Buckland, etc., 38p. 8vo. 1756
Note: SABIN 18763. First printed Philadelphia, 1755, (EVANS 7403). Also Glasgow, 1756 (L;).
Locations: L; DLC, RPJCB, MiU-C

1756#20
DAVIES, Samuel. *Virginia's danger and remedy. Two discourses, occasioned by the severe drought in sundry parts of the country; and the defeat of General Braddock.* Glasgow. J.Bryce and D.Paterson, 48p. 8vo. 1756

Note: First published Williamsburg, 1756 (EVANS 7644).
Locations: L; CSmH

1756#21
A dutiful address to the *throne; upon the present state of G t B n...* London. J. Scott, 28p. 8vo. 1756
Note: Ministerial corruption the source of all misfortunes since Braddock's defeat. Young men sent like galley slaves to North America; Hessians and Hanoverians take their place in Britain.
Locations: L; NN, CtY, CSmH

1756#22
An enquiry into the present *system.* London. A. and C. Corbett, 58p. 8vo. 1756
Note: KRESS SUPP. 4044. Doubts the necessity of the American war.
Locations: C; DLC, RPJCB, CSmH

1756#23
ERSKINE, John. *The influence of religion on national happiness. A sermon preached... 5 January 1756...* Edinburgh. 46p. 8vo. 1756
Note: Society in Scotland for Propagating Christian Knowledge sermon for 1756 with state of the Society and extensive references to missions in North America.
Locations: L; RPJCB; NjR, MH-AH

1756#24
An essay on the times... London. M. Cooper, G. Woodfall, J. Langford, 54p. 8vo. 1756
Note: French and Indian wars.
Locations: L; RPJCB, MiU-C

1756#25
EVANS, Lewis. *Geographical, historical, political, philosophical and mechanical essays. Number II. Containing a letter, representing the impropriety of sending forces to Virginia...* London. J. and R. Dodsley, 35p. 8vo. 1756
Note: SABIN 123176. First printed Philadelphia, 1755 in three parts; in 1756 as single volume (EVANS 7411-13, 7652). Some of the Philadelphia publications were distributed by the Dodsleys in London.
Locations: L; DLC, CtY, Vi

1756#26
A fair representation of his *majesty's right to Nova-Scotia or Acadie. Briefly stated from the memorials of the English commissaries...* London. E. Owen, 64p. 8vo. 1756
Note: SABIN 56129, HIGGS 1250. Also Dublin, 1756. Sometimes attributed to W. Mildmay.
Locations: L; E; O; DLC, NN, RPJCB, MiU-C

1756

1756#26A
The fatal consequences which may arise from the want of system in the conduct of public affairs. [London]. 55p. 8vo. 1756
Note: Reissued in 1757. Refers to want of system in America.
Locations: L; C: CSmH, NNC

1756#27
FAUQUIER, Francis. *An essay on ways and means for raising money for the support of the present war...* London. M. Cooper, 35p. 8vo. 1756
Note: HIGGS 1272.
Locations: L; DLC, RPJCB, CSmH

1756#28
FAWCETT, Benjamin. *A compassionate address to the Christian Negroes in Virginia With an appendix, containing some account of the rise and progress of Christianity among that poor people...* Shrewsbury? J. Eddowes and J. Cotton, sold by J. Buckland, 40p. 12mo. 1756
Note: HIGGS 1261. Fawcett was a dissenting minister of Kidderminster, Worcs. The price is stated at 3d or '18s per Hundred to those that give them to the Negroes'.
Locations: L; Vi

1756#29
A fifth letter to the people of England. On m—l influence. And management of national treasure. London. 32p. 8vo. 1756
Note: Refutes Shebbeare's *A fourth letter on the conduct... Ohio*, below, 1756 and his views on Minorca and America.
Locations: L; C; NIC, NNC, CSmH

1756#30
A fourth letter to the people of England... London. M. Cooper, 43p. 8vo. 1756
Note: HIGGS 1246. A criticism of John Shebbeare's letters and not to be confused with Shebbeare's *A fourth letter on the conduct... Ohio*, below, 1756.
Locations: L;

1756#31
A full and particular answer to... the fourth letter to the people of England... since the first difficulties on the Ohio... London. T. Harris, 61p. 8vo. 1756
Note: KRESS SUPP. 4047.
Locations: L; DLC, MH, RPJCB

1756#32
Further objections to the establishment of a constitutional militia... London. C. Henderson, 44p. 8vo. 1756
Note: Cites America experience, Braddock's defeat, nature of colonial militia.
Locations: L; ICN, MH, CtY

1756#33
The genius of Britain. An iambic ode. Addressed to the Right Hon. William Pitt, Esq. London. M. Cooper, 12p. 4to. 1756
Note: Also Dublin, 1756. But see! upon his wasted shores/America's sad genius lies/ Each wasted province he deplores, etc. CSmH 180775. By John Gilbert Cooper.
Locations: L; C; NjP, CSmH

1756#34
GEORGE, II, KING OF GREAT BRITAIN. *The royal conference or a dialogue between... G*** the IId. of E***d. and L**s the XV. of F***e.* London], 28p. 8vo. 1756
Note: With regard to the line between the French and English possessions in Canada.
Locations: L;

1756#35
GIBBONS, Thomas. *Our duty as patriots, protestants and Christians... a sermon preached... May 23... on occasion of the public declaration of war against the French king, May 18, 1756.* London. J. Buckland, etc. 46p. 8vo. 1756
Note: References to North America, Indian barbarities, etc.
Locations: L; MH, MiD

1756#36
GREAT BRITAIN. PARLIAMENT. *An act for extending the act... for amending... the laws relating to the government of His Majesty's ships... in North America.* London. 1756
Locations: MB

1756#37
GREAT BRITAIN. PARLIAMENT. *An act for the better recruiting of His Majesty's forces on the continent of America; and for the better regulation of the army, and prevention of desertion there.* London. 1756
Locations: MB

1756#38
GREAT BRITAIN. PARLIAMENT. *An act further continuing an act... for securing... the trade of his majesties sugar colonies in America...* London. 1756
Locations: MB

1756#39
GREAT BRITAIN. PARLIAMENT. *An act to enable His Majesty to grant commissions to a certain number of foreign Protestants who have served abroad as offices... to act or rank as officers, or engineers, in America...* London. 1756
Note: L; Lpro; and CSmH also have *A bill to enable...*
Locations: MB, RPJCB, MiU-C

1756#40
GREAT BRITAIN. PARLIAMENT. HOUSE OF LORDS. *The humble address of the right honourable the Lords. . . in Parliament. . . to his majesty on Friday the third day of December, 1756. With his majesty's gracious answer.* London. T. Baskett, Assigns of R. Baskett, 4p. 2o. 1756
Note: Relates to defence of American colonies.
Locations: L; MRu; RPJCB

1756#41
GREAT BRITAIN. SOVEREIGN. GEORGE II. *Proclamation. Declaration of war against the French King. [17 May 1756].* London. T. Baskett and assigns of R. Baskett, s.sh. F. 1756
Note: BRIGHAM, 203, CRAWFORD p. 85 lists (L; LS;) a 'first edition' with a typographical error, which had to be reprinted at great expense for dispatch to America.
Locations: L; MHi

1756#42
HILL, John. *The naval history of Britain, from the earliest periods. . . to. . . M.DCC.LVI. Compiled from the papers of the late honourable captain George Berkeley.* London. T. Osborne, J.Shipton, etc., 706p. 2o. 1756
Note: HIGGS 1176. Originally published in parts.
Locations: L; DLC, CtY, NN

1756#43
A historical account of the *rise and establishment of the people called Quakers. . . By a Friend.* London. J. Newberry, 32p. 8vo. 1756
Note: SABIN 32055, SMITH I, 64.
Locations: DLC, PHC, NIC

1756#44
HOWARD, Leonard. *A collection of letters and state papers, from the original manuscript of many princes, great personages and statesmen. . .* London. 2 vols. 4to. 1756
Note: SABIN 33263. Long letter by William Penn included.
Locations: DLC, CU

1756#45
An humble apology for the *Quakers. . . to which are added Observations on a new pamphlet, entituled A brief view of the conduct of Pennsylvania for the year 1755. . .* London. S. Crowder and H. Woodgate, 12p. 12mo. 1756
Note: SABIN 33694, SMITH, I, 65.
Locations: NN, CSmH

1756#46
HUNTER, Thomas. *An historical account of earthquakes, extracted from the most authentick historians. And a sermon preached at Weaverham, in Cheshire, on. . . 6 February. . . [1756]. . .* Liverpool. R. Williamson, 159p. 8vo. 1756
Note: Cf. SABIN 33931.
Locations: L; C; DLC, TxU, CSt

1756#47
An impartial view of the *conduct of the M – ry, in regard to the war in America; the engagements entered into with Russia, Hesse-Cassel, and Prussia. . .* London. 52p. 8vo. 1756
Note: SABIN 34386, HIGGS 1242.
Locations: L; MRu; DLC, RPJCB, MiU-C

1756#48
A letter from a citizen *of Port-Royal in Jamaica, to a citizen in New York. . .* London. J. Johnson, 16p. 8vo. 1756
Note: SABIN 40271, HIGGS 1266. Also Dublin, 1756.
Locations: L; RPJCB, MiU-C, IU

1756#49
A letter from a cobler *to the people of England, on affairs of importance. . .* London. 17p. 12mo. 1756
Note: SABIN 10271, HIGGS 1237, KRESS 5535. Treats war in America, etc.
Locations: O; DLC, RPJCB, CtY

1756#50
A letter from a Frenchman *at Paris, to his countryman at the Hague, on the present dispute between France and Great Britain. . .* London. S. Bladon, 56p. 8vo. 1756
Note: On Acadia and Seven Years War. Purports to be translated from the French.
Locations: L; DLC, RPJCB, MiU-C

1756#51
A letter of the right *honourable William Pitt, esq. being an impartial vindication of the conduct of his ministry.* London. P. Hodges, 47p. 1756
Note: HIGGS 1238.
Locations: RPJCB, CtY, MiU-C

1756#52
A letter to the King *of *****. By an Englishman not a member of the House of Commons. . .* London. A. and C. Corbett, 39p. 8vo. 1756
Note: SABIN 40491. To King of France. On Canada, etc.
Locations: RPJCB, MiU-C, MH

1756#53
MAYHEW, Jonathan. *Sermons upon the following subjects. . .* London. Boston printed, London reprinted. A. Millar, 392p. 8vo. 1756
Note: First printed Boston, 1755, EVANS 7488.
Locations: L; RPJCB, NN, CtY

1756

1756#54
A modest address to the Commons of Great Britain... the ill success of our present naval war with France, and the want of a militia bill. London. J. Scott, 36p. 8vo. 1756
Locations: L; RPJCB, CtY, N

1756#55
A new scheme for increasing the Protestant religion, and improving the kingdom of Ireland... Dublin. 46p. 8vo. 1756
Note: KRESS 5548. Discusses reasons for American population growth and Irish emigration to North America.
Locations: C; RPJCB, CSmH, MH-BA

1756#56
Party spirit in times of publick danger, considered... London. T. Waller, 55p. 8vo. 1756
Note: KRESS 5552. French threat in America.
Locations: L; DLC, RPJCB, MiU-C

1756#57
PAYNE, J. *The French encroachments exposed: or, Britain's original right to all that part of the American continent claimed by France fully asserted... In two letters, from a merchant...* London. G. Keith, 44p. 8vo. 1756
Note: SABIN 25883.
Locations: RPJCB, CSmH, MiU-C

1756#58
PEMBERTON, Israel. *An account of conferences held, and treaties made, between Major-General Sir William Johnson, Bart. and the chief Sachems and Warriours of the... Indian Nations... at their meeting at Fort Johnson... New York, in the years 1755 and 1756... With a letter... a preface... notes... an appendix...* London. A. Millar, 77p. 8vo. 1756
Locations: L; C; O; DLC, RPJCB, MiU-C

1756#59
PEMBERTON, Israel. *Several conferences between some of the principal... Quakers in Pennsylvania, and the deputies from the six Indian Nations in alliance with Britain... to which is prefixed... two addresses from said Quakers... to Lieutenant-governor... and... General Assembly... and Lieutenant-governor's declaration of war against... Indians...* Newcastle. J. Thompson and Company, 28p. 4to. 1756
Note: SABIN 59612.
Locations: L; DLC, RPJCB, MiU-C

1756#60
POSTLETHWAYT, Malachy. *A short state of the progress of the French trade and navigation, wherein is shown the great foundation that France has laid...* London. J. Knapton, 86p. 8vo. 1756

Note: SABIN 64568, HIGGS 1150, KRESS 5557.
Locations: L; DLC, RPJCB, MiU-C

1756#61
POWNALL, Thomas. *Considerations towards a general plan of measures for the English provinces. Laid before the Board of commissioners at Albany, by Mr Pownall.* Edinburgh. New York printed, Edinburgh reprinted. Hamilton and Balfour, 19p. 12mo. 1756
Note: First printed New York, 1756, (EVANS 7641, SABIN 16029).
Locations: RPJCB, DLC, CtY

1756#62
The progress of the French, in their views of universal monarchy... London. W. Owen, 58p. 8vo. 1756
Note: HIGGS 1362, KRESS 5558. Discusses France's American policy since time of Richelieu.
Locations: L; DLC, NN, CtY

1756#63
Reasons for allowing the importation of bar-iron from America. London. 4p. F. [1756]
Note: ESTC lists under 1755.
Locations: Lpro; DLC, NNC

1756#64
Reasons humbly offered to prove that the letter printed at the end of the French memorial of justification is a forgery... London. M. Collyer, 61p. 8vo. 1756
Note: SABIN 62823, HIGGS 1256. Letter at end of the French Memorial was from Duke of Cumberland to General Braddock. See Moreau, *The mystery revealed...*, below, 1759.
Locations: L; DLC, RPJCB, MiU-C

1756#65
Reflections on the welfare and prosperity of Great Britain in the present crisis. London. S. Crowder, H. Woodgate, 58p. 8vo. 1756
Note: KRESS 5563, HIGGS 1193. Against war. Discusses North America, New England militia, etc.
Locations: DLC, RPJCB, CSmH

1756#66
Remarks on the French memorials concerning the limits of Acadia... with two maps. London. T. Jefferys, 110p. 8vo. 1756
Note: SABIN 69463, HIGGS 1239.
Locations: L; DLC, RPJCB, MiU-C

1756#67
The resignation: or the fox out of the pit, and the geese in, with B—g at the bottom. London. 24p. 8vo. 1756
Note: SABIN 70065, HIGGS 1262. Relates to Braddock's defeat, etc.
Locations: L; RPJCB, MiU-C, DLC

1756#68
ROLT, Richard. *A new dictionary of trade and commerce...* London. T. Osborne, etc. [c. 700]p. 2o. 1756
Note: HIGGS 1156. Entries on British America, rice, tobacco, etc.
Locations: L; CtY, DLC, MiU

1756#69
A sequel to Hosier's ghost: or, Old Blakeney's reception into the Elysian Fields. A ballad written by a patriot of Ireland. Dublin. 2p. 1/2o. 1756
Note: Also London, 1756. (CtY, OCU) 'On th'Ohio, though neglected/ I deplored Old-England's shame' etc.
Locations: L; O;

1756#70
SHEBBEARE, John. *An answer to a pamphlet call'd, The conduct of the ministry impartially examined.* London. M. Cooper, 100p. 8vo. 1756
Note: HIGGS 1241. Also issued as *A fifth letter, by the author of the four former letters.* (1757).
Locations: L; DLC, RPJCB, MiU-C

1756#71
SHEBBEARE, John. *A fourth letter to the people of England on the conduct of the M——rs... since the first differences on the Ohio...* London. M. Collier, 111p. 8vo. 1756
Note: HIGGS 1294, KRESS 5570. Other issues in 1756, some with addition of Nos. LII and LIII of *The Monitor*.
Locations: L; DLC, RPJCB, MiU-C

1756#72
SHEBBEARE, John? *A prophetic fragment of a future chronicle. By the author of the Four Letters to the People of England.* London. M. Collier, 23p. 8vo. 1756
Note: Some American references.
Locations: CSmH, CtY, IaU

1756#73
SHEBBEARE, John. *A third letter to the people of England on liberty, taxes, and the application of public money...* London. J. Scott, 60p. 8vo. 1756
Note: KRESS 5573-4. Cf. HIGGS 1923. Other editions in 1756. Attack on Hanover subsidies. American references.
Locations: L; MH, CtY, MiU-C

1756#74
SMITH, William (1727–1803). *A brief view of the conduct of Pennsylvania, for the year 1755; so far as it affected the general service of the British colonies, particularly the expedition under the late General Braddock...* London. R. Griffiths, 88p. 8vo. 1756
Note: SABIN 84594, HIGGS 1252.
Locations: L; C; E; DLC, MH, NN, Vi

1756#75
SMITH, William (1727–1803). *A letter to a gentleman in London, to his friend in Pennsylvania; with a satire... upon... Quakers...* London. J. Scott, 23p. 8vo. 1756
Note: SABIN 40287, 66930. SMITH AQ. 406.
Locations: DLC, RPJCB, NN

1756#76
SMITHSON, Isaac. *A sermon, occasioned by the declaration of war against France. Preached at Harleston, May the 23d, 1756.* London. J. Waugh and W. Fenner, 23p. 8vo. 1756
Note: Cites France's American attacks before war was declared and its ambitions for a universal empire.
Locations: L;

1756#77
SOCIETY FOR THE PROPAGATION OF THE GOSPEL. *Instructions from the Society... to their missionaries in North-America.* London. E. Owen, 8p. 8vo. 1756
Note: SABIN 85938.
Locations: MSaE, RPJCB, CSmH

1756#78
THOMPSON, Thomas. *A letter from New Jersey, in America, giving some account... of that province. By a gentleman late of Christ's College, Cambridge.* London. M. Cooper, 26p. 8vo. 1756
Note: SABIN 40331, HIGGS 1268.
Locations: DLC, RPJCB, NN, CSmH

1756#79
Entry cancelled.

1756#80
TRUE ANTIGALLIGAN. *Britain, strike home. A poem humbly inscribed to every Briton...* London. T. Legg, 11p. 4to. 1756
Note: 'No sacred compacts can confine their pride;/They want America, and then the world beside!' etc.
Locations: L; NN

1756#81
TUCKER, Josiah. *The case of the importation of bar-iron, from our own colonies of North America... recommended to... Parliament, by the iron manufacturers of Great Britain.* London. T. Trye, 29p. 8vo. 1756
Note: SABIN 11316, KRESS 5496, HIGGS 1231.
Locations: L; O; DLC, MH, RPJCB

1756#82
The voice of liberty. An occasional essay... London. R. Withy, 23p. 8vo. 1756
Note: In praise of Pitt, with frequent American references.
Locations: L; DLC, CSmH, NIC

1756

1756#83
The voice of the people: *A collection of addresses to his Majesty, and instructions to members of Parliament by their constituents, upon the unsuccessful management of the present war.*.. London. J. Payne, 56p. 8vo. 1756
Note: SABIN 100674.
Locations: L; RPJCB, MiU-C, NN

1756#84
W., J. *A letter from a gentleman in Nova-Scotia, to a person of distinction on the continent. Describing the present state of government in that colony.*.. London. 12p. 4to. 1756
Note: Dated at Halifax, March 1, 1756.
Locations: L; MH

1756#85
WESLEY, John. *Hymns occasioned by the earthquake, March 8, 1750. To which are added an hymn for the English in America, and another for the year 1756. Part II. The second edition.* Bristol. Printed by E. Farley, 24p. 12mo. 1756
Note: The first edition, London, 1750, *Hymns occasioned by the earthquake, March 8, 1750.* Also published London, 1756 'To which are added an hymn upon the pouring out of the seventh vial.' A third edition, London, 1756. Published anonymously.
Locations: MRu; DWT, CtY-D, CCC

1756#86
WHITEFIELD, George. *A short address to persons of all denominations, occasioned by the alarm of an intended invasion.*.. London. W. Strahan, etc., 20p. 8vo. 1756
Note: SABIN 103592. Discusses the war in America. Other editions, London (2), Edinburgh, Boston, New York, Philadelphia.
Locations: L; C; RPJCB, MiU-C, CtY

1756#87
WHITEFIELD, George. *The two first parts of his life, with his journals... corrected...* London. W. Strahan, etc, 446p. 12mo. 1756
Note: SABIN 103603.
Locations: L; C; DLC, RPJCB, NN

1756#88
WINTER, Richard. *The importance and necessity of his majesty's declaration of war with France considered... in a sermon... May 23, 1756.* London. E. Dilly, etc., 32p. 8vo. 1756
Note: SABIN 104824. Dissenter's sermon.
Locations: L; DLC, NN, CtY

1756#89
WITHERSPOON, John. *Essay on the connection between the doctrine of justification by the imputed righteousness of Christ...* Glasgow. J. Bryce and D. Paterson, 72p. 8vo. 1756
Note: Also Edinburgh, 1756 (L;) and 1757 (NN, RPJCB, NjP).
Locations: L; RPJCB

1757#1
BALL, Nathaniel. *True religion, loyalty and union recommended... sermon preached at Pleshey, Feb. 11, 1757...* London. J. Buckland; and T. Toft in Chelmsford, 19p. 8vo. 1757
Note: War-time fast sermon.
Locations: L; OO

1757#2
Britain, a poem; in three *books...* Edinburgh. W. Ruddiman, etc. for the author. 86p. 12mo. 1757
Note: Poetic survey of the war: 'Behold the ghost of Braddoc [sic], brave in fight, /With generous Halket, stalking round/Ohio's red streams, unburied, unavenged' etc. etc.
Locations: L; NjP, CU, OClW-Hi

1757#3
BROWN, John. *An estimate of the manners and principles of the times...* London. For L. Davis and C. Reyners, 221p. 8vo. 1757
Note: HIGGS 1588. Also Dublin 1757. Nine or more editions by 1758. Refers to French successes in North America and American degeneracy.
Locations: L; DLC, CSmH, MH

1757#4
BULFINCH, Thomas. *Dissertatio medica inauguralis, de crisibus...* Edinburgh. Hamilton, Balfour et Neill, 21p. 8vo. 1757
Note: Bulfinch was a Bostonian.
Locations: DLC, CtY-M, NN

1757#5
BURKE, William. *An account of the European settlements in America. In six parts...* London. R. and J. Dodsley, 2 vols. 8vo. 1757
Note: SABIN 9282, HIGGS 1499. Other editions, 1758, 1760, etc.
Locations: L; C; E; DLC, RPJCB, MH

1757#6
DAVIES, Samuel. *The crisis: or, the uncertain doom of kingdoms... with reference to Great-Britain and her colonies in their present circumstances. A sermon, preached in Hanover, Virginia, October 28, 1756...* London. J. Buckland, etc., 36p. 8vo. 1757
Note: SABIN 18757. Possibly EVANS 7644: *Virginia's danger and remedy...*, (Williamsburgh, 1756?).
Locations: L; C; DLC, RPJCB, MiU-C

1757#7
DAVIES, Samuel. *Letters from the Rev. Samuel Davies... shewing the present state of religion in Virginia, particularly among the Negroes...* London. R. Pardon, 44p. 12mo. 1757
Note: SABIN 18761. A second edition in 1757: RPJCB, PPPrHi.
Locations: L; DLC, MiU-C, MH

1757#8
DICKINSON, Jonathan. *Familiar letters to a gentleman, upon a variety of seasonable and important subjects in religion...* Edinburgh. William Gray, 380p. 12mo. 1757
Note: SABIN 20058. First printed Boston, 1745, (EVANS 5572). Two other Edinburgh editions in 1757. Reprinted Dundee, 1772, Glasgow, 1775.
Locations: L; E;

1757#9
DODD, William. *Thoughts on the glorious epiphany of the Lord Jesus Christ...* London. W. Fadden and E. Dilly, 46p. 8vo. 1757
Note: Inspired by the fate of French neutrals from North America.
Locations: L; CtY, MH

1757#10
DONALDSON, William. *North America, a descriptive poem. Representing the voyage to America; a sketch of that beautiful country; with remarks upon the political humour and singular conduct of its inhabitants...* London. J. Shepheard, 19p. 4to. 1757
Note: SABIN 20591.
Locations: L; CSmH; DLC, MB

1757#11
DU PLESSIS, ——. *Duplessis's memoirs, or, a variety of adventures in England and America... and a description of some strolling players, with whom he travelled...* Dublin. 2 vols. 12mo. 1757
Note: SABIN 21366. Fictitious.
Locations: L; DLC, ICN, MH

1757#12
DUNBAR, Charles. *Charles Dunbar, of the Island of Antigua... appellant. Daniel Parke Custis, son and heir, and also sole executor of the last will and testament of John Custis of Virginia... The appellant's case.* London. 7p. F. [1757]
Locations: NN

1757#13
DYER, John. *The fleece: a poem. In four books.* London. R. and J. Dodsley, 156p. 4to. 1757
Note: HIGGS 1387. Substantial references to colonies.
Locations: L; RPB, CtY, CSmH

1757#14
An enquiry into the causes of our ill success in the present war... London. R. Griffiths, 47p. 8vo. 1757
Note: HIGGS 1485.
Locations: L; RPJCB, MiU-C, N

1757#15
ENTICK, John. *A new naval history: or, A compleat view of the British marine...* London. R. Manby, etc., 887p. F. 1757
Note: HIGGS 1410.
Locations: L; DLC, MH, CtY

1757#16
GILBERT, Robert. *An alarm to Great Britain; with an invitation to repentance... sermon... at Northampton, February 11th, 1757...* London. J. Buckland, 36p. 8vo. 1757
Note: Sees providential rebukes in transatlantic defeats.
Locations: L; O;

1757#17
GREAT BRITAIN. PARLIAMENT. *An act to extend the liberty... of importing bar iron from... America.* London. T. Baskett, 4p. F. 1757
Locations: RPJCB

1757#18
GREAT BRITAIN. PARLIAMENT. *An act to prohibit... the exportation of corn, grain... victual... from his majesty's colonies and plantations in America...* London. T. Baskett, 11p. F. 1757
Locations: RPJCB

1757#19
KEENE, Edmund. *A sermon preached... February 18, 1757...* London. E. Owen, T.Harrison, 83p. 4to. 1757
Note: SABIN 37154. SPG sermon for 1757, with abstract, etc.
Locations: L; DLC, RPJCB, CtY

1757#20
A letter from a merchant of the city of London to the R—t H—ble W— P— Esq; upon the affairs and commerce of North America, and the West Indies... London. J. Scott, 98p. 8vo. 1757
Note: SABIN 40307, HIGGS 1492, KRESS 5621. Second edition in 1757 (O; CaOTU).
Locations: E; MRu; DLC, MB, NN

1757#21
A letter from Lewis XV. To G—l M—t. London. I. Pottenger, 23p. 8vo. 1757
Note: Satire on French expansionist ambitions.
Locations: L; C; O;

NORTH AMERICA,

A

Descriptive Poem.

I.

FAR from the (1) silky Sons of soft Delight,
  Where Folly-Fools disseminate;
 Far from Debauchery's intemp'rate Night,
  And flutt'ring Joys effeminate.
Far from ignoble Strife,—ungen'rous Jars;
Domestic (2) Clamours, and domestic Wars.

---

(1) *Silky Sons*, &c. This Insinuation seems rather the Production of Prejudice, than the Offspring of Truth; for it is impossible that *England* should so lose its Property, as to raise up such enervate Sons of Foppery to disgrace its Records, as our peevish Author would wish you to believe.

(2) *Domestic Clamours*, &c. Sedition raised some invidious Clamour against great Men, how far Reason directed, or the Voice of Patriotism was concerned in the Tumult, I will not take upon me to determine; but this I know, that it ever has been the Opinion

1757#22
A letter from Sir William **** *Deputy Lieutenant of the County of ***** to his tenants and neighbours.* London. M. Cooper, 24p. 8vo. 1757
Note: The French 'are aiming to cut off our colonies at a stroke' etc.
Locations: CSmH, MoU, IU

1757#23
A letter to a member of Parliament, on the importance of the American colonies, and the best means of making them useful to the mother country. London. J. Scott, 24p. 8vo. 1757
Note: SABIN 40401, HIGGS 1480, KRESS SUPP. 4088.
Locations: L; MRu; DLC, CSmH, MiU-C

1757#24
LIVINGSTON, William. *A review of the military operations in North-America; from the commencement of the French hostilities on the frontiers of Virginia in 1753, to the surrender of Oswego. . . 1756. . .* London. R. and J. Dodsley, 144p. 4to. 1757
Note: SABIN 41649. Also Dublin, 1757, 'To which are added, Colonel Washington's journal. . . and several letters and other papers. . . found in the cabinet of Major General Braddock. . .' (D; MHi, DLC. Reprinted in 'New-England', 1758, (EVANS 8163).
Locations: L; DLC, RPJCB, MnU, NN

1757#25
LONG, Edward. *The Anti-Gallican; or, the history and adventures of Harry Cobham, Esq. Inscribed to Louis XVth, by the Author.* [London]. T. Lownds, 240p. 8vo. 1757
Note: A novel with violent anti-French theme and colonial references.
Locations: L; MH, DFo, CtY

1757#26
McCULLOH, Henry. *Proposals for uniting the English colonies on the continent of America so as to enable them to act with force and vigour against their enemies.* London. J. Wilkie, 38p. 8vo. 1757
Note: SABIN 66040.
Locations: L; DLC, MiU-C, CSmH

1757#27
The military history of Great Britain, for 1756, 1757. Containing a letter from an English officer at Canada, taken prisoner at Oswego. Exhibiting the cruelty and infidelity of the French, and their savage Indians. . . London. J. Millar, 125p. 8vo. 1757
Note: SABIN 48965. With journal of siege of Oswego, etc.
Locations: D; DLC, RPJCB, MiU-C

1757#28
MITCHELL, John. *The contest in America between Great Britain and France. . . giving an account of the views and designs of the French, with the interests of Great Britain, and the situation of the British and French colonies. . .* London. A. Millar, 260p. 8vo. 1757
Note: HIGGS 1491.
Locations: L; E; DLC, NN, RPJCB, MiU-C

1757#29
MOREAU, Jacob Nicolas. *The conduct of the late ministry, or, A memorial; containing a summary of facts with their vouchers, in answer to the Observations, sent by the English ministry, to the courts of Europe. . .* London. W. Bizet, 319p. 8vo. 1757
Note: SABIN 15205, HIGGS 1992. Contains North American documents.
Locations: DLC, RPJCB, MiU-C

1757#30
Motives for a peace with England. By an old sea officer. Translated from the French. London. 32p. 8vo. 1757
Locations: CSmH, ICN, MiU-C

1757#31
Entry cancelled.

1757#32
POSTLETHWAYT, Malachy. *Britain's commercial interest explained and improved. . . containing a candid enquiry into the secret causes of the present misfortunes of the nation. . .* London. D. Browne, etc., 2 vols. 8vo. 1757
Note: HIGGS 1375, KRESS 5638. A second edition in 1758, *Great Britain's commercial interest. . . With a clear view of the state of our plantations in America. . .* , (L; DLC, CtY, MH-BA).
Locations: L; DLC, RPJCB, CtY

1757#33
POSTLETHWAYT, Malachy. *Great-Britain's true system. . .* London. A. Millar, etc., 363p. 8vo. 1757
Note: KRESS 5639, HIGGS 1514.
Locations: L; DLC, RPJCB, CSmH

1757#34
Reflections on the importation of bar-iron, from our own colonies of North-America. In answer to a late pamphlet. Humbly submitted to. . . consideration of. . . the House of Commons, March 14, 1757. London. 23p. 8vo. [1757]
Note: SABIN 68701, HIGGS 1453, KRESS SUPP. 4094.
Locations: L; DLC, RPJCB, MiU-C

1757#35
Remarks upon a letter published in the London Chronicle, or Universal Evening Post, no. 115. Containing an enquiry into the causes of the failure of the late expedition

against Cape Breton. In a letter to a member of Parliament. London. M. Cooper, 30p. 8vo. 1757
Note: SABIN 10732.
Locations: L; DLC, RPJCB, MiU-C

1757#36
RICHARDSON, John. *An account of the life of that ancient servant of Jesus Christ, John Richardson...* London. L. Hinde, 236p. 8vo. 1757
Note: SABIN 71023, SMITH II, 485, HIGGS 1483. Reprinted Philadelphia, 1759.
Locations: L; DLC, RPJCB, CtY

1757#37
RIMIUS, Heinrich. *A second solemn call on Mr Zinzendorf, otherwise call'd Count Zinzendorf...* London. A. Linde, 58, 76p. 4to. 1757
Note: SABIN 71407.
Locations: L; C; MH, NN, ICN

1757#38
RUFFHEAD, Owen. *Proposals for carrying on the war with vigour, raising the supplies within the year, and forming a national militia...* London. M. Cooper, 54p. 8vo. 1757
Note: HIGGS 1510, KRESS 5641.
Locations: L; RPJCB

1757#39
SCOTT, Thomas. *Great Britain's danger and remedy. Represented in a discourse... on the day appointed for a general fast, February the 11th, 1757.* Ipswich. W. Craighton, 26p. 8vo. 1757
Note: French represented as antichrist. Loss of colonies would mean loss of wealth, invasion, etc.
Locations: L; RPJCB

1757#40
SHEBBEARE, John. *A letter to the people of England upon the militia, continental connections, neutralities and secret expeditions...* London. J. Scott, 41p. 8vo. 1757
Note: HIGGS 1580.
Locations: L; NNC

1757#41
SHEBBEARE, John. *A sixth letter to the people of England, on the progress of the national ruin...* London. J. Morgan, 121p. 8vo. 1757
Note: HIGGS 1373, KRESS 5648-9. Several editions in 1757. Discussion of trade and colonies.
Locations: L; MB, NN, CSmH

1757#42
SHEBBEARE, John? *A letter to his grace the D - of N-e, on the duty he owes himself, his king, his country...* London. J. Morgan, 47p. 8vo. 1757
Note: HIGGS 1572. Other issues.
Locations: L; RPJCB, DLC, NN

1757#43
SHEBBEARE, John? *A fifth letter to the people of England, on the subversion of the constitution...* London. J. Morgan, 99p. 8vo. 1757
Note: Other issues in 1757. Minor American reference.
Locations: L; MH, ViU, RPJCB

1757#44
SHIRLEY, William. *Memoirs of the principal transactions of the last war between the English and the French in North America... in 1744... to the... Treaty at Aix la Chapelle... an account of the importance of Nova Scotia or Acadia and the island of Cape Breton to both nations.* London. R. and J. Dodsley, 102p. 8vo. 1757
Note: SABIN 80550-1, HIGGS 1488. Other editions, including Bath, 1759. Reprinted Boston, 1758.
Locations: MRu; O; DLC, MH, RPJCB

1757#45
SMITH, William (1728–1793). *The history of the province of New York, from the first discovery to the year MDCCXXXII.* London. T. Wilcox, 255p. 4to. 1757
Note: SABIN 84566, HIGGS 1490.
Locations: L; DLC, RPJCB, MiU-C

1757#46
SOCIETY OF FRIENDS. *From our yearly meeting in London... 1757. To our friends and brethren... New Jersey and Pennsylvania...* London. 2p. [1757]
Locations: PHC, MB

1757#47
TAYLOR, John. *A sermon preached before the Hon. House of Commons... 11th day of February 1757...* London. C. Bathurst, 23p. 4to. 1757
Note: Fast sermon. French and Indian war.
Locations: L; DLC, NN

1757#48
TOWNSHEND, George. *Extract of a letter from Vice-Admiral Townshend at Jamaica, to Mr Cleveland, dated the 22d of March 1757.* London. 4p. F. 1757
Note: SABIN 96404. Infamous proceedings of the privateers of New York and other northern colonies.
Locations: CSmH, RPJCB

1757#49
Virtue triumphant; or, Elizabeth Canning *in America; being a circumstantial narrative of her adventures, from her setting sail for transportation, to the present time...* London. Boston printed, London reprinted. J. Cooke, 78p. 8vo. 1757
Note: SABIN 100592. No Boston imprint has been found.
Locations: RPJCB, NN, MH

1757#50
WILLIAMSON, Peter. *French and Indian cruelty; exemplified in the life... of P. W... written by himself...* York. N. Nickson, 103p. 8vo. 1757
Note: Second edition, York, with additions and corrections in 1758: DLC, RPJCB, NN. Other editions Glasgow, 1758, London, 1759, and later editions. Some editions have a discourse on kidnapping added.
Locations: L; DLC, RPJCB, NN

1758#1
An account of the customs *and manners of the Micmakis and Maricheets savage nations, now dependent on the government of Great Britain... several pieces relative to the savages in Nova-Scotia, and to North America in general.* London. S. Hooper, A. Morley, 138p. 8vo. 1758
Note: SABIN 94. 'From an original French manuscript letter'. Edited anonymously; editorship sometimes ascribed to Antoine-Simon Maillard.
Locations: L; DLC, RPJCB, MB

1758#2
An address to the great *man: with advice to the public.* London. J. Robinson, 54p. 8vo. 1758
Note: SABIN 63079, HIGGS 1740, KRESS SUPP. 4105.
Locations: L; RPJCB, MiU-C

1758#3
ALEXANDER, William. *The conduct of Major-General Shirley, late general and commander in chief of his majesty's forces in North America. Briefly stated.* London. R. and J. Dodsley, 130p. 8vo. 1758
Note: SABIN 15205, 80544.
Locations: L; MRu; RPJCB, CSmH, MH

1758#4
An authentic account of the *reduction of Louisbourg, in June and July 1758... By a spectator.* London. W. Owen, 60p. 8vo. 1758
Note: SABIN 42174.
Locations: L; RPJCB, MiU-C

1758#5
Authentic memoirs of the life *and treasonable practices of Doctor Florence Hensey, who received sentence of death on Wednesday the 14th day of June, 1758... for high treason...* London. Printed for G. Burnet, 44p. 8vo. 1758
Note: Sentenced to death for spying on 14 June, 1758; transmitted materials relating to North American operations, among others.
Locations: Luk; O; CSmH; NNNAM, KU-S

1758#6
CHURCH OF ENGLAND. *A form of prayer and thanksgiving... to be used... on Sunday the twentieth day of August, 1758... in all churches... throughout England... for the taking of Louisbourg...* London. T. Baskett, etc., 4p. 4to. 1758
Locations: L; NN, MB

1758#7
CLAYTON, Thomas. *Dissertatio medica inauguralis, de parca et simplici medicina, quam... pro gradu doctoratus... eruditorum examini subjicit Thomas Clayton...* Edinburgh. Hamilton, Balfour, and Neill, 23p. 8vo. 1758
Note: Clayton is described as 'Virginiensis'.
Locations: MRu; Eu; DNLM, PPL, PPL

1758#8
COADE, George. *A letter to the right honourable W. P., esq; by an Englishman.* Exeter. Andrew Brice and sold by A. Tozer, 132p. 8vo. 1758
Note: References to American trade and need to preserve American colonies.
Locations: L; RPJCB

1758#9
The conduct of a noble *commander in America, impartially reviewed. With the genuine causes of the discontents at New-York and Halifax...* London. R. Baldwin, 45p. 8vo. 1758
Note: SABIN 15197. The noble commander was the Earl of Loudoun. Another issue and a second edition in 1758.
Locations: MRu; DLC, CSmH, CtY

1758#10
Considerations upon war, upon cruelty *in general, and religious cruelty in particular.* London. T. Osborne, 468p. 8vo. 1758
Note: Some discussion of North American Indians.
Locations: L; ICN, MiU

1758#11
The cruel massacre of Protestants *in North-America; shewing how the French and Indians joined together to scalp the English and the manner of their scalping...* London. Aldermary churchyard, 8p. 8vo. [1758?]
Note: A chapbook, based on Peter Williamson's writings. CSmH version is *The Cruell massacre* with illustration of distinctly non-Indian 'massacerers'; text dwells on English rights, Indian cruelty, etc. RPJCB dates 1761.
Locations: L; RPJCB, DLC, CSmH

1758#12
DAVIES, Samuel. *The curse of cowardice: a sermon preached to the militia in Hanover county, Virginia, at a general muster, May 8, 1758...* London. J. Buckland and others, 36p. 12mo. 1758
Note: SABIN 18758. For later American editions see EVANS 8333–6.
Locations: L; RPJCB, MiU-C N

FRENCH *and* INDIAN *Cruelty;*

Exemplified in the

LIFE

And various Vicissitudes of Fortune, of

PETER WILLIAMSON,

A DISBANDED SOLDIER.

CONTAINING

A particular Account of the *Manners, Customs,* and *Dress,* of the SAVAGES; of their *scalping, burning,* and other *Barbarities,* committed on the ENGLISH, in NORTH-AMERICA, during his Residence among them: Being at eight Years of Age, *stolen* from his *Parents* and sent to PENSYLVANIA, where he was sold as a SLAVE: Afterwards married and settled as a *Planter,* 'till the *Indians* destroy'd his House and every Thing he had, and carried him off a *Captive;* from whom, after several Months Captivity, he made his Escape, and serv'd as a *Volunteer* and *Soldier* in many Expeditions against them.

COMPREHENDING IN THE WHOLE,

A SUMMARY of the Transactions of the several Provinces of PENSYLVANIA (including PHILADELPHIA), NEW-YORK, NEW-ENGLAND, NEW-JERSEY, &c &c From the Commencement of the War in these Parts; particularly, those relative to the *intended* Attack on CROWN POINT and NIAGARA.

And, an accurate and succinct Detail, of the Operations of the FRENCH and ENGLISH Forces, at the Siege of OSWEGO, where the AUTHOR was wounded and taken Prisoner; and being afterwards sent to ENGLAND, was, on his Arrival at *Plymouth,* discharg'd as *incapable* of FURTHER Service.

Written by HIMSELF.

Y O R K:
Printed for the AUTHOR, by N. NICKSON. 1757.
And Sold at his Shops in *Stonegate* and *Coffee-Yard.*
[Price ONE SHILLING]

1758

1758#13
DAVIES, Samuel. *The duty of Christians to propagate their religion among heathens, earnestly recommended to the masters of negro slaves in Virginia. A sermon preached in Hanover, January 8, 1757.* London. J. Oliver, 46p. 12mo. 1758
Locations: L; DLC, RPJCB, MiU-C

1758#14
DAVIES, Samuel. *Little children invited to Jesus Christ: sermon. . . in Hanover county, Virginia, May 8, 1757. With a short account. . . late remarkable religious impressions among the students in the College of New-Jersey.* London. J. Buckland, 36p. 12mo. 1758
Note: SABIN 18762. Reprinted Boston 1759, (EVANS 833).
Locations: L; RPJCB, MiU-C, MWA

1758#15
DAVIES, Samuel. *The vessels of mercy and the vessels of wrath. . . sermon first preached in New-Kent, Virginia, August 22, 1756. . .* London. J. Buckland, etc., 35p. 8vo. 1758
Note: SABIN 18769.
Locations: L; RPJCB, MiU-C

1758#16
DILWORTH, W. H. *The history of the bucanniers of America. . . adorned with copper plates. . .* London. G. Wright, 144p. 12mo. 1758
Note: SABIN 20182. The 'fourth edition' (1759) in RPJCB, MH.
Locations: L; MWA

1758#17
EDWARDS, Jonathan. *Remarks on the Essays on the principles of morality, and natural religion. In a letter to a minister of the Church of Scotland. . .* Edinburgh. 19p. 8vo. 1758
Note: The *Essays* were by Henry Home, Lord Kames.
Locations: DLC, NjP, MiU-C

1758#18
An eighth and last letter, or address, to the Parliament as well as the people of Great Britain. . . London. 16p. 8vo. [1758]
Note: Caption page has slip 'An eighth and last' pasted over original 'A seventh and last. . . '.
Locations: CSmH

1758#19
Facts, records, authorities and arguments; concerning the claims of liberty and the obligations of military service. . . London. W. Faden, 108p. 8vo. 1758
Note: References to America.
Locations: L; DLC, RPJCB, MiU-C

1758#20
FALQUES, Marianne-Agnès. *The last war of the beasts. A fable. To serve for the history of the eighteenth century. In two parts. Translated from the original French of the author of Abassai.* London. Printed for C. G. Seyffert, vii, [1], 244p. 8vo. 1758
Note: On the dispute between Great Britain and France over Nova Scotia. Also issued in French (L; E; MnU, MH-H) in 1758, with a London imprint, though the place of publication was probably Geneva.
Locations: DLC, MB

1758#21
FURNEAUX, Philip. *A sermon preached at Clapham in Surry, on Friday the 17th February, 1758. . .* London. J. Buckland, etc., 46p. 8vo. 1758
Note: Discusses war in America.
Locations: L; MH

1758#22
A genuine account of the proceedings on the trial of Florence Hensey, M. D. . . for high treason. London. H. Owen, 64p. 8vo. 1758
Note: See above, *Authentic memoirs,* 1758
Locations: L; DNLM

1758#23
Genuine memoirs of the life and treasonable practices of Dr. Florence Hensey. . . London. Bailey's printing and register office, 32p. 8vo. 1758
Note: See above, *Authentic memoirs,* 1758.
Locations: L; CSmH, CaOHM

1758#24
GREAT BRITAIN. LORDS COMMISSIONERS FOR OPENING PARLIAMENT. *The speech of the Lords Commissioners to both Houses of Parliament, on Tuesday the twentieth day of June, 1758.* London. T. Baskett and assigns of R.Baskett, 4p. F. 1758
Note: War and North America.
Locations: RPJCB

1758#25
Great Britain's glory. Being a loyal song on the taking of Cape Breton from the French 26 of July by Admiral Boscawen. . . [London]. s.sh. F. 1758
Note: Madden collection.
Locations: C;

1758#26
HANWAY, Jonas. *Two letters. . .* London. R. and J. Dodsley, 35p. 4to. 1758
Note: Partly about augmenting the number of seamen in the colonies.
Locations: L; NNC, MH-BA

1758

1758#27
The independent freeholder's letter to *the people of England, upon the one thing needfull at this present crisis.* London. C. Corbett, 44p. 8vo. 1758
Note: References to effects of political system in and on America.
Locations: L; NIC, NN, InU

1758#28
IRELAND. LORDS JUSTICES. *Proclamation continuing embargo on ships carrying provisions... [13 September 1758].* Dublin. 2p. F. 1758
Note: Embargo not to extend to ships carrying provisions to American colonies.
Locations: DPR;

1758#29
JOHNSON, James. *A sermon preached... Friday, February 24, 1758...* London. E. Owen, T. Harrison, 77p. 4to. 1758
Note: SPG sermon for 1758, with abstract, etc.
Locations: L; DLC, RPJCB, CtY

1758#30
LA DREVETIERE, Louis L'Isle de. *Tombo-Chiqui: or, the American savage. A dramatic entertainment. In three acts.* London. S. Hooper, A. Morley, 55p. 8vo. 1758
Note: SABIN 13616. Translated by John Cleland.
Locations: L; C; E; DLC, MiU-C, CSmH

1758#31
A letter of consolation to *Dr Shebbeare.* London. E. Cabe, 45p. 8vo. 1758
Note: Attack on Shebbeare. Cites Ministry's American victories, etc.
Locations: MH, RPJCB, CaOTP

1758#32
The life and authentick trial *of Doctor Hensey, for high-treason, in giving intelligence to the French. Taken on Monday, the 12th of June, at the Court of King's Bench...* London. Printed by Larkin Howe, 8p. 8vo. 1758
Note: See above, *Authentic Memoirs*, 1758.
Locations: NIC

1758#33
NEVILL, Valentine. *The reduction of Louisbourg. A poem, wrote on board his majesty's ship Orford in Louisbourg harbour...* Portsmouth for J. Wilkinson; and sold by T. Osborne and W. Owen, London. 16p. F. 1758
Note: Cf. SABIN 52417.
Locations: DLC, RPJCB, MH

1758#33A
OFFICER. *Six plans of the different disposition of the English army, under the command of the late General Braddock, in North America... By an officer.* London printed for T. Jefferys, [2]p., plates; 20. 1758
Locations: NN, ICN

1758#34
PERCEVAL, John. *Things as they are [part 1].* London. S. Hooper, etc., 112p. 8vo. 1758
Note: Part 2 was published in 1761.
Locations: L; RPJCB, DLC, MiU-C

1758#35
POSTLETHWAYT, Malachy. *In Honour to the administration. The importance of the African expedition considered...* London. C. Say and sold by M. Cooper, xxiv, 99p. 8vo. 1758
Note: SABIN 64566, KRESS 5748. Discussion of North America and North American Indians.
Locations: L; DLC, CtY, MH

1758#36
PULLEIN, Samuel. *The culture of silk, or, an essay on its rational practice and improvement... For the use of the American colonies.* London. A. Millar, 299p. 8vo. 1758
Note: SABIN 66625, HIGGS 1640, KRESS 5750.
Locations: C; RPJCB, MiU-C, CtY

1758#37
RADCLIFF, Ebenezer. *The crisis: or, the decisive period of British power and liberty... In two sermons preached at Boston in the county of Lincoln, February 17, 1758.* London. R. Griffiths, 30p. 8vo. 1758
Note: Remarks on French plunder of Britain's American possessions and on Indian savagery.
Locations: L;

1758#38
RAILTON, John. *Proposals to the public, especially those in power... to save Great-Britain, likewise to regain... Minorca, besides our late possessions in America...* London. 15p. 8vo. 1758
Note: SABIN 67513. For a 'brisk militia'—military training in schools.
Locations: MRu; Lhl; RPJCB, MH, CSmH

1758#39
A review of the sixth *letter to the people of England; wherein the principal passages of that malignant piece are quoted at large, and refuted...* London. 64p, 8vo. 1758
Note: HIGGS 1836. Attacks Shebbeare's views, including those on the war, with some American references.
Locations: L; MH, CtY, CSmH

1758#40
The rocking of the cradle... to which is added... The sailor's return from Cape Breton. London. Entered according to order, 8p. [1758?]
Note: A chapbook. Various issues at L; and C
Locations: EN;

1758#41
A seventh letter to the people of England. Upon political writing, true patriotism... London. J. Single, 57p. 8vo. 1758
Note: Attack on John Shebbeare; ridicules his geographical knowledge, including that of North America.
Locations: L; CtY, RPJCB, NN

1758#42
SHEBBEARE, John. *A letter to the people of England. Letter VII.* London. [119]p. 8vo. [1758]
Note: Bound with letter I in RPJCB. A unique(?) copy of a work seized before publication. References to Florida; mostly about war in Europe.
Locations: RPJCB

1758#43
SOCIETY FOR THE ENCOURAGEMENT OF ARTS. *Premiums by the Society, established at London, for the encouragement of arts, manufactures and commerce...* London. 31p. 8vo. 1758
Note: SABIN 65052. Cf. HIGGS 1938. Includes premiums for the advantage of the British colonies. Later editions 1759, 1760.
Locations: L; CtY, PPL

1758#44
SOCIETY FOR THE ENCOURAGEMENT OF ARTS. *Rules and orders of the Society, established at London...* London. Printed by order of the Society, 53p. 8vo. 1758
Note: Contains list of members, including Benjamin Franklin, Alexander Garden, and other Americans. The premiums were to apply to North America and the society established a subcommittee on colonies and trade. Subsequent rules and membership lists were published annually.
Locations: L; CtY, CSmH

1758#45
STEPHENS, Thomas d. 1780. *The rise and fall of pot-ash in America, addressed to the Right Honourable the Earl of Halifax.* London. 43p. 4to. 1758
Note: SABIN 91309, HIGGS 1997, KRESS SUPP. 4146.
Locations: MRu; Lu; RPJCB, MiU-C, NN

1758#46
TEMPLE, William. *A vindication of commerce and the arts; proving that they are the source of the greatness... of a state...* London. J. Nourse, 137p. 8vo. 1758
Note: HIGGS 1703, KRESS 5760. Attacks W. Bell, *A dissertation on... causes... to render a nation populous*, above, 1756. References to North American Indians, etc.
Locations: L; MH-BA, CtY, NN

1758#47
THOMPSON, Thomas. *An account of two missionary voyages by appointment of the Society for the Propagation of the Gospel in Foreign Parts. The one to New Jersey in North America, the other from America to the coast of Guiney.* London. B. Dod, 87p. 8vo. 1758

Locations: L; C; MRu; DLC, RPJCB, NN

1758#48
TOWGOOD, Micaiah. *Britons invited to rejoice... sermon preach'd at Exeter, August the 27th, 1758... after receiving the account of the taking of the islands of Cape-Breton and St. John.* [London]. J. Noon and sold by A. Tozer, Exeter, 30p. 8vo. 1758
Note: SABIN 96355.
Locations: L; DLC, MiU-C, NN

1758#49
WILLIAMSON, Peter. *Authentic instances of French and Indian cruelty, exemplified in the sufferings of Peter Williamson... written by himself.* York. J. Jackson, 104p. 8vo. 1758
Note: First printed in Grand Magazine? Editions in London, [1758?] (L; ICN) and in 1759, *French and Indian cruelty exemplified...*, the fourth edition, with 'considerable improvements.' (L; RPJCB).
Locations: O; Ep; RPJCB

1758#50
WILLIAMSON, Peter. *Occasional reflections on the importance of the war in America, and the reasonableness and justice of supporting the King of Prussia, etc...* London. J. Whitestone, B. White, 139p. 8vo. 1758
Locations: L; DLC, RPJCB, CSmH

1758#51
WILLIAMSON, Peter. *Some considerations on the present state of affairs. Wherein the defenceless state of Great-Britain is, pointed out... interspersed with an account of the first settlement of Pensylvania... with... detail of... manners... of the Indians...* York. Printed for the author, 58p. 8vo. 1758
Locations: L; Ct; E; NN, MiU-C, CSmH, MB

1758#52
WITHERSPOON, John. *The absolute necessity of salvation through Christ. A sermon, preached... January*

2. *1758.* . . Edinburgh. Printed for W. Miller, [2], 90p. 8vo. 1758
Note: Society in Scotland for Propagating Christian Knowledge sermon for 1758 with short account of the state of the Society.
Locations: L; RPJCB, NNUT, NjP

1758#53
YOUNG, Arthur. *The theatre of the present war in North America: with candid reflections on the great improvement of the war in that part of the world.* London. J. Coote, 56p. 8vo. 1758
Note: SABIN 106065.
Locations: L; MRu; DLC, MiU-C, RPJCB, CtY

1759#1
An abstract of the form of prayer and thanksgiving. . . to be used on. . . the 29th day of November, 1759. . . Edinburgh. 14p. 8vo. 1759
Note: SABIN 66982. Thanksgiving for military successes, especially in Canada.
Locations: MB

1759#2
An account of the constitution and present state of Great Britain, together with a view of its trade, policy, and interest. . . London. J. Newberry, 291p. 18mo. 1759
Note: KRESS 5764. For young people. Substantial discussion of North America.
Locations: L; DLC, NcU, NNC

1759#3
BALL, Nathaniel. *The divine goodness and human gratitude properly consider'd, in a sermon preach'd at West-Horsley. . . November 29, 1759.* . . London. J. Buckland; Chelmsford. K. Lobb, 36p. 12mo. 1759
Note: Quebec thanksgiving sermon.
Locations: L; OO

1759#4
BOSTWICK David. *Self disclaimed, and Christ exalted: a sermon preached at Philadelphia. . . May 25, 1758.* . . London. Philadelphia printed, London reprinted. For E. Dilly, 38p. 8vo. 1759
Note: SABIN 6789. Preface by G. Tennent; with extract of character of Jonathan Edwards.
Locations: L; RPJCB, MH, CSmH

1759#5
BRADBURY, Charles. *Hymns for the general thanksgiving day, Thursday, November 19, 1759.* . . London. Sold at the Chapel, in King John's Court Bermondsey; and at Glovers Hall, 12p. 12mo. 1759
Locations: CtHT-W

1759#6
BRADSTREET, John. *An impartial account of Lieut. Col. Bradstreet's expedition to Fort Frontenac. . . By a volunteer on the expedition.* London. T. Wilcox, etc. 60p. 8vo. 1759
Note: SABIN 7301, HIGGS 2000.
Locations: L; DLC, RPJCB, MiU-C

1759#7
BRECKNOCK, Timothy. *A plan for establishing the general peace of Europe upon honourable terms to Great Britain.* . . London. W. Griffith, 95p. 8vo. 1759
Note: HIGGS 2109, KRESS SUPP. 4150. Another edition in 1759.
Locations: DLC, CtY

1759#8
BREWSTER, Richard. *A sermon, preached in the Church of St. Nicholas, in Newcastle upon Tyne, on Thursday, the 29th day of November.* . . Newcastle. John White, [4], 28p. 4to. 1759
Note: Quebec thanksgiving sermon.
Locations: Npl; O; TxU

1759#9
BRICE, Andrew. *A universal geographical dictionary; or, grand gazetteer; including a comprehensive view of. . . Europe. . . and America; more especially of the British dominions and settlements.* . . London. J. Robinson, etc. 2 vols. F. 1759
Note: SABIN 7791. Another London issue in 1759? Also Exeter, 1759 as *The grand gazetteer.* . . , 1759.
Locations: L; BAT; ScCC, CtY

1759#10
Britain in tears, for the loss of the brave General Wolfe. Tune, The lamentation of Jane Shore. London. s.sh., ill., 1/4 F. 1759
Note: 'If ancient Romans did lament'.
Locations: C;

1759#11
BRUCE, Alexander. *An inquiry into the cause of the pestilence. In three parts.* . . Edinburgh. A. Kincaid and J. Bell, London, A Millar. 154p. 8vo. 1759
Note: HIGGS 2084. Frequent references to North America and North American Indians.
Locations: L; DLC, PPULC, PU

1759#12
BULKLEY, Charles. *The signs of the times, illustrated and improved. In a sermon preached. . . October 21, 1759. On occasion of the surrender of Quebec.* . . London. J. Noon and C.Henderson, 30p. 8vo. 1759
Note: SABIN 9098.
Locations: L; MRu; NN, PPl

1759#13
CARLYLE, Alexander. *Plain reasons for removing a certain great man from his m——y's presence and councils for ever.* London. M. Cooper, 51p. 8vo. 1759
Note: Satirical attack on (i.e. a defence of) Pitt, including his American policies.
Locations: L; DLC, RPJCB, FU

1759#14
CATTON, William. *Sacred to the memory of that renowned hero, Major General Wolfe...* London. s.sh. F. [1759?]
Locations: L;

1759#15
CHURCH OF ENGLAND. *A form of prayer and thanksgiving... to be used... on Sunday the twenty first of October 1759...* London. T. Baskett, 4p. 4to. 1759
Note: To be used in London and Westminster and elsewhere within the bills of mortality. Thanksgiving for defeat of French in Canada and taking of Quebec.
Locations: L; E; CSmH

1759#16
CHURCH OF ENGLAND. *Abstract of a form of prayer and thanksgiving to almighty God; to be used in all churches and chapels... on Thursday the 29th of November instant, being the day appointed by proclamation for a general thanksgiving to God; for vouchsafing such signal successes to His Majesty's arms, both by sea and land, particularly by the defeat of the French army in Canada, and the taking of Quebeck; and for most seasonably granting us at this time an uncommonly plentiful harvest.* London. T. Baskett, 15p. 4to. 1759
Note: SABIN 67003. To be used in England and Wales and Berwick upon Tweed. Several issues.
Locations: L; O; E; RPJCB, CSmH, NN

1759#17
CHURCH OF IRELAND. *A form of prayer, and thanksgiving to Almighty God; to be used in all churches and chapels throughout the kingdom of Ireland, on Thursday the twenty ninth day of November, being the day appointed by proclamation for a general thanksgiving to Almighty God,... By the special command of his Grace the Lord Lieutenant.* Cork, Dublin printed, and, Cork reprinted by Eugene Swiney, by permission of Boulter Grierson, 16p. 8vo. 1759
Locations: Dt; CSmH

1759#18
CLARKE, Richard. *An essay on the number seven. Wherein the duration of the Church of Rome... are attempted to be shewn.* London. J. Rivington and J. Fletcher, 2 vols in one. 4to. 1759

Note: Clarke was minister at St. Philips, Charleston, S. C. Contains an attack on the slave trade. The second part is an answer to his critics.
Locations: L; FU; MiU

1759#19
CLARKE, Richard. *A warning to the world; or the prophetical numbers of Daniel and John calculated...* London. Charlestown printed, London reprinted, J. Townsend, 24p. 4to. 1759
Note: See Clarke, *Essay*, above, 1759. First printed Charleston, 1759: MWA notes to EVANS. Second edition with additions Charleston, 1759, (EVANS 8317). Other editions Boston, Philadelphia, 1759.
Locations: Llp; RPJCB, DNLM

1759#20
Considerations on the importance of *Canada, and the Bay and River of St. Lawrence; and of the American fisheries...* London. W. Owen, 23p. 8vo. 1759
Note: HIGGS 1993, KRESS 5774.
Locations: L; E; DLC, RPJCB, CtY

1759#21
CRAVEN, Charles. *The case of Major Charles Craven, of the late Fifty-first regiment, in North America, now on half pay...* London. s.sh. F. [1759?]
Locations: RPJCB

1759#22
CROOKSHANKS, John. *The conduct and treatment of John Crookshanks... late commander of... the Lark.* London. J. Scott, 156p. 8vo. 1759
Note: Crookshank's court martial for acts at Louisbourg in 1747.
Locations: RPJCB

1759#23
CROOKSHANKS, John. *The reply of John Crookshanks, Esq; to a pamphlet lately set forth by Admiral Knowles...* London. M. Cooper, 46p. 8vo. 1759
Note: Crookshank's court martial for acts at Louisbourg in 1747.
Locations: L; CSmH

1759#24
Daphnis and Menalcas: a pastoral. *Sacred to the memory of the late General Wolfe...* London. R. and J. Dodsley, J. Scott, 20p. 4to. 1759
Note: SABIN 104989n.
Locations: L; DLC, CtY, PHi

1759#25
DAYRELL, Richard. *A sermon preached before the honourable House of Commons, at St. Margaret's Westminster, on Thursday November 19, 1759...* London. J. Walter, 32p. 4to. 1759

1759

Note: Quebec thanksgiving sermon.
Locations: L; InU

1759#26
A dialogue betwixt General Wolfe, and the Marquis Montcalm, in the Elysian Fields. London. Printed. . . and sold by E. Jopson in Coventry; Messrs. Rivington and Fletcher, London, 20p. 8vo. 1759
Note: SABIN 19937.
Locations: L; CaQMM

1759#27
DILWORTH, W. H. *The conquest of Peru. . . Together with the voyages of the first adventurers, particularly Ferdinand de Soto, for the discovery of Florida.* . . London. G. Wright, 164p. 18mo. 1759
Note: SABIN 20183. Florida is discussed on pps. 127–64.
Locations: L; RPJCB, NN, MWA

1759#28
DUNCOMBE, John. *A sermon preached in. . . St Anne's, Westminster. . . November 29, 1759.* London. J. Whiston and D. White, 23p. 4to. 1759
Note: Quebec thanksgiving sermon.
Locations: L; C; NjR

1759#29
ELLIS, William. *London and Country Brewer. . . in three parts. . .* London. T. Astley, 332p. 8vo. 1759
Note: Cf. SABIN 41861. The seventh edition. Contains Philadelphia and South Carolina methods of brewing. Earlier editions not checked.
Locations: L; C; DeU, ICU

1759#30
ELLYS, Anthony. *A sermon preached. . . February 23, 1759. . .* London. E. Owen and T. Harrison, 95p. 4to. 1759
Note: SABIN 22289. SPG sermon for 1759.
Locations: L; DLC, RPJCB, MHi

1759#31
The encouraging general, a song sung by that truly gallant officer, General Wolfe, the evening before he received the mortal wound which occasioned his death. London. s.sh. ill. 1/4 F. 1759
Note: 'How stands the glass around'.
Locations: C;

1759#32
The English Pericles; or, the four qualifications necessary to make a true statesman, exemplified in the character and conduct of Mr. Secretary Pitt. London. G. Woodfall, 2, 62p. 8vo. [1759]
Note: Panegyric, discussing American successes.
Locations: L; CSmH, InU-Li, NIC

1759#33
ERSKINE, Robert. *The facts and accusations set forth in a late pamphlet, intituled: The conduct of John Crookshanks, proved to be false and groundless.* . . London. S. Bladen, 36p. 8vo. 1759
Note: SABIN 22796. Crookshank's court martial for acts at Louisbourg in 1747.
Locations: BRu; RPJCB, NN, CSmH

1759#34
FRANKLIN, Benjamin. *A parable against persecution.* . . London? 2p. 8vo. [1759?]
Note: Begins 'And it came to pass'.
Locations: Lmh; DLC

1759#35
FRANKLIN, Benjamin. *Some account of the success of inoculation for the small-pox in England and America. Together with Plain Instructions.* . . London. W. Strahan, 8, 12p. 4to. 1759
Note: SABIN 25589, 31198. FORD 256. Perhaps always printed with Heberden's *Plain Instructions.* . . (1759), which has separate title-page.
Locations: DLC, RPJCB, CSmH

1759#36
GENTLEMAN IN AN EMINENT STATION ON THE SPOT. *An accurate and authentic journal of the siege of Quebec, 1759.* . . London. J. Robinson, 44p. 8vo. 1759
Note: SABIN 66987, HIGGS 1999. Also Dublin, 1759.
Locations: L; MRu; DLC, RPJCB, MiU-C

1759#37
GERARD, Alexander. *National blessings an argument for reformation. A sermon, preached at Aberdeen, November 29, 1759.* . . Aberdeen, printed by J. Chalmers, 2, 26p. 8vo. 1759
Note: Quebec thanksgiving sermon. Also sold by A. Millar in the Strand.
Locations: L; N

1759#38
GILBERT, Robert. *Britain revived. . . A sermon delivered at Northampton. . . Nov. 29, 1759.* . . London. J. Buckland, 36p. 8vo. 1759
Note: SABIN 27354. Quebec thanksgiving sermon.
Locations: L; MRu; MH-AH, MdBJ-G

1759#39
GREAT BRITAIN. LORDS COMMISSIONERS OF APPEALS IN PRIZE CAUSES. *America. Ferret, master. Before the Right Honourable the Lords Commissioners of Appeals for Prizes. America, Louis Ferret, master. . . Appellant's case.* London, 4p. 2o. [1759]

Note: Also *Case on behalf of the respondents* and *Appendix to the respondents case.*
Locations: L; Lpro;

1759#40
GREAT BRITAIN. SOVEREIGN. GEORGE II. *Proclamation. For a public thanksgiving in England and Wales for defeat of French. [23 October 1759].* London. T. Baskett and R. Baskett, s.sh. F. 1759
Note: BRIGHAM 207, CRAWFORD p. 94.
Locations: MHi, RPJCB

1759#41
GREAT BRITAIN. SOVEREIGN. GEORGE II. *Proclamation. For a public thanksgiving in Ireland for defeat of French. [30 October 1759].* London. 1759
Note: CRAWFORD, p. 94. Possibly no longer extant?
Locations: DPR; (?)

1759#42
GREAT BRITAIN. SOVEREIGN. GEORGE II. *Proclamation. For a public thanksgiving in Scotland for the defeat of French. [23 October 1759].* London. 1p. F. 1759
Note: BRIGHAM 208, CRAWFORD, VIII, 93.
Locations: L;

1759#43
GREEN, John. *A sermon preached before the honourable the House of Commons, at St. Margaret's Westminster.* London. Benj. Dodd, 19p. 4to. 1759
Note: Fast sermon preached 16 February 1759. French encroachments, etc.
Locations: L; CSmH

1759#44
GROVE, Joseph. *A letter to a right honourable patriot; upon the glorious success at Quebec... with a postcript, which enumerates the other conquests mentioned in the London address.* London. J. Burd, 58p. 8vo. 1759
Note: SABIN 28987.
Locations: DLC, RPJCB, MiU-C

1759#45
HARRIS, John. *A thanksgiving-sermon, preached in the parish church of Greensted, in Essex, on Thursday November 29, 1759... By John Harris...* London prited [sic] by E. Owen and T. Harrison, [2], 13, [1]p. 4to. 1759
Locations: L; Llp;

1759#46
HEBERDEN, William. *Plain instructions for inoculation in the small-pox; by which any person may be enabled to perform the operation, and conduct the patient through the distemper.* London. Printed at the expence of the author, to be given away in America, 12p. 4to. 1759

Note: Anonymous. By William Heberden. Perhaps always a part of Franklin, *Some account*, above, 1759.
Locations: NNNAM

1759#47
HENRY, William. *The triumphs and hopes of Great-Britain and Ireland. A sermon, preached... Thursday November the 29th, 1759...* Dublin. For Peter Wilson, 23p. 8vo. 1759
Note: Quebec thanksgiving sermon.
Locations: L; LLp;

1759#48
HITCHIN, Edward. *A sermon preached at the New Meeting... Spital-Fields... 29 November 1759...* London. J. Buckland, etc. 30p. 8vo. 1759
Note: Quebec thanksgiving sermon.
Locations: L; CtY

1759#49
HOGG, John. *A sermon preached to a congregation of Protestant dissenters at Sidmouth in Devonshire... Nov. 29, 1759...* London. J. Buckland; and A. Tozer, Exeter, 32p. 4to. 1759
Note: Quebec thanksgiving sermon.
Locations: MRu; MH-AH

1759#50
The honest grief of a *Tory, expressed in a genuine letter...* London. J. Angel, 39p. 8vo. 1759
Note: HIGGS 2101. Attack on corruption, denying ministry's credit for American successes.
Locations: L; DLC, RPJCB, CtY

1759#51
A horrid and barberous [sic] murder *committed by a negroe on three white persons in America who was hung up in chains alive, who lived three days in that deplorable condition. With another shocking account, how a lady was murdered by her niece at London, Feb. 26th 1759.* Edinburgh. s.sh. 1/2o. F. [1759]
Note: Originally published in the *Edinborough Courant* of 5th of March, 1759. The second murder was that of Mrs. Susanna Walker by her niece, Mary Edmondson.
Locations: Gu;

1759#52
JACKSON, Richard. *An historical review of the constitution and government of Pennsylvania, from its origin... Founded on authentic documents.* London. R. Griffiths, 444p. 8vo. 1759
Note: SABIN 25512, HIGGS 1995. Sometimes attributed to Benjamin Franklin.
Locations: L; DLC, RPJCB, MiU-C

1759#53
JOHN-THE-GIANT-KILLER. *Food for the mind, or a new riddle book; compiled for the use of the great and*

the little good boys and girls in England, Scotland, and Ireland. By John-the-Giant-Killer, Esq; The third edition. London. Printed for the booksellers of Europe, Asia, Africa and America, [and John Newbery] and sold at the Bible and Sun in St. Paul's Church-yard, viii, 112, [8]p. 24o. 1759
Note: With four final advertisement leaves. Publisher's name from S. Roscoe, *John Newbery and his successors* (Wormley, Herts., 1973) J190B(3).
Locations: NRU, OChHi

1759#54
JOHNSON, James. *A sermon preached before the right honourable the House of Lords. . . November 29, 1759. . .* London. G. Hawkins, 23p. 4to. 1759
Note: Quebec thanksgiving sermon.
Locations: L; CLU-S/C

1759#55
JUSTICE, James. *The British gardener's calendar. . .* Edinburgh. R. Fleming, 412p. 8vo. 1759
Note: Contains list of American tree seeds, etc.
Locations: L; DNAL, MH-A

1759#56
KENNEDY, Gilbert. *The ambitious designs of wicked men. . . a sermon preach'd at Belfast, on Thursday, Nov. 29th, 1759. . .* Belfast. D. Blow, 27p. 8vo. 1759
Note: Quebec thanksgiving sermon.
Locations: C;

1759#57
KIPPIS, Andrew. *A sermon preached at the Chapel in Long-Ditch, Westminster on. . . November 29, 1759.* London. C. Henderson, 40p. 8vo. 1759
Note: Quebec thanksgiving sermon.
Locations: MRu; Lmh; MH-AH

1759#58
KNOX, Thomas. *A letter from Mr Knox, of Bristol, to the honourable William Nelson, Esq. of Virginia.* Bristol. E.Ward, 16p. 8vo. 1759
Note: SABIN 38175.
Locations: MBAt

1759#59
A letter from a gentleman in the country, to a member of Parliament. . . containing remarks on a book lately published. . . 'The conduct and treatment of John Crookshank's. . . late commander of. . . the Lark.'. London. 36p. 8vo. 1759
Note: Crookshank's court martial for acts at Louisbourg in 1747.
Locations: L; O; RPJCB, CSmH

1759#60
A letter from the Duchess of M—r—gh in the shades, to the great man. London. S. Hooper, 79p. 8vo. 1759
Note: References to Cape Breton, etc.
Locations: L; DLC, RPJCB, CtY

1759#61
A letter to the right honourable William Pitt esq., from an officer at Fort Frontenac. London. J. Fleming, 4, 38p. 8vo. 1759
Note: SABIN 40533.
Locations: C; DLC, RPJCB, MiU-C

1759#62
LOCKMAN, John. *A history of the cruel sufferings of the Protestants, and others by popish persecutions, in various countries. . .* London. J. Clarke, 345p. 12mo. [1759]
Locations: L; DLC, NjP, PPL

1759#63
LOCKMAN, John. *To the Honourable General Townshend, on his arrival from Quebec.* London. s.sh. F. [1759]
Note: Verse broadside, with MS inscription dated 28 December, 1759.
Locations: MH

1759#64
MACQUEEN, Daniel. *A sermon. . . preached. . . January 1 1759. . . the present state of the said society.* Edinburgh. Hamilton, Balfour and Neill, 76p. 8vo. 1759
Note: SABIN 44458. Society in Scotland for Propagating Christian Knowledge sermon for 1759 with state of Society.
Locations: E; NN, MH, RPJCB

1759#65
MASON, John. *The wicked taken in their own net. A sermon, preached at Cheshunt in Hertfordshire. . . Nov. 29th 1759. . .* London. J. Buckland, 26p. 8vo. 1759
Note: Quebec thanksgiving sermon.
Locations: L; MH-AH

1759#66
MASSIE, Joseph. *A state of the British sugar-colony trade. . .* London. T. Payne, 40p. 4to. 1759
Note: North American references.
Locations: L; RPJCB, DLC, MiU-C

1759#67
Memoirs of the pillory, being a consolatory epistle to Dr Shebbeare. . . London. 50p. 8vo. 1759
Note: SABIN 47576, HIGGS 2095. Minor references to Ministry's American successes.
Locations: L; C; CaOHM

1759#68
MERCER, John. *An exact abridgement of all the public acts of assembly of Virginia, in force and use. January 1, 1758. Together with a proper table.* Glasgow. J. Bryce and D. Paterson, 482p. 8vo. 1759
Note: SABIN 100390.
Locations: RPJCB, CtY, CSmH

1759#69
MOLYNEUX, Thomas More. *Conjunct expeditions: or, expeditions that have been carried on jointly by the fleet and army...* London. R. and J. Dodsley, 2 vols. in one. 8vo. 1759
Locations: L; RPJCB, DLC, NN

1759#70
A monody on the death of Major-Genl. James Wolfe. To which is added some particulars of his life... London. M. Thrush, 19p. 4to. 1759
Note: SABIN 104989n.
Locations: RPJCB, CaOTU

1759#71
MOREAU, Jacob Nicolas (compiler). *The mystery revealed; or, Truth brought to light.* London. W. Cater, etc. 319p. 8vo. 1759
Note: SABIN 51661. A translation of *Mémoire contenant le précis des faits, avec leurs pièces justificatives...* a work by French government to show British aggression in North America: (Paris, 1756).
Locations: L; DLC, RPJCB, MiU-C

1759#72
Motives to return to God with all the heart, drawn from the consideration of his providential goodness towards Great-Britain in the year past... London. J. Waugh, 3p. F. [1759]
Note: Victories in North America.
Locations: L; RPJCB

1759#73
A new song, sung by Mr. Beard. [London]. [1759]
Note: Madden collection. 'On America's strand Amherst limits the land/Boscawen gives Laws on the Main.'
Locations: C;

1759#74
The Northumberland garland. Containing four excellent new songs. [London]. 8p. 12mo. [1759?]
Note: Verses on 'Britain's conquest' mention Cape Breton, Crown Point, Senegal, etc. and 'Quedec's [sic] mighty fall'.
Locations: L;

1759#75
Observations from the law of nature and nations, and the civil law; shewing that the British nation have an undoubted right... London. J. and R. Dodsley, etc., 12p. 4to. 1759
Note: SABIN 56475, KRESS 5803, HIGGS 1964. On seizure of French goods in neutral bottoms, especially from French America.
Locations: L; RPJCB, MiU-C, MH

1759#76
OBOURN, Thomas. *A sermon preached in the parish church of Kingsclere, Hants, on Thursday the 29th of November, 1759, being the day appointed for a general thanksgiving. By Thomas Obourn, A.M...* Reading: printed and sold by C. Pocock sold also by Mr. Owen, at London; Messrs. Collins and Easton at Salisbury; Mr. Aillen at Basingstoke; Mr. Wimpey in Newbury; and Mr. Greenville in Winchester, 16p. 8vo. 1759
Note: Quebec thanksgiving sermon.
Locations: MRu;

1759#77
An ode, sacred to the memory of General Wolfe. London printed for J. Millan, 8p. 2o. 1759
Locations: CSmH

1759#78
PIERS, Henry. *Victory and plenty great subjects of thanksgiving. A sermon preached in... Bexley... Kent. On Thursday the 29th of November, 1759...* London. M. Lewis, 22p. 8vo. 1759
Note: SABIN 62788. Quebec thanksgiving sermon.
Locations: MRu; Llp; DLC

1759#79
POST, Christian Frederick. *The second journal of Christian Frederick Post, on a message from the governor of Pennsylvania to the Indians on the Ohio.* London. J. Wilkie, 67p. 8vo. 1759
Note: HIGGS 2004.
Locations: MRu; DLC, RPJCB, MiU-C

1759#80
PREVOST, James. *Case on behalf of Colonel Prevost, and other foreign officers, in the Royal American Regiment.* London. 4p. 2vo. 1759
Note: Heard before the House of Lords. Signed and dated Owen Ruffhead. 28th Nov. 1759.
Locations: L;

1759#81
PRICE, Richard. *Britain's happiness, and the proper improvement of it... a sermon... at Newington-Green, Middlesex... Nov. 29. 1759.* London. A. Millar and R. Griffiths, 24p. 8vo. 1759
Note: Quebec thanksgiving sermon.
Locations: L; C; CtY, MdBJ-G

1759

1759#82
PULLEIN, Samuel. *An essay towards a method of preserving the seeds of plants in a state fit for vegetation, during long voyages. For the improvement of the British colonies in America.* London. A. Millar, T. Pote, 15p. 8vo. 1759
Note: SABIN 66626.
Locations: RPJCB, MiU-C, CSmH

1759#83
The Raree Show, or the sad case of Monsieur Ragou... [London]. s.sh. F. 1759
Note: 'Oh where is my Louisburg, where is Quebec...', etc.
Locations: C;

1759#84
Reasons for a general peace. Addressed to the legislature... London. Printed for G. Kearsley, 20p. 8vo. 1759
Locations: RPJCB, NIC

1759#85
The recommendation of William Smith, provost of the College of Philadelphia... to the University of Oxford, by the archbishop of Canterbury and others... [Oxford?]. 1759
Note: SABIN 84646. Only known in reprint of 1865.
Locations: NO COPY LOCATED.

1759#86
RICH, Edward Pickering. *A sermon preached... Nov. 29, 1759...* London. Printed for the author, 10p. 4to. 1759
Note: Quebec thanksgiving sermon. Rich was rector of Bagendon, Glos.
Locations: L; MRu;

1759#87
SCOTT, Thomas. *The reasonableness, pleasure, and benefit of national thanksgiving. A sermon preached Nov. 29, 1759 at Ipswich... Suffolk...* Ipswich. W. Craighton, sold by T. Longman, 19p. 8vo. 1759
Note: Quebec thanksgiving sermon.
Locations: L; MRu; NN

1759#88
A sermon preached... 29th of November 1759... London. R. and J. Dodsley, 20p. 4to. 1759
Note: Quebec thanksgiving sermon. Author not given.
Locations: L; CtY

1759#89
The siege of Quebec. [London]. s.sh. F. 1759
Note: Six verses; begins 'Sound your silver trumpets, now, brave boys'.
Locations: C;

1759#90
A simile. London. Printed for B. Williams, 6p. 2o. [1759?]
Note: Verse. 'Political verse directed against the elder Pitt's policies in regard to the hiring of German mercenaries and the sending of British troops to Germany in 1758–59 to oppose the French and Russians under the pretext of "fighting for America."' (NUC).
Locations: E; LEu; CLU-C, CU-BANC, OCU, TxU

1759#91
SMITH, William (1727–1803). *Discourses on several public occasions during the war in America, preached chiefly with a view to explaining the importance of the Protestant cause, in the British colonies... With an appendix...* London. A. Millar, 246p. 8vo. 1759
Note: SABIN 84601, HIGGS 2001.
Locations: L; O; DLC, RPJCB, MiU-C

1759#92
SOCIETY OF FRIENDS. *From our yearly meeting in London... the 4th to the 9th day of the 6th month, 1759. To our Friends and brethren at their ensuing yearly meeting, to be held at Philadelphia, for Pennsylvania and New Jersey.* London. 2p. F. 1759
Locations: L; PHC, MB

1759#93
The soldier's delight. Being a choice collection of songs. London. Aldermary church yard, 8p. 4to. [1759?]
Note: Contain's 'Britannia's glory' with verses on Boscawen, Amherst and Cape Breton.
Locations: L; E;

1759#94
A song on the taking of Mont-real by General Amherst. Sung by Mr. Lowe. [London]. s.sh. F. [1759?]
Note: 'The French are undone; And now Canada's won/Britannia there shall fix her throne.'.
Locations: CSmH

1759#95
Spartan lessons; or, the praise of valour; in the verses of Tyrtaeus... Glasgow. R. and A. Foulis, 30p. 4to. 1759
Note: Inscribed to 'young gentlemen... serving their country, as officers of the Highland battalions now in America'.
Locations: L; MiU-C

1759#96
SPENCER, James. *An essay on the large common American aloe, with a particular account of that which is now in bloom in the gardens of George Montgomerie, Esq;...* Bury St. Edmunds. William Green, 30p. 8vo. 1759

Note: Montgomery was of Chippenham, near Newmarket.
Locations: Lrcs; RPJCB

1759#97
STEPHENS, Thomas fl. 1759. *The castle builders: or, The history of William Stephens of the Isle of Wight, Esq; lately deceased. A political novel*. . . London. xiv, 198p. 8vo. 1759
Note: Second edition with large additions, 1759. Less a novel than a biography. William Stephens lived for 16 years in Georgia.
Locations: L; RPJCB, NN, GU

1759#98
STONE, George. *A sermon preached in Christ-Church, Dublin; on Thursday, Nov. 29, 1759*. . . Dublin. Printed for H.Bradley, [19?]p. 4to. 1759
Note: BRADSHAW 1328. The third edition. Also London, 1760 (L;).
Locations: C;

1759#99
THOMPSON, Charles. *An enquiry into the causes of the alienation of the Delaware and Shawanese Indians from the British interest*. . . *Together with the remarkable journal of Charles Frederic Post*. . . London. J. Wilkie, 184p. 8vo. 1759
Note: SABIN 95562, HIGGS 2005.
Locations: L; DLC, RPJCB, MiU-C

1759#100
TOWNLEY, James. *A sermon preached*. . . *on Thursday, November 29, 1759*. . . London. H. Kent, etc., 19p. 8vo. 1759
Note: SABIN 96373. Quebec thanksgiving sermon.
Locations: L; NN, CtY, CSmH

1759#101
VENEGAS, Miguel. *A natural and civil history of California:*. . . *translated from the original Spanish*. . . London. J. Rivington, J. Fletcher, 2 vols. 8vo. 1759
Note: HIGGS 1994.
Locations: L; DLC, RPJCB, MiU-C

1759#102
WELTON, James. *A sermon, preached at*. . . *Norwich*. . . *Nov. 29. 1759*. . . Norwich. W. Chase; sold also by Mrs Cooper, London; Mr Merrill, Cambridge; Mr Green, Bury; Mr Hollingworth, Lynn; Mr Carr, Yarmouth; Mr Fortin, Swaffham, 12p. 4to. 1759
Note: Quebec thanksgiving sermon.
Locations: L; Lampeter: St David's;

1759#103
WESLEY, John. *Hymns to be used on the Thanksgiving-day, Nov. 29, 1759. And after it*. London. [23]p. 12mo. [1759]

Note: Pagination continues from Wesley's *Hymns on the expected invasion*, London, 1759 though probably issued separately.
Locations: L; IU

1759#104
WILLIAMS, J. *The favours of providence to Britain in 1759. A sermon preached at Wokingham*. . . *Berks*. . . *29th*. . . *November 1759*. . . London. C. Henderson, R. Griffiths; Reading, S. Blackman, 30p. 8vo. 1759
Note: Quebec thanksgiving sermon.
Locations: L; MdBj-G

1759#105
WINTER, Richard. *A sermon preached at New-Court, Carey-Street; on*. . . *November 29, 1759*. . . London. J. Buckland, etc., 39p. 8vo. 1759
Note: SABIN 104825. Quebec thanksgiving sermon.
Locations: L; MRu; DLC, RPJCB, MiU-C

1759#106
The world displayed; or a *curious collection of voyages and travels*. . . London. J. Newberry, 20 vols. 18mo. 1759
Note: SABIN 105485. Compiled by Oliver Goldsmith, Samuel Johnson and Christopher Smart. Published 1759–1761. Vols I-VI have American material.
Locations: L; NN, MH, CtY

1759#107
WYNNE, R. *A sermon preached at the parish-church of St. Vedast, Foster Lane, on November 29, 1759*. . . London. T. Field, 16p. 8vo. 1759
Note: Quebec thanksgiving sermon. CSmH 306371.
Locations: CSmH

1759#108
The year 59. [London]. s.sh. F. 1759
Note: Eight verses. Celebration of Canadian conquests.
Locations: C;

1759#109
YOUNG, Arthur. *Reflections on the present state of affairs at home and abroad*. . . London. J. Coote, 51p. 8vo. 1759
Note: SABIN 106064, KRESS SUPP. 4176.
Locations: L; RPJCB, CSmH

1760#1
ALMON, John. *A new military dictionary; or, the field of war*. . . London. J. Cooke, [435]p. F. 1760
Note: SABIN 53286. Account of battles and sieges etc., 'such as relate to Great Britain and her dependencies'. First published in 80 weekly numbers.
Locations: L; DLC

1760

1760#2
An answer to the letter to two great men... London. A. Henderson, 22p. 8vo. 1760
Note: In part defends Loudoun's American campaign.
Locations: L; DLC, RPJCB, MH

1760#3
Answers to the queries, in defense of the malt distillery. Wherein the matter is attempted to be stated clearly and briefly with respect to the trading and landed interest of Great-Britain and her colonies... London. Printed for T. Payne, [4], 23, [1]p. 4to. 1760
Note: A reply to Queries in defence of the malt distillery by Sir Joseph Mawbey.
Locations: L; NNC, DLC, IU

1760#4
ASHBURNHAM, William. *A sermon preached...* February 15, 1760... London. E. Owen, etc. 88p. 4to. 1760
Note: SPG sermon for 1760, with abstract, etc.
Locations: L; DLC, RPJCB

1760#5
ASSOCIATES OF DR BRAY. *An account of the designs of the Associates of the late Dr. Bray; with an abstract of their proceedings.* London. B. Dod, 22, 16p. 8vo. 1760
Note: SABIN 7470.
Locations: L; NN

1760#6
An authentic register of the British successes... from the taking of Louisbourg... to the defeat of the French fleet... Nov. 21, 1759... London. G. Kearsley, 126p. 12mo. 1760
Note: SABIN 30930. A second edition, London, 1760 'to which is now added, Gen. Wolfe's letter to Mr. Pitt, a few days before the taking of Quebec...'.
Locations: L; DLC, RPJCB

1760#7
BEATTY, Charles. *To the pious, charitable, and well-disposed Christians, inhabitants of Great Britain... the humble memorial of Charles Beatty.* London. s.sh. F. 1760
Note: For poor distressed dissenting ministers in Pennsylvania, Virginia, etc., attacked by Indians.
Locations: RPJCB

1760#8
The Beavers: A fable. London. Printed for S. Hooper, 23p. 4to. 1760
Note: Verse satire on Seven Years War.
Locations: L; CSmH

1760#9
BELSHAM, Jacobus. *Canadia. Ode...* London. 18p. 4to. 1760
Note: Latin verses on taking of Quebec.
Locations: L; Ldw; DLC, RPJCB, MiU-C

1760#10
BOWNAS, Samuel. *An account of the captivity of Elizabeth Hanson, now or late of Kachecky; in New England: who, with four of her children and servant-maid, was taken captive by the Indians, and carried into Canada... Taken in substance from her own mouth by Samuel Bownas...* London. S. Clark, 28p. 8vo. 1760
Note: SABIN 30265, SMITH I, 309, HIGGS 2231. First printed Philadelphia, 1728, (EVANS 2996). A second edition in 1760.
Locations: ABu; DLC, NN, ICN

1760#11
Britannia, or the death of Wolfe. Newcastle. 8p. [1760?]
Note: A chapbook.
Locations: GU;

1760#12
BRITISH FREEHOLDER. *Unanswerable arguments against a peace.* Dublin. S. Smith, 24p. 8vo. 1760
Note: Also printed London, 1760. British should drive French entirely from the Americas.
Locations: L; CSmH, N

1760#13
BRYAN, Hugh. *Living Christianity delineated, in the diaries and letters of... Mr Hugh Bryan and Mrs Mary Hutson, both of South Carolina... preface by the Reverend Mr John Cander and the Reverend Mr Thomas Gibbons.* London. J. Buckland, 171p. 12mo. 1760
Locations: L; DLC, RPJCB, MB

1760#14
BURKE, William. *Remarks on the letter addressed to two great men. In a letter to the author of that piece.* London. R. and J. Dodsley, 64p. 8vo. [1760]
Note: SABIN 96404, HIGGS 2241, KRESS 5835. Two or more other London editions in 1760. Also Dublin, 1760. A section on British rights in North America.
Locations: L; DLC, CtY, N

1760#15
A candid and fair examination of the remarks on the letter to two great men... London. For A. Henderson, 24p. 8vo. 1760
Locations: RPJCB, MH, CSmH

1760#16
CARLYLE, Alexander. *The question relating to a Scots militia considered...* Edinburgh. G. Hamilton and J. Balfour, 45p. 8vo. 1760

Note: HIGGS 2380. Also a corrected second edition in 1760. A militia would release troops for America; other references to the American war.
Locations: L; CtY, MH, NN

1760#17
CARTER, Landon. *A letter to the Right Reverend Father in God the Lord B—p of L—n. Occasioned by a letter of his lordship's to the L—ds of T-e, on the subject of the Act of Assembly passed in the year 1758, intituled, An act to enable the inhabitants of this colony to discharge their publick dues, etc. in money for the ensuing year. From Virginia.* London. Printed in Virginia, and reprinted in London. 2, 60p. 8vo. 1760
Note: SABIN 40537. First printed [Williamsburgh, 1759], EVANS 41028, BRISTOL B2016. ESTC lists another issue (?), 56, 2p. in 1760 at Lu; (Porteous collection).
Locations: CSmH

1760#18
CATO. *Reasons for not restoring Guadeloupe at a peace. In a letter addressed to the Right Honourable the Earl of Hallifax. . . In answer to certain animadversions contained in a letter to two great men.* London. J. Williams, 46p. 8vo. 1760
Note: SABIN 290043, HIGGS 2240.
Locations: NN, MHi, MiU-C, NN

1760#19
CATTON, William. *A poem on the taking of Cape Breton and Cherbourg. . .* London. s.sh. 1o [1760]
Note: Mentions Louisbourg, Crown Point, etc. Dedicated to Wolfe's memory.
Locations: L;

1760#20
Chapter of Admirals. To which *are added. . . Patrick O'Neal's return from drubbing the French. An Anacreonic song.* [London]. 8p. [1760?]
Note: A chapbook. The date is notional. Mockery of Irish boasting.
Locations: EN;

1760#21
CHURCH OF ENGLAND. *A form of prayer and thanksgiving. . . to be used. . . on Sunday the twelfth of October 1760. . . on occasion of the late successes of his majesty's arms in North-America. . .* London. J. Baskett, etc., 4p. 4to. 1760
Locations: L; Llp; O; CSmH

1760#22
CLARKE, Richard. *A second warning to the world, by the spirit of prophecy. . .* London. J. Townsend, 250p. 8vo. 1760
Note: Clarke was rector of St. Philips, Charleston, S. C.
Locations: L; Ldw;

1760#23
CLARKE, Richard. *A spiritual voice to the Christian church, and to the Jews. . . in which the approaching millennium is supported. . .* London. J. Townshend, 140p. 8vo. 1760
Note: Predicts freeing of 'servants' after 6 years of the millennium. Clarke was rector of St. Philip's, Charleston, S. C.
Locations: L;

1760#24
COADE, George. *A letter to a noble Lord: wherein it is demonstrated, that all difficulties in obtaining an honourable and lasting peace. . . are. . . imaginary.* London. G. Kearsly, 46p. 8vo. 1760
Note: SABIN 40419.
Locations: RPJCB, MiU-C, ICN

1760#25
COCKINGS, George. *War: an heroic poem. From the taking of Minorca by the French, to the raising of the siege of Quebec. . .* London. C. Say for the author; and sold by J. Cook, xiv, 174p. 8vo. 1760
Note: Expanded editions in 1762, 1765. Reprinted Boston and Portsmouth, New Hampshire, 1762, etc.
Locations: CSmH; NN

1760#26
A collection of testimonies concerning *several ministers of the gospel among the people called Quakers. . .* London. L. Hinde, 372p. 8vo. 1760
Note: SABIN 66920, SMITH, II, 720.
Locations: L; C; O; DLC, RPJCB

1760#27
A copy of a letter *from a gentleman in Guadaloupe, to his friend in London. . .* London. 19p. 8vo. 1760
Note: SABIN 16723 says privately printed. On value of Guadaloupe against Canada. Forecasts rebellion in North America. Reply to a *Gentleman's Magazine* article of May 1760.
Locations: RPJCB

1760#28
CUMING, Patrick. *A sermon preached. . . February 4. 1760.* Edinburgh. A. Kincaid, 86p. 8vo. 1760
Note: Society in Scotland for Propagating Christian Knowledge sermon for 1760. Discusses war in America, Scots contribution, and progress of gospel there as a result of victories.
Locations: L; NN, MH

1760#29
DAWSON, Eli. *A discourse, delivered at Quebec, in the chappel belonging to the convent of the Ursulins, September 27th, 1759; occasioned by the success of our arms in the*

1760

reduction of that capital... London. R. Griffiths, 14p. 4to. 1760
Note: SABIN 18929.
Locations: L; Ct; MH, RPJCB, MiU-C

1760#30
DILWORTH, W. H. *The history of the present war... to the conclusion of the year 1759...* London. H. Woodgate, S. Brooks, 166p. 18mo. 1760
Note: SABIN 20185.
Locations: C; MB, MiU-C, CSmH

1760#31
DOUGLAS, John. *A letter addressed to two great men, on the prospect of the peace; and the terms necessary to be insisted upon in the negociation...* London. A. Millar, 56p. 8vo. 1760
Note: SABIN 20684, 40263, HIGGS 2238, KRESS 5846. Also two Dublin editions in 1760. Reprinted Boston, 1760.
Locations: L; RPJCB, MiU-C

1760#32
FLETCHER, William. *A sermon, preached in St. Andrew's, Dublin; before the Honourable House of Commons: on Thursday, Nov. 29, 1759...* Dublin. Printed for Cornelius Wynne, 19, [1]p. 4to. 1760
Note: Quebec thanksgiving sermon.
Locations: L; Llp; Lmh; MoU

1760#33
FLLOYD, Thomas. *Bibliotheca biographica: a synopsis of universal biography...* London. J. Hinton, etc. 3 vols. 8vo. 1760
Note: Wolfe's biography included.
Locations: L; CtY, DLC, CU

1760#34
FORTESCUE, J. *A sermon preach'd at Topsham on Thursday November the 29th, 1759...* Exeter. A. Brice and sold by B. Thorn and E. Stone, 30p. 8vo. 1760
Note: Quebec thanksgiving sermon.
Locations: L; MSaE

1760#35
FRANKLIN, Benjamin. *The interest of Great Britain considered, with regard to her colonies, and the acquisitions of Canada and Guadaloupe. To which are added, Observations concerning the increase of mankind, peopling of countries...* London. T. Becket, 58p. 8vo. 1760
Note: SABIN 35450, HIGGS 2268, KRESS 5854. Reprinted in 1760 in Dublin, Boston and Philadelphia.
Locations: L; C; E; DLC, CtY, RPJCB

1760#36
A full and candid answer to a pamphlet, entitled, Considerations on the present German war. London. J. Pridden, etc. 86p. 8vo. 1760
Note: Discusses Prussia, Hanover, France and America. Another edition in 1760.
Locations: L; DLC, NN, MH

1760#37
A garland of new songs... General Wolfe's song... Newcastle. 8p. [1760?]
Note: A chapbook.
Locations: GU;

1760#38
A garland of new songs. The world's a stage... Britannia, or the death of General Wolfe. Newcastle. 8p. [1760?]
Note: A chapbook.
Locations: Gp;

1760#39
General reflections occasioned by the letter addressed to two great men, and the remarks on that letter. London. E. Dilly, 23p. 8vo. 1760
Note: SABIN 26900.
Locations: L; DLC, RPJCB, MHi

1760#40
GODDARD, Peter Stephen. *A sermon preached November 29, 1759... at Fornham... and Edmondsbury...* London. Bury St. Edmunds. Crowder and Co., etc. 20p. 8vo. 1760
Note: Quebec thanksgiving sermon.
Locations: L; Ct; Llp;

1760#41
GREAT BRITAIN. LORDS COMMISSIONERS OF APPEAL IN PRIZE CAUSES. *Elizabeth Galley. New York. The case of the respondents.* London. 4p. 1760
Note: Also *The case of the claimant and appellant* 4p. and *Appendix to the respondents case*, 4p.
Locations: L;

1760#42
GREAT BRITAIN. PARLIAMENT. *An Act for permitting tea to be exported to Ireland, and... America, without paying the inland duties... (That is, so much therof as relates to the exportation of tea).* London. Printed by Thomas Baskett; and by the assigns of Robert Baskett, [2], 5–21, [1]p. 12mo. 1760
Note: This act was passed in 1747.
Locations: L;

1760#43
GREAT BRITAIN. PARLIAMENT. *An act for vesting certain estates in Pennsylvania, New-Jersey, and Maryland, belonging to the proprietors of a partnership commonly called the Pennsylvania Land-Company in London...* London. 31p. F. [1760]
Locations: L; RPJCB

1760#44
GREAT BRITAIN. SOVEREIGN. GEORGE III. *By the King, A proclamation [for continuing officers in plantations till his majesty's pleasure shall be further signified... 27 October 1760].* London. T. Baskett, etc. s.sh. F. 1760
Note: BRIGHAM 210. Cf. CRAWFORD p. 97.
Locations: L; DLC, MiU-C

1760#45
GREAT BRITAIN. SOVEREIGN. GEORGE III. *His Majesty's most gracious speech to both Houses of Parliament, on Tuesday the eighteenth day of November, 1760.* London. Printed by Thomas Baskett; and by the assigns of Robert Baskett: sold by John Bowles and son; and Thomas Kitchen, s.sh. F. 1760
Note: Refers to the total reduction of Canada.
Locations: MH-H, CaQMM

1760#46
HANWAY, Jonas. *An account of the Society for the encouragement of the British troops, in Germany and North America...* London. 91, 55p. 8vo. 1760
Note: SABIN 100, 30276, HIGGS 2338, KRESS 5859.
Locations: L; C; O; DLC, RPJCB, MiU-C

1760#47
HEATH, John. *God's blessing on a people's just endeavours... A sermon preached at Writtle in Essex, on Thursday the 29th of November, 1759...* London. J. Shuckburgh, 14p. 4to. 1760
Note: Quebec thanksgiving sermon.
Locations: L;

1760#48
The hero's garland. Being a collection of new songs... London. 8p. 8vo. [1760?]
Note: L; copy is missing but probably American material.
Locations: L;

1760#49
The Highlander's march a garland. Composed of several new songs viz. 1. The Highlander's march to America... Edinburgh? 1760
Note: Damaged part of an 8p. chapbook. 'O the French like Foxes do lie in the Wood', etc.
Locations: E;

1760#50
A hint to the fair sex. A garland, containing six new songs. Leominster, P. Davis; Worcester, E. Elcox; Gloucester, R. Netherwood, 8p. 12mo. [1760]
Note: Chapbook. Patriotic verses refer to Amherst, Wolfe, etc.
Locations: L;

1760#51
The history of the war: A new British medley. Proper to be said or sung in all companies of true Britons. London. 2mo 1760
Locations: NO COPY LOCATED.

1760#52
Hymen: an accurate description of the ceremonies used in marriage, by every nation in the known world... Dedicated to the ladies of Great-Britain and Ireland. London. I. Pottinger, 206p. 12mo. 1760
Note: SABIN 34131. Florida, Hudson Bay, Mississippi and other Indians.
Locations: L; RPJCB, MiU-C, NN

1760#53
JEFFERYS, Thomas. *Directions for navigating the gulf and river of St. Laurence; with a particular account of the bays, roads... Published by command of the Right Hon. the Lords Commissioners of the Admiralty.* London. For Thomas Jefferys, 31p. 4to. 1760
Note: SABIN 35961.
Locations: L; O; MH, RPJCB

1760#54
JEFFERYS, Thomas. *The natural and civil history of the French dominions in North and South America...* London. T. Jefferys, 2 vols. 2o. 1760
Note: SABIN 35964, HIGGS 2226.
Locations: L; LEu; MHi, RPJCB, MiU-C

1760#55
JOHNSTONE, Charles. *Chrysal: or, the adventures of a guinea. Wherein are exhibited views of several striking scenes,... in America, England, Holland, Germany and Portugal. By an adept...* London. Printed for T. Becket, 2 vols. 12mo. 1760
Note: Also Dublin, 1760. The American references are mainly to Jamaica and Peru, but there are some general remarks on French encroachments in North America.
Locations: L; C; CtY, DFo, ICN, RPJCB

1760#56
A journal of the siege of Quebec. To which is annexed, a correct plan of the environs of Quebec... London. 16p. 4to. [1760]
Note: SABIN 67008.
Locations: DLC, RPJCB, MB

1760#57
KIDDELL, John. *A sermon preached at Tiverton, Devon, November 29, 1759...* London. J. Ward; sold also by Mr. Tozer in Exon. 31p. 8vo. 1760
Note: Quebec thanksgiving sermon.
Locations: L; MRu;

1760

1760#58
LAVINGTON, Samuel. *God the giver of victory: a sermon, preached at Bideford, Devon, being the day appointed for a general thanksgiving... for the success of His Majesty's arms...* London. Printed for J. Buckland, J. Ward; and A. Tozer at Exeter, 2, 38p. 8vo. 1760
Note: Quebec thanksgiving sermon.
Locations: MRu; E;

1760#59
A letter from a gentleman in the country to his friend in town, on his perusal of a pamphlet addressed to Two Great Men... London. R. Davis, 20p. 8vo. 1760
Note: SABIN 40293.
Locations: L; DLC, RPJCB, CtY

1760#60
A letter to an honourable brigadier general, commander in chief of his majesty's forces in Canada. London. J. Burd, 31p. 8vo. 1760
Note: SABIN 36903, CHURCH 1034.
Locations: L; C; E; RPJCB, MiU-C, CSmH

1760#61
A letter to the great man, occasioned by the Letter to two great men... By a citizen of London... London. W. Bristow, 61p. 8vo. 1760
Note: SABIN 40479.
Locations: DLC, RPJCB, MiU-C

1760#62
LYTTELTON, George. *Dialogues of the dead.* London. W. Sandby, 320p. 8vo. 1760
Note: Contains 'dialogue' with Wolfe. Several editions and issues.
Locations: L; DLC, RPJCB, CtY

1760#63
LOCKMAN, John. *Verses on the demise of the late king and the accession of his present majesty...* London. R. and J. Dodsley, 8p. F. 1760
Note: 'Freed Canada from her corroding chains/And gave her bliss beneath a British reign' etc.
Locations: CSmH, MH

1760#64
MAUDUIT, Israel. *Considerations on the present German war.* London. J. Wilkie, 137p. 8vo. [1760]
Note: SABIN 46916, HIGGS 2366. Six London and one Dublin editions in 1760–1.
Locations: L; DLC, RPJCB, MiU-C

1760#65
MAYHEW, Jonathan. *Two discourses delivered... October the 25th, 1759, being the day appointed by authority... as a day of thanksgiving for the success of his majesty's arms... reduction of Quebec...* Boston and London, A. Millar, [84]p. 8vo. 1760
Note: First printed Boston 1759, (EVANS 8192). Quebec thanksgiving sermon.
Locations: L; Cq; MnU, RPJCB

1760#66
MERCHANT OF LONDON. *A state of the trade carried on with the French, on the island of Hispaniola, by the merchants in North America, under colour of flags of truce...* London. W. Owen, 29p. 8vo. 1760
Note: Cf. SABIN 90634. KRESS 5904, HIGGS 2207.
Locations: L; MRu; RPJCB, NN, MH

1760#67
Military maxims, or the standard of generalship. Addressed to a British commander. By an officer in a marching regiment. London. A. Morley, 46p. 8vo. 1760
Note: Wolfe and Quebec.
Locations: CSmH, N

1760#68
MILLER, Philip. *Figures of the most beautiful, useful, and uncommon plants described in the gardeners dictionary.* London. J. Rivington, 2 vols. 2o. 1760
Note: Originally published in parts, from 1755.
Locations: L; MH-A, CtY, NN

1760#69
The naval chronicle; or voyages, travels, expeditions... of the most celebrated English navigators... London. J. Fuller, 3 vols. 8vo. 1760
Note: SABIN 52075. Considerable American material.
Locations: L; O; DLC, DN, PPL

1760#70
NEWCOMB, Thomas. *Novus epigrammatum delectus: or, Original State epigrams and minor odes...* London. G. Kearsly, 96p. 8vo. 1760
Note: SABIN 54939. Several poems on conquest of North America.
Locations: L; DLC

1760#71
An ode, in two parts, humbly inscrib'd to... William Pitt... London. J. Hart, 19p. 4to. 1760
Note: SABIN 63095. Quebec campaign.
Locations: O; DLC, RPJCB, CtY

1760#72
One thousand seven hundred and fifty nine: a poem, inscribed to every Briton who bore a part in the service of that distinguished year... London. R. Baldwin, 122p. 4to. 1760
Locations: CSmH, MiU-C

1760#73
PATRICK J. *Quebec: a poetical essay, in imitation of the Miltonic style: Being a regular narrative of... transactions... under... Saunders and... Wolfe...* London. P. Whitridge, T. Becket, 30p. 4to. 1760
Note: SABIN 59075.
Locations: CaOTP

1760#74
PATRIOT. *A political essay upon the English and French colonies in northern and southern America, considered in a new light...* London. G. Woodfall, 15p. 8vo. 1760
Locations: L; RPJCB, CtY

1760#75
PHILLMORE, J. *Two dialogues on the man-trade.* London. J. Waugh, etc. 68p. 8vo. 1760
Note: Attack on slave trade and slavery in plantations.
Locations: L; NN, NIC

1760#76
PICHON, Thomas. *Genuine letters and memoirs, relating to the natural, civil, and commercial history of the islands of Cape Breton, and Saint John... to... 1758... By an impartial Frenchman...* London. J. Nourse. 400p. 8vo. 1760
Note: SABIN 62611, HIGGS 2229, KRESS SUPP. 4203.
Locations: L; DLC, RPJCB, MiU-C

1760#77
Political thoughts. Printed in the year 1760. London. 68p. 8vo. 1760
Note: Some discussion of Canada versus Guadeloupe; and North American back country.
Locations: L; E; INU-Li

1760#78
PRINGLE, Sir John. *The life of General James Wolfe, the conqueror of Canada, or, the eulogium of that renowned hero...* London. G. Kearsly, 24p. 4to. 1760
Note: SABIN 58057.
Locations: L; E; Ob; DLC, RPJCB, CSmH

1760#79
PRYCE, David. *To the King's most excellent Majesty. The petition of David Pryce, Esq. master and commander in your Majesty's Royal Navy, and late agent to transports, in North America, under the direction of the then General, (now Lord) Amherst.* London. 8, [2]p. 4to. 1760?
Locations: Lpro

1760#80
Remarks on a pamphlet entitled, Reasons why the approaching treaty of peace should be debated in Parliament, etc. In a letter to the author. London. M. Cooper, 24p. 8vo. 1760
Locations: MRu; RPJCB, MiU-C, CSmH

1760#81
Remarks on two popular pamphlets viz, the Considerations on the present German war; and the Full and candid answer to the Considerations. London. 4, 27, 1p. 8vo. 1760
Note: HIGGS 2370, KRESS 5896. The considerations was by Israel Mauduit, above, 1759.
Locations: L; RPJCB, MH-BA, NIC

1760#82
Resolute Dick's garland. Composed of several excellent new songs. [London]. [1760?]
Note: Contains 'General Wolfe's dying words; or, the conquest of Quebeck.'.
Locations: MH

1760#83
RUFFHEAD, Owen. *Reasons why the approaching treaty of peace should be debated in Parliament... In a letter addressed to a great man... occasioned by... a letter addressed to two great men...* London. R. Griffiths, 49p. 8vo. 1760
Note: SABIN 68296.
Locations: L; RPJCB, MiU-C

1760#84
SHEBBEARE, John. *The history of the excellence and decline of the constitution, religion, laws... of the Sumatrans...* London. G. Shearsley, 2 vols. 8vo. [1760]
Note: A satire on English affairs. References to colonies and suggestions for reforms.
Locations: L; NN, CtY, RPB

1760#85
SHEBBEARE, John. *A letter to the people of England, on the necessity of putting an immediate end to the war; and the means of obtaining an advantageous peace.* London. R. Griffiths, 54p. 8vo. 1760
Note: SABIN 40507, HIGGS 2282.
Locations: L; DLC, RPJCB, MiU-C

1760#86
Short animadversions on the difference now set up between gin and rum, and our mother country and colonies... London. C. Henderson, 19p. 4to. 1760
Note: HIGGS 2237, KRESS 5900.
Locations: L; DLC, RPJCB, MH-BA

1760#87
SMITH, Thomas. *The terrible calamities that are occasioned by war... a sermon... November the 29th, 1759...* London. 35p. 8vo. 1760
Note: SABIN 84347. Quebec thanksgiving sermon.
Locations: L;

1760#88
SOCIETY OF FRIENDS. *Epistles from the yearly meeting of the people called Quakers, held in London, to the*

1760

quarterly and monthly meetings in Great Britain, Ireland, and elsewhere; from the year 1675, to 1759, inclusive... London. S. Clark, 275p. F. 1760
Note: SABIN 66923.
Locations: L; PHC, NN, CtY

1760#89
Some remarks on the Royal *Navy. To which are annexed some short but interesting reflections on a future peace.* London. R. Davis, 57p. 8vo. [1760]
Note: SABIN 86748. Many American references.
Locations: NN, MH

1760#90
STRATIOTICUS. *A scheme for the general good of the nation... and for the effectual security of our commerce and possessions abroad...* London. S. Hooper, 15p. 8vo. 1760
Note: KRESS SUPP. 4212. Regiments in America ought to be disbanded and given land there.
Locations: MH-BA, ICN

1760#91
TAGG, Tommy. *A collection of pretty poems for the amusement of children three foot high. By Tommy Tagg, Esq; The fifty seventh edition, adorned with above sixty cuts.* London. Printed for the booksellers of Europe, Asia, Africa and America, and sold at the Bible and Sun in St. Paul's Church-Yard [by J. Newbery], [4], 104p. 24o 1760
Note: Also, *A collection of pretty poems for the amusement of children six foot high,* London, 1757, 1760, with same imprint. Included because of the imprint.
Locations: NNPM

1760#92
THORNTON, Bonnell. *City Latin; or, Critical and political remarks...* London. R. Stevens, 35p. 8vo. 1760
Note: 'By the Rev. Busby Birch.' Satire on Latin of dedication on stone at Blackfriars bridge to William Pitt 'qui vigore ingenii, animi constantia/Imperium Britannicum/in Asia, Africa et America/restituit, auxit et stabilvit...'.
Locations: L; MH, CtY, NN

1760#93
Thoughts on present war and *future peace; wherein our present measures and alliances, are candidly considered...* London. M. Cooper, 42p. 8vo. 1760
Note: Mainly about Europe. Supports the views on America in Douglas's *Letter to two great men,* above, 1760.

Locations: C; MRu; RPJCB, MH, PU

1760#94
THUMB, Thomas. *Proposals for printing by subscription, the history of the publick life and distinguished actions of Vice-Admiral Sir Thomas Brazen, commander of an American squadron in the last age... In three volumes in quarto, adorn'd throughout with cuts...* London. 18, [4]p. 8vo. 1760
Note: Thomas Brazen was supposedly Thomas Pownall.
Locations: MBAt, MeB

1760#95
THURLOW, Edward. *A refutation of the letter to an honble. brigadier-general, commander of His Majesty's forces in Canada. By an officer.* London. R. Stevens, 52p. 8vo. 1760
Note: SABIN 36904, 95766. CHURCH 1036. The general was George Townshend. Four editions in 1760.
Locations: L; C; MRu; NN, RPJCB, MiU-C

1760#96
The travels and adventures of *John Thomson, who was taken and carried to America...* Edinburgh? 12p. [1760?]
Note: A chapbook. Kidnapped from Aberdeen; captured by savages in 1759. Based on Peter Williamson? Date is uncertain.
Locations: E;

1760#97
A vindication of the conduct *of the present war; in a letter to ******.* London. J. and R. Tonson, 43p. 8vo. 1760
Note: SABIN 99804. Also Dublin, 1761.
Locations: L; DLC, RPJCB, MiU-C

1760#98
VOLUNTEER IN THE BRITISH SERVICE. *Genuine letters from a volunteer, in the British service, at Quebec.* London. H. Whitridge, A. and C. Corbett, 39p. 8vo. [1760]
Note: SABIN 26962.
Locations: L; C; RPJCB, MiU-C, NN

1760#99
The voyages and cruises of *Commodore Walker, during the late Spanish and French Wars. In two volumes.* London. A. Millar, 2 vols., 12mo. 1760
Note: References to Carolinas.
Locations: L; DLC, RPJCB, NN

1760#100
WALLACE, George. *A system of the principles of the laws of Scotland...* London. A. Millar, etc. 592p. 2o. 1760
Note: Stated to be in two volumes but only one published. Discusses slavery and colonies.
Locations: L; C; MH-L

1760#101
WALLIN, Benjamin. *The joyful sacrifice of a prosperous nation. A sermon preached at the meeting-house near Maze Pond, Southwark. . . November 29, 1759. . .* London. Printed for the author. Sold by G. Keith, etc. 34p. 8vo. 1760
Note: SABIN 101123. Quebec thanksgiving sermon.
Locations: L; CtY, MWA

1760#102
WILLIAMSON, Peter. *A brief account of the war in N. America. . . the necessity and advantage of keeping Canada. . . the maintaining of friendly correspondence with the Indians. To which is added a description of the natives. . .* Edinburgh. Printed for the author, 38p. 8vo. [1760]
Note: SABIN 104465.
Locations: RPJCB, CtY, PHi 1

INDEX OF TITLES

Abel being dead yet speaketh; or, The life and death of... Mr. John Cotton... —NORTON, John. 1658#10

An abreviate of Hollands deliverance by, and ingratitude to the Crown of England... —CLIFFE, Edward. 1665#14

An abridgment of Mr Baxter's History of his life and times. With an account of the ministers who were ejected, after the Restauration... —CALAMY, Edmund, D. D. 1702#5

An abridgement of the laws in force and use in her majesty's plantations... —1704#1

An abridgement of the life of... Dr Cotton Mather... Taken from the account... published by his son, the Reverend Mr. Samuel Mather... —JENNINGS, David. 1744#28

An abridgement of the publick laws of Virginia, in force and use, June 10, 1720... —BEVERLEY, Robert. 1722#1

An abridgement of the statutes and rules of the Society... —SOCIETY IN SCOTLAND FOR PROPAGATING CHRISTIAN KNOWLEDGE. 1732#37

An abridgment of Mr. David Brainerd's Journal among the Indians. Or, the rise and progress of a remarkable work of grace among... —BRAINERD, David. 1748#1

An abridgment of several acts and clauses of acts of Parliament, relating to the trade and navigation of Great Britain to, from... —1739#1

The abrogation of the Jewish sabbath. —ASPINWALL, William. 1657#1

The absolute necessity of salvation through Christ. A sermon, preached... January 2. 1758... —WITHERSPOON, John. 1758#52

An abstract of a charter granted by his majesty... —1683#1

Abstract of a form of prayer and thanksgiving to almighty God; to be used in all churches and chapels... on Thursday the 29th... —CHURCH OF ENGLAND. 1759#16

An abstract, of a letter from a person of eminency and worth in [New] Caledonia, to a friend in Boston in New England... —PATERSON, William. 1699#13

An abstract of a letter from Thomas Paskell of Pensilvania to his friend J. J. of Chippenham. —PASKELL, Thomas. 1683#16

An abstract of all the statutes made concerning aliens... Also, all the laws made for securing our plantation trade to our selves... —HAYNE, Samuel. 1685#17

An abstract of laws and government... Collected and digested by... Mr. John Cotton... published after his death, by William Aspinwall... —COTTON, John. 1655#6

An abstract of some of the printed laws of New England which are either contrary or not agreeable to the laws of England... —1689#1

An abstract of the case of James Annesley, Esq. Veritas Praevalebit. Printed in the year 1751... —1751#1

An abstract of the case of the Honourable James Annesley... humbly submitted to the consideration of all disinterested persons... —1754#1

An abstract of the Charter granted to the Society for the Propagation of the Gospel in Foreign Parts; with a short account of what... —SOCIETY FOR THE PROPAGATION OF THE GOSPEL. 1702#25

An abstract of the form of prayer and thanksgiving... to be used on... the 29th day of November, 1759... —1759#1

An abstract of the proceedings of the Society for the Propagation of the Gospel... 1715. —SOCIETY FOR THE PROPAGATION OF THE GOSPEL. 1716#8

An abstract of the scheme of government so far as it relates to the grantees in trust, for settling the land lying between Nova-Scotia... —1721#1

An abstract or abbreviation of some few of the many (later and former) testimonys from the inhabitants of Jersey, and other eminent persons... —1681#1

An abstract or [sic] the lawes of New England as they are now established. —COTTON, John. 1641#5

The academy of armory. —HOLME, Randle. 1688#8

The acccomplish'd vagabond, or, The compleat mumper: exemplifyed in the... enterprizes of Bampfylde Carew... —1745#1

An accidence to the English tongue... —JONES, Hugh. 1724#10

An account of a great fight, between the Christians, and the Quakers, and also how they blew themselves up, with a magazine of there... —1701#1

An account of a remarkable work of grace, or the great success of the gospel, in Virginia. In a letter... to the Rev. Mr. Bellamy... —DAVIES, Samuel. 1752#5

An account of a voyage for the discovery of North-West Passage by Hudson's Streights, to the Western and Southern Ocean of America... —CLERK OF THE CALIFORNIA. 1748#4

An account of conferences held and treaties made, between Major-General Sir William Johnson, Bart. and the chief Sachems and Warriours... —PEMBERTON, Israel. 1756#58

An account of money received and disbursed for the orphan-house in Georgia... To which is prefixed A plan of the building. —WHITEFIELD, George. 1741#48

An account of money, received and expended by the Rev. Mr Whitefield, for the poor of Georgia. —WHITEFIELD, George. 1739#72

An account of Monsieur de la Salle's last expedition and discoveries in North America... Made English from the Paris original. —1698#1

An account of six years residence in Hudson's Bay, from 1733 to 1736, and 1744 to 1747... —ROBSON, Joseph. 1752#15

An account of some of the labours, exercises, travels and perils by sea and land, of John Taylor, of York... —TAYLOR, John. 1710#22

An account of the captivity of Elizabeth Hanson, now or late of Kachecky; in New England: who, with four of her children and servant-maid... —BOWNAS, Samuel. 1760#10

An account of the colony in Nova Scotia. —1751#2

An account of the commitment, arraignment, tryal and condemnation of Nicholas Bayard, Esq; for high treason, in endeavouring... —BAYARD, Nicholas. 1703#3

An account of the constitution and present state of Great Britain, together with a view of its trade, policy, and interest... —1759#2

An account of the countries adjoining to Hudson's Bay... With an abstract of Captain Middleton's journal, and observations upon his behaviour... —DOBBS, Arthur. 1744#15

An account of the customs and manners of the Micmakis and Maricheets savage nations, now dependent on the government of Great... —1758#1

An account of the designs of the Associates of the late Dr. Bray; with an abstract of their proceedings. —ASSOCIATES OF DR BRAY. 1760#5

An account of the Earl of Bellomont's proceedings at New-York. Offer'd to be proved before the Committee of Trade and Plantations... —1701#2

An account of the endeavours... by the Society for the Propagation of the Gospel... to instruct... slaves in New York. Together... —HUMPHREYS, David. 1730#15

An account of the European settlements in America. In six parts... —BURKE, William. 1757#5

An account of the expedition to Carthagena... —KNOWLES, Charles, Admiral Sir. 1743#21

An account of the fair and impartial proceedings of the Lords Proprietors, governour and council of... South Carolina, in answer to... —SOUTH CAROLINA. PROPRIETORS, GOVERNOR AND COUNCIL. 1706#19

An account of the foundation, and establishment of a design now on foot, for a settlement on the Golden Islands, to the south of Port Royal in Carolina... —BARNWELL, John. 1720#4

An account of the great divisions amongst the Quakers in Pensilvania, etc. As appears by their own book... printed 1692... intituled... The plea of the innocent... —KEITH, George. 1692#7

An account of the late action of the New-Englanders, under... Sir William Phips, against the French at Canada... —SAVAGE, Thomas. 1691#18

An account of the late revolution in New-England. Together with the declaration of the gentlemen, merchants, and inhabitants of Boston, and the country adjacent... —BYFIELD, Nathaniel. 1689#4

An account of the life and travels in the work of the ministry, of J. F. To which are added, divers epistles to friends in Great Britain and America... —FOTHERGILL, John. 1753#6

An account of the life of that ancient servant of Jesus Christ, John Richardson... —RICHARDSON, John. 1757#36

An account of the life, travels and Christian experiences in the work of the ministry of Samuel Bownas. —BOWNAS, Samuel. 1756#10

An account of the method and success of inoculating for the small-pox in Boston in New-England. In a letter from a gentleman there, to his friend in London. —MATHER, Cotton. 1722#21

An account of the present state of Nova-Scotia: in two letters to a noble lord: one from a gentleman in the navy newly arrived... —1756#1

An account of the progress of the reformation of manners, in England and Ireland, and other parts of the world... —WOODWARD, Josiah. 1701#45

An account of the propagation of the gospel in foreign parts. Continued to... 1705... —SOCIETY FOR THE PROPAGATION OF THE GOSPEL. 1705#18

An account of the propagation of the gospel in foreign parts, what the Society hath done... in her majesty's plantations, colonies and factories... —SOCIETY FOR THE PROPAGATION OF THE GOSPEL. 1704#25

An account of the province of Carolina in America. Together with an abstract of the patent, and several other necessary and useful... —WILSON, Samuel. 1682#30

An account of the Quakers politicks. —KEITH, George. 1700#20

An account of the rise, constitution, and management of the Society... —SOCIETY IN SCOTLAND FOR PROPAGATING CHRISTIAN KNOWLEDGE. 1714#19

An account of the societies for reformation of manners in London and Westminster... —WOODWARD, Josiah. 1699#20

An account of the Society for promoting Christian Knowledge. —SOCIETY FOR PROMOTING CHRISTIAN KNOWLEDGE. 1738#22

An account of the Society for Propagating the gospel in foreign parts. . . with their proceedings and success, and hopes of continual progress. . . —SOCIETY FOR THE PROPAGATION OF THE GOSPEL. 1706#17

An account of the Society for the encouragement of the British troops, in Germany and North America. . . —HANWAY, Jonas. 1760#46

An account of two missionary voyages by appointment of the Society for the Propagation of the Gospel in Foreign Parts. The one to. . . —THOMPSON, Thomas. 1758#47

An account of two voyages to New England, wherein you have the setting out of a ship, with the charges; the prices of all necessaries. . . —JOSSELYN, John. 1674#6

An account shewing the progress of the colony of Georgia in America from its first establishment. —MARTYN, Benjamin. 1741#26

An account shewing what money has been received by the Trustees for the use of the colony of Georgia. —STEPHENS, Thomas. fl. 1742. 1742#41

Accounts relating to the orphan house in Georgia. —WHITEFIELD, George. 1746#29

An accurate and authentic journal of the siege of Quebec, 1759. . . —GENTLEMAN IN AN EMINENT STATION ON THE SPOT. 1759#36

An accurate journal and account of the proceedings of the New-England land-forces, during the late expedition against the French settlements on Cape Breton. . . —PEPPERRELL, William. 1746#15

Act discharging the importation of tobacco. —ENGLAND AND WALES. PARLIAMENT. 1705#10

Act for ascertaining the rates of foreign coins in her majesties plantations in America. —GREAT BRITAIN. PARLIAMENT. 1708#6

Act for avoiding and putting an end to certain doubts. . . relating to. . . wills and codicils, concerning real estates, in. . . England. . . —GREAT BRITAIN. PARLIAMENT. 1752#8

Act for better preservation of his Majesty's woods in America, and for the encouragement of the importation of naval stores from thence. . . —GREAT BRITAIN. PARLIAMENT. 1729#12

Act for better securing and encouraging trade of His Majesty's sugar colonies in America. —GREAT BRITAIN. PARLIAMENT. 1733#17

Act for charging of tobacco brought from New-England with custome and excise. —ENGLAND AND WALES. PARLIAMENT. 1650#4

Act for continuing an act. . . intituled, An act for encouraging the importation of naval stores from. . . plantations in America. . . —GREAT BRITAIN. PARLIAMENT. 1712#11

Act for continuing an act made in the twelfth year of. . . Queen Anne. . . An act for incouraging the tobacco trade. —GREAT BRITAIN. PARLIAMENT. 1719#3

Act for continuing several impositions. . . and concerning certain drugs of America. . . to be imported from her majesties plantations. —GREAT BRITAIN. PARLIAMENT. 1709#8

Act for continuing several laws. . . relating to the praemiums upon the importation of masts, yards, and bowsprits, tar, pitch and turpentine. . . —GREAT BRITAIN. PARLIAMENT. 1751#16

Act for continuing the act for encouraging the growth of coffee in his majesty's plantations in America. . . —GREAT BRITAIN. PARLIAMENT. 1752#9

Act for continuing the liberty of exporting Irish lining [sic] cloth to British plantations in America duty-free. . . —GREAT BRITAIN. PARLIAMENT. 1717#6

Act for encouragement of silk manufacture. . . for reducing the duties on beaver skins. . . imported; and for all furs products of the. . . —GREAT BRITAIN. PARLIAMENT. 1722#15

Act for encouraging the growth and culture of raw silk in. . . colonies or plantations in America.. —GREAT BRITAIN. PARLIAMENT. 1750#19

Act for encouraging the importation of naval stores. . . from her majesty's plantations in America. . . —ENGLAND AND WALES. PARLIAMENT. 1704#14

Act for encouraging the making of indico in the British plantations in America. —GREAT BRITAIN. PARLIAMENT. 1748#8

Act for encouraging the making of pot ashes and pearl ashes in the British plantations in America. —GREAT BRITAIN. PARLIAMENT. 1751#17

Act for encouraging the people known by the name of Unitas Fratrum or United Brethren, to settle in his majesty's colonies in America. —GREAT BRITAIN. PARLIAMENT. 1749#19

Act for encouraging the tobacco trade. —GREAT BRITAIN. PARLIAMENT. 1714#8

Act for establishing a general post office for all her majesties dominions. . . —GREAT BRITAIN. PARLIAMENT. 1711#8

Act for establishing an agreement with seven of the lords proprietors of Carolina, for the surrender of their title. . . —GREAT BRITAIN. PARLIAMENT. 1729#13

Act for extending the act. . . for amending. . . the laws relating to the government of His Majesty's ships. . . in North America. —GREAT BRITAIN. PARLIAMENT. 1756#36

Act for further preventing robbery, burglary. . . and for the more effectual transportation of felons. —GREAT BRITAIN. PARLIAMENT. 1720#14

Act for further regulating the plantation trade; and for relief of merchants importing prize goods from America. —GREAT BRITAIN. PARLIAMENT. 1742#20

Act for granting liberty to carry rice from. . . Carolina. . . directly to any part of Europe, South of Cape Finisterre. —GREAT BRITAIN. PARLIAMENT. 1730#14

257

Act for importing from his majesty's plantations in America, direct into Ireland, goods not enumerated in any act of parliament... —GREAT BRITAIN. PARLIAMENT. 1731#15

Act for importing salt from Europe, into the colony of New York... —GREAT BRITAIN. PARLIAMENT. 1729#14

Act for increase of shipping, and encouragement of the navigation of this nation... the ninth of October, 1651... — ENGLAND AND WALES. PARLIAMENT. 1651#8

Act for maintaining the peace with the Indians in the province of Georgia, prepared by the Honourable trustees for establishing... —GEORGIA TRUSTEES. 1735#4

Act for naturalizing such foreign Protestants, and others... as are settled, or shall settle in any of his majesty's colonies in America. —GREAT BRITAIN. PARLIAMENT. 1739#30

Act for permitting tea to be exported to Ireland, and... plantations in America, without paying the inland duties... —GREAT BRITAIN. PARLIAMENT. 1748#9

Act for permitting tea to be exported to Ireland, and... America, without paying the inland duties... (That is, so much therof... —GREAT BRITAIN. PARLIAMENT. 1760#42

Act for preventing frauds and regulating abuses in the plantation trade. —ENGLAND AND WALES. PARLIAMENT. 1696#11

Act for rendring the colony of Georgia more defencible, by prohibiting the importation and use of black slaves or negroes into... —GEORGIA TRUSTEES. 1735#5

Act for the better recruiting of His Majesty's forces on the continent of America; and for the better regulation of the army, and prevention of desertion there. —GREAT BRITAIN. PARLIAMENT. 1756#37

Act for the better securing and encouraging the trade of His Majesty's sugar colonies in America. —GREAT BRITAIN. PARLIAMENT. 1731#16

Act for the encouragement of the trade to America... —GREAT BRITAIN. PARLIAMENT. 1708#7

Act for the further encouragment and enlargement of the whale fishery. —GREAT BRITAIN. PARLIAMENT. 1749#20

Act for the more easy securing of debts in his majesty's plantations and colonies in America. —GREAT BRITAIN. PARLIAMENT. 1732#16

Act for the more effectual securing and encouraging the trade of his majesty's British subjects to America... —GREAT BRITAIN. PARLIAMENT. 1739#31

Act for the more effectual securing and encouraging the trade of America... —GREAT BRITAIN. PARLIAMENT. 1740#15

Act for the preservation of white and other pine trees... in... New Hampshire, in Massachusetts Bay,... Main, Rhode Island, and Providence-Plantation... —GREAT BRITAIN. PARLIAMENT. 1711#9

Act for the promoting and propagating the gospel of Jesus Christ in New-England. —ENGLAND AND WALES. PARLIAMENT. 1649#2

Act for vesting certain estates in Pennsylvania, New-Jersey, and Maryland, belonging to the proprietors of a partnership commonly... —GREAT BRITAIN. PARLIAMENT. 1760#43

Act for vesting the parts or shares late belonging to Benjamin Brain, merchant, deceased, of and in one twenty-fourth part... — GREAT BRITAIN. PARLIAMENT. 1753#9

Act further continuing an act... for securing... the trade of his majesties sugar colonies in America... —GREAT BRITAIN. PARLIAMENT. 1756#38

Act giving a licence for transporting fish in forreigne bottoms. — ENGLAND. PARLIAMENT. 1657#7

The Act of Tonnage and Poundage, and Book of Rates; with several statutes at large relating to the Customs... With an abridgment... —CARKESSE, Charles (compiler). 1675#3

Act prohibiting trade with the Barbada's, Virginia, Bermudas and Antego... [30 October 1650. —ENGLAND AND WALES. PARLIAMENT. 1650#5

Act to apply five hundred thousand pounds out of sinking fund... by paying off... and ten thousand pounds to the Trustees for... Georgia... —GREAT BRITAIN. PARLIAMENT. 1733#18

Act to continue an act... intituled, An act for granting liberty to carry rice from His Majesty's province of Carolina... —GREAT BRITAIN. PARLIAMENT. 1729#15

Act to enable His Majesty to grant commissions to a certain number of foreign Protestants who have served abroad as offices... — GREAT BRITAIN. PARLIAMENT. 1756#39

Act to encourage the importation of pig and bar iron from... colonies in America; and to prevent erection of any mill... in any... colony. —GREAT BRITAIN. PARLIAMENT. 1750#20

Act to explain an act made in the last session of Parliament, intituled, An act for importing from... America, directly into Ireland, goods not enumerated... —GREAT BRITAIN. PARLIAMENT. 1732#17

Act to extend the liberty... of importing bar iron from... America. —GREAT BRITAIN. PARLIAMENT. 1757#17

Act to extend the provisions of an act... intituled An act for naturalizing foreign Protestants... in... his majesty's colonies... —GREAT BRITAIN. PARLIAMENT. 1747#8

Act to prevent the exportation of hats out of any of His Majesty's colonies in America, and to restrain the number of apprentices... —GREAT BRITAIN. PARLIAMENT. 1732#18

Act to prevent the importation and use of rum and brandies in the Province of Georgia... approved by... George the Second, in Council... —GEORGIA TRUSTEES. 1735#6

Act to prohibit... the exportation of corn, grain... victual... from his majesty's colonies and plantations in America... — GREAT BRITAIN. PARLIAMENT. 1757#18

Act to regulate and restrain paper-bills of credit in his majesty's colonies or plantations of Rhode-Island, and Providence plantations... —GREAT BRITAIN. PARLIAMENT. 1751#18

Act to repeal a clause in an act made in the ninth year of his late Majesty's reign, which prohibts the importation of tobacco... —GREAT BRITAIN. PARLIAMENT. 1729#16

Act to revive several acts... turnpikes... and to continue severalacts relating to rice to frauds in the customs, to the clandestine... —GREAT BRITAIN. PARLIAMENT. 1742#21

Acts and laws passed by... assembly of the province of... Massachusetts Bay... from 1692 to 1719. —MASSACHUSETTS GENERAL COURT. 1724#14

The acts and negotiations, together with the particular articles at large, of the general peace concluded at Ryswick. —BERNARD, Jacques. 1699#4

The acts made in the first parliament of our... soveraigne Charles... at Edinburgh... —SCOTLAND. PARLIAMENT. 1633#5

Acts of Assembly, passed in the colony of Virginia, from 1622, to 1715. Volume I. —VIRGINIA ASSEMBLY. 1727#25

Acts of assembly, passed in the province of Maryland, from 1692 to 1715. —MARYLAND ASSEMBLY. 1723#7

Acts of Assembly, passed in the province of New-York from 1691, to 1718. —NEW YORK ASSEMBLY. 1719#6

The acts of Dr. Bray's visitation. held at Annopolis [sic] in Mary-land, May 23, 24, 25, anno 1700. —BRAY, Thomas. 1700#3

Adam in Eden: or, Nature in Paradise. The history of plants, fruits, herbs and flowers... —COLES, William. 1657#5

Adam in his innocence. —BLOYS, William. 1638#8

An addition or postscript to the Vindication... —HUDSON, Samuel. 1658#8

An additional brief narrative of a late bloody design against the Protestants in Ann Arundel County, and Severn, in Maryland in the Country of Virginia... —HEAMAN, Roger. 1655#14

An address to persons of quality and estate... —NELSON, Robert. 1715#18

An address to the British army and navy. Intended to remind our brave warriors of the important interests, in which they are engaged... —1756#2

An address to the electors, and other free subjects of Great Britain... In which is contained a particular account of all our negociations with Spain... —ROBINS, Benjamin. 1739#61

An address to the great man with advice to the public. —1758#2

An address to the merchants of Great-Britain: or, a review of the conduct of the administration, with regard to our trade and navigation... —MERCHANT RETIR'D. 1739#48

Address'd to the merchants of London. A genuine narrative of the transactions in Nova Scotia, since the settlement, June 1749, till August the 5th, 1751... —WILSON, John. 1751#36

The admirable and indefatigable adventures of the nine pious pilgrims... Written in America... by a zealous lover of truth. —FRANCK, Richard. 1707#8

Admirable curiosities, rarities and wonders... —CROUCH, Nathaniel. 1682#10

The advantage of Great Britain considered in the tobacco trade... humbly offered to the Parliament of Great Britain... —NICOLL, John. 1727#18

The advantages of the difinitive [sic] treaty to the people of Great-Britain demonstrated. —1749#1

The advantages of the revolution illustrated, by a view of the present state of Great Britain... —B., G. 1753#1

The adventures of Pomponius, a Roman knight, or the history of our own times... —LABADIE, ———. 1726#10

The adventures of Robert Chevalier, called de Beauchene, Captain of a privateer in New-France. —LE SAGE, Alain René. 1745#27

An advertisement concerning East-New-Jersey —1685#1

An advertisement concerning the province of East-New-Jersey in America. Published for information of such as are desirous to be concerned therein... —PERTH, James Drummond. 1685#21

Advertisement. February 4, 1702. There will be speedily published some New voyages to North-America, perform'd by the Baron de la Hontan... — 1703#1

Advertisement. There is lately brought forth to this place from America, a savage: being a canibal-Indian... —1720#1

Advertisements for the unexperienced planters of New-England, or any where. Or, the path-way to experience to erect a plantation —SMITH, John. 1631#3

Advice to a son. A discourse at the request of a gentleman in New-England, upon his son's going to Europe... —PEMBERTON, EBENEZER. 1705#16

AE. M. S. eximij pietate, eruditione, pudentia' viri D. Ebenezrae Pembertoni, apud Bostoniensis Americanos praedicatoris vere... —CHARMION, John. 1717#4

Afer baptizatus: or the negro turned Christian... I. The necessity of instruction, and baptizing slaves... a sermon —HILL, Anthony. 1702#13

An affidavit taken and sworn at York... the 14th. day of Feb: 1701. Setting forth... the hardships of several merchants in the said... —SMITH, Thomas. 1701#37

The African trade, the great pillar and support of the British plantation trade in America... —POSTLETHWAYT, Malachy. 1745#33

An alarm to Great Britain; with an invitation to repentance... sermon... at Northampton, February 11th, 1757... —GILBERT, Robert. 1757#16

An alarm to the priests, or, a message from heaven... —ELLWOOD, Thomas. 1660#5

All the workes of John Taylor the Water-poet... —TAYLOR, John. 1630#9

The allegations against proprietary governments considered, and their merit and benefit to the Crown briefly observed... —PENN, William. 1701#32

An almanack for the provinces of Virginia and Maryland... —SELLER, John. 1685#26

The almost Christian. A sermon preached... in England. Added, a poem on his design for Georgia. —WHITEFIELD, George. 1738#30

An alphabetical list of the subscribers in nomination for deputy-governor and assistants for the first government of the company... —COMPANY FOR MINES AND MINERALS IN NEW-ENGLAND. 1688#3

Altamira's ghost; or, justice triumphant. A new ballad. Occasion'd by a certain nobleman's cruel usage of his nephew. Done extempore. —BOYD, Elizabeth. 1744#7

The ambitious designs of wicked men... a sermon preached at Belfast, on Thursday, Nov. 29th, 1759... —KENNEDY, Gilbert. 1759#56

America: being the latest, and most accurate description of the new world... —OGILBY, John. 1670#10

America dissected, being a full and true account of all the American colonies... Published as a caution to unsteady people who may be tempted to leave their native country. —MACSPARRAN, James. 1753#15

America. Ferret, master. Before the Right Honourable the Lords Commissioners of Appeals for Prizes. America, Louis Ferret, master... Appellant's case. —GREAT BRITAIN. LORDS COMMISSIONERS OF APPEALS IN PRIZE CAUSES. 1759#39

America: or an exact description of the West Indies... —N., N. 1655#17

America painted to the life. The true history... —GORGES, Ferdinando. 1659#16

America. Translated from the French. —1720#2

The American physitian; or, a Treatise of the roots, plants, trees, shrubs, fruits, herbs, etc. growing in the English plantations in America... —HUGHES, William. 1672#4

Americans no Jewes, or improbabilities, that the Americans are of that race... —LESTRANGE, Hamon [L'ESTRANGE]. 1652#7

Anabaptism, the true fountaine of independency... a second part of The disswasive from the errors of the time... —BAILLIE, Robert. 1647#2

The analysis of innoculation: comprising the history, theory and practice of it... —KIRKPATRICK, James. 1754#21

An anatomy of independency, or, A brief commentary, and moderate discourse upon the Apologeticall narration... —FORBES, Alexander. 1644#7

Andrew Wiggin, and others, petitioners. Against Jonathan Belcher, Esq: -Respondent. The Respondent's case... 12th day of November, 1739. —GREAT BRITAIN. PRIVY COUNCIL. 1739#36

Anguis flagellatus; or, a switch for the snake. Being an answer to the third and last edition of the Snake in the Grass... —WYETH, Joseph. 1699#21

Animadversions on George Whitehead's book. —CRISP, Thomas. 1694#4

The annales... of England... Continued unto 1631. By Edmund Howes —STOW, John. 1631#4

An answer of the elders of the severall churches in New-England unto nine positions... written in the year 1639 —DAVENPORT, John. 1643#6

An answer to a letter from Dr. Bray, directed to such as have contributed towards the propagating Christian knowledge in the plantations... —WYETH, Joseph. 1700#38

An answer to a libell intituled, A coole conference... —STEUART, Adam. 1644#17

An answer to a pamphlet, called a Second Letter to the People... In which the subsidiary system is fairly stated... —1755#2

An answer to a pamphlet called, The conduct of the ministry impartially examined. —SHEBBEARE, John. 1756#70

An answer to a scandalous paper... therein is found many lies and slanders, and false accusations against those people called Quakers... —BRECK, Edward. 1656#2

An answer to an invidious pamphlet, intituled, A brief state of the province of Pennsylvania... —CROSS, -. 1755#12

An answer to George Keith's narrative of his proceedings at Turner's Hall. —ELLWOOD, Thomas. 1696#10

An answer to Joseph Jenk's reply to William Wilkinson's treatise, entituled, the baptism of the holy spirit... —WILKINSON, William. 1721#24

An answer to Reasons (so call'd) against the bill for exporting Irish linen to the British plantations duty-free. —1717#1

An answer to several new laws and orders made by the rulers of Boston in New England... —FOX, George. 1678#4

An answer to some considerations on the bill for encouraging the importation of pig and bar iron from America... —1750#2

An answer to the letter to two great men... —1760#2

An answer to the reasons against Leisler's bill... offerd to the, consideration of the... Commons. —1695#1

An answer to the reasons offered against restraining the use and wearing of printed callicoes in England, Ireland and the plantations. —1704#2

The answer to The call to humiliation, or. A vindication of the Church of England, from the reproaches of W. Woodward. —1690#1

The answer to Tom-Tell-Troth. The practise of princes and the lamentations of the kirke. —CALVERT, George. 1642#2

An answer to two treatises of Mr John Cann, the leader of the English Brownists in Amsterdam —BALL, John. 1642#1

An answer to W. R. his Narration of the opinions and practises of the churches lately erected in New-England. . . —WELD, Thomas. 1644#19

Answers for Andrew Anderson merchant in Virginia and his factor, to petition of Arthur Nasmith. . . [signed] Arch. Murray. June 1, 1749. —1749#3

Answers for Robert Rae of Little-Govan, to the petition of John Jamieson merchants in Glasgow. —RAE, Robert. 1747#21

Answers to all the objections made to the bill for supporting the sugar colonies. —1732#2

Answers to the queries, in defense of the malt distillery. Wherein the matter is attempted to be stated clearly and briefly with. . . —1760#3

Antapologia: or, A full answer to the Apologeticall narration. . . —EDWARDS, Thomas. 1644#6

The anti-Christs and Saducees detected among a sort of Quakers; or Caleb Pusie, of Pennsylvania, and John Pennington. . . — KEITH, George. 1696#14

The Anti-Craftsmen: being an answer to the Craftsmen extraordinary. . . —1729#2

The Anti-Gallican; or, the history and adventures of Harry Cobham, Esq. Inscribed to Louis XVth, by the Author. —LONG, Edward. 1757#25

Anti-Socinianism, or a brief explication. . . for the confutation of. . . gross errors and Socinian heresies, lately published. . . — CHEWNEY, Nicholas. 1650#2

An antidote against the common plague of the world. Or, an answer to a small treatise. . . intitul'd Saltmarsh returned from the dead. . . —GORTON, Sam. 1657#9

An antidote against the infectious contagion of popery and tyranny. . . —1745#2

Antidotum Lincolniense. Or, an answer to a book entituled, The holy table, name and thing. . . —HEYLYN, Peter. 1637#2

Antinomians and Familists condemned by the synod of elders in New-England. . . —WINTHROP, John. 1644#24

The antithelemite, or an answer to certain queries. . . and to the Considerations of an unknown author concerning toleration. — MAURICE, Henry. 1685#18

An apologie of the churches in New-England for church covenant. . . Sent over in answer to Master Bernard, in the year 1639. . . —MATHER, Richard. 1643#13

An apology for a late resignation in a letter from an English gentleman to. . . friend at the Hague. —STANHOPE, Philip Dormer. 1748#28

An apology for Congregational divines. . . —YOUNG, Samuel. 1698#26

An apology for the builder; or, a discourse shewing the causes and effects of the increase of building. —BARBON, Nicholas. 1685#3

An apology for the discipline of the ancient church. . . especially. . . our mother the Church of England. . . —NICOLSON, William. 1659#25

An apology for the life of Bampfylde-Moore Carew, (son of the Rev. Mr. Carew of Bickley). . . his many comical adventures, travels. . . —1749#4

An apology or vindication of Francis Nicholson. . . governor of South Carolina from the unjust aspersions cast on him by some of the members of the Bahama company. . . —NICHOLSON, Francis. 1724#16

An apostate exposed or, George Keith's contradicting himself. . . —PENINGTON, John. 1695#24

Apostolick charity, its nature and excellence considered. . . Preached. . . Decemb. 19. 1697. at the ordination of some Protestant. . . —BRAY, Thomas. 1698#2

An appeal to the sense of the people, on the present posture of affairs. Wherein the nature of the late treaties are inquired into. . . — 1756#4

An appeal to the unprejudiced, concerning the present discontents occasioned by the late convention with Spain. —GORDON, Thomas 1739#29

An appendix to. . . New England judged; being certain writings (never yet printed) of those persons which were there executed. . . —ROBINSON, William. 1661#15

Appendix to the report of the Committee of both houses of Assembly. . . appointed to enquire into the causes of the disappointment. . . — SOUTH CAROLINA ASSEMBLY. COMMITTEE OF BOTH HOUSES. 1743#37

The application of redemption, by the effectual work of the word, and spirit of Christ. . . —HOOKER, Thomas. 1656#7A

An argument for union, taken from the true interest of those dissenters in England, who profess, and call themselves Protestants. — TENISON, Thomas. 1683#22

The arguments of the Quakers, more particularly, of George Whitehead, William Penn. . . against baptism and the supper. — KEITH, George. 1698#10

Arms of the baronets of England, and Nova Scotia. With crests, supporters, mottos, family honours. . . By John Millan. . . corrected to September 1753. —MILLAN, John, d. 1782. 1753#18

The arraignment, tryal, and condemnation, of Capt. John Quelch, and others. . . for sundry piracies, robberies, and murder. . . — 1704#3

The arraignment, tryal, and condemnation of Captain William Kidd, for murther and piracy. . . —1701#4

The art of making common salt, as now practiced in most parts of the world; with several improvements proposed in that art, for the use of the British dominions. —BROWNRIGG, William. 1748#2

Articles of agreement, for carrying on an expedition, by Hudson's Streights, for the discovery of a North-West passage. . . March 30, 1745. . . —1745#3

Articles of agreement made the 10th day of October... 1695. Between the... Earl of Bellomont... and Robert Levingston... and Captain William Kidd... —1701#5

Articles of impeachment of high treason... against Robert, etc... —1739#4

Articles of peace and alliance... —ENGLAND AND WALES. TREATIES. 1662#5

Articles of peace and alliance... —ENGLAND AND WALES. TREATIES. 1667#4

Articles of peace and alliance... —ENGLAND AND WALES. TREATIES. 1667#3

Articles of peace between... Charles II... and several Indian Kings and Queens... 29th day of May, 1677... —ENGLAND AND WALES. SOVEREIGN. CHARLES II. 1677#2

Articles of peace, friendship and entercourse... —1655#1

The articles, settlement, and offices of the Free Society of Traders in Pennsilvania: Agreed upon by divers merchants and others... —1682#1

Ashton's memorial: or, an authentick account of the strange adventures... of Mr. Philip Ashton... To which is added, a sermon on Dan. III, 17, by J. Barnard... —BARNARD, John. 1726#1

The ass: or, the serpent. A comparison between the tribes of Issachar and Dan, in their regard for civil liberty. —BRADBURY, Thomas. 1712#1

An astronomical description of the late comet. —DANFORTH, Samuel. 1666#4

At Punch's theatre. For the entertainment of the four Indian kings... this present Munday [sic], May 1. at seven a-clock —1710#1

At the Court at St. James, the second day of February, 1717... Upon reading this day a report from the... Committee for hearing of appeals from the Plantations... —GREAT BRITAIN. PRIVY COUNCIL. 1718#9

At the Court at Whitehall, the 20th of July, 1683. —ENGLAND AND WALES. PRIVY COUNCIL. 1683#9

At the Court... 16 February 1680[-1]. To regulate and encourage trade with the colonies. —ENGLAND AND WALES. PRIVY COUNCIL. 1681#6

Athenae Oxoniensis... —WOOD, Anthony. 1691#23

Atheomastix clearing foure truthes against atheists. —FOTHERBY, Martin. 1622#14

Atlas geographus: or, a compleat system of geography, ancient and modern... With the discoveries and improvements of the best modern authors to this time... —MOLL, Herman. 1711#17

Atlas manuale: or, a new sett of maps of all the parts of the earth, as well Asia, Africa and America, as Europe... Mostly perform'd by Herman Moll. —MOLL, Herman. 1709#16

Atlas maritimus & commercialis; or, A general view of the world... together with a large account of the commerce carried on by... —CUTLER, Nathaniel. 1728#6

Atlas minimus, or a book of geography. —SELLER, John. 1679#4

August 1. 1706. Yesterday arriv'd an express from the West Indies, with the following news from Rhoad-Island, April 5. —1706#1

Aulicus coquinariae; or Vindication, in answer to a pamphlet... —SANDERSON, William. 1650#11

An authentic account of the reduction of Louisbourg, in June and July 1758... By a spectator. —1758#4

Authentic instances of French and Indian cruelty, exemplified in the sufferings of Peter Williamson... written by himself. —WILLIAMSON, Peter. 1758#49

An authentic journal of the proceedings in the great cause tried at Dublin, between the Honourable James Annesley plaintiff, and a noble person, defendant... —CRAIG, Campbell. 1743#9

Authentic memoirs of the life and treasonable practices of Doctor Florence Hensey, who received sentence of death on Wednesday... —1758#5

Authentic papers relating to the expedition against Carthagena... —1744#1

An authentic register of the British successes... from the taking of Louisbourg... to the defeat of the French fleet... Nov. 21, 1759... —1760#6

An authentick list of the house of peers; as they voted for and against the Convention... —1739#5

An authentick narrative of the success of tar-water... —PRIOR, Thomas. 1746#19

Authentick papers, concerning a late remarkable transaction. —1746#2

Babylon's fall in Maryland; a fair warning to Lord Baltimore. Or, a relation of an assault made by divers Papists... against the Protestants... —STRONG, Leonard. 1655#20

A Ballad. Addres'd to the Reverend Members of the Convocation, held at Man's Ordinary, at Williamsburgh, in Virginia;... —1704#4

The baptism of the holy spirit, without elementary water, demonstratively proved to be the true baptism of Christ... —WILKINSON, William. 1718#22

Batavia illustrata: or, A view of the policy and commerce of the United Provinces... of the rise and progress of their East and West India Companies... —BURRISH, Onslow. 1728#2

Batchelors hall. A poem... —WEBB, George. 1731#34

The battaile of Agincourt. —DRAYTON, Michael. 1627#1

Batteries upon the kingdom of the Devil. Seasonable discourses upon some common but woful, instances, wherein men gratifie the grand enemy of their salvation. —MATHER, Cotton. 1695#18

Beames of eternal brightness, or branches of everlasting blessings, to be spread over India and all the nations of the earth, by John, who is called a Quaker. —PERROT, John. 1661#14

The Beavers: A fable —1760#8

The Belgicke pismire. —SCOTT, Thomas. 1623#4

A bemoaning letter of an ingenious Quaker. . . —MUCKLOWE, William. 1700#30

The benefit and comfort of the Christian revelation. . . —BROWN, William. 1736#5

Bibliotheca biographica: a synopsis of universal biography. . . —FLLOYD, Thomas. 1760#33

Bibliotheca parochialis Part I. —BRAY, Thomas. 1697#1

Bibliothecae Americanae primordia. An attempt towards laying the foundations of an American library, in several books, papers, and writings. . . —KENNETT, White. 1713#5

A bill for better preservation of his majesty's woods in America, and for the encouragement of the importation of naval stores from thence. . . —GREAT BRITAIN. PARLIAMENT. HOUSE OF COMMONS. 1729#17

A bill for encouraging the people known by the name of Unitas Fratum, or United Brethren, to settle in his majesty's colonies in America. —GREAT BRITAIN. PARLIAMENT. HOUSE OF COMMONS. 1749#21

A bill for establishing a method to bar entails upon the province of Maryland. —GREAT BRITAIN. PARLIAMENT. HOUSE OF COMMONS. 1754#14

A bill for explaining and amending an act of the thirteenth year of his majesty's present reign, intituled, an act for the more. . . —GREAT BRITAIN. PARLIAMENT. HOUSE OF COMMONS. 1746#10

A bill for importing salt, from Europe, into the province of Pensylvania in America. —GREAT BRITAIN. PARLIAMENT. HOUSE OF COMMONS. 1727#11

A bill for registering all seamen, watermen, fishermen, lightermen. . . *capable of service at sea, throughout his majesty's dominions.* . . —GREAT BRITAIN. PARLIAMENT. HOUSE OF COMMONS. 1739#32

A bill for the better protecting and securing the trade and navigation of this kingdom, in times of war. —GREAT BRITAIN. PARLIAMENT. HOUSE OF COMMONS. 1746#11

A bill for the more easy and effectual conviction of persons returning from transportation [to any part of America. —GREAT BRITAIN. PARLIAMENT. HOUSE OF COMMONS. 1720#15

A bill for the speedy and effectual recruiting of his majesty's regiments of foot serving in Flanders, Minorca, Gibraltar, and the plantations, and regiments of marines. —GREAT BRITAIN. PARLIAMENT. HOUSE OF COMMONS. 1745#25

A bill, intituled, An act for naturalizing such foreign protestants, and others therein mentioned, as are settled, or shall settle in any of His Majesty's colonies in America. —GREAT BRITAIN. PARLIAMENT. HOUSE OF COMMONS. 1739#33

A bill, intituled, an act for restraining and preventing several unwarrantable schemes. . . *in his majesty's colonies.* . . *in America.* —GREAT BRITAIN. PARLIAMENT. HOUSE OF COMMONS. 1741#20

A bill, intituled, an act for the better securing and encouraging the trade of His Majesty's Sugar colonies in America. —GREAT BRITAIN. PARLIAMENT. HOUSE OF COMMONS. 1733#19

A bill, intituled, An act for the better securing and encouraging the trade of His Majesty's sugar colonies in America. —GREAT BRITAIN. PARLIAMENT. HOUSE OF COMMONS. 1732#19

A bill, intituled, An act for the more effectual securing and encouraging the trade of his Majesty's British subjects in America. . . —GREAT BRITAIN. PARLIAMENT. HOUSE OF COMMONS. 1739#34

A bill, intituled, An act to encourage the importation of pig and bar iron from his majesty's colonies in America; and to prevent. . . —GREAT BRITAIN. PARLIAMENT. HOUSE OF COMMONS. 1750#21

A bill to explain and amend. . . *an act made in the sixth year of the reign of.* . . *George the first.* . . —GREAT BRITAIN. PARLIAMENT. HOUSE OF COMMONS. 1742#22

A bill to prevent the issuing of paper bills of credit in the British colonies and plantations in America, to be legal tenders in payments for money. —GREAT BRITAIN. PARLIAMENT. HOUSE OF COMMONS. 1744#20

A bill to regulate and restrain paper bills of credit in the British colonies and plantations in America, and to prevent the same being legal tenders. . . —GREAT BRITAIN. PARLIAMENT. HOUSE OF COMMONS. 1749#22

The block and yard arm. A new ballad, on the loss of Minorca, and the danger of our American, rights and possessions. —1756#8

Bloody news from Carolina: or, the English sailors tragedy. . . —1742#4

The bloody tenant yet more bloody: by Mr. Cotton's endevour to wash it white in the blood of the lambe. . . —WILLIAMS, Roger. 1652#18

The bloudy tenent, of persecution, for cause of conscience, discussed, in a conference between truth and peace. . . —WILLIAMS, Roger. 1644#20

The bloudy tenent, washed. . . —COTTON, John. 1647#5

Boanerges. or The humble supplication of the ministers of Scotland. —1624#3

A bomb thrown amongst the Quakers in Norwich, which will. . . *set fire on [sic] the combustible matter thorow their whole camp in England, Wales and America.* —BUGG, Francis. 1702#3

A book of funds. —HOUGHTON, Thomas. 1695#12

The book of James. . . —BELSHAZZER, Kapha the Jew. 1743#4

The book of psalmes with the new translation in English. . . —LEUSDEN, John. 1688#9

A book of the continuation of forreign passages. . . —1657#2

The books and divers epistles of the faithful servant of the Lord Josiah Coale. . . —COALE, Josiah. 1671#4

263

Boreland, Francis, respondent. . . The respondent's case. . . —BORELAND, Francis 1737#1

Both sides of the question: or, a candid and impartial enquiry into a certain doubtful character in a letter to a General-Officer. . . —1749#6

Bowells of compassion towards the scattered seed. . . Written to the scattered people in America. . . —PINDER, Richard. 1659#29

A brand pluck'd from the burning. . . —KEIMER, Samuel. 1718#13

The bravo turn'd bully; or, the depredators. A dramatic entertainment. Founded on some late transactions in America. —1740#5

A brief account concerning several of the agents of New-England. . . —MATHER, Increase. 1691#13

A brief account of the case of John Tennent, M. D. —TENNENT, John, M. D. 1742#46

A brief account of the causes that have retarded the progress of the colony of Georgia. . . attested upon oath. Being a proper contrast. . . —STEPHENS, Thomas. fl. 1742. 1743#39

A brief account of the life and death and some of the gospel labours of. . . William Ellis. . . —1710#2

A brief account of the occasion, process, and issue of a late trial at the assize held at Gloucester. —WHITEFIELD, George. 1744#44

A brief account of the province of East: New: Jersey in America: Published by the Scots Proprietors having interest there. . . —1683#2

A brief account of the province of Pennsylvania, lately granted by the King, under the great seal of England, to William Penn and his heirs and assigns.— PENN, William. 1681#17

A brief account of the rise, principles, and discipline of the people call'd Quakers in America, and elsewhere, extracted from a system of geography, lately published. —RANDALL, Joseph. 1747#22

A brief account of the rise, progress and present situation of the orphan-house in Georgia. In a letter to a friend. —WHITEFIELD, George. 1748#36

A brief account of the situation and advantages of the new-intended settlement in. . . Azilia; a late erected British province on the South of Carolina. —MONTGOMERY, Robert, Sir. 1717#12

A brief account of the war in N. America. . . the necessity and advantage of keeping Canada. . . the maintaining of friendly correspondence. . . —WILLIAMSON, Peter. 1760#102

A brief advertisment, concerning East-New-Jersey, in America. —SCOTT, George. 1685#24

A brief, and plain apology by John Wheelwright: Wherein he doth vindicate himself, from al [sic] those errors. . . layed to his charge by Mr. Thomas Welde. . . —WHEELWRIGHT, John. 1658#12

A brief and true narration of the late wars risen in New-England: occasioned by the quarrelsom [sic] disposition. . . of the barbarous, savage and heathenish natives there. . . —1675#1

A brief description of New-York; formerly called New-Netherlands. . . —DENTON, Daniel. 1670#3

A brief description of the fifth monarchy, or kingdome that shortly is to come into the world. . . —ASPINWALL, William. 1653#1

A brief description of the province of Carolina on the coasts of Floreda. . . —1666#2

A brief discourse concerning that ceremony of laying the hand on the Bible in swearing.— WILLARD, Samuel. 1689#30

A brief discourse concerning the lawfulness of worshipping God by the Common-Prayer. . . —WILLIAMS, John. 1693#19

A brief discourse concerning the unlawfulness of the Common-prayer worship and the laying the hand on, and kissing the booke in swearing. —MATHER, Increase. 1689#18

A brief discovery of some of the blasphemous and seditious principles and practices of the people, called Quakers. —BECKHAM, Edward. 1699#1

A brief essay on the advantages and disadvantages which respectively attend France and Great Britain, with regard to trade. . . —TUCKER, Josiah. 1749#43

A brief exposition of the whole book of Canticles, or, the Song of Solomon —COTTON, John. 1642#4

A brief exposition with practicall observations upon the whole book of Canticles.— COTTON, John. 1655#7

A brief exposition with practicall observations upon the whole book of Ecclesiastes. —COTTON, John. 1654#6

A brief historical relation of the life of Mr J. Livingston. . . written by himself. —LIVINGSTONE, John. 1727#16

A brief history of the Episcopal Church of the Moravian brethren, from their first beginning. Together with the reasons for and against. . . —1750#5

A brief history of the poor Palatine refugees lately arrived in England. —DEFOE, Daniel. 1709#7

A brief history of the Protestant Episcopal Church, known by the name of Unitas Fratrum. . . the reasons for and against the priviledges. . . —1750#6

A brief history of the rise, growth, and progress of Quakerism. —BUGG, Francis. 1697#5

A brief history of the war with the Indians in New-England. From June 24. 1675. . . to August 12, 1676. . . —MATHER, Increase. 1676#12

A brief journal of the life, travels, labours of love, in the work of the ministry of. . . T. Wilson. . . —WILSON, Thomas. (1655?-1725). 1728#16

A brief manifestation of the state and case of the Quakers presented to all people. . . also to all planters or occupiers of land in the English and forreign plantations. . . —DAVENPORT, Thomas. 1664#5

A brief narration of the original undertakings. —GORGES, Ferdinando. 1658#6

A brief narration of the practices of the churches in New-England, in their solemne worship of God. . . —WELD, Thomas. 1645#19

A brief narrative of some considerable passages concerning the first gathering, and further progress of a Church of Christ, in gospel-order. . . —RUSSELL, John. 1680#10

A brief narrative of the proceedings of William Pen. —1701#13

A brief narrative of the progress of the gospel amongst the Indians in New-England, as in the year 1670. . . —ELIOT, John. 1671#7

A brief relation of the adventures of M. Bampfylde Carew. —1746#4

A brief relation of the discovery and plantation of New-England: and of sundry accidents therein occurring. . . —COUNCIL FOR NEW ENGLAND. 1622#9

A brief relation of the state of New England, from the beginning of that plantation to this present year, 1689. . . —MATHER, Increase. 1689#19

A brief state of the province of Pennsylvania, in which the conduct of their assemblies. . . is. . . examined, and the true cause of. . . —SMITH, William (1727-1803). 1755#51

A brief survey of the prophetical and evangelical events of the last times. . . —BROWNE, John. 1653#2

A brief treatise of the use of the globe celestiall and terrestriall. . . —T[ANNER]., R[obert]. 1647#16

A brief view of the conduct of Pennsylvania, for the year 1755; so far as it affected the general service of the British colonies. . . —SMITH, William. (1727-1803). 1756#74

Briefe considerations concerning the advancement of trade. —ROBINSON, Henry. 1650#10

A briefe description of the whole worlde. . . —ABBOT, George. 1624#1

A briefe discovery or description of the most famous island of Madagascar. —BOOTHBY, Richard. 1646#1

A briefe exposition of the Lord's prayer. . . —HOOKER, Thomas. 1645#9A

A briefe narration of some church courses held in opinion and practise in the churches lately erected in New England. —RATHBAND, William. 1644#14

Britain, a poem; in three books. . . —1757#2

Britain in tears, for the loss of the brave General Wolfe. Tune, The lamentation of Jane Shore. —1759#10

Britain revived. A sermon delivered at Northampton. . . Nov. 29, 1759. . . —GILBERT, Robert. 1759#38

Britain strike home. A poem humbly inscribed to every Briton. . . —TRUE ANTIGALLIGAN. 1756#80

Britain's commercial interest explained and improved. . . containing a candid enquiry into the secret causes of the present misfortunes of the nation. . . —POSTLETHWAYT, Malachy. 1757#32

Britain's glory: or, ship-building unvail'd. —SUTHERLAND, William. 1717#17

Britain's golden mines discovered: or the fishery trade considered. . . —FISHER, Sally. 1720#11

Britain's happiness, and the proper improvement of it. . . a sermon. . . at Newington-Green, Middlesex. . . Nov. 29.ˆ 1759. —PRICE, Richard. 1759#81

Britain's mercies, and Britain's duty. Represented in a sermon. . . at Philadelphia. . . August 24, 1746. And occasioned by the suppression of the late unnatural rebellion. . . —WHITEFIELD, George. 1746#30

Britain's mistakes in the commencement and conduct of the present war. By a merchant and citizen of London. . . —1740#7

Britannia and the Gods in council, a dramatic poem: wherein. . . the causes of the present disputes in Europe and America are debated. . . —AVERAY, Robert. 1756#5

Britannia languens; or a discourse of trade. —PETYT, William. 1680#8

Britannia major: the new scheme, or essay, for discharging the debts, improving the lands, and enlarging the trade of the British dominions in Europe and America. —1732#7

Britannia: or A geographical description of the kingdom's of England, Scotland and Ireland, with the Isles and territories there to belonging. . . —BLOME, Richard. 1673#3

Britannia or the death of Wolfe. —1760#11

Britannia triumphalis; a brief history of the warres and other state-affaires of Great Britain. . . —1654#3

Britanniae Speculum; or a short view of the ancient and modern state of Great Britain. . . and of all other dominions and territories. . . —1683#3

The British bell-man. Printed in the year of the saints fear. Anno Domini, 1648. . . —1648#2

The British empire in America, consider'd. In a second letter, from a gentleman of Barbadoes. . . —ASHLEY, John. 1732#3

The British empire in America, containing the history of the discovery, settlement, progress and present state of all the British. . . —OLDMIXON, John. 1708#12

The British gardener's calendar. . . —JUSTICE, James. 1759#55

The British merchant. —1721#2

The British monarchy: or a new chorographical description of all the dominions subject to the king of Great Britain. . . —BICKHAM, George. 1743#5

The British sailor's discovery : or the Spanish pretensions confuted. . . —1739#8

Britons invited to rejoice. . . sermon preached at Exeter, August the 27th, 1758. . . after receiving the account of the taking of the islands of Cape- Breton and St. John. —TOWGOOD, Micaiah. 1758#48

Brontologia sacra: the voice of the glorious God in the thunder. . . —MATHER, Cotton. 1695#19

The Bubbler's mirrour: or England's folley. —1720#8

Burnbank and George Fachney's last shift or, a strange plot at a dead lift. —1722#6

Burnbank's farewell to Edinburgh, at his departure for the Indies, with his last will and testament.—PENNECUIK, Alexander. 1721#16

By Captain Joseph Taylour, commander of her majesty's ship Litchfield, and commander in chief of all her majesty's forces in Newfoundland...—TAYLOUR, Joseph. 1711#31

By his majesties commissioners for Virginia... —ENGLAND AND WALES. COMMISSIONERS FOR VIRGINIA. 1624#5

By order of the Mineral Master General, at the New-England Coffee-House behind the Royal Exchange, London. —1712#2

By the Commissioners for collecting and receiving the six pence a month out of seamens wages, for the use of Greenwich Hospital... —ROYAL HOSPITAL FOR SEAMEN AT GREENWICH. 1727#23

By the Commissioners for Executing the Office of Lord High Admiral of Great Britain and Ireland... His Majesty hath been pleased... —GREAT BRITAIN. ROYAL NAVY. 1728#9

By the Corporation of London Assurance... Proposals for assuring... from loss and damage by fire, in England... and all other parts of his majesties dominions beyond the seas. —LONDON ASSURANCE, CORPORATION OF. 1722#18

C. C. the covenanter vindicated from perjurie... —1644#1

Caesar's due rendred unto him according to his image and superscription—FOX, George. 1679#3

Cain against Abel, representing New England's Church hirarchy [sic], in opposition to her Christian Protestant dissenters... —FOX, George. 1675#7

A calculation of the species and value of the manufactures and products of Great-Britain, Newfoundland, and Ireland, annually exported to the port of Leghorn. —1713#1

A call from death to life, and out of the dark wayes and worships of the world... —STEPHENSON, Marmaduke. 1659#32

A call to the unfaithful professors of truth... —ESTAUGH, John. 1745#20

Cambrensium Caroleia... —VAUGHAN, William. 1625#13

Canadia. Ode... —BELSHAM, Jacobus. 1760#9

Canary-birds naturalized in Utopia. A canto... —1709#1

A candid and fair examination of the remarks on the letter to two great men... —1760#15

A candid narrative of the rise and progress of the Herrnhuters, commonly called Moravians... —RIMIUS, Heinrich. 1753#19

The Canninad. Or, Betty's soliloquy in Newgate, on the night destin'd for her departure to her American settlement, but luckily... —1754#4

The capitall laws of New-England. —1643#3

Captain Bilton's journal of his unfortunate voyage from Lisbon to Virginia in the year 1707...—BILTON, Thomas. 1715#4

Captain Fayrer Hall's evidence, before a Committee of the House of Commons, in April 1731 concerning the sugar colony bill. Remarks... —HALL, Fayrer. 1732#20

Captain Leisler's case. —1695#5

The captive... visited with the day-spring from on high... Given forth especially for the scattered people in America...—PINDER, Richard. 1660#24

Caribbeana. Containing letters and dissertations, together with poetical essays... —KEIMER, Samuel. 1741#23

Carigueya, seu Marsupiale Americanum, or the Anatomy of an Opossum, dissected at Gresham-college. —TYSON, Edward. 1698#25

Carolina described more fully than heretofore, being an impartial collection from the several relations of that place... from... —1684#2

Carolina; or A description of the present state of that country, and the natural excellencies thereof... —ASH, Thomas. 1682#2

Case and tryal of John Peter Zenger, of New-York, printer... —1750#7

Case of Benjamin Harris, bookseller, lately come from New England... —HARRIS, Benjamin. 1681#12

Case of Benjamin Withall, gent. In his majesty's victualling office... —WITHALL, Benjamin. 1715#25

Case of British merchants, owners of ships and others relative to the employment and increase of British shipping... —1750#8

Case of Charles Lord Baltemore, a minor, with relation to his government of Maryland, granted by King Charles I, to Cecil Lord Baltemore... —CALVERT, George. 1689#5

Case of Charles Lord Baltemore [sic], a minor, with relation to his government of Maryland. —1715#7

Case of Great Britain's manufacturers of iron and steel, for her majesty's plantations and colonies... —1711#1

Case of Hannah Penn, the widow and executrix of William Penn Esq; late proprietor and governour of Pensilvania.—PENN, Hannah. 1730#25

Case of Henry Armistead, esq;... a native of Virginia... —ARMISTEAD, HENRY. 1740#2

Case of his majesty's colony of Conneticut [sic] in New England, with respect to their Charter, which is intended to be taken... —1715#8

Case of his majesty's province of New Hampshire upon two appeals... —1739#12

Case of his majesty's province of the Massachusetts Bay, touching the dispute between that province, and the colony of Rhode-Island... —1743#8

Case of his majesty's province of the Massachusetts Bay. . . with respect to the expences. . . in taking and securing Cape Breton. —1746#5

Case of inoculating the small-pox considered, and its advantages asserted; in a review of Dr. Wagstaffe's letter. . . —CRAWFORD, J. 1722#11

Case of J. Degrave. . . and others, owners of the seven sail of transports taken up to carry provisions to Newfoundland. — 1700#11

Case of Job Mathew. —1712#3

Case of lay-communion with the Church of England considered. . . —WILLIAMS, John. 1683#24

Case of Lewis Morris, esq; lord chief justice in of the province of New York. . . to be heard before. . . the lords of the committee of the Privy Council. . . —MORRIS, Lewis. 1735#13

Case of Mainwaring, Hawes, Payne and others, concerning a depredation. . . upon the ship Elizabeth, going. . . to Virginia. . . —MAINWARING, Randall. 1646#15

Case of Major Charles Craven, of the late Fifty-first regiment, in North America, now on half pay. . . —CRAVEN, Charles. 1759#21

Case of Messieurs Penn, and the people of Pensilvania, and the three lower counties of Newcastle, Kent, and Sussex, on Delaware. . . —1737#5

Case of Michael Wicks, Esq. late receiver of the plantation-duty. —WICKS, Michael. 1709#24

Case of Mr William P———s, an unfortunate young gentleman who is now confin'd in Newgate for returning from transportation. Shewing. . . —PARSONS, William. 1750#37

Case of Protestant dissenters in Carolina, shewing how a law to prevent occasional conformity there, has ended in the total subversion. . . —DEFOE, Daniel. 1706#10

Case of Robert Wise, late of London, tobacco-merchant. —WISE, Robert. 1714#22

Case of Scots-men residing in England and in the English plantations. Containing an account of the reasons in law, why they. . . —RIDPATH, George. 1702#24

Case of small twist roll tobacco. —1709#2

Case of the British northern colonies. —1731#4

Case of the British northern colonies. —1732#8

Case of the British northern colonies. —1733#5

Case of the British northern colonies. —1750#9

Case of the British sugar colonies. —1739#13

Case of the British sugar-colonies. —1731#6

Case of the British sugar colonies. —1731#5

Case of the British sugar colonies. —1737#6

Case of the British sugar colonies. —1733#6

Case of the chaplains of her majesty's navy, most humbly submitted to the honourable House of Commons. . . —1713#2.

Case of the Church of England in Carolina, humbly offered to the consideration of both houses of Parliament. In the year 1663. . . —1706#6

Case of the clergy of Maryland. . . —HENDERSON, Jacob. 1729#19

Case of the colony of Connecticott, upon its establishment under the charter of K. Charles II. —1701#16

Case of the colony of Rhoad Island, and Providence Plantations, and the province of New Jersey in America; with respect. . . — 1733#7

Case of the colony of Rhode Island, with respect to the bill depending in Parliament to regulate and restrain paper bills of credit. . . —1751#8

Case of the colony of South-Carolina in America: humbly offered to the consideration of both houses of Parliament. —1717#3

Case of the deputies of the Moravian Brethren. —UNITED BRETHREN IN CHRIST. 1749#44

Case of the exporters of tea to Ireland, and the British plantations in America. —1744#9

Case of the felt-makers, against the bill now depending, for confirming the charter of the Hudson's Bay Company. —1690#4

Case of the French Protestant refugees, settled in and about London, and in the English plantations in America. —1696#3

Case of the German protestant churches settled in the province of Pensylvania, and in North America. —1752#3

Case of the heir at law and executrix of the late proprietor of Pensilvania. . . —1725#3

Case of the honest exporters of Great Britain's manufactured iron and steel to her majesty's plantations and collonies. —1711#2

Case of the honourable James Annesley, Esq. being a sequel to the memoirs of an unfortunate young nobleman. . . —1745#8

Case of the honourable James Annesley, esq.; humbly offered to all lovers of truth and justice. . . —1756#11

Case of the Hudson's-Bay Company. —1693#4

Case of the Hudson's-Bay Company. —1749#7

Case of the Hudson's Bay Company of England, In referrence to the Canada Company of France, and their servant Gabriel de la Forest. . . —1696#4

Case of the Hudson's-Bay Company. Reasons for the continuance of the former act. —HUDSON'S BAY COMPANY. 1690#10

Case of the Hudson's-Bay-Company. The Kings of England by right of discovery. . . —1696#5

Case of the importation of bar-iron, from our own colonies of North America. . . recommended to. . . Parliament, by the iron manufacturers of Great Britain. —TUCKER, Josiah. 1756#81

Case of the importers of common turpentine, from Her Majesty's plantations, briefly stated. —1712#4

Case of the inhabitants in Pensilvania. . . —1749#8

Case of the manufacturers, and others, concerned in the making and vending of beaver hats. . . —1752#4

Case of the merchants, and others, of the City of Bristol, trading to the British Colonies in America. —1736#6

Case of the merchants, and planters, trading to, and residing in, Virginia and Maryland. —1713#3

Case of the merchants, and planters, trading to, and residing in, Virginia, and Maryland. —1728#4

Case of the merchants of London, and manufacturers of wheat and biscuit. —1732#9

Case of the merchants trading in tobacco, with relation to the bill now depending in. . . Commons, for lessening the drawback on tobacco exported for Ireland. —1714#1

Case of the merchants trading to and from America. —1731#7

Case of the merchants trading to New England, and of others residing there, with relation to the bills of exchange drawn for the Canada expedition. . . —1715#9

Case of the merchants trading to New England, and of others residing there, with relation to the bills of exchange drawn for the Canada expedition. . . —1716#2

Case of the merchants who export tobacco. . . —1714#2

Case of the officers, victuallers and clothiers of the four independent companies of New-York. . . —1704#9

Case of the officers who served in America, at the reduction of Anapolis Royal, and on several other commands. —1718#2

Case of the owners and proprietors of the ship and goods, Charles, seized by order of the Hudson's bay company, as the said ship. . . —1690#5

Case of the petitioner, Richard Budge, late Commander and part-owner of the ship Hope, and sole- owner of her cargo of logwood. —1709#3

Case of the planters of tobacco in Virginia, as represented by themselves; signed by the President of the Council, and Speaker. . . —1733#9

Case of the planters of tobacco in Virginia, as represented by themselves, signed by the President of the Council and Speaker of the House of Burgesses. . . Williamsburg, June 28, 1732. —1733#8

Case of the planters of Virginia, and the merchants trading thither humbly represented to the Parliament. —1729#3

Case of the province of Maryland, touching the outrageous riots which have been committed in the borders of that province, by the inhabitants of Pensilvania. —1737#7

Case of the province of New York, one of the British northern colonies. . . —1733#10

Case of the province of the Massachusets-Bay in New England with relation to their charter, and some observations thereon. —1715#10

Case of the province of Virginia, one of the British northern [sic] colonies. . . —1733#11

Case of the provinces of the Massachusetts-Bay, and New-Hampshire, and the colonies of Rhoad-Island with Providence plantations. . . —1731#8

Case of the provinces of the Massachusets-Bay and New Jersy [sic], and the colonies of Connecticut and Rhode Island, and the Providence. . . —1729#4

Case of the tobacco-merchants, who are become insolvent, and are bound to her majesty for duties. . . —1714#3

Case of the tobacco planters in his Majesty's Colony of Virginia, as to the bill now depending in the House of Lords, for the more. . . —1732#10

Case of Thomas Byfield, and Company, owners of the ship Dove. . . relating to the bill for importing naval stores from the plantations. —BYFIELD, Thomas. 1705#3

Case of Thomas Lewis, Elizabeth Jorden, Owen Griffith, Elizabeth Mackay, and Thomas Joy, and others. . . —1709#4

Case of William Atwood, esq; by the late King William. . . constituted chief justice of the province of New York. . . With a true. . . —ATWOOD, William. 1703#2

Case of William Penn, esq; as to the proprietary government of Pensilvania; which, together with Carolina, New York, etc is intended to be taken away by a bill in Parliament. —PENN, William. 1701#33

Case of William Penn, Esq; Proprietary-Governor of Pensilvania and of Joshua Gee, Henry Gould, Silvanus Grove, John Woods, and others, mortgagees under the said William Penn. —PENN, William. 1720#25

Case of William Penn, proprietary, and governor in chief of the province of Pennsylvania, and territories, against the Lord Baltimore's. . . —PENN, William. 1709#18

Case of William Tipton. . . —TIPTON, William. 1717#18

Case on behalf of Colonel Prevost, and other foreign officers, in the Royal American Regiment. —PREVOST, James. 1759#80

Case re-stated; or, An examine of a late pamphlet, intituled, The state of the nation for the year 1747. —1748#3

The castle builders: or, The history of William Stephens of the Isle of Wight, Esq; lately deceased. A political novel. . . —STEPHENS, Thomas. 1759#96

Catalogue of American trees and shrubs that will endure the climate of England. —GRAY, Christopher. 1737#13

Catalogue of divers rich and valuable effects, being a collection of Elihu Yale. Part 4. . . Will be sold by auction on Thursday the 15th of. . . November. . . —COCK, Christopher. 1722#7

Catalogue of divers rich and valuable effects, being a collection of Elihu Yale. part 5. A fifth sale of Elihu Yale. . . Will. . . —COCK, Christopher. 1723#3

Catalogue of English and foreign trees. —FURBER, Robert. 1727#7

Catalogue of Friend's books; written by many of the people called Quakers. . . —WHITING, John. 1708#18

Catalogue of many natural rarities. . . to be seen at the place called the Musick-House near the west end of St. Paul's church. . . —HUBERT, Robert. 1664#10

Catalogue of some narratives, vouchers, and other papers. . . from the United Moravian churches. —1749#9

Catalogue of the books belonging to the Charles-Town Library Society. . . —CHARLESTON, SOUTH CAROLINA. LIBRARY COMPANY. 1750#10

Catalogue of the damages for which the English demand reparation from the United Provinces. . . —1664#3

Catalogue of the libraries of the several gentlemen undermentioned, viz. . . II. The Hon. Governor Winthorp [sic] Fellow of the Royal Society. . . —OSBORNE, Thomas. 1748#18

Catalogus classicus et topicus, omnium rerum figuratarum in V. decadibus, seu primo [-secundo] volumine Gazophylacii naturae et artis. —PETIVER, James. 1709#19

Catalogus plantarum officinalium. . . —MILLER, Philip. 1730#21

Catalogus plantarum. Part I. —MILLER, Philip. 1730#22

Catalogus plantarum, tum exoticarum tum domesticarum. . . —LONDON. SOCIETY OF GARDENERS. 1730#19

Catechetical discourses on the whole doctrine of the covenant of grace. . . design'd to be read in the plantations. —BRAY, Thomas. 1701#9

A catechisme containing the chief heads. . . for the church of Christ at New-Haven. . . —DAVENPORT, John. 1659#9

A catechisme or, the grounds and principles of Christian religion, set forth by way of question and answer. . . —MATHER, Richard. 1650#7

Cato Major; or a treatise on old age, by M. Tullius Cicero. With explanatory notes. . . —LOGAN, James. 1750#29

Cato's letters. . . —TRENCHARD, John. 1723#11

The causeless ground of surmises. . . in relation to the late religious differences and breaches among some of the people called Quakers in America. —KEITH, George. 1694#10

A caveat against infidelity. —WATTS, Isaac. 1729#25

A censure of that learned and reverend. . . Mr John Cotton. . . upon the way of Mr Henden, of Benenden, in Kent. . . —1656#3

Certain certificates received from America, on behalf of Samuel Jennings. . . —PENINGTON, John. 1695#25

Certain miscellany tracts —BROWNE, Thomas. 1683#4

Certain proposalls in order to the peoples freedome and accommodation in some particulars. . . —ROBINSON, Henry. 1652#11

Certain queres [sic] modestly (though plainly) propounded. . . to such as affect the Congregationall-Way. . . —HOLLINGWORTH, Richard. 1646#14

Certain queries concerning the ordination of ministers. —ASPINWALL, William. 1647#1

Certain queries published by a friend. . . —COTTON, John. 1654#7

Certain select cases resolved. Specially, tending to the right ordering of the heart, that we may comfortably walk with God in our general and particular callings. —SHEPARD, Thomas. 1648#13

Certain verses written by severall of the authors friends; to be reprinted with the second edition of Gondibert. —DENHAM, Sir John. 1653#6

The certainty of the world of spirits, fully evinced by the unquestionable histories of apparations and witchcrafts. . . —BAXTER, Richard. 1691#1

A chaine of scripture chronologie from the creation of the world to the death of Jesus Christ. —ALLEN, Thomas. 1658#1

Chapter of Admirals. To which are added. . . Patrick O'Neal's return from drubbing the French. An Anacreonic song. —1760#20

The character of a rebellion, and what England may expect by one. . . —NALSON, John. 1681#14

A character of the province of Mary-land. . . also a small treatise on the wilde and naked Indians. . . Together with a collection of historical letters. —ALSOP, George. 1666#1

The character, preaching, etc. of the Reverend Mr George Whitefield impartially represented and supported. . . —SMITH, Josiah. 1741#34

The charge delivered from the bench to the Grand Inquest at a Court. . . Philadelphia, April 13th, 1736. —LOGAN, James. 1737#16

Charles Dunbar, of the Island of Antigua. . . appellant. Daniel Parke Custis, son and heir, and also sole executor of the last. . . —DUNBAR, Charles. 1757#12

The Charter granted by Charles II, to William Penn, Esq. Proprietor and Governor of Pennsylvania (4th March 1681). —1681#3

The Charter granted by Their majesties King William and Queen Mary, to the inhabitants of the. . . Massachusetts Bay. —1692#2

Charter of incorporation of Society for the Propagation of the Gospel in Foreign Parts, dated 16th June 1701. —ENGLAND AND WALES. SOVEREIGN. WILLIAM III. 1701#18

The Charter of Maryland. —1677#1

Charter of Maryland. Dated the 20th June, in 8th of Car. I. 1632. —1715#11

The chimera: or, the French way of paying national debts. . . the Mississippi stock. —DEFOE, Daniel. 1720#10

Chirurgus marinus; or, The sea chirurgion. . . —MOYLE, John. 1693#15

A chorographicall description of. . . Great Britain. . . Digested into a poem. . . —DRAYTON, Michael. 1622#12

Christ the fountaine of life. . . —COTTON, John. 1651#7

Christ triumphing and Satan raging: a sermon. . . first preached at Nottingham in Pensilvania. . . —FINLEY, Samuel. 1741#13

Christ victorious over the powers of darkness. . . A sermon preached in Boston, December 12, 1733. —SEWALL, Joseph. 1734#20

Christenings make not Christians, or A brief discourse concerning that name heathen, commonly given to the Indians. —WILLIAMS, Roger. 1646#20

The Christian commonwealth: or, The civil policy of the rising kingdom of Jesus Christ. . . —ELIOT, John. 1659#10

A Christian directory: or, A summ of practical theology, and cases of conscience. . . —BAXTER, Richard. 1673#1

The Christian doctrine and society of the people called Quakers, cleared from the reproach of the late division of a few in some parts of America. . . —WHITEHEAD, George. 1693#18

The Christian history; or, a general account of the progress of the gospel, in England, Wales, Scotland, and America: so far as the. . . —1747#3

The Christian philosopher: A collection of the best discoveries in nature, with religious improvements. —MATHER, Cotton. 1721#11

The Christian progress of. . . G. W; historically relating his experience. . . and service in defence of the truth, and of. . . Quakers. —WHITEHEAD, George. 1725#11

The Christian Quaker: or, George Keith's eyes opened. Good news from Pensilvania. . . —KEITH, George. 1693#8

The Christian traveller: A farewel-sermon preached. . . on the 20th of January, 1710. To the Palatines. Before their going out of England. . . —TRIBBECHOV, Johann. 1710#23

The Christian's two chief lessons. . . —HOOKER, Thomas. 1640#3

The Christianity of the people called Quakers, asserted, by George Keith: in answer to a sheet, called, A serious call to the Quakers. —FIELD, John. 1700#16

Christianographie. or The description of the multitude and sundry sort of Christians in the world not subject to the Pope. . . —PAGITT, Ephraim. 1635#2

Christophori Helvici, v. c. theatrum historicum. . . —HELWIG, Cristoph. 1651#11

Christ's fidelity the only shield against Satan's malignity. . . sermon. . . Salem-village the 24th of March, 1692. —LAWSON, Deodat. 1704#17

Chrysal: or, the adventures of a guinea. Wherein are exhibited views of several striking scenes,. . . in America, England, Holland, Germany and Portugal. By an adept. . . —JOHNSTONE, Charles. 1760#55

Church government and church-covenant discussed, in an answer of the elders of the severall churches in New England. . . —MATHER, Richard. 1643#14

Church members set in joynt. Or, a discovery of the unwarrantable and disorderly practice of private Christians, in usurping. . . —WOODBRIDGE, Benjamin. 1648#17

The church militant, historically continued. —VAUGHAN, William. 1640#6

The churches resurrection, or the opening of the fift and sixt verses of the 20th. chap. of the Revelation. —COTTON, John. 1642#5

A circular letter to the clergy of Maryland. . . —BRAY, Thomas. 1700#4

City Latin; or, Critical and political remarks. . . —THORNTON, Bonnell. 1760#92

The citye match. A comoedye. —MAYNE, Jasper. 1639#3

The civil law in its natural order. . . translated. . . by William Strahan. . . —DOMAT, Jean. 1722#13

The civil magistrates power in matters of religion modestly debated. . . with a brief answer to a certain slanderous pamphlet. . . Ill news from New England. . . —COBBET, Thomas. 1653#3

A clear and succinct account of North America, historical, geographical, etc. so far as it respects the arguments of the present time. . . —1755#8

The clear sun-shine of the Gospel breaking forth upon the Indians in New England. . . —SHEPARD, Thomas. 1648#14

A cloud of witnesses. . . —BESSE, Joseph. 1732#6

Coach and sedan. . . —PEACHAM, Henry. 1636#4

A coale from the altar. . . —HEYLYN, Peter. 1636#1

The coat of armes of Sir John Presbyter—1658#2

A collection for the improvement of husbandry and trade. . . Now revised, corrected, and published. . . by Richard Bradley. —HOUGHTON, John, ed. 1727#8

A collection of all the proclamations, declarations, articles and ordinances. . . —ENGLAND. 1654#5

A collection of curious observations on the manners, customs, usages. . . of the several nations of Asia, Africa, and America. Translated from the French. . . by John Dunn. . . —LAMBERT, Claude François. 1750#26

A collection of letters and state papers, from the original manuscript of many princes, great personages and statesmen. . . —HOWARD, Leonard. 1756#44

A collection of many select and Christian epistles, letters and testimonies. . . —FOX, George. 1698#7

A collection of pamphlets: containing the way and manner of inoculating the small-pox both in Britain and New-England. To which is added, a letter by Dr. D. Cumyng. —1722#8

A collection of papers. . . —SOCIETY FOR THE PROPAGATION OF THE GOSPEL. 1741#36

A collection of papers and other tracts, written occasionally on various subjects. —KEITH, William. 1740#21

A collection of papers, lately printed in the Daily Advertiser. . . —WHITEFIELD, George. 1740#39

A collection of papers, printed by order. . . viz. the Charter, the request, etc. . . —SOCIETY FOR THE PROPAGATION OF THE GOSPEL. 1706#18

A collection of poems in four volumes. By several hands. —DODSLEY, Robert. 1755#16

A collection of poems on various subjects. —ELLWOOD, Thomas. 1750#12A

A collection of pretty poems for the amusement of children three foot high. By Tommy Tagg, Esq; The fifty seventh edition, adorned with above sixty cuts. —TAGG, Tommy. 1760#91

A collection of Psalms and Hymns. —WESLEY, Charles and John. 1744#41

A collection of several pieces never before printed or not extant in his works. —LOCKE, John. 1720#19

A collection of State Tracts, published on occasion of the late revolution in 1688. . . —1705#5

A collection of sundry messages and warnings to the inhabitants of the city of Bristol. . . —BURY, Richard. 1728#3

A collection of testimonies concerning several ministers of the gospel among the people called Quakers. . . —1760#26

A collection of the epistles and works of Benjamin Holme. . . his life and travels in the work of the ministry, through several parts of Europe and America. . . —HOLME, Benjamin. 1753#12

A collection of the lives of ten eminent divines. . . —CLARKE, Samuel. 1662#2

A collection of the several writings. . . of Humphrey Smith, who dyed. . . 4th day of the 3d moneth. . . 1663. . . —SMITH, Humphry. 1683#20

A collection of the tracts of a certain free inquirer, noted for his sufferings for his opinions. . . —ANNET, Peter. 1750#1

A collection of the works of Thomas Chalkley. In two parts. . . —CHALKLEY, Thomas. 1751#9

A collection of the works of William Penn. In two volumes. To which is prefixed a journal of his life with many original letters and papers. . . —PENN, William. 1726#14

A collection of treaties, alliances, and conventions, relating to the security, commerce and navigation of the British dominions. . . —1717#5

A collection of voyages and travels. —CHURCHILL, Awnsham. 1704#10

A collection of voyages and travels, in three parts [Part III]. . . A description of the English province of Carolana. . . —COXE, Daniel. 1741#8

A collection of voyages undertaken by the Dutch East-India Company, for the improvement of trade and navigation. . . —COMMELIN, Izaak. 1703#6

Columna rostrata: or, a critical history of the English sea-affairs. . . —COLLIBER, Samuel. 1727#4

The comical history of the. . . states and empires of the moon and the sun. —CYRANO DE BERGERAC, Savinien. 1687#3

A comment upon Christ's last prayer in the seventeenth of John. . . —HOOKER, Thomas. 1656#8

Commissio Regia pro exercendâ jurisdictione spirituali et ecclesiasticâ in plantationibus Americanis. —GREAT BRITAIN. SOVEREIGN. GEORGE II). 1728#10

A commission for the well governing of our people, inhabiting in New-found-land. . . —ENGLAND AND WALES. SOVEREIGN. CHARLES I. 1634#1

Common-good: or, the improvement of commons, forests, and chases, by inclosure. . . —TAYLER, Silvanus. 1652#15

Common sense: its nature and use. With the manner of bringing all disputable cases. . . Applied to the Spanish affair. —1738#5

The Common-wealth's great ship. . . —1653#4

A comparison between the British sugar colonies and New England, as they relate to the interest of Great Britain. With some. . . —1732#11

A comparison between the doctrines taught by the clergy of the Church of England, and. . . Whitefield. . . To which is added, The wisdom of fleeing. . . —1741#7

A compassionate address to the Christian Negroes in Virginia With an appendix, containing some account of the rise and progress of Christianity among that poor people. . . —FAWCETT, Benjamin. 1756#28

A compendious account of the whole art of breeding, nursing, and the right ordering of the silk-worm. Illustrated with figures engraven. . . —1733#12

A compendious history of the rise and progress of the reformation of the church here in England. . . —DISNEY, Daniel. 1715#13

Compendium geographicum: Or, a more exact, plain, and easie introduction into all geography. . . —CHAMBERLAYNE, Peregrine. 1682#7

A compendium of the laws and government. . . of England and dominions, plantations, and territories thereto belonging. —CURSON, Henry. 1699#6

The complaint of M. Tenter-hooke the projector —TAYLOR, John. 1641#22

A compleat collection of papers. In twelve parts. . . —1689#7

The compleat Country Dancing-Master. . . —1718#3

The compleat gentleman. . . third impression much, inlarged. . . —PEACHAM, Henry. 1661#13

The compleat herbal of physical plants. . . —PECHEY, John. 1694#18

A compleat history of magick, sorcery, and witchcraft. . . —BOULTON, Richard. 1715#6

A compleat history of the most remarkable providences, both of judgement and mercy, which have hapned [sic] in this present age. . . —TURNER, William. 1697#12

The compleat ship-wright. —BUSHNELL, Edmund. 1664#2

A compleat system of general geography. . . —VAREN, Bernhard. 1733#36

A complete answer to the clergyman's letter to the right honourable the Earl of —— concerning the affair of Elizabeth Canning. . . —1753#3

A complete collection of all the laws of Virginia now in force. . . —1684#4

271

The complete English tradesman. —DEFOE, Daniel. 1725#4

A complete guide to the officers of His Majesty's customs in the out-ports. Being forms, precedents, and instructions. . . —CROUCH, Henry. 1732#13

A complete history of England. —1706#19

The complete merchant's clerk: or, British and American compting-house. In two parts. . . To which is added, an appendix. . . —WESTON, William. 1754#42

A complete system of geography. Being a description of all the countries. —BOWEN, Emanuel. 1744#6

A complete view of the British Customs. . . —CROUCH, Henry. 1724#6

A concise description of the English and French possessions in North-America, for the better explaining of the map published with that title. —PALAIRET, Jean. 1755#40

A concise history of the Spanish America. . . —CAMPBELL, John. 1741#4

The conduct and treatment of John Crookshanks. . . late commander of. . . the Lark. —CROOKSHANKS, John. 1759#22

The conduct of a noble commander in America, impartially reviewed. With the genuine causes of the discontents at New-York and Halifax. . . —1758#9

The conduct of Major-General Shirley, late general and commander in chief of his majesty's forces in North America. Briefly stated. —ALEXANDER, William. 1758#3

The conduct of the allies, and of the late ministry, in beginning and carrying on the present war —SWIFT, Jonathan. 1711#30

The conduct of the French, with regard to Nova Scotia; from its first settlement to the present time. . . In a letter to a member of Parliament. —JEFFERYS, Thomas. 1754#17

The conduct of the late administration, with regard to foreign affairs. —1742#11

The conduct of the late ministry, or, A memorial; containing a summary of facts with their vouchers, in answer to the Observations. . . —MOREAU, Jacob Nicolas. 1757#29

The conduct of the ministry impartially examined. In a letter to the merchants of London. . . —1756#12

A conference between a Bensalian Bishop and an English doctor, concerning church-government. —1681#4

A conference Mr. John Cotton held at Boston with the elders of New-England. . . —CORNWELL, Francis. 1646#5

A conference of. . . J. Belcher, Esq. . . with Edewakenk Chief Sachem of the Penobscut tribe, Loron one of the chief captains of the same tribe. . . —MASSACHUSETTS. GOVERNOR. 1732#29

The conformists reasons for hearing and joining with the nonconformists. . . —1691#6

A confutation of a late pamphlet intituled, A letter ballancing the necessity of keeping a land-force. —JOHNSON, Samuel. 1698#9

A confutation of infants baptisme, or an answer to a treatise written by Georg [sic] Phillips, of Wattertowne in New England. . . —LAMBE, Thomas. 1643#12

A congregational church is a catholike visible church. . . —STONE, Samuel. 1652#14

A congratulatory poem upon the noble feast made by the ancient and renouned families of the Smiths. — 1680#1A

Conjunct expeditions: or, expeditions that have been carried on jointly by the fleet and army. . . —MOLYNEUX, Thomas More. 1759#69

The conquest of Peru. . . Together with the voyages of the first adventurers, particularly Ferdinand de Soto, for the discovery of Florida. . . —DILWORTH, W. H. 1759#27

The conquests and triumphs of grace. . . —MAYHEW, Matthew. 1695#20

The consequences of the bill now depending in favour of the sugar colonies, impartially considered. —1731#10

Considerations humbly offered to the parliament shewing that those charters relating to the plantations. . . —1689#8

Considerations in relation to trade considered. —DONALDSON, James. 1706#11

Considerations on the addresses lately presented to his majesty on occasion of the loss of Minorca, in a letter to a member of Parliament. —1756#13

Considerations on the bill for a general naturalization, as it may conduce to the improvement of our manufactures and traffic. . . —SALMON, Thomas. 1748#23

Considerations on the bill for prohibiting the exportation of corn, etc. from North America. —1730#5

Considerations on the bill for prohibiting the exportation of corn, &c. from North America. . . —1740#8

Considerations on the bill now depending before the honourable House of Commons, for encouraging the importation of pig and bar iron from America, etc. —1750#11

Considerations on the bill now depending in Parliament concerning the British sugar colonies in America. . . —HALL, Fayrer. 1731#17

Considerations on the dispute now depending before the Honourable House of Commons, between the British, southern and northern plantations. . . In a letter to ———. —Z———h, A———r. 1731#35

Considerations on the great advantages which would arise from the discovery of the North west passage, and a clear account of the most practical method for attempting that discovery. —ELLIS, Henry. 1750#12

Considerations on the importance of Canada, and the Bay and River of St. Lawrence; and of the American fisheries. . . —1759#20

Considerations on the present German war. —MAUDUIT, Israel. 1760#64

Considerations on the present state of affairs, with some reflections of the Dutch observator. —1756#14

Considerations on the state of the British fisheries in America... With proposals for their security, by the reduction of Cape-Breton... January 1744-5... —1745#10

Considerations on the trade to Newfoundland. —THOMPSON, Thomas. 1711#32

Considerations relating to the laying any additional duty on sugar from the British plantations. Wherein is shewn, that such... —1747#6

Considerations touching the new contract for tobacco, as the same hath been propounded by Maister Ditchfield, and other undertakers. —DITCHFIELD, Master. 1625#2

Considerations towards a general plan of measures for the English provinces. Laid before the Board of commissioners at Albany, by Mr Pownall. —POWNALL, Thomas. 1756#61

Considerations upon the present state of our affairs, at home and abroad. In a letter to a member of Parliament from a friend in the country. —LYTTELTON, George. 1739#47

Considerations upon the white herring and cod fisheries... —VERNON, Edward. 1749#45

Considerations upon war, upon cruelty in general, and religious cruelty in particular. —1758#10

Consolation for our grammar schools, or a Comfortable encouragement for laying of a sure foundation of all good learning... —BRINSLEY, John. 1622#4

A constituent's answer to the reflexions of a member of Parliament upon the present state of affairs at home and abroad; particularly... —1755#9

Consuetudo, vel, Lex mercatoria, or, The antient law-merchant. —MALYNES, Gerard de. 1636#3

The contents of a folio history of the Moravians or United Brethren... humbly dedicated to the pious of every denomination of in Europe and America... —LOVER OF LIGHT. 1750#30

The contest in America between Great Britain and France... giving an account of the views and designs of the French, with the interests... —MITCHELL, John. 1757#28

A continuation of the account of the orphan-house in Georgia, from January 1740/1 to June 1742... —WHITEFIELD, George. 1742#50

A continuation of the account of the orphan-house in Georgia, from January 1740/1, to January 1742/3... —WHITEFIELD, George. 1743#44

A continuation of the friendly debate. By the same author. —PATRICK, Simon 1669#2

A continuation of the Reverend Mr Whitefield's journal, after his arrival at Georgia, to a few days after his second return thither from Philadelphia... —WHITEFIELD, George. 1741#49

A continuation of the Reverend Mr Whitefield's journal, during the time he was detained in England by the embargo... —WHITEFIELD, George. 1739#73

A continuation of the Reverend Mr Whitefield's journal, from a few days after his return to Georgia to his arrival at Falmouth... —WHITEFIELD, George. 1741#50

A continuation of the Reverend Mr. Whitefield's journal, from his arrival at London, to his departure, from thence on his way to Georgia... —WHITEFIELD, George. 1739#74

A continuation of the Reverend Mr. Whitefield's journal, from his arrival at Savannah, to his return to London. —WHITEFIELD, George. 1739#75

A continuation of the Reverend Mr Whitefield's journal from his embarking after the embargo, to his arrival at Savannah in Georgia. —WHITEFIELD, George. 1740#40

A continuation of the state of New-England; being a further account of the Indian warr... —1676#1

The controversie concerning liberty of conscience in matters of religion, truly stated... —COTTON, John. 1646#6

The controversy between the Northern colonies and the sugar islands, respectively considered... —1732#12

Controversy ended: or the sentence himself given against himself by George Fox... ratified and aggravated by W. Penn... —HEDWORTH, Henry. 1673#6

The Convention. An excellent new ballad. To which is added the king of Spain's protest, and a new epitaph. —1739#16

The Convention vindicated from the misrepresentations of the enemies of our peace. —WALPOLE, Horatio. 1739#68

A coole conference between the Scottish commissioners cleared reformation, and the Holland ministers Apologeticall narration... —1644#3

Copies of Pennsylvania assembly's present address to his majesty, and of the royal instructions given in 1740... —1755#10

Copies of several publick papers, which have passed in the province of Pensilvania in the month of November, 1755. —1756#15

Copies of the lieutenant-governor of Pennsylvania, his speeches to the assembly, their addresses in answer thereto, and several messages and answers, between them. —1755#11

A coppy of a letter of Mr Cotton of Boston, in New England, sent in answer of certaine objections made against their discipline and order there —COTTON, John. 1641#6

A copy of a letter from a gentleman in Guadaloupe to his friend in London... —1760#27

Copy of a letter from Mr. Caleb Spurrier to his correspondent in Cornwall. —SPURRIER, Caleb. 1721#19

A copy of a letter from Quebeck in Canada, to a Pr-M-r in France, dated October 11. 1747. —NE—L, Mc-O—. 1747#16

The copy of a letter written by Mr. Thomas Parker, pastor of the church in Newbury in New-England, to his sister... Novemb. 22. 1649... —PARKER, Thomas. 1650#9

Copy of a petition from the governor and company of the Sommer Islands... with a short collection of the most remarkable passages... —1651#6

The copy of a reference. . . [12 April 1622.] —WHITBOURNE, Richard. 1622#25

The Copy of an act lately passed in Carolina, and sent over to be continued here. . . which would be highly prejudicial to her Majesty's. . . —CAROLINA. 1704#8

Copy of three letters, the first written by Dr John Nicol at New York. . . the second by a dissenting minister in England. . . the third. . . —NICOL, John and others. 1740#25

Copy of two letters, the first written by a gentleman at New York. . . the second by a dissenting minister in England. . . progress and success of the gospel in foreign parts. . . —NICOL, John and others. 1740#26

Cosmographie in four books. . . —HEYLYN, Peter. 1652#4

Cosmography and geography in two parts. —BLOME, Richard. 1682#4

Cotejo de la conducta. . . His Catholick Majesty's conduct compared with that of his Britannick Majesty's. . . —1739#18

The countermine: or, a short but true discovery of the dangerous principles, and secret practices of the dissenting party. . . —NALSON, John. 1677#14

The counterpart to the state dunces. By a native of New-York. —NATIVE OF NEW-YORK. 1733#25

The counterpoise. Being thoughts on a militia and a standing army. . . —THORNTON, William. 1752#23

The countryman's companion. . . —TRYON, Thomas. 1684#10

The court and city kalendar; or, Gentleman's Register, for England, Scotland, Ireland, and America for the year. —1745#11

The court of Atalantis. . . in verse and prose. . . —1714#4

The cov—ous mother, or, the terrible overthrow of Two Loyal Lovers. —1685#7

The covenant of Gods free grace. . . Whereunto is added A profession of faith. . . by John Davenport. . . —COTTON, John. 1645#4

The covenant of grace, not absolute but conditional. . . —1692#4

The covenant of grace opened: wherein these particulars are handled. . . —HOOKER, Thomas. 1649#3

The covenant of grace. . . Whereunto are added: Certain queries. . . also a discussion of the civil magistrates power. . . —COTTON, John. 1655#8

The Crisis. —1756#17

The crisis: or, the decisive period of British power and liberty. . . In two sermons preached at Boston in the county of Lincoln, February 17, 1758. —RADCLIFF, Ebenezer. 1758#37

The crisis: or, the uncertain doom of kingdoms. . . with reference to Great-Britain and her colonies in their present circumstances. . . —DAVIES, Samuel. 1757#6

A critical essay concerning marriage. . . to which is added, an historical account of the marriage rites and ceremonies. . . —SALMON, Thomas. 1724#20

A critical history of the administration of Sr Robert Walpole, now earl of Orford. . . —RALPH, James. 1743#29

The cruel massacre of Protestants in North-America; shewing how the French and Indians joined together to scalp the English and the. . . —1758#11

The cry of the innocent and oppressed for justice. —1664#4

The culture of silk, or, an essay on its rational practice and improvement. . . For the use of the American colonies. —PULLEIN, Samuel. 1758#36

The curious and profitable gardener. . . To which is added, an exact description of the great American aloe. . . together with the culture of that, and many other rare exotic plants. . . —COWELL, John. 1730#6

Curious enquiries. Being six brief discourses. . . —1688#13

The curse of cowardice: a sermon preached to the militia in Hanover county, Virginia, at a general muster, May 8, 1758. . . —DAVIES, Samuel. 1758#12

The danger of desertion: or a Farwel sermon —HOOKER, Thomas. 1641#15

The danger of the church and kingdom from foreigners considered. . . —OWEN, Charles. 1721#15

Daphnis and Menalcas: a pastoral. Sacred to the memory of the late General Wolfe. . . —1759#24

The dawnings of the gospel-day, and its light and glory discovered. . . —HOWGILL, Francis. 1676#10

The day of doom: or, A description of the great and last judgement. . . —WIGGLESWORTH, Michael. 1666#7

The day-breaking, if not the sun-rising of the gospell with the Indians in New-England. —WILSON, John. 1647#20

De Baptismate. . . —MATHER, Samuel. 1715#17

De Christiana liberate, or liberty of conscience. . . In two parts. . . To which is added, a word of advice to the Pensilvanians. —BUGG, Francis. 1682#5

De jure maritimo et navali: or a treatise of affaires maritime. . . —MOLLOY, Charles. 1676#13

De rebus liturgicis oratio pro gradu doctoratûs in S. S. theologia. . . A Io. Sharp ecclesiae Anglicanae apud Americanos prebytero. —SHARP, John. 1714#18

De successu evangelii apud Indos in Nova-Anglia epistola. . . —MATHER, Increase. 1688#11

Death made easie and happie. Two brief discourses on the prudent apprehensions of death. . . together with serious thoughts in dying times. . . —MATHER, Cotton. 1701#30

The deceiver of the nations discovered. . . his cruel works of darkness. . . in Maryland in Virginia. —HOWGILL, Francis. 1660#14

A declaration how the monies. . . were disposed, which was gathered (by Mr Patrick Copland. . .). . . (towards the building of a free schoole in Virginia). . . —COPLAND, Patrick. 1622#7

A declaration of his highnes by the advice of his council... —ENGLAND. LORD PROTECTOR. 1655#10

A declaration of the General Court of the Massachusetts... October 18. 1659. Concerning the execution of two Quakers... Reprinted in London... —MASSACHUSETTS GENERAL COURT. 1659#19

A declaration of the Lord Baltemore's plantation in Mary-land, nigh upon Virginia: manifesting the nature, quality, condition, and rich utilities it contayneth. —WHITE, Andrew. 1633#6

The declaration of the reasons and motives for the present appearing in arms of their majesties protestant subjects in Maryland. —PROTESTANT ASSOCIATION. 1689#25

A declaration of the sad and great persecution of and martyrdom of the people of God, called Quakers, in New-England... —BURROUGH, Edward. 1661#5

A declaration of the state of the colony and affairs in Virginia. With a relation of the barbarous massacre in the time of peace... —WATERHOUSE, Edward. 1622#24

A deduction of the right and title of the Crown of Great Britain, and therein of... Queen Anne, to all the streights, bays... —1709#6

A defence of a book intituled The snake in the grass... —LESLIE, Charles. 1700#25

A defence of church-government exercised in prebyteriall, classical and synodall assemblies. —PAGIT, John. 1641#18

A defence of Mr John Cotton from the imputation of selfe contradiction... —COTTON, John. 1658#3

A defence of natural and revealed religion... With a general index... —BURNET, Gilbert. 1737#4

A defence of the answer made unto the nine questions or positions sent from New-England... —ALLIN, John and SHEPARD, Thomas. 1648#1

A defence of the Dutch, against the imputations of fraud, cruelty and perfidiousness... the encroachments of France, and the untractableness... —1749#10

A defence of the examination of a book entituled, A brief account of many of the prosecutions of the people called Quakers... —1737#10

A defence of the New-England charters... —DUMMER, Jeremiah. 1721#4

A defence of the principles of love, which are necessary to the unity and concord of Christians... —BAXTER, Richard. 1671#1

A defence of The resolution of this case... —FOWLER, Edward. 1684#5

A defense of sundry positions & scriptures alledged to justifie the Congregationall way... —EATON, Samuel and TAYLOR, Timothy. 1645#6

A defense of the Christian revelation... —WEST, Gilbert. 1748#33

A demonstration of true love unto you the rulers of the colony of the Massachusets... —CODDINGTON, William. 1674#1

The deplorable state of New - England; by reason of a covetous and treacherous governor, and pusillanimous counsellors with a vindication... —1708#4

The description and use of his Majesties dials in White-Hall Garden. —GUNTER, Edmund. 1624#8

A description of a great sea-storm, that happened to some ships in the gulph of Florida, in September last... —1671#6

A description of a new-invented stove-grate, shewing its uses... over all others... —DURNO, J. 1753#5

A description of Georgia, by a gentleman who has resided there upwards of seven years, and was one of the first settlers. —CHRISTIE, Thomas. 1741#5

A description of Holland... Wherein is contained, a particular account of... commerce, in... America. —1743#11

A description of New-England in general... —JOSSELYN, John. 1682#18

A description of some curious and uncommon creatures, omitted in the Description of 300 animals, and likewise in the supplement to that book. —BOREMAN, Thomas. 1739#7

A description of the coast, tides and currents, in Button's Bay and in the Welcome: being the north-west coast of Hudson's Bay... —1745#13

A description of the English and French territories in North America: being an explanation of a new map of the same. Shewing all the encroachments of the French... —1755#15

A description of the English province of Carolana, by the Spaniards called Florida, and by the French, La Louisiane... —COXE, Daniel. 1722#10

A description of the famous new colony of Georgia, in South Carolina (established by the present majesty,) of which Colonel David... —GRADY, ———. 1734#7

A description of the four parts of the world, viz. Europe, Africa, Asia, America, with the several kingdoms, etc. —1695#9

A description of the Golden islands, with an account of the undertaking now on foot for making a settlement there... —MONTGOMERY, Robert, Sir. 1720#22

A description of the island of Jamaica... —BLOME, Richard. 1672#1

A description of the new world. Or, America islands, and continent: and by what people those regions are now inhabited... —GARDYNER, George. 1651#9

A description of the province of New Albion. And a direction for adventurers with small stock to get two for one, and good land freely... —PLANTAGENET, Beauchamp. 1648#10

The description of the province of West-Jersey, in America: as also proposals to such who desire to have any propriety therein. —PENN, William. 1676#16

A description of the whole world... —FAGE, Robert. 1658#4

A description of the Windward passage, and Gulf of Florida, with the course of the British trading-ships to, and from the island... —COWLEY, J. 1739#19

A description of three hundred animals; viz. beasts, birds, fishes, serpents and insects. With a particular account of the whale-fishery... —BOREMAN, Thomas. 1730#2

Description du pays nommé Caroline. —1679#1

The destruction of the French foretold by Ezekiel; or, a commentary on the thirty-fifth chapter of that prophet... —DOUGLAS, John (1721-1807). 1755#17

Detection of a conspiracy to suppress a general good in physic, and to promote error... —TENNENT, John, M. D. 1743#42

A detection of the court and state of England during the last few reigns. —COKE, Roger. 1694#3

A detection of the state and situation of the present sugar planters of Barbadoes and the Leeward islands... —ROBERTSON, Robert. 1732#35

A detection of the views of those who would... engage... in a ruinous expensive land war... —1746#8

A determination of the case of Mr. Thomas Story, and Mr. James Hoskins, relating to an affair of the Pennsilvania Company... —BOCKETT, Elias. 1724#3

The devil turn'd Round-head: or, Pluto become a Brownist — TAYLOR, John. 1642#13

A dialogue about the French government... between Tom and Dick, two seamen... —1690#9

A dialogue between an English-man and a Dutch-man on the subject of trade... —1737#11

Dialogue between the ghost of Captain Kidd, and the napper in the Strand, napt. —1702#8

A dialogue betwixt General Wolfe, and the Marquis Montcalm, in the Elysian Fields. —1759#26

Dialogues of the dead. —LYTTELTON, George. 1760#62

A diamond or rich jewel, presented to the Common wealth of England, for inriching the Nation —CHAPPEL, Samuel. 1651#4

The DIATRIBE proved to be PARADIATRIBE, Or A Vindication of the judgement of Reformed Churches... —SEAMAN, Lazurus. 1647#14

Dictionarium rusticum and urbanicum: or, A dictionary of all sorts of country affairs. —1704#12

Dictionarium sacrum seu religiosum. A dictionary of all religions, ancient and modern. —1704#13

A dictionary of the Hudson's Bay Indian language. —BOWREY, Thomas. 1701#8

Die Sabatti 23 Januarii 1646. Whereas the severall plantations in Virginia, Bermudas, Barbados, and other places of America... —ENGLAND AND WALES. PARLIAMENT. 1647#8

A digest of all the laws relating to the customs, to trade, and navigation. —FORSTER, Samuel. 1727#6

A direction for adventurers... with small stock to get two for one, and good land freely... true description of the healthiest... — EVELYN, Robert. 1641#11

Directions for navigating the gulf and river of St. Laurence; with a particular account of the bays, roads... Published... —JEFFERYS, Thomas. 1760#53

A discourse about trade. —CHILD, Josiah. 1690#6

A discourse and a view of Virginia. By Sir William Berkeley (governor of Virginia). —BERKELEY, William. 1663#1

A discourse and discovery of New-found-land, with many reasons how a plantation may there be made... —WHITBOURNE, Richard. 1622#26

A discourse concerning faith and fervency in prayer... — MATHER, Increase. 1713#7

A discourse concerning the currencies of the British plantations in America. Especially with regard to their paper money... — DOUGLASS, William. 1741#9

A discourse concerning the designed establishment of a new colony to the south of Carolina, in the most delightful country in the universe. —MONTGOMERY, Robert, Sir. 1717#13

A discourse concerning the maintenance, due to those that preach the gospel... —MATHER, Increase. 1709#14

A discourse concerning the origine and properties of wind. With a historicall account of hurricanes. —BOHUN, Ralph. 1671#3

A discourse concerning the plague, with some preservatives against it. By a lover of mankind. —BYRD, William II ?. 1721#3

A discourse containing a loving invitation... to all such as shall be adventurers, either in person, or purse, for the advancement... —WHITBOURNE, Richard. 1622#27

A discourse, delivered at Quebec, in the chappel belonging to the convent of the Ursulins, September 27th, 1759; occasioned by the success of our arms in the reduction of that capital... — DAWSON, Eli. 1760#29

A discourse how to render the plantations on the continent of America, and Islands adjacent; more beneficial... to this Kingdom. —RANDOLPH, Edward. 1697#11

A discourse of the laws relating to pirates and piracies, and the marine affairs of Great Britain. —1726#6

A discourse of the plurality of worlds... —FONTENELLE, Bernard Le Bovyer de. 1687#4

A discourse of trade, by N. B... —BARBON, Nicholas. 1690#2

A discourse on trade; more particularly on sugar and tobacco: shewing the true and natural means of their support, and the unreasonableness of depending upon the legislature for their relief. —1733#13

A discourse showing the great advantages that new-buildings, and the enlarging of towns and cities do bring to a nation... —1678#3

A discourse written by Sir Geo. Downing vindicating his royal master... —DOWNING, George. 1664#6

Discourses concerning government... —SIDNEY, Algernon. 1698#18

Discourses on several public occasions during the war in America, preached chiefly with a view to explaining the importance... — SMITH, William (1727-1803). 1759#90

Discourses on the publick revenues, and on the trade of England... —DAVENANT, Charles. 1698#6

The discoveries of John Lederer, in three several marches from Virginia, to the west of Carolina, and other parts of the continent... —LEDERER, John. 1672#6

A discovery of a large, rich, and plentiful country, in North America... —HENNEPIN, Louis. 1720#16

The discovery of New Brittaine. Began August 27. Anno Dom. 1650... From Fort Henry... in Virginia... to the fals of Blandina... in New Brittaine... —BLAND, Edward. 1651#1

A discovery of subterraneall treasure, viz, Of all manner of mines and mineralls from the gold to the coal. —PLATTES, Gabriel. 1639#5

The discovery of the accursed thing found in the Foxonian Quakers camp. —CRISP, Thomas. 1695#8

A discussion of that great point in divinity, the sufferings of Christ... —NORTON, John. 1653#14

A disquisition concerning the... souls of men... —TEXT QUERY MATHER, Increase. 1707#query

A disputation concerning church-members and their children, in answer to XXI. questions... —MATHER, Richard. 1659#20

The dispute between the northern colonies and the sugar islands, set in a clear view. —1731#12

The dissenting gentleman's answer to the Reverend Mr White's three letters. —TOWGOOD, Micaiah. 1746#26

The dissenting gentleman's second letter to the Reverend Mr White. —TOWGOOD, Micaiah. 1747#28

Dissertatio medica inauguralis de abortu... —PEYTON, Valentine. 1754#28

Dissertatio medica inauguralis, de crisibus... —BULFINCH, Thomas. 1757#4

Dissertatio medica inauguralis, de febre maligna biliosa Americae... pro gradu doctoratus... Joannes Moultrie, ex Meridionali Carolinae provincia... —MOULTRIE, John. 1749#31

Dissertatio medica inauguralis, de fluoro albo... —JAY, James (1732-1815). 1753#13

Dissertatio medica inauguralis, de parca et simplici medicina, quam... pro gradu doctoratus... eruditorum examini subjicit Thomas Clayton... —CLAYTON, Thomas. 1758#7

A dissertation concerning the future conversion of the Jewish nation... —MATHER, Increase. 1709#15

A dissertation on... causes... to render a nation populous. —BELL, William. 1756#6

A dissertation on enthusiasm... —GREEN, Thomas. 1755#26

A dissertation on liberty and necessity, pleasure and pain. —FRANKLIN, Benjamin. 1725#6

A dissertation on the numbers of mankind in antient and modern times: in which the superior populousness of antiquity is maintained... —WALLACE, Robert. 1753#22

A dissertation on the origin of the venereal disease; proving that it was not brought from America, but began in Europe by an epidemical... —1751#13

A dissertation on the plan, use, and importance, of the Universal dictionary of trade and commerce, translated from the French... —POSTLETHWAYT, Malachy. 1749#34

A dissertation on the present conjuncture, particularly with regard to trade... —1739#20

A dissertation wherein the strange doctrine... —TEXT QUERY MATHER, Increase. number 1708#query

Dissertations on the prophecies, which have remarkably been fulfilled, and at this time are fulfilling in the world. —NEWTON, Thomas. 1754#27

A dissuasive from the errours of the time: wherein the tenets of the principall sects, especially of the Independents, are drawn together in one map... —BAILLIE, Robert. 1645#1

The disswasive from the errors of the time, vindicated from the exceptions of Mr Cotton and Mr Tombes... —BAILLIE, Robert. 1655#4

The distinguishing marks of a work of the spirit of God... lately appeared... in New-England... —EDWARDS, Jonathan. 1742#12

The divine goodness and human gratitude properly considered, in a sermon preached at West-Horsley... November 29, 1759... —BALL, Nathaniel. 1759#3

The divine right of church-government and excommunication... —RUTHERFORD, Samuel. 1646#18

The divine right of infant baptism examined... —GILL, John. 1749#18

Doctor Pinfold's state of the case of the petitioner's for settling his majesties waste land, lying between Nova-Scotia, and the province of Maine... —PINFOLD, Charles. 1721#17

The doctrine of devils, proved to be the grand apostacy of the times... —ORCHARD, N. 1676#15

The doctrine of instituted churches explained and proved from the word of God... —STODDARD, Solomon. 1700#34

The doctrine of life, or of mans redemtion [sic]... —HOLYOKE, Edward. 1658#7

The doctrine of the church. —COTTON, John. 1643#4

The doctrine of the sacrament —CHAUNCY, Charles (1592-1672). 1642#3

Dr. Houstoun's memoirs of his own life-time... Containing... VIII. The importance of Cape Breton to the British nation. —HOUSTOUN, James. 1747#10

The due right of presbyteries... wherein is examined 1. The way of the church of Christ in New England. —RUTHERFORD, Samuel. 1644#16

Duplessis's memoirs, or, a variety of adventures in England and America... and a description of some strolling players, with whom he travelled... —DU PLESSIS, ——. 1757#11

The duties, difficulties and reward of the faithful minister. A sermon, preached at the installation of the Revd. Mr. John Todd... —DAVIES, Samuel. 1754#7

A dutiful address to the throne upon the present state of G t B n... —1756#21

The duty and manner of propagating the gospel shewn in a sermon... on requiring a collection to be made for the use of the Society for propagating the Gospel in Foreign Parts. —WATTS, Robert. 1711#34

The duty and reward of propagating principles of religion and virtue... A sermon preach'd... March 15, 1732... —BURTON, John. 1733#4

The duty of all Christians to read the scriptures... in two sermons. —WEBSTER, Charles. 1743#43

The duty of Christians to propagate their religion among heathens, earnestly recommended to the masters of negro slaves in Virginia. A sermon preached in Hanover, January 8, 1757. —DAVIES, Samuel. 1758#13

The duty of public spirit recommended in a sermon preach'd... March 20, 1739-40... —CROWE, William. 1740#9

A dying father's last legacy. —PETER, Hugh. 1660#22

The early conversion of islanders, a wise expedient for propagating Christianity. A sermon preached... 19th of Feb. 1713-14... —STANHOPE, George. 1714#20

Early piety, exemplified in the life and death of Nathaniel Mather... —MATHER, Cotton. 1689#16

An earnest dissuasive from intemperance in meats and drinks... sermon... Lambeth... —GIBSON, Edmund. 1745#22

An easie and familiar method whereby to judge the effects depending on eclipses... —LILLY, William. 1652#8

Ebenezer: or a monument of thankfulness. Being a true account of a late miraculous preservation of nine men in a small boat... —GEARE, Allen. 1708#5

Edifying and curious letters of some missioners of the Society of Jesus, from foreign missions... —LE GOBIEN, Charles. 1707#11

Edinburgh, 20 May 1731. R.D.B. [Reverend and Dear Brethren]... —SCOTLAND. CHURCH OF SCOTLAND. GENERAL ASSEMBLY. 1731#32

Edinburgh, November 14, 1728. R.D.B. [Reverend and Dear Brethren]... —SCOTLAND. CHURCH OF SCOTLAND. GENERAL ASSEMBLY. 1728#14

An eighth and last letter, or address, to the Parliament as well as the people of Great Britain... —1758#18

An elegy on the death of Capt. William Kidd... —1701#17

Elegy on the mournful banishment, of James Campbell of Burnbank, to the West Indies. —1721#5

The elements of commerce, and the theory of taxes... —TUCKER, Josiah. 1755#58

The elements of philosophy... to which is added, an original letter concerning the settlement of bishops in America... the third edition... —JOHNSON, Samuel. (1696-1772). 1754#18

Eleothriambos, or, The triumph of mercy... —LEE, Samuel. 1677#11

Eleutheria: or, An idea of the Reformation in England: and a History of Non-Conformity in and since that Reformation. With predictions... —MATHER, Cotton. 1698#13

Elizabeth Galley. New York. The case of the respondents. —GREAT BRITAIN. LORDS COMMISSIONERS OF APPEAL IN PRIZE CAUSES. 1760#41

Emblems of rarities; or Choice observations out of worthy histories... —LUPTON, Donald. 1636#2

The emissary instructed, or the wiles of popery represented... —1742#13

Enchiridion geographicum. Or, A manual of geography. Being a description of all the empires, kingdoms, and dominions of the earth. —SYMSON, Matthias. 1704#27

An encouragement to colonies. —ALEXANDER, William, 1st Earl of Stirling. 1624#2

Encouragements. For such as shall have intention to bee under-takers in the new plantations of Cape Breton... — GORDON, Robert. 1625#7

The encouraging general, a song sung by that truly gallant officer, General Wolfe, the evening before he received the mortal wound which occasioned his death. —1759#31

An endevour after the reconcilement of that... difference between the godly Presbyterians and the godly Independents... —1648#5

Englands appeale from the private cabal at White-hall to the great council of the nation... —LISOLA, François. 1673#7

Englands bane: or, The description of drunkennesse. —YOUNG, Thomas. 1634#9

England's danger by Indian manufactures. —SMITH, Thomas. 1700#33

England's duty, under the present gospel liberty... —FLAVELL, John. 1689#11

England's-exchequer. or A discourse of the sea... —HAGTHORPE, John. 1625#8

Englands grandeur, and way to get wealth; or, promotion of trade made easy... —TRYON, Thomas. 1699#18

England's great happiness or, A dialogue between content and complaint... — HOUGHTON, John. 1677#6

England's happiness increased, or a sure and easie remedy against all succeeding dear years; by a plantation of the roots called potatoes... —FORSTER, John. 1664#7

England's improvements. In two parts... —COKE, Roger. 1675#4

England's monarchs... —CROUCH, Nathaniel. 1685#8

England's royall fishing revived. —SHARPE, Edward. 1630#7

England's safety, in trades encrease. —ROBINSON, Henry. 1641#21

England's safety: or, A bridle to the French king. . . — SAINT LO, George. 1693#17

England's shame: or the unmasking of a political atheist. . . the life and death of. . . Hugh Peters. . . —YONGE, William. 1663#3

England's treasure by forraign trade. . . —MUN, Thomas. 1664#11

Englands wants; or several proposals probably beneficial to England, humbly offered to. . . both houses of Parliament. —CHAMBERLAYNE, Edward. 1667#2

The English Baronetage. . . To which are added, an account of such Nova-Scotia baronets as are of English families. . . —WOTTON, Thomas. 1741#54

The English cotejo, or the cruelties. . . charged upon the English in a Spanish libel. . . —COPITHORNE, Richard. 1739#17

The English empire in America: or, A View of the dominions of the Crown of England in the West-Indies. . . —B., R. [i. e. CROUCH, Nathaniel]. 1685#2

The English Pericles; or, the four qualifications necessary to make a true statesman, exemplified in the character and conduct of Mr. Secretary Pitt. —1759#32

The English rogue, described in the life of Meriton Latroon. A witty extravangant. Being a compleat history of the most eminent cheats of both sexes. . . —HEAD, Richard and KIRKMAN, Francis. 1665#18

The English sailors resolution to fight the Spaniards Guarda Costas. —1739#22

Englishmen's eyes opened; or All made to see. —1733#15

Enquiries touching the diversity of languages and religions through the chief parts of the world. . . —BREREWOOD, Edward. 1622#3

An enquiry into the causes of our ill success in the present war. . . —1757#14

An enquiry into the causes of the alienation of the Delaware and Shawanese Indians from the British interest. . . Together with the remarkable journal of Charles Frederic Post. . . —THOMPSON, Charles. 1759#99

An enquiry into the melancholy circumstances of Great Britain. —1730#10

An enquiry into the present system. —1756#22

An enquiry into the state of the bills of credit of the province of the Massachusetts Bay. . . in a letter from a gentleman in Boston to a merchant in London. —1743#15

An enquiry whether a general practice of virtue tends to be the wealth or poverty, benefit or disadvantage of a people. . . —BLEWITT, George. 1725#1

The epilogue, to be spoken before the four Indian kings, at the Queen's Theatre. . . the 24th of April. —1710#3

An epistle, containing a salutation to all faithful friends, a reproof to all the unfaithfull; and a visitation to the enquiring. . . —PENN, William. 1682#21

An epistle from Benjamin Holme, being a salutation to friends in Great Britain and Ireland. . . —HOLME, Benjamin. 1718#11

An epistle from James Janney to Friends of Cheshire, and by them desired to be made publick. . . —JANNEY, Thomas. 1694#13

An epistle general to them who are of the royal priest-hood and chosen generation. . . to be sent abroad among the saints. . . in Old and New England. . . Barbados, and Virginia. . . —FOX, George. 1660#11

An epistle of love and tender advice, to friends and brethren in America, or elswhere. . . —BINGLEY William. 1689#3

An epistle of love to all the saints. —BISHOP, George. 1661#2

An epistle to Alexander Pope esq; from South Carolina. . . —KIRKPATRICK, James. 1737#14

An epistle to all professors in New-England, Germany, and other parts of the called Christian world. . . —FOX, George. 1673#4

An epistle to Dr. Richard Mead concerning the epidemical diseases of Virginia, particularly, a pleurisy and peripneumony, wherein. . . —TENNENT, John, M. D. 1738#27

An epistle to Friends and tender-minded people in America. . . —HOLME, Benjamin. 1722#17

An epistle to Friends. . . and warning them to beware of that spirit of contention. . . in George Keith, and some few others. . . who have. . . —ELLWOOD, Thomas. 1694#5

An epistle to Friends in Maryland, Virginia, Barbadoes, and the other colonies. . . Dear Friends. . . John Bell. Bromley near London, 3d Month 1741. —BELL, John. 1741#2

An epistle to the Hon. Arthur Dobbs, esq; in Europe. From a clergyman in America. . . —STERLING, James. 1752#22

An epistle to the inhabitants of South Carolina; containing sundry observations proper to be consider'd by every professor of Christianity in general. —HUME, Sophia. 1754#16

The epistles of Mr Robert Rich to the seven churches. . . —RICH, Robert. 1680#9

Epistles from the yearly meeting of the people called Quakers, held in London, to the quarterly and monthly meetings in Great. . . —SOCIETY OF FRIENDS. 1760#88

An epitome of Mr. J. Speed's theatre of the empire. . . —SPEED, John.. 1676#18

An epitome of navigation. . . —GELLIBRAND, Henry. 1674#4

An essay against the transportation and selling of men to the plantations of forreigners; with special regard to Scotland. . . —1699#8

An essay concerning humane understanding —LOCKE, John. 1690#12

An essay concerning inland and foreign trade. . . showing how a company for national trade, may be constituted in Scotland. . . —PATERSON, William. 1704#21

An essay concerning the multiplication of mankind: together with another essay in political arithmetick —PETTY, William. 1686#3

An essay for the recording of illustrious providences, wherein an account is given of many remarkable and memorable events. . . especially in New-England. . . —MATHER, Increase. 1684#7

An essay humbly offer'd for an act of Parliament to prevent capital crimes. . . —OLLYFFE, George. 1731#27

An essay on inoculation, occasioned by the small-pox being brought into South Carolina in the year 1738. . . with an appendix, containing a faithful account of the event there. —KIRKPATRICK, James. 1743#20

An essay on maritime power and commerce. —DESLANDES, André F. B. 1743#12

An essay on the causes of the decline of foreign trade. . . —DECKER, Matthew. 1744#14

Essay on the connection between the doctrine of justification by the imputed righteousness of Christ. . . —WITHERSPOON, John. 1756#89

An essay on the large common American aloe, with a particular account of that which is now in bloom in the gardens of George Montgomerie, Esq;. . . —SPENCER, James. 1759#96

An essay on the management of the present war with Spain. . . —1740#10

An essay on the merchandise of slaves and the souls of men. . . With an application thereof to the Church of Rome. —DUDLEY, Paul. 1732#14

An essay on the number seven. Wherein the duration of the Church of Rome are attempted to be shewn. —CLARKE, Richard. 1759#18

An essay on the state of England, in relation to its trade. —CARY, John. 1695#6

An essay on the times. . . —1756#24

An essay on the trade and improvement of Ireland. —DOBBS, Arthur. 1729#7

An essay on ways and means for raising money for the support of the present war. . . —FAUQUIER, Francis. 1756#27

An essay presented; or a method humbly proposed, to the consideration of. . . both Houses. . . by an English woolen manufacturer. . . —WEBB, Daniel. 1744#40

An essay towards a method of preserving the seeds of plants in a state fit for vegetation, during long voyages. For the improvement of the British colonies in America. —PULLEIN, Samuel. 1759#82

An essay towards an instruction for the Indians; explaining the most essential doctrines of Christianity. . . Together with directions. . . —WILSON, Thomas 1663-1755. 1740#45

An essay towards promoting all necessary and useful knowledge. —BRAY, Thomas. 1697#2

An essay, towards regulating the trade, and employing the poor of this kingdom. . . —CARY, John. 1717#2

Essay upon industry and trade. . . —BLACK, David. 1706#2

An essay upon projects. —DEFOE, Daniel. 1697#8

An essay upon the government of the English plantations in America. Together with some remarks upon the discourse on the plantation. . . —AMERICAN. 1701#3

An essay upon the present interest of England. . . —STEPNEY, George. 1701#40

The essayes or counsels, civill and morall. . . —BACON, Francis. 1625#1

Essays about the poor, manufactures, trade, plantations and immorality. . . —BELLERS, John. 1699#3

Essays and observations, read before a Society in Edinburgh, and published by them. . . —EDINBURGH PHILOSOPHICAL SOCIETY. 1754#11

Essays on several subjects. —BLOUNT, Sir Thomas Pope. 1691#3

Essays on trade and navigation. In five parts. The first part. —BREWSTER, Francis. 1695#4

The essence and unitie of the church catholike visible. —HUDSON, Samuel. 1645#12

An estimate of the manners and principles of the times. . . —BROWN, John. 1757#3

The eternity of hell torments. A sermon preached at Savannah in Georgia. . . —WHITEFIELD, George. 1738#31

An exact abridgement of all the public acts of assembly of Virginia, in force and use. January 1, 1758. Together with a proper table. —MERCER, John. 1759#68

An exact and most impartial accompt. . . of the trial. . . of twenty nine regicides. . . —NOTTINGHAM, Heneage. 1660#20

An exact and true list [of] the names of all the persons that was sentenced to be hanged, trasported [sic]. . . at the Old-Bailey. . . —1731#13

An exact list of all those who voted for and against the Convention in the House of Commons. . . —1739#23

An exact list of the lords spiritual and temporal. . . To which is added the names of the Trustees for Georgia, and the places of their abode. . . —1735#3

An exact list of the Lords spiritual and temporal; to which is added, the Trustees for Georgia. —1736#7

An exact narrative of the proceedings at Turner' Hall. . . —KEITH, George. 1696#15

An examination of a pamphlet, entitled his Catholic Majesty's manifesto. . . —1739#24

An examination of sundry scriptures, alleadged by our brethren (of New England) in defence of some particulars of their church-way. . . —HOLLINGWORTH, Richard. 1645#8

An examination of the grounds or causes, which are said to induce the court of Boston. . . to make that order against the Quakers. . . —PENINGTON, Isaac. 1660#21

An examination of the principles, and an enquiry into the conduct, of the two b———rs. . . —PERCEVAL, John. 1749#32

The excellency and advantage of doing good. . . a sermon preached. . . to which is annexe'd a letter of Samuel Lloyd. . . concerning the nature and goodness of the Georgia silk. —THORESBY, Ralph. 1748#30

An excellent new song; entituled, The farmer's glory. —1750#13

An exhortation to the inhabitants of. . . South Carolina, to bring their deeds to the light of Christ. . . —HUME, Sophia. 1750#22

An exhortation to the inhabitants of the South Parish of Glasgow. . . Wednesday September 26th, 1750. —GILLIES, John. 1751#15

An exhortation to the restoring of brotherly communion —DAVENPORT, John. 1641#9

The expedition of Major General Braddock to Virginia; with the two regiments of Hacket and Dunbar. . . extracts of letters from an officer to his friend in London. . . —1755#20

Experimenta et meletemata de plantarum generatione. Autore Jacobo Logan. . . Experiments and considerations on the generation of plants. . . —LOGAN, James. 1747#15

An experimentall discoverie of Spanish practises or the counsell of a well-wishing soldier. —SCOTT, Thomas. 1623#5

Experiments and observations on electricity, made at Philadelphia. . . and communicated in several letters to Mr. P. Collinson, of London, F.R.S. —FRANKLIN, Benjamin. 1751#14

Experiments of spiritual life and health, and their preservatives in which the weakest child of God may get assurance of his spirituall life. . . —WILLIAMS, Roger. 1652#19

Explanation for the new map of Nova Scotia and Cape Breton, with the adjacent parts of New England and Canada. —GREEN, John and JEFFERYS, Thomas. 1755#25

An explication and application of the seventh chapter of Daniel. . . —ASPINWALL, William. 1654#1

An explication of the first causes of action in matter, and of the cause of gravitation. —COLDEN, Cadwallader. 1746#6

An exposition of the Assemblies catechism. . . —FLAVELL, John. 1692#6

An exposition of the principles of Religion. — HOOKER, Thomas. 1645#9B

An exposition upon the thirteenth chapter of the Revelation. —COTTON, John. 1655#9

An expostulatory letter, addressed to Nicholas Lewis, Count Zinzendorff. . . —WHITEFIELD, George. 1753#23

An expostulatory letter to Mr. Daniel Neal, upon occasion of his publishing the History of the Puritans. . . —B., A. 1732#4

The expounder expounded: or, Annotations upon that incomparable piece, intitled, A short account of God's dealings with. . . —JEPHSON, Ralph. 1740#20

Extract of a letter from Mr Thomas Lowndes, to the honourable the Commissioners for victualling his majesty's navy, dated 18 April, 1748. —LOWNDES, Thomas. 1748#14

Extract of a letter from Vice-Admiral Townshend at Jamaica, to Mr Cleveland, dated the 22d of March 1757. —TOWNSHEND, George. 1757#48

An extract of sundry passages taken out of Mr Whitefield's printed sermons, journals, and letters; together with some scruples. . . —EVANS, Thomas?. 1741#11

An extract of the journals of Mr Commissary Von Reck, who conducted the first Saltzburgers to Georgia; and of the Reverend Mr Bolzius, one of their ministers. . . —RECK, Philipp G. and BOLTZIUS, John Martin. 1734#17

An extract of the preface to. . . Whitefield's account of the orphan-house in Georgia. Together with. . . some letters sent to him from the superintendents. . . and some of the children. —WHITEFIELD, George. 1741#51

An extract of the Rev. Mr John Wesley's journal, from February 1, 1737-8, to his return from Germany. —WESLEY, John. 1740#38

An extract of the Revd. Mr John Wesley's Journal from August 12, 1738, to Nov. 1, 1739. —WESLEY, John. 1742#49

An extract of the Rev. Mr John Wesley's journal from his embarking for Georgia to his return to London. . . edited by Nehemiah Curnock. —WESLEY, John. 1739#71

An extract of the Reverend Mr John Wesley's journal, from Sept. 3, 1741 to October 27, 1743. —WESLEY, John. 1749#46

An extract of the Reverend Mr Wesley's journal, from November 1, 1739, to September 3, 1741. —WESLEY, John. 1744#42

An extract out of the bishop of Oxford's sermon before the Society for propagating the gospel in foreign parts. The state of our colonies. —SECKER, Thomas. 1741#31

Extraordinary events the doings of God and marvellous in pious eyes. . . seen on. . . taking the city of Louisbourg, on the Isle of Cape Breton. . . —PRINCE, Thomas. 1746#18

Faction detected by the evidence of facts. —PERCEVAL, John. 1743#28

The facts and accusations set forth in a late pamphlet, intituled: The conduct of John Crookshanks, proved to be false and groundless. . . —ERSKINE, Robert. 1759#33

Facts, records, authorities and arguments concerning the claims of liberty and the obligations of military service. . . —1758#19

A fair and impartial testimony essayed in name of a number of ministers. . . —WILLISON, John. 1744#46

A fair representation of his majesty's right to Nova-Scotia or Acadie. Briefly stated from the memorials of the English commissaries. . . —1756#26

The fair traders objections, against the bill, entituled, a bill for preventing clandestine trading, as it relates to the plantations of Virginia and Maryland. —1680#2

The faith and testimony of the martyrs and suffering servants of Christ Jesus persecuted in New England vindicated... — HOLDER, Christopher. 1670#8

The faithful convenanter: A sermon... By... Mr. Tho. Hooker... now in New England. — HOOKER, Thomas. 1644#11A

A faithful narrative of the conversion of many hundred souls in Northampton... New England. In a letter to Dr. B. Colman... and published with a preface by Dr Watts and Dr Guyse... —EDWARDS, Jonathan. 1737#12

A faithful narrative of the life and character of the Reverend Mr Whitefield... his motives for going to Georgia... —1739#27

A faithful testimony for God and my country. —BILLING, Edward. 1664#1

Faithful souls shall be with Christ. —BAXTER, Richard. 1681#2

The false accusers accused or the undeceived Englishman: being an important enquiry into the general conduct of the administration... —1741#12

Familiar letters to a gentleman, upon a variety of seasonable and important subjects in religion... —DICKINSON, Jonathan. 1757#8

A farewel epistle, by way of exhortation to Friends... On his departure to America... —THOMPSON, Thomas. 1715#21

A farther account of the great divisions among the Quakers in Pensilvania, etc. As appears by another of their books... intituled, Some reasons and causes... —KEITH, George. 1693#9

A farther brief and true narration of the late wars risen in New-England... with an account of the fight, the 19th of December last, 1675. —1676#3

A farther discussion of that great point in divinity the sufferings of Christ... —PYNCHON, William. 1655#19

Farther considerations touching the sugar colonies, with additional observations in respect to trade... By the author of Some... —AUTHOR OF 'SOME CONSIDERATIONS TOUCHING THE SUGAR COLONIES'. 1734#1

The fatal consequences which may arise from the want of system in the conduct of public affairs. —1756#26A

The favours of providence to Britain in 1759. A sermon preached at Wokingham... Berks... 29th... November 1759... —WILLIAMS, J. 1759#104

The females advocate: or, an essay to prove that the sisters in every church of Christ, have a right to church-government as well as the brethren. —E., N. 1718#4

A fifth letter to the people of England. On m——l influence. And management of national treasure. —1756#29

A fifth letter to the people of England, on the subversion of the constitution... —SHEBBEARE, John?. 1757#43

Figures of the most beautiful, useful, and uncommon plants described in the gardeners dictionary. —MILLER, Philip. 1760#68

First, a bitt and a knock for under-sheriffs... secondly, with a preservative against fraudulent executors... by William Leach... —LEACH, William. 1652#6

The first charter granted by King Charles II to the proprietors of Carolina. —1706#12

The first principles of the oracles of God... —SHEPARD, Thomas. 1648#15

Five pastoral letters to the people of his diocese. —GIBSON, Edmund. 1749#17

Five sermons on the following subjects... With a preface by the Rev. Mr. Gilbert Tennent... —WHITEFIELD, George. 1747#29

The fleece, a poem. In four books. —DYER, John. 1757#13

Flora: seu, De florum cultura... —REA, John. 1665#19

Florus Anglicus or an exact history of England, from the reign of William the Conqueror to the death of Charles I. —BOS, Lambert van den. 1657#3

The flower-garden displayed. —FURBER, Robert. 1732#15

The flower garden enlarged... To which is now added a treatise of all the roots, plants, trees, shrubs, fruits, herbs, etc., growing in his majesties plantations, etc. —HUGHES, William. 1677#8

The following verses were composed by a pious clergyman in Virginia, who preaches to seven congregations... —DAVIES, Samuel. 1755#13

Food for the mind, or a new riddle book; compiled for the use of the great and the little good boys and girls in England, Scotland... —JOHN-THE-GIANT-KILLER. 1759#53

The Fool's Opera; or, the taste of the age. Written by Mat. Medley... To which is prefixed, a sketch of the author's life, written by himself. —ASTON, Anthony. 1730#1

For the King and both houses of Parliament... —1660#10

For the King and both houses of Parliament... —1661#7

Forgery detected, and Innocency vindicated. Being a full discovery of an horrid... slander raisd on the Anabaptists of New-England... —BAXTER, Benjamin. 1673#2

Forgery detected. By which is evinced how groundless are all the calumnies cast upon the editor, in a pamphlet published under the name of Arthur Dobbs... —MIDDLETON, Christopher. 1745#29

A form of prayer, and thanksgiving to Almighty God; to be used in all churches and chapels throughout the kingdom of Ireland... —CHURCH OF IRELAND. 1759#17

A form of prayer and thanksgiving... to be used... on Sunday the twelfth of October 1760... on occasion of the late successes of his majesty's arms in North-America... —CHURCH OF ENGLAND. 1760#21

A form of prayer and thanksgiving... to be used... on Sunday the twentieth day of August, 1758... in all churches... throughout

England. . . for the taking of Louisbourg. . . —CHURCH OF ENGLAND. 1758#6

A form of prayer and thanksgiving. . . to be used. . . on Sunday the twenty first of October 1759. . . —CHURCH OF ENGLAND. 1759#15

Form of a certificate for a ship that gives bond in the plantations to return to England, Wales, or Berwick only. —1685#13

Form of a certificate for a ship that hath produced a certificate in the plantations of bond given in England, to return to England, Wales, or Berwick only. —1685#14

The fortunate transport; or, the secret history of the life and adventures of the celebrated Polly Haycock. . . —1750#14

Fortune's fickle distribution; in three parts. . . —DEFOE, Daniel. 1730#12

The fortunes and misfortunes of the famous Moll Flanders. . . —DEFOE, Daniel. 1722#12

The fortunes and misfortunes of Moll Flanders, who was born in Newgate. . . 8 years a transport in Virginia. —1730#11

Fortunes favourite; containing memoirs of the many hardships and sufferings of Jacobo Anglicano, a young nobleman. . . trepanned into slavery. —1744#17

The four kings of Canada. Being a succinct account of the four Indian princes lately arriv'd from North America. . . —1710#6

The Four gospels and the Acts of the Holy Apostles, translated into the Malayan tongue. . . —1677#3

The Four Indian Kings garland; being a faithful. . . account of how. . . a young lady conquered the heart of one of the four Indian Kings. —1736#8

Four Indian Kings. Part I. How a beautiful lady. . . Part II. The lady's answer. . . —1710#4

The Four Indian King's speech to her majesty. London, April 20. 1710. Yesterday the four princes. . . —1710#5

Foure learned and godly treatises. —HOOKER, Thomas. 1638#10A

Four letters etc. taken from the London Weekly History of the progress of the gospel; with a large postcript vindicating the late revival and the promoters. —SMITH, Josiah. 1743#36

Four letters from Mr. Gilbert Tennent, the Secretary of New-England, and Dr. Colman, concerning the great success of the gospel abroad. —TENNENT, Gilbert. 1741#40

Four sermons, upon the great and indispensible duty of Christian masters and mistresses to bring up their negro slaves in the. . . —BACON, Thomas. 1750#3

A fourth letter to the people of England. . . —1756#30

A fourth letter to the people of England on the conduct of the M————rs. . . since the first differences on the Ohio. . . —SHEBBEARE, John. 1756#71

The fourth paper, presented by Major Butler, to the. . . committee of Parliament, for the propagating of the gospel. . . —WILLIAMS, Roger. 1652#20

The Foxonian Quakers, dunces, lyars and slanderers. . . —YOUNG, Samuel. 1697#13

The Frame of the government of the province of Pennsylvania in America; together with certain laws agreed upon in England by the governour and divers freemen of the aforesaid province. . . —1682#14

Francis Lynch, merchant, appellant. Martin Killikelly, of Dublin, merchant, and Arthur Lynch and company, of Bilbao in Spain, merchants. . . respondents. The case of the respondents. —LYNCH, Francis. 1738#15

Francis Lynch, of Dublin, merchant appellant. Martin Killikelly, of Dublin, Merchant, Arthur Lynch and Company, of Bilbao. . . —LYNCH, Francis. 1738#16

The free and impartial examiner: being a candid enquiry into the causes of our present melancholy situation, with regard to both domestick and foreign affairs. . . —1745#21

A free disputation against pretended liberty of conscience. . . —RUTHERFORD, Samuel. 1649#6

Free trade. or, The meanes to make trade flourish. —MISSELDEN, Edward. 1622#16

The Freedom of commerce of the subjects of the Austrian Nether-lands asserted and vindicated. Being a confutation of the arguments. . . —MACNENY, Patrick. 1725#8

French and Indian cruelty exemplified in the life. . . of P. W. . . written by himself. . . —WILLIAMSON, Peter. 1757#50

French counsels destructive to Great Britain. . . —AMHURST, Nicholas. 1739#2

The French encroachments exposed: or, Britain's original right to all that part of the American continent claimed by France. . . —PAYNE, J. 1756#57

French influence upon English counsels demonstrated from an impartial examination of our measures. . . —1740#12

The French intrigues discovered. With the method and art to retrench the potency of France. —1681#9

French policy defeated. Being an account of all the proceedings of the French, against the inhabitants of the British colonies. . . —TRUE BRITON. 1755#57

Friends, These are to satisfie you. . . that New Cesarea, or New Jersey. . . is a healthy, pleasant and plentiful country. . . dated this 8th of the 1st month, 1675. —FENWICK, John. 1675#6

From our yearly-meeting, held at Philadelphia, for Pennsylvania, and New Jersey, from the 17th to the 21st day of the 7th. . . —SOCIETY OF FRIENDS. 1737#24

From our yearly meeting in London. . . 1757. To our friends and brethren. . . New Jersey and Pennsylvania. . . —SOCIETY OF FRIENDS. 1757#46

From our yearly meeting in London. . . the 4th to the 9th day of the 6th month, 1759. To our Friends and brethren at their ensuing. . . —SOCIETY OF FRIENDS. 1759#92

From the London Gazette, of December 25, 1742. An account of the late invasion of Georgia, drawn out by Lieutenant P. S... —SUTHERLAND, Patrick. 1743#40

A fruitfull and usefull discourse... —COBBET, Thomas. 1656#4

The fulfilling of the Scripture, or an essay shewing the exact accomplishment of the word of God in his works of providence... —FLEMING, Robert. 1681#8

A full account of the proceedings in relation to Captain Kidd. In two letters... to a kinsman of the Earl of Bellomont... —1701#21

A full and candid answer to a pamphlet, entitled, Considerations on the present German war. —1760#36

A full and exact description of the island of Cape Breton, which was taken from the French, by Admiral Warren, upon the 16th of June... —1745#23

A full and faithful account of the life of James Bather, late... of... Nightingale Brig... —BATHER, James. 1755#3

A full and impartial account of all the secret consults... of the Romish party in Ireland... —1689#12

A full and impartial account of the Company of Mississippi, otherwise called the French East-India Company, projected and settled by Mr. Law... —LAW, John. 1720#17

A full and particular answer to... the fourth letter to the people of England... since the first difficulties on the Ohio... —1756#31

A full and true discovery of all the robberies, pyracies... of that famous English pyrate Capt James Kelly... With an account of his... —1700#17

A full answer to The country-parson's plea against the Quaker tythe-bill. —BESSE, Joseph. 1736#4

A full answer to the Letter from a by-stander... —CARTE, Thomas. 1742#7

A full reply to Lieut. Cadogan's Spanish hireling and Lieut. Mackay's letter... wherein the Impartial account of the late expedition to St. Augustine is clearly vindicated... —OGLETHORPE, James Edward. 1743#27

The fundamental constitutions of Carolina, in number a hundred and twenty... dat. the first day of March, 1669. —LOCKE, John. 1670#9

A further accompt of the progresse of the gospel amongst the Indians in New-England, and of the means used effectually to advance the same... —ELIOT, John. 1659#11

A further account of East-New-Jersay by a letter write to one of the proprietors therof, by a countrey-man, who has a great plantation there... —LOCKHART, George. 1683#13

A further account of God's dealings with the Reverend Mr George Whitefield, from the time of his ordination to his embarking for Georgia. —WHITEFIELD, George. 1747#30

A further account of New Jersey. In an abstract of letters lately writ from thence, by several inhabitants there resident. —HARTSHORNE, Richard, and others. 1676#8

A further account of the province of Pennsylvania and its improvements. For the satisfaction of those that are adventurers, and enclined to be so. —PENN, William. 1685#20

A further account of the tryals of the New-England witches. With the observations of a person who was upon the place... To which... —MATHER, Increase. 1693#14

Further considerations for encouraging the woollen manufactures of this kingdom, humbly offered to the Lords and Commons... —1704#16

A further discovery of that spirit of contention and division... in George Keith, etc. Being a reply to two late printed pieces of his... —ELLWOOD, Thomas. 1694#6

A further discovery of the spirit of falshood [sic] and persecution in Sam. Jennings and his party... in Pensilvania... —KEITH, George. 1694#11

A further justification of the present war against the United Netherlands... —STUBBE, Henry. 1673#11

Further objections to the establishment of a constitutional militia... —1756#32

Further observations intended for improving the culture and curing of indigo, etc in South-Carolina. —CROKATT, James. 1747#7

Further reasons for inlarging the trade to Russia, humbly offered by the merchants and planters trading to and interested in the... —PERRY, Micaiah. 1698#14

A further vindication of New-England from false suggestions in a late scandalous pamphlet, pretending to shew, The inconvenience... —MATHER, Increase. 1689#20

Gangraena: or a catalogue and discovery of many of the errours... —EDWARDS, Thomas. 1646#9

The gardeners and florists dictionary. —MILLER, Philip. 1724#15

The gardeners dictionary. —MILLER, Philip. 1731#25

A garland of new songs... General Wolfe's song... —1760#37

A garland of new songs. The world's a stage... Britannia, or the death of General Wolfe. —1760#38

The gazetteer's or newsman's interpreter. Being a geographical index of... Asia, Africa and America. —ECHARD, Laurence. 1703#8

Gazophylacii naturae et artis decas sexta [-nona]. —PETIVER, James. 1711#19

Gazophylacii naturae et artis prima [-quinta] —PETIVER, James. 1702#20

The general accompt of all monies and effects recieved and expended by the Trustees for... Georgia... from the ninth day of June.. 1735, to the ninth day of June... 1736. —GEORGIA TRUSTEES. 1736#9

The general account of all monies and effects received and expended by the Trustees for... Georgia... from... ninth... June... 1732... to ninth... June... 1733... —GEORGIA TRUSTEES. 1733#16

The general account of all monies and effects received and expended by the Trustees for. . . Georgia. . . from the ninth day of June. . . 1733. to the ninth day of June. . . 1734. . . —GEORGIA TRUSTEES. 1734#6

A general account of the rise and state of the College, lately established in the province of New-Jersey, in America. . . Originally. . . —TENNENT, Gilbert and DAVIES, Samuel. 1754#40

A general and particular description of America. . . with very particular accounts of the English plantations; and maps. . . —LUYTS, Jan. 1701#28

General heads for the natural history of country great or small; drawn out for the use of travellers and navigators. . . —BOYLE, Robert. 1692#1

A general history of all voyages and travels throughout the old and new world. . . by Monsr. Du Perier. . . —BELLEGARDE, Jean Baptiste Morvan de. 1708#1

A general history of discoveries and improvements, in useful arts, particularly in the great branches of commerce, navigation and plantation. . . —DEFOE, Daniel. 1725#5

A general history of the lives and actions of the most famous highwaymen, murderers, street-robbers. . . To which is added, A genuine. . . —JOHNSON, Charles. 1734#12

The general history of the Quakers. . . —CROESE, Gerard. 1696#8

A general history of the robberies and murders of the most notorious pyrates, and also their policies, discipline and government. . . by Captain Charles Johnson. —DEFOE, Daniel. 1724#7

A general natural history; or, New and accurate descriptions of the animals, vegetables and minerals. . . —HILL, John. 1748#10

General reflections occasioned by the letter addressed to two great men, and the remarks on that letter. —1760#39

The general shop book: or, the tradesman's universal director. . . explaining the domestic and foreign trade of Great Britain and the plantations. . . —1753#8

General thoughts on the construction, use and abuse of the great offices. . . —McCULLOH, Henry. 1754#25

A general treatise of monies and exchanges; in which those of all trading nations are particularly describ'd and consider'd. . . By a well-wisher to trade. —JUSTICE, Alexander. 1707#10

A general treatise of naval trade and commerce. . . —1738#8

The generall historie of Virginia, New-England, and the Summer Isles. . . —SMITH, John. 1624#11

The generall history of Virginia, the Somer Iles, and New England, with the names of the adventurers, and their adventures. . . —SMITH, John. 1623#6

The genius of Britain. An iambic ode. Addressed to the Right Hon. William Pitt, Esq. —1756#33

The gentlemans guide, in three discourses. First, of travel. . . —LEIGH, Edward. 1680#5

The gentlemen who at the request of the Society. . . are trustees for. . . Saltzburg Protestants. . . appointed to transport them to Georgia. . . —SOCIETY FOR PROMOTING CHRISTIAN KNOWLEDGE. 1734#22

A genuine account of Nova Scotia: containing, a description of its situation, air, climate, soil and its produce. . . his majesty's. . . —1750#17

A genuine account of the burning the Nightingale Brig, lately belonging to Thomas Benson. . . —LANCEY, John. 1754#23

A genuine account of the proceedings on the trial of Florence Hensey, M. D. . . for high treason. —1758#22

A genuine, impartial, and authentick account of the life of William Parsons, esq; executed at Tyburn, Monday Feb. 11, 1751, for returning from transportation. . . —PARSONS, William. 1751#24

A genuine letter from Mr. John Brainard [sic], employed by the Scotch Society for Propagating the Gospel, a missionary to the Indians. . . —BRAINERD, John. 1753#2

Genuine letters and memoirs, relating to the natural, civil, and commercial history of the islands of Cape Breton, and Saint John. . . to. . . 1758. . . By an impartial Frenchman. . . —PICHON, Thomas. 1760#76

Genuine letters from a volunteer, in the British service, at Quebec. —VOLUNTEER IN THE BRITISH SERVICE. 1760#98

Genuine memoirs of the life and treasonable practices of Dr. Florence Hensey. . . —1758#23

Geodaesia: or, The art of surveying and measuring of land. . . —LOVE, John. 1688#10

Geographia universalis: The present state of the whole world. . . —DUVAL, Pierre. 1685#9

A geographical and historical description of the principal objects of the present war in the West Indies. viz. Cartagena, Puerto Belo. . . and San Augustin, etc. —1741#14

A geographical description of the four parts of the world. . . —BLOME, Richard. 1670#1

A geographical description of the world. . . —MERITON, George. 1674#8

A geographical dictionary, representing the present and ancient names of all countries. . . —BOHUN, Edmund. 1688#1

Geographical, historical, political, philosphical and mechanical essays. Number II. Containing a letter, representing the impropriety of sending forces to Virginia. . . —EVANS, Lewis. 1756#25

A geographical history of Nova Scotia. Containing an account of the situation, extent and limits thereof. As also the various struggles. . . —1749#14

A geographicall and anthologicall description of all the empires. . . —STAFFORD, Robert. 1634#6

A geographicall description of all the countries in the known world. . . and of the four chiefest English plantations in America. . . —CLARKE, Samuel. 1657#4

Geography anatomized: or, a compleat geographical grammer. . . —GORDON, Patrick. 1693#7

285

Geography epitomiz'd: or, the London gazetteer. Being a geographical and historical treatise of Europe, Asia, Africa and America. . . To which are added, an introduction to geography. —G., J. 1718#8

Geography rectified: or, a description of the world. . . —MORDEN, Robert. 1680#7

George Keith's challenge to William Penn and Geor. Whitehead; two eminent Quakers. . . — KEITH, George. 1696#16

George Keith's explications of divers passages contained in his former books. —KEITH, George. 1697#9

George Keith's fifth narrative, of his proceedings at Turners-Hall; detecting the Quakers errors —KEITH, George. 1701#25

George Keith's fourth narrative, of his proceedings at Turner's Hall. —KEITH, George. 1700#21

Georgia, a poem. Tomo Chachi, an ode. A copy of verses on Mr Oglethorpe's second voyage to Georgia. . . —1736#10

Georgia bill of exchange payable in England. . . —1749#16

A German diet: or, the ballance of Europe. . . —HOWELL, James. 1653#11

The German spy. In familiar letters. . . written by a gentleman. . . to his friend in England. . . —1738#9

Gillam Phillips, only brother of Henry Phillips deceased intestate. appellant. Faith Savage widow. . . and others, respondents. The case of Faith Savage. —PHILLIPS, Gillam. 1737#21

A glass for the people of New-England, in which they may see themselves and spirits, and if not too late repent, and turn away from their abominable ways. . . —GROOME, Samuel. 1676#7

The glorious progress of the Gospel, amongst the Indians in New England. Manifested by three letters. . . —WINSLOW, Edward. 1649#10

Glory to be God on High. . . A rare and new discovery of a speedy way. . . for the feeding of silk worms in the woods, on the mulberry-tree-leaves in Virginia. . . —HARTLIB, Samuel. 1652#3

God the giver of victory: a sermon, preached at Bideford, Devon, being the day appointed for a general thanksgiving. . . for the success of His Majesty's arms. . . —LAVINGTON, Samuel. 1760#58

God's blessing on a people's just endeavours. . . A sermon preached at Writtle in Essex, on Thursday the 29th of November, 1759. . . —HEATH, John. 1760#47

God's mercie mixed with his justice, or, his people's deliverance in times of danger. . . in severall sermons. —COTTON, John. 1641#7

Gods mighty power magnified: as manifested. . . in his faithful handmaid Joan Vokins. . . —VOKINS, Joan. 1691#22

God's promise; a grand incentive to Christian liberality. A sermon preached at Walmer in Kent, on. . . 12 of July 1752. —RUDD, Sayer. 1752#16

God's promise to His plantation, 2 Sam. 7. 10; in a sermon. —COTTON, John. 1630#1

God's protecting providence, man's surest help and defence. . . remarkable deliverance. . . from devouring waves. . . also from. . . inhumane cannibals of Florida. . . —DICKINSON, Jonathan. 1700#14

God's wonders in the great deep, or the seaman's danger and deliverance exemplified. Containing several wonderful and amazing relations. . . —1710#7

The golden fleece divided into three parts. . . the errours of religion, the vices and decayes of the kingdome. . . the wayes to get wealth, and to restore trading. —VAUGHAN, William. 1626#3

The golden glover's garland. . . new songs. —1750#18

Good newes from New-England: or A true relation of things very remarkable at. . . Plimoth. —WINSLOW, Edward. 1624#12

Good newes from Virginia, sent from James his towne this present moneth of March, 1623, by a gentleman in that country. To the tune of, All those that be good fellowes. —1624#7

Good news from New-England: with an exact relation of the first planting that countrey. . . With the names of the severall towns, and who be preachers to them. —JOHNSON, Edward. 1648#7

The good soldier. Extracted from a sermon preached to a company of volunteers, raised in Virginia. . . —DAVIES, Samuel. 1756#18

The gospel-covenant; or The covenant of grace opened. . . Preached in Concord in New-England. —BULKELEY, Peter. 1646#2

Gospel conversion together with some reasons against stinted forms of praising God. . . —COTTON, John. 1646#7

Gospel family order, being a short discourse concerning the ordering of families, both of whites, blacks, and Indians. . . —FOX, George. 1676#4

Gospel ministers must be fit for the master's use. . . sermon preached at Deerfield, August 31. 1735. . . with special reference to the Indians of the Houssattonic. . . —APPLETON, Nathaniel. 1736#2

Gospel musick. or, The singing of David's Psalms, etc., in the publick congregations, or private families asserted, and vindicated. . . —HOLMES, Nathaniel. 1644#11

The grand concern of England explained; in several proposals offered to the consideration of parliament. . . —1673#5

The grand pyrate, or the life and death of Capt. George Cusack the great sea-robber. . . —1676#6

The grand question, whether war or no war with Spain, impartially considered: in defence of the present measures against those that delight in war. . . —WALPOLE, Horatio. 1739#69

Grant and release of one eighth part of Carolina, from his majesty to Lord Carteret. . . —GREAT BRITAIN. SOVEREIGN. GEORGE II. 1744#21

Great Britain's complaints against Spain impartially examined. And the conduct of each nation, from the treaty of Utrecht to the late declaration of war, compared. . . —1740#17

Great Britain's danger and remedy. Represented in a discourse... on the day appointed for a general fast, February the 11th, 1757. —SCOTT, Thomas. 1757#39

Great Britain's glory. Being a loyal song on the taking of Cape Breton from the French 26 of July by Admiral Boscawen... —1758#25

Great-Britain's true system... —POSTLETHWAYT, Malachy. 1757#33

The great duty of family religion: a sermon preached... —WHITEFIELD, George. 1738#32

The great historical geographical, genealogical and poetical dictionary... —MORERI, Louis. 1694#17

The great importance of Cape Breton, demonstrated... by extracts from the best writers... With the reasons that induced the people... —1746#12

A great victory obtained by the English against Dutch... Also, the number of ships... richly laden from the east-Indies, the Straights, Virginia and the Barbadoes. —STOAKES, John. 1652#13

Greene's Tu quoque, or the cittie gallant. —COOKE, John. 1622#6

Greevous grones for the poore. Done by a well-wisher, who wisheth, that the poore of England might be so provided for, as none should neede to go a begging within this realme... —SPARKE, Michae.—1621#5

Gross error and hypocrisie detected, in George Whitehead, and some of his brethren. —KEITH, George. 1695#14

The grounds and ends of the baptisme... —COTTON, John. 1647#6

Gulliver's flight: or The man mountain. A dream. —1739#41

Hammond versus Heamans. Or, an answer to an audacious pamphlet... by... Roger Heamans... his murthers and treacheries committed in the Province of Maryland... —HAMMOND, John. 1655#11

The happiness of a holy life, exemplified in the sickness and death of... Mrs Martha Gerrish, of Boston in New-England... with a collection... —APPLETON, Nathaniel. 1740#1

The happiness of man the glory of God. A sermon... March 15, 1743... —BRUCE, Lewis. 1744#8

The hard case of the distressed people of Georgia. —STEPHENS, Thomas fl. 1742. 1742#42

The Harleian miscellany: or, A collection of scarce, curious and entertaining pamphlets and tracts... found in the late earl of Oxford's library. —1744#25

The hat-makers case. —1721#9

The hatmakers case. Shewing that the present exporting of beaver hats of the manufacture of the colonies in America, hath been... —1732#23

Have at you blind harpers. Three ballads concerning the times. Consisting of, I. The royal embassy: or, A ballad on the progress of the four Indians kings. —1710#8

Heads of some of those advantages this nation might enjoy, by encouraging the tobacco trade to Russia... —HEATHCOTE, Samuel. 1700#18

A healing question propounded and resolved... in order to love and union amongst the honest party... —VANE, Henry. 1656#12

The heart of New-England hardned [sic] through wickednes... —HOWGILL, Francis. 1659#17

The heart of New-England rent at the blasphemies of the present generation... doctrine of the Quakers... —NORTON, John. 1660#19

A heart-melting exhortation, together with a cordiall consolation, presented in a letter from New-England... —MATHER, Richard. 1650#8

Heautonaparnumenos: or a treatise of self-denyall... —HOOKER, tHOMAS. 1646#14a

Heaven's treasury opened in a fruitfull exposition of the Lords Prayer. —HOOKER, Thomas. 1645#9C

The heinous sin of drunkenness; a sermon preached on board the Whitaker. —WHITEFIELD, George. 1739#76

Hell broke loose: or an history of the Quakers both old and new. —UNDERHILL, Thomas. 1660#28

The herball or Generall historie of plantes... very much enlarged and amended by Thomas Johnson —GERARD, John. 1633#1

Heresiography: or, A description of the heretickes and sectaries of these latter times... —PAGITT, Ephraim. 1645#14

The heros garland. —1760#48

The Highlander's march a garland. Composed of several new songs viz. 1. The Highlander's march to America... —1760#49

A hint to the fair sex. A garland, containing six new songs. —1760#50

The hireling ministry none of Christs, or, A curse touching the propagating of the gospel of Jesus... —WILLIAMS, Roger. 1652#21

His Catholic majesty's most Christian manifesto... —1739#44

His Catholick majesty's manifesto justifying his conduct in relation to the late convention... —1739#43

His excellency, Governour Penn's speech, to the assembly, held at Philadelphia in Pensilvania; September the 15th 1701. With... —PENNSYLVANIA Assembly. 1701#34

His majesties gracious letter to the Earl of South-hampton, treasurer, and to the Councell and Company of Virginia heere: commanding... —BONOEIL, John. 1622#2

His majesties most gracious speech to both houses of Parliament... on... the thirteenth day of November 1755. —GREAT BRITAIN. SOVEREIGN. GEORGE II. 1755#24

His majesties propriety, and dominion on the Brittish seas asserted. —CODRINGTON, Robert. 1665#13

His majesty's declaration concerning the province of East-New Jersey. —ENGLAND AND WALES. SOVEREIGN. CHARLES II. 1683#10

His majesty's most gracious speech to both houses of Parliament, on Thursday the first day of February 1738. —GREAT BRITAIN. SOVEREIGN. GEORGE II. 1738#11

His majesty's most gracious speech to both Houses of Parliament, on Tuesday the eighteenth day of November, 1760. —GREAT BRITAIN. SOVEREIGN. GEORGE III). 1760#45

Histoire et commerce des colonies angloises, dans l'Amerique... —BUTEL-DUMONT, Georges. 1755#4

Histoire géographique de la Nouvelle Ecosse... —LAFARGUE, Etienne. 1754#22

Historia plantarum rariorum. —MARTYN, John. 1728#11

Historia plantarum; species hacteus editas aliasque insuper multas naviter inventas et descriptas complectens... —RAY, John. 1686#4

Historia vitae & mortis. —BACON, Francis. 1623#2

The historians guide, in two parts... Summary account of all... remarkable passages in his majesty's dominions from 1600 until 1676... —1676#9

An historical account of earthquakes, extracted from the most authentick historians. And a sermon preached at Weaverham, in Cheshire, on... 6 February... [1756].... —HUNTER, Thomas. 1756#46

A historical account of some memorable actions, particularly in Virginia... —GRANTHAM, Thomas, Sir. 1714#7

An historical account of the Incorporated Society for the Propagation of the Gospel in Foreign Parts... to the year 1728. —HUMPHREYS, David. 1730#16

A historical account of the rise and establishment of the people called Quakers... By a Friend. —1756#43

An historical account of the rise and growth of the West-Indies collonies. —THOMAS, Dalby. 1690#24

An historical account of the small-pox inoculated in New England, upon all sorts of persons... —BOYLSTON, Zabdiel. 1726#3

An historical and critical account of Hugh Peters. After the manner of Mr Beyle. —HARRIS, William. 1751#19

An historical and geographical account of the province and country of Pensilvania; and of West-New-Jersey in America... —THOMAS, Gabriel. 1698#20

Historical collections relating to remarkable periods of the success of the Gospel, and eminent instruments employed in promoting it. —GILLIES, John. 1754#12

An historical description of Carolina North, and South... With the advantageous proposals offered by the assembly to such as will settle in that colony. —1717#9

An historical essay concerning witchcraft... And also two sermons... —HUTCHINSON, Francis. 1718#12

An historical essay on the rise and progress of the small-pox. —CLINCH, William. 1724#5

An historical essay upon the ballance of civil power in England. —SQUIRE, Samuel. 1748#27

An historical, physiological and theological treatise of spirits, apparitions, witchcrafts... —BEAUMONT, John. 1705#1

An historical review of the constitution and government of Pennsylvania, from its origin... Founded on authentic documents. —JACKSON, Richard. 1759#52

Historico-political geography; or, A description of the... several countries in the world... —PASCHOUD, ——, schoolmaster. 1722#22

The historie of the raigne of King Henry the seventh —BACON, Francis. 1622#1

Histories novels and translations. The second volume. —BEHN, Aphra. 1700#2

The history and constitutions of the... Free and Accepted Masons. —ANDERSON, James. 1746#1

The history and present state of Virginia, in four parts... By a native and inhabitant of the place. —BEVERLEY, Robert. 1705#2

The history and progress of the four Indian kings to the kingdom of England... also the four Indian kings speech to her majesty... —1710#9

The history and remarkable life of the truly honourable Col. Jacque, commonly called Col. Jack... —DEFOE, Daniel. 1723#4

The history of Autonous... —KIRKBY, John. 1736#12

The history of conformity. —COLLINGES, John. 1681#5

The history of England: during the reigns of K. William, Q. Anne and K. George I. —RALPH, James. 1744#37

The history of Independency... —WALKER, Clement. 1648#16

The history of modern enthusiasm from the Reformation to the present times. —EVANS, Theophilus. 1752#6

The history of New-England containing an impartial account of the civil and ecclesiastical affairs of the country to... 1700. To which is added the present state of New-England... —NEAL, Daniel. 1720#23

A history of New England. From the English planting in the yeere 1628 untill the yeere 1652... —JOHNSON, Edward. 1654#12

The history of the Babylonish cabal; or the intrigues... of the Daniel-Catchers. In a poem. —STEERE, Richard. 1682#26

The history of the British plantations in America. With a chronological account of the most remarkable things... —KEITH, Sir William. 1738#13

The history of the bucanniers of America... adorned with copper plates... —DILWORTH, W. H. 1758#16

A history of the cruel sufferings of the Protestants, and others by popish persecutions, in various countries... —LOCKMAN, John. 1759#62

The history of the excellence and decline of the constitution, religion, laws... of the Sumatrans... —SHEBBEARE, John. 1760#84

The history of the first discovery and settlement of Virginia... —STITH, William. 1753#21

The history of the five Indian nations of Canada, which are dependent on the province of New-York in America, and are the barrier... —COLDEN, Cadwallader. 1747#5

The history of the four Indian kings from the continent of America, between New-Eengland [sic] and Canada. Who came to begg [sic]... —1710#10

History of the life and adventures of Mr. Anderson. Containing his strange varieties of fortune in Europe and America... —KIMBER, Edward. 1754#20

The history of the life and death of Hugh Peters, that archtraytor, from the cradell to the gallowes. —1661#9

The history of the life of Thomas Ellwood, or, an account of his birth, education, etc. with divers observations... To which is added a supplement By Joseph Wyeth. —ELLWOOD, Thomas. 1714#6

The history of the Moravians, from their first settlement at Herrnhaag... —RIMIUS, Heinrich. 1754#33

The history of the peace with France, and the war with Holland, in the year 1672... —1712#12

The history of the present parliament, and convocation. With the debates... relating to the conduct of the war abroad... —PITTIS, William. 1711#20

The history of the present war... to the conclusion of the year 1759... —DILWORTH, W. H. 1760#30

The history of the propagation of Christianity, and the overthrow of paganism... —MILLAR, Robert. 1723#8

The history of the province of New York, from the first discovery to the year MDCCXXXII. —SMITH, William (1728-1793). 1757#45

The history of the puritans or protestant nonconformists... to the death of Queen Elizabeth... —NEAL, Daniel. 1732#30

The history of the rise, increase and progress of the people called Quakers... written originally in low-Dutch... now revised... —SEWEL, William. 1722#27

The history of the Royal Society of London for improving natural knowledge... —BIRCH, Thomas. 1756#7

A history of the voyages and travels of Capt. Nathaniel Uring... —URING, Nathaniel. 1726#16

The history of the war: A new British medley. Proper to be said or sung in all companies of true Britons. —1760#51

The history of the world: the second part... —ROSS, Alexander. 1653#15

The history of the world... Together with a geographicall description... —PETAVIUS, Dionysius or PETAU, Denis. 1659#27

The history of witches and wizards: giving a true account of all their tryals in England, Scotland, Sweedland, France and New England; with their confession and condemnation. —P., W. 1750#36

The holy seed: or, The life of Mr Thomas Beard, wrote by himself: with some account of his death, September 15, 1710... —PORTER, Joseph. 1711#21

The honest grief of a Tory, expressed in a genuine letter... —1759#50

The honest mans companion: or, the family's safeguard... some hints relating to the clergy... our plantations... —HODSHON, Read. 1736#11

An honest scheme for improving the trade and credit of the nation... —1727#14

The honest Welch-cobler, for her do scorne to call her selfe the simple Welch-cobler... —SHINKIN ap SHONE [psued.]. 1647#15

Honesty the truest policy, shewing the sophistry, envy and perversion of George Keith. —COOLE, Benjamin. 1700#12

A horrid and barberous [sic] murder committed by a negroe on three white persons in America who was hung up in chains alive, who lived... —1759#51

Hudson's Bay. A general collection of treatys, declarations of war, manifestoes, and other papers relating to peace and war... —HUDSON'S BAY COMPANY. 1710#11

The humble address of the House of Commons to the King... —GREAT BRITAIN. PARLIAMENT. HOUSE OF COMMONS. 1721#7

The humble address of the Lords... to his majesty, in relation to the petition of Charles Desborow, employed in the trade to New-foundland... —ENGLAND AND WALES. PARLIAMENT. LORDS. 1699#7

The humble address of the publicans of New England, to which king you please; with some remarks upon it... —1691#8

The humble address of the right honourable Lords spiritual and temporal, in Parliament assembled, presented to her majesty on... —BOONE, Joseph. 1706#5

The humble address of the Right Honourable the Lords... in Parliament... presented to His Majesty... the fourth day of May, 1738. With his majesty's answer... —GREAT BRITAIN. PARLIAMENT. HOUSE OF LORDS. 1738#10

The humble address of the... Lords... presented to his majesty... November, 1755... —GREAT BRITAIN. PARLIAMENT. HOUSE OF LORDS. 1755#23

The humble address of the right honourable the Lords... in Parliament... to his majesty on Friday the third day of December, 1756. With his majesty's gracious answer. —GREAT BRITAIN. PARLIAMENT. HOUSE OF LORDS. 1756#40

An humble apology for the Quakers... to which are added Observations on a new pamphlet, entituled A brief view of the conduct of Pennsylvania for the year 1755... —1756#45

The humble petition and address of the General Court sitting at Boston in New England, unto Prince Charles the second: presented Feb. 11, 1660.— MASSACHUSETTS GENERAL COURT. 1660#16

The humble petition of divers inhabitants of New-England. —1643#11

A humble proposal to the people of England, for the encrease of their trade. . . By the author of the Compleat Tradesman. —DEFOE, Daniel. 1729#6

The humble request of his majesties loyall subjects, the governour and company late gone for New-England; to the rest of their brethren, in and of the Church of England. . . —PHILLIPS, George?. 1630#6

The humble submission of the kings, princes, generals, etc. to the Crown of England. Lately presented to. . . Sir Nathaniel Johnston, the present governour of Carolina. . . —COWETA INDIANS. 1707#4

Humorous and diverting dialogues between Monsieur Baboon, a French dancing-master, (but lately come-over:) and Jack Tar, an English sailor. —1755#28

Hurlo-Thrumbo's lucubrations. . . Very proper to be bound up with a pamphlet. . . A true state of the case between the British northern colonies and the sugar-islands. . . —1732#24

Hymen: an accurate description of the ceremonies used in marriage, by every nation in the known world. . . Dedicated to the ladies of Great-Britain and Ireland. —1760#52

Hymns for the general thanksgiving-day, Thursday, November 29, 1759. . . BRADBURY, Charles. 1759#5

Hymns occasioned by the earthquake, March 8, 1750. To which are added an hymn for the English in America, and another for the year 1756. Part II. The second edition. —WESLEY, John. 1756#85

Hymns to be used on the Thanksgiving-day, Nov. 29, 1759. And after it. —WESLEY, John. 1759#103

Hypocrosie unmasked: by a true relation of the proceedings of the Governour and Company of the Massachusetts against Samuel Gorton. . . —WINSLOW, Edward. 1646#21

Ignorance and superstition a source of violence and cruelty, and in particular the cause of the present rebellion. . . —WALLACE, Robert. 1746#28

Ill-judged bounties tend to beggary on both sides: or, Observations on a paper, intituled, Reasons for laying a duty on French. . . —1748#11

Ill newes from New England: or A narrative of New - Englands persecution. . . Also four proposals to. . . Parliament and Councel of State. . . —CLARK, John. 1652#1

Illuminatio Britannicae; or, a true and faithful narrative of what passed at a conference held at the Admiralty Office. . . January 11, 1740-41. . . —1742#24

The immortality of the soule. . . —HOOKER, Thomas. 1645#10

An impartial account of Lieut. Col. Bradstreet's expedition to Fort Frontenac. . . By a volunteer on the expedition. —BRADSTREET, John. 1759#6

An impartial account of the late expedition against St. Augustine under General Oglethorpe. Occasioned by the suppression of the. . . —OGLETHORPE, James Edward. 1742#31

An impartial account of the present state of the Hudson-Bay Company, as they stand incorporated. . . —1696#13

An impartial account of the state of New England; or, the late government there, vindicated. . . —PALMER, John. 1690#19

An impartial enquiry into the state and utility of the province of Georgia. —MARTYN, Benjamin. 1741#27

An impartial examination of the fourth volume of Mr. Daniel Neal's history of the Puritans. —GREY, Zachary. 1739#40

An impartial representation of the conduct of the several powers of Europe, engaged in the late general war. . . To. . . 1748. —ROLT, Richard. 1749#35

An impartial trial of the spirit. . . a sermon preached at New London-derry, October 14th 1741. . . —CALDWELL, John. 1742#5

An impartial view of the conduct of the M - ry, in regard to the war in America; the engagements entered into with Russia, Hesse-Cassel, and Prussia. . . —1756#47

The impartialiste satyre. . . —TAYLOR, John. 1652#16

The importance and advantage of Cape Breton, truly stated, and impartially considered. With proper maps. . . —BOLLAN, William. 1746#3

The importance and necessity of his majesty's declaration of war with France considered. . . in a sermon. . . May 23, 1756. —WINTER, Richard. 1756#88

The importance of Cape Breton to the British nation. Humbly represented by Robert Aucknuty, judge of his majesty's court of vice-admiralty. . . —AUCKMUTY, Robert. 1745#5

The importance of gaining and preserving the friendship of the Indians to the British interest considered. . . —KENNEDY, Archibald. 1752#11

The importance of Jamaica to Great-Britain. . . the advantages. . . to Great-Britain, Ireland, and the colonies in North-America. . . —1741#22

The importance of religious knowledge to the happiness of mankind. A sermon preached. . . January 1, 1750. . . —BLAIR, Hugh. 1750#4

The importance of settling and fortifying Nova Scotia: with a particular account of the climate, soil and native inhabitants of that country. . . —1751#20

The importance of the British plantations in America to this kingdom. . . —HALL, Fayrer. 1731#18

The importance of the sugar colonies to Great-Britain stated, and some objections against the sugar colony bill answer'd. . . —1731#23

The important question concerning invasions, a sea war, raising the militia. . . impartially stated. . . —TUCKER, Josiah. 1755#59

In canc' John Penn. Thomas Penn, and Richard Penn Esqrs. Plaintiffs. Charles Calvert Esq. Lord Baltimore. . . Defendant. The Plaintiffs case. —1742#25

In Chancery. Breviate. John Penn, Thomas Penn, and Richard Penn, plaintiffs. . . For the plaintiffs. —PENN, John. 1742#34

In Honour to the administration. The importance of the African expedition considered. . . —POSTLETHWAYT, Malachy. 1758#35

In the eleventh month, on the nineth day. . . the Spirit of the Lord then signified. . . saying, Arise and take up a lamentation. . . —BROWNE, John, Quaker. 1678#1

The inconsistencie of the independent way, with scripture, and it self. Manifested in a three fold discourse. . . —CAWDREY, Daniel. 1651#3

The inconveniencies that have happened to some persons that have transported themselves from England to Virginia, without provisions necessary to sustaine themselves. . . —VIRGINIA COMPANY. 1622#22

Independency accused by nine severall arguments; written by a godly learned minister. —1645#13

The independent freeholders letter to the people of England, upon the one thing needfull at this present crisis. —1758#27

An index to the report of the Secret Committee. . . In a letter to a friend. —1715#16

Index Vectigalium; or, an abbreviated collection of the Laws, Edicts, Rules and Practices, touching the Customs. . . —ENGLAND AND WALES. FARMERS OF HIS MAJESTIES CUSTOMS. 1670#5

Indian converts. . . lives and dying speeches of. . . Christianized Indians of Martha's Vineyard. . . some account of. . . English ministers. . . in that and the adjacent islands. . . —MAYHEW, Experience. 1727#17

The Indian lover's garland; or, an account of how one of the Indian king's fell in love with a lady that was walking in St. James's park. —1730#17

The influence of religion on national happiness. A sermon preached. . . 5 January 1756. . . —ERSKINE, John. 1756#23

Information and direction to such persons as are inclined to America, more especially those related to the province of Pennsylvania. —PENN, William. 1684#8

The infortunate: or, the voyage and adventures of William Moraley. . . Containing, whatever is curious and remarkable in. . . —MORALEY, William. 1743#25

Inoculation of the small pox as practiced in Boston. —DOUGLASS, William. 1722#14

An inquiry into the cause of the pestilence in three parts. . . —BRUCE, Alexander. 1759#11

An inquiry into the causes of our naval miscarriages; with some thoughts on the interest of this nation, as to a naval war, and of the only true way of manning the fleet. . . —1707#9

Insectorum, sive minimorum animalium theatrum. —MOFFETT, Thomas. 1634#5

Instructions by the Commissioners for Managing and Causing to be Levied and Collected His Majesty's Customs. . . to [blank] who is established collector of His Majesty's customs at [blank] in America. —GREAT BRITAIN. CUSTOMS COMMISSIONERS. 1741#17

Instructions by the Commissioners for managing. . . his majesty's customs. . . in England, to [blank] who is established collector of his majesty's customs at [blank] in America —GREAT BRITAIN. COMMISSIONERS OF CUSTOMS. 1734#9

Instructions for the clergy employed by the Society. —SOCIETY FOR THE PROPAGATION OF THE GOSPEL. 1704#26

Instructions from the Society. . . to their missionaries in North-America. —SOCIETY FOR THE PROPAGATION OF THE GOSPEL. 1756#77

Instructions to ministers: in three parts. . . I. Two discourses. . . by. . . John Jennings. II. A letter. . . by. . . Augustus. . . —JENNINGS, David. 1744#29

The interest of Great Britain considered, with regard to her colonies, and the acquisitions of Canada and Guadaloupe. To which are added. . . —FRANKLIN, Benjamin. 1760#35

The interest of Great Britain in supplying herself with iron: impartially considered. . . —1747#13

The interest of Holland as to their alliances. . . —COURT VAN DER VOORT, Pieter de la. 1712#6

The interest of princes and states. —BETHEL, Slingsby. 1680#1

The interest of Scotland considered. . . —LINDSAY, Patrick. 1733#23

The interest of the nation as it respects all the sugar-plantations abroad. —1691#9

Introductio ad latinam blasonium. . . —GIBBON, John. 1682#16

An introduction to geography, astronomy, and dialling. —GORDON, George. 1726#7

An introduction to the history of. . . Asia, Africa, and America, both ancient and modern, according to the method of Samuel Pufendorf. . . —CRULL, Jodocus. 1705#6

An introduction to the history of the principal states. . . —PUFENDORF, Samuel von. 1695#27

An introductory discourse to catechetical instruction. . . In a Pastoral Letter to the clergy of Maryland. . . containing a Course. . . —BRAY, Thomas. 1704#5

An invitation of love. . . With a word to the wise. . . and a lamentation for New-England. . . —BROOKSOP, Joan. 1662#1

Invocation of Neptune, and his attendant Nereids, to Britannia, on the dominion of the sea. —1652#5

Ireland disgraced; or, the island of saints become an island of sinners clearly proved in a dialogue... —1755#31

Irenicum; or, an essay towards a brotherly peace and union, between those of the Congregational and Presbyterian way... —NEWCOMEN, Matthew. 1659#24

The iron-trade of Great-Britain impartially considered... —1730#18

The irregular and disorderly state of the plantation trade, discussed and humbly offered to... the Lords and Commons... —1695#13

Jemmy Gay's garland, consisting of a variety of new songs... —1750#23

The Jenny Wren. Part IV. being a choice collection of favourite songs... —1740#19

Jewes in America, or, Probabilities that the Americans are of that race... —THOROWGOOD, Thomas. 1650#13

The Jewes Synagogue: or, a treatise concerning the ancient orders and manners of worship used by the government truly and plainly stated. —PYNCHON, William. 1652#10

Journal of a voyage from Gibraltar to Georgia... —WHITEFIELD, George. 1738#33

Journal of a voyage from London to Savannah in Georgia. In two parts. Part I. From London to Gibraltar. Part II. From Gibraltar to Savannah. —WHITEFIELD, George. 1738#34

Journal of a voyage from Savannah to Philadelphia, and from Philadelphia to England... —SEWARD, William. 1740#33

Journal of an expedition under the command of Francis Nicholson... for the reduction of Port-Royal in Nova-Scotia... —NICHOLSON, Francis. 1711#18

Journal of Major George Washington, sent by... Robert Dinwiddie... lieutenant-governor of Virginia, to the commandant of the French forces on the Ohio... with a new map... —WASHINGTON, George. 1754#41

Journal of the expedition to Carthagena, with notes. In answer to a late pamphlet... An account of the expedition to Carthagena. —1744#30

Journal of the last voyage perform'd by Monsr. de La Sale, to the Gulph of Mexico, to find out the mouth of the Missisippi river... —JOUTEL, Henri. 1714#11

Journal of the late actions of the French at Canada. With the manner of their being repulsed... —BAYARD, Nicholas and LODOWICK, Charles. 1693#1

Journal of the late siege by the troops from North-America, against the French at Cape Breton, the city of Louisbourg... —GIBSON, James. 1745#24

Journal of the life of that ancient servant of Christ, John Gratton... —GRATTON, John. 1720#13

Journal of the life of Thomas Story containing an account of his... embracing the principles... held by the Quakers... —STORY, Thomas. 1747#26

Journal of the life, travels, and labour of love in the work of the ministry of... James Dickinson... —DICKINSON, James. 1745#14

Journal of the life, travels, sufferings and labour of love in the work of the ministry of... William Edmundson, who departed this life... 1712. —EDMUNDSON, William. 1715#14

Journal of the proceedings in Georgia, beginning October 20, 1737... A state of the province, as attested on oath in the court of Savannah, November 10, 1740... —STEPHENS, William. 1742#43

Journal of the proceedings in the detection of the conspiracy formed by some white people, in conjunction with negro and other slaves, for burning the city of New-York... —HORSMANDEN, Daniel. 1747#9

Journal of the siege of Quebec. To which is annexed, a correct plan of the environs of Quebec... —1760#56

Journal of travels from New-Hampshire to Caratuck, on the continent of North-America. —KEITH, George. 1706#13

Journal: or full account of the late expedition to Canada. With an appendix... —WALKER, Hovenden. 1720#39

Journal, or, historical account of the life, travels and Christian experiences of... Thomas Chalkley... —CHALKLEY, Thomas. 1751#10

Journal or historical account of the life, travels, sufferings... of... George Fox... The first volume... —FOX, George. 1694#7

Journal received February 4, 1741. By the Trustees for establishing the colony of Georgia... commencing September 22, 1741, and ending October 28 following. —STEPHENS, William. 1742#44

A journey to Paris in the year 1698... —LISTER, Martin. 1698#12

The jovial gamester's Garland, composed of several excellent new songs... —1750#24

The joyful sacrifice of a prosperous nation. A sermon preached at the meeting-house near Maze Pond, Southwark... November 29, 1759... —WALLIN, Benjamin. 1760#101

Judas and the chief priests... in answer to G. Keith's fourth... narrative... —WHITING, John. 1701#44

The judgement given forth by twenty eight Quakers against George Keith, and his friends, with answers to the said judgement... —1694#15

A judicious observation of that dreadful comet, which appeared on November by J. W. in New-England... —WISWALL, Ichabod. 1683#25

A just and cleere refutation of a false and scandalous pamphlet, entituled, Babylon's fall in Maryland, etc... To which is added... —LANGFORD, John. 1655#16

A just and lawful tryal of the Foxonian chief priests... —CRISP, Thomas. 1697#7

The just defence of James Hoskins, against the proceedings, and judgements, of Westminster monthly meeting. . . —HOSKINS, James. 1724#9

A just reprehension of Cotton Mather. London, the 11th of the 12th month, 1709. —WHITING, John. 1710#26

A just vindication of my earnest expostulation. . . —KEITH, George. 1696#17

A just vindication of the covenant and church-estate of children of church members. . . —COBBET, Thomas. 1648#3

Justification by faith: or a confutation of that antinomian error, that justification is before faith. . . —WOODBRIDGE, Benjamin. 1652#22

The justification of the independent churches of Christ. Being an answer to Mr Edwards his booke. —CHIDLEY, Katherine. 1641#4

A justification of the present war against the United Netherlands. . . —STUBBE, Henry. 1672#7

A key into the language of America: or, An help to the language of the natives. . . *in New-England.* . . *with brief observations of the customes.* . . *of the afore-said natives.* . . —WILLIAMS, Roger. 1643#19

The key of the revelation, searched and demonstrated. . . *whereunto is added A conjecture concerning Gog and Magog by the same author.* . . —MEDE, Joseph. 1643#15

A key to the Church catechism. . . *recommended as useful for schools and families.* . . —1719#5

A key to the present politics of the principal powers of Europe. . . —1743#18

The keyes of the kingdom of heaven, and power thereof, according to the word of God. . . —COTTON, John. 1644#4

The kid-napper trapan'd. . . *being a pleasant relation of a man that would have sold his wife to Virginia.* . . —1675#8

The king of pirates. . . *an account of the famous enterprises of Captain Avery, the mock king of Madagasgar.* . . —DEFOE, Daniel. 1719#2

The king of Spain's cabinet council divulged. . . *for obtaining the universal monarchy.* —1658#9

The king of Spain's reasons for not paying the 95,000l. stipulated in the convention signed at the Pardo, 14 Jan. 1739. . . —1739#45

The kingdom of darkness. . . —CROUCH, Nathaniel. 1688#4

The kingdoms divisions anatomized. . . —LISLE, Francis. 1649#4

The kings most excellent majesties wellcome to his own house. . . —TAYLOR, John. 1647#17

The knowledge of Christ. . . —DAVENPORT, John. 1653#5

The knowledge of the heavens and the earth made easy. —WATTS, Isaac. 1726#17

A large dictionary, in three parts. —HOLYOAKE, Thomas. 1677#5

The last war of the beasts. A fable. To serve for the history of the eighteenth century. In two parts. Translated from the original French of the author of Abassai. —FALQUES, Marianne-Agnès. (1721-1773). 1758#20

The last will of that impostor, George Fox (with a letter from Josiah Coale of Maryland). . . —BUGG, Francis. 1701#14

A late and further manifestation of the progress of the gospel among the Indians, in New-England. . . *Pub. by the corporation.* . . *for propagating the gospel there.* . . —ELIOT, John. 1654#11

Late memorable providences relating to witchcrafts and possessions. . . —MATHER, Cotton. 1691#11

A law of Maryland concerning religion. —1689#14

The lawes of Virginia now in force. . . —MORYSON, Francis. 1662#12

The laws of the British plantations in America, relating to the church and clergy, religion and learning. Collected in one volume. —TROTT, Nicholas. 1721#21

Leah and Rachel, or, The two fruitful sisters Virginia, and Maryland: their present condition, impartially stated and related. . . —HAMMOND, John. 1656#7

A learned treatyse of globes. . . *made English.* . . *by John Chilmead.* —HUES, Robert. 1638#15

Leather: a discourse, tendered to the high court of Parliament. . . —1629#1

A legacy for children, being some of the last expressions and dying sayings of Hannah Hill, junr., of. . . *Philadelphia.* . . *aged eleven years and near three months.* —HILL, Hannah. 1719#4

The legend of captaine Jones. —LLOYD, David. 1631#2

The legislative power is Christ's. . . —ASPINWALL, William. 1656#1

A letetr [sic] written. . . *to Sir G. Calvert his Majesties principall secretary: from Feryland in Newfoundland.* . . —WINNE, Edward. 1621#10

The lets and impediments in planting. . . *the gospel.* . . *A sermon preached.* . . *Friday the 15th of February, 1711/12* SEE KENNETT, White. 1712#13

Letter addressed to every honest man in Britain. . . —FERGUSON, C. 1738#7

Letter addressed to two great men, on the prospect of the peace; and the terms necessary to be insisted upon in the negociation. . . —DOUGLAS, John. 1760#31

Letter from a citizen of Port-Royal in Jamaica, to a citizen in New York. . . —1756#48

Letter from a cobler to the people of England on affairs of importance. . . —1756#49

Letter from a Dissenter in the city to a Dissenter in the country. Second edition. —1710#12

Letter from a Frenchman at Paris, to his countryman at the Hague, on the present dispute between France and Great Britain... — 1756#50

Letter from a friend in Edinburgh to a gentleman in the country:... concerning the wonderful progress and success of the glorious... —FRIEND IN EDINBURGH. 1742#16

Letter from a gentleman in America, to his friend in Scotland... —1699#10

Letter from a gentleman in Boston, to Mr. George Wishart, one of the ministers in Edinburgh, concerning the state of religion in New-England. —CHAUNCY, Charles (1705-87). 1742#8

Letter from a gentleman in Nova-Scotia, to a person of distinction on the continent. Describing the present state of government in that colony... —W., J. 1756#84

Letter from a gentleman in the country to a member of Parliament... containing remarks on a book lately published... 'The... — 1759#59

Letter from a gentleman in the country, to his friend in Edinburgh, concerning Mr Wh——f——d... —1741#24

Letter from a gentleman in the country to his friend in town, on his perusal of a pamphlet addressed to Two Great Men... — 1760#59

Letter from a gentleman in the North of Ireland, to a person in an eminent post under his majesty; concerning the transportation... —1729#22

Letter from a gentleman in Virginia, to the merchants of Great Britain, trading to that colony. —CARTER, Landon. 1754#5

Letter from a gentleman out of England, to his country men, the people called the Galloway Levellers. —A.B.C. 1724#1

*Letter from a member of Parliament to... the Duke of ****** upon the present situation of affairs.* —1755#33

Letter from a member of the Society for promoting Christian knowledge in London, to his friend in the country, newly chosen a corresponding member of that Society. —1709#12

Letter from a member of the Society for the propagation of Christian knowledge in London, to a correspondent in the country. —1702#15

Letter from a member of the Society for propagating the gospel... to an inhabitant of the City of London... —CHAMBERLAYNE, John. 1711#3

Letter from a merchant of the city of London to the R——t H——ble W——m P—— Esq; upon the affairs and commerce of North America, and the West Indies. —1757#20

Letter from a merchant who has left off trade, to a member of parliament, in which the case of the British and Irish manufacture of linen, threads, and tape is fairly stated... —BINDON, David. 1738#2

Letter from a Russian sea-officer... relative to the new discoveries northward and eastward from Kamatschatka. Together with... —DOBBS, Arthur. 1754#9

Letter from a West-India merchant to a gentleman at Tunbridg, concerning the part of the French proposals, which relates to North-America, and particularly Newfoundland... —1712#14

Letter from an old Whig in town, to a modern Whig in the country, upon the late expedition to Canada. —Z., X. 1711#35

Letter from Doctor More, with passages out of several letters from persons of good credit, relating to the state and improvement of the province of Pennsylvania... —MORE, Nicholas. 1687#7

Letter from Dr. Bray to such as have contributed towards the propagating Christian knowledge in the plantations... —BRAY, Thomas. 1700#5

Letter from James Murray, in New-York in America, to the Reverend Mr. Baptist Boyd, minister of the gospel, in the Parish of Aughelow... —1736#13

Letter from John Ray of New York, to Peter Ennis of Colraine, Pedlar. —1738#14

Letter from Lewis XV. To G——l M——t. —1757#21

Letter from Lieut. Hugh MacKay, of General Oglethorpe's regiment. —MACKAY, Hugh. 1742#28

Letter from Mr Habersham, (superintendent... at the orphan-house in Georgia,) to... Mr Whitefield... —HABERSHAM, James. 1744#24

Letter from Mr Knox, of Bristol, to the honourable William Nelson, Esq. of Virginia. —KNOX, Thomas. 1759#58

Letter from New-England, concerning the state of religion there. —OLIPHANT, Andrew. 1742#33

Letter from New-England concerning their customs, manners and religion. Written upon occasion of a report about a Quo Warranto brought against the government. —W., J. 1682#28

Letter from New Jersey, in America, giving some account... of that province. By a gentleman late of Christ's College, Cambridge. — THOMPSON, Thomas. 1756#78

Letter from Quebeck, in Canada, to M. L'Maine, a French officer. Which contains a particular account of the present designs of the French upon the English in North-America... —DE LA ROCHE, ——. 1755#14

*Letter from Sir William **** Deputy Lieutenant of the County of ***** to his tenants and neighbours.* —1757#22

Letter from South Carolina; giving an account of the soil, air, product, trade... together with the manner of necessary charges of settling a plantation there... by a Swiss gentleman... —NAIRNE, Thomas. 1710#14

Letter from the chancellour of Mary-land, to Col. Henry Meese, merchant in London: concerning the late troubles in Maryland... From Patuxent riverside, this 28 December, 1681. —CALVERT, Philip. 1682#6

Letter from the Duchess of Marlborough in the shades, to the great man. —1759#60

Letter from the famous Dr. Ph——ps Mountebank, to the Reverend Mr G——e Whitefield, A. B. —1741#25

Letter from the Grecian coffee-house, in answer to the Taunton-Dean letter to which is added, a paper of queries sent from Worcester. —J., F. 1701#24

Letter from the Lord Bishop of London, to his clergy within the bills of mortality. . . 14 May 1711. . . —COMPTON, Henry. 1711#4

Letter from the Lord Bishop of London, to the clergy and people. . . —SHERLOCK, Thomas. 1750#45

Letter from the Lord Bishop of Sarum, to the clergy of his diocese. —SHERLOCK, Thomas. 1742#38

Letter from the Lord Bishop of Winchester, to his clergy within the bills of mortality. . . —TRELAWNY, Jonathan. 1711#33

Letter from the Rev. Mr Dawson. . . to the clergy of Virginia in America. —DAWSON, William. 1745#12

Letter from the Rev. Mr George Whitefield to the religious societies, lately set on foot in several parts of England and Wales. —WHITEFIELD, George. 1740#41

Letter from the Reverend Mr. George Whitefield to a friend in London, dated at New-Brunswick in New-Jersey, April 27, 1740. —WHITEFIELD, George. 1740#42

Letter from W. A., a minister in Virginia, to his friend T. B., merchant, of Gracious street, London, declaring the advantages to those minded to transport themselves thither. —A. W. 1623#1

Letter from William Penn, proprietary and governour of Pennsylvania. . . to the committee of the Free Society of Traders of that. . . —PENN, William. 1683#17

Letter from William Shirley. . . to. . . the Duke of Newcastle: with a journal of the siege of Louisbourg. . . —SHIRLEY, William. 1746#23

Letter of advice to the churches of the non-conformists in the English nation: endeavouring their satisfaction in that point, Who are the true Church of England? —MATHER, Cotton. 1700#28

Letter of advice written by Sr. Thomas Bacon to the Duke of Buckingham. . . —BACON, Francis. 1661#1

Letter of consolation to Dr Shebbeare. —1758#31

Letter of many ministers in Old England, requesting the judgement of their reverend brethren in New England concerning nine. . . —ASHE, Simeon and BALL, John. 1643#1

Letter of Mr. John Cottons, teacher of the church of Boston in New-England, to Mr [Roger] Williams —COTTON, John. 1643#5

Letter of the Lord Bishop of London to the masters and mistresses of families in the English plantations abroad; exhorting. . . —GIBSON, Edmund. 1727#9

Letter of the right honourable William Pitt, esq. being an impartial vindication of the conduct of his ministry. —1756#51

Letter sent to London from a spie at Oxford. —TAYLOR, John. 1643#18

Letter to a friend; giving a concise but just account. . . of the Ohio defeat. . . —CHAUNCY, Charles. 1755#5

Letter to a friend in the country, upon the news of the town. —JONES, John. 1755#32

Letter to a friend in America; wherein is clearly held forth the peculiar interest that the elect have in the death of Christ, by virtue. . . —R., P. 1754#31

Letter to a friend in the country, on the late expedition to Canada. . . —DUMMER, Jeremiah. 1712#8

Letter to a gentleman, concerning the boundaries of the province of Maryland. Wherein is shewn, that no part of the 40th degree. . . —1732#25

Letter to a gentleman in London, to his friend in Pennsylvania; with a satire. . . upon. . . Quakers. . . —SMITH, William (1727-1803). 1756#75

Letter to a gentleman in Scotland, containing remarks upon. . . Mr George Whitefield. —BISSET, John. 1742#2

Letter to a Member of Parliament, concerning The naval-store bill brought in last session. With observations on the plantation-trade. . . —1720#18

Letter to a member of Parliament. Concerning the present state of affairs at home and abroad. . . —1740#23

Letter to a member of Parliament for incouraging offices of insurance for ships. . . particularly for incouraging the British fishery. . . —B., A. 1720#3

Letter to a member of parliament in the country, concerning the present posture of affairs in Christendom. —1700#27

Letter to a member of Parliament, on the importance of the American colonies, and the best means of making them useful to the mother country. —1757#23

Letter to a member of Parliament, on the regulation of the plantation trade. —B., J. 1701#6

Letter to a Member of Parliament, relating to the relief of poor insolvent prisoners for debt. . . And a proposal for strengthning the British plantations in America. —1724#13

Letter to a member of the P———t of G———t B———n, occasioned by the priviledge granted by the French King to Mr. Crozat. —CROZAT, Anthony. 1713#4

Letter to a noble lord, concerning the late expedition to Canada. —DUMMER, Jeremiah. 1712#9

Letter to a noble Lord: wherein it is demonstrated that all difficulties in obtaining an honourable and lasting peace. . . are. . . imaginary. —COADE, George. 1760#24

Letter to a noble peer, relating to the Bill in favour of the sugar planters. —1733#22

Letter to a nobleman in the country, on the affair of Mr Annesley. . . —1744#32

Letter to a right honourable patriot; upon the glorious success at Quebec. . . with a postcript, which enumerates the other conquests mentioned in the London address. —GROVE, Joseph. 1759#44

Letter to a West-country clothier and free holder, concerning the country's rejecting the French treaty of commerce. . . —1713#5A

295

Letter to an honourable brigadier general, commander in chief of his majesty's forces in Canada. —1760#60

Letter to Dr Freind; showing the danger and uncertainty of inoculating the small pox. —WAGSTAFFE, William. 1722#28

Letter to George Keith, concerning his late religious differences with William Penn and his party. . . —1696#19

Letter to his grace the D - of N-e on the duty he owes himself, his king, his country. . . —SHEBBEARE, John?. 1757#42

Letter to Mr Penn. With his answer. —POPPLE, Will. 1688#15

Letter to Mr. Law, upon his arrival in Great Britain. —1721#10

Letter to Mr. Tho. Edwards. . . Scavenger Generall, throughout Great Britaine, New-England, and the United Provinces. . . —1647#10

Letter to the great man, occasioned by the Letter to two great men. . . By a citizen of London. . . —1760#61

Letter to the Honourable A———r M———re, Com———ner of Trade and Plantation. —1714#12

Letter to the honourable the Lords Commissioners of trade and plantations. Wherein the grand concern of trade is asserted and maintained. . . —COADE, George. 1747#4

Letter to the King of *****. By an Englishman not a member of the House of Commons. . . —1756#52

Letter to the learned Caleb Cotesworth, M. D. . . containing a comparison between the mortality of the natural smallpox, and that given by inoculation. . . —JURIN, James. 1723#5

Letter to the Negroes lately converted to Christ in America. And particularly to those, lately called out of darkness. . . at Mr. Jonathan Bryan's in South Carolina. . . —1742#26

Letter to the people of England. Letter VII. —SHEBBEARE, John. 1758#42

Letter to the people of England, on the necessity of putting an immediate end to the war; and the means of obtaining an advantageous peace. —SHEBBEARE, John. 1760#85

Letter to the people of England, on the present situation and conduct of national affairs. Letter I. —SHEBBEARE, John. 1755#47

Letter to the people of England upon the militia, continental connections, neutralities and secret expeditions. . . —SHEBBEARE, John. 1757#40

Letter to the Reverend John Wesley, in answer to his sermon, entituled, Free-grace. . . —WHITEFIELD, George. 1741#52

Letter to the Reverend Mr Thomas Church. . . in answer to his serious and expostulatory letter to. . . Whitefield. . . —WHITEFIELD, George. 1744#45

Letter to the right honourable Sir R W etc., upon the present posture of affairs. . . —AMHURST, Nicholas. 1739#3

Letter to the right honourable the Lords Commissioners of Trade and Plantations; or, a short essay on the principle branches of the trade of New England. . . —BANISTER, Thomas. 1715#2

Letter to the right honourable W. P., esq; by an Englishman. —COADE, George. 1758#8

Letter to the right honourable William Pitt esq., from an officer at Fort Frontenac. —1759#61

Letter to the Right Reverend Father in God the Lord B———p of L———n. Occasioned by a letter of his lordship's to the L———ds of T-e. . . —CARTER, Landon. 1760#17

A letter to the West-India merchants, in answer to their petition now before the Honble House of Commons, praying for a prohibition. . . —B., M 1751#3

Letter to. . . Whitefield. Designed to correct his mistaken account of regeneration. . . now published to prevent his doing mischief. . . —LAND, Tristram. 1739#46

Letter which was delivered to the King. . . —MAYLINS, Robert. 1661#10

Letter written to a member of Parliament relating to trade. —EGLETON, John. 1702#9

Letters and negotiations of Count d'Estrades. . . from MDXXVIII to MDCLXIII, containing an account of. . . troubles that happened. . . —ESTRADES, Godefroi Louis. 1755#19

Letters concerning the English Nation. . . —VOLTAIRE, François Marie Arouet de. 1733#37

Letters from a gentleman in the north of Scotland to his friend in London. . . In two volumes. —BURT, Edward. 1754#2

Letters from the Rev. Samuel Davies. . . shewing the present state of religion in Virginia, particularly among the Negroes. . . —DAVIES, Samuel. 1757#7

Letters of Samuel Holden, Esquire, to Dr. Benjamin Coleman of Boston, New-England. —HOLDEN, Samuel. 1741#21

Letters on the English nation. . . —ANGELONI, Battista. [pseudonym for J. Shebbeare]. 1755#1

Letters patent graunted by the states of the United Netherlands Provinces, to the West Indian company of merchants. . . —UNITED PROVINCES. STATES GENERAL. 1621#8

Lettre pastorale de Monseigneur l'éveque de Londres. . . —GIBSON, Edmund. 1729#10

Leviathan, Or the matter, forme, and power of a Commonwealth. —HOBBES, Thomas. 1651#12

Lex mercatoria rediviva: or the merchant's directory. . . Containing an account of our trading companies and colonies, with their. . . —BEAWES, Wyndham. 1751#7

The liberty and property of British subjects asserted: in a letter from an assembly-man in Carolina, to his friend in London. —N., J. 1726#13

Liberty asserted. A tragedy. As it is acted at the New Theatre in Little Lincoln's-Inn-Fields. —DENNIS, John. 1704#11

The liberty of the gospel explained, and recommended. A sermon. . . 15 February, 1716. . . —HAYLEY, Thomas. 1717#8

The life and actions of James Dalton, (the noted street-robber.). . . With a particular account of his running away with the ship when he was first transported. . . —DALTON, James. 1730#7

The life and adventures of Bampfylde-Moore Carew, the noted Devon-shire stroller and dog-stealer, as related by himself, during his passage to the plantations in America. . . —CAREW, Bampfylde Moore? 1745#7

The life and adventures of Joe Thompson. —KIMBER, Edward. 1750#25

Life and adventures of Matthew Bishop, of Deddington in Oxford-shire, containing an account of several actions by sea, battles. . . —BISHOP, Matthew. 1744#4

The life and authentick trial of Doctor Hensey, for high-treason, in giving intelligence to the French. Taken on Monday, the 12th of June, at the Court of King's Bench. . . — 1758#32

The life and character of a strange He-Monster, lately arriv'd in London from an English Colony in America. And is often to be seen on the Royal Exchange, Gratis. —1726#12

The life and death of Sir Henry Vane, Kt. Or, a short narrative of the main passages of his earthly pilgrimage. . . —SIKES, George. 1662#15

The life and death of the renowned Mr John Eliot. . . — MATHER, Cotton. 1691#12

The life and death, travels and suffering of Robert Widders. . . —WIDDERS, Robert. 1688#18

The life and errors of John Dunton late citizen of London. . . —DUNTON, John. 1705#9

The life and particular proceedings of George Whitefield. . . to his embarking for Pensilvania. . . —TUCKER, Josiah. 1739#66

The life of Charlotta du Pont, an English lady. . . Giving an account of how she was trepan'd by her stepmother to Virginia. . . —AUBIN, Penelope. 1723#1

The life of faith, exemplified and recommended, in a letter found in the study of J. Belcher, late of Dedham in New-England. . . —ELIOT, Joseph. 1741#10

The life of General James Wolfe, the conqueror of Canada, or, the eulogium of that renowned hero. . . —PRINGLE, John, Sir. 1760#78

The life of Harriot Stuart, written by herself. —LENNOX, Charlotte. 1751#21

The life of Henry Simms, alias Young gentleman Harry. . . to his death at Tyburn. . . June 17, 1747. . . robberies. . . and extraordinary adventures. . . at home and abroad. . . —SIMMS, Henry. 1747#25

The life of Michael Adrian de Ruyter Admiral of Holland. — 1677#12

The life of Mr Cleveland, natural son of Oliver Cromwell, written by himself. Giving a particular account of. . . his great sufferings in Europe and America. . . —PREVOST D'EXILES, Antoine François. 1731#28

The life of Oliver Cromwell. —KIMBER, Isaac. 1724#12

Life of Sir John Leake. . . admiral of the fleet. —LEAKE, Stephen Martin. 1750#27

The life of the honourable Robert Boyle. —BIRCH, Thomas. 1744#3

The life of the valiant and learned Sir Walter Raleigh, Knight. . . London —SHIRLEY, John. 1677#17

The life of. . . White Kennett. . . with several original letters. . . papers and records. . . —NEWTON, William. 1730#23

Light and truth. . . reply to. . . 'A plain discovery of many gross falsehoods, etc. . .' by George Keith. . . —FIELD, John. 1701#20

Light and truth triumphant. —WHITEHEAD, George. 1712#26

The light appearing more and more towards the perfect day. Or, a farther discovery of the present state of the Indians in New England. . . —WHITFIELD, Henry. 1651#15

Light for the Jews, or the means to convert them. . . —EVANS, Arise. 1656#6

List of copies of charters, from the Commissioners for Trade and Plantations, presented to the Honourable the House of Commons. . . —GREAT BRITAIN. BOARD OF TRADE. 1741#16

A list of such the names of the nobility. . . of England and Ireland. . . attainted for high treason. . . together with. . . copies of the acts of the said pretended Parliament. . . —1690#11

A list of the absentees of Ireland. —PRIOR, Thomas. 1729#23

A list of the adventurers of England trading into Hudson's Bay and of their respective shares in the general stock. November 1, 1675. —1675#9

A list of the names and stocks, of the governour and company of the adventurers of England trading to Hudson's bay. . . —1673#8

A list of the public offices and officers ecclesiastical and civil employed in his majesty's government. . . —1737#15

A list of those members of the late parliament, that voted for the passing of the Act for naturalising foreign Protestants; and consequently, for the bringing over the Palatines. . . —1711#14

Lithobolia: or, the stone throwing devil. . . account of infernal spirits. . . and the great disturbance they gave to George Walton's. . . —CHAMBERLAYNE Richard. 1698#5

Little children invited to Jesus Christ: sermon. . . in Hanover county, Virginia, May 8, 1757. With a short account. . . late. . . — DAVIES, Samuel. 1758#14

The lives of sundry eminent persons in this later age. In two parts. —CLARKE, Samuel. 1683#5

Lives of the admirals. . . a new and accurate naval history. . . with passages relating to our discoveries, plantations, and commerce. —CAMPBELL, John. 1742#6

The lives of the most remarkable criminals, who have been condemn'd and executed; for murder,. . . or other offences; from the year. . . —1732#26

Living Christianity delineated, in the diaries and letters of. . . Mr Hugh Bryan and Mrs Mary Hutson, both of South Carolina. . . —BRYAN, Hugh. 1760#13

London and Country Brewer. . . in three parts. . . —ELLIS, William. 1759#29

London triumphant: Or, the City in jollity and splendour. . . —JORDAN, Thomas. 1672#8

London's triumphs, celebrated the nine and twentieth day of. . . October, 1657. . . —TATHAM, John. 1657#13

A looking glass for the times, etc. to which is added the report from the Lords of the Committee of Councils, and the King's Orders relating to Quakers in New England. —BISHOP, George. 1668#1

The Lord Baltemores case, concerning the province of Maryland. —1653#12

The Lord Haversham's speech in the House of Peers, on Thursday, November 23, 1704. —THOMPSON, John, first baron Haversham. 1704#28

The Lords protest against the convention-treaty. —GREAT BRITAIN. PARLIAMENT. HOUSE OF LORDS. 1739#35

The Lord's protest in the last session of Parliament, viz. . . IV. On the representation of the state of the colonies in America. . . [26 March 1734]. —GREAT BRITAIN. PARLIAMENT. HOUSE OF LORDS. 1734#10

The loyal address of the clergy of Virginia. . . —1702#16

Luck at last or the happy unfortunate. . . —BLACKAMORE, Arthur. 1723#2

LXXX sermons. —DONNE, John. 1640#1

Lydia, or Filial Piety: a novel. . . —SHEBBEARE, John. 1755#48

M. S. to A. S. with a plea for libertie of conscience against the cavils of A. S. —GOODWIN, John. 1644#8

Mafteah leshon hakodesh clavis linguae sanctae. . . —TROTT, Nicholas. 1721#22

Magnalia Christi Americana: or; the ecclesiastical history of New-England, from its first planting in the year 1620 unto the year of our Lord, 1698. . . —MATHER, Cotton. 1702#17

The maintenance of free trade. —MALYNES, Gerard. 1622#15

Manly Christianity. A brief essay on the signs of good growth and strength in the most lovely Christianity. . . —MATHER, Cotton. 1711#15

A mapp of New Jersey, in America. . . The description of the province of West-Jersey. . . As also, Proposals to such as desire to have any property there. —SELLER, John. 1677#16

Mare clausum, seu De dominio maris libri duo. . . —SELDEN, John. 1635#3

The mariage of Oceanus and Brittania. —FLECKNOE, Richard. 1665#17

The mariner's compass rectified. . . —WAKELY, Andrew. 1665#21

Marvellous things done by the right hand. . . of God in getting him the victory. . . —CHAUNCY, Charles (1705-87). 1745#9

Maryland. Benjamin Tasker appellant. John Simpson, lessee of William Brent, respondent. The appellants case.. to be heard. . . 25th. . January 1739. . . —GREAT BRITAIN. PRIVY COUNCIL. 1739#37

Maryland. Benjamin Tasker, esq. . . appellant. John Simpson, lessee of William Brent, respondent. The respondent's case. To be heard. . . 25th. . January 1739. . . —GREAT BRITAIN. PRIVY COUNCIL. 1739#38

Maryland. Charles Carroll. . . appellant. John Parran. . . and Mary Parran. . . respondents. The appellant's case. —CARROLL, Charles. 1739#11

The mayden's of London, brave adventures, or, a boon voyage intended for the sea. . . —PRICE, Laurence. 1655#18

Medicina Britannica; or, a treatise on such physical plants, as are generally to be found in. . . Great Britain. . . —SHORT, Thomas. 1746#24

Meditations and spiritual experiences of Mr T. Shepard. . . —SHEPARD, Thomas. 1749#37

Melius inquirendum, or, An answer to a book of Edward Cockson .. mis-intituled, Rigid Quakers cruel persecutors. —CLARIDGE, Richard. 1706#7

Mémoire présenté à Sa. Gr. Mylord Duc de Newcastle. . . sur l'état présent de la Caroline et sur les moyens de l'améliorer. —PURRY, Jean Pierre. 1724#18

Memoirs and considerations concerning the trade and revenues of the British colonies in America. With proposals for rendering those colonies more beneficial to Great Britain. —ASHLEY, John. 1740#3

The memoirs, life, and character of the great Mr Law. . . with an accurate. . . account of the establishment of the Missippi [sic] Company in France. . . Written by a Scots gentleman. —GRAY, ——. 1721#6

Memoirs of an unfortunate young nobleman, in which is continued the history of Count Richard, concluding with a summary view. . . —ANNESLEY, James. 1743#1

Memoirs of an unfortunate young nobleman, return'd from a thirteen years slavery in America. . . Vol III which completes the work, and is a key to the other two volumes. —ANNESLEY, James. 1747#1

Memoirs of an unfortunate young nobleman, return'd from a thirteen years slavery in America, where he had been sent by the wicked. . . —ANNESLEY, James. 1743#2

The memoirs of John Ker of Kersland, in North Britain. . . with an account of the. . . Ostend Company. . . —KER, John. 1726#9

Memoirs of Queen Anne: being a compleat supplement to the history of her reign. —GIBSON, ——. 1729#11

Memoirs of the English affairs, chiefly naval from the year 1660, to 1673. —JAMES II. 1729#20

Memoirs of the life and adventures of William Parsons, esq; from the time of his entering into life, to his death. . . Written by himself and corrected (with additions) by a gentleman. —PARSONS, William. 1751#25

Memoirs of the life and death of... Mrs Jane Turell, who died at Medford, March 26, 1735... to which is added two sermons... by... B. Colman, D. D. —TURELL, Ebenezer. 1741#46

Memoirs of the life of the late reverend Increase Mather... With a preface by... Edmund Calamy... —MATHER, Cotton. 1725#9

Memoirs of the pillory, being a consolatory epistle to Dr Shebbeare... —1759#67

Memoirs of the principal transactions of the last war between the English and the French in North America... in 1744... to... —SHIRLEY, William. 1757#44

Memoirs of the right villainous John Hall, the late famous and notorious robber... —HALL, John. 1708#9

The memorable works of a son of thunder and consolation... Edward Burroughs... —BURROUGH, Edward. 1672#2

A memorial, humbly shewing the past and present state of the land lying waste and un-inhabited between Nova-Scotia, and the Province of Main in New England in America. —1721#14

A memorial of several aggrievances and oppressions of his majesty's subjects... in the colony of New-York... —MULFORD, Samuel. 1717#15

A Memorial of the case of the German emigrants settled in the British colonies of Pensilvania, and the back parts of Maryland, Virginia, etc... —1754#26

A memorial of the present deplorable state of New-England with the many disadvantages it lyes under, by the male-administration... —MATHER, Cotton. 1707#12

Memorial or state of the process at the instance of William Lauder of Wine-Park... —LAUDER, William. 1718#14

A memorial presented to... Duke of Newcastle... concerning the present state of Carolina, and the means of improving it. —PURRY, Jean Pierre. 1724#19

A memorial relating to the tobacco trade... —MACKERCHER, Daniel. 1737#17

A memorial representing the present case of the church in Mary-Land, with relation to its establishment by law. —BRAY, Thomas. 1701#10

A memorial, representing the present state of religion, on the continent of North-America. —BRAY, Thomas. 1700#6

The memorialls of Margaret de Valoys, first wife to Henry the fourth, King of France. —1641#16

Memorials of the English affairs... —WHITELOCKE, Bulstrode. 1682#29

Memorials of the English affairs... with some account of his life and writings by William Penn... —WHITELOCKE, Bulstrode. 1709#23

The memorials of the French and English commissaries concerning the limits of Nova Scotia or Acadia. —GREAT BRITAIN.

BOARD OF TRADE. COMMISSION FOR ADJUSTING BOUNDARIES. 1755#22

The merchant's complaint against Spain... the pretensions of Spain to Georgia... —ROBINS, Benjamin. 1738#21

The merchant's magazine: or, Trades-man's treasury... —HATTON, Edward. 1695#11

The merchants mappe of commerce... —ROBERTS, Lewes. 1638#16

Mercurius Americanus, Mr Welds his Antitype, or, Massachusetts great apologie examined... —WHEELWRIGHT, John. 1645#20

The merit and reward of a good intention. A sermon preached... March 18. 1741-2... in which some notice is taken of a late... —BEST, William. 1742#1

Merry drollery, or a collection of jovial poems, merry songs... —1661#11

The messiah magnified by the mouths of babes in America... —MATTHEWS, Marmaduke. 1659#21

The method and plain process for making pot-ash, equal if not superior to the best foreign pot-ash... —STEPHENS, Thomas d. 1780. 1755#55

A method for determining the best climate of the earth, on a principle to which all geographers and historians have been hitherto strangers... —PURRY, Jean Pierre. 1744#36

The method of grace... —WOODBRIDGE, Benjamin. 1656#13

The method used by the Society to encourage the distribution of good books... —SOCIETY FOR THE PROPAGATION OF THE GOSPEL. 1727#24

The Methodists, an humorous burlesque poem; addressed to... Whitefield and his followers: proper to be bound up with his sermons, and the journals of his voyage to Georgia... —1739#49

Methodus gratiae divinae in traductione hominis peccatoris ad vitam, septuaginta thesibus succincta et elaborate explicate. —PARKER, Thomas. 1657#11

Methodus plantarum nova... —RAY, John. 1682#23

Methodus procedendi contra clericos irregulares in plantationibus Americanis. —GIBSON, Edmund. 1728#8

Microcosmus; or A little description of the great world... —HEYLYN, Peter. 1621#3

The military history of Great Britain, for 1756, 1757. Containing a letter from an English officer at Canada, taken prisoner... —1757#27

Military maxims, or the standard of generalship. Addressed to a British commander. By an officer in a marching regiment. —1760#67

The militia reform'd... —TOLAND, John. 1698#21

Milk for babes... —COTTON, John. 1646#8

Ministerial artifices detected, or, A full answer to a pamphlet... The interests of the empress queen, the Kings of France... —1749#28

Ministerial prejudices in favour of the Convention, examined and answered. —1739#50

Miracles of art and nature, or, a brief description of the several varieties of birds, beasts, fishes, plants, and fruits of other countreys... —CROUCH, Nathaniel. 1678#2

A mirrour or looking-glass, both for saints and sinners... By... examples... —CLARKE, Samuel. 1646#4

Miscellanea Aurea; or the Golden Medley... —1720#21

Miscellanea; consisting of three treatises... —HOMES, Nathaniel. 1664#9

Miscellanea Curiosa. Being a collection of some of the principal phaenomena in nature... —HALLEY, Edmond. 1705#11

A miscellaneous essay concerning the courses pursued by Great Britain in the affairs of her colonies: with some observations on the... —McCULLOH, Henry. 1755#34

Miscellaneous poems compos'd at Newfoundland, on board His Majesty's ship the Kinsale... —LACY, B [sic]. 1729#21

Miscellaneous reflections upon the peace, and its consequences... —1749#29

Miscellaneous works consisting of essays political and moral. —PHILIPS, Erasmus. 1751#27

A miscellany, containing several tracts on various subjects... —BERKELEY, George. 1752#1

The misery of ignorant and unconverted sinners. A sermon preached in the High Church of Edinburgh, Monday, January 1. 1733... —SMITH, James. 1733#33

Missionalia, or a collection of missionary pieces relating to the conversion of the heathen; both the African negroes and American Indians. In two parts. —BRAY, Thomas. 1727#3

The mitre and crown; or Great Britain's true interest... —1748#15

Mock Songs and joking poems... —1675#10

A model for erecting a bank of credit; with a discourse in explanation thereof. Adapted to the use of any trading countrey... —1688#21

The model of the government of the province of East-New-Jersey in America. —SCOTT, George. 1685#25

A moderate and safe expedient to remove jealousies and feares, of any danger... by the Roman Catholickes of this kingdome... —CALVERT, Cecil. 1646#3

The modern gazetteer: or, a short view of the several nations of the world... —SALMON, Thomas. 1746#22

Modern history, or The present state of all nations. —SALMON, Thomas. 1725#10

A modest account from Pensylvania, of the principal differences in point of doctrine, between George Keith and... —PUSEY, Caleb. 1696#23

A modest address to the Commons of Great Britain... the ill success of our present naval war with France, and the want of a militia bill. —1756#54

A modest and brotherly answer to Mr. Charles Herle his book, against the independency of churches... —MATHER, Richard. 1644#12

A modest and cleere answer to Mr Ball's discourse of set formes of prayer —COTTON, John. 1642#6

A modest and impartial narrative of several grievances... that the peacable and most considerable inhabitants of New-York... —1690#16

A modest answer to a malicious libel against his excellency Francis Nicholson... or an examination of that part of Mr Blair's affidavit... —NICHOLSON, Francis. 1705#17

A modest defence of my book, entituled, Quakerism exposed... —BUGG, Francis. 1700#9

A modest enquiry into the grounds and occasions of a late pamphlet, intituled, A memorial of the present deplorable state of New-England. By a disinterested hand. —DUDLEY, Joseph?. 1707#5

A modest enquiry into the present state of foreign affairs... By a lover of his country. —1742#30

A modest examination of the resolution of this case of conscience... —1683#14

The Mohocks; a tragi-comical farce. —GAY, John. 1712#10

Money and trade considered, with a proposal for supplying the nation with money... —LAW, John. 1705#14

Money answers all things: or, an essay to make money sufficiently plentiful... —VANDERLINT, Jacob. 1734#24

The Monitor: a speech... by the Honourable W——m P——t. —PITT, William. 1755#41

A monody on the death of Major-Genl. James Wolfe. To which is added some particulars of his life... —1759#70

The monstrous injustice and unmercifulness of Nicholas Trott, late governour of the Bahama-Islands in America... —BULKLEY, Thomas. 1698#4

Moral instructions of a father to his son, upon his departure for a long voyage... —SYLVESTRE DUFOUR, Philippe. 1683#21

Moravian heresy, wherein the principal errors of that doctrine, as taught throughout several parts of Europe and America... are proved and refuted. —ROCHE, John. 1751#31

More divisions among the Quakers... —KEITH, George and BUDD, Thomas. 1693#11

More excellent observations of the estate and affaires of Holland... —1622#18

More news from Virginia, being a full and true relation of all occurrences in that countrey, since the death of Nath. Bacon with... —1677#13

More wonders of the invisible word: or The wonders of the invisible world displayed... To which is added, a postcript relating to a book intitled, The life of Sir William Phips. . . —CALEF, Robert. 1700#10

Moro-Mastix: Mr John Goodwin whipt with his own rod. Or the dissecting of the sixteenth section of his book. . . so far as it. . . mentions a. . . disputation in Christ-Church parish. . . — 1647#12

Moses and Aaron: or, the rights of church and state. . . —NOYES, James. 1661#12

A most compleat compendium of geography. . . —ECHARD, Laurence. 1691#7

A most exact and accurate map of the whole world: or, The orb terrestial described in four plain maps, (viz.) Asia, Europe, Africa, and America. —LUPTON, Donald. 1676#11

A most grave, and modest confutation of the errors of the sect commonly called Brownists. . . —RATHBAND, William. 1644#15

A most humble proposal to the Most Honourable the Lords Regents. . . for an effectual method to prevent piracy, and make the trade of America safe. . . —PHILOPATRIS. 1723#9

Motives for a peace with England. By an old sea officer. Translated from the French. —1757#30

Motives to return to God with all the heart, drawn from the consideration of his providential goodness towards Great-Britain in the year past. . . —1759#72

Mourning Virginia. —1622#17

Mourt's relation. A relation or journall of the beginning and proceedings of the English plantation setled at Plimoth in New England. . . —1622#19

Mr Baxter baptiz'd in bloud, or, a sad history of the unparallel'd cruelty of the Anabaptists in New England. . . —PARKER, Samuel. 1673#9

Mr. Baxter's vindication of the church of England. —BAXTER, Richard. 1682#3

Mr Cottons letter lately printed, examined and answered: by Roger Williams of Providence in New-England. —WILLIAMS, Roger. 1644#21

Mr Dummers account of the West India correspondence, how it was propounded, and how since performed. Received 15 October 1705. —DUMMER, Jeremiah. 1705#8

Mr James Janeway's legacy. . . twenty seven famous instances of God's providences in and about sea-dangers and deliverances. . . a sermon on the same subject. . . —JANEWAY, James. 1674#5

Mr. Maitland's account of inoculating the small pox vindicated, from Dr. Wagstaffe's misrepresentations. . . —MAITLAND, Charles. 1722#19

Mr Peters last report of the English wars. . . —PETER, Hugh. 1646#17

Mr Robe's first letter to the Reverend James Fisher. . . —ROBE, James. 1742#36

Mr Robe's fourth letter to the Reverend James Fisher. . . —ROBE, James. 1743#31

Mr Robe's second letter to the Reverend James Fisher. . . —ROBE, James. 1743#32

Mr Robe's third letter to the Reverend James Fisher. . . —ROBE, James. 1743#33

Mr. Worlidge's two treatises —WORLIDGE, John. 1694#20

Musaeum regalis societatis. Or a catalogue and description of the natural and artificial rarities belonging to the Royal Society and preserved at Gresham Colledge —GREW, Nehemiah. 1681#11

Musaeum tradescantianum: or, A collection of Rarities preserved at South-Lambeth neer London —TRADESCANT, John. 1656#11

Musei Petiveriani prima [-octavia]. —PETIVER, James. 1695#26

My Lord, The Bill upon which I was examined last year. . . —HALL, Fayrer. 1732#21

The mystery of Israel's salvation, explained and applyed. . . —MATHER, Increase. 1669#1

The mystery revealed; or, Truth brought to light. —MOREAU, Jacob Nicolas. (compiler). 1759#71

The Naked Truth. Number I. . . addressed to the people of Great Britain, Ireland and America. —OGLETHORPE, William. 1755#39

The names of the lords and gentlemen, entrusted with the moneys collected for the use of the German emigrants in Pensilvania, and other provinces of North America. —1755#36

A narrative of the imprisonment of two non-conformist ministers, and prosecution or trial of one of them, for preaching a sermon in. . . New York. —MAKEMIE, Francis. 1708#11

A narrative of the late proceed's [sic] at White-Hall concerning the Jews. . . —JESSEY, Henry. 1656#9

A narrative of the late work of God, at and near Northampton, in New-England, extracted from Mr Edward's letter. . . —WESLEY, John. 1744#43

A narrative of the method and success of inoculating the small pox in New England. . . With a reply to the objections. . . in letter from a minister at Boston. . . a historical introduction by Daniel Neal. . . —COLMAN, Benjamin. 1722#9

A narrative of the miseries of New England, by reason of an arbitrary government erected there. . . —MATHER, Increase. 1688#12

A narrative of the proceedings of Sir E. Androsse printed in the year 1691. . . —STOUGHTON, William. 1691#20

A narrative of the proceedings of the people of South-Carolina, in the year 1719. . . motives that induced them to renounce their obedience to the Lords Proprietors. . . —YONGE, Francis. 1726#19

A narrative of the sufferings of. . . Captain John Dean. . . in the Nottingham-Galley of London, cast away on Boon island, near New England, December 11 1710. —DEAN, John. 1711#5

A narrative of the wicked plots carried on by Seignior Gondamore for advancing the popish religion and Spanish faction. . . —DUGDALE, Richard. 1679#2

National blessings an argument for reformation. A sermon, preached at Aberdeen, November 29, 1759. . . —GERARD, Alexander. 1759#37

National considerations upon importing iron in bars from America, etc. —1750#34

The national dispute; or, The history of the convention treaty: containing the full substance of all the proceedings, debates, journals, pamphlets. . . —1739#51

National expectations on the late change in the ministry. . . —1751#22

The national merchant: or, discourses on commerce and colonies; being an essay for regulating and improving the trade and plantations. . . —BENNET, John. 1736#3

National prejudice, opposed to national interest, candidly considered in the detention or yielding up Gibraltar and Cape-Breton. . . —1748#16

A natural and civil history of California:. . . *translated from the original Spanish.* . . —VENEGAS, Miguel. 1759#101

The natural and civil history of the French dominions in North and South America. . . —JEFFERYS, Thomas. 1760#54

The natural and moral government and agency of God, in causing droughts and rains. —PRINCE, Thomas. 1750#39

A natural history: containing many not common observations; extracted out of the best modern writers. . . —BLOUNT, Sir Thomas Pope. 1693#2

A natural history of birds. . . —EDWARDS, George. 1743#13

A natural history of birds. Illustrated with a hundred and one copper plates. . . —ALBIN, Eleazar. 1731#1

The natural history of Carolina, Florida, and the Bahama Islands. . . *with remarks upon agriculture.* . . —CATESBY, Mark. 1731#9

The natural history of North-Carolina; with an account of the trade, manners, and customs of the Christian and Indian inhabitants. . . —BRICKELL, John. 1737#2

The nature and necessity of a religious education. A sermon. . . *January 6. 1752.* . . —BONAR, John. 1752#2

The nature of regeneration opened, and absolute necessity demonstrated. . . *a sermon.* . . *with expostulatory address.* . . *by G. Tennent.* . . —TENNENT, John.(1706-1732). 1741#41

The naval chronicle; or voyages, travels, expeditions. . . *of the most celebrated English navigators.* . . —1760#69

The naval history of Britain, from the earliest periods. . . *to.* . . *M.DCC.LVI. Compiled from the papers of the late honourable captain George Berkeley.* —HILL, John. 1756#42

The naval history of England, in all its branches; from. . . *1066, to the conclusion of 1734.* . . —LEDIARD, Thomas. 1735#11

Navigantium atque itinerantium bibliotheca: or, A compleat collection of voyages and travels. . . *To which is prefixed, A history of the peopling.* . . —HARRIS, John. 1705#12

Navigation and commerce, their original and progress. . . —EVELYN, John. 1674#3

A necessary companion; or the English interest discovered and promoted. . . —REYNELL, Carew. 1685#23

The necessity of contending for revealed religion. . . *to which is prefixed, a letter from the Reverend Cotton Mather.* . . —BRADBURY, Thomas. 1720#6

The negociators magazine. . . *to which are added, curious calculations of great use in the West-India, Carolina and New-England trades.* . . —HAYES, Richard. 1739#42

The Negro's and Indian's advocate, suing for their admission into the church. . . *To which is added, A brief account of religion in Virginia.* —GODWIN, Morgan. 1680#4

Neonomianism unmask'd: or, the ancient gospel pleaded, against the other, called a new law, or gospel. —CHAUNCY, Isaac. 1692#3

A net for a night-raven; or, A trap for a scold. —1674#9

A new account of some parts of Guinea, and the slave-trade. . . —SNELGRAVE, William. 1734#21

A new and accurate account of the provinces of South-Carolina and Georgia. With many curious and useful observations on the trade, navigation and plantations of Great-Britain. . . —MARTYN, Benjamin. 1732#27

A new and complete history of the British empire in America. . . —1755#37

A new and further narrative of the state of New-England, being a continued account of the bloudy Indian-war from March till August, 1676. . . —S., N. 1676#17

A new and most exact account of the fertile and famous colony of Carolina. . . *the whole being the compendious account of a voyage.* . . —CRAFFORD, John. 1683#6

A new collection of voyages and travels. . . *None of them before ever printed.* . . —STEVENS, John. 1711#29

The new covenant, or, a treatise, unfolding the order and manner of giving and receiving the covenant of grace. . . —COTTON, John. 1654#8

The new creature described and considered as the sure characteristick of a man's being in Christ. . . —CHAUNCY, Charles (1705-87). 1742#9

A new description of that fertile and pleasant province of Carolina with a brief account of its discovery, settling, and the government thereof. —ARCHDALE, John. 1707#1

A new description of the world. . . —CURSON, Henry. 1706#9

A new description of the world, or a compendious treatise. . . *of Europe, Asia, Africa and America.* . . —CLARKE, Samuel. 1689#6

A new dictionary of trade and commerce. . . —ROLT, Richard. 1756#68

The new discoverer discover'd. . . *By way of an answer to Mr. Baxter.* . . —PIERCE, Thomas. 1659#28

A new discoverie of an old traveller lately arrived from Port-Dul... —1675#11

A new discovery of a vast country in America, extending above four thousand miles, between New France and New Mexico... —HENNEPIN, Lewis. 1698#8

New-England a degenerate plant. Who having forgot their former sufferings, and lost their ancient tenderness, are now become... —ROUS, John. 1659#30

New-England almanack... for xxx. years —SELLER, John. 1685#27

A New-England fire brand quenched, being something in answer unto... book entituled: George Fox digged out of his burrows, etc... —FOX, George, and BURNYEAT, John. 1678#6

New England judged... and the summe sealed up of New-England's persecutions... —BISHOP, George. 1661#3

New England judged... in two parts... Formerly published by G. Bishop, and now somewhat abbreviated. With an appendix... Also an answer... —BISHOP, George. 1703#4

New England judged. The second part... a relation of the cruel and bloody sufferings of... Quakers, in the jurisdiction chiefly of the Massachusetts... —BISHOP, George. 1667#1

New-England, or a brief enarration of the ayre, earth, water, fish and fowles of that country... in Latine and English verse. —MORRELL, William. 1625#10

New-England vindicated from the unjust aspersions cast on the former government there, by some late Considerations, pretending... —MATHER, Increase. 1689#21

New-England's ensigne: it being the account of cruelty, the professors pride, and the articles of new faith; signified in characters written in blood... —NORTON, Humphrey. 1659#26

New England's faction discovered; or a brief and true account of their persecution of the Church of England... —D., C. 1690#7

New Englands first fruits; in respect. First of the conversion of some, convictions of diverse, preparation of sundry of the... —ELIOT, John. 1643#7

New-Englands Jonas cast up in London: or, A relation of the proceedings of the court at Boston in New-England against divers honest and godly persons... —CHILD, John. 1647#4

New Englands lamentation for the late firing of the city of London. —COUCH, Robert. 1666#3

New Englands lamentations for old Englands present errours and divisions... —SHEPARD, Thomas. 1645#16

New-Englands plantation. Or, A short and true description of that countrey... —HIGGINSON, Francis. 1630#5

New-England's present sufferings, under their cruel neighbouring Indians. Represented in two letters, lately written from Boston to London. —WHARTON, Edward. 1675#15

New-England's pretended Christians, who contrary to Christ, have destroyed the lives of men. —SMITH, Humphrey. 1660#26

New England's prospect. A true, lively, and experimentall description of that part of America, commonly called New England... —WOOD, William. 1634#8

New Englands rarities discovered; in birds, beasts, fishes, serpents, and plants of that country... —JOSSELYN, John. 1672#5

New-Englands salamander, discovered by an irreligious and scornefull pamphlet, called New-England's Jonas... —WINSLOW, Edward. 1647#21

New-Englands sence, of old-England and Ireland sorrowes. A sermon preached upon a day of generall humiliation in the churches of New-England. —HOOKE, William. 1645#9

New Englands teares, for old Englands feares... sermon... July 23. 1640. —HOOKE, William. 1641#14

New England's tears for her present miseries: or, A late and true relation of the calamities of New-England since April last past... —TOMPSON, Benjamin. 1676#19

New Englands trials. Declaring the successe of 80 ships employed thither within these eight yeares... With the present estate... —SMITH, John. 1622#21

New English Canaan or New Canaan. Containing an abstract of New England, composed in three bookes... —MORTON, Thomas. 1637#5

A new essay on civil power in things sacred. —WATTS, Isaac. 1739#70

New essays on trade. —BREWSTER, Sir Francis. 1702#2

A new general English dictionary... Together with a supplement of the proper names of the most noted foreign kingdoms, provinces, cities, towns, rivers, etc... —DYCHE, Thomas. 1735#2

The new general history of birds... —1745#32

A new geographical and historical grammar... —SALMON, Thomas. 1749#36

New Hampshire. The (late) House of Representatives there, complainants. Jonathan Belcher esq, the governour there, respondent... —GREAT BRITAIN. PRIVY COUNCIL. 1739#9

New-Haven's settling in New-England. And some lawes for government: published for the use of their colony... —1656#10

A new military dictionary; or, the field of war... —ALMON, John. 1760#1

A new naval history: or, A compleat view of the British marine... —ENTICK, John. 1757#15

The new pilgrim's progress; or, the pious Indian convert... Together with a narrative of his... travels among the savage Indians for their conversion... —WALCOT, James. 1748#31

A new poetical translation of the Psalmes of David... —CRADOCK, Thomas. 1754#6

A new project to make England a florishing [sic] kingdom —1702#18

New Rome arraigned, and out of her own mouth condemned... —BUGG, Francis. 1693#3

A new scheme for increasing the Protestant religion, and improving the kingdom of Ireland... —1756#55

A new song. —1755#38

A new song sung by Mr. Beard. —1759#73

A new systeme of geography... — SELLER, John. 1685#28

A new voyage to Carolina; containing the exact description and natural history of that country... and a journal of a thousand mile travelled through several nations of Indians... —LAWSON, John. 1709#11

A new voyage to Georgia. By a young gentleman... his travels to South Carolina and part of North Carolina... —1735#14

New voyages to North-America. Containing an account of the several nations of that vast continent... Done into English... —LAHONTAN, Louis Armand de Lom d'Arce. 1703#9

A new wind-mil, a new. —CANNE, Abednego. 1643#2

The new world, or the new reformed church. Discovered out of the second epistle of Peter the third chap. verse 13 —HOMES, Nathaniel. 1641#13

Newes from America; or A new and experimentall discoverie of New England; containing, a true relation of their war-like proceedings... with a figure of the Indian fort, or palizado... —UNDERHILL, John. 1638#17

Newes from New-England in a letter written to a person of quality... —1690#18

Newes from New-England: of a most strange and prodigious birth, brought to Boston in New-England... Also other relations of six strange and prodigious births —1642#12

The Newlanders cure. As well of those violent sicknesses... as also by a cheape and newfound dyet, to preserve the body sound and free from all diseases... —VAUGHAN, William. 1630#10

News from New-England, being a true and last account of the present bloody wars carried on betwixt the infidels, natives, and the English Christians, and converted Indians of New-England... —1676#14

News from New-England: in a letter... —1689#22

News from New Rome, occasioned by the Quakers challenging of Francis Bug... News, Numb. I. —BUGG, Francis. 1701#12

News from Pensilvania: or a brief narrative of several remarkeable passages in the government of the Quakers in that province... —BUGG, Francis. 1703#5

The Newsman's interpreter, or a description of several Spanish territories in America; particularly of those places against which, it is supposed, the English have a design... —1741#28

Ninian Brice, John Orr of Barrowfield, Esq.... — BRYCE, William. 1740#7A

Ninian Brice, ship-master in Glasgow, and others, Apellants. William Brice, Merchant in Glasgow, Respondent. The Appellants Case. —BRICE, Ninian. 1740#6

The non-conformists plea for uniformity... judgement of... provincial assembly... and... preachers, English, Scottish, and New English, concerning toleration and uniformity... —1674#10

North America, a descriptive poem. Representing the voyage to America; a sketch of that beautiful country; with remarks upon the political humour and singular conduct of its inhabitants... —DONALDSON, William. 1757#10

North-West Fox or, Fox from the North-west passage... —FOX, Luke. 1635#1

The Northumberland garland. Containing four excellent new songs. —1759#74

A note of the shipping, men, and provisions, sent and provided for Virginia, by... Earle of Southampton, and the Company, and other private adventurers, in the yeere 1621... —VIRGINIA COMPANY. 1622#23

A note of the shipping, men, and provisions, sent and provided for Virginia, by... Earle of Southampton and the Company, this yeare, 1620. —VIRGINIA COMPANY. 1621#9

Nova Francia, or the description of that part of New France, which is one continent with Virginia... —LESCARBOT, Marc. 1625#9

The Nova Scotia's garland; furnished with three merry, new songs... —1750#35

Novus epigrammatum delectus: or, Original State epigrams and minor odes... —NEWCOMB, Thomas. 1760#70

Nummi Britannici Historia or An historical account of English money... —LEAKE, Stephen. 1726#11

Nuptial rites, or the several marriage ceremonies practised amongst all the nations of the world... —GAYA, Louis de. 1685#15

The objections against paying the remainder of the Canada bills of exchange, answered... —1716#5

Observations and reflections on the present practice, errors and mismanagement of the Governors and their Naval Officers, and the Clerks... —PARMYTER, Paroculus. 1720#24

Observations arising from the declaration of war against Spain, and the future management of it by Great Britain... —1739#53

Observations concerning indigo and cochineal... —CROKATT, James. 1746#7

Observations from the law of nature and nations, and the civil law; shewing that the British nation have an undoubted right... —1759#75

Observations occasion'd by reading a pamphlet, intitled, A discourse concerning the currencies of the British plantations in America. In a letter to ——. —SMITH, Wavell. 1741#35

Observations on Monsieur de Sorbier's voyage into England... —SPRAT, Thomas. 1665#20

Observations on the case of the northern colonies. —1731#26

Observations on The case of the planters of Virginia. In a letter to ——. —1733#27

Observations on the course of proceeding in admiralty courts in prize causes. —1747#17

Observations on the inhabitants, climate, soil, rivers... In his travels from Pensilvania to Onondago, Oswego and the Lake Ontario... —BARTRAM, John. 1751#6

Observations on the late and present conduct of the French, with regard to their encroachments upon the British colonies in North America. . . . —CLARKE, William. 1755#7

Observations on the present convention with Spain. —ROBINS, Benjamin. 1739#62

Observations on the probable issue of the Congress at Aix La-Chapelle. In a letter to a friend. —1748#17

Observations on the report of the Committee of Secrecy. —BANISTER, Thomas. 1715#3

Observations on the trade between Ireland, and the English and foreign colonies in America. In a letter to a friend. —PRIOR, Thomas. 1731#29

Observations on the trade carried on between our plantations and the foreign colonies in America: occasioned by a petition lately. . . . —HALL, Fayrer. 1731#19

Observations on trade and taxes; shewing what is required and necessary to rescue and increase the wealth and power of the British nation. . . . —POSTLETHWAYT, Malachy. 1751#28

Observations upon Prince Rupert's white dogge, called Boye, carefully taken by T. B. . . . —1643#16

Observations upon Remarks upon Mr. Whitefield; containing an answer thereto, and a vindication. . . . —1741#29

Observation upon the manifesto of his catholick majesty; with an answer to his reasons for not paying the ninety-five thousand pounds. . . . —1739#52

Occasional reflections on the importance of the war in America, and the reasonableness and justice of supporting the King of Prussia, etc. . . . —WILLIAMSON, Peter. 1758#50

An ode, in two parts, humbly inscribed to. . . William Pitt. . . . —1760#71

An ode, sacred to the memory of General Wolfe. —1759#77

An ode to the right honourable Sir Peter Warren. . . occasioned by the late signal success of the British navy. —1747#18

Of publick spirit in regard to publick works. An epistle to Frederick, Prince of Wales. —SAVAGE, Richard. 1737#23

Of regeneration and baptism, Hebrew and Christian, with their rites, etc. —ELDERFIELD, Christopher. 1653#7

Of schism. Parochial congregations in England, and ordination. . . . —FIRMIN, Giles. 1658#5

Of the conversion of five thousand and nine hundred East Indians. . . with a post-script of the Gospel's good successe also amongst the West-Indians, in New-England. . . . —SIBELIUS, Caspar. 1650#12

Of the holinesse of church-members. . . . —COTTON, John. 1650#3

Of the propagation of the gospel in foreign parts. A sermon preach'd. . . Feb. 18. 1703/4. . . . —BURNET, Gilbert. 1704#7

Of the propagation of the gospel in foreign parts. A sermon preached. . . Feb. 16 1704/5. . . . —HOUGH, John. 1705#13

Of the reconcileableness of the specifick medicines to the corpuscular philosophy. . . . —BOYLE, Robert. 1685#4

Of the truth and excellency of the gospel. A sermon preached. . . Friday the 20th of February 1712/13. . . . —MOORE, John. 1713#8

The offers of France explained. . . . —1712#20

The old paths restored. . . . —MATHER, Cotton. 1712#17

Old England for ever, or Spanish cruelty display'd; wherein the Spaniards right to America is impartially examined and found defective, their pretensions founded in blood. . . . —1740#27

Old John Uncas and the greater part of the tribe of Moheagan Indians, by Samuel Mason, their Guardian, Appellants. . . To be heard before. . . Privy Council. . . . —1700#31

One thousand seven hundred and fifty nine: a poem, inscribed to every Briton who bore a part in the service of that distinguished year. . . . —1760#72

The operations of the war for the first twelve months, examined and accounted for: from a late ministerial piece called, the grand question. —1740#28

The order of the gospel, professed and practised by the churches of Christ in New England. . . . —MATHER, Increase. 1700#29

Orders and articles granted by the. . . States General of the United Provinces, concerning the erecting of a West India Companie. . . . —UNITED PROVINCES. STATES GENERAL. 1621#7

Orders that tobacco on British ships should be of the growth of British colonies. —GREAT BRITAIN. COMMISSIONERS OF ADMIRALTY. 1725#7

An ordinance of the Lords and Commons. . . whereby Robert earle of Warwicke is made governour in chiefe, and lord high admirall of all. . . . —ENGLAND AND WALES. LORDS AND COMMONS. 1643#8

The ordinary, a comedy. —CARTWRIGHT, William. 1651#2

The ordinary of Newgate his account of the behaviour, confessions and dying words of Captain William Kidd, and other pyrates. . . . —LORRAIN, Paul. 1701#27

The origin of death, and of immortal life, considered. . . . —JENNINGS, David. 1743#17

Original and growth of the Spanish monarchy. . . . —PHILIPOT, Thomas. 1664#12

Original letters and papers of state, addressed to Oliver Cromwell. . . . —NICKOLLS, John. 1743#26

Original letters to an honest sailor. . . . —VERNON, Edward. 1746#27

The original manuscript account of the kingdom of Aacaniba, given by the affidavit of Mathieu Sagean a Frenchman. . . Englished by Quin Mackenzie. . . . —SAGEAN, Mathieu. 1755#45

Original paprrs [sic] relating to the expedition to Carthagena. . . . —VERNON, Edward. 1744#39

Origines sacrae: or, A rational account of the grounds of the Christian faith. —STILLINGFLEET, Edward. 1662#16

Ornaments for the daughters of Zion, or The character and happiness of a virtuous woman... —MATHER, Cotton. 1694#16

Ornithologia libri tres... —WILLUGHBY, Francis. 1686#6

The ornithology of Francis Willughby... —WILLUGHBY, Francis. 1678#7

Orphan-letters. Being a collection of letters wrote by the orphans in the hospital of Georgia. To the Reverend Mr George Whitefield... —WHITEFIELD, George. 1741#53

The orthodox evangelist. Or a treatise wherein many great evangelical truths... are briefly discussed... —NORTON, John. 1654#13

Our ancient testimony renewed... occasioned... by several unjust charges... by G. Keith... Given forth... at Philadelphia... —OWEN, Griffith?. 1695#21

Our duty as patriots, protestants and Christians... a sermon preached... May 23... on occasion of the public declaration of war against the French king, May 18, 1756. —GIBBONS, Thomas. 1756#35

Our saviour's divine sermon on the mount... explained... —BLAIR, James. 1722#2

Ovid's Metamorphosis Englished by G. S... —SANDYS, George. 1626#2

Owaneko, chief Sachem or prince of the Mohegan-Indians in New-England, his letter to a gentleman now in Lond: faithfully translated... —1704#20

Pacata Britannia. A panegyrick to the queen, on the peace... —NEWCOMB, Thomas. 1713#9

A pack of patentees. opened. shuffled. cut. dealt. and played. —1641#17

The Palatine's catechism, or A true description of their camps at Blackheath and Camberwell. In a dialogue between an English tradesman and a High-Dutchman —1709#17

The Pancronometer, or universal Georgian calendar... —JONES, Hugh. 1753#14

Panourgia. A brief review of Mr Davis's vindication... —FIRMIN, Giles. 1693#6

Pansebeia: or, a view of all religions in the world... throughout Asia, Africa, America, and Europe. —ROSS, Alexander. 1653#16

The panther-prophesy, or, a premonition to all people... —LLOYD, Owen. 1662#10

Paper currency in North-America. —1751#23

A paper to William Penn, at the departure of that gentleman to his territory... —HUMFREY, John. 1700#19

Papers presented to the committee appointed to inquire into the state and condition of the countries adjoining to Hudson's Bay, and of the trade carried on there. —GREAT BRITAIN. PARLIAMENT. HOUSE OF COMMONS COMMITTEE. 1749#23

Papers relating to an affidavit made by... James Blair... against Francis Nicholson... Printed in the year 1727. —1727#19

Papers relating to the Quakers tythe bill. —1736#15

A parable against persecution... —FRANKLIN, Benjamin. 1759#34

The parable of the ten virgins opened and applied: being the substance of divers sermons on Matth. 25. 1, — 13... —SHEPARD, Thomas. 1660#25

Paradisi in sole paradisus terrestris... —PARKINSON, John. 1629#2

A paraenetick or humble addresse to the Parliament and assembly for (not loose, but) Christian libertie. —WILLIAMS, Roger. 1644#22

A parallel between the faith and doctrine of the present Quakers and that of the chief hereticks in all ages... —LESLIE, Charles. 1700#26

The parallel... the renewal of our Prussian treaty. —MAUDUIT, Israel. 1742#29

A paraphrase upon the Psalmes of David... —SANDYS, George. 1636#5

Part of Du Bartas, English and French... Englished... —DU BARTAS, Guillaume de Salluste. 1625#3

A particular account of the taking Cape Breton... by Admiral Warren and Sir W. Pepperell, 17th June, 1745, with... a letter from... —DURRELL, Philip. 1745#17

The particulars of an Indian treaty at Conestogoe, between... Sir William Keith, governor of Pennsylvania, and the deputies of the Five nations... —PENNSYLVANIA PROVINCE. 1722#23

Party spirit in times of publick danger, considered... —1756#56

Party-tyranny: or, an occasional bill in miniature as now practised in Carolina. Humbly offered to the consideration of... Parliament. —DEFOE, Daniel. 1705#7

The paterne of perfection: exhibited in Gods image on Adam... —HOOKER, Thomas. 1640#5

The pay of the garrisons in Ireland Gibraltar Minorca & ye plantations. The half-pay of the officers of the Navy & of the Army... —GREAT BRITAIN. ARMY. REGULATIONS. 1740. 1741#15

Peculium Dei. A discourse about the Jews. —HICKES, George. 1681#13

The Pensilv[ania] Bubble bubbled by the Treasurer, or, an account of his admitting purchasers for shares... —HOSKINS, James. 1726#8

The people called Quakers cleared by Geo. Keith from the false doctrines charged on them by G. Keith... —PENINGTON, John. 1696#22

A perfect description of Virginia: being, a full and true relation of the present state of the plantation... Also, a narration... —1649#5

The perfect politician. —FLETCHER, Henry. 1660#9

The perfidious brethren, or, the religious triumvirate: displayed in three ecclesiastic novels. . . —BLACKAMORE, Arthur. 1720#5

The perpetuity of the Christian religion, a sermon preached in the High Church of Edinburgh, Monday January 3d, 1737; upon occasion. . . —NISBET, James. 1737#20

Persecution exposed, in some memoirs relating to the sufferings of John Whiting, and many. . . *Quakers.* . . —WHITING, John. 1715#24

Peters patern newly revived. . . *a funeral sermon preached at the internment of Mr Hugh Peters.* . . —CARYL, Joseph?. 1659#3

Petition for Thomas Breakenrig messenger in Edinburgh; against [blank] Newlands and others. —BREAKENRIG, Thomas. 1725#2

The petition of Mr Kenneth Gordon of Cluny, advocate. 26 November 1731. —GORDON, Kenneth. 1731#14

A petition of W. C. exhibited to the high court of Parliamen[t] now assembled, for the propagating of the gospel in America. . . —CASTELL, William. 1641#2

Pharmacologia, seu Manuductio ad materiam medicam. . . —DALE, Samuel. 1693#5

The phenix: or, A revival of scarce and valuable pieces from the remotest antiquity down to the present time. —DUNTON, John, comp. 1707#6

The philosophical grammar; being a view of the present state of experimental physiology. —MARTIN, Benjamin. 1735#12

A philosophical treatise of the original and production of things. Writ in America in a time of solitudes. . . —FRANCK, Richard. 1687#5

The philosophy of earthquakes, natural and religious. —STUKELEY, William. 1750#49

Phylomythie or phylomythologie. . . *Second edition, much inlarged.* —SCOT, Thomas. 1622#20

Physical disquisitions: demonstrating the real causes of the blood's morbid rarefaction and stagnation. . . —TENNENT, John, M. D. 1745#36

Physical enquiries: discovering the mode of translation in the constitutions of northern inhabitants, on going to, and for some time after arriving in southern climates. . . —TENNENT, John, M. D. 1742#47

The picture of Quakerism drawn to the life. . . —BUGG, Francis. 1697#6

Pietas Hallensis: or, an abstract of the marvellous foot-steps of divine providence, attending the management and improvement. . . —FRANCKE, August Hermann. 1716#3

Pietas in patrium: the life of his excellency Sir William Phips, Knt. . . —MATHER, Cotton. 1697#10

Piety promoted, in a collection of dying sayings of many of the people called Quakers. With a brief account of some of their labours in the Gospel, and sufferings. . . —TOMKINS, John. 1701#41

The pilgrim's progress, from Quakerism, to Christianity. —BUGG, Francis. 1698#3

A pindaric poem on the propagation of the gospel in foreign parts. —SETTLE, Elkanah(?). 1711#28

A plain and friendly perswasive to the inhabitants of Virginia and Maryland, for promoting towns and cohabitation. . . —MAKEMIE, Francis. 1705#15

A plain discovery of many gross falshoods, cheats and impostures —KEITH, George. 1701#26

Plain dealing: or, Newes from New-England. . . *A short view of New-Englands present government, both ecclesiastical and civil* —LECHFORD, Thomas. 1642#11

Plain instructions for inoculation in the small-pox; by which any person may be enabled to perform the operation, and conduct the patient through the distemper. —HEBERDEN, William, 1710-1801. 1759#46

Plain reasons for removing a certain great man from his m———y's presence and councils for ever. —CARLYLE, Alexander. 1759#13

A plaine path-way to plantations. —EBURNE, Richard. 1624#4

A plan for establishing and disciplining a national militia in Great Britain, Ireland, and in all the British dominions of America. —MARTIN, Samuel. 1745#28

A plan for establishing the general peace of Europe upon honourable terms to Great Britain. . . —BRECKNOCK, Timothy. 1759#7

A plan of the English commerce. . . —DEFOE, Daniel. 1728#7

Plantation work the work of this generation. Written in true-love to all such as are weightily inclined to transplant themselves. . . —LODDINGTON, William. 1682#19

Planter's charity. —MANDEVILLE, Bernard. 1704#18

The planter's plea. Or the grounds of plantations examined, and usual objections answered. Together with a manifestation of the causes. . . —WHITE, John. 1630#11

The planter's speech to his neighbors and country-men of Pennsylvania, East and West-Jersey, and to all such as have transported themselves into new colonies. . . —TRYON, Thomas. 1684#11

A platform of church discipline. . . —MATHER, Richard. 1652#9

A platform of church discipline. . . *agreed upon by the elders and messengers.* . . *at Cambridge in New-England.* . . —MATHER, Richard. 1653#13

Plays written by the late ingenious Mrs. Behn, entire in two volumes. . . —BEHN, Aphra. 1702#1

The pleasant art of money-catching. —H., N. 1684#6

Plus ultra: or, the progress and advancement of knowledge since the days of Aristotle. —GLANVILL, Joseph. 1668#3

A poem. Inscrib'd to the Right Honourable Sir Robert Walpole, on the success of His Majesty's arms in America. —C-, H. 1741#3

A poem on the death of His Highness the Duke of Gloucester. Written by a gentleman in New-England. —GENTLEMAN IN NEW-ENGLAND. 1701#22

A poem on the death of the late Thomas Hollis, Esq., humbly inscribed to Mr John Hollis, brother of the deceased... —RUDD, Sayer. 1731#31

A poem on the late massacre in Virginia. With particular mention of those men of note that suffered in that disaster. —BROOKE, Christopher. 1622#5

A poem on the taking of Cape Breton and Cherbourg... —CATTON, William. 1760#19

A poem, to his excellency the Lord Privy-Seal, on the prospect of peace. —TICKELL, Thomas. 1713#14

A poem. To the memory of Aquila Rose, who dyed at Philadelphia, August the 22d, 1723... —BOCKETT, Elias. 1724#4

Poems moral and divine, on the following subjects... To which is added some account of the author. —AMERICAN GENTLEMAN. 1756#3

Poems on several occasions. —LENNOX, Charlotte. 1747#14

A political essay upon commerce. Written in French by Monsieur M———. Tr., with some annotation and remarks by David Bindon, esq. —MELON, Jean François. 1738#17

A political essay upon the English and French colonies in northern and southern America, considered in a new light... —PATRIOT. 1760#74

Political Arithmetick, or a discourse concerning, the extent and value of lands people... —PETTY, William. 1690#21

Political thoughts. Printed in the year 1760. —1760#77

The politicks on both sides, with regard to foreign affairs, stated from their own writings... —PULTENEY, William. 1734#16

The poor unhappy transported felon's sorrowful account of fourteen years transportation, at Virginia in America. In six parts... —REVEL, James. 1750#42

The popish inquisition newly erected in New-England, whereby their church is manifested to be a daughter of mysterie Babylon... —HOWGILL, Francis. 1659#18

Popular prejudices against the convention and treaty with Spain, examined and answered... —1739#54

The possibility and reality of magick, sorcery and witchcraft... In answer to Dr. Hutchinson's Historical essay... —BOULTON, Richard. 1722#4

The power of Christ vindicated, against the magick of apostacy: in answer to George Keith's book... The magick of Quakerism. —WHITEHEAD, George. 1708#17

The power of Congregational churches asserted and vindicated. —DAVENPORT, John. 1672#3

The powring out of the seven vials: or, An exposition of the 16. chapter of the Revelation —COTTON, John. 1642#7

A practical commentary, or an exposition... upon the first epistle generall of John... —COTTON, John. 1656#5

A practical discourse of prayer... by Thomas Cobbet, minister of the word at Lyn. —COBBET, Thomas. 1654#4

Practical discourses upon the parable of the ten virgins... —COLMAN, Benjamin. 1707#3

A practical essay concerning the small-pox. —DOUGLASS, William. 1730#8

The practical husbandman and planter... —1733#28

A practical treatise upon several different and useful subjects... IV. A rational way for the promulgation of the gospel in America... —TATE, Robert. 1732#41

Premiums by the Society, established at London, for the encouragement of arts, manufactures and commerce... —SOCIETY FOR THE ENCOURAGEMENT OF ARTS. 1758#43

A premonition of sundry sad calamities... —ASPINWALL, William. 1655#2

Presbyterial ordination vindicated. In a brief and sober discourse concerning episcopacy... —FIRMIN, Giles. 1660#8

The presbyterian and independent churches in New-England and elsewhere brought to the test... —KEITH, George. 1691#10

The present embargo on cheese and butter prevents the same from being exported to any of his majesty's dominions abroad, likewise to Holland and Hambro... —1746#17

The present interest of England stated... —BETHEL, Slingsby. 1671#2

The present state of Carolina with advice to the setlers... —F., R. 1682#13

The present state of Christendome and the interest of England, with regard to France —1677#15

The present state of his majesties isles and territories in America, viz. Jamaica... New Jersey, Pensilvania... Carolina, Virginia... —BLOME, Richard. 1687#1

The present state of Ireland —1673#10

The present state of Mr. Wood's partnership —1720#26

The present state of New-England. Being a narrative of the troubles with the Indians... To which is added a discourse about the war with the Pequods in the year 1677... —HUBBARD, William. 1677#7

The present state of NEW-ENGLAND, with respect to the Indian War. Wherein is an account of the true reason thereof... Licenced December 13, 1675... —1675#12

The present state of North America... Part I. —HUSKE, Ellis. 1755#29

The present state of popery in England... —E., R. 1733#14

The present state of the British and French sugar colonies, and our own northern colonies, considered... —PERRIN, William. 1740#29

The present state of the British and French trade to Africa and America consider'd and compar'd... —ASHLEY, John. 1745#4

The present state of the British sugar colonies consider'd: in a letter from a gentleman of Barbadoes to his friend in London. —ASHLEY, John?. 1731#2

The present state of the colony of West-Jersey, in America —1681#19

The present state of the country and inhabitants, Europeans and Indians, of Louisiana, on the north continent of America. By an officer of New Orleans to his friend at Paris. —CHAMPIGNY, Jean. 1744#10

The present state of the Islands in the Archipelago, (or Arches) Sea of Constantinople, and Gulf of Smyrna. . . —RANDOLPH, Bernard. 1687#8

The present state of the Protestant religion in Maryland, under the government of Francis Nicholson Esq. by Dr Bray. . . —BRAY, Thomas. 1700#7

The present state of the revenue and forces. . . of France and Spain. . . —1740#30

The present state of the tobacco-plantations in America —1709#20

The present state of the tobacco-trade, as the late act affects the London-manufacturers considered; in a letter to a friend. —1751#29

The present state of Virginia, and the college; by Messieurs Hartwell, Blair and Chilton. . . the charter for erecting the said college. . . —HARTWELL, Henry, BLAIR, James and CHILTON, Edward. 1727#13

The present state of Virginia. Giving a particular and short account of the Indian, English, and negroe inhabitants of that colony. . . —JONES, Hugh. 1724#11

Presumptive reasons why the governments of the provinces of South and North Carolina, and the Bahama and Lucaios Islands being. . . —1715#20

A pretended voice from heaven, proved to bee the voice of men, and not of God. . . —CHARKE, Ezekiel. 1659#4

The pretended yearly meeting of the Quakers. . . the evil and wicked practises of them in Pensilvania. —KEITH, George. 1695#15

The primitive origination of mankind, considered and examined according to the light of nature. —HALE, Matthew. 1677#4

The principles of action in matter, the gravitation of bodies, and the motion of the planets, explained from their principles. —COLDEN, Cadwallader. 1751#11

Principles of polity, being the grounds and reasons of civil empire. . . —POWNALL, Thomas. 1752#14

The principles of the leading Quakers truly represented. —S., T. 1732#36

The principles of the Quakers further shewn to be blasphemous and seditious. . . —BECKHAM, Edward. 1700#1

The private character of Admiral Anson. —HUTCHINSON, J. Mrs. 1747#12

Private-men no pulpit men: or, A modest examination of lay-mens preaching. . . —WORKMAN, Giles. 1646#22

Private virtue and publick spirit displayed. In a succinct essay on the character of Capt. Thomas Coram. . . —1751#30

The proceedings of the Kings commission of the peace. . . held for the tryal of Captain William Kidd. . . May 1701. —1701#36

Proclamation against the disorderly transporting his majesties subjects. . . to America. —ENGLAND AND WALES. SOVEREIGN. CHARLES I. 1637#1

Proclamation. Appointing distribution of prizes taken before His Majesty's declaration of war 18 June 1741. —GREAT BRITAIN. LORD JUSTICES. 1741#18

Proclamation. Appointing distribution of prizes taken since the declaration of war. [18 June 1741]. —GREAT BRITAIN. LORDS JUSTICES. 1741#19

Proclamation. At the Court at Kensington, the second day of October, 1721. . . —GREAT BRITAIN. SOVEREIGN. GEORGE I. 1721#8

Proclamation. By the Lords Justices. Hardwicke, C. Hartington, Granville, P. Holdernesse. —GREAT BRITAIN. LORDS JUSTICES. 1752#7

Proclamation by the Rt. Honourable William Beeston, Kt. Governor of Jamaica. . . 8th day of April 1699.—BEESTON, William. 1699#2

Proclamation completing number of Nova Scotia baronets. —SCOTLAND. PRIVY COUNCIL. 1625#12

Proclamation concerning tobacco. . . —ENGLAND AND WALES. SOVEREIGN. CHARLES I. 1634#2

Proclamation concerning tobacco. . . —ENGLAND AND WALES. SOVEREIGN. CHARLES I. 1639#2

Proclamation concerning tobacco. . . —ENGLAND AND WALES. SOVEREIGN. CHARLES I. 1638#10

Proclamation concerning tobacco. . . —ENGLAND AND WALES. SOVEREIGN. CHARLES I. 1631#1

Proclamation concerning tobacco. . . —ENGLAND AND WALES. SOVEREIGN. JAMES I. 1624#6

Proclamation continuing embargo on ships carrying provisions. . . [13 September 1758]. —IRELAND. LORDS JUSTICES. 1758#28

Proclamation declaring. . . a free port at his city of Tanger. . . [16 November 1662.] —ENGLAND AND WALES. SOVEREIGN. CHARLES II. 1662#4

Proclamation, declaring what ensigns or colours shall be born at sea in merchant ships or vessels belonging to any of her majesties. . . —ENGLAND AND WALES. SOVEREIGN. ANNE. 1707#7

Proclamation discharging transporting of persons to the plantations of forraigners. . . [27 December 1698.] —SCOTLAND. PRIVY COUNCIL. 1698#16

Proclamation dispensing with clauses in Navigation Act [22 March 1664/5.] —ENGLAND AND WALES. SOVEREIGN. CHARLES II. 1665#16

Proclamation for a public thanksgiving in England and Wales for defeat of French. [23 October 1759]. —GREAT BRITAIN. SOVEREIGN. GEORGE II. 1759#40

Proclamation for a public thanksgiving in Ireland for defeat of French. [30 October 1759]. —GREAT BRITAIN. SOVEREIGN. GEORGE II. 1759#41

Proclamation for a public thanksgiving in Scotland for the defeat of French. [23 October 1759]. —GREAT BRITAIN. SOVEREIGN. GEORGE II. 1759#42

Proclamation for apprehension of pirates [6 March 1700/1]. —ENGLAND AND WALES. SOVEREIGN. WILLIAM III. 1701#19

Proclamation for continuing all officers in their places. 9 March 1701/2]. —ENGLAND AND WALES. SOVEREIGN. ANNE. 1702#10

Proclamation for continuing officers in colonies. [6 February 1684/5.] —ENGLAND AND WALES. SOVEREIGN. JAMES II. 1685#11

Proclamation for continuing officers in His majesty's Plantations... [5 July 1727]. —GREAT BRITAIN. SOVEREIGN. GEORGE II. 1727#12

Proclamation for continuing officers in plantations till his majesty's pleasure shall be further signified... 27 October 1760]. —GREAT BRITAIN. SOVEREIGN. GEORGE III. 1760#44

Proclamation for continuing the officers in... plantations [22 November 1714]. —GREAT BRITAIN. SOVEREIGN. GEORGE I. 1714#9

Proclamation for encouraging trade to Newfoundland. [26 June 1708]. —GREAT BRITAIN. SOVEREIGN. ANNE. 1708#8

Proclamation for enforcing act establishing General Post Office in Dominions 23 June 1711]. —GREAT BRITAIN. SOVEREIGN. ANNE. 1711#10

Proclamation for Newfoundland. Whereas, William and Mary [have been proclaimed King and Queen of England, France and Ireland... —1689#24

Proclamation for prohibiting the importation of commodities of Europe into any of his majesties plantations in Africa, Asia, or America... —ENGLAND AND WALES. SOVEREIGN. CHARLES II. 1675#5

Proclamation for protection of Royal African Company [30 November 1674.] —ENGLAND AND WALES. SOVEREIGN. CHARLES II. 1674#2

Proclamation for recalling dispensations in the Navigation Acts [23 August 1667.] —ENGLAND AND WALES. SOVEREIGN. CHARLES II. 1667#5

Proclamation for setling the plantation of Virginia. —ENGLAND AND WALES. SOVEREIGN. CHARLES I. 1625#4

Proclamation for settling and ascertaining the current rates of coin in her majesties colonies and plantations in America [18 June 1704]. —ENGLAND AND WALES. SOVEREIGN. ANNE. 1704#15

Proclamation for suppressing pirates in West Indies or adjoining to our plantations [5 September 1717]. —GREAT BRITAIN. SOVEREIGN. GEORGE I. 1717#7

Proclamation for suppressing pirates in West Indies or adjoining to our plantations [21 December 1718]. —GREAT BRITAIN. SOVEREIGN. GEORGE I. 1718#10

Proclamation for suppressing the lottery in Virginia and all others... —ENGLAND AND WALES. SOVEREIGN. JAMES I. 1621#1

Proclamation for the due observation of certain statutes made for the suppressing of rogues, vagabonds... [9 May 1661.] —ENGLAND AND WALES. SOVEREIGN. CHARLES II. 1661#6

Proclamation for the more effectual reducing and suppressing of pirates and privateers in America... [20 January 1687/8.] —ENGLAND AND WALES. SOVEREIGN. JAMES II. 1688#6

Proclamation for the ordering of tobacco... —ENGLAND AND WALES. SOVEREIGN. CHARLES I. 1627#2

Proclamation for the suppressing a rebellion lately raised... Virginia... [27 October 1676.] —ENGLAND AND WALES. SOVEREIGN. CHARLES II. 1676#2

Proclamation for the utter prohibiting the importation of... all tobacco... not of... Virginia and the Summer Islands... —ENGLAND AND WALES. SOVEREIGN. JAMES I. 1625#6

Proclamation forbidding the disorderly trading with the salvages in New England... —ENGLAND AND WALES. SOVEREIGN. CHARLES I. 1630#3

Proclamation of declaration of war against France. [29 March 1744]. —GREAT BRITAIN. SOVEREIGN. GEORGE II. 1744#22

Proclamation of declaration of war against the French King. [17 May 1756]. —GREAT BRITAIN. SOVEREIGN. GEORGE II. 1756#41

Proclamation of grant of Pennsylvania to William Penn [2 April 1681.] —ENGLAND AND WALES. SOVEREIGN. CHARLES II. 1681#7

Proclamation on institution of Nova Scotia baronets. —SCOTLAND. PRIVY COUNCIL. 1624#10

Proclamation prohibiting interloping and disorderly trading to New England in America... the sixty [sic] of November... [1622]. —ENGLAND AND WALES. SOVEREIGN. JAMES I. 1622#13

Proclamation prohibiting trade within limits of the Hudson's Bay Company. [31 March 1688.] —ENGLAND AND WALES. SOVEREIGN. JAMES II. 1688#7

Proclamation providing for distribution of prize money. [19 June 1740]. —GREAT BRITAIN. LORDS JUSTICES. 1740#14

Proclamation regarding distribution of prizes [14 June 1744]. —GREAT BRITAIN. SOVEREIGN. GEORGE II. 1744#23

Proclamation, requiring all ships and vessels, trading from the plantations in the way of the Algerines, to furnish themselves with passes [4 October 1714]. —GREAT BRITAIN. SOVEREIGN. GEORGE I. 1714#10

Proclamation requiring passes formerly granted for ships trading in way of Algerine cruizers to be returned for reissue [19 July 1722]. —GREAT BRITAIN. SOVEREIGN. GEORGE I. 1722#16

Proclamation requiring passes formerly granted to ships trading in way of Algerine cruizers to be returned for reissue [31 December 1729]. —GREAT BRITAIN. SOVEREIGN. GEORGE II. 1729#18

Proclamation restraining the abusive venting of tobacco... —ENGLAND AND WALES. SOVEREIGN. CHARLES I. 1634#3

Proclamation that if any protected person is murdered and the murderers go free four papists shall be transported in their place to America [18 April 1655.] —IRELAND. BY THE LORD DEPUTY AND COUNCIL. 1655#15

Proclamation to give assurance unto all his majesties subjects in the islands and continent of America. —ENGLAND AND WALES. SOVEREIGN. CHARLES I. 1643#9

Proclamation to prohibit his majesties subjects from trading within the limits assigned to the Royal African Company... [1 April 1685.] —ENGLAND AND WALES. SOVEREIGN. JAMES II. 1685#10

Proclamation to restraine the transporting of passengers and provisions to New England, without licence... [1 May 1638.] —ENGLAND AND WALES. SOVEREIGN. CHARLES I. 1638#9

Proclamation touching the sealing of tobacco. —ENGLAND AND WALES. SOVEREIGN. CHARLES I. 1627#3

Proclamation touching tobacco. —ENGLAND AND WALES. SOVEREIGN. CHARLES I. 1627#4

Proclamation touching tobacco. —ENGLAND AND WALES. SOVEREIGN. CHARLES I. 1625#5

Proclamation voiding all orders and licences for transportation of idle and vagabond persons to the West Indies. [4 March 1656/7.] —IRELAND. LORD DEPUTY AND COUNCIL. 1657#10

Proclamation. Whereas by an act passed this present session... for the more effectual securing and encouraging the trade... GREAT BRITAIN. SOVEREIGN. GEORGE II. 1740#16

The profession of faith of... Mr J. D... Made publiquely before the congregation at his admission into one of the churches of God in New-England. —DAVENPORT, John. 1642#9

The profit and loss of Great Britain and Spain, from the commencement of the present war to this time, impartially stated... —PHILALETHES. 1742#35

Profitable advice for rich and poor. In a dialogue between James Freeman, a Carolina planter, and Simon Question, a West-Country... —NORRIS, John. 1712#19

The progress of the French in their views of universal monarchy... —1756#62

The prologue and epilogue to the History of Bacon in Virginia. —DRYDEN, John. 1689#9

Prolusio inauguralis, de usu vesicantium, quae cantharides recipiunt, in febribus... —MOORE, Charles. 1752#12

The promise of God proclaimed... preached by the apostles and by his servants and messengers sent forth since for Barbados, New-England, Virginia... to go to them all... —FOX, George. 1660#12

A proper reply to a late scurrilous libel; intituled Sedition and defamation displayed... —PULTENEY, William. 1731#30

A prophetic fragment of a future chronicle. By the author of the Four Letters to the People of England. —SHEBBEARE, John?. 1756#72

A proposal for humbling Spain. Written in 1711. By a person of distinction. And now first printed... —1739#55

A proposal for propagating the Christian religion... offered to the Queen's most excellent majesty, who by those... means may now be the foundress of a new empire... —1710#15

A proposal for putting a speedy end to the war, by ruining the commerce of the French and the Spaniards... —DENNIS, John. 1703#7

Proposal for raising a stock, and settling a new colony in Azilia... —MONTGOMERY, Robert, Sir. 1717#14

A proposal for raising a stock not exceeding forty thousand pounds sterling; by subscriptions for forming a settlement, in a large... —MARSH, Henry. 1716#4

A proposal for the better supplying of churches in our foreign plantations, and for converting the savage Americans to Christianity... —BERKELEY, George. 1724#2

A proposal humbly offered to the... Commons... for improving the woollen manufacture, for raising 3000000L on funds never yet imposed in this reign... and for other ends and purposes... —1710#16

Proposals by the proprietors of East-Jersey in America; for the building of a town on Ambo-Point, and for the disposition of lands... And for the encouragement of artificers and labourers... —1682#22

Proposals, concerning the propagating of Christian knowledge, in... Scotland and foreign parts of the world. —KIRKWOOD, James. 1706#14

Proposals for carrying on an effectual war in America, against the French and Spaniards. —1702#21

Proposals for carrying on the war with vigour, raising the supplies within the year, and forming a national militia. . . — RUFFHEAD, Owen. 1757#38

Proposals for clearing land in Carolina, Pennsylvania, East Jersey, West Jersey: or any other parts of America. . . August 9, 1682. —SOMERS, Nathan. 1682#25

Proposals for printing an essay towards a natural history of Florida, Carolina, and the Bahama islands; containing twelve coloured plates. . . —CATESBY, Mark. 1730#3

Proposals for printing by subscription, in one volume in folio, A. De La Motraye's voyages lately performed through Maryland. . . —1730#26

Proposals for printing by subscription, the history of the publick life and distinguished actions of Vice-Admiral Sir Thomas Brazen. . . —THUMB, Thomas. 1760#94

Proposals for settling a colony in Florida. —1698#15

Proposals for the incouragement and promoting of religion. . . —BRAY, Thomas. 1695#3

Proposals for uniting the English colonies on the continent of America so as to enable them to act with force and vigour against their enemies. —McCULLOH, Henry. 1757#26

Proposals to the legislature, for preventing the frequent execution and exportations of convicts. . . —STUDENT IN POLITICS. 1754#38

Proposals to the public, especially those in power. . . to save Great-Britain, likewise to regain. . . Minorca, besides our late possessions in America. . . —RAILTON, John. 1758#38

A proposition of provisions needfull for such as intend to plant themselves in New England, for one whole yeare. Collected by the adventurers, with the advice of the planters. —COUNCIL FOR NEW ENGLAND. 1630#2

Propositions concerning the subject of baptism and consociation of churches. . . by a synod. . . of the churches in Massachusetts-colony. . . —MITCHEL, Jonathan. 1662#11

A prospect of the most famous parts of the world. Together with that large theater of Great Brittaines empire —SPEED, John. 1627#7

A prospective plan of the battle near Lake George, on the eighth day of September, 1755. With an explanation thereof; Containing. . . —BLODGET, Samuel. 1756#9

The pr-t-st of the m——ch——ts of G——t B——n against the Pr-1-m——ry A-t—— s for a peace lately signed at A-x la Ch-pp—le. —1748#20

The providences of God observed through several ages towards this nation. —BETHEL, Slingsby. 1691#2

Pteri-graphia americana; icones continens filicum nec non muscos, lichenes, fungos, corallia. . . ex insulis nostra Charibbaeis. . . —PETIVER, James. 1712#21

Publick good without private interest. . . —GATFORD, Lionel. 1657#8

The publick having been imposed on, by several very imperfect and erroneous lists. . . —1739#56

The publick spirit; a poem. . . —FOX, John. 1718#5

Publick spirit, illustrated in the life and designs of the Reverend Thomas Bray D. D. —SMITH, Samuel. 1746#25

Purchas his pilgrim. Microcosmus, or The historie of man. —PURCHAS, Samuel. 1627#5

Purchase his Pilgrimage. Or Relations of the world and all ages and places discovered. —PURCHAS, Samuel. 1626#1

Purchas his pilgrimes. —PURCHAS, Samuel. 1625#11

The Quaker and Methodist compared, in an abstract of Geo. Fox's journal, with his will, and the Rev. Geo. Whitefiel ''; journal, with historical notes. —GREY, Zachary. 1740#18

Quakerism withering, and Christianity reviving or, A brief reply to the Quakers pretended vindication. . . —BUGG, Francis. 1694#1

The Quakers cleared from being apostates. . . —COOLE, Benjamin. 1696#7

The Quakers confuted. . . —EATON, Samuel. 1654#10

The Quakers downfal. . . also a brief narration of the Quakers conference with us the second of July 1659. wherein we made it appear. . . —CLARKSON [or CLAXTON], Laurence. 1659#6

The Quakers farewel to England, or their voyage to New Jersey, scituate on the continent of Virginia, and bordering upon New England. . . —1675#13

A Quakers Sea-Journal: being a true relation of a voyage to New-England. Performed by Robert Fowler of the Town of Burlington in Yorkshire, in the year 1658. . . —FOWLER, Robert. 1659#12

The Quakers set in their true light. . . —BUGG, Francis. 1696#2

Quaternio, or A fourefold way to a happie life. . . —NASH, Thomas. 1633#4

Quebec: a poetical essay, in imitation of the Miltonic style: Being a regular narrative of. . . transactions. . . under. . . Saunders and. . . Wolfe. . . . —PATRICK J. 1760#73

Queries of highest consideration proposed to Mr Thomas Goodwin. . . And to the Commissioners of the General Assembly (so-called) of the Church of Scotland. . . —WILLIAMS, Roger. 1644#23

The question relating to a Scots militia considered. . . —CARLYLE, Alexander. 1760#16

Quodlibets, lately come over from New Britaniola, Old Newfoundland. Epigrams and other small parcels, both morall and divine. . . —HAYMAN, Robert. 1628#1

Rabshakeh's retreat. A sermon preached. . . December 18, 1745. —STENNETT, Joseph. 1745#35

The Raree show ballad or the English Missisippi. . . —1720#27

The Raree Show, or the sad case of Monsieur Ragou. . . —1759#83

The real and true case of the planters in Virginia. —B., L. 1733#1

The real Christian, or a Treatise of effectual calling. . . —FIRMIN, Giles. 1670#7

The real crisis: or, the necessity of giving immediate and powerful succour to the emperor against France. . . —REVOLUTION, William. 1735#17

Reasonable religion: or the truths of the Christian religion demonstrated. . . —MATHER, Cotton. 1713#6

The reasonableness, pleasure and benefit of national thanksgiving. A sermon preached Nov. 29, 1759 at Ipswich. . . Suffolk. . . —SCOTT, Thomas. 1759#87

Reasons against a general prohibition of the iron manufacture in his Majesty's plantations. —1719#8

Reasons against making barr-iron in America. —1718#15

Reasons against the independent government of particular congregations. . . as also against the toleration of such churches. —EDWARDS, Thomas. 1641#10

Reasons for a general peace. Addressed to the legislature. . . —1759#84

Reasons for a war against Spain. In a letter from a merchant of London trading to America, to a member of the House of Commons. . . —D., L. 1737#9

Reasons for a war with France. —PITTIS, William. 1715#19

Reasons for allowing the importation of bar-iron from America. —1756#63

Reasons for an immediate war against France. . . —1740#31

Reasons for encourageing the making of iron in our plantations, and the objections answer'd. —1719#9

Reasons for encouraging the importation of iron from our plantations. . . —1720#28

Reasons for encouraging the importation of iron in bars from His Majesty's plantations in America. —1737#22

Reasons for encouraging the importation of timber, plank, boards, and other wood, from her majesty's plantations, by taking off the custom, or allowing a bounty money thereon. . . —1711#22

Reasons for establishing the colony of Georgia, with regard to the trade of Great Britain, the increase of our people. . . employment. . . —MARTYN, Benjamin. 1733#24

Reasons for giving encouragement to the sea-faring people of Great-Britain, in times of peace or war. . . —1739#58

Reasons for importing naval stores from our own plantations, and the employing of our people there. —1720#29

Reasons for laying a duty on French and Spanish Indico, and granting a bounty on what is made in the British plantations. —1748#21

Reasons for leave to import Tarr, otherwise than from the places of its growth. —1704#22

Reasons for making of bar, as well as pig or sow-iron in His Majesty's plantations. —1720#30

Reasons for making pigg-iron, and against making barr-iron in America. —1720#31

Reasons for not restoring Guadeloupe at a peace. In a letter addressed to the Right Honourable the Earl of Hallifax. . . In answer to certain animadversions. . . —CATO. 1760#18

Reasons for the confirmation of the charter belonging to the Massachusetts colony in New-England. —1691#17

Reasons for the confirmation of the charters belonging to the several corporations in New-England. —MATHER, Increase. 1691#14

Reasons for the encouragement of making raw silk in America. —1750#40

Reasons for the present application to Parliament for liberty to import salt from any part of Europe directly into his majesty's colonies in America. —1750#41

Reasons for the reversal of Leister's attainder. Humbly presented to the. . . House of Commons. —1694#19

Reasons grounded on facts. . . —1748#22

Reasons hnmbly [sic] offered for the encouragement of making iron and copper, in His Majesty's plantations of America. —1718#16

Reasons humbly offered against a clause in the bill for the encouraging the importation of naval stores from the plantations. —1710#17

Reasons humbly offer'd against encouraging the making of iron in America. —1718#17

Reasons humbly offered against general certificates for the conveyance of tobaccos, etc. —1722#24

Reasons humbly offered against restraining the using and wearing of printed callicoes in England, Ireland and the plantations. —1704#23

Reasons humbly offered against the bill, for continuing a former act, for the confirming to the Hudson's bay company, their priviledges and trade. . . —1690#22

Reasons humbly offered. . . against the bill now depending in the. . . Commons, for exporting Irish linens, to the British plantations in America. —1717#16

Reasons humbly offered against the encouragement of making iron in his majesty's plantations. —1718#18

Reasons humbly offer'd by the merchants trading in pitch and tar, from His Majesty's plantations. —1720#32

Reasons humbly offered by the merchants trading to Virginia and Maryland, for incouraging the exportation of tobacco, and bringing in of French wine in return —1708#13

Reasons humbly offr'd for allowing the merchants etc. of New-England, New-York and Carolina, relief upon the dutys paid on prize-goods. . . —1713#11

Reasons humbly offered, for not doubling the subsidy on tobacco from Virginia and Maryland. . . —1720#33

Reasons humbly offered for permitting rice of the growth of the British plantations, to be transported to Spain, Portugal, and other. . . —1730#27

313

Reasons humbly offered for regulating the importation of tobacco into this kingdom, for the preservation of the revenue, and the better carrying on of the said trade. —1722#25

Reasons humbly offered for taking off the enumeration of rice, made in His Majesty's plantations in America. —1730#28

Reasons humbly offered for the encouragement of making iron in his majesty's plantations of America. —1718#19

Reasons humbly offered in behalf of the Hudson-Bay Company, that they may be exempted in the clause that will be offer'd for suppressing the insurance offices. —1712#22

Reasons humbly offer'd in behalf of the plantations, against the bill for settling the trade to Affrica. . . —1695#28

Reasons humbly offered to prove that the letter printed at the end of the French memorial of justification is a forgery. . . —1756#64

Reasons humbly offered to. . . Commons, by the merchants and traders in tobacco, with relation to the bill, now depending, for the lessening the drawback, on tobacco exported to Ireland. —1714#15

Reasons humbly offered to. . . Commons, by the tobacco and wine merchants, against payment of interest for the time past on their bonds at the Custom-house, where the principal is paid. —1714#16

Reasons humbly offered to. . . Commons for passing the clause in the bill for the better encouragement of trade to America; whereby. . . —1710#21

Reasons humbly offer'd to the. . . Commons. . . against the passing the bill for the reversing the Attainder of Jacob Leisler, Jacob Milburn, Abraham Governour and others. —1695#29

Reasons humbly offer'd to the. . . Commons, by the merchants trading in tobacco, against a clause relating to the exportation of goods entitled to a draw-back. . . —1710#18

Reasons humbly offered to the. . . House of Commons by the merchants and traders in tobacco, with relation to the bill. . . for lessening the drawback, on tobacco. . . —1730#29

Reasons humbly offered to the Honourable House of Commons, for passing the bill for the better encouragement and protection of the trade to America. —1710#19

Reasons humbly offered to the honourable House of Commons, to obviate the objections made by the East-India Company against the amendments. . . —1710#20

Reasons humbly offered to the honourable the Commons of England in Parliament for laying an easie duty on whale-finns of the fishery of New-England, New York, and Pensilvania. —1708#14

Reasons humbly proposed to the Honourable House of Commons, for laying a duty upon East-India silks, etc. Exported into Her Majesties. . . —1714#17

Reasons most humbly offered to the Honourable the House of Commons, for carrying on an American fishery, upon the coast of New England and North Carolina. . . —1720#34

Reasons humbly offer'd to the. . . Lords for passing the bill, entituled, A Bill for relief of merchants, importers of tobacco and wine. . . —1714#14

Reasons most humbly proposed for encouraging the British coinage, and preventing the melting and exporting that which is, and shall be coined. . . —1746#20

Reasons offered to. . . Commons, relating to the bill. . . for laying an additional duty on all commodities imported, as far as it relates to the trade of Virginia and Maryland. —1704#24

Reasons proposed to the House of Commons for laying a duty on East India stock, and that no drawback be allowed on articles exported to America. . . —1730#30

Reasons prov'd to be unreasonable: or, An answer to the reasons against a war with France. —1702#22

Reasons shewing that it is the landed interest, as well as the interest of the nation to encourage the importation of iron from. . . —1740#32

Reasons to shew, that there is a great probability of a navigable passage to the American western ocean, through the Hudson's streights. . . —DOBBS, Arthur. 1749#11

Reasons why the approaching treaty of peace should be debated in Parliament. . . In a letter addressed to a great man. . . occasioned by. . . a letter addressed to two great men. . . —RUFFHEAD, Owen. 1760#83

The reception of the Palatines vindicated: in a fifth letter to a Tory member. . . —HARE, Francis. 1711#11

The recommendation of William Smith, provost of the College of Philadelphia. . . to the University of Oxford, by the archbishop of Canterbury and others. . . —1759#85

The reduction of Louisbourg. A poem, wrote on board his majesty's ship Orford in Louisbourg harbour. . . —NEVILL, Valentine. 1758#33

Reflections and considerations occasioned by the petition. . . to. . . House of Commons, for taking off the drawback on foreign linens, etc. —1738#18

Reflections on courtship and marriage. . . in two letters to a friend. —FRANKLIN, Benjamin. 1750#16

Reflections on the conduct of divine providence in the series and conclusion of the late war; a sermon. —DODDRIDGE, Philip. 1749#13

Reflections on the expediency of a law for the naturalization of foreign protestants. In two parts. —TUCKER, Josiah. 1751#35

Reflections on the importation of bar-iron, from our own colonies of North-America. In answer to a late pamphlet. Humbly submitted. . . —1757#34

Reflections on the present state of affairs at home and abroad. . . —YOUNG, Arthur. 1759#109

Reflections on the printed case of William Penn, esq; in a letter from some gentlemen of Pensilvania. . . —1702#23

Reflections on the welfare and prosperity of Great Britain in the present crisis. —1756#65

Reflections upon East-Indy and Royal African companies. . . —COKE, Roger. 1695#7

Reflections upon the present state of affairs, at home and abroad. . . In a letter from a member of Parliament to a constituent. . . —1755#42

The reformed common wealth of bees. Presented in severall letters and observations. . . With the reformed Virginian silk-worm. . . —HARTLIB, Samuel. 1655#12

The reformed Virginian silk-worms, or, a rare and new discovery. . . for the feeding of silk-worms. . . on the mulberry tree-leaves in Virginia. . . —HARTLIB, Samuel. 1655#13

A refutation of the letter to an honble. brigadier- general, commander of His Majesty's forces in Canada. By an officer. —THURLOW, Edward. 1760#95

A rejoinder to Mr. Dobb's reply to Captain Middleton. . . —MIDDLETON, Christopher. 1745#30

A relation of a discovery lately made on the coast of Florida, (from lat. 31 to 33 deg. 45 min. north lat.). . . with proposals. . . —HILTON, William. 1664#8

A relation of some speciall points concerning the state of Holland. . . —SCOTT, Thomas. 1621#4

A relation of some yeares travaile, begunne anno 1626. . . —HERBERT, Sir Thomas. 1634#4

A relation of the Christians in the world. . . —PAGITT, Ephraim. 1639#4

A relation of the great sufferings and strange adventures of Henry Pitman. . . —PITMAN, Henry. 1689#23

A relation of the invasion and conquest of Florida by the Spaniards, under the command of Fernando de Soto. . . —1686#5

A relation of the labour, travail and suffering of that faithful servant of the Lord Alice Curwen. . . —MARTINDELL, Anne. 1680#6

A relation of the successfull beginnings of the Lord Baltemore's plantation in Mary-land. . . extract of certain letters written. . . —WHITE, Andrew. 1634#7

A relation, or journal, of a late expedition to the gates of St. Augustine, on Florida; conducted by. . . James Oglethorpe. . . —KIMBER, Edward. 1744#31

The relief of the persecuted protestants of Saltzburgh, and the support of the colony of Georgia, recommended in a sermon preach'd. . . January 13, 1734. . . —BEST, William. 1734#2

Religion a treasure to men, and the strength and glory of a nation. A sermon. . . January 7. 1754. . . —PLENDERLEATH, David. 1754#29

Religion and patriotism. . . sermon. . . to. . . volunteers, raised in Hanover county, Virginia, August 17, 1755. —DAVIES, Samuel. 1756#19

The religious ceremonies and customs of the several nations of the known world. . . —BERNARD, Jean Frederic, editor. 1731#3

Reliquiae Baxterianae: or Mr Richard Baxter's narrative of. . . his life. . . —BAXTER, Richard. 1696#1

Remarks, in support of the new chart of North and South America; in six sheets. —GREEN, John. 1753#10

Remarks on a false, scandalous, and seditious libel. —1711#23

Remarks on a pamphlet entitled, Reasons why the approaching treaty of peace should be debated in Parliament, etc. In a letter to the author. —1760#80

Remarks on Dr Bray's memorial, etc. with brief observations on some passages in the Acts of his Visitation in Maryland, and on his circular letter to the clergy there. . . —WYETH, Joseph. 1701#47

Remarks on Mr. Whitefield. —1741#30

Remarks on several Acts of Parliament relating more especially to the colonies abroad; as also on diverse acts of assemblies there. . . —BLENMAN, Jonathan. 1742#3

Remarks on the advantages and disadvantages of France and of Great Britain with respect to commerce. . . —PLUMARD DE DANGEUL, Louis Joseph. 1754#30

Remarks on the common topicks of conversation in town, at the meeting of Parliament. . . 1734-5. —1735#16

Remarks on the continuation of Mr. Whitefield's Journal. Pointing out the many direct inconsistencies. . . —1738#19

Remarks on the Craftsman's vindication of his two honble patrons. . . —HERVEY, John. 1731#21

Remarks on the Essays on the principles of morality, and natural religion. In a letter to a minister of the Church of Scotland. . . —EDWARDS, Jonathan. 1758#17

Remarks on the French memorials concerning the limits of Acadia. . . with two maps. —1756#66

Remarks on the letter addressed to two great men. In a letter to the author of that piece. —BURKE, William. 1760#14

Remarks on the Reverend Mr Whitefield's journal, his many inconsistencies are pointed out and his tenets considered; the whole showing the dangerous tendency of his doctrine. . . —GIB, T. 1740#13

Remarks on the trial of John-Peter Zenger. . . —1738#20

Remarks on those passages of the letters of the Spanish ministers. . . which relate to the hostilities committed by the Spanish Guarda-Costas. . . —1727#22

Remarks on two popular pamphlets viz, the Considerations on the present German war; and the Full and candid answer to the Considerations. —1760#81

Remarks upon a book, entituled, The present state of the sugar colonies considered. . . —HALL, Fayrer. 1731#20

Remarks upon a late pamphlet, intitul'd The two great questions consider'd. —1700#32

Remarks upon a letter published in the London Chronicle, or Universal Evening Post, no. 115. Containing an enquiry into the causes. . . —1757#35

Remarks upon a pamphlet, intitled, The considerations in relation to trade considered, and a short view of our present trade and taxes reviewed. —BLACK, William. 1706#3

Remarks upon Capt. Middleton's defence: wherein his conduct during his late voyage for discovering a passage from Hudson's Bay to... —DOBBS, Arthur. 1744#16

Remarks upon some queries handed about by the separate traders to Africa... —1711#24.

Remarks upon the present negotiations of peace begun between Britain and France. —1711#25

Remarks upon the trials of Edward Fitzharris... —HAWLES, Sir John. 1689#13

Remonstrance on behalf of the merchants trading to Spain, East Indies, and Newfoundland. —1648#11

The rending church-member regularly called back, to Christ, and to his church... —MATTHEWS, Marmaduke. 1659#22

The reply of John Crookshanks, Esq; to a pamphlet lately set forth by Admiral Knowles... —CROOKSHANKS, John. 1759#23

A reply of Sir George Downing... to the remarks of the deputies of the Estates-general, upon his memorial of December 20. 1664... —DOWNING, George. 1665#15

A reply of two of the brethren to A. S. wherein you have observations on his considerations... upon the Apologeticall narration... —GOODWIN, John. 1644#9

A reply to a book entitled Anguis flagellatus, or, A switch for the snake. The opus palmare of the Quakers. —LESLIE, Charles. 1702#14

A reply to a confutation of some grounds for infants baptisme: as also concerning the form of a church... —PHILLIPS, George. 1645#15

A reply to a pamphlet entitled 'Observations arising from the declaration of war against Spain, etc.' —1739#59

A reply to a pamphlet intitled, Popular prejudices against the Convention and Treaty with Spain, examined and answered. In a letter to a member of Parliament. —1739#60

A reply to Capt. Middleton's answer to the remarks on his vindication of his conduct, in a late voyage made by him in the Furnace... —DOBBS, Arthur. 1745#15

A reply to Mr. Dobb's answer to a pamphlet, entitled, Forgery detected... —MIDDLETON, Christopher. 1745#31

A reply to Mr Rutherford. —MATHER, Richard. 1647#11

A reply to the Remarks of Arthur Dobbs Esq; on Capt Middleton's Vindication of his conduct. —MIDDLETON, Christopher. 1744#33

A reply to the Vindication of the Representation of the Case of the planters of tobacco in Virginia. In a letter to Sir J. R. from the merchants or factors of London... —1733#29

A report from the Committee appointed to inquire into the state and condition of the countries adjoining to Hudson's Bay, and of the trade carried on there. —GREAT BRITAIN. PARLIAMENT. HOUSE OF COMMONS COMMITTEE. 1749#24

A report from the Committee appointed to inspect and examine the several returns (made to the House) of the felons and vagabonds ordered for transportation... —IRELAND. PARLIAMENT. HOUSE OF COMMONS. COMMITTEE. 1744#27

A report from the committee of secrecy, appointed by order of the House of Commons to examine several books and papers... relating... —GREAT BRITAIN. PARLIAMENT. HOUSE OF COMMONS. PROCEEDINGS. 1715#15

Report from the committee to whom the petition of the deputies of the united Moravian churches... was referred; together... — GREAT BRITAIN. PARLIAMENT. HOUSE OF COMMONS COMMITTEE. 1749#25

The report of the committee of both houses of Assembly of the province of South Carolina, appointed to enquire into... the late expedition against St. Augustine... —SOUTH CAROLINA ASSEMBLY. COMMITTEE OF BOTH HOUSES. 1743#38

Report on the petitions relating to the manufacture of hats... —GREAT BRITAIN. PARLIAMENT. HOUSE OF COMMONS COMMITTEE. 1752#10

Report relating to the finding of a north-west passage. —GREAT BRITAIN. PARLIAMENT. HOUSE OF COMMONS COMMITTEE. 1745#25A

A report to the Honourable Commissioners for putting in execution the Act... —DAVENANT, Charles. 1712#7

The report, with appendix, from committee of... Commons appointed to enquire into the frauds and abuses in the customs... Published by order of the House of Commons. —GREAT BRITAIN. PARLIAMENT. HOUSE OF COMMONS COMMITTEE. 1733#20

Representation from the Commissioners for Trade and Plantations, to the... Lords... in pursuance of their Lordships addresses... —GREAT BRITAIN. COMMISSIONERS FOR TRADE AND PLANTATIONS. 1735#8

Representation of the Board of Trade relating to the laws made, manufactures set up, and trade carried on, in His Majesty's plantations in America —GREAT BRITAIN. COMMISSIONERS FOR TRADE AND PLANTATIONS. 1734#8

The representation of the committee of the English congregations in union with the Moravian church. —1754#32

A representation of the state of the trade of Ireland, laid before the House of Lords of England... —PERCEVAL, John. 1750#38

A representation to king and parliament, of... Quakers in New-England... —1669#3

The request of the Society for the Propagation of the Gospel... concerning fit ministers to be sent abroad for that good purpose. —SOCIETY FOR THE PROPAGATION OF THE GOSPEL. 1702#26

The resignation: or the fox out of the pit, and the geese in, with B——g at the bottom. —1756#67

Resolute Dick's garland. Composed of several excellent new songs. —1760#82

The resolutions of Trustees for... Georgia... this eight day of March... relating to the grants and tenure of lands within the said colony... —GEORGIA TRUSTEES. 1742#17

Responsio ad totam quaestionum syllogen a... Guilielmo Apollonio... —NORTON, John. 1648#9

The result of a synod... —COTTON, John. 1654#9

The retraction of... written in his own hand before his going to New England, in the yeer, 1637. —CHAUNCY, Charles (1592-1672). 1641#3

A review of all that hath passed between the courts of Great Britain and Spain, relating to our trade and navigation, from the year 1721, to the present convention... —PULTENEY, William. 1739#57

A review of the military operations in North-America; from the commencement of the French hostilities on the frontiers of Virginia in 1753, to the surrender of Oswego... 1756... —LIVINGSTON, William. 1757#24

A review of the preface to a narrative of the extraordinary work at Kilsyth, and other congregations in the neighbourhood, written by the Reverend Mr James Robe... —FISHER, James. 1742#15

A review of the principal facts objected to the first volume of the History of the Puritans... —NEAL, Daniel. 1734#15

A review of the short view; and of the remarks on the treaty with Spain... —1730#31

A review of the sixth letter to the people of England; wherein the principal passages of that malignant piece are quoted at large, and refuted... —1758#39

A review of the whole political conduct of a late eminent patriot, and his friends; for twenty years last past... —1743#30

The revival: or Directions for a sculpture, describing the extraordinary care and diligence of our nation, in publishing the faith... —GODWIN, Morgan. 1682#17

Rhode Island. Daniel Coggeshall, Esq.,... appellant. Mary Coggeshall... respondent... The appellant's case. —COGGESHALL, Daniel. 1739#15

Rhode Island. James Mac Sparran... of... Rhode Island, plaintiff and appellant... The appellants case. —MACSPARRAN, James. 1737#18

Rhode Island. Peleg Browne... Collector of... Customs for Newport... appellant. Ezekiel Cheevers, of Boston... and James Allen... respondents. The respondent's case. —CHEEVER, Ezekiel. 1738#4

Rhode Island. Peleg Browne, Collector of Customs... Rhode Island... appellant. James Allen, and Ezekiel Chever... respondents. The appellant's case. —BROWNE, Peleg. 1738#3

Rhode Island. The Reverend James McSparran of North Kingston... plaintiff... The respondent's case. —MACSPARRAN, James. 1737#19

The right honourable the Earl of Arlington's letters to Sir W. Temple, Bar... All printed from the originals and never before publish'd. —BENNET, Henry, earl of Arlington. 1701#7

The right honourable Thomas Lord Fairfax, petitioner. against the governor and council of Virginia, in right of the Crown, defendents. The case of the petitioner the Lord Fairfax. —FAIRFAX, Thomas, Lord. 1739#25

Right thoughts in sad hours, representing the comforts and duties of good men under all their afflictions; and particularly that one, the untimely death of Children... —MATHER, Cotton. 1689#17

The right way to shake off a viper. An essay, on a case, too commonly calling for consideration. What shall good men do, when they are evil spoke. With a preface by Dr. Increase Mather... —MATHER, Cotton. 1711#16

Rigid Quakers, cruel persecutors... together with a short abridgement of the history of the Quakers persecutions for religion... —COCKSON, Edward. 1705#4

The rise and fall of pot-ash in America, addressed to the Right Honourable the Earl of Halifax. —STEPHENS, Thomas d. 1780. 1758#45

The rise and progress of religion in the soul. —DODDRIDGE, Philip. 1745#16

Rites of Funeral. Ancient and modern, in use through the known world... —MURET, Pierre. 1683#15

The rock of ages exalted above Rome's imagined rock... —HOWGILL, Francis. 1662#8

The rocking of the cradle... to which is added... The sailor's return from Cape Breton. —1758#40

*The royal conference or a dialogue between... G*** the IId. of E***d. and L**s the XV. of F***e.* —GEORGE, II, KING OF GREAT BRITAIN. 1756#34

The royal fishing revived. Wherein is demonstrated from what causes the Dutch have upon the matter ingrossed the fishing trade of his majesty's seas... —1670#12

Royal genealogies... Part I... the genealogies of the earliest great families, and most ancient sovereigns of Asia, Europe, Africa and America... —ANDERSON, James. 1732#1

Royal institutions: being proposals for articles to establish and confirm laws... of silver and gold mines... in... Africa and America. —HOUGHTON, Thomas. 1694#9

Royal remarks: or, The Indian king's observations on the most fashionable follies now reigning in the kingdom of Great Britain... —1711#26

The ruinous condition of the tobacco trade, and the causes thereof mathematically demonstrated... —1752#17

Rules and articles for the better government of his majesty's horse and footguards... in Great Britain and Ireland, and dominions beyond the seas... —GREAT BRITAIN. ARMY. REGULATIONS. 1718#7

317

Rules and orders of the Society, established at London... —SOCIETY FOR THE ENCOURAGEMENT OF ARTS. 1758#44

Rules and orders respecting the Charity left by the will of the hon. Robert Boyle... —COMPANY FOR PROPAGATION OF THE GOSPEL IN NEW ENGLAND AND THE PARTS ADJACENT IN AMERICA. 1691#5

Rules for the year 1735. —GEORGIA TRUSTEES. 1735#7

Rules of the St. Andrew's Club at Charles-Town, in South Carolina. —ST. ANDREWS CLUB, CHARLES-TOWN, SOUTH CAROLINA. 1750#43

The Rump or a collection of songs and ballads... —BROME, Alexander. 1660#3

Sacred to the memory of that renowned hero, Major General Wolfe... —CATTON, William. 1759#14

Sad and deplorable newes from New England... —TOMPSON, Benjamin. 1676#20

Sad and dreadful news from New England, being a true relation of the barbarous cruelty lately committed by the Spaniards upon the English... —1684#9

The Sailor's advocate... —1722#26

The sailors danger and hardship at sea. Giving a full and true description of the late expedition to Quebeck... Likewise, a full... account... —1711#27

The Sailor's Warning Piece... Being a dreadful relation of 7 English Sailors... as also another astonishing relation of the Gloucester Merchant-ship from Virginia... —1706#15

Saint Paul the tent-maker: in a discourse shewing how religion has in all ages, been promoted by the industrious mechanick. —1690#23

The saints anchor-hold —DAVENPORT, John. 1642#10

The saints dignitie and dutie... —HOOKER, Thomas. 1651#13

The saint's guide —HOOKER, Thomas. 1645#11

Salt and fishery. A discourse thereof... —COLLINS, John. 1682#8

A salutation of love, and tender invitation, to all people; but more especially to the inhabitants of New-England, Road-Island and Long- Island, to come unto Shiloh... —THOMPSON, Thomas. 1713#13

A salutation of love to the seed of God everywhere. —DICKINSON, James. 1696#9

A salutation to the Britains, to call them from many things, to the one thing needful, for the saving of their souls... translated from the British language. —PUGH, Ellis. 1732#34

The salvations of God in 1746. In part set forth in a sermon at the South Church in Boston, Nov... 27, 1746... —PRINCE, Thomas. 1747#19

Samuel Hartlib, his legacie; or an enlargement of the discourse of husbandry used in Brabant and Flanders... —HARTLIB, Samuel. 1651#10

Samuel Waldo - appellant. Hannah Fayrweather, widow and John Fayrweather, executors, respondents. The respondents case. To be heard... 10th of December, 1734. —WALDO, Samuel. 1734#25

The saviour with his rainbow. A discourse concerning the covenant which God will remember, in the times of danger passing over his church. —MATHER, Cotton. 1714#13

A sceene of sceenes. Extract of a letter from a merchant in Boston, to his correspondent in London, dated Nov. 5. 1754. —1755#46

A scheme for improving the mines, the mineral and the battery works, in New England. —1712#23

A scheme for the general good of the nation... and for the effectual security of our commerce and possessions abroad. —STRATIOTICUS. 1760#90

A scheme to drive the French out of all the continent of America... —C., T. 1754#3

The Scotch marine, or memoirs of the life of Celestina, who... spent two years... as a man... her marriage afterwards with Cario, a North Briton, in New-England... —1752#19

The Scots gard'ner in two parts... —REID, John. 1683#19

The scourge in vindication of the Church of England. —LEWIS, Thomas. 1717#11

A sea grammar, with the plaine exposition of Smith's Accidence for young seamen enlarged... —SMITH, John. 1627#6

The seaman's opinion of a standing army in England, in opposition to a Fleet at Sea, as the best security of this nation. —1699#15

The sea-mans practice, contayning a fundamentall probleme in navigation... —NORWOOD, Richard. 1637#6

The sea-piece, a poetical narration of a voyage from Europe to America. Canto II. —KIRKPATRICK, James. 1749#27

A seasonable caveat against the prevalency of Quakerism... a hint also of arbitrary government in Pensilvania... —BUGG, Francis. 1701#15

Seasonable considerations on the expediency of a war with France... To which are added... a short comparison between the British and French dominions... —BURRINGTON, George. 1743#6

A seasonable information and caveat against a scandalous book of Thomas Ellwood, called, An epistle to Friends. — KEITH, George. 1694#12

Seasonable observations on the naturalization bill... —1748#24

Seasonable reflections and discourses, in order to the conviction and cure of the... age... —GLANVILL, Joseph. 1676#5

Seasonable remarks on trade. —BROWNE, John. 1728#1

The second book of James... —BELSHAZZER, Kapha the Jew. 1744#2

A second defence of the Three letters to a gentleman dissenting from the Church of England... —WHITE, John. 1748#34

The second journal of Christian Frederick Post, on a message from the governor of Pennsylvania to the Indians on the Ohio. —POST, Christian Frederick. 1759#79

A second letter from a member of the Society for the Propagation of the Gospel. . .—SOCIETY FOR THE PROPAGATION OF THE GOSPEL. 1713#12

A second letter to a gentleman dissenting from the Church of England. —WHITE, John. 1745#37

A second letter to the people of England, on foreign subsidies, subsidiary armies, and their consequences. . . —SHEBBEARE, John. 1755#49

A second narrative of the proceedings at Turners-Hall. . . — KEITH, George. 1700#22

The second part of Babel's builders unmask't. —CRISP, Thomas. 1683#7

The second part of Gangraena. —EDWARDS, Thomas. 1646#10

The second part of Memoirs and considerations concerning the trade and revenues of the British colonies in America. . . —ASHLEY, John. 1743#3

The second part of that book call'd Independency not God's ordinance: or the post-script. . . —BASTWICK, John. 1645#2

The second part of the duply to M. S. alias Two brethren. . . —STEUART, Adam. 1644#18

The second part of The fortunate transport. Being a continuation. . . *from the time of her arrival in England, to her death.* —1750#44

The second parts of Systema agriculturae, or The mystery of husbandry. . . —WORLIDGE, John. 1689#31

A second series of facts and arguments, tending to prove that the abilities of the two b———s, are not more extraordinary than their virtues. . . —PERCEVAL, John. 1749#33

A second solemn call on Mr Zinzendorf, otherwise called Count Zinzendorf. . . —RIMIUS, Heinrich. 1757#37

The second volume of the writings of the author of the London Spy. —WARD, Edward. 1703#11

A second warning to the world, by the spirit of prophecy. . . —CLARKE, Richard. 1760#22

Second pastoral letter to the people of his diocese. . . —GIBSON, Edmund. 1730#13

Secret memoirs of the new treaty of alliance with France. —1716#6

The secret workes of a cruel people made manifest. . . —FOX, George. 1659#13

Select tracts relating to colonies. . . —OGLETHORPE, James Edward. 1732#31

Select trials at the Sessions House in the Old Bailey, for murder, robberies, rapes, sodomy, coining,. . . *To which are added.* . . —1742#37

Select trials for murders, robberies, rapes, sodomy, coining,. . . *at the Sessions House in the Old Bailey. To which are added.* . . —1734#19

Selemnarchia. Or the government of the world in the moon. — CYRANO DE BERGERAC, Savinien. 1659#8

Self disclaimed, and Christ exalted: a sermon preached at Philadelphia. . . *May 25, 1758.* . . —BOSTWICK David. 1759#4

Separation examined: or, a treatise wherein the grounds for separation from the ministry and churches of England are weighed and found to be too light. . . —FIRMIN, Giles. 1652#2

Septima pars patentium de Anno Regis Jacobi Secundi Quarto. —1688#24

A sequel to Hosier's ghost: or, Old Blakeney's reception into the Elysian Fields. A ballad written by a patriot of Ireland. —1756#69

A series of wisdom and policy being a full justification of all our measures ever since the year 1721. . . *and.* . . *our late most honourable convention with Spain.* . . —1735#18

A serious address to lay-methodists, to beware of the false pretences of their teachers. With an appendix, containing an account. . . —GREY, Zachary. 1745#26

A serious call to the City of London, and thro' them to the whole nation, to the relief of the persecuted Protestants of Saltzburg. . . —1732#36A

The serious Christian: or three great points of practical Christianity. . . *By an American.* —MATHER, Cotton. 1699#11

Serious considerations on the present state of the affairs of the northern colonies. —KENNEDY, Archibald. 1754#19

A sermon delivered at the South-Church in Boston. . . *August 14, 1746.* . . *Thanksgiving for.* . . *glorious and happy victory near Culloden.* . . —PRINCE, Thomas. 1747#20

A sermon. . . *February 17, 1737-8.* . . —HERRING, Thomas. 1738#12

A sermon. . . *February 20, 1735.* . . —LYNCH, John. 1736#14

A sermon. . . *March 17, 1742-3.* . . —KING, James. 1743#19

A sermon occasioned by the declaration of war against France. Preached at Harleston, May the 23d, 1756. —SMITHSON, Isaac. 1756#76

A sermon. . . *on Friday the 21st February, 1717.* . . —BISSE, Philip. 1718#1

A sermon preached. . . *20 February 1701/2.* . . —WILLIS, Richard. 1702#27

A sermon preached. . . *16th February, 1710/11.* . . —FLEETWOOD, William. 1711#6

A sermon preached. . . *18th February, 1714.* . . —ASHE, St. George. 1715#1

A sermon preached. . . *20th February, 1718.* . . —CHANDLER, Edward. 1719#1

A sermon preached. . . *19th February, 1719.* . . —BRADFORD, Samuel. 1720#7

A sermon preached. . . *16th February 1727.* . . — REYNOLDS, Richard. 1728#13

A SERMON PREACHED... 21ST FEBRUARY 1728...

A sermon preached... 21st February 1728... —EGERTON, Henry. 1729#8

A sermon preached... 21st February, 1734... —HARE, Francis. 1735#10

A sermon preached... 16th of February, 1721... —BOULTER, Hugh. 1722#3

A sermon preached... 18th of February, 1725. —WILCOCKS, Joseph. 1726#18

A sermon preached... 29th of November 1759... —1759#88

A sermon preached... April the 17th 1735 to which is annexed an account of the origin and design of the society for promoting Christian Knowledge... —PEARCE, Zachary. 1735#15

A sermon preached at Clapham in Surry, on Friday the 17th February, 1758... —FURNEAUX, Philip. 1758#21

A sermon preached at Henrico, 29 April 1753. And at Canongate, 26th May 1754. —DAVIES, Samuel. 1754#8

A sermon preached at Little-Wild-Street on Tuesday, April 25, 1749. Being the day... for a general thanksgiving... for the peace. —STENNET, Joseph. 1749#41

A sermon, preached at... Norwich... Nov. 29. 1759... —WELTON, James. 1759#102

A sermon preached at Plimmoth in New-England December 9. 1621 in an assemblie of his majesties faithfull subjects, there inhabiting... —CUSHMAN, Robert. 1622#10

A sermon preached at the Chapel in Long-Ditch, Westminster on... November 29, 1759. —KIPPIS, Andrew. 1759#57

A sermon preached at the New Meeting... Spital-Fields... 29 November 1759... —HITCHIN, Edward. 1759#48

A sermon preached at the parish church of St Peter's, in Talbot County, Maryland: on Sunday the 14th of October, 1750. for the benefit... —BACON, Thomas. 1751#4

A sermon preached at the parish-church of St. Vedast, Foster Lane, on November 29, 1759... —WYNNE, R. 1759#107

A sermon preached at Tiverton, Devon, November 29, 1759... —KIDDELL, John. 1760#57

A sermon preached at Topsham on Thursday November the 29th, 1759... —FORTESCUE, J. 1760#34

A sermon preached at Trinity-Church in New-York... August 13, 1706. At the funeral of the right honourable Katherine Lady Cornbury... —SHARP, John. 1706#16

A sermon preach'd at Turner's Hall... 5th. of May, 1700. —KEITH, George. 1700#23

A sermon preached before his grace the Duke of Marlborough... March 5 1752... To which is added a postcript, containing an account of the small-pox... —MADDOX, Isaac. 1753#16

A sermon preached before the Hon. House of Commons... 11th day of February 1757... —TAYLOR, John. 1757#47

A sermon preached before the honourable the House of Commons, at St. Margaret's Westminster.. —GREEN, John. 1759#43

A sermon preached before the honourable House of Commons, at St. Margaret's Westminster, on Thursday November 19, 1759... —DAYRELL, Richard. 1759#25

A sermon preached before the right honourable the House of Lords... November 29, 1759... —JOHNSON, James. 1759#54

A sermon preach'd before the Trustees for... Georgia... and Associates of... Bray... February 23, 1730-1... —SMITH, Samuel. 1733#34

A sermon preached before the trustees... Thursday, March 21, 1734... —HALES, Stephen. 1734#11

A sermon preached before the Trustees... Thursday, March 18. 1735... —WATTS, George. 1736#18

A sermon preach'd before... Trustees for... Georgia... and the associates of... Bray... March 15, 1738-9... —BERRIMAN, William. 1739#6

A sermon preached... Feb. 1724. —WYNNE, John. 1725#12

A sermon preached... Feb. 20, 1740-1... —SECKER, Thomas. 1741#32

A sermon preached... Feb. 16, 1749... —TREVOR, Richard. 1750#50

A sermon preached... February 15. 1705/6... —WILLIAMS, John. 1706#21

A sermon preached... February 21st 1706... —BEVERIDGE, William. 1707#2

A sermon preached... February 20th, 1707/8... —STANLEY, William. 1708#16

A sermon preached... February 18, 1708-9... —DAWES, William. 1709#5

A sermon preached... February 21, 1723... —GREENE, Thomas. 1724#8

A sermon preached... February 16, 1732... —SMALBROKE, Richard. 1733#32

A sermon preached... February 18, 1736... —CLAGETT, Nicholas. 1737#8

A sermon preached... February 16, 1738-9. —BUTLER, Joseph. 1739#9

A sermon preached... February 15, 1739-40. —BENSON, Martin. 1740#4

A sermon preached... February 19, 1741/2... —STEBBING, Henry. 1742#40

A sermon preached... February 18, 1742-3... —MAWSON, Matthias. 1743#23

A sermon preached... February 17, 1743-4... —GILBERT, John. 1744#18

A sermon preached... February 15, 1744... —BEARCROFT, Philip. 1745#6

A sermon preached... February 21, 1745... —HUTTON, Matthew. 1746#13

A sermon preached... February 20, 1746... —THOMAS, John 1691-1766. 1747#27

A sermon preached. . . February 19, 1747. . . —LISLE, Samuel. 1748#12

A sermon preached. . . February 17, 1748. —GEORGE, William. 1749#15

A sermon preached. . . February 15, 1750. . . —THOMAS, John. (1696-1781). 1751#34

A sermon preached. . . February 16, 1753. . . —CRESSET, Edward. 1753#4

A sermon preached. . . February 15, 1754. . . —DRUMMOND, Robert Hay. 1754#10

A sermon preached. . . February 21, 1755. . . —HAYTER, Thomas. 1755#27

A sermon preached. . . February 20, 1756. . . —CORNWALLIS, Frederick. 1756#16

A sermon preached. . . February 18, 1757. . . —KEENE, Edmond. 1757#19

A sermon preached. . . February 23, 1759. . . —ELLYS, Anthony. 1759#30

A sermon preached. . . February 4. 1760. —CUMING, Patrick. 1760#28

A sermon preached. . . February 15, 1760. . . —ASHBURNHAM, William. 1760#4

A sermon preached. . . February 17, 1733/4. to recommend the charity for establishing the new colony of Georgia. —RUNDLE, Thomas. 1734#18

A sermon preached. . . Friday, February 24, 1758. . . —JOHNSON, James. 1758#29

A sermon preached. . . Friday the 17th of February, 1709/10. . . —TRIMNELL, Charles. 1710#24

A sermon preached. . . Friday the 17th of February, 1720. . . —WADDINGTON, Edward. 1721#23

A sermon preached in Christ-Church, Dublin; on Thursday, Nov. 29, 1759. . . —STONE, George. 1759#98

A sermon preached in Christ-Church, Philadelphia before the Provincial Grand Master. . . 24th June 1755. . . —SMITH, William (1727-1803). 1755#52

A sermon, preached in St. Andrew's, Dublin; before the Honourable House of Commons: on Thursday, Nov. 29, 1759. . . —FLETCHER, William. 1760#32

A sermon preached in St Anne's, Westminster. . . November 29, 1759. —DUNCOMBE, John. 1759#28

A sermon preach'd in the audience of His Excellency William Shirley, . . . the Honourable His Majesty's council, and the. . . House. . . —MAYHEW, Jonathan. 1754#24

A sermon, preached in the Church of St. Nicholas, in Newcastle upon Tyne, on Thursday, the 29th day of November. . . —BREWSTER, Richard. 1759#8

A sermon preached in the parish church of Kingsclere, Hants, on Thursday the 29th of November, 1759, being the day appointed for a general thanksgiving. By Thomas Obourn, A.M. . . . —OBOURN, Thomas, b. 1717 or 18. 1759#76

A sermon. . . preached. . . January 1 1759. . . the present state of the said society. —MACQUEEN, Daniel. 1759#64

A sermon preached. . . March 16, 1737-8. . . —BEARCROFT, Philip. 1738#1

A sermon preached. . . March 19, 1740-1. . . —BATEMAN, Edmund. 1741#1

A sermon preached. . . March 20, 1745-6. . . —RIDLEY, Glocester. 1746#21

A sermon preached. . . March 16, 1748-9. . . —HARVEST, George. 1749#26

A sermon preached. . . March 16, 1749,50. . . —FRANCKLIN, Thomas. 1750#15

A sermon preached. . . Nov. 29, 1759. . . —RICH, Edward Pickering. 1759#86

A sermon preached November 29, 1759. . . at Fornham. . . and Edmondsbury. . . . —GODDARD, Peter Stephen. 1760#40

A sermon preached. . . on. . . February 18, 1731. . . —BERKELEY, George. 1732#5

A sermon preached. . . on Friday February 2l, 1752. . . —OSBALDESTON, Richard. 1752#13

A sermon preached. . . on Friday, the 17th of February 1726. . . —LENG, John. 1727#15

A sermon preached. . . on Friday the 20th of February, 1729. . . —PEARCE, Zachary. 1730#24

A sermon preached. . . on Friday the 15th of February, 1733. . . —MADDOX, Isaac. 1734#13

A sermon preached. . . on November 29, 1759. . . —WINTER, Richard. 1759#105

A sermon preached. . . on Thursday, November 29, 1759. . . —TOWNLEY, James. 1759#100

A sermon preached. . . the 17th of February, 1715. —SHERLOCK, Thomas. 1716#7

A sermon. . . preached. . . the 15th February, 1722. —WAUGH, John. 1723#12

A sermon preached. . . the 19th of February 1730 [i.e. 1731]. —DENNE, John. 1731#11

A sermon preached. . . Thursday May 4th 1738. . . to which is annexed. . . —CONYBEARE, John. 1738#6

A sermon preached. . . Thursday May 3d, 1739. . . —CLAGETT, Nicholas. 1739#14

A sermon preached. . . Thursday May the 8th 1740. . . —THOMAS, John, (1691-1766) 740#34

A sermon preached to a congregation of Protestant dissenters at Sidmouth in Devonshire. . . Nov. 29, 1759. . . —HOGG, John. 1759#49

A sermon shewing that the present dispensations of providence declare that wonderful revolutions in the world are near at hand. . . —MATHER, Increase. 1710#13

A sermon upon the VIII. verse of the I. chapter of the Actes of the Apostles. Preached to the honourable company of the Virginian plantation. —DONNE, John. 1622#11

Sermons and discourses on several occasions. By the late... Ebenezer Pemberton... in Boston... —PEMBERTON, Ebenezer, (1671-1717). 1727#20

Sermons on several subjects... —BARNARD, John. 1727#1

Sermons on the following subjects... with an abstract of Consul Dean's narrative, relating to his suffering shipwreck... in the year 1710 —WILSON, Samuel. 1735#19

Sermons upon the following subjects... —MAYHEW, Jonathan. 1756#53

Sermons wherein those eight characters... called the beatitudes, are opened... —MATHER, Increase. 1721#13

Seven sermons upon the following subjects... —MAYHEW, Jonathan. 1750#32

A seventh collection of papers relating to the Parliament and the penal laws... —1689#26

A seventh letter to the people of England upon political writing, true patriotism... —1758#41

Several circular letters to the clergy of Mary-Land, subsequent to their late visitation, to enforce such resolutions as were taken therein. —BRAY, Thomas. 1701#11

Several conferences between some of the principal... Quakers in Pennsylvania, and the deputies from the six Indian Nations in alliance... —PEMBERTON, Israel. 1756#59

Several epistles given forth by two of the Lord's faithful servants, whom he sent to New-England... William Robinson, William Leddra... —ROBINSON, William. 1669#4

Several essays in political arithmetick. —PETTY, William. 1699#14

Several living testimonies given forth... —1698#17

Several new, pressing and weighty considerations for an immediate war with Spain... —1739#63

Several treaties of peace and commerce... —ENGLAND AND WALES. TREATIES. 1685#12

Severall considerations, offered to the Parliament, concerning the improvement of trade... —CAREW, George. 1675#2

Ship Catherina... John Paasch, master' appellant. John Sweet. Commander of the Defiance, Privateer, Respondent. The Appellant's case. —1752#20

Ship Charles... James Crokatt and others... appellants. His Majesty's Procurator-General, and Peter Warren, Esq., and the Hon. Henry Aylmer, Esq... respondents... —1743#34

Ship King's Meadow. Jamaica... —1748#25

Ship Le Grand Juste... Peter Vincent Duplessis master... appellant... Bradwarden Thompson, Esq. respondent. The appellant's case. —1743#35

Ship Notre Dame de Deliverance... Philip Durell, Esq. and others Appellants. William Bollan... and others Respondents. The Case of Captain John Wickham and others... —1749#38

Ship South Kingston. Rhode Island. Benjamin Hassard and others, appellants. John Rous, Respondent. The case of the... appellants... —1748#26

Ship Victory. Solomon de Medina, Mosesson and others, appellants. Matthew Norris Esq; and Edward Greenly, Esq. Respondents. The Appellants Case. —1736#16

Ship Vrow Dorothea. Michael Goolde Master of the... Trelawny Galley... Appellants. Pieter Black master of the vrow Dorothea... Respondent. The case of the... appellants... —1755#50

A short account of God's dealings with the Reverend Mr. George Whitefield... from his infancy, to the time of his entring into Holy Orders... —WHITEFIELD, George. 1740#43

A short account of iron, made in the colonies of Virginia and Maryland, only. With the opinion of the iron-merchants and manufacturers thereon. —1747#23

A short account of the first settlement of the provinces of Virginia, Maryland, New-York, New-Jersey, and Pennsylvania, by the English... —HALL, Fayrer. 1735#9

A short account of the late application to Parliament made by the merchants of London upon the neglect of their trade... —GLOVER, Richard. 1742#19

A short account of the life and sufferings of Elias Neau... —MORIN, J. 1749#30

A short account of the present state of New-England. Anno Domini 1690 —N. N. 1690#17

A short account of the rise, progress, and present state of the Society in Scotland for propagating Christian knowledge. With a sermon prefix'd to it; preached... Monday January 4. 1748... —WALKER, Robert. 1748#32

A short account of the several kinds of societies, set up in late years... —BRAY, Thomas. 1700#8

A short address to persons of all denominations, occasioned by the alarm of an intended invasion... —WHITEFIELD, George. 1756#86

A short and easie method with the deists... The eighth edition. —LESLIE, Charles. 1723#6

A short and plain account of inoculation. With some remarks on the main arguments... by Mr. Maitland and others... —MASSEY, Isaac. 1722#20

Short animadversions on the difference now set up between gin and rum, and our mother country and colonies... —1760#86

A short answer to A. S. alias Adam Stewart's second part of his overgrown duply to the two brethren... —GOODWIN, John. 1644#10

A short answer to an elaborate pamphlet, entitled, The Importance of the sugar plantations, etc... In a letter to a noble peer. —1731#33

A short collection of the most remarkable passages from the originall to the dissolution of the Virginia Company. —WOODNOTH, Arthur. 1651#16

A short confession of faith of the Church of Christ at Newport in Rhode Island, under the care of Mr Daniel White... —1747#24

A short description of the American colonies, belonging to the crown of Great Britain. Engrave'd by George Bickham... —BICKHAM, George. 1747#2

A short discourse of the New-found-land; Contaynig [sic] diverse reasons and inducements, for the planting of that countrey... —C., T. 1623#3

A short discourse, shewing the great inconvenience of joyning the plantation charters with those of England, etc. Containing a full... —1689#27

A short discourse upon the doctrine of our baptismal covenant... —BRAY, Thomas. 1697#3

A short discoverie of the coasts and continent of America, from the equinoctiall northward, and of the adjacent isles... Whereunto is prefixed... —CASTELL, William. 1644#2

A short essay upon trade in general... —1741#33

A short history of standing armies... —TRENCHARD, John. 1698#22

A short history of the Bohemian-Moravian Protestant church of the United Brethren... —GRADIN, Arvid. 1743#16

A short introduction to moral philosophy, in three books... —HUTCHESON, Francis. 1747#11

A short narrative and justification of the proceedings of the committee appointed by the Adventurers, to prosecute the discovery... —1749#40

Short notes and observations drawn from the present decaying condition of this kingdom in point of trade... —1662#14

Short observations on the bill at present depending in favour of the sugar-islanders... —1733#31

A short state of the countries and trade of North America. Claimed by the Hudson's Bay company, under a pretence of a charter... shewing the illegality of said grant... —1749#39

A short state of the progress of the French trade and navigation, wherein is shown the great foundation that France has laid... —POSTLETHWAYT, Malachy. 1756#60

A short state of the Society... —SOCIETY IN SCOTLAND FOR PROPAGATING CHRISTIAN KNOWLEDGE. 1732#38

A short supply or amendment to the propositions for the new representative, for the perpetual peace... of this nation... written and proposed by Edmund Leach of New-England, merchant. —LEACH, Edmund. 1651#14

A short view of the countries and trade carried on by the Company in Hudson's-Bay, shewing the prejudice of that exclusive trade... —DOBBS, Arthur. 1749#12

A short view of the encroachments of France in America; and of the British commerce with Spain. —1750#46

A short view of the evidence upon which the Christian religion... is established... —MIDDLETON, Patrick. 1734#14

A short view of the smuggling trade, carried on by the British northern colonies, in violation of the act of navigation, and several other acts of Parliament —1750#47

A short way to know the world: or, The rudiments of geography. —1707#13

The siege of Quebec. —1759#89

The signs of the times considered: or, the high probability, that the present appearances in New-England, and the west of Scotland... —ERSKINE, John. 1742#14

The signs of the times, illustrated and improved. In a sermon preached... October 21, 1759. On occasion of the surrender of Quebec... —BULKLEY, Charles. 1759#12

The signs of the times: or, wonderful signs of wonderful times... a faithful collection of... signs and wonders... in the heavens, on the earth and on the waters... this last year 1680. —NESSE, Christopher. 1681#15

A simile. —1759#90

The simple cobler of Aggawam in America. Willing to help 'mend his native country... —WARD, Nathaniel. 1647#18

Simplicities defence against seven-headed policy. or, Innocency vindicated... —GORTON, Samuel. 1646#13

The sincere convert: discovering the small numbers of true believers; and the great difficulty of saving-conversion. —SHEPARD, Thomas. 1640#5

Singing of psalmes... —COTTON, John. 1647#7

Sinners in the hands of an angry God... preached at Enfield, July 8, 1741... With a preface by... John Willison Minister of the Gospel at Dundee... —EDWARDS, Jonathan. 1745#18

The sins of a gainsaying and rebellious people laid before them... Written at the command of the Lord... —ROUS, John. 1659#31

Sion's travellers comforted. —MARSHALL, Charles. 1704#19

Sir H. Mackworth's proposal in miniature, as it has been put in practice in New-York, in America. —MACKWORTH, Sir Humphrey. 1720#20

Sir, may it please you to be at the Hudson's-Bay House. on [blank] the [blank] day of [blank] 170[blank]... at a committee there to be held —HUDSON'S BAY COMPANY. 1701#23

The situation of the world at the time of Christ's appearance... sermon... January 6, 1755... —ROBERTSON, William. 1755#44

Six dialogues about sea-services. —BUTLER, Nathaniel. 1685#6

Six plans of the different dispositions of the English army, under the command of the late General Braddock, in North America... By an officer. —OFFICER. 1758#33A

Six sermons on the following subjects. . . With a preface by the Reverend Mr Gilbert Tennent. —WHITEFIELD, George. 1750#51

Six sermons on the several duties of masters, mistresses, slaves, etc. Preached. . . in Talbot county. . . Maryland. . . —BACON, Thomas. 1751#5

Sixteene questions of serious and necessary consequence, propounded unto Mr John Cotton. . . —COTTON, John. 1644#5

A sixth collection of papers relating to the present juncture of affairs in England. —1689#28

A sixth letter to the people of England, on the progress of the national ruin. . . —SHEBBEARE, John. 1757#41

The skilful doctor; or the compleat mountebank. . . —PILKINGTON, R. 1685#22

The snake in the grass. . . discovering the deep and unexpected subtilty. . . of the principal leaders of those people called Quakers. . . —LESLIE, Charles. 1696#18

A sober dialogue between a country friend, a London friend, and one of G. K.'s friends, concerning the great differences. . . betwixt many Quakers. . . —1699#16

A sober reply to the sober answer of reverend Mr Cawdrey. . . also, the question of Reverend Mr Hooker concerning the baptisme of infants. . . —FIRMIN, Giles. 1653#10

Social bliss considered: In marriage and divorce. . . with the speech of Miss Polly Baker. . . —ANNET, Peter. 1749#2

The Society for promoting Christian knowledge and the members chosen by them to be trustees for the poor Saltzburgers. . . to go to Georgia. . . —SOCIETY FOR PROMOTING CHRISTIAN KNOWLEDGE. 1734#23

Society for promoting Christian knowledge. This presents you by order of the Society. . . with the continuation of the account of receipts. . . —SOCIETY FOR PROMOTING CHRISTIAN KNOWLEDGE. 1736#17

The soldier's delight. Being a choice collection of songs. —1759#93

A solemn call on Count Zinzendorf, the author and advocate of the sect of Herrnhuters, commonly called Moravians. . . —RIMIUS, Heinrich. 1754#34

Some account of the designs of the Trustees for establishing the colony of Georgia in America. —MARTYN, Benjamin. 1732#28

Some account of the North-America Indians. . . To which are added Indian Miscellanies. . . by a learned and ingenious gentleman of the province of Pennsylvania. . . —SMITH, William. (1727-1803). 1754#35

Some account of the principles of the Moravians; chiefly collected from several conversations with Count Zinzendorf; and from some sermons preached by him. . . —TENNENT, Gilbert. 1743#41

Some account of the province of Pensilvania in America. . . —PENN, William. 1681#18

Some account of the success of inoculation for the small-pox in England and America. Together with Plain Instructions. . . —FRANKLIN, Benjamin. 1759#35

Some brief observations upon George Keith's earnest expostulations. . . —PENINGTON, Edward. 1696#21

Some buds and blossoms of piety. . . —ANTROBUS, Benjamin. 1684#1

Some considerations humbly offered to demonstrate how prejudicial it would be to the English plantations. . . —1699#17

Some considerations humbly offer'd upon the bill now depending in the House of Lords, relating to the trade between the Northern Colonies and the Sugar-Islands. . . —1732#39

Some considerations in relation to trade. —BLACK, William. 1706#4

Some considerations on the consequences of the French settling colonies on the Mississippi, with respect to the trade and safety. . . —GENTLEMAN OF AMERICA [SMITH, James?]. 1720#12

Some considerations on the importation and exportation of beaver, with remarks on the hatter's case. —1752#21

Some considerations on the present state of affairs. Wherein the defenceless state of Great-Britain is pointed out. . . interspersed. . . —WILLIAMSON, Peter. 1758#51

Some considerations on the prohibiting the exportation of corn and provisions from the northern colonies. . . —1741#38

Some considerations relating to the payment of the publick debts, humbly offered to the Commons. . . —HUTCHESON, Archibald. 1717#10

Some considerations touching the present debate between owners and fishermen, relating to the New-found-land trade. By the impartial pen of an eye witness. . . —1671#9

Some considerations touching the sugar colonies, with political observations in respect to trade. . . —PERSON WELL ACQUAINTED WITH THE SUGAR TRADE. 1732#33

Some considerations touching the usefulnesse of experimental naturall philosophy —BOYLE, Robert. 1663#2

Some further considerations of the consequences of the bill now depending in the House of Lords, relating to the dispute of the trade of the British colonies in America. . . —PHILO-AMERICUS. 1733#26

Some further remarks on a late pamphlet, intitled, Observations on the conduct of Great-Britain. . . —AMHURST, Nicholas. 1729#1

Some general considerations offered, relating to our present trade. —TRYON, Thomas. 1698#23

Some gospel-treasures opened: or the holiest of the unvailing —EVERARD, John. 1653#9

Some important truths about conversion, delivered in sundry sermons. . . —MATHER, Increase. 1674#7

Some letters and an abstract of letters from Pennsylvania, containing the state and improvement of that province. Published to prevent mis-reports. —1691#19

Some material and very important remarks concerning the present situation of affairs between Great Britain, France and Spain... —1755#53

Some memoires for a natural history... —PERRAULT, Claude. 1688#14

Some memoirs of the life of Job, the son of Solomon the high priest of Boonda in Africa; who was a slave about two years in Maryland;... —BLUETT, Thomas. 1734#3

Some observations and annotations upon the Apologeticall narration, submitted to Parliament... —STEUART, Adam. 1643#17

Some observations for improvement of trade, by establishing the fishery of Great Britain... —PECK, Philip. 1732#32

Some observations made upon the herb cassiny; imported from Carolina; shewing its admirable virtues in curing the small pox... —PECHEY, John?. 1695#23

Some observations made upon the Virginian nutts, imported from the Indies: showing their admirable virtue against the scurvy... —PECHEY, John?. 1682#20

Some observations on a direct exportation of sugar from the British islands... —ASHLEY, John. 1735#1

Some observations on extracts taken out of the report from the Lords Commissioners for Trade and Plantations. —1708#15

Some observations on the assiento trade, as it has been exercised by the South-Sea Company; proving the damage, which will... —PERSON WHO RESIDED SEVERAL YEARS AT JAMAICA. 1728#12

Some observations on the conduct of the famous Mr Whitefield... —1742#39

Some observations on the Northern colonie trade with the French sugar colonies with respect to our acts of Parliament now in force in a letter to a noble Lord. —1732#40

Some observations on the occasional writer numb. IV. Wherein the following... —1738#24

Some of the glories of our Lord and Saviour... in twenty sacramental discourses, preached at Boston... —COLMAN, Benjamin. 1728#5

Some philosophical considerations touching the being of witches... —GLANVILL, Joseph. 1667#6

Some proposals for a second settlement in the province of Pennsylvania. —PENN, William. 1690#20

Some proposals towards promoting the propagation of the Gospel in our American plantations. —BROKESBY, Francis. 1708#2

Some reasons for a farther encouragement for bringing naval stores from America, for supplying the Royal Navy... —1712#24

Some reasons humbly offered to the Honourable the House of Commons for passing the Newfoundland bill. —1701#38

Some reasons offered by the late ministry in defence of their administration. —DEFOE, Daniel. 1715#12

Some receipts of medicines, for the most part parable and simple... sent to a friend in America. —BOYLE, Robert. 1688#2

Some remarks on a late pamphlet entitled, the state of religion in New-England, since the Rev. Mr George Whitefield's arrival there... —WHITEFIELD, George. 1742#51

Some remarks on a pretended answer to a discourse concerning the common-prayer worship with an exhortation to the churches in New-England to hold forth to their faith without wavering... —MATHER, Increase. 1712#18

Some remarks on the present state of the iron-trade of Great Britain. —1738#25

Some remarks on the Royal Navy. To which are annexed some short but interesting reflections on a future peace. —1760#89

Some remarks upon Dr. Wagstaffe's letter, and Mr. Massey's sermon against inoculating the small-pox... —BRADY, Samuel. 1722#5

Some thoughts concerning the present revival of religion in New England, and the way it ought to be acknowledged and promoted... —EDWARDS, Jonathan. 1743#14

Some thoughts upon America, and upon the danger from Roman Catholicks there. —1739#64

Some treasure fetched out of rubbish. —COTTON, John. 1660#4

Some useful observations on the consequences of the present war with Spain. —KEITH, William. 1740#22

Something in answer to a letter (which I have seen) of John Leverat Governor of Boston to William Coddington... dated 1677... —FOX, George. 1678#5

A song of Sion. Written by a citizen thereof, whose outward habitation is in Virginia... with an additional postscript from another hand. —GRAVE, John. 1662#6

A song of the judgements and mercies of the lord: wherein the things seen in secret, are declared openly... —COALE, Josiah. 1662#3

A song [on Louis XIV, Marshal Belle-Isle, and Prince Charles Edward Stuart...] —1745#34

A song on the taking of Mont-real by General Amherst. Sung by Mr. Lowe. —1759#94

Sophistry detected or an answer to George Keith's synopsis... —COOLE, Benjamin. 1699#5

The sorrowful lamentation, of James Campbell of Burnbank. Who is banished to the West Indians, for carrying on that horrid murder, of Margaret Hall, with his last farewell to Scotland. —1721#18

The sot-weed factor: or, a voyage to Maryland. A satyr. In which is described, the laws, government, courts and constitutions of the country... —COOK, Ebenezer. 1708#3

The soules exaltation... —HOOKER, Thomas. 1638#11

The soules humiliation... —HOOKER, Thomas. 1637#2A

The soules implantation... —HOOKER, Thomas. 1637#3

The soules ingrafting into Christ... —HOOKER, Thomas. 1637#4

The soules possession of Christ... —HOOKER, Thomas. 1638#12

The soules preparation for Christ, or a treatise of contrition. —HOOKER, Thomas. 1632#1

The soules vocation or effectual calling to Christ... —HOOKER, Thomas. 1638#13

Souls flying to Jesus Christ, pleasant and admirable to behold. A sermon preached... at the opening evening lecture, in... Boston... October 21, 1740. —COLMAN, Benjamin. 1741#6

The sound beleever. Or, a treatise of evangelicall conversion. —SHEPARD, Thomas. 1645#17

South-Carolina, George the Second by the grace of God... —GREAT BRITAIN. SOVEREIGN. GEORGE II. 1733#21

The Spanish hireling detected: being a refutation of the several calumnies and falsehoods in a late pamphlet, entituled an impartial account... —CADOGAN, George. 1743#7

Spartan lessons; or, the praise of valour; in the verses of Tyrtaeus... —1759#95

A specimen towards a new and compleat plan for regulating and settling the military power of Great Britain... by incorporating the Land and Sea-Forces... —1730#32

Speculum mundi. or A glasse representing the face of the world. —SWAN, John. 1635#4

A speech delivered by an Indian chief, in reply to a sermon by a Swedish missionary in order to convert the Indians to the Christian religion. —1753#20

A speech delivered in Parliament, by a worthy member thereof. —PYM, John. 1641#19

The speech of a Creek-Indians [sic], against the immoderate use of spirituous liquors. Delivered in a national assembly of the Creeks... —SMITH, William. (1727-1803). 1754#36

The speech of Mr. John Checkley upon his tryal, at Boston in New-England, for publishing the Short and easy method with the deists... —CHECKLEY, John. 1730#4

The speech of the Lord Commissioners to both Houses of Parliament... 1 June 1754. —GREAT BRITAIN. LORDS COMMISSIONERS FOR OPENING PARLIAMENT. 1754#13

The speech of the Lords Commissioners to both Houses of Parliament, on Tuesday the twentieth day of June, 1758. —GREAT BRITAIN. LORDS COMMISSIONERS FOR OPENING PARLIAMENT. 1758#24

The speech of the right honourable the Lord Viscount Gage, in parliament, against the convention with Spain. —GAGE, Thomas. 1739#28

The spirit of laws. Translated from the French of M. de Secondat... —MONTESQUIEU, Charles Louis de Secondat, Baron Montesquieu. 1750#33

The spirit of the martyrs revived in the doctrines of the Reverend George Whitefield, and the judicious and faithful methodists... Part I. —WARNE, Jonathan. 1740#36

A spiritual voice to the Christian church and to the Jews... in which the approaching millennium is supported... —CLARKE, Richard. 1760#23

Spiritual milk for babes. —COTTON, John. 1668#2

Spiritual milk for Boston Babes. —COTTON, John. 1657#6

St. Foine improved. —PETTUS, John. 1671#8

The standard of the Lord lifted up in New-England... —NICHOLSON, Joseph. 1660#18

State of British and French colonies in North America, with respect to number of people, forces, forts, Indians, trade and other advantages... —1755#54

The state of religion in New-England, since the Reverend George Whitefield's arrival there. In a letter from a gentleman in New-England... —M., A. 1742#27

A state of the British sugar-colony trade... —MASSIE, Joseph. 1759#66

The state of the case... betwixt the... Quakers, in Pennsylvania... and George Keith... —JENNINGS, Samuel. 1694#14

State of the Constitution of the colonies —1720#36

The state of the nation considered, in a letter to a member of Parliament. —GRANVILLE, John Carteret. 1746#9

The state of the nation for 1747-8 with a general balance of the publick accompts. —1748#29

The state of the nation for the year 1747, and respecting 1748. Inscribed to a member of the present Parliament. —GRANVILLE, John Carteret. 1748#6

A state of the national debt, as it stood December... 1716, with the payments... out of the sinking fund, &c. compared with... 1725. —PULTENEY, William. 1727#21

The state of the Palatines, for fifty years past to this present time —1709#21

A state of the province of Georgia, attested upon oath... in the court of Savannah, Nov. 10, 1740. —STEPHENS, William. 1742#45

A state of the rise and progress of our disputes with Spain, and of the conduct of our ministers... —CAMPBELL, Hugh Hume. 1739#10

A state of the proceedings in the House of Commons, with relation to the impeached Lords... —1701#39

The state of the Society in Scotland, for Propagating Christian Knowledge, anno 1729. Published by order of the general meeting of the foresaid society. —SOCIETY IN SCOTLAND FOR PROPAGATING CHRISTIAN KNOWLEDGE. 1729#24

State of the Society in Scotland for propagating Christian knowledge... together with some account of this Society's missionaries for converting the native Indians of America. —SOCIETY IN

SCOTLAND FOR PROPAGATING CHRISTIAN KNOWLEDGE. 1741#37

The state of the trade and manufactory of iron in Great-Britain considered... —1750#48

A state of the trade carried on with the French, on the island of Hispaniola, by the merchants in North America, under colour of flags of truce... —MERCHANT OF LONDON. 1760#66

The state of trade of the northern colonies considered; with an account of their produce, and a particular description of Nova Scotia... —LITTLE, Otis. 1748#13

A stiptick for a bleeding nation. —1721#20

The strange and dangerous voyage of Captaine Thomas James, in his intended discovery of the Northwest Passage into the South Sea... —JAMES, Thomas. 1633#3

Strange and prodigious religious customs and manners of sundry nations... —CROUCH, Nathaniel. 1683#8

Strange newes from Virginia, being a true relation of a great tempest. —1667#7

Strange news from Virginia; being a full and true account of the life and death of Nathanael Bacon Esquire. —1677#18

Strength out of weaknesse; or A glorious manifestation of the further progress of the gospel among the Indians in New-England... —WHITFIELD, Henry. 1652#17

Strenuous motives for an immediate war against Spain... Inscribed to the merchants of Great-Britain trading to America. —1738#26

Subjection to Christ in all his ordinances and appointments, the best means to preserve our liberty... —SHEPARD, Thomas. 1652#12

A subsidy granted to the King, of Tonnage and Poundage, and other sums of money payable upon merchandize exported and imported. Together with a book of rates... —ENGLAND AND WALES. PARLIAMENT. 1660#7

The substance of a letter from Mr. Davies... to Mr Bellamy of Bethlem, in New England, concerning the state of religion in Virginia... —DAVIES, Samuel. 1751#12

A succinct view of the Society in Scotland for propagating Christian knowledge... —SOCIETY IN SCOTLAND FOR THE PROPAGATION OF CHRISTIAN KNOWLEDGE. 1738#23

The sufferings of the people called Quakers... from the year 1650 to the year 1660. —BESSE, Joseph. 1733#3

A summary, historical and political, of the first planting, progressive improvements, and present state of the British settlements in North America... —DOUGLASS, William. 1755#18

Supernatural revelation the only sure hope of sinners. A sermon preached... —WEBSTER, Alexander. 1741#47

Supplement to the Bibliotheca parochialis. —BRAY, Thomas. 1697#4

A supplement to the candid narrative of the rise and progress of the Herrnhuters, commonly called Moravians... in which the political schemes... of their patriarch are disclosed... —RIMIUS, Heinrich. 1755#43

A supplement to the detection of the state and situation of the present sugar planters... —ROBERTSON, Robert. 1733#30

A supplement to the first edition of The detection of the court of England. —COKE, Roger. 1696#6

A supplement to the Negro's and Indian's advocate: Or, some further considerations and proposals for the effectual and speedy carrying on of the Negro's Christianity... —GODWIN, Morgan. 1681#10

A supplement to the State of the Nation; being free-thoughts on the present critical conjuncture. —GRANVILLE, John Carteret. 1748#7

Surrender of seven eighth parts of Carolina, from Lord Carteret to his majesty... —GRANVILLE, John Carteret. 1744#19

A survay of that foolish, seditious, scandalous, prophane libell, The protestation protested. —HALL, Joseph. 1641#12

A survey of the spirituall antichrist. —RUTHERFORD, Samuel. 1648#12

A survey of the summe of church-discipline. Wherein, the way of the churches of New-England is warranted out of the Word. —HOOKER, Thomas. 1648#6

A survey of the Survey of that summe of church discipline, penned by Mr Thomas Hooker, late pastor... in New England... —RUTHERFORD, Samuel. 1658#11

A survey of trade, in four parts... Together with considerations on our money and bullion... —WOOD, William. 1718#23

Sylva, or a discourse of forest trees, and the propagation of timber in his majesty's dominions. —EVELYN, John. 1660#6

Sympathy with our suffering brethren... two discourses... To which are prefixed, some serious reflections on the present situation of these nations, and our American colonies. —GIBBONS, Thomas. 1755#21

Synopsis methodica animalium quadrupedum et serpentini generis... —RAY, John. 1693#16

A system of geography, or, A new and accurate description of the earth in all its empires, kingdoms and states... —MOLL, Herman. 1701#31

A system of moral philosophy in three books... —HUTCHESON, Francis. 1755#30

A system of the principles of the laws of Scotland... —WALLACE, George. 1760#100

Table of meteorological observations from 1721 to 1729 in nine voyages to Hudson's Bay. —MIDDLETON, Christopher?. 1730#20

A tale of Two Tubs: or, the b———s in querpo... —1749#42

The tales and jests of Mr Hugh Peters, collected in one volume... —PETER, Hugh. 1660#23

Taxes no charge: in a letter from a gentleman, to a person of quality... —DEFOE, Daniel. 1690#8

Tears of repentance: or, A further narrative of the progress of the gospel amongst the Indians in New England... —ELIOT, John. 1653#8

Telliamed: or, Discourses between an Indian philosopher and a French missionary, on the diminution of the sea, formation of the earth, the origin of men... —MAILLET, Benoît de. 1750#31

The temple... —HERBERT, George. 1633#2

The temple measured: or, a brief survey of the temple mystical, which is the instituted church of Christ... —NOYES, James. 1647#13

Ten practical discourses. —BRADLEY, Richard. 1727#2

Ten sermons preached on the following subjects... —WHITEFIELD, George. 1751#35A

The tenth muse lately sprung up in America. Or severall poems... Also a dialogue between old England and new, concerning the late troubles. —BRADSTREET, Anne. 1650#1

The terrible calamities that are occasioned by war... a sermon... November the 29th, 1759... —SMITH, Thomas. 1760#87

A testimony against John Fenwick, concerning his proceeding about New-Cesaria, or New-Jersey... Also John Fenwick's letter of condemnation... —1675#14

A testimony against several prophane and superstitions customs, now practised by some in New-England... —MATHER, Increase. 1687#6

The testimony and advice of an assembly of pastors of churches in New England, at a meeting in Boston, July 7, 1743. Occasioned by the late happy revival of religion. —BOSTON. ASSEMBLY OF PASTORS. 1744#5

A testimony concerning our dear and well-beloved friend and brother in the truth, William Coale... —1682#27

A testimony concerning the life, death, travels... of Edward Burroughs... —HOWGILL, Francis. 1662#9

Thankfulness for mercies received... farewel sermon... on board Whitaker, at anchor near Savannah... May the 17th, 1738... —WHITEFIELD, George. 1738#35

A thanksgiving sermon preach'd at Boston... December, 1705. On the return of a gentleman from his travels. —WILLARD, Samuel 1640-1707. 1709#25

A thanksgiving-sermon, preached in the parish church of Greensted, in Essex, on Thursday November 29, 1759... By John Harris... —HARRIS, John. 1759#45

A theatre of politicall flying insects. Wherein especially the nature... of the bee, is discovered and described... —PURCHAS, Samuel. 1657#12

The theatre of the present war in North America: with candid reflections on the great improvement of the war in that part of the world. —YOUNG, Arthur. 1758#53

Theatrum botanicum: The theater of plants —PARKINSON, John. 1640#4

Their majesties declaration against the French King... [7 May 1689.] —ENGLAND AND WALES. SOVEREIGN. WILLIAM AND MARY. 1689#10

The theological works... —BOYLE, Robert. 1715#5

Theses Sabbaticae. Or, The doctrine of the Sabbath. —SHEPARD, Thomas. 1649#7

Things as they are [part 1]. —PERCEVAL, John. 1758#34

The third and last letter to a gentleman dissenting from the Church of England. —WHITE, John. 1745#38

A third collection of papers relating to the present juncture of affairs in England. —1688#25

A third letter from a member of the Society. —SOCIETY FOR THE PROPAGATION OF THE GOSPEL. 1718#20

A third letter to the people of England on liberty, taxes, and the application of public money... —SHEBBEARE, John. 1756#73

A third narrative of the proceedings at Turners-Hall... —KEITH, George. 1698#11

The third part of Gangraena. —EDWARDS, Thomas. 1646#11

The third part of the present state of England... To which is likewise added England's guide to industry: or, the improvement of trade for the good of all people in general. —PETTY, William. 1683#18

The third volume of the Compleat History of the lives and robberies of the most notorious high-way men... —SMITH, Alexander. 1720#35

Thoughts concerning the present revival of religion in New England... Abridged by John Wesley. —EDWARDS, Jonathan. 1745#19

Thoughts on present war and future peace; wherein our present measures and alliances, are candidly considered... —1760#93

Thoughts on the glorious epiphany of the Lord Jesus Christ... —DODD, William. 1757#9

Thoughts on trade, and a publick spirit. —BASTON, Thomas. 1716#1

Three godly sermons... —HOOKER, Thomas. 1638#13A

Three letters from New-England, relating to the controversy of the present time. —MATHER, Cotton. 1721#12

Three letters... III. To the inhabitants of Maryland, Virginia, and North and South Carolina, concerning their Negroes. —WHITEFIELD, George. 1740#44

Three letters of thanks to the Protestant reconciler. 1. From the Anabaptists at Munster. 2. From the congregations in New-England. 3. From the Quakers in Pensilvania. —1683#23

Three letters to a gentleman dissenting from the Church of England. —WHITE, John. 1748#35

Three letters wrote from Boston in New-England to a correspondent in the Gorbels of Glasgow... —1741#43

Thunder from heaven against the back-sliders... —ASPINWALL, William. 1654#2

The time when the first sabbath was ordained... —PYNCHON, William. 1654#14

Time's telescope universal and perpetual... with a general view of the four parts of the world. —CAMPBELL, Duncan. 1734#4

To Friends in Barbadoes, Virginia, Maryland, New-England, and elsewhere. —FOX, George. 1661#8

To friends in England, Ireland, Scotland, Holland, New-England... London. —PENINGTON, Isaac. 1666#5

To our reverend and deare brethren the ministers of England and Wales. —1649#8

To our reverend brethren the ministers of the Gospel in England and Wales. —1649#9

To the councill of officers of the Armie, and the Heads of the nation; and for the inferior officers and souldiers to read. —FOX, George. 1659#14

To the Governor and Council of East New Jersey and the inhabitants etc. ordering their obedience to the proprietors, the Earl of Perth... —ENGLAND AND WALES. SOVEREIGN. CHARLES II. 1683#11

To the honourable General Townshend, on his arrival from Quebec. —LOCKMAN, John. 1759#63

To the honorable the House of Commons. Reasons (humbly offered) against laying a further duty on linnens to be imported in England;... —1714#21

To the King's most excellent majesty... an essay for recovery of trade. —SMITH, William. 1661#17

To the King's most excellent majesty. The humble address of divers gentry, merchants, and others... in Boston, Charlestown and places adjacent... —1691#21

To the King's most excellent majesty, the humble petition of... —WILLIAMS, Roger, mariner. 1681#21

To the King's most excellent majesty. The humble petition of William Dyre gent... —DYRE, William. 1670#4

To the Kings most excellent majesty, the humble remonstrance of John Blande... on the behalf of the inhabitants and planters in Virginia and Mariland... —BLAND, John. 1661#4

To the King's most excellent Majesty. The petition of David Pryce, Esq. master and commander in your Majesty's Royal Navy, and late... —PRYCE, David. 1760#79

To the most noble prince Henry duke of Beaufort... Palatine of the province of South Carolina in America. —MARSTON, Edward. 1712#16

To the Parliament of England, the case of the poor English protestants in Mary-land under the arbitrary power of their popish governour the Lord Baltimore... —1681#20

To the pious, charitable, and well-disposed Christians, inhabitants of Great Britain... the humble memorial of Charles Beatty. —BEATTY, Charles. 1760#7

To the quarterly and monthly meetings of Friends, in Great Britain, Ireland, and America... From the meeting for sufferings in London, the sixth day of the seventh month, 1751... —SOCIETY OF FRIENDS. 1751#33

To the quarterly and monthly meetings of Friends in Pennsylvania and elsewhere in America... —SOCIETY OF FRIENDS. 1754#37

To the right honourable the Parliament of the Commonwealth of England... Humble petition of Edward Godfrey... and sundry others... of the Provinces of Mayne and Liconia... —GODFREY, Edward. 1659#15

To the Right Honourable the Lords Commissioners of Trade and Plantations the following supplement to my essay on trade is most humbly offered. —1741#44

To the right honourable William, Earl of Craven... being proprietors of Carolina, and the Bahama Islands... —BULKLEY, Thomas. 1694#2

To the Right Reverend, and Reverend the Bishops, and Clergy of the Province of Canterbury... in Convocation... petition of many... —1689#29

To the supreme authority of this nation, the Commons of England assembled in Parliament... The humble petition of the merchants and others of the cities of London and Bristol... —1650#14

To the worthy and generous friends of religion and learning; the petition of Gilbert Tennent and Samuel Davies, in the name of the... —TENNENT, Gilbert. 1754#39

A token for mariners, containing many famous and wonderful instances of God's providence in sea dangers and deliverances... —JANEWAY, James. 1708#10

Toleration and liberty of conscience considered, and proved impracticable, impossible... sinful and unlawful. —NALSON, John. 1685#19

Tombo-Chiqui: or, the American savage. A dramatic entertainment. In three acts. —LA DREVETIERE, Louis L'Isle de. 1758#30

Torism and trade never agree. To which is added, an account and character of the Mercator... In a letter to Sir G- H-. —OLDMIXON, John. 1713#10

The total consequences which may arise from the want of system in the conduct of public affairs. —1756#79

A total rout, or a brief discovery of a pack of knaves and drabs... —1653#18

The trade and navigation of Great-Britain considered: shewing that the surest way for a nation to increase in riches, is to prevent... —GEE, Joshua. 1729#9

Trade preferred before religion, and Christ made to give way to Mammon... a sermon relating to the plantations... —GODWIN, Morgan. 1685#16

Trade revived, or a way proposed to restore, increase inrich, strengthen and preserve the decayed... trade of this our English nation... —BLAND, John. 1659#2

The trappan'd maiden: or, the distressed damsel... —1700#35

The trappan'd Welsh man, sold to Virginia. —1685#29

The travels and adventures of John Thomson, who was taken and carried to America... —1760#96

Travels and voyages into Africa, Asia, and America, and the East and West-Indies... —MOCQUET, Jean. QUERY DATE 1696#20

Travels of the Jesuits into various parts of the world; compiled from their letters... —LOCKMAN, John. 1743#22

The treasure of traffike. or a discourse of forraigne trade. —ROBERTS, Lewes. 1641#20

A treatise concerning the motion of the seas... —VOSSIUS, Isaac. 1677#20

A treatise of liturgies... in answer to... Mr. John Ball... —SHEPARD, Thomas. 1653#17

A treatise of Mr Cottons... concerning predestination... —TWISSE, William. 1646#19

A treatise of New England published in anno Dom. 1637. and now reprinted. —1650#15

A treatise of the covenant of Grace... —COTTON, John. 1659#7

A treatise on maritime affairs: or a comparison between the naval power of England and France... —HORSLEY, William. 1744#26

A treatise wherein is demonstrated, that the Church and state of England, are in equal danger with the trade of it. —COKE, Roger. 1671#5

A treaty for the composing of differences, and the establishing of peace in America, between the Crowns of Great Britain and Spain. —ENGLAND AND WALES. TREATIES. 1670#6

The treaty held with the Indians of the Six Nations at Philadelphia, in July 1742. —PENNSYLVANIA PROVINCE. 1744#35

Treaty of peace, good correspondence and neutrality in America, between... James II... of Great Britain, and... Lewis XIV... —ENGLAND AND WALES. SOVEREIGN. JAMES II. 1686#1

The trial and remarkable life of William Parsons, who was executed at Tyburn near London, on Monday the 11th of February 17501... —PARSONS, William. 1751#26

The trial at bar, between Campbell Craig... and... Richard earl of Anglesey... at the King's Courts, Dublin... 1743. —CRAIG, Campbell. 1743#10

The trial at bar, between Campbell Craig, lessee of James Annesley, Esq: plaintiff, and... Richard Earl of Anglesey, defendant... —CRAIG, Campbell. 1744#11

The trial at large, between James Annesley, Esq. and the Rt. Hon. Earl of Anglesea... —CRAIG, Campbell. 1744#12

The trial in ejectment (at large) between Campbell Craig, lessee of James Annesley... and... Richard Earl of Anglesea... Friday, November 11, 1743... —CRAIG, Campbell. 1744#13

The trial of James Annesley and Joseph Redding, at the Sessions-House in the Old Bailey, on Thursday the 15th July, 1742 for the murder of Thomas Egglestone... —1742#48

The trial of Mr Whitefield's spirit. In some remarks upon his fourth Journal... —WELLER, Samuel. 1740#37

The trial of the Right Honourable Richard Earl of Anglesey... For an assault on the Honourable James Annesley... —1744#38

A trip to New-England. With a character of the country and people, both English and Indians. —WARD, Edward. 1699#19

The triumphs and hopes of Great-Britain and Ireland. A sermon preached... Thursday November the 29th, 1759... —HENRY, William. 1759#47

Trodden down strength, by the God of strength, or Mrs Drake revived... —HART, John. 1647#9

A true account of the Aloe Americana or Africana, which is niw in blossom in Mr. Cowell's garden at Hoxton... —COWELL, John. 1729#5

A true account of the behaviour, confession and dying speeches, of Captain William Kidd, and the rest of the pyrates that were executed... 23rd of May, 1701 —1701#42

A true account of the dying words of Ockanickon, an Indian King... by John Cripps of Burlington, N. J. —CRIPPS, John. 1682#9

A true account of the most considerable occurences that have hapned [sic] in the warre between the English and the Indians in New England... —1676#21

A true account of the proceedings... of... Quakers in London... to... end... divisions and differences among some of the people... —HANNAY, Robert. 1694#8

A true account of the tryals, examinations, confessions, condemnations, and executions of divers witches, at Salem, in New-England... —M., C. 1693#12

The true account of the voyage of the Nottingham-galley of London, John Dean Commander... —LANGMAN, Christopher. 1711#13

A true and accurate account of the disposal of the one hundred shares or proprieties of the province of West-New-Jersey, by Edward Bylling... —BUDD, Thomas. 1685#5

A true and authentic account of A. F., concerning the occasion of his coming among the Herrnhuters or Moravians... —FREYEN, ANDREAS. 1753#7

A true and exact list, of all the criminals in Newgate, who were transported this day being Thursday the 28th of August. 1718. —1718#21

A true and exact list of all the malefactors, both men and women, who pleaded to His Majesty's most gracious pardon, at the sessions-house... —1715#22

A true, and faithful account of the four chiefest plantations of the English in America... Virginia, New-England, Bermudas, Bar-

bados... as also... the natives of Virginia, and New-England... —CLARKE, Samuel. 1670#2

A true and genuine account of the life and doctrine of the Reverend Mr. George Whitefield —1741#45

A true and historical narrative of the colony of Georgia in America, from the first settlement thereof until this present present period... —TAILFER, Patrick. 1741#39

A true and particular history of earthquakes... —PHILOTHEUS. 1748#19

A true believers testimony of the work of true faith... —ROFE, George. 1661#16

The true character of the Rev. Mr. Whitefield. —1739#65

The true constitution of a particular visible church —COTTON, John. 1642#8

True copies of I. the agreement between Lord Baltimore and Messieurs Penn, dated 10 May 1732. II. The commissions... to mark out the... —1733#35

The true copy of a letter: written by Mr. Thomas Parker... in New-England... touching the government practised in the churches of New-England. —PARKER, Thomas. 1644#13

The true copy of a paper... together with a short list of... vile and gross errors... (being of the same sort and nature... charged on some in Pensilvania... —KEITH, George. 1695#16

A true copy of eight pages out of the History of the present State of Virginia... containing an account of the actions of Francis Nicholson... —1720#37

A true description of Carolina. —GASCOYNE, Joel. 1682#15

The true English interest. —REYNELL, Carew. 1674#11

A true history of the captivity and restoration of Mrs Mary Rowlandson, a minister's wife in New England... annexed, a sermon... by Mr. Joseph Rowlandson... —ROWLANDSON, Mary. 1682#24

The true interest and political maxims of the republick of Holland and West-Friesland... Written by John de Witt and other great men in Holland... —COURT VAN DER VOORT, Pieter de la. 1702#6

The true interest of Great Britain, Ireland and our plantations: or, a proposal for making such an union... as that already made betwixt Scotland and England... —MURRAY, Alexander. 1740#24

A true list of the several ships arrived at Leghorne from Great Britain, Ireland, and Newfoundland, in one year, commencing at Lady-Day, 1712, to Lady-Day, 1713... —1713#15

The true lover's joy: or, a dialogue between a seaman and his love. —1670#13

The true picture of an ancient Tory. —DAVENANT, Charles. 1702#7

A true relation of of [sic] a wonderfull sea fight betweene two... Spanish ships... and a small... English ship... in her passage to Virginia... —1621#6

A true relation of the late battell fought in New England, between the English, and the salvages: with the present state of things there. —VINCENT, Philip. 1637#7

A true relation of the proceedings against certain Quakers, at the generall court of the Massachusetts... October 18, 1659... —1660#27

A true relation of Virginia and Mary-land; with the commodities therein, which in part the author saw, the rest he had from credible persons... anno 1669. —SHRIGLEY, Nathaniel. 1669#5

True religion, loyalty and union recommended... sermon preached at Pleshey, Feb. 11, 1757... —BALL, Nathaniel. 1757#1

A true representation of the state of the case of the sugar islands... fully answering a paper entitled, The dispute between the northern settlements and the sugar colonies... —1732#42

A true state of the Bishop of London's jurisdiction in the plantations abroad. —1728#15

The true state of the case between John Fenwick Esq., and John Eldridge and Edmund Warner, concerning Mr. Fenwick's ten parts of his land in West New Jersey in America. —1677#19

A true state of the case between the British Northern-Colonies, and the sugar islands in America... with respect... —1732#43

A true state of the case between the inhabitants of South Carolina, and the Lords Proprietors of that province; containing an account of the grievances under which they labour. —1720#38

A true state of the tobacco trade I. As it relates to the plantations in America,... V. As it relates to the incouragement of the said plantations... —1707#15.

The true travels, adventures, and observations of Captaine John Smith, in Europe, Asia, Affrika, and America, from anno Domini 1593. to 1629... —SMITH, John. 1630#8

A trumpet sounded out of the wilderness of America... —LEEDS, Daniel. 1699#9

The truth and economy of the Christian religion. A sermon preached... January 3, 1732. —HAMILTON, William. 1732#22

The truth and excellency of the gospel-revelation... —KINLOCH, Robert. 1731#24

The truth exalted in the writings of that eminent and faithful servant of Christ, John Burnyeat, collected into this ensuing volume... —BURNYEAT, John. 1691#4

Truth and innocence the armour and defence of the people called Quakers... Being an answer to part of a book, entituled, The man of God furnished. —HENDERSON, Patrick. 1709#9

Truth and inocency defended; against falsehood and envy... In answer to Cotton Mather... his late Church-History of New-England... —WHITING, John. 1703#12

Truth defended: and the friends thereof cleared, from the false charges... by George Keith... in two books... —ELLWOOD, Thomas. 1695#10

Truth further defended, and William Penn vindicated... —WIGHT, Thomas. 1700#37

Truth prevalent; and the Quakers discharged from the Norfolk rector's furious charge. —WHITEHEAD, George. 1701#43

Truth rescued from imposture. Or a brief reply to. . . a pretented answer, to the tryal of W. Penn, and W. Mead, etc. . . —PENN, William. 1670#11

Truth stifled, and an appeal to the genius of the ancient Romans. Being the case of Dr John Tennent, with respect to his free publication. . . —TENNENT, John M.D. 1741#42

Truth the strongest of all: or, An apostate further convicted, and truth defended; in reply to George Keith's Fifth narrative. —WHITING, John. 1706#20

Truth, Truth, Truth. . . —1715#23

The tryal of John Peter Zenger, of New-York, printer. . . With the pleadings and arguments on both sides. . . —1738#29

The tryall of travell. . . In three bookes epitomized. . . —GOODALL, Baptist. 1630#4

The tryals of Peter Boss, George Keith, Thomas Budd, and William Bradford, Quakers. . . at Philadelphia in Pennsylvania, the ninth, tenth and twelfth days of December, 1692. . . —KEITH, George. 1693#10

The tryals of Major Stede Bonnet, and other pirates. . . at the Admiralty Sessions held at Charles-Town. . . the 28th of October, 1718. . . —1719#10

Tryon's letters, domestic and foreign to several persons of quality. . . —TRYON, Thomas. 1700#36

Tunbridgalia: or, The pleasures of Tunbridge. A poem. In Latin and English. —CAUSTON, Peter. 1684#3

A turbulent spirit troubled with his our confutations. In reply to George Keith's pretended Answer to seventeen queries. . . —NICKOLLS, Thomas. 1702#19

A tutor to astronomie and geographie: or an easie. . . —MOXON, Joseph. 1659#23

Two addresses from the governour, council and convention of the Massachusetts colony. . . Presented to his majesty at Hampton-Court, August 7, 1689. . . —MASSACHUSETTS GOVERNOR, COUNCIL AND CONVENTION. 1689#15

Two bookes of epigrammes and epitaphs. . . —BANCROFT, Thomas. 1639#1

The two charters granted by King Charles IId. to the proprietors of Carolina. With the first and fundamfntal [sic] constitutions of that colony. —1698#24

Two dialogues on the man-trade. —PHILLMORE, J. 1760#75

Two discourses delivered. . . October the 25th, 1759, being the day appointed by authority. . . as a day of thanksgiving for the success of his majesty's arms. . . reduction of Quebec. . . —MAYHEW, Jonathan. 1760#65

Two essays sent from Oxford to a nobleman in London, concerning some errors about the creation, general flood and peopling of the world. . . —P., L. 1695#22

The two first parts of his life, with his journals. . . —WHITEFIELD, George. 1756#87

The two great questions consider'd. —DEFOE, Daniel. 1700#13

Two letters. . . —HANWAY, Jonas. 1758#26

Two letters, concerning some farther advantages and improvements that may been necessary to be made on the taking and keeping of Cape Breton. . . —PHILOLAOS. 1746#16

Two letters of the Lord Bishop of London: the first, to the masters and mistresses of families in the English plantations abroad. . . The second, to the missionaries there. . . —GIBSON, Edmund. 1727#10

Two letters to a friend, on the present critical conjuncture of affairs in North America; particularly on the vast importance of the victory. . . —CHAUNCY, Charles. (1705-1787). 1755#6

Two ordinances of the Lords and Commons. . . the one dated November 2. 1643. . . the other March 21. 1645. . . —ENGLAND AND WALES. LORDS AND COMMONS. 1646#12

Two plain and practical discourses. Concerning 1. Hardness of Heart. . . —MATHER, Increase. 1699#12

Two sermons preach'd at the parish-church of St. George. . . London May the 12th. 1700. —KEITH, George. 1700#24

Two sermons, preached to a congregation of black slaves, at the parish church of S. P., in the province of Maryland. By an American pastor. —BACON, Thomas. 1749#5

Two treatises of government. —LOCKE, John. 1690#13

A two years journal in New-York: and part of its territories in America. . . —WOOLEY, Charles. 1701#46

Tythe no gospel maintenance, for gospel ministers. . . —LODDINGTON, William. 1695#17

Unanswerable arguments against a peace. —BRITISH FREEHOLDER. 1760#12

The unbeleevers-preparing for Christ. . . —HOOKER, Thomas. 1638#14

The undoubted art of thriving, showing that a million. . . may be raised. . . how the Indian and African Company may propagate their. . . —DONALDSON, James. 1700#15

The unhappiness of England, as to its trade by sea and land. . . —POVEY, Charles. 1701#35

Unio reformantium sive examen Hoornbecki de indepentismo apologeticum. . . —BEVERLEY, John. 1659#1

The universal dictionary of trade and commerce. Translated from the French. . . by Malachy Postlethwayt. —SAVARY DES BRUSLONS, Jacques. 1751#32

A universal geographical dictionary; or, grand gazetteer; including a comprehensive view of Europe. . . and America; more especially of the British dominions and settlements. . . —BRICE, Andrew. 1759#9

An universal, historical, geographical, chronological and poetical dictionary —1703#10

The universal merchant: containing a rationale of commerce, in theory and practice. —MAGENS, Nikolaus. 1753#17

The universal pocket-book... Containing... I. A map of the world. —1740#35

The universal traveller: or, a compleat description of the several nations of the world... —SALMON, Thomas. 1752#18

The universal traveller: or, A complete account of the most remarkable voyages and travels. —BARCLAY, Patrick. 1733#2

The unlawfulnes and danger of limited episcopacie. —BAILLIE, Robert. 1641#1

Unto the Right Honourable, the Lords of Council and Session, the petition of John Jamieson merchant in Glasgow. —JAMIESON, John. 1746#14

Upon the joyfull and welcome return of Charles the second... to his... government over these his majesties kingdoms and dominions... —MAYHEW, Thomas. 1660#17

Upon Wednesday the 18th day of November 1696. —HUDSON'S BAY COMPANY. 1696#12

Useful miscellanies, or Serious reflections, respecting mens duty to God. —DOVER, William. 1739#21

The vain prodigal life, and tragical penitential death of Thomas Hellier... executed according to law at Westover, in Charles-City, in the Country of Virginia... 5th August 1678... —G., R. 1680#3

The vast importance of the herring fishery to these kingdoms... —LOCKMAN, John. 1750#28

Vectigalium systema: or, a complete view of that part of the revenue of Great Britain, commonly called Customs. Wherein... IV. The laws... —EDGAR, William. 1714#5

Verses on the demise of the late king and the accession of his present majesty... —LOCKMAN, John. 1760#63

The vessels of mercy and the vessels of wrath... sermon first preached in New-Kent, Virginia, August 22, 1756... —DAVIES, Samuel. 1758#15

Victory... A sermon... January 31st 1730... Death of Thomas Hollis, Esq... —HUNT, Jeremiah. 1731#22

Victory and plenty great subjects of thanksgiving. A sermon preached in... Bexley... Kent. On Thursday the 29th of November, 1759... —PIERS, Henry. 1759#78

A view of the political transactions of Great Britain since the Convention was approved by Parliament. In a letter to an absenting member... —1739#67

A view of the Queen and kingdom's enemies, in the case of the poor Palatines... —1709#22

A view of the trade of South Carolina, with proposals humbly offerrd for improving the same. —YONGE, Francis. 1722#29

A vindication of commerce and the arts; proving that they are the source of the greatness... of a state... —TEMPLE, William. 1758#46

A vindication of the conduct of Captain Christopher Middleton, in a late voyage on board His Majesty's ship the Furnace... —MIDDLETON, Christopher. 1743#24

A vindication of the conduct of the present war; in a letter to ******. —1760#97

A vindication of the essence and unity of the Church Catholike visible... in answer to... Mr Hooker... —HUDSON, Samuel. 1650#6

A vindication of the rights of the Commons of England. By a member. —MACKWORTH, Humphrey, Sir. 1701#29

A vindication of William Penn, proprietary of Pennsilvania, from the late aspersions... 12th. 12 Month, 1682... —FORD, Philip. 1683#12

Vindiciae anti-Baxterianiae, or some animadversions on a book, entitled Reliquiae Baxterianiae, or the life of Mr. R. Baxter... —YOUNG, Samuel. 1696#24

Vindiciae clavium, or, A vindication of the keyes of the kingdome of heaven... Being some animadversions on a tract of Mr J.[ohn] C.[otton]... —CAWDREY, Daniel. 1645#3

Vindiciae Judaeorum, or a true account of the Jews... —THOROWGOOD, Thomas. 1666#6

Vindiciae ministerii evangelici... —COLLINGES, John. 1651#5

A vindication of New-England.% —MATHER, Increase? 1690#14

Virginia and Maryland. Or, the Lord Baltamore's [sic] printed case, uncased and answered. Shewing, the illegality of his patent... —1655#21

Virginia impartially examined, and left to publick view, to be considered by all judicious and honest men... —BULLOCK, William. 1649#1

Virginia ss. Pleas at the capitol in Williamsburgh... —BURGES, Frances. 1737#3

Virginia. The right honourable Thomas Lord Fairfax petitioner, the governor and council of Virginia, in right of the Crown defendents. The case on behalf of the Crown. —FAIRFAX, Thomas, Lord. 1739#26

The Virginia trade stated... —1680#11

Virginia's cure: or an advisive narrative concerning Virginia. Discovering the true ground of that churches unhappiness... —GRAY, Robert. 1662#7

Virginia's danger and remedy. Two discourses, occasioned by the severe drought in sundry parts of the country; and the defeat of General Braddock. —DAVIES, Samuel. 1756#20

Virginia's discovery of silke-wormes, with their benefit. And the implanting of mulberry trees... —WILLIAMS, Edward. 1650#16

Virginia's God be thanked, or A sermon of thanksgiving for the happie successe of the affayres in Virginia this last yeare. Preached by Patrick Copland... 18. of April 1622... —COPLAND, Patrick. 1622#8

Virgo triumphans: or, Virginia richly and truly valued; more especially the south part thereof: viz the fertile Carolina, and no lesse excellent isle of Roanoak. . . —WILLIAMS, Edward. 1650#17

Virtue triumphant; or, Elizabeth Canning in America; being a circumstantial narrative of her adventures, from her setting sail for transportation, to the present time. . . . —1757#49

The virtues and excellency of the American tobacco plant, for cure of diseases, and preservation of health: And the noxious qualities of the tobacco growing in northern countries. —1712#25

The visions and prophecies of Daniel. . . —PARKER, Thomas. 1646#16

A visitation of tender love (once more) from the Lord unto Charles the II . —RIGGE, Ambrose. 1662#13

The voice of liberty. An occasional essay. . . —1756#82

The voice of the people: A collection of addresses to his Majesty, and instructions to members of Parliament by their constituents. . . —1756#83

Vox populi: or, A cloud of witnesses, proving the leading Quakers great impostors. —BUGG, Francis. 1702#4

A voyage into New England begun in 1623 and ended in 1624. Performed by Christopher Levett, his majesties woodward of Somersetshire, and one of the Councell of New England. . . —LEVETT, Christopher. 1624#9

A voyage round the world. . . in the years 1719, 20, 21, 22 in the Speedwell of London. . . —SHELVOCKE, George. 1726#15

The voyage, shipwreck, and miraculous escape of Richard Castleman. . . With a description of Pennsylvania. . . and. . . Philadelphia. . . —CHETWOOD, William Rufus. 1726#4

A voyage to England. . . as also Observations on the same voyage, by Dr. Thomas Sprat. . . with a letter of Monsieur Sorbiere's concerning the war. . . in 1652. —KING, WILLIAM. 1709#10

A voyage to Georgia. Begun in the year 1735. Containing, an account of the settling the town of Frederica. . . —MOORE, Francis. 1744#34

A voyage to Hudson's-Bay, by the Dobbs galley and California, in the years 1746 and 1747, for discovering a North-West Passage with. . . a short natural history of the country. . . —ELLIS, Henry. 1748#5

A voyage to the islands. . . with some relations concerning the neighbouring continent and islands of America. . . —SLOANE, Hans. 1707#14

A voyage to the South Sea, and round the world. . . —COOKE, Edward. 1712#5

A voyage to Virginia: or, the valliant souldiers' farewel to his love. . . —1685#30

The voyages and adventures of Captain Robert Boyle. . . To which is added the voyage, shipwreck, and miraculous escape of Richard Castleman. . . —CHETWOOD, William Rufus. 1726#5

The voyages and adventures of Miles Philips. . . the inhuman treatment he met. . . at Mexico, and the salvage Indians of Canada. . . —PHILIPS, Miles. 1724#17

The voyages and cruises of Commodore Walker, during the late Spanish and French Wars. In two volumes. —1760#99

The voyages, dangerous adventures and imminent escapes of Captain Richard Falconer: containing the laws, customs and manners of the Indians. . . —CHETWOOD, William Rufus. 1720#9

The wanderer. With all the motto's in Latin and English: to which is added The publick spirit, an heroick poem. By Mr. Fox. —FOX, John. 1718#6

The wandring whore continued. A dialogue between Magdalena. . . —GARFIELD, John. 1660#13

War: an heroic poem. From the taking of Minorca by the French, to the raising of the siege of Quebec. . . —COCKINGS, George. 1760#25

A warning against countenancing the ministrations of Mr G. Whitefield. . . —GIB, Adam. 1742#18

A warning to all the lovers of Christ in Scotland to be upon their guard against the spreading contagion broken out from Mr. Adam Gib. . . —OLD DRUMCLOG SOLDIER. 1742#32

A warning to the world; or the prophetical numbers of Daniel and John calculated. . . —CLARKE, Richard. 1759#19

The warnings of the Lord to the men of this generation. —BISHOP, George. 1660#2

The warr in New-England visibly ended. King Philip that barbarous Indian now beheaded, and most of his bloudy adherents submitted to mercy. . . —HUTCHINSON, Richard. 1677#9

The way cast up, and the stumbling-blocks removed. . . —KEITH, George. 1677#10

The way of congregational churches cleared. —COTTON, John. 1648#4

The way of life. Or, God's way and course, in bringing the soule into, keeping it in, and carrying it on, in the wayes of life and peace. . . in foure severall treatises. —COTTON, John. 1641#8

The way of the churches of Christ in New-England. —COTTON, John. 1645#5

Ways and means to raise the value of land; or, the landlords companion: with political discourses on the land-tax, war, and other subjects. —ALLEN, William. 1736#1

Ways and means whereby his majesty may man his navy with ten thousand able sailors. . . To which is added a collection of some political essays. By Eboranos. —EBORANOS. 1734#5

Weighty questions discussed. . . —FIRMIN, Giles. 1692#5

The West-India almanack for the year 1719. —PARKER, George. 1719#7

Whereas by Her Majesties directions, a monthly correspondence is settled, between Great Britain, and Her Majesties dominions on the mainland of America. —WARREN, William. 1710#25

Whereas... by reason... abuses of a lewd sort of people called spirits, in seducing many of his majesties subjects to go on shipboard... [December 13 1682.] —ENGLAND AND WALES. SOVEREIGN. CHARLES II. KING IN COUNCIL. 1682#12

Whereas... by reason... abuses of a lewd sort of people, called spirits, in seducing many of his majesties subjects to go on shipboard... —ENGLAND AND WALES. SOVEREIGN. JAMES II. 1686#2

Whereas it hath pleased Almighty God, to call to His mercy our late sovereign lord King William the Third... —ENGLAND AND WALES. SOVEREIGN. ANNE. 1702#11

Whereas some doubts have arisen with regard to the rank and command, which officers and troops raised by the governors of our provinces in North-America, should have... —GREAT BRITAIN. SOVEREIGN. GEORGE II. 1754#15

Whereas the Queen has been pleased to direct, that a monthly correspondence be established between this kingdom, and... the continent of America... —GREAT BRITAIN. GENERAL POST OFFICE. 1711#7

Whereas wee are credibly informed... —ENGLAND AND WALES. SOVEREIGN. JAMES I. 1621#2

Whereas we are credibly informed, that in many of our plantations... —ENGLAND AND WALES. SOVEREIGN. WILLIAM III. 1702#12

The whole book of psalmes, faithfully translated into English metre; whereunto is prefixed a discourse... —BIBLE. OLD TESTAMENT. PSALMS. 1647#3

The whole course of catechetical institution, through three classes of catechumens, consisting of I. An introductory discourse... —BRAY, Thomas. 1704#6

The whole prophecie of Daniel explained, by a paraphrase, analysis and briefe comment... —HUIT, Ephraim. 1643#10

Wholesome severity reconciled with Christian liberty. or, The true resolution of a present controversie concerning liberty of conscience... —GILLESPIE, George. 1645#7

The wicked taken in their own net. A sermon, preached at Cheshunt in Hertfordshire... Nov. 29th 1759... —MASON, John. 1759#65

The widdow ranter or, the history of Bacon in Virginia. A tragi-comedy. —BEHN, Aphra. 1690#3

The William Galley, ship. Lords Commissioners of Prizes... The appellants case. —1752#24x

William Penn and the Quakers either impostors, or apostates... —YOUNG, Samuel. 1696#25

Winthropi Justa. A sermon at the funeral of the Honble John Winthrop, Esq... —MATHER, Cotton. 1709#13

The wisdom and policy of the French in the construction of their great offices... With some observations on... disputes... English and French colonies... America. —McCULLOH, Henry. 1755#35

The wisdom of God manifested in the works of the creation... —RAY, John. 1691#16

The wit and honesty of James Hoskins, etc. considered in Remarks on their late Pamphlet, called the Pa. Bubble. By the translator of the Pattern of Modesty. —BOCKETT, Elias. 1726#2

Wit in a constable. A comedy. —GLAPTHORNE, Henry. 1640#2

The woman outwitted: or, the weaver's wife cunningly catched in a trap, by her husband, who sold her for ten pounds, and sent her to Virginny... —1685#31

The wonderful narrative; or, a faithful account of the French prophets... several other instances of persons under the influence of the like spirit... particularly in New-England... —CHAUNCY, Charles (1705-87). 1742#10

Wonderful predictions of Nostredamus, Grebner, David Pareus and Antonio Torquatus, wherein the grandeur of their present majesties... —ATWOOD, William. 1689#2

Wonderful prodigies of judgement and mercy... —CROUCH, Nathaniel. 1682#11

The wonders of free-grace: Or, A compleat history of all the most remarkable penitents that have been executed at Tyburn, and elsewhere, for these last thirty years... —MATHER, Increase. 1690#15

The wonders of nature and art; being an account of... natural history. —1750#52

The wonders of the invisible world: being an account of the tryals of several witches lately excuted [sic] in New England... —MATHER, Cotton. 1693#13

The Worcestershire garland; composed of three excellent new songs. —1718#24

A word to Mr. Peters, and two words for the Parliament and Kingdom. Or, an answer to a scandalous pamphlet, entituled, A word for the armie... —WARD, Nathaniel. 1647#19

A word to the well-inclined of all persuasions. Together with a copy of a letter from William Penn to George Keith... —STORY, Thomas. 1698#19

The work of the age... —ASPINWALL, William. 1655#3

The works of John Cleveland... —CLEVELAND, John. 1687#2

The works of Mr. Thomson. Volume the second. Containing Liberty: a poem in five parts. —THOMSON, James. 1738#28

The works of the late Aaron Hill, Esq; consisting of letters on various subjects, and of original poems... —HILL, Aaron. 1753#11

The works of the long-mournfull and sorely distressed Isaac Penington... —PENINGTON, Isaac. 1681#16

The works of the pious and profoundly learned Joseph Mede... —MEDE, Joseph. 1648#8

The world bewitch'd... —BEKKER, Balthasar. 1695#2

The world displayed; or a curious collection of voyages and travels... —1759#106

The world in miniature; or the entertaining traveller... —FRANSHAM, John. 1740#11

The world surveyed: or, the famous voyages and travailes of Vincent Le Blanc. —LE BLANC, Vincent. 1660#15

The year 59. —1759#108

Yet one warning more, to thee, O England... with a very tender lamentation... which may echo and ring again in the ears of New-England... —BAKER, Daniel. 1660#1

You are desired to accompany the Corps of Sir William Phipps from Salters Hall... to the parish-church of St. Mary Woolnoth... —1695#31

Zeal against the enemies of our country pathetically recommended. In a... sermon preached before... governor of Maryland... —STERLING, James. 1755#56

Zerubbabel to Sanballat and Tobiah: or, the first part of the duply to M. S. alias Two Brethren... concerning Independents... —STEUART, Adam. 1645#18

[Hebrew] or the doctrin [sic] of the justification of a sinner in the sight of God... —CHAUNCY, Charles (1592-1672). 1659#5

INDEX OF AUTHORS

A.B.C. *Letter from a gentleman out of England, to his country men, the people called the Galloway Levellers.*—1724#1

A. W. *Letter from W. A., a minister in Virginia, to his friend T. B., merchant, of Gracious street, London, declaring the advantages to those minded to transport themselves thither.*—1623#1

ABBOT, George. *A briefe description of the whole worlde...*—1624#1

ALBIN, Eleazar. *A natural history of birds. Illustrated with a hundred and one copper plates...*—1731#1

ALEXANDER, William. *An encouragement to colonies.*—1624#2

ALEXANDER, William. *The conduct of Major-General Shirley, late general and commander in chief of his majesty's forces in North America. Briefly stated.*—1758#3

ALLEN, Thomas. *A chaine of scripture chronologie from the creation of the world to the death of Jesus Christ.*—1658#1

ALLEN, William. *Ways and means to raise the value of land; or, the landlords companion: with political discourses on the land-tax, war, and other subjects.*—1736#1

ALLIN, John and SHEPARD, Thomas. *A defence of the answer made unto the nine questions or positions sent from New-England...*—1648#1

ALMON, John. *A new military dictionary; or, the field of war...*—1760#1

ALSOP, George. *A character of the province of Mary-land... also a small treatise on the wilde and naked Indians... Together with a collection of historical letters.*—1666#1

AMERICAN. *An essay upon the government of the English plantations in America. Together with some remarks upon the discourse on the plantation...*—1701#3

AMERICAN GENTLEMAN. *Poems moral and divine, on the following subjects... To which is added some account of the author.*—1756#3

AMHURST, Nicholas.
French counsels destructive to Great Britain...—739#2
Letter to the right honourable Sir R W etc., upon the present posture of affairs...—1739#3
Some further remarks on a late pamphlet, intitled, Observations on the conduct of Great-Britain...—1729#1

ANDERSON, James.
The history and constitutions of the... Free and Accepted Masons.—1746#1

Royal genealogies... Part I... the genealogies of the earliest great families, and most ancient sovereigns of Asia, Europe, Africa and America...—1732#1

ANGELONI, Battista. [pseudonym for J. Shebbeare]. *Letters on the English nation...*—1755#1

ANNESLEY, James.
Memoirs of an unfortunate young nobleman, in which is continued the history of Count Richard, concluding with a summary view...—1743#1
Memoirs of an unfortunate young nobleman, return'd from a thirteen years slavery in America... Vol III which completes the work, and is a key to the other two volumes.—1747#1
Memoirs of an unfortunate young nobleman, return'd from a thirteen years slavery in America, where he had been sent by the wicked...—1743#2

ANNET, Peter.
A collection of the tracts of a certain free inquirer, noted for his sufferings for his opinions...—1750#1
Social bliss considered: In marriage and divorce... with the speech of Miss Polly Baker...—1749#2

ANTROBUS, Benjamin. *Some buds and blossoms of piety...*—1684#1

APPLETON, Nathaniel.
Gospel ministers must be fit for the master's use... sermon preached at Deerfield, August 31. 1735... with special reference to the Indians of the Houssattonic...—1736#2
The happiness of a holy life, exemplified in the sickness and death of... Mrs Martha Gerrish, of Boston in New-England... with a collection...—1740#1

ARCHDALE, John. *A new description of that fertile and pleasant province of Carolina with a brief account of its discovery, settling, and the government thereof.*—1707#1

ARMISTEAD, HENRY. *Case of Henry Armistead, esq;... a native of Virginia...*—1740#2

ASH, Thomas. *Carolina; or A description of the present state of that country, and the natural excellencies thereof...*—1682#2

ASHBURNHAM, William. *A sermon preached... February 15, 1760...*—1760#4

ASHE, St. George. *A sermon preached... 18th February, 1714...*—1715#1

ASHE, Simeon and BALL, John. *Letter of many ministers in Old England, requesting the judgement of their reverend brethren in New England concerning nine...*—1643#1

ASHLEY, John.
The British empire in America, consider'd. In a second letter, from a gentleman of Barbadoes. . .—1732#3
Memoirs and considerations concerning the trade and revenues of the British colonies in America. With proposals for rendering those colonies more beneficial to Great Britain.—1740#3
The present state of the British and French trade to Africa and America consider'd and compar'd. . .—1745#4
The present state of the British sugar colonies consider'd: in a letter from a gentleman of Barbadoes to his friend in London.—1731#2
The second part of Memoirs and considerations concerning the trade and revenues of the British colonies in America. . .—1743#3
Some observations on a direct exportation of sugar from the British islands. . .—1735#1

ASPINWALL, William.
The abrogation of the Jewish sabbath.—1657#1
A brief description of the fifth monarchy, or kingdome that shortly is to come into the world. . .—1653#1
Certain queries concerning the ordination of ministers.—1647#1
An explication and application of the seventh chapter of Daniel. . .—1654#1
The legislative power is Christ's. . .—1656#1
A premonition of sundry sad calamities. . .—1655#2
Thunder from heaven against the back-sliders. . .—1654#2
The work of the age. . .—1655#3

ASSOCIATES OF DR BRAY. An account of the designs of the Associates of the late Dr. Bray; with an abstract of their proceedings.—1760#5

ASTON, Anthony. The Fool's Opera; or, the taste of the age. Written by Mat. Medley. . . To which is prefixed, a sketch of the author's life, written by himself.—1730#1

ATWOOD, William.
Case of William Atwood, esq; by the late King William. . . constituted chief justice of the province of New York. . . With a true. . .—1703#2
Wonderful predictions of Nostredamus, Grebner, David Pareus and Antonio Torquatus, wherein the grandeur of their present majesties. . .—1689#2

AUBIN, Penelope. The life of Charlotta du Pont, an English lady. . . Giving an account of how she was trepan'd by her stepmother to Virginia. . .—1723#1

AUCKMUTY, Robert. The importance of Cape Breton to the British nation. Humbly represented by Robert Auckmuty, judge of his majesty's court of vice-admiralty. . .—1745#5

AUTHOR OF 'SOME CONSIDERATIONS TOUCHING THE SUGAR COLONIES'. Farther considerations touching the sugar colonies, with additional observations in respect to trade. . . By the author of Some. . .—1734#1

AVERAY, Robert. Britannia and the Gods in council, a dramatic poem: wherein. . . the causes of the present disputes in Europe and America are debated. . .—1756#5

B., A. An expostulatory letter to Mr. Daniel Neal, upon occasion of his publishing the History of the Puritans. . .—1732#4

B., A. Letter to a member of Parliament for incouraging offices of insurance for ships. . . particularly for incouraging the British fishery. . .—1720#3

B., G. The advantages of the revolution illustrated, by a view of the present state of Great Britain. . .—1753#1

B., J. Letter to a member of Parliament, on the regulation of the plantation trade.—1701#6

B., L. The real and true case of the planters in Virginia.—1733#1

B., M. A letter to the West-India merchants, in answer to their petition now before the Honble House of Commons, praying for a prohibition. . .—1751#3

B., R. [i. e. CROUCH, Nathaniel]. The English empire in America: or, a View of the dominions of the Crown of England in the West-Indies. . .—1685#2

BACON, Francis.
The essayes or counsels, civill and morall. . .—1625#1
Historia vitae & mortis.—1623#2
The historie of the raigne of King Henry the seventh—1622#1
Letter of advice written by Sr. Thomas Bacon to the Duke of Buckingham. . .—1661#1

BACON, Thomas.
Four sermons, upon the great and indispensible duty of Christian masters and mistresses to bring up their negro slaves in the. . .—1750#3
A sermon preached at the parish church of St Peter's, in Talbot County, Maryland: on Sunday the 14th of October, 1750. for the benefit. . .—1751#4
Six sermons on the several duties of masters, mistresses, slaves, etc. Preached. . . in Talbot county. . . Maryland. . .—1751#5
Two sermons, preached to a congregation of black slaves, at the parish church of S. P., in the province of Maryland. By an American pastor.—1749#5

BAILLIE, Robert.
Anabaptism, the true fountaine of independency. . . a second part of A dissuasive from the errours of the time: wherein the tenets of the principall sects, especially of the Independents, are drawn together in one map. . . —1645#1
The disswasive from the errors of the time. . .—1647#2
The disswasive from the errors of the time, vindicated from the exceptions of Mr Cotton and Mr Tombes. . .—1655#4
The unlawfulnes and danger of limited episcopacie.—1641#1

BAKER, Daniel. Yet one warning more, to thee, O England. . . with a very tender lamentation. . . which may echo and ring again in the ears of New-England. . .—1660#1

BALL, John. An answer to two treatises of Mr John Cann, the leader of the English Brownists in Amsterdam—1642#1
See also ASHE, Simeon.

BALL, Nathaniel.
The divine goodness and human gratitude properly considered, in a sermon preached at West-Horsley. . . November 29, 1759. . .—1759#3

True religion, loyalty and union recommended... sermon preached at Pleshey, Feb. 11, 1757...—1757#1

BANCROFT, Thomas. *Two bookes of epigrammes and epitaphs...*—1639#1

BANISTER, Thomas.
Letter to the right honourable the Lords Commissioners of Trade and Plantations; or, a short essay on the principle branches of the trade of New England...—1715#2
Observations on the report of the Committee of Secrecy.—1715#3

BARBON, Nicholas.
An apology for the builder; or, a discourse shewing the causes and effects of the increase of building.—1685#3
A discourse of trade, by N. B...—1690#2

BARCLAY, Patrick. *The universal traveller: or, A complete account of the most remarkable voyages and travels.*—1733#2

BARNARD, John.
Ashton's memorial: or, an authentick account of the strange adventures... of Mr. Philip Ashton... To which is added, a sermon on Dan. III, 17, by J. Barnard...—1726#1
Sermons on several subjects...—1727#1

BARNWELL, John. *An account of the foundation, and establishment of a design now on foot, for a settlement on the Golden Islands, to the south of Port Royal in Carolina...*—1720#4

BARTRAM, John. *Observations on the inhabitants, climate, soil, rivers... In his travels from Pensilvania to Onondago, Oswego and the Lake Ontario...*—1751#6

BASTON, Thomas. *Thoughts on trade, and a publick spirit.*—1716#1

BASTWICK, John. *The second part of that book call'd Independency not God's ordinance: or the post-script...*—1645#2

BATEMAN, Edmund. *A sermon preached... March 19, 1740-1...*—1741#1

BATHER, James. *A full and faithful account of the life of James Bather, late... of... Nightingale Brig...*—1755#3

BAXTER, Benjamin. *Forgery detected, and Innocency vindicated. Being a full discovery of an horrid... slander rais'd on the Anabaptists of New-England...*—1673#2

BAXTER, Richard.
The certainty of the world of spirits, fully evinced by the unquestionable histories of apparations and witchcrafts...—1691#1
A Christian directory: or, A summ of practical theology, and cases of conscience...—1673#1
A defence of the principles of love, which are necessary to the unity and concord of Christians...—1671#1
Faithful souls shall be with Christ.—1681#2
Mr. Baxter's vindication of the church of England...—1682#3
Reliquiae Baxterianiae: or Mr Richard Baxter's narrative of... his life...—1696#1

BAYARD, Nicholas. *An account of the commitment, arraignment, tryal and condemnation of Nicholas Bayard, Esq; for high treason, in endeavouring...*—1703#3

BAYARD, Nicholas and LODOWICK, Charles. *Journal of the late actions of the French at Canada. With the manner of their being repulsed...*—1693#1

BEARCROFT, Philip.
A sermon preached... February 15, 1744...—1745#6
A sermon preached... March 16, 1737-8...—1738#1

BEATTY, Charles. *To the pious, charitable, and well-disposed Christians, inhabitants of Great Britain... the humble memorial of Charles Beatty.*—1760#7

BEAUMONT, John. *An historical, physiological and theological treatise of spirits, apparitions, witchcrafts...*—1705#1

BEAWES, Wyndham. *Lex mercatoria rediviva: or the merchant's directory... Containing an account of our trading companies and colonies, with their...*—1751#7

BECKHAM, Edward.
A brief discovery of some of the blasphemous and seditious principles and practices of the people, called Quakers.—1699#1
The principles of the Quakers further shewn to be blasphemous and seditious...—1700#1

BEESTON, William. *Proclamation by the Rt. Honourable William Beeston, Kt. Governor of Jamaica... 8th day of April 1699.*—1699#2

BEHN, Aphra.
Histories novels and translations. The second volume.—1700#2
Plays written by the late ingenious Mrs. Behn, entire in two volumes...—1702#1
The widdow ranter or, the history of Bacon in Virginia. A tragi-comedy.—1690#3

BEKKER, Balthasar. *The world bewitch'd...*—1695#2

BELL, John. *An epistle to Friends in Maryland, Virginia, Barbadoes, and the other colonies... Dear Friends... John Bell. Bromley near London, 3d Month 1741.*—1741#2

BELL, William. *A dissertation on... causes... to render a nation populous...*—1756#6

BELLEGARDE, Jean Baptiste Morvan de. *A general history of all voyages and travels throughout the old and new world... by Monsr. Du Perier...*—1708#1

BELLERS, John. *Essays about the poor, manufactures, trade, plantations and immorality...*—1699#3

BELSHAM, Jacobus. *Canadia. Ode...*—1760#9

BELSHAZZER, Kapha the Jew.
The book of James...—1743#4
The second book of James...—1744#2

BENNET, Henry, earl of Arlington. *The right honourable the Earl of Arlington's letters to Sir W. Temple, Bar... All printed from the originals and never before publish'd.*—1701#7

BENNET, John. *The national merchant: or, discourses on commerce and colonies; being an essay for regulating and improving the trade and plantations...*—1736#3

BENSON, Martin. *A sermon preached... February 15, 1739-40.*—1740#4

BERKELEY, George.
*A miscellany, containing several tracts on various subjects. . .—*1752#1

*A proposal for the better supplying of churches in our foreign plantations, and for converting the savage Americans to Christianity. . .—*1724#2

*A sermon preached. . . on. . . February 18, 1731. . .—*1732#5

BERKELEY, Sir William. *A discourse and a view of Virginia. By Sir William Berkeley (governor of Virginia).*—1663#1

BERNARD, Jacques. *The acts and negotiations, together with the particular articles at large, of the general peace concluded at Ryswick.*—1699#4

BERNARD, Jean Frederic, editor. *The religious ceremonies and customs of the several nations of the known world. . .—*1731#3

BERRIMAN, William. *A sermon preach'd before. . . Trustees for. . . Georgia. . . and the associates of. . . Bray. . . March 15, 1738–9. . .—*1739#6

BESSE, Joseph.
*A cloud of witnesses. . .—*1732#6

A full answer to The country-parson's plea against the Quaker tythe-bill.—1736#4

The sufferings of the people called Quakers. . . from the year 1650 to the year 1660.—1733#3

BEST, William.
*The merit and reward of a good intention. A sermon preached. . . March 18. 1741–2. . . in which some notice is taken of a late. . .—*1742#1

*The relief of the persecuted protestants of Saltzburgh, and the support of the colony of Georgia, recommended in a sermon preach'd. . . January 13, 1734. . .—*1734#2

BETHEL, Slingsby.
The interest of princes and states.—1680#1
*The present interest of England stated. . .—*1671#2
The providences of God observed through several ages towards this nation.—1691#2

BEVERIDGE, William. *A sermon preached. . . February 21st 1706. . .—*1707#2

BEVERLEY, John. *Unio reformantium sive examen Hoornbecki de indepentismo apologeticum. . .—*1659#1

BEVERLEY, Robert.
*An abridgement of the publick laws of Virginia, in force and use, June 10, 1720. . .—*1722#1

The history and present state of Virginia, in four parts. . . By a native and inhabitant of the place.—1705#2

BIBLE. OLD TESTAMENT. PSALMS. *The whole book of psalmes, faithfully translated into English metre; whereunto is prefixed a discourse. . .—*1647#3

BICKHAM, George.
*The British monarchy: or a new chorographical description of all the dominions subject to the king of Great Britain. . .—*1743#5

*A short description of the American colonies, belonging to the crown of Great Britain. Engrave'd by George Bickham. . .—*1747#2

BILLING, Edward. *A faithful testimony for God and my country.*—1664#1

BILTON, Thomas. *Captain Bilton's journal of his unfortunate voyage from Lisbon to Virginia in the year 1707. . .—*1715#4

BINDON, David. *Letter from a merchant who has left off trade, to a member of parliament, in which the case of the British and Irish manufacture of linen, threads, and tape is fairly stated. . .—*1738#2

BINGLEY William. *An epistle of love and tender advice, to friends and brethren in America, or elswhere. . .—*1689#3

BIRCH, Thomas.
*The history of the Royal Society of London for improving natural knowledge. . .—*1756#7

The life of the honourable Robert Boyle.—1744#3

BISHOP, George.
An epistle of love to all the saints.—1661#2

A looking glass for the times, etc. to which is added the report from the Lords of the Committee of Councils, and the King's Orders relating to Quakers in New England.—1668#1

*New England judged. . . and the summe sealed up of New-England's persecutions. . .—*1661#3

*New England judged. . . in two parts. . . Formerly published by G. Bishop, and now somewhat abbreviated. With an appendix. . . Also an answer. . .—*1703#4

*New England judged. The second part. . . a relation of the cruel and bloody sufferings of. . . Quakers, in the jurisdiction chiefly of the Massachusetts. . .—*1667#1

The warnings of the Lord to the men of this generation.—1660#2

BISHOP, Matthew. *Life and adventures of Matthew Bishop, of Deddington in Oxfordshire, containing an account of several actions by sea, battles. . .—*1744#4

BISSE, Philip. *A sermon. . . on Friday the 21st February, 1717. . .—*1718#1

BISSET, John. *Letter to a gentleman in Scotland, containing remarks upon. . . Mr George Whitefield.*—1742#2

BLACK, David. *Essay upon industry and trade. . .—*1706#2

BLACK, William.
Remarks upon a pamphlet, intitled, The considerations in relation to trade considered, and a short view of our present trade and taxes reviewed.—1706#3

Some considerations in relation to trade.—1706#4

BLACKAMORE, Arthur.
*Luck at last or the happy unfortunate. . .—*1723#2

*The perfidious brethren, or, the religious triumvirate: displayed in three ecclesiastic novels. . .—*1720#5

BLAIR, Hugh. *The importance of religious knowledge to the happiness of mankind. A sermon preached. . . January 1, 1750. . .—*1750#4

BLAIR, James.
Our saviour's divine sermon on the mount. . . explained. . .— 1722#2
See also HARTWELL, Henry.

BLAND, Edward. *The discovery of New Brittaine. Began August 27. Anno Dom. 1650. . . From Fort Henry. . . in Virginia. . . to the fals of Blandina. . . in New Brittaine. . .*—1651#1

BLAND, John.
To the Kings most excellent majesty, the humble remonstrance of John Blande. . . on the behalf of the inhabitants and planters in Virginia and Mariland. . .—1661#4
Trade revived, or a way proposed to restore, increase inrich, strengthen and preserve the decayed. . . trade of this our English nation. . .—1659#2

BLENMAN, Jonathan. *Remarks on several Acts of Parliament relating more especially to the colonies abroad; as also on diverse acts of assemblies there. . .*—1742#3

BLEWITT, George. *An enquiry whether a general practice of virtue tends to be the wealth or poverty, benefit or disadvantage of a people. . .*—1725#1

BLODGET, Samuel. *A prospective plan of the battle near Lake George, on the eighth day of September, 1755. With an explanation thereof; Containing. . .*—1756#9

BLOME, Richard.
Britannia: or A geographical description of the kingdom's of England, Scotland and Ireland, with the Isles and territories there to belonging. . .—1673#3
Cosmography and geography in two parts.—1682#4
A description of the island of Jamaica. . .—1672#1
A geographical description of the four parts of the world. . .—1670#1
The present state of his majesties isles and territories in America, viz. Jamaica. . . New Jersey, Pensilvania. . . Carolina, Virginia. . .—1687#1

BLOUNT, Sir Thomas Pope.
Essays on several subjects.—1691#3
A natural history: containing many not common observations; extracted out of the best modern writers. . .—1693#2

BLOYS, William. *Adam in his innocence.*—1638#8

BLUETT, Thomas. *Some memoirs of the life of Job, the son of Solomon the high priest of Boonda in Africa; who was a slave about two years in Maryland;. . .*—1734#3

BOCKETT, Elias.
A determination of the case of Mr. Thomas Story, and Mr. James Hoskins, relating to an affair of the Pennsylvania Company. . .—1724#3
A poem. To the memory of Aquila Rose, who dyed at Philadelphia, August the 22d, 1723. . .—1724#4
The wit and honesty of James Hoskins, etc. considered in Remarks on their late Pamphlet, called the Pa. Bubble. By the translator of the Pattern of Modesty.—1726#2

BOHUN, Edmund. *A geographical dictionary, representing the present and ancient names of all countries. . .*—1688#1

BOHUN, Ralph. *A discourse concerning the origine and properties of wind. With a historicall account of hurricanes.*—1671#3

BOLLAN, William. *The importance and advantage of Cape Breton, truly stated, and impartially considered. With proper maps. . .*—1746#3

Boltzius, John Martin.
See RECK, Philip G.

BONAR, John. *The nature and necessity of a religious education. A sermon. . . January 6. 1752. . .*—1752#2

BONOEIL, John. *His majesties gracious letter to the Earl of South-hampton, treasurer, and to the Councell and Company of Virginia heere: commanding. . .*—1622#2

BOONE, Joseph. *The humble address of the right honourable Lords spiritual and temporal, in Parliament assembled, presented to her majesty on. . .*—1706#5

BOOTHBY, Richard. *A briefe discovery or description of the most famous island of Madagascar.*—1646#1

BORELAND, Francis. *Boreland, Francis, respondent. . . The respondent's case. . .*—1737#1

BOREMAN, Thomas.
A description of some curious and uncommon creatures, omitted in the Description of 300 animals, and likewise in the supplement to that book.—1739#7
A description of three hundred animals; viz. beasts, birds, fishes, serpents and insects. With a particular account of the whale-fishery. . .—1730#2

BOS, Lambert van den. *Florus Anglicus or an exact history of England, from the reign of William the Conqueror to the death of Charles I.*—1657#3

BOSTON. ASSEMBLY OF PASTORS. *The testimony and advice of an assembly of pastors of churches in New England, at a meeting in Boston, July 7, 1743. Occasioned by the late happy revival of religion.*—1744#5

BOSTWICK David. *Self disclaimed, and Christ exalted: a sermon preached at Philadelphia. . . May 25, 1758. . .*—1759#4

BOULTER, Hugh. *A sermon preached. . . 16th of February, 1721. . .*—1722#3

BOULTON, Richard.
A compleat history of magick, sorcery, and witchcraft. . .—1715#6
The possibility and reality of magick, sorcery and witchcraft. . . In answer to Dr. Hutchinson's Historical essay. . .—1722#4

BOWEN, Emanuel. *A complete system of geography. Being a description of all the countries.*—1744#6

BOWNAS, Samuel.
An account of the captivity of Elizabeth Hanson, now or late of Kachecky; in New England: who, with four of her children and servant-maid. . .—1760#10
An account of the life, travels and Christian experiences in the work of the ministry of Samuel Bownas.—1756#10

BOWREY, Thomas. *A dictionary of the Hudson's Bay Indian language.*—1701#8

BOYD, Elizabeth. *Altamira's ghost; or, justice triumphant. A new ballad. Occasion'd by a certain nobleman's cruel usage of his nephew. Done extempore.*—1744#7

BOYLE, Robert.
General heads for the natural history of country great or small; drawn out for the use of travellers and navigators...—1692#1
Of the reconcileableness of the specifick medicines to the corpuscular philosophy...—1685#4
Some considerations touching the usefulnesse of experimental naturall philosophy—1663#2
Some receipts of medicines, for the most part parable and simple... sent to a friend in America.—1688#2
The theological works...—1715#5

BOYLSTON, Zabdiel. *An historical account of the small-pox inoculated in New England, upon all sorts of persons...*—1726#3

BRADBURY, Charles. *Hymns for the general thanksgiving day, Thursday, November 29, 1759...*—1759#5

BRADBURY, Thomas.
The ass: or, the serpent. A comparison between the tribes of Issachar and Dan, in their regard for civil liberty.—1712#1
The necessity of contending for revealed religion... to which is prefixed, a letter from the Reverend Cotton Mather...—1720#6

BRADFORD, Samuel. *A sermon preached... 19th February, 1719...*—1720#7

BRADLEY, Richard. *Ten practical discourses.*—1727#2

BRADSTREET, Anne. *The tenth muse lately sprung up in America. Or severall poems... Also a dialogue between old England and new, concerning the late troubles.*—1650#1

BRADSTREET, John. *An impartial account of Lieut. Col. Bradstreet's expedition to Fort Frontenac... By a volunteer on the expedition.*—1759#6

BRADY, Samuel. *Some remarks upon Dr. Wagstaffe's letter, and Mr. Massey's sermon against inoculating the small-pox...*—1722#5

BRAINERD, David. *An abridgment of Mr. David Brainerd's Journal among the Indians. Or, the rise and progress of a remarkable work of grace among...*—1748#1

BRAINERD, John. *A genuine letter from Mr. John Brainard [sic], employed by the Scotch Society for Propagating the Gospel, a missionary to the Indians...*—1753#2

BRAY, Thomas.
The acts of Dr. Bray's visitation. held at Annopolis [sic] in Maryland, May 23, 24, 25, anno 1700.—1700#3
Apostolick charity, its nature and excellence considered... Preached... Decemb. 19. 1697. at the ordination of some Protestant...—1698#2
Bibliotheca parochialis Part I.—1697#1
Catechetical discourses on the whole doctrine of the covenant of grace... design'd to be read in the plantations.—1701#9
A circular letter to the clergy of Maryland...—1700#4
An essay towards promoting all necessary and useful knowledge.—1697#2
An introductory discourse to catechetical instruction... In a Pastoral Letter to the clergy of Maryland... containing a Course...—1704#5
Letter from Dr. Bray to such as have contributed towards the propagating Christian knowledge in the plantations...—1700#5
A memorial representing the present case of the church in Mary-Land, with relation to its establishment by law.—1701#10
A memorial, representing the present state of religion, on the continent of North-America.—1700#6
Missionalia, or a collection of missionary pieces relating to the conversion of the heathen; both the African negroes and American Indians. In two parts.—1727#3
The present state of the Protestant religion in Maryland, under the government of Francis Nicholson Esq. by Dr Bray...—1700#7
Proposals for the incouragement and promoting of religion...—1695#3
Several circular letters to the clergy of Mary-Land, subsequent to their late visitation, to enforce such resolutions as were taken therein.—1701#11
A short account of the several kinds of societies, set up in late years...—1700#8
A short discourse upon the doctrine of our baptismal covenant...—1697#3
Supplement to the Bibliotheca parochialis.—1697#4
The whole course of catechetical institution, through three classes of catechumens, consisting of I. An introductory discourse...—1704#6

BREAKENRIG, Thomas. *Petition for Thomas Breakenrig messenger in Edinburgh; against [blank] Newlands and others.*—1725#2

BRECK, Edward. *An answer to a scandalous paper... therein is found many lies and slanders, and false accusations against those people called Quakers...*—1656#2

BRECKNOCK, Timothy. *A plan for establishing the general peace of Europe upon honourable terms to Great Britain...*—1759#7

BREREWOOD, Edward. *Enquiries touching the diversity of languages and religions through the chief parts of the world...*—1622#3

BREWSTER, Francis.
Essays on trade and navigation. In five parts. The first part.—1695#4
New essays on trade.—1702#2

BREWSTER, Richard. *A sermon, preached in the Church of St. Nicholas, in Newcastle upon Tyne, on Thursday, the 29th day of November...*—1759#8

BRICE, Andrew. *A universal geographical dictionary; or, grand gazetteer; including a comprehensive view of Europe... and America; more especially of the British dominions and settlements...*—1759#9

BRICE, Ninian. *Ninian Brice, ship-master in Glasgow, and others, Apellants. William Brice, Merchant in Glasgow, Respondent. The Appellants Case.*—1740#6

BRICKELL, John. *The natural history of North-Carolina; with an account of the trade, manners, and customs of the Christian and Indian inhabitants. . .*—1737#2

BRINSLEY, John. *Consolation for our grammar schools, or a Comfortable encouragement for laying of a sure foundation of all good learning. . .*—1622#4

BRITISH FREEHOLDER. *Unanswerable arguments against a peace.*—1760#12

BROKESBY, Francis. *Some proposals towards promoting the propagation of the Gospel in our American plantations.*—1708#2

BROME, Alexander. *The Rump or a collection of songs and ballads. . .*—1660#3

BROOKE, Christopher. *A poem on the late massacre in Virginia. With particular mention of those men of note that suffered in that disaster.*—1622#5

BROOKSOP, Joan. *An invitation of love. . . With a word to the wise. . . and a lamentation for New-England. . .*—1662#1

BROWN, John. *An estimate of the manners and principles of the times. . .*—1757#3

BROWN, William. *The benefit and comfort of the Christian revelation. . .*—1736#5

BROWNE, John, Captain. *A brief survey of the prophetical and evangelical events of the last times. . .*—1653#2

BROWNE, John, Quaker. *In the eleventh month, on the nineth day. . . the Spirit of the Lord then signified. . . saying, Arise and take up a lamentation. . .*—1678#1

BROWNE, John. *Seasonable remarks on trade.*—1728#1

BROWNE, Peleg. *Rhode Island. Peleg Browne, Collector of Customs. . . Rhode Island. . . appellant. James Allen, and Ezekiel Chever. . . respondents. The appellant's case.*—1738#3

BROWNE, Thomas. *Certain miscellany tracts*—1683#4

BROWNRIGG, William. *The art of making common salt, as now practiced in most parts of the world; with several improvements proposed in that art, for the use of the British dominions.*—1748#2

BRUCE, Alexander. *An inquiry into the cause of the pestilence in three parts. . .*—1759#11

BRUCE, Lewis. *The happiness of man the glory of God. A sermon. . . March 15, 1743. . .*—1744#8

BRYAN, Hugh. *Living Christianity delineated, in the diaries and letters of. . . Mr Hugh Bryan and Mrs Mary Hutson, both of South Carolina. . .*—1760#13

BRYCE, William. *Ninian Brice, John Orr of Barrowfield, Esq . . .*—1740#7A

BUDD, Thomas.
A true and accurate account of the disposal of the one hundred shares or proprieties of the province of West-New-Jersey, by Edward Bylling. . .—1685#5

See also KEITH, George.

BUGG, Francis.
A bomb thrown amongst the Quakers in Norwich, which will. . . set fire on [sic] the combustible matter thorow their whole camp in England, Wales and America.—1702#3
A brief history of the rise, growth, and progress of Quakerism.—1697#5
De Christiana liberate, or liberty of conscience. . . In two parts. . . To which is added, a word of advice to the Pensilvanians.—1682#5
The last will of that impostor, George Fox (with a letter from Josiah Coale of Maryland). . .—1701#14
A modest defence of my book, entituled, Quakerism exposed. . .—1700#9
New Rome arraigned, and out of her own mouth condemned. . .—1693#3
News from New Rome, occasioned by the Quakers challenging of Francis Bug. . . News, Numb. I.—1701#12
News from Pensilvania: or a brief narrative of several remarkable passages in the government of the Quakers in that province. . .—1703#5
The picture of Quakerism drawn to the life. . .—1697#6
The pilgrim's progress, from Quakerism, to Christianity.—1698#3
Quakerism withering, and Christianity reviving or, A brief reply to the Quakers pretended vindication. . .—1694#1
The Quakers set in their true light. . .—1696#2
A seasonable caveat against the prevalency of Quakerism. . . a hint also of arbitrary government in Pensilvania. . .—1701#15
Vox populi: or, A cloud of witnesses, proving the leading Quakers great impostors.—1702#4

BULFINCH, Thomas. *Dissertatio medica inauguralis, de crisibus. . .*—1757#4

BULKELEY, Peter. *The gospel-covenant; or The covenant of grace opened. . . Preached in Concord in New-England. . .*—1646#2

BULKLEY, Charles. *The signs of the times, illustrated and improved. In a sermon preached. . . October 21, 1759. On occasion of the surrender of Quebec. . .*—1759#12

BULKLEY, Thomas.
The monstrous injustice and unmercifulness of Nicholas Trott, late governour of the Bahama-Islands in America. . .—1698#4
To the right honourable William, Earl of Craven. . . being proprietors of Carolina, and the Bahama Islands. . .—1694#2

BULLOCK, William. *Virginia impartially examined, and left to publick view, to be considered by all judicious and honest men. . .*—1649#1

BURGES, Frances. *Virginia ss. Pleas at the capitol in Williamsburgh. . .*—1737#3

BURKE, William.
An account of the European settlements in America. In six parts. . .—1757#5
Remarks on the letter addressed to two great men. In a letter to the author of that piece.—1760#14

BURNET, Gilbert.
A defence of natural and revealed religion. . . With a general index. . .—1737#4
Of the propagation of the gospel in foreign parts. A sermon preach'd. . . Feb. 18. 1703/4. . .—1704#7

BURNYEAT, John.
The truth exalted in the writings of that eminent and faithful servant of Christ, John Burnyeat, collected into this ensuing volume. . .—1691#4
See also FOX, George.

BURRINGTON, George. *Seasonable considerations on the expediency of a war with France. . . To which are added. . . a short comparison between the British and French dominions. . .*—1743#6

BURRISH, Onslow. *Batavia illustrata: or, A view of the policy and commerce of the United Provinces. . . of the rise and progress of their East and West India Companies. . .*—1728#2

BURROUGH, Edward.
A declaration of the sad and great persecution of and martyrdom of the people of God, called Quakers, in New-England. . .—1661#5
The memorable works of a son of thunder and consolation. . . Edward Burroughs. . .—1672#2

BURT, Edward. *Letters from a gentleman in the north of Scotland to his friend in London. . . In two volumes.*—1754#2

BURTON, John. *The duty and reward of propagating principles of religion and virtue. . . A sermon preach'd. . . March 15, 1732. . .*—1733#4

BURY, Richard. *A collection of sundry messages and warnings to the inhabitants of the city of Bristol. . .*—1728#3

BUSHNELL, Edmund. *The compleat ship-wright.*—1664#2

BUTEL-DUMONT, Georges. *Histoire et commerce des colonies angloises, dans l'Amerique. . .*—1755#4

BUTLER, Joseph. *A sermon preached. . . February 16, 1738-9.*—1739#9

BUTLER, Nathaniel. *Six dialogues about sea-services.*—1685#6

BYFIELD, Nathaniel. *An account of the late revolution in New-England. Together with the declaration of the gentlemen, merchants, and inhabitants of Boston, and the country adjacent. . .*—1689#4

BYFIELD, Thomas. *Case of Thomas Byfield, and Company, owners of the ship Dove. . . relating to the bill for importing naval stores from the plantations.*—1705#3

BYRD, William II ?. *A discourse concerning the plague, with some preservatives against it. By a lover of mankind.*—1721#3

C-, H. *A poem. Inscrib'd to the Right Honourable Sir Robert Walpole, on the success of His Majesty's arms in America.*—1741#3

C., T. *A scheme to drive the French out of all the continent of America. . .*—1754#3

C., T. *A short discourse of the New-found-land; Contaynig [sic] diverse reasons and inducements, for the planting of that countrey. . .*—1623#3

CADOGAN, George. *The Spanish hireling detected: being a refutation of the several calumnies and falsehoods in a late pamphlet, entituled an impartial account. . .*—1743#7

CALAMY Edmund, D. D. *An abridgment of Mr Baxter's History of his life and times. With an account of the ministers who were ejected, after the Restauration. . .*—1702#5

CALDWELL, John. *An impartial trial of the spirit. . . a sermon preached at New London-derry, October 14th 1741. . .*—1742#5

CALEF, Robert. *More wonders of the invisible word: or The wonders of the invisible world displayed. . . To which is added, a postcript relating to a book intitled, The life of Sir William Phips. . .*—1700#10

CALVERT, Cecil. *A moderate and safe expedient to remove jealousies and feares, of any danger. . . by the Roman Catholickes of this kingdome. . .*—1646#3

CALVERT, George.
The answer to Tom-Tell-Troth. The practise of princes and the lamentations of the kirke.—1642#2
Case of Charles Lord Baltemore, a minor, with relation to his government of Maryland, granted by King Charles I, to Cecil Lord Baltemore. . .—1689#5

CALVERT, Philip. *Letter from the chancellour of Mary-land, to Col. Henry Meese, merchant in London: concerning the late troubles in Maryland. . . From Patuxent riverside, this 28 December, 1681.*—1682#6

CAMPBELL, Duncan. *Time's telescope universal and perpetual. . . with a general view of the four parts of the world.*—1734#4

CAMPBELL, Hugh Hume. *A state of the rise and progress of our disputes with Spain, and of the conduct of our ministers. . .*—1739#10

CAMPBELL, John.
A concise history of the Spanish America. . .—1741#4
Lives of the admirals. . . a new and accurate naval history. . . with passages relating to our discoveries, plantations, and commerce.—1742#6

CANNE, Abednego. *A new wind-mil, a new.*—1643#2

CAREW, Bampfylde Moore?. *The life and adventures of Bampfylde-Moore Carew, the noted Devon-shire stroller and dog-stealer, as related by himself, during his passage to the plantations in America. . .*—1745#7

CAREW, George. *Severall considerations, offered to the Parliament, concerning the improvement of trade. . .*—1675#2

CARKESSE, Charles (compiler). *The Act of Tonnage and Poundage, and Book of Rates; with several statutes at large relating to the Customs. . . With an abridgment. . .*—1675#3

CARLYLE, Alexander.
Plain reasons for removing a certain great man from his m———y's presence and councils for ever.—1759#13
The question relating to a Scots militia considered. . .—1760#16

CAROLINA. *The Copy of an act lately passed in Carolina, and sent over to be continued here. . . which would be highly prejudicial to her Majesty's. . .*—1704#8

CARROLL, Charles. *Maryland. Charles Carroll. . . appellant. John Parran. . . and Mary Parran. . . respondents. The appellant's case.*—1739#11

CARTE, Thomas. *A full answer to the Letter from a by-stander. . .*—1742#7

CARTER, Landon.
Letter from a gentleman in Virginia, to the merchants of Great Britain, trading to that colony.—1754#5
Letter to the Right Reverend Father in God the Lord B———p of L———n. Occasioned by a letter of his lordship's to the L———ds of T———e. . .—1760#17

CARTWRIGHT, William. *The ordinary, a comedy.*—1651#2

CARY, John.
An essay on the state of England, in relation to its trade.—1695#6
An essay, towards regulating the trade, and employing the poor of this kingdom. . .—1717#2

CARYL, Joseph? *Peters patern newly revived. . . a funeral sermon preached at the internment of Mr Hugh Peters. . .*—1659#3

CASTELL, William.
A petition of W. C. exhibited to the high court of Parliamen[t] now assembled, for the propagating of the gospel in America. . .—1641#2
A short discoverie of the coasts and continent of America, from the equinoctiall northward, and of the adjacent isles. . . Whereunto is prefixed. . .—1644#2

CATESBY, Mark.
The natural history of Carolina, Florida, and the Bahama Islands. . . with remarks upon agriculture. . .—1731#9
Proposals for printing an essay towards a natural history of Florida, Carolina, and the Bahama islands; containing twelve coloured plates. . .—1730#3

CATO. *Reasons for not restoring Guadeloupe at a peace. In a letter addressed to the Right Honourable the Earl of Hallifax. . . In answer to certain animadversions. . .*—1760#18

CATTON, William.
A poem on the taking of Cape Breton and Cherbourg. . .—1760#19
Sacred to the memory of that renowned hero, Major General Wolfe. . .—1759#14

CAUSTON, Peter.
Tunbridgalia: or, The pleasures of Tunbridge. A poem. In Latin and English.—1684#3

CAWDREY, Daniel.
The inconsistencie of the independent way, with scripture, and it self. Manifested in a three fold discourse. . .—1651#3
Vindiciae clavium, or, A vindication of the keyes of the kingdome of heaven. . . Being some animadversions on a tract of Mr J.[ohn] C.[otton]. . .—1645#3

CHALKLEY, Thomas.
A collection of the works of Thomas Chalkley. In two parts. . .—1751#9
Journal, or, historical account of the life, travels and Christian experiences of. . . Thomas Chalkley. . .—1751#10

CHAMBERLAYNE, Edward. *Englands wants; or several proposals probably beneficial to England, humbly offered to. . . both houses of Parliament.*—1667#2

CHAMBERLAYNE, John. *Letter from a member of the Society for propagating the gospel. . . to an inhabitant of the City of London. . .*—1711#3

CHAMBERLAYNE, Peregrine. *Compendium geographicum: Or, a more exact, plain, and easie introduction into all geography. . .*—1682#7

CHAMBERLAYNE, Richard. *Lithobolia: or, the stone throwing devil. . . account of infernal spirits. . . and the great disturbance they gave to George Walton's. . .*—1698#5

CHAMPIGNY, Jean. *The present state of the country and inhabitants, Europeans and Indians, of Louisiana, on the north continent of America. By an officer of New Orleans to his friend at Paris.*—1744#10

CHANDLER, Edward. *A sermon preached. . . 20th February, 1718. . .*—1719#1

CHAPPEL, Samuel. *A diamond or rich jewel, presented to the Common wealth of England, for inriching the Nation*—1651#4

CHARKE, Ezekiel. *A pretended voice from heaven, proved to bee the voice of men, and not of God. . .*—1659#4

CHARLESTON, SOUTH CAROLINA. LIBRARY COMPANY. *Catalogue of the books belonging to the Charles-Town Library Society. . .*—1750#10

CHARMION, John. *AE. M. S. eximij pietate, eruditione, pudentia' viri D. Ebenezrae Pembertoni, apud Bostoniensis Americanos praedicatoris vere. . .*—1717#4

CHAUNCY, Charles (1592–1672).
The doctrine of the sacrament—1642#3
[Hebrew] or the doctrin [sic] of the justification of a sinner in the sight of God. . .—1659#5
The retraction of. . . written in his own hand before his going to New England, in the yeer, 1637.—1641#3

CHAUNCY, Charles (1705–87).
Letter from a gentleman in Boston, to Mr. George Wishart, one of the ministers in Edinburgh, concerning the state of religion in New-England.—1742#8
Letter to a friend; giving a concise but just account. . . of the Ohio defeat. . .—1755#5

Marvellous things done by the right hand... of God in getting him the victory...—1745#9

The new creature described and considered as the sure characteristick of a man's being in Christ...—1742#9

Two letters to a friend, on the present critical conjuncture of affairs in North America; particularly on the vast importance of the victory...—1755#6

The wonderful narrative; or, a faithful account of the French prophets... several other instances of persons under the influence of the like spirit... particularly in New - England...—1742#10

CHAUNCY, Isaac. *Neonomianism unmask'd: or, the ancient gospel pleaded, against the other, called a new law, or gospel.*—1692#3

CHECKLEY, John. *The speech of Mr. John Checkley upon his tryal, at Boston in New-England, for publishing the Short and easy method with the deists...*—1730#4

CHEEVER, Ezekiel. *Rhode Island. Peleg Browne... Collector of... Customs for Newport... appellant. Ezekiel Cheevers, of Boston... and James Allen... respondents. The respondent's case.*—1738#4

CHETWOOD, William Rufus.

The voyage, shipwreck, and miraculous escape of Richard Castleman... With a description of Pennsylvania... and... Philadelphia...—1726#4

The voyages and adventures of Captain Robert Boyle... To which is added the voyage, shipwreck, and miraculous escape of Richard Castleman...—1726#5

The voyages, dangerous adventures and imminent escapes of Captain Richard Falconer: containing the laws, customs and manners of the Indians...—1720#9

CHEWNEY, Nicholas. *Anti-Socinianism, or a brief explication... for the confutation of... gross errors and Socinian heresies, lately published...*—1650#2

CHIDLEY, Katherine. *The justification of the independent churches of Christ. Being an answer to Mr Edwards his booke.*—1641#4

CHILD, John. *New-Englands Jonas cast up in London: or, A relation of the proceedings of the court at Boston in New-England against divers honest and godly persons...*—1647#4

CHILD, Josiah. *A discourse about trade.*—1690#6

CHILTON, Edward: See HARTWELL, Henry.

CHRISTIE, Thomas. *A description of Georgia, by a gentleman who has resided there upwards of seven years, and was one of the first settlers.*—1741#5

CHURCH OF ENGLAND.

Abstract of a form of prayer and thanksgiving to almighty God; to be used in all churches and chapels... on Thursday the 29th...—1759#16

A form of prayer and thanksgiving... to be used... on Sunday the twentieth day of August, 1758... in all churches... throughout England... for the taking of Louisbourg...—1758#6

A form of prayer and thanksgiving... to be used... on Sunday the twenty first of October 1759...—1759#15

A form of prayer and thanksgiving... to be used... on Sunday the twelfth of October 1760... on occasion of the late successes of his majesty's arms in North-America...—1760#21

CHURCH OF IRELAND. *A form of prayer, and thanksgiving to Almighty God; to be used in all churches and chapels throughout the kingdom of Ireland...*—1759#17

CHURCHILL, Awnsham. *A collection of voyages and travels.*—1704#10

CLAGETT, Nicholas.

A sermon preached... February 18, 1736...—1737#8

A sermon preached... Thursday May 3d, 1739...—1739#14

CLARIDGE, Richard. *Melius inquirendum, or, An answer to a book of Edward Cockson... mis-intituled, Rigid Quakers cruel persecutors.*—1706#7

CLARK, John. *Ill newes from New England: or A narrative of New - Englands persecution... Also four proposals to... Parliament and Councel of State...*—1652#1

CLARKE, Richard.

An essay on the number seven. Wherein the duration of the Church of Rome are attempted to be shewn.—1759#18

A second warning to the world, by the spirit of prophecy...—1760#22

A spiritual voice to the Christian church and to the Jews... in which the approaching millennium is supported...—1760#23

A warning to the world; or the prophetical numbers of Daniel and John calculated...—1759#19

CLARKE, Samuel.

A collection of the lives of ten eminent divines...—1662#2

A geographicall description of all the countries in the known world... and of the four chiefest English plantations in America...—1657#4

The lives of sundry eminent persons in this later age. In two parts.—1683#5

A mirrour or looking-glasse, both for saints and sinners... By... examples...—1646#4

A new description of the world, or a compendious treatise... of Europe, Asia, Africa and America...—1689#6

A true, and faithful account of the four chiefest plantations of the English in America... Virginia, New-England, Bermudas, Barbados... as also... the natives of Virginia, and New-England...—1670#2

CLARKE, William. *Observations on the late and present conduct of the French, with regard to their encroachments upon the British colonies in North America...*—1755#7

CLARKSON [or CLAXTON], Laurence. *The Quakers downfal... also a brief narration of the Quakers conference with us the second of July 1659. wherein we made it appear...*—1659#6

CLAYTON, Thomas. *Dissertatio medica inauguralis, de parca et simplici medicina, quam... pro gradu doctoratus... eruditorum examini subjicit Thomas Clayton...*—1758#7

CLERK OF THE CALIFORNIA. *An account of a voyage for the discovery of North-West Passage by Hudson's Streights, to the Western and Southern Ocean of America...*—1748#4

CLEVELAND, John. *The works of John Cleveland...*—1687#2

CLIFFE, Edward. *An abreviate of Hollands deliverance by, and ingratitude to the Crown of England...*—1665#14

CLINCH, William. *An historical essay on the rise and progress of the small-pox.*—1724#5

COADE, George.
Letter to a noble Lord: wherein it is demonstrated that all difficulties in obtaining an honourable and lasting peace... are... imaginary.—1760#24
Letter to the honourable the Lords Commissioners of trade and plantations. Wherein the grand concern of trade is asserted and maintained...—1747#4
Letter to the right honourable W. P., esq; by an Englishman.—1758#8

COALE, Josiah.
The books and divers epistles of the faithful servant of the Lord Josiah Coale...—1671#4
A song of the judgements and mercies of the lord: wherein the things seen in secret, are declared openly...—1662#3

COBBET, Thomas.
The civil magistrates power in matters of religion modestly debated... with a brief answer to a certain slanderous pamphlet... Ill news from New England...—1653#3
A fruitfull and usefull discourse...—1656#4
A just vindication of the covenant and church-estate of children of church members...—1648#3
A practical discourse of prayer... by Thomas Cobbet, minister of the word at Lyn.—1654#4

COCK, Christopher.
Catalogue of divers rich and valuable effects, being a collection of Elihu Yale. Part 4... Will be sold by auction on Thursday the 15th of... November...—1722#7
Catalogue of divers rich and valuable effects, being a collection of Elihu Yale. part 5. A fifth sale of Elihu Yale... Will...—1723#3

COCKINGS, George. *War: an heroic poem. From the taking of Minorca by the French, to the raising of the siege of Quebec...*—1760#25

COCKSON, Edward. *Rigid Quakers, cruel persecutors... together with a short abridgement of the history of the Quakers persecutions for religion...*—1705#4

CODDINGTON, William. *A demonstration of true love unto you the rulers of the colony of the Massachusetts...*—1674#1

CODRINGTON, Robert. *His majesties propriety, and dominion on the Brittish seas asserted.*—1665#13

COGGESHALL, Daniel. *Rhode Island. Daniel Coggeshall, Esq.,... appellant. Mary Coggeshall... respondent... The appellant's case.*—1739#15

COKE, Roger.
A detection of the court and state of England during the last few reigns.—1694#3
England's improvements. In two parts...—1675#4
Reflections upon East-Indy and Royal African companies...—1695#7
A supplement to the first edition of The detection of the court of England.—1696#6
A treatise wherein is demonstrated, that the Church and state of England, are in equal danger with the trade of it.—1671#5

COLDEN, Cadwallader.
An explication of the first causes of action in matter, and of the cause of gravitation.—1746#6
The history of the five Indian nations of Canada, which are dependent on the province of New-York in America, and are the barrier...—1747#5
The principles of action in matter, the gravitation of bodies, and the motion of the planets, explained from their principles.—1751#11

COLES, William. *Adam in Eden: or, Nature in Paradise. The history of plants, fruits, herbs and flowers...*—1657#5

COLLIBER, Samuel. *Columna rostrata: or, a critical history of the English sea-affairs...*—1727#4

COLLINGES, John.
The history of conformity.—1681#5
Vindiciae ministerii evangelici...—1651#5

COLLINS, John. *Salt and fishery. A discourse thereof...*—1682#8

COLMAN, Benjamin.
A narrative of the method and success of inoculating the small pox in New England... With a reply to the objections... in letter from a minister at Boston... a historical introduction by Daniel Neal...—1722#9
Practical discourses upon the parable of the ten virgins...—1707#3
Some of the glories of our Lord and Saviour... in twenty sacramental discourses, preached at Boston...—1728#5
Souls flying to Jesus Christ, pleasant and admirable to behold. A sermon preached... at the opening evening lecture, in... Boston... October 21, 1740.—1741#6

COMMELIN, Izaak. *A collection of voyages undertaken by the Dutch East-India Company, for the improvement of trade and navigation...*—1703#6

COMPANY FOR MINES AND MINERALS IN NEW-ENGLAND. *An alphabetical list of the subscribers in nomination for deputy-governor and assistants for the first government of the company...*—1688#3

COMPANY FOR PROPAGATION OF THE GOSPEL IN NEW ENGLAND AND THE PARTS ADJACENT IN AMERICA. *Rules and orders respecting the Charity left by the will of the hon. Robert Boyle...*—1691#5

COMPTON, Henry. Letter from the Lord Bishop of London, to his clergy within the bills of mortality. . . 14 May 1711. . .—1711#4

CONYBEARE, John. A sermon preached. . . Thursday May 4th 1738. . . to which is annexed. . .—1738#6

COOK, Ebenezer. The sot-weed factor: or, a voyage to Maryland. A satyr. In which is described, the laws, government, courts and constitutions of the country. . .—1708#3

COOKE, Edward. A voyage to the South Sea, and round the world. . .—1712#5

COOKE, John. Greene's Tu quoque, or the cittie gallant.—1622#6

COOLE, Benjamin.
Honesty the truest policy, shewing the sophistry, envy and perversion of George Keith.—1700#12
The Quakers cleared from being apostates. . .—1696#7
Sophistry detected or an answer to George Keith's synopsis. . .—1699#5

COPITHORNE, Richard. The English cotejo, or the cruelties. . . charged upon the English in a Spanish libel. . .—1739#17

COPLAND, Patrick.
A declaration how the monies. . . were disposed, which was gathered (by Mr Patrick Copland. . .). . . (towards the building of a free schoole in Virginia). . .—1622#7
Virginia's God be thanked, or A sermon of thanksgiving for the happie successe of the affayres in Virginia this last yeare. Preached by Patrick Copland. . . 18. of April 1622. . .—1622#8

CORNWALLIS, Frederick. A sermon preached. . . February 20, 1756. . .—1756#16

CORNWELL, Francis. A conference Mr. John Cotton held at Boston with the elders of New-England. . .—1646#5

COTTON, John.
An abstract of laws and government. . . Collected and digested by. . . Mr. John Cotton. . . published after his death, by William Aspinwall. . .—1655#6
An abstract or [sic] the lawes of New England as they are now established.—1641#5
The bloudy tenent, washed. . .—1647#5
A brief exposition of the whole book of Canticles, or, the Song of Solomon—1642#4
A brief exposition with practicall observations upon the whole book of Canticles.—1655#7
A brief exposition with practicall observations upon the whole book of Ecclesiastes.—1654#6
Certain queries published by a friend. . .—1654#7
Christ the fountaine of life. . .—1651#7
The churches resurrection, or the opening of the fift and sixt verses of the 20th. chap. of the Revelation.—1642#5
The controversie concerning liberty of conscience in matters of religion, truly stated. . .—1646#6
A coppy of a letter of Mr Cotton of Boston, in New England, sent in answer of certaine objections made against their discipline and order there—1641#6
The covenant of Gods free grace. . . Whereunto is added A profession of faith. . . by John Davenport. . .—1645#4
The covenant of grace. . . Whereunto are added: Certain queries. . . also a discussion of the civil magistrates power. . .—1655#8
A defence of Mr John Cotton from the imputation of selfe contradiction. . .—1658#3
The doctrine of the church.—1643#4
An exposition upon the thirteenth chapter of the Revelation.—1655#9
God's mercie mixed with his justice, or, his people's deliverance in times of danger. . . in severall sermons.—1641#7
God's promise to His plantation, 2 Sam. 7. 10; in a sermon.—1630#1
Gospel conversion together with some reasons against stinted forms of praising God. . .—1646#7
The grounds and ends of the baptisme. . .—1647#6
The keyes of the kingdom of heaven, and power thereof, according to the word of God. . .—1644#4
Letter of Mr. John Cottons, teacher of the church of Boston in New-England, to Mr [Roger] Williams—1643#5
Milk for babes. . .—1646#8
A modest and cleere answer to Mr Ball's discourse of set formes of prayer—1642#6
The new covenant, or, a treatise, unfolding the order and manner of giving and receiving the covenant of grace. . .—1654#8
Of the holinesse of church-members. . .—1650#3
The powring out of the seven vials: or, An exposition of the 16. chapter of the Revelation—1642#7
A practical commentary, or an exposition. . . upon the first epistle generall of John. . .—1656#5
The result of a synod. . .—1654#9
Singing of psalmes. . .—1647#7
Sixteene questions of serious and necessary consequence, propounded unto Mr John Cotton. . .—1644#5
Some treasure fetched out of rubbish.—1660#4
Spiritual milk for babes.—1668#2
Spiritual milk for Boston Babes.—1657#6
A treatise of the covenant of Grace. . .—1659#7
The true constitution of a particular visible church—1642#8
The way of congregational churches cleared.—1648#4
The way of life. Or, God's way and course, in bringing the soule into, keeping it in, and carrying it on, in the wayes of life and peace. . . in foure severall treatises.—1641#8
The way of the churches of Christ in New-England.—1645#5

COUCH, Robert. New Englands lamentation for the late firing of the city of London.—1666#3

COUNCIL FOR NEW ENGLAND.
A brief relation of the discovery and plantation of New-England: and of sundry accidents therein occurring. . .—1622#9
A proposition of provisions needfull for such as intend to plant themselves in New England, for one whole yeare. Collected by the adventurers, with the advice of the planters.—1630#2

COURT VAN DER VOORT, Pieter de la.
The interest of Holland as to their alliances...—1712#6
The true interest and political maxims of the republick of Holland and West-Friesland... Written by John de Witt and other great men in Holland...—1702#6

COWELL, John.
The curious and profitable gardener... To which is added, an exact description of the great American aloe... together with the culture of that, and many other rare exotic plants...—1730#6
A true account of the Aloe Americana or Africana, which is now in blossom in Mr. Cowell's garden at Hoxton...—1729#5

COWETA INDIANS. *The humble submission of the kings, princes, generals, etc. to the Crown of England. Lately presented to... Sir Nathaniel Johnston, the present governour of Carolina...*—1707#4

COWLEY, J. *A description of the Windward passage, and Gulf of Florida, with the course of the British trading-ships to, and from the island...*—1739#19

COXE, Daniel.
A collection of voyages and travels, in three parts [Part III]... A description of the English province of Carolana...—1741#8
A description of the English province of Carolana, by the Spaniards called Florida, and by the French, La Louisiane...—1722#10

CRADOCK, Thomas. *A new poetical translation of the Psalmes of David...*—1754#6

CRAFFORD, John. *A new and most exact account of the fertile and famous colony of Carolina... the whole being the compendious account of a voyage...*—1683#6

CRAIG, Campbell.
An authentic journal of the proceedings in the great cause tried at Dublin, between the Honourable James Annesley plaintiff, and a noble person, defendant...—1743#9
The trial at bar, between Campbell Craig... and... Richard earl of Anglesey... at the King's Courts, Dublin... 1743.—1743#10
The trial at bar, between Campbell Craig, lessee of James Annesley, Esq: plaintiff, and... Richard Earl of Anglesey, defendant...—1744#11
The trial at large, between James Annesley, Esq. and the Rt. Hon. Earl of Anglesea...—1744#12
The trial in ejectment (at large) between Campbell Craig, lessee of James Annesley... and... Richard Earl of Anglesea... Friday, November 11, 1743...—1744#13

CRAVEN, Charles. *Case of Major Charles Craven, of the late Fifty-first regiment, in North America, now on half pay...*—1759#21

CRAWFORD, J. *Case of inoculating the small-pox considered, and its advantages asserted; in a review of Dr. Wagstaffe's letter...*—1722#11

CRESSET, Edward. *A sermon preached... February 16, 1753...*—1753#4

CRIPPS, John. *A true account of the dying words of Ockanickon, an Indian King... by John Cripps of Burlington, N. J.*—1682#9

CRISP, Thomas.
Animadversions on George Whitehead's book.—1694#4
The discovery of the accursed thing found in the Foxonian Quakers camp.—1695#8
A just and lawful tryal of the Foxonian chief priests...—1697#7
The second part of Babel's builders unmask't.—1683#7

CROESE, Gerard. *The general history of the Quakers...*—1696#8

CROKATT, James.
Further observations intended for improving the culture and curing of indigo, etc in South-Carolina.—1747#7
Observations concerning indigo and cochineal...—1746#7

CROOKSHANKS, John.
The conduct and treatment of John Crookshanks... late commander of... the Lark.—1759#22
The reply of John Crookshanks, Esq; to a pamphlet lately set forth by Admiral Knowles...—1759#23

CROSS, -. *An answer to an invidious pamphlet, intituled, A brief state of the province of Pennsylvania...*—1755#12

CROUCH, Henry.
A complete guide to the officers of His Majesty's customs in the out-ports. Being forms, precedents, and instructions...—1732#13
A complete view of the British Customs...—1724#6

CROUCH, Nathaniel.
Admirable curiosities, rarities and wonders...—1682#10
England's monarchs...—1685#8
The kingdom of darkness...—1688#4
Miracles of art and nature, or, a brief description of the several varieties of birds, beasts, fishes, plants, and fruits of other countreys...—1678#2
Strange and prodigious religious customs and manners of sundry nations...—1683#8
Wonderful prodigies of judgement and mercy...—1682#11
See also B., R.

CROWE, William. *The duty of public spirit recommended in a sermon preach'd... March 20, 1739-40...*—1740#9

CROZAT, Anthony. *Letter to a member of the P——t of G——t B——n, occasioned by the priviledge granted by the French King to Mr. Crozat.*—1713#4

CRULL, Jodocus. *An introduction to the history of... Asia, Africa, and America, both ancient and modern, according to the method of Samuel Pufendorf...*—1705#6

CUMING, Patrick. *A sermon preached... February 4. 1760.*—1760#28

CURSON, Henry.
A compendium of the laws and government... of England and dominions, plantations, and territories thereto belonging.—1699#6
A new description of the world...—1706#9

CUSHMAN, Robert. *A sermon preached at Plimmoth in New-England December 9. 1621 in an assemblie of his majesties faithfull subjects, there inhabiting...*—1622#10

CUTLER, Nathaniel. *Atlas maritimus & commercialis; or, A general view of the world... together with a large account of the commerce carried on by...*—1728#6

CYRANO DE BERGERAC, Savinien.
The comical history of the... states and empires of the moon and the sun.—1687#3
Selemnarchia. Or the government of the world in the moon.—1659#8

D., C. *New England's faction discovered; or a brief and true account of their persecution of the Church of England...*—1690#7

D., L. *Reasons for a war against Spain. In a letter from a merchant of London trading to America, to a member of the House of Commons...*—1737#9

DALE, Samuel. *Pharmacologia, seu Manuductio ad materiam medicam...*—1693#5

DALTON, James. *The life and actions of James Dalton, (the noted street-robber.)... With a particular account of his running away with the ship when he was first transported...*—1730#7

DANFORTH, Samuel. *An astronomical description of the late comet.*—1666#4

DAVENANT, Charles.
Discourses on the publick revenues, and on the trade of England...—1698#6
A report to the Honourable Commissioners for putting in execution the Act...—1712#7
The true picture of an ancient Tory.—1702#7

DAVENPORT, John.
An answer of the elders of the severall churches in New-England unto nine positions... written in the year 1639—1643#6
A catechisme containing the chief heads... for the church of Christ at New-Haven...—1659#9
An exhortation to the restoring of brotherly communion—1641#9

The knowledge of Christ...—1653#5
The power of Congregational churches asserted and vindicated.—1672#3
The profession of faith of... Mr J. D... Made publiquely before the congregation at his admission into one of the churches of God in New-England.—1642#9
The saints anchor-hold—1642#10

DAVENPORT, Thomas. *A brief manifestation of the state and case of the Quakers presented to all people... also to all planters or occupiers of land in the English and forreign plantations...*—1664#5

DAVIES, Samuel.
An account of a remarkable work of grace, or the great success of the gospel, in Virginia. In a letter... to the Rev. Mr. Bellamy...—1752#5

The crisis: or, the uncertain doom of kingdoms... with reference to Great-Britain and her colonies in their present circumstances...—1757#6
The curse of cowardice: a sermon preached to the militia in Hanover county, Virginia, at a general muster, May 8, 1758...—1758#12
The duties, difficulties and reward of the faithful minister. A sermon, preached at the installation of the Revd. Mr. John Todd...—1754#7
The duty of Christians to propagate their religion among heathens, earnestly recommended to the masters of negro slaves in Virginia. A sermon preached in Hanover, January 8, 1757.—1758#13
The following verses were composed by a pious clergyman in Virginia, who preaches to seven congregations...—1755#13
The good soldier. Extracted from a sermon preached to a company of voluntiers, raised in Virginia...—1756#18
Letters from the Rev. Samuel Davies... shewing the present state of religion in Virginia, particularly among the Negroes...—1757#7
Little children invited to Jesus Christ: sermon... in Hanover county, Virginia, May 8, 1757. With a short account... late...—1758#14
Religion and patriotism... sermon... to... volunteers, raised in Hanover county, Virginia, August 17, 1755.—1756#19
A sermon preached at Henrico, 29 April 1753. And at Canongate, 26th May 1754.—1754#8
The substance of a letter from Mr. Davies... to Mr Bellamy of Bethlem, in New England, concerning the state of religion in Virginia...—1751#12
The vessels of mercy and the vessels of wrath... sermon first preached in New-Kent, Virginia, August 22, 1756...—1758#15
Virginia's danger and remedy. Two discourses, occasioned by the severe drought in sundry parts of the country; and the defeat of General Braddock.—1756#20
See also TENNENT, Gilbert.

DAWES, William. *A sermon preached... February 18, 1708–9...*—1709#5

DAWSON, Eli. *A discourse, delivered at Quebec, in the chappel belonging to the convent of the Ursulins, September 27th, 1759; occasioned by the success of our arms in the reduction of that capital...*—1760#29

DAWSON, William. *Letter from the Rev. Mr Dawson... to the clergy of Virginia in America.*—1745#12

DAYRELL, Richard. *A sermon preached before the honourable House of Commons, at St. Margaret's Westminster, on Thursday November 19, 1759...*—1759#25

DE LA ROCHE, ——. *Letter from Quebeck, in Canada, to M. L'Maine, a French officer. Which contains a particular account of the present designs of the French upon the English in North-America...*—1755#14

DEAN, John. *A narrative of the sufferings of... Captain John Dean... in the Nottingham-Galley of London, cast away on Boon island, near New England, December 11 1710.*—1711#5

DECKER, Matthew. *An essay on the causes of the decline of foreign trade.* . .—1744#14

DEFOE, Daniel.
A brief history of the poor Palatine refugees lately arrived in England.—1709#7
Case of Protestant dissenters in Carolina, shewing how a law to prevent occasional conformity there, has ended in the total subversion. . .—1706#10
The chimera: or, the French way of paying national debts. . . the Mississippi stock.—1720#10
The complete English tradesman.—1725#4
An essay upon projects.—1697#8
The fortunes and misfortunes of the famous Moll Flanders. . .—1722#12
Fortune's fickle distribution; in three parts. . .—1730#12
A general history of discoveries and improvements, in useful arts, particularly in the great branches of commerce, navigation and plantation. . .—1725#5
A general history of the robberies and murders of the most notorious pyrates, and also their policies, discipline and government. . . by Captain Charles Johnson.—1724#7
The history and remarkable life of the truly honourable Col. Jacque, commonly called Col. Jack. . .—1723#4
A humble proposal to the people of England, for the encrease of their trade. . . By the author of the Compleat Tradesman.—1729#6
The king of pirates. . . an account of the famous enterprises of Captain Avery, the mock king of Madagascar. . .—1719#2
Party-tyranny: or, an occasional bill in miniature as now practised in Carolina. Humbly offered to the consideration of. . . Parliament.—1705#7
A plan of the English commerce. . .—1728#7
Some reasons offered by the late ministry in defence of their administration.—1715#12
Taxes no charge: in a letter from a gentleman, to a person of quality. . .—1690#8
The two great questions consider'd.—1700#13

DENHAM, Sir John. *Certain verses written by severall of the authors friends; to be reprinted with the second edition of Gondibert.*—1653#6

DENNE, John. *A sermon preached. . . the 19th of February 1730 [i.e. 1731].*—1731#11

DENNIS, John.
Liberty asserted. A tragedy. As it is acted at the New Theatre in Little Lincoln's-Inn-Fields.—1704#11
A proposal for putting a speedy end to the war, by ruining the commerce of the French and the Spaniards. . .—1703#7

DENTON, Daniel. *A brief description of New-York; formerly called New-Netherlands.* . .—1670#3

DESLANDES, André F. B. *An essay on maritime power and commerce.*—1743#12

DICKINSON, James.
Journal of the life, travels, and labour of love in the work of the ministry of. . . James Dickinson. . .—1745#14
A salutation of love to the seed of God everywhere.—1696#9AUTH

DICKINSON, Jonathan.
Familiar letters to a gentleman, upon a variety of seasonable and important subjects in religion. . .—1757#8
God's protecting providence, man's surest help and defence. . . remarkable deliverance. . . from devouring waves. . . also from. . . inhumane cannibals of Florida. . .—1700#14

DILWORTH, W. H.
The conquest of Peru. . . Together with the voyages of the first adventurers, particularly Ferdinand de Soto, for the discovery of Florida. . .—1759#27
The history of the bucanniers of America. . . adorned with copper plates. . .—1758#16
The history of the present war. . . to the conclusion of the year 1759. . .—1760#30

DISNEY, Daniel. *A compendious history of the rise and progress of the reformation of the church here in England.* . .—1715#13

DITCHFIELD, Master. *Considerations touching the new contract for tobacco, as the same hath been propounded by Maister Ditchfield, and other undertakers.*—1625#2

DOBBS, Arthur.
An account of the countries adjoining to Hudson's Bay. . . With an abstract of Captain Middleton's journal, and observations upon his behaviour. . .—1744#15
An essay on the trade and improvement of Ireland.—1729#7
Letter from a Russian sea-officer. . . relative to the new discoveries northward and eastward from Kamatschatka. Together with. . .—1754#9
Remarks upon Capt. Middleton's defence: wherein his conduct during his late voyage for discovering a passage from Hudson's Bay to. . .—1744#16
Reasons to shew, that there is a great probability of a navigable passage to the American western ocean, through the Hudson's streights. . .—1749#11
A reply to Capt. Middleton's answer to the remarks on his vindication of his conduct, in a late voyage made by him in the Furnace. . .—1745#15
A short view of the countries and trade carried on by the Company in Hudson's-Bay, shewing the prejudice of that exclusive trade. . .—1749#12

DODD, William. *Thoughts on the glorious epiphany of the Lord Jesus Christ.* . .—1757#9

DODDRIDGE, Philip.
Reflections on the conduct of divine providence in the series and conclusion of the late war; a sermon.—1749#13
The rise and progress of religion in the soul.—1745#16

DODSLEY, Robert. *A collection of poems in four volumes. By several hands.*—1755#16

DOMAT, Jean. *The civil law in its natural order. . . translated. . . by William Strahan.* . .—1722#13

DONALDSON, James.
Considerations in relation to trade considered.—1706#11

The undoubted art of thriving, showing that a million. . . may be raised. . . how the Indian and African Company may propagate their. . .—1700#15

DONALDSON, William. *North America, a descriptive poem. Representing the voyage to America; a sketch of that beautiful country; with remarks upon the political humour and singular conduct of its inhabitants. . .*—1757#10

DONNE, John.
LXXX sermons.—1640#1
A sermon upon the VIII. verse of the I. chapter of the Actes of the Apostles. Preached to the honourable company of the Virginian plantation.—1622#11

DOUGLAS, John.
The destruction of the French foretold by Ezekiel; or, a commentary on the thirty-fifth chapter of that prophet. . .—1755#17
Letter addressed to two great men, on the prospect of the peace; and the terms necessary to be insisted upon in the negociation. . .—1760#31

DOUGLASS, William.
A discourse concerning the currencies of the British plantations in America. Especially with regard to their paper money. . .—1741#9
Inoculation of the small pox as practiced in Boston.—1722#14
A practical essay concerning the small-pox.—1730#8
A summary, historical and political, of the first planting, progressive improvements, and present state of the British settlements in North America. . .—1755#18

DOVER, William. *Useful miscellanies, or Serious reflections, respecting mens duty to God.*—1739#21

DOWNING, George.
A discourse written by Sir Geo. Downing vindicating his royal master. . .—1664#6
A reply of Sir George Downing. . . to the remarks of the deputies of the Estates-general, upon his memorial of December 20. 1664. . .—1665#15

DRAYTON, Michael.
The battaile of Agincourt.—1627#1
A chorographicall description of. . . Great Britain. . . Digested into a poem. . .—1622#12

DRUMMOND, Robert Hay. *A sermon preached. . . February 15, 1754. . .*—1754#10

DRYDEN, John. *The prologue and epilogue to the History of Bacon in Virginia.*—1689#9

DU BARTAS, Guillaume de Salluste. *Part of Du Bartas, English and French. . . Englished. . .*—1625#3

DU PLESSIS, ——. *Duplessis's memoirs, or, a variety of adventures in England and America. . . and a description of some strolling players, with whom he travelled. . .*—1757#11

DUDLEY, Joseph?. *A modest enquiry into the grounds and occasions of a late pamphlet, intituled, A memorial of the present deplorable state of New-England. By a disinterested hand.*—1707#5

DUDLEY, Paul. *An essay on the merchandise of slaves and the souls of men. . . With an application thereof to the Church of Rome.*—1732#14

DUGDALE, Richard. *A narrative of the wicked plots carried on by Seignior Gondamore for advancing the popish religion and Spanish faction. . .*—1679#2

DUMMER, Jeremiah.
A defence of the New-England charters. . .—1721#4
Letter to a friend in the country, on the late expedition to Canada. . .—1712#8
Letter to a noble lord, concerning the late expedition to Canada.—1712#9
Mr Dummers account of the West India correspondence, how it was propounded, and how since performed. Received 15 October 1705.—1705#8

DUNBAR, Charles. *Charles Dunbar, of the Island of Antigua. . . appellant. Daniel Parke Custis, son and heir, and also sole executor of the last. . .*—1757#12

DUNCOMBE, John. *A sermon preached in. . . St Anne's, Westminster. . . November 29, 1759.*—1759#28

DUNTON, John.
The life and errors of John Dunton late citizen of London. . .—1705#9
The phenix: or, A revival of scarce and valuable pieces from the remotest antiquity down to the present time.—1707#6

DURNO, J. *A description of a new-invented stove-grate, shewing its uses. . . over all others. . .*—1753#5

DURRELL, Philip. *A particular account of the taking Cape Breton. . . by Admiral Warren and Sir W. Pepperell, 17th June, 1745, with. . . a letter from. . .*—1745#17

DUVAL, Pierre. *Geographia universalis: The present state of the whole world. . .*—1685#9

DYCHE, Thomas. *A new general English dictionary. . . Together with a supplement of the proper names of the most noted foreign kingdoms, provinces, cities, towns, rivers, etc. . .*—1735#2

DYER, John. *The fleece, a poem. In four books.*—1757#13

DYRE, William. *To the King's most excellent majesty. The humble petition of William Dyre gent. . .*—1670#4

E., N. *The females advocate: or, an essay to prove that the sisters in every church of Christ, have a right to church-government as well as the brethren.*—1718#4

E., R. *The Present state of popery in England. . .*—1733#14

EATON, Samuel and TAYLOR, Timothy. *A defense of sundry positions & scriptures alledged to justify the Congregationall way. . .*—1645#6

EATON, Samuel. *The Quakers confuted. . .*—1654#10

EBORANOS. *Ways and means whereby his majesty may man his navy with ten thousand able sailors. . . To which is added a collection of some political essays. By Eboranos.*—1734#5

EBURNE, Richard. *A plaine path-way to plantations.*—1624#4

ECHARD, Laurence.
The gazetteer's or newsman's interpreter. Being a geographical index of. . . Asia, Africa and America.—1703#8
A most compleat compendium of geography. . .—1691#7

EDGAR, William. *Vectigalium systema: or, a complete view of that part of the revenue of Great Britain, commonly called Customs. Wherein. . . IV. The laws. . .*—1714#5

EDINBURGH PHILOSOPHICAL SOCIETY. *Essays and observations, read before a Society in Edinburgh, and published by them. . .*—1754#11

EDMUNDSON, William. *Journal of the life, travels, sufferings and labour of love in the work of the ministry of. . . William Edmundson, who departed this life. . . 1712.*—1715#14

EDWARDS, George. *A natural history of birds. . .*—1743#13

EDWARDS, Jonathan.
The distinguishing marks of a work of the spirit of God. . . lately appeared. . . in New-England. . .—1742#12
A faithful narrative of the conversion of many hundred souls in Northampton. . . New England. In a letter to Dr. B. Colman. . . and published with a preface by Dr Watts and Dr Guyse. . .—1737#12
Remarks on the Essays on the principles of morality, and natural religion. In a letter to a minister of the Church of Scotland. . .—1758#17
Sinners in the hands of an angry God. . . preached at Enfield, July 8, 1741. . . With a preface by. . . John Willison Minister of the Gospel at Dundee. . .—1745#18
Some thoughts concerning the present revival of religion in New England, and the way it ought to be acknowledged and promoted. . .—1743#14
Thoughts concerning the present revival of religion in New England. . . Abridged by John Wesley.—1745#19

EDWARDS, Thomas.
Antapologia: or, A full answer to the Apologeticall narration. . .—1644#6
Gangraena: or a catalogue and discovery of many of the errours. . .—1646#9
Reasons against the independent government of particular congregations. . . as also against the toleration of such churches.—1641#10
The second part of Gangraena.—1646#10
The third part of Gangraena.—1646#11

EGERTON, Henry. *A sermon preached. . . 21st February 1728. . .*—1729#8

EGLETON, John. *Letter written to a member of Parliament relating to trade.*—1702#9

ELDERFIELD, Christopher. *Of regeneration and baptism, Hebrew and Christian, with their rites, etc.*—1653#7

ELIOT, John.
A brief narrative of the progress of the gospel amongst the Indians in New-England, as in the year 1670. . .—1671#7
The Christian commonwealth: or, The civil policy of the rising kingdom of Jesus Christ. . .—1659#10
A further accompt of the progresse of the gospel amongst the Indians in New-England, and of the means used effectually to advance the same. . .—1659#11
A late and further manifestation of the progress of the gospel among the Indians, in New-England. . . Pub. by the corporation. . . for propagating the gospel there. . .—1654#11
New Englands first fruits; in respect. First of the conversion of some, convictions of diverse, preparation of sundry of the. . .—1643#7
Tears of repentance: or, A further narrative of the progress of the gospel amongst the Indians in New England. . .—1653#8

ELIOT, Joseph. *The life of faith, exemplified and recommended, in a letter found in the study of J. Belcher, late of Dedham in New-England. . .*—1741#10

ELLIS, Henry.
Considerations on the great advantages which would arise from the discovery of the North west passage, and a clear account of the most practical method for attempting that discovery.—1750#12
A voyage to Hudson's-Bay, by the Dobbs galley and California, in the years 1746 and 1747, for discovering a North-West Passage with. . . a short natural history of the country. . .—1748#5

ELLIS, William. *London and Country Brewer. . . in three parts. . .*—1759#29

ELLWOOD, Thomas.
An alarm to the priests, or, a message from heaven. . .—1660#5
An answer to George Keith's narrative of his proceedings at the Turner's Hall.—1696#10
A collection of poems on various subjects.—1750#12A
An epistle to Friends. . . and warning them to beware of that spirit of contention. . . in George Keith, and some few others. . . who have. . .—1694#5
A further discovery of that spirit of contention and division. . . in George Keith, etc. Being a reply to two late printed pieces of his. . .—1694#6
The history of the life of Thomas Ellwood, or, an account of his birth, education, etc. with divers observations. . . To which is added a supplement By Joseph Wyeth.—1714#6
Truth defended: and the friends thereof cleared, from the false charges. . . by George Keith. . . in two books. . .—1695#10

ELLYS, Anthony. *A sermon preached. . . February 23, 1759. . .*—1759#30

ENGLAND. *A collection of all the proclamations, declarations, articles and ordinances. . .*—1654#5

ENGLAND. LORD PROTECTOR. *A declaration of his highnes by the advice of his council. . .*—1655#10

ENGLAND AND WALES: See GREAT BRITAIN.

ENTICK, John. *A new naval history: or, A compleat view of the British marine. . .*—1757#15

ERSKINE, John.
The influence of religion on national happiness. A sermon preached. . . 5 January 1756. . .—1756#23

*The signs of the times considered: or, the high probability, that the present appearances in New-England, and the west of Scotland...—*1742#14

ERSKINE, Robert. *The facts and accusations set forth in a late pamphlet, intituled: The conduct of John Crookshanks, proved to be false and groundless...—*1759#33

ESTAUGH, John. *A call to the unfaithful professors of truth...—*1745#20

ESTRADES, Godefroi Louis. *Letters and negotiations of Count d'Estrades... from MDXXVIII to MDCLXIII, containing an account of... troubles that happened...—*1755#19

EVANS, Arise. *Light for the Jews, or the means to convert them...—*1656#6

EVANS, Lewis. *Geographical, historical, political, philosphical and mechanical essays. Number II. Containing a letter, representing the impropriety of sending forces to Virginia...—*1756#25

EVANS, Theophilus. *The history of modern enthusiasm from the Reformation to the present times.—*1752#6

EVANS, Thomas?. *An extract of sundry passages taken out of Mr Whitefield's printed sermons, journals, and letters; together with some scruples...—*1741#11

EVELYN, John.
*Navigation and commerce, their original and progress...—*1674#3
*Sylva, or a discourse of forest trees, and the propagation of timber in his majesty's dominions.—*1660#6

EVELYN, Robert. *A direction for adventurers... with small stock to get two for one, and good land freely... true description of the healthiest...—*1641#11

EVERARD, John. *Some gospel-treasures opened: or the holiest of the unvailing—*1653#9

F., R. *The present state of Carolina with advice to the setlers...—*1682#13

FAGE, Robert. *A description of the whole world...—*1658#4

FAIRFAX, Thomas, Lord.
*The right honourable Thomas Lord Fairfax, petitioner. against the governor and council of Virginia, in right of the Crown, defendents. The case of the petitioner the Lord Fairfax.—*1739#25
*Virginia. The right honourable Thomas Lord Fairfax petitioner, the governor and council of Virginia, in right of the Crown defendents. The case on behalf of the Crown.—*1739#26

FALQUES, Marianne-Agnès. *The last war of the beasts. A fable. To serve for the history of the eighteenth century. In two parts. Translated from the original French of the author of Abassai.—*1758#20

FAUQUIER, Francis. *An essay on ways and means for raising money for the support of the present war...—*1756#27

FAWCETT, Benjamin. *A compassionate address to the Christian Negroes in Virginia With an appendix, containing some account of the rise and progress of Christianity among that poor people...—*1756#28

FENWICK, John. *Friends, These are to satisfie you... that New Cesarea, or New Jersey... is a healthy, pleasant and plentiful country... dated this 8th of the 1st month, 1675.—*1675#6

FERGUSON, C. *Letter addressed to every honest man in Britain...—*1738#7

FIELD, John.
*The Christianity of the people called Quakers, asserted, by George Keith: in answer to a sheet, called, A serious call to the Quakers.—*1700#16
*Light and truth... reply to... 'A plain discovery of many gross falsehoods, etc...' by George Keith...—*1701#20

FINLEY, Samuel. *Christ triumphing and Satan raging: a sermon... first preached at Nottingham in Pensilvania...—*1741#13

FIRMIN, Giles.
*Of schism. Parochial congregations in England, and ordination...—*1658#5
*Panourgia. A brief review of Mr Davis's vindication...—*1693#6
*Presbyterial ordination vindicated. In a brief and sober discourse concerning episcopacy...—*1660#8
*The real Christian, or a Treatise of effectual calling...—*1670#7
*Separation examined: or, a treatise wherein the grounds for separation from the ministry and churches of England are weighed and found to be too light...—*1652#2
*A sober reply to the sober answer of reverend Mr Cawdrey... also, the question of Reverend Mr Hooker concerning the baptisme of infants...—*1653#10
*Weighty questions discussed...—*1692#5

FISHER, James. *A review of the preface to a narrative of the extraordinary work at Kilsyth, and other congregations in the neighbourhood, written by the Reverend Mr James Robe...—*1742#15

FISHER, Sally. *Britain's golden mines discovered: or the fishery trade considered...—*1720#11

FLAVELL, John.
*England's duty, under the present gospel liberty...—*1689#11
*An exposition of the Assemblies catechism...—*1692#6

FLECKNOE, Richard. *The mariage of Oceanus and Brittania.—*1665#17

FLEETWOOD, William. *A sermon preached... 16th February, 1710/11...—*1711#6

FLEMING, Robert. *The fulfilling of the Scripture, or an essay shewing the exact accomplishment of the word of God in his works of providence...—*1681#8

FLETCHER, Henry. *The perfect politician.—*1660#9

FLETCHER, William. *A sermon, preached in St. Andrew's, Dublin; before the Honourable House of Commons: on Thursday, Nov. 29, 1759...—*1760#32

FLOYD, Thomas. *Bibliotheca biographica: a synopsis of universal biography...—*1760#33

FONTENELLE, Bernard Le Bovyer de. *A discourse of the plurality of worlds...—*1687#4

FORBES, Alexander. *An anatomy of independency, or, A brief commentary, and moderate discourse upon the Apologeticall narration...*—1644#7

FORD, Philip. *A vindication of William Penn, proprietary of Pennsylvania, from the late aspersions... 12th. 12 Month, 1682...*—1683#12

FORSTER, John. *England's happiness increased, or a sure and easie remedy against all succeeding dear years; by a plantation of the roots called potatoes...*—1664#7

FORSTER, Samuel. *A digest of all the laws relating to the customs, to trade, and navigation.*—1727#6

FORTESCUE, J. *A sermon preached at Topsham on Thursday November the 29th, 1759...*—1760#34

FOTHERBY, Martin. *Atheomastix clearing foure truthes against atheists.*—1622#14

FOTHERGILL, John. *An account of the life and travels in the work of the ministry, of J. F. To which are added, divers epistles to friends in Great Britain and America...*—1753#6

FOWLER, Edward. *A defence of The resolution of this case...*—1684#5

FOWLER, Robert. *A Quakers Sea-Journal: being a true relation of a voyage to New-England. Performed by Robert Fowler of the Town of Burlington in Yorkshire, in the year 1658...*—1659#12

FOX, George, and BURNYEAT, John. *A New-England fire brand quenched, being something in answer unto... book entituled: George Fox digged out of his burrows, etc...*—1678#6

FOX, George.
An answer to several new laws and orders made by the rulers of Boston in New England...—1678#4
Caesar's due rendred unto him according to his image and superscription—1679#3
Cain against Abel, representing New England's Church hirarchy [sic], in opposition to her Christian Protestant dissenters...—1675#7
A collection of many select and Christian epistles, letters and testimonies...—1698#7
An epistle general to them who are of the royal priest-hood and chosen generation... to be sent abroad among the saints... in Old and New England... Barbados, and Virginia..—1660#11
An epistle to all professors in New-England, Germany, and other parts of the called Christian world...—1673#4
Gospel family order, being a short discourse concerning the ordering of families, both of whites, blacks, and Indians...—1676#4
Journal or historical account of the life, travels, sufferings... of... George Fox... The first volume...—1694#7
The promise of God proclaimed... preached by the apostles and by his servants and messengers sent forth since for Barbados, New-England, Virginia... to go to them all...—1660#12
The secret workes of a cruel people made manifest...—1659#13
Something in answer to a letter (which I have seen) of John Leverat Governor of Boston to William Coddington... dated 1677...—1678#5
To Friends in Barbadoes, Virginia, Maryland, New-England, and elsewhere.—1661#8
To the council of officers of the Armie, and the Heads of the nation; and for the inferior officers and souldiers to read.—1659#14

FOX, John.
The publick spirit; a poem...—1718#5
The wanderer. With all the motto's in Latin and English: to which is added The publick spirit, an heroick poem. By Mr. Fox.—1718#6

FOX, Luke. *North-West Fox or, Fox from the North-west passage...*—1635#1

FRANCK, Richard.
The admirable and indefatigable adventures of the nine pious pilgrims... Written in America... by a zealous lover of truth.—1707#8
A philosophical treatise of the original and production of things. Writ in America in a time of solitudes...—1687#5

FRANCKE, August Hermann. *Pietas Hallensis: or, an abstract of the marvellous foot-steps of divine providence, attending the management and improvement...*—1716#3

FRANCKLIN, Thomas. *A sermon preached... March 16, 1749,50...*—1750#15

FRANKLIN, Benjamin.
A dissertation on liberty and necessity, pleasure and pain.—1725#6
Experiments and observations on electricity, made at Philadelphia... and communicated in several letters to Mr. P. Collinson, of London, F.R.S.—1751#14
The interest of Great Britain considered, with regard to her colonies, and the acquisitions of Canada and Guadaloupe. To which are added...—1760#35
A parable against persecution...—1759#34
Reflections on courtship and marriage... in two letters to a friend.—1750#16
Some account of the success of inoculation for the small-pox in England and America. Together with Plain Instructions...—1759#35

FRANSHAM, John. *The world in miniature; or the entertaining traveller...*—1740#11

FRIEND IN EDINBURGH. *Letter from a friend in Edinburgh to a gentleman in the country:... concerning the wonderful progress and success of the glorious...*—1742#16

FREYEN, ANDREAS. *A true and authentic account of A. F., concerning the occasion of his coming among the Herrnhuters or Moravians...*—1753#7

FURBER, Robert.
Catalogue of English and foreign trees.—1727#7
The flower-garden displayed.—1732#15

FURNEAUX, Philip. *A sermon preached at Clapham in Surry, on Friday the 17th February, 1758...*—1758#21

G., J. *Geography epitomiz'd: or, the London gazetteer. Being a geographical and historical treatise of Europe, Asia, Africa and America... To which are added, an introduction to geography.*—1718#8

G., R. *The vain prodigal life, and tragical penitential death of Thomas Hellier... executed according to law at Westover, in Charles-City, in the Country of Virginia... 5th August 1678...*—1680#3

GAGE, Thomas. *The speech of the right honourable the Lord Viscount Gage, in parliament, against the convention with Spain.*—1739#28

GARDYNER, George. *A description of the new world. Or, America islands, and continent: and by what people those regions are now inhabited...*—1651#9

GARFIELD, John. *The wandring whore continued. A dialogue between Magdalena...*—1660#13

GASCOYNE, Joel. *A true description of Carolina.*—1682#15

GATFORD, Lionel. *Publick good without private interest...*—1657#8

GAY, John. *The Mohocks; a tragi-comical farce.*—1712#10

GAYA, Louis de. *Nuptial rites, or the several marriage ceremonies practised amongst all the nations of the world...*—1685#15

GEARE, Allen. *Ebenezer: or a monument of thankfulness. Being a true account of a late miraculous preservation of nine men in a small boat...*—1708#5

GEE, Joshua. *The trade and navigation of Great-Britain considered: shewing that the surest way for a nation to increase in riches, is to prevent...*—1729#9

GELLIBRAND, Henry. *An epitome of navigation...*—1674#4

GENTLEMAN IN AN EMINENT STATION ON THE SPOT. *An accurate and authentic journal of the siege of Quebec, 1759...*—1759#36

GENTLEMAN IN NEW-ENGLAND. *A poem on the death of His Highness the Duke of Gloucester. Written by a gentleman in New-England.*—1701#22

GENTLEMAN OF AMERICA [SMITH, James?]. *Some considerations on the consequences of the French settling colonies on the Mississippi, with respect to the trade and safety...*—1720#12

GEORGE II, KING OF GREAT BRITAIN. *The royal conference or a dialogue between... G*** the IId. of E***d. and L**s the XV. of F***e.*—1756#34

GEORGE, William. *A sermon preached... February 17, 1748.*—1749#15

GEORGIA TRUSTEES.
Act for maintaining the peace with the Indians in the province of Georgia, prepared by the Honourable trustees for establishing...—1735#4
Act for rendring the colony of Georgia more defencible, by prohibiting the importation and use of black slaves or negroes into...—1735#5
Act to prevent the importation and use of rum and brandies in the Province of Georgia... approved by... George the Second, in Council...—1735#6
The general accompt of all monies and effects recieved and expended by the Trustees for... Georgia... from the ninth day of June... 1735, to the ninth day of June... 1736.—1736#9
The general account of all monies and effects received and expended by the Trustees for... Georgia... from... ninth... June... 1732... to ninth... June... 1733...—1733#16
The general account of all monies and effects received and expended by the Trustees for... Georgia... from the ninth day of June... 1733. to the ninth day of June... 1734...—1734#6
The resolutions of Trustees for... Georgia... this eight day of March... relating to the grants and tenure of lands within the said colony...—1742#17
Rules for the year 1735.—1735#7

GERARD, Alexander. *National blessings an argument for reformation. A sermon, preached at Aberdeen, November 29, 1759...*—1759#37

GERARD, John. *The herball or Generall historie of plantes... very much enlarged and amended by Thomas Johnson*—1633#1

GIB, Adam. *A warning against countenancing the ministrations of Mr G. Whitefield...*—1742#18

GIB, T. *Remarks on the Reverend Mr Whitefield's journal, his many inconsistencies are pointed out and his tenets considered; the whole showing the dangerous tendency of his doctrine...*—1740#13

GIBBON, John. *Introductio ad latinam blasonium...*—1682#16

GIBBONS, Thomas.
Our duty as patriots, protestants and Christians... a sermon preached... May 23... on occasion of the public declaration of war against the French king, May 18, 1756.—1756#35
Sympathy with our suffering brethren... two discourses... To which are prefixed, some serious reflections on the present situation of these nations, and our American colonies.—1755#21

GIBSON, ——. *Memoirs of Queen Anne: being a compleat supplement to the history of her reign.*—1729#11

GIBSON, Edmund.
An earnest dissuasive from intemperance in meats and drinks... sermon... Lambeth...—1745#22
Five pastoral letters to the people of his diocese.—1749#17
Letter of the Lord Bishop of London to the masters and mistresses of families in the English plantations abroad; exhorting...—1727#9
Lettre pastorale de Monseigneur l'éveque de Londres...—1729#10

Methodus procedendi contra clericos irregulares in plantationibus Americanis.—1728#8

Second pastoral letter to the people of his diocese. . .—1730#13

Two letters of the Lord Bishop of London: the first, to the masters and mistresses of families in the English plantations abroad. . . The second, to the missionaries there. . .—1727#10

GIBSON, James. *Journal of the late siege by the troops from North-America, against the French at Cape Breton, the city of Louisbourg. . .*—1745#24

GILBERT, John. *A sermon preached. . . February 17, 1743-4. . .*—1744#18

GILBERT, Robert.
An alarm to Great Britain; with an invitation to repentance. . . sermon. . . at Northampton, February 11th, 1757. . .—1757#16
Britain revived. A sermon delivered at Northampton. . . Nov. 29, 1759. . .—1759#38

GILL, John. *The divine right of infant baptism examined. . .*—1749#18

GILLESPIE, George. *Wholesome severity reconciled with Christian liberty. or, The true resolution of a present controversie concerning liberty of conscience. . .*—1645#7

GILLIES, John.
An exhortation to the inhabitants of the South Parish of Glasgow. . . Wednesday September 26th, 1750.—1751#15
Historical collections relating to remarkable periods of the success of the Gospel, and eminent instruments employed in promoting it.—1754#12

GLANVILL, Joseph.
Plus ultra: or, the progress and advancement of knowledge since the days of Aristotle.—1668#3
Seasonable reflections and discourses, in order to the conviction and cure of the. . . age. . .—1676#5
Some philosophical considerations touching the being of witches. . .—1667#6

GLAPTHORNE, Henry. *Wit in a constable. A comedy.*—1640#2

GLOVER, Richard. *A short account of the late application to Parliament made by the merchants of London upon the neglect of their trade. . .*—1742#19

GODDARD, Peter Stephen. *A sermon preached November 29, 1759. . . at Fornham. . . and Edmondsbury. . .*—1760#40

GODFREY, Edward. *To the right honourable the Parliament of the Commonwealth of England. . . Humble petition of Edward Godfrey. . . and sundry others. . . of the Provinces of Mayne and Liconia. . .*—1659#15

GODWIN, Morgan.
The Negro's and Indian's advocate, suing for their admission into the church. . . To which is added, A brief account of religion in Virginia.—1680#4
The revival: or Directions for a sculpture, describing the extraordinary care and diligence of our nation, in publishing the faith. . .—1682#17

A supplement to the Negro's and Indian's advocate: Or, some further considerations and proposals for the effectual and speedy carrying on of the Negro's Christianity. . .—1681#10

Trade preferred before religion, and Christ made to give way to Mammon. . . a sermon relating to the plantations. . .—1685#16

GOODALL, Baptist. *The tryall of travell. . . In three bookes epitomized. . .*—1630#4

GOODWIN, John.
M. S. to A. S. with a plea for libertie of conscience against the cavils of A. S.—1644#8
A reply of two of the brethren to A. S. wherein you have observations on his considerations. . . upon the Apologeticall narration. . .—1644#9
A short answer to A. S. alias Adam Stewart's second part of his overgrown duply to the two brethren. . .—1644#10

GORDON, George. *An introduction to geography, astronomy, and dialling.*—1726#7

GORDON, Kenneth. *The petition of Mr Kenneth Gordon of Cluny, advocate. 26 November 1731.*—1731#14

GORDON, Patrick. *Geography anatomized: or, a compleat geographical grammer. . .*—1693#7

GORDON, Robert. *Encouragements. For such as shall have intention to bee under-takers in the new plantations of Cape Breton. . .*—1625#7

GORDON, Thomas. *An appeal to the unprejudiced, concerning the present discontents occasioned by the late convention with Spain.*—1739#29

GORGES, Ferdinando.
America painted to the life. The true history. . .—1659#16
A brief narration of the original undertakings.—1658#6

GORTON, Samuel.
An antidote against the common plague of the world. Or, an answer to a small treatise. . . intitul'd Saltmarsh returned from the dead. . .—1657#9
Simplicities defence against seven-headed policy. or, Innocency vindicated. . .—1646#13

GRADIN, Arvid. *A short history of the Bohemian-Moravian Protestant church of the United Brethren. . .*—1743#16

GRADY, ——. *A description of the famous new colony of Georgia, in South Carolina (established by the present majesty,) of which Colonel David. . .*—1734#7

GRANTHAM, Sir Thomas. *A historical account of some memorable actions, particularly in Virginia. . .*—1714#7

GRANVILLE, John Carteret.
The state of the nation considered, in a letter to a member of Parliament.—1746#9
The state of the nation for the year 1747, and respecting 1748. Inscribed to a member of the present Parliament.—1748#6
A supplement to the State of the Nation; being free-thoughts on the present critical conjuncture.—1748#7

GRATTON, JOHN.

Surrender of seven eighth parts of Carolina, from Lord Carteret to his majesty...—1744#19

GRATTON, John. *Journal of the life of that ancient servant of Christ, John Gratton...*—1720#13

GRAVE, John. *A song of Sion. Written by a citizen thereof, whose outward habitation is in Virginia... with an additional postscript from another hand.*—1662#6

GRAY, ——. *The memoirs, life, and character of the great Mr Law... with an accurate... account of the establishment of the Missippi [sic] Company in France... Written by a Scots gentleman.*—1721#6

GRAY, Christopher. *Catalogue of American trees and shrubs that will endure the climate of England.*—1737#13

GRAY, Robert. *Virginia's cure: or an advisive narrative concerning Virginia. Discovering the true ground of that churches unhappiness...*—1662#7

GREAT BRITAIN.
ARMY. REGULATIONS.
The pay of the garrisons in Ireland Gibraltar Minorca & ye plantations. The half-pay of the officers of the Navy & of the Army...—1741#15

Rules and articles for the better government of his majesty's horse and footguards... in Great Britain and Ireland, and dominions beyond the seas...—1718#7

COMMISSION FOR ADJUSTING BOUNDARIES.
The memorials of the French and English commissaries concerning the limits of Nova Scotia or Acadia.—1755#22

COMMISSIONERS FOR TRADE AND PLANTATIONS.
List of copies of charters, from the Commissioners for Trade and Plantations, presented to the Honourable the House of Commons...—1741#16

Representation from the Commissioners for Trade and Plantations, to the... Lords... in pursuance of their Lordships addresses...—1735#8

Representation of the Board of Trade relating to the laws made, manufactures set up, and trade carried on, in His Majesty's plantations in America—1734#8

COMMISSIONERS FOR VIRGINIA.
By his majesties commissioners for Virginia...—1624#5

COMMISSIONERS OF ADMIRALTY.
Orders that tobacco on British ships should be of the growth of British colonies.—1725#7

COMMISSIONERS OF CUSTOMS.
Instructions by the Commissioners for Managing and Causing to be Levied and Collected His Majesty's Customs... to [blank] who is established collector of His Majesty's customs at [blank] in America.—1741#17

Instructions by the Commissioners for managing... his majesty's customs... in England, to [blank] who is established collector of his majesty's customs at [blank] in America—1734#9

FARMERS OF HIS MAJESTIES CUSTOMS.
Index Vectigalium; or, an abbreviated collection of the Laws, Edicts, Rules and Practices, touching the Customs...—1670#5

GENERAL POST OFFICE.
Whereas the Queen has been pleased to direct, that a monthly correspondence be established between this kingdom, and... the continent of America...—1711#7

LORDS COMMISSIONERS FOR OPENING PARLIAMENT.
The speech of the Lord Commissioners to both Houses of Parliament... 1 June 1754.—1754#13

The speech of the Lords Commissioners to both Houses of Parliament, on Tuesday the twentieth day of June, 1758.—1758#24

LORDS COMMISSIONERS OF APPEAL IN PRIZE CAUSES.
Elizabeth Galley. New York. The case of the respondents.—1760#41

America. Ferret, master. Before the Right Honourable the Lords Commissioners of Appeals for Prizes. America, Louis Ferret, master... Appellant's case.—1759#

LORDS JUSTICES.
Proclamation. Appointing distribution of prizes taken before His Majesty's declaration of war 18 June 1741.—1741#1839

Proclamation. Appointing distribution of prizes taken since the declaration of war. [18 June 1741].—1741#19

Proclamation providing for distribution of prize money. [19 June 1740].—1740#14

Proclamation. By the Lords Justices. Hardwicke, C. Hartington, Granville, P. Holdernesse.—1752#7

NAVY.
By the Commissioners for Executing the Office of Lord High Admiral of Great Britain and Ireland... His Majesty hath been pleased....—1728#9

PARLIAMENT. ACTS
Act discharging the importation of tobacco.—1705#10

Act for ascertaining the rates of foreign coins in her majesties plantations in America.—1708#6

Act for avoiding and putting an end to certain doubts... relating to... wills and codicils, concerning real estates, in... England...—1752#8

Act for better preservation of his Majesty's woods in America, and for the encouragement of the importation of naval stores from thence...—1729#12

Act for better securing and encouraging trade of His Majesty's sugar colonies in America.—1733#17

Act for charging of tobacco brought from New-England with custome and excise.—1650#4

Act for continuing an act... intituled, An act for encouraging the importation of naval stores from... plantations in America...—1712#11

Act for continuing an act made in the twelfth year of... Queen Anne... An act for incouraging the tobacco trade.—1719#3

358

GREAT BRITAIN.

Act for continuing several impositions. . . and concerning certain drugs of America. . . to be imported from her majesties plantations.—1709#8

Act for continuing several laws. . . relating to the praemiums upon the importation of masts, yards, and bowsprits, tar, pitch and turpentine. . . —1751#16

Act for continuing the act for encouraging the growth of coffee in his majesty's plantations in America. . . —1752#9

Act for continuing the liberty of exporting Irish lining [sic] cloth to British plantations in America duty-free. . . —1717#6

Act for encouragement of silk manufacture. . . for reducing the duties on beaver skins. . . imported; and for all furs products of the. . . —1722#15

Act for encouraging the growth and culture of raw silk in. . . colonies or plantations in America. . . —1750#19

Act for encouraging the importation of naval stores. . . from her majesty's plantations in America. . . —1704#14

Act for encouraging the making of indico in the British plantations in America.—1748#8

Act for encouraging the making of pot ashes and pearl ashes in the British plantations in America.—1751#17

Act for encouraging the people known by the name of Unitas Fratrum or United Brethren, to settle in his majesty's colonies in America.—1749#19

Act for encouraging the tobacco trade.—1714#8

Act for establishing a general post office for all her majesties dominions. . . —1711#8

Act for establishing an agreement with seven of the lords proprietors of Carolina, for the surrender of their title. . . —1729#13

Act for extending the act. . . for amending. . . the laws relating to the government of His Majesty's ships. . . in North America.—1756#36

Act for further preventing robbery, burglary. . . and for the more effectual transportation of felons.—1720#14

Act for further regulating the plantation trade; and for relief of merchants importing prize goods from America.—1742#20

Act for granting liberty to carry rice from. . . Carolina. . . directly to any part of Europe, South of Cape Finisterre.—1730#14

Act for importing from his majesty's plantations in America, direct into Ireland, goods not enumerated in any act of parliament. . . —1731#15

Act for importing salt from Europe, into the colony of New York. . . —1729#14

Act for increase of shipping, and encouragement of the navigation of this nation. . . the ninth of October, 1651. . . —1651#8

Act for naturalizing such foreign Protestants, and others. . . as are settled, or shall settle in any of his majesty's colonies in America.—1739#30

Act for permitting tea to be exported to Ireland, and. . . America, without paying the inland duties. . . (That is, so much therof. . . —1760#42

Act for permitting tea to be exported to Ireland, and. . . plantations in America, without paying the inland duties. . . —1748#9

Act for preventing frauds and regulating abuses in the plantation trade.—1696#11

Act for the better recruiting of His Majesty's forces on the continent of America; and for the better regulation of the army, and prevention of desertion there.—1756#37

Act for the better securing and encouraging the trade of His Majesty's sugar colonies in America.—1731#16

Act for the encouragement of the trade to America. . .—1708#7

Act for the further encouragment and enlargement of the whale fishery.—1749#20

Act for the more easy securing of debts in his majesty's plantations and colonies in America.—1732#16

Act for the more effectual securing and encouraging the trade of his majesty's British subjects to America. . .—1739#31

Act for the more effectual securing and encouraging the trade of America. . .—1740#15

Act for the preservation of white and other pine trees. . . in. . . New Hampshire, in Massachusetts Bay,. . . Main, Rhode Island, and Providence-Plantation. . .—1711#9

Act for the promoting and propagating the gospel of Jesus Christ in New-England.—1649#2.

Act for vesting certain estates in Pennsylvania, New-Jersey, and Maryland, belonging to the proprietors of a partnership commonly. . .—1760#43

Act for vesting the parts or shares late belonging to Benjamin Brain, merchant, deceased, of and in one twenty-fourth part. . .—1753#9

Act further continuing an act. . . for securing. . . the trade of his majesties sugar colonies in America. . .—1756#38

Act giving a licence for transporting fish in forreigne bottoms.—1657#7

Act prohibiting trade with the Barbada's, Virginia, Bermudas and Antego. . . [30 October 1650].—1650#5

Act to apply five hundred thousand pounds out of sinking fund. . . by paying off. . . and ten thousand pounds to the Trustees for. . . Georgia. . .—1733#18

Act to continue an act. . . intituled, An act for granting liberty to carry rice from His Majesty's province of Carolina. . .—1729#15

Act to enable His Majesty to grant commissions to a certain number of foreign Protestants who have served abroad as offices. . .—1756#39

Act to encourage the importation of pig and bar iron from. . . colonies in America; and to prevent erection of any mill. . . in any. . . colony.—1750#20

Act to explain an act made in the last session of Parliament, intituled, An act for importing from. . . America, directly into Ireland, goods not enumerated. . .—1732#17

Act to extend the liberty. . . of importing bar iron from. . . America.—1757#17

Act to extend the provisions of an act. . . intituled An act for naturalizing foreign Protestants. . . in. . . his majesty's colonies. . .—1747#8

359

GREAT BRITAIN.

Act to prevent the exportation of hats out of any of His Majesty's colonies in America, and to restrain the number of apprentices. . .—1732#18

Act to prohibit. . . the exportation of corn, grain. . . victual. . . from his majesty's colonies and plantations in America. . .—1757#18

Act to regulate and restrain paper-bills of credit in his majesty's colonies or plantations of Rhode-Island, and Providence plantations. . .—1751#18

Act to repeal a clause in an act made in the ninth year of his late Majesty's reign, which prohibts the importation of tobacco. . .—1729#16

Act to revive several acts. . . turnpikes. . . and to continue severalacts relating to rice to frauds in the customs, to the clandestine. . .—1742#21

Die Sabatti 23 Januarii 1646. Whereas the severall plantations in Virginia, Bermudas, Barbados, and other places of America. . .—1647#8

Ordinance of the Lords and Commons. . . whereby Robert earle of Warwicke is made governour in chiefe, and lord high admirall of all. . .—1643#8

Subsidy granted to the King, of Tonnage and Poundage, and other sums of money payable upon merchandize exported and imported. Together with a book of rates. . . .—1660#7

Two ordinances of the Lords and Commons. . . the one dated November 2. 1643. . . the other March 21. 1645. . . —1646#12

PARLIAMENT. BILLS.

A bill for better preservation of his majesty's woods in America, and for the encouragement of the importation of naval stores from thence. . .—1729#17

A bill for establishing a method to bar entails upon the province of Maryland.—1754#14

A bill for encouraging the people known by the name of Unitas Fratum, or United Brethren, to settle in his majesty's colonies in America.—1749#21

A bill for explaining and amending an act of the thirteenth year of his majesty's present reign, intituled, an act for the more. . .—1746#10

A bill for importing salt, from Europe, into the province of Pensylvania in America.—1727#11

A bill for registering all seamen, watermen, fishermen, lightermen. . . capable of service at sea, throughout his majesty's dominions. . .—1739#32

A bill for the better protecting and securing the trade and navigation of this kingdom, in times of war.—1746#11

A bill for the more easy and effectual conviction of persons returning from transportation [to any part of America].—1720#15

A bill for the speedy and effectual recruiting of his majesty's regiments of foot serving in Flanders, Minorca, Gibraltar, and the plantations, and regiments of marines.—1745#25

A bill, intituled, An act for the better securing and encouraging the trade of His Majesty's sugar colonies in America.—1732#19

A bill, intituled, An act for naturalizing such foreign protestants, and others therein mentioned, as are settled, or shall settle in any of His Majesty's colonies in America.—1739#33

A bill, intituled, an act for restraining and preventing several unwarrantable schemes. . . in his majesty's colonies. . . in America.—1741#20

A bill, intituled, an act for the better securing and encouraging the trade of His Majesty's Sugar colonies in America.—1733#19

A bill, intituled, An act for the more effectual securing and encouraging the trade of his Majesty's British subjects in America. . .—1739#34

A bill, intituled, An act to encourage the importation of pig and bar iron from his majesty's colonies in America; and to prevent. . .—1750#21

A bill to explain and amend. . . an act made in the sixth year of the reign of. . . George the first. . .—1742#22

A bill to prevent the issuing of paper bills of credit in the British colonies and plantations in America, to be legal tenders in payments for money.—1744#20

A bill to regulate and restrain paper bills of credit in the British colonies and plantations in America, and to prevent the same being legal tenders. . .—1749#22

The humble address of the House of Commons to the King. . .—1721#7

PARLIAMENT. HOUSE OF COMMONS COMMITTEES.

Papers presented to the committee appointed to inquire into the state and condition of the countries adjoining to Hudson's Bay, and of the trade carried on there.—1749#23

A report from the Committee appointed to inquire into the state and condition of the countries adjoining to Hudson's Bay, and of the trade carried on there.—1749#24

A report from the committee of secrecy, appointed by order of the House of Commons to examine several books and papers. . . relating. . .—1715#15

Report from the committee to whom the petition of the deputies of the united Moravian churches. . . was referred; together. . .—1749#25

Report on the petitions relating to the manufacture of hats. . .—1752#10

Report relating to the finding of a north-west passage.—1745#25A

The report, with appendix, from committee of. . . Commons appointed to enquire into the frauds and abuses in the customs. . . Published by order of the House of Commons.—1733#20

PARLIAMENT. HOUSE OF LORDS.

The humble address of the. . . Lords. . . presented to his majesty. . . November, 1755. . .—1755#23

The humble address of the Lords. . . to his majesty, in relation to the petition of Charles Desborow, employed in the trade to Newfoundland. . .—1699#7

The humble address of the Right Honourable the Lords. . . in Parliament. . . presented to His Majesty. . . the fourth day of May, 1738. With his majesty's answer. . .—1738#10

The humble address of the right honourable the Lords. . . in Parliament. . . to his majesty on Friday the third day of December, 1756. With his majesty's gracious answer.—1756#40

The Lords protest against the convention-treaty.—1739#35

The Lord's protest in the last session of Parliament, viz. . . IV. On the representation of the state of the colonies in America. . . [26 March 1734].—1734#10

PRIVY COUNCIL.

Andrew Wiggin, and others, petitioners. Against Jonathan Belcher, Esq: -Respondent. The Respondent's case. . . 12th day of November, 1739.—1739#36

At the Court at St. James, the second day of February, 1717. . . Upon reading this day a report from the. . . Committee for hearing of appeals from the Plantations. . .—1718#9

Maryland. Benjamin Tasker appellant. John Simpson, lessee of William Brent, respondent. The appellants case. . . to be heard. . . 25th. . . January 1739. . .—1739#37

Maryland. Benjamin Tasker, esq. . . appellant. John Simpson, lessee of William Brent, respondent. The respondent's case. To be heard. . . 25th. . . January 1739. . .—1739#38

New Hampshire. The (late) House of Representatives there, complainants. Jonathan Belcher esq, the governour there, respondent. . .—1739#39

SOVEREIGN. JAMES I.

Proclamation concerning tobacco. . .—1624#6

Proclamation for suppressing the lottery in Virginia and all others. . .—1621#1

Proclamation for the utter prohibiting the importation of. . . all tobacco. . . not of. . . Virginia and the Summer Islands. . .—1625#6

Proclamation prohibiting interloping and disorderly trading to New England in America. . . the sixty [sic] of November. . . [1622].—1622#13

Whereas wee are credibly informed. . .—1621#2

SOVEREIGN. CHARLES I.

A commission for the well governing of our people, inhabiting in New-found-land. . .—1634#1

Proclamation against the disorderly transporting his majesties subjects. . . to America.—1637#1

Proclamation concerning tobacco. . .—1631#1

Proclamation concerning tobacco. . .—1634#2

Proclamation concerning tobacco. . .—1638#10

Proclamation concerning tobacco. . .—1639#2

Proclamation for setling the plantation of Virginia.—1625#4

Proclamation for the ordering of tobacco. . .—1627#2

Proclamation forbidding the disorderly trading with the salvages in New England. . .—1630#3

Proclamation restraining the abusive venting of tobacco. . .—1634#3

Proclamation to give assurance unto all his majesties subjects in the islands and continent of America.—1643#9

Proclamation to restrain the transporting of passengers and provisions to New England, without licence. . . [1 May 1638].—1638#9

Proclamation touching the sealing of tobacco.—1627#3

Proclamation touching tobacco.—1625#5

Proclamation touching tobacco.—1627#4

SOVEREIGN. CHARLES II.

Articles of peace between. . . Charles II. . . and several Indian Kings and Queens. . . 29th day of May, 1677. . .—1677#2

At the Court at Whitehall, the 20th of July, 1683.—1683#9

at the court. . . 16 february 1680[-1]. to regulate and encourage trade with the colonies.—1681#6

At the Court. . . 16 February 1680[-1]. To regulate and encourage trade with the colonies.—1681#6

His majesty's declaration concerning the province of East-New Jersey.—1683#10

Proclamation declaring. . . a free port at his city of Tanger. . . [16 November 1662].—1662#4

Proclamation dispensing with clauses in Navigation Act [22 March 1664/5].—1665#16

Proclamation for protection of Royal African Company [30 November 1674].—1674#2

Proclamation for prohibiting the importation of commodities of Europe into any of his majesties plantations in Africa, Asia, or America. . .—1675#5

Proclamation for recalling dispensations in the Navigation Acts [23 August 1667].—1667#5

Proclamation for the due observation of certain statutes made for the suppressing of rogues, vagabonds. . . [9 May 1661].—1661#6

Proclamation for the suppressing a rebellion lately raised. . . Virginia. . . [27 October 1676].—1676#2

Proclamation of grant of Pennsylvania to William Penn [2 April 1681].—1681#7

To the Governor and Council of East New Jersey and the inhabitants etc. ordering their obedience to the proprietors, the Earl of Perth. . .—1683#11

Whereas. . . by reason. . . abuses of a lewd sort of people called spirits, in seducing many of his majesties subjects to go on shipboard. . . [December 13 1682].—1682#12

SOVEREIGN. JAMES II.

Proclamation for continuing officers in colonies. [6 February 1684/5].—1685#11

Proclamation for the more effectual reducing and suppressing of pirates and privateers in America. . . [20 January 1687/8].—1688#6

Proclamation prohibiting trade within limits of the Hudson's Bay Company. [31 March 1688].—1688#7

Proclamation to prohibit his majesties subjects from trading within the limits assigned to the Royal African Company. . . [1 April 1685].—1685#10

GREEN, JOHN.

Treaty of peace, good correspondence and neutrality in America, between. . . James II. . . of Great Britain, and. . . Lewis XIV. . .—1686#1

Whereas. . . by reason. . . abuses of a lewd sort of people, called spirits, in seducing many of his majesties subjects to go on shipboard. . .—1686#2

SOVEREIGN. WILLIAM AND MARY.
Their majesties declaration against the French King. . . [7 May 1689].—1689#10

SOVEREIGN. WILLIAM III.
Charter of incorporation of Society for the Propagation of the Gospel in Foreign Parts, dated 16th June 1701.—1701#18

Proclamation for apprehension of pirates [6 March 1700/1].—1701#19.

Whereas we are credibly informed, that in many of our plantations. . .—1702#12

SOVEREIGN. ANNE.
Proclamation, declaring what ensigns or coloursshall be born at sea in merchant ships or vessels belonging to any of her majesties. . .—1707#7

Proclamation for continuing all officers in their places. 9 March 1701/2.—1702#10

Proclamation for enforcing act establishing General Post Office in Dominions 23 June 1711.—1711#10

Proclamation for settling and ascertaining the current rates of coin in her majesties colonies and plantations in America [18 June 1704].—1704#15

Whereas it hath pleased Almighty God, to call to His mercy our late sovereign lord King William the Third. . .—1702#11

Proclamation for encouraging trade to Newfoundland. [26 June 1708].—1708#8

SOVEREIGN. GEORGE I.
Proclamation. At the Court at Kensington, the second day of October, 1721. . .—1721#8

Proclamation for continuing the officers in. . . plantations [22 November 1714].—1714#9

Proclamation for suppressing pirates in West Indies or adjoining to our plantations [5 September 1717].—1717#7

Proclamation for suppressing pirates in West Indies or adjoining to our plantations [21 December 1718].—1718#10

Proclamation, requiring all ships and vessels, trading from the plantations in the way of the Algerines, to furnish themselves with passes [4 October 1714].—1714#10

Proclamation requiring passes formerly granted for ships trading in way of Algerine cruizers to be returned for reissue [19 July 1722].—1722#16

SOVEREIGN. GEORGE II.
Commissio Regia pro exercendâ jurisdictione spirituali et ecclesiasticâ in plantationibus Americanis.—1728#10

Grant and release of one eighth part of Carolina, from his majesty to Lord Carteret. . .—1744#21

His majesties most gracious speech to both houses of Parliament. . . on. . . the thirteenth day of November 1755.—1755#24

His majesty's most gracious speech to both houses of Parliament, on Thursday the first day of February 1738.—1738#11

Proclamation for a public thanksgiving in England and Wales for defeat of French. [23 October 1759].—1759#40

Proclamation for a public thanksgiving in Ireland for defeat of French. [30 October 1759].—1759#41

Proclamation for a public thanksgiving in Scotland for the defeat of French. [23 October 1759].—1759#42

Proclamation for continuing officers in His majesty's Plantations. . . [5 July 1727].—1727#12

Proclamation of declaration of war against France. [29 March 1744].—1744#22

Proclamation of declaration of war against the French King. [17 May 1756].—1756#41

Proclamation regarding distribution of prizes [14 June 1744].—1744#23

Proclamation requiring passes formerly granted to ships trading in way of Algerine cruizers to be returned for reissue [31 December 1729].—1729#18

Proclamation. Whereas by an act passed this present session. . . for the more effectual securing and encouraging the trade. . .—1740#16

South-Carolina, George the Second by the grace of God. . .—1733#21

Whereas some doubts have arisen with regard to the rank and command, which officers and troops raised by the governors of our provinces in North-America, should have. . .—1754#15

SOVEREIGN. GEORGE III.
His majesty's most gracious speech to both Houses of Parliament, on Tuesday the eighteenth day of November, 1760.—1760#45

Proclamation for continuing officers in plantations till his majesty's pleasure shall be further signified. . . 27 October 1760.—1760#44

TREATIES.
Articles of peace and alliance. . .—1667#3
Articles of peace and alliance. . .—1667#4
Articles of peace and alliance. . .—1662#5
Articles of peace between. . . Charles II. . . and several Indian Kings and Queens. . . 29th day of May, 1677. . .—1677#2

Several treaties of peace and commerce. . .—1685#12

A treaty for the composing of differences, and the establishing of peace in America, between the Crowns of Great Britain and Spain.—1670#6

GREEN, John. *A sermon preached before the honourable the House of Commons, at St. Margaret's Westminster. . .*—1759#43

GREEN, John. *Remarks, in support of the new chart of North and South America; in six sheets.*—1753#10

GREEN, John and JEFFERYS, Thomas. *Explanation for the new map of Nova Scotia and Cape Breton, with the adjacent parts of New England and Canada.*—1755#25

GREEN, Thomas. *A dissertation on enthusiasm...*—1755#26

GREENE, Thomas. *A sermon preached... February 21, 1723...*—1724#8

GREW, Nehemiah. *Musaeum regalis societatis. Or a catalogue and description of the natural and artificial rarities belonging to the Royal Society and preserved at Gresham Colledge*—1681#11

GREY, Zachary.
An impartial examination of the fourth volume of Mr. Daniel Neal's history of the Puritans.—1739#40

The Quaker and Methodist compared, in an abstract of Geo. Fox's journal, with his will, and the Rev. Geo. Whitefield's journal, with historical notes.—1740#18

A serious address to lay-methodists, to beware of the false pretences of their teachers. With an appendix, containing an account...—1745#26

GROOME, Samuel. *A glass for the people of New-England, in which they may see themselves and spirits, and if not too late repent, and turn away from their abominable ways...*—1676#7

GROVE, Joseph. *Letter to a right honourable patriot; upon the glorious success at Quebec... with a postcript, which enumerates the other conquests mentioned in the London address.*—1759#44

GUNTER, Edmund. *The description and use of his Majesties dials in White-Hall Garden.*—1624#8

H., N. *The pleasant art of money-catching.*—1684#6

HABERSHAM, James. *Letter from Mr Habersham, (superintendent... at the orphan-house in Georgia,) to... Mr Whitefield...*—1744#24

HAGTHORPE, John. *England's-exchequer. or A discourse of the sea...*—1625#8

HALE, Matthew. *The primitive origination of mankind, considered and examined according to the light of nature.*—1677#4

HALES, Stephen. *A sermon preached before the trustees... Thursday, March 21, 1734...*—1734#11

HALL, Fayrer.
Captain Fayrer Hall's evidence, before a Committee of the House of Commons, in April 1731 concerning the sugar colony bill. Remarks...—1732#20

Considerations on the bill now depending in Parliament concerning the British sugar colonies in America...—1731#17

The importance of the British plantations in America to this kingdom...—1731#18

My Lord, The Bill upon which I was examined last year...—1732#21

Observations on the trade carried on between our plantations and the foreign colonies in America: occasioned by a petition lately...—1731#19

Remarks upon a book, entituled, The present state of the sugar colonies considered...—1731#20

A short account of the first settlement of the provinces of Virginia, Maryland, New-York, New-Jersey, and Pennsylvania, by the English...—1735#9

HALL, John. *Memoirs of the right villainous John Hall, the late famous and notorious robber...*—1708#9

HALL, Joseph. *A survay of that foolish, seditious, scandalous, prophane libell, The protestation protested.*—1641#12

HALLEY, Edmond. *Miscellanea Curiosa. Being a collection of some of the principal phaenomena in nature...*—1705#11

HAMILTON, William. *The truth and economy of the Christian religion. A sermon preached... January 3, 1732.*—1732#22

HAMMOND, John.
Hammond versus Heamans. Or, an answer to an audacious pamphlet... by... Roger Heamans... his murthers and treacheries committed in the Province of Maryland...—1655#11

Leah and Rachel, or, The two fruitful sisters Virginia, and Maryland: their present condition, impartially stated and related...—1656#7

HANNAY, Robert. *A true account of the proceedings... of... Quakers in London... to... end... divisions and differences among some of the people...*—1694#8

HANWAY, Jonas.
An account of the Society for the encouragement of the British troops, in Germany and North America...—1760#46

Two letters...—1758#26

HARE, Francis.
The reception of the Palatines vindicated: in a fifth letter to a Tory member...—1711#11

A sermon preached... 21st February, 1734...—1735#10

HARRIS, Benjamin. *Case of Benjamin Harris, bookseller, lately come from New England...*—1681#12

HARRIS, John. *Navigantium atque itinerantium bibliotheca: or, A compleat collection of voyages and travels... To which is prefixed, A history of the peopling...*—1705#12

HARRIS, John. *A thanksgiving-sermon, preached in the parish church of Greensted, in Essex, on Thursday November 29, 1759... By John Harris...*—1759#45

HARRIS, William. *An historical and critical account of Hugh Peters. After the manner of Mr Beyle.*—1751#19

HART, John. *Trodden down strength, by the God of strength, or Mrs Drake revived...*—1647#9

HARTLIB, Samuel.
Glory to be God on High... A rare and new discovery of a speedy way... for the feeding of silk worms in the woods, on the mulberry-tree-leaves in Virginia...—1652#3

The reformed common wealth of bees. Presented in severall letters and observations... With the reformed Virginian silk-worm...—1655#12

The reformed Virginian silk-worms, or, a rare and new discovery... for the feeding of silk-worms... on the mulberry tree-leaves in Virginia...—1655#13

Samuel Hartlib, his legacie; or an enlargement of the discourse of husbandry used in Brabant and Flanders...—1651#10

HARTSHORNE, Richard, and others. *A further account of New Jersey. In an abstract of letters lately writ from thence, by several inhabitants there resident.*—1676#8

HARTWELL, Henry, BLAIR, James and CHILTON, Edward. *The present state of Virginia, and the college; by Messieurs Hartwell, Blair and Chilton. . . the charter for erecting the said college. . .*—1727#13

HARVEST, George. *A sermon preached. . . March 16, 1748–9. . .*—1749#26

HATTON, Edward. *The merchant's magazine: or, Tradesman's treasury. . .*—1695#11

HAWLES, Sir John. *Remarks upon the trials of Edward Fitzharris. . .*—1689#13

HAYES, Richard. *The negociators magazine. . . to which are added, curious calculations of great use in the West-India, Carolina and New-England trades. . .*—1739#42

HAYLEY, Thomas. *The liberty of the gospel explained, and recommended. A sermon. . . 15 February, 1716. . .*—1717#8

HAYMAN, Robert. *Quodlibets, lately come over from New Britaniola, Old Newfound-land. Epigrams and other small parcels, both morall and divine. . .*—1628#1

HAYNE, Samuel. *An abstract of all the statutes made concerning aliens. . . Also, all the laws made for securing our plantation trade to our selves. . .*—1685#17

HAYTER, Thomas. *A sermon preached. . . February 21, 1755. . .*—1755#27

HEAD, Richard and KIRKMAN, Francis. *The English rogue, described in the life of Meriton Latroon. A witty extravagant. Being a compleat history of the most eminent cheats of both sexes. . .*—1665#18

HEAMAN, Roger. *An additional brief narrative of a late bloody design against the Protestants in Ann Arundel County, and Severn, in Maryland in the Country of Virginia. . .*—1655#14

HEATH, John. *God's blessing on a people's just endeavours. . . A sermon preached at Writtle in Essex, on Thursday the 29th of November, 1759. . .*—1760#47

HEATHCOTE, Samuel. *Heads of some of those advantages this nation might enjoy, by encouraging the tobacco trade to Russia. . .*—1700#18

HEBERDEN, William. *Plain instructions for inoculation in the small-pox; by which any person may be enabled to perform the operation, and conduct the patient through the distemper.*—1759#46

HEDWORTH, Henry. *Controversy ended: or the sentence himself given against himself by George Fox. . . ratified and aggravated by W. Penn. . .*—1673#6

HELWIG, Cristoph. *Christophori Helvici, v. c. theatrum historicum. . .*—1651#11

HENDERSON, Jacob. *Case of the clergy of Maryland. . .*—1729#19

HENDERSON, Patrick. *Truth and innocence the armour and defence of the people called Quakers. . . Being an answer to part of a book, entituled, The man of God furnished.*—1709#9

HENNEPIN, Lewis.
A discovery of a large, rich, and plentiful country, in the North America. . .—1720#16
A new discovery of a vast country in America, extending above four thousand miles, between New France and New Mexico. . .—1698#8

HENRY, William. *The triumphs and hopes of Great-Britain and Ireland. A sermon preached. . . Thursday November the 29th, 1759. . .*—1759#47

HERBERT, George. *The temple. . .*—1633#2

HERBERT, Sir Thomas. *A relation of some yeares travaile, begunne anno 1626. . .*—1634#4

HERRING, Thomas. *A sermon. . . February 17, 1737–8. . .*—1738#12

HERVEY, John. *Remarks on the Craftsman's vindication of his two honble patrons. . .*—1731#21

HEYLYN, Peter.
Antidotum Lincolniense. Or, an answer to a book entituled, The holy table, name and thing. . .—1637#2
A coale from the altar. . .—1636#1
Cosmographie in four books. . .—1652#4
Microcosmus; or A little description of the great world. . .—1621#3

HICKES, George. *Peculium Dei. A discourse about the Jews.*—1681#13

HIGGINSON, Francis. *New-Englands plantation. Or, A short and true description of that countrey. . .*—1630#5

HILL, Aaron.
Afer baptizatus: or the negro turned Christian. . . I. The necessity of instruction, and baptizing slaves. . . a sermon—1702#13
The works of the late Aaron Hill, Esq; consisting of letters on various subjects, and of original poems. . .—1753#11

HILL, Hannah. *A legacy for children, being some of the last expressions and dying sayings of Hannah Hill, junr., of. . . Philadelphia. . . aged eleven years and near three months.*—1719#4

HILL, John.
A general natural history; or, New and accurate descriptions of the animals, vegetables and minerals. . .—1748#10
The naval history of Britain, from the earliest periods. . . to. . . M.DCC.LVI. Compiled from the papers of the late honourable captain George Berkeley.—1756#42

HILTON, William. *A relation of a discovery lately made on the coast of Florida, (from lat. 31 to 33 deg. 45 min. north lat.). . . with proposals. . .*—1664#8

HITCHIN, Edward. *A sermon preached at the New Meeting. . . Spital-Fields. . . 29 November 1759. . .*—1759#48

HOBBES, Thomas. *Leviathan, Or the matter, forme, and power of a Commonwealth.*—1651#12

HODSHON, Read. *The honest mans companion: or, the family's safeguard... some hints relating to the clergy... our plantations...*—1736#11

HOGG, John. *A sermon preached to a congregation of Protestant dissenters at Sidmouth in Devonshire... Nov. 29, 1759...*—1759#49

HOLDEN, Samuel. *Letters of Samuel Holden, Esquire, to Dr. Benjamin Coleman of Boston, New-England.*—1741#21

HOLDER, Christopher. *The faith and testimony of the martyrs and suffering servants of Christ Jesus persecuted in New England vindicated...*—1670#8

HOLLINGWORTH, Richard.
Certain queres [sic] modestly (though plainly) propounded... to such as affect the Congregationall-Way...—1646#14
An examination of sundry scriptures, alleadged by our brethren (of New England) in defence of some particulars of their church-way...—1645#8

HOLME, Benjamin.
A collection of the epistles and works of Benjamin Holme... his life and travels in the work of the ministry, through several parts of Europe and America...—1753#12
An epistle from Benjamin Holme, being a salutation to friends in Great Britain and Ireland...—1718#11
An epistle to Friends and tender-minded people in America...—1722#17

HOLME, Randle. *The academy of armory.*—1688#8

HOLMES, Nathaniel. *Gospel musick. or, The singing of David's Psalms, etc., in the publick congregations, or private families asserted, and vindicated...*—1644#11

HOLYOAKE, Thomas. *A large dictionary, in three parts.*—1677#5

HOLYOKE, Edward. *The doctrine of life, or of mans redemtion [sic]...*—1658#7

HOMES, Nathaniel.
Miscellanea; consisting of three treatises...—1664#9
The new world, or the new reformed church. Discovered out of the second epistle of Peter the third chap. verse 13—1641#13

HOOKE, William.
New-Englands sence, of old-England and Ireland sorrowes. A sermon preached upon a day of generall humiliation in the churches of New-England.—1645#9
New Englands teares, for old Englands feares... sermon... July 23. 1640.—1641#14

HOOKER, Thomas.
The application of redemption, by the effectual work of the word, and spirit of Christ...—1656#7A
A briefe exposition of the Lord's prayer...—1645#9A
The Christian's two chief lessons...—1640#3
A comment upon Christ's last prayer in the seventeenth of John...—1656#8
The covenant of grace opened: wherein these particulars are handled...—1649#3
The danger of desertion: or a Farwel sermon—1641#15
An exposition of the principles of Religion.—1645#9B
The faithful covenanter: A sermon...—1644#11A
Four learned and godly treatises.—1638#10A
Heautonaparnumenos: or a treatise of self-denyall...—1646#14A
Heaven's treasury opened in a fruitfull exposition of the Lords Prayer...—1645#9C
The immortality of the soule...—1645#10
The paterne of perfection...—1640#5
The saints dignitie and dutie...—1651#13
The saint's guide—1645#11
The soules exaltation...—1638#11
The soules humiliation...—1637#2A
The soules implantation...—1637#3
The soules ingrafting into Christ...—1637#4
The soules possession of Christ...—1638#12
The soules preparation for Christ, or a treatise of contrition.—1632#1
The soules vocation or effectual calling to Christ...—1638#13
A survey of the summe of church-discipline. Wherein, the way of the churches of New-England is warranted out of the Word.—1648#6
Three godly sermons...—1638#13A
The unbeleevers-preparing for Christ...—1638#14

HORSLEY, William. *A treatise on maritime affairs: or a comparison between the naval power of England and France...*—1744#26

HORSMANDEN, Daniel. *Journal of the proceedings in the detection of the conspiracy formed by some white people, in conjunction with negro and other slaves, for burning the city of New-York...*—1747#9

HOSKINS, James.
The just defence of James Hoskins, against the proceedings, and judgements, of Westminster monthly meeting...—1724#9
The Pensilv[ania] Bubble bubbled by the Treasurer, or, an account of his admitting purchasers for shares...—1726#8

HOUGH, John. *Of the propagation of the gospel in foreign parts. A sermon preached... Feb. 16 1704/5...*—1705#13

HOUGHTON, John, ed.
A collection for the improvement of husbandry and trade... Now revised, corrected, and published... by Richard Bradley.—1727#8
England's great happiness or, A dialogue between content and complaint...—1677#6

HOUGHTON, Thomas.
A book of funds.—1695#12
Royal institutions: being proposals for articles to establish and confirm laws... of silver and gold mines... in... Africa and America.—1694#9

HOUSTOUN, James. *Dr. Houstoun's memoirs of his own life-time... Containing... VIII. The importance of Cape Breton to the British nation.*—1747#10

HOWARD, Leonard. *A collection of letters and state papers, from the original manuscript of many princes, great personages and statesmen...*—1756#44

HOWELL, James. *A German diet: or, the ballance of Europe...*—1653#11

HOWGILL, Francis.
The dawnings of the gospel-day, and its light and glory discovered...—1676#10
The deceiver of the nations discovered... his cruel works of darkness... in Maryland in Virginia...—1660#14
The heart of New-England hardned [sic] through wickednes...—1659#17
The popish inquisition newly erected in New-England, whereby their church is manifested to be a daughter of mysterie Babylon...—1659#18
The rock of ages exalted above Rome's imagined rock...—1662#8
A testimony concerning the life, death, travels... of Edward Burroughs...—1662#9

HUBBARD, William. *The present state of New-England. Being a narrative of the troubles with the Indians... To which is added a discourse about the war with the Pequods in the year 1677...*—1677#7

HUBERT, Robert. *Catalogue of many natural rarities... to be seen at the place called the Musick-House near the west end of St. Paul's church...*—1664#10

HUDSON, Samuel.
An addition or postscript to the Vindication...—1658#8
The essence and unitie of the church catholike visible.—1645#12
A vindication of the essence and unity of the Church Catholike visible... in answer to... Mr Hooker...—1650#6

HUDSON'S BAY COMPANY.
Case of the Hudson's-Bay Company. Reasons for the continuance of the former act.—1690#10
Hudson's Bay. A general collection of treatys, declarations of war, manifestoes, and other papers relating to peace and war...—1710#11
Reasons humbly offered in behalf of the Hudson-Bay Company, that they may be exempted in the clause that will be offer'd for suppressing the insurance offices.—1712#22
Sir, may it please you to be at the Hudson's-Bay House. on [blank] the [blank] day of [blank] 170[blank]... at a committee there to be held—1701#23
Upon Wednesday the 18th day of November 1696.—1696#12

HUES, Robert. *A learned treatyse of globes... made English... by John Chilmead.*—1638#15

HUGHES, William.
The American physitian; or, a Treatise of the roots, plants, trees, shrubs, fruits, herbs, etc. growing in the English plantations in America...—1672#4
The flower garden enlarged... To which is now added a treatise of all the roots, plants, trees, shrubs, fruits, herbs, etc., growing in his majesties plantations, etc.—1677#8

HUIT, Ephraim. *The whole prophecie of Daniel explained, by a paraphrase, analysis and briefe comment...*—1643#10

HUME, Sophia.
An epistle to the inhabitants of South Carolina; containing sundry observations proper to be consider'd by every professor of Christianity in general.—1754#16
An exhortation to the inhabitants of... South Carolina, to bring their deeds to the light of Christ...—1750#22

HUMFREY, John. *A paper to William Penn, at the departure of that gentleman to his territory...*—1700#19

HUMPHREYS, David.
An account of the endeavours... by the Society for the Propagation of the Gospel... to instruct... slaves in New York. Together...—1730#15
An historical account of the Incorporated Society for the Propagation of the Gospel in Foreign Parts... to the year 1728.—1730#16

HUNT, Jeremiah. *Victory... A sermon... January 31st 1730... Death of Thomas Hollis, Esq...*—1731#22

HUNTER, Thomas. *An historical account of earthquakes, extracted from the most authentick historians. And a sermon preached at Weaverham, in Cheshire, on... 6 February... [1756]...*—1756#46

HUSKE, Ellis. *The present state of North America... Part I.*—1755#29

HUTCHESON, Archibald. *Some considerations relating to the payment of the publick debts, humbly offered to the Commons...*—1717#10

HUTCHESON, Francis.
A short introduction to moral philosophy, in three books...—1747#11
A system of moral philosophy in three books...—1755#30

HUTCHINSON, Francis. *An historical essay concerning witchcraft... And also two sermons...*—1718#12

HUTCHINSON, J. Mrs. *The private character of Admiral Anson.*—1747#12

HUTCHINSON, Richard. *The warr in New-England visibly ended. King Philip that barbarous Indian now beheaded, and most of his bloudy adherents submitted to mercy...*—1677#9

HUTTON, Matthew. *A sermon preached... February 21, 1745...*—1746#13

IRELAND.
  LORD DEPUTY AND COUNCIL.
  Proclamation that if any protected person is murdered and the murderers go free four papists shall be transported in their place to America [18 April 1655].—1655#15
  Proclamation voiding all orders and licences for transportation of idle and vagabond persons to the West Indies. [4 March 1656/7].—1657#10
  LORDS JUSTICES.
  Proclamation continuing embargo on ships carrying provisions... [13 September 1758].—1758#28

PARLIAMENT. HOUSE OF COMMONS COMMITTEE.
A report from the Committee appointed to inspect and examine the several returns (made to the House) of the felons and vagabonds ordered for transportation. . .—1744#27

J., F. *Letter from the Grecian coffee-house, in answer to the Taunton- Dean letter to which is added, a paper of queries sent from Worcester.*—1701#24

JACKSON, Richard. *An historical review of the constitution and government of Pennsylvania, from its origin. . . Founded on authentic documents.*—1759#52

JAMES II. *Memoirs of the English affairs, chiefly naval from the year 1660, to 1673.*—1729#20

JAMES, Thomas. *The strange and dangerous voyage of Captaine Thomas James, in his intended discovery of the Northwest Passage into the South Sea. . .*—1633#3

JAMIESON, John. *Unto the Right Honourable, the Lords of Council and Session, the petition of John Jamieson merchant in Glasgow.*—1746#14

JANEWAY, James.
Mr James Janeway's legacy. . . twenty seven famous instances of God's providences in and about sea-dangers and deliverances. . . a sermon on the same subject. . .—1674#5
A token for mariners, containing many famous and wonderful instances of God's providence in sea dangers and deliverances. . .—1708#10

JANNEY, Thomas. *An epistle from James Janney to Friends of Cheshire, and by them desired to be made publick. . .*—1694#13

JAY, James (1732–1815). *Dissertatio medica inauguralis, de fluoro albo. . .*—1753#13

JEFFERYS, Thomas.
The conduct of the French, with regard to Nova Scotia; from its first settlement to the present time. . . In a letter to a member of Parliament.—1754#17
Directions for navigating the gulf and river of St. Laurence; with a particular account of the bays, roads. . . Published. . .—1760#53
The natural and civil history of the French dominions in North and South America. . .—1760#54
See also GREEN, John.

JENNINGS, David.
An abridgement of the life of. . . Dr Cotton Mather. . . Taken from the account. . . published by his son, the Reverend Mr. Samuel Mather. . .—1744#28
Instructions to ministers: in three parts. . . I. Two discourses. . . by. . . John Jennings. II. A letter. . . by. . . Augustus. . .—1744#29
The origin of death, and of immortal life, considered. . .—1743#17

JENNINGS, Samuel. *The state of the case. . . betwixt the. . . Quakers, in Pennsylvania. . . and George Keith. . .*—1694#14

JEPHSON, Ralph. *The expounder expounded: or, Annotations upon that incomparable piece, intitled, A short account of God's dealings with. . .*—1740#20

JESSEY, Henry. *A narrative of the late proceed's [sic] at White-Hall concerning the Jews. . .*—1656#9

JOHN-THE-GIANT-KILLER. *Food for the mind, or a new riddle book; compiled for the use of the great and the little good boys and girls in England, Scotland. . .*—1759#53

JOHNSON, Charles. *A general history of the lives and actions of the most famous highwaymen, murderers, street-robbers. . . To which is added, A genuine. . .*—1734#12

JOHNSON, Edward.
Good news from New-England: with an exact relation of the first planting that countrey. . . With the names of the severall towns, and who be preachers to them.—1648#7
A history of New England. From the English planting in the yeere 1628 untill the yeere 1652. . .—1654#12

JOHNSON, James.
A sermon preached before the right honourable the House of Lords. . . November 29, 1759. . .—1759#54
A sermon preached. . . Friday, February 24, 1758. . .—1758#29

JOHNSON, Samuel. *A confutation of a late pamphlet intituled, A letter ballancing the necessity of keeping a land-force.*—1698#9

JOHNSON, Samuel. (1696–1772). *The elements of philosophy. . . to which is added, an original letter concerning the settlement of bishops in America. . . the third edition. . .*—1754#18

JOHNSTONE, Charles. *Chrysal: or, the adventures of a guinea. Wherein are exhibited views of several striking scenes,. . . in America, England, Holland, Germany and Portugal. By an adept. . .*—1760#55

JONES, Hugh.
An accidence to the English tongue. . .—1724#10
The Pancronometer, or universal Georgian calendar. . .—1753#14
The present state of Virginia. Giving a particular and short account of the Indian, English, and negroe inhabitants of that colony. . .—1724#11

JONES, John. *Letter to a friend in the country, upon the news of the town.*—1755#32

JORDAN, Thomas. *London triumphant: Or, the City in jollity and splendour. . .*—1672#8

JOSSELYN, John.
An account of two voyages to New England, wherein you have the setting out of a ship, with the charges; the prices of all necessaries. . .—1674#6
A description of New-England in general. . .—1682#18
New Englands rarities discovered; in birds, beasts, fishes, serpents, and plants of that country. . .—1672#5

JOUTEL, Henri. *Journal of the last voyage perform'd by Monsr. de La Sale, to the Gulph of Mexico, to find out the mouth of the Missisippi river. . .*—1714#11

JURIN, James. *Letter to the learned Caleb Cotesworth, M. D. . . containing a comparison between the mortality of the natural smallpox, and that given by inoculation. . .*—1723#5

JUSTICE, Alexander. *A general treatise of monies and exchanges; in which those of all trading nations are particularly describ'd and consider'd. . . By a well-wisher to trade.*—1707#10

JUSTICE, James. *The British gardener's calendar. . .*—1759#55

KEENE, Edmond. *A sermon preached. . . February 18, 1757. . .*—1757#19

KEIMER, Samuel.
Brand pluck'd from the burning. . .—1718#13
Caribbeana. Containing letters and dissertations, together with poetical essays. . .—1741#23

KEITH, George.
An account of the great divisions amongst the Quakers in Pensilvania, etc. As appears by their own book. . . printed 1692. . . intituled. . . The plea of the innocent. . .—1692#7
An account of the Quakers politicks.—1700#20
The anti-Christs and Saducees detected among a sort of Quakers; or Caleb Pusie, of Pennsylvania, and John Pennington. . .—1696#14
The arguments of the Quakers, more particularly, of George Whitehead, William Penn. . . against baptism and the supper.—1698#10
The causeless ground of surmises. . . in relation to the late religious differences and breaches among some of the people called Quakers in America.—1694#10
The Christian Quaker: or, George Keith's eyes opened. Good news from Pensilvania. . .—1693#8
An exact narrative of the proceedings at Turner' Hall. . .—1696#15
A farther account of the great divisions among the Quakers in Pensilvania, etc. As appears by another of their books. . . intituled, Some reasons and causes. . .—1693#9
A further discovery of the spirit of falshood [sic] and persecution in Sam. Jennings and his party. . . in Pensilvania. . .—1694#11
George Keith's challenge to William Penn and Geor. Whitehead; two eminent Quakers. . .—1696#16
George Keith's explications of divers passages contained in his former books.—1697#9
George Keith's fifth narrative, of his proceedings at Turners-Hall; detecting the Quakers errors—1701#25
George Keith's fourth narrative, of his proceedings at Turner's Hall.—1700#21
Gross error and hypocrisie detected, in George Whitehead, and some of his brethren.—1695#14
Journal of travels from New-Hampshire to Caratuck, on the continent of North-America.—1706#13
A just vindication of my earnest expostulation. . .—1696#17

A plain discovery of many gross falshoods, cheats and impostures—1701#26
The presbyterian and independent churches in New-England and elsewhere brought to the test. . .—1691#10
The pretended yearly meeting of the Quakers. . . the evil and wicked practises of them in Pensilvania.—1695#15
A seasonable information and caveat against a scandalous book of Thomas Ellwood, called, An epistle to Friends.—1694#12
A second narrative of the proceedings at Turners-Hall. . .—1700#22
A sermon preach'd at Turner's Hall. . . 5th. of May, 1700.—1700#23
A third narrative of the proceedings at Turners-Hall. . .—1698#11
The true copy of a paper. . . together with a short list of. . . vile and gross errors. . . (being of the same sort and nature. . . charged on some in Pensilvania. . .—1695#16
The tryals of Peter Boss, George Keith, Thomas Budd, and William Bradford, Quakers. . . at Philadelphia in Pennsylvania, the ninth, tenth and twelfth days of December, 1692. . .—1693#10
Two sermons preach'd at the parish-church of St. George. . . London May the 12th. 1700.—1700#24
The way cast up, and the stumbling-blockes removed. . .—1677#10

KEITH, George and BUDD, Thomas. *More divisions among the Quakers. . .*—1693#11

KEITH, William.
A collection of papers and other tracts, written occasionally on various subjects.—1740#21
The history of the British plantations in America. With a chronological account of the most remarkable things. . .—1738#13
Some useful observations on the consequences of the present war with Spain.—1740#22

KENNEDY, Archibald.
The importance of gaining and preserving the friendship of the Indians to the British interest considered. . .—1752#11
Serious considerations on the present state of the affairs of the northern colonies.—1754#19

KENNEDY, Gilbert. *The ambitious designs of wicked men. . . a sermon preached at Belfast, on Thursday, Nov. 29th, 1759. . .*—1759#56

KENNETT, White.
Bibliothecae Americanae primordia. An attempt towards laying the foundations of an American library, in several books, papers, and writings. . .—1713#5
The lets and impediments in planting. . . the gospel. . . A sermon preached. . . Friday the 15th of February, 1711/12—1712#13

KER, John. *The memoirs of John Ker of Kersland, in North Britain. . . with an account of the. . . Ostend Company. . .*—1726#9

KIDDELL, John. *A sermon preached at Tiverton, Devon, November 29, 1759. . .*—1760#57

KIMBER, Edward.
History of the life and adventures of Mr. Anderson. Containing his strange varieties of fortune in Europe and America. . .—1754#20

The life and adventures of Joe Thompson.—1750#25

A relation, or journal, of a late expedition to the gates of St. Augustine, on Florida; conducted by. . . James Oglethorpe. . .—1744#31

KIMBER, Isaac. *The life of Oliver Cromwell.*—1724#12

KING, James. *A sermon. . . March 17, 1742–3. . .*—1743#19

KING, William. *A voyage to England. . . as also Observations on the same voyage, by Dr. Thomas Sprat. . . with a letter of Monsieur Sorbiere's concerning the war. . . in 1652.*—1709#10

KINLOCH, Robert. *The truth and excellency of the gospel-revelation. . .*—1731#24

KIPPIS, Andrew. *A sermon preached at the Chapel in Long-Ditch, Westminster on. . . November 29, 1759.*—1759#57

KIRKBY, John. *The history of Autonous. . .*—1736#12

KIRKMAN, Francis: See HEAD, Richard.

KIRKPATRICK, James.
The analysis of inoculation: comprising the history, theory and practice of it. . .—1754#21

An epistle to Alexander Pope esq; from South Carolina. . .—1737#14

An essay on innoculation, occasioned by the small-pox being brought into South Carolina in the year 1738. . . with an appendix, containing a faithful account of the event there.—1743#20

The sea-piece, a poetical narration of a voyage from Europe to America. Canto II.—1749#27

KIRKWOOD, James. *Proposals, concerning the propagating of Christian knowledge, in. . . Scotland and foraign parts of the world.*—1706#14

KNOWLES, Charles, Admiral Sir. *An account of the expedition to Carthagena. . .*—1743#21

KNOX, Thomas. *Letter from Mr Knox, of Bristol, to the honourable William Nelson, Esq. of Virginia.*—1759#58

LABADIE, ———. *The adventures of Pomponius, a Roman knight, or the history of our own times. . .*—1726#10

LACY, B [sic]. *Miscellaneous poems compos'd at Newfoundland, on board His Majesty's ship the Kinsale. . .*—1729#21

LA DREVETIERE, Louis L'Isle de. *Tombo-Chiqui: or, the American savage. A dramatic entertainment. In three acts.*—1758#30

LAFARGUE, Etienne. *Histoire géographique de la Nouvelle Ecosse. . .*—1754#22

LAHONTAN, Louis Armand de Lom d'Arce. *New voyages to North-America. Containing an account of the several nations of that vast continent. . . Done into English. . .*—1703#9

LAMBE, Thomas. *A confutation of infants baptisme, or an answer to a treatise written by Georg [sic] Phillips, of Wattertowne in New England. . .*—1643#12

LAMBERT, Claude François. *A collection of curious observations on the manners, customs, usages. . . of the several nations of Asia, Africa, and America. Translated from the French. . . by John Dunn. . .*—1750#26

LANCEY, John. *A genuine account of the burning the Nightingale Brig, lately belonging to Thomas Benson. . .*—1754#23

LAND, Tristram. *Letter to. . . Whitefield. Designed to correct his mistaken account of regeneration. . . now published to prevent his doing mischief. . .*—1739#46

LANGFORD, John. *A just and cleere refutation of a false and scandalous pamphlet, entituled, Babylon's fall in Maryland, etc. . . To which is added. . .*—1655#16

LANGMAN, Christopher. *The true account of the voyage of the Nottingham-galley of London, John Dean Commander. . .*—1711#13

LAUDER, William. *Memorial or state of the process at the instance of William Lauder of Wine-Park. . .*—1718#14

LAVINGTON, Samuel. *God the giver of victory: a sermon, preached at Bideford, Devon, being the day appointed for a general thanksgiving. . . for the success of His Majesty's arms. . .*—1760#58

LAW, John.
A full and impartial account of the Company of Mississippi, otherwise called the French East-India Company, projected and settled by Mr. Law. . .—1720#17

Money and trade considered, with a proposal for supplying the nation with money. . .—1705#14

LAWSON, Deodat. *Christ's fidelity the only shield against Satan's malignity. . . sermon. . . Salem-village the 24th of March, 1692.*—1704#17

LAWSON, John. *A new voyage to Carolina; containing the exact description and natural history of that country. . . and a journal of a thousand mile travelled through several nations of Indians. . .*—1709#11

LE BLANC, Vincent. *The world surveyed: or, the famous voyages and travailes of Vincent Le Blanc.*—1660#15

LE GOBIEN, Charles. *Edifying and curious letters of some missioners of the Society of Jesus, from foreign missions. . .*—1707#11

LE SAGE, Alain René. *The adventures of Robert Chevalier, called de Beauchene, Captain of a privateer in New-France.*—1745#27

LEACH, Edmund. *A short supply or amendment to the propositions for the new representative, for the perpetual peace. . . of this nation. . . written and proposed by Edmund Leach of New-England, merchant.*—1651#14

LEACH, William. *First, a bitt and a knock for under-sheriffs. . . secondly, with a preservative against fraudulent executors. . . by William Leach. . .*—1652#6

LEAKE, Stephen.
Life of Sir John Leake. . . admiral of the fleet.—1750#27

LECHFORD, THOMAS.

Nummi Britannici Historia or An historical account of English money... —1726#11

LECHFORD, Thomas. *Plain dealing: or, Newes from New-England... A short view of New-Englands present government, both ecclesiastical and civil*—1642#11

LEDERER, John. *The discoveries of John Lederer, in three several marches from Virginia, to the west of Carolina, and other parts of the continent...*—1672#6

LEDIARD, Thomas. *The naval history of England, in all its branches; from... 1066, to the conclusion of 1734...*—1735#11

LEE, Samuel. *Eleothriambos, or, The triumph of mercy...*—1677#11

LEEDS, Daniel. *A trumpet sounded out of the wilderness of America...*—1699#9

LEIGH, Edward. *The gentlemans guide, in three discourses. First, of travel...*—1680#5

LENG, John. *A sermon preached... on Friday, the 17th of February 1726...*—1727#15

LENNOX, Charlotte.
The life of Harriot Stuart, written by herself.—1751#21
Poems on several occasions.—1747#14

LESCARBOT, Marc. *Nova Francia, or the description of that part of New France, which is one continent with Virginia...*—1625#9

LESLIE, Charles.
A defence of a book intituled The snake in the grass...—1700#25
A parallel between the faith and doctrine of the present Quakers and that of the chief hereticks in all ages...—1700#26
A reply to a book entitled Anguis flagellatus, or, A switch for the snake. The opus palmare of the Quakers.—1702#14
A short and easie method with the deists... The eighth edition.—1723#6
The snake in the grass... discovering the deep and unexpected subtilty... of the principal leaders of those people called Quakers...—1696#18

LESTRANGE, Hamon [L'ESTRANGE]. *Americans no Jewes, or improbabilities, that the Americans are of that race...*—1652#7

LEUSDEN, John. *The book of psalmes with the new translation in English...*—1688#19

LEVETT, Christopher. *A voyage into New England begun in 1623 and ended in 1624. Performed by Christopher Levett, his majesties woodward of Somersetshire, and one of the Councell of New England...*—1624#9

LEWIS, Thomas. *The scourge in vindication of the Church of England.*—1717#11

LILLY, William. *An easie and familiar method whereby to judge the effects depending on eclipses...*—1652#8

LINDSAY, Patrick. *The interest of Scotland considered...*—1733#23

LISLE, Francis. *The kingdoms divisions anatomized...*—1649#4

LISLE, Samuel. *A sermon preached... February 19, 1747...*—1748#12

LISOLA, François. *Englands appeale from the private cabal at White-hall to the great council of the nation...*—1673#7

LISTER, Martin. *A Journey to Paris in the year 1698...*—1698#12

LITTLE, Otis. *The state of trade of the northern colonies considered; with an account of their produce, and a particular description of Nova Scotia...*—1748#13

LIVINGSTON, William. *A review of the military operations in North-America; from the commencement of the French hostilities on the frontiers of Virginia in 1753, to the surrender of Oswego... 1756...*—1757#24

LIVINGSTONE, John. *A brief historical relation of the life of Mr J. Livingston... written by himself.*—1727#16

LLOYD, David. *The legend of captaine Jones.*—1631#2

LLOYD, Owen. *The panther-prophesy, or, a premonition to all people...*—1662#10

LOCKE, John.
A collection of several pieces never before printed or not extant in his works.—1720#19
An essay concerning humane understanding—1690#12
The fundamental constitutions of Carolina, in number a hundred and twenty... dat. the first day of March, 1669.—1670#9
Two treatises of government.—1690#13

LOCKHART, George. *A further account of East-New-Jersay by a letter write to one of the proprietors therof, by a countrey-man, who has a great plantation there...*—1683#13

LOCKMAN, John.
A history of the cruel sufferings of the Protestants, and others by popish persecutions, in various countries...—1759#62
To the Honourable General Townshend, on his arrival from Quebec.—1759#63
Travels of the Jesuits into various parts of the world; compiled from their letters...—1743#22
The vast importance of the herring fishery to these kingdoms...—1750#28
Verses on the demise of the late king and the accession of his present majesty...—1760#63

LODDINGTON, William.
Plantation work the work of this generation. Written in true-love to all such as are weightily inclined to transplant themselves...—1682#19
Tythe no gospel maintenance, for gospel ministers...—1695#17

LODOWICK, Charles: see BAYARD, Nicholas.

LOGAN, James.
Cato Major; or a treatise on old age, by M. Tullius Cicero. With explanatory notes...—1750#29
The charge delivered from the bench to the Grand Inquest at a Court... Philadelphia, April 13th, 1736.—1737#16

Experimenta et meletemata de plantarum generatione. Autore Jacobo Logan. . . Experiments and considerations on the generation of plants. . .—1747#15

LONDON ASSURANCE, CORPORATION OF. *By the Corporation of London Assurance. . . Proposals for assuring. . . from loss and damage by fire, in England. . . and all other parts of his majesties dominions beyond the seas.*—1722#18

LONDON. SOCIETY OF GARDENERS. *Catalogus plantarum, tum exoticarum tum domesticarum. . .*—1730#19

LONG, Edward. *The Anti-Gallican; or, the history and adventures of Harry Cobham, Esq. Inscribed to Louis XVth, by the Author.*—1757#25

LORRAIN, Paul. *The ordinary of Newgate his account of the behaviour, confessions and dying words of Captain William Kidd, and other pyrates. . .*—1701#27

LOVE, John. *Geodaesia: or, The art of surveying and measuring of land. . .*—1688#10

LOVER OF LIGHT. *The contents of a folio history of the Moravians or United Brethren. . . humbly dedicated to the pious of every denomination of in Europe and America. . .*—1750#30

LOWNDES, Thomas. *Extract of a letter from Mr Thomas Lowndes, to the honourable the Commissioners for victualling his majesty's navy, dated 18 April, 1748.*—1748#14

LUPTON, Donald.
Emblems of rarities; or Choice observations out of worthy histories. . .—1636#2
A most exact and accurate map of the whole world: or, The orb terrestial described in four plain maps, (viz.) Asia, Europe, Africa, and America.—1676#11

LUYTS, Jan. *A general and particular description of America. . . with very particular accounts of the English plantations; and maps. . .*—1701#28

LYNCH, Francis.
Francis Lynch, merchant, appellant. Martin Killikelly, of Dublin, merchant, and Arthur Lynch and company, of Bilbao in Spain, merchants. . . respondents. The case of the respondents.—1738#15
Francis Lynch, of Dublin, merchant appellant. Martin Killikelly, of Dublin, Merchant, Arthur Lynch and Company, of Bilbao. . .—1738#16

LYNCH, John. *A sermon. . . February 20, 1735. . .*—1736#14

LYTTELTON, George.
Considerations upon the present state of our affairs, at home and abroad. In a letter to a member of Parliament from a friend in the country.—1739#47
Dialogues of the dead.—1760#62

M., A. *The state of religion in New-England, since the Reverend George Whitefield's arrival there. In a letter from a gentleman in New-England. . .*—1742#27

M., C. *A true account of the tryals, examinations, confessions, condemnations, and executions of divers witches, at Salem, in New-England. . .*—1693#12

MACKAY, Hugh. *Letter from Lieut. Hugh MacKay, of General Oglethorpe's regiment.*—1742#28

MACKERCHER, Daniel. *A memorial relating to the tobacco trade. . .*—1737#17

MACKWORTH, Sir Humphrey.
Sir H. Mackworth's proposal in miniature, as it has been put in practice in New-York, in America.—1720#20
A vindication of the rights of the Commons of England. By a member.—1701#29

MACNENY, Patrick. *The Freedom of commerce of the subjects of the Austrian Nether-lands asserted and vindicated. Being a confutation of the arguments. . .*—1725#8

MACQUEEN, Daniel. *A sermon. . . preached. . . January 1 1759. . . the present state of the said society.*—1759#64

MACSPARRAN, James.
America dissected, being a full and true account of all the American colonies. . . Published as a caution to unsteady people who may be tempted to leave their native country.—1753#15
Rhode Island. James Mac Sparran. . . of. . . Rhode Island, plaintiff and appellant. . . The appellants case.—1737#18
Rhode Island. The Reverend James McSparran of North Kingston. . . plaintiff. . . The respondent's case.—1737#19

MADDOX, Isaac.
A sermon preached before his grace the Duke of Marlborough. . . March 5 1752. . . To which is added a postcript, containing an account of the small-pox. . .—1753#16
A sermon preached. . . on Friday the 15th of February, 1733. . .—1734#13

MAGENS, Nikolaus. *The universal merchant: containing a rationale of commerce, in theory and practice.*—1753#17

MAILLET, Benoît de. *Telliamed: or, Discourses between an Indian philosopher and a French missionary, on the diminution of the sea, formation of the earth, the origin of men. . .*—1750#31

MAINWARING, Randall. *Case of Mainwaring, Hawes, Payne and others, concerning a depredation. . . upon the ship Elizabeth, going. . . to Virginia. . .*—1646#15

MAITLAND, Charles. *Mr. Maitland's account of inoculating the small pox vindicated, from Dr. Wagstaffe's misrepresentations. . .*—1722#19

MAKEMIE, Francis.
A narrative of the imprisonment of two non-conformist ministers, and prosecution or trial of one of them, for preaching a sermon in. . . New York.—1708#11
A plain and friendly perswasive to the inhabitants of Virginia and Maryland, for promoting towns and cohabitation. . .—1705#15

MALYNES, Gerard de.
Consuetudo, vel, Lex mercatoria, or, The antient law-merchant.—1636#3

The maintenance of free trade.—1622#15

MANDEVILLE, Bernard. *Planter's charity.*—1704#18

MARSH, Henry. *A proposal for raising a stock not exceeding forty thousand pounds sterling; by subscriptions for forming a settlement, in a large...*—1716#4

MARSHALL, Charles. *Sion's travellers comforted.*—1704#19

MARSTON, Edward. *To the most noble prince Henry duke of Beaufort... Palatine of the province of South Carolina in America.*—1712#16

MARTIN, Benjamin. *The philosophical grammar; being a view of the present state of experimental physiology.*—1735#12

MARTIN, Samuel. *A plan for establishing and disciplining a national militia in Great Britain, Ireland, and in all the British dominions of America.*—1745#28

MARTINDELL, Anne. *A relation of the labour, travail and suffering of that faithful servant of the Lord Alice Curwen...*—1680#6

MARTYN, Benjamin.
An account shewing the progress of the colony of Georgia in America from its first establishment.—1741#26
An impartial enquiry into the state and utility of the province of Georgia.—1741#27
A new and accurate account of the provinces of South-Carolina and Georgia. With many curious and useful observations on the trade, navigation and plantations of Great-Britain...—1732#27
Reasons for establishing the colony of Georgia, with regard to the trade of Great Britain, the increase of our people... employment...—1733#24
Some account of the designs of the Trustees for establishing the colony of Georgia in America.—1732#28

MARTYN, John. *Historia plantarum rariorum.*—1728#11

MARYLAND ASSEMBLY. *Acts of assembly, passed in the province of Maryland, from 1692 to 1715.*—1723#7

MASON, John. *The wicked taken in their own net. A sermon, preached at Cheshunt in Hertfordshire... Nov. 29th 1759...*—1759#65

MASSACHUSETTS.
GENERAL COURT.
Acts and laws passed by... assembly of the province of... Massachusetts Bay... from 1692 to 1719.—1724#14
A declaration of the General Court of the Massachusetts... October 18. 1659. Concerning the execution of two Quakers... Reprinted in London...—1659#19
The humble petition and address of the General Court sitting at Boston in New England, unto Prince Charles the second: presented Feb. 11, 1660.—1660#16
GOVERNOR.
A conference of... J. Belcher, Esq... with Edewakenk Chief Sachem of the Penobscut tribe, Loron one of the chief captains of the same tribe...—1732#29

GOVERNOR, COUNCIL AND CONVENTION.
Two addresses from the governour, council and convention of the Massachusetts colony... Presented to his majesty at Hampton-Court, August 7, 1689...—1689#15

MASSEY, Isaac. *A short and plain account of inoculation. With some remarks on the main arguments... by Mr. Maitland and others...*—1722#20

MASSIE, Joseph. *A state of the British sugar-colony trade...*—1759#66

MATHER, Cotton.
An account of the method and success of inoculating for the small-pox in Boston in New-England. In a letter from a gentleman there, to his friend in London.—1722#21
Batteries upon the kingdom of the Devil. Seasonable discourses upon some common but woful, instances, wherein men gratifie the grand enemy of their salvation.—1695#18
Brontologia sacra: the voice of the glorious God in the thunder...—1695#19
The Christian philosopher: A collection of the best discoveries in nature, with religious improvements.—1721#11
Death made easie and happie. Two brief discourses on the prudent apprehensions of death... together with serious thoughts in dying times...—1701#30
Early piety, exemplified in the life and death of Nathaniel Mather...—1689#16
Eleutheria: or, An idea of the Reformation in England: and a History of Non-Conformity in and since that Reformation. With predictions...—1698#13
Late memorable providences relating to witchcrafts and possessions...—1691#11
Letter of advice to the churches of the non-conformists in the English nation: endeavouring their satisfaction in that point, Who are the true Church of England?—1700#28
The life and death of the renowned Mr John Eliot...—1691#12
Magnalia Christi Americana: or; the ecclesiastical history of New-England, from its first planting in the year 1620 unto the year of our Lord, 1698...—1702#17
Manly Christianity. A brief essay on the signs of good growth and strength in the most lovely Christianity...—1711#15
Memoirs of the life of the late reverend Increase Mather... With a preface by... Edmund Calamy...—1725#9
A memorial of the present deplorable state of New-England with the many disadvantages it lyes under, by the male-administration...—1707#12
The old paths restored...—1712#17
Ornaments for the daughters of Zion, or The character and happiness of a virtuous woman...—1694#16
Pietas in patrium: the life of his excellency Sir William Phips, Knt...—1697#10
Reasonable religion: or the truths of the Christian religion demonstrated...—1713#6
Right thoughts in sad hours, representing the comforts and duties of good men under all their afflictions; and particularly that one, the untimely death of Children...—1689#17

The right way to shake off a viper. An essay, on a case, too commonly calling for consideration. What shall good men do, when they are evil spoke. With a preface by Dr. Increase Mather...—1711#16

The saviour with his rainbow. A discourse concerning the covenant which God will remember, in the times of danger passing over his church.—1714#13

The serious Christian: or three great points of practical Christianity... By an American.—1699#11

Three letters from New-England, relating to the controversy of the present time.—1721#12

Winthropi Justa. A sermon at the funeral of the Honble John Winthrop, Esq...—1709#13

The wonders of the invisible world: being an account of the tryals of several witches lately excuted [sic] in New England...—1693#13

MATHER, Increase.

A brief account concerning several of the agents of New-England...—1691#13

A brief discourse concerning the unlawfulness of the Common-prayer worship and the laying the hand on, and kissing the booke in swearing.—1689#18

A brief history of the war with the Indians in New-England. From June 24. 1675... to August 12, 1676...—1676#12

A brief relation of the state of New England, from the beginning of that plantation to this present year, 1689...—1689#19

De successu evangelii apud Indos in Nova-Anglia epistola...—1688#11

A discourse concerning faith and fervency in prayer...—1713#7

A discourse concerning the maintenance, due to those that preach the gospel...—1709#14

A dissertation concerning the future conversion of the Jewish nation...—1709#15

An essay for the recording of illustrious providences, wherein an account is given of many remarkable and memorable events... especially in New-England...—1684#7

A further account of the tryals of the New-England witches. With the observations of a person who was upon the place... To which...—1693#14

A further vindication of New-England from false suggestions in a late scandalous pamphlet, pretending to shew, The inconvenience...—1689#20

The mystery of Israel's salvation, explained and applyed...—1669#1

A narrative of the miseries of New England, by reason of an arbitrary government erected there...—1688#12

New-England vindicated from the unjust aspersions cast on the former government there, by some late Considerations, pretending...—1689#21

The order of the gospel, professed and practised by the churches of Christ in New England...—1700#29

Reasons for the confirmation of the charters belonging to the several corporations in New-England.—1691#14

A sermon shewing that the present dispensations of providence declare that wonderful revolutions in the world are near at hand...—1710#13

Sermons wherein those eight characters... called the beatitudes, are opened...—1721#13

Some important truths about conversion, delivered in sundry sermons...—1674#7

Some remarks on a pretended answer to a discourse concerning the common-prayer worship with an exhortation to the churches in New-England to hold forth to their faith without wavering...—1712#18

A testimony against several prophane and superstitions customs, now practised by some in New-England...—1687#6

Two plain and practical discourses. Concerning 1. Hardness of Heart...—1699#12

The wonders of free-grace: Or, A compleat history of all the most remarkable penitents that have been executed at Tyburn, and elsewhere, for these last thirty years...—1690#15

MATHER, Richard.

An apologie of the churches in New-England for church covenant... Sent over in answer to Master Bernard, in the year 1639...—1643#13

A catechisme or, the grounds and principles of Christian religion, set forth by way of question and answer...—1650#7

Church government and church-covenant discussed, in an answer of the elders of the severall churches in New England...—1643#14

A disputation concerning church-members and their children, in answer to XXI. questions...—1659#20

A heart-melting exhortation, together with a cordiall consolation, presented in a letter from New-England...—1650#8

A modest and brotherly answer to Mr. Charles Herle his book, against the independency of churches...—1644#12

A platform of church discipline...—1652#9

A platform of church discipline... agreed upon by the elders and messengers... at Cambridge in New-England...—1653#13

A reply to Mr Rutherford.—1647#11

MATHER, Samuel. *De Baptismate...*—1715#17

MATTHEWS, Marmaduke.

The messiah magnified by the mouths of babes in America...—1659#21

The rending church-member regularly called back, to Christ, and to his church...—1659#22

MAUDUIT, Israel.

Considerations on the present German war.—1760#64

The parallel... the renewal of our Prussian treaty.—1742#29

MAURICE, Henry. *The antithelemite, or an answer to certain queries... and to the Considerations of an unknown author concerning toleration.*—1685#18

MAWSON, Matthias. *A sermon preached... February 18, 1742-3...*—1743#23

MAYHEW, Experience. *Indian converts... lives and dying speeches of... Christianized Indians of Martha's Vineyard...*

some account of. . . English ministers. . . . in that and the adjacent islands. . . .—1727#17

MAYHEW, Jonathan.
A sermon preach'd in the audience of His Excellency William Shirley,. . . the Honourable His Majesty's council, and the. . . House. . .—1754#24
Sermons upon the following subjects. . .—1756#53
Seven sermons upon the following subjects. . .—1750#32
Two discourses delivered. . . October the 25th, 1759, being the day appointed by authority. . . as a day of thanksgiving for the success of his majesty's arms. . . reduction of Quebec. . .—1760#65

MAYHEW, Matthew. The conquests and triumphs of grace. . .—1695#20

MAYHEW, Thomas. Upon the joyfull and welcome return of Charles the second. . . to his. . . government over these his majesties kingdoms and dominions. . .—1660#17

MAYLINS, Robert. Letter which was delivered to the King. . .—1661#10

MAYNE, Jasper. The citye match. A comoedye.—1639#3

McCULLOH, Henry.
General thoughts on the construction, use and abuse of the great offices. . .—1754#25
A miscellaneous essay concerning the courses pursued by Great Britain in the affairs of her colonies: with some observations on the. . .—1755#34
Proposals for uniting the English colonies on the continent of America so as to enable them to act with force and vigour against their enemies.—1757#26
The wisdom and policy of the French in the construction of their great offices. . . With some observations on. . . disputes. . . English and French colonies. . . America.—1755#35

MEDE, Joseph.
The key of the revelation, searched and demonstrated. . . whereunto is added A conjecture concerning Gog and Magog by the same author. . .—1643#15
The works of the pious and profoundly learned Joseph Mede. . .—1648#8

MELON, Jean François. A political essay upon commerce. Written in French by Monsieur M———. Tr., with some annotation and remarks by David Bindon, esq.—1738#17

MERCER, John. An exact abridgement of all the public acts of assembly of Virginia, in force and use. January 1, 1758. Together with a proper table.—1759#68

MERCHANT OF LONDON. A state of the trade carried on with the French, on the island of Hispaniola, by the merchants in North America, under colour of flags of truce. . .—1760#66

MERCHANT RETIR'D. An address to the merchants of Great-Britain: or, a review of the conduct of the administration, with regard to our trade and navigation. . .—1739#48

MERITON, George. A geographical description of the world. . .—1674#8

MIDDLETON, Christopher.
Forgery detected. By which is evinced how groundless are all the calumnies cast upon the editor, in a pamphlet published under the name of Arthur Dobbs. . .—1745#29
A rejoinder to Mr. Dobb's reply to Captain Middleton. . .—1745#30
A reply to Mr. Dobb's answer to a pamphlet, entitled, Forgery detected. . .—1745#31
A reply to the Remarks of Arthur Dobbs Esq; on Capt Middleton's Vindication of his conduct.—1744#33
Table of meteorological observations from 1721 to 1729 in nine voyages to Hudson's Bay.—1730#20
A vindication of the conduct of Captain Christopher Middleton, in a late voyage on board His Majesty's ship the Furnace. . .—1743#24

MIDDLETON, Patrick. A short view of the evidence upon which the Christian religion. . . is established. . .—1734#14

MILLAN, John, d. 1782. Arms of the baronets of England, and Nova Scotia. With crests, supporters, mottos, family honours. . . By John Millan. . . corrected to September 1753.—1753#18

MILLAR, Robert. The history of the propagation of Christianity, and the overthrow of paganism. . .—1723#8

MILLER, Philip.
Catalogus plantarum officinalium. . .—1730#21
Catalogus plantarum. Part I.—1730#22
Figures of the most beautiful, useful, and uncommon plants described in the gardeners dictionary.—1760#68
The gardeners and florists dictionary.—1724#15
The gardeners dictionary.—1731#25

MISSELDEN, Edward. Free trade. or, The meanes to make trade flourish.—1622#16

MITCHEL, Jonathan. Propositions concerning the subject of baptism and consociation of churches. . . by a synod. . . of the churches in Massachusetts-colony. . .—1662#11

MITCHELL, John. The contest in America between Great Britain and France. . . giving an account of the views and designs of the French, with the interests. . .—1757#28

MOCQUET, Jean. Travels and voyages into Africa, Asia, and America, and the East and West-Indies. . .—1696#20

MOFFETT, Thomas. Insectorum, sive minimorum animalium theatrum.—1634#5

MOLL, Herman.
Atlas geographus: or, a compleat system of geography, ancient and modern. . . . With the discoveries and improvements of the best modern authors to this time. . .—1711#17
Atlas manuale: or, a new sett of maps of all the parts of the earth, as well Asia, Africa and America, as Europe. . . Mostly perform'd by Herman Moll.—1709#16
A system of geography, or, A new and accurate description of the earth in all its empires, kingdoms and states. . .—1701#31

MOLLOY, Charles. De jure maritimo et navali: or a treatise of affaires maritime. . .—1676#13

MOLYNEUX, Thomas More. *Conjunct expeditions: or, expeditions that have been carried on jointly by the fleet and army...*—1759#69

MONTESQUIEU, Charles Louis de Secondat, Baron Montesquieu. *The spirit of laws. Translated from the French of M. de Secondat...*—1750#33

MONTGOMERY, Sir Robert.
A brief account of the situation and advantages of the new-intended settlement in... Azilia; a late erected British province on the South of Carolina.—1717#12
A description of the Golden islands, with an account of the undertaking now on foot for making a settlement there...—1720#22
A discourse concerning the designed establishment of a new colony to the south of Carolina, in the most delightful country in the universe.—1717#13
Proposal for raising a stock, and settling a new colony in Azilia...—1717#14

MOORE, Charles. *Prolusio inauguralis, de usu vesicantium, quae cantharides recipiunt, in febribus...*—1752#12

MOORE, Francis. *A voyage to Georgia. Begun in the year 1735. Containing, an account of the settling the town of Frederica...*—1744#34

MOORE, John. *Of the truth and excellency of the gospel. A sermon preached... Friday the 20th of February 1712/13...*—1713#8

MORALEY, William. *The infortunate: or, the voyage and adventures of William Moraley... Containing, whatever is curious and remarkable in...*—1743#25

MORDEN, Robert. *Geography rectified: or, a description of the world...*—1680#7

MORE, Nicholas. *Letter from Doctor More, with passages out of several letters from persons of good credit, relating to the state and improvement of the province of Pennsylvania...*—1687#7

MOREAU, Jacob Nicolas.
The conduct of the late ministry, or, A memorial; containing a summary of facts with their vouchers, in answer to the Observations...—1757#29
The mystery revealed; or, Truth brought to light.—1759#71

MORERI, Louis. *The great historical geographical, genealogical and poetical dictionary...*—1694#17

MORIN, J. *A short account of the life and sufferings of Elias Neau...*—1749#30

MORRELL, William. *New-England, or a brief enarration of the ayre, earth, water, fish and fowles of that country... in Latine and English verse.*—1625#10

MORRIS, Lewis. *Case of Lewis Morris, esq; lord chief justice in of the province of New York... to be heard before... the lords of the committee of the Privy Council...*—1735#13

MORTON, Thomas. *New English Canaan or New Canaan. Containing an abstract of New England, composed in three bookes...*—1637#5

MORYSON, Francis. *The lawes of Virginia now in force...*—1662#12

MOULTRIE, John. *Dissertatio medica inauguralis, de febre maligna biliosa Americae... pro gradu doctoratus... Joannes Moultrie, ex Meridionali Carolinae provincia...*—1749#31

MOXON, Joseph. *A tutor to astronomie and geographie: or an easie...*—1659#23

MOYLE, John. *Chirurgus marinus; or, The sea chirurgion...*—1693#15

MUCKLOWE, William. *A bemoaning letter of an ingenious Quaker...*—1700#30

MULFORD, Samuel. *A memorial of several aggrievances and oppressions of his majesty's subjects... in the colony of New-York...*—1717#15

MUN, Thomas. *England's treasure by forraign trade...*—1664#11

MURET, Pierre. *Rites of Funeral. Ancient and modern, in use through the known world...*—1683#15

MURRAY, Alexander. *The true interest of Great Britain, Ireland and our plantations: or, a proposal for making such an union... as that already made betwixt Scotland and England...*—1740#24

N., J. *The liberty and property of British subjects asserted: in a letter from an assembly-man in Carolina, to his friend in London.*—1726#13

N., N. *America: or an exact description of the West Indies...*—1655#17

N., N. *A short account of the present state of New-England. Anno Domini 1690*—1690#17

NAIRNE, Thomas. *Letter from South Carolina; giving an account of the soil, air, product, trade... together with the manner of necessary charges of settling a plantation there... by a Swiss gentleman...*—1710#14

NALSON, John.
The character of a rebellion, and what England may expect by one...—1681#14
The countermine: or, a short but true discovery of the dangerous principles, and secret practices of the dissenting party...—1677#14
Toleration and liberty of conscience considered, and proved impracticable, impossible... sinful and unlawful.—1685#19

NASH, Thomas. *Quaternio, or A fourefold way to a happie life...*—1633#4

NATIVE OF NEW-YORK. *The counterpart to the state dunces. By a native of New-York.*—1733#25

NE——L, Mc-O——. *A copy of a letter from Quebeck in Canada, to a Pr-M-r in France, dated October 11. 1747.*—1747#16

NEAL, Daniel.
The history of New-England containing an impartial account of the civil and ecclesiastical affairs of the country to... 1700. To

which is added the present state of New-England...—1720#23

The history of the puritans or protestant nonconformists... to the death of Queen Elizabeth...—1732#30

A review of the principal facts objected to the first volume of the History of the Puritans...—1734#15

NELSON, Robert. An address to persons of quality and estate...—1715#18

NESSE, Christopher. The signs of the times: or, wonderful signs of wonderful times... a faithful collection of... signs and wonders... in the heavens, on the earth and on the waters... this last year 1680.—1681#15

NEVILL, Valentine. The reduction of Louisbourg. A poem, wrote on board his majesty's ship Orford in Louisbourg harbour...—1758#33

NEW YORK ASSEMBLY. Acts of Assembly, passed in the province of New-York from 1691, to 1718.—1719#6

NEWCOMB, Thomas.

Novus epigrammatum delectus: or, Original State epigrams and minor odes...—1760#70

Pacata Britannia. A panegyrick to the queen, on the peace...—1713#9

NEWCOMEN, Matthew. Irenicum; or, an essay towards a brotherly peace and union, between those of the Congregational and Presbyterian way...—1659#24

NEWTON, Thomas. Dissertations on the prophecies, which have remarkably been fulfilled, and at this time are fulfilling in the world.—1754#27

NEWTON, William. The life of... White Kennett... with several original letters... papers and records...—1730#23

NICHOLSON, Francis.

An apology or vindication of Francis Nicholson... governor of South Carolina from the unjust aspersions cast on him by some of the members of the Bahama company...—1724#16

Journal of an expedition under the command of Francis Nicholson... for the reduction of Port-Royal in Nova-Scotia...—1711#18

A modest answer to a malicious libel against his excellency Francis Nicholson... or an examination of that part of Mr Blair's affidavit...—1705#17

NICHOLSON, Joseph. The standard of the Lord lifted up in New-England...—1660#18

NICKOLLS, John. Original letters and papers of state, addressed to Oliver Cromwell...—1743#26

NICKOLLS, Thomas. A turbulent spirit troubled with his our confutations. In reply to George Keith's pretended Answer to seventeen queries...—1702#19

NICOL, John and others.

Copy of three letters, the first written by Dr John Nicol at New York... the second by a dissenting minister in England... the third...—1740#25

Copy of two letters, the first written by a gentleman at New York... the second by a dissenting minister in England... progress and success of the gospel in foreign parts...—1740#26

NICOLL, John. The advantage of Great Britain considered in the tobacco trade... humbly offered to the Parliament of Great Britain...—1727#18

NICOLSON, William. An apology for the discipline of the ancient church... especially... our mother the Church of England...—1659#25

NISBET, James. The perpetuity of the Christian religion, a sermon preached in the High Church of Edinburgh, Monday January 3d, 1737; upon occasion...—1737#20

NORRIS, John. Profitable advice for rich and poor. In a dialogue between James Freeman, a Carolina planter, and Simon Question, a West-Country...—1712#19

NORTON, Humphrey. New-England's ensigne: it being the account of cruelty, the professors pride, and the articles of new faith; signified in characters written in blood...—1659#26

NORTON, John.

Abel being dead yet speaketh; or, The life and death of... Mr. John Cotton...—1658#10

A discussion of that great point in divinity, the sufferings of Christ...—1653#14

The heart of New-England rent at the blasphemies of the present generation... doctrine of the Quakers...—1660#19

The orthodox evangelist. Or a treatise wherein many great evangelical truths... are briefly discussed...—1654#13

Responsio ad totam quaestionum syllogen a... Guilielmo Apollonio...—1648#9

NORWOOD, Richard. The sea-mans practice, contayning a fundamentall probleme in navigation...—1637#6

NOTTINGHAM, Heneage. An exact and most impartial accompt... of the trial... of twenty nine regicides...—1660#20

NOYES, James.

Moses and Aaron: or, the rights of church and state...—1661#12

The temple measured: or, a brief survey of the temple mystical, which is the instituted church of Christ...—1647#13

OBOURN, Thomas, b. 1717 or 18. A sermon preached in the parish church of Kingsclere, Hants, on Thursday the 29th of November, 1759, being the day appointed for a general thanksgiving. By Thomas Obourn, A.M...—1759#76

OFFICER. Six plans of the different dispositions of the English army, under the command of the late General Braddock, in North America... By an officer.—1758#33A

OGILBY, John. America: being the latest, and most accurate description of the new world...—1670#10

OGLETHORPE, James Edward.

A full reply to Lieut. Cadogan's Spanish hireling and Lieut. Mackay's letter... wherein the Impartial account of the late expedition to St. Augustine is clearly vindicated...—1743#27

An impartial account of the late expedition against St. Augustine under General Oglethorpe. Occasioned by the suppression of the...—1742#31

Select tracts relating to colonies...—1732#31

OGLETHORPE, William. *The Naked Truth. Number I... addressed to the people of Great Britain, Ireland and America.*—1755#39

OLD DRUMCLOG SOLDIER. *A warning to all the lovers of Christ in Scotland to be upon their guard against the spreading contagion broken out from Mr. Adam Gib...*—1742#32

OLDMIXON, John.
The British empire in America, containing the history of the discovery, settlement, progress and present state of all the British...—1708#12
Torism and trade never agree. To which is added, an account and character of the Mercator... In a letter to Sir G- H-.—1713#10

OLIPHANT, Andrew. *Letter from New-England, concerning the state of religion there.*—1742#33

OLLYFFE, George. *An essay humbly offer'd for an act of Parliament to prevent capital crimes...*—1731#27

ORCHARD, N. *The doctrine of devils, proved to be the grand apostacy of the times...*—1676#15

OSBALDESTON, Richard. *A sermon preached... on Friday February 2l, 1752...*—1752#13

OSBORNE, Thomas. *Catalogue of the libraries of the several gentlemen undermentioned, viz... II. The Hon. Governor Winthrop [sic] Fellow of the Royal Society...*—1748#18

OWEN, Charles. *The danger of the church and kingdom from foreigners considered...*—1721#15

OWEN, Griffith?. *Our ancient testimony renewed... occasioned... by several unjust charges... by G. Keith... Given forth... at Philadelphia...*—1695#21

P., L. *Two essays sent from Oxford to a nobleman in London, concerning some errors about the creation, general flood and peopling of the world...*—1695#22

P., W. *The history of witches and wizards: giving a true account of all their tryals in England, Scotland, Sweedland, France and New England; with their confession and condemnation.*—1750#36

PAGIT, John. *A defence of church-government exercised in presbyteriall, classical and synodall assemblies.*—1641#18

PAGITT, Ephraim.
Christianographie. or The description of the multitude and sundry sort of Christians in the world not subject to the Pope...—1635#2
Heresiography: or, A description of the heretickes and sectaries of these latter times...—1645#14
A relation of the Christians in the world...—1639#4

PALAIRET, Jean. *A concise description of the English and French possessions in North-America, for the better explaining of the map published with that title.*—1755#40

PALMER, John. *An impartial account of the state of New England; or, the late government there, vindicated...*—1690#19

PARKER, George. *The West-India almanack for the year 1719.*—1719#7

PARKER, Samuel. *Mr Baxter baptiz'd in bloud, or, a sad history of the unparallel'd cruelty of the Anabaptists in New England...*—1673#9

PARKER, Thomas.
The copy of a letter written by Mr. Thomas Parker, pastor of the church in Newbury in New-England, to his sister... Novemb. 22. 1649...—1650#9
Methodus gratiae divinae in traductione hominis peccatoris ad vitam, septuaginta thesibus succincta et elaborate explicate.—1657#11
The true copy of a letter: written by Mr. Thomas Parker... in New-England... touching the government practised in the churches of New-England.—1644#13
The visions and prophecies of Daniel...—1646#16

PARKINSON, John.
Paradisi in sole paradisus terrestris...—1629#2
Theatrum botanicum: The theater of plants—1640#4

PARMYTER, Paroculus. *Observations and reflections on the present practice, errors and mismanagement of the Governors and their Naval Officers, and the Clerks...*—1720#24

PARSONS, William.
Case of Mr William P——s, an unfortunate young gentleman who is now confin'd in Newgate for returning from transportation. Shewing...—1750#37
A genuine, impartial, and authentick account of the life of William Parsons, esq; executed at Tyburn, Monday Feb. 11, 1751, for returning from transportation...—1751#24
Memoirs of the life and adventures of William Parsons, esq; from the time of his entering into life, to his death... Written by himself and corrected (with additions) by a gentleman.—1751#25
The trial and remarkable life of William Parsons, who was executed at Tyburn near London, on Monday the 11th of February 17501...—1751#26

PASCHOUD, ——, schoolmaster. *Historico-political geography; or, A description of the... several countries in the world...*—1722#22

PASKELL, Thomas. *An abstract of a letter from Thomas Paskell of Pensilvania to his friend J. J. of Chippenham.*—1683#16

PATERSON, William.
An abstract, of a letter from a person of eminency and worth in [New] Caledonia, to a friend in Boston in New England...—1699#13
An essay concerning inland and foreign trade... showing how a company for national trade, may be constituted in Scotland...—1704#21

PATRICK J. *Quebec: a poetical essay, in imitation of the Miltonic style: Being a regular narrative of... transactions... under... Saunders and... Wolfe...*—1760#73

PATRICK, Simon. *A continuation of the friendly debate. By the same author.*—1669#2

PATRIOT. *A political essay upon the English and French colonies in northern and southern America, considered in a new light. . .*—1760#74

PAYNE, J. *The French encroachments exposed: or, Britain's original right to all that part of the American continent claimed by France. . .*—1756#57

PEACHAM, Henry.
Coach and sedan. . .—1636#4
The compleat gentleman. . . third impression much, inlarged. . .—1661#13

PEARCE, Zachary.
A sermon preached. . . April the 17th 1735 to which is annexed an account of the origin and design of the society for promoting Christian Knowledge. . .—1735#15
A sermon preached. . . on Friday the 20th of February, 1729. . .—1730#24

PECHEY, John.
The compleat herbal of physical plants. . .—1694#18
Some observations made upon the herb cassiny; imported from Carolina; shewing its admirable virtues in curing the small pox. . .—1695#23
Some observations made upon the Virginian nutts, imported from the Indies: showing their admirable virtue against the scurvy. . .—1682#20

PECK, Philip. *Some observations for improvement of trade, by establishing the fishery of Great Britain. . .*—1732#32

PEMBERTON, Ebenezer, (1671–1717).
Advice to a son. A discourse at the request of a gentleman in New-England, upon his son's going to Europe. . .—1705#16
Sermons and discourses on several occasions. By the late. . . Ebenezer Pemberton. . . in Boston. . .—1727#20

PEMBERTON, Israel.
An account of conferences held and treaties made, between Major-General Sir William Johnson, Bart. and the chief Sachems and Warriours. . .—1756#58
Several conferences between some of the principal. . . Quakers in Pennsylvania, and the deputies from the six Indian Nations in alliance. . .—1756#59

PENINGTON, Edward. *Some brief observations upon George Keith's earnest expostulations. . .*—1696#21

PENINGTON, Isaac.
An examination of the grounds or causes, which are said to induce the court of Boston. . . to make that order against the Quakers. . .—1660#21
To friends in England, Ireland, Scotland, Holland, New-England. . . London.—1666#5
The works of the long-mournfull and sorely distressed Isaac Penington. . .—1681#16

PENINGTON, John.
An apostate exposed or, George Keith's contradicting himself. . .—1695#24
Certain certificates received from America, on behalf of Samuel Jennings. . .—1695#25
The people called Quakers cleared by Geo. Keith from the false doctrines charged on them by G. Keith. . .—1696#22

PENN, Hannah. *Case of Hannah Penn, the widow and executrix of William Penn Esq; late proprietor and governour of Pensilvania.*—1730#25

PENN, John. *In Chancery. Breviate. John Penn, Thomas Penn, and Richard Penn, plaintiffs. . . For the plaintiffs.*—1742#34

PENN, William.
The allegations against proprietary governments considered, and their merit and benefit to the Crown briefly observed. . .—1701#32
A brief account of the province of Pennsylvania, lately granted by the King, under the great seal of England, to William Penn and his heirs and assigns.—1681#17
Case of William Penn, esq; as to the proprietary government of Pensilvania; which, together with Carolina, New York, etc is intended to be taken away by a bill in Parliament.—1701#33
Case of William Penn, Esq; Proprietary-Governor of Pensilvania and of Joshua Gee, Henry Gould, Silvanus Grove, John Woods, and others, mortgagees under the said William Penn.—1720#25
Case of William Penn, proprietary, and governor in chief of the province of Pennsylvania, and territories, against the Lord Baltimore's. . .—1709#18
A collection of the works of William Penn. In two volumes. To which is prefixed a journal of his life with many original letters and papers. . .—1726#14
The description of the province of West-Jersey, in America: as also proposals to such who desire to have any propriety therein.—1676#16
An epistle, containing a salutation to all faithful friends, a reproof to all the unfaithfull; and a visitation to the enquiring. . .—1682#21
A further account of the province of Pennsylvania and its improvements. For the satisfaction of those that are adventurers, and enclined to be so.—1685#20
Information and direction to such persons as are inclined to America, more especially those related to the province of Pennsylvania.—1684#8
Letter from William Penn, proprietary and governour of Pennsylvania. . . to the committee of the Free Society of Traders of that. . .—1683#17
Some account of the province of Pensilvania in America. . .—1681#18
Some proposals for a second settlement in the province of Pennsylvania.—1690#20
Truth rescued from imposture. Or a brief reply to. . . a pretented answer, to the tryal of W. Penn, and W. Mead, etc. . .—1670#11

PENNECUIK, Alexander. *Burnbank's farewel to Edinburgh, at his departure for the Indies, with his last will and testament.*—1721#16

PENNSYLVANIA
   ASSEMBLY.
   His excellency, Governour Penn's speech, to the assembly, held at Philadelphia in Pensilvania; September the 15th 1701. With...—1701#34
   PROVINCE.
   The particulars of an Indian treaty at Conestogoe, between... Sir William Keith, governor of Pennsylvania, and the deputies of the Five nations...—1722#23
   The treaty held with the Indians of the Six Nations at Philadelphia, in July 1742.—1744#35

PEPPERRELL, William. *An accurate journal and account of the proceedings of the New-England land-forces, during the late expedition against the French settlements on Cape Breton...*—1746#15

PERCEVAL, John.
An examination of the principles, and an enquiry into the conduct, of the two b——rs...—1749#32
Faction detected by the evidence of facts.—1743#28
A representation of the state of the trade of Ireland, laid before the House of Lords of England...—1750#38
A second series of facts and arguments, tending to prove that the abilities of the two b——s, are not more extraordinary than their virtues...—1749#33
Things as they are [part 1].—1758#34

PERRAULT, Claude. *Some memoires for a natural history...*—1688#14

PERRIN, William. *The present state of the British and French sugar colonies, and our own northern colonies, considered...*—1740#29

PERROT, John. *Beames of eternal brightness, or branches of everlasting blessings, to be spread over India and all the nations of the earth, by John, who is called a Quaker.*—1661#14

PERRY, Micaiah. *Further reasons for inlarging the trade to Russia, humbly offered by the merchants and planters trading to and interested in the...*—1698#14

PERSON WELL ACQUAINTED WITH THE SUGAR TRADE. *Some considerations touching the sugar colonies, with political observations in respect to trade...*—1732#33

PERSON WHO RESIDED SEVERAL YEARS AT JAMAICA. *Some observations on the assiento trade, as it has been exercised by the South-Sea Company; proving the damage, which will...*—1728#12

PERTH, James Drummond. *An advertisement concerning the province of East-New-Jersey in America. Published for information of such as are desirous to be concerned therein...*—1685#21

PETAVIUS, Dionysius or PETAU, Denis. *The history of the world... Together with a geographicall description...*—1659#27

PETER, Hugh.
A dying father's last legacy.—1660#22
Mr Peters last report of the English wars...—1646#17

The tales and jests of Mr Hugh Peters, collected in one volume...—1660#23

PETIVER, James.
Catalogus classicus et topicus, omnium rerum figuratarum in V. decadibus, seu primo [-secundo] volumine Gazophylacii naturae et artis.—1709#19
Gazophylacii naturae et artis decas sexta [-nona].—1711#19
Gazophylacii naturae et artis prima [-quinta].—1702#20
Musei Petiveriani prima [-octavia].—1695#26
Pteri-graphia americana; icones continens filicum nec non muscos, lichenes, fungos, corallia... ex insulis nostra Charibbaeis...—1712#21

PETTUS, John. *St. Foine improved.*—1671#8

PETTY, William.
An essay concerning the multiplication of mankind: together with another essay in political arithmetick—1686#3
Political Arithmetick, or a discourse concerning, the extent and value of lands people...—1690#21
Several essays in political arithmetick.—1699#14
The third part of the present state of England... To which is likewise added England's guide to industry: or, the improvement of trade for the good of all people in general.—1683#18

PETYT, William. *Britannia languens; or a discourse of trade.*—1680#8

PEYTON, Valentine. *Dissertatio medica inauguralis de abortu...*—1754#28

PHILALETHES. *The profit and loss of Great Britain and Spain, from the commencement of the present war to this time, impartially stated...*—1742#35

PHILIPOT, Thomas. *Original and growth of the Spanish monarchy...*—1664#12

PHILIPS, Erasmus. *Miscellaneous works consisting of essays political and moral.*—1751#27

PHILIPS, Miles. *The voyages and adventures of Miles Philips... the inhuman treatment he met... at Mexico, and the salvage Indians of Canada...*—1724#17

PHILLIPS, George.
The humble request of his majesties loyall subjects, the governour and company late gone for New-England; to the rest of their brethren, in and of the Church of England...—1630#6
A reply to a confutation of some grounds for infants baptisme: as also concerning the form of a church...—1645#15

PHILLIPS, Gillam. *Gillam Phillips, only brother of Henry Phillips deceased intestate. appellant. Faith Savage widow... and others, respondents. The case of Faith Savage.*—1737#21

PHILLMORE, J. *Two dialogues on the man-trade.*—1760#75

PHILO-AMERICUS. *Some further considerations of the consequences of the bill now depending in the House of Lords, relating to the dispute of the trade of the British colonies in America...*—1733#26

PHILOLAOS. Two letters, concerning some farther advantages and improvements that may seem necessary to be made on the taking and keeping of Cape Breton. . .—1746#16

PHILOPATRIS. A most humble proposal to the Most Honourable the Lords Regents. . . for an effectual method to prevent piracy, and make the trade of America safe. . .—1723#9

PHILOTHEUS. A true and particular history of earthquakes. . .—1748#19

PICHON, Thomas. Genuine letters and memoirs, relating to the natural, civil, and commercial history of the islands of Cape Breton, and Saint John. . . to. . . 1758. . . By an impartial Frenchman. . .—1760#76

PIERCE, Thomas. The new discoverer discover'd. . . By way of an answer to Mr. Baxter. . .—1659#28

PIERS, Henry. Victory and plenty great subjects of thanksgiving. A sermon preached in. . . Bexley. . . Kent. On Thursday the 29th of November, 1759. . .—1759#78

PILKINGTON, R. The skilful doctor; or the compleat mountebank. . .—1685#22

PINDER, Richard.
Bowells of compassion towards the scattered seed. . . Written to the scattered people in America. . .—1659#29
The captive. . . visited with the day-spring from on high. . . Given forth especially for the scattered people in America. . .—1660#24

PINFOLD, Charles. Doctor Pinfold's state of the case of the petitioner's for settling his majesties waste land, lying between Nova-Scotia, and the province of Maine. . .—1721#17

PITMAN, Henry. A relation of the great sufferings and strange adventures of Henry Pitman. . .—1689#23

PITT, William. The Monitor: a speech. . . by the Honourable W——m P—t.—1755#41

PITTIS, William.
The history of the present parliament, and convocation. With the debates. . . relating to the conduct of the war abroad. . .—1711#20
Reasons for a war with France.—1715#19

PLANTAGENET, Beauchamp. A description of the province of New Albion. And a direction for adventurers with small stock to get two for one, and good land freely. . .—1648#10

PLATTES, Gabriel. A discovery of subterraneall treasure, viz, Of all manner of mines and mineralls from the gold to the coal.—1639#5

PLENDERLEATH, David. Religion a treasure to men, and the strength and glory of a nation. A sermon. . . January 7. 1754. . .—1754#29

PLUMARD DE DANGEUL, Louis Joseph. Remarks on the advantages and disadvantages of France and of Great Britain with respect to commerce. . .—1754#30

POPPLE, William. Letter to Mr Penn. With his answer.—1688#15

PORTER, Joseph. The holy seed: or, The life of Mr Thomas Beard, wrote by himself: with some account of his death, September 15, 1710. . .—1711#21

POST, Christian Frederick. The second journal of Christian Frederick Post, on a message from the governor of Pennsylvania to the Indians on the Ohio.—1759#79

POSTLETHWAYT, Malachy.
The African trade, the great pillar and support of the British plantation trade in America. . .—1745#33
Britain's commercial interest explained and improved. . . containing a candid enquiry into the secret causes of the present misfortunes of the nation. . .—1757#32
A dissertation on the plan, use, and importance, of the Universal dictionary of trade and commerce, translated from the French. . .—1749#34
Great-Britain's true system. . .—1757#33
In Honour to the administration. The importance of the African expedition considered. . .—1758#35
Observations on trade and taxes; shewing what is required and necessary to rescue and increase the wealth and power of the British nation. . .—1751#28
A short state of the progress of the French trade and navigation, wherein is shown the great foundation that France has laid. . .—1756#60

POVEY, Charles. The unhappiness of England, as to its trade by sea and land. . .—1701#35

POWNALL, Thomas.
Considerations towards a general plan of measures for the English provinces. Laid before the Board of commissioners at Albany, by Mr Pownall.—1756#61
Principles of polity, being the grounds and reasons of civil empire. . .—1752#14

PREVOST, James. Case on behalf of Colonel Prevost, and other foreign officers, in the Royal American Regiment.—1759#80

PREVOST D'EXILES, Antoine François. The life of Mr Cleveland, natural son of Oliver Cromwell, written by himself. Giving a particular account of. . . his great sufferings in Europe and America. . .—1731#28

PRICE, Laurence. The mayden's of London, brave adventures, or, a boon voyage intended for the sea. . .—1655#18

PRICE, Richard. Britain's happiness, and the proper improvement of it. . . a sermon. . . at Newington-Green, Middlesex. . . Nov. 29. 1759.—1759#81

PRINCE, Thomas.
Extraordinary events the doings of God and marvellous in pious eyes. . . seen on. . . taking the city of Louisbourg, on the Isle of Cape Breton. . .—1746#18
The natural and moral government and agency of God, in causing droughts and rains.—1750#39
The salvations of God in 1746. In part set forth in a sermon at the South Church in Boston, Nov. . . 27, 1746. . .—1747#19

A sermon delivered at the South-Church in Boston. . . August 14, 1746. . . Thanksgiving for. . . glorious and happy victory near Culloden. . .—1747#20

PRINGLE, Sir John. *The life of General James Wolfe, the conqueror of Canada, or, the eulogium of that renowned hero. . .*—1760#78

PRIOR, Thomas.
An authentick narrative of the success of tar-water. . .—1746#19
A list of the absentees of Ireland.—1729#23
Observations on the trade between Ireland, and the English and foreign colonies in America. In a letter to a friend.—1731#29

PROTESTANT ASSOCIATION. *The declaration of the reasons and motives for the present appearing in arms of their majesties protestant subjects in Maryland.*—1689#25

PRYCE, David. *To the King's most excellent Majesty. The petition of David Pryce, Esq. master and commander in your Majesty's Royal Navy, and late. . .*—1760#79

PUFENDORF, Samuel von. *An introduction to the history of the principal states. . .*—1695#27

PUGH, Ellis. *A salutation to the Britains, to call them from many things, to the one thing needful, for the saving of their souls. . . translated from the British language.*—1732#34

PULLEIN, Samuel.
The culture of silk, or, an essay on its rational practice and improvement. . . For the use of the American colonies.—1758#36
An essay towards a method of preserving the seeds of plants in a state fit for vegetation, during long voyages. For the improvement of the British colonies in America.—1759#82

PULTENEY, William.
The politicks on both sides, with regard to foreign affairs, stated from their own writings. . .—1734#16
A proper reply to a late scurrilous libel; intituled Sedition and defamation displayed. . .—1731#30
A review of all that hath passed between the courts of Great Britain and Spain, relating to our trade and navigation, from the year 1721, to the present convention. . .—1739#57
A state of the national debt, as it stood December. . . 1716, with the payments. . . out of the sinking fund, &c. compared with. . . 1725.—1727#21

PURCHAS, Samuel.
Purchas his pilgrim. Microcosmus, or The historie of man.—1627#5
Purchase his Pilgrimage. Or Relations of the world and all ages and places discovered.—1626#1
Purchas his pilgrimes.—1625#11
A theatre of politicall flying insects. Wherein especially the nature. . . of the bee, is discovered and described. . .—1657#12

PURRY, Jean Pierre.
Mémoire présenté à Sa. Gr. Mylord Duc de Newcastle. . . sur l'état présent de la Caroline et sur les moyens de l'améliorer.—1724#18

A memorial presented to. . . Duke of Newcastle. . . concerning the present state of Carolina, and the means of improving it.—1724#19
A method for determining the best climate of the earth, on a principle to which all geographers and historians have been hitherto strangers. . .—1744#36

PUSEY, Caleb. *A modest account from Pensylvania, of the principal differences in point of doctrine, between George Keith and. . .*—1696#23

PYM, John. *A speech delivered in Parliament, by a worthy member thereof.*—1641#19

PYNCHON, William.
A farther discussion of that great point in divinity the sufferings of Christ. . .—1655#19
The Jewes Synagogue: or, a treatise concerning the ancient orders and manners of worship used by the government truly and plainly stated.—1652#10
The time when the first sabbath was ordained. . .—1654#14

R., P. *Letter to a friend in America; wherein is clearly held forth the peculiar interest that the elect have in the death of Christ, by virtue. . .*—1754#31

RADCLIFF, Ebenezer. *The crisis: or, the decisive period of British power and liberty. . . In two sermons preached at Boston in the county of Lincoln, February 17, 1758.*—1758#37

RAE, Robert. *Answers for Robert Rae of Little-Govan, to the petition of John Jamieson merchants in Glasgow.*—1747#21

RAILTON, John. *Proposals to the public, especially those in power. . . to save Great-Britain, likewise to regain. . . Minorca, besides our late possessions in America. . .*—1758#38

RALPH, James.
A critical history of the administration of Sr Robert Walpole, now earl of Orford. . .—1743#29
The history of England: during the reigns of K. William, Q. Anne and K. George I.—1744#37

RANDALL, Joseph. *A brief account of the rise, principles, and discipline of the people call'd Quakers in America, and elsewhere, extracted from a system of geography, lately published.*—1747#22

RANDOLPH, Bernard. *The present state of the Islands in the Archipelago, (or Arches) Sea of Constantinople, and Gulf of Smyrna. . .*—1687#8

RANDOLPH, Edward. *A discourse how to render the plantations on the continent of America, and Islands adjacent; more beneficial. . . to this Kingdom.*—1697#11

RATHBAND, William.
A briefe narration of some church courses held in opinion and practise in the churches lately erected in New England.—1644#14
A most grave, and modest confutation of the errors of the sect commonly called Brownists. . .—1644#15

RAY, John.
Historia plantarum; species hacteus editas aliasque insuper multas naviter inventas et descriptas complectens. . .—1686#4
Methodus plantarum nova. . .—1682#23

Synopsis methodica animalium quadrupedum et serpentini generis...—1693#16

The wisdom of God manifested in the works of the creation...—1691#16

REA, John. *Flora: seu, De florum cultura...*—1665#19

RECK, Philipp G. and BOLTZIUS, John Martin. *An extract of the journals of Mr Commissary Von Reck, who conducted the first Saltzburgers to Georgia; and of the Reverend Mr Bolzius, one of their ministers...*—1734#17

REID, John. *The Scots gard'ner in two parts...*—1683#19

REVEL, James. *The poor unhappy transported felon's sorrowful account of fourteen years transportation, at Virginia in America. In six parts...*—1750#42

REVOLUTION, William. *The real crisis: or, the necessity of giving immediate and powerful succour to the emperor against France...*—1735#17

REYNELL, Carew.
A necessary companion; or the English interest discovered and promoted...—1685#23
The true English interest.—1674#11

REYNOLDS, Richard. *A sermon preached... 16th February 1727...*—1728#13

RICH, Edward Pickering. *A sermon preached... Nov. 29, 1759...*—1759#86

RICH, Robert. *The epistles of Mr Robert Rich to the seven churches...*—1680#9

RICHARDSON, John. *An account of the life of that ancient servant of Jesus Christ, John Richardson...*—1757#36

RIDLEY, Glocester. *A sermon preached... March 20, 1745-6...*—1746#21

RIDPATH, George. *Case of Scots-men residing in England and in the English plantations. Containing an account of the reasons in law, why they...*—1702#24

RIGGE, Ambrose. *A visitation of tender love (once more) from the Lord unto Charles the II.*—1662#13

RIMIUS, Heinrich.
A candid narrative of the rise and progress of the Herrnhuters, commonly called Moravians...—1753#19
The history of the Moravians, from their first settlement at Herrnhaag...—1754#33
A second solemn call on Mr Zinzendorf, otherwise called Count Zinzendorf...—1757#37
A solemn call on Count Zinzendorf, the author and advocate of the sect of Herrnhuters, commonly called Moravians...—1754#34
A supplement to the candid narrative of the rise and progress of the Herrnhuters, commonly called Moravians... in which the political schemes... of their patriarch are disclosed...—1755#43

ROBE, James.
Mr Robe's first letter to the Reverend James Fisher...—1742#36
Mr Robe's fourth letter to the Reverend James Fisher...—1743#31
Mr Robe's second letter to the Reverend James Fisher...—1743#32
Mr Robe's third letter to the Reverend James Fisher...—1743#33

ROBERTS, Lewes.
The merchants mappe of commerce...—1638#16
The treasure of traffike. or a discourse of forraigne trade.—1641#20

ROBERTSON, Robert.
A detection of the state and situation of the present sugar planters of Barbadoes and the Leeward islands...—1732#35
A supplement to the detection of the state and situation of the present sugar planters...—1733#30

ROBERTSON, William. *The situation of the world at the time of Christ's appearance... sermon... January 6, 1755...*—1755#44

ROBINS, Benjamin.
An address to the electors, and other free subjects of Great Britain... In which is contained a particular account of all our negociations with Spain...—1739#61
The Merchant's complaint against Spain... the pretensions of Spain to Georgia...—1738#21
Observations on the present convention with Spain.—1739#62

ROBINSON, Henry.
Briefe considerations concerning the advancement of trade.—1650#10
Certain proposalls in order to the peoples freedome and accommodation in some particulars...—1652#11
England's safety, in trades encrease.—1641#21

ROBINSON, William.
An appendix to... New England judged; being certain writings (never yet printed) of those persons which were there executed...—1661#15
Several epistles given forth by two of the Lord's faithful servants, whom he sent to New-England... William Robinson, William Leddra...—1669#4

ROBSON, Joseph. *An account of six years residence in Hudson's Bay, from 1733 to 1736, and 1744 to 1747...*—1752#15

ROCHE, John. *Moravian heresy, wherein the principal errors of that doctrine, as taught throughout several parts of Europe and America... are proved and refuted.*—1751#31

ROFE, George. *A true believers testimony of the work of true faith...*—1661#16

ROLT, Richard.
An impartial representation of the conduct of the several powers of Europe, engaged in the late general war... To... 1748.—1749#35
A new dictionary of trade and commerce...—1756#68

ROSS, Alexander.
The history of the world: the second part...—1653#15
Pansebeia: or, a view of all religions in the world... throughout Asia, Africa, America, and Europe.—1653#16

ROUS, John.
New-England a degenerate plant. Who having forgot their former sufferings, and lost their ancient tenderness, are now become...—1659#30
The sins of a gainsaying and rebellious people laid before them... Written at the command of the Lord...—1659#31

ROWLANDSON, Mary. *A true history of the captivity and restoration of Mrs Mary Rowlandson, a minister's wife in New England... annexed, a sermon... by Mr. Joseph Rowlandson...*—1682#24

ROYAL HOSPITAL FOR SEAMEN AT GREENWICH. *By the commissioners for collecting and receiving the six pence a month out of seamens wages, for the use of Greenwich Hospital...*—1727#23

RUDD, Sayer.
God's promise; a grand incentive to Christian liberality. A sermon preached at Walmer in Kent, on... 12 of July 1752.—1752#16
A poem on the death of the late Thomas Hollis, Esq., humbly inscribed to Mr John Hollis, brother of the deceased...—1731#31

RUFFHEAD, Owen.
Proposals for carrying on the war with vigour, raising the supplies within the year, and forming a national militia...—1757#38
Reasons why the approaching treaty of peace should be debated in Parliament... In a letter addressed to a great man... occasioned by... a letter addressed to two great men...—1760#83

RUNDLE, Thomas. *A sermon preached... February 17, 1733/4. to recommend the charity for establishing the new colony of Georgia.*—1734#18

RUSSELL, John. *A brief narrative of some considerable passages concerning the first gathering, and further progress of a Church of Christ, in gospel-order...*—1680#10

RUTHERFORD, Samuel.
The divine right of church-government and excommunication...—1646#18
The due right of presbyteries... wherein is examined 1. The way of the church of Christ in New England.—1644#16
A free disputation against pretended liberty of conscience...—1649#6
A survey of the spirituall antichrist.—1648#12
A survey of the Survey of that summe of church discipline, penned by Mr Thomas Hooker, late pastor... in New England...—1658#11

S., N. *A new and further narrative of the state of New-England, being a continued account of the bloudy Indian-war from March till August, 1676...*—1676#17

S., T. *The principles of the leading Quakers truly represented.*—1732#36

SAGEAN, Mathieu. *The original manuscript account of the kingdom of Aacaniba, given by the affidavit of Mathieu Sagean a Frenchman... Englished by Quin Mackenzie...*—1755#45

SAINT LO, George. *England's safety: or, A bridle to the French king...*—1693#17

SALMON, Thomas.
Considerations on the bill for a general naturalization, as it may conduce to the improvement of our manufactures and traffic...—1748#23
A critical essay concerning marriage... to which is added, an historical account of the marriage rites and ceremonies...—1724#20
The modern gazetteer: or, a short view of the several nations of the world...—1746#22
Modern history, or The present state of all nations.—1725#10
A new geographical and historical grammar...—1749#36
The universal traveller: or, a compleat description of the several nations of the world...—1752#18

SANDERSON, William. *Aulicus coquinariae; or Vindication, in answer to a pamphlet...*—1650#11

SANDYS, George.
Ovid's Metamorphosis Englished by G. S...—1626#2
A paraphrase upon the Psalmes of David...—1636#5

SAVAGE, Richard. *Of publick spirit in regard to publick works. An epistle to Frederick, Prince of Wales.*—1737#23

SAVAGE, Thomas. *An account of the late action of the New-Englanders, under... Sir William Phips, against the French at Canada...*—1691#18

SAVARY DES BRUSLONS, Jacques. *The universal dictionary of trade and commerce. Translated from the French... by Malachy Postlethwayt.*—1751#32

SCOT, Thomas. *Phylomythie or phylomythologie... Second edition, much inlarged.*—1622#20

SCOTLAND.
CHURCH OF SCOTLAND. GENERAL ASSEMBLY.
Edinburgh, 20 May 1731. R.D.B. [Reverend and Dear Brethren]...—1731#32
Edinburgh, November 14, 1728. R.D.B. [Reverend and Dear Brethren]...—1728#14
PARLIAMENT.
The acts made in the first parliament of our... soveraigne Charles... at Edinburgh...—1633#5
PRIVY COUNCIL.
Proclamation completing number of Nova Scotia baronets.—1625#12
Proclamation discharging transporting of persons to the plantations of forraigners... [27 December 1698].—1698#16
Proclamation on institution of Nova Scotia baronets.—1624#10

SCOTT, George.
A brief advertisment, concerning East-New-Jersey, in America.—1685#24
The model of the government of the province of East-New-Jersey in America.—1685#25

SCOTT, Thomas.
The Belgicke pismire.—1623#4
An experimentall discoverie of Spanish practises or the counsell of a well-wishing soldier.—1623#5
A relation of some speciall points concerning the state of Holland. . .—1621#4

SCOTT, Thomas.
Great Britain's danger and remedy. Represented in a discourse. . . on the day appointed for a general fast, February the 11th, 1757.—1757#39
The reasonableness, pleasure and benefit of national thanksgiving. A sermon preached Nov. 29, 1759 at Ipswich. . . Suffolk. . .—1759#87

SEAMAN, Lazurus. *The DIATRIBE proved to be PARA-DIATRIBE, Or A Vindication of the judgement of Reformed Churches. . .*—1647#14

SECKER, Thomas.
An extract out of the bishop of Oxford's sermon before the Society for propagating the gospel in foreign parts. The state of our colonies.—1741#31
A sermon preached. . . Feb. 20, 1740–1. . .—1741#32

SELDEN, John. *Mare clausum, seu De dominio maris libri duo. . .*—1635#3

SELLER, John.
An almanack for the provinces of Virginia and Maryland. . .—1685#26
Atlas minimus, or a book of geography.—1679#4
A mapp of New Jersey, in America. . . The description of the province of West-Jersey. . . As also, Proposals to such as desire to have any property there.—1677#16
New-England almanack. . . for xxx. years.—1685#27
A new systeme of geography. . .—1685#28

SETTLE, Elkanah(?). *A pindaric poem on the propagation of the gospel in foreign parts.*—1711#28

SEWALL, Joseph. *Christ victorious over the powers of darkness. . . A sermon preached in Boston, December 12, 1733.*—1734#20

SEWARD, William. *Journal of a voyage from Savannah to Philadelphia, and from Philadelphia to England. . .*—1740#33

SEWEL, William. *The history of the rise, increase and progress of the people called Quakers. . . written originally in low-Dutch. . . now revised. . .*—1722#27

SHARP, John.
De rebus liturgicis oratio pro gradu doctoratûs in S. S. theologia. . . A Io. Sharp ecclesiae Anglicanae apud Americanos prebytero.—1714#18
A sermon preached at Trinity-Church in New-York. . . August 13, 1706. At the funeral of the right honourable Katherine Lady Cornbury. . .—1706#16

SHARPE, Edward. *England's royall fishing revived.*—1630#7

SHEBBEARE, John.
An answer to a pamphlet called, The conduct of the ministry impartially examined.—1756#70
A fifth letter to the people of England, on the subversion of the constitution. . .—1757#43
A fourth letter to the people of England on the conduct of the M——rs. . . since the first differences on the Ohio. . .—1756#71
The history of the excellence and decline of the constitution, religion, laws. . . of the Sumatrans. . .—1760#84
Letter to his grace the D - of N-e on the duty he owes himself, his king, his country. . .—1757#42
Letter to the people of England. Letter VII.—1758#42
Letter to the people of England, on the necessity of putting an immediate end to the war; and the means of obtaining an advantageous peace.—1760#85
Letter to the people of England, on the present situation and conduct of national affairs. Letter I.—1755#47
Letter to the people of England upon the militia, continental connections, neutralities and secret expeditions. . .—1757#40
Lydia, or Filial Piety: a novel. . .—1755#48
A prophetic fragment of a future chronicle. By the author of the Four Letters to the People of England.—1756#72
A second letter to the people of England, on foreign subsidies, subsidiary armies, and their consequences. . .—1755#49
A sixth letter to the people of England, on the progress of the national ruin. . .—1757#41
A third letter to the people of England on liberty, taxes, and the application of public money. . .—1756#73
See also ANGELONI, Battista

SHELVOCKE, George. *A voyage round the world. . . in the years 1719, 20, 21, 22 in the Speedwell of London. . .*—1726#15

SHEPARD, Thomas.
Certain select cases resolved. Specially, tending to the right ordering of the heart, that we may comfortably walk with God in our general and particular callings.—1648#13
The clear sun-shine of the Gospel breaking forth upon the Indians in New England. . .—1648#14
The first principles of the oracles of God. . .—1648#15
Meditations and spiritual experiences of Mr T. Shepard. . .—1749#37
New Englands lamentations for old Englands present errours and divisions. . .—1645#16
The parable of the ten virgins opened and applied: being the substance of divers sermons on Matth. 25. 1, —— 13. . .—1660#25
The sincere convert: discovering the small numbers of true believers; and the great difficulty of saving-conversion.—1640#6
The sound beleever. Or, a treatise of evangelicall conversion.—1645#17
Subjection to Christ in all his ordinances and appointments, the best means to preserve our liberty. . .—1652#12
Theses Sabbaticae. Or, The doctrine of the Sabbath.—1649#7
A treatise of liturgies. . . in answer to. . . Mr. John Ball. . .—1653#17

See also ALLIN, John.

SHERLOCK, Thomas. *Letter from the Lord Bishop of London, to the clergy and people...*—1750#45

Letter from the Lord Bishop of Sarum, to the clergy of his diocese.—1742#38

A sermon preached... the 17th of February, 1715.—1716#7

SHINKIN ap SHONE [psued]. *The honest Welch-cobler, for her do scorne to call her selfe the simple Welch-cobler...*—1647#15

SHIRLEY, John. *The life of the valiant and learned Sir Walter Raleigh, Knight... London*—1677#17

SHIRLEY, William. *Letter from William Shirley... to... the Duke of Newcastle: with a journal of the siege of Louisbourg...*—1746#23

Memoirs of the principal transactions of the last war between the English and the French in North America... in 1744... to...—1757#44

SHORT, Thomas. *Medicina Britannica; or, a treatise on such physical plants, as are generally to be found in... Great Britain...*—1746#24

SHRIGLEY, Nathaniel. *A true relation of Virginia and Mary-land; with the commodities therein, which in part the author saw, the rest he had from credible persons... anno 1669.*—1669#5

SIBELIUS, Caspar. *Of the conversion of five thousand and nine hundred East Indians... with a post-script of the Gospel's good successe also amongst the West-Indians, in New-England...*—1650#12

SIDNEY, Algernon. *Discourses concerning government...*—1698#18

SIKES, George. *The life and death of Sir Henry Vane, Kt. Or, a short narrative of the main passages of his earthly pilgrimage...*—1662#15

SIMMS, Henry. *The life of Henry Simms, alias Young gentleman Harry... to his death at Tyburn... June 17, 1747... robberies... and extraordinary adventures... at home and abroad...*—1747#25

SLOANE, Hans. *A voyage to the islands... with some relations concerning the neighbouring continent and islands of America...*—1707#14

SMALBROKE, Richard. *A sermon preached... February 16, 1732...*—1733#32

SMITH, Alexander. *The third volume of the Compleat History of the lives and robberies of the most notorious high-way men...*—1720#35

SMITH, Humphry. *A collection of the several writings... of Humphrey Smith, who dyed... 4th day of the 3d moneth... 1663...*—1683#20

New-England's pretended Christians, who contrary to Christ, have destroyed the lives of men.—1660#26

SMITH, James. *The misery of ignorant and unconverted sinners. A sermon preached in the High Church of Edinburgh, Monday, January 1. 1733...*—1733#33

SMITH, John. *Advertisements for the unexperienced planters of New-England, or any where. Or, the path-way to experience to erect a plantation*—1631#3

The generall historie of Virginia, New-England, and the Summer Isles...—1624#11

The generall history of Virginia, the Somer Iles, and New England, with the names of the adventurers, and their adventures...—1623#6

New Englands trials. Declaring the successe of 80 ships employed thither within these eight yeares... With the present estate...—1622#21

A sea grammar, with the plaine exposition of Smith's Accidence for young seamen enlarged...—1627#6

The true travels, adventures, and observations of Captaine John Smith, in Europe, Asia, Affrika, and America, from anno Domini 1593. to 1629...—1630#8

SMITH, Josiah. *The character, preaching, etc. of the Reverend Mr George Whitefield impartially represented and supported...*—1741#34

Four letters etc. taken from the London Weekly History of the progress of the gospel; with a large postcript vindicating the late revival and the promoters.—1743#36

SMITH, Samuel. *Publick spirit, illustrated in the life and designs of the Reverend Thomas Bray D. D.*—1746#25

A sermon preach'd before the Trustees for... Georgia... and Associates of... Bray... February 23, 1730–1...—1733#34

SMITH, Thomas. *An affidavit taken and sworn at York... the 14th. day of Feb: 1701. Setting forth... the hardships of several merchants in the said...*—1701#37

England's danger by Indian manufactures.—1700#33

SMITH, Thomas. *The terrible calamities that are occasioned by war... a sermon... November the 29th, 1759...*—1760#87

SMITH, Wavell. *Observations occasion'd by reading a pamphlet, intitled, A discourse concerning the currencies of the British plantations in America. In a letter to ———.*—1741#35

SMITH, William. *To the King's most excellent majesty... an essay for recovery of trade.*—1661#17

SMITH, William (1727–1803). *A brief state of the province of Pennsylvania, in which the conduct of their assemblies... is... examined, and the true cause of...*—1755#51

A brief view of the conduct of Pennsylvania, for the year 1755; so far as it affected the general service of the British colonies...—1756#74

SMITH, WILLIAM.

Discourses on several public occasions during the war in America, preached chiefly with a view to explaining the importance...—1759#90

Letter to a gentleman in London, to his friend in Pennsylvania; with a satire... upon... Quakers...—1756#75

A sermon preached in Christ-Church, Philadelphia before the Provincial Grand Master... 24th June 1755...—1755#52

Some account of the North-America Indians... To which are added Indian Miscellanies... by a learned and ingenious gentleman of the province of Pennsylvania...—1754#35

The speech of a Creek-Indians [sic], against the immoderate use of spirituous liquors. Delivered in a national assembly of the Creeks...—1754#36

SMITH, William (1728–1793).

The history of the province of New York, from the first discovery to the year MDCCXXXII.—1757#45

SMITHSON, Isaac.
A sermon occasioned by the declaration of war against France. Preached at Harleston, May the 23d, 1756.—1756#76

SNELGRAVE, William.
A new account of some parts of Guinea, and the slave-trade...—1734#21

SOCIETY FOR PROMOTING CHRISTIAN KNOWLEDGE.

An account of the Society for promoting Christian Knowledge.—1738#22

The gentlemen who at the request of the Society... are trustees for... Saltzburg Protestants... appointed to transport them to Georgia...—1734#22

Society for promoting Christian knowledge. This presents you by order of the Society... with the continuation of the account of receipts...—1736#17

The Society for promoting Christian knowledge and the members chosen by them to be trustees for the poor Saltzburgers... to go to Georgia...—1734#23

SOCIETY FOR THE ENCOURAGEMENT OF ARTS.

Premiums by the Society, established at London, for the encouragement of arts, manufactures and commerce...—1758#43

Rules and orders of the Society, established at London...—1758#44

SOCIETY FOR THE PROPAGATION OF THE GOSPEL.

An abstract of the Charter granted to the Society for the Propagation of the Gospel in Foreign Parts; with a short account of what...—1702#25

An abstract of the proceedings of the Society for the Propagation of the Gospel... 1715.—1716#8

An account of the propagation of the gospel in foreign parts. Continued to... 1705...—1705#18

An account of the propagation of the gospel in foreign parts, what the Society hath done... in her majesty's plantations, colonies and factories...—1704#25

An account of the Society for Propagating the gospel in foreign parts... with their proceedings and success, and hopes of continual progress...—1706#17

A collection of papers...—1741#36

A collection of papers, printed by order... viz. the Charter, the request, etc...—1706#18

Instructions for the clergy employed by the Society.—1704#26

Instructions from the Society... to their missionaries in North-America.—1756#77

The method used by the Society to encourage the distribution of good books...—1727#24

The request of the Society for the Propagation of the Gospel... concerning fit ministers to be sent abroad for that good purpose.—1702#26

A second letter from a member of the Society for the Propagation of the Gospel...—1713#12

A third letter from a member of the Society.—1718#20

SOCIETY IN SCOTLAND FOR PROPAGATING CHRISTIAN KNOWLEDGE.

An abridgement of the statutes and rules of the Society...—1732#37

An account of the rise, constitution, and management of the Society...—1714#19

A short state of the Society...—1732#38

The state of the Society in Scotland, for Propagating Christian Knowledge, anno 1729. Published by order of the general meeting of the foresaid society.—1729#24

State of the Society in Scotland for propagating Christian knowledge... together with some account of this Society's missionaries for converting the native Indians of America.—1741#37

A succinct view of the Society in Scotland for propagating Christian knowledge...—1738#23

SOCIETY OF FRIENDS.

Epistles from the yearly meeting of the people called Quakers, held in London, to the quarterly and monthly meetings in Great...—1760#88

From our yearly meeting in London... the 4th to the 9th day of the 6th month, 1759. To our Friends and brethren at their ensuing...—1759#92

From our yearly-meeting, held at Philadelphia, for Pennsylvania, and New Jersey, from the 17th to the 21st day of the 7th...—1737#24

From our yearly meeting in London... 1757. To our friends and brethren... New Jersey and Pennsylvania...—1757#46

To the quarterly and monthly meetings of Friends, in Great Britain, Ireland, and America... From the meeting for sufferings in London, the sixth day of the seventh month, 1751...—1751#33

To the quarterly and monthly meetings of Friends in Pennsylvania and elsewhere in America...—1754#37

SOMERS, Nathan.
Proposals for clearing land in Carolina, Pennsylvania, East Jersey, West Jersey: or any other parts of America... August 9, 1682.—1682#25

SOUTH CAROLINA.
ASSEMBLY. COMMITTEE OF BOTH HOUSES.
Appendix to the report of the Committee of both houses of Assembly... appointed to enquire into the causes of the disappointment...—1743#37

The report of the committee of both houses of Assembly of the province of South Carolina, appointed to enquire into... the late expedition against St. Augustine...—1743#38

PROPRIETORS, GOVERNOR AND COUNCIL.
An account of the fair and impartial proceedings of the Lords Proprietors, governour and council of... South Carolina, in answer to...—1706#19

SPARKE, Michael. *Greevous grones for the poore. Done by a well-wisher, who wisheth, that the poore of England might be so provided for, as none should neede to go a begging within this realme...—1621#5*

SPEED, John.
An epitome of Mr. J. Speed's theatre of the empire...—1676#18
A prospect of the most famous parts of the world. Together with that large theater of Great Brittaines empire—1627#7

SPENCER, James. *An essay on the large common American aloe, with a particular account of that which is now in bloom in the gardens of George Montgomerie, Esq;...—1759#96*

SPRAT, Thomas. *Observations on Monsieur de Sorbier's voyage into England...—1665#20*

SPURRIER, Caleb. *Copy of a letter from Mr. Caleb Spurrier to his correspondent in Cornwall.—1721#19*

SQUIRE, Samuel. *An historical essay upon the ballance of civil power in England.—1748#27*

ST. ANDREWS CLUB, CHARLES-TOWN, SOUTH CAROLINA. *Rules of the St. Andrew's Club at Charles-Town, in South Carolina.—1750#43*

STAFFORD, Robert. *A geographicall and anthologicall description of all the empires...—1634#6*

STANHOPE, George. *The early conversion of islanders, a wise expedient for propagating Christianity. A sermon preached... 19th of Feb. 1713–14...—1714#20*

STANHOPE, Philip Dormer. *An apology for a late resignation in a letter from an English gentleman to... friend at the Hague.—1748#28*

STANLEY, William. *A sermon preached... February 20th, 1707/8... SEE Number: 1708#16*

STEBBING, Henry. *A sermon preached... February 19, 1741/2...—1742#40*

STEERE, Richard. *The history of the Babylonish cabal; or the intrigues... of the Daniel-Catchers. In a poem.—1682#26*

STENNET, Joseph.
Rabshakeh's retreat. A sermon preached... December 18, 1745.—1745#35

A sermon preached at Little-Wild-Street on Tuesday, April 25, 1749. Being the day... for a general thanksgiving... for the peace.—1749#41

STEPHENS, Thomas. fl. 1742.
An account shewing what money has been received by the Trustees for the use of the colony of Georgia.—1742#41
A brief account of the causes that have retarded the progress of the colony of Georgia... attested upon oath. Being a proper contrast...—1743#39
The hard case of the distressed people of Georgia.—1742#42

STEPHENS, Thomas d. 1780.
The method and plain process for making pot-ash, equal if not superior to the best foreign pot-ash...—1755#55
The rise and fall of pot-ash in America, addressed to the Right Honourable the Earl of Halifax.—1758#45

STEPHENS, Thomas. fl. 1759. *The castle builders: or, The history of William Stephens of the Isle of Wight, Esq; lately deceased. A political novel...—1759#96*

STEPHENS, William.
Journal of the proceedings in Georgia, beginning October 20, 1737... A state of the province, as attested on oath in the court of Savannah, November 10, 1740...—1742#43
Journal received February 4, 1741. By the Trustees for establishing the colony of Georgia... commencing September 22, 1741, and ending October 28 following.—1742#44
A state of the province of Georgia, attested upon oath... in the court of Savannah, Nov. 10, 1740.—1742#45

STEPHENSON, Marmaduke. *A call from death to life, and out of the dark wayes and worships of the world...—1659#32*

STEPNEY, George. *An essay upon the present interest of England...—1701#40*

STERLING, James.
An epistle to the Hon. Arthur Dobbs, esq; in Europe. From a clergyman in America...—1752#22
Zeal against the enemies of our country pathetically recommended. In a... sermon preached before... governor of Maryland...—1755#56

STEUART, Adam.
An answer to a libell intituled, A coole conference...—1644#17
The second part of the duply to M. S. alias Two brethren...—1644#18
Some observations and annotations upon the Apologeticall narration, submitted to Parliament...—1643#17
Zerubbabel to Sanballat and Tobiah: or, the first part of the duply to M. S. alias Two Brethren... concerning Independents...—1645#18

STEVENS, John. *A new collection of voyages and travels... None of them before ever printed...—1711#29*

STILLINGFLEET, Edward. *Origines sacrae: or, A rational account of the grounds of the Christian faith.—1662#16*

STITH, William. *The history of the first discovery and settlement of Virginia...—1753#21*

STOAKES, John. *A great victory obtained by the English against Dutch. . . Also, the number of ships. . . richly laden from the east-Indies, the Straights, Virginia and the Barbadoes.*—1652#13

STODDARD, Solomon. *The doctrine of instituted churches explained and proved from the word of God. . .*—1700#34

STONE, George. *A sermon preached in Christ-Church, Dublin; on Thursday, Nov. 29, 1759. . .*—1759#98

STONE, Samuel. *A congregational church is a catholike visible church. . .*—1652#14

STORY, Thomas.
Journal of the life of Thomas Story containing an account of his. . . embracing the principles. . . held by the Quakers. . .—1747#26

A word to the well-inclined of all persuasions. Together with a copy of a letter from William Penn to George Keith. . .—1698#19

STOUGHTON, William. *A narrative of the proceedings of Sir E. Androsse printed in the year 1691. . .*—1691#20

STOW, John. *The annales. . . of England. . . Continued unto 1631. By Edmund Howes*—1631#4

STRATIOTICUS. *A scheme for the general good of the nation. . . and for the effectual security of our commerce and possessions abroad.*—1760#90

STRONG, Leonard. *Babylon's fall in Maryland; a fair warning to Lord Baltimore. Or, a relation of an assault made by divers Papists. . . against the Protestants. . .*—1655#20

STUBBE, Henry.
A further justification of the present war against the United Netherlands. . .—1673#11

A justification of the present war against the United Netherlands. . .—1672#7

STUDENT IN POLITICS. *Proposals to the legislature, for preventing the frequent execution and exportations of convicts. . .*—1754#38

STUKELEY, William. *The philosophy of earthquakes, natural and religious.*—1750#49

SUTHERLAND, Patrick. *From the London Gazette, of December 25, 1742. An account of the late invasion of Georgia, drawn out by Lieutenant P. S. . .*—1743#40

SUTHERLAND, William. *Britain's glory: or, ship-building unvail'd.*—1717#17

SWAN, John. *Speculum mundi. or A glasse representing the face of the world.*—1635#4

SWIFT, Jonathan. *The conduct of the allies, and of the late ministry, in beginning and carrying on the present war*—1711#30

SYLVESTRE DUFOUR, Philippe. *Moral instructions of a father to his son, upon his departure for a long voyage. . .*—1683#21

SYMSON, Matthias. *Enchiridion geographicum. Or, A manual of geography. Being a description of all the empires, kingdoms, and dominions of the earth.*—1704#27

TAGG, Tommy. *A collection of pretty poems for the amusement of children three foot high. By Tommy Tagg, Esq; The fifty seventh edition, adorned with above sixty cuts.*—1760#91

TAILFER, Patrick. *A true and historical narrative of the colony of Georgia in America, from the first settlement thereof until this present present period. . .*—1741#39

T[ANNER]., R[obert]. *A brief treatise of the use of the globe celestiall and terrestiall. . .*—1647#16

TATE, Robert. *A practical treatise upon several different and useful subjects. . . IV. A rational way for the promulgation of the gospel in America. . .*—1732#41

TATHAM, John. *London's triumphs, celebrated the nine and twentieth day of. . . October, 1657. . .*—1657#13

TAYLER, Silvanus. *Common-good: or, the improvement of commons, forests, and chases, by inclosure. . .*—1652#15

TAYLOR, John. *An account of some of the labours, exercises, travels and perils by sea and land, of John Taylor, of York. . .*—1710#22

TAYLOR, John.
All the workes of John Taylor the Water-poet. . .—1630#9
The complaint of M. Tenter-hooke the projector—1641#22
The devil turn'd Round-head: or, Pluto become a Brownist—1642#13
The impartialiste satyre. . .—1652#16
The Kings most excellent majesties wellcome to his own house. . .—1647#17
Letter sent to London from a spie at Oxford.—1643#18

TAYLOR, John. *A sermon preached before the Hon. House of Commons. . . 11th day of February 1757. . .*—1757#47

TAYLOR, Timothy.
See EATON, Samuel.

TAYLOUR, Joseph. *By Captain Joseph Taylour, commander of her majesty's ship Litchfield, and commander in chief of all her majesty's forces in Newfoundland. . .*—1711#31

TEMPLE, William. *A vindication of commerce and the arts; proving that they are the source of the greatness. . . of a state. . .*—1758#46

TENISON, Thomas. *An argument for union, taken from the true interest of those dissenters in England, who profess, and call themselves Protestants.*—1683#22

TENNENT, Gilbert.
Four letters from Mr. Gilbert Tennent, the Secretary of New-England, and Dr. Colman, concerning the great success of the gospel abroad.—1741#40

Some account of the principles of the Moravians; chiefly collected from several conversations with Count Zinzendorf; and from some sermons preached by him. . .—1743#41

To the worthy and generous friends of religion and learning; the petition of Gilbert Tennent and Samuel Davies, in the name of the. . .—1754#39

TENNENT, Gilbert and DAVIES, Samuel. *A general account of the rise and state of the College, lately established in the province of New-Jersey, in America... Originally...*—1754#40

TENNENT, John, M. D.
A brief account of the case of John Tennent, M. D.—1742#46
Detection of a conspiracy to suppress a general good in physic, and to promote error...—1743#42
An epistle to Dr. Richard Mead concerning the epidemical diseases of Virginia, particularly, a pleurisy and peripneumony, wherein...—1738#27
Physical disquisitions: demonstrating the real causes of the blood's morbid rarefaction and stagnation...—1745#36
Physical enquiries: discovering the mode of translation in the constitutions of northern inhabitants, on going to, and for some time after arriving in southern climates...—1742#47
Truth stifled, and an appeal to the genius of the ancient Romans. Being the case of Dr John Tennent, with respect to his free publication...—1741#42

TENNENT, John (1706–1732). *The nature of regeneration opened, and absolute necessity demonstrated... a sermon... with expostulatory address... by G. Tennent...*—1741#41

THOMAS, Dalby. *An historical account of the rise and growth of the West-Indies collonies.*—1690#24

THOMAS, Gabriel. *An historical and geographical account of the province and country of Pensilvania; and of West-New-Jersey in America..*—1698#20

THOMAS, John (1691–1766).
A sermon preached... February 20, 1746...—1747#27
A sermon preached... Thursday May the 8th 1740...—1740#34

THOMAS, John. (1696–1781). *A sermon preached... February 15, 1750...*—1751#34

THOMPSON, Charles. *An enquiry into the causes of the alienation of the Delaware and and Shawanese Indians from the British interest... Together with the remarkable journal of Charles Frederic Post...*—1759#99

THOMPSON, John, first baron Haversham. *The Lord Haversham's speech in the House of Peers, on Thursday, November 23, 1704.*—1704#28

THOMPSON, Thomas. *Considerations on the trade to New-foundland.*—1711#32

THOMPSON, Thomas. (1632–1704)
A farewel epistle, by way of exhortation to Friends... On his departure to America...—1715#21
A salutation of love, and tender invitation, to all people; but more especially to the inhabitants of New-England, Road-Island and Long- Island, to come unto Shiloh...—1713#13

THOMPSON, Thomas. (1708–1773)
An account of two missionary voyages by appointment of the Society for the Propagation of the Gospel in Foreign Parts. The one to...—1758#47

Letter from New Jersey, in America, giving some account... of that province. By a gentleman late of Christ's College, Cambridge.—1756#78

THOMSON, James. *The works of Mr. Thomson. Volume the second. Containing Liberty: a poem in five parts.*—1738#28

THORESBY, Ralph. *The excellency and advantage of doing good... a sermon preached... to which is annexe'd a letter of Samuel Lloyd... concerning the nature and goodness of the Georgia silk.*—1748#30

THORNTON, Bonnell. *City Latin; or, Critical and political remarks...*—1760#92

THORNTON, William. *The counterpoise. Being thoughts on a militia and a standing army...*—1752#23

THOROWGOOD, Thomas.
Jewes in America, or, Probabilities that the Americans are of that race...—1650#13
Vindiciae Judaeorum, or a true account of the Jews...—1666#6

THUMB, Thomas. *Proposals for printing by subscription, the history of the publick life and distinguished actions of Vice-Admiral Sir Thomas Brazen...*—1760#94

THURLOW, Edward. *A refutation of the letter to an honble. brigadier- general, commander of His Majesty's forces in Canada. By an officer.*—1760#95

TICKELL, Thomas. *A poem, to his excellency the Lord Privy-Seal, on the prospect of peace.*—1713#14

TIPTON, William. *Case of William Tipton...*—1717#18

TOLAND, John. *The militia reform'd...*—1698#21

TOMKINS, John. *Piety promoted, in a collection of dying sayings of many of the people called Quakers. With a brief account of some of their labours in the Gospel, and sufferings...*—1701#41

TOMPSON, Benjamin.
New England's tears for her present miseries: or, A late and true relation of the calamities of New-England since April last past...—1676#19
Sad and deplorable newes from New England...—1676#20

TOWGOOD, Micaiah.
Britons invited to rejoice... sermon preached at Exeter, August the 27th, 1758... after receiving the account of the taking of the islands of Cape- Breton and St. John.—1758#48
The dissenting gentleman's answer to the Reverend Mr White's three letters.—1746#26
The dissenting gentleman's second letter to the Reverend Mr White.—1747#28

TOWNLEY, James. *A sermon preached... on Thursday, November 29, 1759...*—1759#100

TOWNSHEND, George. *Extract of a letter from Vice-Admiral Townshend at Jamaica, to Mr Cleveland, dated the 22d of March 1757.*—1757#48

TRADESCANT, John. *Musaeum tradescantianum: or, A collection of Rarities preserved at South-Lambeth neer London*—1656#11

TRELAWNY, Jonathan. *Letter from the Lord Bishop of Winchester, to his clergy within the bills of mortality...*—1711#33

TRENCHARD, John.
Cato's letters...—1723#11
A short history of standing armies....—1698#22

TREVOR, Richard. *A sermon preached... Feb. 16, 1749...*—1750#50

TRIBBECHOV, Johann. *The Christian traveller: A farewel-sermon preached... on the 20th of January, 1710. To the Palatines. Before their going out of England...*—1710#23

TRIMNELL, Charles. *A sermon preached... Friday the 17th of February, 1709/10....*—1710#24

TROTT, Nicholas.
The laws of the British plantations in America, relating to the church and clergy, religion and learning. Collected in one volume.—1721#21
Mafteah leshon hakodesh clavis linguae sanctae...—1721#22

TRUE ANTIGALLIGAN. *Britain strike home. A poem humbly inscribed to every Briton...*—1756#80

TRUE BRITON. *French policy defeated. Being an account of all the proceedings of the French, against the inhabitants of the British colonies...*—1755#57

TRYON, Thomas.
The countryman's companion...—1684#10
Englands grandeur, and way to get wealth; or, promotion of trade made easy...—1699#18
The planter's speech to his neighbors and country-men of Pennsylvania, East and West-Jersey, and to all such as have transported themselves into new colonies...—1684#11
Some general considerations offered, relating to our present trade.—1698#23
Tryon's letters, domestic and foreign to several persons of quality...—1700#36

TUCKER, Josiah.
A brief essay on the advantages and disadvantages which respectively attend France and Great Britain, with regard to trade...—1749#43
Case of the importation of bar-iron, from our own colonies of North America... recommended to... Parliament, by the iron manufacturers of Great Britain.—1756#81
The elements of commerce, and the theory of taxes...—1755#58
The important question concerning invasions, a sea war, raising the militia... impartially stated...—1755#59
The life and particular proceedings of George Whitefield... to his embarking for Pensilvania...—1739#66
Reflections on the expediency of a law for the naturalization of foreign protestants. In two parts.—1751#35

TURELL, Ebenezer. *Memoirs of the life and death of... Mrs Jane Turell, who died at Medford, March 26, 1735... to which is added two sermons... by... B. Colman, D. D.*—1741#46

TURNER, William. *A compleat history of the most remarkable providences, both of judgement and mercy, which have hapned [sic] in this present age...*—1697#12

TWISSE, William. *A treatise of Mr Cottons... concerning predestination...*—1646#19

TYSON, Edward. *Carigueya, seu Marsupiale Americanum, or the Anatomy of an Opossum, dissected at Gresham-college.*—1698#25

UNDERHILL, John. *Newes from America; or A new and experimentall discoverie of New England; containing, a true relation of their war-like proceedings... with a figure of the Indian fort, or palizado...*—1638#17

UNDERHILL, Thomas. *Hell broke loose: or an history of the Quakers both old and new.*—1660#28

UNITED BRETHREN IN CHRIST. *Case of the deputies of the Moravian Brethren.*—1749#44

UNITED PROVINCES. STATES GENERAL.
Letters patent graunted by the states of the United Netherlands Provinces, to the West Indian company of merchants...—1621#8
Orders and articles granted by the... States General of the United Provinces, concerning the erecting of a West India Companie...—1621#7

URING, Nathaniel. *A history of the voyages and travels of Capt. Nathaniel Uring...*—1726#16

VANDERLINT, Jacob. *Money answers all things; or, an essay to make money sufficiently plentiful...*—1734#24

VANE, Henry. *A healing question propounded and resolved... in order to love and union amongst the honest party...*—1656#12

VAREN, Bernhard. *A compleat system of general geography...*—1733#36

VAUGHAN, William.
Cambrensium Caroleia...—1625#13
The church militant, historically continued.—1640#7
The golden fleece divided into three parts... the errours of religion, the vices and decayes of the kingdome... the wayes to get wealth, and to restore trading.—1626#3
The Newlanders cure. As well of those violent sicknesses... as also by a cheape and newfound dyet, to preserve the body sound and free from all diseases...—1630#10

VENEGAS, Miguel. *A natural and civil history of California:... translated from the original Spanish...*—1759#101

VERNON, Edward.
Considerations upon the white herring and cod fisheries...—1749#45
Original letters to an honest sailor...—1746#27
Original paprrs [sic] relating to the expedition to Carthagena...—1744#39

VINCENT, Philip. *A true relation of the late battell fought in New England, between the English, and the salvages: with the present state of things there.*—1637#7

VIRGINIA.
  ASSEMBLY.
  Acts of Assembly, passed in the colony of Virginia, from 1622, to 1715. Volume I.—1727#25
  COMPANY.
  The inconveniencies that have happened to some persons that have transported themselves from England to Virginia, without provisions necessary to sustaine themselves...—1622#22
  A note of the shipping, men, and provisions, sent and provided for Virginia, by... Earle of Southampton and the Company, this yeare, 1620.—1621#9
  A note of the shipping, men, and provisions, sent and provided for Virginia, by... Earle of Southampton, and the Company, and other private adventurers, in the yeere 1621...—1622#23

VOKINS, Joan. *Gods mighty power magnified: as manifested... in his faithful handmaid Joan Vokins...*—1691#22

VOLTAIRE, François Marie Arouet de. *Letters concerning the English Nation...*—1733#37

VOLUNTEER IN THE BRITISH SERVICE. *Genuine letters from a volunteer, in the British service, at Quebec.*—1760#98

VOSSIUS, Isaac. *A treatise concerning the motion of the seas...*—1677#20

W., J. *Letter from a gentleman in Nova-Scotia, to a person of distinction on the continent. Describing the present state of government in that colony...*—1756#84

W., J. *Letter from New-England concerning their customs, manners and religion. Written upon occasion of a report about a Quo Warranto brought against the government.*—1682#28

WADDINGTON, Edward. *A sermon preached... Friday the 17th of February, 1720...*—1721#23

WAGSTAFFE, William. *Letter to Dr Freind; showing the danger and uncertainty of inoculating the small pox.*—1722#28

WAKELY, Andrew. *The mariner's compass rectified...*—1665#21

WALCOT, James. *The new pilgrim's progress; or, the pious Indian convert... Together with a narrative of his... travels among the savage Indians for their conversion...*—1748#31

WALDO, Samuel. *Samuel Waldo - appellant. Hannah Fayrweather, widow and John Fayrweather, executors, respondents. The respondents case. To be heard... 10th of December, 1734.*—1734#25

WALKER, Clement. *The history of Independency...*—1648#16

WALKER, Hovenden. *Journal: or full account of the late expedition to Canada. With an appendix...*—1720#39

WALKER, Robert. *A short account of the rise, progress, and present state of the Society in Scotland for propagating Christian knowledge. With a sermon prefix'd to it; preached... Monday January 4. 1748...*—1748#32

WALLACE, George. *A system of the principles of the laws of Scotland...*—1760#100

WALLACE, Robert.
A dissertation on the numbers of mankind in antient and modern times: in which the superior populousness of antiquity is maintained...—1753#22
Ignorance and superstition a source of violence and cruelty, and in particular the cause of the present rebellion...—1746#28

WALLIN, Benjamin. *The joyful sacrifice of a prosperous nation. A sermon preached at the meeting-house near Maze Pond, Southwark... November 29, 1759...*—1760#101

WALPOLE, Horatio.
The Convention vindicated from the misrepresentations of the enemies of our peace.—1739#68
The grand question, whether war or no war with Spain, impartially considered: in defence of the present measures against those that delight in war...—1739#69

WARD, Edward.
The second volume of the writings of the author of the London Spy.—1703#11
A trip to New-England. With a character of the country and people, both English and Indians.—1699#19

WARD, Nathaniel.
The simple cobler of Aggawam in America. Willing to help 'mend his native country...—1647#18
A word to Mr. Peters, and two words for the Parliament and Kingdom. Or, an answer to a scandalous pamphlet, entituled, A word for the armie...—1647#19

WARNE, Jonathan. *The spirit of the martyrs revived in the doctrines of the Reverend George Whitefield, and the judicious and faithful methodists... Part I.*—1740#36

WARREN, William. *Whereas by Her Majesties directions, a monthly correspondence is settled, between Great Britain, and Her Majesties dominions on the mainland of America.*—1710#25

WASHINGTON, George. *Journal of Major George Washington, sent by... Robert Dinwiddie... lieutenant-governor of Virginia, to the commandant of the French forces on the Ohio... with a new map...*—1754#41

WATERHOUSE, Edward. *A declaration of the state of the colony and affaires in Virginia. With a relation of the barbarous massacre in the time of peace...*—1622#24

WATTS, George. *A sermon preached before the Trustees... Thursday, March 18. 1735...*—1736#18

WATTS, Isaac.
A caveat against infidelity.—1729#25
The knowledge of the heavens and the earth made easy.—1726#17
A new essay on civil power in things sacred.—1739#70

WATTS, Robert. *The duty and manner of propagating the gospel shewn in a sermon... on requiring a collection to be made for the use of the Society for propagating the Gospel in Foreign Parts.*—1711#34

WAUGH, John. *A sermon... preached... the 15th February, 1722.*—1723#12

WEBB, Daniel. *An essay presented; or a method humbly proposed, to the consideration of. . . both Houses. . . by an English woolen manufacturer. . .*—1744#40

WEBB, George. *Batchelors hall. A poem. . .*—1731#34

WEBSTER, Alexander. *Supernatural revelation the only sure hope of sinners. A sermon preached. . .*—1741#47

WEBSTER, Charles. *The duty of all Christians to read the scriptures. . . in two sermons.*—1743#43

WELD, Thomas.
An answer to W. R. his Narration of the opinions and practises of the churches lately erected in New-England. . .—1644#19
A brief narration of the practices of the churches in New-England, in their solemne worship of God. . .—1645#19

WELLER, Samuel. *The trial of Mr Whitefield's spirit. In some remarks upon his fourth Journal. . .*—1740#37

WELTON, James. *A sermon, preached at. . . Norwich. . . Nov. 29. 1759. . .*—1759#102

WESLEY, Charles and John. *A collection of Psalms and Hymns.*—1744#41

WESLEY, John.
An extract of the Rev. Mr John Wesley's journal, from February 1, 1737–8, to his return from Germany.—1740#38
An extract of the Rev. Mr John Wesley's journal from his embarking for Georgia to his return to London. . . edited by Nehemiah Curnock.—1739#71
An extract of the Revd. Mr John Wesley's Journal from August 12, 1738, to Nov. 1, 1739.—1742#49
An extract of the Reverend Mr John Wesley's journal, from Sept. 3, 1741 to October 27, 1743.—1749#46
An extract of the Reverend Mr Wesley's journal, from November 1, 1739, to September 3, 1741.—1744#42
Hymns occasioned by the earthquake, March 8, 1750. To which are added an hymn for the English in America, and another for the year 1756. Part II. The second edition.—1756#85
Hymns to be used on the Thanksgiving-day, Nov. 29, 1759. And after it.—1759#103
A narrative of the late work of God, at and near Northampton, in New-England, extracted from Mr Edward's letter. . .—1744#43

WEST, Gilbert. *A defense of the Christian revelation. . .*—1748#33

WESTON, William. *The complete merchant's clerk: or, British and American compting-house. In two parts. . . To which is added, an appendix. . .*—1754#42

WHARTON, Edward. *New-England's present sufferings, under their cruel neighbouring Indians. Represented in two letters, lately written from Boston to London.*—1675#15

WHEELWRIGHT, John.
A brief, and plain apology by John Wheelwright: Wherein he doth vindicate himself, from al [sic] those errors. . . layed to his charge by Mr. Thomas Welde. . .—1658#12
Mercurius Americanus, Mr Welds his Antitype, or, Massachusetts great apologie examined. . .—1645#20

WHITBOURNE, Richard.
The copy of a reference. . . [12 April 1622].—1622#25
A discourse and discovery of New-found-land, with many reasons how a plantation may there be made. . .—1622#26
A discourse containing a loving invitation. . . to all such as shall be adventurers, either in person, or purse, for the advancement. . .—1622#27

WHITE, Andrew.
A declaration of the Lord Baltemore's plantation in Mary-land, nigh upon Virginia: manifesting the nature, quality, condition, and rich utilities it contayneth.—1633#6
A relation of the successfull beginnings of the Lord Baltemore's plantation in Mary-land. . . extract of certain letters written. . .—1634#7

WHITE, John. *The planter's plea. Or the grounds of plantations examined, and usual objections answered. Together with a manifestation of the causes. . .*—1630#11

WHITE, John.
A second defence of the Three letters to a gentleman dissenting from the Church of England. . .—1748#34
A second letter to a gentleman dissenting from the Church of England.—1745#37
The third and last letter to a gentleman dissenting from the Church of England.—1745#38
Three letters to a gentleman dissenting from the Church of England.—1748#35

WHITEFIELD, George.
An account of money received and disbursed for the orphan-house in Georgia. . . To which is prefixed A plan of the building.—1741#48
An account of money, received and expended by the Rev. Mr Whitefield, for the poor of Georgia.—1739#72
Accounts relating to the orphan house in Georgia.—1746#29
The almost Christian. A sermon preached. . . in England. Added, a poem on his design for Georgia.—1738#30
A brief account of the occasion, process, and issue of a late trial at the assize held at Gloucester.—1744#44
A brief account of the rise, progress and present situation of the orphan-house in Georgia. In a letter to a friend.—1748#36
Britain's mercies, and Britain's duty. Represented in a sermon. . . at Philadelphia. . . August 24, 1746. And occasioned by the suppression of the late unnatural rebellion. . .—1746#30
A collection of papers, lately printed in the Daily Advertiser. . .—1740#39
A continuation of the account of the orphan-house in Georgia, from January 1740/1, to January 1742/3. . .—1743#44
A continuation of the account of the orphan-house in Georgia, from January 1740/1 to June 1742. . .—1742#50
A continuation of the Reverend Mr Whitefield's journal, after his arrival at Georgia, to a few days after his second return thither from Philadelphia. . .—1741#49
A continuation of the Reverend Mr Whitefield's journal, during the time he was detained in England by the embargo. . .—1739#73

A continuation of the Reverend Mr Whitefield's journal, from a few days after his return to Georgia to his arrival at Falmouth...—1741#50

A continuation of the Reverend Mr. Whitefield's journal, from his arrival at London, to his departure, from thence on his way to Georgia...—1739#74

A continuation of the Reverend Mr. Whitefield's journal, from his arrival at Savannah, to his return to London.—1739#75

A continuation of the Reverend Mr Whitefield's journal from his embarking after the embargo, to his arrival at Savannah in Georgia.—1740#40

The eternity of hell torments. A sermon preached at Savannah in Georgia...—1738#31

An expostulatory letter, addressed to Nicholas Lewis, Count Zinzendorff...—1753#23

An extract of the preface to... Whitefield's account of the orphanhouse in Georgia. Together with... some letters sent to him from the superintendents... and some of the children.—1741#51

Five sermons on the following subjects... With a preface by the Rev. Mr. Gilbert Tennent...—1747#29

A further account of God's dealings with the Reverend Mr George Whitefield, from the time of his ordination to his embarking for Georgia.—1747#30

The great duty of family religion: a sermon preached...—1738#32

The heinous sin of drunkenness; a sermon preached on board the Whitaker.—1739#76

Journal of a voyage from Gibraltar to Georgia...—1738#33

Journal of a voyage from London to Savannah in Georgia. In two parts. Part I. From London to Gibraltar. Part II. From Gibraltar to Savannah.—1738#34

Letter from the Reverend Mr. George Whitefield to a friend in London, dated at New-Brunswick in New-Jersey, April 27, 1740.—1740#42

Letter from the Reverend Mr George Whitefield to the religious societies, lately set on foot in several parts of England and Wales.—1740#41

Letter to the Reverend John Wesley, in answer to his sermon, entituled, Free-grace...—1741#52

Letter to the Reverend Mr Thomas Church... in answer to his serious and expostulatory letter to... Whitefield...—1744#45

Orphan-letters. Being a collection of letters wrote by the orphans in the hospital of Georgia. To the Reverend Mr George Whitefield...—1741#53

A short account of God's dealings with the Reverend Mr. George Whitefield... from his infancy, to the time of his entring into Holy Orders...—1740#43

A short address to persons of all denominations, occasioned by the alarm of an intended invasion...—1756#86

Six sermons on the following subjects... With a preface by the Reverend Mr Gilbert Tennent.—1750#51

Some remarks on a late pamphlet entitled, the state of religion in New-England, since the Rev. Mr George Whitefield's arrival there...—1742#51

Ten sermons preached on the following subjects...—1751#35A

Thankfulness for mercies received... farewel sermon... on board Whitaker, at anchor near Savannah... May the 17th, 1738...—1738#35

Three letters... III. To the inhabitants of Maryland, Virginia, and North and South Carolina, concerning their Negroes.—1740#44

The two first parts of his life, with his journals...—1756#87

WHITEHEAD, George.

The Christian doctrine and society of the people called Quakers, cleared from the reproach of the late division of a few in some parts of America...—1693#18

The Christian progress of... G. W; historically relating his experience... and service in defence of the truth, and of... Quakers.—1725#11

Light and truth triumphant.—1712#26

The power of Christ vindicated, against the magick of apostacy: in answer to George Keith's book... The magick of Quakerism.—1708#17

Truth prevalent; and the Quakers discharged from the Norfolk rector's furious charge.—1701#43

WHITELOCKE, Bulstrode.

Memorials of the English affairs...—1682#29

Memorials of the English affairs... with some account of his life and writings by William Penn...—1709#23

WHITFIELD, Henry.

The light appearing more and more towards the perfect day. Or, a farther discovery of the present state of the Indians in New England...—1651#15

Strength out of weaknesse; or A glorious manifestation of the further progress of the gospel among the Indians in New-England...—1652#17

WHITING, John.

Catalogue of Friend's books; written by many of the people called Quakers...—1708#18

Judas and the chief priests... in answer to G. Keith's fourth... narrative...—1701#44

A just reprehension of Cotton Mather. London, the 11th of the 12th month, 1709.—1710#26

Persecution exposed, in some memoirs relating to the sufferings of John Whiting, and many... Quakers...—1715#24

Truth and inocency defended; against falsehood and envy... In answer to Cotton Mather... his late Church-History of New-England...—1703#12

Truth the strongest of all: or, An apostate further convicted, and truth defended; in reply to George Keith's Fifth narrative.—1706#20

WICKS, Michael. *Case of Michael Wicks, Esq. late receiver of the plantation-duty.*—1709#24

WIDDERS, Robert. *The life and death, travels and suffering of Robert Widders...*—1688#18

WIGGLESWORTH, Michael. *The day of doom: or, A description of the great and last judgement...*—1666#7

WIGHT, Thomas. *Truth further defended, and William Penn vindicated...*—1700#37

WILCOCKS, Joseph. *A sermon preached... 18th of February, 1725.*—1726#18

WILKINSON, William.
An answer to Joseph Jenk's reply to William Wilkinson's treatise, entituled, the baptism of the holy spirit...—1721#24
The baptism of the holy spirit, without elementary water, demonstratively proved to be the true baptism of Christ...—1718#22

WILLARD, Samuel.
A brief discourse concerning that ceremony of laying the hand on the Bible in swearing.—1689#30
A thanksgiving sermon preach'd at Boston... December, 1705. On the return of a gentleman from his travels.—1709#25

WILLIAMS, Edward.
Virginia's discovery of silke-wormes, with their benefit. And the implanting of mulberry trees...—1650#16
Virgo triumphans: or, Virginia richly and truly valued; more especially the south part thereof: viz the fertile Carolina, and no lesse excellent isle of Roanoak...—1650#17

WILLIAMS, J. *The favours of providence to Britain in 1759. A sermon preached at Wokingham... Berks... 29th... November 1759...*—1759#104

WILLIAMS, John.
A brief discourse concerning the lawfulness of worshipping God by the Common-Prayer...—1693#19
Case of lay-communion with the Church of England considered...—1683#24
A sermon preached... February 15. 1705/6...—1706#21

WILLIAMS, Roger, mariner. *To the King's most excellent majesty, the humble petition of...*—1681#21

WILLIAMS, Roger.
The bloody tenent yet more bloody: by Mr. Cotton's endevour to wash it white in the blood of the lambe...—1652#18
The bloudy tenent, of persecution, for cause of conscience, discussed, in a conference between truth and peace...—1644#20
Christenings make not Christians, or A brief discourse concerning that name heathen, commonly given to the Indians.—1646#20
Experiments of spiritual life and health, and their preservatives in which the weakest child of God may get assurance of his spirituall life...—1652#19
The fourth paper, presented by Major Butler, to the... committee of Parliament, for the propagating of the gospel...—1652#20
The hireling ministry none of Christs, or, A curse touching the propagating of the gospel of Jesus...—1652#21
A key into the language of America: or, An help to the language of the natives... in New-England... with brief observations of the customes... of the afore-said natives...—1643#19
Mr Cottons letter lately printed, examined and answered: by Roger Williams of Providence in New-England.—1644#21

A paraenetick or humble addresse to the Parliament and assembly for (not loose, but) Christian libertie.—1644#22
Queries of highest consideration proposed to Mr Thomas Goodwin... And to the Commissioners of the General Assembly (so-called) of the Church of Scotland...—1644#23

WILLIAMSON, Peter.
Authentic instances of French and Indian cruelty, exemplified in the sufferings of Peter Williamson... written by himself.—1758#49
A brief account of the war in N. America... the necessity and advantage of keeping Canada... the maintaining of friendly correspondence...—1760#102
French and Indian cruelty exemplified in the life... of P. W... written by himself...—1757#50
Occasional reflections on the importance of the war in America, and the reasonableness and justice of supporting the King of Prussia, etc...—1758#50
Some considerations on the present state of affairs. Wherein the defenceless state of Great-Britain is pointed out... interspersed...—1758#51

WILLIS, Richard. *A sermon preached... 20 February 1701/2...*—1702#27

WILLISON, John. *A fair and impartial testimony essayed in name of a number of ministers...*—1744#46

WILLUGHBY, Francis.
Ornithologia libri tres...—1686#6
The ornithology of Francis Willughby...—1678#7

WILSON, John. *Address'd to the merchants of London. A genuine narrative of the transactions in Nova Scotia, since the settlement, June 1749, till August the 5th, 1751...*—1751#36

WILSON, John. *The day-breaking, if not the sun-rising of the gospell with the Indians in New-England.*—1647#20

WILSON, Samuel.
An account of the province of Carolina in America. Together with an abstract of the patent, and several other necessary and useful...—1682#30

WILSON, Samuel. *Sermons on the following subjects... with an abstract of Consul Dean's narrative, relating to his suffering shipwreck... in the year 1710*—1735#19

WILSON, Thomas (1663–1755). *An essay towards an instruction for the Indians; explaining the most essential doctrines of Christianity... Together with directions...*—1740#45

WILSON, Thomas. (1655?–1725). *A brief journal of the life, travels, labours of love, in the work of the ministry of... T. Wilson...*—1728#16

WINNE, Edward. *A letetr [sic] written... to Sir G. Calvert his Majesties principall secretary: from Feryland in Newfoundland...*—1621#10

WINSLOW, Edward.
The glorious progress of the Gospel, amongst the Indians in New England. Manifested by three letters...—1649#10
Good newes from New-England: or A true relation of things very remarkable at... Plimoth.—1624#12

Hypocrosie unmasked: by a true relation of the proceedings of the Governour and Company of the Massachusetts against Samuel Gorton...—1646#21

New-Englands salamander, discovered by an irreligious and scornefull pamphlet, called New-England's Jonas...—1647#21

WINTER, Richard.
The importance and necessity of his majesty's declaration of war with France considered... in a sermon... May 23, 1756.—1756#88

A sermon preached... on November 29, 1759...—1759#105

WINTHROP, John. *Antinomians and Familists condemned by the synod of elders in New-England...*—1644#24

WISE, Robert. *Case of Robert Wise, late of London, tobacco-merchant.*—1714##22

WISWALL, Ichabod. *A judicious observation of that dreadful comet, which appeared on November by J. W. in New-England...*—1683#25

WITHALL, Benjamin. *Case of Benjamin Withall, gent. In his majesty's victualling office...*—1715#25

WITHERSPOON, John.
The absolute necessity of salvation through Christ. A sermon, preached... January 2. 1758...—1758#52

Essay on the connection between the doctrine of justification by the imputed righteousness of Christ...—1756#89

WOOD, Anthony. *Athenae Oxoniensis...*—1691#23

WOOD, William. *New England's prospect. A true, lively, and experimentall description of that part of America, commonly called New England...*—1634#8

WOOD, William. *A survey of trade, in four parts... Together with considerations on our money and bullion...*—1718#23

WOODBRIDGE, Benjamin.
Church members set in joynt. Or, a discovery of the unwarrantable and disorderly practice of private Christians, in usurping...—1648#17

Justification by faith: or a confutation of that antinomian error, that justification is before faith...—1652#22

The method of grace...—1656#13

WOODNOTH, Arthur. *A short collection of the most remarkable passages from the originall to the dissolution of the Virginia Company.*—1651#16

WOODWARD, Josiah.
An account of the progress of the reformation of manners, in England and Ireland, and other parts of the world...—1701#45

An account of the societies for reformation of manners in London and Westminster...—1699#20

WOOLEY, Charles. *A two years journal in New-York: and part of its territories in America...*—1701#46

WORKMAN, Giles. *Private-men no pulpit men: or, A modest examination of lay-mens preaching...*—1646#22

WORLIDGE, John.
Mr. Worlidge's two treatises—1694#20

The second parts of Systema agriculturae, or The mystery of husbandry...—1689#31

WOTTON, Thomas. *The English Baronetage... To which are added, an account of such Nova-Scotia baronets as are of English families...*—1741#54

WYETH, Joseph.
Anguis flagellatus; or, a switch for the snake. Being an answer to the third and last edition of the Snake in the Grass...—1699#21

An answer to a letter from Dr. Bray, directed to such as have contributed towards the propagating Christian knowledge in the plantations...—1700#38

Remarks on Dr Bray's memorial, etc. with brief observations on some passages in the Acts of his Visitation in Maryland, and on his circular letter to the clergy there...—1701#47

WYNNE, John. *A sermon preached... Feb. 1724.*—1725#12

WYNNE, R. *A sermon preached at the parish-church of St. Vedast, Foster Lane, on November 29, 1759...*—1759##107

YONGE, Francis.
A narrative of the proceedings of the people of South-Carolina, in the year 1719... motives that induced them to renounce their obedience to the Lords Proprietors...—1726#19

A view of the trade of South Carolina, with proposals humbly offerrd for improving the same.—1722#29

YONGE, William. *England's shame: or the unmasking of a political atheist... the life and death of... Hugh Peters...*—1663#3

YOUNG, Arthur.
Reflections on the present state of affairs at home and abroad...—1759#109

The theatre of the present war in North America: with candid reflections on the great improvement of the war in that part of the world.—1758#53

YOUNG, Samuel.
An apology for Congregational divines...—1698#26

The Foxonian Quakers, dunces, lyars and slanderers...—1697#13

Vindiciae anti-Baxterianiae, or some animadversions on a book, entitled Reliquiae Baxterianiae, or the life of Mr. R. Baxter...—1696#24

William Penn and the Quakers either impostors, or apostates...—1696#25

YOUNG, Thomas. *Englands bane: or, The description of drunkennesse.*—1634#9

Z., X. *Letter from an old Whig in town, to a modern Whig in the country, upon the late expedition to Canada.*—1711#35

Z——h, A——r. *Considerations on the dispute now depending before the Honourable House of Commons, between the British, southern and northern plantations... In a letter to ——.*—1731#35

18098